MGMT¹¹

PRINCIPLES OF MANAGEMENT

CHUCK WILLIAMS
Butler University

CENGAGE

Australia • Brazil • Mexico • Singapore • United Kingdom • United States

MGMT 11e

Chuck Williams

Senior Vice President, Higher Ed Product, Content, and Market Development: Erin Joyner

Product Director: Bryan Gambrel

Content/Media Developer: Patricia Hempel

Product Assistant: Rhett Ransom

Marketing Manager: Charisse Darin

Senior Content Project Manager: Martha Conway

Senior Art Director: Bethany Bourgeois

Text Designer: Tippy McIntosh

Cover Designer: Lisa Kuhn, Curio Press, LLC / Chris Miller, Cmiller Design

Cover Image: Hilvaria Images / Alamy Stock Photo

Internal Design Images: Checkmark, Zorana Matijasevic/Shutterstock.com

Intellectual Property Analyst: Diane Garrity

Intellectual Property Project Manager: Sarah Shainwald

Production Service: MPS Limited

For product information and technology assistance, contact us at **Cengage Customer & Sales Support, 1-800-354-9706** or **support.cengage.com.**

For permission to use material from this text or product, submit all requests online at **www.cengage.com/permissions**.

Library of Congress Control Number: 2017954065

Student Edition ISBN: 978-1-337-40747-2
Student Edition with MindTap ISBN: 978-1-337-40746-5

Cengage
20 Channel Center Street
Boston, MA 02210
USA

Cengage is a leading provider of customized learning solutions with employees residing in nearly 40 different countries and sales in more than 125 countries around the world. Find your local representative at **www.cengage.com.**

Cengage products are represented in Canada by Nelson Education, Ltd.

To learn more about Cengage platforms and services, visit **www.cengage.com.**

To register or access your online learning solution or purchase materials for your course, visit **www.cengagebrain.com.**

Printed in the United States of America
Print Number: 05   Print Year: 2020

CHUCK WILLIAMS
MGMT¹¹ BRIEF CONTENTS

Hilvaria Images / Alamy Stock Photo

Contents

Part 2
Planning

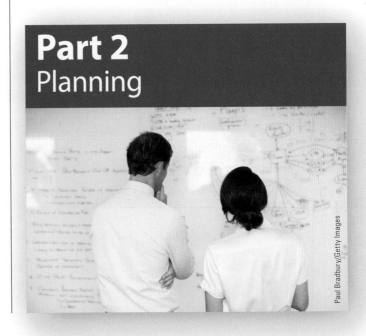

Paul Bradbury/Getty Images

Part 3
Organizing

canbedone/Shutterstock.com

Part 4
Leading

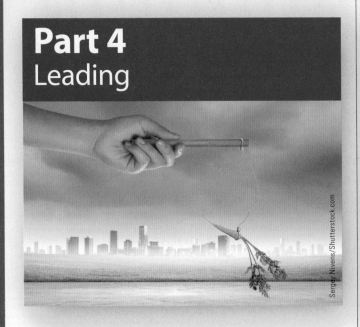

Sergej Nivens/Shutterstock.com

Part 5
Controlling

mikulas1/E+/Getty Images

1 | Management

LEARNING OUTCOMES

1-1 Describe what management is.

1-2 Explain the four functions of management.

1-3 Describe different kinds of managers.

1-4 Explain the major roles and subroles that managers perform in their jobs.

1-5 Explain what companies look for in managers.

1-6 Discuss the top mistakes that managers make in their jobs.

1-7 Describe the transition that employees go through when they are promoted to management.

1-8 Explain how and why companies can create competitive advantage through people.

After you finish this chapter, go to **PAGE 21** for **STUDY TOOLS**

Graiki/Moment/Getty Images

1-1 MANAGEMENT IS ...

Management issues are fundamental to any organization: How do we plan to get things done, organize the company to be efficient and effective, lead and motivate employees, and put controls in place to make sure our plans are followed and our goals met? Good management is basic to starting a business, growing a business, and maintaining a business after it has achieved some measure of success.

To understand how important *good* management is, think about this. Sears, one of the oldest retailers in the United States, has lost $10.45 billion since 2011. Recent results are just as bad. Sears lost $1.1 billion in 2015 and closed 562 stores. In 2016, it lost $2.25 billion and closed 200 stores. In 2017, it plans to close another 250 stores.[1] Without the $10.4 billion it raised from selling Lands End clothing, Sears Hometown and Outlet Stores, 327 profitable Sears stores and its Craftsman tool brand (to Stanley Black & Decker), Sears would be filing for bankruptcy.

Robert Futterman, CEO of RKF, a retail leasing and consulting company, said, "Retailers invest in their best stores and refurbish them, they don't sell them."[2]

Ah, bad managers and bad management. Is it any wonder that companies pay management consultants nearly $210 billion a year for advice on basic management issues such as how to outperform competitors to earn customers' business, lead people effectively, organize the company efficiently, and manage large-scale projects and processes?[3] This textbook will help you understand some of the basic issues that management consultants help companies resolve. (And it won't cost you billions of dollars.)

Many of today's managers got their start welding on the factory floor, clearing dishes off tables, helping customers fit a suit, or wiping up a spill in aisle 3. Similarly, lots of you will start at the bottom and work your way up. There's no better way to get to know your competition, your customers, and your business. But whether you begin your career at the entry level or as a supervisor, your job as a manager is not to do the work but to help others do theirs. **Management** is getting work done through others.

Vineet Nayar, CEO of IT services company HCL Technologies, doesn't see himself as the guy who has to do everything or have all the answers. Instead, he sees himself as "the guy who is obsessed with enabling employees to create value." Rather than coming up with solutions himself, Nayar creates opportunities for collaboration, for peer review, and for employees to give feedback on ideas and work processes. Says Nayar, "My job is to make sure everybody is enabled to do what they do well."[4]

Nayar's description of managerial responsibilities suggests that managers also have to be concerned with efficiency and effectiveness in the work process. **Efficiency**

Sears is so cash strapped that it has sacrificed future earnings for short-term needs by selling hundreds of profitable stores.

is getting work done with a minimum of effort, expense, or waste. At aircraft manufacturer Airbus, lasers help workers join massive fuselage pieces together

Management getting work done through others

Efficiency getting work done with a minimum of effort, expense, or waste

30 percent faster (and 40 percent cheaper). Similarly, rather than reaching up for hours to assemble and install overhead luggage bins, workers now assemble these parts at waist-high benches and then bolt them to the plane's ceiling. Besides being easier for workers, this process is 30 percent faster. When testing a plane's electrical circuitry, engineers previously used probes to validate electrical connections, hand recording the results of 35,000 such tests on each plane's paper blueprints. Today, wireless probes paired to computer tablets test each connection, automatically recording the results onto the plane's digital blueprints. Finally, by using a massive ink-jet printer, Airbus has cut the time it takes to paint airline logos on plane tail fins from 170 to 17 hours.[5]

Efficiency alone, however, is not enough to ensure success. Managers must also strive for **effectiveness**, which is accomplishing tasks that help fulfill organizational objectives such as customer service and satisfaction. Spectrum (formerly Time Warner Cable) recently reduced its eight-hour service-call window to just one hour by outfitting technicians with iPads that geolocate the nearest customer needing service. Company spokesman Bobby Amirshahi said, "We know when a tech is finishing up at one home, the one-hour window somewhere near them is starting to open for another customer, so we can dynamically dispatch that technician to the next job."[6] The focus on improving customer service is paying off. Today, technicians arrive within the set one-hour window 98 percent of the time. A special app provides customers with the technician's arrival time, name, identification number, and photo. Thanks to improvements in company reliability, repair-related visits dropped by 15 percent and the number of pay-TV subscribers increased.[7]

1-2 MANAGEMENT FUNCTIONS

Henri Fayol, who was a managing director (CEO) of a large steel company in the early 1900s, was one of the founders of the field of management. You'll learn more about Fayol and management's other key contributors when you read about the history of management in Chapter 2. Based on his 20 years of experience as a CEO, Fayol argued that "the success of an enterprise generally depends much more on the administrative ability of its leaders than on their technical ability."[8] A century later, Fayol's arguments still hold true.

During a two-year study code-named Project Oxygen, Google analyzed performance reviews and feedback surveys to identify the traits of its best managers. According to Laszlo Bock, Google's vice president for people operations, "We'd always believed that to be a manager, particularly on the engineering side, you need to be as deep or deeper a technical expert than the people who work for you. It turns out that that's absolutely the least important thing." What was most important? "Be a good coach." "Empower; Don't micromanage." "Be product and results-oriented." "Be a good communicator and listen to your team." "Be interested in [your] direct reports' success and well-being." In short, Google found what Fayol observed: administrative ability, or management, is key to an organization's success.[9]

According to Fayol, managers need to perform five managerial functions in order to be successful: planning, organizing, coordinating, commanding, and controlling.[10] Most management textbooks today have updated this list by dropping the coordinating function and referring to Fayol's commanding function as "leading." Fayol's management functions are thus known today in this updated form as planning, organizing, leading, and controlling. Studies indicate that managers who perform these management functions well are more successful, gaining promotions for themselves and profits for their companies. For example, the more time CEOs spend planning, the more profitable their companies are.[11] A 25-year study at AT&T found that employees with better planning and decision-making skills were more likely to be promoted into management jobs, to be successful as managers, and to be promoted into upper levels of management.[12]

The evidence is clear. Managers serve their companies well when they plan, organize, lead, and control. So we've organized this textbook based on these functions of management, as shown in Exhibit 1.1.

Now let's take a closer look at each of the management functions: 1-2a planning, 1-2b organizing, 1-2c leading, and 1-2d controlling.

1-2a Planning

Planning involves determining organizational goals and a means for achieving them. As you'll learn in Chapter 5, planning is one of the best ways to improve performance. It encourages people to work harder, to work for extended periods, to engage in behaviors directly related to goal accomplishment, and to think of better ways to do their jobs. But most importantly, companies that plan have larger profits and faster growth than companies that don't plan.

For example, the question "What business are we in?" is at the heart of strategic planning. You'll learn about

Effectiveness accomplishing tasks that help fulfill organizational objectives

Exhibit 1.1
The Four Functions of Management

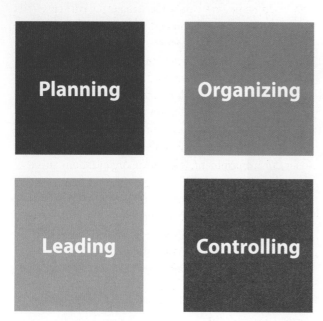

Planning	Organizing
Leading	**Controlling**

You'll learn more about planning in Chapter 5 on planning and decision making, Chapter 6 on organizational strategy, Chapter 7 on innovation and change, and Chapter 8 on global management.

1-2b Organizing

Organizing is deciding where decisions will be made, who will do what jobs and tasks, and who will work for whom in the company. In other words, organizing is about determining how things get done. In the retail industry, that usually means matching staffing levels to customer traffic, increasing staffing when busy, and then decreasing staffing when slow. Walmart recently implemented software to match the schedules of its 2.2 million associates with the flows of its 260 million weekly customers. While this dynamic, just-in-time approach sounds like a great idea, it resulted in highly fragmented schedules for thousands of store employees who could be sent home from work after just a few hours (due to unexpectedly slow customer traffic) or called back unexpectedly (when customer traffic increased). These unpredictable work schedules, which effectively put many associates perpetually on call, produced backlash from employees, advocacy groups, and unions alike. In response, Walmart reconfigured its schedules using three types of shifts: open, fixed, and flex. Managers schedule open shift employees during times that they previously indicated that they would be available for. Fixed shifts, which are offered first to long-time employees, guarantee the same weekly hours for up to a year. Finally, flex shifts let employees build their own schedules in two- to three-week blocks. Walmart is also developing an app that will allow employees to view, update, and set their schedules using a smartphone. Walmart managers have high hopes for the new shift structures, which reduced absenteeism by 11 percent and employee turnover by 14 percent during a two-year test.[15]

this in Chapter 6. If you can answer the question "What business are you in?" in two sentences or fewer, chances are you have a very clear plan for your business. But getting a clear plan is not so easy. As the manufacturer of backpacks for industry leading brands like JanSport, North Face, Timberland, and Eastpak, VF Corporation dominates the $2.7 billion backpack business. The increasing digitalization of textbooks and other documents has led VF to reassess how customers use its backpacks. According to JanSport director of research and design Eric Rothenhaus, "We realized we needed to forget everything we knew about the category.... We started to ask: What are the things we carry with us? How do we carry them? And how is that changing?"[13] VF studied college students, homeless people, and extreme mountaineers, learning that they had surprisingly similar requirements: water-resistance, flexibility, storage for electronics, and the ability to pack and unpack several times a day. So rather than making bags to carry things from point A to point B, VR's JanSport backpacks are designed for people who move *and* work in multiple locations—classrooms, coffee shops, shared office spaces, and beyond. "When you need to be on the go," Rothenhaus said, "you need a backpack."[14]

You'll learn more about organizing in Chapter 9 on designing adaptive organizations, Chapter 10 on managing teams, Chapter 11 on managing human resources, and Chapter 12 on managing individuals and a diverse workforce.

Planning determining organizational goals and a means for achieving them

Organizing deciding where decisions will be made, who will do what jobs and tasks, and who will work for whom

MANAGEMENT TIPS FROM THE PROS

The functions of planning, organizing, leading, and controlling all seem straightforward enough, but how do managers do all of them simultaneously? Today's managers are busy; as you'll learn later in the chapter, managers spend as little as two minutes on a task before having to switch to another! Here are some techniques seasoned managers use to be more efficient and effective as they execute on the four functions of management.

» *Planning*: Carlos Ghosn is CEO of two automakers with headquarters halfway around the world from each other: Nissan (in Japan) and Renault (in France). He is also the chairman of a third—AvtoVaz (in Russia). To balance all his responsibilities, he plans his schedule out more than a year in advance.

» *Organizing*: One of the ways Adora Cheung, CEO of Homejoy, stays organized

PepsiCo CEO Indra Nooyi.

is by crowdsourcing meeting agendas. She asks coworkers to add agenda items to an online spreadsheet, and then during the meeting, covers only the topics listed—no more.

» *Leading*: Indra Nooyi, CEO of PepsiCo, handwrites notes to roughly 200 of the company's top employees and even to top recruits. She also sends notes to the parents of her direct reports, thanking them for their child.

» *Controlling*: Birchbox CEO Katia Beauchamp insists her coworkers give her a deadline for every question they ask her, no matter how simple. That way, she can prioritize her responses and stay on track.

Source: J. McGregor, "How 10 CEOs Work Smarter, Manage Better, and Get Things Done Faster," *Washington Post*, January 2, 2015, https://www.washingtonpost.com/news/on-leadership/wp/2015/01/02/how-10-ceos-work-smarter-manage-better-and-get-things-done-faster/.

iStock.com/EdStock

1-2c Leading

Our third management function, **leading**, involves inspiring and motivating workers to work hard to achieve organizational goals. Eileen Martinson, CEO of software developer Sparta Systems, believes that it is important for leaders to clearly communicate what an organization's goals are. She says, "A boss taught me a long time ago that people are going to remember only two to three things." So at her first company-wide meeting, she communicated just one goal—doubling revenues over the next few years.[16] Martinson says, "The employees completely understand where we are going, and we've built a culture around that. If you have to come in and show me 45 charts and go through a lot of mumbo jumbo that neither of us understands, it's not going to work."[17]

You'll learn more about leading in Chapter 13 on motivation, Chapter 14 on leadership, and Chapter 15 on managing communication.

Leading inspiring and motivating workers to work hard to achieve organizational goals

Controlling monitoring progress toward goal achievement and taking corrective action when needed

1-2d Controlling

The last function of management, **controlling**, is monitoring progress toward goal achievement and taking corrective action when progress isn't being made. The basic control process involves setting standards to achieve goals, comparing actual performance to those standards, and then making changes to return performance to those standards. When traveling, Indians are much more likely to stay with friends or family than in a hotel. In fact, there are just two hotel rooms for every 10,000 people in India (compared to 40 in China and 200 in the United States). Why is this? Analyst Chetan Kapoor says, "There are lots of hotels where customers go in thinking, 'Will there be rats in my room?'"[18] Roughly 60 percent of those rooms are located in independent budget hotels, which vary dramatically in quality. Oyo Rooms is aiming to change that with its new hotel inspection service. Oyo inspects hotels across 200 dimensions, including linen quality, mattress comfort, cleanliness, shower water temperature, and staff appearance. Hotels agree to maintain those standards as a condition of staying in Oyo's 175 city database. Oyo Rooms founder Ritesh Agarwal says that inspections encourage hoteliers to make repairs and upgrade facilities. As a result, he says, "When you book a room through Oyo, you know exactly what you're going to get."[19]

You'll learn more about the control function in Chapter 16 on control, Chapter 17 on managing information, and Chapter 18 on managing service and manufacturing operations.

1-3 KINDS OF MANAGERS

Not all managerial jobs are the same. The demands and requirements placed on the CEO of Facebook are significantly different from those placed on the manager of your local Chipotle restaurant.

*As shown in Exhibit 1.2, there are four kinds of managers, each with different jobs and responsibilities: **1-3a top managers, 1-3b middle managers, 1-3c first-line managers,** and **1-3d team leaders.***

1-3a Top Managers

Top managers hold positions such as chief executive officer (CEO), chief operating officer (COO), chief financial officer (CFO), and chief information officer (CIO) and are responsible for the overall direction of the organization. Top managers have three major responsibilities.[20]

First, they are responsible for creating a context for change.

CEO Doug McMillon explains why Walmart's board of directors hired him, "The company needs to go through quite a bit of change. So don't just run it. Don't just maintain it. Get it prepared for the future."[21] And that future is one in which Walmart's online sales ($13.7 billion in 2016) parallel its sales in its brick-and-mortar stores. McMillon says, "To do that, we need to build a strong and capable e-commerce business—but also to strengthen what we're doing in stores. Customers want to save money and time and have the broadest assortment of items, and we think that by bringing e-commerce and digital capabilities together with the stores, we can do things that a pure e-commerce player can't."[22]

Indeed, in both Europe and the United States, 35 percent of all CEOs are eventually fired because of their inability to successfully change their companies.[23] Creating a context for change includes forming a long-range vision or mission for the company. When Satya Nadella was appointed CEO of **Microsoft**, the company was perceived as a shortsighted, lumbering behemoth. Nadella reoriented the company with a series of acquisitions and innovations, including purchasing **Mojang**, maker of the **Minecraft** video game, and a 3D-hologram feature for controlling Windows. After

following Microsoft for years, one analyst noted about Nadella's new direction for the company, "Microsoft hasn't really shown any sort of vision like this in a long, long time."[24] As one CEO said, "The CEO has to think about the future more than anyone."[25]

After that vision or mission is set, the second responsibility of top managers is to develop employees' commitment to and ownership of the company's performance. That is, top managers are responsible for creating employee buy-in. Third, top managers must create a positive organizational culture through language and action, actively managing internal communication. Top managers impart company values, strategies, and lessons through what they do and say to others both inside and outside the company. Indeed, no matter what they communicate, it's critical for them to send and reinforce clear, consistent messages.[26] When Mark Fields became Ford Motor Company's CEO, the clear, consistent message from his predecessor, Alan Mulally, was "One Ford," which was meant to pull together a fractionalized company characterized by "infighting and fiefdom-building."[27] Said Mulally, "Our single most important strategy is to continue to integrate Ford around the world."[28] By contrast, Fields made clear that the message under his leadership is "Two Fords." One Ford was "foundational," but the company needs to "evolve" to being an auto *and* mobility company. Fields explains that total revenue from, "the traditional automotive industry is around $2.3 trillion today and growing; Ford, he says, gets about 6 percent of this. Fields notes that, "transportation products and services revenue is already around $5.4 trillion [per year]. We and the traditional auto industry get 0 percent of this today. That's why being an auto and a mobility company makes business sense [for Ford]."[29]

Finally, top managers are responsible for monitoring their business environments. This means that top managers must closely monitor customer needs, competitors' moves, and long-term business, economic, and social trends.

1-3b Middle Managers

Middle managers hold positions such as plant manager, regional manager, or divisional manager. They are responsible for setting objectives consistent with

Leszek Glasner/Shutterstock.com

Top managers executives responsible for the overall direction of the organization

Middle managers responsible for setting objectives consistent with top management's goals and for planning and implementing subunit strategies for achieving these objectives

Exhibit 1.2
What the Four Kinds of Managers Do

Jobs		Responsibilities

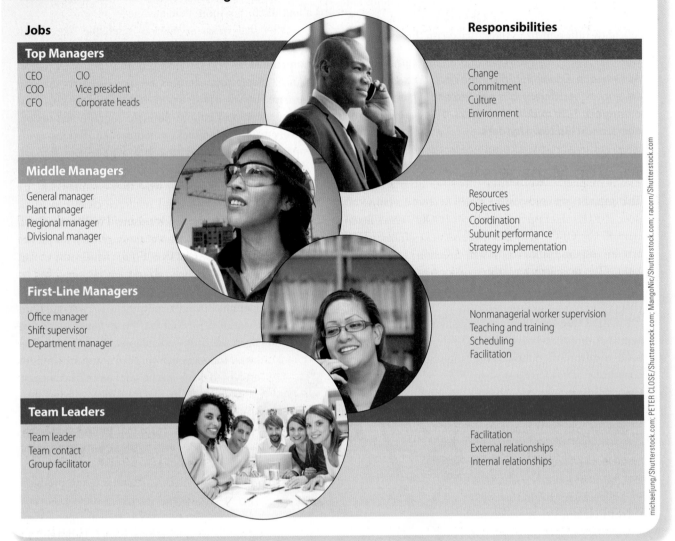

Top Managers

CEO	CIO
COO	Vice president
CFO	Corporate heads

Change
Commitment
Culture
Environment

Middle Managers

General manager
Plant manager
Regional manager
Divisional manager

Resources
Objectives
Coordination
Subunit performance
Strategy implementation

First-Line Managers

Office manager
Shift supervisor
Department manager

Nonmanagerial worker supervision
Teaching and training
Scheduling
Facilitation

Team Leaders

Team leader
Team contact
Group facilitator

Facilitation
External relationships
Internal relationships

michaeljung/Shutterstock.com; PETER CLOSE/Shutterstock.com; MangoNic/Shutterstock.com; racorn/Shutterstock.com

---

top management's goals and for planning and implementing subunit strategies for achieving those objectives.[30] Or as one middle manager put it, a middle manager is, "the implementer of the company's strategy" who figures out the "how" to do the "what."[31] Ryan Carson founded online learning company Treehouse Island without managers because he believed that his 100 employees could make decisions better and faster by themselves. However, that decision was severely tested when rapid growth resulted in 100,000 students enrolled in Treehouse Island's online courses. Employees, unsure of their responsibilities, became increasingly frustrated as endless meetings never seemed to result in meaningful action or decisions. Tasks and projects that were necessary to keep up with demand started to fall behind schedule. Carson fixed the situation by creating roles for middle managers. "That [managerless] experiment broke," said Carson. "I just had to admit it."[32]

One specific middle management responsibility is to plan and allocate resources to meet objectives. A second major responsibility is to coordinate and link groups, departments, and divisions within a company. One middle manager described his job as, "A man who can discuss strategy with [the] CXO at breakfast and [then] eat lunch with workers."[33]

A third responsibility of middle management is to monitor and manage the performance of the subunits and individual managers who report to them. Finally, middle managers are also responsible for implementing the changes or strategies generated by top managers. Why? Because they're closer to the managers and employees who work on a daily basis with suppliers to effectively and efficiently deliver the company's product or service. In short, they're closer to the people who can best solve problems and implement solutions. How important are middle managers to company performance? A study of nearly 400 video-game companies conducted at the University of Pennsylvania's Wharton School of Business found that middle managers' effectiveness accounted for 22 percent of the differences in performance across companies. In fact, middle managers were three times as important as the video-game designers who develop game characters and storylines. Professor Ethan Mollick, who conducted the study, said that middle managers are the key to "making sure the people at the bottom and the top [of the organization] are getting what they need."[34] As for Treehouse Island, revenue is up, the number of instructional videos has increased, and response times to student questions have been cut in half. According to teacher Craig Dennis, things are "light years better" with middle managers in place.[35]

1-3c First-Line Managers

First-line managers hold positions such as office manager, shift supervisor, or department manager. The primary responsibility of first-line managers is to manage the performance of entry-level employees who are directly responsible for producing a company's goods and services. Thus, first-line managers are the only managers who don't supervise other managers. The responsibilities of first-line managers include monitoring, teaching, and short-term planning.

First-line managers encourage, monitor, and reward the performance of their workers. First-line managers are also responsible for teaching entry-level employees how to do their jobs. They also make detailed schedules and operating plans based on middle management's intermediate-range plans. In contrast to the long-term plans of top managers (three to five years out) and the intermediate plans of middle managers (six to eighteen months out), first-line managers engage in plans and actions that typically produce results within two weeks.[36] Consider the typical convenience store manager (e.g., 7-Eleven) who starts the day by driving past competitors' stores to inspect their gasoline prices and then checks the outside of his or her store for anything that might need maintenance, such as burned-out lights or

wirojsid/123RF

signs, or restocking, such as windshield washer fluid and paper towels. Then comes an inside check, where the manager determines what needs to be done for that day. (Are there enough donuts and coffee for breakfast or enough sandwiches for lunch?) After the day is planned, the manager turns to weekend orders. After accounting for the weather (hot or cold) and the sales trends at the same time last year, the manager makes sure the store will have enough beer, soft drinks, and snack foods on hand. Finally, the manager looks seven to ten days ahead for hiring needs. Because of strict hiring procedures (basic math tests, drug tests, and background checks), it can take that long to hire new employees. Said one convenience store manager, "I have to continually interview, even if I am fully staffed."[37]

1-3d Team Leaders

The fourth kind of manager is a team leader. This relatively new kind of management job developed as companies shifted to self-managing teams, which, by definition, have no formal supervisor. In traditional management hierarchies, first-line managers are responsible for the performance of nonmanagerial employees and have the authority to hire and fire workers, make job assignments, and control resources. In this new structure, the teams themselves perform nearly all of the functions performed by first-line managers under traditional hierarchies.[38]

Team leaders are primarily responsible for facilitating team activities toward accomplishing a goal. This doesn't mean team leaders are

First-line managers responsible for training and supervising the performance of nonmanagerial employees who are directly responsible for producing the company's products or services

Team leaders managers responsible for facilitating team activities toward goal accomplishment responsible for team performance. They aren't. The team is. So how do team leaders help their teams accomplish their goals? Avinoam Nowogrodski, CEO at Clarizen, a software company, says, "Great leaders ask the right questions. They recognize . . . that a team is much better at figuring out the answers."[39] Team leaders help their team members plan and schedule work, learn to solve problems, and work effectively with each other. Management consultant Franklin Jonath says, "The idea is for the team leader to be at the service of the group." It should be clear that the team members own the outcome. The leader is there to bring intellectual, emotional, and spiritual resources to the team. Through his or her actions, the leader should be able to show the others how to think about the work that they're doing in the context of their lives. It's a tall order, but the best teams have such leaders.[40]

Relationships among team members and between different teams are crucial to good team performance and must be well managed by team leaders, who are responsible for fostering good relationships and addressing problematic ones within their teams. Getting along with others is much more important in team structures because team members can't get work done without the help of teammates. Clarizen CEO Avinoam Nowogrodski agrees, saying, "Innovation is created with people who you respect. It will never happen in a group of people who hate each other. If you want to have innovation within your company, you need to have a culture of respect."[41] And, Nowogrodski adds, that starts with the team leader. "If you respect other people, they'll respect you."[42] In other words, team leaders need to foster *civil behavior* based on politeness, respect, and positive regard. For two decades, Professor Christine Porath has studied the effects of workplace incivility. She stress that leaders set the tone for their teams: "A study of cross-functional product teams revealed that when leaders treated members of their team well and fairly, the team members were more productive individually and as a team. They also were more likely to go above and beyond their job requirements. It all starts at the top. When leaders are civil, it increases performance and creativity, allows for early mistake detection and the initiative to take actions, and reduces emotional exhaustion."[43]

Team leaders are also responsible for managing external relationships. Team leaders act as the bridge or liaison between their teams and other teams, departments, and divisions in a company. For example, if a member of Team A complains about the quality of Team B's work, Team A's leader is responsible for solving the problem by initiating a meeting with Team B's leader. Together, these team leaders are responsible for getting members of both teams to work together to solve the problem. If it's done right, the problem is solved without involving company management or blaming members of the other team.[44]

In summary, because of these critical differences, team leaders who don't understand how their roles are different from those of traditional managers often struggle in their jobs.

You will learn more about teams in Chapter 10.

 # 1-4 MANAGERIAL ROLES

Although all four types of managers engage in planning, organizing, leading, and controlling, if you were to follow them around during a typical day on the job, you would probably not use these terms to describe what they actually do. Rather, what you'd see are the various roles managers play. Professor Henry Mintzberg followed five American CEOs, shadowing each for a week and analyzing their mail, their conversations, and their actions. He concluded that managers fulfill three major roles while performing their jobs—interpersonal, informational, and decisional.[45]

In other words, managers talk to people, gather and give information, and make decisions. Furthermore, as shown in Exhibit 1.3, these three major roles can be subdivided into 10 subroles.

*Let's examine each major role—**1-4a interpersonal roles**, **1-4b informational roles**, and **1-4c decisional roles**—and their 10 subroles.*

1-4a Interpersonal Roles

More than anything else, management jobs are people-intensive. When asked about her experience as a first-time CEO, Kim Bowers, CEO of CST Brands, said, "We have 12,000 employees. [So,] I spend a lot of time out in the field with them."[46] Estimates vary with the level of management, but most managers spend between two-thirds and four-fifths of their time in face-to-face communication with others.[47] If you're a loner, or if you consider dealing with people a pain, then you may not be cut out for management work. In fulfilling the interpersonal role of management, managers perform three subroles: figurehead, leader, and liaison.

Interpersonal Roles

- Figurehead
- Leader
- Liaison

Informational Roles

- Monitor
- Disseminator
- Spokesperson

Decisional Roles

- Entrepreneur
- Disturbance Handler
- Resource Allocator
- Negotiator

Source: Adapted from "The Manager's Job: Folklore and Fact," by Mintzberg, H. *Harvard Business Review*, July–August 1975.

In the **figurehead role**, managers perform ceremonial duties such as greeting company visitors, speaking at the opening of a new facility, or representing the company at a community luncheon to support local charities. When **Fendi**, the Italian fashion house, launched a design initiative to raise money for charity, CEO Pietro Beccari hosted a gala at the company's recently opened flagship store in New York City.[48]

In the **leader role**, managers motivate and encourage workers to accomplish organizational objectives. One way managers can act as leaders is to establish challenging goals. Ken Switzer, CFO of Marcos Pizza, a 1,000-store pizza franchiser, says, "Franchisee profitability is what we call our WIG—our wildly important goal. Some people call it their BHAG—the big hairy audacious goal. It's the thing that drives us."[49] The BHAG for Marcos Pizza is growing franchisees' store sales by 20 percent a year.

In the **liaison role**, managers deal with people outside their units. Studies consistently indicate that managers spend as much time with outsiders as they do with their own subordinates and their own bosses. For example, CEOs often sit on other companies' boards. CEO Stephen Zarrilli, of Safeguard Scientifics, which invests in high-growth health care and technology firms, says, "When you sit on another company's board, you gain perspective—not only about the company and its industry—but, more importantly, about other operating methodologies, governance, and viewpoints that can be very beneficial when you bring them back to your company."[50] Indeed, companies in low-growth, highly competitive industries whose CEOs sit on outside boards earn an average return on assets 15 percent higher than companies with CEOs who don't sit on outside boards![51]

1-4b Informational Roles

Not only do managers spend most of their time in face-to-face contact with others, they spend much of it obtaining and sharing information. Mintzberg found that the managers in his study spent 40 percent of their time giving and getting information from others. In this regard, management can be viewed as gathering information by scanning the business environment and listening to others in face-to-face conversations, processing that information, and then sharing it with people both inside and outside the company. Mintzberg described three informational subroles: monitor, disseminator, and spokesperson.

In the **monitor role**, managers scan their environment for information, actively contact others for information, and, because of their personal contacts, receive a great deal of unsolicited information. Besides receiving firsthand information, managers monitor their environment by reading local newspapers and the *Wall Street Journal* to keep track of customers, competitors, and technological changes that may affect their businesses. Today's managers can subscribe to electronic monitoring and distribution services that track the news wires (Associated Press, Reuters, and so on) for stories and social media posts related to their businesses. These services deliver customized news that only includes topics the managers specify. Business Wire (http://www.businesswire.com) monitors and distributes daily news headlines from major industries (for example automotive, banking and financial, health, high tech).[52] Glean (http://www.glean.info) does real-time monitoring of Twitter, Facebook, LinkedIn, and Instagram

Figurehead role the interpersonal role managers play when they perform ceremonial duties

Leader role the interpersonal role managers play when they motivate and encourage workers to accomplish organizational objectives

Liaison role the interpersonal role managers play when they deal with people outside their units

Monitor role the informational role managers play when they scan their environment for information

Companies Must Improve at Spotting Management Talent

If you work in a large organization, getting anointed as a HIPO (high potential) is a mark of early success, as it indicates a strong belief in your management potential. Typically, HIPOs are thought to be in top 5 percent of those with management potential. However, follow-up research of 1,964 HIPOs from three organizations indicated that 12 percent were in the bottom quarter and that 42 percent overall were below average in management potential! What went wrong?

While these non-HIPOs had technical and professional expertise, took initiative and produced results, honored their commitments, and fit their organizations' cultures, they weren't strategic and had difficulty motivating others. Were they bad employees? No, they were great individual contributors. But, they weren't well suited for management. And putting them in managerial roles not only hurt them, it hurt employees and the company.

Ilia Uriadnikov/123RF

Source: J. Zenger & J. Folkman, "Companies Are Bat at Identifying High-Potential Employees," *Harvard Business Review*, February 20, 2017, accessed March 9, 2017, https://hbr.org/2017/02/companies-are-bad-at-identifying-high-potential-employees.

---

feeds, as well as 60,000 global news outlets in 250 languages in 191 countries.[53] It also offers CyberAlert Social, which monitors roughly 25 million individual social media posts daily across 190 million social media sources worldwide. Brandwatch and ViralHeat are additional tools. Another site, Federal News Service (http://fednews.com), provides subscribers with precision alerts and monitoring of federal hearings (via complete transcripts), bills, and policy proposals that may affect their company or industry.[54]

Because of their numerous personal contacts and their access to subordinates, managers are often hubs for the distribution of critical information. In the **disseminator role**, managers share the information they have collected with their subordinates and others in the company. At Qualtrics, a software company that provides sophisticated online survey research tools, CEO Ryan Smith makes sure that everyone in the company is clear on company goals and plans. Every Monday, employees are asked via email to respond to two questions: "What are you going to get done this week? And what did you get done last week that you said you were going to do?" Smith says, "Then that rolls up into one email that the entire organization gets. So if someone's got a question, they can look at that for an explanation. We share other information, too—every time we have a meeting, we release meeting notes to the organization. When we have a board meeting, we write a letter about it afterward and send it to the organization." Qualtrics also uses an internal database where each quarter

AP Images/Keith Srakocic

H.J. Heinz Company CEO Bernardo Hees acts as a spokesperson for his company.

Disseminator role the informational role managers play when they share information with others in their departments or companies employees enter their plans for meeting the company's objectives. Those plans are then made visible to everyone else at Qualtrics.[55]

In contrast to the disseminator role, in which managers distribute information to employees inside the company, managers in the **spokesperson role** share information with people outside their departments or companies. One of the most common ways that CEOs act as spokespeople for their companies is speaking at annual meetings and on conference calls with shareholders or boards of directors. CEOs also serve as spokespeople to the media when their companies are involved in major news stories. After Foxconn Technology Group, best known as the manufacturer of Apple iPhones, paid $3.88 billion for a 60 percent ownership of Sharp, the maker of home appliances, document systems (multifunctional printers and copiers), robotics and TV/audio equipment, new CEO Tai Jeng-wu, who became CEO as part of the takeover, announced, "My mission as the leader of Sharp is to turn around this company without any further delay."[56] With losses of more than $2 billion a year, Mr. Tai also indicated that Sharp would restructure and that layoffs would be needed to reduce costs. Tai said that Sharp would also seek to cancel licensing deals, in which Sharp had licensed its name to other companies, permitting them to sell consumer electronics, such as TVs, using Sharp's brand name. Tai said, "We want to polish Sharp's brand value by ourselves and make it shine globally."[57]

1-4c Decisional Roles

Mintzberg found that obtaining and sharing information is not an end in itself. Obtaining and sharing information with people inside and outside the company is useful to managers because it helps them make good decisions. According to Mintzberg, managers engage in four decisional subroles: entrepreneur, disturbance handler, resource allocator, and negotiator.

In the **entrepreneur role**, managers adapt themselves, their subordinates, and their units to change. Faced with near zero interest rates, glacially slow economic growth, and an aging customer base, Ogaki Kyoritsu Bank (OKB) in Ogaki, Japan, has been forced to innovate to grow its business. President Takashi Tsuchiya says, "With these interest rates, you might make more money selling 10 OKB chocolates instead of managing a million yen (about US$8,600) in deposits."[58] OKB chocolates? Yes, and an OKB farm,

OKB rice, and OKB radio studio. Legally, OKB can't run those businesses, so it pays them to use the OKB brand name. To encourage customer growth, OKB uses roulette, dice, pinball and slot machines to dispense cash awards when customers make deposits or withdrawals. Says Tsuchiya, "We're not a bank, we're a service company. If you're going to go to the bank, it should be fun."[59]

In the **disturbance handler role**, managers respond to pressures and problems so severe that they demand immediate attention and action. When hurricanes threaten Waffle House restaurants, the Waffle House Index indicates if a restaurant is open and serving a full menu (green), open, serving water and a reduced menu, but without power (yellow), or not open (red). Vice president Pat Warner says, "We're a 24-hour restaurant, so oddly enough shutting down is a big deal for us."[60] Jump teams from headquarters are sent ahead of the storms with emergency supplies and generators. Warner said, "A lot of times, especially after a big storm, we're the only ones still open because we've got generators. Right after storms, business is brisk. We have a lot of people come in and are only able to get their first hot meal at a Waffle House."[61]

In the **resource allocator role**, managers decide who will get what resources and how many resources they will get. After Apple, Alphabet (formerly Google) is the second most profitable company in the world. For years, it grew so fast, with revenues greatly exceeding costs, that budgets, much less budget discipline, didn't matter (if ever used at all). When founders Larry Page and Sergey Brin hired CFO Ruth Porat, they did so to get Alphabet's businesses to make and stick to their budgets. Alphabet Chairman Eric Schmidt admits, "Before she was there, we had lost discipline."[62] Alphabet makes 95 percent of its revenue from online ads, meaning Google search, YouTube, and mobile ads (mostly on Android phones). But

Ken Wolter/123RF

Spokesperson role the informational role managers play when they share information with people outside their departments or companies

Entrepreneur role the decisional role managers play when they adapt themselves, their subordinates, and their units to change

Disturbance handler role the decisional role managers play when they respond to severe pressures and problems that demand immediate action

Resource allocator role the decisional role managers play when they decide who gets what resources and in what amounts in the rest of Alphabet (Nest thermostats, Google Ventures, Google Fiber), expenses far exceed revenues. So Porat is instilling discipline by cutting budgets, by approving video conferences rather than business travel, by charging the business units for using Alphabet's functions (legal, human resources, and public relations). Chairman Schmidt says, "The cost cutting is real, and it's the right thing to be done, and it's driven by [Porat]."[63]

In the **negotiator role**, managers negotiate schedules, projects, goals, outcomes, resources, and employee raises. Twenty of the US's largest companies, including American Express, IBM, Marriott, Shell Oil, and Verizon Communications, have formed the Health Transformation Alliance (HTA) to negotiate lower drug and medical costs. Kevin Cox, chief human resource office at American Express, says, "Even the most successful companies won't be able to afford the rising costs of health care in the not too distant future."[64] At a time when health care spending is increasing 6 to 8 percent per year, the HTA expects to lower drug costs by 15 percent for their 6 million employees. Kyu Rhee, IBM's chief health officer says, "This is the group that's paying the bill. We're not waiting for the public sector to come up with the solution—we have the skills and expertise to do this ourselves."[65]

1-5 WHAT COMPANIES LOOK FOR IN MANAGERS

I didn't have the slightest idea what my job was. I walked in giggling and laughing because I had been promoted and had no idea what principles or style to be guided by. After the first day, I felt like I had run into a brick wall. (Sales Representative #1)

Suddenly, I found myself saying, boy, I can't be responsible for getting all that revenue. I don't have the time. Suddenly you've got to go from [taking care of] yourself and say

now I'm the manager, and what does a manager do? It takes awhile thinking about it for it to really hit you . . . a manager gets things done through other people. That's a very, very hard transition to make. (Sales Representative #2)[66]

The preceding statements were made by two star sales representatives who, on the basis of their superior performance, were promoted to the position of sales manager. At first they did not feel confident about their ability to do their jobs as managers. Like most new managers, these sales managers suddenly realized that the knowledge, skills, and abilities that led to success early in their careers (and were probably responsible for their promotion into the ranks of management) would not necessarily help them succeed as managers. As sales representatives, they were responsible only for managing their own performance. But as sales managers, they were now directly responsible for supervising all of the sales representatives in their sales territories. Furthermore, they were now directly accountable for whether those sales representatives achieved their sales goals. If performance in nonmanagerial jobs doesn't necessarily prepare you for a managerial job, then what does it take to be a manager?

When companies look for employees who would be good managers, they look for individuals who have technical skills, human skills, conceptual skills, and the motivation to manage.[67] Exhibit 1.4 shows the relative importance of these four skills to the jobs of team leaders, first-line managers, middle managers, and top managers.

Technical skills are the specialized procedures, techniques, and knowledge required to get the job done. For the sales managers described previously, technical skills involve the ability to find new sales prospects, develop accurate sales pitches based on customer needs, and close sales. For a nurse supervisor, technical skills include being able to insert an IV or operate a crash cart if a patient goes into cardiac arrest.

Technical skills are most important for team leaders and lower-level managers because they supervise the workers who produce products or serve

Negotiator role the decisional role managers play when they negotiate schedules, projects, goals, outcomes, resources, and employee raises

Technical skills the specialized procedures, techniques, and knowledge required to get the job done

LOVE THE JOB? YOUR BOSS HAS TECHNICAL SKILLS

When companies look for employees who could be good managers, they look for technical, human and conceptual skills, and the motivation to manage. Technical skills are the specialized procedures, techniques, and knowledge required to get the job done. Technical skills are most important for team leaders and lower-level managers, and for training new employees and helping them solve problems. Generally, technical skills become less important as managers rise through the managerial ranks, but they are still important. The question is, why?

It turns out, employees are much happier if they work for a boss with technical skills. A study of 35,000 randomly selected employees in the United States and the United Kingdom found that, "having a highly competent boss is easily the largest positive influence on a typical worker's level of job satisfaction." Highly competent was defined as being able to do the employees job, working one's way up inside the company, and whether the employee felt the boss possessed technical competence.

So, yes, technical skills become less important the higher you go. But, they always matter to those you manage.

Source: B. Artz, A. Goodall & A. Oswald, "If Your Boss Could Do Your Job, You're More Likely to Be Happy at Work," Harvard Business Review, December 29, 2016, accessed March 9, 2017, https://hbr.org/2016/12/if-your-boss-could-do-your-job-youre-more-likely-to-be-happy-at-work.

customers. Team leaders and first-line managers need technical knowledge and skills to train new employees and help employees solve problems. Technical knowledge and skills are also needed to troubleshoot problems that employees can't handle. Technical skills become less important as managers rise through the managerial ranks, but they are still important.

Human skills can be summarized as the ability to work well with others. Managers with human skills work effectively within groups, encourage others to express their thoughts and feelings, are sensitive to others' needs and viewpoints, and are good listeners and communicators. Human skills are equally important at all levels of management, from team leaders to CEOs. However, because lower-level managers spend much of their time solving technical problems, upper-level managers may actually spend more time dealing directly with people. On average, first-line managers spend 57 percent of their time with people, but that percentage increases to 63 percent for middle managers and 78 percent for top managers.[68]

Conceptual skills are the ability to see the organization as a whole, to understand how the different parts of the company affect each other, and to recognize how the company fits into or is affected by its external environment such as the local community, social and economic forces, customers, and the competition. Good managers have to be able to recognize, understand, and reconcile multiple complex problems and perspectives. In other words, managers have to be smart! In fact, intelligence makes so much difference for managerial performance that managers with above-average intelligence typically outperform managers of average intelligence by approximately 48 percent.[69] Clearly, companies need to be careful to promote smart workers into management. Conceptual skills increase in importance as managers rise through the management hierarchy.

Good management involves much more than

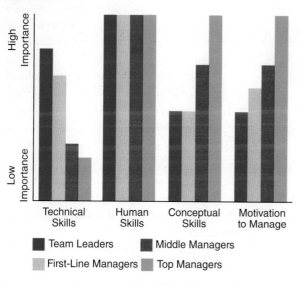

Exhibit 1.4
Management Skills

High Importance / Low Importance

Technical Skills | Human Skills | Conceptual Skills | Motivation to Manage

■ Team Leaders   ■ Middle Managers
▫ First-Line Managers   ▪ Top Managers

Human skills the ability to work well with others

Conceptual skills the ability to see the organization as a whole, understand how the different parts affect each other, and recognize how the company fits into or is affected by its environment intelligence, however. For example, making the department genius a manager can be disastrous if that genius lacks technical skills, human skills, or one other factor known as the motivation to manage. **Motivation to manage** is an assessment of how motivated employees are to interact with superiors, participate in competitive situations, behave assertively toward others, tell others what to do, reward good behavior and punish poor behavior, perform actions that are highly visible to others, and handle and organize administrative tasks. Managers typically have a stronger motivation to manage than their subordinates, and managers at higher levels usually have a stronger motivation to manage than managers at lower levels. Furthermore, managers with a stronger motivation to manage are promoted faster, are rated as better managers by their employees, and earn more money than managers with a weak motivation to manage.[70]

1-6 MISTAKES MANAGERS MAKE

Another way to understand what it takes to be a manager is to look at the mistakes managers make. In other words, we can learn just as much from what managers shouldn't do as from what they should do. Exhibit 1.5 lists the top 10 mistakes managers make.

Several studies of U.S. and British managers have compared "arrivers," or managers who made it all the way to the top of their companies, with "derailers," or managers who were successful early in their careers but were knocked off the fast track by the time they reached the middle to upper levels of management.[71] The researchers found that there were only a few differences between arrivers and derailers. For the most part, both groups were talented, and both groups had weaknesses. But what distinguished derailers from arrivers was that derailers possessed two or more fatal flaws with respect to the way they managed people. Although arrivers were by no means perfect, they usually had no more than one fatal flaw or had found ways to minimize the effects of their flaws on the people with whom they worked.

The top mistake made by derailers was that they were insensitive to others by virtue of their abrasive, intimidating, and bullying management style. The authors of one study described a manager who walked into his

Motivation to manage
an assessment of how enthusiastic employees are about managing the work of others

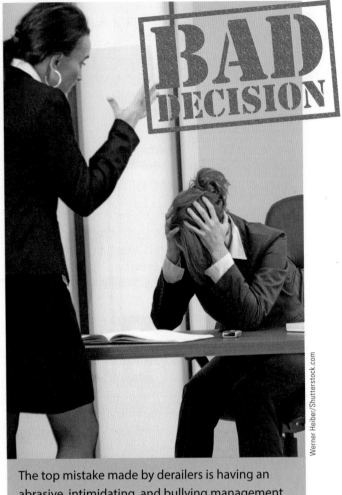

Chrisdorney/Shutterstock.com

Werner Heiber/Shutterstock.com

The top mistake made by derailers is having an abrasive, intimidating, and bullying management style.

Exhibit 1.5
Top 10 Mistakes Managers Make

1. Insensitive to others: abrasive, intimidating, bullying style
2. Cold, aloof, arrogant
3. Betrays trust
4. Overly ambitious: thinking of next job, playing politics
5. Specific performance problems with the business
6. Overmanaging: unable to delegate or build a team
7. Unable to staff effectively
8. Unable to think strategically
9. Unable to adapt to boss with different style
10. Overdependent on advocate or mentor

Source: M. W. McCall, Jr., and M. M. Lombardo, "What Makes a Top Executive?" *Psychology Today*, February 1983, 26–31.

subordinate's office and interrupted a meeting by saying, "I need to see you." When the subordinate tried to explain that he was not available because he was in the middle of a meeting, the manager barked, "I don't give a damn. I said I wanted to see you now."[72] Not surprisingly, only 25 percent of derailers were rated by others as being good with people, compared to 75 percent of arrivers.

The second mistake was that derailers were often cold, aloof, or arrogant. Although this sounds like insensitivity to others, it has more to do with derailed managers being so smart, so expert in their areas of knowledge, that they treated others with contempt because they weren't experts, too.[73] For example, AT&T called in an industrial psychologist to counsel its vice president of human resources because she had been blamed for "ruffling too many feathers" at the company.[74] Interviews with the vice president's coworkers and subordinates revealed that they thought she was brilliant, was "smarter and faster than other people," "generates a lot of ideas," and "loves to deal with complex issues." Unfortunately, these smarts were accompanied by a cold, aloof, and arrogant management style. The people she worked with complained that she does "too much too fast," treats coworkers with "disdain," "impairs teamwork," "doesn't always show her warm side," and has "burned too many bridges."[75]

The third mistake made by derailers involved betraying a trust. Betraying a trust doesn't mean being dishonest. Instead, it means making others look bad by not doing what you said you would do when you said you would do it. That mistake, in itself, is not fatal because managers and their workers aren't machines. Tasks go undone in every company every day. There's always too much to do and not enough time, people, money, or resources to do it. The fatal betrayal of trust is failing to inform others when things will not be done right or on time. This failure to admit mistakes, failure to quickly inform others of the mistakes, failure to take responsibility for the mistakes, and failure to fix the mistakes without blaming others clearly distinguished the behavior of derailers from arrivers.

The fourth mistake was being overly political and ambitious. Managers who always have their eye on their next job rarely establish more than superficial relationships with peers and coworkers. In their haste to gain credit for successes that would be noticed by upper management, they make the fatal mistake of treating people as though they don't matter. An employee with an overly ambitious boss described him this way: "He treats employees coldly, even cruelly. He assigns

blame without regard to responsibility, and takes all the credit for himself. I once had such a boss, and he gave me a new definition of shared risk: If something I did was successful, he took the credit. If it wasn't, I got the blame."[76]

The fatal mistakes of being unable to delegate, build a team, and staff effectively indicate that many derailed managers were unable to make the most basic transition to managerial work: to quit being hands-on doers and get work done through others. In fact, according to an article in *Harvard Business Review*, up to 50 percent of new managers fail because they cannot make the transition from producing to managing.[77] Two things go wrong when managers make these mistakes. First, when managers meddle in decisions that their subordinates should be making—when they can't stop being doers—they alienate the people who work for them. Rich Dowd, founder of Dowd Associates, an executive search firm, admits to constantly monitoring and interrupting employees because they weren't doing the job "in the way I saw fit, even when their work was outstanding." According to Richard Kilburg of Johns Hopkins University, when managers interfere with workers' decisions, "You . . . have a tendency to lose your most creative people. They're able to say, 'Screw this. I'm not staying here.'"[78] Indeed, one employee told Dowd that if he was going to do her job for her, she would quit. Second, because they are trying to do their subordinates' jobs in addition to their own, managers who fail to delegate will not have enough time to do much of anything well. An office assistant to a Washington politician came in to work every day to find a long to-do list waiting on her desk, detailing everything she was expected to get done that day, along with how to do it, who to call, and when to give her boss updates on her progress. She said, "Sometimes, this list was three or four pages long. It must have taken him at least an hour to create."[79]

1-7 THE TRANSITION TO MANAGEMENT: THE FIRST YEAR

In her book *Becoming a Manager: Mastery of a New Identity*, Harvard Business School professor Linda Hill followed the development of 19 people in their first year as managers. Her study found that becoming a manager produced a profound psychological transition that changed the way these managers viewed

Exhibit 1.6
Stages in the Transition to Management

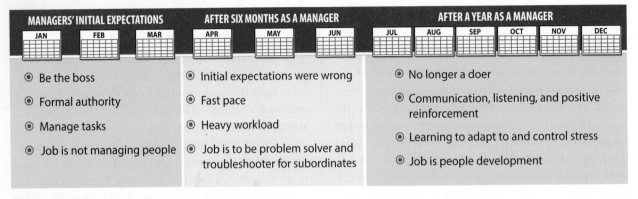

MANAGERS' INITIAL EXPECTATIONS			AFTER SIX MONTHS AS A MANAGER			AFTER A YEAR AS A MANAGER					
JAN	FEB	MAR	APR	MAY	JUN	JUL	AUG	SEP	OCT	NOV	DEC

MANAGERS' INITIAL EXPECTATIONS
- Be the boss
- Formal authority
- Manage tasks
- Job is not managing people

AFTER SIX MONTHS AS A MANAGER
- Initial expectations were wrong
- Fast pace
- Heavy workload
- Job is to be problem solver and troubleshooter for subordinates

AFTER A YEAR AS A MANAGER
- No longer a doer
- Communication, listening, and positive reinforcement
- Learning to adapt to and control stress
- Job is people development

Source: L.A. Hill, *Becoming a Manager: Mastery of a New Identity* (Boston: Harvard Business School Press, 1992).

themselves and others. As shown in Exhibit 1.6, the evolution of the managers' thoughts, expectations, and realities over the course of their first year in management reveals the magnitude of the changes they experienced.

Initially, the managers in Hill's study believed that their job was to exercise formal authority and to manage tasks—basically being the boss, telling others what to do, making decisions, and getting things done. One of the managers Hill interviewed said, "Being the manager means running my own office, using my ideas and thoughts." Another said, "[The office is] my baby. It's my job to make sure it works."[80] In fact, most of the new managers were attracted to management positions because they wanted to be in charge. Surprisingly, the new managers did not believe that their job was to manage people. The only aspects of people management mentioned by the new managers were hiring and firing.

After six months, most of the new managers had concluded that their initial expectations about managerial work were wrong. Management wasn't just about being the boss, making decisions, and telling others what to do. The first surprise was the fast pace and heavy workload involved. Said one of Hill's managers, "This job is much harder than you think. It is 40 to 50 percent more work than being a producer! Who would have ever guessed?" The pace of managerial work was startling, too. Another manager said, "You have eight or nine people looking for your time . . . coming into and out of your office all day long." A somewhat frustrated manager declared that management was "a job that never ended . . . a job you couldn't get your hands around."[81]

Informal descriptions like these are consistent with studies indicating that the average first-line manager spends no more than two minutes on a task before being interrupted by a request from a subordinate, a phone call, or an email. The pace is somewhat less hurried for top managers, who spend an average of approximately nine minutes on a task before having to switch to another. In practice, this means that supervisors may perform 30 tasks per hour, while top managers perform seven tasks per hour, with each task typically different from the one that preceded it. A manager described this frenetic level of activity by saying, "The only time you are in control is when you shut

IQoncept/Shutterstock.com

your door, and then I feel I am not doing the job I'm supposed to be doing, which is being with the people."[82]

The other major surprise after six months on the job was that the managers' expectations about what they should do as managers were very different from their subordinates' expectations. Initially, the managers defined their jobs as helping their subordinates perform their jobs well. For the managers, who still defined themselves as doers rather than managers, assisting their subordinates meant going out on sales calls or handling customer complaints. One manager said, "I like going out with the rep, who may need me to lend him my credibility as manager. I like the challenge, the joy in closing. I go out with the reps and we make the call and talk about the customer; it's fun."[83] But when new managers "assisted" in this way, their subordinates were resentful and viewed their help as interference. The subordinates wanted their managers to help them by solving problems that they couldn't solve themselves. After the managers realized this distinction, they embraced their role as problem solver and troubleshooter. Thus, they could help without interfering with their subordinates' jobs.

After a year on the job, most of the managers thought of themselves as managers and no longer as doers. In making the transition, they finally realized that people management was the most important part of their job. One of Hill's interviewees summarized the lesson that had taken him a year to learn by saying, "As many demands as managers have on their time, I think their primary responsibility is people development. Not production, but people development."[84] Another indication of how much their views had changed was that most of the managers now regretted the rather heavy-handed approach they had used in their early attempts to manage their subordinates. "I wasn't good at managing . . . , so I was bossy like a first-grade teacher." "Now I see that I started out as a drill sergeant. I was inflexible, just a lot of how-tos." By the end of the year, most of the managers had abandoned their authoritarian approach for one based on communication, listening, and positive reinforcement.

Finally, after beginning their year as managers in frustration, the managers came to feel comfortable with their subordinates, with the demands of their jobs, and with their emerging managerial styles. While being managers had made them acutely aware of their limitations and their need to develop as people, it also provided them with an unexpected reward of coaching and developing the people who worked for them. One manager said, "It gives me the best feeling to see somebody do something well after I have helped them. I get excited." Another stated, "I realize now that when I accepted the position of branch manager that it is truly an exciting vocation. It is truly awesome, even at this level; it can be terribly challenging and terribly exciting."[85]

1-8 COMPETITIVE ADVANTAGE THROUGH PEOPLE

If you walk down the aisle of the business section in your local bookstore, you'll find hundreds of books that explain precisely what companies need to do to be successful. Unfortunately, the best-selling business books tend to be faddish, changing dramatically every few years. One thing that hasn't changed, though, is the importance of good people and good management: companies can't succeed for long without them. Apple CEO Tim Cook agrees, saying, "I think about my day and weeks and months and years—I put them in three buckets: people, strategy, and execution. I sort of move between those on a daily basis as to where I put my time. I always think the most important one of those is people. If you don't get that one right, it doesn't matter what kind of energy you have in the other two—it's not enough."[86]

In his books *Competitive Advantage through People: Unleashing the Power of the Work Force* and *The Human Equation: Building Profits by Putting People First*, Stanford University business professor Jeffrey Pfeffer contends that what separates top-performing companies from their competitors is the way they treat their workforces—in other words, their management style.[87]

Pfeffer found that managers in top-performing companies used ideas such as employment security, selective hiring, self-managed teams and decentralization, high pay contingent on company performance, extensive training, reduced status distinctions (between managers and employees), and extensive sharing of financial information to achieve financial performance that, on average, was 40 percent higher than that of other companies. These ideas, which are explained in detail in Exhibit 1.7, help organizations develop workforces that are smarter, better trained, more motivated, and more committed than their competitors' workforces. And—as indicated by the phenomenal growth and return on investment earned by these companies—smarter, better trained, more motivated, and more committed workforces provide superior products and service to customers. Such customers keep buying and, by telling others about their positive experiences, bring in new customers.

According to Pfeffer, companies that invest in their people will create long-lasting competitive advantages that are difficult for other companies to duplicate. Other studies also clearly demonstrate that sound management practices can produce substantial advantages in four critical

Exhibit 1.7
Competitive Advantage Through People: Management Practices

1. Employment Security—Employment security is the ultimate form of commitment companies can make to their workers. Employees can innovate and increase company productivity without fearing the loss of their jobs.

2. Selective Hiring—If employees are the basis for a company's competitive advantage, and those employees have employment security, then the company needs to aggressively recruit and selectively screen applicants in order to hire the most talented employees available.

3. Self-Managed Teams and Decentralization—Self-managed teams are responsible for their own hiring, purchasing, job assignments, and production. Self-managed teams can often produce enormous increases in productivity through increased employee commitment and creativity. Decentralization allows employees who are closest to (and most knowledgeable about) problems, production, and customers to make timely decisions. Decentralization increases employee satisfaction and commitment.

4. High Wages Contingent on Organizational Performance—High wages are needed to attract and retain talented workers and to indicate that the organization values its workers. Employees, like company founders, shareholders, and managers, need to share in the financial rewards when the company is successful. Why? Because employees who have a financial stake in their companies are more likely to take a long-run view of the business and think like business owners.

5. Training and Skill Development—Like a high-tech company that spends millions of dollars to upgrade computers or research and development labs, a company whose competitive advantage is based on its people must invest in the training and skill development of its people.

6. Reduction of Status Differences—A company should treat everyone, no matter what the job, as equal. There are no reserved parking spaces. Everyone eats in the same cafeteria and has similar benefits. The result is improved communication as employees focus on problems and solutions rather than on how they are less valued than managers.

7. Sharing Information—If employees are to make decisions that are good for the long-term health and success of the company, they need to be given information about costs, finances, productivity, development times, and strategies that was previously known only by company managers.

Source: J. Pfeffer, *The Human Equation: Building Profits by Putting People First* (Boston: Harvard Business School Press, 1996).

areas of organizational performance: sales revenues, profits, stock market returns, and customer satisfaction.

In terms of sales revenues and profits, a study of nearly 1,000 U.S. firms found that companies that use *just some* of the ideas shown in Exhibit 1.7 had $27,044 more sales per employee and $3,814 more profit per employee than companies that didn't. For a 100-person company, these differences amount to $2.7 million more in sales and nearly $400,000 more in annual profit! For a 1,000-person company, the difference grows to $27 million more in sales and $4 million more in annual profit![88]

Another study that considers the effect of investing in people on company sales found that poorly performing companies were able to improve their average return on investment from 5.1 percent to 19.7 percent and increase sales by $94,000 per employee. They did this by adopting management techniques as simple as setting performance expectations (establishing goals, results, and schedules), coaching (informal, ongoing discussions between managers and subordinates about what is being done well and what could be done better), reviewing employee performance (annual, formal discussion about results), and rewarding employee performance (adjusting salaries and bonuses based on employee performance and results).[89] Two decades of research across 92 companies indicates that the average increase in company performance from using these management practices is typically around

20 percent.[90] That fits with another study of 2,000 firms showing that an average improvement in management practices can produce a 10-20 percent increase in the total value of a company.[91] In addition to significantly improving the profitability of healthy companies, sound management practices can also turn around failing companies.

To determine how investing in people affects stock market performance, researchers matched companies on *Fortune* magazine's list of "100 Best Companies to Work for in America" with companies that were similar in industry, size, and—this is key—operating performance. Both sets of companies were equally good performers; the key difference was how well they treated their employees. For both sets of companies, the researchers found that employee attitudes such as job satisfaction changed little from year to year. The people who worked for the "100 Best" companies were consistently much more satisfied with their jobs and employers year after year than were employees in the matched companies. More importantly, those stable differences in employee attitudes were strongly related to differences in stock market performance. Over a three-year period, an investment in the "100 Best" would have resulted in an 82 percent cumulative stock return compared with just 37 percent for the matched companies.[92] This difference is remarkable given that both sets of companies were equally good performers at the beginning of the period.

No Shortcuts: Manage for the Long Run

It's frequently said that good managers "manage for the long run." That means incurring costs or making investments that might hurt short-term financial performance, but that benefit customers and the firm's competitive position in the long run. But, does "managing for the long run" actually work?

A 15-year study of 615 firms found that only 25 percent of companies actually manage for the long run by investing more in research and development or by being willing to miss short-term financial targets (short-term pain for long-term gain). But, compared to industry competitors, companies that managed for the long run had 47 percent higher revenues, 36 percent larger profits, and added 12,000 more jobs over 15 years.

Good management matters, but it makes a big difference when companies are managed for the long run. Don't manage for next quarter. Manage for the long run.

Source: D. Barton, J. Manyika & S. Heohane Williamson, "Finally, Proof That Managing for the Long Term Pays Off," *Harvard Business Review*," February 7, 2017, accessed March 9, 2017, https://hbr.org/2017/02/finally-proof-that-managing-for-the-long-term-pays-off.

Finally, research also indicates that managers have an important effect on customer satisfaction. Many people find this surprising. They don't understand how managers, who are largely responsible for what goes on inside the company, can affect what goes on outside the company. They wonder how managers, who often interact with customers under negative conditions (when customers are angry or dissatisfied), can actually improve customer satisfaction. It turns out that managers influence customer satisfaction through employee satisfaction. When employees are satisfied with their jobs, their bosses, and the companies they work for, they provide much better service to customers.[93] In turn, customers are more satisfied, too. In fact, customers of companies on *Fortune*'s list of "100 Best," where employees are much more satisfied with their jobs and their companies, have much higher customer satisfaction scores than do customers of comparable companies that are not on *Fortune*'s list. Over an eight-year period, that difference in customer satisfaction also resulted in a 14 percent annual stock market return for the "100 Best" companies compared to a 6 percent return for the overall stock market.[94]

You will learn more about the service-profit chain in Chapter 18 on managing service and manufacturing operations.

STUDY TOOLS 1

LOCATED IN TEXTBOOK

☐ Rip out and review chapter review card.

LOCATED AT WWW.CENGAGEBRAIN.COM

☐ Gain unique perspectives on key concepts with new 4LTR concept videos in the e-book.

☐ Increase your comprehension with Aplia for MGMT11.

☐ Complete interactive content within the e-book.

2 | The History of Management

After you finish this chapter, go to **PAGE 43** for **STUDY TOOLS**

LEARNING OUTCOMES

2-1 Explain the origins of management.

2-2 Explain the history of scientific management.

2-3 Discuss the history of bureaucratic and administrative management.

2-4 Explain the history of human relations management.

2-5 Discuss the history of operations, information, systems, and contingency management.

Mark Brodkin Photography/Moment/Getty Images

2-1 THE ORIGINS OF MANAGEMENT

Each day, managers are asked to solve challenging problems with limited time, people, and resources. Yet it's still their responsibility to get things done on schedule and within budget. Tell today's managers to "reward workers for improved production or performance," "set specific goals to increase motivation," or "innovate to create and sustain a competitive advantage," and they'll respond, "Duh! Who doesn't know that?" A mere 125 years ago, however, business ideas and practices were so different that today's widely accepted management ideas would have been as self-evident as space travel, smart phones, and flying drones. In fact, management jobs and careers didn't exist 125 years ago, so management was not yet a field of study. Now, of course, managers and management are such an important part of the business world that it's hard to imagine organizations without them.

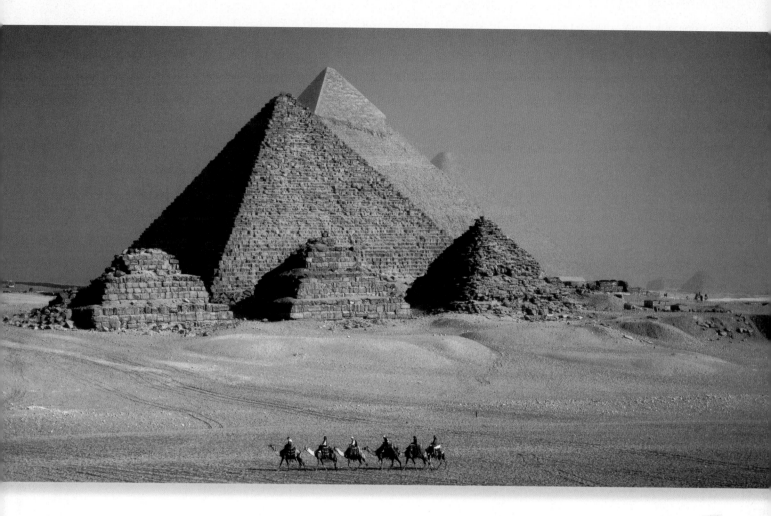

So if there were no managers 125 years ago, but you can't walk down the hall today without bumping into one, where did management come from?

Although we can find the seeds of many of today's management ideas throughout history, not until the past few centuries did systematic changes in the nature of work and organizations create a compelling need for managers.

2-1a Management Ideas and Practices throughout History

Examples of management thought and practice can be found throughout history.[1] For example, the earliest recorded instance of information management dates to ancient Sumer (modern Iraq), *circa* 8000–3000 BCE. Sumerian businesses used small clay tokens to calculate quantities of grain and livestock—and later, value-added goods such as perfume or pottery—that they owned and traded in temples and at city gates. Different shapes and sizes represented different types and quantities of goods. The tokens were also used to store data. They were kept in small clay envelopes, and the token shapes were impressed on the outside of the envelope to indicate what was inside. Eventually, someone figured out that it was easier to just write these symbols with a stylus on a tablet instead of using the tokens. In the end, the new technology of *writing* led to more efficient management of the business of Sumerian temples.[2]

A task as enormous as building the great pyramids in Egypt was bound to present practical problems that would lead to the development of management ideas. Egyptians recognized the need for planning, organizing, and controlling; for submitting written requests; and for consulting staff for advice before making decisions. The enormity of the task they faced is evident in the pyramid of King Khufu, which contains 2.3 million blocks of stone. Each block had to be quarried, cut to precise size and shape, cured (hardened in the sun), transported by boat for two to three days, moved to the construction site, numbered to identify where it would be placed, and then shaped and smoothed so that it would fit perfectly into place. It took 20,000 workers 23 years to complete this pyramid; more than 8,000 were needed just to quarry and transport the stones. A typical quarry expedition might include 100 army officers, 50 government and religious officials, and 200 members of the king's court to lead; 130 stonemasons to cut the stones; and 5,000 soldiers, 800 barbarians, and 2,000 bond servants to load and unload the stones from the ships.[3]

Exhibit 2.1 shows how other management ideas and practices throughout history relate to the management functions we discuss in this textbook.

2-1b Why We Need Managers Today

Working from 8:00 a.m. to 5:00 p.m., coffee breaks, lunch hours, crushing rush hour traffic, and endless emails and nonstop meetings are things we associate with today's working world. Work hasn't always been this way, however. In fact, the design of jobs and organizations has changed dramatically over the past 500 years. For most of humankind's history, for example, people didn't commute to work.[4] Work usually occurred in homes or on farms. In 1720, almost 80 percent of the 5.5 million people in England lived and worked in the country. And as recently as 1870, two-thirds of Americans earned their living from agriculture. Even most of those who didn't earn their living from agriculture didn't commute to work. Blacksmiths, furniture makers, leather goods makers, and other skilled tradespeople or craftspeople who formed trade guilds (the historical predecessors of labor unions) in England as early as 1093 typically worked out of shops in or next to their homes.[5] Likewise, cottage workers worked with each other out of small homes that were often built in a semicircle. A family in each cottage would complete a different production step, and work passed from one cottage to the next until production was complete. With small, self-organized work groups, no commute, no bosses, and no common building, there wasn't a strong need for management.

Exhibit 2.1
Management Ideas and Practices throughout History

Time	Individual or Group	Planning	Organizing	Leading	Controlling	Contributions to Management Thought and Practice
5000 BCE	Sumerians				√	Written record keeping
4000 BCE to 2000 BCE	Egyptians	√	√		√	Planning, organizing, and controlling to build the pyramids; submitting requests in writing; making decisions after consulting staff for advice
1800 BCE	Hammurabi				√	Controls and using witnesses in legal cases
600 BCE	Nebuchadnezzar		√	√		Wage incentives and production control
500 BCE	Sun Tzu	√		√		Strategy and identifying and attacking opponents' weaknesses
400 BCE	Xenophon	√	√	√	√	Management as separate art
400 BCE	Cyrus		√	√	√	Human relations and motion study
175	Cato		√			Job descriptions
284	Diocletian		√			Delegation of authority
900	al-Farabi			√		Leadership traits
1100	Ghazali			√		Managerial traits
1418	Barbarigo		√			Different organizational forms/structures
1436	Venetians				√	Numbering, standardization, and interchangeability of parts
1500	Sir Thomas More			√		Critique of poor management and leadership
1525	Machiavelli	√	√			Cohesiveness, power, and leadership in organizations

Source: C. S. George Jr., *The History of Management Thought* (Englewood Cliffs, NJ: Prentice Hall, 1972).

During the Industrial Revolution (1750–1900), however, jobs and organizations changed dramatically.[6] First, unskilled laborers running machines began to replace high-paid, skilled artisans. This change was made possible by the availability of power (steam engines and, later, electricity) as well as numerous related inventions, including Darby's coke-smelting process and Cort's puddling and rolling process (both for making iron), as well as Hargreaves's spinning jenny and Arkwright's water frame (both for spinning cotton). Whereas artisans made entire goods by themselves by hand, this new production system was based on a division of labor: each worker, interacting with machines, performed separate, highly specialized tasks that were but a small part of all the steps required to make manufactured goods. Mass production was born as rope- and chain-driven assembly lines moved work to stationary workers who concentrated on performing one small task over and over again. While workers focused on their singular tasks, managers were needed to coordinate the different parts of the production system and optimize its overall performance. Productivity skyrocketed at companies that understood this. At **Ford Motor Company**, where the assembly line was developed, the time required to assemble a car dropped from 12.5 work hours to just 93 minutes after switching to mass production.[7]

Second, instead of being performed in fields, homes, or small shops, jobs occurred in large, formal organizations where hundreds, if not thousands, of people worked under one roof.[8] In 1849, for example, **Chicago Harvester** (the predecessor of International Harvester) ran the largest factory in the United States with just 123 workers. Yet by 1913, Henry Ford employed 12,000 employees in his Highland Park, Michigan, factory alone. Because the number of people working in manufacturing quintupled from 1860 to 1890, and individual factories employed so many workers under one roof, companies now had a strong need for disciplinary rules to impose order and structure. For the first time, they needed managers who knew how to organize large groups, work with employees, and make good decisions.

2-2 SCIENTIFIC MANAGEMENT

Before 1880, business educators taught only basic bookkeeping and secretarial skills, and no one published books or articles about management.[9] Today if you have a question about management, you can turn to dozens of academic journals (such as the Academy of Management's *Journal* or *Review*, *Administrative Science Quarterly*, the *Strategic Management Journal*, and the *Journal of Applied Psychology*), hundreds of business school and practitioner journals (such as *Harvard Business Review*, *MIT Sloan Management Review*, and the *Academy of Management Perspectives*), and thousands of other books and articles. In the next four sections, you will learn about some important contributors to the field of management and how their ideas shaped our current understanding of management theory and practice.

Bosses, who were hired by the company owner or founder, used to make decisions by the seat of their pants—haphazardly, without any systematic study, thought, or collection of information. If the bosses decided that workers should work twice as fast, little or no thought was given to worker motivation. If workers resisted, the bosses often resorted to physical beatings to get workers to work faster, harder, or longer. With no incentives for bosses and workers to cooperate with one another, both groups played the system by trying to take advantage of each other. Moreover, each worker did the same job in his or her own way with different methods and different tools. In short, there were no procedures to standardize operations, no standards by which to judge whether performance was good or bad, and no follow-up to determine whether productivity or quality actually improved when changes were made.[10]

This all changed, however, with the advent of **scientific management**, which involved thorough study and testing of different work methods to identify the best, most efficient ways to complete a job.

Let's find out more about scientific management by learning about 2-2a Frederick W. Taylor, the father of scientific management; 2-2b Frank and Lillian Gilbreth and motion studies; and 2-2c Henry Gantt and his Gantt charts.

2-2a Father of Scientific Management: Frederick W. Taylor

Frederick W. Taylor (1856–1915), the father of scientific management, began his career as a worker at **Midvale Steel Company**. He was promoted to patternmaker, supervisor, and then chief engineer. At Midvale, Taylor was deeply affected by his three-year struggle to get the men who worked for him to do, as he called it, "a fair day's work." Taylor, who had worked alongside the men as a coworker before becoming their boss, said,

Scientific management thoroughly studying and testing different work methods to identify the best, most efficient way to complete a job

Frederick W. Taylor was affected by his three-year struggle to get the men who worked for him to do, as he called it, "a fair day's work."

"We who were the workmen of that shop had the quantity output carefully agreed upon for everything that was turned out in the shop. We limited the output to about, I should think, one third of what we could very well have done." Taylor explained that, as soon as he became the boss, "the men who were working under me . . . knew that I was onto the whole game of **soldiering**, or deliberately restricting output."[11] When Taylor told his workers, "I have accepted a job under the management of this company and I am on the other side of the fence . . . I am going to try to get a bigger output," the workers responded, "We warn you, Fred, if you try to bust any of these rates [a **rate buster** was someone who worked faster than the group] we will have you over the fence in six weeks."[12]

Over the next three years, Taylor tried everything he could think of to

improve output. By doing the job himself, he showed workers that it was possible to produce more output. He hired new workers and trained them himself, hoping they would produce more. But "very heavy social pressure" from the other workers kept them from doing so. Pushed by Taylor, the workers began breaking their machines so that they couldn't produce. Taylor responded by fining them every time they broke a machine and for any violation of the rules, no matter how small, such as being late to work. Tensions became so severe that some of the workers threatened to shoot Taylor. Looking back at the situation, Taylor reflected, "It is a horrid life for any man to live, not to be able to look any workman in the face all day long without seeing hostility there and feeling that every man around one is his virtual enemy." He said, "I made up my mind either to get out of the business entirely and go into some other line of work or to find some remedy for this unbearable condition."[13]

The remedy that Taylor eventually developed was scientific management. Taylor, who once described scientific management as "seventy-five percent science and twenty-five percent common sense," emphasized that the goal of scientific management was to use systematic study to find the "one best way" of doing each task. To do that, managers had to follow the four principles shown in Exhibit 2.2. The first principle was to "develop a science" for each element of work. Study it. Analyze it. Determine the "one best way" to do the work. For example, one of Taylor's controversial proposals at the time was to give rest breaks to factory workers doing physical labor. We take morning, lunch, and afternoon breaks for granted, but in Taylor's day, factory workers were expected to work without stopping.[14] When Taylor said that breaks would increase worker productivity, no one believed him. Nonetheless, through systematic experiments, he showed that workers receiving frequent rest breaks were able to greatly increase their daily output.

Second, managers had to scientifically select, train, teach, and develop workers to help them reach their full potential. Before Taylor, supervisors often hired on the basis of favoritism and nepotism. Who you knew was often more important than what you could do. By contrast, Taylor instructed supervisors to hire "first-class" workers on the basis of their aptitude to do a job well. In one of the first applications of this principle, physical reaction times were used to select bicycle ball-bearing inspectors, who had to be able to examine ball bearings as fast as they were produced on a production line. For similar reasons, Taylor also recommended that companies train and develop their workers—a rare practice at the time.

ullstein bild/Getty Images

Exhibit 2.2
Taylor's Four Principles of Scientific Management

First:	Develop a science for each element of a man's work, which replaces the old rule-of-thumb method.
Second:	Scientifically select and then train, teach, and develop the workman, whereas in the past, he chose his own work and trained himself as best he could.
Third:	Heartily cooperate with the men so as to ensure all of the work being done is in accordance with the principles of the science that has been developed.
Fourth:	There is an almost equal division of the work and the responsibility between the management and the workmen. The management take over all the work for which they are better fitted than the workmen, while in the past, almost all of the work and the greater part of the responsibility were thrown upon the men.

Source: F. W. Taylor, *The Principles of Scientific Management* (New York: Harper, 1911).

The third principle instructed managers to cooperate with employees to ensure that the scientific principles were actually implemented. Labor unrest was widespread at the time; the number of labor strikes against companies doubled between 1893 and 1904. As Taylor knew from personal experience, workers and management more often than not viewed each other as enemies. Taylor's advice ran contrary to the common wisdom of the day. He said, "The majority of these men believe that the fundamental interests of employees and employers are necessarily antagonistic. Scientific management, on the contrary, has for its very foundation the firm conviction that the true interests of the two are one and the same; that prosperity for the employer cannot exist through a long term of years unless it is accompanied by prosperity for the employee and vice versa; and that it is possible to give the workman what he most wants—high wages—and the employer what he wants—a low labor cost for his manufactures."[15]

The fourth principle of scientific management was to divide the work and the responsibility equally between management and workers. Prior to Taylor, workers alone were held responsible for productivity and performance. But, said Taylor, "Almost every act of the workman should be preceded by one or more preparatory acts of the management, which enable him to do his work better and quicker than he otherwise could. And each man should daily be taught by and receive the most friendly help from those who are over him, instead of being, at the one extreme, driven or coerced by his bosses, and at the other left, to his own unaided devices."[16]

Above all, Taylor believed these principles could be used to determine a "fair day's work," that is, what

Taylor's Rest Break Now Includes Napping

While rest breaks traditionally involve sitting or taking a brief walk, some employers now see a rest break as an opportunity for a quick snooze. Lampooned in movies, television, and even the business press, napping at work is nonetheless a proven way to increase focus, memory, and alertness on the job. A recent study from the University of Michigan found that a one-hour nap during the workday produced all those benefits—and more. As numerous as the benefits of napping are said to be, the challenges of napping at work are even more so. Not only is it difficult to break pace during the workday long enough to actually fall asleep, but finding a *place* to sleep can be challenging as well. Only 6 percent of companies have dedicated spaces for napping, and many employees work in loud, crowded spaces with stiff, uncomfortable chairs. Sleep experts do have some advice for people working at companies that embrace workday naps. First, when deciding what time to close your eyes, figure out the midpoint of your previous night's rest and add 12 hours. (For example, if you slept from 11 p.m. to 7 a.m., then your ideal nap time the next day is 3 p.m.) Once you know when to nap, sleep either for 20 or 90 minutes—ideal times for a re-energizing nap. Anything in between or beyond those two durations will leave the napper feeling groggy and ineffective, counteracting the point of the nap in the first place.

Source: R. Greenfield, "Napping at Work Can Be So Exhausting," *Bloomberg Businessweek*, August 20, 2015, http://www.bloomberg.com/news/articles/2015-08-20/napping-at-work-can-be-so-exhausting, accessed March 26, 2016.

an average worker could produce at a reasonable pace, day in and day out. After that was determined, it was management's responsibility to pay workers fairly for that fair day's work. In essence, Taylor was trying to align management and employees so that what was good for employees was also good for management. In this way, he believed, workers and managers could avoid the conflicts he had experienced at Midvale Steel.

Although Taylor remains a controversial figure among some academics who believe that his ideas were bad for workers, his key ideas have stood the test of time.[17] These include using systematic analysis to identify the best methods; scientifically selecting, training, and developing workers; promoting cooperation between management and labor; developing standardized approaches and tools; setting specific tasks or goals and then rewarding workers with financial incentives; and giving workers shorter work hours and frequent breaks. In fact, his ideas are so well accepted and widely used that we take most of them for granted. As eminent management scholar Edwin Locke said, "The point is not, as is often claimed, that he was 'right in the context of his time,' but is now outdated, but that *most of his insights are still valid today.*"[18]

2-2b Motion Studies: Frank and Lillian Gilbreth

The husband and wife team of Frank and Lillian Gilbreth are best known for their use of motion studies to simplify work, but they also made significant contributions to the employment of disabled workers and to the field of industrial psychology. Like Taylor, their early experiences significantly shaped their interests and contributions to management.

Though admitted to MIT, Frank Gilbreth (1868–1924) began his career as an apprentice bricklayer. While learning the trade, he noticed the bricklayers using three different sets of motions—one to teach others how to lay bricks, a second to work at a slow pace, and a third to work at a fast pace.[19] Wondering which was best, he studied the various approaches and began eliminating unnecessary motions. For example, by designing a stand that could be raised to waist height, he eliminated the need to bend over to pick up each brick. Turning to grab a brick was faster and easier than bending down. By having lower-paid workers place all the bricks with their most attractive side up, bricklayers didn't waste time turning a brick over to find it. By mixing a

Motion study breaking each task or job into its separate motions and then eliminating those that are unnecessary or repetitive

Frank and Lillian Gilbreth are best known for their use of motion studies to simplify work.

George Rinhart/Corbis Historical/Getty Images

more consistent mortar, bricklayers no longer had to tap each brick numerous times to put it in the right position. Together, Gilbreth's improvements raised productivity from 120 to 350 bricks per hour and from 1,000 bricks to 2,700 bricks per day.

As a result of his experience with bricklaying, Gilbreth and his wife, Lillian, developed a long-term interest in using motion study to simplify work, improve productivity, and reduce the level of effort required to safely perform a job. Indeed, Frank Gilbreth said, "The greatest waste in the world comes from needless, ill-directed, and ineffective motions."[20] **Motion study** broke each task or job into separate motions and then eliminated those that were unnecessary or repetitive. Because many motions were completed very quickly, the Gilbreths used motion-picture films, then a relatively new technology, to analyze jobs. Most film cameras at that time were hand cranked and thus variable in their film speed, so Frank invented the microchronometer, a large clock that could record time to 1/2,000th of a second. By placing the microchonometer next to the worker in the camera's field of vision and attaching a flashing strobe light to the worker's hands to better identify the direction and sequence of key movements, the Gilbreths could use film to detect and precisely time even the slightest, fastest movements.

Exhibit 2.3
Gantt Chart for Starting Construction on a New Headquarters

Tasks	Weeks	23 Sep to 29 Sep	30 Sep to 6 Oct	7 Oct to 13 Oct	14 Oct to 20 Oct	21 Oct to 27 Oct	28 Oct to 3 Nov	4 Nov to 10 Nov	11 Nov to 17 Nov	18 Nov to 25 Nov
Interview and select architectural firm		Architect by October 7								
Hold weekly planning meetings with architects				Planning with architects by November 4						
Obtain permits and approval from city							Permits and approval by November 11			
Begin preparing site for construction								Site preparation done by November 18		
Finalize loans and financing									Financing finalized by November 18	
Begin construction										Start building

Motion study typically yielded production increases of 25–300 percent.[21]

Taylor also strove to simplify work, but he did so by managing time rather than motion as the Gilbreths did.[22] Taylor developed time study to put an end to soldiering and to determine what could be considered a fair day's work. **Time study** worked by timing how long it took a "first-class man" to complete each part of his job. A standard time was established after allowing for rest periods, and a worker's pay would increase or decrease depending on whether the worker exceeded or fell below that standard.

Lillian Gilbreth (1878–1972) was an important contributor to management in her own right. She was the first woman to receive a PhD in industrial psychology as well as the first woman to become a member of the Society of Industrial Engineers and the American Society of Mechanical Engineers. When Frank died in 1924, she continued the work of their management consulting company (which they had shared for over a dozen years). Lillian, who was concerned with the human side of work, was one of the first contributors to industrial psychology, originating ways to improve office communication, incentive programs, job satisfaction, and management training. Her work also convinced the government to enact laws regarding workplace safety, ergonomics, and child labor.

2-2c Charts: Henry Gantt

Henry Gantt (1861–1919) was first a protégé and then an associate of Frederick W. Taylor. Gantt is best known for the Gantt chart, but he also made significant contributions to management with respect to pay-for-performance plans and the training and development of workers. As shown in Exhibit 2.3, a **Gantt chart** visually indicates what tasks must be completed at which times in order to complete a project. It accomplishes this by showing time in various units on the x-axis and tasks on the y-axis. For example, Exhibit 2.3 shows that the following tasks must be completed by the following dates: in order to start construction on a new company headquarters by the week of November 18, the architectural firm must be selected by October 7, architectural planning done by November 4, permits obtained from the city by November 11, site preparation finished by November 18, and loans and financing finalized by November 18.

Though simple and straightforward, Gantt charts were revolutionary in the era of seat-of-the-pants management

> **Time study** timing how long it takes good workers to complete each part of their jobs
>
> **Gantt chart** a graphical chart that shows which tasks must be completed at which times in order to complete a project or task

because of the detailed planning information they provided. As Gantt wrote, "By using the graphical forms, its [the Gantt chart's] value is very much increased, for the general appearance of the sheet is sufficient to tell how closely the schedule is being lived up to; in other words, whether the plant is being run efficiently or not."[23] Gantt said, "Such sheets show at a glance where the delays occur, and indicate what must have our attention in order to keep up the proper output." The use of Gantt charts is so widespread today that nearly all project management software and computer spreadsheets have the capability to create charts that track and visually display the progress being made on a project.

Finally, Gantt, along with Taylor, was one of the first to strongly recommend that companies train and develop their workers.[24] In his work with companies, he found that workers achieved their best performance levels if they were trained first. At the time, however, supervisors were reluctant to teach workers what they knew for fear that they could lose their jobs to more knowledgeable workers. Gantt overcame the supervisors' resistance by rewarding them with bonuses for properly training all of their workers. Said Gantt, "This is the first recorded attempt to make it in the financial interest of the foreman to teach the individual worker, and the importance of it cannot be overestimated, for it changes the foreman from a driver of men to their friend and helper."[25] Gantt's approach to training was straightforward: "(1) A scientific investigation in detail of each piece of work, and the determination of the best method and the shortest time in which the work can be done. (2) A teacher capable of teaching the best method and the shortest time. (3) Reward for both teacher and pupil when the latter is successful."[26]

2-3 BUREAUCRATIC AND ADMINISTRATIVE MANAGEMENT

The field of scientific management developed quickly in the United States between 1895 and 1920 and focused on improving the efficiency of manufacturing facilities and their workers. At about the same time, equally important ideas about bureaucratic and administrative management were developing in Europe. German sociologist Max Weber presented a new way to run entire organizations (bureaucratic management) in *The Theory of Social and Economic Organization*, published in 1922. Henri Fayol, an experienced French CEO, published his ideas about how and what managers should do in their jobs (administrative management) in *General and Industrial Management* in 1916.

*Let's find out more about the contributions Weber and Fayol made to management by learning about **2-3a bureaucratic management** and **2-3b administrative management**.*

2-3a Bureaucratic Management: Max Weber

Today, when we hear the term *bureaucracy*, we think of inefficiency and red tape, incompetence and ineffectiveness, and rigid administrators blindly enforcing nonsensical rules. When German sociologist Max Weber (1864–1920) first proposed the idea of bureaucratic organizations, however, these problems were associated

Many Managers! Bureaucracy's "Iron Cage" Costs Companies Trillions

While Max Weber's ideas (fairness, efficiency, rules, and procedures) advanced business management, he correctly predicted bureaucracy's downside, saying, "Once fully established, bureaucracy is among those social structures which are the hardest to destroy."

So how much does bureaucracy's inefficiency, red tape, and incompetence cost companies? According to management professors Gary Hamel and Michele Zanini, in the United States alone, its cost is $3 trillion a year, or 17 percent of GDP!

If management ideas were supposed to improve business functioning and productivity, how is this so? Too many managers!

Twenty-four million U.S. managers results in 1 manager for every 4.7 workers. Hamel and Zanini estimate that companies could easily double that to 1 manager for every 10 workers. With more people manufacturing products, providing services or directly dealing with customers, and millions fewer managers pushing red tape rather than company goals, productivity could jump by 15 percent!

Sources: G. Hamel & M. Zanini, "Excess Management Is Costing the U.S. $3 Trillion Per Year," *Harvard Business Review Digital Articles*, September 5, 2016, accessed March 4, 2017, https://hbr.org/2016/09/excess-management-is-costing-the-us-3-trillion-per-year; M. Weber, *The Protestant Ethic and the Spirit of Capitalism* (New York: Scribner's, 1958).

Christian Delbert/Shutterstock.com

Exhibit 2.4
Elements of Bureaucratic Organizations

Maxx-Studio/Shutterstock.com; Wavebreakmedia/Shutterstock.com; ImageFlow/Shutterstock.com; Lucky Business/Shutterstock.com; XRoigs/Shutterstock.com; Pressmaster/Shutterstock.com; Andy Dean Photography/Shutterstock.com

Qualification-based hiring:	Employees are hired on the basis of their technical training or educational background.
Merit-based promotion:	Promotion is based on experience or achievement. Managers, not organizational owners, decide who is promoted.
Chain of command:	Each job occurs within a hierarchy, the chain of command, in which each position reports and is accountable to a higher position. A grievance procedure and a right to appeal protect people in lower positions.
Division of labor:	Tasks, responsibilities, and authority are clearly divided and defined.
Impartial application of rules and procedures:	Rules and procedures apply to all members of the organization and will be applied in an impartial manner, regardless of one's position or status.
Recorded in writing:	All administrative decisions, acts, rules, and procedures will be recorded in writing.
Managers separate from owners:	The owners of an organization should not manage or supervise the organization.

Source: M. Weber, *The Theory of Social and Economic Organization*, trans. A. Henderson and T. Parsons (New York: The Free Press, 1947), 329–334.

with monarchies and patriarchies rather than bureaucracies. In monarchies, where kings, queens, sultans, and emperors ruled, and patriarchies, where a council of elders, wise men, or male heads of extended families ruled, the top leaders typically achieved their positions by virtue of birthright. For example, when the queen died, her oldest son became king, regardless of his intelligence, experience, education, or desire. Likewise, promotion to prominent positions of authority in monarchies and patriarchies was based on who you knew (politics), who you were (heredity), or ancient rules and traditions.

It was against this historical background of monarchical and patriarchal rule that Weber proposed the then-new idea of bureaucracy. *Bureaucracy* comes from the French word *bureaucratie*. Because *bureau* means desk or office and *cratie* or *cracy* means to rule, *bureaucracy* literally means to rule from a desk or office. According to Weber, **bureaucracy** is "the exercise of control on the basis of knowledge."[27] Rather than ruling by virtue of favoritism or personal or family connections, people in a bureaucracy would lead by virtue of their rational-legal authority—in other words, their knowledge, expertise, or experience. Furthermore, the aim of bureaucracy is not to protect authority but to achieve an organization's goals in the most efficient way possible.

Exhibit 2.4 shows the seven elements that, according to Weber, characterize bureaucracies. First, instead of hiring people because of their family or political connections

> **Bureaucracy** the exercise of control on the basis of knowledge, expertise, or experience

or personal loyalty, they should be hired because their technical training or education qualifies them to do the job well. Second, along the same lines, promotion within the company should no longer be based on who you know (politics) or who you are (heredity) but on your experience or achievements. And to further limit the influence of personal connections in the promotion process, *managers* rather than organizational owners should decide who gets promoted. Third, each position or job is part of a chain of command that clarifies who reports to whom throughout the organization. Those higher in the chain of command have the right, if they so choose, to give commands, take action, and make decisions concerning activities occurring anywhere below them in the chain. Unlike in many monarchies or patriarchies, however, those lower in the chain of command are protected by a grievance procedure that gives them the right to appeal the decisions of those in higher positions. Fourth, to increase efficiency and effectiveness, tasks and responsibilities should be separated and assigned to those best qualified to complete them. Authority is vested in these task-defined positions rather than in people, and the authority of each position is clearly defined in order to reduce confusion and conflict. If you move to a different job in a bureaucracy, your authority increases or decreases commensurate with the responsibilities of that job. Fifth, because of his strong distaste for favoritism, Weber believed that an organization's rules and procedures should apply to all the members regardless of their position or status. Sixth, to ensure consistency and fairness over time and across different leaders and supervisors, all rules, procedures, and decisions should be recorded in writing. Finally, to reduce favoritism, "professional" managers rather than company owners should manage or supervise the organization.

When viewed in historical context, Weber's ideas about bureaucracy represent a tremendous improvement in how organizations should be run. Fairness supplanted favoritism, the goal of efficiency replaced the goal of personal gain, and logical rules and procedures took the place of traditions or arbitrary decision making.

Today, however, after more than a century of experience, we recognize that bureaucracy has limitations as well. Weber called bureaucracy the "iron cage" and said, "Once fully established, bureaucracy is among those social structures which are the hardest to destroy."[28] In bureaucracies, managers are supposed to influence employee behavior by fairly rewarding or punishing employees for compliance or noncompliance with organizational policies, rules, and procedures. In reality, however, most employees would argue that bureaucratic managers emphasize punishment for noncompliance much more than rewards for compliance. Ironically, bureaucratic management was created to prevent just this type of managerial behavior.

2-3b Administrative Management: Henri Fayol

Though his work was not translated and widely recognized in the United States until 1949, Frenchman Henri Fayol (1841–1925) was as important a contributor to the field of management as Taylor. Like Taylor and the Gilbreths, Fayol's work experience significantly shaped his thoughts and ideas about management. But, whereas Taylor's ideas changed companies from the shop floor up, Fayol's ideas were shaped by his experience as a managing director (CEO) and generally changed companies from the board of directors down.[29] Fayol is best known for developing five functions of managers and 14 principles of management, as well as for his belief that management can and should be taught to others.

The most formative events in Fayol's business career came during his 20+ years as the managing director of Compagnie de Commentry-Fourchambault et Décazeville, commonly known as **Comambault**, a vertically integrated steel company that owned several coal and iron ore mines and employed 10,000–13,000 workers. Fayol was initially hired by the board of directors to shut down the "hopeless" steel company. The company was facing increased competition from English and German steel companies, which had lower costs, and from new steel mills in northern and eastern France, which were closer to major markets and thus could avoid the high shipping costs incurred by Fayol's company, located in central France.[30] In the five years before Fayol became CEO, production had dropped more than 60 percent, from 38,000 to 15,000 annual metric tons. Comambault had exhausted a key supply of coal needed for steel production, had already shut down one steel mill, and was losing money at another.[31] The company had quit paying dividends to shareholders and had no cash to invest in new technology, such as blast furnaces, that could lower its costs and increase productivity.

So the board hired Fayol as CEO to quickly dissolve and liquidate the business. But, after "four months of reflection and study," he presented the board with a plan, backed by detailed facts and figures, to save the company.[32] With little to lose, the board agreed. Fayol then began the process of turning the company around by obtaining supplies of key resources such as coal and iron ore; using research to develop new steel alloy products;

carefully selecting key subordinates in research, purchasing, manufacturing, and sales and then delegating responsibility to them; and cutting costs by moving the company to a better location closer to key markets.[33] Looking back 10 years later, Fayol attributed his and the company's success to changes in management practices. He wrote, "When I assumed the responsibility for the restoration of Décazeville, I did not rely on my technical superiority. . . . I relied on my ability as an organizer [and my] skill in handling men."[34]

Based on his experience as a CEO, Fayol argued that "the success of an enterprise generally depends much more on the administrative ability of its leaders than on their technical ability."[35] And, as you learned in Chapter 1, Fayol argued that managers need to perform five managerial functions if they are to be successful: planning, organizing, coordinating, commanding, and controlling.[36] Because most management textbooks have dropped the coordinating function and now refer to Fayol's commanding function as "leading," these functions are widely known as planning (determining organizational goals and a means for achieving them), organizing (deciding where decisions will be made, who will do what jobs and tasks, and who will work for whom), leading (inspiring and motivating workers to work hard to achieve organizational goals), and controlling (monitoring progress toward goal achievement and taking corrective action when needed). In addition, according to Fayol, effective management is based on the 14 principles in Exhibit 2.5.

Exhibit 2.5
Fayol's 14 Principles of Management

1. **Division of work**
   Increase production by dividing work so that each worker completes smaller tasks or job elements.

2. **Authority and responsibility**
   A manager's authority, which is the "right to give orders," should be commensurate with the manager's responsibility. However, organizations should enact controls to prevent managers from abusing their authority.

3. **Discipline**
   Clearly defined rules and procedures are needed at all organizational levels to ensure order and proper behavior.

4. **Unity of command**
   To avoid confusion and conflict, each employee should report to and receive orders from just one boss.

5. **Unity of direction**
   One person and one plan should be used in deciding the activities to be carried out to accomplish each organizational objective.

6. **Subordination of individual interests to the general interests**
   Employees must put the organization's interests and goals before their own.

7. **Remuneration**
   Compensation should be fair and satisfactory to both the employees and the organization; that is, don't overpay or underpay employees.

8. **Centralization**
   Avoid too much centralization or decentralization. Strike a balance depending on the circumstances and employees involved.

9. **Scalar chain**
   From the top to the bottom of an organization, each position is part of a vertical chain of authority in which each worker reports to just one boss. For the sake of simplicity, communication outside normal work groups or departments should follow the vertical chain of authority.

10. **Order**
    To avoid confusion and conflict, order can be obtained by having a place for everyone and having everyone in his or her place; in other words, there should be no overlapping responsibilities.

11. **Equity**
    Kind, fair, and just treatment for all will develop devotion and loyalty. This does not exclude discipline, if warranted, and consideration of the broader general interests of the organization.

12. **Stability of tenure of personnel**
    Low turnover, meaning a stable work force with high tenure, benefits an organization by improving performance, lowering costs, and giving employees, especially managers, time to learn their jobs.

13. **Initiative**
    Because it is a "great source of strength for business," managers should encourage the development of initiative, or the ability to develop and implement a plan, in others.

14. *Esprit de corps*
    Develop a strong sense of morale and unity among workers that encourages coordination of efforts.

Sources: H. Fayol, *General and Industrial Management* (London: Pittman & Sons, 1949); M. Fells, "Fayol Stands the Test of Time," *Journal of Management History* 6 (2000): 345–360; C. Rodrigues, "Fayol's 14 Principles of Management Then and Now: A Framework for Managing Today's Organizations Effectively," *Management Decision* 39 (2001): 880–889.

DOING THE RIGHT THING

C.C. Spaulding: "Mr. Cooperation," African-American CEO, and Early Contributor to Management

Thanks to new archival research by Professors Leon Prieto and Simone Phipps, Charles Clinton (C.C.) Spaulding is now recognized as a significant early contributor to the field of management. Spaulding, a successful African American business executive, was born 10 years (1874) after the end of the American Civil War and died 12 years (1952) before passage of the 1964 Civil Rights Act outlawing discrimination.

Like Henry Fayol and Chester Barnard, Spaulding's experience as president of the North Carolina Mutual Life Insurance Company—then the largest African American insurance company in the United States—shaped his views about management. However, Spaulding wrote his eight fundamental necessities of business administration in a 1927 article titled "The Administration of Big Business" before Barnard's (1938) and Fayol's (1949) ideas were first published in the United States. His ideas on conflict and cooperation are consistent with those of Mary Parker Follett, which were also published during the 1920s. Spaulding's eight fundamental necessities of management are, in the author's own words:

C.C. Spaulding is shown at left in this undated photo with Jessie Matthews Vann, editor and publisher of *The Pittsburgh Courier*.

» Necessity 1: Cooperation and Teamwork. "Not only should executives confer daily with each other, disclosing all the facts and circumstances attendant upon their operations, but they ought to keep constant check upon the activities and liabilities of their associates . . . "

» Necessity 2: Authority and Responsibility. "There must always be some responsible executive who must pass upon every issue that is fundamental; he must be the final authority from whom there is no appeal except to the entire group in conference."

» Necessity 3: Division of Labor. "Departmental divisions function separately under the direction of experts who may or may not be executive officers."

» Necessity 4: Adequate Manpower. "First and foremost success in business depends upon adequate manpower. Our schools are turning out only partially trained young people with no business experience whatsoever, and while many of them are good technicians they are for the most part helpless in their new jobs because there is little correlation between the classroom and the business office."

» Necessity 5: Adequate Capital. "Initial capital must not only be sufficient to commence operations, but must be sustaining over a given period . . . Even large scale corporations frequently dissipate their surplus earnings in hurried dividends instead of re-investing the surplus for the extension of the business."

» Necessity 6: Feasibility Analysis. "Frequently it happens that as soon as one person or group appears successful in a given line [of business] another person or group organizes a new enterprise in the same line without ascertaining the advisability of such a move, as reflected in the needs and resources of the community."

» Necessity 7: Advertising Budget. "[. . .] when it comes to advertising, a large number of our organizations are depriving themselves of the most effective means of propagation . . . Very few of these have an annual appropriation for advertisement."

» Necessity 8: Conflict Resolution. "Personal contact and business contact, if not properly directed and if not based on mutual goodwill and intelligence derived from a common sense education, will develop personal conflict and business conflict instead of personal cooperation and business cooperation."

Sources: L.C. Prieto & S.T.A. Phipps, "Re-discovering Charles Clinton Spaulding's 'The Administration of Big Business,' Insight Into Early 20th Century African-American Management Thought," *Journal of Management History* 22 (1) (2016): 73–90; A. Rutledge, "They call him 'Co-operation,'" *The Saturday Evening Post*, March 27, 1943, p. 15; C.C. Spaulding, "The Administration of Big Business," *The Pittsburgh Courier*, August, 13, 1927, 4; C.C. Spaulding, "The Administration of Big Business," *The Pittsburgh Courier*, August, 20, 1927, 8; H. Fayol, *General and Industrial Management* (London: Pittman & Sons, 1949); P. Graham, ed., *Mary Parker Follett—Prophet of Management: A Celebration of Writings from the 1920s* (Boston: Harvard Business School Press, 1995); C. I. Barnard, *The Functions of the Executive* (Cambridge, MA: Harvard University Press, 1938).

Jonathan McHugh//Ikon Images/Getty Images

2-4 HUMAN RELATIONS MANAGEMENT

As we have seen, scientific management focuses on improving efficiency; bureaucratic management focuses on using knowledge, fairness, and logical rules and procedures; and administrative management focuses on how and what managers should do in their jobs. The human relations approach to management focuses on *people*, particularly the psychological and social aspects of work. This approach to management sees people not as just extensions of machines but as valuable organizational resources in their own right. Human relations management holds that people's needs are important and that their efforts, motivation, and performance are affected by the work they do and their relationships with their bosses, coworkers, and work groups. In other words, efficiency alone is not enough. Organizational success also depends on treating workers well.

Let's find out more about human relations management by learning about 2-4a Mary Parker Follett's theories of constructive conflict and coordination, 2-4b Elton Mayo's Hawthorne Studies, and 2-4c Chester Barnard's theories of cooperation and acceptance of authority.

2-4a Constructive Conflict and Coordination: Mary Parker Follett

Mary Parker Follett (1868–1933) was a social worker with a degree in political science who, in her 50s, after 25 years of working with schools and nonprofit organizations, began lecturing and writing about management and working extensively as a consultant for business and government leaders in the United States and Europe. Although her contributions were overlooked for decades, perhaps because she was a woman or perhaps because they were so different, many of today's "new" management ideas can clearly be traced to her work.

Follett believed that the best way to deal with conflict was not **domination**, where one side wins and the other loses, or **compromise**, where each side gives up some of what it wants, but integration. Said Follett, "There is a way beginning now to be recognized at least, and even occasionally followed: when two desires are *integrated*, that means that a solution has been found in which both desires have found a place that neither side has had to sacrifice anything."[37] So, rather than one side dominating the other or both sides compromising, the point of **integrative conflict resolution** is to have

both parties indicate their preferences and then work together to find an alternative that meets the needs of both. According to Follett, "Integration involves invention, and the clever thing is to recognize this, and not to let one's thinking stay within the boundaries of two alternatives which are mutually exclusive." Indeed, Follett's ideas about the positive use of conflict and an integrative approach to conflict resolution predate accepted thinking in the negotiation and conflict resolution literature by six decades (see the best-selling book *Getting to Yes: Negotiating Agreement without Giving In* by Roger Fisher, William Ury, and Bruce Patton).

Exhibit 2.6 summarizes Follett's contributions to management in her own words. She casts power as "with" rather than "over" others. Giving orders involves discussing instructions and dealing with resentment. Authority flows from job knowledge and experience rather than position. Leadership involves setting the tone for the team rather than being aggressive and dominating, which may be harmful. Coordination and control should be based on facts and information. In the end, Follett's contributions added significantly to our understanding of the human, social, and psychological sides of management. Peter Parker, the former chairman of the London School of Economics, said about Follett: "People often puzzle about who is the father of management. I don't know who the father was, but I have no doubt about who was the mother."[38]

2-4b Hawthorne Studies: Elton Mayo

Australian-born Elton Mayo (1880–1948) is best known for his role in the famous Hawthorne Studies

Domination an approach to dealing with conflict in which one party satisfies its desires and objectives at the expense of the other party's desires and objectives

Compromise an approach to dealing with conflict in which both parties give up some of what they want in order to reach an agreement on a plan to reduce or settle the conflict

Integrative conflict resolution an approach to dealing with conflict in which both parties indicate their preferences and then work together to find an alternative that meets the needs of both

Exhibit 2.6

Mary Parker Follett says . . .

On constructive conflict...

"As conflict—difference—is here in this world, as we cannot avoid it, we should, I think, use it to work for us. Instead of condemning it, we should set it to work for us."

On power...

"It seems to me that whereas power usually means power-over, the power of some person or group over some other person or group, it is possible to develop the conception of power-with, a jointly developed power, a co-active, not a coercive power."

On the giving of orders...

"An advantage of not exacting blind obedience, of discussing your instructions with your subordinates, is that if there is any resentment, any come-back, you get it out into the open, and when it is in the open, you can deal with it."

On authority...

"Authority should go with knowledge and experience, that is where obedience is due, no matter whether it is up the line or down."

On leadership...

"Of the greatest importance is the ability to grasp a total situation. . . . Out of a welter of facts, experience, desires, aims, the leader must find the unifying thread. He must see a whole, not a mere kaleidoscope of pieces. . . . The higher up you go, the more ability you have to have of this kind."

On coordination...

"The most important thing to remember about unity is—that there is no such thing. There is only unifying. You cannot get unity and expect it to last a day—or five minutes. Every man in a business should be taking part in a certain process and that process is unifying."

On control...

"Central control is coming more and more to mean the co-relation of many controls rather than a superimposed control."

Source: M. Parker Follett, *Mary Parker Follett—Prophet of Management: A Celebration of Writings from the 1920s*, ed. P. Graham (Boston: Harvard Business School Press, 1995).

at the **Western Electric Company**. The Hawthorne Studies were conducted in several stages between 1924 and 1932 at a Western Electric plant in Chicago. Although Mayo didn't join the studies until 1928, he played a significant role thereafter, writing about the results in his book, *The Human Problems of an Industrial Civilization*.[39] The first stage of the Hawthorne Studies investigated the effects of lighting levels and incentives on employee productivity in the Relay Test Assembly Room, where workers took approximately a minute to put "together a coil, armature, contact springs, and insulators in a fixture and secure the parts by means of four machine screws."[40]

Two groups of six experienced female workers, five to do the work and one to supply needed parts, were separated from the main part of the factory by a 10-foot partition and placed at a standard work bench with the necessary parts and tools. Over the next five years, the experimenters introduced various levels and combinations of lighting, financial incentives, and rest pauses (work breaks) to study the effect on productivity. Curiously, however, production levels increased whether the experimenters increased or decreased the lighting, paid workers based on individual production or group production, or increased or decreased the number and length of rest pauses. In fact, Mayo and his fellow researchers were surprised that production steadily increased from 2,400 relays per day at the beginning of the study to 3,000 relays per day five years later. The question was: Why?

Mayo and his colleagues eventually concluded that two things accounted for the results. First, substantially more attention was paid to these workers than to workers in the rest of the plant. Mayo wrote, "Before every change of program [in the study], the group is consulted. Their comments are listened to and discussed; sometimes their objections are allowed to negate a suggestion. The group unquestionably develops a sense of participation in the critical determinations and becomes something of a social unit."[41]

For years, the "Hawthorne Effect" has been *incorrectly* defined as increasing productivity by paying more attention to workers.[42] But it is not simply about attention from management. The Hawthorne Effect cannot be understood without giving equal importance to the social units, which became intensely cohesive groups. Mayo said, "What actually happened was that six individuals became a team and the team gave itself wholeheartedly and spontaneously to cooperation in the experiment. The consequence was that they felt themselves to be participating freely and without afterthought, and they were happy in the knowledge that they were working without coercion from above or limits from below."[43]

For the first time, human factors related to work were found to be more important than the physical conditions or design of the work. Together, the increased attention from management and the development of a cohesive work group led to significantly higher levels of job satisfaction and productivity. In short, the Hawthorne Studies found that workers' feelings and attitudes affected their work.

The next stage of the Hawthorne Studies was conducted in the Bank Wiring Room, where "the group consisted of nine wiremen, three solderers, and two inspectors. Each of these groups performed a specific task and collaborated with the other two in completion of each unit of equipment. The task consisted of setting up the banks of terminals side-by-side on frames, wiring the corresponding terminals from bank to bank, soldering the connections, and inspecting with a test set for short circuits or breaks in the wire. One solderman serviced the work of the three wiremen."[44] While productivity increased in the Relay Test Assembly Room no matter what the researchers did, productivity dropped in the Bank Wiring Room. Again, the question was: Why?

Mayo and his colleagues found that the differences in performance were due to group dynamics. The workers in the Bank Wiring Room had been an existing work group for some time and had already developed strong negative norms that governed their behavior. For instance, despite a group financial incentive for production, the group members decided that they would wire only 6,000–6,600 connections a day (depending on the kind of equipment they were wiring), well below the production goal of 7,300 connections that management had set for them. Individual workers who worked at a faster pace were socially ostracized from the group or "binged" (hit on the arm) until they slowed their work pace. Thus, the group's behavior was reminiscent of the soldiering that Taylor had observed. Mayo concluded, "Work [was] done in accord with the group's conception of a day's work; this was exceeded by only one individual who was cordially disliked."[45]

In the end, the Hawthorne Studies demonstrated that the workplace was more complex than previously

The Hawthorne Effect showed that when management paid more attention to workers, productivity increased. But equal importance should be given to the social units, or teams, that were created, which demonstrated that human factors were more important than physical conditions or the work itself.

thought, that workers were not just extensions of machines, and that financial incentives weren't necessarily the most important motivator for workers. By highlighting the crucial role, positive or negative, that groups, group norms, and group behavior play at work, Mayo strengthened Follett's point about coordination—make just one change in an organization and others, some expected and some unexpected, will occur. Thanks to Mayo and his colleagues and their work on the Hawthorne Studies, managers better understood the effect that group social interactions, employee satisfaction, and attitudes had on individual and group performance.

2-4c Cooperation and Acceptance of Authority: Chester Barnard

Like Fayol, Chester Barnard (1886–1961) had experiences as a top executive that shaped his views of management. Barnard began his career in 1909 as an engineer and translator for **AT&T**, becoming a general manager at Pennsylvania Bell Telephone in 1922 and then president of New Jersey Bell Telephone in 1927.[46] Barnard's ideas, published in his classic book, *The Functions of the Executive*, influenced companies from the board of directors down. He is best known for his ideas about cooperation and the acceptance of authority.

Barnard proposed a comprehensive theory of cooperation in formal organizations. In fact, he defines an **organization** as a "system of consciously coordinated activities or forces of two or more persons."[47] In other words, organization occurs whenever two people work together for some purpose, whether it be classmates working together to complete a class project, Habitat for Humanity volunteers donating their time to build a house, or managers working with subordinates to reduce costs, improve quality, or increase sales. Barnard placed so much emphasis on cooperation because cooperation is *not* the normal state of affairs: "Failure to cooperate, failure of cooperation, failure of organization, disorganization, disintegration, destruction of organization—and reorganization—are characteristic facts of human history."[48]

According to Barnard, the extent to which people willingly cooperate in an organization depends on how workers perceive executive authority and whether they're willing to accept it. Many managerial requests or directives fall within a *zone of indifference* in which acceptance of managerial authority is automatic.

Organization a system of consciously coordinated activities or forces created by two or more people

For example, if your supervisor asks you for a copy of the monthly inventory report, and compiling and writing that report is part of your job, you think nothing of the request and automatically send it. In general, people will be indifferent to managerial directives or orders if they (1) are understood, (2) are consistent with the purpose of the organization, (3) are compatible with the people's personal interests, and (4) can actually be carried out by those people. Acceptance of managerial authority (that is, cooperation) is not automatic, however. Ask people to do things contrary to the organization's purpose or to their own benefit and they'll put up a fight. While many people assume that managers have the authority to do whatever they want, Barnard, referring to the "fiction of superior authority," believed that workers ultimately grant managers their authority.

2-5 OPERATIONS, INFORMATION, SYSTEMS, AND CONTINGENCY MANAGEMENT

In this last section, we review four other significant historical approaches to management that have influenced how today's managers produce goods and services on a daily basis, gather and manage the information they need to understand their businesses and make good decisions, understand how the different parts of the company work together as a whole, and recognize when and where particular management practices are likely to work.

*To better understand these ideas, let's learn about **2-5a operations management, 2-5b information management, 2-5c systems management,** and **2-5d contingency management.***

2-5a Operations Management

In Chapter 18, you will learn about *operations management*, which involves managing the daily production of goods and services. In general, operations management uses a quantitative or mathematical approach to find ways to increase productivity, improve quality, and manage or reduce costly inventories. The most commonly used operations management tools and methods are quality control, forecasting techniques, capacity planning, productivity measurement and improvement, linear programming, scheduling systems, inventory systems, work measurement techniques (similar to the Gilbreths' motion studies), project management (similar to Gantt's charts), and cost-benefit analysis.[49]

Since the sixteenth century, skilled craftspeople made the lock, stock, and barrel of a gun by hand. After each part was made, a skilled gun finisher assembled the parts into a complete gun. But the gun finisher did not simply screw the different parts of a gun together, as is done today. Instead, each handmade part required extensive finishing and adjusting so that it would fit together with the other handmade gun parts. Hand-fitting was necessary because, even when made by the same skilled craftspeople, no two parts were alike. In fact, gun finishers played a role similar to that of fine watchmakers who meticulously assembled expensive watches—without them, the product simply wouldn't work. Today, we would say that these parts were low quality because they varied so much from one part to another.

All this changed in 1791 when the U.S. government, worried about a possible war with France, ordered 40,000 muskets from private gun contractors. All but one contractor built handmade muskets assembled by skilled gun finishers who made sure that all the parts fit together. Thus, each musket was unique. If a part broke, a replacement part had to be handcrafted. But one contractor, Eli Whitney of New Haven, Connecticut (who is better known for his invention of the cotton gin), determined that if gun parts were made accurately enough, guns could be made with standardized, interchangeable parts. So he designed machine tools that allowed unskilled workers to make each gun part the same as the next. Said Whitney, "The tools which I contemplate to make are similar to an engraving on copper plate from which may be taken a great number of impressions perceptibly alike."[50] Years passed before Whitney delivered his 10,000 muskets to the U.S. government. But he demonstrated the superiority of interchangeable parts to President-elect Thomas Jefferson in 1801 by quickly and easily assembling complete muskets from randomly picked piles of musket parts. Today, because of Whitney's ideas, most products, from cars to toasters to space shuttles, are manufactured using standardized, interchangeable parts.

But even with this advance, manufacturers still could not produce a part unless they had seen or examined it

firsthand. Thanks to Gaspard Monge, a Frenchman of modest beginnings, this soon changed. Monge's greatest achievement was his book *Descriptive Geometry*.[51] In it, he explained techniques for drawing three-dimensional objects on paper. For the first time, precise drawings permitted manufacturers to make standardized, interchangeable parts without first examining a prototype. Today, thanks to Monge, manufacturers rely on CAD (computer-aided design) and CAM (computer-aided manufacturing) to take three-dimensional designs straight from the computer to the factory floor.

Once standardized, interchangeable parts became the norm, and after parts could be made from design drawings alone, manufacturers ran into a costly problem that they had never faced before: too much inventory. *Inventory* is the amount and number of raw materials, parts, and finished products that a company has in its possession. In fact, large factories were accumulating parts inventories sufficient for two to three months, much more than they needed on a daily basis to run their manufacturing operations. A solution to this problem was found in 1905 when the Oldsmobile Motor Works in Detroit burned down.[52] Management rented a new production facility to get production up and running as quickly as possible after the fire. But because the new facility was much smaller, there was no room to store large stockpiles of inventory (which the company couldn't afford anyway as it was short on funds). Therefore, the company made do with what it called "hand-to-mouth inventories," in which each production station had only enough parts on hand to do a short production run. Because all of its parts suppliers were close by, Oldsmobile could place orders in the morning and receive them in the afternoon (even without telephones), just as with today's computerized just-in-time inventory systems. So, contrary to common belief, just-in-time inventory systems were not invented by Japanese manufacturers. Instead, they were invented out of necessity more than a century ago because of a fire.

2-5b Information Management

For most of recorded history, information has been costly, difficult to obtain, and slow to spread. Because of the immense labor and time it took to hand copy

FROM INDEX CARDS TO THE INTERNET AND GOOGLE

From 1735 to 1770, naturalist Carl Linnaeus, the founder of modern taxonomy, categorized 12,000 minerals, plants, and animals across 13 editions of his book, *Systema Naturae*. Rather than use notebooks to record his observations and data, he invented and used separate notecards. In a quickly changing field exploding with new information (sound familiar?), notecards provided flexibility to easily recategorize, add, or update information without having to change his other 12,000 observations.

The advantages of managing information by index cards were so great they gave birth in 1910 to Google's nondigital ancestor, Belgium's Mundaneum, which used 18 million index cards in 15,000 drawers for the purpose—like Google—of categorizing "all the information in the world."

In 1935, Paul Otlet, co-founder of the Mundaneum, clearly envisioned how notecards could lead to today's Internet, writing, "From a distance, everyone will be able to read text, enlarged and limited to the desired subject, projected on an individual screen. In this way, everyone from his

armchair will be able to contemplate the whole of creation, in whole or in certain parts."

Sources: "History | Archives Centre," Mundaneum," accessed March 4, 2017, http://archives.mundaneum.org/en/history; "Google and Mundaneum Are Proud to Announce Their Collaboration," Mundaneum, accessed March 4, 2017, http://expositions.mundaneum.org/en/google-and-mundaneum-are-proud-announce-their-collaboration; British Society for the History of Science, "Carl Linnaeus Invented The Index Card," *ScienceDaily*, June 16, 2009, accessed March 4, 2017, https://www.sciencedaily.com/releases/2009/06/090616080137.htm; J. Schifman, "How the Humble Index Card Foresaw the Internet," *Popular Mechanics*, February 11, 2016, accessed March 4, 2017, http://www.popularmechanics.com/culture/a19379/a-short-history-of-the-index-card/.

information, books, manuscripts, and written documents of any kind were rare and extremely expensive. Word of Joan of Arc's death in 1431 took 18 months to travel from France across Europe to Constantinople (now Istanbul, Turkey).

Consequently, throughout history, organizations have pushed for and quickly adopted new information technologies that reduce the cost or increase the speed with which they can acquire, store, retrieve, or communicate information. The first technologies to truly revolutionize the business use of information were paper and the printing press. In the fourteenth century, water-powered machines were created to pulverize rags into pulp to make paper. Paper prices, which were already lower than those of animal-skin parchments, dropped dramatically. Less than a half-century later, Johannes Gutenberg invented the printing press, which greatly reduced the cost and time needed to copy written information. In fifteenth-century Florence, Italy, a scribe would charge one florin (an Italian unit of money) to hand copy one document page. By contrast, a printer would set up and print 1,025 copies of the same document for just three florins. Within 50 years of its invention, Gutenberg's printing press cut the cost of information by 99.8 percent!

What Gutenberg's printing press did for publishing, the manual typewriter did for daily communication. Before 1850, most business correspondence was written by hand and copied using the letterpress. With the ink still wet, the letter would be placed into a tissue-paper book. A hand press would then be used to squeeze the book and copy the still-wet ink onto the tissue paper. By the 1870s, manual typewriters made it cheaper, easier, and faster to produce and copy business correspondence. Of course, in the 1980s, slightly more than a century later, typewriters were replaced by personal computers and word processing software with the same results.

Finally, businesses have always looked for information technologies that would speed access to timely information. The Medici family, which opened banks throughout Europe in the early 1400s, used post messengers to keep in contact with their more than 40 branch managers. The post messengers, who predated the U.S. Postal Service Pony Express by 400 years, could travel 90 miles per day, twice what average riders could cover, because the Medicis were willing to pay for the expense of providing them with fresh horses. This need for timely information also led companies to quickly adopt the telegraph in the 1860s, the telephone in the 1880s, and, of course, Internet technologies in the past three decades.

AVOIDING THE PITFALLS OF MERGERS

Managers interested in growth and scale often hope to reach their goals through mergers and acquisitions. Although mergers are a traditional path toward growth, several common problems arise when trying to achieve synergy through a merger.

» **Assuming you know what you're doing.** Managers often assume that their past experiences with mergers will automatically translate to any future merger they pursue ("I've done this before, so I can do it again—no problem."). Unfortunately, past experience is not always a predictor of future success because the strategies needed to create synergy in one merger are not necessarily universally applicable. Solve this problem by mixing up your team. A team whose members have diverse merger experiences will have a more panoramic view of the current opportunity and will be more likely to identify pitfalls early.

» **Breaking the bank.** Merger activity increases when companies have cash to spend. Managers who feel like their money is burning a hole in their pockets tend to overpay. Resist that urge by focusing on the metrics and logic of the merger. Ask yourself how the acquisition will create value for your company; whether your company is, in fact, the right buyer; and if the merger makes sense for your company strategically.

» **Understanding the real costs and benefits.** Not all synergies are equal. Synergies derived from cost savings are typically the most successful, while those related to cross-selling or vertical integration are more difficult to achieve. To avoid this pitfall, pay close attention to the costs associated with the merger (such as management time, severance for laid-off workers, and additional investments). According to experts, producing annual savings of any amount can, over time, cost twice as much to achieve. (That is, if you expect to gain $100 million in synergistic cost savings, also expect to spend $200 million over time to achieve them.)

Source: S. Finkelstein, "How to Avoid Four Common Problems in Mergers," *Wall Street Journal*, February 22, 2016, R7.

2-5c Systems Management

Today's companies are much more complex than they used to be. They are larger and employ more people. They most likely manufacture, service, *and* finance what they sell, not only in their home markets but in foreign markets throughout the world, too. They also operate in complex, fast-changing, competitive, global environments that can quickly turn competitive advantages into competitive disadvantages. How, then, can managers make sense of this complexity, both within and outside their organizations?

One way to deal with organizational and environmental complexity is to take a systems view of organizations. The systems approach is derived from theoretical models in biology and social psychology developed in the 1950s and 1960s.[53] A **system** is a set of interrelated elements or parts that function as a whole. Rather than viewing one part of an organization as separate from the other parts, a systems approach encourages managers to complicate their thinking by looking for connections between the different parts of the organization. Indeed, one of the more important ideas in the systems approach to management is that organizational systems are composed of parts or **subsystems**, which are simply smaller systems within larger systems. Subsystems and their connections matter in systems theory because of the possibility for managers to create synergy. **Synergy** occurs when two or more subsystems working together can produce more than they can working apart. In other words, synergy occurs when 1 + 1 = 3.

Systems can be open or closed. **Closed systems** can function without interacting with their environments. But nearly all organizations should be viewed as **open systems** that interact with their environments and depend on them for survival. Therefore, rather than viewing what goes on within the organization as separate from what goes on outside it, the systems approach encourages managers to look for connections between the different parts of the organization and the different parts of its environment. Exhibit 2.7 illustrates how the elements of systems management work together.

A systems view of organizations offers several advantages. First, it forces managers to view their organizations as part of and subject to the competitive, economic, social, technological, and legal/regulatory forces in their environments.[54] Second, it forces managers to be

System a set of interrelated elements or parts that function as a whole

Subsystems smaller systems that operate within the context of a larger system

Synergy when two or more subsystems working together can produce more than they can working apart

Closed systems systems that can sustain themselves without interacting with their environments

Open systems systems that can sustain themselves only by interacting with their environments, on which they depend for their survival

Exhibit 2.7
Systems View of Organizations

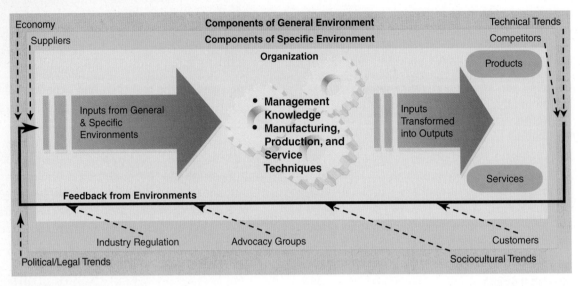

aware of how the environment affects specific parts of the organization. Third, because of the complexity and difficulty of trying to achieve synergies among different parts of the organization, the systems view encourages managers to focus on better communication and cooperation within the organization. Finally, it makes managers acutely aware that good internal management of the organization may not be enough to ensure survival. Survival also depends on making sure that the organization continues to satisfy critical environmental stakeholders such as shareholders, employees, customers, suppliers, governments, and local communities.

2-5d Contingency Management

Earlier, you learned that the goal of scientific management was to use systematic study to find the one best way of doing each task and then use that one best way everywhere. The problem, as you may have gathered from reading about the various approaches to management, is that no one in management seems to agree on what that one best way is. Furthermore, more than 100 years of management research has shown that there are clear boundaries or limitations to most management theories and practices. No management ideas or practices are universal. Although

> **Contingency approach** holds that there are no universal management theories and that the most effective management theory or idea depends on the kinds of problems or situations that managers are facing at a particular time and place

any theory or practice may work much of the time, none works all the time. How, then, is a manager to decide what theory to use? Well, it depends on the situation. The **contingency approach** to management clearly states that there are no universal management theories and that the most effective management theory or idea depends on the kinds of problems or situations that managers or organizations are facing at a particular time and place.[55] In short, the best way depends on the situation.

One of the practical implications of the contingency approach to management is that management is much harder than it looks. In fact, because of the clarity

Wavebreakmedia/Shutterstock.com

and obviousness of management theories (OK, most of them), students and workers often wrongly assume that a company's problems would be quickly and easily solved if management would take just a few simple steps. If this were true, few companies would have problems.

A second implication of the contingency approach is that managers need to look for key contingencies that differentiate today's situation or problems from yesterday's situation or problems. Moreover, it means that managers need to spend more time analyzing problems, situations, and employees before taking action to fix them. Finally, it means that as you read this text and learn about management ideas and practices, you need to pay particular attention to qualifying phrases such as "usually," "in these situations," "for this to work," and "under these circumstances." Doing so will help you identify the key contingencies that will help you become a better manager.

STUDY TOOLS 2

LOCATED IN TEXTBOOK

☐ Rip out and review chapter review card.

LOCATED AT WWW.CENGAGEBRAIN.COM

☐ Gain unique perspectives on key concepts with new 4LTR concept videos in the e-book.

☐ Increase your comprehension with Aplia for MGMT11.

☐ Complete interactive content within the e-book.

3 | Organizational Environments and Cultures

LEARNING OUTCOMES

3-1 Discuss how changing environments affect organizations.

3-2 Describe the four components of the general environment.

3-3 Explain the five components of the specific environment.

3-4 Describe the process that companies use to make sense of their changing environments.

3-5 Explain how organizational cultures are created and how they can help companies be successful.

After you finish this chapter, go to **PAGE 67** for **STUDY TOOLS**

Lisa Valder-E+/Getty Images

3-1 CHANGING ENVIRONMENTS

This chapter examines the internal and external forces that affect business. We begin by explaining how the changes in external organizational environments affect the decisions and performance of a company. Next, we examine the two types of external organizational environment: the general environment that affects all organizations and the specific environment unique to each company. Then, we learn how managers make sense of their changing general and specific environments. The chapter finishes with a discussion of internal organizational environments by focusing on organizational culture. But first, let's see how the changes in external organizational environments can affect a company's decisions and performance.

External environments are the forces and events outside a company that have the potential to influence or affect it. "Eat out or stay in tonight?" "Let's go out!" Americans now spend more money at restaurants and bars than at grocery stores. Even worse, hypercompetition is shrinking grocery stores' already weak profits. In the last decade, Walmart added nearly 2,300 grocery-selling super stores. Convenience stores and dollar stores have moved aggressively into groceries, accounting for 81 percent of the 6,500 new food retailers opened in the last three years.[1] Amazon hopes to disrupt the grocery industry by opening drive-in stores where consumers can pick up groceries preordered on amazon.com. License plate scanning will speed processing and reduce waiting times. Established grocers are fighting back. Walmart will have curbside pick up at 25 percent of its stores by 2018. Meijer, the inventor of the superstore, is offering one-hour home delivery at a cost of just $99 a year.[2] Finally, innovative grocers are serving alcohol at in-store bars, earning additional revenues and increasing how long customers shop. Some even have cart drink holders for drinking while shopping. Whole Foods' Chris Kopperud says, "When customers find out that they can sip and shop, a lot of times it's a light-bulb moment."[3] There's no doubt that the grocery industry is being affected by major changes in its external environment. Marty Siewert, Nielsen's senior vice president for consumer and shopper analytics, says, "I don't think we've seen shopping change so dramatically ever."[4]

*Let's examine the three basic characteristics of changing external environments: **3-1a environmental change; 3-1b environmental complexity; 3-1c resource scarcity;** and **3-1d the uncertainty that environmental change, complexity, and resource scarcity can create for organizational managers.***

External environments
all events outside a company that have the potential to influence or affect it

3-1a Environmental Change

Environmental change is the rate at which a company's general and specific environments change. In **stable environments**, the rate of environmental change is slow. The funeral business changes little from year to year. Families arrange for services for their loved ones with a funeral home, which then obtains a casket from one of three U.S. manufacturers, cares for the remains, hosts a visitation or memorial service, and organizes the burial or cremation, by perhaps connecting the family with the cemetery or columbarium for purchase of a final resting place—all for an average price of $7,181 for viewing and burial and $6,078 for viewing and cremation. Although there have been some changes—such as cremation increasing from 4 percent in 1960 to 43 percent today, advances in embalming that are healthier (for the embalmer and the environment), and a small percentage of imported caskets (less than 10%)—the basic business of preparing bodies for burial, internment, or cremation hasn't changed significantly in over a century.[5]

Whereas the funeral industry has a stable environment, SiriusXM satellite radio competes in an extremely dynamic external environment. In **dynamic environments**, the rate of environmental change is fast. SiriusXM satellite radio makes money directly through the $15-a-month fees paid by 24 million subscribers, and indirectly via subsidies and revenue sharing paid to automakers (so that 75% of new cars have satellite radios that come with several free months of access to SiriusXM's 175 channels). But with telecom companies switching to unlimited data plans, will consumers continue to pay $15 a month if they can stream Spotify, Pandora, or Apple Music in their cars at no extra cost?[6] Also, thanks to the ubiquity of smartphones, podcast listening is growing 20 percent per month, and dedicated podcast listeners listen to five podcasts per week, mostly in their cars.[7]

Amazon Go grocery stores have implemented technology that allows shoppers to select groceries and leave without waiting in line or scanning them. Preordered groceries can be picked up in drive-throughs.

David Ryder/ Bloomberg/Getty Images

Although you might think that a company's external environment would be either stable or dynamic, research suggests that companies often experience both. According to **punctuated equilibrium theory**, companies go through long periods of stability (equilibrium) during which incremental changes occur; followed by short, complex periods of dynamic, fundamental change (revolutionary periods); and finishing with a return to stability (new equilibrium).[8]

The U.S. airline industry is a classic example of punctuated equilibrium, as three times in the past 30 years it has experienced revolutionary periods followed by a temporary return to stability. The first, from mid-1979 to mid-1982, occurred immediately after airline deregulation in 1978. Prior to deregulation, the federal government controlled where airlines could fly, how much they could charge, when they could fly, and the number of flights they could have on a particular route. After deregulation, these choices were left to the airlines. The large financial losses during this period clearly indicate that the airlines had trouble adjusting to the intense competition from new airlines that occurred after deregulation. By mid-1982, however, profits returned to the industry and held steady until mid-1989.

Then, after experiencing record growth and profits, U.S. airlines lost billions of dollars between 1989 and 1993 as the industry went through dramatic changes. Key expenses, including jet fuel and employee salaries, which had held steady for years, suddenly increased.

Environmental change the rate at which a company's general and specific environments change

Stable environment an environment in which the rate of change is slow

Dynamic environment an environment in which the rate of change is fast

Punctuated equilibrium theory the theory that companies go through long periods of stability (equilibrium), followed by short periods of dynamic, fundamental change (revolutionary periods), and then a new equilibrium

Furthermore, revenues, which had grown steadily year after year, suddenly dropped because of dramatic changes in the airlines' customer base. Business travelers, who had typically paid full-price fares, made up more than half of all passengers during the 1980s. However, by the late 1980s, the largest customer base had changed to leisure travelers, who wanted the cheapest flights they could get.[9]

With expenses suddenly up, and revenues suddenly down, the airlines responded to these changes in their business environment by laying off 5 to 10 percent of their workers, canceling orders for new planes, and eliminating unprofitable routes. Starting in 1993 and lasting until 1998, these changes helped the airline industry achieve profits far in excess of their historical levels. The industry began to stabilize, if not flourish, just as punctuated equilibrium theory predicts.[10]

The third revolutionary period for the U.S. airline industry began with the terrorist attacks of September 11, 2001, in which planes were used as missiles to bring down the World Trade Center towers and damage the Pentagon. The immediate effect was a 20 percent drop in scheduled flights, a 40 percent drop in passengers, and losses so large that the U.S. government approved a $15 billion bailout to keep the airlines in business. Heightened airport security also affected airports, the airlines themselves, and airline customers. Five years after the 9/11 attacks, United Airlines, U.S. Airways, Delta, and American Airlines had reduced staffing by 169,000 full-time jobs to cut costs after losing a combined $42 billion.[11] Due to their financially weaker position, the airlines restructured operations to take advantage of the combined effect of increased passenger travel, a sharply reduced cost structure, and a 23 percent reduction in the fleet to return their businesses to profitability.[12] But, just as the airlines were heading toward a more stable period of equilibrium in 2006 and 2007, the price of oil jumped dramatically, doubling, if not tripling, the price of jet fuel, which prompted the airlines to charge for luggage (to increase revenues and discourage heavy baggage) and cut flights using older, fuel-inefficient jets.

In 2013, however, stability and profitability largely returned. Compared to 2007, the airlines cut total seat capacity 14 percent; filled 83 percent of seats, up from 80 percent; and with stronger demand and fewer flights, saw round-trip fares rise by 4 percent, even after adjusting for inflation. In 2008, U.S. airlines collectively lost

Digital music services such as Pandora, Spotify, and Apple Music have changed the way that we consume music.

Thomas Trutschel / Photothek/Getty Images

$23.7 billion, but by the end of 2016, they had logged their sixth consecutive year of profits.[13] Multiple airline mergers—Delta and Northwest, United and Continental, Southwest and AirTran, and U.S. Airways and American Airlines—reduced competition and routes even further. As a result, the number of domestic flights dropped 6.8 percent from 2012 to 2015, while the number of available seats increased by 2.2 percent.[14] Indeed, in 2016 half of Boeing's new large planes were 10 seats across, 1 more than the standard 9 seat configuration.[15] Why are airlines instituting these changes? So they can fly fewer flights in larger, fuller planes. Smaller U.S. airports, many in the Midwest and South, have seen dramatic cuts in flights. These hubs traditionally flew smaller planes with low passenger loads—that is—too many empty seats. Dan Landson, spokesperson for Southwest, recently justified the reduced flight traffic to these locations, saying, "We have a responsibility to maximize the productivity and profitability of our fleet."[16]

3-1b Environmental Complexity

Environmental complexity refers to the number and the intensity of external factors in the environment that affect organizations. **Simple environments** have few environmental factors, whereas **complex environments** have many environmental factors. The dairy industry is an excellent example of a relatively simple external environment. Even accounting for decades-old advances in processing, automatic milking machines, and breeding techniques, where the latter has increased annual yield from 5,000 pounds of milk per cow in 1942 to 22,774 pounds today, milk is produced the same way today as it was 100 years ago.[17] So while food manufacturers introduce dozens of new dairy-based products each year, U.S. milk production has grown a modest 1.7 percent per year over the past decade. In short, producing milk is a highly competitive industry with a few key environmental factors.[18]

Environmental complexity the number and the intensity of external factors in the environment that affect organizations

Simple environment an environment with few environmental factors

Complex environment an environment with many environmental factors

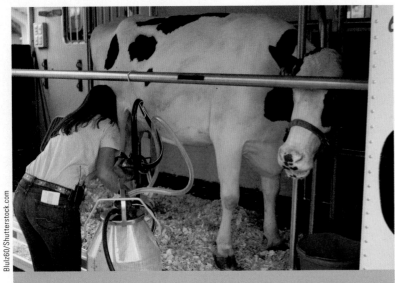

Bluiz60/Shutterstock.com

The dairy industry is an excellent example of a simple external environment.

At the other end of the spectrum, we find "less-than-truckload" (LTL) distribution companies with surprisingly complex environments. Order a home safe or other items too big or too heavy for UPS, FedEx, or the USPS, and they'll be delivered to your home by LTL trucking companies that traditionally deliver to business' loading docks. With LTL deliveries up 20 percent thanks to e-commerce, LTL firms are struggling with how to quickly and cheaply deliver heavy, bulky items via full-sized trucks that are too large for small neighborhood streets. Paul Dugent, vice president of Estes Express Lines says, "Chances are, we're going to take out a mailbox."[19] Furthermore, LTL truck drivers pull double duty by also unloading the heavy shipments by themselves. Steven Gast, president of Wilson trucking says, "If you're the [online] seller, you're happy. If you're the guy delivering it, you're pulling your hair out." Wilson says, "Nobody's figured out the cost side. Everyone is scrambling."[20]

3-1c Resource Scarcity

The third characteristic of external environments is resource scarcity. **Resource scarcity** is the abundance or shortage of critical organizational resources in an organization's external

Resource scarcity the abundance or shortage of critical organizational resources in an organization's external environment

Uncertainty extent to which managers can understand or predict which environmental changes and trends will affect their businesses

General environment the economic, technological, sociocultural, and political/legal trends that indirectly affect all organizations

environment. Thanks to the sweet tooths of the growing middle classes in India and China, global demand for chocolate is up, but with global production down because of antiquated farming methods and aging, less-productive cocoa trees, cocoa prices have risen 40 percent since 2012. The 10 largest chocolate producers have combined efforts to increase supply by dedicating $1 billion toward sharing ways to improve crop yields. Yea Amekudzi, who works for Mondelez International, which makes Cadbury Dairy Milk bars, says that producers in Ghana (which is the second largest cocoa exporter in the world), "…need to change the way they farm. We don't have the forest cover we had, we don't have the rain our grandfathers had, and the soil isn't as fertile…"[21] With the right methods, chocolate companies believe that Ghana's farmers can triple yields.

3-1d Uncertainty

As Exhibit 3.2 shows, environmental change, environmental complexity, and resource scarcity affect environmental **uncertainty**, which is how well managers can understand or predict the external changes and trends affecting their businesses. Starting at the left side of the exhibit, environmental uncertainty is lowest when environmental change and environmental complexity are at low levels, and resource scarcity is low (that is, resources are plentiful). In these environments, managers feel confident that they can understand, predict, and react to the external forces that affect their businesses. By contrast, the right side of the exhibit shows that environmental uncertainty is highest when environmental change and complexity are extensive, and resource scarcity is a problem. In these environments, managers may not be confident that they can understand, predict, and handle the external forces affecting their businesses.

3-2 GENERAL ENVIRONMENT

As Exhibit 3.3 shows, two kinds of external environments influence organizations: the general environment and the specific environment. The **general environment** consists of the economy and the technological,

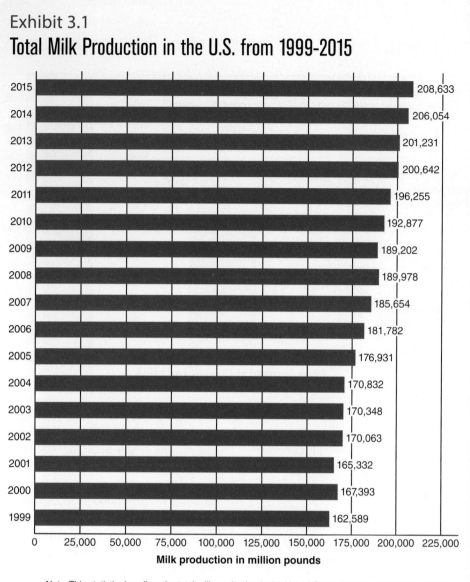

Exhibit 3.1
Total Milk Production in the U.S. from 1999-2015

Year	Milk production in million pounds
2015	208,633
2014	206,054
2013	201,231
2012	200,642
2011	196,255
2010	192,877
2009	189,202
2008	189,978
2007	185,654
2006	181,782
2005	176,931
2004	170,832
2003	170,348
2002	170,063
2001	165,332
2000	167,393
1999	162,589

Milk production in million pounds

Note: This statistic describes the total milk production in the United States from 1999 to 2015. In 1999, approximately 163 billion pounds of milk were produced. This figure excludes milk sucked by calves.

Source: http://www.statista.com/statistics/194937/total-US-milk-production-since-1999/

sociocultural, and political/legal trends that indirectly affect *all* organizations. Changes in any sector of the general environment eventually affect most organizations. For example, when the Federal Reserve lowers its prime lending rate, most businesses benefit because banks and credit card companies often lower the interest rates they charge for loans. Consumers, who can then borrow money more cheaply, might borrow more to buy homes, cars, refrigerators, and large-screen LCD TVs.

Each organization also has a **specific environment** that is unique to that firm's industry and directly affects the way it conducts day-to-day business.

Specific environment the customers, competitors, suppliers, industry regulations, and advocacy groups that are unique to an industry and directly affect how a company does business

Exhibit 3.2
Environmental Change, Environmental Complexity, and Resource Scarcity

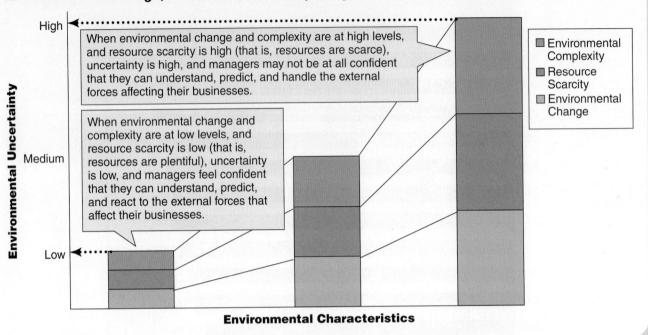

When environmental change and complexity are at high levels, and resource scarcity is high (that is, resources are scarce), uncertainty is high, and managers may not be at all confident that they can understand, predict, and handle the external forces affecting their businesses.

When environmental change and complexity are at low levels, and resource scarcity is low (that is, resources are plentiful), uncertainty is low, and managers feel confident that they can understand, predict, and react to the external forces that affect their businesses.

Legend:
- Environmental Complexity
- Resource Scarcity
- Environmental Change

Y-axis: Environmental Uncertainty (Low, Medium, High)
X-axis: Environmental Characteristics

The specific environment, which will be discussed in detail in Section 3-3 of this chapter, includes customers, competitors, suppliers, industry regulation, and advocacy groups.

But first let's take a closer look at the four components of the general environment: 3-2a the economy and 3-2b the technological, 3-2c sociocultural, and 3-2d political/legal trends that indirectly affect all organizations.

3-2a Economy

The current state of a country's economy affects virtually every organization doing business there. In general, in a growing economy, more people are working, and wages are growing, and therefore consumers have relatively more money to spend. More products are bought and sold in a growing economy than in a static or shrinking economy. Although an individual firm's sales will not necessarily increase, a growing economy does provide an environment favorable to business growth. In contrast, in a shrinking economy, consumers have less money to spend, and relatively fewer products are bought and sold. Thus, a shrinking economy makes growth for individual businesses more difficult.

For three decades, the Chinese economy averaged 10 percent annual growth. This consistent growth spurred cargo companies to buy new ships to transport goods to and from China.[22] In 2008, however, China's growth rate began declining. China's growth slowed so much that by 2015, several global shipping companies started storing, selling, or scrapping much of their fleets.[23] In 2016, roughly 1,000 ships capable of transporting 52 million metric tons were dismantled and sold for scrap.[24] From 2015 to 2016, **International Shipcare** doubled its number of ships in dry dock from 51 to 102.[25] **Scorpio Bulkers**, which spent $1.5 billion in 2013 and 2014 to acquire new cargo ships, has had to sell them all at a loss of $400 million.[26] Regarding the shift in China's economy, Maritime advisor Basil Karatzas says, "It's a bloodbath, which calls into question the survival of many dry-bulk shipping companies."[27]

Because the economy influences basic business decisions, such as whether to hire more employees, expand production, or take out loans to purchase equipment, managers scan their economic environments for signs of significant change. Unfortunately, the economic statistics that managers rely on when making these decisions are notoriously poor predictors of *future* economic activity. Scott Wine, CEO of Polaris Industries, which makes motorcycles, snowmobiles, and off-road vehicles, says, "The so-called experts and global economists are proven as often to be wrong as right these days."[28] Steve Miller, CEO of International Automotive Components Group, agrees, saying, "You can't run your business with only

Exhibit 3. 3
General and Specific Environments

one track in mind—which is the direction that forecasters and experts are telling you it will go."[29] So a manager who hired 10 more employees because forecasts suggested future growth, could very well have had to lay off those workers when the forecasted economic growth did not occur.

Because economic statistics can be poor predictors, some managers try to predict future economic activity by keeping track of business confidence. **Business confidence indices** show how confident actual managers are about future business growth. For example, the Conference Board's CEO Confidence Index is a quarterly survey of 100 CEOs in large companies across a variety of different industries that examines attitudes regarding future growth in the economy or particular industries.[30] Another useful index is the *Wall Street Journal (WSJ)*/Vistage Small Business CEO Survey, which surveys small business CEOS about their sentiments regarding their general economy and how optimistic they are about future revenues, profitability, and business spending.[31] Managers often prefer business confidence indices to economic statistics because they know that other managers make business decisions that are in line with their expectations concerning the economy's

future. So if the Conference Board or *WSJ*/Vistage Small Business CEO Survey business confidence indices are dropping, a manager might decide against hiring new employees, increasing production, or taking out additional loans to expand the business.

3-2b Technological Component

Technology is the knowledge, tools, and techniques used to transform inputs (raw materials, information, and so on) into outputs (products and services). For example, the inputs of authors, editors, and artists (knowledge) and the use of equipment such as computers and printing presses (technology) transformed paper, ink, and glue (raw materials) into this book (the finished product). In the case of a service company such as an airline, the technology consists of equipment, including airplanes, repair tools, and computers, as well as the knowledge of

Business confidence indices indices that show managers' level of confidence about future business growth

Technology the knowledge, tools, and techniques used to transform inputs into outputs mechanics, ticketers, and flight crews. The output is the service of transporting people from one place to another.

Changes in technology can help companies provide better products or produce their products more efficiently. Although technological changes can benefit a business, they can also threaten it. For example, the insurance industry earns about $200 billion annually in premiums for auto insurance. When self-driving cars arrive, they could, much like technology in passenger jet cockpits, reduce accidents by 80 percent. Furthermore, does the passenger who is *not* driving pay the insurance? Allstate Corporation CEO Tom Wilson says, "Change is coming, and we need to get ahead of it."[32] Companies must embrace new technology and find effective ways to use it to improve their products and services or decrease costs. If they don't, they will lose out to companies that do.

3-2c Sociocultural Component

The sociocultural component of the general environment refers to the demographic characteristics, general behavior, attitudes, and beliefs of people in a particular society. Sociocultural changes and trends influence organizations in two important ways.

First, changes in demographic characteristics, such as the number of people with particular skills or the growth of or decline in the number of people with particular population characteristics (marital status, age, gender, ethnicity), affect how managers staff their businesses. With the cruise industry growing just 3–4 percent per year, Carnival Cruise Lines has increased the number of cruises sailing out of China, the industry's fastest growing market, from one in 2011 to four today. While 700,000 Chinese took cruises last year, compared to 10 million Americans, Carnival expects 20–30 percent annual growth in China, which will result in 5 million Chinese taking cruises by 2020.[33]

Second, sociocultural changes in behavior, attitudes, and beliefs also affect the demand for a business's products and services. For example, urban dwellers in their twenties and early thirties who follow the latest styles, trends, and fashions—often referred to as *hipsters*—spend more of their income on food than their parents did at the same age. But rather than buying from the commercial food and beverage companies that their parents made into household names, these young adults gravitate toward organic foods, exotic ingredients, and craft beers, spirits, and mixers. Consequently, markets that used to be considered niche are booming. Sales of organic food have doubled in little over a decade; U.S. craft beers account for 19 percent of the total U.S. beer

TRUST EXPERTS, BUT NOT ABOUT THE FUTURE

"If I were a gambler, I would take even money that England will not exist in the year 2000." After 20 years of testing 28,000 predictions made by experts, Professor Philip Tetlock clearly found that experts are not much better than chance when it comes to predicting the future. Why? Because they rely on assumptions that explain the past, but not the future. That 1971 prediction, by the way, was made by an expert, Stanford biologist Paul Erich, who, like England, is still around.

Source: M. Ridley, "Experts and the Future," Matt Ridley, July 31, 2016, accessed March 8, 2017, http://www.rationaloptimist.com/blog/experts-and-the-future/.

market; and sales of male grooming products, such as beard balm, are up nearly 10 percent.[34] Despite the economic impact that hipsters have in these markets, large consumer product companies find it difficult to get and keep their purchasing loyalty. Economist Douglas McWilliams says that hipsters have "identifiable spending patterns and homogeneous tastes. But they don't want others to copy them, so they keep up by changing their tastes, by moving on to the next things. You have to watch that if you're a consumer products company.[35]

3-2d Political/Legal Component

The political/legal component of the general environment includes the legislation, regulations, and court decisions that govern and regulate business behavior. New laws and regulations continue to impose additional responsibilities on companies. Unfortunately, many managers are unaware of these new responsibilities. For example, under the 1991 Civil Rights Act (http://www.eeoc.gov/policy/cra91.html), if an employee is sexually harassed by anyone at work (a supervisor, a coworker, or even a customer), the company—not just the harasser—is potentially liable for damages, attorneys' fees, and back pay.[36] Under the Family and Medical Leave Act (https://www.dol.gov/general/topic/benefits-leave/fmla), which applies to employers with 50 or more employees, employees who have been on the job one year are guaranteed 12 weeks of unpaid leave per year to tend to their own illnesses or to their elderly parents, a newborn baby, or a newly adopted child. Employees are guaranteed the same job, pay, and benefits when they return to work.[37] The most recent major regulation to affect U.S. businesses is the Patient Protection and Affordable Care Act (https://www.hhs.gov/healthcare/about-the-law/index. html), which requires businesses with more than 100 full-time employees to offer affordable health care insurance to full-time employees and their families. To demonstrate that they are in compliance, companies must file tax forms showing their individual employees' health care costs on a monthly basis. Penalties for not filing proper tax forms can be up to $3,000 per employee.[38]

Many managers are also unaware of the potential legal risks associated with traditional managerial decisions about recruiting, hiring, and firing employees. Increasingly, businesses and managers are being sued for negligent hiring and supervision, defamation, invasion of privacy, emotional distress, fraud, and misrepresentation during employee recruitment.[39] More than 14,000 suits for wrongful termination (unfairly firing employees) are filed each year.[40] In fact, wrongful termination lawsuits increased by 77 percent during the 1990s.[41] Likewise, Equal Employment Opportunity Commission filings alleging wrongful discharge average around 23,500 cases per year.[42] One in four employers will at some point be sued for wrongful termination. It can cost $300,000 to settle such a case after it goes to court, but employers lose 50 percent to 70 percent of court cases,[43] and the former employee is awarded, on average, $1 million or more.[44] On the other hand, employers who settle before going to court typically pay just $10,000–$100,000 per case.[45]

Not everyone agrees that companies' legal risks are too severe. Indeed, many believe that the government should do more to regulate and restrict business behavior and that it should be easier for average citizens to sue dishonest or negligent corporations. From a managerial perspective, the best medicine against legal risk is prevention. As a manager, it is your responsibility to educate yourself about the laws, regulations, and potential lawsuits that could affect your business. Failure to do so may put you and your company at risk of sizable penalties, fines, or legal charges.

3-3 SPECIFIC ENVIRONMENT

As you just learned, changes in any sector of the general environment (economic, technological, sociocultural, and political/legal) eventually affect most organizations. Each organization also has a specific environment that is unique to that firm's industry and directly affects the way it conducts day-to-day business. For instance, if your

customers decide to use another product, your main competitor cuts prices 10 percent, your best supplier can't deliver raw materials, federal regulators mandate reductions in pollutants in your industry, or environmental groups accuse your company of selling unsafe products, the impact from the specific environment on your business is immediate.

*Let's examine how the **3-3a customer, 3-3b competitor, 3-3c supplier, 3-3d industry regulation,** and **3-3e advocacy group** components of the specific environment affect businesses.*

3-3a Customer Component

Customers purchase products and services. Companies cannot exist without customer support. Monitoring customers' changing wants and needs is critical to business success. There are two basic strategies for monitoring customers: reactive and proactive.

Reactive customer monitoring involves identifying and addressing customer trends and problems after they occur. One reactive strategy is to listen closely to customer complaints and respond to customer concerns. **Listen360** is a company that helps businesses monitor customer satisfaction and complaints by contacting their customers and asking two questions, "How likely are you to recommend this business?" followed by an open-ended question to explain why. Customer responses fall into three categories: "promoters," who would recommend the business to others; "passives," who are neither negative nor positive; and "detractors," unhappy customers who would not recommend the business. When customers are unhappy, the business receives a report detailing what products and services the customer purchased, what it would cost the company if it lost that customer's business, and a "voice of the customer" report that scans the answers to the open-ended question for key words about specific likes, dislikes, and concerns. According to Heather Anderson, director of marketing for The Little Gym, a children's fitness franchise, "Many owners have also chosen to get an immediate notification via text message if they receive a detractor comment, so they can respond within minutes of receiving the feedback."[46]

Companies that respond quickly to customer letters of complaint (that is, reactive customer monitoring) are viewed much more favorably than companies that are slow to respond or never respond.[47] In particular, studies have shown that customers are much more likely to purchase products or services again from a company when that company sends a follow-up letter

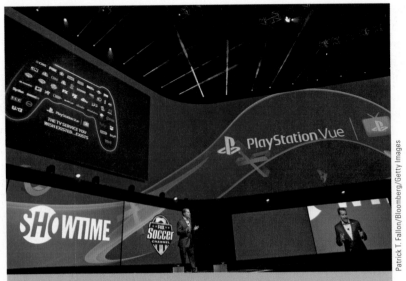

Cable and satellite providers face new competition from streaming television options like Sony's PlayStation Vue. Launched nationwide in March, 2016, Vue offers live streaming television, cloud-based DVR, and no contracts for less than $30 a month.

to thank the customer for writing; offers a sincere, specific response to the complaint (not a form letter, but an explanation of how the problem will be handled); and offers a small gift, coupons, or a refund to make up for the problem.[48]

Proactive monitoring of customers means identifying and addressing customer needs, trends, and issues *before* they occur. **Spotify** is the world's most popular subscription music service, with 20 million paying subscribers and 55 million ad-supported users. Spotify Fan Insights, a data analytics tool, helps musical artists better understand their listeners and convert their fans' enthusiasm into deeper engagement. Fan Insights lists listeners' geographic locations, demographic information (such as gender and age), how they are listening (for example, to a Spotify-curated playlist or to their own collections), when they are listening (down to the time of day), and even which playlists contain the artists' music. In addition, artists can now sell concert tickets and merchandise directly through Spotify. For Spotify Chief Revenue Officer Jeff Levick, supporting artists with metrics and selling tools helps them understand their own audiences. "For artists, this can even give them the ability to better manage their tours. They can have the knowledge about where they should

be playing certain songs, for example, rather than just doing the same set list everywhere."[49] This kind of information is particularly helpful for finding and catering to superfans. According to Spotify's vice president of product, Charlie Hellman, these fans "have a disproportionate impact on revenue: they're the people who'll buy tickets, VIP packages, merchandise, and will be the social evangelists for the band."[50]

3-3b Competitor Component

Competitors are companies in the same industry that sell similar products or services to customers. Ford, Toyota, Honda, Nissan, Hyundai, and Kia all compete for automobile customers. NBC, ABC, CBS, and Fox (along with hundreds of cable channels) compete for TV viewers' attention. McDonald's, Burger King, Wendy's, Hardee's, Chick-fil-A, and a host of others compete for fast-food customers' dollars. Often the difference between business success and failure comes down to whether your company is doing a better job of satisfying customer wants and needs than the competition. Consequently, companies need to keep close track of what their competitors are doing. To do this, managers perform a **competitive analysis**, which involves deciding who your competitors are, anticipating competitors' moves, and determining competitors' strengths and weaknesses.

Surprisingly, managers often do a poor job of identifying potential competitors because they tend to focus on only two or three well-known competitors with similar goals and resources.[51]

Another mistake managers may make when analyzing the competition is to underestimate potential competitors' capabilities. When this happens, managers don't take the steps they should to continue to improve their products or services. Yellow Cab Cooperative (YCC), San Francisco's largest taxi company, has filed for bankruptcy protection (to reorganize its finances). President Pamela Martinez said, "We are in the midst of serious financial setbacks. Some are due to business challenges beyond our control, and others are of our own making."[52] What are the challenges supposedly beyond YCC's control? San Francisco-based

Competitors companies in the same industry that sell similar products or services to customers

Competitive analysis a process for monitoring the competition that involves identifying competition, anticipating their moves, and determining their strengths and weaknesses

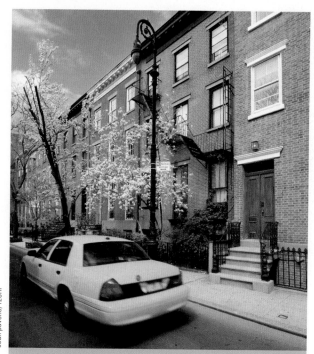

Services like Uber and Lyft have brought serious competition to traditional yellow taxis.

Staples is a prime example of a supplier.

Uber and Lyft, the ride sharing companies, are popular for their easy-to-use apps that make clear your price, driver, and how long you'll have to wait for your ride to arrive. Yellow Cab taxi service in Chicago has also filed for bankruptcy for similar reasons, citing competition from, "on-demand app-based private transportation network."[53] YCC finally released Yo Taxi, a ride-hailing app to compete with Uber and Lyft. Why did it wait so long to do so?

3-3c Supplier Component

Suppliers are companies that provide material, human, financial, and informational resources to other companies. U.S. Steel buys iron ore from suppliers to make steel products. When IBM sells a mainframe computer, it also provides support staff, engineers, and other technical consultants to the company that bought the computer. If you're shopping for desks, chairs, and office supplies, chances are that Staples will be glad to help your business open a revolving charge account to pay for your purchases. When a clothing manufacturer has spent $100,000 to purchase new high-pressure water drills to cut shirt and pant patterns to precise sizes, the water drill manufacturer, as part of the purchase, will usually train the workers to use the machinery.

A key factor influencing the impact and quality of the relationship between companies and their suppliers is how dependent they are on each other.[54] **Supplier dependence** is the degree to which a company relies on that supplier because of the importance of the supplier's product to the company and the difficulty of finding other sources for that product. Over the last decade, China has produced 75 to 95 percent of all rare-earth metals.[55] That dominance made automotive companies almost exclusively dependent on Chinese suppliers for heavy rare-earth metals used to manufacture the magnets used in hybrid car engines.

Buyer dependence is the degree to which a supplier relies on a buyer because of the importance of that buyer to the supplier's sales and the difficulty of finding other buyers of its products. While South Korea-based Samsung dominates the OLED market for smartphone screens (that is, supplier dependence), it's also the case that Samsung's growing OLED business is highly dependent on Apple, which purchased 100 million 5.5 inch OLED screens for $2.6 billion from Samsung for 2017 and another order of $4.3 billion for OLED screens in 2018 and beyond. Apple's tenth anniversary iPhone, released in fall 2017, will have curved OLED screens.[56]

A high degree of buyer or seller dependence can

Suppliers companies that provide material, human, financial, and informational resources to other companies

Supplier dependence the degree to which a company relies on a supplier because of the importance of the supplier's product to the company and the difficulty of finding other sources of that product

Buyer dependence the degree to which a supplier relies on a buyer because of the importance of that buyer to the supplier and the difficulty of finding other buyers for its products

Federal Regulatory Agencies and Commissions

Consumer Product Safety Commission
Reduces risk of injuries and deaths associated with consumer products, sets product safety standards, enforces product recalls, and provides consumer education **http://www.cpsc.gov**

Department of Labor
Collects employment statistics and administers labor laws concerning safe working conditions, minimum hourly wages and overtime pay, employment discrimination, and unemployment insurance **http://www.dol.gov**

Environmental Protection Agency
Reduces and controls pollution through research, monitoring, standard setting, and enforcement activities **http://www.epa.gov**

Equal Employment Opportunity Commission
Promotes fair hiring and promotion practices **http://www.eeoc.gov**

Federal Communications Commission
Regulates interstate and international communications by radio, television, wire, satellite, and cable **http://www.fcc.gov**

Federal Reserve System
As the nation's central bank, controls interest rates and money supply and monitors the U.S. banking system to produce a growing economy with stable prices **http://www.federalreserve.gov**

Federal Trade Commission
Restricts unfair methods of business competition and misleading advertising and enforces consumer protection laws **http://www.ftc.gov**

Food and Drug Administration
Protects the nation's health by making sure food, drugs, and cosmetics are safe **http://www.fda.gov**

National Labor Relations Board
Monitors union elections and stops companies from engaging in unfair labor practices **http://www.nlrb.gov**

Occupational Safety and Health Administration
Saves lives, prevents injuries, and protects the health of workers **http://www.osha.gov**

Securities and Exchange Commission
Protects investors in the bond and stock markets, guarantees access to information on publicly traded securities, and regulates firms that sell securities or give investment advice **http://www.sec.gov**

---

lead to **opportunistic behavior,** in which one party benefits at the expense of the other. Because of its market dominance, when China cut rare-earth exports by 40 percent, prices rose by a factor of 10 because there were few alternative sources. Motivated by the opportunistic behavior of Chinese rare-earth producers, Honda successfully completed a decade-long effort in 2017 to manufacture hybrid car engines that drastically reduced the use of rare earth metals. Honda's new hybrid engine uses just one rare-earth metal, neodymium, but since that can be obtained from North America and Australia, Honda is no longer dependent on China as the sole supplier.[57]

In contrast to opportunistic behavior, **relationship behavior** focuses on establishing a mutually beneficial, long-term relationship between buyers and suppliers.[58] General Motors has a well-earned reputation for opportunistic behavior toward its suppliers. Steve Kiefer, GM's purchasing chief, admits that GM's supplier relationships have been one sided in GM's favor. If material costs or currency exchange rates changed, significantly raising suppliers costs, GM expected them to absorb the losses because they previously agreed to lower prices. But Kiefer, who used to work for Delphi Automotive PLC, one of GM's largest suppliers, is encouraging a mutually beneficial relationship by allowing suppliers to renegotiate their contracts when market conditions change significantly. Kiefer says that with GM's new relationship behavior is, "…adopting a simple formula that is more predictable and allows both sides to share in the ups and downs of those costs."[59] Scott Paradise, of Magna International, a GM supplier, welcomes the change, saying, "We now have a chance to recoup some of the costs you just weren't planning on hitting your business."[60]

Opportunistic behavior
a transaction in which one party in the relationship benefits at the expense of the other

Relationship behavior
the establishment of mutually beneficial, long-term exchanges between buyers and suppliers

3-3d Industry Regulation Component

Whereas the political/legal component of the general environment affects all businesses, the **industry regulation** component consists of regulations and rules that govern the practices and procedures of specific industries, businesses, and professions. Airbnb, the home-sharing website, that helps homeowners earn extra money through short-term rentals of rooms, apartments, or homes, is facing regulatory push back from major cities. Regulators argue that Airbnb rentals reduce the supply of housing that could go to full-time renters or owners, thus driving expensive housing prices even higher. Accordingly, London makes Airbnb limit homeowners to no more than 90 rental days a year. Amsterdam does the same, but the limit is 60 rental days a year. Regulators believe that limiting rental days should discourage home owners from purchasing properties for the purpose of renting them out all year via Airbnb. Not surprisingly, Airbnb disagrees with these regulations and frequently takes regulators to court. In New York, Airbnb's largest market, where it's illegal to rent an entire apartment for less than 30 days, Airbnb has filed with a court appeal, arguing that the law, "would impose significant immediate burdens and irreparable harm" to its business.[61]

The nearly 100 federal agencies and regulatory commissions can affect almost any kind of business. For example, according to the Consumer Products Safety Commission (CPSC), a child is injured every 24 minutes, or killed every two weeks, from furniture and TVs tipping over. In 2016, the CPSC announced a recall of 29 million Ikea chests and dressers that were tip-over hazards.

Airbnb has frequently gone to court in an attempt to challenge regulators.

Accordingly, Ikea offered consumers a full refund or a free wall anchoring kit.[62]

3-3e Advocacy Groups

Advocacy groups are groups of concerned citizens who band together to try to influence the business practices of specific industries, businesses, and professions. The members of a group generally share the same point of view on a particular issue. For example, environmental advocacy groups might try to get manufacturers to reduce smokestack pollution emissions. Unlike the industry regulation component of the specific environment, advocacy groups cannot force organizations to change their practices. Nevertheless, they can use a number of techniques to try to influence companies, including public communications, media advocacy, web pages, blogs, and product boycotts.

The **public communications** approach relies on *voluntary* participation by the news media and the advertising industry to send out an advocacy group's message. Media advocacy is much more aggressive than the public communications approach. A **media advocacy** approach typically involves framing the group's concerns as public issues (affecting everyone); exposing questionable, exploitative, or unethical practices; and creating controversy that is likely to receive extensive news coverage.

A **product boycott** is a tactic in which an advocacy group actively tries to persuade consumers not to purchase a company's product or service. Often times, advocacy groups will combine media advocacy with boycotts. This not only draws attention to concerns a group has with a company's practices or products, it also decreases the company's revenues and profits. This was the case with the LEGO Group, a family-owned Danish company that makes LEGO block and toys. While 90 percent of LEGO players are boys,

Industry regulation regulations and rules that govern the business practices and procedures of specific industries, businesses, and professions

Advocacy groups concerned citizens who band together to try to influence the business practices of specific industries, businesses, and professions

Public communications an advocacy group tactic that relies on voluntary participation by the news media and the advertising industry to get the advocacy group's message out

Media advocacy an advocacy group tactic that involves framing issues as public issues; exposing questionable, exploitative, or unethical practices; and forcing media coverage by buying media time or creating controversy that is likely to receive extensive news coverage

Product boycott an advocacy group tactic that involves protesting a company's actions by persuading consumers not to purchase its product or service the company has launched four girl-focused toy lines since 1979—mostly for building jewelry, beach houses, and stables in pink and purple. Feminist groups criticized each line for being less challenging than the traditional LEGO bricks aimed at boys and for perpetuating gender stereotypes through "pinkification." Before making another attempt at appealing to girls, LEGO spent five years conducting observation research to better understand how they assembled and played with LEGO products. LEGO also researched how girls and their parents make purchase decisions. (As it turns out, when given the choice, they still opted for pinks and purples over gender-neutral packaging.)

The research led to the development and launch of LEGO Friends, which design director Rosario Costa described as, "a real construction toy—not dumbing it down."[63] But as with prior product lines aimed at girls,

LEGO Friends was harshly criticized and boycotted. Advocacy group Spark Movement published an open letter to LEGO, beginning, "We represent the girls, the parents, the children, the fans, the hobbyists, the collectors, the friends, the big sisters and brothers, the grandparents, and your future. And we are very disappointed."[64] LEGO ultimately modified some of the LEGO Friends marketing materials, but the product remained unchanged—pink and purple bricks for building pop star houses, cupcake cafés, and a supermarket. Overall, LEGO Friends has been a tremendous success. The boycott had no effect on sales, and independent research firm NPD Group credits LEGO Friends with increasing the market for girls' building toys from $300 million to $900 million in just three years.[65] According to LEGO Senior Design Manager Benedikte Schinkel Stamp, "We just had to wait for the controversy to die out."[66]

Kari Haraldsdatter Høglund/123RF

Despite being harshly criticized and boycotted, LEGO friends has been a tremendous success.

3-4 MAKING SENSE OF CHANGING ENVIRONMENTS

In Chapter 1, you learned that managers are responsible for making sense of their business environments. As our discussions of the general and specific environments have indicated, however, making sense of business environments is not an easy task.

Because external environments can be dynamic, confusing, and complex, managers use a three-step process to make

*sense of the changes in their external environments: **3-4a environmental scanning, 3-4b interpreting environmental factors,** and **3-4c acting on threats and opportunities.***

3-4a Environmental Scanning

Environmental scanning involves searching the environment for important events or issues that might affect an organization. Managers scan the environment to stay up-to-date on important factors in their industry and to reduce uncertainty. They want to know if demand will increase, prices for key components will rise, and whether competitors sales are rising or falling. WeWork is a co-working office space company (meaning people from different small firms work in the same offices) with locations in 20 US cities and 17 international cities. WeWork plans start at $45 per month for 2 days per month, to $220 per month for a hot desk (use any empty desk), $350 per month for a dedicated desk in an open space or $400 per month for a private office. WeWork provides high-speed Internet, common areas for socializing, printers, free coffee, tea and beer, on site staff, and phone booths for private calls. Unfortunately, WeWork's competitors are multiplying like rabbits, from 250 co-working offices in the US in 2010, the year WeWork began business, to 3,000 co-working offices today. Fending off competitors could be difficult because of how easy it is for existing office developers to copy WeWork's business model. Indeed, co-founder Miguel McKelvey admits that close to WeWork's new Shanghai, China office, "there are quite a few derivations" of co-working nearly identical to WeWork.

Organizational strategies also affect environmental scanning. In other words, managers pay close attention to trends and events that are directly related to their company's ability to compete in the marketplace.[68] A key trend affecting many businesses is declining birthrates, down from 2.12 babies per woman before 2007, to 1.9 babies per woman from 2007 onward. While seemingly small, in the United States alone that results in half a million fewer babies born each year. Jennifer Olson, vice president of strategy and business development at Children's Hospitals and Clinics of Minnesota, says, "We're just in a new era nationally and even globally where people are having fewer children."[69] Reg McLay, senior vice president of Babies "R" Us, says, "The assumption we'll make is that the market is not going to grow."[70] So Babies "R" Us will try to grow by taking market share from competitors. Hospitals are adapting, too, by adding neonatal care units as career women delay childbirth into their late 30s.[71]

Finally, environmental scanning is important because it contributes to organizational performance. Environmental scanning helps managers detect environmental changes and problems before they become organizational crises.[72] Furthermore, companies whose CEOs do more environmental scanning have higher profits.[73] CEOs in better-performing firms scan their firms' environments more frequently and scan more key factors in their environments in more depth and detail than do CEOs in poorer-performing firms.[74]

3-4b Interpreting Environmental Factors

After scanning, managers determine what environmental events and issues mean to the organization. Typically, managers view environmental events and issues as either threats or opportunities. When managers interpret environmental events as threats, they take steps to protect the company from further harm. For more than a century, dry cereal was found on nearly every breakfast table in the United States. At its peak, Kellogg's and its cast of cartoon cereal mascots held a dominating 45 percent share of the market. Today, however, Kellogg's sales are dropping. Instead of having cereal for breakfast, many Americans now prefer a variety of alternatives, such as a piece of fruit, a breakfast sandwich, a granola bar, or a protein shake, all of which they can eat in their car or at their desk. Kellogg's CEO John Bryant acknowledges the threat to the company, saying, "The good news is that more people are eating breakfast; the bad news is that there are more alternatives."[75] Kellogg's CEO John Bryant implemented Project K, a cost-cutting program, from which a percentage of the savings would be invested in product innovation. Kellogg's also hired additional sales people to create more attractive in-store product displays. And, the company changed how it markets some of its cereals. For example, sales of Fruit Loops rose 3 percent after they were marketed to adults as a late-night snack.[76]

Valentina_S/Shutterstock.com

> **Environmental scanning** searching the environment for important events or issues that might affect an organization

With the world's population projected to grow from 7.3 billion in 2016 to 9.7 billion by 2050, farmers and food producers will need to produce an additional 455 million metric tons of meat to keep up with demand. Chicken is expected to account for the majority of that increase because of its mild taste, universal religious acceptance, and efficiency. Bringing a full-grown chicken to market requires just 30 percent of the water and feed needed to bring a cow to market.[77] Hoping to take advantage of the growing population and increased preference for chicken, Cargill has invested several billion dollars in new and expanded facilities. These high-tech operations feature automated, high-speed processing lines for breast deboning and production-line software that ensures that chicken portions are consistent in size and weight.[78] In Thailand, the company's network of more than 100 animal-friendly poultry farms has increased production 300 percent in just 10 years. Cargill is now able to ship 2.6 million birds from its Thailand operations to customers in Asia and Europe every week. This amounts to an additional 100 metric tons of chicken per year, or roughly 22 percent of the amount needed to feed an additional 2.4 billion people by 2050. Cargill expects to increase its capacity in Thailand another 30 percent in the near future, and also plans to develop a similarly sized network in sub-Saharan Africa to meet growing demand for meat across Africa's swelling urban centers.[79]

3-4c Acting on Threats and Opportunities

After scanning for information on environmental events and issues and interpreting them as threats or opportunities, managers have to decide how to respond to these environmental factors. Deciding what to do

Exhibit 3.4
Cognitive Maps

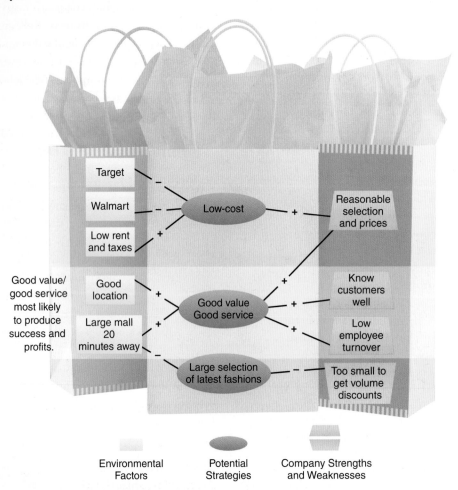

Environmental Factors   Potential Strategies   Company Strengths and Weaknesses

under conditions of uncertainty is always difficult. Managers can never be completely confident that they have all the information they need or that they correctly understand the information they have.

Because it is impossible to comprehend all the factors and changes, managers often rely on simplified models of external environments called cognitive maps. **Cognitive maps** summarize the perceived relationships between environmental factors and possible organizational actions. For example, the cognitive map shown in Exhibit 3.4 represents a small clothing-store owner's interpretation of her business environment. The map shows three kinds of variables. The first variables, shown as rectangles, are environmental factors, such as a Walmart or a large mall 20 minutes away. The second variables, shown in ovals, are potential actions that the store owner might take, such as a low-cost strategy; a good-value, good-service strategy; or a "large selection of the latest fashions" strategy. The third variables, shown as trapezoids, are company strengths, such as low employee turnover, and weaknesses, such as small size.

The plus and minus signs on the map indicate whether the manager believes there is a positive or negative relationship between variables. For example, the manager believes that a low-cost strategy won't work because Walmart and Target are nearby. Offering a large selection of the latest fashions would not work, either—not with the small size of the store and that large nearby mall. However, the manager believes that a good-value, good-service strategy would lead to success and profits due to the store's low employee turnover, good knowledge of customers, reasonable selection of clothes at reasonable prices, and good location.

Dealership culture can have an impact on auto sales.

Mary Rawson/123RF

3-5 ORGANIZATIONAL CULTURES: CREATION, SUCCESS, AND CHANGE

We have been looking at trends and events outside of companies that have the potential to affect them. By contrast, the **internal environment** consists of the trends and events *within* an organization that affect the management, employees, and **organizational culture**. Internal environments are important because they affect what people think, feel, and do at work. The key component in internal environments is organizational culture, or the set of key values, beliefs, and attitudes shared by members of the organization.

Creating, maintaining, and changing organizational culture matters because research shows that positive, consistent cultures improves company performance. In a six-year study of 95 automobile dealerships, Professor Michael Gillespie says, "We found that culture causes performance, not vice versa." Culture clearly comes first. Dealerships whose cultures did not improve were less profitable over the course of the study.[80] But dealerships, with positive cultures in the study's first few years usually had higher profits in the later years. It usually took, however, several years of change to an organizational culture to improve dealership performance as measured by customer satisfaction and dealer sales. "The culture of a sales department right now is to influence the customer satisfaction from that department two years from now, and that customer satisfaction is going to drive vehicle sales two years from that point," says Gillespie.[81] Gillespie and his co-authors concluded, "…that strong culture at the foundation can be a unique point of leverage for winning and retaining customers over time."[82] Leadership consultant David Grossman concludes, "Culture change today is at the heart of winning because it's so difficult for [other] employers to copy."[83]

Let's take a closer look at **3-5a how organizational**

Cognitive maps graphic depictions of how managers believe environmental factors relate to possible organizational actions

Internal environment the events and trends inside an organization that affect management, employees, and organizational culture

Organizational culture the values, beliefs, and attitudes shared by organizational members *cultures are created and maintained, 3-5b the characteristics of successful organizational cultures, and 3-5c how companies can accomplish the difficult task of changing organizational cultures.*

3-5a Creation and Maintenance of Organizational Cultures

A primary source of organizational culture is the company founder. Founders like Walt Disney (Disney) and Steve Jobs (Apple) created organizations in their own images and imprinted them with their beliefs, attitudes, and values. According to Professor Zeynep Ton, "The founder is in a better position than anyone else to say this is what our business is about, this is what we won't give up. They have to stick to their values 100 percent of the time, not 95 percent of the time." Founder Kip Tindell infused the **Container Store** with his personal philosophy, "Pay employees well and treat them with respect; consider suppliers and customers as family; have fun."[84] Tindell has turned that philosophy into seven Foundational Principles (see http://standfor.containerstore.com/our-foundation-principles/) that drive the Container Store's culture and actions. Not only are full-time employees given a week of training on the principles, the principles have been printed on company shopping bags, t-shirts, and packing tape. One strong sign that the principles have shaped the company culture is the low rate of employee turnover. Whereas the median turnover rate for part-time retail workers is 75 percent, at the Container Store, it is only 10 percent.[85] How are values, attitudes, and beliefs sustained in organizational cultures? Answer: stories, heroes, and celebrations.

People tell **organizational stories** to make sense of organizational events and changes and to emphasize culturally consistent assumptions, decisions, and actions.[86] CFO Ken Switzer has spent 27 years at Marco's Pizza, a pizza franchiser with 1,000 stores. Switzer says, "About three years ago, we embarked on a road to develop a culture of accountability at all levels of the organization. Accountability starts at a very personal level and that's true for everyone at the organization. It's been a long time since I heard somebody say 'It's not my job.'"[87] Monday meetings at headquarters and stores are critical to reinforcing the right assumptions, decisions, and actions in Marco's Pizza's organizational culture. Switzer explains, "Every Monday, for example, we have a pep rally for 10 minutes. We talk about new stores that have opened and stores that have hit new record levels of sales, new hires and personal achievements. We read recognition cards about people in the organization who have achieved something. It sounds a little hokey. There is clapping and cheering. It was awkward at first. It took a little time for people to be comfortable, but now it's a start-your-week-right attitude. Now some of the stores also hold their own weekly pep rallies."[88]

A second way in which organizational culture is sustained is by recognizing and celebrating heroes. By definition, **organizational heroes** are organizational people admired for their qualities and achievements within the organization. When Marco's Pizza reads recognition cards each Monday and applauds store managers and store crews that have hit record sales and achievements, they're recognizing and celebrating heroes.

Finally, the last way of sustaining organizational culture is through ceremonies. **Organizational ceremonies** are gatherings in which symbolic acts commemorate or celebrate notable achievements or changes. Patti Sanchez, senior vice president at Duarte, a communications consulting firm, explains that organizations, "… rely on ceremonies to anticipate new beginnings, demarcate endings, and help everyone understand or navigate the changes at hand."[89] Sanchez describes a famous organizational ceremony at Apple in which co-founder and CEO Steve Jobs held a mock funeral for the Mac OS 9 operating system (which could only run one application at a time) nine months after Apple released the unix-based Mac OS X capable of running multiple applications simultaneously. "With sad music playing in the background, Jobs placed a large box labeled 'Mac OS 9' into a coffin on stage and then delivered a eulogy for the operating system that had been 'a friend to us all.'"[90] Though done tongue-in-cheek, Jobs Mac OS 9 funeral was an important signal to Apple's customer and software developers that it would never go back to OS 9's outdated computing standards.

Organizational stories stories told by organizational members to make sense of organizational events and changes and to emphasize culturally consistent assumptions, decisions, and actions

Organizational heroes people celebrated for their qualities and achievements within an organization

Organizational ceremonies gatherings in which symbolic acts commemorate or celebrate notable achievements or changes

Markus Mainka/123RF

3-5b Successful Organizational Cultures

Preliminary research shows that organizational culture is related to organizational success. As shown in Exhibit 3.5, cultures based on adaptability, involvement, a clear mission, and consistency can help companies achieve higher sales growth, return on assets, profits, quality, and employee satisfaction.[91]

Adaptability is the ability to notice and respond to changes in the organization's environment. Cultures need to reinforce important values and behaviors, but a culture becomes dysfunctional if it prevents change. Unfortunately, that was the case at **Mattel**, the toy company, where Barbie sales were down 18 percent after dropping 13 percent the year before. Sales of Fisher-Price toys have declined three straight years. With revenues shrinking, Mattel cut $550 million in expenses just to maintain profits. CEO Bryan Stockton tried turning things around by changing the PowerPoint-presentation, meeting-driven, slow-to-make decisions culture. For example, it took eight meetings and 30 design iterations to approve the school crest for the Monster High toy line. As such, Mattel drifted from its creative roots focused on fun and play toward a conservative culture focused on the bottom line. To jump-start culture change, CEO Stockton generated new rules for meetings: No more than 10 participants (except for training meetings), every meeting must have a specific purpose,

and, "There should be no more than a TOTAL of three meetings to make any decision."[92] Change is slow, but it took just one meeting to approve the new package designs for the 2016 Hot Wheels toys. Unfortunately, Mattel subsequently lost a $300 million-a-year Disney toy licensing agreement to Hasbro. CEO Stockton resigned in January 2015. Interim CEO Christopher Sinclair led a two-year turnaround that saw global Barbie doll sales rebound 20 percent. Sinclair relinquished his interim CEO responsibilities in April 2017 when Google executive Margaret Georgiadis became Mattel's new CEO.[93]

Company mission is the business's purpose or reason for existing. In organizational cultures with a clear company mission, the organization's strategic purpose and direction are apparent to everyone in the company. When managers are uncertain about their business environments, the mission helps guide the discussions, decisions, and behavior of the people in the company. BPV Capital Management is a Knoxville, Tennessee, mutual fund with 38 employees. Alluding to the common dream of owning a retirement home with wonderful weather and a great view, founder Mike West explains that "BPV" stands for "back porch vista"; BPV exists "to help American families retire well." More specifically, its mission is, "To ensure that investors who work hard and save have the opportunity to retire comfortably, regardless of net worth." Says West, "Our values and the promise that we make to every advisor and investor are driven by that core ideology."[94]

Finally, in **consistent organizational cultures**, the company actively defines and teaches organizational values, beliefs, and attitudes. With 520 Olympic medals (220 gold), the U.S. Olympic team has dominated swimming for 25 years (Australia is a distant second with 171 medals). In 2015, **USA Swimming**, which governs the sport, commissioned a study to find out why. Said Executive Director Chuck Wielgus, "We wanted to know, what is **USA Swimming** doing so right?" The answer wasn't superior athletes or facilities, but a consistent three-part culture:

1. Build the base (develop a team environment and create a talent pipeline).
2. Promote the sport (mentor young swimmers and support mature swimmers so they can devote time to training).
3. Achieve competitive success (pair swimmers with experts and cultivate the value of serving swimming as a sport).

Exhibit 3.5
Keys to an Organizational Culture That Fosters Success

de2marco/Shutterstock.com

Adaptability

Employee Involvement

Clear Mission

Consistency

> **Company mission** a company's purpose or reason for existing
>
> **Consistent organizational culture** a company culture in which the company actively defines and teaches organizational values, beliefs, and attitudes

Hardcore Tech Culture

Crunchtime at a software development firm can be so intense that employees spend several days at the office without even going home. As journalist Joel Stein puts it, "Sleeping in the office is as Silicon Valley as startups in garages." Spending the night at work can be seen as a badge of commitment and dedication; not so much to a company, but to the occupation of computer coding itself. It's said that even after he was a billionaire, Yahoo! co-founder David Filo would doze in a sleeping bag under his desk. Elon Musk of PayPal (and now Tesla and SpaceX) would do the same on a beanbag alongside Filo's sleeping bag. Aaron Levie, founder of Box.com, even moved his bed to his new office when his company (and his staff) outgrew his home. But workers who actually *live* on site are in another category altogether.

Google programmer Matthew Weaver lived in an RV in the company's parking lot for 54 weeks, eating at the Googleplex and showering in the company gym. His record stood until programmer Ben Discoe joined Google and lived out of a GMC van in the company parking lot for 56 weeks. Following Weaver's strategy, Discoe ate at the Googleplex, charged his electronics

Stock-Asso/Shutterstock.com

at the office, and "badged" into the building in the middle of the night if he needed the restroom. According to Discoe, "Only a fool would pay rent in the Bay Area."

Source: J. Stein, "The Man Who Lived at Google: Thirteen Months of Working, Eating, Sleeping, and Bathing at the Googleplex. The Saga of Ben Discoe," *Bloomberg BusinessWeek*, July 27–August 2, 2015, 57–59.

According to Wielgus, "Consistency is underrated. If you have consistency across your culture, you will always at least be in the top 80 percent. Then, from time to time, you might have a huge star pop up, but even if you don't, you still have your 80 percent."[95] USA Swimming's consistent culture paid dividends again in August 2016 as USA swimmers won 16 gold, 8 silver, and 9 bronze medals. Australia was the next closest team, with 3 gold, 4 silver, and 3 bronze.[96]

Having a consistent or strong organizational culture doesn't guarantee good company performance. When core beliefs are widely shared and strongly held, it is very difficult to bring about needed change. Consequently, companies with strong cultures tend to perform poorly when they need to adapt to dramatic changes in their external environments. Their consistency sometimes prevents them from adapting to those changes.[97]

3-5c Changing Organizational Cultures

Behavioral addition the process of having managers and employees perform new behaviors that are central to and symbolic of the new organizational culture that a company wants to create

As shown in Exhibit 3.6, organizational cultures exist on three levels.[98] On the first, or surface, level are the reflections of an organization's

culture that can be seen and observed, such as symbolic artifacts (for example, dress codes and office layouts) and workers' and managers' behaviors. Next, just below the surface, are the values and beliefs expressed by people in the company. You can't see these values and beliefs, but they become clear if you carefully listen to what people say and observe how decisions are made or explained. Finally, unconsciously held assumptions and beliefs about the company are buried deep below the surface. These are the unwritten views and rules that are so strongly held and so widely shared that they are rarely discussed or even thought about unless someone attempts to change them or unknowingly violates them. Changing such assumptions and beliefs can be very difficult. Instead, managers should focus on the parts of the organizational culture they can control. These include observable surface-level items, such as workers' behaviors, symbolic artifacts, and expressed values and beliefs, which can be influenced through employee selection. Let's see how these can be used to change organizational cultures.

One way of changing a corporate culture is to use behavioral addition or behavioral substitution to establish new patterns of behavior among managers and employees. **Behavioral addition** is the process of having managers and employees perform a new behavior, while

Exhibit 3.6
Three Levels of Organizational Culture

SEEN
(Surface level)

- Symbolic artifacts such as dress codes
- Workers' and managers' behaviors
- What people say

HEARD
(Expressed values and beliefs)

- How decisions are made and explained

BELIEVED
(Unconscious assumptions and beliefs)

- Widely shared assumptions and beliefs
- Buried deep below surface
- Rarely discussed or thought about

Anton Zabielskyi/Shutterstock.com

CULTURAL FIT: GOOD IDEA OR LEGAL PROBLEM?

Zappos, the online shoe retailer, only hires people who fit its quirky culture. Zappos' Rick Jordan, head of talent acquisition, says, "People who are true fits to the culture and believe what we believe—they'll do anything for the business." While hiring for cultural fit makes sense, companies like Facebook see it as a "bias trap," and discourage managers from using it as a hiring criterion. Professor Lauren Rivera says, "In many organizations, it is this catchall for, 'I don't feel right about this person.'" If you use cultural fit, clearly define it and get approval from company attorneys so it helps make good, legal hiring decisions.

Source: R. Feintzeig, "'Culture Fit' May Be the Key to Your Next Job," *Wall Street Journal*, October 12, 2017, accessed March 8, 2017, https://www.wsj.com/articles/culture-fit-may-be-the-key-to-your-next-job-1476239784.

behavioral substitution is having managers and employees perform a new behavior in place of another behavior. The key in both instances is to choose behaviors that are central to and symbolic of the old culture you're changing and the new culture that you want to create.[99] Unfortunately, reward systems sometimes encourage behaviors that run counter to desired cultural changes. When this happens, behavioral addition and substitution can produce the wrong behaviors. Professor Daniel Barron explains that, "When you're given a strong incentive, when a lot of money is on the line, you're going to move your behavior toward that."[100] Because of aggressive sales goals, 5,300 Wells Fargo bank employees and branch managers were fired after opening 2.1 million bank accounts and services that customers never approved. CFO John Shrewsberry admitted the problems were caused by "people trying to meet minimum goals to hang onto their jobs."[101] CEO John Stumpf said incentives

Behavioral substitution
the process of having managers and employees perform new behaviors central to the new organizational culture in place of behaviors that were central to the old organizational culture

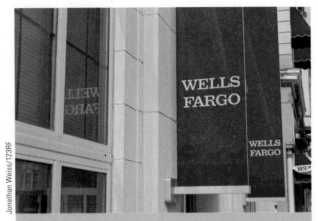

Some 5,300 Wells Fargo bank employees and branch managers were fired after opening 2.1 million bank accounts and services that customers never approved.

would no longer be linked to branch-level sales goals. "We think to the extent that some team members used a sales goal as a motivation to something that is inconsistent with our culture… [it's] just not worth it."[102] Mary Mack, Wells Fargo's head of retail banking, said, "The primary focus [of the new reward system] will be on customer service and growth."[103] Mack noted it will take time to "communicate the plan and train thousands," but that company leadership will be "closely monitoring results after the plan is in place to ensure behaviors are appropriate and we're achieving the results we expect."[104]

Another way in which managers can begin to change corporate culture is to change the **visible artifacts** of their old culture, such as the office design and layout, company dress code, and recipients (or nonrecipients) of company benefits and perks such as stock options, personal parking spaces, or the private company dining room. Recall from Chapter 1 that Ryanair is a Dublin-based airline that offers incredibly low rates. Ryanair led the way in charging passengers for every part of the flight experience, including $50 to print a boarding pass at the airport and a "no refunds" policy for canceled flights. Ryanair's brazen policies originate from its brash CEO, Michael O'Leary. Regarding passengers who forget to print boarding passes at home, O'Leary says, "We think they should pay 60 euros for being so stupid." Regarding canceled flights, he says, "You're not getting a refund, so **** off. We don't want to hear your sob stories. What part of 'no refund'

Visible artifacts visible signs of an organization's culture, such as the office design and layout, company dress code, and company benefits and perks, such as stock options, personal parking spaces, or the private company dining room

don't you understand?"[105] Unfortunately, O'Leary's unabashed statements have rubbed off on the company's staffers, whose similarly negative attitudes discourage customers from choosing the airline. To address the problem, Ryanair recently introduced the "Always Getting Better" campaign (also called the "Being Nicer" campaign) to change the company's focus from being cheap to providing a superior customer experience. The company reduced or eliminated some (but not all) of its fees; simplified online booking to require only 5 mouse clicks instead of 17; and introduced fully allocated seating to minimize congestion at the boarding gate. Previously, its "first come, first served" boarding strategy encouraged travelers to rush the gates to get better seats.[106] Crews were issued new, brightly colored uniforms, and the company moved its headquarters from a tired, dull facility to a cheerful building with colorful art on the walls. The changes dramatically improved company performance. In just one year, the number of Ryanair passengers increased 10 percent, and the load factor (the measurement of how full a jet is) reached 95 percent. O'Leary said, "If I'd known being nicer to customers was going to work so well, I'd have done it ages ago."[107]

Cultures can also be changed by hiring and selecting people with values and beliefs consistent with the company's desired culture. *Selection* is the process of gathering information about job applicants to decide who should be offered a job. As discussed in Chapter 11 on human resources, most selection instruments measure whether job applicants have the knowledge, skills, and abilities needed to succeed in their jobs. But companies are increasingly testing job applicants to determine how they fit with the company's desired culture by using selection tests, instruments, and exercises to measure these values and beliefs in job applicants. (See Chapter 11 for a complete review of applicant and managerial selection.) During the hiring process, Amazon uses a group of employees called "Bar Raisers," who interview job candidates from other areas of the company, asking difficult and unexpected questions. Bar Raisers, who spend two to three hours on each job candidate, conducting phone and face-to-face interviews and participating in evaluation meetings, have the power to veto any applicant they've assessed. Founder Jeff Bezos started the Bar Raiser program to create a consistent corporate culture by "raising the bar" when it came to hiring talent. Rather than hiring people for particular jobs, Bezos asks Bar Raisers to focus on hiring people who can succeed in Amazon's culture. John Vlastelica, an HR consultant who worked at Amazon in its early days, says, "You want someone who can adapt to new roles in the company,

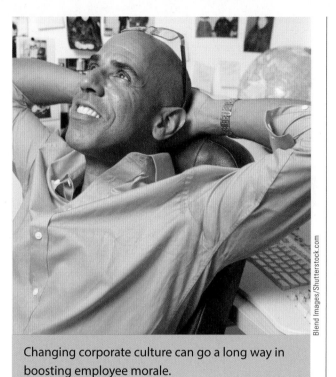
Changing corporate culture can go a long way in boosting employee morale.

not just someone who can fill the role that's vacant." Susan Harker, Amazon's vice president of global talent acquisition, says, "We want to be as objective and scientific in our hiring as possible. The point is to optimize our chances of having long-term employees." And, unlike many companies, that means hiring talented people who fit Amazon's culture. Human resource consultant Valerie Frederickson says, "There is no company that sticks to its process like Amazon does. They don't just hire the best of what they see; they're willing to keep looking and looking for the right talent."[108]

Corporate cultures are very difficult to change. Consequently, there is no guarantee that any one approach—changing visible cultural artifacts, using behavioral substitution, or hiring people with values consistent with a company's desired culture—will change a company's organizational culture. The best results are obtained by combining these methods. Together, these are some of the best tools managers have for changing culture because they send the clear message to managers and employees that "the accepted way of doing things" has changed.

STUDY TOOLS 3

LOCATED IN TEXTBOOK

☐ Rip out and review chapter review card.

LOCATED AT WWW.CENGAGEBRAIN.COM

☐ Gain unique perspectives on key concepts with new **4LTR** concept videos in the e-book.

☐ Increase your comprehension with Aplia for MGMT11.

☐ Complete interactive content within the e-book.

4 | Ethics and Social Responsibility

After you finish this chapter, go to **PAGE 89** for **STUDY TOOLS**

LEARNING OUTCOMES

4-1 Identify common kinds of workplace deviance.

4-2 Describe the U.S. Sentencing Commission Guidelines for Organizations, and explain how they both encourage ethical behavior and punish unethical behavior by businesses.

4-3 Describe what influences ethical decision making.

4-4 Explain what practical steps managers can take to improve ethical decision making.

4-5 Explain to whom organizations are socially responsible.

4-6 Explain for what organizations are socially responsible.

4-7 Explain how organizations can respond to societal demands for social responsibility.

4-8 Explain whether social responsibility hurts or helps an organization's economic performance.

D-BASE/Exactostock-1598/Superstock

4-1 WORKPLACE DEVIANCE

Today, it's not enough for companies to make a profit. We also expect managers to make a profit by doing the right things. Unfortunately, no matter what managers decide to do, someone or some group will be unhappy with the outcome. Managers don't have the luxury of choosing theoretically optimal, win-win solutions that are obviously desirable to everyone involved. In practice, solutions to ethical and social responsibility problems aren't optimal. Often, managers must be satisfied with a solution that just makes do or does the least harm. Rights and wrongs are rarely crystal clear to managers charged with doing the right thing. The business world is much messier than that.

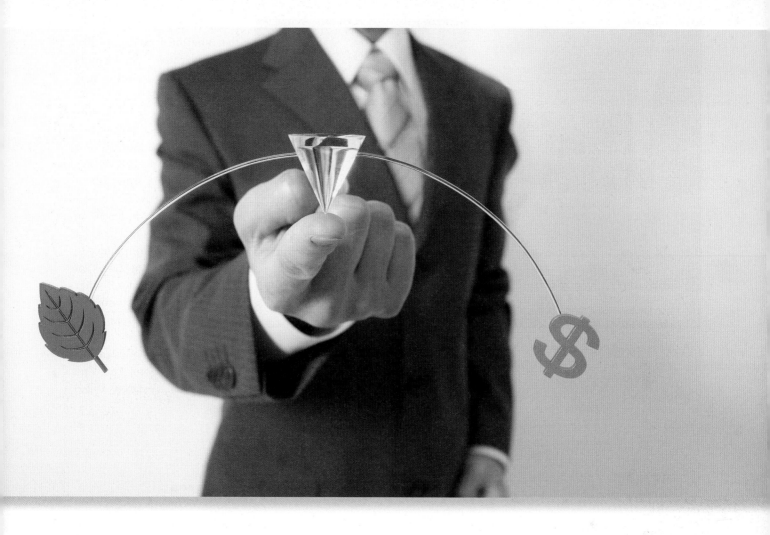

Ethics is the set of moral principles or values that defines right and wrong for a person or group. Unfortunately, numerous studies have consistently produced distressing results about the state of ethics in today's business world. One global ethics study found that, even though business is substantially more trusted than government and that 65 percent of employees trust the company where they work, just 40 percent believe the companies they work for are ethical, and only 37 percent believe that CEOs can be believed.[1] Another study found that just 25 percent trust business leaders to honestly correct mistakes and that less than 20 percent believed that business leaders would be truthful and make ethical decisions.[2] The Ethics & Compliance Initiative's *Global* Business Ethics Survey across 13 countries found that:

» 22 percent of employees were pressured to commit unethical acts.

» 33 percent of employees observed unethical behavior.

» 59 percent of employees observing unethical behavior reported it to company officials.

» 36 percent of those reporting unethical behavior experienced retaliation for doing so (see the discussion of whistle-blowing in section 4-4d).[3]

The Ethics & Compliance Initiative's *National* Business Ethics Survey (for US companies) also found that 24 percent of unethical behavior was committed by senior managers, while 60 percent was committed by managers (of all kinds).[4]

Fortunately, some studies contain good news about workplace ethics. When people believe their work environment is ethical, they are six times more likely to stay with that company than if they believe they work in an unethical environment.[5] In fact, a survey by Deloitte reported that employees who were considering leaving their jobs cited "loss of

> **Ethics** the set of moral principles or values that defines right and wrong for a person or group

Matthias Mueller, CEO of the Volkswagen group, has called for the company to learn from its mistakes following the devastating financial impact of an emission test cheating scandal.

really sick. Experts estimate that unethical behaviors like these, which researchers call *workplace deviance*, may cost companies as much as $3.7 trillion a year, or roughly 5 percent of their revenues.[9]

Workplace deviance is unethical behavior that violates organizational norms about right and wrong. As Exhibit 4.1 shows, workplace deviance can be categorized by how deviant the behavior is, from minor to serious, and by the target of the deviant behavior, either the organization or particular people in the workplace.[10]

Company-related deviance can affect both tangible and intangible assets. One kind of workplace deviance, called

trust" as the greatest factor.[6] One study asked 444 white-collar workers which qualities they considered to be important in company leaders. The results? Honesty (30%) and communication (22%) ranked by far the highest. Interestingly, these two qualities also ranked highest as areas in which business leaders needed to improve—16 percent of respondents said that leaders need to improve their honesty, and 11 percent cited communication.[7] Michael Gould, Bloomingdale's CEO of 22 years, agrees, saying, "To me, the fundamental basis of leadership is trust. If you don't have trust, you have no leadership."[8] In short, much needs to be done to make workplaces more ethical, but—and this is very important—most managers and employees want this to happen.

Ethical behavior follows accepted principles of right and wrong. Depending on which study you look at, one-third to three-quarters of all employees admit that they have stolen from their employers, committed computer fraud, embezzled funds, vandalized company property, sabotaged company projects, faked injuries to receive workers' compensation benefits or insurance, or been "sick" from work when they weren't

Ethical behavior behavior that conforms to a society's accepted principles of right and wrong

Workplace deviance unethical behavior that violates organizational norms about right and wrong

Exhibit 4.1
Types of Workplace Deviance

Organizational

Production Deviance
- Leaving early
- Taking excessive breaks
- Intentionally working slowly
- Wasting resources

Property Deviance
- Sabotaging equipment
- Accepting kickbacks
- Lying about hours worked
- Stealing from company

Minor ← → **Serious**

Political Deviance
- Showing favoritism
- Gossiping about coworkers
- Blaming coworkers
- Competing nonbeneficially

Personal Aggression
- Sexual harassment
- Verbal abuse
- Stealing from coworkers
- Endangering coworkers

Interpersonal

Source: Adapted from "A Typology of Deviant Workplace Behaviors" (Figure), S. L. Robinson and R. J. Bennett. *Academy of Management Journal* 38 (1995).

production deviance, hurts the quality and quantity of work produced. Examples include leaving early, taking excessively long work breaks, intentionally working slower, or wasting resources. A Salary.com study found that 89 percent of employees admit to wasting time at work, with 62 percent wasting 30 minutes to an hour, 22 percent wasting 2 to 3 hours, and 4 percent wasting 4 to 5 hours per day.[11] The most accomplished time wasters secretly brought their pet birds to the office, hid under boxes to scare co-workers, and held wrestling matches with other employees. A female employee wasted time by shaving her legs in the women's restroom.[12] The biggest source of workplace deviance, however, is probably *cyberloafing*, wasting time on the job with non-work-related social-media sites and apps like Facebook, Twitter, Instagram, or SnapChat, as well as surfing non-work-related retail sites like Amazon.com. Amazingly, participants in a Kansas State University study admitted to wasting 60 percent to 80 percent of their work time online! Cyberloafing is estimated to cost U.S. businesses $85 billion a year in loss productivity.[13]

Property deviance is unethical behavior aimed at company property or products. Examples include sabotaging, stealing, or damaging equipment or products, and overcharging for services and then pocketing the difference. A study of 1 million visits to self-service checkout lanes, in which customers and not store employees scanned products at store registers, found that only 86 percent of items were scanned. Consumers did not scan 850,000 items out of the 6 million items brought to the self-service checkout lanes, leaving retailers 4 percent short of what they should have been paid. Study researchers concluded, "Retailers could find themselves accused of making theft so easy that some customers who would normally—and happily—pay are tempted to commit crime, especially when they feel 'justified' in doing it."[14]

Blue ocean photo/Shutterstock.com

The biggest type of workplace deviance is spending time on personal social media sites and surfing non-work related retail sites.

Organizational employees, however, do a significant amount of property deviance themselves. **Employee shrinkage**, when employees steal company merchandise, accounts for 43 percent of theft from U.S. retailers and costs $18 billion a year. In fact, employee theft costs U.S. retailers more than shoplifters do![15] A survey of 25 large retailers across 21,288 stores found that 1 out of 38 employees is caught stealing each year and that a dishonest employee steals 4.4 times as much as the typical shoplifter.[16] Likewise, 58 percent of office workers acknowledge taking company property for personal use, according to a survey conducted for lawyers.com. "Sweethearting" occurs when employees discount or don't ring up merchandise their family or friends bring to the cash register. Sweethearting costs the retail service industry (that is, restaurants, hotels, hair salons, car washes, and so on) $80 billion annually. Sixty-seven percent of employees admit to sweethearting, primarily in hopes of receiving similar deals and discounts from the customers to whom they had extended a sweetheart deal.[17] In "dumpster diving," employees unload trucks, stash merchandise in a dumpster, and then retrieve it after work.[18]

Whereas production and property deviance harm companies, political deviance and personal aggression are unethical behaviors that hurt particular people within companies. **Political deviance** is using one's influence to harm others in the company. Examples include making decisions based on favoritism rather than performance, spreading rumors about coworkers, or blaming others for mistakes they didn't make. **Personal aggression** is hostile or aggressive behavior toward others. Examples include sexual harassment, verbal abuse, stealing from coworkers, or personally threatening coworkers. Another kind of personal aggression is workplace violence. Fortunately, like nearly all kinds of crime, workplace violence has dropped significantly since 1993, when 16 of every 1,000 employees experienced nonfatal workplace violence. Today, the rate has dropped to just 3.1 incidents per 10,000 full-time workers. Furthermore, the rate of workplace violence is one-third the level of nonworkplace violence. So, overall, you are less likely to encounter violence at work. Still, 417 people were killed at work in 2015, the most recent year for which data are available. That means 8.6 percent of

Production deviance unethical behavior that hurts the quality and quantity of work produced

Property deviance unethical behavior aimed at the organization's property or products

Employee shrinkage employee theft of company merchandise

Political deviance using one's influence to harm others in the company

Personal aggression hostile or aggressive behavior toward others workplace deaths are homicides.[19] For more information on workplace violence, see the Bureau of Labor Statistics website, http://www.bls.gov/iif/osh_wpvs.htm.

4-2 U.S. SENTENCING COMMISSION GUIDELINES FOR ORGANIZATIONS

A male supervisor is sexually harassing female coworkers. A sales representative offers a $25,000 kickback to persuade an indecisive customer to do business with his company. A company president secretly meets with the CEO of her biggest competitor, and they agree not to compete in markets where the other has already established customers. Each of these behaviors is clearly unethical (and, in these cases, also illegal). Historically, if management was unaware of such activities, the company could not be held responsible for them. Since 1991, however, when the U.S. Sentencing Commission Guidelines for Organizations were established, companies can be prosecuted and punished *even if management didn't know about the unethical behavior*. Penalties can be substantial, with maximum fines approaching a whopping $600 million.[20] Later changes to the Guidelines resulted in much stricter ethics training requirements and emphasized the importance of creating a legal and ethical company culture.[21]

Let's examine 4-2a to whom the guidelines apply and what they cover and 4-2b how, according to the guidelines, an organization can be punished for the unethical behavior of its managers and employees.

4-2a Who, What, and Why?

Nearly all businesses are covered by the U.S. Sentencing Commission's guidelines. This includes nonprofits, partnerships, labor unions, unincorporated organizations and associations, incorporated organizations, and even pension funds, trusts, and joint stock companies. If your organization can be characterized as a business (remember, nonprofits count, too), then it is subject to the guidelines.[22] For example, World Vision, a nonprofit Christian humanitarian aid organization, has a compliance program based on the U.S. sentencing guidelines. The program includes regular audits, a code of conduct, ethics standards, and anti-bribery and corruption policies (because much of its humanitarian work is carried out in third-world countries).[23]

The guidelines cover offenses defined by federal laws such as invasion of privacy, price fixing, fraud, customs violations, antitrust violations, civil rights violations, theft, money laundering, conflicts of interest, embezzlement, dealing in stolen goods, copyright infringements, extortion, and more. But it's not enough merely to stay within the law. The purpose of the guidelines is not just to punish companies *after* they or their employees break the law but also to encourage companies to take proactive steps that will discourage or prevent white-collar crime *before* it happens. The guidelines also give companies an incentive to cooperate with and disclose illegal activities to federal authorities.[24]

4-2b Determining the Punishment

The guidelines impose smaller fines on companies that take proactive steps to encourage ethical behavior or voluntarily disclose illegal activities to federal authorities. Essentially, the law uses a carrot-and-stick approach. The stick is the threat of heavy fines that can total millions of dollars. The carrot is a greatly reduced fine, but only if the company has started an effective compliance program (discussed next) to encourage ethical behavior *before* the illegal activity occurs.[25] The method used to determine a company's punishment illustrates the importance of establishing a compliance program, as illustrated in Exhibit 4.2.

The first step is to compute the *base fine* by determining what *level of offense* (that is, its seriousness) has occurred. The level of the offense varies depending on the kind of crime, the loss incurred by the victims, and how much planning went into the crime. For example, simple fraud is a level 6 offense (there are 38 levels in all). But if the victims of that fraud lost more than $5 million, that level 6 offense becomes a level 22 offense. Moreover, anything beyond minimal planning to commit the fraud results in an increase of two levels to a level 24 offense. How much difference would this make to a company? As Exhibit 4.2 shows, crimes at or below level 6 incur a base fine of $8,500, whereas the base fine for level 24 is $3.5 million, a difference of $3,491,500! The base fine for level 38, the top-level offense, is a hefty $150 million.

After assessing a *base fine*, the judge computes a culpability score, which is a way of assigning blame to the company. The culpability score can range from 0.05 to 4.0. The greater the corporate responsibility in conducting, encouraging, or sanctioning illegal or unethical activity, the higher the culpability score. A company that already has a compliance program and voluntarily reports the offense to authorities will incur a culpability score of 0.05. By contrast, a company whose management secretly plans, approves, and participates in illegal or unethical activity will receive the maximum score of 4.0.

Exhibit 4.2

Offense Levels, Base Fines, Culpability Scores, and Possible Total Fines under the U.S. Sentencing Commission Guidelines for Organizations

Offense Level	Base Fine	Total Fine with a Culpability Score of					
		0.05	0.5	1.0	2.0	3.0	4.0
6 or less	$ 8,500	$ 425	$ 4,250	$ 8,500	$ 17,000	$ 25,500	$ 34,000
7	15,000	750	7,500	15,000	30,000	45,000	60,000
8	15,000	750	7,500	15,000	30,000	45,000	60,000
9	25,000	1,250	12,500	25,000	50,000	75,000	100,000
10	35,000	1,750	17,500	35,000	70,000	105,000	140,000
11	50,000	2,500	25,000	50,000	100,000	150,000	200,000
12	70,000	3,500	35,000	70,000	140,000	210,000	280,000
13	100,000	5,000	50,000	100,000	200,000	300,000	400,000
14	150,000	7,500	75,000	150,000	300,000	450,000	600,000
15	200,000	10,000	100,000	200,000	400,000	600,000	800,000
16	300,000	15,000	150,000	300,000	600,000	900,000	1,200,000
17	450,000	22,500	225,000	450,000	900,000	1,350,000	1,800,000
18	600,000	30,000	300,000	600,000	1,200,000	1,800,000	2,400,000
19	850,000	42,500	425,000	850,000	1,700,000	2,550,000	3,400,000
20	1,000,000	50,000	500,000	1,000,000	2,000,000	3,000,000	4,000,000
21	1,500,000	75,000	750,000	1,500,000	3,000,000	4,500,000	6,000,000
22	2,000,000	100,000	1,000,000	2,000,000	4,000,000	6,000,000	8,000,000
23	3,000,000	150,000	1,500,000	3,000,000	6,000,000	9,000,000	12,000,000
24	3,500,000	175,000	1,750,000	3,500,000	7,000,000	10,500,000	14,000,000
25	5,000,000	250,000	2,500,000	5,000,000	10,000,000	15,000,000	20,000,000
26	6,500,000	325,000	3,250,000	6,500,000	13,000,000	19,500,000	26,000,000
27	8,500,000	425,000	4,250,000	8,500,000	17,000,000	25,500,000	34,000,000
28	10,000,000	500,000	5,000,000	10,000,000	20,000,000	30,000,000	40,000,000
29	15,000,000	750,000	7,500,000	15,000,000	30,000,000	45,000,000	60,000,000
30	20,000,000	1,000,000	10,000,000	20,000,000	40,000,000	60,000,000	80,000,000
31	25,000,000	1,250,000	12,500,000	25,000,000	50,000,000	75,000,000	100,000,000
32	30,000,000	1,500,000	15,000,000	30,000,000	60,000,000	90,000,000	120,000,000
33	40,000,000	2,000,000	20,000,000	40,000,000	80,000,000	120,000,000	160,000,000
34	50,000,000	2,500,000	25,000,000	50,000,000	100,000,000	15,000,0000	200,000,000
35	65,000,000	3,250,000	32,500,000	65,000,000	130,000,000	195,000,000	260,000,000
36	80,000,000	4,000,000	40,000,000	80,000,000	160,000,000	240,000,000	320,000,000
37	100,000,000	5,000,000	50,000,000	100,000,000	200,000,000	300,000,000	400,000,000
38 or more	150,000,000	7,500,000	75,000,000	150,000,000	300,000,000	450,000,000	600,000,000

Source: U.S. Sentencing Commission, *Guidelines Manual*, §3E1.1 (November 2015), accessed August 4, 2016. http://www.ussc.gov/sites/default/files/pdf/guidelines-manual/2015/GLMFull.pdf.

iStock.com/Terry Hankin

The culpability score is critical because the total fine is computed by multiplying the base fine by the culpability score. Going back to our level 24 fraud offense, the left point of the upper arrow in Exhibit 4.2 shows that a company with a compliance program that turns itself in will be fined only $175,000 ($3,500,000 × 0.05). In contrast, a company that secretly planned, approved, and participated in illegal activity will be fined $14 million ($3,500,000 × 4.0), as shown by the right point of the upper arrow. The difference is even greater for level 38 offenses. As shown by the left point of the bottom arrow, a company with a compliance program and a 0.05 culpability score is fined only $7.5 million, whereas a company with the maximum 4.0 culpability score is fined a whopping $600 million, as indicated by the right point of the bottom arrow. These differences clearly show the importance of having a compliance program in place. In 2015, the last year for which data are available, 181 companies, up 11.7 percent from 2014, were charged under the U.S. Sentencing Commission Guidelines. Ninety-eight percent pleaded guilty. Twenty-eight percent were ordered to develop a compliance program (see next paragraph). Sixty-five percent were ordered to pay fines, with an average fine of nearly $23 million.[26]

Fortunately for companies that want to avoid paying these stiff fines, the U.S. Sentencing Guidelines clearly spell out the seven necessary components of an effective compliance program.[27] Exhibit 4.3 lists those components. Caremark International, a managed-care service provider in Delaware, pleaded guilty to criminal charges related to its physician contracts and improper patient referrals. When shareholders sued the company for negligence and poor management, the Delaware court dismissed the case, ruling that the company's ethics compliance program, built on the components described in Exhibit 4.3, was a good-faith attempt to monitor employees and that the company did not knowingly allow illegal and unethical behavior to occur. The court went on to rule that a compliance program based on the U.S. Sentencing Guidelines was enough to shield the company from liability.[28]

Exhibit 4.3
Compliance Program Steps from the U.S. Sentencing Commission Guidelines for Organizations

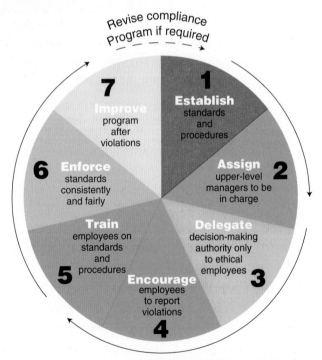

Sources: D. R. Dalton, M. B. Metzger, and J. W. Hill, "The 'New' U.S. Sentencing Commission Guidelines: A Wake-up Call for Corporate America," *Academy of Management Executive* 8 (1994): 7–16; "U.S. Sentencing Commission, Guidelines Manual, Chapter Eight - Sentencing of Organizations," U.S. Sentencing Commission, November 1, 2014, accessed March 19, 2017, www.ussc.gov/sites/default/files/pdf/guidelines-manual/2014/CHAPTER_8.pdf.

4-3 INFLUENCES ON ETHICAL DECISION MAKING

Consider this case study, based on a real-life dilemma regarding an experimental antivral drug called brincidofovir, made by Chimerix. This drug could be an effective treatment for a range of virulent viruses, including Ebola, smallpox, and the adenovirus, which is thought to cause the common cold. The CEO of Chimerix was contacted by the family of Josh Hardy, a seven-year-old boy who underwent a marrow stem cell transplant to treat kidney cancer. While being treated for cancer, Josh contracted a life-threatening respiratory virus that the family hoped could be treated with brincidofovir. Unfortunately, drug companies must often reserve their limited drug supply for clinical trials needed to secure FDA approval and bring drugs to market. After being declined three times for the drug, the family decided to conduct a social media campaign. More than 32,000 tweets using the hashtag #savejosh were posted worldwide. Nonprofit group Kids v Cancer publicized the campaign, and its director made a public statement that it is "profoundly unethical" for

Chimerix to not give Josh the drug. The company was lambasted on social media, and according to the FBI, the CEO Kenneth Moch received several credible death threats.[29] As Chimerix's CEO, what would be the ethical thing to do?

Although some ethical issues are easily solved, many do not have clearly right or wrong answers. But even though the answers are rarely clear, managers do need to have a clear sense of *how* to arrive at an answer in order to manage this ethical ambiguity well. The following sections will examine this case study from several perspectives to consider how a situation like this might be resolved.

The ethical answers that managers choose depend on **4-3a the ethical intensity of the decision, 4-3b the moral development of the manager,** *and* **4-3c the ethical principles used to solve the problem.**

4-3a Ethical Intensity of the Decision

Managers don't treat all ethical decisions the same. Chimerix's CEO, who has to decide if the company's drug treatment will go to Josh or to another ill (perhaps dying) person who has been waiting for the company's clinical trial to begin, is going to treat that decision much more seriously than the decision of how to deal with an assistant who has been taking paper home for personal use. These decisions differ in their **ethical intensity**, or the degree of concern people have about an ethical issue. When addressing an issue of high ethical intensity, managers are more aware of the impact their decision will have on others. They are more likely to view the decision as an ethical or moral decision than as an economic decision. They are also more likely to worry about doing the right thing.

Six factors must be taken into account when determining the ethical intensity of an action, as shown in Exhibit 4.4.

Exhibit 4.4
Six Factors That Contribute to Ethical Intensity

Magnitude of consequences
Social consensus
Probability of effect
Temporal immediacy
Proximity of effect
Concentration of effect

Source: Republished with permission of Academy of Management; P.O. Box 3020, Briar Cliff Manor, NY, 10510-8020. T.M. Jones, "Ethical Decision Making by Individuals in Organizations: An Issue Contingent Model," *Academy of Management Review* 16 (1991) 366–395; Reproduced by permission of the publisher via Copyright Clearance Center, Inc.

HOW CONVENIENCE COMPROMISES ETHICS

E-signatures are tremendously convenient. There's no need to print, sign, scan, or return anything. Just type your name in a digital field or check a box, and you're done! Because they are so fast and easy, e-signatures increase ease of use, meaning that fewer signatures are missing from key documents. However, e-signatures can also make people feel less committed to the (sometimes legally binding) documents they are signing. A recent study in the *Journal of Experimental Psychology* found that people are more likely to sign their name to a dishonest statement if they use an e-signature than if they sign traditionally with a pen. So if you want the honest truth, ask your clients to sign with a pen (or a stylus).

Source: P. Anand, "The Lies E-Sigs Tell: Research suggests people are more honest if signing by hand," *Wall Street Journal*, October 14, 2015, R5.

Magnitude of consequences is the total harm or benefit derived from an ethical decision. The more people who are harmed or the greater the harm to those people, the larger the consequences. **Social consensus** is agreement on whether behavior is bad or good. **Probability of effect** is the chance that something will happen that results in harm to others. If we combine these factors, we can see the effect they can have on ethical intensity. For example, if there is *clear agreement* (social consensus) that a managerial decision or action is *certain* (probability of effect) to have *large negative consequences* (magnitude of consequences) in some way, then people will be highly concerned about that managerial decision or action, and ethical intensity will be high.

Temporal immediacy is the time between an act and the consequences the act produces. Temporal immediacy is stronger if a manager has to lay off workers next week as opposed to three months from now. **Proximity of effect** is the social, psychological, cultural, or physical distance of a decision maker from those affected by his or her decisions. Thus, proximity of effect is greater when a manager lays off employees

Ethical intensity the degree of concern people have about an ethical issue

Magnitude of consequences the total harm or benefit derived from an ethical decision

Social consensus agreement on whether behavior is bad or good

Probability of effect the chance that something will happen that results in harm to others

Temporal immediacy the time between an act and the consequences the act produces

Proximity of effect the social, psychological, cultural, or physical distance between a decision maker and those affected by his or her decisions

Exhibit 4.5
Kohlberg's Stages of Moral Development

Stage 1	Stage 2	Stage 3	Stage 4	Stage 5	Stage 6
Punishment and Obedience	Instrumental Exchange	Good Boy, Nice Girl	Law and Order	Social Contract	Universal Principle
Preconventional		**Conventional**		**Postconventional**	
Self-Interest		**Societal Expectations**		**Internalized Principles**	

he knows than when he lays off employees he doesn't know. Finally, whereas the magnitude of consequences is the total effect across all people, **concentration of effect** is how much an act affects the average person. For instance, eliminating health care coverage for 100 employees has a greater concentration of effect than reducing the health care benefits for 1,000 employees by 10 percent.

Which of these six factors has the most impact on ethical intensity? Studies indicate that managers are much more likely to view decisions as ethical issues when the magnitude of consequences (total harm) is high and there is a social consensus (agreement) that a behavior or action is bad.[30]

4-3b Moral Development

It's Friday. Another long week of classes and studying is over, and all you want to do is sit down and relax. "A movie sounds good," you think to yourself, but you don't want to spend $12 to trek down to the megaplex. And, while it would cost less than a $1.50 to rent a DVD, you're too tired to make the short trip down to the corner drugstore's Redbox machine. Your roommate says he's got the perfect solution and gives you the URL of a website that streams all the latest blockbuster movies and TV shows for free. The writers, actors, and producers won't earn a dime if you watch the pirated copy of the movie. Furthermore, it's illegal to download or watch streamed copies of pirated shows. But how will the movie studios ever find out? Are the cops going to come through your door because you watched a pirated copy of *Pirates of the Caribbean: Dead Men Tell No Tales*? Will you watch the movie? What are you going to do?

In part, according to psychologist Lawrence Kohlberg, your decision will be based on your level of moral development. Kohlberg identified three phases of moral development, with two stages in each phase (see Exhibit 4.5).[31] At the **preconventional level of moral development**, people decide based on selfish reasons. For example, if you are in Stage 1, the punishment and obedience stage, your primary concern will be to avoid trouble for yourself. So you won't watch the pirated movie because you are afraid of being caught and punished. Yet, in Stage 2, the instrumental exchange stage, you worry less about punishment and more about doing things that directly advance your wants and needs. So you will watch the pirated movie.

People at the **conventional level of moral development** make decisions that conform to societal expectations. In other words, they look outside themselves to others for guidance on ethical issues. In Stage 3, the "good boy, nice girl" stage, you normally do what the other "good boys" and "nice girls" are doing. If everyone else is watching the pirated movie, you will, too. But if they aren't, you won't either. In the law and order stage, Stage 4, you again look for external guidance and do whatever the law permits, so you won't watch the movie.

People at the **postconventional level of moral development** use internalized ethical principles to solve ethical dilemmas. In Stage 5, the social contract stage, you will refuse to watch the pirated movie because, as a whole, society is better off when the rights of others—in this case, the rights of actors, producers, directors, and writers—are not violated. In Stage 6, the universal principle stage, you might or might not watch the pirated movie, depending on your principles of right and wrong. Moreover, you will stick to your principles even if your decision conflicts with the law (Stage 4) or what others believe is best for society (Stage 5). For example, those with socialist or communist beliefs would probably choose to watch the pirated movie because they believe goods and services should be owned by society rather than by individuals and corporations.

Concentration of effect the total harm or benefit that an act produces on the average person

Preconventional level of moral development the first level of moral development, in which people make decisions based on selfish reasons

Conventional level of moral development the second level of moral development, in which people make decisions that conform to societal expectation

Postconventional level of moral development the third level of moral development, in which people make decisions based on internalized principles

Unethical Amnesia: Why Unethical Workers Can Live with Themselves

"I hope you can sleep at night!" is what we might (or would like) to say to someone acting unethically or making unethical decisions. But, thanks to *unethical amnesia*, people who are repeatedly unethical generally forget that they were, which makes it easier to continue being unethical. When recalled, memories of unethical behavior are remembered less clearly than ethical behavior, which is easily and accurately remembered. So why do unethical workers have a "clear conscious?" Because they can't remember.

Source: F. Gina & M. Kouchaki, "We're Unethical at Work Because We Forget Our Misdeeds," *Harvard Business Review*, May 18, 2016, accessed March 21, 2017, https://hbr.org/2016/05/were-unethical-at-work-because-we-forget-our-misdeeds.

Patramansky Oleg/Shutterstock.com

(who might not receive treatment because of limited supply). Because of these violations, Chimerix should not give Josh Hardy the treatment.

The **principle of personal virtue** holds that you should never do anything that is not honest, open, and truthful and that you would not be glad to see reported in the newspapers or on TV. Using the principle of personal virtue, Chimerix would have quietly allocated treatment doses of brincidofovir for Josh Hardy. Had it done so, it might have avoided the social media firestorm and the subsequent publication of an article in *Bloomberg BusinessWeek*, which brought the story to even more people.

Under the **principle of distributive justice**, you should never take any action that harms the least fortunate among us in some way. This principle is designed to protect the poor, the uneducated, and the unemployed. Josh Hardy could certainly be considered vulnerable. Having fought kidney cancer since he was a baby, he contracted a life-threatening virus after receiving a marrow stem cell transplant targeting the cancer. Chimerix had a drug on hand that had been shown effective in the treatment of such viruses. Would the company want to be seen as one that had a cure and intentionally withheld it? The principle of distributive justice says it would not.

Finally, the **principle of utilitarian benefits** states that you should never take an action that does not result in greater good for society. In short, you should do whatever creates the greatest good for the greatest number. Chimerix has previously given 430 patients brincidofovir for compassionate use. That program, however, was funded by the government. When funding ended, Chimerix reallocated all of its remaining doses of the drug to the formal trials required for FDA approval. Allocating any doses to Josh might have jeopardized the FDA approval process by reducing the number of doses available for use in the formal trials. Fewer individuals would be able to participate in the trials, potentially requiring additional trial rounds, delaying approval, and preventing distribution of the life-saving drug to even more people suffering from life-threatening viral infections. Thus, according to the principle of utilitarian benefit, Chimerix would be obligated to put the larger group's interests first and deny the Hardy family's request. Chimerix CEO Kenneth Moch echoed this principle, saying, "If it were my child, would I do what the Hardys did? Absolutely, yes. As the CEO, I have to think about not just the individual but the many."[37]

So, what did Moch decide to do? He factored in many of the concerns raised by these ethical principles and worked with the FDA to create a separate clinical trial for brincidofovir with Josh Hardy as its first patient. Within a week of receiving the drug, Josh's condition improved and he was discharged from the hospital. Three weeks into the trial, however, Moch was replaced as CEO of Chimerix. He said he would have "loved to continue to be the CEO, but the board thought otherwise."[38] Josh Hardy died two years later, at the age of 10, from complications related to his cancer.[39]

4-4 PRACTICAL STEPS TO ETHICAL DECISION MAKING

Companies are putting more emphasis on ethical decision making. Eighty-one percent now provide ethics

Principle of personal virtue an ethical principle that holds that you should never do anything that is not honest, open, and truthful and that you would not be glad to see reported in the newspapers or on TV

Principle of distributive justice an ethical principle that holds that you should never take any action that harms the least fortunate among us: the poor, the uneducated, the unemployed

Principle of utilitarian benefits an ethical principle that holds that you should never take any action that does not result in greater good for society training. Sixty-seven percent include ethical conduct as a standard part of performance evaluations. And, seventy-four percent communicate internally about disciplinary actions that are taken when unethical behavior occurs.[40]

*Managers can encourage more ethical decision making in their organizations by **4-4a carefully selecting and hiring ethical employees, 4-4b establishing a specific code of ethics, 4-4c training employees to make ethical decisions,** and **4-4d creating an ethical climate.***

4-4a Selecting and Hiring Ethical Employees

As an employer, how can you increase your chances of hiring honest employees, the kind who would return a wallet filled with money to its rightful owner? **Overt integrity tests** estimate job applicants' honesty by asking them directly what they think or feel about theft or about punishment of unethical behaviors.[41] For example, an employer might ask an applicant, "Would you ever consider buying something from somebody if you knew the person had stolen the item?" or "Don't most people steal from their companies?" Surprisingly, unethical people will usually answer "yes" to such questions because they believe that the world is basically dishonest and that dishonest behavior is normal.[42]

Personality-based integrity tests indirectly estimate job applicants' honesty by measuring psychological traits such as dependability and conscientiousness. For example, prison inmates serving time for white-collar crimes (counterfeiting, embezzlement, and fraud) scored much lower than a comparison group of middle-level managers on scales measuring reliability, dependability, honesty, conscientiousness, and abiding by rules.[43] These results show that companies can selectively hire and promote people who will be more ethical.

4-4b Codes of Ethics

Today, almost all large corporations have an ethics code in place. In fact, to be listed on the New York Stock Exchange, a company must "adopt and disclose a code of business conduct and ethics for directors, officers, and employees."[44] Even if a company has a code of ethics, two things must still happen if those codes are to encourage ethical decision making and behavior.[45] First, a company must communicate its code to others both inside and outside the company.

Second, in addition to having an ethics code with general guidelines such as "do unto others as you would have others do unto you," management must also develop practical ethical standards and procedures specific to the company's line of business. ADP (Automatic Data Processing), a global provider of HR, payroll, time tracking, tax and benefits solutions, does business in 110 countries. Visitor's to ADP's website can download its "Code of Business Conduct & Ethics" or its "Anti-Bribery Policy." The code and other extensive policies set specific ethical standards on topics ranging from conflicts of interest to gifts, bribes, and kickbacks to covering up mistakes and falsifying records. For example, the code specifically states, "Mistakes should never be covered up, but should be immediately fully disclosed and corrected. Falsification of any ADP, client or third-party record is prohibited. If you are uncertain about whether a mistake has been made, you should seek guidance from your immediate supervisor or manager." ADP has a strict anti-bribery policy against "improper and unethical payments" to influence business decisions. However, items not exceeding $25 in value, "such as ADP logo pen and pencil sets, shirts, hats and other similar items" may be given to government officials, but not more than once per year.[46] Specific codes of ethics such as this make it much easier for employees to decide what to do when they want to do the right thing.

4-4c Ethics Training

In addition to establishing ethical standards for the company, managers must sponsor and be involved in ethics and compliance training in order to create an ethical company culture.[47] The first objective of ethics training is to develop employees' awareness of ethics.[48] This means helping employees recognize which issues are ethical issues and then avoiding rationalizing unethical behavior by thinking, "This isn't really illegal or immoral" or "No one will ever find out." Several companies have created board games, produced videos, or invited special speakers to improve awareness of ethical issues.[49] Howard Winkler, project manager for ethics and compliance at Southern Co., an Atlanta-based energy provider, even had a convicted felon come in to talk about how small

> **Overt integrity test** a written test that estimates job applicants' honesty by directly asking them what they think or feel about theft or about punishment of unethical behaviors
>
> **Personality-based integrity test** a written test that indirectly estimates job applicants' honesty by measuring psychological traits, such as dependability and conscientiousness

> "When I first began prosecuting corruption, I expected to walk into rooms and find the vilest people. I was shocked to find ordinarily good people I could well have had coffee with that morning."
>
> **Why Ethical People Make Unethical Choices**

ethical compromises eventually lead to bigger unethical behavior, such as fraud, the charges that sent him to jail for five years. "It created an enormous impression," Winkler says, because, "This person didn't start out his career looking to commit fraud. The main message was that once you make the first ethical compromise, you are embarking on a path that can lead all the way to a prison cell."[50] Winkler also regularly creates opportunities for senior executives to speak with employees about ethics issues. This multifaceted approach appears to be working, as internal surveys indicate that 93 percent of employees recognize that their continued career at Southern "depends on my ethical behavior."

The second objective for ethics training programs is to achieve credibility with employees. Not surprisingly, employees can be highly suspicious of management's reasons for offering ethics training. Some companies have hurt the credibility of their ethics programs by having outside instructors and consultants conduct the classes.[51] Employees often complain that outside instructors and consultants are teaching theory that has nothing to do with their jobs and the practical dilemmas they actually face on a daily basis. CA Technologies made its ethics training practical and relevant by creating a series of comical training videos with a fictional manager, Griffin Peabody. Chief ethics officer Joel Katz says, "Over the years, we have created a library of funny videos involving Griffin that cover topics ranging from appropriate workplace conduct to anti-corruption to insider trading. While some of the videos are admittedly silly and a bit over the top, we have received overwhelmingly positive feedback from our employees about the Griffin character. Employees

also reported that they had retained more from the Griffin videos because they were fully engaged in the course content due to the use of humor. We have also gotten many YouTube hits on these videos (search for "Griffin Peabody") along with requests from other companies to use them in their own compliance training offerings."[52]

Ethics training becomes even more credible when top managers teach the initial ethics classes to their subordinates who in turn teach their subordinates.[53] At Intuitive Research and Technology Corp., an engineering services company in Huntsville, Alabama, Harold "Hal" Brewer, the company's co-founder and president, is the company's ethics champion. Every new employee attends a session called "Let's Talk Ethics with Hal," led by Brewer and the director of human resources, Juanita Phillips. Brewer explains how employees' decisions impact the company, situations they will likely encounter with outside organizations they do business with, and then how to respond. What effect does having the co-founder and president talk to every employee about ethics? Philips says about Hal, "He makes it clear that he is the ethics officer. His strength is that he means every word of it, and he shows it in how he lives every day in terms of running the company.[54] Michael Hoffman, executive director for the Center for Business Ethics at Bentley University, says that having managers teach ethics courses greatly reinforces the seriousness with which employees treat ethics in the workplace.[55]

The overarching goals of ethics training are to develop employees' awareness of ethics, achieve credibility with employees, and teach employees a practical model of ethical decision making.

Mangostar/Shutterstock.com

The third objective of ethics training is to teach employees a practical model of ethical decision making. A basic model should help them think about the consequences their choices will have on others and consider how they will choose between different solutions. Exhibit 4.6 presents a basic model of ethical decision making.

4-4d Ethical Climate

Organizational culture is key to fostering ethical decision making. The 2015 National Business Ethics Survey reported that only 33 percent of employees who work at companies with a strong ethical culture (where core beliefs are widely shared and strongly held) have observed

CALLING ALL TIPSTERS!

The Securities and Exchange Commission (SEC) and the Commodities Futures Trading Commission (CFTC) are looking for whistle-blowers. To encourage reports of fraud and wrongdoing, these two agencies launched programs to pay bounties for information that leads to sanctions or fines. The similarities between the two programs end there, however. While the SEC's program is working smoothly, the CFTC has paid more in administrative costs to keep its whistle-blowing program operational than it has paid bounties to actual whistle-blowers. By 2016, the SEC had paid out more than $55 million in bounties to the CFTC's $530,000. The SEC leads on the overall tip count as well—14,116 to 655 as of September 2015. Still, head of the CFTC whistle-blower office Christopher Ehrman is undeterred: "The program will continue onward. We'll get what we get and hope for the best."

Borja Andreu/Shutterstock.com

Source: J. Eaglesham, "CFTC Can't Give Whistleblower Money Away," *Wall Street Journal*, February 8, 2016, accessed February 22, 2016, www.wsj.com/articles /cftc-cant-give-whistleblower-money-away-1454876128.

Exhibit 4.6
A Basic Model of Ethical Decision Making

1. **Identify the problem.** What makes it an ethical problem? Think in terms of rights, obligations, fairness, relationships, and integrity. How would you define the problem if you stood on the other side of the fence?

2. **Identify the constituents.** Who has been hurt? Who could be hurt? Who could be helped? Are they willing players, or are they victims? Can you negotiate with them?

3. **Diagnose the situation.** How did it happen in the first place? What could have prevented it? Is it going to get worse or better? Can the damage now be undone?

4. **Analyze your options.** Imagine the range of possibilities. Limit yourself to the two or three most manageable. What are the likely outcomes of each? What are the likely costs? Look to the company mission statement or code of ethics for guidance.

5. **Make your choice.** What is your intention in making this decision? How does it compare with the probable results? Can you discuss the problem with the affected parties before you act? Could you disclose without qualm your decision to your boss, the CEO, the board of directors, your family, or society as a whole?

6. **Act.** Do what you have to do. Don't be afraid to admit errors. Be as bold in confronting a problem as you were in causing it.

Source: L. A. Berger, "Train All Employees to Solve Ethical Dilemmas," *Best's Review—Life-Health Insurance Edition* 95 (1995): 70–80.

others engaging in unethical behavior, whereas 62 percent of those who work in organizations with weak ethical cultures (where core beliefs are not widely shared or strongly held) have observed others engaging in unethical behavior.[56] Employees of companies with strong ethical cultures are also more likely to report misconduct that they observe (87% versus 32% in weak ethical cultures).[57]

The first step in establishing an ethical climate is for managers, especially top managers, to act ethically themselves. It's no surprise that in study after study, when researchers ask, "What is the most important influence on your ethical behavior at work?" the answer comes back, "My manager."

A second step in establishing an ethical climate is for top management to be active in and committed to the company ethics program.[58] Top managers who consistently talk about the importance of ethics and back up that talk by participating in their companies' ethics programs send the clear message that ethics matter. When management engages and communicates about ethical issues, employees are less likely to break rules and more likely to report ethical violations.[59] Business writer Dayton Fandray says, "You can have ethics offices and officers and training programs and reporting systems, but if the CEO doesn't seem to care, it's all just a sham. It's not surprising to find that the companies that really do care about ethics make a point of including senior management in all of their ethics and compliance programs."[60]

A third step is to put in place a reporting system that encourages managers and employees to report potential ethics violations. **Whistle-blowing**, that is, reporting others' ethics violations, is a difficult step for most people to take.[61] Professor Elizabeth Morrison says, "You have to confront the two fundamental challenges preventing employees from speaking up. The first is the natural feeling of futility—feeling like speaking up isn't worth the effort or that on one wants to hear it. The second is the natural fear that speaking up will lead to retribution or harsh reactions."[62] Indeed, in large companies without an effective compliance program, 62 percent of workers have observed unethical behavior, 32 percent of those have reported the misconduct, and 59 percent of those who reported the unethical behavior experienced some kind of retaliation.[63]

Johnny Burris, a JPMorgan broker, was fired after pushing back against managers who insisted he sell JPMorgan investments that he thought were too risky for his oldest clients (who typically focus on less risky income-based investments).[64] Brad Scott, a former JPMorgan financial advisor who quit to work at LPL Financial, agreed with Burris, saying, "We were not able to do the right things for our clients."[65] Burris went public with his complaints in a *New York Times* article, after which his boss added unsubstantiated customer complaints to Burris' regulatory files. JPMorgan was ordered to pay Burris back wages and $100,000 in damages. The bank also agreed to a Securities and Exchange Commission settlement of $307 million for, as alleged by Burris, pushing the wrong kind of JPMorgan investments to clients. Burris said he is considering filing his, "case before the U.S. District Court to receive a trial by my peers."[66]

A 2014 ruling by the U.S. Supreme Court greatly expands protections for whistle-blowers. The Court declared that the strong whistle-blowers' protections built into the 2002 Sarbanes-Oxley Act, which apply to employees of publicly traded companies, should also apply to the employees of contractors and subcontractors that work with those public companies. This ruling extends whistle-blowers protection laws beyond the 5,000 publicly traded companies covered by Sarbanes-Oxley to an additional 6 million private companies.[67]

To encourage employees to report ethics violations, that is, to act as whistle-blowers, many companies have installed confidential ethics hotlines. Employees at ADP, which has the extensive code of ethics discussed earlier, can anonymously report ethics violations via phone or website, both of which are staffed by EthicsPoint, an independent, third-party provider.[68] Anonymous reporting is critical as it helps whistle-blowers avoid retaliation by their companies or managers. Retaliation typically occurs within three weeks of reporting an ethical violation.[69]

The factor that does the most to discourage whistle-blowers from reporting problems is lack of company action on their complaints.[70] Thus, the final step in developing an ethical climate is for management to fairly and consistently punish those who violate the company's code of ethics. The key, says Paychex CEO Martin Mucci, is "to deal with it quickly, severely, and publicize it."[71] Says Mucci, "Our employees know that if they are caught cheating in any way, even if only to make a few dollars or improve their scores, they will most likely be terminated. Then we review that with the entire management team. We have done that with managers of locations, top sales representatives–we don't treat anyone differently."[72] Amazingly, though, not all companies fire ethics violators. In fact, 8 percent of surveyed companies admit that they would promote top performers even if they violated ethical standards.[73]

4-5 TO WHOM ARE ORGANIZATIONS SOCIALLY RESPONSIBLE?

Social responsibility is a business's obligation to pursue policies, make decisions, and take actions that

Whistle-blowing reporting others' ethics violations to management or legal authorities

Social responsibility a business's obligation to pursue policies, make decisions, and take actions that benefit society benefit society.[74] Unfortunately, because there are strong disagreements over to whom and for what in society organizations are responsible, it can be difficult for managers to know what is or will be perceived as socially responsible corporate behavior. After a terrorist attack that killed 14 people, the U.S. government asked Apple to break into the attacker's encrypted iPhone. In a public letter to its customers (see http://www.apple.com/customer-letter/), CEO Tim Cook stated, "While we believe the FBI's intentions are good, it would be wrong for the government to force us to build a backdoor into our products. And ultimately, we fear that this demand would undermine the very freedoms and liberty our government is meant to protect." District Attorney Cyrus Vance, Jr. criticized Apple, saying, "Apple and Google are their own sheriffs. There are no rules." Was Apple's refusal principled and to society's benefit, or will its lack of cooperation harm, if not eventually endanger others?[75]

There are two perspectives regarding to whom organizations are socially responsible: the shareholder model and the stakeholder model. According to the late Nobel Prize–winning economist Milton Friedman, the only social responsibility that organizations have is to satisfy their owners, that is, company shareholders. This view—called the **shareholder model**—holds that the only social responsibility that businesses have is to maximize profits. By maximizing profit, the firm maximizes shareholder wealth and satisfaction. More specifically, as profits rise, the company stock owned by shareholders generally increases in value.

Friedman argued that it is socially irresponsible for companies to divert time, money, and attention from maximizing profits to social causes and charitable organizations. The first problem, he believed, is that organizations cannot act effectively as moral agents for all company shareholders. Although shareholders are likely to agree on investment issues concerning a company, it's highly unlikely that they have common views on what social causes a company should or should not support.

The second major problem, Friedman said, is that the time, money, and attention diverted to social causes undermine market efficiency.[76] In competitive markets, companies compete for raw materials, talented workers, customers, and investment funds. A company that spends money on social causes will have less money to purchase quality materials or to hire talented workers who can produce a valuable product at a good price. If customers find the company's product less desirable, its sales and profits will fall. If profits fall, the company's stock price will decline, and the company will have difficulty attracting investment funds that could be used to fund long-term growth. In the end, Friedman argues,

diverting the firm's money, time, and resources to social causes hurts customers, suppliers, employees, and shareholders. Russell Roberts, an economist and research fellow at Stanford University's Hoover Institution, agrees, saying, "Doesn't it make more sense to have companies do what they do best, make good products at fair prices, and then let consumers use the savings for the charity of their choice?"[77]

By contrast, under the **stakeholder model**, management's most important responsibility is the firm's long-term survival (not just maximizing profits), which is achieved by satisfying the interests of multiple corporate stakeholders (not just shareholders).[78] **Stakeholders** are persons or groups with a legitimate interest in a company.[79] Because stakeholders are interested in and affected by the organization's actions, they have a stake in what those actions are. Marc Benioff, founder and CEO of SalesForce.com, says, "The next generation of CEOs must advocate for all stakeholders—employees, customers, community, the environment, everybody. . .not just shareholders."[80] "I even consider the communities that we live in are stakeholders. The environment is a stakeholder."[81] Because of the importance that Benioff places on stakeholders, SaleForce has a "1-1-1" philosophy in which it donates 1 percent of its founding stock (for grants supporting technology innovation in nonprofit and youth programs), 1 percent of employees' time (giving each employee 6 paid days of volunteer time each year), and 1 percent of its product (donation or discounting of SalesForce's customer relationship management services) each year.[82] So far, says Benioff, "…we've put software in 26,000 nonprofits and schools, provided $100 million in grants, and our people have done over 1.1 million volunteer hours around the world."[83]

Stakeholder groups may try to influence the firm to advance their interests. Exhibit 4.7 shows the various stakeholder groups that the organization must satisfy to assure its long-term survival. Being responsible to multiple stakeholders raises two basic questions. First, how does a company identify organizational stakeholders? Second, how does a company balance the needs of different stakeholders? Distinguishing between primary and secondary stakeholders can help to answer these questions.[84]

Shareholder model a view of social responsibility that holds that an organization's overriding goal should be profit maximization for the benefit of shareholders

Stakeholder model a theory of corporate responsibility that holds that management's most important responsibility, long-term survival, is achieved by satisfying the interests of multiple corporate stakeholders

Stakeholders persons or groups with a stake, or legitimate interest, in a company's actions

Exhibit 4.7
Stakeholder Model of Corporate Social Responsibility

PRIMARY STAKEHOLDERS:
SECONDARY STAKEHOLDERS:

SECONDARY STAKEHOLDERS

PRIMARY STAKEHOLDERS

Governments

Local Communities

Special Interest Groups

Suppliers

FIRM

Shareholders

Media

Employees

Customers

Trade Associations

Source: Republished with permission of Academy of Management, P.O. Box 3020, Briar Cliff Manor, NY, 10510-8020. "The Stakeholder Theory of the Corporation: Concepts, Evidence and Implications" (Figure), T. Donaldson and L. E. Preston, *Academy of Management Review* 20 (1995). Reproduced by permission of the publisher via Copyright Clearance Center, Inc.

Some stakeholders are more important to the firm's survival than others. **Primary stakeholders** are groups on which the organization depends for its long-term survival; they include shareholders, employees, customers, suppliers, governments, and local communities. When managers are struggling to balance the needs of different stakeholders, the stakeholder model suggests that the needs of primary stakeholders take precedence over the needs of secondary stakeholders. But among primary stakeholders, are some more important than others? According to the life cycle theory of organizations, the answer is yes. In practice, the answer is also yes, as CEOs typically give somewhat higher priority to shareholders, employees, and customers than to suppliers, governments, and local communities, no matter what stage of the life cycle a company is in.[85] Addressing the concerns of primary stakeholders is important because if a stakeholder group becomes dissatisfied and terminates its relationship with the company, the company could be seriously harmed or go out of business.

Secondary stakeholders, such as the media and special interest groups, can influence or be influenced by the company. Unlike the primary stakeholders, however, they do not engage in regular transactions with the company and are not critical to its long-term survival. Meeting the needs of primary stakeholders is therefore usually more important than meeting the needs of secondary stakeholders. Nevertheless, secondary stakeholders are still important because they can affect public perceptions and opinions about socially responsible behavior.

Antibacterial gels, soaps, cleansers, and sanitizers make up a large segment of the $30 billion U.S. cleaning products industry. But according to nonprofit special-interest group the Natural Resources Defense Council, the key ingredient has a number of serious side effects. Triclosan, which weakens bacterial strains, is believed to alter thyroid production, aggravate asthma, decrease muscle function, and, thanks to its pervasive use, actually increase resistance to antibiotics.[86] Kaiser Permanente has banned triclosan and 13 other antimicrobials from its hospitals because, as Environmental-Stewardship Officer Kathy Gerwig says, "We want to use our purchasing power to send a message that it's not OK to use ingredients that might be harmful to our health." Soap manufacturers have begun to take notice of the debate. Henkel (the maker of Dial), Procter & Gamble, Johnson & Johnson, and Colgate Palmolive have all begun eliminating triclosan from some or all of their cleansing products in response to consumer concerns.[87]

So, to whom are organizations socially responsible? Many commentators, especially economists and financial analysts, continue to argue that organizations are responsible only to shareholders. Increasingly, however, top managers have come to believe that they and their companies must be socially responsible to their stakeholders. Today, surveys show that as many as 80 percent of top-level managers believe that it is unethical to focus just

Primary stakeholder any group on which an organization relies for its long-term survival

Secondary stakeholder any group that can influence or be influenced by a company and can affect public perceptions about the company's socially responsible behavior on shareholders. Twenty-nine states have changed their laws to allow company boards of directors to consider the needs of employees, creditors, suppliers, customers, and local communities, as well as those of shareholders.[88] Although there is not complete agreement, a majority of opinion makers would argue that companies must be socially responsible to their stakeholders.

4-6 FOR WHAT ARE ORGANIZATIONS SOCIALLY RESPONSIBLE?

If organizations are to be socially responsible to stakeholders, what are they to be socially responsible *for*? Companies can best benefit their stakeholders by fulfilling their economic, legal, ethical, and discretionary responsibilities. Economic and legal responsibilities are at the bottom of the pyramid because they play a larger part in a company's social responsibility than do ethical and discretionary responsibilities. However, the relative importance of these various responsibilities depends on society's expectations of corporate social responsibility at a particular point in time.[89] A century ago, society expected businesses to meet their economic and legal responsibilities and little else. Today, when society judges whether businesses are socially responsible, ethical and discretionary responsibilities are considerably more important than they used to be.

Historically, **economic responsibility**, or making a profit by producing a product or service valued by society, has been a business's most basic social responsibility. Organizations that don't meet their financial and economic expectations come under tremendous pressure. For example, company boards are quick these days to fire CEOs. Typically, all it takes is two or three bad quarters in a row. **Spirit Airlines** is known for its extremely low cost "Bare Fare" pricing. Spirit customers get cheap prices, but they don't get snacks (not even water), are charged for carry-on luggage (which is free on most other airlines), and sit in crowded, nonreclining seats (more people equals lower prices). Spirit grew steadily, went public, and by September 2015, had revenues of $1.6 billion, up

Minerva Studio/Shutterstock.com

11 percent over 2014. More impressively, profits rose 43 percent to nearly $243 million during that same period. Competing airlines noticed. Helped by low oil prices, they aggressively slashed fares. In turn, Spirit cut fares 17 percent to stay competitive. Its revenues, profits and stock price all declined. Three months later, CEO Ben Baldanza was abruptly replaced.[90] William Rollnick, who became acting chairman of Mattel after the company fired its previous CEO, says, "There's zero forgiveness. You screw up and you're dead."[91] According to the Conference Board, 16–29 percent of CEOs of large companies are fired each year.[92]

Legal responsibility is a company's social responsibility to obey society's laws and regulations as it tries to meet its economic responsibilities. Volkswagen clearly violated its legal responsibilities after admitting to using software to falsify emissions tests (turning emissions controls on during testing to meet standards and then turning them off during driving for better mileage). It agreed to pay $22 billion in settlements and fines in the United States, including payments of $5,000 to $10,000 to each owner of a VW diesel car and $4.3 billion in civil and criminal penalties. "Volkswagen deeply regrets the behavior that gave rise to the diesel crisis," the company said in a statement. "The agreements that we have reached with the U.S. government reflect our determination to address misconduct that went against all of the values Volkswagen holds so dear."[93]

Ethical responsibility is a company's social responsibility to not violate accepted principles of right and wrong when conducting its business. When pepper costs spiked, spice company McCormick & Co. reduced the amount of pepper in its aluminum tins from four ounces to three ounces. McCormick relabeled the product contents on the front label, so consumers were technically informed of the change. Still, consumers could easily have assumed that they were buying four ounces of pepper since the overall design and size of the package didn't change. The food industry calls this strategy—putting less product into the same-sized package—*weight-out*. Marketing professor and former Federal Trade Commission official Thomas J. Maronick says that legally, "the critical thing is that [McCormick & Co.] told the truth.[94]

By contrast, consumer-fraud attorney

Economic responsibility
a company's social responsibility to make a profit by producing a valued product or service

Legal responsibility
a company's social responsibility to obey society's laws and regulations

Ethical responsibility
a company's social responsibility not to violate accepted principles of right and wrong when conducting its business

Galaxy Note 7 Phones Catch Fire

In October 2016, global airlines banned Samsung Galaxy Note 7 phones. The phones, 300 of which had caught fire or exploded, were not even to be stored turned off in passengers' luggage. Samsung recalled the phones, used software to "brick" every Note 7 by preventing charging and mobile functions, and then offered customers free versions of its other phones, as well as other financial incentives.

After pulling Note 7s from the market, Samsung assigned 700 research and development staff to test 200,000 phones and 30,000 batteries. The result? Batteries made by its suppliers overheated (an independent lab agreed).

Samsung blamed its own poor quality controls for the problem, and installed an eight-point quality plan, including five days of testing and X-raying every battery, to prevent these problems.

Did Samsung handle the crisis responsibly? Did it do right by customers and fix the problem for the long term? Would you buy a Samsung phone now?

Travelers who used Galaxy 7 Notes were able to exchange the phones at special Samsung booths set up at busy U.S. airports; airlines did not allow the smartphones to be carried on board.

Sources: G. Fowler & J. Stern, "Why Samsung's Battery Fix Gets a Grade C, For Now," *Wall Street Journal*, January 22, 2017, accessed March 21, 2017, https://www.wsj.com/articles/why-samsungs-battery-fix-gets-a-grade-c-for-now-1485133200; S. Gibbs, "Samsung Galaxy Note 7: Airlines Across Asia, the US and Europe Ban Exploding Smartphone," *Guardian*, October 17, 2016, accessed March 21, 2017, https://www.theguardian.com/technology/2016/oct/17/samsung-galaxy-note-7-airlines-asia-us-europe-ban-exploding-smartphone; T. Martin & E-Y Jeong, "Samsung Blames Galaxy Note 7 Overheating on Problems at Suppliers," *Wall Street Journal*, January 22, 2017, accessed March 21, 2017, https://www.wsj.com/articles/samsung-blames-galaxy-note-7-overheating-on-problems-at-suppliers-1485136013; C. Warren, "Samsung Is About to Brick Every Galaxy Note 7 in America," December 16, 2017, accessed March 21, 2017, http://gizmodo.com/samsung-is-about-to-brick-every-galaxy-note-7-in-americ-1789913643.

Christopher Dilts/ Bloomberg/Getty Images

Janine Pollack says, "When it tips the balance over to where you're kind of cheating a bit, that's when the law needs to step in."[95] Indeed, several companies have been caught going too far with weight-out, including Procter & Gamble's Old Spice and Olay brands, L'Oréal, CVS, Johnson & Johnson, Unilever's Axe brand, and ConAgra's Slim Jim brand.[96] While McCormick informed retailers and changed the bar code used for scanning, would it not have been more ethical to add a distinctive sticker informing customers as well?

Discretionary responsibilities pertain to the social roles that businesses play in society beyond their economic, legal, and ethical responsibilities. When a million-acre wild fire destroyed the town of Fort McMurray in Alberta, Canada, 88,000 citizens were ordered to evacuate from their homes. Twenty-four hundred buildings, including 1,800 homes, were destroyed.[97] Thankfully, no one died. As recovery efforts began, local companies stepped in with donations, contributions, and other forms of valuable assistance. According to Professor Steven Horowitz, "The oil companies provided free food and shelter to over 25,000 people. When the fires cut off easy road access to the small community of Fort McKay First Nation, Brion Energy began trucking in perishable foods daily. Imperial Oil donated 20,000 liters of gasoline to the relief efforts and Shell Albian Aerodrome rounded up evacuees on buses and, along with Suncor's Firebag Aerodrome, evacuated over 7,000 people on company-chartered commercial jets using their private airstrips."[98] Reporter Tristin Hopper says that, "Alberta's oil producers effectively turned themselves into multi-million-dollar humanitarian organizations at the drop of a hat."[99]

Carrying out discretionary responsibilities such as these is voluntary. Companies are not considered unethical if they don't perform them. Today, however, corporate stakeholders expect companies to do much more than in the past to meet their discretionary responsibilities.

Discretionary responsibilities the social roles that a company fulfills beyond its economic, legal, and ethical responsibilities

4-7 RESPONSES TO DEMANDS FOR SOCIAL RESPONSIBILITY

Social responsiveness refers to a company's strategy to respond to stakeholders' economic, legal, ethical, or discretionary expectations concerning social responsibility. A social responsibility problem exists whenever company actions do not meet stakeholder expectations. One model of social responsiveness identifies four strategies for responding to social responsibility problems: reactive, defensive, accommodative, and proactive. These strategies differ in the extent to which the company is willing to act to meet or exceed society's expectations.

A company using a **reactive strategy** will do less than society expects. For nearly two decades, the National Transportation Safety Board (NTSB) has been pressuring the helicopter industry to adopt tougher fuel-tank standards that would reduce the likelihood of fires erupting after a crash. The NTSB estimates that with these upgrades, hundreds of fatalities and serious burns caused by post-impact fires could have been prevented. The industry balked at the expense of the upgrades ($100,000 per helicopter, or $500 million industry-wide). Until, that is, a series of high-profile accidents and fatal crashes made it impossible to ignore the issue any longer. Matthew Zuccaro, president of industry trade association Helicopter Association International, acknowledges that attitudes have finally changed. "There is a major cultural shift in the international helicopter community. You got our attention, and we're going to participate," he said.[100] Prompted by two fatal crashes in a three-year period, **Air Methods**, the largest operator of air ambulances in the United States, has begun the process by retrofitting the fuel systems on 130 of its 400 helicopters.

By contrast, a company using a **defensive strategy** would admit responsibility for a problem but would do the least required to meet societal expectations. Defective Takata airbags are responsible for 13 deaths worldwide. Moisture unexpectedly triggers the bags to open, exposing drivers to damaging and sometimes deadly metal shards. Four auto manufacturers, Fiat Chrysler, Mitsubishi, Toyota, and Volkswagen, admit to still making new cars with these defective airbags. Since it takes time for moisture to build up, the new air bags are considered safe in the short run. All four automakers have until 2018 to replace the defective airbags with functional airbags (which are in short supply because of manufacturing issues). But only Volkswagen and Mitsubishi are telling consumers which cars have the defective airbags. Toyota and Fiat Chrysler are not. Karl Brauer, senior analyst at Kelley Blue Book, an automotive research company, said, "I find it bizarre on multiple levels. Multiple mainstream automakers essentially know that they are selling cars that already have a defective part in them. And it's not a defective windshield wiper or sun visor hinge. It's an airbag, a primary safety device. If a company is unwilling to disclose which models, I as a consumer would hesitate buying any of their cars until I know which ones are affected."[101]

A company using an **accommodative strategy** will accept responsibility for a problem and take a progressive approach by doing all that could be expected to solve the problem. Chipotle once ridiculed rivals for using artificial ingredients and boasted that it served "food with integrity." In 2015, however, the fast-casual restaurant chain was hit with a foodborne illnesses outbreak that crippled the brand's sparkling image. Between July and December 2015, hundreds of customers across nine states contracted *E. coli* and noroviruses after eating Chipotle food. In response, Chipotle not only closed the stores where outbreaks occurred but also neighboring stores. Managers and employees across the country scoured their stores to sterilize them, and thousands of ingredient samples were submitted to the Centers for Disease Control (CDC) for testing. Ultimately, the CDC could not point to a particular cause or source. Chipotle director of public relations Chris Arnold said, however, "If there's a silver lining in this, it is that by not knowing for sure what the cause is, it's prompted us to look at every ingredient we use with an eye to improving our practices."[102] Chipotle's beef supplier now tests meat for pathogens before shipping, and Chipotle has adopted new labeling protocols, such as unique item numbers for all its ingredients, to allow full traceability from the field to food suppliers to restaurants. To ensure that these changes stick, half of all bonuses given to Chipotle managers are now tied to food safety.[103]

Finally, a company using a **proactive strategy** will anticipate responsibility for a problem before it occurs, do more than expected to address the problem, and lead

---

Social responsiveness a company's strategy to respond to stakeholders' economic, legal, ethical, or discretionary expectations concerning social responsibility

Reactive strategy a social responsiveness strategy in which a company does less than society expects

Defensive strategy a social responsiveness strategy in which a company admits responsibility for a problem but does the least required to meet societal expectations

Accommodative strategy a social responsiveness strategy in which a company accepts responsibility for a problem and does all that society expects to solve that problem

Proactive strategy a social responsiveness strategy in which a company anticipates a problem before it occurs and does more than society expects to take responsibility for and address the problem

RESPONDING TO COMPETING SOCIAL RESPONSIBILITIES

The Colorado Correctional Industries (CCI) considers it part of its core mission to provide inmates with job and life skills as a way to facilitate their return to society and reduce recidivism. In furtherance of that mission, CCI collaborated with several companies to give inmates the opportunity to train for a variety of jobs. One such company, Haystack Mountain Goat Dairy, sells goat cheese to the national grocery chain Whole Foods. According to Whole Foods spokesperson Michael Silverman, "We felt that supporting supplier partners who found a way to be part of paid, rehabilitative work being done by inmates would help people get back on their feet." Michael Allen of End Mass Incarceration Houston disagrees, however. Allen believes that Whole Foods' support of products made with inmate labor is exploitative rather than socially responsible, saying, "People are incarcerated and then forced to work for pennies on the dollar—compare that to what the products are sold for." Although Whole Foods asked Haystack Mountain Goat Dairy to find an alternate source for the goat milk that

goes into its cheeses, CCI and Haystack Mountain stand by the program. Haystack considers the arrangement a model prison-labor program because inmates not only earn up to $2,500 a year, they also receive teamwork and job training, giving them a new set of skills for when they are released.

Source: A. Aubrey, "Whole Foods Says It Will Stop Selling Foods Made with Prison Labor," *National Public Radio*, October 1, 2015, www.npr.org/sections/thesalt/2015/09/30/444797169/whole-foods-says-it-will-stop-selling-foods-made-by-prisoners (Accessed February 23, 2016).

the industry in its approach. McDonald's CEO Steve Easterman announced that at its 14,350 U.S. stores, it will stop selling menu items made from chickens treated with antibiotics. Scientists and doctors have long warned that treating livestock with antibiotics to prevent infections before they occur is accelerating the development of antibiotic-resistant bacteria. Indeed, 2 million Americans a year develop bacterial infections resistant to antibiotics, and, according to the Centers for Disease Control and Prevention, 23,000 of them will die. McDonald's is making these changes even though it will significantly increase its costs (antibiotic-free chickens are two to three times more expensive to raise). McDonald's size is expected to broadly influence the chicken-growing industry to stop raising chicken with antibiotics. Gail Hansen of the Pew Charitable Trust, an organization critical of the use of antibiotics in meat, said McDonald's new policy, "Will have a ripple effect probably throughout the entire food industry."[104]

 ## 4-8 SOCIAL RESPONSIBILITY AND ECONOMIC PERFORMANCE

One question that managers often ask is, "Does it pay to be socially responsible?" In previous editions of this textbook, the answer was no, as early research indicated that there was not an inherent relationship between social responsibility and economic performance.[105] Recent research, however, leads to different conclusions. There is no trade-off between being socially responsible and economic performance.[106] And there is a small, positive relationship between being socially responsible and economic performance that strengthens with corporate reputation.[107] Let's explore what each of these results means.

First, as noted earlier, there is no trade-off between being socially responsible and economic performance.[108] Being socially responsible usually won't make a business less profitable. What this suggests is that the costs of being socially responsible—and those costs can be high, especially early on—can be offset by a better product or corporate reputation, which results in stronger sales or higher profit margins. When businesses enhance their reputations by being socially responsible, they hope to maximize *willingness to pay,* that is, customers paying more for products and services that are socially responsible. The market for organic, grass-fed, antibiotic-free beef has grown over 300 percent in the last five years. While it takes longer (20 to 24 months versus 16 to 18 months) for organically raised cattle to make weight, and it costs more (due to the extra time, which raises feed and medical costs, and to the audits and paperwork required to prove the cattle were raised naturally), organic grass-fed beef sells for 30 to 80 percent more per pound. In other words, consumers and restaurants like Chipotle are clearly maximizing a willingness to pay for socially responsible beef.[109]

Second, it usually *does* pay to be socially responsible, and that relationship becomes stronger, particularly when a company or its products have a strong reputation for social responsibility.[110] Finally, even if there is generally a small positive relationship between social responsibility and economic performance that becomes stronger when a company or its products have a positive reputation for social responsibility, and even if there is no trade-off between being socially responsible and

economic performance, there is no guarantee that socially responsible companies will be profitable. Simply put, socially responsible companies experience the same ups and downs in economic performance that traditional businesses do. For all of the positive press that Tesla gets for its high-performing, environmentally friendly, very expensive cars (*without options*, Model S prices range from $71,000 to $137,800 while Model X prices range from $89,000 to $139,000), few people realize that Tesla has reported a quarterly profit just twice since going public in 2010 (Tesla was founded in 2003). Every other quarter resulted in millions of dollars of losses. Part of this is because Tesla is a startup automotive company, which is a cash-intensive business. As of February 2017, Tesla reported 10 straight quarters of negative free cash flow, which means that Tesla was burning more cash than it was generating.[111] Indeed, as Tesla finally delivers its more reasonably priced $35,000 Model 3 in 2018, five years late to market, founder Elon Musk explained that Tesla's cash will drop "close to the edge."[112] Musk further projects that Tesla will not be profitable until 2020 when it reaches full production capacity on all three of its cars.[113] Tesla could ultimately disrupt the automotive industry and be wildly profitable. But if it does so on Musk's estimated schedule, it will have taken 17 years just to get to consistent profitability. Being socially responsible may be the right thing to do, and it is usually associated with increased profits, but it doesn't guarantee business success.

Ahturner/Shutterstock.com

STUDY TOOLS 4

LOCATED IN TEXTBOOK
☐ Rip out and review chapter review card.

LOCATED AT WWW.CENGAGEBRAIN.COM
☐ Gain unique perspectives on key concepts with new 4LTR concept videos in the e-book.

☐ Increase your comprehension with Aplia for MGMT11.
☐ Complete interactive content within the e-book.

5 | Planning and Decision Making

LEARNING OBJECTIVES

5-1 Discuss the benefits and pitfalls of planning.

5-2 Describe how to make a plan that works.

5-3 Discuss how companies can use plans at all management levels, from top to bottom.

5-4 Explain the steps and limits to rational decision making.

5-5 Explain how group decisions and group decision-making techniques can improve decision making.

After finishing this chapter go to **PAGE 111** for **STUDY TOOLS.**

Paul Bradbury/Getty Images

5-1 BENEFITS AND PITFALLS OF PLANNING

Even inexperienced managers know that planning and decision making are central parts of their jobs. Figure out what the problem is. Generate potential solutions or plans. Pick the best one. Make it work. Experienced managers, however, know how hard it really is to make good plans and decisions. One seasoned manager says, "I think the biggest surprises are the problems. Maybe I had never seen it before. Maybe I was protected by my management when I was in sales. Maybe I had delusions of grandeur, I don't know. I just know how disillusioning and frustrating it is to be hit with problems and conflicts all day and not be able to solve them very cleanly."[1]

Planning choosing a goal and developing a strategy to achieve that goal

Planning is choosing a goal and developing a method or strategy to achieve that goal. Seventy dollars is the break-even price for a barrel of off-shore, deep-water oil. But with innovative fracking technologies, a barrel of (on ground) shale oil can be profitable at $50 or less. So Royal Dutch Shell's new plan is to significantly cut the costs and time it takes to deliver oil from its off-shore, deep-water platforms. "Chief irritants" have been assigned in each department to challenge, question and simplify how business gets done. Shell now takes 40 percent less equipment onto deep-water platforms, reducing costs and complexity. The number of support ships taking equipment and supplies to platforms has dropped from 61 to 16. Once-routine $10,000 helicopter trips to overnight parts to platforms are now used only for emergencies. Annual savings on logistics alone should reduce costs $300 million a year. Kevin McMahon, who manages an offshore platform, says, "This is not a cut-and-cope exercise. This is our new reality."[2]

Are you one of those naturally organized people who always makes a daily to-do list, writes everything down so you won't forget, and never misses a deadline because you keep track of everything with written lists, a spreadsheet, or task management apps like Todoist or WunderList on your smartphone, tablet, or computer? Or are you one of those flexible, creative, go-with-the-flow people who dislikes planning and organizing because it restricts your freedom, energy, and performance? Some

people are natural planners. They love it and can see only its benefits. Others dislike planning and can see only its disadvantages. It turns out that *both* views have real value.

*Planning has advantages and disadvantages. Let's learn about **5-1a the benefits** and **5-1b the pitfalls of planning.***

5-1a Benefits of Planning

Planning offers several important benefits: intensified effort, persistence, direction, and creation of task strategies.[3] First, managers and employees put forth greater effort when following a plan. Take two workers. Instruct one to "do your best" to increase production, and instruct the other to achieve a 2 percent increase in production each month. Research shows that the one with the specific plan will work harder.[4]

Second, planning leads to persistence, that is, working hard for long periods. In fact, planning encourages persistence even when there may be little chance of short-term success.[5] McDonald's founder Ray Kroc, a

As American President Calvin Coolidge said, "Nothing in the world can take the place of persistence."

keen believer in the power of persistence, had this quotation from President Calvin Coolidge hung in all of his executives' offices: "Nothing in the world can take the place of persistence. Talent will not; nothing is more common than unsuccessful men with talent. Genius will not; unrewarded genius is almost a proverb. Education will not; the world is full of educated derelicts. Persistence and determination alone are omnipotent."[6]

The third benefit of planning is direction. Alex Macedo, President of BK North America, said, "In a moment when a lot of brands in quick service are trying to become more fast-casual, we're taking an opposite view."[7] After struggling to maintain sales with new menu items like cranberry salads and low calories "satisfries," Burger King (BK) is returning to its fast food roots by focusing its menu on flame-grilled burgers, french fries, hot dogs, and chicken fries. David Harper who runs 72 BK restaurants says, "We know who we are now."[8] Same-store sales are now growing 5.6 percent a year.

The fourth benefit of planning is that it encourages the development of task strategies. In other words, planning not only encourages people to work hard for extended periods and to engage in behaviors directly related to goal accomplishment, it also encourages them to think of better ways to do their jobs. Finally, perhaps the most compelling benefit of planning is that it has been proven to work for both companies and individuals. On average, companies with plans have larger profits and grow much faster than companies without plans.[9] The same holds true for individual managers and employees:

There is no better way to improve the performance of the people who work in a company than to have them set goals and develop strategies for achieving those goals.

5-1b Pitfalls of Planning

Despite the significant benefits associated with planning, it is not a cure-all. Plans won't fix all organizational problems. In fact, many management authors and consultants believe that planning can harm companies in several ways.[10]

The first pitfall of planning is that it can impede change and prevent or slow needed adaptation. Sometimes companies become so committed to achieving the goals set forth in their plans or on following the

Analysts estimate that Apple sold nearly 12 million Apple Watches in 2016, accounting for half the global market share in smart watches.

strategies and tactics spelled out in them that they fail to see that their plans aren't working or that their goals need to change. In 2015, only 25 percent of the makers of luxury Swiss mechanical watches thought Apple's new smart watch would have a "meaningful impact" on sales.[11] But by the end of 2015, sales had dropped by $2 billion, or 1.6 percent. By the end of 2016, sales had fallen again, by 9.9 percent, or nearly or $19 billion.[12] To avoid price discounts, Swiss watch makers bought back nearly 10 percent of unsold watch inventory from retailers and dismantled those watches for parts.[13] Analysts estimate that Apple sold nearly 12 million Apple Watches in 2016, accounting for half the market share and 80 percent of the profits in global smart watches.[14] Will luxury buyers come back to mechanical watches? Hong Kong's Jai Ignacio says, "This [Apple Watch] is more practical for me. I can change the bracelet to steel links when I need to dress up."[15] Canalysis, a market research company, estimates that smart watch sales may total 67 percent of Swiss watch sales by the end of 2017.[16]

The second pitfall is that planning can create a false sense of certainty. Planners sometimes feel that they know exactly what the future holds for their competitors, their suppliers, and their companies. However, all plans are based on assumptions. "National home prices never go down. Eurozone countries don't default. Saudi Arabia won't let the price of oil crash. China's demand for raw materials is infinite." For plans to work, the assumptions on which they are based must hold true. If the assumptions turn out to be false, then the plans based on them are likely to fail. Indeed, according to the *Wall Street Journal's* Greg Ip, the four assumptions just listed were "some of the most cherished assumptions of investors and policy makers in the past decade, assumptions that have underpinned trillions of dollars of investment and debt."[17] And they were all completely wrong.

The third potential pitfall of planning is the detachment of planners. In theory, strategic planners and top-level managers are supposed to focus on the big picture and not concern themselves with the details of implementation (that is carrying out the plan). According to management professor Henry Mintzberg, detachment leads planners to plan for things they don't understand.[18] Plans are meant to be guidelines for action, not abstract theories. Consequently, planners need to be familiar with the daily details of their businesses if they are to produce plans that can work.

When she became PepsiCo's CEO, Indra Nooyi declared that healthy snacks represented one of Pepsi-Co's "biggest growth opportunities."[19] So PepsiCo began removing calories, redoing recipes, and delivering new products like Lemon Lemon (carbonated lemonade with real lemon juice), Quaker Real Medleys (oatmeal in portable packages that can be eaten anywhere), and Mountain Dew Kickstart (with half the regular calories). While great in theory, Nooyi's plans ignored Pepsi's own research that snackers care about taste and not health. Greg Yep, PepsiCo's former senior vice president of long-term research, said, "I don't know too many consumers who compromise on taste for something that's more nutritious."[20] Norman Deschamps, a market researcher at Packaged Facts, agreed, saying when people socialize, "they have snacks like potato chips and pretzels. They don't all sit around and snack on granola bars." In other words, Pepsi's business is growing because consumers are reaching for the latest flavors of Fritos, Cheetos, and Lay's potato chips. In fact, at the beginning of 2017, chips produced 52 percent of PepsiCo's profits, up from 43 percent in 2010.[21]

5-2 HOW TO MAKE A PLAN THAT WORKS

Planning is a double-edged sword. If done right, planning brings about tremendous increases in individual and organizational performance. If planning is done wrong, however, it can have just the opposite effect and harm individual and organizational performance.

*In this section, you will learn how to make a plan that works. As depicted in Exhibit 5.1, planning consists of **5-2a setting goals**, **5-2b developing commitment to the goals**, **5-2c developing effective action plans**, **5-2d tracking progress toward goal achievement**, and **5-2e maintaining flexibility in planning**.*

5-2a Setting Goals

The first step in planning is to set goals. To direct behavior and increase effort, goals need to be specific and challenging.[22] For example, deciding to "increase sales this year" won't direct and energize workers as much as deciding to "increase North American sales by 4 percent in the next six months." Specific, challenging goals provide a target for which to aim and a standard against which to measure success.

One way of writing effective goals for yourself, your job, or your company is to use the S.M.A.R.T. guidelines. **S.M.A.R.T. goals** are **S**pecific, **M**easurable, **A**ttainable, **R**ealistic, and **T**imely.[23] With annual sales of $83 billion,

> **S.M.A.R.T. goals** goals that are specific, measurable, attainable, realistic, and timely

Exhibit 5.1
How to Make a Plan That Works

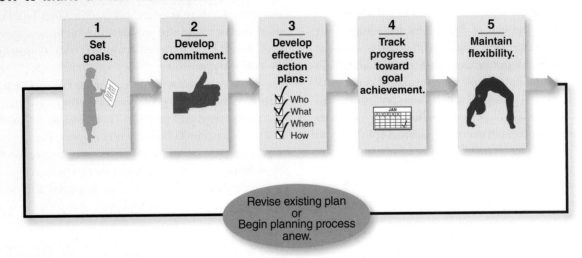

Cincinnati-based **Procter & Gamble** is a global leader in consumer products in 180 countries. It's size, however, makes managing growth difficult. To combat this difficulty, in 2013, CEO A.G. Lafley established a goal of cutting P&G's massive brand portfolio of roughly 165 brands to 65 core brands, organized into 10 key categories, by 2016.[24] Let's see how P&G's objectives measure up to the S.M.A.R.T. guidelines for goals.

First, is the goal *Specific*? Yes, as opposed to saying that it wants to be smaller, P&G identified exactly how many brands it wanted in its portfolio by 2016—its 65 best-selling brands. Is the goal *Measurable*? Yes, P&G's best-performing brands generate 95 percent of its profits, which are growing faster than the rest of P&G, while its poorer performing brands haves sales and profits that are shrinking 3 percent and 16 percent per year, respectively.[25] Whether the goal is *Attainable* or not depends on many factors. First, P&G needs to find potential buyers for the 100 brands it is selling. After it identifies potential buyers, they must agree on a purchase price (a complex task with billion-dollar businesses). Then, it must clear the financial and legal hurdles involved in transferring ownership of each brand. But, major merger and acquisitions transactions aren't new, certainly for P&G, and it's unlikely these issues will be problematic. Finally, while the goals are ambitious, they are *Timely*. When P&G announced the goal in 2013, it gave itself three years to divest 50 of the 100 brands it has identified for sale. In 2016, it had successfully sold 43 beauty brands, including Clairol and Cover Girl, to Coty for $12.5 billion.[26] By March 2017, P&G had settled on 65 key brands in 10 different businesses (http://us.pg.com/our-brands).

5-2b Developing Commitment to Goals

Just because a company sets a goal doesn't mean that people will try to accomplish it. If workers don't care about a goal, that goal won't encourage them to work harder or smarter. Thus, the second step in planning is to develop commitment to goals.[27]

Goal commitment is the determination to achieve a goal. Commitment to achieve a goal is not automatic. Managers and workers must choose to commit themselves to a goal. Edwin Locke, professor emeritus of management at the University of Maryland and the foremost expert on how, why, and when goals work, tells a story about an overweight friend who lost 75 pounds. Locke says, "I asked him how he did it, knowing how hard it was for most people to lose so much weight." His friend responded, "Actually, it was quite simple. I simply decided that I *really wanted* to do it."[28] Put another way, goal commitment is really wanting to achieve a goal.

So how can managers bring about goal commitment? The most popular approach is to set goals participatively. Rather than assigning goals to workers ("Johnson, you've got till Tuesday of next week to redesign the flux capacitor so it gives us 10 percent more output"), managers

Goal commitment the determination to achieve a goal

and employees choose goals together. The goals are more likely to be realistic and attainable if employees participate in setting them. Another technique for gaining commitment to a goal is to make the goal public. For example, college students who publicly communicated their semester grade goals ("This semester, I'm shooting for a 3.5") to important people in their lives (usually a parent or sibling) were much more committed to achieving their grades than those who did not. Still another way to increase goal commitment is to obtain top management's support. Top management can show support for a plan or program by providing funds, speaking publicly about the plan, or participating in the plan itself.

5-2c Developing Effective Action Plans

The third step in planning is to develop effective action plans. An **action plan** lists the specific steps (how), people (who), resources (what), and time period (when) for accomplishing a goal. It takes a blackberry bush three years to produce fruit, so to add a salad with blackberries to its 2016 summer menu, Wendy's started planning well in advance, especially since sourcing blackberries was a significant challenge. Wendy's usually interviews two to five potential suppliers before selecting one, but for blackberries, its procurement team spent 14 months reviewing over 30 growers before finding two that could supply its needs. Since most U.S. blackberries end up in supermarkets, with little left for restaurants, Wendy's worked with those two growers to plant the blackberry bushes to grow the nearly 2 million extra berries, or 10 percent of the total U.S. blackberry crop, needed to serve a summer's worth of salads at its nearly 6,700 North American restaurants. Wendy's COO Bob Wright admits the plan was challenging to put into action, saying, "Just to have a salad on a menu is a very difficult thing to achieve."[29]

5-2d Tracking Progress

The fourth step in planning is to track progress toward goal achievement. There are two accepted methods of tracking progress. The first is to set proximal goals and distal goals. **Proximal goals** are short-term goals or subgoals, whereas **distal goals** are long-term or primary goals.[30]

When General Motors launched a plan to produce a driverless car by 2025 (the distal goal), managers identified three proximal goals to get there:

1. In 2010, driver is in charge.
2. In 2015, driver is mostly in charge.
3. In 2020, car is mostly in charge.[31]

DOES "PLAN B" KILL GOAL COMMITMENT?

Standard advise is to have a "Plan B" in in case "Plan A" doesn't work. However, developing "Plan B" might reduce your commitment — and chance of success — with Plan A.

In three studies, Professors Jihae Shin and Katherine Milkman had college students do a series of tasks for which they could be rewarded with a snack. But some of the students were told to think about other places on campuses where they might get free food if they weren't successful at their tasks, that is, Plan B. Milkman said, ""When people were prompted to think about another way to achieve the same high-level outcome in case they failed in their primary goal, they worked less hard and did less well."

So, if you really want to succeed with Plan A, be cautious when asked, "What's Plan B?" At the very least says Shin, "You might want to delay making a backup plan until after you have done everything you can to achieve your primary goal."

Source: Knowledge@ Wharton, "The Downside of a Backup Plan – and What to Do About It," University of Pennsylvania, The Wharton School of Business, June 2, 2016, accessed March 25, 2017, http://knowledge.wharton.upenn.edu/article/the-downsideof-making-a-backup-plan/; R. Silverman, "Plan A' Works Better When There's No 'Plan B," *Wall Street Journal*, August 16, 2016, accessed March 25, 2017, https://www.wsj.com/articles/plan-a-works-better-when-theres-no-plan-b-1471356000.

The second method of tracking progress is to gather and provide performance feedback. Regular, frequent performance feedback allows workers and managers to track their progress toward goal achievement and make adjustments in effort, direction, and strategies.[32] Exhibit 5.2 shows the impact of feedback on safety behavior at a large bakery company with a worker safety record that was two-and-a-half times worse than the industry average. During the baseline period, workers in the wrapping department, who measure and mix ingredients, roll the bread dough, and put it into baking pans, performed their jobs safely about 70 percent of the time (see 1 in Exhibit 5.2). The baseline safety record for workers in the makeup department, who bag and seal baked bread and assemble, pack, and tape cardboard cartons for shipping, was somewhat better at 78 percent (see 2). The company then

> **Action plan** a plan that lists the specific steps, people, resources, and time period needed to attain a goal
>
> **Proximal goals** short-term goals or subgoals
>
> **Distal goals** long-term or primary goals

gave workers 30 minutes of safety training, set a goal of 90 percent safe behavior, and then provided daily feedback (such as a chart similar to Exhibit 5.2). Performance improved dramatically. During the intervention period, safely performed behaviors rose to an average of 95.8 percent for wrapping workers (see 3) and 99.3 percent for workers in the makeup department (see 4), and never fell below 83 percent. Thus, the combination of training, a challenging goal, and feedback led to a dramatic increase in performance. The importance of feedback alone can be seen in the reversal stage, when the company quit posting daily feedback on safe behavior. Without daily feedback, the percentage of safely performed behaviors returned to baseline levels—70.8 percent for the wrapping department (see 5) and 72.3 percent for the makeup department (see 6). For planning to be effective, workers need both a specific, challenging goal and regular feedback to track their progress. In

Exhibit 5.2
Effects of Goal Setting, Training, and Feedback on Safe Behavior in a Bread Factory

Source: J. Komaki, K. D. Barwick, and L. R. Scott. "A Behavioral Approach to Occupational Safety: Pinpointing and Reinforcing Safe Performance in a Food Manufacturing Plant," *Journal of Applied Psychology* 63 (1978).

Canadapanda/Shutterstock.com

Максим Кузубов/123RF

fact, additional research indicates that the effectiveness of goal setting can be doubled by the addition of feedback.[33]

5-2e Maintaining Flexibility

Because action plans are sometimes poorly conceived and goals sometimes turn out not to be achievable, the last step in developing an effective plan is to maintain flexibility. One method of maintaining flexibility while planning is to adopt an options-based approach.[34] The goal of **options-based planning** is to keep options open by making small, simultaneous investments in many alternative plans. Then, when one or a few of these plans emerge as likely winners, you invest even more in these plans while discontinuing or reducing investment in the others. With revenues flat, layoffs at headquarters, and an unsuccessful effort to duplicate Amazon.com's prime membership plan (ShippingPass offered free two-day shipping for $49 a year), Walmart is using options-based planning to jump start its online sales which grew 7 percent last year, compared to 31 percent for amazon.com. Walmart is making numerous, simultaneous investments by acquiring promising online retailers, such as jet.com, which is growing by 400,000 customers a month. Jet sells products for 10 to 15 percent less than competitors by discounting prices for volume purchasing, opting out of costly free returns and paying with debit cards (which avoid credit card transaction fees). Walmart also bought ModCloth.com, a hipster clothing site, Moosejaw,com, which sells outdoor clothes and gear, and ShoeBuy.com, an online shoe retailer. And, in contrast to previous acquisitions that were absorbed into the company, Walmart will run these online sites as separate businesses. CEO Doug McMillion said, "I don't think it's an exaggeration to say we are going through a transformative period."[35]

In part, options-based planning is the opposite of traditional planning. Whereas the purpose of an action plan is to commit people and resources to a particular course of action, the purpose of options-based planning is to leave those commitments open by maintaining **slack resources**—that is, a cushion of resources, such as extra time, people, money, or production capacity, that can be used to address and adapt to unanticipated changes, problems, or opportunities.[36] Holding options open gives you choices. And choices, combined with slack resources, give you flexibility. Because it can take a year and a half to receive new equipment, U.S. power companies are funding Grid Assurance, LLC, which will buy and hold extra electrical transformers and circuit breakers to be used for emergencies when damaged power generating and transmission equipment needs replacing. Grid Assurance will also locate key equipment in secure, undisclosed locations. In case of terrorist attack, "The last thing we want is for someone to do a physical attack and wipe out our spares," says Scott Moore, vice president of transmission engineering for American Electric Power.[37] Grid Assurance will need a minimum of 100 transformers, which can cost from $2 million to $10 million each. Grid Assurance provides the equivalent of catastrophic insurance, giving power companies the extra resources needed to survive unanticipated disruptions and breakdowns.

5-3 PLANNING FROM TOP TO BOTTOM

Planning works best when the goals and action plans at the bottom and middle of the organization support the goals and action plans at the top of the organization. In other words, planning works best when everybody pulls in the same direction. Exhibit 5.3 illustrates this planning continuity, beginning at the top with a clear definition of the company purpose and ending at the bottom with the execution of operational plans.

Let's see how 5-3a top managers create the organization's purpose statement and strategic objective, 5-3b middle managers develop tactical plans and use management by objectives to motivate employee efforts toward the overall purpose and strategic objective, and 5-3c first-level managers use operational, single-use, and standing plans to implement the tactical plans.

Options-based planning maintaining planning flexibility by making small, simultaneous investments in many alternative plans

Slack resources a cushion of extra resources that can be used with options-based planning to adapt to unanticipated changes, problems, or opportunities

Exhibit 5.3
Planning from Top to Bottom

5-3a Starting at the Top

Top management is responsible for developing long-term **strategic plans** that make clear how the company will serve customers and position itself against competitors in the next two to five years. Recall that P&G recently set a goal of cutting 100 of its brands. That goal was part of a strategic plan developed under former CEO A.G. Lafley. During his first term as CEO, the now twice-retired Lafley. Lafley focused on acquisitions and growth. His strategic focus turned P&G into the world's largest consumer-products company. When he returned to serve as CEO for a second time, Lafley began purposefully shrinking the giant company. The reason? The company had grown too large to compete. Lafley sold Camay and Zest brands to archrival Unilever and exited the battery business by selling Duracell and the pet-food business by selling Iams. He also looked to sell Wella and Clairol, two brands that he acquired during his first term as P&G's CEO. "Decade after decade, we have to find the strategy and the business model that wins with consumers," Lafley said, and trimming P&G's portfolio "strategically resets P&G's where-to-play choices for at least the next five years."[38]

Strategic planning begins with the creation of an organizational purpose. A **purpose statement**, which is often referred to as an organizational mission or vision, is a statement of a company's purpose or reason for existing.[39] Purpose statements should be brief—no more than two sentences. They should also be enduring, inspirational, clear, and consistent with widely shared company beliefs and values. An excellent example of a well-crafted purpose statement is that of cosmetics company Avon: "To be the company that best understands and satisfies the product, service and self-fulfillment needs of women—globally."[40] It guides everyone in the organization and provides a focal point for the delivery of beauty products and

Strategic plans overall company plans that clarify how the company will serve customers and position itself against competitors over the next two to five years

Purpose statement a statement of a company's purpose or reason for existing

Daniel Acker/AFP/Getty Images

services to the customers, women around the world. The purpose is the same whether Avon is selling lipstick to women in India, shampoo packets to women in the Amazon, or jewelry to women in the United States. Despite these regional differences in specific strategy, the overall goal—understanding the needs of women globally—does not change. Other examples of organizational purpose statements that have been particularly effective include Walt Disney Company's "to make people happy", Schlage Lock Company's "to make the world more secure," and *Highlights for Children*, the long running magazine for children, "fun with a purpose."[41]

The **strategic objective**, which flows from the purpose, is a more specific goal that unifies company-wide efforts, stretches and challenges the organization, and possesses a finish line and a time frame.[42] Collins and Porras explain that: "A mission is a clear and compelling goal that serves to unify an organization's efforts. An effective mission must stretch and challenge the organization, yet be achievable." However, many others define *mission* as an organization's purpose. In this edition, to be more specific and avoid confusion, we use Collins and Porras's term *purpose statement*, meaning a clear statement of an organization's purpose or reason for existence. Furthermore, we will continue to use Collins and Porras's definition of a mission (that is "a clear and compelling goal . . .") but instead call it "the strategic objective."

After two bankruptcies, Sbarro, a chain of Italian restaurants located in shopping mall food courts, will return to its New York–style pizza roots. CEO David Karam says, "The essence of this brand is pizza. It's what consumers buy from Sbarro and how they view Sbarro."[43] In other words, Sbarro's reason for existence (that is, it's purpose) is pizza. Sbarro's strategic objective, which flows from that purpose, is to establish neighborhood pizza restaurants that also deliver pizza. Karam explained, "There are 900 malls in the U.S. with food courts, and we're in a third of them. But instead of them representing 90 percent of our sites, I'd like them to represent less than half."[44]

Once the strategic objective has been accomplished, a new one should be chosen. However, the new strategic objective must grow out of the organization's purpose, which does not change significantly over time. Intuit started three decades ago with Quicken, its top-selling checkbook and budgeting software. Consistent with its purpose to "power prosperity around the world," it then developed QuickBooks, accounting software for small businesses, and TurboTax, for individuals and businesses. So it was surprising when Intuit sold Quicken last year!

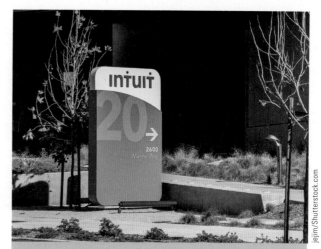

Intuit saw its customers moving to cloud-based services and developed new strategic initiatives to meet the challenge.

jejim/Shutterstock.com

Intuit, however, saw its customers and competitive environment moving to cloud-based services like Xero. Xero, which is cloud-based accounting software for small businesses, not only offers anywhere accessibility but also direct connections to corporate bank accounts (eliminating hand entry of data) and secure access for outside accounting firms (which no longer need company book-keepers to prepare accounting data). In response to those changes, Intuit developed a new strategic objective, "being the operating system behind small business success and doing the nations' taxes in the U.S. and Canada." Which meant that Quicken, a standalone app without cloud-based capabilities no longer fit. So Intuit sold Quicken and then revamped QuickBooks into QuickBooks Online, which connects to 2,000 apps. QuickBooks Online subscriptions are up 49 percent in just one year. UBS analyst Brent Thrill said, "Whenever Intuit makes a wrong turn, they quickly get off the gravel and back onto the blacktop. That's why the company has done so well for such a long time."[45]

5-3b Bending in the Middle

Middle management is responsible for developing and carrying out tactical plans to accomplish the organization's strategic objective. **Tactical plans** specify how a company will use resources, budgets,

Strategic objective a more specific goal that unifies company-wide efforts, stretches and challenges the organization, and possesses a finish line and a time frame

Tactical plans plans created and implemented by middle managers that direct behavior, efforts, and attention over the next six months to two years and people to accomplish specific goals related to its strategic objective for the next five years. Whereas strategic plans and objectives are used to focus company efforts over the next two to five years, tactical plans and objectives are used to direct behavior, efforts, and attention over the next six months to two years. Hostess sells nearly $1.3 billion a year in Twinkies, Cupcakes, HoHos, Ding Dongs, and other snack cakes in more than 100,000 convenience stores across the United States. Still, says CEO Bill Toler, Hostess is 20,000 stores shy of reaching its strategic objective: "To be sold everywhere a candy bar is sold, whether it's an airport kiosk, or a vending machine."[46] To achieve that objective, Hostess's tactical plans include expanding in the United States, broadening distribution in Europe and the Caribbean, and launching new distribution in Mexico and Canada. Hostess has extended its brand name by placing bread and sandwich buns in drug, dollar, and convenience stores, and is also considering entering the $400 million brownie category (and perhaps the cookie category as well). These expansions have limits, however. Toler wants to keep Hostess close to its roots as a maker of treats. According to him, "We have a mindful eye into healthier trends . . . but our primary focus is on being an indulgent snack."[47]

Management by objectives is a management technique often used to develop and carry out tactical plans. **Management by objectives** is a four-step process in which managers and their employees (1) discuss possible goals; (2) collectively select goals that are challenging, attainable, and consistent with the company's overall goals; (3) jointly develop tactical plans that lead to the accomplishment of tactical goals and objectives; and (4) meet regularly to review progress toward accomplishment of those goals. Kimberly-Clark, the maker of diapers, tissues, and other consumer products, was a low-pressure workplace in which, according to retired sales director Rick Herbert, "A lot of people [meaning poor performers] could and would hide in the weeds."[48] But the company has now switched to a performance management system, a variant of MBO, in which personalized goals and tracking data are used to closely monitor performance. Says Herbert, "People can't duck and hide in the same way they could in the past." Instead of once-a-year reviews, feedback regarding goal progress and personal improvement is real-time and continuous. Engineer Stephanie Martin said, says, "We have to routinely shuffle the resources and say, what's the most important thing we need to do today, this week, this month, to drive this objective?"[49]

5-3c Finishing at the Bottom

Lower-level managers are responsible for developing and carrying out **operational plans**, which are the day-to-day plans for producing or delivering the organization's products and services. Operational plans direct the behavior, efforts, and priorities of operative employees for periods ranging from 30 days to six months. There are three kinds of operational plans: single-use plans, standing plans, and budgets.

Single-use plans deal with unique, one-time-only events. In 1905, **General Electric Co.** set up a banking division to finance the sale of its equipment to utility companies. By the 1930s, it financed appliances sales to consumers. By 2015, GE Capital had $500 billion in assets and was the seventh-largest U.S. bank. To sharpen its strategic focus and return to its industrial roots, GE aims to obtain 90 percent of earnings from industrial businesses in 2016, up from 58 percent in 2014. Accordingly, GE created a single-use plan, called "Project Hubble," to dismantle and sell off GE Capital. Over a two-year period, GE will sell its $74 billion lending unit, including roughly $165 million in loans to companies such as Wendy's, and liquidate $26.5 billion in commercial real estate. GE will use the proceeds from this one-time only event to invest further in its remaining industrial businesses, while also rewarding shareholders with $90 billion in dividends and stock buybacks.[50]

Unlike single-use plans that are created, carried out once, and then never used again, **standing plans** save managers time because after the plans are created, they can be used repeatedly to handle frequently recurring

Management by objectives a four-step process in which managers and employees discuss and select goals, develop tactical plans, and meet regularly to review progress toward goal accomplishment

Operational plans day-to-day plans, developed and implemented by lower-level managers, for producing or delivering the organization's products and services over a 30-day to six-month period

Single-use plans plans that cover unique, one-time-only events

Standing plans plans used repeatedly to handle frequently recurring events

events. If you encounter a problem that you've seen before, someone in your company has probably written a standing plan that explains how to address it. When a snowstorm hit Atlanta in 2014, **Delta Airlines** transformed a Boeing 767 into sleeping quarters for stranded employees. Instead of going to the airport hotel—or to uncomfortable cots in the terminal—employees slept on the plane's business class lie-flat seats and were rested and ready when the runways were clear in the morning. The contingency plan was so successful that Delta added it to its standard storm-response planning in 2015. Using a standing plan rather than reinventing the wheel allows Delta to save time. Delta's senior vice president of operations, Dave Holtz, says, "We don't want to limit our ability to get customers going because employees can't get there."[51] There are three kinds of standing plans: policies, procedures, and rules and regulations.

Policies indicate the general course of action that company managers should take in response to a particular event or situation. A well-written policy will also specify why the policy exists and what outcome the policy is intended to produce[52]. When bad weather threatened flights, the old policy followed by the airlines was to take care of frequent fliers first, finding them alternative routes to their destinations. As for everyone else, well, with limited seats available on any particular travel day, large numbers of travelers were guaranteed to be stuck at the airport. Now, however, the policy is to electronically issue passengers flexible weather waivers several days in advance of disruptive weather. The waivers allow passengers to cancel their flights (with a full refund), fly several days before or after their ticketed travel date, or, even fly out of or to nearby airports where flights are still operating, all without typical changes fees of $200 or more per ticket. Delta spokesperson Michael Thomas explained, "We used to just rebook passengers on the next available flight. Now we let them choose."[53]

Procedures are more specific than policies because they indicate the series of steps that should be taken in response to a particular event. All commercial airplanes require regular cleaning. With no regulatory standards, airlines set their own procedures. At **Singapore Airlines**, which flies longer international flights, a 12-person team takes roughly 40 minutes to clean a Boeing 777-300 jet during a normal stopover. At **United Airlines**, most domestic flights require a quick turn (30 minutes or less), so the cleaning procedures focus on the following tasks:

» Removing visible trash and cleaning out the seat-back pockets

» Cleaning and restocking the bathrooms and galleys

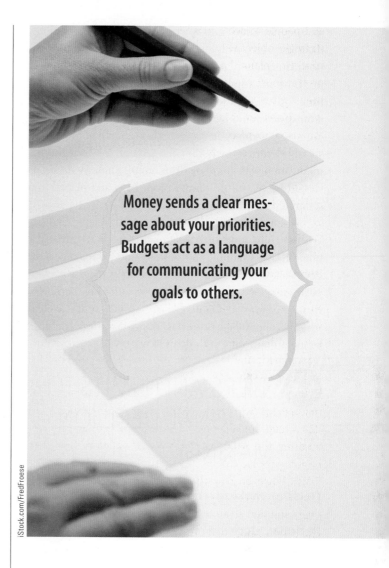

> Money sends a clear message about your priorities. Budgets act as a language for communicating your goals to others.

iStock.com/FredFroese

» Pulling up the armrests

» Wiping crumbs off seats

» Cleaning large spills

In addition to between flights, United conducts more thorough overnight cleanings (vacuuming and cleaning restrooms and galleys) and "deep cleanings," in which the plane is "scrubbed from nose to tail," every 35 to 55 days.[54]

Rules and regulations are even more specific than procedures because they specify what must happen or not happen. They describe precisely how a particular action should be performed. For example,

Policies standing plans that indicate the general course of action that should be taken in response to a particular event or situation

Procedures standing plans that indicate the specific steps that should be taken in response to a particular event

Rules and regulations standing plans that describe how a particular action should be performed or what must happen or not happen in response to a particular event for security issues and worries about drug interactions, most hospitals prohibit patients from bringing medications from home. At the MD Anderson Cancer Center in Houston, admitting nurses must follow this regulation: "All medications brought into the hospital upon admission should be returned home whenever possible. Nursing personnel carrying out the admission procedure should determine whether the patient has brought any medication with him/her from home. Such medications should be placed in tamper-proof bags and placed in a secured area in the nursing unit."[55]

After single-use plans and standing plans, budgets are the third kind of operational plan. **Budgeting** is quantitative planning because it forces managers to decide how to allocate available money to best accomplish company goals. According to Jan King, author of *Business Plans to Game Plans*, "Money sends a clear message about your priorities. Budgets act as a language for communicating your goals to others."

5-4 STEPS AND LIMITS TO RATIONAL DECISION MAKING

Decision making is the process of choosing a solution from available alternatives.[56] **Rational decision making** is a systematic process in which managers define problems, evaluate alternatives, and choose optimal solutions that provide maximum benefits to their organizations. Thus, for example, your boss comes to you requesting that you define and evaluate the various options for the company's social media strategy; after all, you tweet and use Facebook, Instagram, SnapChat, Reddit, and so on and he doesn't even know how to reboot his computer. Furthermore, your solution has to be optimal. Because budgets and expertise are limited, the company gets one, maybe two, tries to make its social media strategy work. If you choose incorrectly, the company's investment will

Gts/Shutterstock.com

just go to waste, without increasing sales and market share. What would you recommend?

Let's learn more about each of these: 5-4a define the problem, 5-4b identify decision criteria, 5-4c weigh the criteria, 5-4d generate alternative courses of action, 5-4e evaluate each alternative, and 5-4f compute the optimal decision. Then we'll consider 5-4g limits to rational decision making.

5-4a Define the Problem

The first step in decision making is identifying and defining the problem. A **problem** exists when there is a gap between a desired state (what is wanted) and an existing state (the situation you are actually facing). You're in charge of ordering the pharmaceutical drugs used in your hospital system. You buy the drugs that doctors and nurses need for treating patients from wholesalers and are paid by insurers who negotiate a fixed reimbursement rate for those patients. When drug prices jump unexpectedly, such as when Valeant Pharmaceuticals increased the price of Nitropress and Isuprel (both used for treating heart-related health issues) by 200 to 500 percent, the hospital end ups absorbing the entire cost increase. In other words, there's a huge gap between what you budgeted to pay for particular drugs like Nitropress and Isuprel, and the much-higher price that you're actually paying when pharmaceutical firms suddenly raise prices.[57]

The presence of a gap between an existing state and a desired state is no guarantee that managers will make decisions to solve problems. Three things must occur for this to happen.[58] First, managers have to be aware of the gap. They have to know there is a problem before they can begin solving it. For example, after noticing that people were spending more money on their pets, a new dog food company created an expensive, high-quality dog food. To emphasize its quality, the dog food was sold in cans and bags with gold labels, red letters, and detailed information about its benefits and nutrients. Yet the product did not sell very well, and the company went out of business in less than a year. Its founders didn't understand why. When they asked a manager at a competing dog food company what their biggest mistake had been, the answer was, "Simple. You didn't have a picture of a dog on the package."[59] This problem would have been easy to solve if management had only been aware of it.

Being aware of a problem isn't enough to begin the decision-making process. Managers have to be motivated to reduce the gap between a desired and an existing state. Sales of carbonated soda have declined as public health concerns over obesity and diabetes have grown. In response, **Pepsi Cola** and **Coca-Cola** diversified by adding water, juice, and energy drinks to their product lines. But after missing its growth target (3–4%) for two straight years, Coke CEO Muhtar Kent settled on a simple strategy to close Coke's sales gap—sell more soda. The company launched Freestyle self-serve soda machines that allow consumers to custom mix more than 100 drink flavors (there are now 27,000 Freestyle machines in U.S. restaurants) and is working with **Keurig Green Mountain Inc.** to develop an in-home counter-top soda machine. Coke also announced a $3 billion cost-cutting program, including some 1,500 layoffs. Soda accounts for 70 percent of Coke's revenue, and Classic Coke and Diet Coke are the top-selling sodas in the United States. With Coke's stalled stock prices making it a potential takeover target, management is highly motivated to address flagging soft drink sales. CEO Kent says, "If we don't do what we need to do quickly, effectively, execute 100 percent, then somebody else will come and do it for us."[60]

Finally, it's not enough to be aware of a problem and be motivated to solve it. Managers must also have the knowledge, skills, abilities, and resources to fix the problem. So how do hospitals solve the problem of sudden price increases for pharmaceuticals (that is, closing the gap between what they budgeted to pay for drugs and the higher prices they actually pay when pharmaceutical companies unexpectedly raise prices). When Nitropress and Isuprel prices jumped 200 to 500 percent, MedStar Washington Hospital Center in Washington, D.C., switched from Nitropress to a cheaper, but identical generic drug and repackaged Isuprel from a one-time use ampule (used for injections), much of which was wasted, into five dosages. Savings amounted to $1.7 million a year.[61]

5-4b Identify Decision Criteria

Decision criteria are the standards used to guide judgments and decisions. Typically, the more criteria a potential solution meets, the better that solution will be. Again, imagine your boss asks you to determine the best options for the company's social media strategy. What general factors would be important when selecting one social media tool over another? Are you trying to increase your search rankings? Provide customer support? Are you trying to

Exhibit 5.4
Absolute Weighting of Decision Criteria for a Car Purchase

5 critically important
4 important
3 somewhat important
2 not very important
1 completely unimportant

1. Predicted reliability		1	2	3	4	(5)
2. Owner satisfaction		1	(2)	3	4	5
3. Predicted depreciation	(1)	2	3	4	5
4. Avoiding accidents		1	2	3	(4)	5
5. Fuel economy		1	2	3	4	(5)
6. Crash protection		1	2	3	(4)	5
7. Acceleration	(1)	2	3	4	5
8. Ride		1	2	(3)	4	5
9. Front seat comfort		1	2	3	4	(5)

reach a particular target market? Is it young single women ages 18–25 or, perhaps, married women ages 25–35? Are you reaching out directly to consumers or to businesses (that is business-to-business)? Will your strategy focus on visual content, demonstrations, or detailed, complex knowledge? Answering questions like these will help you identify the criteria that will guide the social media strategy you recommend.

5-4c Weigh the Criteria

After identifying decision criteria, the next step is deciding which criteria are more or less important. Although there are numerous mathematical models for weighing decision criteria, all require the decision maker to provide an initial ranking of the criteria. Some use **absolute comparisons**, in which each criterion is compared with a standard or is ranked on its own merits. For example, *Consumer Reports* uses nine criteria when it rates

> **Decision criteria** the standards used to guide judgments and decisions
>
> **Absolute comparisons** a process in which each decision criterion is compared to a standard or ranked on its own merits

Exhibit 5.5
Relative Comparison of Home Characteristics

Home Characteristics	L	SSQ	IP	SR	QS	NBH
Daily commute (L)		+1	−1	−1	−1	0
School system quality (SSQ)	−1		−1	−1	−1	−1
In-ground pool (IP)	+1	+1		0	0	+1
Sun room (SR)	+1	+1	0		0	0
Quiet street (QS)	+1	+1	0	0		0
Newly built house (NBH)	0	+1	−1	0	0	
Total weight	+2	+5	−3	−2	−2	0

Exhibit 5.5 shows six criteria that someone might use when buying a house. Moving down the first column of Exhibit 5.5, we see that the time of the daily commute has been rated less important (−1) than school system quality; more important (+1) than having an in-ground pool, a sun room, or a quiet street; and just as important as the house being brand new (0). Total weights, which are obtained by summing the scores in each column, indicate that the school system quality and daily commute are the most important factors to this home buyer, while an in-ground pool, sun room, and a quiet street are the least important. So with relative comparison, criteria are directly compared with each other.

and recommends new cars: predicted reliability, current owners' satisfaction, predicted depreciation (the price you could expect if you sold the car), ability to avoid an accident, fuel economy, crash protection, acceleration, ride, and front seat comfort.[62]

Different individuals will rank these criteria differently, depending on what they value or require in a car. Exhibit 5.4 shows the absolute weights that someone buying a car might use. Because these weights are absolute, each criterion is judged on its own importance using a five-point scale, with 5 representing "critically important" and 1 representing "completely unimportant." In this instance, predicted reliability, fuel economy, and front seat comfort were rated most important, and acceleration and predicted depreciation were rated least important.

Another method uses **relative comparisons**, in which each criterion is compared directly with every other criterion.[63] Professor Jordan Ellenberg emphasizes that not *comparing* the data associated with each option is a fundamental mistake. He says, "A number by itself is often meaningless; it is the comparison between numbers that carries the force."[64]

Relative comparisons a process in which each decision criterion is compared directly with every other criterion

iStock.com/Jason Walton

5-4d Generate Alternative Courses of Action

After identifying and weighting the criteria that will guide the decision-making process, the next step is to identify possible courses of action that could solve the problem. In general, at this step, the idea is to generate as many alternatives as possible. Let's assume that you're trying to select a city in Europe to be the location of a major office. After meeting with your staff, you generate a list of possible alternatives: Amsterdam, the Netherlands; Barcelona or Madrid, Spain; Berlin, Dusseldorf, Frankfurt, or Munich, Germany; Brussels, Belgium; London, England; and Paris, France.

5-4e Evaluate Each Alternative

The next step is to systematically evaluate each alternative against each criterion. Because of the amount of information that must be collected, this step can take much longer and be much more expensive than other steps in the decision-making process. When selecting a European city for your office, you could contact economic development offices

Exhibit 5.6
Criteria Ratings Used to Determine the Best Location for a New Office

Criteria Weights:	Access to Markets 0.60	Qualified Staff 0.53	Telecom-munications 0.52	Easy to Travel to/from City 0.42	Cost & Value of Office Space 0.33	Cost of Staff 0.32	Available Office Space 0.25	Languages Spoken 0.21	Business Climate 0.20	Travel within City 0.20	Quality of Life 0.16	Freedom from Pollution 0.16	Weighted Average	Ranking
Amsterdam	0.42	0.40	0.39	0.68	0.30	0.19	0.30	0.96	0.47	0.34	0.44	0.63	1.72	5
Barcelona	0.23	0.32	0.16	0.29	0.52	0.59	0.52	0.23	0.31	0.47	1.08	0.42	1.45	8
Berlin	0.44	0.39	0.41	0.35	0.78	0.40	0.79	0.50	0.34	0.78	0.38	0.29	1.85	4
Brussels	0.46	0.43	0.37	0.48	0.44	0.17	0.42	0.98	0.37	0.29	0.41	0.27	1.65	7
Dusseldorf	0.30	0.30	0.23	0.21	0.37	0.14	0.28	0.18	0.17	0.22	0.20	0.26	0.97	10
Frankfurt	0.68	0.57	0.70	1.17	0.38	0.11	0.44	0.57	0.38	0.35	0.17	0.18	2.16	3
London	1.50	1.36	1.27	1.79	0.27	0.10	0.42	1.48	0.55	1.26	0.46	0.15	4.03	1
Madrid	0.45	0.46	0.27	0.41	0.52	0.61	0.67	0.22	0.29	0.53	0.67	0.13	1.70	6
Munich	0.34	0.47	0.48	0.37	0.18	0.03	0.18	0.30	0.22	0.47	0.62	0.57	1.36	9
Paris	1.09	0.84	0.89	1.36	0.22	0.10	0.37	0.58	0.30	1.07	0.52	0.12	2.83	2

Source: "European Cities Monitor 2011," *Cushman & Wakefield*, 2011, accessed 27 May 2013. http://www.berlin-partner.de/fileadmin/user_upload/01_chefredaktion/02_pdf /studien-rankings/2011/Cushman%20&%20Wakefield%20-%20European%20Cities%20Monitor%20%282011%20english%29.pdf

in each city, systematically interview businesspeople or executives who operate there, retrieve and use published government data on each location, or rely on published studies such as Cushman & Wakefield's *European Cities Monitor*, which conducted a survey of more than 500 senior European executives who rated 34 European cities on 12 business-related criteria.[65]

No matter how you gather the information, once you have it, the key is to use that information systematically to evaluate each alternative against each criterion. Exhibit 5.6 shows how each of the 10 cities on your staff's list fared with respect to each of the 12 criteria (higher scores are better), from qualified staff to freedom from pollution. Although London has the most qualified staff, the best access to markets and telecommunications, and is the easiest city to travel to and from, it is also one of the most polluted and expensive cities on the list. Paris offers excellent access to markets and clients, but if your staff is multilingual, Brussels might be a better choice.

5-4f Compute the Optimal Decision

The final step in the decision-making process is to compute the optimal decision by determining the optimal value of each alternative. This is done by multiplying the rating for each criterion (Step 5-4e) by the weight for that criterion (Step 5-4c), and then summing those scores for each alternative course of action that you generated (Step 5-4d). For example, the 500 executives participating in Cushman & Wakefield's survey of the best European cities for business rated the 12 decision criteria in terms of importance, as shown in the first row of Exhibit 5.6. Access to markets, qualified staff, telecommunications, and easy travel to and from the city were the four most important factors, while quality of life and freedom from pollution were the least important factors. To calculate the optimal value for Paris, the weight for each category is multiplied by its score in each category (.53 × .84 in the qualified staff category, for example).

Then all of these scores are added together to produce the optimal value, as follows:

$$(.60 \times 1.09) + (.53 \times .84) + (.52 \times .89) +$$
$$(.42 \times 1.36) + (.33 \times .22) + (.32 \times .10) +$$
$$(.25 \times .37) + (.21 \times .58) + (.20 \times .30) +$$
$$(.20 \times 1.07) + (.16 \times .52) + (.16 \times .12) = 2.83$$

Because London has a weighted average of 4.03 compared to 2.83 for Paris and 2.16 for Frankfurt (the cities with the next-best ratings), London clearly ranks as the best location for your company's new European office because of its large number of qualified staff; easy access to markets; outstanding ease of travel to, from, and within the city; excellent telecommunications; and top-notch business climate.

5-4g Limits to Rational Decision Making

In general, managers who diligently complete all six steps of the rational decision-making model will make better decisions than those who don't. So, when they can, managers should try to follow the steps in the rational decision-making model, especially for big decisions with long-range consequences. Chapter 17, Managing Information, also addresses the limits of rational decisions, but does so by examining how models and algorithms can help managers make better, faster decisions (see section 17-4c on sharing knowledge and expertise).

To make completely rational decisions, managers would have to operate in a perfect world with no real-world constraints. Of course, it never actually works like that in the real world. Managers face time and money constraints. They often don't have time to make extensive lists of decision criteria. And they often don't have the resources to test all possible solutions against all possible criteria.

In theory, fully rational decision makers **maximize** decisions by choosing the optimal solution. In practice, however, limited resources along with attention, memory, and expertise problems make it nearly impossible for managers to maximize decisions. Consequently, most managers don't maximize—they satisfice. Whereas maximizing is choosing the best alternative, **satisficing** is choosing a "good-enough" alternative.

In the opening to this section, your boss comes to you asking for a recommendation on the best options for the company's social media strategy. With so many options and the fast pace of change, deciding isn't easy. In other words, there's no optimal solution that will satisfy all criteria. For instance, if you're trying to

Maximize choosing the best alternative

Satisficing choosing a "good-enough" alternative

increase your search rankings, you should use Facebook and YouTube, both of which are directly linked to Facebook and Google search algorithms. If you're interested in providing customer support, then pay close attention to what your customers are saying on Facebook and Twitter, and reach out to them when they're having problems or are dissatisfied. If your target market is teenagers, use Instagram and SnapChat. If it is young single women ages 18–25, use Facebook, SnapChat, or Instagram. If it's married women ages 25–35, use Pinterest. If reaching out directly to consumers, use Pinterest and Facebook, but if reaching out to businesses, use LinkedIn and Twitter. Finally, if your strategy focuses on visual content, use Pinterest; if your intent is to demonstrate what your product or service does, use YouTube; and if you've got detailed, complex knowledge, use Twitter and blogs.[66] Your decision will be complete when you find a "good-enough alternative" that does the best job of meeting your decision criteria.

5-5 USING GROUPS TO IMPROVE DECISION MAKING

A survey of 2,044 human resources and organizational leaders found that 84 percent of companies used teams for special projects, while 74 percent used teams to address departmental issues and innovation.[67] In other words, groups were used to solve problems and make decisions. Companies rely so heavily on groups to make decisions because when done properly, group decision making can lead to much better decisions than those typically made by individuals. In fact, numerous studies show that groups consistently outperform individuals on complex tasks.

*Let's explore the **5-5a advantages and pitfalls of group decision making** and see how the following group decision-making methods—**5-5b structured conflict, 5-5c the nominal group technique, 5-5d the Delphi technique,** and **5-5e electronic brainstorming**—can be used to improve decision making.*

5-5a Advantages and Pitfalls of Group Decision Making

Groups can do a much better job than individuals in two important steps of the decision-making process: defining the problem and generating alternative solutions. Still, group decision making is subject to some pitfalls that can quickly erase these gains. One possible pitfall is groupthink. **Groupthink** occurs in highly cohesive groups when group members feel intense pressure to agree with each other so that the group can approve a proposed solution.[68] Because groupthink leads to consideration of a limited number of solutions and restricts discussion of any considered solutions, it usually results in poor decisions. Groupthink is most likely to occur under the following conditions:

» The group is insulated from others with different perspectives.

» The group leader begins by expressing a strong preference for a particular decision.

» The group has no established procedure for systematically defining problems and exploring alternatives.

» Group members have similar backgrounds and experiences.[69]

A second potential problem with group decision making is that it takes considerable time. Reconciling schedules so that group members can meet takes time. Furthermore, it's a rare group that consistently holds productive, task-oriented meetings to effectively work through the decision-making process. Some of the most common complaints about meetings (and thus group decision making) are that the meeting's purpose is unclear, participants are unprepared, critical people are absent or late, conversation doesn't stay focused on the problem, and no one follows up on the decisions that were made.

A third possible pitfall to group decision making is that sometimes one or two people, perhaps the boss or a strong-willed, vocal group member, can dominate group discussions and limit the group's consideration of different problem definitions and alternative solutions. This may be more likely to happen when subject matter experts are part of groups. The pitfall is that subject matter experts dominate and limit group discussion as non-experts in the group defer to "expert" judgment. Doing so often results in much poorer quality decisions.[70] And, unlike individual decisions where people feel personally responsible for making a good choice, another potential problem is that group members may not feel accountable for the decisions made and actions taken by the group. Ironically, a fourth pitfall to group decision making is equality bias, which causes individuals to treat all group members as equally competent. More highly competent people tend to underestimate their abilities, while less competent people overestimate theirs. A recent study showed that even though the

"Today's theme is 'Getting Beyond Group Think'."

more competent person in a pair of study participants was correct over 70 percent of the time, the more competent person would agree to the less competent partner's decision roughly 40 percent of the time. Likewise, the less competent person in the pair would agree with the more competent partner's choice only 50 percent of the time—even though the other person was correct over 70 percent of the time. Study author Professor Bahudar Bahrami noted, "Even when we showed them exactly how competent they each were, they still gave each other more or less equal say. Incredibly, this still continued when people were rewarded with real money for making correct decisions." Bahrami suggests two key reasons for equality bias. First, individuals do not want to exclude the other group members by asserting their competence. Second, individuals may be reluctant to take responsibility for group decisions.[71]

Although these pitfalls can lead to poor decision making, this doesn't mean that managers should avoid using groups to make decisions. When done properly, group decision making can lead to much better decisions. The pitfalls of group decision making are not inevitable. Managers can overcome most of them by using the various techniques described next.

5-5b Structured Conflict

Most people view conflict negatively. Yet the right kind of conflict can lead to much better group decision making. **C-type conflict**, or "cognitive conflict," focuses on problem- and issue-related differences of opinion.[72] In c-type conflict,

Groupthink a barrier to good decision making caused by pressure within the group for members to agree with each other

C-type conflict (cognitive conflict) disagreement that focuses on problem- and issue-related differences of opinion group members disagree because their different experiences and expertise lead them to view the problem and its potential solutions differently. C-type conflict is also characterized by a willingness to examine, compare, and reconcile those differences to produce the best possible solution. Victor Ho, the CEO and co-founder of Five Stars, a customer loyalty network for small and medium businesses, who worked for McKinsey & Company, a global consulting firm, said, "The strongest lesson I learned at McKinsey that I now share with every new hire is what they call the 'obligation to dissent.' It means that the youngest, most junior person in any given meeting is the most capable to disagree with the most senior person in the room."[73] Amit Singh, president of Google for Work, agrees saying, "Some of the best discussions are passionate but respectful, so that you leave a meeting without feeling like you've lost something, even though your point of view may not have been the one that was adopted. That is what fosters innovation in a company — a clash of ideas, but a respectful clash."[74]

By contrast, **a-type conflict**, meaning "affective conflict," refers to the emotional reactions that can occur when disagreements become personal rather than professional. A-type conflict often results in hostility, anger, resentment, distrust, cynicism, and apathy. Unlike c-type conflict, a-type conflict undermines team effectiveness by preventing teams from engaging in the activities characteristic of c-type conflict that are critical to team effectiveness. Examples of a-type conflict statements are "your idea," "our idea," "my department," "you don't know what you are talking about," or "you don't understand our situation." Rather than focusing on issues and ideas, these statements focus on individuals.[75]

The **devil's advocacy** approach can be used to create c-type conflict by assigning an individual or a subgroup the role of critic. The following five steps establish a devil's advocacy program:

1. Generate a potential solution.

2. Assign a devil's advocate to criticize and question the solution.

3. Present the critique of the potential solution to key decision makers.

4. Gather additional relevant information.

5. Decide whether to use, change, or not use the originally proposed solution.[76]

When properly used, the devil's advocacy approach introduces c-type conflict into the decision-making process. Contrary to the common belief that conflict is bad, studies show that these methods lead not only to less a-type conflict but also to improved decision quality and greater acceptance of decisions after they have been made.[77]

Another method of creating c-type conflict is **dialectical inquiry**, which creates c-type conflict by forcing decision makers to state the assumptions of a proposed solution (a thesis) and then generate a solution that is the opposite (antithesis) of the proposed solution. The five steps of the dialectical inquiry process are:

1. Generate a potential solution.

2. Identify the assumptions underlying the potential solution.

3. Generate a conflicting counterproposal based on the opposite assumptions.

4. Have advocates of each position present their arguments and engage in a debate in front of key decision makers.

5. Decide whether to use, change, or not use the originally proposed solution.[78]

5-5c Nominal Group Technique

Nominal means "in name only." Accordingly, the **nominal group technique** (NGT) received its name because it begins with a quiet time in which group members independently write down as many problem definitions and alternative solutions as possible. In other words, the NGT begins by having group members act as individuals. After the quiet time, the group leader asks each member to share one idea at a time with the group. As they are read aloud, ideas are posted on flip charts or wallboards for all to see. This step continues until all ideas have been shared. In the next step, the group discusses the advantages and disadvantages of the ideas. The NGT closes with a second quiet time in which group members independently rank the ideas presented. Group members then read their rankings aloud, and the idea with the highest average rank is selected.[79]

IBM manager Phil Gilbert used the NGT when his team developed a new email tool called IBM Verse. Instead of instructing them to come up with the next big thing in email, Gilbert had them spend ten minutes

A-type conflict (affective conflict) disagreement that focuses on individuals or personal issues

Devil's advocacy a decision-making method in which an individual or a subgroup is assigned the role of critic

Dialectical inquiry a decision-making method in which decision makers state the assumptions of a proposed solution (a thesis) and generate a solution that is the opposite (antithesis) of that solution

Nominal group technique a decision-making method that begins and ends by having group members quietly write down and evaluate ideas to be shared with the group quietly writing down what they disliked about email on sticky notes—one idea per note, and no talking. As people finished writing, they stuck their notes on a big whiteboard until there weren't any more to post. The team leader then organized the sticky notes into logical groupings for review. Then the team left (Gilbert says sometimes briefly or for days). When they returned to the whiteboard, they brought additional ideas. Regarding the NGT process, Gilbert says, "It makes for better teams, and it leads to better outcomes. When you give voice to more people, the best ideas win, not the loudest ones."[80]

The nominal group technique improves group decision making by decreasing a-type conflict. But it also restricts c-type conflict. Consequently, the nominal group technique typically produces poorer decisions than the devil's advocacy and dialectical inquiry approaches. Nonetheless, more than eighty studies have found that nominal groups produce better ideas than those produced by traditional groups.[81]

5-5d Delphi Technique

In the **Delphi technique**, the members of a panel of experts respond to questions and to each other until reaching agreement on an issue. The first step is to assemble a panel of experts. Unlike other approaches to group decision making, however, it isn't necessary to bring the panel members together in one place. Because the Delphi technique does not require the experts to leave their offices or disrupt their schedules, they are more likely to participate.

The second step is to create a questionnaire consisting of a series of open-ended questions for the group. In the third step, the group members' written responses are analyzed, summarized, and fed back to the group for reactions until the members reach agreement. Asking group members why they agree or disagree is important because it helps uncover their unstated assumptions and beliefs. Again, this process of summarizing panel feedback and obtaining reactions to that feedback continues until the panel members reach agreement.

5-5e Electronic Brainstorming

Brainstorming, in which group members build on others' ideas, is a technique for generating a large number of alternative solutions. Brainstorming has four rules:

1. The more ideas, the better.
2. All ideas are acceptable, no matter how wild or crazy they might seem.
3. Other group members' ideas should be used to come up with even more ideas.
4. Criticism or evaluation of ideas is not allowed.

Although brainstorming is great fun and can help managers generate a large number of alternative solutions, it does have a number of disadvantages. Fortunately, **electronic brainstorming**, in which group members use computers to communicate and generate alternative solutions, overcomes the disadvantages associated with face-to-face brainstorming.[82]

The first disadvantage that electronic brainstorming overcomes is **production blocking**, which occurs when you have an idea but have to wait to share it because someone else is already presenting an idea to the group. During this short delay, you may forget your idea or decide that it really wasn't worth sharing. Production blocking doesn't happen with electronic brainstorming. All group members are seated at computers, so everyone can type in ideas whenever they occur. There's no waiting for your turn to be heard by the group.

The second disadvantage that electronic brainstorming overcomes is **evaluation apprehension**, that is, being afraid of what others will think of your ideas. An employee suffering from evaluation apprehension described this incident: "...for the thousandth time, I was in a meeting where I thought I had a great solution to a

Creativa Images/Shutterstock.com

Delphi technique a decision-making method in which members of a panel of experts respond to questions and to each other until reaching agreement on an issue

Brainstorming a decision-making method in which group members build on each others' ideas to generate as many alternative solutions as possible

Electronic brainstorming a decision-making method in which group members use computers to build on each others' ideas and generate as many alternative solutions as possible

Production blocking a disadvantage of face-to-face brainstorming in which a group member must wait to share an idea because another member is presenting an idea

Evaluation apprehension fear of what others will think of your ideas

Maximize Your Life Decisions Using a Spreadsheet

Maximizers, according to the *Wall Street Journal's* Elizabeth Bernstein, "like to take their time and weigh a wide range of options—sometimes every possible one—before choosing." Satisficers, on the other hand, "would rather be fast than thorough; they prefer to quickly choose the option that fills the minimum criteria." Most of us are satisficers. But should we really make major life decisions based on what meets "minimum criteria?"

Probably not. When it comes to the decisions that matter, it is in your best interest to weigh the costs and benefits of all available choices. This may sound like a daunting task, but a simple spreadsheet can help you evaluate your alternatives quickly and easily. Suppose you're looking for a new apartment. First, list the criteria you're looking for (location, cost, spaciousness) in the left-hand column and list your various alternatives at the top. As you gather information, rate each alternative against the criteria on a scale of 1–5 (1 being worst and 5 being best). Psychologist Fjola Helgadottir has used this spreadsheet method to "run 4 marathons, climb Mt Kilimanjaro, travel the world, and complete 4 university degrees." What could a spreadsheet help you decide to do with your life?

Sources: F. Helgadottir, "How Excel Can Help You Achieve Goals," The *AI-Therapy Blog*, August 27, 2012, accessed May 7, 2016, https://www.ai-therapy.com/blog/how-excel-can-help-you-achieve-goals/; R. Sanghani, "How Excel Spreadsheets Can Help You Make Major Life Decisions," *The Telegraph*, January 4, 2016, accessed May 7, 2016, http://www.telegraph.co.uk/women/life/how-excel-spreadsheets-can-help-you-make-major-life-decisions/; E. Bernstein, "How You Make Decisions Says a Lot About How Happy You Are," *Wall Street Journal*, October 6, 2014, accessed May 7, 2016, http://www.wsj.com/articles/how-you-make-decisions-says-a-lot-about-how-happy-you-are-1412614997.

complicated problem my team is facing, and I was right. How do I know? Because I didn't say a word, but the guy sitting next to me suggested the same thing I was thinking—and, as a result, got put in charge of a project I'd love to have been assigned."[83]

With electronic brainstorming, all ideas are anonymous. When you type in an idea and press the Enter key to share it with the group, group members see only the idea. Furthermore, many brainstorming software programs also protect anonymity by displaying ideas in random order. So if you laugh maniacally when you type "Cut top management's pay by 50 percent!" and then press the Enter key, it won't show up immediately on everyone's screen. This makes it doubly difficult to determine who is responsible for which comments.

In the typical layout for electronic brainstorming, all participants sit in front of computers around a U-shaped table. This configuration allows them to see their computer screens, the other participants, a large main screen, and a meeting leader or facilitator. Step 1 in electronic brainstorming is to anonymously generate as many ideas as possible. Groups commonly generate 100 ideas in a half-hour period. Step 2 is to edit the generated ideas, categorize them, and eliminate redundancies. Step 3 is to rank the categorized ideas in terms of quality. Step 4, the last step, has three parts: generate a series of action steps, decide the best order for accomplishing these steps, and identify who is responsible for each step. All four steps are accomplished with computers and electronic brainstorming software.[84]

Studies show that electronic brainstorming is much more productive than face-to-face brainstorming. Four-person electronic brainstorming groups produce 25 to 50 percent more ideas than four-person regular brainstorming groups, and 12-person electronic brainstorming groups produce 200 percent more ideas than regular groups of the same size! In fact, because production blocking (having to wait your turn) is not a problem in electronic brainstorming, the number and quality of ideas generally increase with group size.[85]

Even though it works much better than traditional brainstorming, electronic brainstorming has disadvantages, too. An obvious problem is the expense of computers, networks, software, and other equipment. As these costs continue to drop, however, electronic brainstorming will become cheaper.

Another problem is that the anonymity of ideas may bother people who are used to having their ideas accepted by virtue of their position (that is the boss). On the other hand, one CEO said, "Because the process is anonymous, the sky's the limit in terms of what you can say, and, as a result, it is more thought-provoking. As a CEO, you'll probably discover things you might not want to hear but need to be aware of."[86]

A third disadvantage is that outgoing individuals who are more comfortable expressing themselves verbally may find it difficult to express themselves in writing. Finally, the most obvious problem is that participants have to be able to type. Those who can't type, or who type slowly, may be easily frustrated and find themselves at a disadvantage compared to experienced typists.

STUDY TOOLS 5

LOCATED IN TEXTBOOK

☐ Rip out and review chapter review card.

LOCATED AT WWW.CENGAGEBRAIN.COM

☐ Gain unique perspectives on key concepts with new 4LTR concept videos in the e-book.

☐ Increase your comprehension with Aplia for MGMT11.

☐ Complete interactive content within the e-book.

6 | Organizational Strategy

LEARNING OBJECTIVES

6-1 Specify the components of sustainable competitive advantage, and explain why it is important.

6-2 Describe the steps involved in the strategy-making process.

6-3 Explain the different kinds of corporate-level strategies.

6-4 Describe the different kinds of industry-level strategies.

6-5 Explain the components and kinds of firm-level strategies.

After finishing this chapter, go to **PAGE 135** for **STUDY TOOLS**

KTSDESIGN/Getty Images

6-1 SUSTAINABLE COMPETITIVE ADVANTAGE

Just seven years ago, there was no market for tablet computers. A number of computer makers sold touchscreen laptops, but other than some programs that allowed users to handwrite notes, there was little to distinguish these machines from traditional laptops. All of that changed when Apple released the iPad, a tablet computer that is controlled by a multitouch display and can run hundreds of thousands of applications allowing users to read books, watch movies, listen to music, check the weather, or play games. With its innovative product, Apple in effect created a new market for portable, touch-based tablet computers. The iPad is not without its competitors, however. There is, for example, the Amazon Kindle Fire, Barnes & Noble's Nook HD, and Samsung's Android-based Galaxy Tab S3. The latest competitor is the

Microsoft Surface, which comes with a touchscreen, a combination cover/detachable keyboard, and the Windows 10 operating system. Critics complain about the higher price ($2,099 for a 256GB Surface Pro 4 with a 12.3-inch screen, keyboard, and Surface Pen versus $1,350 for a 256GB iPad Pro with a 12.9-inch screen, keyboard, and the Apple Pencil), and the Surfaces's 40 percent shorter battery life. Despite its competitors, Apple still dominates tablet sales, selling 45.6 million iPads in 2016 compared to just 3.9 million Surfaces, 26.5 million Galaxies, and 12.1 million Kindle fires.[1]

How can a company like Apple, which dominates a particular industry, maintain its competitive advantage as strong, well-financed competitors enter the market? What steps can Apple and other companies take to better manage their strategy-making process?

Resources are the assets, capabilities, processes, employee time, information, and knowledge that an organization controls. Firms use their resources to improve organizational effectiveness and efficiency. Resources are critical to organizational strategy because they can help companies create and sustain an advantage over competitors.[2]

> **Resources** the assets, capabilities, processes, employee time, information, and knowledge that an organization uses to improve its effectiveness and efficiency and create and sustain competitive advantage

VS.

Organizations can achieve a **competitive advantage** by using their resources to provide greater value for customers than competitors can. For example, the iPad's initial competitive advantage came partly from its sleek, attractive design and partly from the reputation of Apple's iPod and iPhone as innovative, easy-to-use products.

The goal of most organizational strategies is to create and then sustain a competitive advantage. A competitive advantage becomes a **sustainable competitive advantage** when other companies cannot duplicate the value a firm is providing to customers. Sustainable competitive advantage is *not* the same as a long-lasting competitive advantage, though companies obviously want a competitive advantage to last a long time. Instead, a competitive advantage is *sustained* if competitors have tried unsuccessfully to duplicate the advantage and have, for the moment, stopped trying to duplicate it. It's the corporate equivalent of your competitors saying, "We give up. You win. We can't do what you do, and we're not even going to try to do it anymore." Four conditions must be met if a firm's resources are to be used to achieve a sustainable competitive advantage. The resources must be valuable, rare, imperfectly imitable, *and* nonsubstitutable.

Valuable resources allow companies to improve their efficiency and effectiveness. Unfortunately, changes in customer demand and preferences, competitors' actions, and technology can make once-valuable resources much less valuable. Before the iPad was introduced, netbooks appeared to be the next big thing in mobile computing. These laptops were small and light, making them ultra portable; were very affordable, averaging anywhere from $200 to $500; and let users run basic programs such as web browsing and word processing on the go. At first, sales were brisk—in 2009, 7.5 million netbooks were sold in the United States and more than 34 million worldwide. But all that changed. The iPad had a touchscreen, an intuitive operating system, and a large selection of app software, while netbooks were often criticized for having small, hard-to-use keyboards, a slow operating system, and a lack of software options. While it took only 28 days for Apple to sell its first 1 million iPads, netbook sales fell by 40 percent in one year.[3] Only one year after netbook sales peaked, tablet sales passed them, and netbook sales have been steadily declining ever since.[4]

For sustained competitive advantage, valuable resources must also be rare resources. Think about it: How can a company sustain a competitive advantage if all of its competitors have similar resources and capabilities? Consequently, **rare resources**, resources that are not controlled or possessed by many competing firms, are necessary to sustain a competitive advantage. One of Apple's rare resources has been its ability to reconfigure existing technology into elegantly designed, easy to use systems. Apple leveraged its experience with the iPod, iPod touch, and iPhone to develop the iOS operating

Competitive advantage providing greater value for customers than competitors can

Sustainable competitive advantage a competitive advantage that other companies have tried unsuccessfully to duplicate and have, for the moment, stopped trying to duplicate

Valuable resource a resource that allows companies to improve efficiency and effectiveness

Rare resource a resource that is not controlled or possessed by many competing firms system into a single platform giving users the same experience across multiple devices. Because of iOS, iPhone users instantly know how to use their new iPads. But, they might have trouble learning the macOS operating system on Apple Mac personal computers, which is substantially different. By contrast, with Windows 10, the Microsoft Surface 4 automatically and seamlessly switches apps from personal computer mode (when a keyboard is attached) to tablet mode. Detach the keyboard and Windows 10 asks if you want to switch into Tablet mode based on touch screen gestures, rather than mouse and keyboard clicks. In other words, Apple is no longer the only software/hardware provider to create an operating system that is easily used across multiple devices or input formats. *PC Magazine* even argues that Windows 10 "leads in innovation when it comes to desktop operating systems."[5]

As this example shows, valuable and rare resources can create temporary competitive advantage. For sustained competitive advantage, however, other firms must be unable to imitate or find substitutes for those valuable, rare resources. **Imperfectly imitable resources** are those resources that are impossible or extremely costly or difficult to duplicate. Microsoft, Google, Amazon, and other Apple competitors buy standard "off the shelf" computer chips from Intel and other chipmakers. Because they all use the same chip architectures, none has an advantage with the "digital engines" that power their devices. By contrast, for over a decade Apple's semiconductor team has designed the unique chips used in Apple iPhones, the latest being the A10 chip used in iPhone 7s. Why does this matter? Because it would take billions in investment and 5 to 10 years for competitors to catch up. Because the A10 chips are faster than the "off the shelf" chips from traditional semiconductor companies.[6] Because Apple takes the chips first designed for iPhones and then reuses them in other devices, such as iPads, Apple TVs, and Apple Watches. Tech analyst Steve Cheney says, "Because of Apple's scale in smart phones, and reuse of chips in other device categories like the watch and TV, Apple has massive influence with suppliers. They can plan three to five years out and decide what to license, build, invest in, or buy."[7] In short, it would be extremely costly and difficult for Apple's competitors to match its chip design capabilities. Apple's chip design advantage may be an imperfectly imitable resource.

Valuable, rare, imperfectly imitable resources can produce sustainable competitive advantage only if they are also **nonsubstitutable resources**, meaning that no other resources can replace them and produce similar value or competitive advantage. From 2007 to 2012, Google Maps was the iPhone's dominant navigation app. In 2012, 91 percent of iPhone owners used Google Maps because it gave them accurate information, voice-guided direction, and the ability to map routes by car, public transportation, and walking.[8] So for five years, nothing else on the iPhone came close to providing the simple, accurate, easy-to-use navigation found in Google Maps. With 7,000 people working on Google Maps as "street view drivers, people flying planes, people drawing maps, people correcting listings, and people building new products," Google Maps was a nonsubstitutable navigation resource on the iPhone.[9] Apple set out to change that in 2012 when the company released the first version of Apple Maps for iOS. However, it was so bad and inaccurate that CEO Tim Cook apologized, saying, "We are extremely sorry for the frustration," and that iPhone users could, while Maps was being improved, "try alternatives by downloading map apps from the App Store or use Google or Nokia (now called Here) maps."[10] By June 2015, after acquiring a number of mapping software companies, fixing incorrect map data, and largely matching the functionality found in Google Maps, Apple reported that iPhone owners used the Apple Maps app 5 billion times per week, 3.5 times more than the "next leading maps app," Google Maps.[11] Does this mean that Apple Maps has a sustainable competitive advantage over Google Maps? No—not even close. But it does mean that Apple Maps is a worthy substitute for Google Maps, and that Google Maps lost its previously sustainable competitive advantage among iPhone users.

In summary, Apple reaped the rewards of a first-mover advantage when it introduced the iPad. The company's history of developing customer-friendly software, the innovative capabilities of the iPad, the ease and uniformity of experience Apple's iOS operating system provides across devices, and its—so far—imperfectly imitable chip design, have made Apple the most profitable business in history. Indeed, in smartphones alone, Apple is estimated to earn 80 percent or more of the profits in the smartphone business! As demonstrated by the rise of Windows 10 and the stumble of Apple Maps, however, past success is no guarantee of future success. Apple needs to continue developing and improving its products or risk being unseated by more nimble competitors whose products are more relevant and have higher perceived value for consumers.

Imperfectly imitable resource a resource that is impossible or extremely costly or difficult for other firms to duplicate

Nonsubstitutable resource a resource that produces value or competitive advantage and has no equivalent substitutes or replacements

6-2 STRATEGY-MAKING PROCESS

To create a sustainable competitive advantage, a company must have a strategy.[12] Exhibit 6.1 displays the three steps of the strategy-making process:

6-2a assess the need for strategic change, 6-2b conduct a situational analysis, and then 6-2c choose strategic alternatives. *Let's examine each of these steps in more detail.*

6-2a Assessing the Need for Strategic Change

The external business environment is much more turbulent than it used to be. With customers' needs constantly growing and changing, and with competitors working harder, faster, and smarter to meet those needs, the first step in creating a strategy is determining the need for strategic change. In other words, the company should determine whether it needs to change its strategy to sustain a competitive advantage.[13]

Determining the need for strategic change might seem easy to do, but it's really not. There's a great deal of uncertainty in strategic business environments. Furthermore, top-level managers are often slow to recognize the need for strategic change, especially at successful companies that have created and sustained competitive advantages. Because they are acutely aware of the strategies that made their companies successful, they continue to rely on those strategies, even as the competition changes. In other words, success often leads to **competitive inertia**—a reluctance to change strategies or competitive practices that have been successful in the past. A decade ago, GameStop sold video game discs for personal computers (PC) and game consoles, such as the PlayStation or Xbox, that could only be purchased and picked up at its then 6,000 stores. GameStop sold each game twice, first as a new game and second as a used game (after the original buyer traded the new game in for

Exhibit 6.1
Three Steps of the Strategy-Making Process

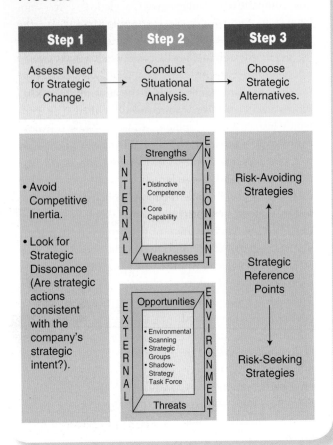

Step 1	Step 2	Step 3
Assess Need for Strategic Change.	Conduct Situational Analysis.	Choose Strategic Alternatives.

- Avoid Competitive Inertia.

- Look for Strategic Dissonance (Are strategic actions consistent with the company's strategic intent?).

INTERNAL ENVIRONMENT
Strengths
- Distinctive Competence
- Core Capability
Weaknesses

EXTERNAL ENVIRONMENT
Opportunities
- Environmental Scanning
- Strategic Groups
- Shadow-Strategy Task Force
Threats

Risk-Avoiding Strategies

Strategic Reference Points

Risk-Seeking Strategies

Northfoto/Shutterstock.com

GameStop closed 150 stores in 2017, in part because of the increase in downloadable and streaming games.

store credit toward another game purchase). Double profit on each game was the competitive inertia that made GameStop reluctant to change. Today, however, video games can also be played online, on smartphones, on streaming devices like the Apple TV, or on budding virtual reality systems. What all of those different gaming platforms have in common is that more often than not, games are downloaded to the device (including the most recent consoles). In 2014, in the United States and 2016 in the United King-

Aldi's business model focuses on selling a limited number of groceries and household items in a small setting.

dom, sales of digitally downloaded and streamed games exceeded sales of game discs for the first time.[14] Likewise, in 2016, sales from mobile games, which are all streamed or downloaded, also exceeded console game sales for the first time.[15] GameStop has diversified into trading and selling collectibles, but its core business of selling games and gaming systems continues to shrink while the gaming industry grows. In 2016, sales dropped 8% and profits sagged 22%. GameStop closed 150 stores in 2017.[16]

Besides being aware of the dangers of competitive inertia, what can managers do to improve the speed and accuracy with which they determine the need for strategic change? One method is to actively look for signs of strategic dissonance. **Strategic dissonance** is a discrepancy between a company's intended strategy and the strategic actions managers take when actually implementing that strategy.[17] Google has long been a leading innovator in voice technology, that is, using voice commands and natural language to interact with computer devices. Indeed, 20 percent of mobile searches ("Hey Google…") are done by voice. So it was surprising that Amazon's Echo, which uses voice commands to search for information ("Hey Alexa, what's the weather today?") and order things on amazon.com ("Hey Alexa, order barbecue potato chips."), beat Google Home, Google's voice-activated assistant, to market by nearly two years. Professor Scott Galloway said, "Amazon got there first, which is super impressive, and it has been a huge hit."[18] Google was seriously invested in bringing voice capabilities to market. Its largest team was working on a stand-alone voice app for different smartphones. The Android team was working on building voice directly into the

Android operating system for phones and tablets. But Google's hardware divisions, which manufacture the phones, tablets, and Chromecast TV devices, never coordinated with those teams. So, in a clear case of strategic dissonance, no one was actually working on a voice device for people's homes, despite Google's strategic commitment to voice processing.[19]

Note, however, that strategic dissonance is not the same thing as when a strategy does not produce the results that it's supposed to. Airbus created the wide-body, double decker A380, the largest passenger jet in the world capable of flying 853 passengers. The idea was that airlines would use the A380 for their most profitable, heavily traveled, long-haul international flights. But even with low jet fuel prices, the A380 is expensive to operate, which means it has to fly as full as possible to cover costs. So airlines are canceling orders and leases for the A380. Airbus delivered 27 planes last year, but will only make 14 in 2017 and 12 in 2018.[20]

6-2b Situational Analysis

A situational analysis can also help managers determine the need for strategic change. A **situational analysis**, also called a **SWOT analysis**,

Competitive inertia a reluctance to change strategies or competitive practices that have been successful in the past

Strategic dissonance a discrepancy between a company's intended strategy and the strategic actions managers take when implementing that strategy

Situational (SWOT) analysis an assessment of the strengths and weaknesses in an organization's internal environment and the opportunities and threats in its external environment

SHADOW-STRATEGY TASK FORCE

When looking for threats and opportunities, many managers focus on competitors in the external environment. Others, however, prefer to examine the internal environment through a **shadow-strategy task force**. This strategy involves a company actively seeking out its own weaknesses and then thinking like its competitors, trying to determine how they can be exploited for competitive advantage. To make sure that the task force challenges conventional thinking, its members should be independent-minded, come from a variety of company functions and levels, and have the access and authority to question the company's current strategic actions and intent.

Source: W. B. Werther, Jr., and J. L. Kerr, "The Shifting Sands of Competitive Advantage," *Business Horizons* (May–June 1995): 11–17.

for *strengths*, *weaknesses*, *opportunities*, and *threats*, is an assessment of the strengths and weaknesses in an organization's internal environment and the opportunities and threats in its external environment.[21] Ideally, as shown in Step 2 of Exhibit 6.1, a SWOT analysis helps a company determine how to increase internal strengths and minimize internal weaknesses while maximizing external opportunities and minimizing external threats.

An analysis of an organization's internal environment, that is, a company's strengths and weaknesses, often begins with an assessment of its distinctive competencies and core capabilities. A **distinctive competence** is something that a company can make, do, or perform better than its competitors. For example, *Consumer Reports* magazine consistently ranks Toyota and Subaru cars as tops in quality, reliability, and owner satisfaction.[22] Similarly, *PC Magazine* ranked Intuit's TurboTax the best tax preparation software for its user experience, thorough coverage of tax topic, and robust help resources.[23]

Shadow-strategy task force a committee within a company that analyzes the company's own weaknesses to determine how competitors could exploit them for competitive advantage

Distinctive competence what a company can make, do, or perform better than its competitors

Core capabilities the internal decision-making routines, problem-solving processes, and organizational cultures that determine how efficiently inputs can be turned into outputs

Strategic group a group of companies within an industry against which top managers compare, evaluate, and benchmark strategic threats and opportunities

Whereas distinctive competencies are tangible—for example, a product or service is faster, cheaper, or better—the core capabilities that produce distinctive competencies are not. **Core capabilities** are the less visible, internal decision-making routines, problem-solving processes, and organizational cultures that determine how efficiently inputs can be turned into outputs. Distinctive competencies cannot be sustained for long without superior core capabilities.

Walmart's distinctive competence, what it does better than competitors, is sell items at low prices. But that's no longer true in groceries, as prices at Aldi grocery stores are consistently 20 percent lower than Walmart's. What core capabilities help Aldi sell at such dramatically lower prices? It focuses on selling a limited number of groceries and household items in a small setting. Aldi stores are just 16 percent the size of a typical Walmart store and carry just 1,500 or so items, compared to 100,000 items in a superstore. Furthermore, most items are private brands—that is, goods that Aldi buys and packages itself. Hundreds of other small decisions keep costs and prices low. Instead of employees returning carts from parking lots, it charges customers a 25-cent deposit, which is paid inside Aldi stores. Likewise, Aldi charges 4 cents for paper bags and $1.99 for reusable shopping bags. Together, these decisions allow Aldi to run a store with just four to five employees. Aldi is growing strongly at 15 to 20 percent a year.[24]

After examining internal strengths and weaknesses, the second part of a situational analysis is to look outside the company and assess the opportunities and threats in the external environment. In Chapter 3, you learned that *environmental scanning* involves searching the environment for important events or issues that might affect the organization, such as pricing trends or new products and technology. In situational analysis, however, managers use environmental scanning to identify specific opportunities and threats that can either improve or harm the company's ability to sustain its competitive advantage. Identification of strategic groups and formation of shadow-strategy task forces are two ways to do this (see box "Shadow-Strategy Task Force").

Strategic groups are not groups that actually work together. They are companies—usually competitors—that managers closely follow. More specifically, a **strategic group** is a group of other companies within an industry against which top managers compare, evaluate, and benchmark their company's strategic threats and opportunities.[25] (*Benchmarking* involves identifying outstanding practices, processes, and standards at other companies and adapting them to your own company.) Typically, managers include companies as part of their strategic group if they compete directly with

Exhibit 6.2
Core and Secondary Firms in the Home Improvement Industry

Home Depot
Lowe's

Ace Hardware   84 Lumber

<small>iStock.com/Tom McNemar</small>

	# of Stores	# of States	Countries	Size of Typical Store (sq. feet)
Home Depot	2,200	50	3	104,000
Lowe's	2,355	50	3	112,000
Ace Hardware	4,800	50	60	10,000–14,000
84 Lumber	249	30	1	33,000

In fact, when scanning the environment for strategic threats and opportunities, managers tend to categorize the different companies in their industries as core, secondary, and transient firms.[27] **Core firms** are the central companies in a strategic group. Home Depot operates 2,200 stores covering all 50 states, Puerto Rico, the U.S. Virgin Islands, Guam, Mexico, and Canada. The company has more than 400,000 employees and annual revenues of $94.6 billion. By comparison, Lowe's has more than 2,129 stores and 285,000 employees in the United States, Canada, and Mexico; stocks about 36,000 products in each store; and has annual revenues of $65 billion.[28] Clearly, Lowe's is the closest competitor to the Home Depot and is the core firm in Home Depot's strategic group. Even though Ace Hardware has more stores (4,800) than Home Depot and appears to be a bigger multinational player (60 different countries), Ace's different franchise structure and small, individualized stores (10,000–14,000 square feet, with each store laid out differently with a different mix of products) with 80,000 employees keep it from being a core firm in Home Depot's strategic group.[29] Likewise, Home Depot's management probably doesn't include Aubuchon Hardware in its core strategic group, because Aubuchon has only 110 stores in New England and upstate New York.[30]

When most managers scan their environments for strategic threats and opportunities, they concentrate on the strategic actions of core firms, not unrelated firms such as Aubuchon. Where does a firm like Ace Hardware fit in? As a retailer-owned cooperative, Ace Hardware is a network of independently owned stores. Ace's 20/20 vision employs a customer-focused strategy to grow the brand and improve store performance.[31]

Secondary firms are firms that use strategies related to but somewhat different from those of core firms. 84 Lumber has roughly 250 stores in 30 states, but even though its stores are open to the public, the company focuses on supplying professional

those companies for customers or if those companies use strategies similar to theirs. The U.S. home improvement industry has annual sales in excess of $364 billion. This market is divided into professional and consumer markets, both of which were forecast to grow roughly 4 percent in 2017.[26] It's likely that the managers at Home Depot, the largest U.S. home improvement and hardware retailer, assess strategic threats and opportunities by comparing their company to a strategic group consisting of the other major home improvement supply companies. Exhibit 6.2 shows the number of stores, the size of the typical new store, and the overall geographic distribution (states, countries) of Home Depot stores compared with Lowe's, Ace Hardware, and 84 Lumber.

Core firms the central companies in a strategic group

Secondary firms the firms in a strategic group that follow strategies related to but somewhat different from those of the core firms contractors, to whom it sells 85 percent of its products. Without the wide variety of products on the shelves or assistance available to the average consumer, people without expertise in building or remodeling probably don't find 84 Lumber stores very accessible. Home Depot would most likely classify 84 Lumber as a secondary firm in its strategic group analysis.[32] Managers need to be aware of the potential threats and opportunities posed by secondary firms, but they usually spend more time assessing the threats and opportunities associated with core firms.

6-2c Choosing Strategic Alternatives

After determining the need for strategic change and conducting a situational analysis, the last step in the strategy-making process is to choose strategic alternatives that will help the company create or maintain a sustainable competitive advantage. According to *strategic reference point theory*, managers choose between two basic alternative strategies. They can choose a conservative, *risk-avoiding strategy* that aims to protect an existing competitive advantage. Or they can choose an aggressive, *risk-seeking strategy* that aims to extend or create a sustainable competitive advantage.

The choice to seek risk or avoid risk typically depends on whether top management views the company as falling above or below strategic reference points. **Strategic reference points** are the targets that managers use to measure whether their firm has developed the core competencies that it needs to achieve a sustainable competitive advantage. If a hotel chain decides to compete by providing superior quality and service, then top management will track the success of this strategy through customer surveys or published hotel ratings such as those provided by the prestigious *Mobil Travel Guide*. If a hotel chain decides to compete on price, it will regularly conduct market surveys to check the prices of other hotels. The competitors' prices are the hotel managers' strategic reference points against which to compare their own pricing strategy. If competitors can consistently underprice them, then the managers need to determine whether their staff and resources have the core competencies to compete on price.

As shown in Exhibit 6.3, when a company is performing above or better than its strategic reference points, top management will typically be satisfied with the company's strategy.

Ironically, this satisfaction tends to make top management conservative and risk-averse. Because the company already has a sustainable competitive advantage, the worst thing that could happen would be to lose it, so new issues or changes in the company's external environment are viewed as threats. By contrast, when a company is performing below or worse than its strategic reference points, top management will typically be dissatisfied with the company's strategy. In this instance, managers are much more likely to choose a daring, risk-taking strategy. If the current strategy is producing substandard results, the company has nothing to lose by switching to risky new strategies in the hope that it can create a sustainable competitive advantage. Managers of companies in this situation view new issues or changes in the external environment as opportunities for potential gain.

Strategic reference point theory is not deterministic, however. Managers are not predestined to choose risk-averse or risk-seeking strategies for their companies. In fact, one of the most important elements of the theory is that managers *can* influence the strategies chosen by their company by *actively changing and adjusting* the strategic reference points they use to judge strategic performance. If a company has become complacent after consistently surpassing its strategic reference points, then top management can change from a risk-averse to a risk-taking orientation by raising or changing the standards of performance (that is, the strategic reference points).

This is just what happened at Comcast Cable, long known for terrible customer service, being late to appointments, aggressively raising rates, and generally not addressing customer concerns. Vice chairman Neil Smit decided this needed to change. "As a company, we haven't always put the customer first and we need to do a better job. We need to look at everything we do through a customer lens."[33] Comcast budgeted $300 million for improving customer service via a 10-point Customer Experience Action Plan. A key point was "Being on Time, Every Time." So Comcast linked a new phone app to improved scheduling software indicating when technicians would arrive. The app also let customers immediately rate the technician's timeliness and service.[34] And, if the technician was still late, customer accounts were credited $20 for the inconvenience. Smit concluded, "Transformation isn't going to happen overnight. In fact, it may take a few years before we can honestly say that a great customer experience is something we're known for. But that is our goal and our number one priority ... and that's what we are going to do."[35]

So even when (perhaps *especially* when) companies have achieved a sustainable competitive advantage, top managers must adjust or change strategic reference

Strategic reference points the strategic targets managers use to measure whether a firm has developed the core competencies it needs to achieve a sustainable competitive advantage

Exhibit 6.3
Strategic Reference Points

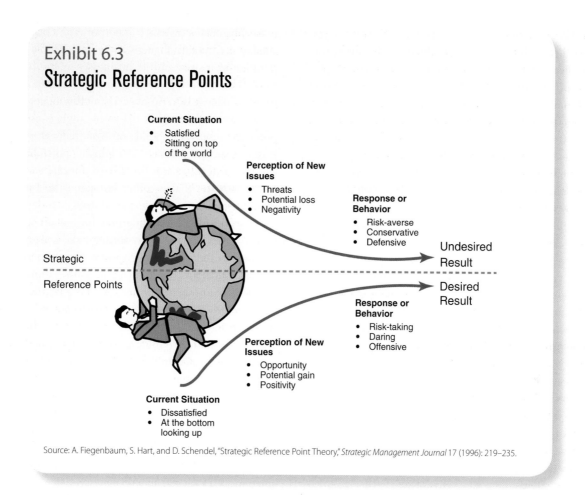

Current Situation
- Satisfied
- Sitting on top of the world

Perception of New Issues
- Threats
- Potential loss
- Negativity

Response or Behavior
- Risk-averse
- Conservative
- Defensive

Undesired Result

Strategic

Reference Points

Desired Result

Response or Behavior
- Risk-taking
- Daring
- Offensive

Perception of New Issues
- Opportunity
- Potential gain
- Positivity

Current Situation
- Dissatisfied
- At the bottom looking up

Source: A. Fiegenbaum, S. Hart, and D. Schendel, "Strategic Reference Point Theory," *Strategic Management Journal* 17 (1996): 219–235.

points to challenge themselves and their employees to develop new core competencies for the future. In the long run, effective organizations will frequently revise their strategic reference points to better focus managers' attention on the new challenges and opportunities that occur in their ever-changing business environments.

6-3 CORPORATE-LEVEL STRATEGIES

To formulate effective strategies, companies must be able to answer these three basic questions:

» What business are we in?

» How should we compete in this industry?

» Who are our competitors, and how should we respond to them?

These simple but powerful questions are at the heart of corporate-, industry-, and firm-level strategies.

Corporate-level strategy is the overall organizational strategy that addresses the question, "What business or businesses are we in or should we be in?" IBM CEO Virginia (Ginni) Rometty knows exactly what business her company is in: "When people say, 'What's IBM?' I say, 'it's an enterprise innovation company.'"[36] Similarly, Dr. Pepper is in the "flavored beverage business."[37]

There are two major approaches to corporate-level strategy that companies use to decide which businesses they should be in: 6-3a portfolio strategy and 6-3b grand strategies.

6-3a Portfolio Strategy

One of the standard strategies for stock market investors is **diversification**, or owning stocks in a variety of companies in different industries. The purpose of this strategy is to reduce risk in the overall stock portfolio (the entire

Corporate-level strategy the overall organizational strategy that addresses the question "What business or businesses are we in or should we be in?"

Diversification a strategy for reducing risk by buying a variety of items (stocks or, in the case of a corporation, types of businesses) so that the failure of one stock or one business does not doom the entire portfolio collection of stocks). The basic idea is simple: if you invest in ten companies in ten different industries, you won't lose your entire investment if one company performs poorly. Furthermore, because they're in different industries, one company's losses are likely to be offset by another company's gains. Portfolio strategy is based on these same ideas. We'll start by taking a look at the theory and ideas behind portfolio strategy and then proceed with a critical review which suggests that some of the key ideas behind portfolio strategy are *not* supported.

Portfolio strategy is a corporate-level strategy that minimizes risk by diversifying investment among various businesses or lines.[38] Just as a diversification strategy guides an investor who invests in a variety of stocks, portfolio strategy guides the strategic decisions of corporations that compete in a variety of businesses. For example, portfolio strategy could be used to guide the strategy of a company such as 3M, which makes 55,000 products for five different business groups: Consumer (Post-its, Scotch tape); Electronics and Energy (electronic devices, telecoms equipment, renewable energy solutions); Health Care (medical, surgical, and dental products, health information systems); Industrial (tapes, abrasives, adhesives, specialty materials, filtration systems); and Safety and Graphics (safety and security products, track and trace solutions, graphic solutions).[39]

Just as investors consider the mix of stocks in their stock portfolio when deciding which stocks to buy or sell, managers following portfolio strategy try to acquire companies that fit well with the rest of their corporate portfolio and to sell those that don't. **Procter & Gamble** used to have a diverse portfolio of food, beverage, household, beauty, health care, pharmaceutical, pet food, and battery brands. However, when it decided to focus on its core business of household, beauty, and health care products, it began selling off brands that did not relate to its core business, a process that included the sale of Duracell to Warren Buffett's **Berkshire Hathaway** for $4.7 billion and Iams and Eukanuba pet foods to **Mars** for $2.9 billion.[40]

First, according to portfolio strategy, the more businesses in which a corporation competes, the smaller its overall chances of failing. Think of a corporation as a stool and its businesses as the legs of the stool. The more legs or businesses added to the stool, the less likely it is to tip over. Using this analogy, portfolio strategy reduces 3M's risk of failing because the corporation's survival depends on essentially five different business sectors. Managers employing portfolio strategy can either develop new businesses internally or look for **acquisitions**, that is, other companies to buy. Either way, the goal is to add legs to the stool.

Second, beyond adding new businesses to the corporate portfolio, portfolio strategy predicts that companies can reduce risk even more through **unrelated diversification**—creating or acquiring companies in completely unrelated businesses (more on the accuracy of this prediction later). According to portfolio strategy, when businesses are unrelated, losses in one business or industry should have minimal effect on the performance of other companies in the corporate portfolio. For example, German-based Merck KGaA, founded in 1668, the world's oldest pharmaceutical and chemical firm, has long sold prescription drugs and over-the-counter medicines. But in the last few years it has embarked on a strategy of unrelated diversification, growing a specialty chemical business that makes liquid crystals used to produce in LCD and OLED display screens, and spending $17 billion to acquire Sigma-Aldrich, which makes laboratory equipment for life sciences research and product development.[41]

Because most internally grown businesses tend to be related to existing products or services, portfolio strategy suggests that acquiring new businesses is the preferred method of unrelated diversification.

Third, investing the profits and cash flows from mature, slow-growth businesses into newer, faster-growing businesses can reduce long-term risk. The best-known portfolio strategy for guiding investment in a corporation's businesses is the Boston Consulting Group (BCG) matrix.[42] The **BCG matrix** is a portfolio strategy that managers use to categorize their corporation's businesses by growth rate and relative market share, which helps them decide how to invest corporate funds. The matrix, shown in Exhibit 6.4, separates businesses into four categories based on how fast the market is growing (high growth or low growth) and the size of the business's share of that market (small or large). **Stars** are companies that have a large share of a fast-growing market. To take advantage of a star's fast-growing market and its strength in that market (large share), the corporation must invest substantially in it. The investment is usually worthwhile, however, because many stars produce

Portfolio strategy a corporate-level strategy that minimizes risk by diversifying investment among various businesses or product lines

Acquisition the purchase of a company by another company

Unrelated diversification creating or acquiring companies in completely unrelated businesses

BCG matrix a portfolio strategy developed by the Boston Consulting Group that categorizes a corporation's businesses by growth rate and relative market share and helps managers decide how to invest corporate funds

Star a company with a large share of a fast-growing market sizable future profits. **Question marks** are companies that have a small share of a fast-growing market. If the corporation invests in these companies, they may eventually become stars, but their relative weakness in the market (small share) makes investing in question marks riskier than investing in stars. **Cash cows** are companies that have a large share of a slow-growing market. Companies in this situation are often highly profitable, hence the name "cash cow." Finally, **dogs** are companies that have a small share of a slow-growing market. As the name suggests, having a small share of a slow-growth market is often not profitable.

Because the idea is to redirect investment from slow-growing to fast-growing companies, the BCG matrix starts by recommending that while the substantial cash flows from cash cows last, they should be reinvested in stars (see 1 in Exhibit 6.4) to help them grow even faster and obtain even more market share. Using this strategy, current profits help produce future profits. Over time, as their market growth slows, some stars may turn into cash cows (see 2). Cash flows should also be directed to some question marks (see 3). Though riskier than stars, question marks have great potential because of their fast-growing market. Managers must decide which question marks are most likely to turn into stars and therefore warrant further investment and which ones are too risky and should be sold. Over time, managers hope some question marks will become stars as their small markets become large ones (see 4). Finally, because dogs lose money, the corporation should "find them new owners" or "take them to the pound." In other words, dogs should either be sold to other companies or closed down and liquidated for their assets (see 5).

Although the BCG matrix and other forms of portfolio strategy are relatively popular among managers, portfolio strategy has some drawbacks. The most significant drawback is that contrary to the predictions of portfolio strategy, the evidence suggests that acquiring unrelated businesses is *not* useful. As shown in Exhibit 6.5, there is a U-shaped relationship between diversification and risk.[43] The left side of the curve shows that single businesses with no diversification are extremely risky (if the single business fails, the entire business fails). So, in part, the portfolio strategy of diversifying is correct—competing in a variety of different businesses can lower risk. However, portfolio strategy is partly wrong, too—the right side of the curve shows that conglomerates composed of completely unrelated businesses are even riskier than single, undiversified businesses.

A second set of problems with portfolio strategy has to do with the dysfunctional consequences that can occur when companies are categorized as stars, cash cows, question marks, or

Exhibit 6.4
Boston Consulting Group Matrix

Question mark a company with a small share of a fast-growing market

Cash cow a company with a large share of a slow-growing market

Dog a company with a small share of a slow-growing market

Question mark - Flat Design/Shutterstock.com / Star - Olga Knutova/Shutterstock.com / Cow - SoRad/Shutterstock.com / Dog - Andresr/Shutterstock.com / Money next to cow - iStock.com/Mosichev / Money in lower left corner - iStock.com/Claudio Baldin / Graph paper background - iStock.com / Post-it notes - iStock.com/subjug

Exhibit 6.5
U-Shaped Relationship between Diversification and Risk

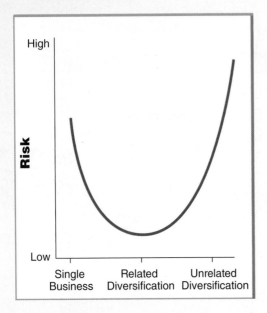

Source: M. Lubatkin & P.J. Lane, "Psst! . . . The Merger Mavens Still Have It Wrong," *Academy of Management* Executive 10 (1996) 21–39.

dogs. Contrary to expectations, the BCG matrix often yields incorrect judgments about a company's potential. In other words, managers using the BCG matrix aren't very good at accurately determining which companies should be categorized as stars, cash cows, questions marks, or dogs. The most common mistake is simply miscategorizing highly profitable companies as dogs.[44] In part, this is because the BCG matrix relies on past performance (previous market share and previous market growth), which is a notoriously poor predictor of future company performance. More worrisome, however, is research that indicates the BCG matrix actually makes managers worse at judging the future profitability of a business. A study conducted in six countries over five years gave managers and business students clear information about the current and future profits (that is, slow or fast growth) of three companies and asked them to select the one that would be most successful in the future.

> **Related diversification**
> creating or acquiring companies that share similar products, manufacturing, marketing, technology, or cultures

Although not labeled this way, one company was clearly a star, another was a dog, and the last was a cash cow. Just exposing people to the ideas in the BCG matrix led them to incorrectly categorize less profitable businesses as the most successful businesses 64 percent of the time, while actually *using* the BCG matrix led to making the same mistake 87 percent of the time.[45]

Furthermore, using the BCG matrix can also weaken the strongest performer in the corporate portfolio: the cash cow. As funds are redirected from cash cows to stars, corporate managers essentially take away the resources needed to take advantage of the cash cow's new business opportunities. As a result, the cash cow becomes less aggressive in seeking new business or in defending its present business.

The Office productivity suite (Word, PowerPoint, Excel) has long been one of Microsoft's two cash cows (the other is its Windows operating system).[46] But with free alternatives, such as Google Docs, Apache's Open Office, and Apple's Pages, Numbers, and Keynote apps (free on every Mac computer, iPhone and iPad), and strongly declining sales of PCs worldwide, Office, while still highly profitable, is facing major challenges that threaten its long-time dominance and ability to throw off cash.[47] These threats come at a time when Microsoft needs to divert cash from Office into its cloud-based file storage and Azure (cloud services, big data, servers, virtual machines, and website hosting) platforms to turn those questions marks into future stars, as well as its Surface tablets, a business which it hopes to transform from a dog to a question mark (and eventually a star). The risk, however, is that diverting cash from Office may make it less able to defend its current business or to grow by seeking new business.[48]

Finally, labeling a top performer as a cash cow can harm employee morale. Cash-cow employees realize that they have inferior status and that instead of working for themselves, they are now working to fund the growth of stars and question marks.

So, what kind of portfolio strategy does the best job of helping managers decide which companies to buy or sell? The U-shaped curve in Exhibit 6.5 indicates that, contrary to the predictions of portfolio strategy, the best approach is probably **related diversification**, in which the different business units share similar products, manufacturing, marketing, technology, or cultures. The key to related diversification is to acquire or create new companies with core capabilities that complement the core capabilities of businesses already in the corporate portfolio. Hormel Foods is an example of related diversification in the food business. The company both manufactures and markets a variety of foods, from deli meats to salsa to the infamous SPAM.

We began this section with the example of 3M and its 55,000 products sold in five different business groups. While seemingly different, most of 3M's product

Hotels Respond: Fighting Back against Expedia and Airbnb

Travelers use Airbnb.com to rent private rooms, flats or houses directly from homeowners. Roughly a third of leisure travelers choose private accommodations, like those through Airbnb, over hotels. Thirty-one percent of business travelers have done the same in the last two years. Likewise, 81 percent of hotel rooms are booked through online travel sites like Expedia.com. When that happens, hotel chains pay travel sites a 15 to 25 percent commission, which means they make make less money per room. Hotels are fighting back by offering discounts and benefits to customers enrolled in hotel member rewards accounts who make direct room reservations using the hotel's website. Hilton's "Stop Clicking Around" plan offered 10 percent member discounts, whereas Marriott's "It Pays to Be Direct" plan offered 2 to 5 percent discounts. Members benefit from "best price guarantees" on hotel websites. Hotels benefit because member discounts are smaller than commissions paid to travel sites. Hotels also offer members additional benefits that are only available through direct reservations on hotel websites, such as free Wi-Fi, digital check-in, and rewards points than can be used to pay for future reservations.

Source: R. Chhatwal, "Marriott And Hilton Fight Back Against Priceline And Expedia," Seeking Alpha, March 21, 2016, accessed April 1, 2017, https://seekingalpha.com/article/3959946-marriott-hilton-fight-back-priceline-expedia; D. Fitzgerald, "Hotels Turn to 'Member' Discounts to Battle Travel Websites," *Wall Street Journal*, July 7, 2016, accessed April 1, 2017, https://www.wsj.com/articles/hotels-turn-to-member-discounts-to-battle-travel-websites-1467907475; E. Glusac, "Hotels vs. Airbnb: Let the Battle Begin," *New York Times*, July 20, 2016, accessed April 1, 2017, https://www.nytimes.com/2016/07/24/travel/airbnb-hotels.html.

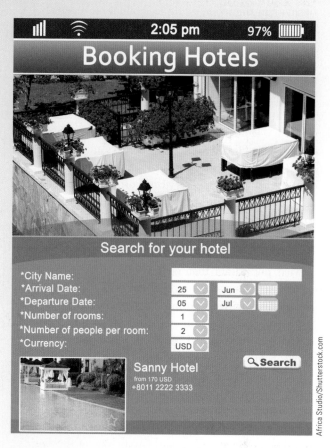

Africa Studio/Shutterstock.com

divisions are based in some fashion on its distinctive competencies in adhesives and tape (for example, wet or dry sandpaper, Post-it notes, Scotchgard fabric protector, transdermal skin patches, and reflective material used in traffic signs). Furthermore, all of 3M's divisions share its strong corporate culture that promotes and encourages risk taking and innovation. In sum, in contrast to a single, undiversified business or unrelated diversification, related diversification reduces risk because the different businesses can work as a team, relying on each other for needed experience, expertise, and support.

6-3b Grand Strategies

A **grand strategy** is a broad strategic plan used to help an organization achieve its strategic goals.[49] Grand strategies guide the strategic alternatives that managers of individual businesses or subunits may use in deciding what businesses they should be in. There are three kinds of grand strategies: growth, stability, and retrenchment/recovery.

The purpose of a **growth strategy** is to increase profits, revenues, market share, or the number of places (stores, offices, locations) in which the company does business. Companies can grow in several ways. They can grow externally by merging with or acquiring other companies in the same or different businesses. Marriott International, with hotel brands such as Marriott, JW Marriott, Courtyard, and Renaissance, paid $12.2 billion to acquire Starwood Hotels & Resorts, which is known for its Westin, St. Regis, Sheraton, and Meridien hotels, among others. Marriott's CEO Arne M. Sorenson said, "We've got an ability to offer just that much more choice. A choice in locations, a choice in the kind of hotel, a choice in

Grand strategy a broad corporate-level strategic plan used to achieve strategic goals and guide the strategic alternatives that managers of individual businesses or subunits may use

Growth strategy a strategy that focuses on increasing profits, revenues, market share, or the number of places in which the company does business the amount a customer needs to spend."[50] Starwood's CEO Adam Aron agreed, noting that, "To be successful in today's lodging space, a wide distribution of brands and hotels across price points is critical. Today, size matters."[51] Together the two firms will be the largest hotel business in the world, with $2.7 billion in revenue, 1.1 million rooms and 30 well-regarded hotel brands.

Another way to grow is internally, directly expanding the company's existing business or creating and growing new businesses. In 2015, Amazon expanded its online e-tail business with several new selling platforms. Handmade at Amazon, a handicraft marketplace similar to Etsy.com, launched with 5,000 artisans from sixty countries selling 80,000 handmade items. Amazon charges vendors a 12 percent commission, but provides them with the same shipping services it offers its Marketplace sellers. Amazon Home Services, a referral service similar to Angie's List, connects consumers with professionals who perform home repairs, upkeep, and upgrades. More than 700 different services can be booked through the service, and rather than charge its customers, Amazon collects a commission on the value of the services from the professionals who provide them. Finally, in its first move away from e-commerce, Amazon recently opened the first of 400 planned brick-and-mortar stores selling books, Kindle e-readers, and Fire tablets.[52]

The purpose of a **stability strategy** is to continue doing what the company has been doing, just doing it better. Companies following a stability strategy try to improve the way in which they sell the same products or services to the same customers. Vanguard Group, one of the world's largest investment firms was designed at its founding in 1975 to offer low-cost investing options. Because it is client-owned, it returns profits to customers by lowering costs. Vanguard's stability strategy to reduce costs means that Vanguard's investment fees have dropped from $0.89 per $100 in 1975 to $0.12 today. Since the typical investment fund charges $1.01 per $100 invested in 2017, an investor with $100,000 invested would save $890 in fees per year with Vanguard.[53]

The purpose of a **retrenchment strategy** is to turn around very poor company performance by shrinking the size or scope of the business or, if a company is in multiple businesses, by closing or shutting down different lines of the business. The first step of a typical retrenchment strategy might include making significant cost reductions: laying off employees; closing poorly performing stores, offices, or manufacturing plants; or closing or selling entire lines of products or services.[54] Before search engines like Google, Yahoo's directories were the fastest way to find things on the Internet.[55] Yahoo's early success led to the company being valued at $125 billion in 2000. Flush with cash, it expanded into dozens of different businesses, and even made an unsuccessful bid to buy Google. But with Google dominating web search and advertising, Yahoo's revenues declining for over a decade, and various strategies to reinvigorate Yahoo's brand not working, CEO Marissa Mayer began shrinking Yahoo, closing down different lines of business. In 2016 alone, Yahoo closed seven digital magazines (most started just 2 years before), laid off 15 percent of employees, took a $230 million accounting write down on blog site Tumblr for which it paid $1 billion in cash three years ago, closed five offices to save $400 million in costs, and then sold its core Internet operations (Yahoo Mail, Yahoo Search, and websites such as Yahoo Finance) to Verizon Communications for $4.8 billion. After the sale closed in 2017, what's left of Yahoo is called Altaba, reflecting a multibillion-dollar investment in China's alibaba.com, and Yahoo Japan, which was not part of the sale to Verizon.[56]

After cutting costs and reducing a business's size or scope, the second step in a retrenchment strategy is recovery. **Recovery** consists of the strategic actions that a company takes to return to a growth strategy. This two-step process of cutting and recovery is analogous to pruning roses. Prior to each growing season, roses should be cut back to two-thirds their normal size. Pruning doesn't damage the roses; it makes them stronger and more likely to produce beautiful, fragrant flowers. The retrenchment-and-recovery process is similar.

Like pruning, the cuts are made as part of a recovery strategy intended to allow companies to eventually return to a successful growth strategy. When company performance drops significantly, a strategy of retrenchment and recovery may help the company return to a successful growth strategy.

After three years of slumping sales due to an overly complex menu and increased competition from fast-casual restaurants, McDonald's returned to basics with a recovery strategy called "Plan to Win." In addition to simplifying its menu, McDonald's took several bold steps under this initiative:

» Renovate existing locations rather than build new ones.

» Increase font sizes on orders so that cooks can read them correctly.

Stability strategy a strategy that focuses on improving the way in which the company sells the same products or services to the same customers

Retrenchment strategy a strategy that focuses on turning around very poor company performance by shrinking the size or scope of the business

Recovery the strategic actions taken after retrenchment to return to a growth strategy

Exhibit 6.6
Porter's Five Industry Forces

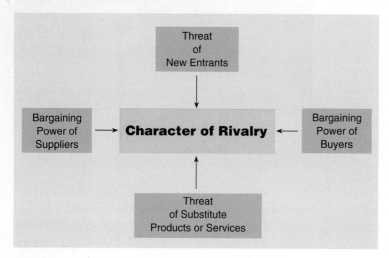

Source: Based on the Simon & Schuster, Inc. Porter, M. E. *Competitive Strategy: Techniques for Analyzing Industries and Competitors.* New York: Free Press, 1980.

» Make the most of the core menu (by, for example, toasting hamburger buns longer and searing hamburgers so they're juicier).

» Institute all-day breakfast (which used to end at 10:30 a.m.).

» Reduce employee turnover by increasing crew pay.

CEO Steve Easterbrook said about the new strategy, "Our goal is net simplification. We want to focus on fewer, bigger decisions that generate bigger reward."[57] After nine months, same-store sales rose 6.2 percent and profits soared by 35 percent.[58]

 INDUSTRY-LEVEL STRATEGIES

Industry-level strategy addresses the question, "How should we compete in this industry?"

Let's find out more about industry-level strategies by discussing **6-4a the five industry forces that determine overall levels of competition in an industry** *as well as* **6-4b the positioning strategies** *and* **6-4c adaptive strategies that companies can use to achieve sustained competitive advantage** *and* **above-average profits.**

6-4a Five Industry Forces

According to Harvard professor Michael Porter, five industry forces determine an industry's overall attractiveness and potential for long-term profitability: the character of the rivalry, the threat of new entrants, the threat of substitute products or services, the bargaining power of suppliers, and the bargaining power of buyers. The stronger these forces, the less attractive the industry becomes to corporate investors because it is more difficult for companies to be profitable. Porter's industry forces are illustrated in Exhibit 6.6. Let's examine how these forces are bringing changes to several kinds of industries.

Character of the rivalry is a measure of the intensity of competitive behavior among companies in an industry. Is the competition among firms aggressive and cutthroat, or do competitors focus more on serving customers than on attacking each other? Both industry attractiveness and profitability decrease when rivalry is cutthroat. For example, selling cars is a highly competitive business. Pick up a local newspaper on Friday, Saturday, or Sunday morning, and you'll find dozens of pages of car advertising ("Anniversary Sale-A-Bration," "Ford March Savings!" and "$99 Down, You Choose!"). In fact, competition in new-car sales is so intense that if it weren't for used-car sales, repair work, and replacement parts, many auto dealers would actually lose money.

The **threat of new entrants** is a measure of the degree to which barriers to entry make it easy or difficult for new companies to get started in an industry. If new companies can enter the industry easily, then competition will increase, and prices and profits will fall. Altos Research provides real-time statistics and analysis of real estate markets for investors and news services such as Bloomberg Financial. Because its business relies on access to terabytes of market data, it leases computing power and data storage from Amazon Web Services (AWS), the market leader in cloud services. Without any negotiation, AWS cut its costs in half, enough to pay for two new programmers. On the other hand, if there are sufficient barriers to entry, such as large capital requirements to buy expensive equipment or plant facilities or the need for specialized knowledge, then competition will be weaker, and prices and profits will generally be higher. The automobile industry has traditionally had a high barrier to entry. So when Tesla entered the market in 2003 to manufacture a completely electric sports car, it was the first new car company in a generation. With billions of dollars in startup funding, the company hired thousands of engineers, built new manufacturing facilities, and created a complex supply chain to source, manufacture, and assemble 10,000 component parts. While its stock is valued at $30 billion, Tesla has never made a profit. In fact, the company has burned through $100 million a month in expenses since going public in 2010. With six new competitors poised to enter the automotive industry (including Apple, Google, and an upstart founded by a team of former Tesla executives), the barrier to entry is falling and competition is rising. Becoming profitable may take longer than Tesla planned as barriers to entry fall and competition rises.[59]

The **threat of substitute products or services** is a measure of the ease with which customers can find substitutes for an industry's products or services. If customers can easily find substitute products or services, the competition will be greater, and profits will be lower. If there are few or no substitutes, competition will be weaker, and profits will be higher. Overnight delivery companies like UPS and DHL deliver millions of items every day. What would happen to these businesses if, instead of buying products and having them delivered, people could use 3-D printers to manufacture what they needed right at work or home? This new technology led UPS chief information officer Dave Barnes to wonder, "Should we be threatened by it or should we endorse it?[60] To answer that question, UPS created a 3-D printing test center at its Louisville, Kentucky hub. There, UPS explored the feasibility of local production and delivery of 3-D printed items. The center's 100 industrial 3-D printers create everything from iPhone cases to replacement parts for UPS's fleet of Airbus A300 jets. DHL's initial studies show that

By leasing its own fleet of trucks, Amazon saves as much as 40 percent on shipping costs.

just 2–4 percent of shipped products can reliably be 3-D printed. UPS, however, is purchasing 900 more 3-D printers for other locations. According to Barnes, "We saw the capability of a logistics company to be challenged on one side but on the other [to] be an enabler."[61]

Bargaining power of suppliers is a measure of the influence that suppliers of parts, materials, and services to firms in an industry have on the prices of these inputs. When companies can buy parts, materials, and services from numerous suppliers, the companies will be able to bargain with the suppliers to keep prices low. On the other hand, if there are few suppliers, or if a company is dependent on a supplier with specialized skills and knowledge, then the suppliers will have the bargaining power to dictate price levels. On the flip side, the **bargaining power of buyers** is a measure of the influence that customers have on the firm's prices. If a company sells a popular product or service to multiple buyers, then the company has more power to set prices. By contrast, if a company is dependent on just a few high-volume buyers, those buyers will typically have enough bargaining power to dictate prices.

We can see how the bargaining power of suppliers and buyers changes by examining the relationship between Amazon and its key delivery suppliers, UPS and FedEx. Since 2009, Amazon's shipping costs have risen each year, from 7.5 percent of sales to 10.8 percent of sales, indicating UPS and FedEx's growing supplier bargaining power. Amazon relies on them for package delivery, especially to Amazon Prime customers, who pay $99 a year for two-day, no charge deliveries. Prime members, who buy three times as much from Amazon as non-Prime customers, drove Amazon's revenue growth from $89 billion in 2014 to $136 billion in 2016.[62] As Amazon has grown, it has reinvested profits into establishing 70 warehouses in 21 states, and leasing 40 Boeing

Threat of substitute products or services a measure of the ease with which customers can find substitutes for an industry's products or services

Bargaining power of suppliers a measure of the influence that suppliers of parts, materials, and services to firms in an industry have on the prices of these inputs

Bargaining power of buyers a measure of the influence that customers have on a firm's prices

767s for "Prime Air" logistics and hundreds of "Prime Now" trucks, the latter of which promise free two-hour delivery. Why does Amazon appear to be establishing its own delivery service capabilities? Perhaps because the average shipping cost of $7.81 a package with FedEx and UPS could be reduced by 40 percent if Amazon delivered packages to customer on its own. With these moves, Amazon's bargaining power as a buyer is clearly getting stronger.[63]

6-4b Positioning Strategies

After analyzing industry forces, the next step in industry-level strategy is to protect your company from the negative effects of industry-wide competition and to create a sustainable competitive advantage. According to Michael Porter, there are three positioning strategies: cost leadership, differentiation, and focus.

Cost leadership means producing a product or service of acceptable quality at consistently lower production costs than competitors so that the firm can offer the product or service at the lowest price in the industry. Cost leadership protects companies from industry forces by deterring new entrants, who will have to match low costs and prices. Cost leadership also forces down the prices of substitute products and services, attracts bargain-seeking buyers, and increases bargaining power with suppliers, who have to keep their prices low if they want to do business with the cost leader. With entry-level surfboards costing $300 and top-of-the-line, handmade longboards going for $1,000 or more, surfing is expensive. Those high prices inspired Matt Zilinskas to create Wavestorm, an 8-foot, mass-produced soft-foam surfboard that sells for $99 at Costco. Now the industry's best-selling surfboard, Wavestorm's sales are so strong that other retailers have stopped selling more expensive soft-foam boards altogether. "Why even bother when you can go to Costco [and get one for] $100?" asked Cody Quarress, manager at the Huntington Surf & Sport.[64] Zilinskas has received complaints from competitors, but he sees his product as beneficial to the industry: "How many of the hundreds of thousands of people who bought our board have moved on to higher-end product? Ask any surfer in the water about Wavestorm. They probably own one."[65]

Differentiation means making your product or service sufficiently different from competitors' offerings that customers are willing to pay a premium price for the extra value or performance that it provides. Differentiation protects companies from industry forces by reducing the threat of substitute products.

It also protects companies by making it easier to retain customers and more difficult for new entrants trying to attract new customers. Would you pay $290 for an Amazon Kindle Oasis ebook reader when the $119 Kindle Paperwhite and the $199 Kindle Voyage have identical high-resolution displays? Perhaps you'd pay more for the included leather cover? Because at 3.4 mm, it's the thinnest ebook reader you can buy? Because it weighs a feather-light 4.6 ounces, versus 6.3 ounces for the Voyage and 7.2 ounces for the Paperwhite? Because it has 60 percent more LED lighting, physical buttons to turn pages, and a battery that lasts twice as long? *Engadget's* Devindra Hardawar says there's no practical reason to pay more for the Oasis, which he describes as, "A feast with the world's finest caviar. It's an all-you-can-eat Wagyu steak dinner. It's an $80 cup of coffee."[66] *ZDNet's* Jason Perlow calls the Oasis the "'Executive Kindle,' much like the

Cost leadership the positioning strategy of producing a product or service of acceptable quality at consistently lower production costs than competitors can, so that the firm can offer the product or service at the lowest price in the industry

Differentiation the positioning strategy of providing a product or service that is sufficiently different from competitors' offerings that customers are willing to pay a premium price for it

Rob Kim/Getty Images Entertainment/Getty Images

HGTV's "Fixer Upper," and hosts Chip and Joanna Gaines, have strong appeal with the cable channel's target customer.

big iPad Pro is the 'Executive iPad.'"[67] Finally, Jason Snell of SixColors.com says, "The Oasis is the ebook reader equivalent of a luxury sedan, but it's overkill for most people."[68]

With a **focus strategy**, a company uses either cost leadership or differentiation to produce a specialized product or service for a limited, specially targeted group of customers in a particular geographic region or market segment. Focus strategies typically work in market niches that competitors have overlooked or have difficulty serving. Cable channel HGTV shows *Property Brothers and Fixer Upper* have a common theme: A couple shops for an outdated house, buying one of the three homes shown to viewers. The contractor takes out a wall, creating an open floor plan, and has an overbudget surprise. The couple moves in, crying with joy at the redesign of their beautiful home. HGTV's target customer is very specific. She's a college educated suburbanite with an $84,000 household income and an insatiable interest in home improvement. Chief programming officer Kathleen Finch says, "We super-serve our viewer what she likes, and we give her more and more of it." HGTV's focus strategy works. As the third-most popular cable network, it deliver twice as much web traffic for

advertisers like Wayfair, an online retailer of furniture, home furnishings, and decor.[69]

6-4c Adaptive Strategies

Adaptive strategies are another set of industry-level strategies. Whereas the aim of positioning strategies is to minimize the effects of industry competition and build a sustainable competitive advantage, the purpose of adaptive strategies is to choose an industry-level strategy that is best suited to changes in the organization's external environment. There are four kinds of adaptive strategies: defenders, prospectors, analyzers, and reactors.[70]

Defenders seek moderate, steady growth by offering a limited range of products and services to a well-defined set of customers. In other words, defenders aggressively "defend" their current strategic position by doing the best job they can to hold on to customers in a particular market segment.

Not surprisingly, ultra-premium carmakers, such as **Ferrari** and **Aston-Martin**, are not as interested in growth as they are in retaining the luxury brand image. That's because higher sales volume leads to ubiquity, which makes it harder to charge premium pricing. The retail price of a new Ferrari California is roughly $200,000, but a new LaFerrari model has an MSRP of $1.4 million. To retain is exclusivity, Ferrari has a self-imposed production cap of 7,000 vehicles a year. At Aston Martin, the level is much lower, at 4,000 cars per year. "This is not a car company that is ever going to be selling a lot of cars," said Andy Palmer, CEO of Aston Martin. "Part of its mystique is its exclusivity."[71]

Prospectors seek fast growth by searching for new market opportunities, encouraging risk taking, and being the first to bring innovative new products to market. Prospectors are analogous to gold miners who "prospect" for gold nuggets (that is, new products) in hope that the nuggets will lead them to a rich deposit of gold (that is, fast growth). 3M has long been known for its innovative products, particularly in the area of adhesives. Since 1904, it has invented sandpaper; masking, cellophane, electrical, and Scotch tapes; the first commercially available audiotapes and videotapes; and its most famous invention, Post-it notes. Lately, 3M has invented a film that increases the brightness of LCD displays on laptop computers; developed a digital system for construction companies to detect underground telecommunication, gas, water, sewer, or electrical lines without digging; and created a pheromone spray that, by preventing harmful insects from mating, will protect apple, walnut, tomato, cranberry, and grape crops. For more on 3M's innovative products,

Focus strategy the positioning strategy of using cost leadership or differentiation to produce a specialized product or service for a limited, specially targeted group of customers in a particular geographic region or market segment

Defenders companies using an adaptive strategy aimed at defending strategic positions by seeking moderate, steady growth and by offering a limited range of high-quality products and services to a well-defined set of customers

Prospectors companies using an adaptive strategy that seeks fast growth by searching for new market opportunities, encouraging risk taking, and being the first to bring innovative new products to market

Aston Martin remains an exclusive automobile by limiting its production to 4,000 cars each year.

see the 3M innovation archive (http://solutions.3m.com /innovation/en_US/).

Analyzers are the blend of the defender and prospector strategies. They seek moderate, steady growth and limited opportunities for fast growth. Analyzers are rarely first to market with new products or services. Instead, they try to simultaneously minimize risk and maximize profits by following or imitating the proven successes of prospectors.

Facebook admits to using an analyzer strategy in copying the key features of Snapchat, the popular social media app in which users share pictures and videos. Facebook product manager Connor Hayes said, "The way people create content is changing to be from text to photos and videos. This is in turn changing the way they're sharing with one another and interacting online. This is something that Snapchat has really pioneered." Facebook has copied Snapchat's features four times. First, Snapchat opens in camera view. Facebook made the camera available with one swipe. Second, it added the one-swipe capability to take and post picture and videos to its Instagram, WhatsApp, and Messenger apps. Third, similar to Snapchat stories, it named these features Facebook Stories. Fourth, just like in SnapChat, users can choose to create photos and stories that only exist for 24 hours. Facebook's adoption of SnapChat features has already slowed Snapchat's user growth. Instagram Stories has 150 million daily users, while Snapchat's daily user base is 158 million.[72]

Finally, unlike defenders, prospectors, or analyzers, **reactors** do not follow a consistent strategy. Rather than anticipating and preparing for external opportunities and threats, reactors tend to react to changes in their external environment after they occur. Not surprisingly, reactors tend to be poorer performers than defenders,

prospectors, or analyzers. A reactor approach is inherently unstable, and firms that fall into this mode of operation must change their approach or face almost certain failure.

6-5 FIRM-LEVEL STRATEGIES

Apple unveils its Apple Watch with advanced fitness tracking and FitBit counters with the Blaze, which has a color touchscreen and syncs automatically with your phone. Starbucks Coffee opens a store, and nearby locally run coffeehouses respond by improving service, increasing portions, and holding the line on prices. In the German luxury car industry, **BMW**, **Audi**, and **Mercedes** have an intense three-way rivalry that goes well beyond sales volume to include investments in technology, quality rankings, and profitability. According to one Audi executive, to get approval for a new project, "I just have to say BMW is already doing it, and it goes through." The rivalry is just as heated over at BMW. When it comes to Audi, one BMW executive said, "We like to stick it to them."[73] Attack and respond, respond and attack. **Firm-level strategy** addresses the question, "How should we compete against a particular firm?"

Let's find out more about the firm-level strategies (direct competition between companies) by reading about 6-5a the basics of direct competition and 6-5b the strategic moves involved in direct competition between companies.

6-5a Direct Competition

Although Porter's five industry forces indicate the overall level of competition in an industry, most companies do not compete directly with all the firms in their industry. For example, McDonald's and Red Lobster are both in the restaurant business, but no one would characterize them as competitors. McDonald's offers low-cost, convenient fast food in a seat-yourself restaurant, while Red Lobster offers mid-priced seafood dinners complete with servers and a bar.

Analyzers companies using an adaptive strategy that seeks to minimize risk and maximize profits by following or imitating the proven successes of prospectors

Reactors companies that do not follow a consistent adaptive strategy but instead react to changes in the external environment after they occur

Firm-level strategy a corporate strategy that addresses the question, "How should we compete against a particular firm?"

Instead of competing with an entire industry, most firms compete directly with just a few companies within it. **Direct competition** is the rivalry between two companies offering similar products and services that acknowledge each other as rivals and take offensive and defensive positions as they act and react to each other's strategic actions.[74] Two factors determine the extent to which firms will be in direct competition with each other: market commonality and resource similarity. **Market commonality** is the degree to which two companies have overlapping products, services, or customers in multiple markets. The more markets in which there is product, service, or customer overlap, the more intense the direct competition between the two companies. **Resource similarity** is the extent to which a competitor has similar amounts and kinds of resources, that is, similar assets, capabilities, processes, information, and knowledge used to create and sustain an advantage over competitors. From a competitive standpoint, resource similarity means that your direct competitors can probably match the strategic actions that your company takes.

Exhibit 6.7 shows how market commonality and resource similarity interact to determine when and where companies are in direct competition.[75] The overlapping area in each quadrant (between the triangle and the rectangle, or between the differently colored rectangles) depicts market commonality. The larger the overlap, the greater the market commonality. Shapes depict resource similarity, with rectangles representing one set of competitive resources and triangles representing another. Quadrant I shows two companies in direct competition because they have similar resources at their disposal and a high degree of market commonality. These companies try to sell similar products and services to similar customers. McDonald's intends to intensify its direct competition with Burger King by partnering with Uber to deliver food via UberEATS. In its top five

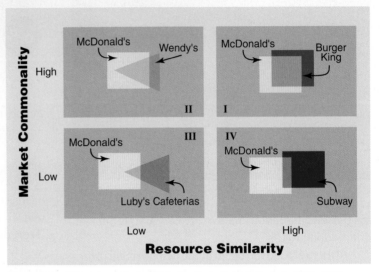

Exhibit 6.7
A Framework of Direct Competition

Source: M. Chen, "Competitor Analysis and InterFirm Rivalry: Toward a Theoretical Integration," *Academy of Management Review* 21 (1996): 100–134.

markets, 75 percent of the population lives within three miles of a McDonald's. Globally, one billion people live within 10 minutes of a McDonald's. Senior vice president Lucy Brady said, "Delivery is the most significant disruption in the restaurant industry in our lifetime."[76]

In Quadrant II, the overlapping parts of the triangle and rectangle show two companies going after similar customers with some similar products or services but doing so with different competitive resources. McDonald's and Wendy's restaurants would fit here. Wendy's is after the same lunchtime and dinner crowds that McDonald's is. Nevertheless, with its more expensive hamburgers, fries, shakes, and salads, Wendy's is less of a direct competitor to McDonald's than Burger King is. For example, Wendy's has recently rebranded itself more like a casual dining restaurant, redesigning its locations with lounge seating, fireplaces, Wi-Fi, and digital menu boards.[77] Wendy's goal is to convert 85 percent of its company-owned locations and 35 percent of its franchised stores by 2017.[78] Even though it competes less directly with Wendy's, McDonald's is taking aim at Wendy's by switching from frozen to fresh beef in its Quarter Pounder hamburgers. Wendy's has long touted its fresh beef as a key difference. Indeed, when McDonald's announced the change to fresh beef, Wendy's tweeted, "So you'll still use frozen beef in MOST of your burgers in ALL of your restaurants? Asking for a friend."[79]

Direct competition the rivalry between two companies that offer similar products and services, acknowledge each other as rivals, and act and react to each other's strategic actions

Market commonality the degree to which two companies have overlapping products, services, or customers in multiple markets

Resource similarity the extent to which a competitor has similar amounts and kinds of resources

McDonald's has partnered with UberEats to beef up its competitive edge.

6-5b Strategic Moves of Direct Competition

While corporate-level strategies help managers decide what business to be in, and industry-level strategies help them determine how to compete within an industry, firm-level strategies help managers determine when, where, and what strategic actions should be taken against a direct competitor. Firms in direct competition can make two basic strategic moves: attack and response. These moves occur all the time in virtually every industry, but they are most noticeable in industries where multiple large competitors are pursuing customers in the same market space.

An **attack** is a competitive move designed to reduce a rival's market share or profits. Gillette dominates the $3.3 billion U.S. shaving business, earning an enormous 32 percent profit on each blade. Dollar Shave Club, an online service selling razor blades via subscription plans, attacked Gillette with substantially lower prices. While Gillette cartridges cost $3.50 to $6.00 each, Dollar Shave Club's entry-level plan, the Humble Twin, charges only $0.20 per cartridge and $2.00 per month for shipping. Dollar Shave Club quickly amassed nearly 53 percent of the online market for razors and blades.[83] Likewise, four-year old Harry's Razor Co., which also sells razors via online monthly plans, already has 2 percent of the overall market for men's razors. However, sales jumped when Target featured Harry's products in its stores. Within weeks, Harry's had 10 percent of Target's cartridges sales and half of its handle sales, mostly at the expense of Gillette.[84]

A **response** is a countermove, prompted by a rival's attack, that is designed to defend or improve a company's market share or profit. There are two kinds of responses.[85] The first is to match or mirror your competitor's move. This is what Gillette did when it launched the online Gillette Shave Club, which offers three subscription plans, free shipping on all orders, loyalty rewards, and sweepstakes for entertainment and major-league sports tickets. Gillette ran ads on Facebook and Twitter promoting the Gillette Shave Club, saying "Going to the store to buy blades is so 2014."[86]

The second kind of response, however, is to respond along a different dimension from your competitor's move or attack. Wireless carriers, such at

In Quadrant III, the very small overlap shows two companies with different competitive resources and little market commonality. McDonald's and Luby's cafeterias fit here. Although both are in the fast-food business, there's almost no overlap in terms of products and customers. Luby's sells baked chicken, turkey, roasts, meat loaf, and vegetables, none of which are available at McDonald's. Furthermore, Luby's customers aren't likely to eat at McDonald's. In fact, Luby's is not really competing with other fast-food restaurants, but with eating at home. Company surveys show that close to half of its customers would have eaten at home, not at another restaurant, if they hadn't come to Luby's.[80]

Finally, in Quadrant IV, the small overlap between the two rectangles shows that McDonald's and Subway compete with similar resources but with little market commonality. In terms of resources, sales at McDonald's are much larger, but Subway has grown substantially in the past decade and now has 44,830 stores in 98 countries, compared to McDonald's with 36,899 stores in more than 100 countries.[81]

Though Subway and McDonald's compete, they aren't direct competitors in terms of market commonality in the way that McDonald's and Burger King are because Subway, unlike McDonald's, sells itself as a provider of healthy fast food. Thus, the overlap is much smaller in Quadrant IV than in Quadrant I. With detailed nutritional information available in its stores, and its close relationships with the American Heart Association, the American College of Cardiologists, and Heart Research UK, Subway has long focused on healthy eating and well being.[82]

Attack a competitive move designed to reduce a rival's market share or profits

Response a competitive countermove, prompted by a rival's attack, to defend or improve a company's market share or profit

T-Mobile has launched a strategic initiative aimed at removing key restrictions found in its competitors' wireless services.

AT&T, Verizon, and Sprint, have typically responded to competitors' attacks by cutting prices, expanding coverage, or speeding up their networks. T-Mobile, the smallest of the major wireless carriers, faired poorly on those dimensions and lost 2 million customers as a result five years ago.[87] In the past three years, however, T-Mobile has grown from 33 million to 71.5 million customers, increasing its share of the U.S. wireless market from 10 to 17 percent. The company achieved this remarkable growth by responding with an "uncarrier" strategy that removes key restrictions found in its competitors' wireless services.[88] Overage charges? Not at T-Mobile, which offers unlimited minutes and texts. Exorbitant roaming charges for international plans? T-Mobile charges a meager 20 cents per minute for international calls, while providing unlimited international data and texts at no extra charge in 140 countries. Moreover, with 35 percent of U.S. international calls and 55 percent of U.S. international travel to Mexico and Canada, T-Mobile has consolidated all three countries into one North American market in which access to data plans, 4G LTE fast connections, and calling are included—at no extra cost—for T-Mobile customers. Finally, are low data caps preventing music and streaming video on your phone? T-Mobile One introduced unlimited data, with music and HD streaming. T-Mobile then cut the price of its unlimited plans by including sales taxes and regulator fees in the advertised prices (not in addition to), and by reducing plans $5 a month if customers used autopay and by $10 a month when a phone uses less than 2GB a month (T-Mobile Kickback.)[89]

Market commonality and resource similarity determine the likelihood of an attack or response, that is, whether a company is likely to attack a direct competitor or to strike back with a strong response when attacked. When market commonality is large, and companies have overlapping products, services, or customers in multiple markets, there is less motivation to attack and more motivation to respond to an attack. The reason for this is straightforward: When firms are direct competitors in a large number of markets, they have a great deal at stake.

Airlines Air France-KLM and Lufthansa once dominated highly lucrative routes between Europe's and Asia's largest cities. That is, until Middle Eastern carriers such as Emirates Airlines and Etihad Airways attacked their market shares and profits by offering high-end amenities such as private suites, onboard showers, and a bar in first class. The European carriers quickly took note, with Air France-KLM CEO Alexandre de Juniac saying, "The Gulf carriers have significantly captured market share."[90] Market commonality is extensive in the airline industry. With so much at stake, Germany-based Lufthansa responded by spending $3.4 billion for 650 new first-class seats, 7,000 business-class seats that lie flat (for sleeping), and upgrades to premium economy seating and in-flight entertainment. Air France-KLM responded similarly, spending $1.1 billion to install private, first-class suites on 44 planes and replace economy-class seating.[91]

Whereas market commonality affects the likelihood of an attack or a response to an attack, resource similarity largely affects response capability, that is, how quickly and forcefully a company can respond to an attack.

When resource similarity is strong, the responding firm will generally be able to match the strategic moves of the attacking firm. Consequently, a firm is less likely to attack firms with similar levels of resources because it is unlikely to gain any sustained advantage when the responding firms strike back. On the other hand, if one firm is substantially stronger than another (that is, there is low resource similarity), then a competitive attack is more likely to produce sustained competitive advantage.

In general, the more moves (that is, attacks) a company initiates against direct competitors, and the greater a company's tendency to respond when attacked, the better its performance. More specifically, attackers and early responders (companies that are quick to launch a retaliatory attack) tend to gain market share and profits at the expense of late responders. This is not to suggest that a full-attack strategy always works best. In fact, attacks can provoke harsh retaliatory responses.

Amazon uses automated pricing algorithms to search competitors' retail websites for prices. When competitors lower prices, Amazon retaliates by aggressively lowering its prices to match or beat competitors' prices. For example, the Star Shower Motion is a light projector sold during holiday season, which projects decorative light patterns on the outside of homes. It sells to retailers for a wholesale price of $30, retails for a suggested price of $49.99, and thus offers the possibility of a $19.99 profit. But once Amazon's algorithm found lower prices on competitors' websites, it began cutting Amazon's price. When competitors repeated lowered prices in response, the algorithm eventually cut Amazon's price to just below $31, or less than a dollar above cost. A. J. Khubani, CEO of Telebrands, which sells the Star Shower Motion, said that traditional brick and mortar retailers were angry that Amazon retaliated by cutting the price to $31. He said, "Keeping everybody happy while we are selling on Amazon has become a challenge."[92]

Amazon's aggressive retaliatory responses, driven by its web search algorithm, followed by competitors' retaliatory price cuts, followed by more retaliatory price cutting from Amazon, eliminated all of the profit [after shipping costs] on the hot-selling Star Shower Motion projector. Because the pricing algorithm does this so often, Amazon calls these CRaP products, meaning "Can't Realize a Profit."[93] Despite the hit to its bottom line, Amazon has no plans to stop selling CRaP products. Amazon spokesperson Julie Law said, "We find the lowest prices and meet or beat them every day."[94] Consequently, when deciding when, where, and what strategic actions to take against a direct competitor, managers should always consider the possibility of retaliation.

STUDY TOOLS 6

LOCATED IN TEXTBOOK
☐ Rip out and review chapter review card.

LOCATED AT WWW.CENGAGEBRAIN.COM
☐ Gain unique perspectives on key concepts with new 4LTR concept videos in the e-book.

☐ Increase your comprehension with Aplia for MGMT11.

☐ Complete interactive content within the e-book.

7 | Innovation and Change

After finishing this chapter, go to **PAGE 156** for **STUDY TOOLS**

LEARNING OUTCOMES

7-1 Explain why innovation matters to companies.

7-2 Discuss the different methods that managers can use to effectively manage innovation in their organizations.

7-3 Discuss why not changing can lead to organizational decline.

7-4 Discuss the different methods that managers can use to better manage change as it occurs.

Todor Tsvetkov/Getty Images

7-1 WHY INNOVATION MATTERS

As you approach your office parking garage, the LED lights inside brighten. Prompted by an app on your smartphone, the garage camera matches your license plate to your personnel record, raises the gate, and locates a parking space. Inside the office, the same app finds a desk based on your schedule and preferences (standing desk, sitting desk, work booth, concentration room, or meeting room). Before setting off to your desk, you drop your coat and personal belongings in an empty locker (indicated by a green light), using your ID badge to unlock it. As you arrive at your desk, the temperature and lighting automatically adjust to the personal preferences you set in the app. A central dashboard collects data on everything from energy usage to when the espresso machines—which, naturally, remember how you like your coffee—need to be refilled. The northfacing exterior wall is glass, while the south-facing exterior wall is composed of an alternating pattern of windows and solar panels that generate more electricity than the building uses. And when everyone leaves for the day, small security robots begin their patrol while other robots clean the rooms that were most heavily used that day. Sound futuristic? It's not. This unbelievable account is routine at **the Edge,** a smart building in Amsterdam where a complex network of cables and 28,000 sensors connects the building, its mechanical structures (heating, ventilation, plumbing, and electricity), technological systems, and occupants via a smartphone app.[1] **Organizational innovation** is the successful implementation of creative ideas, like the construction of the Edge office building in Amsterdam (http://ovgrealestate.com/project-development/the-edge).

Organizational innovation the successful implementation of creative ideas in organizations

We can only guess what changes technological innovations will bring in the next 20 years. Will we carry computers in our pockets? Today's smartphones are a step in that direction. Will solar power and wind power get cheap and efficient enough so that your home can have a standalone power source off the main electrical grid? Will fully automated, self-driving cars chauffeur you (working in the back seat on a computing tablet via high-speed Internet) to work? Who knows? The only thing we do know about the next 20 years is that innovation will continue to change our lives.

*Let's begin our discussion of innovation by learning about **7-1a technology cycles** and **7-2b innovation streams.***

7-1a Technology Cycles

In Chapter 3, you learned that technology consists of the knowledge, tools, and techniques used to transform inputs (raw materials and information) into outputs (products and services). A **technology cycle** begins with the birth of a new technology and ends when that technology reaches its limits and dies as it is replaced by a newer, substantially better technology.[2] For example, technology cycles occurred when air conditioners supplanted fans, when Henry Ford's Model T replaced horse-drawn carriages, when planes replaced trains as a means of cross-country travel, when vaccines that prevented diseases replaced medicines designed to treat them, and when battery-powered wristwatches replaced mechanically powered, stem-wound wristwatches.

From Gutenberg's invention of the printing press in 1448 to the rapid advance of the Internet, studies of hundreds of technological innovations have shown that nearly all technology cycles follow the typical **S-curve pattern of innovation** shown in Exhibit 7.1.[3] Early in a technology cycle, there is still much to learn, so progress is slow, as depicted by point A on the S-curve. The flat slope indicates that increased effort (in terms of money or research and development) brings only small improvements in technological performance.

Fortunately, as the new technology matures, researchers figure out how to get better performance from it. This is represented

Technology cycle a cycle that begins with the birth of a new technology and ends when that technology reaches its limits and is replaced by a newer, substantially better technology

S-curve pattern of innovation a pattern of technological innovation characterized by slow initial progress, then rapid progress, and then slow progress again as a technology matures and reaches its limits

Exhibit 7.1
S-Curves and Technological Innovation

Source: R. N. Foster, *Innovation: The Attacker's Advantage* (New York: Summitt, 1986).

by point B of the S-curve in Exhibit 7.1. The steeper slope indicates that small amounts of effort will result in significant increases in performance. At point C, the flat slope again indicates that further efforts to develop this particular technology will result in only small increases in performance. More importantly, however, point C indicates that the performance limits of that particular technology are being reached. In other words, additional significant improvements in performance are highly unlikely.

Intel's technology cycles have followed this pattern. Intel spends billions to develop new computer chips and to build new facilities to produce them. Intel has found that the technology cycle for its integrated circuits is about three years. In each three-year cycle, Intel spends billions to introduce a new chip, improves the chip by making it a little bit faster each year, and then replaces that chip at the end of the cycle with a brand-new, different chip that is substantially faster than the old chip. At first, though (point A), the billions Intel spends typically produce only small improvements in performance. But after six months to a year with a new chip design, Intel's engineering and production people typically figure out how to make the new chips much faster than they were initially (point B). Yet, despite impressive gains in performance, Intel is unable to make a particular computer chip run any faster because the chip reaches its design limits.

After a technology has reached its limits at the top of the S-curve, significant improvements in performance usually come from radical new designs or new performance-enhancing materials. In Exhibit 7.1, that new technology is represented by the second S-curve. The changeover or discontinuity between the old and new technologies is represented by the dotted line. At first, the old and new technologies will likely coexist. Eventually, however, the new technology will replace the old technology. When that happens, the old technology cycle will be complete, and a new one will have started. The changeover between newer and older computer chip designs typically takes about one year. Over time, improving existing technology (tweaking the performance of the current technology cycle), combined with replacing old technology with new technology cycles (that is, new, faster computer chip designs replacing older ones), has increased the speed of Intel's computer processors by a factor of 300. Today's super-powerful Kaby Lake processors, which provide instantaneous processing and results, have 7.2 billion transistors compared to 3.1 million transistors for 1990s 32-bit processors, 275,000 transistors for the earliest 1980s 32-bit processors, or just 4,500 transistors for the 8-bit processors, which began personal computing in the 1970s.[4]

Though the evolution of Intel's chips has been used to illustrate S-curves and technology cycles, it's important to note that technology cycles and technological innovation don't necessarily involve faster computer chips or cleaner-burning automobile engines. Remember, *technology* is simply the knowledge, tools, and techniques used to transform inputs into outputs. So a technology cycle occurs whenever there are major advances or changes in the *knowledge*, *tools*, and *techniques* of a field or discipline, whatever it may be.

For example, one of the most important technology cycles in the history of civilization occurred in 1859, when 1,300 miles of central sewer line were constructed throughout London to carry human waste to the sea more than 11 miles away. This extensive sewer system replaced the widespread practice of dumping raw sewage directly into streets, where people walked through it and where it drained into public wells that supplied drinking water. Though the relationship between raw sewage and cholera wasn't known at the time, preventing waste runoff from contaminating water supplies stopped the spread of that disease, which had killed millions of people for centuries in cities throughout the world.[5] Safe water supplies immediately translated into better health and longer life expectancies. In fact, the water you drink today is safe thanks to this technological breakthrough. So, when you think about technology cycles, don't automatically think "high tech." Instead, broaden your perspective by considering advances or changes in *any* kind of knowledge, tools, and techniques.

7-1b Innovation Streams

In Chapter 6, you learned that organizations can create *competitive advantage* for themselves if they have a *distinctive competence* that allows them to make, do, or perform something better than their competitors. A competitive advantage becomes sustainable if other companies cannot duplicate the benefits obtained from that distinctive competence. Technological innovation, however, can enable competitors to duplicate the benefits obtained from a company's distinctive advantage. It can also quickly turn a company's competitive advantage into a competitive disadvantage.

Twenty-five years ago, digital cameras replaced film-based technology. But with digital camera sales having peaked at 120 million cameras in 2008 and crashed to 24.4 million cameras in 2016, digital camera makers are losing their competitive advantage to smartphones with HD photo and video capabilities far better than basic digital cameras. Shigenobu Nagamori, CEO of Nidec, which makes electric motors used in consumer electronics, says that thanks to smartphones, we should, "assume that the inexpensive cameras are dead, just like PCs."[6] Tsugio Tsuchiya, a general manager at Tamron that makes lenses for more advanced DSLRs (digital single-lens reflex cameras), worries that, "Smartphones pose a threat not just to compact cameras but entry-level DSLRs," which start at $400 and use interchangeable lenses, such as telescoping zooms.[8] Indeed, in fall of 2016 Apple's iPhone 7 Plus incorporated two 12-megapixel sensors to work with two lenses, a 28mm for "normal" pictures and a 56mm 2x optical zoom, which makes objects look twice as big. Both of those lenses can also be zoomed further with a 10x software zoom function.[9]

Companies that want to sustain a competitive advantage must understand and protect themselves from the strategic threats of innovation. Over the long run, the best way for a company to do that is to create a stream of its own innovative ideas and products year after year. Consequently, we define **innovation streams** as patterns of innovation over time that can create sustainable competitive advantage.[10] Exhibit 7.2 shows a typical innovation consisting of a series of technology cycles. Recall that a technology cycle begins with a new technology and ends when that technology is replaced by a newer, substantially better technology. The innovation stream in Exhibit 7.2 shows three such technology cycles.

An innovation stream begins with a **techno- logical discontinuity**,

Innovation streams patterns of innovation over time that can create sustainable competitive advantage

Technological discontinuity the phase of an innovation stream in which a scientific advance or unique combination of existing technologies creates a significant breakthrough in performance or function

Exhibit 7.2
Innovation Streams: Technology Cycles over Time

Source: Adapted from M. L. Tushman, P. C. Anderson, and C. O'Reilly, "Technology Cycles, Innovation Streams and Ambidextrous Organizations: Organization Renewal Through Innovation Streams and Strategic Change," *On Managing Strategic Innovation and Change*, eds. M. L. Tushman and P. C. Anderson (New Oxford Press, 1997) 3–23.

in which a scientific advance or a unique combination of existing technologies creates a significant breakthrough in performance or function. Imagine the inefficiency of just one train running on the train track between two cities. It goes to the first, returns to the second, and so on. That, however, is exactly how elevators work, up to the top, down to the bottom, just one car per elevator shaft. **ThyssenKrupp**, maker of the Multi elevator, hopes to solve that problem by replacing the steel safety cable and pulleys used to move elevators with magnetic levitation (similar to that used on high-speed trains) that allows elevators cars to "float" to their destinations. This not only reduces the space needed for elevators by half, but without cables, multiple cars can use the same shaft, just like a subway line, and they can even move horizontally,

from one side of a building to another, all of which will allow the design of wider, uniquely shaped buildings.[11]

Technological discontinuities are followed by a **discontinuous change**, which is characterized by technological substitution and design competition. **Technological substitution** occurs when customers purchase new technologies to replace older technologies. For example, just 20 years ago, nearly all phone calls were made via hardwired landline telephones. But, according to the U.S. National Health Interview Survey, half of U.S. homes don't have landline phones.[12] That's up from 17 percent in 2008.[13] However, wireless only rates are much higher among renters (68.8%) and those 25–29 in age (72.6%) and 30–34 in age (69%).[14] Finally, with AT&T and Verizon replacing their old cable-based phone systems with wireless IP-based networks, landline phones won't even be an option within several years.[15] Indeed, Verizon's 10.5 million residential landline customers are already only a small fraction of its 112.1 million individual cellphone connections. Ironically, the growing number of free wifi hotspots may also pose a threat to wireless carriers by making it easy to use a smartphone without a mobile network. Charissa Struble canceled her contract with Verizon and switched to wifi only, saying, "I just got tired of paying an exorbitant bill."[16]

Discontinuous change is also characterized by **design competition,** in which the old technology and several different new technologies compete to establish a new technological standard or dominant design. Because of large investments in old technology and because the new and old technologies are often incompatible with each other, companies and consumers are reluctant to switch to a different technology during a design competition. For example, the telegraph was so widely used as a means of communication in the late 1800s that at first almost no one understood why telephones would be a better way to communicate. It's hard to envision today, with everyone constantly checking cell phones for email, texts, tweets, and voice mail, but as Edwin Schlossberg explains in his book *Interactive Excellence*, "People could not imagine why they would want or need to talk immediately to someone who was across town or, even more absurdly, in another town. Although people could write letters to one another, and some could

Discontinuous change the phase of a technology cycle characterized by technological substitution and design competition

Technological substitution the purchase of new technologies to replace older ones

Design competition competition between old and new technologies to establish a new technological standard or dominant design send telegraph messages, the idea of sending one's voice to another place and then instantly hearing another voice in return was simply not a model that existed in people's experience. They also did not think it was worth the money to accelerate sending or hearing a message."[17] In addition, during design competition, the older technology usually improves significantly in response to the competitive threat from the new technologies; this response also slows the changeover from older to newer technologies.

Discontinuous change is followed by the emergence of a **dominant design**, which becomes the new accepted market standard for technology.[18] Dominant designs emerge in several ways. One is critical mass, meaning that a particular technology can become the dominant design simply because most people use it, for example, Blu-ray beating out HD-DVD. Critical mass will likely determine the dominant design for wireless device charging, where instead of plugging in your device to recharge, you simply place it on top of a recharging station containing magnetic charging coils. Over the last few years, three different wireless technologies were trying to become the dominant standard: the Power Matters Alliance (PMA) backing Duracell's Powermat, a Duracell and Procter & Gamble joint venture supported by Google, AT&T, Starbucks, and McDonald's; the Alliance for Wireless Power (A4WP) and its Rezence charging mats, backed by Samsung, Broadcom, Deutsche Telekom, and Texas Instruments; and the Wireless Power Consortium (WPC) and its Qi charging mats, supported by LG Electronics, Energizer, and Nokia. However, PMA and A4WP joined forces to create a new, combined standard for wireless charging devices.[19] Again, why does this matter? It matters because the market for wireless charging, estimated at $785 million, is projected to increase to $12.6 billion by 2020. In other words, becoming the dominant standard is worth billions to the winner.[20]

Tomislav Pinter/Shutterstock.com

The best technology doesn't always become the dominant design because a number of other factors come into play. For instance, a design can become dominant if it solves a practical problem. The QWERTY keyboard (named for the top left line of letters) became the dominant design for typewriters because it slowed typists who, by typing too fast, caused mechanical typewriter keys to jam. Though computers can easily be switched to the Dvorak keyboard layout, which doubles typing speed and cuts typing errors in half, QWERTY lives on as the standard keyboard. In this instance, the QWERTY keyboard solved a problem that, with computers, is no longer relevant. Yet it remains the dominant design not because it is the best technology, but because most people learned to type that way and continue to use it.

Dominant designs can also emerge through independent standards bodies. The International Telecommunication Union (ITU) (www.itu.ch) is an independent organization that establishes standards for the communications industry. The ITU was founded in Paris in 1865 because European countries all had different telegraph systems that could not communicate with each other. Messages crossing borders had to be transcribed from one country's system before they could be coded and delivered on another. After three months of negotiations, 20 countries signed the International Telegraph Convention, which standardized equipment and instructions, enabling telegraph messages to flow seamlessly from country to country. Today, as in 1865, various standards are proposed, discussed, negotiated, and changed until agreement is reached on a final set of standards that communication industries (Internet, telephony, satellites, radio) will follow worldwide.

For example, the telecommunications industry has yet to agree on standards for 5G, or fifth-generation, service on mobile devices, but the ITU is scheduled to finalize global standards in November 2017.[21] Telecom operators are hoping for a 5G standard data-transmission speed of 10–20 gigabits per second, fast enough to download high-def movies within seconds. Another desired 5G standard is for two 5G devices to communicate with each other with a latency (or wait time) of just 4 millisecond, down from 50 milliseconds with 4G. Shorter 5G latencies would allow doctors in remote hospitals to conduct lifesaving robotics-based surgeries on patients in other locations and the operation of driverless cars. It's estimated that it will take seven years and $275 billion for U.S. wireless providers to make the change from 4G to 5G.[22]

No matter how it happens, the emergence of a dominant design is a key

Dominant design a new technological design or process that becomes the accepted market standard

THE CHALLENGES OF CLIMBING THE STACK

Why do some companies with seemingly endless resources and brainpower fail when they try to innovate? Venture capitalist Anshu Sharma says that it's because of the stack fallacy—the tendency of successful companies to overvalue what they know in one area and misjudge what they need to know to innovate in another.

Imagine technology as a layer cake of capabilities. These capabilities stack on top of each other until they ultimately reach the end user. The Minecraft app on your laptop is the top of a technology stack undergirded by layers—from the operating system, to the server, to the microprocessor, to the electricity powering the device. Just because a company is successful in one layer, say, microprocessors, doesn't mean it can jump up to a higher level, such as the operating system, and have the same success. When Google tried to move from search up to social networking, the result was the failed Google+. IBM saw its revenues shrink four years in a row as it tried to move up from hardware to services. Going down the stack, however, tends to yield positive results. Google moved down the stack by creating its own data farms and servers, which solidified the company's dominance in search. Why is climbing the technology stack so much harder than descending it? Companies don't fully understand what customers on

svetlana foote/123RF

the level above theirs actually want. However, because companies often buy products and services at the level *below* their own, they understand what customers want out of that lower layer of technology. According to Anshu Sharma, the fundamental question of who will win in a given market is, "Who understands the user better?"

Sources: C. Mims, "Why Big Companies Keep Getting Disrupted," *Wall Street Journal*, January 25, 2016, accessed March 22, 2016, http://www.wsj.com/articles/why-bigcompanies-keep-getting-disrupted-1453698061; E. Kim, "Dropbox Is Falling Prey to a Common Fallacy," *Business Insider*, March 17, 2016, accessed May 11, 2016, http://www.businessinsider.com/this-vc-says-dropboxs-recent-moves-show-why-big-companies-often-fail-to-innovate-2016-3.

event in an innovation stream. First, the emergence of a dominant design indicates that there are winners and losers. Technological innovation is both competence enhancing and competence destroying. Companies that bet on the now-dominant design usually prosper. By contrast, when companies bet on the wrong design or the old technology, they may experience **technological lockout**, which occurs when a new dominant design (that is, a significantly better technology) prevents a company from competitively selling its products or makes it difficult to do so.[23] Adobe's Flash software, which supports animation and video on web pages and ads, was once ubiquitous in website design, including video streaming platforms YouTube and Netflix. In 2010, due to resource intensity and security issues, Apple stopped supporting Flash on iPhones and iPads. By 2015, YouTube, Facebook, and Netflix had removed Flash, opting for the new HTML5 video standard.[24] As of 2017, Google's Chrome Browser will not automatically run Flash (unless users configure it).[25] Scott Symonds, managing director at AQKA advertising firm said, "It takes a kick in the pants from a major player like Google to really accelerate a switch over that could have taken years."[26] Today, Flash is now used on just 6 percent of Internet homepages.[27] Technological lockout is a serious threat, as more companies are likely to go out of business in a time of discontinuous change and changing standards than in an economic recession or slowdown.

Second, the emergence of a dominant design signals a shift from design experimentation and competition to **incremental change,** a phase in which companies innovate by lowering the cost and improving the functioning and performance of the dominant design. For example, manufacturing efficiencies enable Intel to cut the cost of its chips by one-half to two-thirds during a technology cycle, while doubling or tripling their speed. This focus on improving the dominant design continues until the next technological discontinuity occurs.

Technological lockout the inability of a company to competitively sell its products because it relies on old technology or a nondominant design

Incremental change the phase of a technology cycle in which companies innovate by lowering costs and improving the functioning and performance of the dominant technological design`

Need Innovation? Offer a Prize

Frustrated with the slow pace of innovation, companies and governments are awarding $2 billion a year in 30,000 innovation competitions. Zeniz Tata of XPrize which runs innovation competitions on behalf of major corporations and foundations says, "A prize allows for crazy open innovation to test a new idea, to take a gamble, to take a risk which you cannot do with grant money." XPrize is currently offering a $20 million prize for turning CO_2 emissions into a valuable product and $7 million to create a handheld "tricorder" which scans peoples' health for 13 conditions. Other competitions offer prizes for creating a delivery drone ($50,000) or a new use for canned tuna fish ($5,000 from a French food supplier). So, need innovation fast? Hold a competition and offer prize money!

Source: L. Chapman, "These Hackathon Hustlers Make Their Living From Corporate Coding Contests," *Bloomberg*, April 4, 2017, accessed April 5, 2017, https://www.bloomberg.com/news/features/2017-04-04/these-hackathon-hustlers-make-their-living-from-corporate-coding-contests; "What is an XPrize?" XPrize, accessed April 5, 2017, http://www.xprize.org/about.

W. Scott McGill//123RF

7-2 MANAGING INNOVATION

One consequence of technology cycles and innovation streams is that managers must be equally good at managing innovation in two very different circumstances. First, during discontinuous change, companies must find a way to anticipate and survive the technological changes that can suddenly transform industry leaders into losers and industry unknowns into powerhouses. Companies that can't manage innovation following technological discontinuities risk quick organizational decline and dissolution. Second, after a new dominant design emerges following discontinuous change, companies must manage the very different process of incremental improvement and innovation. Companies that can't manage incremental innovation slowly deteriorate as they fall further behind industry leaders.

Unfortunately, what works well when managing innovation during discontinuous change doesn't work well when managing innovation during periods of incremental change (and vice versa).

Consequently, to successfully manage innovation streams, companies need to be good at three things: 7-2a managing sources of innovation, 7-2b managing innovation during discontinuous change, and 7-2c managing innovation during incremental change.

7-2a Managing Sources of Innovation

Innovation comes from great ideas. So a starting point for managing innovation is to manage the sources of innovation, that is, where new ideas come from. One place where new ideas originate is with brilliant inventors. But only a few companies have the likes of a Thomas Edison or Alexander Graham Bell. Given that great thinkers and inventors are in short supply, what might companies do to ensure a steady flow of good ideas?

Well, when we say that innovation begins with great ideas, we're really saying that innovation begins with creativity. As we defined it at the beginning of this chapter, creativity is the production of novel and useful ideas.[28] Although companies can't command employees to be creative ("You *will* be more creative!"), they can jump-start innovation by building **creative work environments** in which workers perceive that creative thoughts and ideas are welcomed

> **Creative work environments** workplace cultures in which workers perceive that new ideas are welcomed, valued, and encouraged

Exhibit 7.3
Components of Creative Work Environments

Source: T. M. Amabile, R. Conti, H. Coon, J. Lazenby, and M. Herron, "Assessing the Work Environment for Creativity," *Academy of Management Journal* 39 (1996): 1154–1184.

and valued. As Exhibit 7.3 shows, creative work environments have six components that encourage creativity: challenging work, organizational encouragement, supervisory encouragement, work group encouragement, freedom, and a lack of organizational impediments.[29]

Work is *challenging* when it requires effort, demands attention and focus, and is perceived as important to others in the organization. According to researcher Mihaly Csikszentmihalyi (pronounced ME-high-ee CHICK-sent-me-high-ee), challenging work promotes creativity because it creates a rewarding psychological experience known as "flow." **Flow** is a psychological state of effortlessness, in which you become completely absorbed in what you're doing and time seems to fly. When flow occurs, who you are and what you're doing become one. Csikszentmihalyi first encountered flow when studying artists: "What struck me by looking at artists at work was their tremendous focus on the work, this enormous involvement, this forgetting of time and body. It wasn't justified by expectation of rewards, like, 'Aha, I'm going to sell this painting.'"[30] Csikszentmihalyi has found that chess players, rock climbers, dancers, surgeons, and athletes regularly experience flow, too. Today, achieving flow is increasingly challenging. A recent study by Professor Gloria Mark at the University of California, Irvine, found that workers focus on their computer screen an average of 1 minute 15 seconds before shifting their attention, down from 2 minutes 18 seconds in 2008. Office furniture maker **Steelcase** has designed a workstation that, according to designer Mark McKenna, encourages flow

Flow a psychological state of effortlessness, in which you become completely absorbed in what you're doing, and time seems to pass quickly

by reducing workers' latent anxiety and distractions from physical surroundings. Mark is skeptical, as her research shows that workers suffer more from digital distractions. Indeed, she found that on a daily basis, workers visited Facebook an average of 21 times and checked email 74 times.[31]

Removing distractions assists in creating an environment conducive to flow. Another key part of creating flow experiences, and thus creative work environments, is to achieve a balance between skills and task challenge. Workers become bored when they can do more than is required of them. Or, they become anxious when their skills aren't sufficient to accomplish a task. When skills and task challenges are balanced, however, flow and creativity can occur.

A creative work environment requires three kinds of encouragement: organizational, supervisory, and work group. *Organizational encouragement* of creativity occurs when management encourages risk taking and new ideas, supports and fairly evaluates new ideas, rewards and recognizes creativity, and encourages the sharing of new ideas throughout different parts of the company. GE Healthcare honors teams who have "dared to try new things and learned from failure." The idea is not to reward failure but risk taking and the sharing of new ideas. GE spokesperson Laura Paredes says that GE Healthcare employees formalized the sharing process through a short event it called "Failcon," at which people shared the lessons they learned from failed ideas and efforts.[32] Likewise, failure is also celebrated at X, Alphabet's (Alphabet is Google's new corporate name) research and development lab, which is also called the "moonshot factory." Because of the extreme difficult of X's projects, from self-driving cars to trying to get fuel from seawater, there is a strong expectation that success will be preceded by multiple failures. So like at GE Healthcare, X encourages risk taking by celebrating failure. One way that's done is by letting employees put stickers of crumpled paper (signifying that it's time to go back to the proverbial drawing board) on their laptops whenever they abandon ideas or methods that weren't working.[33] Astro Teller, X's Captain of Moonshots, says, "We keep people brave by rewarding teams that kill their projects. We see killing projects as a normal part of doing business because it means we can go faster and take on ideas that are more promising."[34]

Supervisory encouragement of creativity occurs when supervisors provide clear goals, encourage open interaction with subordinates, and actively support development teams' work and ideas. When it comes to clear goals, MIT's

Andrew McAfee says be specific. He says goals such as, "We need to figure out why so many people are leaving our site before completing a transaction," or, "How can we increase sales to women in their 30s?" are much better at generating innovations than broad goals such as, "What should our next great idea be?"[35] When **General Electric** launched the Ecomagination initiative to emphasize energy efficiency and ecologically friendly products, the company knew that clear goals were important. According to Lorraine Bolsinger, the GE executive running the program, "At a company full of engineers, a business initiative can't just be a feel-good plan. Setting hard targets made it an honest GE initiative."[36] Bolsinger's hard targets for this initiative included doubling the $700 million budget for researching clean technology, doubling the $10 million annual revenue from Ecomagination products (such as wind turbines, efficient jet engines, MRI systems, and hybrid locomotives), cutting water usage by 20 percent, and cutting greenhouse-gas emissions by 1 percent—all within five to seven years. Within five years, investment in clean technology research reached $5 billion, annual revenues from Ecomagination products hit an amazing $85 billion, water usage dropped 42 percent, and greenhouse gases dropped 31 percent.[37]

Work group encouragement occurs when group members have diverse experience, education, and backgrounds, and the group fosters mutual openness to ideas; positive, constructive challenge to ideas; and shared commitment to ideas. *Freedom* means having autonomy over one's day-to-day work and a sense of ownership and control over one's ideas. Numerous studies have indicated that creative ideas thrive under conditions of freedom.

To foster creativity, companies may also have to *remove impediments* to creativity from their work environments. Internal conflict and power struggles, rigid management structures, and a conservative bias toward the status quo can all discourage creativity. They create the perception that others in the organization will decide which ideas are acceptable and deserve support. Geography was a key impediment to creativity for **Levi Strauss**. While Levi is headquartered in San Francisco, its research and development facility used to be located 7,000 miles away in Corlu, Turkey (a facility that, incidentally, reported to a regional office in Brussels, Belgium). California-based designers regularly shipped samples back and forth and traveled to Turkey twice a year, staying for just two weeks each trip. Levi's CEO Chip Bergh said about the arrangement, "We probably spent enough on airfare to buy a 747 just to be managing product back and forth over the ocean."[38] In 2013, Levi's senior director for technical innovation Bart

Levi Strauss brought its research and development team back to its headquarters in San Francisco, California to save money and improve company-wide collaboration.

Sights moved his team from Corlu to San Francisco. The move allowed Sights's team to work closely with designers to develop a new stretch-denim jean with a more comfortable, flattering fit. The Levi's 700 line, featuring the new fabric, launched in 2015 to help Levi compete against Lululemon yoga pants, whose surging popularity had led to an 8 percent decline in sales of women's jeans.

7-2b Experiential Approach: Managing Innovation during Discontinuous Change

A study of 72 product-development projects (that is, innovation) in 36 computer companies across the United States, Europe, and Asia sheds light on how to manage innovation. Companies that succeeded in periods of discontinuous change (characterized by technological substitution and design competition, as described earlier) typically followed an experiential approach to innovation.[39] The **experiential approach to innovation** assumes that innovation is occurring within a highly uncertain environment and that the key to fast product innovation is to use intuition, flexible options, and hands-on experience to reduce uncertainty and accelerate learning and understanding. The experiential approach to innovation has five aspects: design iterations, testing, milestones, multifunctional teams, and powerful leaders.[40]

> **Experiential approach to innovation** an approach to innovation that assumes a highly uncertain environment and uses intuition, flexible options, and hands-on experience to reduce uncertainty and accelerate learning and understanding

FORGET MOONSHOTS—APPLE MAKES A BIG BANG WITH FEWER BUCKS

Tech companies are placing big bets on what they hope will be breakthrough innovations. IBM is focusing on artificial intelligence software Watson; Microsoft on augmented reality glasses HoloLens; Facebook on virtual-reality headsets and drones that will beam the Internet directly to devices; and Alphabet on animal-look-alike robots. While exciting, these outsized innovations come at a cost. Google spends roughly 15 percent of its $66 billion annual revenue on innovation, while Facebook spends 21 percent of its $12.5 billion revenue on innovation. While much of Silicon Valley is spending heavily on so-called *moonshots*, Apple takes a decidedly different, and thrifty, approach, spending only 3.5 percent of its $233 billion annual revenue on innovation in 2015. And even *that* amount is nearly double what the company spent in 2013. Apple co-founder Steve Jobs once said that "innovation has nothing to do with how many R&D dollars you have." And it seems that the company still embraces that less-is-more philosophy.

Source: A. Satariano, "Apple Gets More Bank for Its R&D Buck," *Bloomberg Business-Week*, November 30–December 6, 2015, 38–39.

Asier Romero/Shutterstock.com

An *iteration* is a repetition. So a **design iteration** is a cycle of repetition in which a company tests a prototype of a new product or service, improves on the design, and then builds and tests the improved product or service prototype. A **product prototype** is a full-scale working model that is being tested for design, function, and reliability. The long-time use of ultrasound to scan lumber for defects inspired dentist Ken Johnson to develop a prototype technology for scanning teeth. Johnson brought his prototype to business-person Steve Baird, who formed the S-Ray company to develop and test subsequent prototypes. S-Ray's ClearView Scan combines 3D-modeling software with ultrasound. Besides showing cavities and cracks, the resulting 3D image is used to design perfectly fitting crowns, veneers, braces, and retainers. Dental professor Joerd van der Meer says, "This is the kind of disruptive technology that may really change the dental world."[41]

Testing is a systematic comparison of different product designs or design iterations. Companies that want to create a new dominant design following a technological discontinuity quickly build, test, improve, and retest a series of different product prototypes. While many companies are developing driverless cars, prototype testing has occurred in controlled environments (Google's driverless car always has a driver at the wheel when on public roads—just in case) that often lack the authenticity—and chaos—of daily driving. That changed in 2015 with the opening of **M City**, a 23-acre mini-metropolis in Ann Arbor, Michigan, with 40 building facades, a bridge, a tunnel, a traffic circle, gravel roads, angled intersections, obstructed views, and even robotic jaywalkers pushing baby carriages. M City allows researchers to test what happens if, say, a red light fails, something they could never do on real city streets. Hideki Hada, an electronics systems manager at **Toyota**, said, "We would never do any dangerous or risky tests on the open road, so this will be a good place to test some of the next technology."[42]

By trying a number of very different designs or making successive improvements and changes in the same design, frequent design iterations reduce uncertainty and improve understanding. Simply put, the more prototypes you build, the more likely you are to learn what works and what doesn't. Also, when designers and engineers build a number of prototypes, they are less likely to fall in love with a particular prototype. Instead, they'll be more concerned with improving the product or technology as much as they can. Testing speeds up and improves

Design iteration a cycle of repetition in which a company tests a prototype of a new product or service, improves on that design, and then builds and tests the improved prototype

Product prototype a full-scale, working model that is being tested for design, function, and reliability

Testing the systematic comparison of different product designs or design iterations the innovation process, too. When two very different design prototypes are tested against each other, or the new design iteration is tested against the previous iteration, product design strengths and weaknesses quickly become apparent. Likewise, testing uncovers errors early in the design process when they are easiest to correct. Finally, testing accelerates learning and understanding by forcing engineers and product designers to examine hard data about product performance. When there's hard evidence that prototypes are testing well, the confidence of the design team grows. Also, personal conflict between design team members is less likely when testing focuses on hard measurements and facts rather than on personal hunches and preferences.

Milestones are formal project review points used to assess progress and performance. For example, a company that has put itself on a 12-month schedule to complete a project might schedule milestones at the three-month, six-month, and nine-month points on the schedule. By making people regularly assess what they're doing, how well they're performing, and whether they need to take corrective action, milestones provide structure to the general chaos that follows technological discontinuities. Regularly meeting milestones gives people a sense of accomplishment and can shorten the innovation process by creating a sense of urgency that keeps people on task. At X, Alphabet's research and development lab known as the "moonshot factory," project milestones must be achieved before receiving additional funding or staff. One of the key milestones is called Foundry because it requires project engineers to develop business plans for their technologies. X also pays team members "failure bonuses" for shutting down projects that won't make it to the Foundry milestone. When a team of 30 engineers shut down a two-year-old project, Astro Teller, X's Captain of Moonshots praised them publicly, saying, "Thank you! By ending their project, this team has done more to speed up innovation at X this month than any other team in this room."[43]

Multifunctional teams are work teams composed of people from different departments. Multifunctional teams accelerate learning and understanding by mixing and integrating technical, marketing, and manufacturing activities. By involving all key departments in development from the start, multifunctional teams speed innovation through early identification of new ideas or problems that would typically not have been generated or addressed until much later. Under the code name "Titan," Apple has a multifunctional project team of 500+ people working to develop the code to control the steering, breaking, safety, and navigation system for self-driving cars. The large project team is composed of software engineers developing apps to link vision sensors to driving systems, regulatory

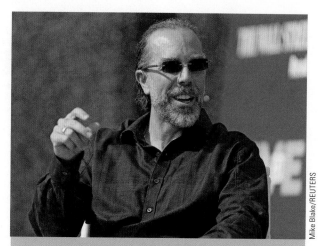

Astro Teller, "Captain of Moonshots" at X, rewards employees for quick failures which speed up overall innovation.

Mike Blake/REUTERS

specialists with experience in auto industry rules, and coding specialists hired away from QNX, which develops automotive "infotainment system" software.[44]

Powerful leaders provide the vision, discipline, and motivation to keep the innovation process focused, on time, and on target. Powerful leaders are able to get resources when they are needed, are typically more experienced, have high status in the company, and are held directly responsible for the products' success or failure. On average, powerful leaders can get innovation-related projects done nine months faster than leaders with little power or influence.

7-2c Compression Approach: Managing Innovation during Incremental Change

Whereas the experiential approach is used to manage innovation in highly uncertain environments during periods of discontinuous change, the compression approach is used to manage innovation in more certain environments during periods of incremental change. Whereas the goals of the experiential approach are significant improvements in performance and the establishment of a *new* dominant design, the goals of the compression approach are lower costs and incremental improvements in the performance and function of the *existing* dominant design.

Milestones formal project review points used to assess progress and performance

Multifunctional teams work teams composed of people from different departments

The general strategies in each approach are different, too. With the experiential approach, the general strategy is to build something new, different, and substantially better. Because there's so much uncertainty—no one knows which technology will become the market leader—companies adopt a winner-take-all approach by trying to create the market-leading, dominant design. With the compression approach, the general strategy is to compress the time and steps needed to bring about small, consistent improvements in performance and functionality. Because a dominant technology design already exists, the general strategy is to continue improving the existing technology as rapidly as possible. For example, after using an experiential approach and investing $50 billion to develop its groundbreaking 787 Dreamliner passenger jet, Boeing is now switching to a compression approach to innovation. Chief Operating Officer Dennis Muilenburg said, "In the past, we may have said our best engineers are working on the new thing. Now we want our best engineers working on innovative reuse."[45] Likewise, Ray Conner, CEO of Boeing's commercial airplane unit said, "It's not to say you don't innovate [but] how do you innovate to make it more producible? How do you innovate to make it more reliable?"[46]

In short, a **compression approach to innovation** assumes that innovation is a predictable process, that incremental innovation can be planned using a series of steps, and that compressing the time it takes to complete those steps can speed up innovation. The compression approach to innovation has five aspects: planning, supplier involvement, shortening the time of individual steps, overlapping steps, and multifunctional teams.[47]

In Chapter 5, *planning* was defined as choosing a goal and a method or strategy to achieve that goal. When *planning for incremental innovation*, the goal is to squeeze or compress development time as much as possible, and the general strategy is to create a series of planned steps to accomplish that goal. Planning for incremental innovation helps avoid unnecessary steps and enables developers to sequence steps in the right order to avoid wasted time and delays between steps. Planning also reduces misunderstandings and improves coordination.

Mircea Maties/123RF

Most planning for incremental innovation is based on the idea of generational change. **Generational change** occurs when incremental improvements are made to a dominant technological design such that the improved version of the technology is fully backward compatible with the older version.[48] Most computers, for instance, have USB (universal serial bus) input slots to connect and power USB thumb drives, monitors, or external hard drives used for backup storage. USB 3.1 (Gen 2), the latest USB standard, can transfer more than 10 Gbps (gigabytes per second), compared to USB 3.0 devices, which operate at 5 Gbps, or USB 2.0 devices, which operate at roughly 1/2 Gbps.[49] What happens if you buy a new computer with USB 3.1 slots, but still own a USB 3.0 external hard drive and a USB 2.0 thumb drive? Both will work, but at slower speeds, because they are backward compatible with USB 3.1.

Because the compression approach assumes that innovation can follow a series of preplanned steps, one of the ways to shorten development time is *supplier involvement*. Delegating some of the preplanned steps in the innovation process to outside suppliers reduces the amount of work that internal development teams must do. Plus, suppliers provide an alternative source of ideas and expertise that can lead to better designs. Even though **Apple** develops most of its innovations in house, it does rely on suppliers for innovation as well. The prospect of landing a large contract and supplying a crucial component to a company like Apple drives suppliers to build out their own research and development capabilities. Professor Ram Mudambi believes that Apple's size and component budget ($29.5 billion in 2016) motivate suppliers to pitch their biggest breakthroughs to the company: "Suppliers are racing with each other to get Apple's business, and part of the racing they are doing is spending more on R&D."[50]

Another way to shorten development time is simply to *shorten the time of individual steps* in the innovation process. Indian cellphone manufacturer **Micromax Informatics** does this by customizing off-the-shelf hardware rather than developing it from scratch. This allows the company to keep up with consumer trends by unveiling a new model every few weeks. In fact, while Apple typically releases two new phones a year and China's Xiaomi releases four, Micromax releases more than 30 new models every year. Because it uses existing hardware imported from China, Micromax only needs three to four months to take a phone from concept to store shelves. Indeed, only four months after deciding

Compression approach to innovation an approach to innovation that assumes that incremental innovation can be planned using a series of steps and that compressing those steps can speed innovation

Generational change change based on incremental improvements to a dominant technological design such that the improved technology is fully backward compatible with the older technology it wanted to launch a handset that could function seamlessly across India's 20 official languages, Micromax released the Unite. Priced at just $110, the 2017 model, the Unite 4 Plus, allows users to communicate using 21 different scripts, including Gujarati, Marathi, and Tamil, as well as English and Hindi. The Unite 4 Plus, which has a fingerprint sensor, a 5-inch HD screen, 4G LTE upload and download speeds, and an 8MP rear camera and a 5MP front camera, is just one of dozens of Micromax cellphones designated for release in 2017. Others include models built on Windows, models with six-inch screens for doodling, models that boast long battery life, no-frills models, and more. According to Micromax CEO Vineet Taneja, "We turn around faster than any other company."[51]

In a sequential design process, each step must be completed before the next step begins. But sometimes multiple development steps can be performed at the same time. *Overlapping steps* shorten the development process by reducing delays or waiting time between steps.

iStock.com/Ermingut

7-3 ORGANIZATIONAL DECLINE: THE RISK OF NOT CHANGING

Founded in 1921 in Boston as a store for ham radio enthusiasts, **RadioShack** grew to more than 7,000 stores by stocking a wide range of components used to build or repair various electronic devices. In fact, before starting **Apple**, co-founders Steve Jobs and Steve Wozniak bought parts at RadioShack to make a "blue box" device that illegally switched on free long distance calling (which mattered when long distance calls were 40 cents a minute).[52] RadioShack's growth was first propelled by hobbyists (nerds like Jobs and Wozniak), then by battery sales, computers, and cell phones. The TRS-80, introduced in 1977, was one of the first broadly popular PCs. Following computers, which it stopped making in 1993, its next growth cycle came from cell phones. The phone companies at first relied on RadioShack to sign up and service customers, but this changed as they eventually established their own retail stores. RadioShack moved

away from its focus on serving technology power users and hobbyists by opening unsuccessful big-box electronics and appliance stores, such as Computer City and Incredible Universe, on which it lost hundreds of millions of dollars in the 1990s. Outmaneuvered by BestBuy in brick-and-mortar retailing, and never really competitive on the Web, RadioShack filed for bankruptcy in spring 2015 after losing $936 million since 2011, the last year it was profitable.[53]

Businesses operate in a constantly changing environment. Recognizing and adapting to internal and external changes can mean the difference between continued success and going out of business. Companies that fail to change run the risk of organizational decline.[54] **Organizational decline** occurs when companies don't anticipate, recognize, neutralize, or adapt to the internal or external pressures that threaten their survival. CEO of **Netflix** Reed Hastings, whose company successfully bridged from its DVD-by-mail business to Internet streaming, said, "Most companies that are great at something—AOL dial-up or Borders bookstores—do not become great at new things people want (streaming for us) because they are afraid to hurt their initial business. Eventually, these companies realize their error of not focusing enough on the new thing, and then the company fights desperately and hopelessly to recover. Companies rarely die from moving too fast, and they frequently die from moving too slowly."[55] In other words, decline occurs when organizations don't recognize the need for change. There are five stages of organizational decline: blinded, inaction, faulty action, crisis, and dissolution.

In the *blinded stage*, decline begins because key managers fail to recognize the internal or external changes that will harm their organizations. This blindness may be due to a simple lack of awareness about changes or an inability to understand their significance. It may also come from the overconfidence that can develop when a company has been successful.

In the *inaction stage*, as organizational performance problems become more visible, management may recognize the need to change but still take no action. The managers may be waiting to see if the problems will correct themselves. Or, they may

> **Organizational decline** a large decrease in organizational performance that occurs when companies don't anticipate, recognize, neutralize, or adapt to the internal or external pressures that threaten their survival

"RadioShacks filed for bankruptcy in 2015 and was acquired by its largest lender, hedge fund, Standard General." And then filed for bankruptcy again in 2017!

find it difficult to change the practices and policies that previously led to success. Possibly, too, they wrongly assume that they can easily correct the problems, so they don't feel the situation is urgent.

In the *faulty action stage*, faced with rising costs and decreasing profits and market share, management will announce belt-tightening plans designed to cut costs, increase efficiency, and restore profits. In other words, rather than recognizing the need for fundamental changes, managers assume that if they just run a tighter ship, company performance will return to previous levels.

In the *crisis stage*, bankruptcy or dissolution (breaking up the company and selling its parts) is likely to occur unless the company completely reorganizes the way it does business. At this point, however, companies typically lack the resources to fully change how they run their businesses. Cutbacks and layoffs will have reduced the level of talent among employees. Furthermore, talented managers who were savvy enough to see the crisis coming will have found jobs with other companies, often with competitors. At this stage, hoping to generate enough cash to fund a much-needed redesign of its remaining stores, RadioShack took out $835 million in loans and closed 1,100 stores, However, during the 2014 holiday season, its corporate finances amounted to the equivalent of just $15,000 cash per store.[56]

In the *dissolution stage*, after failing to make the changes needed to sustain the organization, the company is dissolved through bankruptcy proceedings or by selling assets to pay suppliers, banks, and creditors. At this point, a new CEO may be brought in to oversee the closing of stores, offices, and manufacturing facilities; the final layoff of managers and employees; and the sale of assets. It is important to note that decline is reversible at each of the first four stages and that not all companies in decline reach final dissolution. RadioShack declared bankruptcy in February 2015, and was acquired by its largest lender, hedge fund Standard General. Initially, 1,700 stores remained open, with 1,400 featuring Sprint/RadioShack signage and branding. Sprint used one-third of each store to sell and display Sprint mobile phones and related products.[57] By 2017, Radio Shack filed for bankruptcy again, laying off headquarters staff, closing 200 stores, and "evaluating options" on the remaining stores.[58]

7-4 MANAGING CHANGE

According to social psychologist Kurt Lewin, change is a function of the forces that promote change and the opposing forces that slow or resist change.[59] **Change forces** lead to differences in the form, quality, or condition of an organization over time. In contrast to change forces, **resistance forces** support the status quo, that is, the existing conditions in an organization. Change is difficult under any circumstances. Production schedules on movie sets have changed dramatically as a result of directors having switched from film to digital recordings. When shooting with film, a new film reel has to be loaded every ten minutes, creating frequent breaks when stars would return to their trailers to read, rehearse, or rest. Because there are no film reels with digital recording, shooting can occur continuously, significantly reducing film production time and costs. A number of famous actors, however, don't like the change. Actor Robert Downey Jr. complained, "I can't work like this. I never get to go to my trailer … I'm on my feet 14 hours a day. I'm shooting all the time."[60]

Resistance to change is caused by self-interest, misunderstanding and distrust, and a general intolerance for change.[61] People resist change out of *self-interest* because they fear that change will cost or deprive them of something they value. Resistance might stem from a fear that the changes will result in a loss of pay, power, responsibility, or even perhaps one's job.

Change forces forces that produce differences in the form, quality, or condition of an organization over time.

Resistance forces forces that support the existing conditions in organizations.

Resistance to change opposition to change resulting from self-interest, misunderstanding and distrust, and a general intolerance for change

People also resist change because of *misunderstanding and distrust*; they don't understand the change or the reasons for it, or they distrust the people—typically management—behind the change. Resistance isn't always visible at first. In fact, some of the strongest resisters may initially support the changes in public, nodding and smiling their agreement, but then ignore the changes in private and do their jobs as they always have. Management consultant Michael Hammer calls this deadly form of resistance the "Kiss of Yes."[62]

Resistance may also come from a generally low tolerance for change. Some people are simply less capable of handling change than others. People with a *low tolerance for change* feel threatened by the uncertainty associated with change and worry that they won't be able to learn the new skills and behaviors needed to successfully negotiate change in their companies.

Because resistance to change is inevitable, successful change efforts require careful management.

*In this section, you will learn about **7-4a managing resistance to change, 7-4b what not to do when leading organizational change,** and **7-4c different change tools and techniques.***

7-4a Managing Resistance to Change

According to psychologist Kurt Lewin, managing organizational change is a basic process of unfreezing, change intervention, and refreezing. **Unfreezing** is getting the people affected by change to believe that change is needed. During the **change intervention** itself, workers and managers change their behavior and work practices. **Refreezing** is supporting and reinforcing the new changes so that they stick.

Resistance to change is an example of frozen behavior. Given the choice between changing and not changing, most people would rather not change. Because resistance to change is natural and inevitable, managers need to unfreeze resistance to change to create successful change programs. The following methods can be used to manage resistance to change: education and communication, participation, negotiation, top-management support, and coercion.[63]

When resistance to change is based on insufficient, incorrect, or misleading information, managers should *educate* employees about the need for change and *communicate* change-related information to them. Managers must also supply the information, funding, or other support employees need to make changes. For example, resistance to change can be particularly strong when one

The Kiss of Yes occurs when some of the strongest resisters support changes in public, but then ignore them in private.

Roman Märzinger/AGE Fotostock

company buys another company. This is because one company in the merger usually has a higher status due to its size or its higher profitability or the fact that it is the acquiring company. These status differences are important to managers and employees, particularly if they're in the lower-status company, who worry about retaining their jobs or influence after the merger. That fear or concern can greatly increase resistance to change.[64] When PMA Companies, an insurance risk management firm, was acquired by Old Republic International, an insurance company, PMA's CEO Vince Donnelly communicated frequently with PMA's employees about the merger. Four months before the acquisition became official, he traveled to each of the company's 20 offices and gave employees a detailed description of how their day-to-day operations would change and why the acquisition was good for everyone involved. He also held quarterly

Unfreezing getting the people affected by change to believe that change is needed

Change intervention the process used to get workers and managers to change their behaviors and work practices

Refreezing supporting and reinforcing new changes so that they stick updates with employees via videoconference. Said Donnelly, "It's not just one and done. Communication needs to be continual. You need to continue to reinforce the messages that you want people to internalize. So you need to understand that communication is a continuous process and not something that you do just once." He went on to say, "What you are asking people to do is trust you, [trust] that you have the best interest of everybody in mind, and [trust that] when there is news to tell, you're going to hear it directly from the CEO—good, bad, or indifferent."[65]

Another way to reduce resistance to change is to have those affected by the change *participate in planning and implementing the change process*. Employees who participate have a better understanding of the change and the need for it. Furthermore, employee concerns about change can be addressed as they occur if employees participate in the planning and implementation process. It took Kaiser Permanente, a large healthcare provider, five years to transition from paper records to digital medical records and telemedicine services (for patients in remote locations). CEO Bernard Tyson said, "The biggest problem was our physicians had a bond with the patient. It was the personal touch, the personal voice, the personal phone call. The physician is the advocate of the patient. Then you have the nurses and others. And they had a way of working. There was a lot of concern about breaking that trusted relationship, a lot of questions as to whether it would really work in the health-care industry. It took a lot of buy-in, and conversations and engaging the physicians in particular but the other health-care workers, too. So, ultimately, it wasn't done to them. They were a part of it. But I would not kid you. It was extremely difficult."[66]

Employees are also less likely to resist change if they are allowed *to discuss and agree on who will do what* after change occurs. Craig Durosko, founder of **Sun Design Home Remodeling Specialists** in Burke, Virginia, says, "Unfortunately, the way most employees find out when a company isn't doing well is when their paychecks bounce or when they show up and the front doors are locked. When changes go down and they don't know about it, they can't do anything about it." So, when Sun Design's business shrank dramatically during the recession, Durosko explained the problem, sharing detailed financial information, and then asked his employees what could be done to minimize losses. He says, "No less than 20 employees gave line-by-line specific *things they could do* to make a difference.[67]

Resistance to change also decreases when change efforts receive *significant managerial support*.

Coercion the use of formal power and authority to force others to change

Managers must do more than talk about the importance of change, though. They must provide the training, resources, and autonomy needed to make change happen. Finally, resistance to change can be managed through **coercion,** or the use of formal power and authority to force others to change. Because of the intense negative reactions it can create (for example, fear, stress, resentment, sabotage of company products), coercion should be used only when a crisis exists or when all other attempts to reduce resistance to change have failed.

7-4b What Not to Do When Leading Change

So far, you've learned about the basic change process (unfreezing, change intervention, refreezing) and managing resistance to change. Harvard Business School professor John Kotter argues that knowing what *not* to do is just as important as knowing what to do when it comes to achieving successful organizational change.[68]

Managers commonly make predictable errors when they lead change. The first two errors occur during the unfreezing phase, when managers try to get the people affected by change to believe that change is really needed. The first and potentially most serious error is *not establishing a great enough sense of urgency*. In fact, Kotter estimates that more than half of all change efforts fail because the people affected are not convinced that change is necessary. People will feel a greater sense of urgency if a leader in the company makes a public, candid assessment of the company's problems and weaknesses.

In 1973, Nordstrom launched Nordstrom Rack, a lower-cost outlet version of its nameplate store. Neiman Marcus Last Call, Filene's Basement, and Saks Off Fifth quickly followed.[69] While Macy's currently accounts for 40 percent of U.S. department store sales, it made a critical mistake by debating what to do about off-price stores for six years before finally opening its own version, Macy's Backstage, in 2015. While the company deliberated, off-price behemoth TJX—parent company of T.J.Maxx, Marshalls, and Homegoods—shot past it on three key financial metrics. TJX has been more profitable than Macy's since 2008 and has had higher sales revenue since 2014. Since 2005, Macy's market capitalization has shrunk by $5 billion, while TJX's has risen by $35 billion, making it three times larger than Macy's. According to researcher Craig Johnson, "Macy's has been so successful for so long with its core format that it blinded them to the ways that consumer shopping behaviors were changing . . . The fix isn't going to happen overnight."[70]

The second mistake that occurs in the unfreezing process is *not creating a powerful enough coalition*. Change often starts with one or two people. But change has to be supported by a critical and growing group of people to build enough momentum to change an entire department, division, or company. Besides top management, Kotter recommends that key employees, managers, board members, customers, and even union leaders be members of a *core change coalition* that guides and supports organizational change. For GE's Ecomagination initiative, that core change coalition included a group of engineers who were responsible for finding ways to achieve the company's overall goals of reducing emissions and water usage while increasing energy efficiency. Initiative leader Lorraine Bolsinger said, "We started doing what we called 'treasure hunts' [to] see if there were ways to use our own products at our own facilities to improve efficiency."[71] Many of these treasure hunts paid off. For example, one team at a jet engine testing facility figured out how to save 3 million gallons of jet fuel per year by moving engine tests indoors, reducing the run times needed for accurate testing, and better calculating the placement of weights used to balance the hundreds of fans on jet engines, resulting in a smoother, easier-turning, more efficient jet engine.[72]

The next four errors that managers make occur during the change phase, when a change intervention is used to try to get workers and managers to change their behavior and work practices. *Lacking a vision* for change is a significant error at this point. As you learned in Chapter 5, a *vision* (defined as a *purpose statement* in Chapter 5) is a statement of a company's purpose or reason for existing. A vision for change makes clear where a company or department is headed and why the change is occurring. Change efforts that lack vision tend to be confused, chaotic, and contradictory. By contrast, change efforts guided by visions are clear, are easy to understand, and can be effectively explained in five minutes or less.

Undercommunicating the vision by a factor of ten is another mistake in the change phase. According to Kotter, companies mistakenly hold just one meeting to announce the vision. Or, if the new vision receives heavy emphasis in executive speeches or company newsletters, senior management then undercuts the vision by behaving in ways contrary to it. Successful communication of the vision requires that top managers link everything the company does to the new vision and that they "walk the talk" by behaving in ways consistent with the vision. Furthermore, even companies that begin change with a clear vision sometimes make the mistake of *not removing obstacles to the new vision.* They leave formidable barriers to change in place by failing to redesign jobs, pay plans, and technology to support the new way of doing things. Chapter 1 discussed how CEO Mark Fields was moving Ford Motor Company toward its new "Smart Mobility" vision as an "auto and mobility"

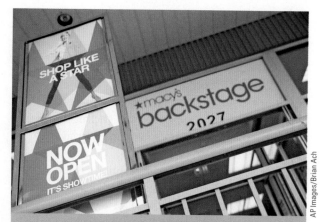

Macy's executives debated off-price stores for six years before finally opening Macy's Backstage in 2015.

company.[73] "Smart Mobility," said Fields, "is our plan to use innovation to take Ford to the next level in connectivity, mobility, autonomous vehicles, the customer experience, and big data."[74] Ford, however, is clearly *avoiding* the mistake of undercommunicating and undercutting this vision. Indeed, Ford's commitment to "Smart Mobility" is evident in the 25 mobility experiments it's conducting, such as in London and Shanghai, where plug-in devices used to track live parking and traffic data are linked to smartphone apps helping drivers find and pay for the nearest available parking space.[75] Likewise, Ford spent $1 billion to become the majority owner in Argo AI, a startup founded by executives who formerly managed self-driving car teams at Uber and Google. Ford will combine its software engineers with Argo AI's to develop the virtual driver system for Ford's self-driving cars. Finally, Ford's board of director's changed CEO Field's financial incentives to reward him for eventually creating a new division, Ford Smart Mobility LLC.[76]

Another error in the change phase is *not systematically planning for and creating short-term wins*. Most people don't have the discipline and patience to wait two years to see if the new change effort works. Change is threatening and uncomfortable, so people need to see an immediate payoff if they are to continue to support it. Kotter recommends that managers create short-term wins by actively picking people and projects that are likely to work extremely well early in the change process.

The last two errors that managers make occur during the refreezing phase, when attempts are made to support and reinforce changes so that they stick. *Declaring victory too soon* is a tempting mistake in the refreezing phase. Managers typically declare victory right after the first large-scale success in the change process. Declaring success too early has the same effect as draining the gasoline out of a car: It stops change efforts dead in their tracks. With success declared, supporters of the change process stop pushing to make change happen. After all, why push when success has been achieved? Rather than declaring victory, managers should use the momentum from short-term wins to push for even bigger or faster changes. This maintains urgency and prevents change supporters from slacking off before the changes are frozen into the company's culture.

The last mistake that managers make is *not anchoring changes in the corporation's culture*. An *organization's culture* is the set of key values, beliefs, and attitudes shared by organizational members that determines the accepted way of doing things in a company. As you learned in Chapter 3, changing cultures is extremely difficult and slow. According to Kotter, two things help anchor changes in a corporation's culture. The first is directly showing people that the changes have actually improved performance. The second is to make sure that the people who get promoted fit the new culture. If they don't, it's a clear sign that the changes were only temporary.

Sara De Marco/Shutterstock.com

7-4c Change Tools and Techniques

Imagine that your boss came to you and said, "All right, genius, you wanted it. You're in charge of turning around the division." Where would you begin? How would you encourage change-resistant managers to change? What would you do to include others in the change process? How would you get the change process off to a quick start? Finally, what approach would you use to promote long-term effectiveness and performance? Results-driven change, the General Electric fastworks approach and organizational development are different change tools and techniques that can be used to address these issues.

One of the reasons that organizational change efforts fail is that they are activity oriented rather than results oriented. In other words, they focus primarily on changing company procedures, management philosophy, or employee behavior. Typically, there is much buildup and preparation as consultants are brought in, presentations are made, books are read, and employees and managers are trained. There's a tremendous emphasis on doing things the new way. But, with all the focus on "doing," almost no attention is paid to *results*, to seeing if all this activity has actually made a difference.

By contrast, **results-driven change** supplants the emphasis on activity with a laser-like focus on quickly measuring and improving results.[77] At Zara, the Spain-based retailer known for "fast fashion," 350 designers send brand new styles to stores and Zara.com twice a week. Because designers get daily data on what's selling, they can react to fashion trends by going from concept to ready-for-sale clothing in just three weeks. If daily reports show surging demand for particular products, Zara airlifts them (the most expensive way to ship) to get them in stores as fast as possible.[78] Furthermore, retailers don't need anyone's approval to make changes. They decide on the spot. Ann Critchlow, an analyst at Société Générale, says, "The root of Inditex's success [Inditex own's Zara] is its predominantly short lead time, which gives a greater level of newness to its collections."[79]

Another advantage of results-driven change is that managers introduce changes in procedures, philosophy, or behavior only if they are likely to improve measured performance. In other words, managers and workers actually test to see if changes make a difference. A third advantage of results-driven change is that quick, visible improvements motivate employees to continue to make additional changes to improve measured performance. Exhibit 7.4 describes the basic steps of results-driven change.

General Electric fastworks approach is a special kind of results-driven change. With fastworks, companies improve results in an uncertain business environment by quickly experimenting with new ideas to solve customer problems and learn from repeated tests and improvements. Because things change quickly in uncertain business environments, the idea is to move as fast, if not faster than competitors. For example, it normally takes GE Healthcare two to four years to bring a new

Results-driven change change created quickly by focusing on the measurement and improvement of results

General Electric fastworks quickly experimenting with new ideas to solve customer problems and learn from repeated tests and improvements

Exhibit 7.4
How to Create a Results-Driven Change Program

1. Set measurable, short-term goals to improve performance.
2. Make sure your action steps are likely to improve measured performance.
3. Stress the importance of immediate improvements.
4. Solicit help from consultants and staffers to achieve quick improvements in performance.
5. Test action steps to see if they actually yield improvements. If they don't, discard them and establish new ones.
6. Use resources you have or that can be easily acquired. It doesn't take much.

Source: R. H. Schaffer and H. A. Thomson, "Successful Change Programs Begin with Results," *Harvard Business Review on Change* (Boston: Harvard Business School Press, 1998), 189–213.

Exhibit 7.5
General Steps for Organizational Development Interventions

1. Entry	A problem is discovered, and the need for change becomes apparent. A search begins for someone to deal with the problem and facilitate change.
2. Startup	A change agent enters the picture and works to clarify the problem and gain commitment to a change effort.
3. Assessment & feedback	The change agent gathers information about the problem and provides feedback about it to decision makers and those affected by it.
4. Action planning	The change agent works with decision makers to develop an action plan.
5. Intervention	The action plan, or organizational development intervention, is carried out.
6. Evaluation	The change agent helps decision makers assess the effectiveness of the intervention.
7. Adoption	Organizational members accept ownership and responsibility for the change, which is then carried out through the entire organization.
8. Separation	The change agent leaves the organization after first ensuring that the change intervention will continue to work.

Source: W. J. Rothwell, R. Sullivan, and G. M. McLean, *Practicing Organizational Development: A Guide for Consultants* (San Diego: Pfeiffer & Co., 1995).

PET/CT scanner to market. But because of customer feedback under fastworks, it cut development time in half.[80]

Fastworks also focuses on solving customer problems. Viv Goldstein, director of innovation acceleration at GE Corporate, says, "We don't assume that we know what features create the best solution. We start speaking to customers much earlier in the cycle so we can test solutions quickly and inexpensively… It's about achieving customer outcomes, as opposed to selling products."[81]

Finally, repeated testing and improvements depend on putting a minimum viable product in front of customers. When GE Appliances was redesigning its high-end Monogram refrigerators, it listened to feedback from home designers and then built a new refrigerator (that is, a minimum viable product). Customers disliked it because the stainless steel was too dark. They fixed that. Next, customers disliked the lighting. GE fixed that. After 6 prototypes, GE built 75 versions for broader testing and feedback. Five versions later, it was ready to begin manufacturing. Fastworks resulted in a refrigerator developed in half the time, for half the cost, and which is selling twice as fast as the typical new model.[82]

Organizational development is a philosophy and collection of planned change interventions designed to improve an organization's long-term health and performance. Organizational development takes a long-range approach to change; assumes that top-management support is necessary for change to succeed; creates change by educating workers and managers to change ideas, beliefs, and behaviors so that problems can be solved in new ways; and emphasizes employee participation in diagnosing, solving, and evaluating problems.[83] As shown in Exhibit 7.5, organizational development interventions begin with the recognition of a problem. Then, the company designates a **change agent** to be formally in charge of guiding the change effort. This person can be someone from within the company or a professional consultant. The change agent clarifies the problem, gathers information, works with decision makers to create and implement an action plan, helps to evaluate the plan's effectiveness, implements the plan throughout the company, and then leaves (if from outside the company) after making sure the change intervention will continue to work.

Organizational development a philosophy and collection of planned change interventions designed to improve an organization's long-term health and performance

Change agent the person formally in charge of guiding a change effort

Exhibit 7.6
Different Kinds of Organizational Development Interventions

Large-System Interventions

Sociotechnical systems	An intervention designed to improve how well employees use and adjust to the work technology used in an organization.
Survey feedback	An intervention that uses surveys to collect information from the members of the system, reports the results of that survey to the members, and then uses those results to develop action plans for improvement.

Small-Group Interventions

Team building	An intervention designed to increase the cohesion and cooperation of work group members.
Unit goal setting	An intervention designed to help a work group establish short- and long-term goals.

Person-Focused Interventions

Counseling/coaching	An intervention designed so that a formal helper or coach listens to managers or employees and advises them on how to deal with work or interpersonal problems.
Training	An intervention designed to provide individuals with the knowledge, skills, or attitudes they need to become more effective at their jobs.

Source: W. J. Rothwell, R. Sullivan, and G. M. McLean, *Practicing Organizational Development: A Guide for Consultants* (San Diego: Pfeiffer & Co., 1995).

Organizational development interventions are aimed at changing large systems, small groups, or people.[84] More specifically, the purpose of *large-system interventions* is to change the character and performance of an organization, business unit, or department. *Small-group intervention* focuses on assessing how a group functions and helping it work more effectively to accomplish its goals. *Person-focused intervention* is intended to increase interpersonal effectiveness by helping people to become aware of their attitudes and behaviors and to acquire new skills and knowledge. Exhibit 7.6 describes the most frequently used organizational development interventions for large systems, small groups, and people.

STUDY TOOLS 7

LOCATED IN TEXTBOOK
☐ Rip out and review chapter review card.

LOCATED AT WWW.CENGAGEBRAIN.COM
☐ Gain unique perspectives on key concepts with new 4LTR concept videos in the e-book.

☐ Increase your comprehension with Aplia for MGMT11.

☐ Complete interactive content within the e-book.

8 | Global Management

After you finish this chapter, go to **PAGE 183** for **STUDY TOOLS**

LEARNING OUTCOMES

8-1 Discuss the impact of global business and the trade rules and agreements that govern it.

8-2 Explain why companies choose to standardize or adapt their business procedures.

8-3 Explain the different ways that companies can organize to do business globally.

8-4 Explain how to find a favorable business climate.

8-5 Discuss the importance of identifying and adapting to cultural differences.

8-6 Explain how to successfully prepare workers for international assignments.

8-1 GLOBAL BUSINESS, TRADE RULES, AND TRADE AGREEMENTS

Business is buying and selling of the goods or services. Buying this textbook was a business transaction. So was selling your first car and getting paid for babysitting or for mowing lawns. **Global business** is the buying and selling of goods and services by people from different countries. The Apple iPhone sitting on my desk while writing this chapter was purchased from an Apple Store in Indiana. The components of that iPhone, the touch screen, camera lenses, microphone, and the hard drive for storage, were made by 200 suppliers around the world. Once assembled in China, my iPhone was flown by UPS or FedEx to Anchorage, Alaska (for refueling), before arriving in Louisville, Kentucky, where it was sorted for truck delivery to the Apple Store.[1]

Global business the buying and selling of goods and services by people from different countries

Global business presents its own set of challenges for managers. How can you be sure that the way you run your business in one country is the right way to run that business in another? This chapter discusses how organizations answer that question. We will start by examining global business in two ways: first exploring its impact on U.S. businesses and then reviewing the basic rules and agreements that govern global trade. Next, we will examine how and when companies go global by examining the trade-off between consistency and adaptation and discussing how to organize a global company. Finally, we will look at how companies decide where to expand globally, including finding the best business climate, adapting to cultural differences, and better preparing employees for international assignments.

Beyond the earlier iPhone example, if you want other demonstrations of the impact of global business, look at the tag on your shirt, the inside of your shoes, and the inside of your digital camera (take out your battery). Chances are, all of these items were made in different places around the world. As I write this, my shirt, shoes,

and digital camera were made in Thailand, China, and Korea. Where were yours made?

*Let's learn more about **8-1a the impact of global business, 8-1b how tariff and nontariff trade barriers have historically restricted global business, 8-1c how today global and regional trade agreements are reducing those trade barriers worldwide**, and **8-1d how consumers are responding to those changes in trade rules and agreements.***

8-1a The Impact of Global Business

Multinational corporations (MNCs) are corporations that own businesses in two or more countries. Motorcycle maker Harley-Davidson is headquartered in Milwaukee, Wisconsin, and has U.S. assembly plants in York, Pennsylvania, and Kansas City, Missouri. But with manufacturing plants in Brazil and India and regional headquarters in

> **Multinational corporation**
> a corporation that owns businesses in two or more countries

England and Singapore, Harley-Davidson, a brand considered to be quintessentially American, is a multinational corporation. While 38 percent of its 2017 sales are outside the United States, up from 22 percent in 2007, Harley-Davidson's goal is to have international sales account for half of its revenues.[2] Harley-Davidson isn't unique. There are 30,000-plus MNCs around the world. The 100 largest MNCs, on average, have 500 foreign facilities/offices located in 50 different countries![3]

Another way to appreciate the impact of global business is by considering direct foreign investment. **Direct foreign investment** occurs when a company builds a new business or buys an existing business in a foreign country. Luxembourg conglomerate JAB Holding Company made a direct foreign investment in the United States when it paid $7.5 billion for Panera restaurants.[4]

Of course, companies from many other countries also own businesses in the United States. As Exhibit 8.1 shows, companies from the United Kingdom, Japan, the Netherlands, Canada, Luxembourg, Switzerland, Germany, and France have the largest direct foreign investment in the United States. Overall, foreign companies invest more than $2.9 trillion a year to do business in the United States.

But direct foreign investment in the United States is only half the picture. U.S. companies also have made large direct foreign investments in countries throughout the world. San Diego-based Qualcomm, which designs and manufacturers smartphone computer chips, is paying $38.5 billion to buy NXP Semiconductors, a Netherlands-based manufacturer of chips used in cars, smartwatches, secure credit cards and appliances. Analyst Mark Hung commented that Qualcomm "is trying to diversify away from smartphones."[5] Qualcomm CEO Steve Mollenkopf said, "It's no secret that we've been looking around. If you look at our growth strategy, it's to grow into adjacent markets at the time that they are being disrupted by the technology of mobile."[6]

As Exhibit 8.2 shows, U.S. companies have made their largest direct foreign investments in the Netherlands, the United Kingdom, Luxembourg, Canada, and Ireland. Overall, U.S. companies invest more than $4.9 trillion a year to do business in other countries.

So, whether foreign companies invest in the United States or U.S. companies invest abroad, direct foreign investment is an increasingly important and common method of conducting global business.

Direct foreign investment
a method of investment in which a company builds a new business or buys an existing business in a foreign country

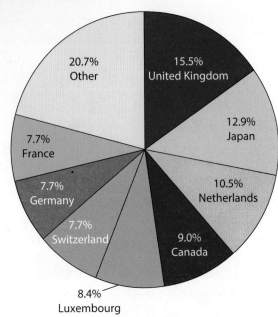

Exhibit 8.1
Direct Foreign Investment in the United States

- 15.5% United Kingdom
- 12.9% Japan
- 10.5% Netherlands
- 9.0% Canada
- 8.4% Luxembourg
- 7.7% Switzerland
- 7.7% Germany
- 7.7% France
- 20.7% Other

Source: D. T. Jenniges and J. J. Fetzer, "Direct Investment Positions for 2014: Country and Industry D etail—Chart 6," *BEA News*, July 2015, accessed April 28, 2016 http://www.bea.gov/scb/pdf/2015/07%20July/0715_direct_investment_positions.pdf.

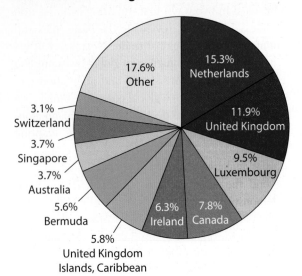

Exhibit 8.2
U.S. Direct Foreign Investment Abroad

- 15.3% Netherlands
- 11.9% United Kingdom
- 9.5% Luxembourg
- 7.8% Canada
- 6.3% Ireland
- 5.8% United Kingdom Islands, Caribbean
- 5.6% Bermuda
- 3.7% Australia
- 3.7% Singapore
- 3.1% Switzerland
- 17.6% Other

Source: D. T. Jenniges and J. J. Fetzer, "Direct Investment Positions for 2014: Country and Industry Detail—Chart 6," *BEA News*, July 2015, accessed April 28, 2016, http://www.bea.gov/scb/pdf/2015/07%20July/0715_direct_investment_positions.pdf.

8-1b Trade Barriers

Although today's consumers usually don't care where the products they buy come from (more on this in Section 8-1d), national governments have traditionally preferred that consumers buy domestically made products in hopes that such purchases would increase the number of domestic businesses and workers. In fact, governments have done much more than hope that you will buy from domestic companies. Historically, governments have actively used **trade barriers** to make it much more expensive or difficult (or sometimes impossible) for consumers to buy or consume imported goods. The Chinese government adds a 25 percent tariff to automobiles imported to China. Imports make up just 4 percent of the 24.4 million cars sold annually in China, a percentage that hasn't changed in 15 years. Consultant Michael Dunne says, "There might as well be a sign saying: Imports not welcome."[7] By establishing these restrictions and taxes, the Chinese government is engaging in **protectionism**, which is the use of trade barriers to protect local companies and their workers from foreign competition. According to trade monitoring group Global Trade Alert, almost 7,000 protectionist measures have been put in place by governments since 2009.[8]

Governments have used two general kinds of trade barriers: tariff and nontariff barriers. A **tariff** is a direct tax on imported goods. Tariffs increase the cost of imported goods relative to that of domestic goods. The Argentinian import tax on electronic products is 35 percent, for example.[9] Countries also place tariffs on exports to discourage manufacturers from sending domestically produced goods overseas. For example, under former president Cristina Fernandez de Kirchner, Argentina placed heavy export tariffs on its agricultural products, including a 35 percent tax on soy exports, 23 percent tax on wheat, and 20 percent tax on corn. This resulted in a stockpile of crops valued at $11.4 billion.[10] When Mauricio Mauri became president in 2015, he eliminated all export tariffs on crops, saying, "We must stop being the world's barn to become the world's supermarket."[11]

Nontariff barriers are nontax methods of increasing the cost or reducing the volume of imported goods. There are five types of nontariff barriers: quotas, voluntary export restraints, government import standards, government subsidies, and customs valuation/classification.

> Countries place tariffs on exports to discourage manufacturers from sending domestically produced goods overseas.

Because there are so many different kinds of nontariff barriers, they can be an even more potent method of shielding domestic industries from foreign competition.

Quotas are specific limits on the number or volume of imported products. For example, the Chinese government only allows 34 imported movies each year. China also limits the amount of foreign content available on video-streaming websites to no more than 30 percent. To get around the quota, films must be at least partially shot in China, co-financed by a Chinese firm, and have some Chinese cultural elements.[12]

Like quotas, **voluntary export restraints** limit the amount of a product that can be imported annually. The difference is that the exporting country rather than the importing country imposes restraints. Usually, however, the "voluntary" offer to limit exports occurs because the importing country has implicitly threatened to impose quotas. For example, to protect Brazilian auto manufacturers from less expensive Mexican-made cars, the Brazilian government convinced Mexico to "voluntarily" restrict auto exports to Brazil to no more than $1.55 billion a year for three years.[13] According to the World Trade Organization (see the discussion in Section 8-1c), however, voluntary export restraints are illegal and should not be used to restrict imports.[14]

In theory, **government import standards** are established to protect the health and safety of citizens. In reality, such standards are often used to restrict or ban imported goods. Europe bans imports of hormone-treated U.S.-raised beef due to alleged health risks to European Union citizens. However, the World Trade Organization (WTO)

Trade barriers government-imposed regulations that increase the cost and restrict the number of imported goods

Protectionism a government's use of trade barriers to shield domestic companies and their workers from foreign competition

Tariff a direct tax on imported goods

Nontariff barriers nontax methods of increasing the cost or reducing the volume of imported goods

Quota a limit on the number or volume of imported products

Voluntary export restraints voluntarily imposed limits on the number or volume of products exported to a particular country

Government import standard a standard ostensibly established to protect the health and safety of citizens but, in reality, is often used to restrict imports ruled that the EU's ban is not based on scientific evidence, and that the European Union should open its markets to American beef imports. Because the EU has not lived up to the WTO ruling, the United States is threatening re-taliation with 100 per-cent tariffs on select EU imports, such as Perrier mineral water, Roquefort cheese, and Vespa scooters. Tracy Brunner, president of the National Cattlemen's Beef Associa-tion, said, "While this is not our preferred choice, retaliation is the only way cattle producers are going to secure our rights for the losses we have incurred over the years due to the EU's hormone ban."[15]

Many nations also use **subsidies**, such as long-term, low-interest loans, cash grants, and tax deferments, to develop and protect companies in special industries. In 2016, the WTO ruled that the European Union illegally provided billions in subsidies to Airbus Group SE, a European conglomerate that designs and manufactures passenger jets. The office of the U.S. Trade Representative said, "The EU did not come into compliance with respect to the subsidies previously found, and it further breached WTO rules by granting more than $4 billion in new subsidized financing for the A350XWB [Airbus's long-haul plane]."[16] U.S. Trade Representative Micheal Froman said, "EU aircraft subsidies have cost American companies tens of billions of dollars in lost revenue."[17] The United States indicated that Airbus received EU subsidies totaling $22 billion and that it would seek $10 billion a year in retaliatory tariffs.[18] The European Union is appealing the fine.

The last type of nontariff barrier is **customs classification**. As products are imported into a country, they are examined by customs agents, who must decide which of nearly 9,000 categories they should be classified into (see

Festive Articles

Apparel

kurhan/Shutterstock.com

the Official Harmonized Tariff Schedule of the United States at www.usitc.gov for more information). The category assigned by customs agents can greatly affect the size of the tariff and whether the item is subject to import quotas. For example, the U.S. Customs Service classifies the various parts of a Santa Claus costume differently. The beard, wig, and hat are classified as "festive articles," which are defined as "flimsy, nondurable, and not normal articles of wearing apparel." Festive articles are exempt from import duties. The jacket, pants, gloves, and toy sacks, however, are considered apparel. They carry tariffs from 10 to 32 percent.[19]

8-1c Trade Agreements

Thanks to the trade barriers described previously, buying imported goods has often been much more expensive and difficult than buying domestic goods. During the 1990s, however, the regulations governing global trade were transformed. The most significant change was that 124 countries agreed to adopt the **General Agreement on Tariffs and Trade (GATT)**. GATT, which existed from 1947 to 1995, was an agreement to regulate trade among (eventually) more than 120 countries, the purpose of which was "substantial reduction of tariffs and other trade barriers and the elimination of preferences."[20] GATT members engaged in eight rounds of trade negotiations, with the Uruguay Round signed in 1994 and going into effect in 1995. Although GATT itself was replaced by the **World Trade Organization (WTO)** in 1995, the changes that it made continue to encourage international trade. Today, the WTO and its member countries are negotiating what's known as the Doha Round, which seeks to advance trade opportunities for developing countries in areas ranging from agriculture to services to intellectual property rights. The WTO, headquartered in Geneva, Switzerland, administers trade agreements, provides a forum for trade negotiations, handles trade disputes, monitors national trade policies, and offers technical assistance and training for developing countries for its 164 member countries.

Through tremendous decreases in tariff and nontariff barriers, the Uruguay round of GATT made it much easier and cheaper for consumers in all countries to buy foreign products. First, tariffs were cut 40 percent

Subsidies government loans, grants, and tax deferments given to domestic companies to protect them from foreign competition

Customs classification a classification assigned to imported products by government officials that affects the size of the tariff and the imposition of import quotas

General Agreement on Tariffs and Trade (GATT) a worldwide trade agreement that reduced and eliminated tariffs, limited government subsidies, and established protections for intellectual property

World Trade Organization (WTO) the successor to GATT; the only international organization dealing with the global rules of trade between nations; its main function is to ensure that trade flows as smoothly, predictably, and freely as possible

Exhibit 8.3
World Trade Organization

✓ **FACT FILE**

WORLD TRADE ORGANIZATION

Location: Geneva, Switzerland
Established: January 1, 1995
Created by: Uruguay Round negotiations (1986–1994)
Membership: 164 countries (on July 29, 2016)
Budget: 197 million Swiss francs for 2015
Secretariat staff: 640
Head: Roberto Azevêdo (Director-General)

Functions:
- Administering WTO trade agreements
- Forum for trade negotiations
- Handling trade disputes
- Monitoring national trade policies
- Technical assistance and training for developing countries
- Cooperation with other international organizations

Source: "Fact File: What Is the WTO?" *World Trade Organization*, accessed April 7, 2017, https://www.wto.org/english/thewto_e/thewto_e.htm.

on average worldwide by 2005. Second, tariffs were eliminated in 10 specific industries: beer, alcohol, construction equipment, farm machinery, furniture, medical equipment, paper, pharmaceuticals, steel, and toys. Third, stricter limits were put on government subsidies (see the discussion of subsidies in Section 8-1b). Fourth, the Uruguay round of GATT established protections for intellectual property, such as trademarks, patents, and copyrights. In 2017, the WTO's Trade Facilitation Agreement (TFA), which simplifies and standardizes customs procedures around the world, went into effect. The WTO estimates the TFA may cut trade costs by 14 percent.[21]

Protection of intellectual property has become an increasingly important issue in global trade because of widespread product piracy. For example, the International Federation of the Phonographic Industry estimates that 20 percent of "fixed-line Internet users worldwide regularly access services offering copyright infringing music."[22] Likewise, according to BSA | The Software Alliance, 39 percent of all software used in the world is pirated, costing companies $52.2 billion in lost sales.[23]

Product piracy is also costly to the movie industry, as movie studios and theaters, as well as video/DVD distributors, lose $18 billion each year to pirates. In fact, digital sales of movies rose 6–10 percent for two movie studios after Megaupload, an illegal site for downloading movies, was closed.[24]

Finally, trade disputes between countries now are fully settled by arbitration panels from the WTO. In the past, countries could use their veto power to cancel a panel's decision. For instance, the French government routinely vetoed rulings that its large cash grants to French farmers constituted unfair subsidies. Now, however, countries that are members of the WTO no longer have veto power. Thus, WTO rulings are complete and final. Exhibit 8.3 provides a brief overview of the WTO and its functions.

The second major development that has reduced trade barriers has been the creation of **regional trading zones**, or zones in which tariff and nontariff barriers are reduced or eliminated for countries within the trading zone. The largest and most important trading zones are:

» Africa: African Free Trade Zone Agreement (AFTZ) and Tripartite Free Trade Area (TFTA)

» Asia: Association of Southeast Asian Nations (ASEAN), Asia-Pacific Economic Cooperation (APEC), and Trans-Pacific Partnership (TPP)

» Central America: Dominican Republic-Central America Free Trade Agreement (CAFTA-DR)

» Europe: The Maastricht Treaty

» North America: North American Free Trade Agreement (NAFTA)

» South America: Union of South American Nations (USAN)

The map in Exhibit 8.4 shows the extent to which free-trade agreements govern global trade.

In 1992, Belgium, Denmark, France, Germany, Greece, Ireland, Italy, Luxembourg, the Netherlands, Portugal, Spain, and the United Kingdom adopted the **Maastricht Treaty of Europe**. The purpose of this treaty was to transform their 12 different economies and 12 currencies into one common economic market, called the European Union (EU), with one

Regional trading zones areas in which tariff and nontariff barriers on trade between countries are reduced or eliminated

Maastricht Treaty of Europe a regional trade agreement among most European countries

Exhibit 8.4
Global Map of Regional Trade Agreements

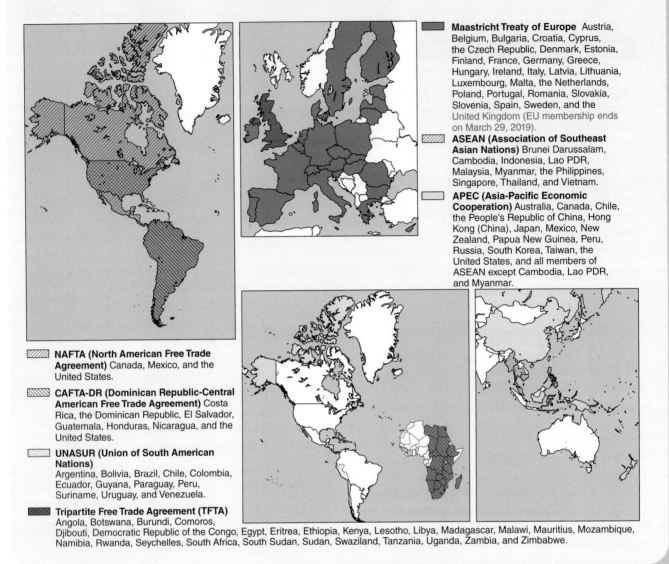

Maastricht Treaty of Europe Austria, Belgium, Bulgaria, Croatia, Cyprus, the Czech Republic, Denmark, Estonia, Finland, France, Germany, Greece, Hungary, Ireland, Italy, Latvia, Lithuania, Luxembourg, Malta, the Netherlands, Poland, Portugal, Romania, Slovakia, Slovenia, Spain, Sweden, and the United Kingdom (EU membership ends on March 29, 2019).

ASEAN (Association of Southeast Asian Nations) Brunei Darussalam, Cambodia, Indonesia, Lao PDR, Malaysia, Myanmar, the Philippines, Singapore, Thailand, and Vietnam.

APEC (Asia-Pacific Economic Cooperation) Australia, Canada, Chile, the People's Republic of China, Hong Kong (China), Japan, Mexico, New Zealand, Papua New Guinea, Peru, Russia, South Korea, Taiwan, the United States, and all members of ASEAN except Cambodia, Lao PDR, and Myanmar.

NAFTA (North American Free Trade Agreement) Canada, Mexico, and the United States.

CAFTA-DR (Dominican Republic-Central American Free Trade Agreement) Costa Rica, the Dominican Republic, El Salvador, Guatemala, Honduras, Nicaragua, and the United States.

UNASUR (Union of South American Nations) Argentina, Bolivia, Brazil, Chile, Colombia, Ecuador, Guyana, Paraguay, Peru, Suriname, Uruguay, and Venezuela.

Tripartite Free Trade Agreement (TFTA) Angola, Botswana, Burundi, Comoros, Djibouti, Democratic Republic of the Congo, Egypt, Eritrea, Ethiopia, Kenya, Lesotho, Libya, Madagascar, Malawi, Mauritius, Mozambique, Namibia, Rwanda, Seychelles, South Africa, South Sudan, Sudan, Swaziland, Tanzania, Uganda, Zambia, and Zimbabwe.

common currency. On January 1, 2002, a single common currency, the euro, went into circulation in 12 of the EU's members (Austria, Belgium, Finland, France, Germany, Greece, Ireland, Italy, Luxembourg, the Netherlands, Portugal, and Spain). Austria, Finland, and Sweden joined the EU in 1995, followed by Cyprus, the Czech Republic, Estonia, Hungary, Latvia, Lithuania, Malta, Poland, Slovakia, and Slovenia in 2004; Bulgaria and Romania in 2007; and Croatia in 2013, bringing the total membership to 28 countries.[25] Albania, Macedonia, Montenegro, Serbia and Turkey have applied and are being considered for membership. In June 2016, the United Kingdom voted to leave the EU. On March 30, 2017, UK prime minister triggered "Article 50," which provides exactly two years to negotiate the UK's exit from the EU.[26]

Prior to the treaty, trucks carrying products were stopped and inspected by customs agents at each border. Furthermore, because the required paperwork, tariffs, and government product specifications could be radically different in each country, companies often had to file 12 different sets of paperwork, pay 12 different tariffs, produce 12 different versions of their basic product to meet various government specifications, and exchange money in 12 different currencies. Likewise, open business travel, which we take for granted in the United States, was complicated by inspections at each border crossing.

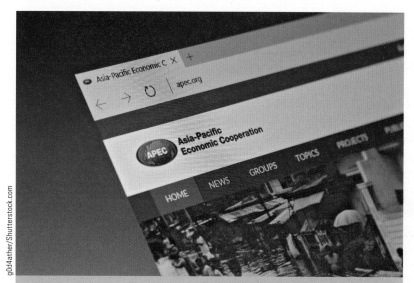
APEC, the Asian-Pacific Economic Cooperation, is one of the two largest regional trading groups in Asia.

If you lived in Germany but worked in Luxembourg, your car was stopped and your passport was inspected twice every day as you traveled to and from work. Also, every business transaction required a currency exchange, for example, from German deutsche marks to Italian lira, or from French francs to Dutch guilders. Imagine all of this happening to millions of trucks, cars, and workers each day, and you can begin to appreciate the difficulty and cost of conducting business across Europe before the Maastricht Treaty. For more information about the Maastricht Treaty, the EU, and the euro, see http://europa.eu

NAFTA, the **North American Free Trade Agreement** among the United States, Canada, and Mexico, went into effect on January 1, 1994. More than any other regional trade agreement, NAFTA has liberalized trade between countries so that businesses can plan for one market (North America) rather than for three separate markets. One of NAFTA's most important achievements was to eliminate most product tariffs *and* prevent the three countries from increasing existing tariffs or introducing new ones. Overall, Mexican and Canadian exports to the United States are up 637 percent and 151 percent, respectively, since NAFTA went into effect. U.S. exports to Mexico and Canada are up 455 percent and 166 percent, growing twice as fast as U.S. exports to any other part of the world. In fact, Mexico and Canada now account for 34 percent of all U.S. exports.[27]

CAFTA-DR, the **Dominican Republic-Central America Free Trade Agreement** among the United States, the Dominican Republic, and the Central American countries of Costa Rica, El Salvador, Guatemala,

Honduras, and Nicaragua, went into effect in August 2005. With a combined population of 52 million, the CAFTA-DR countries together are the sixteenth-largest U.S. export market in the world. U.S. companies export nearly $29 billion in goods each year to the CAFTA-DR countries.[28]

On May 23, 2008, 12 South American countries signed the **Union of South American Nations (UNASUR)** Constitutive Treaty, which united the countries of the Mercosur trade group (Argentina, Brazil, Paraguay, Uruguay, and Venezuela) and the countries of the Andean Community (Bolivia, Colombia, Ecuador, and Peru) with Guyana, Suriname, and Chile. UNASUR aims to create a unified South America by permitting free movement between nations, creating a common infrastructure that includes an interoceanic highway, and establishing the region as a single market by eliminating all tariffs by 2019. UNASUR is one of the largest trading zones in the world, encompassing 418 million people in South America with a combined gross domestic product (GDP) of nearly $4.2 trillion.[29]

ASEAN, the **Association of Southeast Asian Nations**, and **APEC**, the **Asia-Pacific Economic Cooperation**, are the two largest and most important regional trading groups in Asia. ASEAN is a trade agreement among Brunei Darussalam, Cambodia, Indonesia, Lao PDR, Malaysia, Myanmar, the Philippines, Singapore, Thailand, and Vietnam, which form a market of more than 629 million people with a combined

North American Free Trade Agreement (NAFTA) a regional trade agreement among the United States, Canada, and Mexico

Dominican Republic-Central America Free Trade Agreement (CAFTA-DR) a regional trade agreement among Costa Rica, the Dominican Republic, El Salvador, Guatemala, Honduras, Nicaragua, and the United States

Union of South American Nations (UNASUR) a regional trade agreement among Argentina, Brazil, Paraguay, Uruguay, Venezuela, Bolivia, Colombia, Ecuador, Peru, Guyana, Suriname, and Chile

Association of Southeast Asian Nations (ASEAN) a regional trade agreement among Brunei Darussalam, Cambodia, Indonesia, Laos, Malaysia, Myanmar, the Philippines, Singapore, Thailand, and Vietnam

Asia-Pacific Economic Cooperation (APEC) a regional trade agreement among Australia, Canada, Chile, the People's Republic of China, Hong Kong, Japan, Mexico, New Zealand, Papua New Guinea, Peru, Russia, South Korea, Taiwan, the United States, and all the members of ASEAN except Cambodia, Lao PDR, and Myanmar

GDP of $2.4 trillion. U.S. trade with ASEAN countries exceeds $234 billion a year.[30]

In fact, the United States is ASEAN's third-largest trading partner (China is its largest), and ASEAN's member nations constitute the fourth-largest trading partner of the United States. An ASEAN free-trade area was established in 2015 for the six original countries (Brunei Darussalam, Indonesia, Malaysia, the Philippines, Singapore, and Thailand), and in 2018 for the newer member countries (Cambodia, Lao PDR, Myanmar, and Vietnam). All 10 nations have committed to develop a "deeply integrated and highly cohesive ASEAN economy" by 2025.[31]

APEC is a broad agreement that includes Australia, Canada, Chile, the People's Republic of China, Hong Kong, Japan, Mexico, New Zealand, Papua New Guinea, Peru, Russia, South Korea, Taiwan, the United States, and all the members of ASEAN except Cambodia, Lao PDR, and Myanmar. APEC's 21 member countries have a total population of 2.8 billion people and combined GDP of more than $43.4 trillion.[32]

APEC countries began reducing trade barriers in 2000, though all the reductions will not be completely phased in until 2020.[33]

The **Tripartite Free Trade Agreement (TFTA)** is an African trade agreement proposed in 2015. Currently signed by 27 member states and awaiting ratification, the TFTA's ultimate goal is to create a free trade area across all 54 African Union states by 2017.[34]

8-1d Consumers, Trade Barriers, and Trade Agreements

The average worker earns nearly $46,550 in Finland, $57,920 in Sweden, $93,740 in Norway, and $55,980 in the United States.[35] Yet after adjusting these incomes for how much they can buy, the Finnish income is worth just $42,600, the Swedish $48,700, the Norwegian 65,430, and the American $57,540.[36] This is the same as saying $1 of income can buy only $0.92 worth of goods in Finland, $0.84 in Sweden, $0.70 in Norway and $1.03 in the United States.[37] In other words, Americans can buy much more with their incomes than those in many other countries.

One reason that Americans get more for their money is that the U.S. marketplace is the third most competitive in the world (behind Switzerland and Singapore). The U.S. economy has historically been one of the easiest for foreign companies to enter.[38] Although some U.S. industries, such as textiles, have been heavily protected from foreign competition by trade barriers, for the most part, American consumers (and businesses) have had plentiful choices among American-made and foreign-made products. More important, the high level of competition between foreign and domestic companies that creates these choices helps keep prices low in the United States. Furthermore, it is precisely the lack of choice and the low level of competition that keep prices higher in countries that have not been as open to foreign companies and products. For example, Japanese trade barriers on agricultural products are high. In fact, over 45 percent of the value of Japan's agricultural industry comes from trade barriers or subsidies. The tariffs on rice alone amount to $8.4 billion in additional costs to Japanese consumers and taxpayers.[39]

So why do trade barriers and free-trade agreements matter to consumers? They're important because free-trade agreements increase choices, competition, and purchasing power and thus decrease what people pay for food, clothing, necessities, and luxuries. Indeed, in the US trade lowers prices 29% for middle income consumers and 62% for the poorest consumers.[40] Accordingly, today's consumers rarely care where their products and services come from. From seafood to diamonds, people don't care where products are from—they just want to know which brand or kind is cheaper.[41] And why do trade barriers and free-trade agreements matter to managers? The reason, as you're about to read, is that while free-trade agreements create new business opportunities, they also intensify competition, and addressing that competition is a manager's job.

Tripartite Free Trade Agreement (TFTA) a regional trade agreement among 27 African countries

iStock.com/kevinjeon00

GLOBAL TASTES INCLUDE SOGGY CORN FLAKES

Cereal sales have been declining for years in the United States, but they have been exploding in many developing nations. While this overall growth is good news for cereal manufacturer Kellogg's, it has also brought a new set of challenges. Yogurt is more widely available than milk in Colombia, so Kellogg's sells cereal attached to packets of yogurt. Kellogg's found that consumers in South Africa were boiling their Corn Flakes to give the cereal a more porridge-like consistency, so it developed Corn Flakes Instant Porridge for that market. Kara Timperley, Kellogg's marketing director for sub-Saharan Africa, said that once they realized consumer differences, reconceiving Corn Flakes as porridge was a "no-brainer." Today, nearly a third of Kellogg's $14.6 billion annual revenue comes from sales of cereal and related products in emerging markets.

Source: J. Revill and A. Gasparro, "Cereal Makers Tweak Recipes for Emerging Markets," *Wall Street Journal*, September 26, 2015, B6.

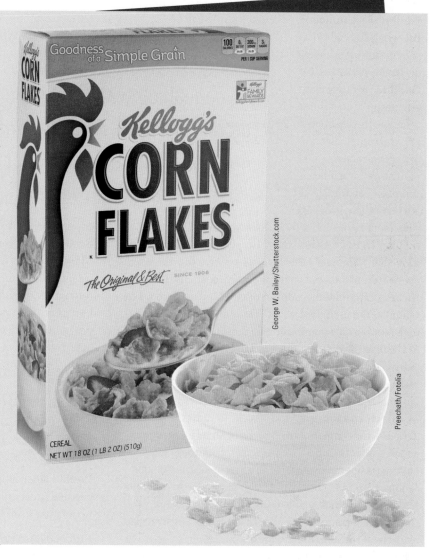

George W. Bailey/Shutterstock.com

Preechath/Fotolia

8-2 CONSISTENCY OR ADAPTATION?

After a company has decided that it *will* go global, it must decide *how* to go global. For example, if you decide to sell in Singapore, should you try to find a local business partner who speaks the language, knows the laws, and understands the customs and norms of Singapore's culture? Or should you simply export your products from your home country? What do you do if you are also entering Eastern Europe, perhaps starting in Hungary? Should you use the same approach in Hungary that you use in Singapore?

In this section, we return to a key issue: How can you be sure that the way you run your business in one country is the right way to run that business in another? In other words, how can you strike the right balance between global consistency and local adaptation?

Global consistency means that a multinational company with offices, manufacturing plants, and distribution facilities in different countries uses the same rules, guidelines, policies, and procedures to run all of those offices, plants, and facilities. Managers at company headquarters value global consistency because it simplifies decisions. For example, rather than stock its new São Paulo, Brazil, store with apparel according to South American seasonality, **Ralph Lauren** followed the North American seasons, putting winter apparel on the shelves during

> **Global consistency** when a multinational company has offices, manufacturing plants, and distribution facilities in different countries and runs them all using the same rules, guidelines, policies, and procedures

the Brazilian summer.[42] By contrast, a company following a policy of **local adaptation** modifies its standard operating procedures to adapt to differences in foreign customers, governments, and regulatory agencies. Amazon chose local adaptation to grow its video services in India by developing new shows specifically for Indian viewers. Roy Price, chief of Amazon Studios, said, "You can have a global service, but there are no global customers. There are only local customers."[43] Amazon is developing a dozen original Indian shows. For example, the animated series "Baahubali: The Lost Legends," based on a popular Indian movie, will be produced in Hindi and English, as well as Tamil and Telugu, two regional languages.[44] Local adaptation is typically preferred by local managers who are charged with making the international business successful in their countries.

If companies lean too much toward global consistency, they run the risk of using management procedures poorly suited to particular countries' markets, cultures, and employees (that is, a lack of local adaptation). Walmart became the world's largest retailer by building hypermarkets with a full-sized grocery and a full-sized discount department store. But that strategy has struggled overseas. Professor Flavio Tayra said, "Ever since it entered Brazil, Wal-Mart has found it difficult to integrate itself into the market. It occupies a modest space here given all the potential it has."[45] Traffic is notoriously bad in Brazil's large cities, so getting to Walmart stores located in city outskirts (because of their large size) is frustrating. Also, bargain-hunting Brazilians prefer "cash and carries" retailers selling heavily discounted goods in bulk. While they might visit cash and carries once a month, Brazilians shop for groceries several times a week at smaller, neighborhood grocers. This makes Walmart's current plans to spend $320 million to upgrade its hypermarkets, and convert two regional chains it bought to hypermarkets with Walmart's name, surprising. Analyst Bruna Pezzin said, "Focusing on a format that is clearly losing market share and is no longer very attractive to Brazilians doesn't seem appropriate."[46]

> Walmart became the world's largest retailer by building hypermarkets with a full-sized grocery and a full-sized discount department store, but the strategy has struggled overseas.

If, however, companies focus too much on local adaptation, they run the risk of losing the cost effectiveness and productivity that result from using standardized rules and procedures throughout the world.[47] While Amazon's video services relies on local adaptation to grow in India, Netflix's concerns for productivity drive its use of global consistency as it slowly expands in India. For now, CEO Reed Hastings said that Netflix's target customers are, "iPhone owners," or "Western-oriented elites" capable of paying $8 a month (500 rupees) for a Netflix subscription. And rather than develop new shows for India, Netflix uses its massive set of viewer data preferences for making local programming decisions. Hastings said, "There's no point in us trying to out-Bollywood Bollywood at this point."[48]

8-3 FORMS FOR GLOBAL BUSINESS

Besides determining whether to adapt organizational policies and procedures, a company must also determine how to organize itself for successful entry into foreign markets.

*Historically, companies have generally followed the phase model of globalization, in which a company makes the transition from a domestic company to a global company in the following sequential phases: **8-3a exporting, 8-3b cooperative contracts, 8-3c strategic alliances,** and **8-3d wholly owned affiliates.** At each step, the company grows much larger, uses those resources to enter more global markets, is less dependent on home-country sales, and is more committed in its orientation to global business. Some companies, however, do not follow the phase model of globalization. Some skip phases on their way to becoming more global and less domestic. Others don't follow the phase model at all. These are known as **8-3e global new ventures.** This section reviews these forms of global business.[49]*

8-3a Exporting

When companies produce products in their home countries and sell those products to customers in foreign countries, they are **exporting**. Exporting as a form of

Local adaptation modifying rules, guidelines, policies, and procedures to adapt to differences in foreign customers, governments, and regulatory agencies

Exporting selling domestically produced products to customers in foreign countries

BMW's plant in Spartanburg, SC, is the largest auto manufacturing plant in the world.

global business offers many advantages. It makes the company less dependent on sales in its home market and provides a greater degree of control over research, design, and production decisions. The largest auto manufacturing plant in the world in Spartanburg, South Carolina, is owned by Germany-based BMW. Opened in 1994, BMW's Spartanburg plant produced 411,000 cars in 2016. Seventy percent of the X3, X4, X5, and X6 BMWs produced there are exported outside the United States, with China being the largest market. Sherry McCraw, vice president of finance at the Spartanburg plant, said that factory workers know when they're producing "Chinese cars," because they're ordered with every possible option.[50]

Though advantageous in a number of ways, exporting also has its disadvantages. The primary disadvantage is that many exported goods are subject to tariff and nontariff barriers that can substantially increase their final cost to consumers. The second disadvantage is that transportation costs can significantly increase the price of an exported product. Chinese regulations require live imported animals to be slaughtered within 55 miles of their point of entry. To meet China's growing demand for fresh beef, Australian ranchers have begun flying cattle on 747 jumbo jets to ports of entry thousands of miles inland. By switching from ships to jets, exporters have been able to expand the market for fresh beef in inland China.[51] The final disadvantage of exporting is that exporters depend on foreign importers for product distribution. If, for example, the foreign importer makes a mistake on the paperwork that accompanies a shipment of imported goods, those goods can be returned to the foreign manufacturer at the manufacturer's expense.

8-3b Cooperative Contracts

When an organization wants to expand its business globally without making a large financial commitment to do so, it may sign a **cooperative contract** with a foreign business owner who pays the company a fee for the right to conduct that business in his or her country. There are two kinds of cooperative contracts: licensing and franchising.

Under a **licensing** agreement, a domestic company, the *licensor*, receives royalty payments for allowing another company, the *licensee*, to produce its product, sell its service, or use its brand name in a particular foreign market. It costs more than $4 million to produce a single episode of a television series like *Blacklist*, *CSI*, or *Gotham*. Payments from U.S. television networks generally only cover 50–65 percent of that, so foreign licensing agreements are critical to covering the remaining production costs. For example, in order to air these shows in the United Kingdom, Britain's Channel 5 (the licensee) pays Warner Bros. (the licensor) a $780,000-per-episode fee.[52] Forty percent of the revenue generated by popular television shows comes from foreign broadcast licenses.[53]

One of the most important advantages of licensing is that it allows companies to earn additional profits without investing more money. As foreign sales increase, the royalties paid to the licensor by the foreign licensee increase. Moreover, the licensee, not the licensor, invests in production equipment and facilities to produce the product. Licensing also helps companies avoid tariff and nontariff barriers. Because the licensee manufactures the product within the foreign country, tariff and nontariff barriers don't apply.

The biggest disadvantage associated with licensing is that the licensor gives up control over the quality of the product or service sold by the foreign licensee. Unless the

> **Cooperative contract** an agreement in which a foreign business owner pays a company a fee for the right to conduct that business in his or her country
>
> **Licensing** an agreement in which a domestic company, the licensor, receives royalty payments for allowing another company, the licensee, to produce the licensor's product, sell its service, or use its brand name in a specified foreign market

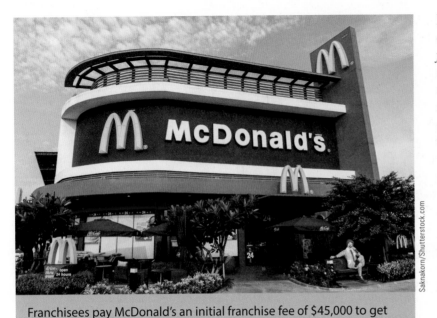

Franchisees pay McDonald's an initial franchise fee of $45,000 to get the rights to operate a restaurant.

licenses the entire business to another person or organization, the *franchisee*. For the price of an initial franchise fee plus royalties, franchisors provide franchisees with training, assistance with marketing and advertising, and an exclusive right to conduct business in a particular location. Most franchise fees run between $5,000 and $35,000. Franchisees pay McDonald's, one of the largest franchisors in the world, an initial franchise fee of $45,000. Another $1,003,000 to $2,228,000 is needed beyond that to pay for food inventory, kitchen equipment, construction, landscaping, and other expenses (the cost varies by location). While franchisees typically borrow part of this cost from a bank, McDonald's requires applicants to have over $500,000 in nonborrowed assets and requires a 25–40 percent down payment in cash for the initial investment.[55] Typical royalties run from 4 percent of gross sales (plus rent at 8.5%) to 15 percent based on location and revenue.[56] So franchisors are well rewarded for the help they provide to franchisees. More than 400 U.S. companies franchise their businesses to foreign franchise partners.

Despite franchising's many advantages, franchisors face a loss of control when they sell businesses to franchisees who are thousands of miles away. Franchising specialist Cheryl Scott says, "One franchisor I know was wondering why the royalties coming from India were so small when he knew the shop was always packed. It was because the franchisee wasn't putting all of the sales through the cash register."[57]

Although there are exceptions, franchising success may be somewhat culture-bound. Because most global franchisors begin by franchising their businesses in similar countries or regions (Canada is by far the first choice for U.S. companies taking their first step into global franchising), and because 65 percent of franchisors make absolutely no change in their business for overseas franchisees, that success may not generalize to cultures with different lifestyles, values, preferences, and technological infrastructures. In Hong Kong Pizza Hut's "flying fish roe salmon cream cheese pizza" is topped with shrimp, crayfish, clams, and scallops. In Australia it serves a hot dog stuffed crust pizza. And in South Korea its serves a dessert stuffed crust (cream cheese, cranberry or cinnamon apple nut) pizza with sausage, steak, bacon and calamari toppings. Burger King offers the "SufganiKing"

licensing agreement contains specific restrictions, the licensee controls the entire business from production to marketing to final sales. Many licensors include inspection clauses in their license contracts, but closely monitoring product or service quality from thousands of miles away can be difficult.

An overeager licensor can dilute the value of a brand or damage the brand's reputation through overexposure. Luxury fashion brands like Louis Vuitton, Celine, Gucci, Yves Saint Laurent, and Burberry recently ended long-term licensing agreements, citing a lack of control over the products sold under their brand names. **Burberry** ended a 45-year agreement with its Japanese licensee, Sanyo Shokai, because the company opened hundreds of stores and flooded Japan with too many moderately-priced items. After canceling the contract, Burberry reduced the number of Japanese stores from more than 400 to two dozen and replaced Sanyo Shokai's mid-tier products with ones costing up to 10 times more. According to CEO for Burberry in Asia, Pascal Perrier, "The license has been suffering from overexposure. We will never do that again."[54] An additional disadvantage is that licensees can eventually become competitors, especially when a licensing agreement includes access to important technology or proprietary business knowledge.

A **franchise** is a collection of networked firms in which the manufacturer or marketer of a product or service, the *franchisor*,

Franchise a collection of networked firms in which the manufacturer or marketer of a product or service, the franchisor, licenses the entire business to another person or organization, the franchisee

In Japan, Burger King offers the "Kuro" (black) burger with a black charred bun, black cheese made from charcoaled bamboo, and black sauce from black squid ink.

whopper with two fried donut halves for the bun in Israel, the "Meatatarian" burger with bacon, chicken, beef, cheese and barbecue sauce in New Zealand, and the "Kuro" (black) burger with a black charred bun, black cheese made from charcoaled bamboo, and black sauce from black squid ink in Japan.[58]

8-3c Strategic Alliances

Companies forming **strategic alliances** combine key resources, costs, risks, technology, and people. Airbnb, the reservation site for people renting rooms, apartments and homes to travelers, makes it easy for Chinese customers to pay for reservations by partnering with Alipay, the Chinese version of PayPal, and with Tencent, the owner of WeChat, the dominant messaging and social group app in China that can also be used to pay bills and make online purchases via TenPay (Tencent's version of PayPal).[59] The most common strategic alliance is a **joint venture**, which occurs when two existing companies collaborate to form a third company. The two founding companies remain intact and unchanged, except that together they now own the newly created joint venture.

One of the advantages of global joint ventures is that, like licensing and franchising, they help companies avoid tariff and nontariff barriers to entry. Another advantage is that companies participating in a joint venture bear only part of the costs and the risks of that business. Many companies find this attractive because of the expense of entering foreign markets or developing new products.

Global joint ventures can be especially advantageous to smaller local partners who link up with larger, more experienced foreign firms that can bring advanced management, resources, and business skills to the joint venture.

Global joint ventures are not without problems, though. Because companies share costs and risks with their joint venture partners, they must also share profits. Managing global joint ventures can also be difficult because they represent a merging of four cultures: the country and the organizational culture of the first partner, and the country and the organizational culture of the second partner. Often, to be fair to all involved, each partner in the global joint venture will have equal ownership and power. But this can result in power struggles and a lack of leadership. Because of these problems, companies forming global joint ventures should carefully develop detailed contracts that specify the obligations of each party. U.S.-based Simon Property, the world's largest shopping mall developer, has had two unsuccessful joint ventures in China. Its first joint venture with U.S.-based investment firm Morgan Stanley and a state-owned Chinese company to build shopping malls in China ended with Simon selling its shares in the business back to its partners. Two years later Simon agreed to form a joint venture with a China-based developer, Bailian Group, to build high end outlet centers in China. But nothing resulted from that agreement, either.[60]

8-3d Wholly Owned Affiliates (Build or Buy)

Approximately one-third of multinational companies enter foreign markets through wholly owned affiliates. In 2015, Chinese firms spent a record $15.7 billion to acquire companies or build new facilities as a way of entering the U.S. market. One of these firms, Golden Dragon Precise Copper Tube Group, entered the U.S. market by building a $120 million pipe factory in Wilcox, Alabama. The company's U.S. subsidiary, GD Copper, is completely owned by the Chinese parentcompany.[61] Unlike licensing arrangements, franchises, or joint ventures, **wholly owned affiliates**, such as American Standard Brands and GROHE,

Strategic alliance an agreement in which companies combine key resources, costs, risks, technology, and people

Joint venture a strategic alliance in which two existing companies collaborate to form a third, independent company

Wholly owned affiliates foreign offices, facilities, and manufacturing plants that are 100 percent owned by the parent company are 100 percent owned by their parent company, in this case, Lixil.

The primary advantage of wholly owned businesses is that the parent company receives all of the profits and has complete control over the foreign facilities. The biggest disadvantage is the expense of building new operations or buying existing businesses. Although the payoff can be enormous if wholly owned affiliates succeed, the losses can be immense if they fail because the parent company assumes all of the risk. After Hong-Kong apparel maker **TAL Group** opened a pants factory in Dongguan, China, employee wages and benefits skyrocketed 31 percent the first year, 28 percent the second year, and then rose 10–12 percent annually thereafter. After nine years, TAL Group closed the pants factory and laid off 2,400 employees. After the shutdown, CEO Roger Lee said that because of the higher labor costs there was no way the Chinese factory could ever be as profitable as factories in Southeast Asia. "We've done the calculation quite a few times," said Lee.[62]

8-3e Global New Ventures

Companies used to evolve slowly from small operations selling in their home markets to large businesses selling to foreign markets. Furthermore, as companies went global, they usually followed the phase model of globalization. Recently, however, three trends have combined to allow companies to skip the phase model when going global. First, quick, reliable air travel can transport people to nearly any point in the world within one day. Second, low-cost communication technologies such as email, teleconferencing and phone conferencing via the Internet, and cloud computing make it easier to communicate with global customers, suppliers, managers, and employees. Third, there is now a critical mass of businesspeople with extensive personal experience in all aspects of global business.[63] This combination of developments has made it possible to start companies that are global from inception. With sales, employees, and financing in different countries, **global new ventures** are companies that are founded with an active strategy.[64]

Purchasing power is growing in countries such as India and China, which have low average levels of income.

Although there are several different kinds of global new ventures, all share two common factors. First, the company founders successfully develop and communicate the company's global vision from inception. Second, rather than going global one country at a time, new global ventures bring a product or service to market in several foreign markets at the same time. U.S.-based Trov sells "on-demand insurance for the things you love." Just two years old, Trov's smartphone app allows consumers to insure cameras and lenses, smartphones and tablets, laptop computers and computer monitors, smartwatches and headphones. Coverage can be bought by the day, month, or year. Everything is handled via Trov's smartphone app. CEO Scott Walcheck says, "From binding a policy to making a claim, the consumer doesn't have to speak to anybody."[65] Trov began offering insurance for Australian and UK customers, will expand coverage to the US in 2017, and has immediate plans to enter Japan and France.

8-4 FINDING THE BEST BUSINESS CLIMATE

When deciding where to go global, companies try to find countries or regions with promising business climates.

An attractive global business climate 8-4a positions the company for easy access to growing markets, 8-4b is an effective but cost-efficient place to build an office or manufacturing facility, and 8-4c minimizes the political risk to the company.

8-4a Growing Markets

The most important factor in an attractive business climate is access to a growing market. Two factors help companies determine the growth potential of foreign markets: purchasing power and foreign competitors.

Purchasing power is measured by comparing the relative cost of a standard set of goods and services in different countries. For example, a Starbucks' grande latte costs $6.96 in Zürich, Switzerland. Because that same grande latte costs $5.08 in the United States, the average American has more purchasing power than the average Swiss.[66] Purchasing power is growing in countries such as India and China, which have low average levels of income. This is because basic living expenses such as food and shelter are very inexpensive in those countries, so consumers still have money to spend after paying for necessities, especially as salaries increase thanks to demand from international trade (see box "Paying for a 'Mac Attack'").

Consequently, countries with high and growing levels of purchasing power are good choices for companies looking for attractive global markets. As Exhibit 8.5 shows, the number of cars per 1,000 people in a country rises directly with purchasing power. For example, in India, China, Israel, and Germany, where the average person earns, respectively $6,030, $14,390, $36,040, and $49,090 per year, the number of cars per 1,000 people increases, respectively, from 32 to 205 to 383 to 572. The more purchasing power people have, the more likely they are to buy cars for themselves and family members. Is purchasing power a perfect predictor of an attractive global market? No. Other factors, such as government regulations,

or the cost and convenience of public transportation, also influence car sales. For instance, while China's car sales have grown from 4 million cars a year in 2005 to 24.3 million cars in 2016 as purchasing power doubled, it's unlikely that additional increases in Chinese purchasing power will lead to similar growth in car sales. Terrible pollution and traffic have prompted city governments in locations like Beijing and Shanghai to strongly limit the number of cars on their roads. So while car sales will continue to grow in China along with purchasing power, the increase will be much slower than before.[67]

The second part of assessing the growth potential of global markets involves analyzing the degree of global competition, which is determined by the number and quality of companies that already compete in a foreign market. Coffee consumption in China is growing 7 percent a year, compared to just 0.9 percent in North America. With this in mind, Starbucks decided to double its Chinese stores to 3,400 by 2019. Likewise, the UK's

Exhibit 8.5
How Car Purchases Vary with Purchasing Power Around the World

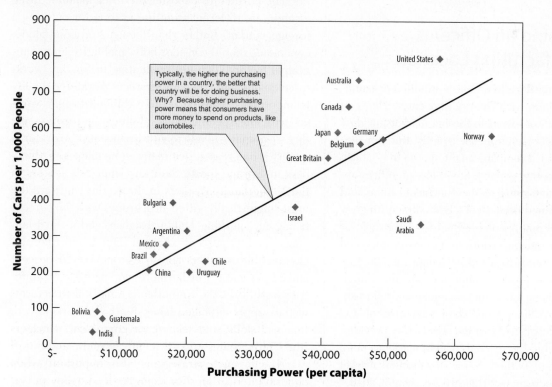

Sources: "GNI Per Capita Ranking, Atlas Method and PPP Based," The World Bank, February 1, 2017, accessed April 9, 2017, http://databank.worldbank.org/data/download/GNIPC.pdf; "All Countries Compared for Transport > Road > Motor Vehicles per 1000 People," NationMaster, accessed April 9, 2017, http://www.nation-master.com/country-info/stats/Transport/Road/Motor-vehicles-per-1000-people.

Paying for a "Mac Attack"

Every year, *The Economist* magazine produces the Big Mac Index to illustrate differences in purchasing power across countries. By comparing the price of a single item, in this case, a Big Mac from McDonald's, the index shows how much (or how little) consumers in each country get for their money. According to the latest index, a Big Mac costs an average of $5.06 in the United States. The average cost jumps to $6.35 in Switzerland, $5.67 in Norway, and $5.26 in Sweden, meaning that residents of these countries get less for their money than U.S. residents do. Conversely, the average cost of a Big Mac is $2.30 in Poland, $2.49 in India, $2.15 in Russia, and just $1.46 in Egypt.

Source: "The Big Mac Index," *Economist*, January 12, 2017, accessed April 10, 2017,, http://www.economist.com/content/big-mac-index/

Tooykrub/Shutterstock.com

Costa Coffee plans to grow from 344 Chinese stores to 900 by 2020. Californian Jim Lee, who moved to Shanghai four years ago to start the Ocean Grounds coffee shop, believes that this incredible growth means that there should be plenty of business for new and old coffee houses alike. "This market is exploding," says Lee.[68]

8-4b Choosing an Office/ Manufacturing Location

Companies do not have to establish an office or manufacturing location in each country they enter. They can license, franchise, or export to foreign markets, or they can serve a larger region from one country. But there are many reasons why a company might choose to establish a location in a foreign country. Some foreign offices are established through global mergers and acquisitions, and some are established because of a commitment to grow in a new market. South Korea-owned LG Electronics is building a $250 million factory in Tennessee to speed time to market, and, to avoid exchange rate fluctuations, which affect products imported into the United States, and tariffs on LG's Chinese manufactured washing machines. William Cho, chief executive of LG North America, explained that the new factory provides, "increased speed to the market[, which] makes us more nimble." LG's share of the U.S. washing machine market grew from 13.2 percent in 2012 to 16.5 percent in 2016.[69]

Other companies choose locations by seeking a tax haven (although this is more difficult for U.S. companies due to legal concerns) or as part of creating a global brand. Ireland is a popular location to establish a company headquarters because of its corporate tax rate of 12.5 percent, which is much lower than the United Kingdom (25%), Germany (30.2%), or the United States (35%), which has the second highest corporate tax rate in the world.[70]

The criteria for choosing an office/manufacturing location are different from the criteria for entering a foreign market. Rather than focusing on costs alone, companies should consider both qualitative and quantitative factors. Two key qualitative factors are workforce quality and company strategy. Workforce quality is important because it is often difficult to find workers with the specific skills, abilities, and experience that a company needs to run its business. Workforce quality is one reason that many companies doing business in Europe locate their customer call centers in the Netherlands. Workers in the Netherlands are the most linguistically gifted in Europe, with 77 percent trilingual (speaking Dutch, English, and a third language) and 90 percent bilingual (Dutch and English). Comparable numbers across Europe are 25 percent and 54 percent.[71] Furthermore, compared to 60 countries worldwide, the Netherlands ranks fourth in terms of the supply of skilled labor, tenth for workers with financial skills, and second for competent managers (the United States ranks fifteenth, seventh, and fifth.[72]

A company's strategy is also important when choosing a location. For example, a company pursuing a low-cost strategy may need plentiful raw materials, low-cost transportation, and low-cost labor. A company pursuing a differentiation strategy (typically

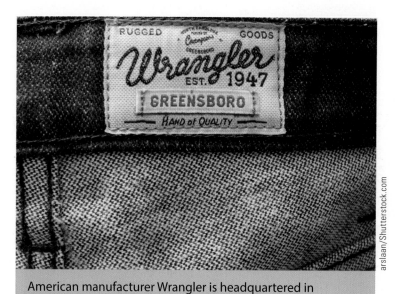
American manufacturer Wrangler is headquartered in Greensboro, NC, but sources products from Ethiopia.

8-4c Minimizing Political Risk

When managers think about political risk in global business, they envision burning factories and riots in the streets. Although political events such as these receive dramatic and extended coverage in the media, the political risks that most companies face usually are not covered as breaking stories on Fox News or CNN. Nonetheless, the negative consequences of ordinary political risk can be just as devastating to companies that fail to identify and minimize that risk.[75]

When conducting global business, companies should attempt to identify two types of political risk: political uncertainty and policy uncertainty.[76] **Political uncertainty** is associated with the risk of major changes in political regimes that can result from war, revolution, death of political leaders, social unrest, or other influential events. **Policy uncertainty** refers to the risk associated with changes in laws and government policies that directly affect the way foreign companies conduct business.

Policy uncertainty is the most common—and perhaps most frustrating—form of political risk in global business, especially when changes in laws and government policies directly undercut sizable investments made by foreign companies. The British exit (Brexit) from the European Union, effective March 29, 2019, has created tremendous uncertainty for British-based firms who don't know how much post-Brexit access, if any, they will have to EU markets. As a result, banks like JP Morgan Chase, which has 16,000 British employees, are studying where to establish sizable offices in Europe. Chase staff have spent nine months studying and visiting 8 European cities, such as Paris, Frankfurt, Luxembourg, and Dublin. CEO Jamie Dimon estimates that 25 percent of Chase's staff may need to move to Europe to maintain Chase's access to EU markets.[77] Likewise, British-based EasyJet would be required by EU law to set up a separate European operating company and have more than half of its publicly held stock be owned by Europeans. The difficulty is that businesses don't know what rules will or won't apply. Companies that wait until specific terms are

a higher-priced, better product or service) may need access to high-quality materials and a highly skilled and educated workforce.

Quantitative factors such as the kind of facility being built, tariff and nontariff barriers, exchange rates, and transportation and labor costs should also be considered when choosing an office/manufacturing location. In the apparel industry, low costs and short distances from field to factory are critical success factors for every manufacturer. That's why VF Corporation, owner of brands such as Wrangler, North Face, and Timberland, is sourcing products from Ethiopia. In addition to having the ability to go from fiber to factory in one country, Ethiopia also boasts a low average salary for garment workers ($21 per month versus up to $297 per month in China), low energy costs, and a free-trade agreement with the United States. The Ethiopian government built a $250 million industrial park exclusively for foreign investors in the apparel industry and is building a railroad through neighboring Djibouti to give its land-locked country access to a sea port. M. Raghuraman, CEO of Brandix, Sri Lanka's largest clothing exporter, is interested in Ethiopia as a manufacturing location because "Ethiopia seems to be the best location from a government, labor, and power point of view."[73] Companies rely on studies such as FM Global's annually published "Resilience Index" to compare business climates throughout the world.[74] Exhibit 8.6 offers a quick overview of the best cities for business based on a variety of criteria. This information is a good starting point if your company is trying to decide where to put an international office or manufacturing plant.

> **Political uncertainty** the risk of major changes in political regimes that can result from war, revolution, death of political leaders, social unrest, or other influential events
>
> **Policy uncertainty** the risk associated with changes in laws and government policies that directly affect the way foreign companies conduct business

Exhibit 8.6
World's Best Countries for Business

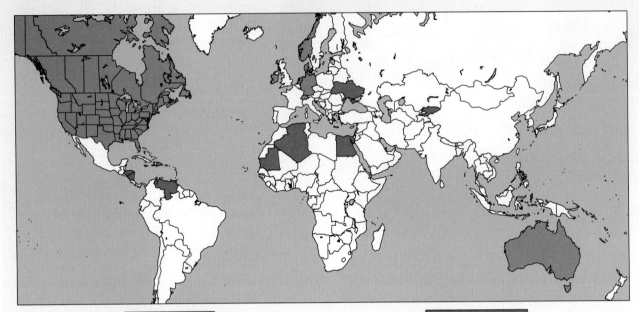

Best 10 Countries

1. Switzerland
2. Norway
3. Ireland
4. Germany
5. Luxembourg
6. The Netherlands
7. United States
8. Canada
9. Australia
10. Denmark

Worst 10 Countries

1. Venezuela
2. Dominican Republic
3. Kyrgyz Republic
4. Nicaragua
5. Mauritania
6. Ukraine
7. Egypt
8. Algeria
9. Jamaica
10. Honduras

Sources: "Table 1: The Top 10 in 2016," Resilience Index 2016, *FM Global*, http://www.fmglobal.com/assets/pdf/Resilience_Methodology.pdf, p. 5; "Table 2: The Bottom 10 in 2016," Resilience Index 2016, *FM Global*, http://www.fmglobal.com/research-and-resources/tools-and-resources/resilienceindex#!year=2016&idx=Index&handler=map.

negotiated for their businesses may not leave themselves enough time to set up operations and relocate staff to Europe. Companies that move staff and operations before Brexit terms are finalized risk incurring unnecessary costs should the EU and UK agree to relatively open access to each others' markets.[78]

Several strategies can be used to minimize or adapt to the political risk inherent in global business. An *avoidance strategy* is used when the political risks associated with a foreign country or region are viewed as too great. If firms are already invested in high-risk areas, they may divest or sell their businesses. If they have not yet invested, they will likely postpone their investment until the risk shrinks. Russia is an attractive market for automakers because it has a growing middle class but ranks fifty-seventh worldwide in terms of the number of cars per 1,000 people (just 300). With the potential of a growing market, General Motors opened a manufacturing facility in St. Petersburg in 2008 to produce 98,000 cars a year. Four years later, GM was hoping to double

production capacity. But by 2015, the Russian car market was shrinking and amid increasingly business-unfriendly regulations, GM closed the plant, taking a $600 million writeoff.[79] GM's president, Daniel Ammann, said, "This decision avoids significant investment into a market that has very challenging long-term prospects."[80]

Exhibit 8.7 shows the long-term political stability of various countries in the Middle East (higher scores indicate less political risk). The following factors, which were used to compile these ratings, indicate greater political risk: government instability, poor socioeconomic conditions, internal or external conflict, military involvement in politics, religious and ethnic tensions, high foreign debt as a percentage of GDP, exchange rate instability, and high inflation.[81] An avoidance strategy would likely be used for the riskiest countries shown in Exhibit 8.7, such as Iran, Lebanon, and Saudi Arabia but might not be needed for the less risky countries, such as Israel or United Arab Emirates. Risk conditions and factors change, so be sure to make risk decisions with

Exhibit 8.7
Overview of Political Risk in the Middle East

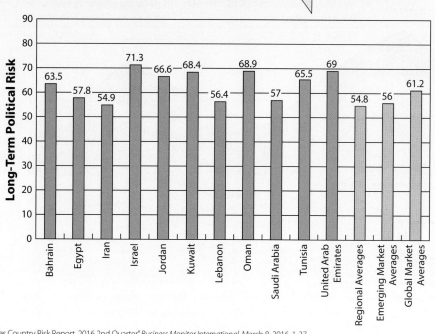

Higher scores indicate less long-term political risk, which is calculated by estimating government instability, socioeconomic conditions, internal or external conflicts, military involvement in politics, religious and ethnic tensions, foreign debt as a percent of gross domestic product, exchange rate instability, and whether there is high inflation.

Country	Long-Term Political Risk
Bahrain	63.5
Egypt	57.8
Iran	54.9
Israel	71.3
Jordan	66.6
Kuwait	68.4
Lebanon	56.4
Oman	68.9
Saudi Arabia	57
Tunisia	65.5
United Arab Emirates	69
Regional Averages	54.8
Emerging Market Averages	56
Global Market Averages	61.2

Source: "United Arab Emirates Country Risk Report, 2016 2nd Quarter," *Business Monitor International*, March 8, 2016, 1-37.

the latest available information from resources such as the PRS Group (www.prsgroup.com), which supplies information about political risk to 80 percent of *Fortune* 500 companies.

Control is an active strategy to prevent or reduce political risks. Firms using a control strategy lobby foreign governments or international trade agencies to change laws, regulations, or trade barriers that hurt their business in that country. **Uber's** low-cost European ride-sharing service, UberPop, has faced a number of setbacks in recent years, including massive protests from professional taxi drivers and restrictive government regulations. UberPop has even been banned outright in France, Germany, and Spain.[82] To deal with these setbacks, Uber hired veteran lobbyist Mark MacGann. MacGann appealed to European Union officials in Belgium, saying, "This is supposed to be a single market [but] what we're finding is that we're getting treated in completely different ways in

different countries, and even within individual countries."[83] Thus far, Uber has made little progress controlling the political risks in these countries.

Another method for dealing with political risk is *cooperation*, which involves using joint ventures and collaborative contracts, such as franchising and licensing. Although cooperation does not eliminate the political risk of doing business in a country, it can limit the risk associated with foreign ownership of a business. For example, a German company forming a joint venture with a Chinese company to do business in China may structure the joint venture contract so that the Chinese company owns 51 percent or more of the joint venture. Doing so qualifies the joint venture as a Chinese company and exempts it from Chinese laws that apply to foreign-owned businesses. However, cooperation cannot always protect against *policy risk* if a foreign government changes its laws and policies to directly affect the way foreign companies conduct business.

Exhibit 8.8
Hofstede's Six Cultural Dimensions

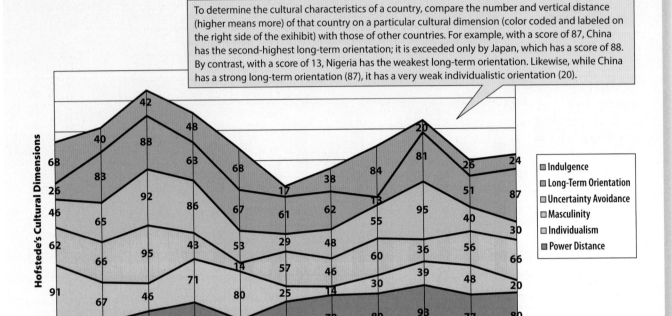

To determine the cultural characteristics of a country, compare the number and vertical distance (higher means more) of that country on a particular cultural dimension (color coded and labeled on the right side of the exihibit) with those of other countries. For example, with a score of 87, China has the second-highest long-term orientation; it is exceeded only by Japan, which has a score of 88. By contrast, with a score of 13, Nigeria has the weakest long-term orientation. Likewise, while China has a strong long-term orientation (87), it has a very weak individualistic orientation (20).

■ Indulgence
■ Long-Term Orientation
■ Uncertainty Avoidance
■ Masculinity
■ Individualism
■ Power Distance

Source: G. H. Hofstede, "Cultural Constraints in Management Theories," *Academy of Management Executive* 7, no. 1 (1993): 81–94; G. Hofstede and G. J. Hofstede, "6 Dimensions for Web Site 2015 12 08 0-100," accessed April 28, 2016, http://www.geerthofstede.eu/dimension-data-matrix.

8-5 BECOMING AWARE OF CULTURAL DIFFERENCES

National culture is the set of shared values and beliefs that affects the perceptions, decisions, and behavior of the people from a particular country. The first step in dealing with culture is to recognize that there are meaningful differences. In recent years, Indian companies have targeted a group of mid-sized, independent, often family-owned, German companies (called Mittlestand) for acquisition. When Rail.One GmbH was acquired by PCM Group, an Indian conglomerate, the new owners didn't change the Bavarian management because, says PCM Chairman Kamal Mittal, "We didn't want to disturb the business."[84] Professor Geert Hofstede spent 20 years studying cultural differences in 53 different countries. His research shows that there are six consistent cultural dimensions across countries: power distance, individualism, masculinity, uncertainty avoidance, short-term versus long-term orientation, and indulgence versus restraint.[85]

Power distance is the extent to which people in a country accept that power is distributed unequally in society and organizations. In countries where power distance is weak, such as Denmark and Sweden, employees don't like their organization or their boss to have power over them or tell them what to do. They want to have a say in decisions that affect them. As Exhibit 8.8 shows, Russia, China and Nigeria, with scores of 93, 80, and 80, respectively, are much stronger in power distance than Germany (35), the Netherlands (38), and the United States (40).

National culture the set of shared values and beliefs that affects the perceptions, decisions, and behavior of the people from a particular country

Individualism is the degree to which societies believe that individuals should be self-sufficient. In individualistic societies, employees put loyalty to themselves first and loyalty to their company and work group second. In Exhibit 8.8, the United States (91), the Netherlands (80), France (71), and Germany (67) are the strongest in individualism, while Indonesia (14), China (20), and Hong Kong (25) are the weakest.

Masculinity and *femininity* capture the difference between highly assertive and highly nurturing cultures. Masculine cultures emphasize assertiveness, competition, material success, and achievement, whereas feminine cultures emphasize the importance of relationships, modesty, caring for the weak, and quality of life. In Exhibit 8.8, Japan (95), Germany (66), and China (66) have the most masculine orientations, while the Netherlands (14) has the most feminine orientation. Manu Parpia, the CEO of Geometric, Ltd., the Indian company that acquired German engineering company 3Cap, noted that, compared to India, "German culture is more precise, very process oriented [and] quite blunt. The emphasis on process in India is much lower, because if you focused on process, nothing would get done."[86]

The cultural difference of *uncertainty avoidance* is the degree to which people in a country are uncomfortable with unstructured, ambiguous, unpredictable situations. In countries with strong uncertainty avoidance, such as Greece and Portugal, people tend to be aggressive and emotional and seek security rather than uncertainty. In Exhibit 8.8, Russia (95), Japan (92), and France (86) are strongest in uncertainty avoidance, while Hong Kong (29) and China (30) are the weakest. Rail.One CEO Jochen Riepl has noticed this dimension playing itself out during meetings with PCM officials. "In India, a 'no' is a kind of invitation to start a discussion. In Germany, a 'no' is a 'no,'" he says.[87]

The cultural dimension of *short-term/long-term orientation* addresses whether cultures are oriented to the present and seek immediate gratification or to the future and defer gratification. Not surprisingly, countries with short-term orientations are consumer-driven, whereas countries with long-term orientations are savings-driven. In Exhibit 8.8, Japan (88) and China (87) have very strong long-term orientations, while Nigeria (13) and the United States (26), have very strong short-term orientations. The cultural dimension of *indulgence versus restraint* addresses the degree to which

While the magical experience of Disney translated easily for visitors, some words and phrases did not as easily bridge the cultural divide at Disneyland Shanghai.

a society allows relatively free gratification of basic drives related to enjoying life and having fun versus strict social norms that regulate and suppress gratification of needs and wants. Nigeria (81), the United States (68), and the Netherlands (68) are strongest in indulgence, while Hong Kong (17), Russia (20), and China (24) practice the most restraint. Part of what makes Mittelstand companies comfortable with new Indian owners is that Indian bidders usually offer long-term commitments. Attorney Christopher Wright says of Indian investors, "They tend to have a long-term vision and [that] gives German companies some assurance.[88]

To generate a graphical comparison of two different countries' cultures, go to http://geert-hofstede.com/countries.html. Select a "Country" from the dropdown list, and then select a "Comparison Country." A graph comparing the countries on each of Hofstede's six cultural differences will be generated automatically.

Cultural differences affect perceptions, understanding, and behavior. Recognizing cultural differences is critical to succeeding in global business. Nevertheless, as Hofstede pointed out, descriptions of cultural differences are based on averages—the average level of uncertainty avoidance in Portugal, the average level of power distance in Argentina, and so forth. Accordingly, says Hofstede, "If you are going to spend time with a Japanese colleague, you shouldn't assume that overall cultural statements about Japanese society automatically apply to this person."[89] Similarly, cultural beliefs may differ significantly from one part of a country to another.[90]

After becoming aware of cultural differences, the second step is deciding how to adapt your company to those differences. Unfortunately, studies investigating the effects of cultural differences on management practices point more to difficulties than to easy solutions.

Another difficulty is that cultural values are changing, albeit slowly, in many parts of the world. The fall of communism in Eastern Europe and the former Soviet Union and the broad economic reforms in China have produced sweeping changes on two continents in the past four decades. Thanks to increased global trade resulting from free-trade agreements, major economic transformations are also under way in India, China, Central America, and South America. Consequently, when trying to adapt management practices to cultural differences, companies must ensure that they are not basing their adaptations on outdated and incorrect assumptions about a country's culture.

8-6 PREPARING FOR AN INTERNATIONAL ASSIGNMENT

When Atlanta native Joanna Maddox was first in Argentina, she was invited to an asado, or Argentinian barbecue, scheduled for 8 p.m. Not wanting to be late, she arrived at 7:30 p.m. The catering chef explained that in Argentina, "you *never* arrive *early* to an asado."[91] When Argentinian guests arrived after 9 p.m., Maddox said, "Not a single apology was given for arriving late."[92] And because drinks and appetizers weren't served until 9:30 p.m., Maddox, who usually ate much earlier, said she was so hungry she could, "eat the tablecloth." Dinner was eventually served at 10:30 p.m. Now, however, Maddox has adjusted to Argentina's cultural expectations regarding time. Today, she says, "when I make plans to meet my Argentine friends for coffee or lunch, all I have to do is add an hour to our meeting time and voila, I will be on time."[93]

If you become an **expatriate**, someone who lives and works outside his or her native country, chances are you'll run into cultural surprises just like Joanna Maddox did in Argentina. The difficulty of adjusting to language, cultural, and social differences is the primary reason for expatriate failure in overseas assignments. For example, although there have recently been disagreements among researchers about these numbers, it is probably safe to say that 5–20 percent of American expatriates sent abroad by their companies will return to the United States before they have successfully completed their assignments.[94] Of those who do complete their international assignments, about one-third are judged by their companies to be no better than marginally effective.[95] Because even well-planned international assignments can cost as much as three to five times an employee's annual salary, failure in those assignments can be extraordinarily expensive.[96] Furthermore, while it is difficult to find reliable indicators, studies typically show that 8–25 percent of expatriate managers leave their companies following an international assignment.[97]

The chances for a successful international assignment can be increased through 8-6a language and cross- cultural training and 8-6b consideration of spouse, family, and dual-career issues.

8-6a Language and Cross-Cultural Training

Predeparture language and cross-cultural training can reduce the uncertainty that expatriates feel, the misunderstandings that take place between expatriates and natives, and the inappropriate behaviors that expatriates unknowingly commit when they travel to a foreign country. In fact, simple things such as using a phone, locating a public toilet, asking for directions, finding out how much things cost, exchanging greetings, or understanding what people want can become tremendously complex when expatriates don't know a foreign language or a country's customs and cultures. Even after spending years in China planning for the opening of Shanghai Disneyland, it was still challenging to clearly translate names, concepts, and ideas from English into Chinese. For example, when Qi Zhu visited Shanghai Disneyland, the slogan "Ignite the magical dream within your heart" translated as "strange dream." Qi said, "What is a strange dream? [And] Why would I want a strange dream in a park?"[98] Fangxing Pitcher, who is part of the park design group for Disney Imagineering, said, "Every time we come up with a name, we had to make sure it has a whimsical Disney feel, it resonates with Chinese people, and it conveys what the experience is. If you just do a straight translation, all of that gets lost."[99]

Expatriates who receive predeparture language and cross-cultural training make faster adjustments to foreign cultures and perform better on their international

Expatriate someone who lives and works outside his or her native country

EXPATS LEAVE AS SQUARES, TRY TO FIT IN AS CIRCLES, AND COME BACK AS TRIANGLES

Working and living abroad changes expatriates. First is the challenge of leaving home, family, and friends, moving from one culture (squares) to fit into a new culture (circles). And that challenge can be harder for the so-called "trailing spouse." Petra Trudell, who gave up her job as a reporter to move with her husband to Japan says, "My own turning point came when I first met the wife of my husband's boss. They are fellow Americans who hadn't been in Japan much longer than us, and we met for dinner while my husband and I were still in temporary housing. She looked at me and asked how I was doing. When I gave the polite answer, dancing around my own insecurities, she did something I didn't expect: She congratulated me. She told me not to feel badly about wanting to stay inside and feeling overwhelmed."

Most expats and their families do adjust to their new cultures. Many thrive and learn to love their new homes and neighbors, eventually taking as their own some of the customs and norms of those new cultures. In that process, they become triangles, a hybrid between their original culture (squares) and their new culture (circles). And that becomes most apparent to them when they return home. Relocation specialist Naomi Hattaway, who moved with her family to

India and then Singapore and back to the United States, says, "During my time abroad, my horizons were expanded, but when we returned home to the U.S., I found myself struggling with fitting in. I felt like a misfit." So she took to blogging to share her thoughts and feelings, forming the "I am a Triangle" group on Facebook, which grew from 30 to 6,300 members. One Facebook participant wrote, "Being home and near family has been great, but outside of that, everything is a challenge. I feel completely foreign to the local culture, and have a hard time connecting with people… [But] I have been reading posts and comments and I already feel better, seeing the community and support here in this group."

Becoming an expat changes you. As Petra Trudell eventually learned in Japan, "it's not always an easy life, but there's no disputing it's a good life." Even when you're a triangle returning home to squares.

Source: N. Hattaway, "Shaping Up in an Expat World: We're All 'Triangles' Now," *Wall Street Journal*, September 13, 2016, accessed April 10, 2017, https://blogs.wsj.com/expat/2016/09/13/shaping-up-in-an-expat-world-were-all-triangles-now/; P. Trudell, "Portrait of a Trailing Spouse: Dependent, Dejected and Learning to Give Herself Some Slack," *Wall Street Journal*, July 6, 2015, accessed April 10, 2017, WSJ, http://blogs.wsj.com/expat/2015/07/06/portrait-of-a-trailing-spouse-dependent-dejected-and-learning-to-give-herself-some-slack/.

assignments.[100] Unfortunately, only a third of the managers who go on international assignments are offered any kind of predeparture training, and only half of those actually participate in the training![101] Suzanne Bernard, director of international mobility at Bombardier Aerospace in Canada, says, "We always offer cross-cultural training, but it's very seldom used by executives leaving in a rush at the last minute."[102] This is somewhat surprising given the failure rates for expatriates and the high cost of those failures. Furthermore, with the exception of some language courses, predeparture training is not particularly expensive or difficult to provide. Three methods can be used to prepare workers for international assignments: documentary training, cultural simulations, and field experiences.

Documentary training focuses on identifying specific critical differences between cultures. France-based fashion company L'Oreal values direct communication so much that it offers a "Managing Confrontation" course for global employees who come from cultures with different communication norms. One Chinese employee said, "We don't do this type of debate traditionally in China, but these trainings have taught us a method of expressing diverging opinions, which we have all come to practice and appreciate, even in meetings made up of only Chinese."[103]

After learning specific critical differences through documentary training, trainees can participate in *cultural simulations*, in which they practice adapting to cultural differences. EMC, a global provider of information storage solutions, uses cultural simulations to train its people. In its early days, EMC was largely based in the United States, but with research labs, offices, and customers on every continent, cross-cultural interactions are a daily part of business. EMC's cultural simulations use photos and audio and video clips to present real-world situations. EMC employees must decide what to do and then learn what happened as a result of their choices. Whether it's interacting with customers or dealing with EMC employees from other countries, at every step they have the opportunity to learn good and bad methods of responding to cultural differences. EMC requires

After learning specific critical differences through documentary training, trainees can participate in cultural simulations, in which they practice adapting to cultural differences.

that how well an expatriate's spouse and family adjust to the foreign culture is the most important factor in determining the success or failure of an international assignment.[105] In fact, a *Harvard Business Review* study found that 32 percent of those offered international assignments turned them down because they did not want their families to have to relocate, while 28 percent turned them down "to protect their marriages."[106] Unfortunately, despite its importance, there has been little systematic research on what does and does not help expatriates' families successfully adapt. A number of companies, however, have found that adaptability screening and intercultural training for families can lead to more successful overseas adjustment.

Adaptability screening is used to assess how well managers and their families are likely to adjust to foreign cultures. For example, Prudential Relocation Management's international division has developed an "Overseas Assignment Inventory" (OAI) to assess a spouse and family's open-mindedness, respect for others' beliefs, sense of humor, and marital communication. The

> **Evidence shows that how well an expatriate's family adjusts to a foreign culture is the most important factor in determining the success of an international assignment.**

its worldwide workforce of 40,500 people to regularly use the cultural simulations. Louise Korver-Swanson, EMC's global head of executive development, said, "This is about ensuring that we're truly a global company. We need everyone in the organization to be tuned in."[104]

Finally, *field simulation* training, a technique made popular by the U.S. Peace Corps, places trainees in an ethnic neighborhood for three to four hours to talk to residents about cultural differences. For example, a U.S. electronics manufacturer prepared workers for assignments in South Korea by having trainees explore a nearby South Korean neighborhood and talk to shopkeepers and people on the street about South Korean politics, family orientation, and day-to-day living.

OAI was initially used to help the U.S. Peace Corps, the U.S. Navy, and the Canadian International Development Agency select people who could adapt well in foreign cultures. Success there led to its use in helping companies assess whether managers and their spouses were good candidates for international assignments.[107] Likewise, Pennsylvania-based AMP, a worldwide producer of electrical connectors, conducts extensive psychological screening of expatriates and their spouses when making international assignments. But adaptability screening does not just involve a company assessing an employee; it can also involve an employee screening international assignments for desirability. Because more employees are becoming aware of the costs of international assignments (spouses having to give up or change jobs, children having to change schools, everyone having

8-6b Spouse, Family, and Dual-Career Issues

Not all international assignments are difficult for expatriates and their families, but the evidence clearly shows to learn a new language), some companies are willing to pay for a preassignment trip so the employee and his or her spouse can investigate the country *before* accepting the international assignment.[108]

Only 40 percent of expatriates' families receive language and cross-cultural training, yet such training is just as important for the families of expatriates as for the expatriates themselves.[109] In fact, it may be more important because, unlike expatriates, whose professional jobs often shield them from the full force of a country's culture, spouses and children are fully immersed in foreign neighborhoods and schools. Households must be run, shopping must be done, and bills must be paid. When Judy Holland's husband was transferred to Shanghai, his company sent the family to a two-day cultural immersion class in the United Kingdom, where the family learned about business etiquette, the cultural importance of the number 8, the Chinese zodiac, and how to eat with chopsticks. The class even prepared the Hollands for differences they might not have anticipated, such as, in China, it's uncommon to find men's shoes in sizes larger than a U.S. 9.5 (Holland's husband wore a U.S. 11.5). Holland was grateful for the instruction, saying, "Nothing can fully prepare you for China, but it certainly took the shock out of arriving." Soon after arriving, however, her sense of confidence eroded. "I remember standing in a house with no furniture, not knowing anyone, and wishing they had buddied me up with someone from my husband's company."[110] In addition to helping families prepare for the cultural differences they will encounter, language and cross-cultural training can help reduce uncertainty about how to act and decrease misunderstandings between expatriates and their families and locals. For example, in the West, people enjoy a fairly large circle of personal space and are only comfortable with family and intimate friends being within inches of their bodies. But in China, where personal space is measured in inches and not feet, the constant jostling by strangers can be perceived as an encroachment and unhinge many Westerners. New Zealander Marita Light, who spent five years in China, found that recalibrating her expectations and being intentionally open helped. "Letting go of my judgments and consciously being more open enabled more creativity in how I dealt with awkward situations. It was a much more rewarding way to live in China."[111]

STUDY TOOLS 8

LOCATED IN TEXTBOOK

☐ Rip out and review chapter review card.

LOCATED AT WWW.CENGAGEBRAIN.COM

☐ Gain unique perspectives on key concepts with new 4LTR concept videos in the e-book.

☐ Increase your comprehension with Aplia for MGMT11.

☐ Complete interactive content within the e-book.

9 | Designing Adaptive Organizations

LEARNING OUTCOMES

9-1 Describe the departmentalization approach to organizational structure.

9-2 Explain organizational authority.

9-3 Discuss the different methods for job design.

9-4 Explain the methods that companies are using to redesign internal organizational processes (that is, intraorganizational processes).

9-5 Describe the methods that companies are using to redesign external organizational processes (that is, interorganizational processes).

After you finish this chapter, go to **PAGE 205** for **STUDY TOOLS**

canbedone/Shutterstock.com

9-1 DEPARTMENTALIZATION

Organizational structure is the vertical and horizontal configuration of departments, authority, and jobs within a company. Organizational structure is concerned with questions such as, "Who reports to whom?" and "Who does what?" and "Where is the work done?" In their 2016 letter to shareholders, Chairman David Thomson and CEO James Smith described the core businesses of Thomson Reuters ("the answer company") like this: "We help investors make smarter investments. We help lawyers practice better law. We help accounting professionals craft the best advice. We do this for some of the biggest companies in the world, as well as some of the smallest."[1] Thomson Reuters is organized into three business units: Financial & Risk ($6 billion in annual revenues), which provides information to traders, investors, and marketplaces;

Organizational structure the vertical and horizontal configuration of departments, authority, and jobs within a company

Legal ($3.4 billion), which provides information to global businesses, law firms, governments, and universities; and Tax & Accounting ($1.5 billion), which provides information to tax professionals, companies, and governments. Those three business units are supported by the Corporate & Other division ($304 million), which provides each business unit help with strategy, funding, technology, and human resources. The "other" in this division is Reuters News, which generates news stories for print, Internet, and TV media outlets.

You can see Thomson Reuters's organizational structure in Exhibit 9.1. In the first half of the chapter, you will learn about the traditional vertical and horizontal approaches to organizational structure, including departmentalization, organizational authority, and job design.

An **organizational process** is the collection of activities that transform inputs into outputs that customers value.[2] Organizational process asks, "How do things get done?" For example, Microsoft uses basic internal and external processes, shown in Exhibit 9.2, to write computer software. The process starts when Microsoft gets feedback from customers through the Windows Insider Program and the Windows Insider Program for Business. This information helps Microsoft understand customers' needs and problems and identify important software issues and needed changes. Microsoft then rewrites the software, testing it internally at the company

Organizational process
the collection of activities that transforms inputs into outputs that customers value

and then externally through its beta testing process in which customers in its Windows Insider programs provide extensive feedback used to improve the software. Ten million people, from every country on earth but two (Cuba and North Korea), participate as Microsoft Insiders. Using the Feedback Hub App they report bugs that crash programs and indicate what changes and functionality they want. After final corrections are made, Microsoft distributes the officially updated version to its broader base of 400 million customers. The feedback process never ends, however, because as soon as Microsoft releases a new version of Windows, that release is followed by a beta version for testing and feedback from Microsoft's 10 million Windows Insiders.[3]

This process view of Microsoft, which focuses on how things get done, is very different from the hierarchical view of Thomson Reuters, which focuses on accountability, responsibility, and positions within the chain of command. In the second half of the chapter, you will learn how companies use reengineering and empowerment to redesign their internal organizational processes. The chapter ends with a discussion about the ways in which companies are redesigning their external processes, that is, how they are changing to improve their interactions with those outside the company. In that discussion, you will explore the basics of modular and virtual organizations.

Traditionally, organizational structures have been based on some form of departmentalization. **Departmentalization** is a method of subdividing work and workers into separate organizational units that take responsibility for completing particular tasks.[4] EBay has separate departments or divisions for payment systems, warehousing and logistics, and marketplaces and selling.[5]

Traditionally, organizational structures have been created by departmentalizing work according to five methods: 9-1a functional, 9-1b product, 9-1c customer, 9-1d geographic, and 9-1e matrix.

9-1a Functional Departmentalization

One of the most common organizational structures is functional departmentalization. Companies tend to use this structure when they are small or just starting out, but nearly a quarter of large companies (50,000 or more employees) also use functional

Departmentalization
subdividing work and workers into separate organizational units responsible for completing particular tasks

Exhibit 9.1
Organizational Chart at Thomson Reuters

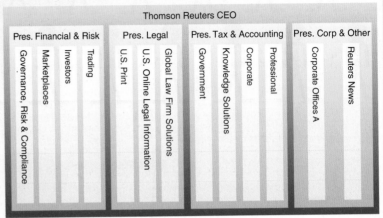

Source: "Thomson Reuters Fact Book 2016," accessed April 11, 2017, http://ir.thomsonreuters.com/phoenix.zhtml?c=76540&p=irol-factbook; "2016 Annual Report," Thomson Reuters, March 9, 2017, accessed April 11, 2017, https://annual-report.thomsonreuters.com/working-like-a-start-up.html.

Exhibit 9.2
Process View of Microsoft's Organization

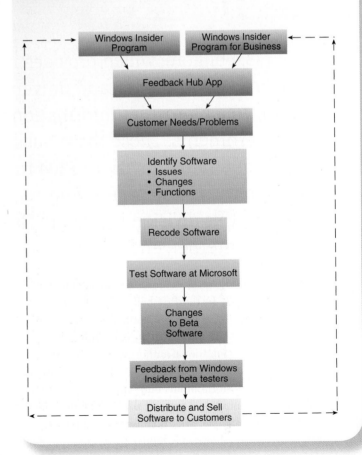

Exhibit 9.3
Functional Departmentalization

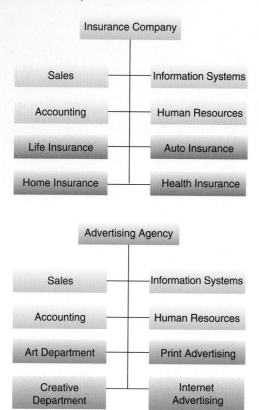

Insurance Company
- Sales
- Information Systems
- Accounting
- Human Resources
- Life Insurance
- Auto Insurance
- Home Insurance
- Health Insurance

Advertising Agency
- Sales
- Information Systems
- Accounting
- Human Resources
- Art Department
- Print Advertising
- Creative Department
- Internet Advertising

Functional departmentalization has some advantages. First, it allows work to be done by highly qualified specialists. While the accountants in the accounting department take responsibility for producing accurate revenue and expense figures, the engineers in research and development can focus their efforts on designing a product that is reliable and simple to manufacture. Second, it lowers costs by reducing duplication. When the engineers in research and development come up with a fantastic new product, they don't have to worry about creating an aggressive advertising campaign to sell it. That task belongs to the advertising experts and sales representatives in marketing. Third, with everyone in the same department having similar work experience or training, communication and coordination are less problematic for departmental managers.

At the same time, functional departmentalization has a number of disadvantages. To start, cross-department coordination can be difficult. Managers and employees are often more interested in doing what's right for their function than in doing what's right for the entire organization. A good example is the traditional conflict between marketing and manufacturing. Marketing typically pushes for spending more money to make more products with more capabilities to meet customer needs. By contrast, manufacturing pushes for fewer products with simpler designs so that manufacturing facilities can ship finished products on time and keep costs within expense budgets. As companies grow, functional departmentalization may also lead to slower decision making and produce managers and workers with narrow experience and expertise.

departmentalization.[6] **Functional departmentalization** organizes work and workers into separate units responsible for particular business functions or areas of expertise. A common functional structure might have individuals organized into accounting, sales, marketing, production, and human resources departments.

Not all functionally departmentalized companies have the same functions. The insurance company and the advertising agency shown in Exhibit 9.3 both have sales, accounting, human resources, and information systems departments, as indicated by the pale orange boxes. The purple and green boxes indicate the functions that are different. As would be expected, the insurance company has separate departments for life, auto, home, and health insurance. The advertising agency has departments for artwork, creative work, print advertising, and Internet advertising. So the functional departments in a company that uses functional structure depend, in part, on the business or industry a company is in.

9-1b Product Departmentalization

Product departmentalization organizes work and workers into separate units responsible for producing particular products or services. Exhibit 9.4 shows the product departmentalization structure used by United Technologies Corporation (UTC), which is organized along four different areas each with its own product line: Climate, Controls & Security (Carrier heating, ventilating, and air-conditioning; Fire safety, security products and services; and food/transport refrigeration), Pratt & Whitney jet engines (Pratt & Whitney Commercial Engines, Pratt & Whitney Military Engines, Pratt & Whitney Canada, and Pratt & Whitney Aero-Power), UTC Aerospace Systems (wing and cockpit controls, landing systems

Functional departmentalization organizing work and workers into separate units responsible for particular business functions or areas of expertise

Product departmentalization organizing work and workers into separate units responsible for producing particular products or services

Exhibit 9.4
Product Departmentalization: UTC

UTC Climate, Controls & Security			Pratt & Whitney				UTC Aerospace Systems	Otis
Carrier HVAC	Fire Safety and Security	Food & Transport Refrigeration	Pratt & Whitney Commercial Engines	Pratt & Whitney Military Engines	Pratt & Whitney Canada	Pratt & Whitney Aero-Power	Wing and cockpit controls, landing systems and sensors, aerostructures, electric power systems and plane interiors.	Elevators, escalators, and moving walkways
— Customer Service — Engineering — Human Resources — Information Technology — Legal — Maintenance & Field Operations — Manufacturing — Marketing & Sales — Sourcing & Logistics			— Administrative Services — Communication & Public Relations — Customer Service & Support — E-Business — Engineering — Enterprise Resource Planning — Environmental Health & Safety — Facilities & Services — Human Resources — Legal — Manufacturing — Procurement — Quality					

Source: "At a Glance," UTC, accessed April 11, 2017, http://www.utc.com/Our-Businesses/Pages/At-A-Glance.aspx.

and sensors, aerostructures, electric power systems, and plane interiors), and Otis (elevators, escalators, and moving walkways).[7]

One of the advantages of product departmentalization is that, like functional departmentalization, it allows managers and workers to specialize in one area of expertise. Unlike the narrow expertise and experiences in functional departmentalization, however, managers and workers develop a broader set of experiences and expertise related to an entire product line. Likewise, product departmentalization makes it easier for top managers to assess work-unit performance. Because of the clear separation of their four different product divisions, UTC's top managers can easily compare the performance of UTC Aerospace Systems division and the Pratt & Whitney aircraft engines division. In 2016, Pratt & Whitney's sales ($15.1 billion) were slightly larger than UTC Aerospace's ($14.5 billion), but UTC Aerospace had a profit of $2.3 billion (a 15.9% margin) compared to Pratt & Whitney's profit of $1.8 billion (11.9% margin).[8]

Finally, decision making should be faster because managers and workers are responsible for the entire product line rather than for separate functional departments; in other words, there are fewer conflicts compared to functional departmentalization.

The primary disadvantage of product departmentalization is duplication. You can see in Exhibit 9.4 that both the UTC Climate, Controls & Security division and the Pratt & Whitney division have customer service, engineering, human resources, legal, manufacturing, and procurement (similar to sourcing and logistics) departments. Duplication like this often results in higher costs. If UTC was organized by function, one legal department would handle matters related to both air conditioners and aircraft engines rather than working on only one or the other.

A second disadvantage is the challenge of coordinating across the different product departments. UTC would probably have difficulty standardizing its policies and procedures in product departments as different as the Carrier (heating, ventilating, and

Exhibit 9.5
Customer Departmentalization: Swisscom AG

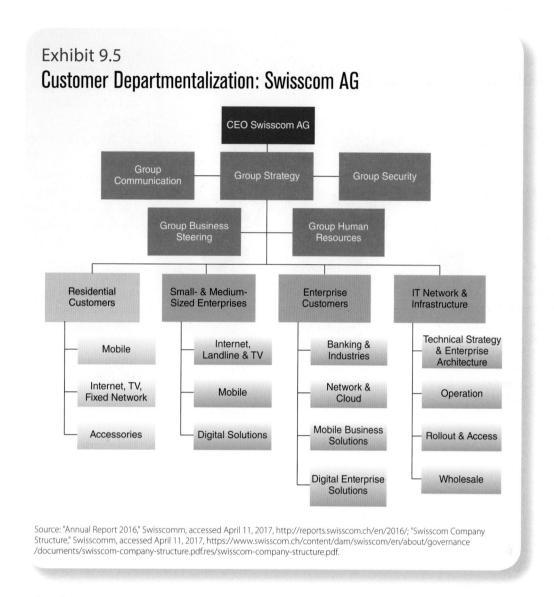

Source: "Annual Report 2016," Swisscomm, accessed April 11, 2017, http://reports.swisscom.ch/en/2016/; "Swisscom Company Structure," Swisscomm, accessed April 11, 2017, https://www.swisscom.ch/content/dam/swisscom/en/about/governance /documents/swisscom-company-structure.pdf.res/swisscom-company-structure.pdf.

air-conditioning) and UTC Aerospace (cockpit controls and landing systems) divisions.

9-1c Customer Departmentalization

Customer departmentalization organizes work and workers into separate units responsible for particular kinds of customers. For example, as Exhibit 9.5 shows, Swisscom AG, Switzerland's leading telecommunications provider, is organized into departments by type of customer: residential customers (mobile, Internet, TV and fixed network, and accessories), small- and medium-sized businesses (Internet, landline and TV, mobile, and digital solutions), enterprise customers (banking and industries, network and cloud, mobile business solutions, and digital enterprise solutions), and IT network and infrastructure (technical strategy and enterprise architecture, operations, rollout and access, and wholesale).[9]

The primary advantage of customer departmentalization is that it focuses the organization on customer needs rather than on products or business functions. Furthermore, creating separate departments to serve specific kinds of customers allows companies to specialize and adapt their products and services to customer needs and problems. The primary disadvantage of customer departmentalization is that, like product departmentalization, it leads to duplication of resources. This is why Swisscom AG also has five "group" functions—communication, strategy, security, business steering, and human resources—that support each of its four customer departments, and avoids the disadvantage of duplication common to customer departmentalization structures. It can be difficult to achieve coordination across different customer departments, as is also the

Customer departmentalization organizing work and workers into separate units responsible for particular kinds of customers

Exhibit 9.6
Geographic Departmentalization: AB InBev Company

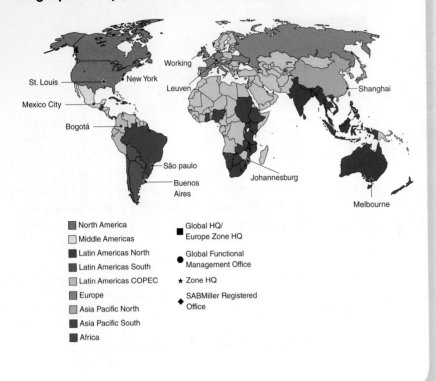

- ■ North America
- □ Middle Americas
- ■ Latin Americas North
- ■ Latin Americas South
- ■ Latin Americas COPEC
- ■ Europe
- ■ Asia Pacific North
- ■ Asia Pacific South
- ■ Africa

- ■ Global HQ/ Europe Zone HQ
- ● Global Functional Management Office
- ★ Zone HQ
- ◆ SABMiller Registered Office

Map labels: St. Louis, New York, Working, Leuven, Mexico City, Bogotá, Shanghai, São paulo, Buenos Aires, Johannesburg, Melbourne

case with product departmentalization. Finally, the emphasis on meeting customers' needs may lead workers to make decisions that please customers but hurt the business.

9-1d Geographic Departmentalization

Geographic departmentalization organizes work and workers into separate units responsible for doing business in particular geographic areas. Exhibit 9.6 shows the geographic departmentalization used by **AB InBev**, the largest beer brewer in the world. AB InBev has operations in 50 countries, 200,000 employees, and annual revenue of $45.5 billion.[10] As shown in

> **Geographic departmentalization** organizing work and workers into separate units responsible for doing business in particular geographic areas

Exhibit 9.6, AB InBev has nine regional groups: North America, Middle Americas, Latin America North, Latin America South, Latin America COPEC, Europe, Asia Pacific North, Asia Pacific South, and Africa. Each of these regions would be a sizable company by itself. The smallest region, Latin America COPEC, for instance, sold 30 million hectoliters of beverages for an estimate annual revenue of $5.5 billion.

The primary advantage of geographic departmentalization is that it helps companies respond to the demands of different markets. This can be especially important when the company sells in different countries. For example, while AB InBev has three brands sold worldwide (Budweiser, Stella Artois, and Corona), and three sold in multiple countries (Beck's, Hoegaarden, and Leffe), most of its brands are local. You'll find the Antarctica and Brahma brands in Brazil, the Belle-Vue and Jupiler brands in Belgium, and the Sibirskaya Korona and Klinskoye brands in Russia.[11]

Another advantage is that geographic departmentalization can reduce costs by locating unique organizational resources closer to customers. For instance, it is cheaper in the long run for AB InBev to build bottling plants in each region than to, for example, transport beer to Mexico, where it has seven beverage plants, after it has been brewed and bottled in Brazil, where it has 25 beverage plants.[12]

The primary disadvantage of geographic departmentalization is that it can lead to duplication of resources. For example, while it may be necessary to adapt products

iStock.com/Micropic

and marketing to different geographic locations, it's doubtful that AB InBev needs significantly different inventory tracking systems from location to location. Also, even more than with the other forms of departmentalization, it can be difficult to coordinate departments that are literally thousands of miles from each other and whose managers have very limited contact with each other.

9-1e Matrix Departmentalization

Matrix departmentalization is a hybrid structure in which two or more forms of departmentalization are used together. The most common matrix combines the product and functional forms of departmentalization, but other forms may also be used. Exhibit 9.7 shows the matrix structure used by Procter & Gamble, which has 105,000 employees working in 70 different countries.[13] Across the top of Exhibit 9.7, you can see that the company uses a product structure where it groups its 22 billion-dollar brands (Pampers, Bounty, Tampax, Crest, Vicks, Gillette, Swiffer, Pantene, and Old Spice are shown for illustration) into four business units: Baby, Feminine & Family Care; Health & Grooming; Fabric & Home Care; and Beauty,

Hair & Personal Care. Each of these units is responsible for developing, manufacturing, and marketing its brands to consumers. As such, each unit operates its own research and development department and product supply initiative. The left side of the figure shows that the company also uses a functional structure based on five functions—finance, human resources (HR), communications, legal, and information technology (IT)—and a set of shared global business services including payroll, purchases, data analytics, benefits, and facilities management. The right side of the figure shows that the selling and market operation functions (SMOs) are external to the brand units but are not part of the other functional groups. SMOs make sure that a product is sold, distributed, shelved, and priced well within a particular region of the world. P&G's SMO regions include Asia Pacific; Europe; Greater China; Latin America; North America; and India, the Middle East, and Africa (IMEA).[14]

The boxes in Exhibit 9.7 represent the matrix structure created by the combination of the

> **Matrix departmentalization**
> a hybrid organizational structure in which two or more forms of departmentalization, most often product and functional, are used together

Exhibit 9.7
Matrix Departmentalization: Procter & Gamble

	Business Units									
	Baby, Feminine, & Family Care			Health & Grooming		Fabric & Home Care			Beauty, Hair, & Personal Care		
	Baby Care	Family Care	Feminine Care	Oral Care	Personal Health Care	Shave Care	Fabric Care	Home Care	Hair Care	Skin & Personal Care	
Finance	Pampers	Bounty	Tampax	Crest	Vicks	Gillette	Tide	Swiffer	Pantene	Old Spice	
Human resources	Pampers	Bounty	Tampax	Crest	Vicks	Gillette	Tide	Swiffer	Pantene	Old Spice	
Communications	Pampers	Bounty	Tampax	Crest	Vicks	Gillette	Tide	Swiffer	Pantene	Old Spice	Selling & Market Operations (SMOs)
Legal	Pampers	Bounty	Tampax	Crest	Vicks	Gillette	Tide	Swiffer	Pantene	Old Spice	
Information technology	Pampers	Bounty	Tampax	Crest	Vicks	Gillette	Tide	Swiffer	Pantene	Old Spice	
Global business services	Pampers	Bounty	Tampax	Crest	Vicks	Gillette	Tide	Swiffer	Pantene	Old Spice	

Source: "Corporate Structure," Procter & Gamble, accessed April 11, 2017, http://us.pg.com/who_we_are/structure_governance/corporate_structure.

Exhibit 9.8
Procter & Gamble's Concentric Matrix

Source: "Corporate Structure," Procter & Gamble, accessed April 11, 2017, http://us.pg.com/who_we_are/structure_governance/corporate_structure.

product and functional structures. For example, P&G's Gillette Group (Gillette is a global brand for men's grooming products within the Shave Care segment of the Health & Grooming unit) would work with SMOs to sell, market, and distribute Gillette products worldwide; use global business services to work with suppliers and keep costs down; and then rely on corporate functions for assistance in hiring employees, billing customers, and paying suppliers. Similar matrix combinations are shown for Pampers, Bounty, Tampax, Crest, Vicks, Tide, Swiffer, Pantene, and Old Spice within each of the segments of P&G's four global business units. As shown in Exhibit 9.8, P&G envisions its complex matrix as a set of concentric circles: the business functions at the core, then the brands, then the selling and market operations on the circle closest to the customer.

Several things distinguish matrix departmentalization from the other traditional forms of departmentalization.[15] First, most employees report to two bosses, one from each core part of the matrix. For example, in Exhibit 9.7 a manager on the Pampers team responsible for marketing would report to a boss in the baby care segment of the Baby, Feminine, & Family Care global business unit as well as to a manager in Selling and Market Operations. Second, by virtue of their hybrid design, matrix structures lead to much more cross-functional interaction than other forms of departmentalization. In

fact, while matrix workers are typically members of only one functional department (based on their work experience and expertise), they are also commonly members of several ongoing project, product, or customer groups. Third, because of the high level of cross-functional interaction, matrix departmentalization requires significant coordination between managers in the different parts of the matrix. In particular, managers have the complex job of tracking and managing the multiple demands (project, product, customer, or functional) on employees' time.

The primary advantage of matrix departmentalization is that it allows companies to manage in an efficient manner large, complex tasks such as researching, developing, and marketing pharmaceuticals or carrying out complex global businesses. Efficiency comes from avoiding duplication. For example, rather than having an entire information technology function for each project, the company simply assigns and reassigns workers from the information technology department at P&G as they are needed at various stages of product completion. More specifically, an employee may simultaneously be part of five different ongoing projects but may be actively completing work on only a few projects at a time. Another advantage is the pool of resources available to carry out large, complex tasks. Because of the ability to quickly pull in expert help from all the functional areas of the company, matrix project managers have a much more diverse set of expertise and experience at their disposal than managers in the other forms of departmentalization.

The primary disadvantage of matrix departmentalization is the high level of coordination required to manage the complexity involved in running large, ongoing projects at various levels of completion. Matrix structures

All Tide products are part of the Fabric & Home Care business unit at P&G.

are notorious for confusion and conflict between project bosses in different parts of the matrix. Disagreements or misunderstandings about schedules, budgets, available resources, and the availability of employees with particular functional expertise are common in matrix structures. Because of these problems, many matrix structures evolve from a **simple matrix**, in which managers in different parts of the matrix negotiate conflicts and resources directly, to a **complex matrix**, in which specialized matrix managers and departments are added to the organizational structure. In a complex matrix, managers from different parts of the matrix might report to the same matrix manager, who helps them sort out conflicts and problems.

9-2 ORGANIZATIONAL AUTHORITY

The second part of traditional organizational structures is authority. **Authority** is the right to give commands, take action, and make decisions to achieve organizational objectives.[16]

Traditionally, organizational authority has been characterized by the following dimensions: 9-2a chain of command, 9-2b line versus staff authority, 9-2c delegation of authority, and 9-2d degree of centralization.

9-2a Chain of Command

Consider again the United Technologies organizational structure. A manager in any of the corporation's divisions ultimately reports to the head of that division. That division head, in turn, reports to the corporation's CEO Gregory Hayes. This line, which vertically connects every job in the company to higher levels of management, represents the chain of command. The **chain of command** is the vertical line of authority that clarifies who reports to whom throughout the organization. People higher in the chain of command have the right, *if they so choose*, to give commands, take action, and make decisions concerning activities occurring anywhere below them in the chain. In the following discussion about delegation and decentralization, you will learn that

managers don't always choose to exercise their authority directly.[17]

One of the key assumptions underlying the chain of command is **unity of command**, which means that workers should report to just one boss.[18] In practical terms, this means that only one person can be in charge at a time. Matrix organizations, in which employees have two bosses, automatically violate this principle. This is one of the primary reasons that matrix organizations are difficult to manage. Unity of command serves an important purpose: to prevent the confusion that might arise when an employee receives conflicting commands from two different bosses. Companies don't necessarily have to have a matrix organization to violate unity of command—they can do so by appointing two CEOs. While co-CEO arrangements sometimes work well, they are rare and often short-lived because, according to research from Professor Lindred Greer, having co-CEOs "causes conflict," leads to "negative performance by [executive] teams," and may likely result in the development of "hostile mindsets" as the co-CEOs struggle to work together.[19] With market share and profits declining, Whole Foods abandoned its co-CEO arrangement. Analyst Brian Yarbrough commented, "When business is going great, there aren't a lot of disagreements, and it can work. But when times get tough, that's when you

Gajus/Shutterstock.com

start to bump heads."[20] Deutsche Bank's co-CEOs resigned abruptly after a series of financial mistakes and regulatory penalties.[21] Finally, Chipotle founder Steve Els became the sole CEO again after co-CEO Monty Moran resigned. Board director Neil Flanzraich said, "Given the ongoing challenges facing the company, the board felt strongly that it was best for Steve to resume leadership of the company going forward."[22]

Simple matrix a form of matrix departmentalization in which managers in different parts of the matrix negotiate conflicts and resources

Complex matrix a form of matrix departmentalization in which managers in different parts of the matrix report to matrix managers, who help them sort out conflicts and problems

Authority the right to give commands, take action, and make decisions to achieve organizational objectives

Chain of command the vertical line of authority that clarifies who reports to whom throughout the organization

Unity of command a management principle that workers should report to just one boss

9-2b Line versus Staff Authority

A second dimension of authority is the distinction between line and staff authority. **Line authority** is the right to command immediate subordinates in the chain of command. For example, Thomson Reuters CEO James C. Smith has line authority over the president of the company's Financial & Risk Information division. Smith can issue orders to that division president and expect them to be carried out. In turn, the president of the Financial & Risk Information division can issue orders to his subordinates, who run the trading, investors, marketplaces, and governance, risk, and compliance divisions, and expect them to be carried out. By contrast, **staff authority** is the right to advise but not command others who are not subordinates in the chain of command. For example, a manager in human resources at Thomson Reuters might advise the manager in charge of the Thomson Reuters Tax & Accounting group on a hiring decision but cannot order him or her to hire a certain applicant.

The terms *line* and *staff* are also used to describe different functions within the organization. A **line function** is an activity that contributes directly to creating or selling the company's products. So, for example, activities that take place within the manufacturing and marketing departments would be considered line functions. A **staff function**, such as accounting, human resources, or legal services, does not contribute directly to creating or selling the company's products but instead supports line activities. For example, marketing managers might consult with the legal staff to ensure the wording of an advertisement is within the law.

Line authority the right to command immediate subordinates in the chain of command

Staff authority the right to advise, but not command, others who are not subordinates in the chain of command

Line function an activity that contributes directly to creating or selling the company's products

Staff function an activity that does not contribute directly to creating or selling the company's products but instead supports line activities

Delegation of authority the assignment of direct authority and responsibility to a subordinate to complete tasks for which the manager is normally responsible

Exhibit 9.9
Delegation: Responsibility, Authority, and Accountability

Source: C. D. Pringle, D. F. Jennings, and J. G. Longenecker, *Managing Organizations: Functions and Behaviors* (Columbus, Ohio: Merrill Publishing, 1984).

9-2c Delegation of Authority

Managers can exercise their authority directly by completing tasks themselves, or they can choose to pass on some of their authority to subordinates. **Delegation of authority** is the assignment of direct authority and responsibility to a subordinate to complete tasks for which the manager is normally responsible.

When a manager delegates work, three transfers occur, as illustrated in Exhibit 9.9. First, the manager transfers full responsibility for the assignment to the subordinate. At Apple, when you've been delegated to a certain task, you become the DRI, or the "directly responsible individual." As a former Apple employee explains, "Any effective meeting at Apple will have an action list. Next to each action item will be the DRI," who of course, is responsible for completing that delegated responsibility. Furthermore, when you're trying to figure out who to contact to get something done in Apple's corporate structure, people simply ask, "Who's the DRI on that?"[23] TripAdvisor's Matthew Mamet says, "When I'm the DRI on a task, it can sometimes come with a bit of apprehension (*Gulp*, not 100% sure how I'm going to do that . . .but ok I'll figure it out), or maybe with a bit of grumbling (oh man, I guess I gotta do that, too), but being the DRI always comes with a sense of responsibility to the team."[24]

Many managers, however, find giving up full responsibility somewhat difficult. When Lori Lord was COO of **Spectrum Health Care**, she stayed up all night writing and reviewing 400-page requests for proposals (RFPs), upon which the company's sales and growth depended. Lord maintained tight control over the RFPs because she considered them critical to the company's success and believed that she was the only person who could do it right. "These were so important for our organization and I wouldn't let anyone else put the document[s] together."[25] One reason it is difficult for some managers to delegate is that they often fear that the task won't be done as well as if they did it themselves. However, one CEO says, "If you can delegate a task to somebody who can do it 75 percent to 80 percent as well as you can today, you delegate it immediately." Why? Many tasks don't need to be done perfectly; they just need to be *done*. And delegating tasks that someone else can do frees managers to assume other important responsibilities. After Lori Lord learned to delegate the RFP review along with other day-to-day activities, she could attend key meetings, focus on the future of the organization, and concentrate on growth, all activities critical to her new role as the company's CEO. She says that she lost five years of her life from not delegating and that now, "I'm glad I don't have to be here at 3 a.m. anymore."[26] Delegating authority can generate a related problem: micromanaging. Sometimes managers delegate only to interfere later with how the employee is performing the task. But delegating full responsibility means that the employee—not the manager—is now completely responsible for task completion. Good managers need to trust their subordinates to do the job.

The second transfer that occurs with delegation is that the manager gives the subordinate full authority over the budget, resources, and personnel needed to do the job. To do the job effectively, subordinates must have the same tools and information at their disposal that managers had when they were responsible for the same task. In other words, for delegation to work, delegated authority must be commensurate with delegated responsibility.

The third transfer that occurs with delegation is the transfer of accountability. The subordinate now has the authority and responsibility to do the job and, in return, is accountable for getting the job done. In other words, managers delegate their managerial authority and responsibility to subordinates in exchange for results.

9-2d Degree of Centralization

Centralization of authority is the location of most authority at the upper levels of the organization. In a centralized organization, managers make most decisions, even the relatively small ones. Store managers at Whole Foods' 430 locations have long been responsible for deciding what to sell in their own stores. To compete more efficiently against Kroger and Costco, however, **Whole Foods** has decided to centralize purchasing responsibilities for meat, produce, and many nonperishable items at the company's Austin, Texas, headquarters. Co-CEO John Mackey says of the change, "We want to evolve the structure in such a way that we take out redundancy and waste."[27]

Decentralization is the location of a significant amount of authority in the lower levels of the organization. An organization is decentralized if it has a high degree of

Volkswagen will apply standardization to decrease costs on production of its popular Golf model.

delegation at all levels. In a decentralized organization, workers closest to problems are authorized to make the decisions necessary to solve the problems on their own.

At Gap, a struggling clothes retailer, CEO Art Peck hopes decentralization produces faster, more effective decisions. Peck first eliminated sign-offs that slowed decisions. So brand merchants acting as fashion collection editors no longer approve every product category. Step two was pushing decision-making authority out to those closest to problems. For example, Gap's foreign suppliers, who make most of the clothes sold in Gap stores, are now authorized to make decisions on items like men's dress shirts.[28]

Decentralization has a number of advantages. It develops employee capabilities throughout the company and leads to faster decision making and more satisfied customers and employees. Furthermore, a study of 1,000 large companies found that companies with a high degree of decentralization outperformed those with a low degree of decentralization in terms of return on assets (6.9% versus 4.7%), return on investment (14.6% versus 9.0%), return on equity (22.8% versus 16.6%), and return on sales (10.3% versus 6.3%). Surprisingly, the same study found that few large companies actually are decentralized. Specifically, only 31 percent of employees in these 1,000 companies were responsible for recommending improvements to management. Overall, just 10 percent of employees received the training and information needed to support a truly decentralized approach to management.[29]

Centralization of authority the location of most authority at the upper levels of the organization

Decentralization the location of a significant amount of authority in the lower levels of the organization

With results like these, the key question is no longer *whether* companies should decentralize, but *where* they should decentralize. One rule of thumb is to stay centralized where standardization is important and to decentralize where standardization is unimportant. **Standardization** is solving problems by consistently applying the same rules, procedures, and processes. Volkswagen (VW) is one of the largest automakers in the world with a dozen brands (Volkswagen Passenger Cars, Audi, SEAT, ŠKODA, Bentley, Bugatti, Lamborghini, Porsche, Ducati, Volkswagen Commercial Vehicles, Scania trucks and buses, and MAN trucks and buses), 620,000 employees, 121 factories, and 330 different vehicles! Running a company this size is enormously complex. For example, the VW Golf, long one of the company's best selling models, can be made with 89 different steering wheels and 24 different radiator grilles. Using that many varieties for the same part not only increases costs (VW is barely profitable), it decreases quality and reliability. So CEO Matthias Mueller is using standardization to address this problem. The goal is to use a small number of standard parts across different car platforms, eliminating 15,000 different parts in the process. That, combined with job cuts, will contribute to reducing costs by $4 billion a year.[30]

9-3 JOB DESIGN

Could you stand to do the same simple tasks an average of 50 times per hour, 400 times per day, 2,000 times per week, 8,000 times per month? Few can. Fast-food workers rarely stay on the job more than six months. In fact, McDonald's and other fast-food restaurants have well over 70 percent employee turnover each year.[31] As a drive-through employee at McDonald's, you would repeatedly perform the following steps:

1. Say, "Welcome to McDonald's. May I have your order please?"

2. Listen to the order. Repeat it for accuracy. State the total cost. "Please drive to the second window."

3. Take the money. Make change.

4. Give customers cups, straws, and napkins.

5. Give customers food.

6. Say, "Thank you for coming to McDonald's."

Standardization solving problems by consistently applying the same rules, procedures, and processes

Job design the number, kind, and variety of tasks that individual workers perform in doing their jobs

Job specialization a job composed of a small part of a larger task or process

In this section, you will learn about **job design**—the number, kind, and variety of tasks that individual workers perform in doing their jobs.

*You will learn **9-3a why companies continue to use specialized jobs such as the McDonald's drive-through job** and **9-3b how job rotation, job enlargement, job enrichment**, and **9-3c the job characteristics model** are being used to overcome the problems associated with job specialization.*

9-3a Job Specialization

Job specialization occurs when a job is composed of a small part of a larger task or process. Specialized jobs are characterized by simple, easy-to-learn steps; low variety; and high repetition, such as the McDonald's drive-through window job just described. One of the clear disadvantages of specialized jobs is that, being so easy to learn, they quickly become boring. This, in turn, can lead to low job satisfaction and high absenteeism and employee turnover, all of which are very costly to organizations.

Why, then, do companies continue to create and use specialized jobs? The primary reason is that specialized jobs are very economical. As we learned from Frederick W. Taylor and Frank and Lillian Gilbreth in Chapter 2, after a job has been specialized, it takes little time to learn and master. Consequently, when experienced workers quit or are absent, the company can replace them with new employees and lose little productivity. For example, next time you're at McDonald's, notice the pictures of the food on the cash registers. These pictures make it easy for McDonald's trainees to quickly learn to take orders. Likewise, to simplify and speed operations at the drive-through, the drink dispensers are set to automatically fill drink cups. Put a medium cup below the dispenser. Punch the medium drink button. The soft-drink machine then fills the cup to within a half-inch of the top, while the worker goes to get your fries. At McDonald's, every task has been simplified in this way. Because the work is designed to be simple, wages can remain low because it isn't necessary to pay high salaries to attract highly experienced, educated, or trained workers.

9-3b Job Rotation, Enlargement, and Enrichment

Because of the efficiency of specialized jobs, companies are often reluctant to eliminate them. Consequently, job redesign efforts have focused on modifying jobs to keep the benefits of specialized jobs while reducing their obvious costs and disadvantages. Three methods—job rotation, job enlargement, and job enrichment—have been used to try to improve specialized jobs.[32]

Job rotation attempts to overcome the disadvantages of job specialization by periodically moving workers from one specialized job to another to give them more variety and the opportunity to use different skills. For example, an office receptionist who does nothing but answer phones could be systematically rotated to a different job, such as typing, filing, or data entry, every day or two. Likewise, the "mirror attacher" in an automobile plant might attach mirrors in the first half of the work shift and then install bumpers during the second half. Because employees simply switch from one specialized job to another, job rotation allows companies to retain the economic benefits of specialized work. At the same time, the greater variety of tasks makes the work less boring and more satisfying for workers.

Another way to counter the disadvantages of specialization is to enlarge the job. **Job enlargement** increases the number of different tasks that a worker performs within one particular job. Instead of being assigned just one task, workers with enlarged jobs are given several tasks to perform. For example, an enlarged "mirror attacher" job might include attaching the mirror, checking to see that the mirror's power adjustment controls work, and then cleaning the mirror's surface. Though job enlargement increases variety, many workers report feeling more stress when their jobs are enlarged. Consequently, many workers view enlarged jobs as simply more work, especially if they are not given additional time to complete the additional tasks.

Job enrichment attempts to overcome the deficiencies in specialized work by increasing the number of tasks *and* by giving workers the authority and control to make meaningful decisions about their work.[33]

9-3c Job Characteristics Model

In contrast to job rotation, job enlargement, and job enrichment, which focus on providing variety in job tasks, the **job characteristics model (JCM)** is an approach to job redesign that seeks to formulate jobs in ways that motivate workers and lead to positive work outcomes.[34]

As shown in Exhibit 9.10, the primary goal of the model is to create jobs that result in positive personal and work outcomes, such as internal work motivation, satisfaction with one's job, and work effectiveness. Of these, the central concern of the JCM is internal motivation. **Internal motivation** is motivation that comes from the job itself rather than from outside rewards such as a raise or praise from the boss. If workers feel that performing the job well is itself rewarding, then the job has internal motivation. Statements such as "I get a nice sense of accomplishment" or "I feel good about myself and what I'm producing" are examples of internal motivation.

In Exhibit 9.10, you can see that the JCM specifies three critical psychological states that must occur for work to be internally motivating. First, workers must *experience the work as meaningful*; that is, they must view their job as being important. Second, they must *experience responsibility for work outcomes*—they must feel personally responsible for the work being done well. Third, workers must have *knowledge of results*; that is, they must know how well they are performing their jobs. All three critical psychological states must occur for work to be internally motivating.

For example, grocery store cashiers usually have knowledge of results. When you're slow, your checkout line grows long. If you make a mistake, customers point it out: "No, I think that's on sale for $2.99, not $3.99." Likewise, cashiers experience responsibility for work outcomes. At the end of the day, the register is totaled, and the money is counted. Ideally, the money matches the total sales in the register. If the money in the till is less than what's recorded in the register, most stores make the cashier pay the difference. Consequently, most cashiers are very careful to avoid being caught short at the end of the day. Nonetheless, despite knowing the results and experiencing responsibility for work outcomes, most grocery store cashiers (at least where I shop) aren't internally motivated because they don't experience the work as meaningful. With scanners, it takes little skill to learn or do the job. Anyone can do it. In addition, cashiers have few decisions to make, and the job is highly repetitive.

What kinds of jobs produce the three critical psychological states? Moving another step to the left in Exhibit 9.10, you can see that these psychological states arise from jobs that are strong on five core job characteristics: skill variety, task identity, task significance, autonomy, and feedback. **Skill variety** is the number of different activities performed in a job. **Task identity** is the

Job rotation periodically moving workers from one specialized job to another to give them more variety and the opportunity to use different skills

Job enlargement increasing the number of different tasks that a worker performs within one particular job

Job enrichment increasing the number of tasks in a particular job and giving workers the authority and control to make meaningful decisions about their work

Job characteristics model (JCM) an approach to job redesign that seeks to formulate jobs in ways that motivate workers and lead to positive work outcomes

Internal motivation motivation that comes from the job itself rather than from outside rewards

Skill variety the number of different activities performed in a job

Task identity the degree to which a job, from beginning to end, requires the completion of a whole and identifiable piece of work

Exhibit 9.10
Job Characteristics Model

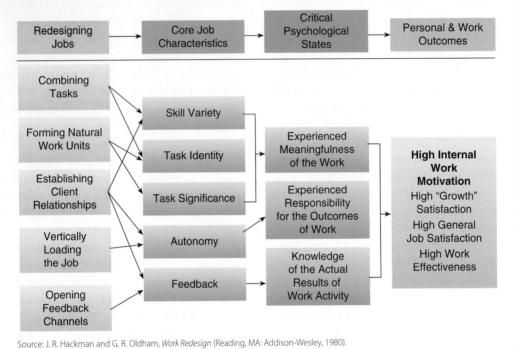

| Redesigning Jobs | → | Core Job Characteristics | → | Critical Psychological States | → | Personal & Work Outcomes |

- Combining Tasks
- Forming Natural Work Units
- Establishing Client Relationships
- Vertically Loading the Job
- Opening Feedback Channels

- Skill Variety
- Task Identity
- Task Significance
- Autonomy
- Feedback

- Experienced Meaningfulness of the Work
- Experienced Responsibility for the Outcomes of Work
- Knowledge of the Actual Results of Work Activity

High Internal Work Motivation
High "Growth" Satisfaction
High General Job Satisfaction
High Work Effectiveness

Source: J. R. Hackman and G. R. Oldham, *Work Redesign* (Reading, MA: Addison-Wesley, 1980).

degree to which a job, from beginning to end, requires completion of a whole and identifiable piece of work. **Task significance** is the degree to which a job is perceived to have a substantial impact on others inside or outside the organization. **Autonomy** is the degree to which a job gives workers the discretion, freedom, and independence to decide how and when to accomplish the work. Finally, **feedback** is the amount of information the job provides to workers about their work performance.

Task significance the degree to which a job is perceived to have a substantial impact on others inside or outside the organization

Autonomy the degree to which a job gives workers the discretion, freedom, and independence to decide how and when to accomplish the job

Feedback the amount of information the job provides to workers about their work performance

PrikGibb/Shutterstock.com

To illustrate how the core job characteristics work together,

let's use them to more thoroughly assess why the McDonald's drive-through window job is not particularly satisfying or motivating. To start, skill variety is low. Except for the size of an order or special requests ("no onions"), the process is the same for each customer. At best, task identity is moderate. Although you take the order, handle the money, and deliver the food, others are responsible for a larger part of the process—preparing the food. Task identity will be even lower if the McDonald's has two drive-through windows because each drive-through window worker will have an even more specialized task. The first is limited to taking the order and making change, while the second just delivers the food.

Task significance, the impact you have on others, is probably low. Autonomy is also very low: McDonald's has strict rules about dress, cleanliness, and procedures. But the job does provide immediate feedback such as positive and negative customer comments, car horns honking, the amount of time it takes to process orders, and the number of cars in the drive-through. With the exception of feedback, the low levels of the core job characteristics show why the drive-through window job is not internally motivating for many workers.

What can managers do when jobs aren't internally motivating? The far left column of Exhibit 9.10 lists five job redesign techniques that managers can use to strengthen a job's core characteristics. *Combining tasks* increases skill variety and task identity by joining separate, specialized tasks into larger work modules. For example, some trucking firms are now requiring truck drivers to load their rigs as well as drive them. The hope is that involving drivers in loading will ensure that trucks are properly loaded, thus reducing damage claims.

Work can be formed into *natural work units* by arranging tasks according to logical or meaningful groups. Although many trucking companies randomly assign drivers to trucks, some have begun assigning drivers to particular geographic locations (for example, the Northeast or Southwest) or to truckloads that require special driving skill (for example, oversized loads or hazardous chemicals). Forming natural work units increases task identity and task significance.

Establishing client relationships increases skill variety, autonomy, and feedback by giving employees direct contact with clients and customers. In some companies, truck drivers are expected to establish business relationships with their regular customers. When something goes wrong with a shipment, customers are told to call drivers directly.

Vertical loading means pushing some managerial authority down to workers. For truck drivers, this means that they have the same authority as managers to resolve customer problems. In some companies, if a late shipment causes problems for a customer, the driver has the authority to fully refund the cost of that shipment without first obtaining management's approval.

The last job redesign technique offered by the model, *opening feedback channels*, means finding additional ways to give employees direct, frequent feedback about their job performance. For example, with advances in electronics, many truck drivers get instantaneous data as to whether they're on schedule and driving their rigs in a fuel-efficient manner. Likewise, the increased contact with customers also means that many drivers now receive monthly data on customer satisfaction.

9-4 INTRAORGANIZA-TIONAL PROCESSES

More than 40 years ago, Tom Burns and G. M. Stalker described how two kinds of organizational designs,

mechanistic and organic, are appropriate for different kinds of organizational environments.[35] **Mechanistic organizations** are characterized by specialized jobs and responsibilities; precisely defined, unchanging roles; and a rigid chain of command based on centralized authority and vertical communication. This type of organization works best in stable, unchanging business environments. By contrast, **organic organizations** are characterized by broadly defined jobs and responsibilities; loosely defined, frequently changing roles; and decentralized authority and horizontal communication based on task knowledge. This type of organization works best in dynamic, changing business environments.

The organizational design techniques described in the first half of this chapter—departmentalization, authority, and job design—are better suited for mechanistic organizations and the stable business environments that were more prevalent before 1980. By contrast, the organizational design techniques discussed in the second part of the chapter, are more appropriate for organic organizations and the increasingly dynamic environments in which today's businesses compete. The key difference between these approaches is that mechanistic organizational designs focus on organizational structure, whereas organic organizational designs are concerned with **intraorganizational process**, which is the collection of activities that take place within an organization to transform inputs into outputs that customers value.

Let's take a look at how companies are using 9-4a reengineering and 9-4b empowerment to redesign intraorganizational processes like these.

9-4a Reengineering

In their best-selling book *Reengineering the Corporation*, Michael Hammer and James Champy define **reengineering** as "the *fundamental* rethinking and *radical* redesign of business *processes* to achieve *dramatic* improvements in critical, contemporary measures of performance, such as cost,

Mechanistic organization an organization characterized by specialized jobs and responsibilities; precisely defined, unchanging roles; and a rigid chain of command based on centralized authority and vertical communication

Organic organization an organization characterized by broadly defined jobs and responsibilities; loosely defined, frequently changing roles; and decentralized authority and horizontal communication based on task knowledge

Intraorganizational process the collection of activities that take place within an organization to transform inputs into outputs that customers value

Reengineering fundamental rethinking and radical redesign of business processes to achieve dramatic improvements in critical measures of performance, such as cost, quality, service, and speed

OPEN FLOORPLAN'S FATAL FLAW: WORKERS WANT PRIVACY

From Silicon Valley to Wall Street, 70 percent of U.S. workplaces have some version of an open floorplan. Open offices save money and space, but they also tend to have a palpable buzz and have long been touted for increasing collaboration, productivity, and transparency while flattening organizational hierarchies. While open floorplans have many benefits, a growing body of research is revealing some significant flaws in them as well. Workers in open offices experience higher levels of job stress and workplace distraction; are more likely to be absent due to illness; and are less productive than are employees who work in private spaces. Perhaps because of these reasons, many workers are interested in returning to more traditional working conditions. In a recent study of 10,000 workers around the world, 95 percent said that they wanted more privacy at work, 85 percent loathed their company's open office plans, and 31 percent said that they had to leave the office to get work done.

Sources: S. Lui, "The Open Plan Office Trap: Why It Pays to Work Alone," *Lifehacker*, January 27, 2016, accessed April 29, 2016, http://www.lifehacker.com.au/2016/01/the-open-plan-office-trap-why-it-pays-to-work-alone/; J. McGregor, "Office Designers Find Open-Plan Spaces Are Actually Lousy for Workers," *Washington Post*, April 22, 2015, accessed April 29, 2016, https://www.washingtonpost.com/news/on-leadership/wp/2015/04/22/office-designers-find-open-plan-spaces-are-actually-lousy-for-workers/; "Privacy Crisis Engulfs the Office," *Steelcase Research*, September 14, 2014, accessed April 29, 2016, http://www.prnewswire.co.uk/news-releases/privacy-crisis-engulfs-the-office-275273621.html.

quality, service and speed."[36] Hammer and Champy further explained the four key words shown in italics in this definition. The first key word is *fundamental*. When reengineering organizational designs, managers must ask themselves, "Why do we do what we do?" and "Why do we do it the way we do?" The usual answer is "Because that's the way we've always done it." The second key word is *radical*. Reengineering is about significant change, about starting over by throwing out the old ways of getting work done. The third key word is *processes*. Hammer and Champy noted that "most business people are not process oriented; they are focused on tasks, on jobs, on people, on structures, but not on processes." The fourth key word is *dramatic*. Reengineering is about achieving quantum improvements in company performance.

An example from IBM Credit's operation illustrates how work can be reengineered.[37] IBM Credit lends businesses money to buy IBM computers. Previously, the loan process began when an IBM salesperson called the home office to obtain credit

approval for a customer's purchase. The first department involved in the process took the credit information over the phone from the salesperson and recorded it on the credit form. The credit form was sent to the credit checking department, then to the pricing department (where the interest rate was determined), and on through a total of five departments. In all, it took the five departments six days to approve or deny the customer's loan. Of course, this delay cost IBM business. Some customers got their loans elsewhere. Others, frustrated by the wait, simply canceled their orders.

Finally, two IBM managers decided to walk a loan straight through each of the departments involved in the process. At each step, they asked the workers to stop what they were doing and immediately process their loan application. They were shocked by what they found. From start to finish, the entire process took just 90 minutes! The six-day turnaround time was almost entirely due to delays in handing off the work from one department to another. The solution:

IBM redesigned the process so that one person, not five people in five separate departments, now handles the entire loan approval process without any handoffs. The results were indeed dramatic. Reengineering the credit process reduced approval time from six days to four hours and allowed IBM Credit to increase the number of loans it handled by a factor of 100!

Reengineering changes an organization's orientation from vertical to horizontal. Instead of taking orders from upper management, lower- and middle-level managers and workers take orders from a customer who is at the beginning and end of each process. Instead of running independent functional departments, managers and workers in different departments take ownership of cross-functional processes. Instead of simplifying work so that it becomes increasingly specialized, reengineering complicates work by giving workers increased autonomy and responsibility for complete processes.

In essence, reengineering changes work by changing **task interdependence**, the extent to which collective action is required to complete an entire piece of work. As shown in Exhibit 9.11, there are three kinds of task interdependence.[38] In **pooled interdependence**, each job or department contributes to the whole independently. In **sequential interdependence**, work must be performed in succession because one group's or job's outputs become the inputs for the next group or job. Finally, in **reciprocal interdependence**, different jobs or groups work together in a back-and-forth manner to complete the process. By reducing the handoffs between different jobs or groups, reengineering decreases sequential interdependence. Likewise, reengineering decreases pooled interdependence by redesigning work so that formerly independent jobs or departments now work together to complete processes. Finally, reengineering increases reciprocal interdependence by making groups or individuals responsible for larger, more complete processes in which several steps may be accomplished at the same time.

As an organizational design tool, reengineering promises big rewards, but it has also come under severe criticism. The most serious complaint is that because it allows a few workers to do the work formerly done by many, reengineering is simply a corporate code word for cost cutting and worker layoffs.[39] For this reason, detractors claim that reengineering hurts morale and performance. Even though ordering times were reduced from three weeks to three days, Levi Strauss ended an $850 million reengineering project because of the fear and turmoil it created

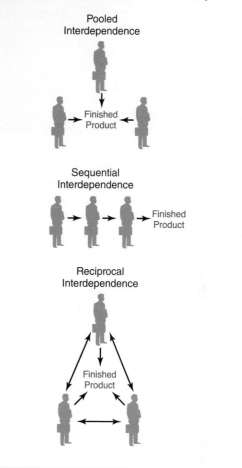

Exhibit 9.11
Reengineering and Task Interdependence

Pooled Interdependence

Finished Product

Sequential Interdependence

Finished Product

Reciprocal Interdependence

Finished Product

in the company's workforce. One low point occurred when Levi management, encouraged by its reengineering consultants, told 4,000 workers that they would have to "reapply for their jobs" as the company shifted from its traditional vertical structure to a process-based form of organizing. Thomas Kasten, Levi Strauss's vice president for reengineering and customer service at that time, says, "We felt the pressure building up [over reengineering efforts], and we were worried about the business."[40] Today,

Task interdependence the extent to which collective action is required to complete an entire piece of work

Pooled interdependence work completed by having each job or department independently contribute to the whole

Sequential interdependence work completed in succession, with one group's or job's outputs becoming the inputs for the next group or job

Reciprocal interdependence work completed by different jobs or groups working together in a back-and-forth manner even reengineering gurus Hammer and Champy admit that roughly 70 percent of all reengineering projects fail because of the effects on people in the workplace. Says Hammer, "I wasn't smart enough about that [the people issues]. I was reflecting my engineering background and was insufficiently appreciative of the human dimension. I've [now] learned that's critical."[41]

9-4b Empowerment

Another way of redesigning intraorganizational processes is through empowerment. **Empowering workers** means permanently passing decision-making authority and responsibility from managers to workers. For workers to be fully empowered, companies must give them the information and resources they need to make and carry out good decisions and then reward them for taking individual initiative.[42] In other words, employees won't feel very empowered if they constantly have someone looking over their shoulders. Warby Parker, the online eyeglasses company, wanted to use computer programmers more effectively. So it empowered employees through its new three-step Warbles system, which was designed by two programming teams. First, anyone can nominate projects that they feel deserve programmers' time and attention. Second, company managers assign points to projects based on perceived value. It's thought that managers' responsibilities make them more likely to identify projects with the broadest impact. Third, programmers decide which projects to work on and are rewarded for choosing higher value projects (with more points). CEO Dave Gilboa says that Warbles, "ensures we're getting a lot of value out of the tech team." Best of all, "Our engineers are much happier; they love the idea that they have autonomy and they can select ideas that they find most interesting."[43]

When workers are given the proper information and resources and are allowed to make good decisions, they experience strong feelings of empowerment. **Empowerment** is a feeling of intrinsic motivation in which workers perceive their work to have meaning and perceive themselves to be competent, having an impact, and capable of self-determination.[44] Work has meaning when it is consistent with personal standards and beliefs. Workers feel competent when they believe they can perform an activity with skill. The belief that they are having an impact comes from a feeling that they can affect work outcomes. A feeling of self-determination arises from workers' belief that they have the autonomy to choose how best to do their work.

Empowerment can lead to changes in organizational processes because meaning, competence, impact, and self-determination produce empowered employees who take active rather than passive roles in their work. At Ritz-Carlton hotels, all employees are empowered to spend up to $2,000 to solve customer service issues. That's not $2,000 per year or $2,000 per day, it's $2,000 per incident. And, employees can spend that $2,000 without asking for managerial approval.[45] Bob Kharazmi, Ritz-Carlton's CEO, shares the powerful story of a wheelchair-bound guest who, overheard by a pool attendant, told her husband she wished they could have dinner on the beach. On his own, without management approval, the pool attendant worked with hotel engineering to build a wooden walkway over the sand and with the kitchen to set up a table to serve the delighted couple dinner.[46]

Warby Parker CEO Dave Gilboa says that allowing the company's tech team to choose which programs it will work on maximizes their happiness and productivity.

Jim Spellman/Getty Images

Empowering workers permanently passing decision-making authority and responsibility from managers to workers by giving them the information and resources they need to make and carry out good decisions

Empowerment feeling of intrinsic motivation in which workers perceive their work to have impact and meaning and perceive themselves to be competent and capable of self-determination

INTERORGANIZA-TIONAL PROCESSES

An **interorganizational process** is a collection of activities that occur *among companies* to transform inputs into outputs that customers value. In other words, many companies work together to create a product or service that keeps customers happy. Nutella, the chocolate and hazelnut spread, is headquartered in Italy, has five factories in Europe, two in South America, and one each in Russia, North America, and Australia. Those factories work with suppliers in Turkey (hazelnuts), Malaysia (palm oil), Nigeria (cocoa), Brazil (sugar), and France (vanillin). The 401,500 tons of Nutella produced each year are then sold to grocers by sales offices and sales brokers in 160 different countries.[47]

*In this section, you'll explore interorganizational processes by learning about **9-5a modular organizations** and **9-5b virtual organizations.***

9-5a Modular Organizations

Virgin America airline's CEO David Cush says, "We will outsource every job that we can that is not customer-facing."[48] Except for the core business activities that they can perform better, faster, and cheaper than others, **modular organizations** outsource all remaining business activities to outside companies, suppliers, specialists, or consultants. The term *modular* is used because the business activities purchased from outside companies can be added and dropped as needed, much like adding pieces to a three-dimensional puzzle. Exhibit 9.12 depicts a modular organization in which the company has chosen to keep training, human resources, sales, product design, manufacturing, customer service, research and development, and information technology as core business activities but has outsourced the noncore activities of product distribution, web page design, advertising, payroll, accounting, and packaging.

The primary advantage of modular organizations is that they can cost significantly less to run than traditional organizations because they pay for outsourced labor, expertise, or manufacturing capabilities only when needed. Due to a surge in online holiday shopping, **Amazon's** fourth quarter revenue is consistently 50 percent higher than that of any other quarter throughout the year. To handle the increase in shipping this creates, Amazon adds 100,000 temporary employees to the 90,000 employees already working at its 70 U.S. warehouses and shipping hubs. Amazon does not hire these seasonal workers itself, however. Instead, it contracts with Integrity Staffing Solutions to provide short-term labor. Integrity handles background checks, tax filings, payroll, unemployment, and other legal issues, saving Amazon roughly $100 million a year on payroll taxes alone. According to former Integrity manager Robert Capo Jr., "If Amazon [was] going to do this themselves, they would have to build an entire different infrastructure."[49] To obtain cost advantages, however, modular organizations need reliable partners—vendors and suppliers with whom they can work closely and can trust.

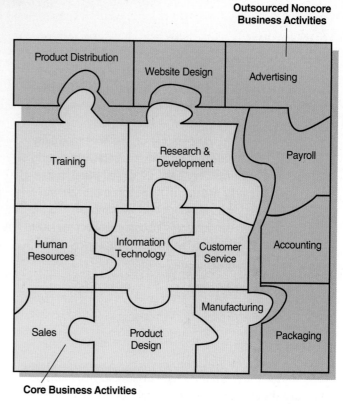

Exhibit 9.12
Modular Organization

Outsourced Noncore Business Activities

Product Distribution | Website Design | Advertising
Training | Research & Development | Payroll
Human Resources | Information Technology | Customer Service | Accounting
Sales | Product Design | Manufacturing | Packaging

Core Business Activities

Interorganizational process a collection of activities that take place among companies to transform inputs into outputs that customers value

Modular organization an organization that outsources noncore business activities to outside companies, suppliers, specialists, or consultants

Democratize the Workplace to Empower Workers?

At some companies, small and large decisions are made not by managers, but by a worker vote. At software company **InContext**, for example, workers recently voted on whether to have standing desks, cubicles, or open tables. After organizing visits to two locations, marketing technology firm **Media-Math** let workers decide the location of its new headquarters. Employees at 1Sale.com voted on whether the company should continue to pay for employee lunches, or whether it should use that money to lower the cost of health insurance. According to 1Sale's Shmuli Bortunk, "They asked us, do you prefer to have your belly full or your wallet full?" While voting can take more time, it can also empower employees and improve morale. With democratized decisions, says InContext Product manager Mackenzie Siren, "People feel like they have a real voice."

Source: R. Silverman, "Workplace Democracy Catches On," *Wall Street Journal*, March 27, 2016, accessed April 29, 2016, http://www.wsj.com/articles/workplace-democracy-catches-on-1459117910.

Rawpixel.com/Shutterstock.com

Modular organizations have disadvantages, too. The primary disadvantage is the loss of control that occurs when key business activities are outsourced to other companies. Also, companies may reduce their competitive advantage in two ways if they mistakenly outsource a core business activity. First, as a result of competitive and technological change, the noncore business activities a company has outsourced may suddenly become the basis for competitive advantage. Second, related to that point, suppliers to whom work is outsourced can sometimes become competitors.

9-5b Virtual Organizations

In contrast to modular organizations, in which the interorganizational process revolves around a central company, a **virtual organization** is part of a network in which many companies share skills, costs, capabilities, markets, and customers with each other. Exhibit 9.13 shows a virtual organization in which, for today, the parts of a virtual company consist of product design, purchasing, manufacturing, advertising, and information technology. Unlike modular organizations, in which the outside organizations are tightly linked to one central company, virtual organizations work with some companies in the network alliance, but not with all. So, whereas a puzzle with various pieces is a fitting metaphor for a modular organization, a potluck dinner is an appropriate metaphor for a virtual organization. All participants bring their finest food dish but eat only what they want.

Another difference is that the working relationships between modular organizations and outside companies tend to be more stable and longer lasting than the shorter, often temporary, relationships found among the virtual companies in a network alliance. The composition of a virtual organization is always changing. The combination of network partners that a virtual corporation has at any one time depends on the expertise needed to solve a particular problem or provide a specific product or service. For instance, today the business might need to focus on advertising and product design, as shown in Exhibit 9.13, but tomorrow, the business could want something completely different. In this sense, the term "virtual organization" means the organization that exists "at the moment."

> **Virtual organization** an organization that is part of a network in which many companies share skills, costs, capabilities, markets, and customers to collectively solve customer problems or provide specific products or services

Exhibit 9.13
Virtual Organizations

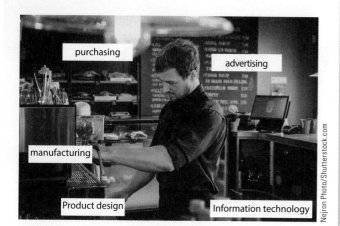

purchasing

advertising

manufacturing

Product design

Information technology

Nejron Photo/Shutterstock.com

Virtual organizations have a number of advantages. They let companies share costs, and because members can quickly combine their efforts to meet customers' needs, they are fast and flexible. Finally, because each member of the network alliance is the best at what it does, virtual organizations should in theory provide better products and services in all respects.

As with modular organizations, a disadvantage of virtual organizations is that after work has been outsourced, it can be difficult to control the quality of work done by network partners. The greatest disadvantage, however, is that tremendous managerial skills are required to make a network of independent organizations work well together, especially because their relationships tend to be short and based on a single task or project. Virtual organizations are using two methods to solve this problem. The first is to use a *broker*. In traditional, hierarchical organizations, managers plan, organize, and control. But with the horizontal, inter-organizational processes that characterize virtual organizations, the job of a broker is to create and assemble the knowledge, skills, and resources from different companies for outside parties, such as customers.[50] The second way to make networks of virtual organizations more manageable is to use a *virtual organization agreement* that, somewhat like a contract, specifies the schedules, responsibilities, costs, payouts, and liabilities for participating organizations.[51]

STUDY TOOLS 9

LOCATED IN TEXTBOOK

☐ Rip out and review chapter review card.

LOCATED AT WWW.CENGAGEBRAIN.COM

☐ Gain unique perspectives on key concepts with new 4LTR concept videos in the e-book.

☐ Increase your comprehension with Aplia for MGMT11.

☐ Complete interactive content within the e-book.

10 | Managing Teams

After you finish this chapter, go to **PAGE 225** for **STUDY TOOLS**

Experience Interiors/Getty Images

LEARNING OUTCOMES

10-1 Explain the good and bad of using teams.

10-2 Recognize and understand the different kinds of teams.

10-3 Understand the general characteristics of work teams.

10-4 Explain how to enhance work team effectiveness.

10-1 THE GOOD AND BAD OF USING TEAMS

Ninety-one percent of organizations are significantly improving their effectiveness by using work teams.[1] Procter & Gamble and Cummins Engine began using teams in 1962 and 1973, respectively. Boeing, Caterpillar, Champion International, Ford Motor Company, 3M, and General Electric established work teams in the mid- to late-1980s. Today, most companies use teams to tackle a variety of issues.[2] "Teams are ubiquitous. Whether we are talking about software development, Olympic hockey, disease outbreak response, or urban warfare, teams represent the critical unit that 'gets things done' in today's world."[3]

Work team a small number of people with complementary skills who hold themselves mutually accountable for pursuing a common purpose, achieving performance goals, and improving interdependent work processes

Work teams consist of a small number of people with complementary skills who hold themselves mutually accountable for pursuing a common purpose, achieving performance goals, and improving interdependent work processes.[4] By this definition, computer programmers working on separate projects in the same department of a company would not be considered a team. To be a team, the programmers would have to be interdependent and share responsibility and accountability for the quality and amount of computer code they produced.[5] Teams are becoming more important in many industries because they help organizations respond to specific problems and challenges. Though work teams are not the answer for every situation or organization, if the right teams are used properly and in the right settings, teams can dramatically improve company performance over more traditional management approaches while also instilling a sense of vitality in the workplace that is otherwise difficult to achieve.

Let's begin our discussion of teams by learning about **10-1a the advantages of teams, 10-1b the disadvantages of teams,** *and* **10-1c when to use and not use teams.**

10-1a The Advantages of Teams

Companies are making greater use of teams because teams have been shown to improve customer satisfaction, product and service quality, speed and efficiency in product development, employee job satisfaction, and decision making.[6] For example, one survey indicated that 80 percent of companies with more than 100 employees use teams, and 90 percent of all U.S. employees work part of their day in a team.[7] In fact, according to recent research, workers spend 50% more time in collaborative activities compared to just 20 years ago![8]

Teams help businesses increase *customer satisfaction* in several ways. One way is to create work teams that are trained to meet the needs of specific customers. 3D printing, also called additive manufacturing because one thin layer is added at a time, is now part of the production process in aviation, energy, pharmaceuticals, cars, and more. A survey of 900 manufacturers found that 14 percent use 3D printing today, and 48 percent plan to use it within a decade. Because legal issues related to additive manufacturing are different from those related to traditional manufacturing, the law practice of **Hunton & Williams** developed a cross-functional team of attorneys to assist clients who are adopting this new technology. Rather than seek out legal advice from several independent lawyers and then try to piece all the information together themselves, clients with significant investments in 3D printing can access a range of experts on product liability, taxes, intellectual property, insurance, litigation—and more—with just one phone call.[9]

Teams also help firms improve *product and service quality* in several ways.[10] In contrast to traditional organizational structures, in which management is responsible

COLLABORATION TOOL OVERLOAD IS KILLING TEAMS

A multitude of ways to communicate, from intranet discussion platforms to company chat programs like Facebook Workplace, and Google Chat, video chat apps like Skype and Google Hangouts, and file-sharing apps like Google Drive and Dropbox overwhelms today's work teams. Forrester Research's Craig Le Clair says, "Workers don't want nine collaboration platforms." Add email to the list and it's the equivalent of having 10 different inboxes!

Seeking a simpler approach, J. Walter Thompson adopted Microsoft Teams, a threaded chat-based tool integrated into Office365, which means that Office Apps like Excel, Word, and PowerPoint, and file storage and sharing like Microsoft's OneDrive, are available without leaving Teams.

Slack, which originated this way of communicating, has even greater functionality. Users can access file storage, task managers, phone and video calls, calendars and meeting scheduling, sales and accounting—1,000 apps in all—without leaving Slack. Slack users report a one-third increase in productivity, a 49 percent drop in email, and 25 percent fewer meetings.

Zull Must/Shutterstock.com

Kill collaboration tool overload. Make your teams more effective.

Source: J. Greene, "Beware Collaboration-Tool Overload," *Wall Street Journal*, March 12, 2017, accessed April 15, 2017, https://www.wsj.com/articles/beware-collaboration-tool-overload-1489370400; J. Nadler, "How to Survive Team Collaboration Tool Overload," Mitel, September 22, 2016, accessed April 15, 2017, http://www.mitel.com/blog/smb/2016/09/how-survive-team-collaboration-tool-overload.

---

for organizational outcomes and performance, teams take direct responsibility for the quality of the products and service they produce and sell. Once considered a solo career, over-the-road (OTR) truck drivers are increasingly pairing up to keep trucks moving more than 20 hours a day. Team driver Gary Helms says that he and his partner only stop for fuel, food, and a shower—otherwise, "We want the truck to move."[11] With state regulations limiting truck drivers to no more than eleven hours a day of driving, a single driver can cover roughly 500 miles per day. Driver teams, however, can cover 1,000 miles a day, which makes them incredibly valuable to online retailers and the organic-grocery industry, both of which promise customers fast delivery and fresh products. Driver teams are so valuable, in fact, that companies are willing to pay them $6 per mile—three times the normal price. According to transportation analyst Donald Broughton, driver teams provide freight speeds at a fraction of the price of alternative delivery methods.[12]

Another reason for using teams is that teamwork often leads to increased *job satisfaction*.[13] Teamwork can be more satisfying than traditional work because it gives workers a chance to improve their skills. This is often accomplished through **cross-training**, in which team members are taught how to do all or most of the jobs performed by the other team members. The advantage for the organization is that cross-training allows a team to function normally when one member is absent, quits, or is transferred. The advantage for workers is that cross-training broadens their skills and increases their capabilities while also making their work more varied and interesting.

Teamwork is also satisfying because work teams often receive proprietary business information that typically is available only to managers. Atomic Object is an employee-owned software company with an "open books" philosophy, which gives team members full access to financial information. Each quarter, founder Carl Erickson shares incomes statements and financial projections and explains how employee bonuses are determined. Financial data are accessible to all via spreadsheets and financial modeling tools to create better understanding about what makes Atomic profitable.

Cross-training training team members to do all or most of the jobs performed by the other team members

Vice president and managing partner Shawn Crowley says each team "has a large key performance indicator (KPI) monitor that displays … marketing and financial metrics. Openly showing our individual contributions allows us to see how we are performing against expectations and keeps us accountable to each other."[14] Which means that Atomic's team members act like business owners. Said team member Brittany Hunter, "I don't mentally check out at 5 p.m. My mind is often going late into the night about things I can do to improve Atomic or promote it to outsiders, ways I can serve my clients better, how to solve hard problems on my projects."[15]

Team members also gain job satisfaction from unique leadership responsibilities that are not typically available in traditional organizations. Finally, teams share many of the advantages of group decision making discussed in Chapter 5. For instance, because team members possess different knowledge, skills, abilities, and experiences, a team is able to view problems from multiple perspectives. This diversity of viewpoints increases the odds that team decisions will solve the underlying causes of problems and not just address the symptoms. The increased knowledge and information available to teams also make it easier for them to generate more alternative solutions, a critical part of improving the quality of decisions. Because team members are involved in decision-making processes, they are also likely to be more committed to making those decisions work. In short, teams can do a much better job than individuals in two important steps of the decision-making process: defining the problem and generating alternative solutions.

10-1b The Disadvantages of Teams

Although teams can significantly improve customer satisfaction, product and service quality, speed and efficiency in product development, employee job satisfaction, and decision making, using teams does not guarantee these positive outcomes. In fact, if you've ever participated in team projects in your classes, you're probably already aware of some of the problems inherent in work teams. Despite all of their promise, teams and teamwork are also prone to these significant disadvantages: initially high turnover, social loafing, and the problems associated with group decision making.

The first disadvantage of work teams is *initially high turnover*. Teams aren't for everyone, and some workers balk at the responsibility, effort, and learning required in team settings. When Zappos, the online shoe company changed from a traditional to a team-based structure where there are no bosses and no titles and employees manage themselves (what it calls Holacracy), it offered everyone in the company three months of severance pay to leave if they decided that it wasn't right for them. Turns out that of its 1,500 employees, 14 percent decided to leave. After 10 months, that figure had risen to 18 percent overall and 38 percent among members of a special technology team charged with migrating Zappos's website to Amazon servers. Zappos's John Bunch, who is managing the transition to Holacracy, said, "Whatever the number of people who took the offer was the right number as they made the decision that was right for them and right for Zappos."[16]

Social loafing is another disadvantage of work teams. **Social loafing** occurs when workers withhold their efforts and fail to perform their share of the work.[17] A nineteenth-century French engineer named Maximilian Ringlemann first documented social loafing when he found that one person pulling on a rope alone exerted an average of 139 pounds of force on the rope. In groups of three, the average

lenetstan/Shutterstock.com

Social loafing behavior in which team members withhold their efforts and fail to perform their share of the work

Exhibit 10.1
When to Use and When Not to Use Teams

Use Teams When . . .

✓ there is a clear, engaging reason or purpose.

✓ the job can't be done unless people work together.

✓ rewards can be provided for teamwork and team performance.

✓ ample resources are available.

Don't Use Teams When . . .

✗ there isn't a clear, engaging reason or purpose.

✗ the job can be done by people working independently.

✗ rewards are provided for individual effort and performance.

✗ the necessary resources are not available.

iStock.com/Tunart

Source: R. Wageman, "Critical Success Factors for Creating Superb Self-Managing Teams," *Organizational Dynamics* 26, no. 1 (1997): 49–61.

force dropped to 117 pounds per person. In groups of eight, the average dropped to just 68 pounds per person. Ringlemann concluded that the larger the team, the smaller the individual effort. In fact, social loafing is more likely to occur in larger groups where identifying and monitoring the efforts of individual team members can be difficult.[18] In other words, social loafers count on being able to blend into the background, where their lack of effort isn't easily spotted.

From team-based class projects, most students already know about social loafers or "slackers," who contribute poor, little, or no work whatsoever. Not surprisingly, a study of 250 student teams found that the most talented students are typically the least satisfied with teamwork because of having to carry slackers and do a disproportionate share of their team's work.[19] A similar study of virtual teams (where team members work remotely) found that social loafing is higher among team members who are stretched by high levels of non-work obligations (such as family, volunteering, and community work).[20] Perceptions of fairness are negatively related to the extent of social loafing within teams.[21]

Finally, teams share many of the *disadvantages of group decision making* discussed in Chapter 5, such as groupthink. In *groupthink*, members of highly cohesive groups feel intense pressure not to disagree with each other so that the group can approve a proposed solution. Because groupthink restricts discussion and leads to consideration of a limited number of alternative solutions, it usually results in poor decisions. Also, team decision making takes considerable time, and team meetings can often be unproductive and inefficient. Another possible pitfall is *minority domination*, where just one or two people dominate team discussions, restricting consideration of different problem definitions and alternative solutions. Minority domination is especially likely to occur when the team leader talks so much during team discussions, effectively discouraging other team members from speaking up. When that happens, team performance drops significantly.[22] Finally, team members may not feel accountable for the decisions and actions taken by the team.

10-1c When to Use Teams

As the two previous subsections made clear, teams have significant advantages *and* disadvantages. Therefore, the question is not whether to use teams, but *when* and *where* to use teams for maximum benefit and minimum cost. As Doug Johnson, associate director at the Center for Collaborative Organizations at the University of North Texas, puts it, "Teams are a means to an end, not an end in themselves. You have to ask yourself questions first. Does the work require interdependence? Will the team philosophy fit company strategy? Will management make a long-term commitment to this process?"[23] Exhibit 10.1 provides some additional guidelines on when to use or not use teams.[24]

First, teams should be used when there is a clear, engaging reason or purpose for using them. Too many companies use teams because they're popular or because the companies assume that teams can fix all problems. Teams are much more likely to succeed if they know why they exist and what they are supposed to accomplish, and they are more likely to fail if they don't.

Second, teams should be used when the job can't be done unless people work together. This typically means that teams are needed when tasks are complex, require multiple perspectives, or require repeated interaction with others to complete. Because of the enormous complexity of today's cars, you would think that auto companies routinely use interconnected design teams. After all, the typical car has 30,000 parts, 80 different computer modules, indicators sensing how close other cars are when parking or going 70 mph, and the ability to automatically adjust braking, cornering, gas mileage, and acceleration. But auto companies don't routinely use interconnected design teams, as most designers are responsible for separate sections or parts of the car. Achim Badstübner, head of **Audi Group** exterior design, says, "We tend to make the mistake that we have an exterior department, an interior department and a technology department, and they all know what they're doing but the connection is not so good." Audi, however, takes a team approach. Badstübner says, "I think it's very important to basically lock them in one room, literally speaking. Then there is an interaction: you talk to the guy who does seats and he tells you something about his expertise and you might take something from him that helps you to develop a new wheel, for example." Badstübner says by connecting the teams, "you get a different result because through this method you get the best of every brain. I think you can't survive if you just depend on one brain to do a complex thing like [design] a car."[25]

Third, teams should be used when rewards can be provided for teamwork and team performance. Rewards that depend on team performance rather than individual performance are the key to rewarding team behaviors and efforts. You'll read more about team rewards later in the chapter, but for now it's enough to know that if the type of reward (individual versus team) is not matched to the type of performance (individual versus team), teams won't work.

10-2 KINDS OF TEAMS

Let's continue our discussion of teams by learning about the different kinds of teams that companies such as Google and Maytag use to make themselves more competitive. We look first at 10-2a how teams differ in terms of autonomy, which is the key dimension that makes one team different from another, and then at 10-2b some special kinds of teams.

10-2a Autonomy, the Key Dimension

Teams can be classified in a number of ways, such as permanent or temporary, or functional or cross-functional.

However, studies indicate that the amount of autonomy possessed by a team is the key difference among teams.[26] *Autonomy* is the degree to which workers have the discretion, freedom, and independence to decide how and when to accomplish their jobs. Exhibit 10.2 shows how five kinds of teams differ in terms of autonomy. Moving left to right across the autonomy continuum at the top of the exhibit, traditional work groups and employee involvement groups have the least autonomy, semi-autonomous work groups have more autonomy, and, finally, self-managing teams and self-designing teams have the most autonomy. Moving from bottom to top along the left side of the exhibit, note that the number of responsibilities given to each kind of team increases directly with its autonomy. Let's review each of these kinds of teams and their autonomy and responsibilities in more detail.

The smallest amount of autonomy is found in **traditional work groups**, where two or more people work together to achieve a shared goal. In these groups, workers are responsible for doing the work or executing the task, but they do not have direct responsibility or control over their work. Workers report to managers, who are responsible for their performance and have the authority to hire and fire them, make job assignments, and control resources. For instance, suppose that an experienced worker blatantly refuses to do his share of the work, saying, "I've done my time. Let the younger employees do the work." In a team with high autonomy, the responsibility of getting this employee to put forth his fair share of effort would belong to his teammates. But, in a traditional work group, that responsibility belongs to the boss or supervisor. The supervisor in this situation calmly confronted the employee and told him, "We need your talent, [and] your knowledge of these machines. But if you won't work, you'll have to go elsewhere." Within days, the employee's behavior improved.[27]

Employee involvement teams, which have somewhat more autonomy, meet on company time on a weekly or monthly basis to provide advice or make suggestions to management concerning specific issues such as plant safety, customer relations, or product quality.[28] Though they offer advice and suggestions, they do not have the authority to make decisions. Membership on these teams is often voluntary, but members may be selected because of their expertise. The idea behind employee involvement teams is that the people closest to the problem or situation are

> **Traditional work group** a group composed of two or more people who work together to achieve a shared goal
>
> **Employee involvement team** team that provides advice or makes suggestions to management concerning specific issues

Exhibit 10.2
Team Autonomy Continuum

Responsibilities	Traditional Work Groups	Employee Involvement Groups	Semi-Autonomous Work Groups	Self-Managing Teams	Self-Designing Teams
Control Design of					
Team					✓
Tasks					✓
Membership					✓
Production/Service Tasks					
Make Decisions				✓	✓
Solve Problems				✓	✓
Major Production/Service Tasks					
Make Decisions			✓	✓	✓
Solve Problems			✓	✓	✓
Information			✓	✓	✓
Give Advice/Make Suggestions		✓	✓	✓	✓
Execute Task	✓	✓	✓	✓	✓

Low Team Autonomy → High Team Autonomy

Sources: R. D. Banker, J. M. Field, R. G. Schroeder, and K. K. Sinha, "Impact of Work Teams on Manufacturing Performance: A Longitudinal Field Study," *Academy of Management Journal* 39 (1996): 867–890; J. R. Hackman, "The Psychology of Self-Management in Organizations," in *Psychology and Work: Productivity, Change, and Employment*, ed. M. S. Pallak and R. Perlof (Washington, DC: American Psychological Association), 85–136.

best able to recommend solutions. For more than three years, production of Boeing's 787 Dreamliner was delayed by multiple problems—parts shortages, improper installation, failed test flights, and more. Because of production delays, Boeing must build ten planes per month, up from the typical two and a half planes. To meet this aggressive goal, it established nearly 200 employee involvement teams to analyze the way 787s are assembled and make changes to maximize efficiency. For example, one employee involvement team found that ducts already installed in the plane were being damaged because workers were kicking and stepping on them while doing other work. The damaged ducts then had to be removed and replaced. The team recommended that temporary covers be placed over the ducts, thus eliminating delays and reducing costs.[29]

Rawpixel.com/Shutterstock.com

Virtual Teams—There's an App for That! Lots, Actually

A host of productivity apps are available to make working remotely easier for people in teams. Keep the following apps in mind next time you have a group project—they might help you all work better together.

» **World Clock** and **Figure It Out** display multiple time zones to help teammates around the globe schedule meetings and avoid calling in the middle of the night.

» **Sqwiggle** takes quick snapshots of each team member via webcam every few seconds, making it easy to tell who is available if you have to call an impromptu meeting across multiple time zones. (The app can be paused during off-hours.)

» With annotation app **Skitch** you can add arrows, text, and more to screenshots and pictures to get your point across quickly and clearly.

» **15Five** lets managers send short sets of company-, project-, or user-specific questions to virtual teams to see what's on everybody's minds.

» With **Meldium**, remote teams can log into apps and tech platforms with a single sign-on. Team members have access to the apps but never see the actual password so the organizer can retain password control and security.

Source: O. Williams, "21 Tools That Will Help Your Remote Team Work Better Together," *The Next Web*, accessed April 20, 2016, http://thenextweb.com/apps/2014/12/06/tools-remote-teams.

Semi-autonomous work groups not only provide advice and suggestions to management but also have the authority to make decisions and solve problems related to the major tasks required to produce a product or service. Semi-autonomous groups regularly receive information about budgets, work quality and performance, and competitors' products. Furthermore, members of semi-autonomous work groups are typically cross-trained in a number of different skills and tasks. In short, semi-autonomous work groups give employees the authority to make decisions that are typically made by supervisors and managers.

That authority is not complete, however. Managers still play a role, though one that is much reduced compared with traditional work groups, in supporting the work of semi-autonomous work groups. The role a manager plays on a team usually evolves over time. "It may start with helping to transition problem-solving responsibilities to the team, filling miscellaneous requests for the team, and doing ad hoc tasks," says Steven Hitchcock, president of Axis Performance Advisors in Portland, Oregon. Later, the team may develop into a mini-enterprise, and the former manager becomes externally focused—sort of an account manager for the customer. Managers have to adjust what they do based on the sophistication of the team.[30] A lot of what managers of semi-autonomous work groups do is ask good questions, provide resources, and facilitate performance of group goals.

Self-managing teams are different from semi-autonomous work groups in that team members manage and control *all* of the major tasks *directly related* to production of a product or service without first getting approval from management. This includes managing and controlling the acquisition of materials, making a product or providing a service, and ensuring timely delivery. Spotify, the streaming music company, organizes its 2,000 employees into self-organizing teams called squads. No larger than 8 people, squads are completely responsible for a particular product function, like search algorithms, and decide what to do, how to do it, who to work with (other squads), and select their leaders. Squads receive feedback from other squads and customers, and conduct postmortems every few weeks to analyze what is or is not working. All of these decisions are made without management's input or approval.[31]

The use of self-managing teams has significantly increased productivity at a number of other companies, increasing quality by 12 percent at AT&T, reducing errors by 13 percent at FedEx, and helping 3M increase production by 300 percent at one of its manufacturing plants.[32] Seventy-two percent of *Fortune* 1,000 companies have at least one self-managing team, up from 28 percent in 1987.[33]

> **Semi-autonomous work group** a group that has the authority to make decisions and solve problems related to the major tasks of producing a product or service
>
> **Self-managing team** a team that manages and controls all of the major tasks of producing a product or service

Self-designing teams have all the characteristics of self-managing teams, but they can also control and change the design of the teams themselves, the tasks they do and how and when they do them, and the membership of the teams. Valve, a Bellevue, Washington, maker of video games, has no managers. In fact, the company defines "manager" in its employee handbook as, "The kind of people we don't have any of. So, if you see one, tell somebody, because it's probably the ghost of whoever was in this building before us."[34] "We do have a founder/ president, but even he isn't your manager. This company is yours to steer—toward opportunities and away from risks. You have the power to green-light projects. You have the power to ship projects."[35] But what makes Valve's team self-designing (and not just self-managing), is that they control and change the teams themselves by deciding who gets hired, fired, promoted, and what they get paid (which is determined by peer rankings regarding contributions to team projects).[36]

10-2b Special Kinds of Teams

Companies are also increasingly using several other kinds of teams that can't easily be categorized in terms of autonomy: cross-functional teams, virtual teams, and project teams. Depending on how these teams are designed, they can be either low- or high-autonomy teams.

Cross-functional teams are intentionally composed of employees from different functional areas of the organization.[37] Because their members have different functional backgrounds, education, and experience, cross-functional teams usually attack problems from multiple perspectives and generate more ideas and alternative solutions, all of which are especially important when trying to innovate or solve problems creatively.[38] Cross-functional teams can be used almost anywhere in an organization and are often used in conjunction with matrix and product organizational structures (see Chapter 9). They can also be used either with part-time or temporary team assignments or with full-time, long-term teams.

Virtual teams are groups of geographically and/ or organization-ally dispersed

coworkers who use a combination of telecommunications and information technologies to accomplish an organizational task.[39] Virtual teams are increasingly common, and are used by 28 percent of U.S.-based corporations and 66 percent of multinational firms.[40] Members of virtual teams rarely meet face-to-face; instead, they use email, video-conferencing, and group communication software. Virtual teams can be employee involvement teams, self-managing teams, or nearly any kind of team discussed in this chapter. Virtual teams are often (but not necessarily) temporary teams that are set up to accomplish a specific task.

Virtual teams are highly flexible because employees can work with each other regardless of physical location or time zones, but they're also much more complex than face-to-face teams when it comes to purpose, communication, and trust. Virtual teams often suffer from a lack of understanding regarding the team's purpose and team member roles. Dave Davis of RedFly Marketing has managed virtual teams for more than a decade and says, "You'd be surprised how many people will wait until halfway through a project to admit they don't understand something."[41] Because of distance and different time zones, 38 percent of virtual team members cite communication as their biggest challenge. Joe McCann says, CEO of NodeSource, a JavaScript software company, says "It's a pain…, I'm gonna be honest. If everybody was in North America, it would be easier. We have an influential gentleman employee in Australia, so every Monday at 6 p.m. when I'd like to be winding down my day I have to have a very focused call."[42] Digital communication (email, IM, virtual conferencing) accounts for 63 percent of communication on virtual teams, yet 23 percent of team members find that long email discussion threads threaten (rather than help) effective project communication.[43] So, it's important for members to know when to use different communication media. Mary Ellen Slater, a manager at **Reputation Capital**, says, "At Rep Cap, we IM each other throughout the day, but there are times when a phone call or face-to-face meeting is better. A new project or something that deviates from our usual process may merit a phone call."[44] Finally, trust is critical for virtual teams to be successful. Andrea Rozman, owner of Your Gal Friday, a company that provides virtual

---

Self-designing team
a team that has the characteristics of self-managing teams but also controls team design, work tasks, and team membership

Cross-functional team
a team composed of employees from different functional areas of the organization

Virtual team a team composed of geographically and/or organizationally dispersed coworkers who use telecommunication and information technologies to accomplish an organizational task

New York   **London**   **Tokyo**

Eskymaks/Shutterstock.com

Exhibit 10.3
Tips for Managing Virtual Teams

1. Establish clear expectations for communication, availability during offices hours, and frequency of check-ins.

2. Establish clear goals and milestones to help remote workers stay on track and accountable to the team.

3. Help team members set clear boundaries between work and family spaces.

4. Assign employees who have many outside obligations to teams whose members mostly have few nonwork obligations.

5. Ensure that team members have access to technology tools such as teleconferencing, file-sharing services, online meeting services, and collaboration portals.

6. Facilitate face-to-face communication with video conferencing or by requiring members of remote teams to work on-site several days each month.

7. Ensure the task is meaningful to the team and the company.

8. When building a virtual team, solicit volunteers as much as possible.

Sources: S. J. Perry, et al., "When Does Virtuality Really Work? Examining the Role of Work-Family and Virtuality in Social Loafing," *Journal of Management* 42 (2016), 449–479; C. Brooks, "4 Ways to Manage Remote Employees," *Business News Daily*, April 23, 2014, accessed April 30, 2016, http://www.businessnewsdaily.com/8895-remote-team-work.html.

personal assistants, says, "You have to take that leap of faith. You have to believe that once you hand them the work, they will do it, and get it done on time."[45] See Exhibit 10.3 for more information on managing virtual teams.

Project teams are created to complete specific, one-time projects or tasks within a limited time.[46] Project teams are often used to develop new products, significantly improve existing products, roll out new information systems, or build new factories or offices. The project team is typically led by a project manager who has the overall responsibility for planning, staffing, and managing the team, which usually includes employees from different functional areas. Effective project teams demand both individual and collective responsibility.[47] One advantage of project teams is that drawing employees from different functional areas can reduce or eliminate communication barriers. In turn, as long as team members feel free to express their ideas, thoughts, and concerns, free-flowing communication encourages cooperation among separate departments and typically speeds up the design process.[48] Another advantage of project teams is their flexibility. When projects are finished, project team members either move on to the next project or return to their functional units. For example, publication of this book required designers, editors, page compositors, and web designers, among others. When

the task was finished, these people applied their skills to other textbook projects. Because of this flexibility, project teams are often used with the matrix organizational designs discussed in Chapter 9.

10-3 WORK TEAM CHARACTERISTICS

"Why did I ever let you talk me into teams? They're nothing but trouble."[49] Lots of managers have this reaction after making the move to teams. Many don't realize that this reaction is normal, both for them and for workers. In fact, such a reaction is characteristic of the *storming* stage of team development (discussed in Section 10-3e). Managers who are familiar with these stages and with the other important characteristics of teams will be better prepared to manage the predictable changes that occur when companies make the switch to team-based structures.

*Understanding the characteristics of work teams is essential for making teams an effective part of an organization. Therefore, in this section you'll learn about **10-3a team norms, 10-3b team cohesiveness, 10-3c team size, 10-3d team conflict**, and **10-3e the stages of team development**.*

10-3a Team Norms

Over time, teams develop **norms**, which are informally agreed-on standards that regulate team behavior.[50] Norms are valuable because they let team members know what is expected of them. One of the key ways in which norms develop is by observing nearby team members. A two-year study in which 2,000 workers were randomly assigned to locations within offices found that ten percent of an employee's productivity, effectiveness, and work quality was determined by who they sat next to. When an average performer was replaced by a top performer, the workers seated nearby increased their performance by ten percent. Likewise, when productive workers (fast, but lacking quality) sat next to quality workers (superior work done slowly), quality workers became 13 percent more productive (faster) and productive workers were 17 percent more effective (higher quality).[51] In other words, one of the

Project team a team created to complete specific, one-time projects or tasks within a limited time

Norms informally agreed-on standards that regulate team behavior ways in which team members know what is expected of them (i.e., norms) is by taking immediate cues from those around them.

Studies indicate that norms are one of the most powerful influences on work behavior because they regulate the everyday actions that allow teams to function effectively. Team norms are often associated with positive outcomes such as stronger organizational commitment, more trust in management, and stronger job and organizational satisfaction.[52] Effective work teams develop norms about the quality and timeliness of job performance, absenteeism, safety, and honest expression of ideas and opinions.

At **Google**, a special task force called Project Aristotle spent four years reviewing published research on teams, as well as analyzing internal data on 180 Google work teams.[53] Unable to find identifiable patterns related to the sizes, skills, or tenures of teams or their team members, Project Aristotle eventually found that Google's most successful teams had positive norms with high levels of psychological safety, a concept that Harvard Business School professor Amy Edmondson defines as "a sense of confidence that the team will not embarrass, reject or punish someone for speaking up . . . the team is safe for interpersonal risk taking."[54] Building on that study, a team of researchers led by Carnegie Mellon professor Anita Woolley found that the best-performing teams engaged in conversational turn-taking. Woolley explained, "As long as everyone got a chance to talk, the team did well. But if only one person or a small group spoke all the time, the collective intelligence [of the team] declined.[55] Woolley's findings are consistent with the previously discussed research showing that overly dominant team

leaders minimized discussion and hurt team performance. See Section 10-1b.

Norms can also influence team behavior in negative ways. For example, most people would agree that damaging organizational property; saying or doing something to hurt someone at work; intentionally doing one's work badly, incorrectly, or slowly; griping about coworkers; deliberately bending or breaking rules; and doing something to harm the company or boss are negative behaviors. A study of workers from 34 teams in 20 different organizations found that teams with negative norms strongly influenced their team members to engage in these negative behaviors. In fact, the longer individuals were members of a team with negative norms and the more frequently they interacted with their teammates, the more likely they were to perform negative behaviors. Because team norms typically develop early in the life of a team, these results indicate how important it is for teams to establish positive norms from the outset.[56]

10-3b Team Cohesiveness

Cohesiveness is another important characteristic of work teams. **Cohesiveness** is the extent to which team members are attracted to a team and motivated to remain in it.[57] What can be done to promote team cohesiveness? First, make sure that all team members are present at team meetings and activities. Team cohesiveness suffers when members are allowed to withdraw from the team and miss team meetings and events.[58] Second, create additional opportunities for teammates to work together by rearranging work schedules and creating common workspaces. Bank of America discovered the value of cohesive teams when it did a study tracking employee

Cohesiveness the extent to which team members are attracted to a team and motivated to remain in it

MINNESOTA VIKINGS' DONUT CLUB RULES

1. Players always buy. The players rotate during the regular season, but the trainers and staff never buy, since the donuts are a nod of appreciation to them.
2. Lateness will not be tolerated.
3. Do not touch the donuts before the designated time. Do not eat the donuts before the designated time. (The boxes open at 7:50 a.m., but no one can touch until 8 a.m. There are penalties.)
4. Finish the donut.
5. Attendance counts.
6. Wear your colors with pride. (There's a club t-shirt.)
7. Once a member of Donut Club, always a member of Donut Club.

iStock.com/pjohnson1

behavior. When Bank of America experimented by having call center employees wear sensors monitoring their movements throughout the office, it found that the most productive employees were in cohesive teams that communicated frequently. So, to encourage more interaction, it scheduled team members to all have breaks at the same time, rather than solo breaks. As a result, worker productivity rose 10 percent.[59] When task interdependence is high, and team members have lots of chances to work together, team cohesiveness tends to increase.[60] Third, engaging in nonwork activities as a team can help build cohesion. The NFL's Minnesota Vikings "Donut Club" is a key way in which the team builds cohesiveness among players. Head trainer Eric Sugarman says, "It's for the guys who aren't injured [who pay for the donuts] to be able to support the guys who get mandatory treatment all week [who eat the donuts]." The Donut Club, which meets every Saturday at 7:50 a.m., has a few key rules. Don't be late. Sugarman says, "The Donut Club waits for nobody." Do not touch or eat the donuts before 8:00 a.m. Sugarman calls this ten minutes, "Basically, a donut viewing." Retired quarterback Gus Frerotte, who started buying the donuts, said, "I love that there are rules. That's what makes the game fun. It's really nice to have a common bond about something stupid like that."[61] Finally, companies build team cohesiveness by making employees feel that they are part of an organization.

10-3c Team Size

The relationship between team size and performance appears to be curvilinear. Very small or very large teams may not perform as well as moderately sized teams. Amazon CEO Jeff Bezos tends to prefer small teams, saying, "If I see more than two pizzas for lunch, the team is too big."[62] For most teams, the right size is somewhere between six and nine members.[63] A team of this size is small enough for the team members to get to know each other and for each member to have an opportunity to contribute in a meaningful way to the success of the team. At the same time, the team is large enough to take advantage of team members' diverse skills, knowledge, and perspectives. It is also easier to instill a sense of responsibility and mutual accountability in teams of this size.[64] The *Wall Street Journal*'s Sue Shellenbarger says managers invite too many people to meetings. For analyzing possible causes of problems, invite 4 to 6 people.[65] Bain & Company's Michael Mankins follows the "rule of seven," which says the chances of making good decisions drop 10 percent for every person beyond seven. Says Mankins, "By the time you get 17 people, the chances of your actually making a decision are zero."[66] So, for making decisions, invite 4 to 7.

Team size has a significant impact on the value of a company as well. Among companies with a market capitalization of $10 billion or more, those with smaller boards of directors outperform their peers by 8.5 percent, and those with larger boards underperform their

SHOOTING THE BOSS: WHEN PAINTBALL WRECKED TEAM BUILDING

"At a previous job, our boss would sometimes take us bowling. This time, though, he wanted to go paint-balling. I'm not a good shot, and I wasn't aiming for him, but my paintball went awry. The next thing I knew, he was on the floor. The game was stopped, the ambulance came, and people started talking about potential liver rupture and damage to his kidneys. He was OK. A preexisting condition had flared up. After the event, he told me it wasn't my fault, but I felt horrible and left the company six weeks later."

Source: K. Morrell, "What's Your Most Awkward Team-Building Experience?" *Bloomberg*, April 5, 2017, accessed April 15, 2017, https://www.bloomberg.com/news/articles/2017-04-05/what-s-your-most-awkward-team-building-experience.

eileen meyer/Shutterstock.com

peers by nearly 11 percent. With only seven directors, Netflix's board was able to spend nine months discussing a potential price increase. Director Jay Hoag says, "We get in-depth. That's easier with a small group." Netflix outperforms its sector peers by 32 percent.[67]

When teams get too large, team members find it difficult to get to know one another, and the team may splinter into smaller subgroups. When this occurs, subgroups sometimes argue and disagree, weakening overall team cohesion. As teams grow, there is also a greater chance of *minority domination*, where just a few team members dominate team discussions. Even if minority domination doesn't occur, larger groups may not have time for all team members to share their input. And when team members feel that their contributions are unimportant or not needed, the result is less involvement, effort, and accountability to the team.[68] Large teams also face logistical problems such as finding an appropriate time or place to meet. Finally, the incidence of social loafing, discussed earlier in the chapter, is much higher in large teams.

Just as team performance can suffer when a team is too large, it can also be negatively affected when a team is too small. Teams with just a few people may lack the diversity of skills and knowledge found in larger teams. Also, teams that are too small are unlikely to gain the advantages of team decision making (multiple perspectives, generating more ideas and alternative solutions, and stronger commitment) found in larger teams.

What signs indicate that a team's size needs to be changed? If decisions are taking too long, if the team has difficulty making decisions or taking action, if a few members dominate the team, or if the commitment or efforts of team members are weak, chances are the team is too big. In contrast, if a team is having difficulty coming up with ideas or generating solutions, or if the team does not have the expertise to address a specific problem, chances are the team is too small.

10-3d Team Conflict

Conflict and disagreement are inevitable in most teams. But this shouldn't surprise anyone. From time to time, people who work together are going to disagree about what and how things get done. What causes conflict in teams? Although almost anything can lead to conflict—casual remarks that unintentionally offend a team member or fighting over scarce resources—the primary cause of team conflict is disagreement over team goals and priorities.[69] Other common causes of team conflict include disagreements over task-related issues, interpersonal incompatibilities, and simple fatigue.

Though most people view conflict negatively, the key to dealing with team conflict is not avoiding it, but rather making sure that the team experiences the right kind of conflict. In Chapter 5, you learned about *c-type conflict*, or *cognitive conflict*, which focuses on problem-related differences of opinion, and *a-type conflict*, or *affective conflict*, which refers to the emotional reactions that can occur when disagreements become personal rather than professional.[70] Cognitive conflict is strongly associated with improvements in team performance, whereas affective conflict is strongly associated with decreases in team performance.[71] Why does this happen? With cognitive conflict, team members disagree because their different experiences and expertise lead them to different views of the problem and solutions. Indeed, managers who participated on teams that emphasized cognitive conflict described their teammates as "smart," "team players," and "best in the business." They described their teams as "open," "fun," and "productive." One manager summed up the positive attitude that team members had about cognitive conflict by saying, "We scream a lot, then laugh, and then resolve the issue."[72] Thus, cognitive conflict is also characterized by a willingness to examine, compare, and reconcile differences to produce the best possible solution.

By contrast, affective conflict often results in hostility, anger, resentment, distrust, cynicism, and apathy. Managers who participated on teams that experienced affective conflict described their teammates as "manipulative," "secretive," "burned out," and "political."[73] Dana Browlee, who runs a corporate training company in Atlanta, gives the example of the naysayer, who, "whatever you bring up, it will never work," and the silent plotter, who she says, "may be the quiet person sitting in the back, but as soon as the [team] meeting is over, they're over by the Coke machine, planning your demise."[74] Not surprisingly, affective conflict can make people uncomfortable and cause them to withdraw and decrease their commitment to a team.[75] Affective conflict also lowers the satisfaction of team members, may lead to personal hostility between coworkers, and can decrease team cohesiveness.[76] So, unlike cognitive conflict, affective conflict undermines team performance by preventing teams from engaging in the kinds of activities that are critical to team effectiveness.

So, what can managers do to manage team conflict? First, they need to realize that emphasizing cognitive conflict alone won't be enough. Studies show that cognitive and affective conflicts often occur together in a given team activity! Sincere attempts to reach agreement on a difficult issue can quickly deteriorate from cognitive to affective conflict if the discussion turns personal, and tempers and emotions flare. While cognitive conflict is clearly the better approach to take, efforts to engage in cognitive conflict should be managed well and checked before they deteriorate, causing the team to become unproductive.

Can teams disagree and still get along? Fortunately, they can. In an attempt to study this issue, researchers examined team conflict in twelve high-tech companies. In four of the companies, work teams used cognitive conflict to address work problems but did so in a way that minimized the occurrence of affective conflict.[77]

There are several ways teams can have a "good fight."[78] First, work with more, rather than less, information. A senior retail executive said, "Disagreement is great as long as it's fact-based."[79] If data are plentiful, objective, and up-to-date, teams will focus on issues, not personalities. Second, develop multiple alternatives to enrich debate. Focusing on multiple solutions diffuses conflict by getting the team to keep searching for a better solution. Positions and opinions are naturally more flexible with five alternatives than with just two. Third, establish common goals. Remember, most team conflict arises from disagreements over team goals and priorities. Therefore, common goals encourage collaboration and minimize conflict over a team's purpose. The late Steve Jobs, former CEO of Apple, explained it this way: "It's okay to spend a lot of time arguing about which route to take to San Francisco when everyone wants to end up there, but a lot of time gets wasted in such arguments if one person wants to go to San Francisco and another secretly wants to go to San Diego."[80] Fourth, inject humor into the workplace. Humor relieves tension, builds cohesion, and just makes being in teams fun. Fifth, maintain a balance of power by involving as many people as possible in the decision process. And, sixth, resolve issues without forcing a consensus. Consensus means that everyone must agree before decisions are finalized. Effectively, requiring consensus gives everyone on the team veto power. Nothing gets done until everyone agrees, which, of course, is nearly impossible. As a result, insisting on consensus usually promotes affective rather than cognitive conflict. If team members can't agree after constructively discussing their options, it's better to have the team leader make the final choice. Most team members can accept the team leader's choice if they've been thoroughly involved in the decision process.

10-3e Stages of Team Development

As teams develop and grow, they pass through four stages of development. As shown in Exhibit 10.4, those stages are forming, storming, norming, and performing.[81] Although not every team passes through each of these stages, teams that do tend to be better performers.[82] This holds true even for teams composed of seasoned executives. After a period of time, however, if a team is not managed well, its performance may start to deteriorate as the team begins a process of decline and progresses through the stages of de-norming, de-storming, and de-forming.[83]

Forming is the initial stage of team development. This is the getting-acquainted stage in which team members

Forming the first stage of team development, in which team members meet each other, form initial impressions, and begin to establish team norms

Exhibit 10.4
Stages of Team Development

Sources: J. F. McGrew, J. G. Bilotta, and J. M. Deeney, "Software Team Formation and Decay: Extending the Standard Model for Small Groups," *Small Group Research* 30, no. 2 (1999): 209–234; B. W. Tuckman, "Development Sequence in Small Groups," *Psychological Bulletin* 63, no. 6 (1965): 384–399.

Storming the second stage of development, characterized by conflict and disagreement, in which team members disagree over what the team should do and how it should do it

Norming the third stage of team development, in which team members begin to settle into their roles, group cohesion grows, and positive team norms develop

Performing the fourth and final stage of team development, in which performance improves because the team has matured into an effective, fully functioning team

De-norming a reversal of the norming stage, in which team performance begins to decline as the size, scope, goal, or members of the team change

De-storming a reversal of the storming phase, in which the team's comfort level decreases, team cohesion weakens, and angry emotions and conflict may flare

---

first meet each other, form initial impressions, and try to get a sense of what it will be like to be part of the team. Some of the first team norms will be established during this stage as team members begin to find out what behaviors will and won't be accepted by the team. During this stage, team leaders should allow time for team members to get to know each other, set early ground rules, and begin to set up a preliminary team structure.

Conflicts and disagreements often characterize the second stage of team development, **storming**. As team members begin working together, different personalities and work styles may clash. Team members become more assertive at this stage and more willing to state opinions. This is also the stage when team members jockey for position and try to establish a favorable role for themselves on the team. In addition, team members are likely to disagree about what the group should do and how it should do it. Team performance is still relatively low, given that team cohesion is weak and team members are still reluctant to support each other. Because teams that get stuck in the storming stage are almost always ineffective, it is important for team leaders to focus the team on team goals and on improving team performance. Team members need to be particularly patient and tolerant with each other in this stage.

During **norming**, the third stage of team development, team members begin to settle into their roles as team members. Positive team norms will have developed by this stage, and teammates should know what to expect from each other. Petty differences should have been resolved, friendships will have developed, and group cohesion will be relatively strong. At this point, team members will have accepted team goals, be operating as a unit, and, as indicated by the increase in performance, be working together effectively. This stage can be very short and is often characterized by someone on the team saying, "I think things are finally coming together." Note, however, that teams may also cycle back and forth between storming and norming several times before finally settling into norming.

In the last stage of team development, **performing**, performance improves because the team has finally matured into an effective, fully functioning team. At this point, members should be fully committed to the team and think of themselves as members of a team and not just employees. Team members often become intensely loyal to one another at this stage and feel mutual accountability for team successes and failures. Trivial disagreements, which can take time and energy away from the work of the team, should be rare. At this stage, teams get a lot of work done, and it is fun to be a team member.

The team should not become complacent, however. Without effective management, its performance may begin to decline as the team passes through the stages of **de-norming**, **de-storming**, and **de-forming**.[84] John Puckett, manufacturing vice president for circuit-board manufacturer XEL Communications, says, "The

To effectively motivate teams:

1. Teams must have a high degree of autonomy.
2. Teams must be empowered with control of resources.
3. Teams need structural accommodation.
4. Teams need bureaucratic immunity.

books all say you start in this state of chaos and march through these various stages, and you end up in this state of ultimate self-direction, where everything is going just great. They never tell you it can go back in the other direction, sometimes just as quickly."[85]

10-4 ENHANCING WORK TEAM EFFECTIVENESS

*Making teams work is a challenging and difficult process. Nonetheless, companies can increase the likelihood that teams will succeed by carefully managing **10-4a the setting of team goals and priorities** and **10-4b how work team members are selected, 10-4c trained, and 10-4d compensated.**[84]*

10-4a Setting Team Goals and Priorities

In Chapter 5, you learned that having specific, measurable, attainable, realistic, and timely (S.M.A.R.T.) goals is one of the most effective means for improving individual job performance. Fortunately, team goals also improve team performance. In fact, team goals lead to much higher team performance 93 percent of the time.[87]

Why is setting *specific* team goals so critical to team success? One reason is that increasing a team's performance is inherently more complex than just increasing one individual's job performance. For instance, consider that any team is likely to involve at least four different kinds of goals: each member's goal for the team, each member's goal for himself or herself on the team, the team's goal for each member, and the team's goal for itself.[88] In other words, without a specific goal for the team itself (the last of the four goals listed), team members may head off in all directions at once pursuing these other goals. Consequently, setting a specific goal *for the team* clarifies team priorities by providing a clear focus and purpose.

Challenging team goals affect how hard team members work. In particular, they greatly reduce the incidence of social loafing. When faced with difficult goals, team members necessarily expect everyone to contribute. Consequently, they are much more likely to notice and complain if a teammate isn't doing his or her share. In fact, when teammates know each other well, when team goals are specific, when team communication is good, and when teams are rewarded for team performance (discussed later in this section), there is only a 1 in 16 chance that teammates will be social loafers.[89]

What can companies and teams do to ensure that team goals lead to superior team performance? One increasingly popular approach is to give teams stretch goals. *Stretch goals* are extremely ambitious goals that workers don't know how to reach.[90] Indian-based Tata Steel's stretch goal is a 25% profit margin. Managing Director TV Narendran said, "Tata Steel has always had a rich history of setting steep targets which we may not know how to achieve. But that is how innovation comes about. Because if we know how to achieve the target, then it is only about execution. If you want to get people to think out of the box, then you have to have those stretch targets."[91] Likewise, CEO Jim Snee says Hormel Foods' goal is to make 15 percent of revenues from products no more than five years old. Says Snee, "The 15 percent is a very aggressive number. It's a stretch goal for our organization."[92] Hormel also aims to increase sales and profits by 5% and 10%, respectively, each year.

Four things must occur for stretch goals to effectively motivate teams.[93] First, teams must have a high degree of autonomy or control over how they achieve their goals. Second,

De-forming a reversal of the forming stage, in which team members position themselves to control pieces of the team, avoid each other, and isolate themselves from team leaders teams must be empowered with control of resources, such as budgets, workspaces, computers, or whatever else they need to do their jobs. Third, teams need structural accommodation. **Structural accommodation** means giving teams the ability to change organizational structures, policies, and practices if doing so helps them meet their stretch goals. Finally, teams need bureaucratic immunity. **Bureaucratic immunity** means that teams no longer have to go through the frustratingly slow process of multilevel reviews and sign-offs to get management approval before making changes. Once granted bureaucratic immunity, teams are immune from the influence of various organizational groups and are accountable only to top management. Experian, a credit reporting company, helps organizations and banks make lending decisions and individuals manage credit scores. Experian's Eric Haller went to his boss with a unique proposal to find out customers' unsolved problems (such as how to lend to people with no credit history), fix them, and turn those solutions into new product lines. His boss replied, "I've wanted to do this for years, so I'll give you the money if you can find the people."[94] With three years of guaranteed funding and just one requirement, a biannual performance report, Haller formed Experian DataLabs and hired his "navy seals of data science."[95] With freedom thanks to bureaucratic immunity, Experian DataLabs has grown in six years from 8 to 40 data scientists and now earns eight-figure revenues.[96]

10-4b Selecting People for Teamwork

University of Southern California management professor Edward Lawler says, "People are very naive about how easy it is to create a team. Teams are the Ferraris of work design. They're high performance but high maintenance and expensive."[97] It's almost impossible to have an effective work team without carefully selecting people who are suited for teamwork or for working on a particular team. A focus on teamwork (individualism-collectivism), team level, and team diversity can help companies choose the right team members.[98]

Are you more comfortable working alone or with others? If you strongly

Building an effective team means selecting people who are suited for teamwork.

prefer to work alone, you may not be well suited for teamwork. Studies show that job satisfaction is higher in teams when team members prefer working with others.[99] An indirect way to measure someone's *preference for teamwork* is to assess the person's degree of individualism or collectivism. **Individualism-collectivism** is the degree to which a person believes that people should be self-sufficient and that loyalty to one's self is more important than loyalty to one's team or company.[100] *Individualists*, who put their own welfare and interests first, generally prefer independent tasks in which they work alone. In contrast, *collectivists*, who put group or team interests ahead of self-interests, generally prefer interdependent tasks in which they work with others. Collectivists would also rather cooperate than compete and are fearful of disappointing team members or of being ostracized from teams. Given these differences, it makes sense to select team members who are collectivists rather than individualists. In fact, many companies use individualism-collectivism as an initial screening device for team members. If team diversity is desired, however, individualists may also be appropriate, as discussed next. To determine your preference for teamwork, take the Team Player Inventory shown in Exhibit 10.5.

Team level is the average level of ability, experience, personality, or any other factor on a team. For example, a high level of team experience means that a team has particularly experienced team members. This does not mean that every member of the team has considerable experience, but that enough team members do to significantly raise the average level of experience on the team. Team level is used to guide selection of teammates when teams need a particular set of skills or capabilities to do their jobs well. For example, **SAP**,

---

Structural accommodation the ability to change organizational structures, policies, and practices in order to meet stretch goals

Bureaucratic immunity the ability to make changes without first getting approval from managers or other parts of an organization

Individualism-collectivism the degree to which a person believes that people should be self-sufficient and that loyalty to one's self is more important than loyalty to team or company

Team level the average level of ability, experience, personality, or any other factor on a team

Exhibit 10.5
The Team Player Inventory

		Strongly Disagree				Strongly Agree
1.	I enjoy working on team/group projects.	1	2	3	4	5
2.	Team/group project work easily allows others to not pull their weight.	1	2	3	4	5
3.	Work that is done as a team/group is better than work done individually.	1	2	3	4	5
4.	I do my best work alone rather than in a team/group.	1	2	3	4	5
5.	Team/group work is overrated in terms of the actual results produced.	1	2	3	4	5
6.	Working in a team/group gets me to think more creatively.	1	2	3	4	5
7.	Teams/groups are used too often when individual work would be more effective.	1	2	3	4	5
8.	My own work is enhanced when I am in a team/group situation.	1	2	3	4	5
9.	My experiences working in team/group situations have been primarily negative.	1	2	3	4	5
10.	More solutions/ideas are generated when working in a team/group situation than when working alone.	1	2	3	4	5

Reverse score items 2, 4, 5, 7, and 9. Then add the scores for items 1 to 10. Higher scores indicate a preference for teamwork, whereas lower total scores indicate a preference for individual work.

Source: T. J. B. Kline, "The Team Player Inventory: Reliability and Validity of a Measure of Predisposition Toward Organizational Team-Working Environments," *Journal for Specialists in Group Work* 24, no. 1 (1999): 102–112.

a German software company, has struggled to deliver cloud-based solutions and hopes to replicate a team approach to innovation pioneered by Xerox Parc in the 1970s. So it hired Alan Kay, a renowned technologist who was a computer scientist at Xerox Parc, to build a similar high-level team. So far, Kay has recruited 20 polymathic technologists, funded their research projects, and then given them the independence to work alone to pursue their research interests.[101] (A polymath is someone who is a genius in more than one field.) Kay understands the risks of having too many "stars." Based on his research on NBA teams, management professor Adam Galinsky says, "If you have too many people [on teams], and they all want to be stars, coordination [on the team] goes down. But if you have a bunch of star programmers all working on their own projects, and they don't need to integrate their programs with each other, then more stars is probably better."[102]

Whereas team level represents the average level or capability on a team, **team diversity** represents the variances or differences in ability, experience, personality, or any other factor on a team.[103] From a practical perspective, why is team diversity important? MIT researcher Alex Pentland's research at MIT's Human Dynamics lab shows that the most successful teams, (1) talk with everyone on the team, balancing talking with listening, (2) have a diversity of ideas and team members who are open to new ideas, and (3) are goal oriented. Pentland says, "You need everyone exploring slightly different things, but doing in the same direction."[104] Team diversity ensures that strong teams not only have talented members (that is, a high team level), but those talented members also have different abilities, experiences, and personalities from which to view and solve problems.

Industrial Light & Magic's Experience Lab (xLAB) has assembled a team of artists, engineers, sound designers, and storytellers to create a virtual reality experience based on *Star Wars: The Force Awakens*. Building the future of immersive cinema requires both dreamers and rocket builders, says Vicki Dobbs Beck, the executive in charge of xLAB. "The dreamers are constantly thinking about what's possible, and the rocket builders figure out how to get us there."[105]

After the right team has been put together in terms of individualism-collectivism, team level, and team diversity, it's important to keep the team together as long as practically possible. Interesting research by the National Transportation

> **Team diversity** the variances or differences in ability, experience, personality, or any other factor on a team

Team-Training Matchmaker

Today's team training events in corporate America go far beyond the stereotypical trust fall. From cooking to caving to paintball to mural painting, team training has become so elaborate that some companies do not have the internal resources needed to organize such exotic events. Instead, these companies outsource to **Wekudo** (pronounced "we could do"), a corporate event matchmaking service that helps companies find the best team-building experiences for their needs and culture. Wekudo draws from a wide range of third-party providers and trains them on how to reframe their activities to align with corporate goals. For example, an improv teacher might create activities for sale pitches, while a laser tag center might focus on team communication. For tea and nutritional supplement company Aloha, Wekudo proposed an outing to an Acroyoga studio. This innovative practice combines yoga and acrobatics and requires heavy doses of both cooperation and communication.

Source: J. Miller, "Mandatory Fun: Companies Are Outsourcing Employee Morale Building," *Bloomberg BusinessWeek*, February 15–21, 2016, 62.

Safety Board shows that 73 percent of serious mistakes made by jet cockpit crews are made the very first day that a crew flies together as a team and that 44 percent of serious mistakes occur on their very first flight together that day (pilot teams fly two to three flights per day). Moreover, research has shown that fatigued pilot crews who have worked together before make significantly fewer errors than rested crews who have never worked together.[106] Their experience working together helps them overcome their fatigue and outperform new teams that have not worked together before. So, after you've created effective teams, keep them together as long as possible.

10-4c Team Training

After selecting the right people for teamwork, you need to train them. To be successful, teams need significant training, particularly in interpersonal skills, decision-making and problem-solving skills, conflict resolution skills, and technical training. Organizations that create work teams *often underestimate the amount of training required to make teams effective*. This mistake occurs frequently in successful organizations where managers assume that if employees can work effectively on their own, they can work effectively in teams. In reality, companies that successfully use teams provide thousands of hours of training to make sure that teams work. Stacy Myers, a consultant who helps companies implement teams, says, "When we help companies move to teams, we also require that employees take basic quality and business knowledge classes as well. Teams must know how their work affects the company, and how their success will be measured.[107]

Most commonly, members of work teams receive training in interpersonal skills. **Interpersonal skills** such as listening, communicating, questioning, and providing feedback enable people to have effective working relationships with others. Consultant Peter Grazier, founder of Teambuilding Inc., says, "Teams have told us that if they had to do it over again, they would have more of the people skills up front. They don't struggle with the technical stuff. They tend to struggle with the people skills."[108] Because of teams' autonomy and responsibility, many companies also give team members training in *decision-making and problem-solving skills* to help them do a better job of cutting costs and improving quality and customer service. Many organizations also teach teams *conflict resolution skills*. Teambuilding Inc.'s Grazier explains that "the diversity of values and personalities makes a team powerful, but it can be the greatest source of conflict. If you're a detail person, and I'm not, and we get on a team, you might say that we need more analysis on a problem before making a decision, [while I] may want to make a decision [right away]. But, if I've been trained in problem-solving and conflict resolution, then I look at your detail [focus] as something that is needed in a team because it's a shortcoming of **mine**.[109] Liane Davey, co-founder of 3COze, a team communication consulting firm, says you see, "…the light bulbs going on as people realize, 'You mean I'm supposed to fight with that person!' Yes! 'And when he's disagreeing with me, it's not because he's a jerk or trying to annoy me?' Right!"[110]

Firms must also provide team members with the *technical training* they need to do their jobs, particularly if they are being cross-trained to perform all of the different jobs on the team. Before teams were created at Milwaukee Mutual Insurance, separate employees performed the tasks of rating, underwriting, and processing insurance policies. After extensive cross-training, however, each team member can now do all three jobs.[111] Cross-training is less appropriate for teams of highly skilled workers. For instance, it is unlikely that a group of engineers, computer programmers, and systems analysts would be cross-trained for each other's jobs.

Interpersonal skills skills, such as listening, communicating, questioning, and providing feedback, that enable people to have effective working relationships with others

Team leaders need training, too, as they often feel unprepared for their new duties. New team leaders face myriad problems ranging from confusion about their new roles as team leaders (compared with their old jobs as managers or employees) to not knowing where to go for help when their teams have problems. The solution is extensive training. Overall, does team training work? One recent study found that across a wide variety of settings, tasks, team types, and 2,650 teams in different organizations, team training was positively related to team performance outcomes.[112]

10-4d Team Compensation and Recognition

Compensating teams correctly is very difficult. For instance, one survey found that only 37 percent of companies were satisfied with their team compensation plans and even fewer, just 10 percent, reported being "very positive."[113] One of the problems, according to Susan Mohrman of the Center for Effective Organizations at the University of Southern California, is that "there is a very strong set of beliefs in most organizations that people should be paid for how well they do. So when people first get put into team-based organizations, they really balk at being paid for how well the team does. It sounds illogical to them. It sounds like their individuality and their sense of self-worth are being threatened."[114] Consequently, companies need to carefully choose a team compensation plan and then fully explain how teams will be rewarded. One basic requirement for team compensation to work is that the level of rewards (individual versus team) must match the level of performance (individual versus team).

Employees can be compensated for team participation and accomplishments in three ways: skill-based pay, gainsharing, and nonfinancial rewards. **Skill-based pay** programs pay employees for learning additional skills or knowledge.[115] These programs encourage employees to acquire the additional skills they will need to perform multiple jobs within a team and to share knowledge with others within their work groups.[116] For example, at the Patience & Nicholson (P&N) drill bit factory in Kaiapoi, New Zealand, workers produce 50,000 drill bits a day for export to Australia, Taiwan, Thailand, and other locations primarily in Asia. P&N uses a skill-based pay system. As employees learn how to run the various machines required to produce drill bits, their pay increases. According to operations manager Rick Smith, workers who are dedicated to learning can increase their pay by $6 an hour over the course of three or four years.[117]

In **gainsharing** programs, companies share the financial value of performance gains, such as productivity increases, cost savings, or quality improvements, with their workers.[118] *Nonfinancial rewards* are another way to reward teams for their performance. These rewards, which can range from vacations to T-shirts, plaques, and coffee mugs, are especially effective when coupled with management recognition, such as awards, certificates, and praise.[119] Nonfinancial awards tend to be most effective when teams or team-based interventions, such as total quality management (see Chapter 18), are first introduced.[120]

Which team compensation plan should your company use? In general, skill-based pay is most effective for self-managing and self-directing teams performing complex tasks. In these situations, the more each team member knows and can do, the better the whole team performs. By contrast, gainsharing works best in relatively stable environments where employees can focus on improving productivity, cost savings, or quality.

Skill-based pay compensation system that pays employees for learning additional skills or knowledge

Gainsharing a compensation system in which companies share the financial value of performance gains, such as increased productivity, cost savings, or quality, with their workers

STUDY TOOLS 10

LOCATED IN TEXTBOOK

☐ Rip out and review chapter review card.

LOCATED AT WWW.CENGAGE.COM/LOGIN

☐ Gain unique perspectives on key concepts with new 4LTR concept videos in the e-book.

☐ Increase your comprehension with Aplia for MGMT11.

☐ Complete interactive content within the e-book.

11 | Managing Human Resource Systems

LEARNING OUTCOMES

11-1 Explain how different employment laws affect human resource practice.

11-2 Explain how companies use recruiting to find qualified job applicants.

11-3 Describe the selection techniques and procedures that companies use when deciding which applicants should receive job offers.

11-4 Describe how to determine training needs, and select the appropriate training methods.

11-5 Discuss how to use performance appraisal to give meaningful performance feedback.

11-6 Describe basic compensation strategies, and discuss the four kinds of employee separations.

After you finish this chapter, go to **PAGE 256** for **STUDY TOOLS**

11-1 EMPLOYMENT LEGISLATION

Human resource management (HRM), or the process of finding, developing, and keeping the right people to form a qualified workforce, is one of the most difficult and important of all management tasks. This chapter is organized around the three parts of the human resource management process shown in Exhibit 11.1: attracting, developing, and keeping a qualified workforce.

This chapter will walk you through the steps of the HRM process. We explore how companies use recruiting and selection techniques to attract and hire qualified employees to fulfill human resource needs. The next part of the chapter discusses how training and performance appraisal can develop the knowledge, skills, and abilities of the workforce. The chapter concludes with a review of compensation and employee separation, that is,

how companies can keep their best workers through effective compensation practices and how they can manage the separation process when employees leave the organization.

Before we explore how human resource systems work, you need to understand the complex legal environment in which they exist. So we'll begin the chapter by reviewing the federal laws that govern human resource management decisions.

"What was your last salary?" used to be the final question asked in the hiring process right before a job offer. Today, employers ask about salary much earlier. Josh Rock,

Human resource management (HRM) the process of finding, developing, and keeping the right people to form a qualified workforce a recruiter at Fairview Health Services which employs 20,000 people, said, "Why not figure out what's going on sooner in the process [rather] than doing a dance?"[1] Unfortunately, says Susan Vitale, chief marketing officer at iCIMS, which makes recruiting software, some companies, "use salary as a prescreening question."[2] For example, she says, "So if the role tops out at $55,000 and they say they want $60,000, it might knock the candidate out of consideration."[3] Out of concern that asking about salary perpetuates smaller salaries for women (who have lower salaries on average) and age discrimination (as older workers with higher salaries are screened out of the hiring process), some cities, like Philadelphia, are passing laws preventing employers from asking job applicants about salary histories. Vice president Christina Wong of Philadelphia-based ESM Productions says not asking about prior salaries will make it difficult for ESM, which hires crews and designers who run conferences and concerts worldwide, to determine appropriate market rates.[4] So, what are employers to do? They don't want to pay overpay employees, exceeding budgets and creating internal equity issues. But they also don't want to violate the law or be accused of gender or age bias.

As the "last salary" example illustrates, the human resource planning process occurs in a very complicated legal environment.

*Let's explore employment legislation by reviewing **11-1a** the major federal employment laws that affect human resource practice, **11-1b** how the concept of adverse impact is related to employment discrimination, and **11-1c** the laws regarding sexual harassment in the workplace.*

11-1a Federal Employment Laws

Exhibit 11.2 lists the major federal employment laws and their websites, where you can find more detailed information. The Fair Labor Standards Act (FLSA), administered by the Department of Labor (DOL), establishes minimum wage, overtime pay, record keeping, and youth employment standards for the private sector, as well as for federal, state, and local governments. (As such, the FLSA pertains to compensation issues discussed in Section 11-6a.) Except for the Family and Medical Leave Act and the Uniformed

Exhibit 11.1
The Human Resource Management Process

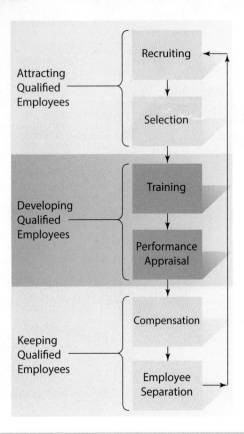

Attracting Qualified Employees
- Recruiting
- Selection

Developing Qualified Employees
- Training
- Performance Appraisal

Keeping Qualified Employees
- Compensation
- Employee Separation

Services Employment and Reemployment Rights Act, which are both administrated by the DOL, All of these laws are administered by the EEOC (www.eeoc.gov). The general effect of this body of law, which is still evolving through court decisions, is that employers may not discriminate in employment decisions on the basis of sex, age, religion, color, national origin, race, disability, or genetic history.[5] The intent is to make these factors irrelevant in employment decisions. Stated another way, employment decisions should be based on factors that are "job related," "reasonably necessary," or a "business necessity" for successful job performance.

The only time that sex, age, religion, and the like can be used to make employment decisions is when they are considered a bona fide occupational qualification.

Title VII of the 1964 Civil Rights Act says that it is legal to hire and employ someone on the basis of sex, religion, or national origin when there is a **bona fide occupational qualification (BFOQ)** that is "reasonably necessary to the normal operation of that particular business." A Baptist church hiring a new minister can reasonably specify that being a Baptist rather than a Catholic or Presbyterian is a BFOQ for the position. However, it's unlikely that the church could specify race or national origin as a BFOQ. In general, the courts and the EEOC take a hard look when a business claims that sex, age, religion, color, national origin, race, or disability is a BFOQ. For example, citing BFOQs, the producers of the Broadway musical *Hamilton*, advertised auditions for "nonwhite performers," claiming, "It is essential to the storytelling… that the principal roles, which were written for nonwhite characters (excepting King George), be performed by nonwhite actors." The EEOC's Compliance Manual clearly states, however, that, "race and color can never be BFOQs."[6] At the urging of the Actor's Equity Association, auditions were opened to actors of all races and colors.[7]

It is important to understand, however, that these laws apply to the entire HRM process and not just to selection decisions (for example, hiring or promotion). These laws also cover all training and development activities, performance appraisals, terminations, and compensation decisions. Employers who use sex, age, race, or religion to make employment-related decisions when those factors are unrelated to an applicant's or employee's ability to perform a job may face charges of discrimination from employee lawsuits or the EEOC.

In addition to the laws presented in Exhibit 11.2, there are two other important sets of federal laws: labor laws and the laws and regulations governing safety standards. Labor laws regulate the interaction between management and labor unions that represent groups of employees. These laws guarantee employees the right to form and join unions of their own choosing. For more information about labor laws, see the National Labor Relations Board at www.nlrb.gov.

The Occupational Safety and Health Act (OSHA) requires that employers provide employees with a workplace that is "free from recognized hazards that are causing or are likely to cause death or serious physical harm." This law is administered by the Occupational Safety and Health Administration (which, like the act, is referred to as OSHA). OSHA sets safety and health standards for employers and conducts inspections to determine whether those standards are being met. Employers who do not meet OSHA standards may be fined.[8] Even though working with wild

Exhibit 11.2
Summary of Major Federal Employment Laws

Fair Labor Standards Act (FLSA) of 1938	http://www.dol.gov/whd/flsa/index.htm	Establishes the federal minimum wage and rules related to overtime pay (eligibility and rates), recordkeeping, and child labor.
Equal Pay Act of 1963	www.eeoc.gov/laws/statutes/epa.cfm	Prohibits unequal pay for males and females doing substantially similar work.
Title VII of the Civil Rights Act of 1964	www.eeoc.gov/laws/statutes/titlevii.cfm	Prohibits employment discrimination on the basis of race, color, religion, gender, or national origin.
Age Discrimination in Employment Act of 1967	www.eeoc.gov/laws/statutes/adea.cfm	Prohibits discrimination in employment decisions against persons age 40 and older.
Pregnancy Discrimination Act of 1978	www.eeoc.gov/laws/statutes/pregnancy.cfm	Prohibits discrimination in employment against pregnant women.
Americans with Disabilities Act of 1990	www.eeoc.gov/laws/statutes/ada.cfm	Prohibits discrimination on the basis of physical or mental disabilities.
Civil Rights Act of 1991	www.eeoc.gov/laws/statutes/cra-1991.cfm	Strengthened the provisions of the Civil Rights Act of 1964 by providing for jury trials and punitive damages.
Family and Medical Leave Act of 1993	www.dol.gov/whd/fmla/index.htm	Permits workers to take up to 12 weeks of unpaid leave for pregnancy and/or birth of a new child, adoption, or foster care of a new child; illness of an immediate family member; or personal medical leave.
Uniformed Services Employment and Reemployment Rights Act of 1994	www.dol.gov/compliance/laws/comp-userra.htm	Prohibits discrimination against those serving in the armed forces reserve, the National Guard, and other uniformed services; guarantees that civilian employers will hold and then restore civilian jobs.
Genetic Information Nondiscrimination Act of 2008	www.eeoc.gov/laws/types/genetic.cfm	Prohibits discrimination on the basis of genetic information.

animals has inherent risks, OSHA found that **Sea World** did not have adequate procedures in place to protect employees and supervisors properly from killer whales while riding on or swimming with the animals. Building fast-rising pool floors and emergency air systems to protect its trainers did not prevent the death of a trainer at a park in Orlando, so OSHA fined the company $25,770.[9]

For more information about OSHA, see www.osha.gov.

11-1b Adverse Impact and Employment Discrimination

The EEOC has investigatory, enforcement, and informational responsibilities. Therefore, it investigates charges of discrimination, enforces the employment discrimination laws in federal court, and publishes guidelines that organizations can use to ensure they are in compliance with the law. One of the most important guidelines,

jointly issued by the EEOC, the U.S. Department of Labor, the U.S. Department of Justice, and the federal Office of Personnel Management, is the *Uniform Guidelines on Employee Selection Procedures*, which can be read in their entirety at www.uniformguidelines.com /uniformguidelines.html. These guidelines define two important criteria, disparate treatment and adverse impact, which are used in determining whether companies have engaged in discriminatory hiring and promotion practices.

Disparate treatment, which is *intentional* discrimination, occurs when people, despite being qualified, are *intentionally* not given the same hiring, promotion, or membership opportunities as

Disparate treatment intentional discrimination that occurs when people are purposely not given the same hiring, promotion, or membership opportunities because of their race, color, sex, age, ethnic group, national origin, or religious beliefs other employees because of their race, color, age, sex, ethnic group, national origin, or religious beliefs.[10] Bobby Nickel, a former facilities manager at Staples, the office supply retailer, was awarded $26 million by a jury that found Staples guilty of harassing him by calling him an "old coot" and an "old goat" and firing him because he was an older employee with a salary.[11]

Legally, a key element of discrimination lawsuits is establishing motive, meaning that the employer intended to discriminate. If no motive can be established, then a claim of disparate treatment may actually be a case of adverse impact. **Adverse impact**, which is *unintentional* discrimination, occurs when members of a particular race, sex, age, or ethnic group are *unintentionally* harmed or disadvantaged because they are hired, promoted, or trained (or any other employment decision) at substantially lower rates than others.

The producers of the Broadway musical *Hamilton* originally advertised auditions for "nonwhite performers," but at the urging of the Actor's Equity Association, auditions were opened to actors of all races and colors.

Joseph Marzullo/WENN.com/AGE Fotostock

At **Texas Roadhouse** restaurants, front-of-house employees (servers, bartenders, and hosts) are required to line dance during shifts, wear jeans, and work nights and weekends. The company hires younger workers for these positions—even though it produces a statistically adverse impact on older workers—because it considers such activities to be BFOQs.[12] The EEOC disagreed, filing a class action lawsuit against the restaurant chain for discrimination. The EEOC noted that only 1.9 percent of Texas Roadhouse's front-of-house employees were over the age of 40, a figure "well below the protected age group's

representation in the general population of defendants' locations, well below the protected age group's representation in Bureau of Labor statistics data for such positions within the industry, and well below the protected age group's representation in the pool of applicants for positions with defendants."[13] How do courts determine what constitutes "well below?"

The courts and federal agencies use the **four-fifths (or 80%) rule** to determine if adverse impact has occurred. Adverse impact is determined by calculating the impact ratio, which divides the decision rate for a protected group of people by the decision rate for a nonprotected group (usually white males). If the impact ratio is less than 80 percent, then adverse impact may have occurred. For example, if 20 out of 100 black applicants are hired (20/100 = 20%), but 60 white applicants are hired (60/100 = 60%), then adverse impact has occurred because the impact ratio is less than 80 percent (.20/.60 = 33%).

Violation of the four-fifths rule is not an automatic indication of discrimination, however. If an employer can demonstrate that a selection procedure or test is valid, meaning that the test accurately predicts job performance or that the test is job related because it assesses applicants on specific tasks actually used in the job, then the organization may continue to use the test. If validity cannot be established, however, then a violation of the four-fifths rule may likely result in a lawsuit brought by employees, job applicants, or the EEOC itself.

11-1c Sexual Harassment

According to the EEOC, **sexual harassment** is a form of discrimination in which unwelcome sexual advances, requests for sexual favors, or other verbal or physical conduct of a sexual nature occurs. From a legal perspective, there are two kinds of sexual harassment, quid pro quo and hostile work environment.[14]

Adverse impact
unintentional discrimination that occurs when members of a particular race, sex, or ethnic group are unintentionally harmed or disadvantaged because they are hired, promoted, or trained (or any other employment decision) at substantially lower rates than others

Four-fifths (or 80%) rule
a rule of thumb used by the courts and the EEOC to determine whether there is evidence of adverse impact; a violation of this rule occurs when the impact ratio (calculated by dividing the decision ratio for a protected group by the decision ratio for a nonprotected group) is less than 80 percent, or four-fifths

Sexual harassment a form of discrimination in which unwelcome sexual advances, requests for sexual favors, or other verbal or physical conduct of a sexual nature occurs while performing one's job

Quid pro quo sexual harassment occurs when employment outcomes, such as hiring, promotion, or simply keeping one's job, depend on whether an individual submits to being sexually harassed. For example, in a quid pro quo sexual harassment lawsuit against Stones River Medical Group, a woman hired as the assistant office manager was pressured for sex by a doctor beginning her first month on the job. The doctor provided her medications, threatened her with violence if she ended the sexual relationship, placing her on leave when she did so, and only hired her back after she resumed their sexual relationship. This made it a quid pro quo case by linking sexual acts to economic outcomes. She again ended their sexual relationship and was fired five days later. A jury awarded her a $2.3 million settlement.[15]

A **hostile work environment** occurs when unwelcome and demeaning sexually related behavior creates an intimidating, hostile, and offensive work environment. In contrast to quid pro quo cases, a hostile work environment may not result in economic injury. However, it can lead to psychological injury when the work environment becomes stressful. Zillow, a real estate website that estimates the value or sales prices of for-sale homes, settled a federal lawsuit alleging a hostile work environment and a "frat house" culture. A sales manager referred to a female worker as "Rachel 2.0," because she was like, "Rachel but with bigger breasts and less miles on her."[16] This sales manager, who was fired by Zillow one day after a hostile work environment lawsuit was filed in federal court, allegedly sent the female worker sexually explicit messages, with one including a picture of a penis. An IT technician, asked to help a female employee reset a password, responded, "Only trade password for boob pix. Haha."[17]

Finally, what should companies do to make sure that sexual harassment laws are followed and not violated?[18] First, respond immediately when sexual harassment is reported. A quick response encourages victims of sexual harassment to report problems to management rather than to lawyers or the EEOC. Furthermore, a quick and fair investigation may serve as a deterrent to future harassment. A lawyer for the EEOC says, "Worse than having no sexual harassment policy is a policy that is not followed. It's merely window dressing. You wind up with destroyed morale when people who come forward are ignored, ridiculed, retaliated against, or nothing happens to the harasser."[19]

Then take the time to write a clear, understandable sexual harassment policy that is strongly worded, gives specific examples of what constitutes sexual harassment, spells outs sanctions and punishments, and is widely publicized within the company. This lets potential harassers and victims know what will not be tolerated and how the firm will deal with harassment should it occur.

Next, establish clear reporting procedures that indicate how, where, and to whom incidents of sexual harassment can be reported. The best procedures ensure that a complaint will receive a quick response, that impartial parties will handle the complaint, and that the privacy of the accused and accuser will be protected. At DuPont, Avon, and Texas Industries, employees can call a confidential hotline 24 hours a day, 365 days a year.[20]

Finally, managers should also be aware that most states and many cities or local governments have their own employment-related laws and enforcement agencies. So compliance with federal law is often not enough. In fact, organizations can be in full compliance with federal law and at the same time be in violation of state or local sexual harassment laws.

11-2 RECRUITING

Frustrated by the high numbers of local candidates declining job offers, executives at **Salesforce.com**'s San Francisco headquarters developed an algorithm to collect the LinkedIn profiles of everyone in Northern California with the technical skills their jobs needed. Finding fewer candidates than anticipated, and realizing that it had already been in contact with 23 percent of them, Salesforce.com decided to look at other cities with larger talent pools. After reviewing the results, Salesforce.com recruiting head

Rommel Canlas/Shutterstock.com

Quid pro quo sexual harassment a form of sexual harassment in which employment outcomes, such as hiring, promotion, or simply keeping one's job, depend on whether an individual submits to sexual harassment

Hostile work environment a form of sexual harassment in which unwelcome and demeaning sexually related behavior creates an intimidating and offensive work environment

Ana Recio said, "Suddenly we were in real-estate discussions."[21]

Recruiting is the process of developing a pool of qualified job applicants.

Let's examine 11-2a what job analysis is and how it is used in recruiting, 11-2b how companies use internal recruiting, and 11-2c external recruiting to find qualified job applicants.

11-2a Defining the Job

Job analysis is a "purposeful, systematic process for collecting information on the important work-related aspects of a job."[22] A job analysis typically collects four kinds of information:

» Work activities, such as what workers do and how, when, and why they do it

» The tools and equipment used to do the job

» The context in which the job is performed, such as the actual working conditions or schedule

» The personnel requirements for performing the job, meaning the knowledge, skills, and abilities (KSAs) needed to do a job well[23]

Job analysis information can be collected by having job incumbents and/or supervisors complete questionnaires about their jobs, by direct observation, by interviews, or by filming employees as they perform their jobs.

Job descriptions and job specifications are two of the most important results of a job analysis. A **job description** is a written description of the basic tasks, duties, and responsibilities required of an employee holding a particular job. **Job specifications**, which are often included as a separate section of a job description, are a summary of the qualifications needed to successfully perform the job. Exhibit 11.3 shows a job description for a firefighter for the city of Portland, Oregon.

Because a job analysis specifies what a job entails as well as the knowledge, skills, and abilities that are needed to do the job well, companies must complete a job analysis *before* beginning to recruit job applicants. Job analyses, job descriptions, and job specifications are the foundation on which all critical human resource activities are built. They are used during recruiting and selection to match applicant qualifications with the requirements of the job. Software company SAP uses machine learning to teach "a computer how to spot patterns and make connections by showing it a massive volume of data."[24] SAP Resume Matching, a machine learning program, reads thousands of job descriptions and specifications on the Internet to identify the KSAs for a variety of jobs. It validated what it learned by using those KSAs to evaluate anonymous resumes (with no names or identifying demographics) of actual job applicants who were rejected, made the first cut of promising candidates, interviewed, or were eventually hired by managers in a variety of companies. SAP's chief innovation officer said, "Recruiters spend 60 percent of their time reading CVs. Why should a person read 300 resumes if a machine can propose the top 10?"[25]

Job descriptions are also used throughout the staffing process to ensure that selection devices and the decisions based on these devices are job related. For example, the questions asked in an interview should be based on the most important work activities identified by a job analysis. Likewise, during performance appraisals, employees should be evaluated in areas that a job analysis has identified as the most important in a job.

Job analyses, job descriptions, and job specifications also help companies meet the legal requirement that their human resource decisions be job related. To be judged *job related*, recruitment, selection, training, performance appraisals, and employee separations must be valid and be directly related to the important aspects of the job, as identified by a careful job analysis. In fact, in *Griggs v. Duke Power Co.* and *Albemarle Paper Co. v. Moody*, the U.S. Supreme Court stated that companies should use job analyses to help establish the job relatedness of their human resource procedures.[26] The EEOC's *Uniform Guidelines on Employee Selection Procedures* also recommend that companies base their human resource procedures on job analysis.

11-2b Internal Recruiting

Internal recruiting is the process of developing a pool of qualified job applicants from people who already work in the company. Internal recruiting, sometimes called "promotion from within," improves employee commitment, morale, and motivation. Recruiting current employees also reduces recruitment start-up time

Recruiting the process of developing a pool of qualified job applicants

Job analysis a purposeful, systematic process for collecting information on the important work-related aspects of a job

Job description a written description of the basic tasks, duties, and responsibilities required of an employee holding a particular job

Job specifications a written summary of the qualifications needed to successfully perform a particular job

Exhibit 11.3
Job Description for a Firefighter for the City of Portland, Oregon

Yes, as a firefighter you will fight fire and provide emergency medical services to your community. But it doesn't end there: your firefighting career offers you the opportunity to expand your skills to include hazardous materials response, specialty response teams (dive, rope rescue, confined space), paramedic care, public education and information, fire investigation, and fire code enforcement.

Teamwork
Professional firefighters work as a team at emergency scenes. The workday also includes training, fire station and equipment maintenance, fire prevention activities, and public education. As a firefighter, you must be in excellent physical condition to meet the demands of the job; this means you must work quickly, handling heavy equipment for long periods of time while wearing special protective gear in hot and hazardous environments. If you can meet the challenge of strenuous work and like the idea of helping people, consider applying for the position of firefighter.

Work Schedule
Portland Fire & Rescue firefighters work a 24-on/48-off shift. This means that Firefighters report to work at 8:00 a.m. the day of their shift and continue working until 8:00 a.m. the following morning. Our firefighters then have the following two days (48 hours) off. Firefighters are required to work shifts on holidays and weekends. Portland Fire & Rescue also has 40-hour-a-week firefighters who work in training, inspections/investigations, public education, logistics, and emergency management. These positions are usually filled after a firefighter has met the minimum requirements for these positions.

Source: Portland Fire and Rescue, accessed July 8, 2016. http://www.portlandoregon.gov/fire/25923.

iStockphoto.com/Kendall Griffin

and costs, and because employees are already familiar with the company's culture and procedures, they are more likely to succeed in new jobs. Crédit Suisse was posting less than half of its open jobs internally until it discovered that those taking a new job within the company were more likely to stay long term. So, it now posts 80 percent of its openings internally—even cold-calling employees to let them know when jobs have opened. Doing so has resulted in promotions for 300 of its people. William Wolf, the bank's global head of talent acquisition and development, says, "We believe we've saved a number of them from taking jobs at other banks."[27] Job posting and career paths are two methods of internal recruiting.

Job posting is a procedure for advertising job openings within the company to existing employees. A job description and requirements are typically posted on a bulletin board, in a company newsletter, or in an internal computerized job bank that is accessible only to employees. Job posting helps organizations discover hidden talent, allows employees to take responsibility for career planning, and makes it easier for companies to retain talented workers who are dissatisfied in their current jobs and would otherwise leave the company.[28] In fact, a LinkedIn survey of workers who changed jobs found that 42 percent would have stayed with their former employers if a relevant position had been available.[29] LinkedIn vice president Parker Barrile says it's often the case that, "People quit their job, not the company."[30] Ally Financial posts jobs via career roundtables in which managers fill openings with internal candidates. Ally Financial's Tony Jefferson got promoted to middle management after discussing his finance skills and managerial aspirations with 12 executives. The roundtable, he says, was, "a good opportunity to get your name and face in front of the senior leadership team."[31]

A study of 70 large global companies found that organizations that formalize internal recruiting and job posting have a lower average rate of turnover (11%) compared to companies that don't (15%).[32] Likewise, a University of Pennsylvania study found external hires generally

> **Internal recruiting** the process of developing a pool of qualified job applicants from people who already work in the company

Job Spotter: The Pokemon Go of Job Postings

Indeed.com is the world's largest job site visited by 200 million people per month seeking employment in 60 countries. Indeed is free for job applicants and employers, but it makes money several ways. When you click on a job near you, you'll find several other "promoted" jobs listed as well. Those promoted jobs are like paid Google Ads, but in this case, companies paid Indeed to "promote" their jobs to make sure they get seen by applicants. The more applicants Indeed brings to its site, the more attractive Indeed becomes to employers. As that happens, standing out in the crowd of employers becomes more difficult, so employers pay for "promoted" jobs.

All of which explains why Indeed is willing to lose money on Job Spotter, it's latest way to get more job openings listed on its website. Job Spotter is an app, like Pokemon Go, in which users score points by finding job openings that aren't listed on Indeed. When you see a "help wanted" sign, take a picture. Submit it with the app. Chris Hyams, Indeed's president, explains that GPS data are used, "to match the photo to a database of businesses to get the name and address, and we use [data from the photo] to automatically extract phone number, email, and other information from the image." Every new job earns 50 points (but only if it's not on Indeed). One hundred points is worth $1 in store credit at Amazon.com. In the six months since launching, users have been paid $250,000 for uploading 500,000 new jobs that Indeed would otherwise have listed.

So next time you're out for a walk or a bike ride, earn some extra spending money by submitting job openings with Job Spotter. You'll earn some pizza money and help someone find their next job!

Sources: C. O'Brien, "Spotting Gap in Jobs Market Works out Very Well Indeed for Ireland," *Irish Times*, February 18, 2017, accessed April 21, 2017, http://www.irishtimes.com/business/retail-and-services/spotting-gap-in-jobs-market-works-out-very-well-indeed-for-ireland-1.2979513; N. Zipkin, "How Indeed's Pokémon Go-Like Job App Almost Didn't Happen," *Entrepreneur*, January 6, 2017, accessed April 21, 2017, https://www.entrepreneur.com/article/287421; No author, "Job Spotter App Gives Small Businesses the Power to Crowdsource Job Advertising," *Indeed Blog*, July 7, 2016, accessed April 21, 2017, http://blog.indeed.com/2016/07/07/indeed-job-spotter-app-helps-small-businesses/; J. Wuerch, "Job Spotter App - Get Paid Taking Pictures Of Help Wanted Signs," *Frugal For Less*, May 31, 2016, https://www.frugalforless.com/job-spotter-app-get-paid-taking-pictures-of-help-wanted-signs/.

are more costly, less reliable hires. Specifically, external hires get paid 18 to 20 percent more than internal hires, are 61 percent more likely to be fired, and are 21 percent more likely to quit their jobs.[33]

A *career path* is a planned sequence of jobs through which employees may advance within an organization. According to Brian Hoyt of RetailMeNot, an online coupon company in Austin, Texas, "Workers were saying, 'It isn't enough for me to work at a fun Internet company,' . . . they wanted to know where their career was going."[34] So the company revamped its internal recruiting system, adding to each job posting a detailed list of responsibilities, required competencies, and skills needed to get each job. Garrett Bircher, an associate product manager, said that when he when was hired, the company lacked a coherent approach. "Now, I feel more secure," he says. "I know four jobs ahead of me now where I want to go and what it takes to get there."[35]

External recruiting the process of developing a pool of qualified job applicants from outside the company

Career paths help employees focus on long-term goals and development while also helping companies increase employee retention. As you can see in Garrett Bircher's case, career paths can also help employees gain a broad range of experience, which is especially useful at higher levels of management.

11-2c External Recruiting

External recruiting is the process of developing a pool of qualified job applicants from outside the company. Headquartered in Canton, Ohio, **Diebold** is the largest manufacturer of ATMs and voting machines in the United States. Diebold needs to expand its software and service offerings to grow, but experts in those areas don't want to move to Canton. To solve this problem, CEO Andy Mattes waived the requirement that executives relocate, saying, "We were fishing in a small pond . . . [so] we expanded the talent pool substantially. As long as they live near an airport, where they work isn't nearly as important as what they can contribute." Now,

Diebold's chief strategist lives in San Jose California, the chief marketing officer in Boston, and the head of software in Dallas. Overall, nearly 40 of Diebold's top 100 executives live outside of Canton.[36]

External recruitment methods include advertising (newspapers, magazines, direct mail, radio, or television), employee referrals (asking current employees to recommend possible job applicants), walk-ins (people who apply on their own), outside organizations (universities, technical/trade schools, professional societies), employment services (state or private employment agencies, temporary help agencies, and professional search firms), special events (career conferences or job fairs), Internet job sites (CareerBuilder .com, Glassdoor.com, Indeed.com, and Monster.com), and social media (LinkedIn and Facebook), as well as career portals on company websites. Which external recruiting method should you use? Historically, studies show that employee referrals, walk-ins, advertisements, and state employment agencies tend to be used most frequently for office/clerical and production/service employees. By contrast, advertisements and college/university recruiting are used most frequently for professional/technical employees. When recruiting managers, organizations tend to rely most heavily on advertisements, employee referrals, and search firms.[37]

Recently, social media sites and industry-specific job boards have been gaining momentum at the expense of generalist job boards and newspapers. **Facebook**'s job search platform is used effectively to recruit lower-skilled workers, and sites such as **LinkedIn** and **theLadders .com** tend to attract more highly skilled or senior-level job seekers.[38] Even though 67 percent of people seeking jobs through social media use Facebook, LinkedIn continues to be where recruiters look for promising candidates. A recent survey found that a whopping 92 percent of recruiters use social media for outreach—87 percent of whom use LinkedIn.[39]

One of the biggest trends in recruiting is identifying passive candidates, people who are not actively seeking a job but who might be receptive to a change. Why pursue passive candidates? About half of all workers would be willing to change jobs if recruited by another company.[40] Apps such as Entelo search 50 sources across the web for information about passive candidates, such as job title, experience, or professional achievements. Recruiters then improve search accuracy after each wave of data matching by indicating whether the identified candidates fit. Becky McCullough, who runs recruiting at digital marketer HubSpot, says, "It has set new benchmarks for response rate," meaning the percentage of passive candidates who respond with interest when contacted by HubSpot, "and we can a/b test various outreach tactics" to see what recruiting methods work best.[41]

Some companies are even hosting virtual job fairs, where job applicants click on recruiting booths to learn about the company, see the kinds of available jobs, and speak with company representatives via video chat or instant message. Because they don't need to send HR representatives on long trips and can interact with potential hires from all over the world, Boeing, Progressive, Citibank, and Amazon have found virtual job fairs to be an efficient, cost-effective way to find qualified candidates. Still an important part of external recruiting, job fairs are being repositioned as branding events. With nearly half of its U.S. workforce expected to retire by 2025, the insurance and risk management industry is aggressively recruiting younger workers. **Allstate** bolsters its campus recruiting and job fairs with trivia nights, free food, and hackathons to attract computer science majors. And instead of wearing business suits, its campus recruiters wear T-shirts emblazoned with "Jobhunting is Mayhem," a reference to the star character in its popular ad campaign.[42]

11-3 SELECTION

After the recruitment process has produced a pool of qualified applicants, the selection process is used to determine which applicants have the best chance of performing well on the job. From the initial review of applicants to phone screening (seven days) to group interviews (six days) to personality and skills testing, it takes an average of 23 to 29 days to screen potential applicants and hire a new employee.[43] Software company **AppDynamics**, however, accomplishes the full selection process in less than a week. A few days after applying, strong candidates have two phone interviews, during which recruiters set expectations about compensation. Applicants then visit the office for seven hours of in-person interviews with roughly six employees. This day ends with a 15-minute interview with a hiring manager who may (or may not) extend an offer. Candidates who receive offers have two days to accept or decline. Luan Lam, AppDynamics' vice president of global talent, says, "Time kills deals," and notes that before implementing this speed-hiring method, AppDynamics needed 30 days to fill every open engineering position.[44]

As this example illustrates, **selection** is the process of gathering information about job applicants to decide who

> **Selection** the process of gathering information about job applicants to decide who should be offered a job

should be offered a job. To make sure that selection decisions are accurate and legally defensible, the EEOC's *Uniform Guidelines on Employee Selection Procedures* recommend that all selection procedures be validated. **Validation** is the process of determining how well a selection test or procedure predicts future job performance. The better or more accurate the prediction of future job performance, the more valid a test is said to be.

Let's examine common selection procedures such as **11-3a application forms and résumés, 11-3b references and background checks, 11-3c selection tests,** *and* **11-3d interviews**.

11-3a Application Forms and Résumés

The first selection devices that most job applicants encounter when they seek a job are application forms and résumés. Both contain similar information about an applicant, such as name, address, job and educational history, and so forth. Though an organization's application form often asks for information already provided by the applicant's résumé, most organizations prefer to collect this information in their own format for entry into a **human resource information system (HRIS)**.

Employment laws apply to application forms just as they do to all selection devices. Application forms may ask applicants only for valid, job-related information. Nonetheless, application forms commonly ask applicants for non-job-related information such as marital status, maiden name, age, or date of high school graduation. One study found that 73 percent of organizations had application forms that violated at least one federal or state law.[45] Likewise, interviewers may not ask about medical histories or genetics, religious beliefs, or citizenship. Exhibit 11.4 provides a more detailed explanation and list of the kinds of information that companies may *not* request in application forms, during job interviews, or in any other part of the selection process.

Courts will assume that you use all of the information you request of

Validation the process of determining how well a selection test or procedure predicts future job performance; the better or more accurate the prediction of future job performance, the more valid a test is said to be

Human resource information system (HRIS) a computerized system for gathering, analyzing, storing, and disseminating information related to the HRM process

Exhibit 11.4
Don't Ask! Topics to Avoid in an Interview

1. **Children.** Don't ask applicants if they have children, plan to have them, or have or need child care. Questions about children can unintentionally single out women.

2. **Age.** Because of the Age Discrimination in Employment Act, employers cannot ask job applicants their age during the hiring process. Because most people graduate high school at the age of 18, even asking for high school graduation dates could violate the law.

3. **Disabilities.** Don't ask if applicants have physical or mental disabilities. According to the Americans with Disabilities Act, disabilities (and reasonable accommodations for them) cannot be discussed until a job offer has been made.

4. **Physical characteristics.** Don't ask for information about height, weight, or other physical characteristics. Questions about weight could be construed as leading to discrimination toward overweight people, and studies show that they are less likely to be hired in general.

5. **Name.** Yes, you can ask an applicant's name, but you cannot ask a female applicant for her maiden name because it indicates marital status. Asking for a maiden name could also lead to charges that the organization was trying to establish a candidate's ethnic background.

6. **Citizenship.** Asking applicants about citizenship could lead to claims of discrimination on the basis of national origin. However, according to the Immigration Reform and Control Act, companies may ask applicants if they have a legal right to work in the United States.

7. **Lawsuits.** Applicants may not be asked if they have ever filed a lawsuit against an employer. Federal and state laws prevent this to protect whistle-blowers from retaliation by future employers.

8. **Arrest records.** Applicants cannot be asked about their arrest records. Arrests don't have legal standing. However, applicants can be asked whether they have been convicted of a crime.

9. **Smoking.** Applicants cannot be asked if they smoke. Smokers might be able to claim that they weren't hired because of fears of higher absenteeism and medical costs. However, they can be asked if they are aware of company policies that restrict smoking at work.

10. **AIDS/HIV.** Applicants can't be asked about AIDS, HIV, or any other medical condition, including genetics. Questions of this nature would violate the Americans with Disabilities Act, as well as federal and state civil rights laws.

11. **Religion.** Applicants can't be asked about religious beliefs. Questions of this nature would violate federal and state civil rights laws.

12. **Genetic information.** Employers should avoid asking about genetic test results or family medical history. This would violate the Genetic Information Nondiscrimination Act, or GINA, which was designed to help encourage people to get more genetic screening done without the fear of employers or insurers using that information to deny employment or coverage.

Sources: J. S. Pouliot, "Topics to Avoid with Applicants," *Nation's Business* 80, no. 7 (1992): 57; M. Trottman, "Employers Beware When Asking about Workers' Health," *Wall Street Journal*, July 22, 2013, accessed July 9, 2014, http://blogs.wsj.com/atwork/2013/07/22/employers-beware-when-asking-about-workers-health/; L. Weber, "Hiring Process Just Got Dicier," *Wall Street Journal*, July 3, 2014, accessed July 9, 2014, http://www.wsj.com/articles/hiring-process-just-got-dicier-1404255998.

applicants even if you actually don't. Be sure to ask only those questions that relate directly to the candidate's ability and motivation to perform the job. Furthermore, using social media such as Facebook and LinkedIn at the initial stage of the hiring process can give employers access to information they're not allowed to obtain directly from applicants. Attorney James McDonald says, "I advise employers that it's not a good idea to use social media as a screening tool. You need to control the information you receive so you're only getting information that is legal for you to take into accounting."[46]

Résumés also pose problems for companies, but in a different way. A CareerBuilder survey of hiring managers found that 58 percent had found a lie on a résumé, with the most common being embellished skills, employment dates, job titles, academic degrees, and the companies for which one has supposedly worked. Applicants in financial services (73%), leisure and hospitality (71%), and IT and health care (both 63%) were the most likely to have lies caught on resumes.[47] Therefore, managers should verify the information collected via résumés and application forms by comparing it with additional information collected during interviews and other stages of the selection process, such as references and background checks, which are discussed next.

11-3b References and Background Checks

In the United States, drivers for the Uber and Lyft ride-sharing services undergo an independent screening by Checkr, a company that runs each applicant's name through seven years of federal and county background checks, sex offender registries, and motor vehicle records. Checkr, which runs 300,000 checks a month, completes background checks in just two days.[48] Commercial truck drivers get an even more thorough background check called "Drive-a-Check," or "DAC." DAC reports, which are completed by HireRight, examine work histories, driving accidents, and reliability in terms of completing scheduled deliveries. One negative incident is usually enough to prevent a hire. Independent trucker Jeff Bailey said, "If a company uses DAC and you have a bad DAC, you're not hired."[49] Nearly all companies ask an applicant to provide **employment references**, such as the names of previous employers or coworkers, whom they can contact to learn more about the candidate. **Background checks** are used to verify the truthfulness and accuracy of information that applicants

provide about themselves and to uncover negative, job-related background information not provided by applicants. Background checks are conducted by contacting "educational institutions, prior employers, court records, police and governmental agencies, and other informational sources, either by telephone, mail, remote computer access, or through in-person investigations."[50]

Unfortunately, previous employers are increasingly reluctant to provide references or background check information for fear of being sued by previous employees for defamation.[51] If former employers provide potential employers with unsubstantiated information that damages applicants' chances of being hired, applicants can (and do) sue for defamation. As a result, 54 percent of employers will not provide information about previous employees.[52] Many provide only dates of employment, positions held, and date of separation.

When previous employers decline to provide meaningful references or background information, they put other employers at risk of *negligent hiring* lawsuits, in which an employer is held liable for the actions of an employee who would not have been hired if the employer had conducted a thorough reference search and background check.[53] Heyl Logistics hired Washington Transportation, a trucking firm, to deliver bottled water, but its driver took drugs, fell asleep, hit a truck, and killed another driver. The killed driver's family sued Heyl Logistics for negligent hiring, alleging it should have known that Washington Transportation operated without a license, did not test its drivers for drug use, and carried no insurance. Heyl was found guilty, Washington Transportation's driver was sent to prison for negligent homicide and driving under the influence, and the family was awarded $5.2 million in punitive damages.[54]

With previous employers generally unwilling to give full, candid references and with negligent hiring lawsuits awaiting companies that don't get such references and background information, what can companies do? They can conduct criminal record checks, especially if the job for which the person is applying involves money, drugs, control over valuable goods, or access to the elderly, people with disabilities, or people's homes.[55] According to CareerBuilder,

Employment references sources such as previous employers or coworkers who can provide job-related information about job candidates

Background checks procedures used to verify the truthfulness and accuracy of information that applicants provide about themselves and to uncover negative, job-related background information not provided by applicants

59 percent of organizations conduct criminal record checks, and 21 percent conduct credit checks.[56] Now that companies provide criminal record checks for $10 an applicant, pulling data from 3,100 court systems nationwide, there's no excuse to not check. Requiring criminal record checks may prompt some applicants to withdraw from the hiring process. Jeff Russow owns Avalanche Roofing & Exteriors in Colorado Springs. He says that for many of the people he recruits to apply for jobs with his company, "As soon as I say 'criminal background check,' 'drug test,' they're out the door."[57] While companies are legally entitled to use criminal background checks at some point in the hiring process, they should follow state laws and EEOC guidelines that may restrict asking applicants about criminal records on initial application forms.[58]

The previous edition of this textbook indicated that recruiters were using public networking sites such as LinkedIn to identify and contact applicants' work colleagues for reference and background checks. LinkedIn, however, has discontinued "Reference Search."[59] Furthermore, fewer companies are using social media (SM) for screening candidates and background checks. Three out of four organizations believe that using SM during recruiting exposes them to legal risk, particularly in regard to information they are not legally entitled to know (See Exhibit 11.4 on topics to avoid in interviews). At this time, companies are advised to not use SM until late in the hiring process, to have HR review SM rather than hiring managers, to look at SM for everyone or no one (be consistent!) and to only review publicly available information.[60]

After doing a background check, dig deeper for more information. Ask references to provide additional references. Next, ask applicants to sign a waiver that permits you to check references, run a background check, or contact anyone else with knowledge of their work performance or history. Likewise, ask applicants if there is anything they would like the company to know or if they expect you to hear anything unusual when contacting references.[61] This in itself is often enough to get applicants to share information they typically withhold. When you've finished checking, keep the findings confidential to minimize the chances of a defamation charge. Always document all reference and background checks, noting who was called and what information was obtained. Document everything, not just information you received. To reduce the likelihood that negligent hiring lawsuits will succeed, it's particularly important to document even which companies and people refused to share reference checks and background information.

Finally, consider hiring private investigators to conduct background checks, which can often uncover information missed by traditional background checks. For example, while traditional background checks should be able to verify applicants' academic credentials, a private investigator hired by the *Wall Street Journal* found that 7 out of 358 senior executives at publicly traded firms had falsified claims regarding the college degrees they had earned."[62] Likewise, private investigators can potentially identify when applicants hire companies that provide fake references from fake bosses (to avoid negative references from previous employers). Indeed, one such business claims, "We can replace a supervisor with a fictitious one, alter your work history, provide you with a positive employment reputation, and give you the glowing reference you need."[63]

11-3c Selection Tests

Selection tests give organizational decision makers a chance to know who will likely do well in a job and who won't. Prehiring assessments are growing in popularity, with 57 percent of large U.S. employers using some sort of prehiring test to ensure a better fit. "The incentives to screen before hiring have increased over time, while costs have declined," says economist Steve Davis. "Both those things are encouraging employers to move away [from] what was essentially a trial employment situation to just screening out people in advance.[64] The basic idea behind selection testing is to have applicants take a test that measures something directly or indirectly related to doing well on the job. The selection tests discussed here are specific ability tests, cognitive ability tests, biographical data, personality tests, work sample tests, and assessment centers.

Specific ability tests measure the extent to which an applicant possesses the particular kind of ability needed to do a job well. Specific ability tests are also called **aptitude tests** because they measure aptitude for doing a particular task well. For example, if you took the SAT to get into college, then you've taken the aptly named Scholastic Aptitude Test, which is one of the best predictors of how well students will do in college (that is, scholastic performances).[65] Specific ability tests also exist for mechanical, clerical, sales, and physical work. For example, clerical workers have to be good at accurately reading and scanning numbers as they type or enter data. Exhibit 11.5 shows items similar to

Specific ability tests (aptitude tests) tests that measure the extent to which an applicant possesses the particular kind of ability needed to do a job well

Exhibit 11.5
Clerical Test Items Similar to Those Found on the Minnesota Clerical Test

	Numbers/Letters		Same	
1.	3468251	3467251	Yes	No
			O	O
2.	4681371	4681371	Yes	No
			O	O
3.	7218510	7218520	Yes	No
			O	O
4.	ZXYAZAB	ZXYAZAB	Yes	No
			O	O
5.	ALZYXMN	ALZYXNM	Yes	No
			O	O
6.	PRQZYMN	PRQZYMN	Yes	No
			O	O

Source: N. W. Schmitt and R. J. Klimoski, *Research Methods in Human Resource Management* (Mason, OH: South-Western, 1991).

the Minnesota Clerical Test, in which applicants have only a short time to determine if the two columns of numbers and letters are identical. Applicants who are good at this are likely to do well as clerical or data entry workers.

Cognitive ability tests measure the extent to which applicants have abilities in perceptual speed, verbal comprehension, numerical aptitude, general reasoning, and spatial aptitude. In other words, these tests indicate how quickly and how well people understand words, numbers, logic, and spatial dimensions. Although specific ability tests predict job performance in only particular types of jobs, cognitive ability tests accurately predict job performance in almost all kinds of jobs.[66] Why is this so? The reason is that people with strong cognitive or mental abilities are usually good at learning new things, processing complex information, solving problems, and making decisions, and these abilities are important in almost all jobs.[67] In fact, cognitive ability tests are almost always the best predictors of job performance. Consequently, if you were allowed to use just one selection test, a cognitive ability test would be the one to use.[68] (In practice, though, companies use a battery of different tests because doing so leads to much more accurate selection decisions.)

Biographical data, or **biodata**, are extensive surveys that ask applicants questions about their personal backgrounds and life experiences. The basic idea behind biodata is that past behavior (personal background and life experience) is the best predictor of future behavior. For example, during World War II, the U.S. Air Force had to test tens of thousands of men without flying experience to determine who was likely to be a good pilot. Because flight training took several months and was very expensive, quickly selecting the right people for training was important. After examining extensive biodata, the Air Force found that one of the best predictors of success in flight school was whether students had ever built model airplanes that actually flew. This one biodata item was almost as good a predictor as the entire set of selection tests that the air force was using at the time.[69]

Most biodata questionnaires have more than 100 items that gather information about habits and attitudes, health, interpersonal relations, money, what it was like growing up in your family (parents, siblings, childhood years, teen years), personal habits, current home (spouse, children), hobbies, education and training, values, preferences, and work.[70] In general, biodata are very good predictors of future job performance, especially in entry-level jobs.

You may have noticed that some of the information requested in biodata surveys is related to those topics employers should avoid in applications, interviews, or other parts of the selection process. This information can be requested in biodata questionnaires provided that the company can demonstrate that the information is job related (that is, valid) and does not result in adverse impact against protected groups of job applicants. Biodata surveys should be validated and tested for adverse impact before they are used to make selection decisions.[71]

An individual's *personality* is made up of a relatively stable set of behaviors, attitudes, and emotions displayed over time. In short, it is personality that makes people different from each other. A **personality test** measures the

Cognitive ability tests tests that measure the extent to which applicants have abilities in perceptual speed, verbal comprehension, numerical aptitude, general reasoning, and spatial aptitude

Biographical data (biodata) extensive surveys that ask applicants questions about their personal backgrounds and life experiences

Personality test an assessment that measures the extent to which an applicant possesses different kinds of job-related personality dimensions extent to which an applicant possesses different kinds of job-related personality dimensions. In Chapter 12, you will learn that there are five major personality dimensions related to work behavior: extraversion, emotional stability, agreeableness, conscientiousness, and openness to experience.[72] Of these, only conscientiousness—the degree to which someone is organized, hardworking, responsible, persevering, thorough, and achievement oriented—predicts job performance across a wide variety of jobs.[73] Conscientiousness tests work especially well in combination with cognitive ability tests, allowing companies to select applicants who are hardworking, organized, responsible, and smart! "Personality tests allow employers to gauge a candidate's personality traits, cultural fit, and even compatibility with a team. **Furstperson**, a prehire test development company, uses a series of statements with agree-disagree scales. Statements which don't have obvious answers, such as "I dislike yelling, but sometimes a little yelling is necessary," make it harder to game the test. Twenty companies using Furstperson assessments saw their rate of 90-day attrition (the percentage of employees who quit or are fired before 90 days) drop from over 40 percent, before using personality tests to 12 percent after using them for two years.[74] Although increasingly prevalent, personality tests are not infallible. Charles Handler, a hiring consultant, admits assessments can't catch everything, saying, "There will be false positives, people who get through who shouldn't, and false negatives, someone who should've got through that didn't."[75]

Work sample tests, also called *performance tests*, require applicants to perform tasks that are actually done on the job. So, unlike specific ability tests, cognitive ability tests, biographical data surveys, and personality tests, which are indirect predictors of job performance, work sample tests directly measure job applicants' capability to do the job. For example, a candidate applying to be a pharmacist might be asked to consult medical databases and accurately fill prescriptions. An applicant for a sales position might have to role-play a sales pitch. The Levenson Group, an advertising firm, had applicants for a junior copywriter job develop an Instagram ad campaign for a vodka company. Fifty designed campaigns. Levensen hired recent college grad Kendall Madden whose ad, which took 16 hours to create, showed hands stretching toward drinks made with

Personality tests measure the extent to which applicants possess different kinds of job-related personality dimensions.

the vodka. Chief product officer Paul McEnany said that without the work sample test, "I'm not certain we would have interviewed her in the first place," because she hadn't studied marketing.[76] Work sample tests are generally very good at predicting future job performance; however, they can be expensive to administer and can be used for only one kind of job. For example, an auto dealership could not use a work sample test for mechanics as a selection test for sales representatives.

Assessment centers use a series of job-specific simulations that are graded by multiple trained observers to determine applicants' ability to perform managerial work. Unlike the previously described selection tests that are commonly used for specific jobs or entry-level jobs, assessment centers are most often used to select applicants who have high potential to be good managers. Assessment centers often last two to five days and require participants to complete a number of tests and exercises that simulate managerial work.

Some of the more common assessment center exercises are in-basket exercises, role-plays, small-group presentations, and leaderless group discussions. An *in-basket exercise* is a paper-and-pencil test in which an applicant is given a manager's in-basket containing memos, phone messages, organizational policies, and other communications normally received by and available to managers. Applicants have a limited time to read through the in-basket, prioritize the items, and decide how to deal with each item. Experienced managers then score the applicants' decisions and recommendations. Exhibit 11.6 shows an item that could be used in an assessment center for evaluating applicants for a job as a store manager.

Work sample tests tests that require applicants to perform tasks that are actually done on the job

Assessment centers a series of managerial simulations, graded by trained observers, that are used to determine applicants' capability for managerial work

In a *leaderless group discussion*, another common assessment center exercise, a group of six applicants is given approximately two hours to solve a problem, but no one is put in charge (hence the name *leaderless* group discussion). Trained observers watch and score each participant on the extent to which he or she facilitates discussion, listens, leads, persuades, and works well with others.

Are tests perfect predictors of job performance? No, they aren't. Some people who do well on selection tests will do poorly in their jobs. Likewise, some people who do poorly on selection tests (and therefore weren't hired) would have been very good performers. Nonetheless, valid tests will minimize selection errors (hiring people who should not have been hired and not hiring people who should have been hired) while maximizing correct selection decisions (hiring people who should have been hired and not hiring people who should not have been hired). Charles Handler, president of Rocket-Hire, a consulting firm on selection tests, says, "Predicting what humans will do is really . . . hard. Tests are a predictor and better than a coin toss, but you have to be realistic about them."[77] In short, tests increase the chances that you'll hire the right person for the job, that is, someone who turns out to be a good performer. So, although tests aren't perfect, almost nothing predicts future job performance as well as the selection tests discussed here.

Exhibit 11.6
In-Basket Item for an Assessment Center for Store Managers

```
February 28
Sam & Dave's Discount Warehouse
Orange, California

Dear Store Manager,

Last week, my children and I were shopping in your store.
After doing our grocery shopping, we stopped in the
electronics department and asked the clerk, whose name
is Donald Block, to help us find a copy of the latest
version of the Madden NFL video game. Mr. Block was rude,
unhelpful, and told us to find it for ourselves as he
was busy.

I've been a loyal customer for over six years and expect
you to immediately do something about Mr. Block's
behavior. If you don't, I'll start doing my shopping
somewhere else.

Sincerely,
Margaret Quinlan
```

Source: Adapted from N. W. Schmitt and R. J. Klimoski, *Research Methods in Human Resource Management* (Mason, OH: South-Western 1991).

11-3d Interviews

In **interviews**, company representatives ask job applicants job-related questions to determine whether they are qualified for the job. Interviews are probably the most frequently used and relied on selection device. There are several basic kinds of interviews: unstructured, structured, and semistructured.

In **unstructured interviews**, interviewers are free to ask applicants anything they want, and studies show that they do. Because interviewers often disagree about which questions should be asked during interviews, different interviewers tend to ask applicants very different questions.[78] Furthermore, individual interviewers even seem to have a tough time asking the same questions from one interview to the next. This high level of variety can make things difficult. As a result, while unstructured interviews do predict job performance with some success, they are about half as accurate as structured interviews at predicting which job applicants should be hired.[79]

By contrast, with **structured interviews**, standardized interview questions are prepared ahead of time so that all applicants are asked the same job-related questions.[80] Structuring interviews also ensures that interviewers ask only for important, job-related information. Not only are the accuracy, usefulness, and validity of the interview improved, but the chances that interviewers will ask

Interview a selection tool in which company representatives ask job applicants job-related questions to determine whether they are qualified for the job

Unstructured interviews interviews in which interviewers are free to ask the applicants anything they want

Structured interviews interviews in which all applicants are asked the same set of standardized questions, usually including situational, behavioral, background, and job-knowledge questions

questions about topics that violate employment laws (see Exhibit 11.4) are reduced.

Laszlo Bock, Google's head of human resources, explains why structured interviews are so effective: "...think about the last five people you interviewed for a similar job. Did you give them similar questions or did each person get different questions? Did you cover everything you needed to with each of them, or did you run out of time? Did you hold them to exactly the same standard, or were you tougher on one because you were tired, cranky, and having a bad day? Did you write up detailed notes so that other interviewers could benefit from your insights? A concise hiring rubric [via structured interviews containing the same questions] addresses all these issues because it distills messy, vague, and complicated work situations down to measurable, comparable results."[51] Four kinds of questions are typically asked in structured interviews. Situational questions ask applicants how they would respond in a hypothetical situation ("What would you do if . . .?"). These questions are more appropriate for hiring new graduates, who are unlikely to have encountered real-work situations because of their limited work experience. Behavioral questions ask applicants what they did in previous jobs that were similar to the job for which they are applying ("In your previous jobs, tell me about . . ."). These questions are more appropriate for hiring experienced individuals. Background questions ask applicants about their work experience, education, and other qualifications ("Tell me about the training you received at . . ."). Job-knowledge questions ask applicants to demonstrate their job knowledge (for example, nurses might be asked, "Give me an example of a time when one of your patients had a severe reaction to a medication. How did you handle it?").[52]

Semistructured interviews lie between structured and unstructured interviews. A major part of the semistructured interview (perhaps as much as 80%) is based

Exhibit 11.7
Guidelines for Conducting Effective Structured Interviews

Interview Stage	What to Do
Planning the Interview	• Identify and define the knowledge, skills, abilities, and other (KSAO) characteristics needed for successful job performance. • For each essential KSAO, develop key behavioral questions that will elicit examples of past accomplishments, activities, and performance. • For each KSAO, develop a list of things to look for in the applicant's responses to key questions.
Conducting the Interview	• Create a relaxed, nonstressful interview atmosphere. • Review the applicant's application form, résumé, and other information. • Allocate enough time to complete the interview without interruption. • Put the applicant at ease; don't jump right into heavy questioning. • Tell the applicant what to expect. Explain the interview process. • Obtain job-related information from the applicant by asking those questions prepared for each KSAO. • Describe the job and the organization to the applicant. Applicants need adequate information to make a selection decision about the organization.
After the Interview	• Immediately after the interview, review your notes and make sure they are complete. • Evaluate the applicant on each essential KSAO. • Determine each applicant's probability of success, and make a hiring decision.

Source: B. M. Farrell, "The Art and Science of Employment Interviews," *Personnel Journal* 65 (1986): 91–94.

Amazon Trains Seasonal Employees in Just Two Days

Amazon hires 120,000 extra warehouse workers in November and December to handle the surge in holiday buying. Amazon's warehouses, which are the size of multiple football fields stuffed with three-story-high shelves containing millions of products and robots and forklifts zipping back and forth, are intimidating and confusing. So how does Amazon train new employees in just two days?

First, an interactive video kiosk shows workers how to pack products by helping them select the right-sized box and spitting out just the right lengths of packing tape. Next workers move to work stations surrounded by shelves to which orange robots bring purchased products. For quick retrieval, computerized screens show workers the precise location on each shelf, including what the product looks like.

New holiday worker Ngcebo Sibiya said, "They demonstrated our job, how it's done. It was pretty easy, just packing packages… decent pay too." John Olsen, Amazon's vice president of human resources, said, "The technology works to walk you through the steps. It automates almost everything."

Source: L. Stevens, "How Amazon Gets Its Holiday Hires Up to Speed in Two Days," *Wall Street Journal*, November 28, 2016, accessed April 21, 2017, https://www.wsj.com/articles/amazon-leans-on-technology-to-speed-training-of-holiday-workers-1480329005..

on structured questions, but some time is set aside for unstructured interviewing to allow the interviewer to probe into ambiguous or missing information uncovered during the structured portion of the interview.

How well do interviews predict future job performance? Contrary to what you've probably heard, recent evidence indicates that even unstructured interviews do a fairly good job.[83] When conducted properly, however, structured interviews can lead to much more accurate hiring decisions than unstructured interviews. In some cases, the validity of structured interviews can rival that of cognitive ability tests.

But even more important, because interviews are especially good at assessing applicants' interpersonal skills, they work particularly well with cognitive ability tests. Combining the two—using structured interviews together with cognitive ability tests to identify smart people who work well with others—leads to even better selection decisions than using either alone.[84] Exhibit 11.7 provides a set of guidelines for conducting effective structured employment interviews.

11-4 TRAINING

According to the American Society for Training and Development, a typical investment in training increases productivity by an average of 17 percent, reduces employee turnover, and makes companies more profitable.[85] Giving employees the knowledge and skills they need to improve their performance is just the first step in developing employees, however. The second step—and not enough companies do this—is giving employees formal feedback about job performance (which we will discuss in section 11-5).

Training means providing opportunities for employees to develop the job-specific skills, experience, and knowledge they need to do their jobs or improve their performance. American companies spend an estimated $189 billion a year on training.[86]

To make sure those training dollars are well spent, companies need to **11-4a determine specific training needs, 11-4b select appropriate training methods,** *and* **11-4c evaluate training.**

11-4a Determining Training Needs

Needs assessment is the process of identifying and prioritizing the learning needs of employees. Needs assessments can be conducted by identifying performance deficiencies, listening to customer complaints, surveying employees and managers, or formally testing employees' skills and knowledge.

> **Training** developing the skills, experience, and knowledge employees need to perform their jobs or improve their performance
>
> **Needs assessment** the process of identifying and prioritizing the learning needs of employees

Note that training should never be conducted without first performing a needs assessment. Sometimes, training isn't needed at all or isn't needed for all employees. Unfortunately, however, many organizations simply require all employees to attend training whether they need to or not. As a result, employees who are not interested or don't need the training may react negatively during or after training. Likewise, employees who should be sent for training but aren't may also react negatively. Consequently, a needs assessment is an important tool for deciding who should or should not attend training. In fact, employment law restricts employers from discriminating on the basis of age, sex, race, color, religion, national origin, or disability when selecting training participants. Just like hiring decisions, the selection of training participants should be based on job-related information.

11-4b Training Methods

Assume that you're a training director for a hospital system and that you're in charge of making sure all employees in the biocontaminant unit can safely treat patients with Ebola.[87] Exhibit 11.8 lists a number of training methods you could use: films and videos, lectures, planned readings, case studies, coaching and mentoring, group discussions, on-the-job training,

Exhibit 11.8
Training Objectives and Methods

Training Objective	Training Methods
Impart Information and Knowledge	▶ *Films and videos.* Films and videos present information, illustrate problems and solutions, and effectively hold trainees' attention.
	▶ *Lectures.* Trainees listen to instructors' oral presentations.
	▶ *Planned readings.* Trainees read about concepts or ideas before attending training.
Develop Analytical and Problem-Solving Skills	▶ *Case studies.* Cases are analyzed and discussed in small groups. The cases present a specific problem or decision, and trainees develop methods for solving the problem or making the decision.
	▶ *Coaching and mentoring.* Coaching and mentoring of trainees by managers involves informal advice, suggestions, and guidance. This method is helpful for reinforcing other kinds of training and for trainees who benefit from support and personal encouragement.
	▶ *Group discussions.* Small groups of trainees actively discuss specific topics. The instructor may perform the role of discussion leader.
Practice, Learn, or Change Job Behaviors	▶ *On-the-job training.* New employees are assigned to experienced employees. The trainee learns by watching the experienced employee perform the job and eventually by working alongside the experienced employee. Gradually, the trainee is left on his or her own to perform the job.
	▶ *Role-playing.* Trainees assume job-related roles and practice new behaviors by acting out what they would do in job-related situations.
	▶ *Simulations and games.* Experiential exercises place trainees in realistic job-related situations and give them the opportunity to experience a job-related condition in a relatively low-cost setting. The trainee benefits from hands-on experience before actually performing the job, where mistakes may be more costly.
	▶ *Vestibule training.* Procedures and equipment similar to those used in the actual job are set up in a special area called a "vestibule." The trainee is then taught how to perform the job at his or her own pace without disrupting the actual flow of work, making costly mistakes, or exposing the trainee and others to dangerous conditions.
Impart Information and Knowledge; Develop Analytical and Problem-Solving Skills; and Practice, Learn, or Change Job Behaviors	▶ *Computer-based learning.* Interactive videos, software, CD-ROMs, PCs, teleconferencing, and the Internet may be combined to present multimedia-based training.

Source: A. Fowler, "How to Decide on Training Methods," *People Management* 25, no. 1 (1995): 36.

Uber drivers in Brazil, Colombia, and Mexico who want to expand their services to English-speaking passengers can use Duolingo to brush up or learn from scratch.

role-playing, simulations and games, vestibule training, and computer-based learning. Which method would be best?

To choose the best method, you should consider a number of factors, such as the number of people to be trained, the cost of training, and the objectives of the training. For instance, if the training objective is to impart information or knowledge to trainees, then you should use films and videos, lectures, and planned readings. In our example, trainees might read a manual or attend a lecture about how to put on and remove personal protective gear.

If developing analytical and problem-solving skills is the objective, then use case studies, coaching and mentoring, and group discussions. In our example, trainees might view a video documenting how a team handled exposure to the disease, talk with first responders who have worked in West Africa, and discuss what they would do in a similar situation.

If practicing, learning, or changing job behaviors is the objective, then use on-the-job training, role-playing, simulations and games, and vestibule training. Employees at the biocontainment unit of the University of Texas Southwestern Medical Center (UTSMC) role-play putting on and taking off their protective gear. Because of the number of steps involved, this is done in teams to ensure compliance so as to prevent the spread of the deadly disease. UTSMC sprays the fake Ebola patients used during the training with spicy, peppery Tabasco sauce. Dr. Bruce Myer says that if doctors and nurses get Tabasco on their skin, "it gives immediate feedback," to let them know a potentially deadly mistake has just been made.[88]

If training is supposed to meet more than one of these objectives, then your best choice may be to combine one of the previous methods with computer-based training. Walmart's Pathways training program uses computer games and videos to teach frontline employees how to read stock labels, the eight-steps used for collecting carts from the parking lot, plus basic information about the retail industry. Pathways supports six months of supervised on-the-job training during which managers help employees prepare to pass "gateway" assessments that can lead to a raise, a promotion to a specialty department, or acceptance into a management training program. Likewise, supervisors are being trained to support their employees and must attend a five-week managerial skills workshop. Jamie Dworackzyk, an apparel manager at the Joplin, Missouri, store for 18 years, appreciates Walmart's new emphasis on training, saying, "In the past we didn't take the time to teach. We just expected them to know. Now I can actually manage my people."[89]

These days, many companies are adopting Internet training, or "computer-based learning." E-learning can offer several advantages. Because employees don't need to leave their jobs, travel costs are greatly reduced. Also, because employees can take training modules when it is convenient (that is, they don't have to fall behind at their jobs to attend week-long training courses), workplace productivity should increase, and employee stress should decrease. And, if a company's technology infrastructure can support it, e-learning can be much faster than traditional training methods. This is especially true of micro-learning apps. With micro-learning, training is accomplished via short, focused lessons that can generally be completed in fewer than five minutes and are often followed by a quiz to check learning. For example, **Uber** drivers in Brazil, Colombia, and Mexico can practice their English skills using **Duolingo**, a foreign language app that delivers micro-instruction through audio, video, text, and pictures. After demonstrating proficiency by advancing to a certain level in the app, a driver's vehicle is listed as an option for English-speaking passengers looking for a driver who speaks their language.[90]

There are, however, several disadvantages to e-learning. First, despite its increasing popularity, it's not always the appropriate training method. E-learning can be a good way to impart information, but it isn't always as effective for changing job behaviors or developing problem-solving and analytical skills. Second, e-learning requires a significant investment in computers and high-speed Internet and network connections for all employees. Finally, though e-learning can be faster, many employees find it so boring and unengaging that they may choose to do their jobs rather than complete e-learning courses when sitting alone at their desks. E-learning may become more interesting, however, as more companies incorporate game-like features such as avatars and competition into their e-learning courses.

11-4c Evaluating Training

After selecting a training method and conducting the training, the last step is to evaluate the training. Training can be evaluated in four ways: on *reactions* (how satisfied trainees were with the program), on *learning* (how much employees improved their knowledge or skills), on *behavior* (how much employees actually changed their on-the-job behavior because of training), or on *results* (how much training improved job performance, such as increased sales or quality, or decreased costs).[91] In general, training provides meaningful benefits for most companies if it is done well. For example, a study by the American Society for Training and Development shows that a training budget as small as $680 per employee can increase a company's total return on investment by 6 percent.[92] Chuck Runyon, CEO of Anytime Fitness, which has 2,500 locations, says, "The only thing worse than training people and having them leave is not training people and having them stay."[93]

11-5 PERFORMANCE APPRAISAL

Performance appraisal is the process of assessing how well employees are doing

their jobs. Most employees and managers intensely dislike the performance appraisal process. In fact, 65 percent of employees are dissatisfied with their performance appraisal process. Likewise, according to the Society for Human Resource Management, 95 percent of human resource managers are dissatisfied with their companies' performance appraisal systems. Sixteen percent of companies, including Accenture, Microsoft Adobe and General Electric (GE), have abolished their performance appraisal systems altogether.[94] GE head of human resources Susan Peters explains the reason for the change this way: "It existed in more or less the same form since I started at the company in 1979, but we think over many years it had become more a ritual than moving the company upwards and forwards."[95]

On the other hand, Paul Rubenstein, a partner at global human resources consulting firm Aon Hewitt, says, "If you get rid of the performance ratings, how are you going to get rid of a fair and equitable and measurable system to blame the distribution of pay on? Because why did performance ratings come into existence? So there's some mechanism to force pay decisions. People wonder, which came first the rating or the pay decision."[96] Consulting firm CEB surveyed 9,000 managers and employees in 18 countries and found that employees were 14 percent less satisfied when companies dropped performance appraisals. The experience, according to CEB's Brian Kropp, "is pretty negative." Managers devote less time to performance issues and, without clarity regarding performance levels, employees often said, "my manager's just going to give more money to the person he likes."[97]

Indeed, performance appraisals are used for four broad purposes: making administrative decisions (for example, pay increase, promotion, retention), providing feedback for employee development (for example, performance, developing career plans), evaluating human resource programs (for example, validating selection systems), and for documentation purposes (for example, documenting performance ratings and decisions based on those ratings).[98]

*Let's explore how companies can avoid some of these problems with performance appraisals by **11-5a accurately measuring job performance** and **11-5b effectively sharing performance feedback with employees**.*

11-5a Accurately Measuring Job Performance

Workers often have strong doubts about the accuracy of their performance appraisals—and they may be right. For example, it's widely known that assessors are prone

Exhibit 11.9
Subjective Performance Appraisal Scales

	Very poor	Poor	Average	Good	Very good
Graphic Rating Scale					
Example 1: Quality of work performed is	1	2	3	4	5

	Very poor (20% errors)	Poor (15% errors)	Average (10% errors)	Good (5% errors)	Very good (less than 5% errors)
Example 2: Quality of work performed is	1	2	3	4	5

Behavioral Observation Scale

Dimension: Customer Service

	Almost Never				Almost Always
1. Greets customers with a smile and a "hello."	1	2	3	4	5
2. Calls other stores to help customers find merchandise that is not in stock.	1	2	3	4	5
3. Promptly handles customer concerns and complaints.	1	2	3	4	5

Dimension: Money Handling

	Almost Never				Almost Always
1. Accurately makes change from customer transactions.	1	2	3	4	5
2. Accounts balance at the end of the day, no shortages or surpluses.	1	2	3	4	5
3. Accurately records transactions in computer system.	1	2	3	4	5

to errors when rating worker performance. Three of the most common rating errors are central tendency, halo, and leniency. *Central tendency error* occurs when assessors rate all workers as average or in the middle of the scale. *Halo error* occurs when assessors rate all workers as performing at the same level (good, bad, or average) in all parts of their jobs. *Leniency error* occurs when assessors rate all workers as performing particularly well. One of the reasons managers make these errors is that they often don't spend enough time gathering or reviewing performance data. Facebook reduces appraisal errors by having managers work together to finalize appraisal ratings. "Managers sit together and discuss their reports face-to-face, defending and championing, debating and deliberating, and incorporating peer feedback. Here, the goal is to minimize the 'idiosyncratic rater effect'—also known as personal opinion. [This way] people aren't unduly punished when individual managers are hard graders or unfairly rewarded when they're easy graders."[99] What can be done to minimize rating errors and improve the accuracy with which job performance is measured? In general, two approaches have been used: improving performance appraisal measures themselves and training performance raters to be more accurate.

One of the ways companies try to improve performance appraisal measures is to use as many objective performance measures as possible. **Objective performance measures** are measures of performance that are easily and directly counted or quantified. Common objective performance measures include output, scrap, waste, sales, customer complaints, and rejection rates.

But when objective performance measures aren't available (and frequently they aren't), subjective performance measures have to be used instead. **Subjective performance measures** require that someone judge or assess a worker's performance. The most common kind of subjective performance measure is the graphic rating scale (GRS), as shown in Exhibit 11.9. Graphic rating scales are most widely used because they are easy to construct, but they are very susceptible to rating errors.

A popular alternative to graphic rating scales is the **behavior observation scale (BOS)**. BOSs requires raters to rate the frequency with which workers perform specific behaviors representative of the job dimensions that are critical to successful job performance. Exhibit 11.9 shows a BOS for two important job dimensions for a retail salesperson: customer service and money handling. Notice that each dimension lists several specific behaviors characteristic of a worker who excels in that dimension of job performance. (Normally, the scale would list 7 to 12 items per dimension, not 3, as in the exhibit.) Notice also that the behaviors are good behaviors, meaning they indicate good performance, and the rater is asked to judge how frequently an employee engaged in those good behaviors. The logic behind the BOS is that better performers engage in good behaviors more often.

Not only do BOSs work well for rating critical dimensions of performance, but studies also show that managers strongly prefer BOSs for giving performance feedback; accurately differentiating between poor, average, and good workers; identifying training needs; and accurately measuring performance. And in response to the statement, "If I were defending a company, this rating format would be an asset to my case," attorneys strongly preferred BOSs over other kinds of subjective performance appraisal scales.[100]

The second approach to improving the measurement of workers' job performance is **rater training**. The most effective is frame-of-reference training, in which a group of trainees learn how to do performance appraisals by watching a video of an employee at work. Next, they evaluate the performance of the person in the video. A trainer (an expert in the subject matter) then shares his or her evaluations, and trainees' evaluations are compared with the expert's. The expert then explains the rationales behind his or her evaluations. This process is repeated until the differences in evaluations given by trainees and evaluations by the expert are minimized. The underlying logic behind the frame-of-reference training is that by adopting the frame of reference used by an expert, trainees will be able to accurately observe, judge, and use relevant appraisal scales to evaluate the performance of others.[101]

11-5b Sharing Performance Feedback

After gathering accurate performance data, the next step is to share performance feedback with employees. Unfortunately, even when performance appraisal ratings are accurate, the appraisal process often breaks down at the feedback stage. Employees become defensive and dislike hearing any negative assessments of their work, no matter how small. Managers become defensive, too, and dislike giving appraisal feedback as much as employees dislike receiving it. In response, many companies are asking managers to ease up on harsh feedback and instead accentuate the positive by focusing on employee strengths. In the past, Michelle Russell of **Boston Consulting Group** says, "We would bring them in and beat them down a bit."[102] Some employees would suffer a crisis of confidence and performance and then quit. At **Intel**, telling employees they "need improvement" deflates morale, says HR manager Devra Johnson, "We call them the walking wounded."[103]

PlusONE/Shutterstock.com

Objective performance measures measures of job performance that are easily and directly counted or quantified

Subjective performance measures measures of job performance that require someone to judge or assess a worker's performance

Behavior observation scales (BOSs) rating scales that indicate the frequency with which workers perform specific behaviors that are representative of the job dimensions critical to successful job performance

Rater training training performance appraisal raters in how to avoid rating errors and increase rating accuracy

What can be done to overcome the inherent difficulties in performance appraisal feedback? First, be mindful of being overly critical and making employees so defensive that they quit listening. The top half of Exhibit 11.10 offers some suggestion for being less negative and more positive in feedback sessions. Also, because performance appraisal ratings have traditionally been the judgments of just one person, the boss, another possibility is to use **360-degree feedback**. In this approach, feedback comes from four sources: the boss, subordinates, peers and coworkers, and the employees themselves. The data, which are obtained anonymously (except for the boss's), are compiled into a feedback report comparing the employee's self-ratings with those of the boss, subordinates, and peers and coworkers. Usually, a consultant or human resource specialist discusses the results with the employee. The advantage of 360-degree programs is that negative feedback ("You don't listen") is often more credible when it comes from several people.

Herbert Meyer, who has been studying performance appraisal feedback for more than 30 years, recommends a list of topics to discuss in performance appraisal feedback sessions (see the bottom half of Exhibit 11.10).[104] Furthermore, managers can do three different things to make performance reviews more comfortable and productive. First, they should separate developmental feedback, which is designed to improve future performance, from administrative feedback, which is used as a reward for past performance, such as for raises. When managers give developmental feedback, they're acting as coaches, but when they give administrative feedback, they're acting as judges. These roles, coaches and judges, are clearly incompatible. As coaches, managers encourage, pointing out opportunities for growth and improvement, and employees are typically open and receptive to feedback. But as judges, managers are evaluative, and employees are typically defensive and closed to feedback.

Second, Meyer suggests that performance appraisal feedback sessions be based on self-appraisals, in which employees carefully assess their own strengths, weaknesses, successes, and failures in writing. Because employees play an active role in the review of their performance, managers can be coaches rather than judges. Also, because the focus is on future goals and development, both employees and managers are likely to be more satisfied with the process and more committed to future plans and changes. Because the focus is on development

and not administrative assessment, studies show that self-appraisals lead to more candid self-assessments than traditional supervisory reviews.[105]

Job search website **Monster.com** has put self-appraisals at the center of its performance feedback system by asking managers to conduct quarterly check-ins with their direct reports. Prior to the meetings, employees must complete a short template that includes one to three professional goals for the upcoming period, what kind of results they hope to achieve in that time frame, and how they plan to achieve them. Monster.com chief human resources officer Kim Mullaney says that "by communicating professional aspirations with their superiors, staffers will be more engaged. Knowing that you're in direct control of your goals is extremely important—as is knowing that your boss is a stakeholder in the plan."[106]

Exhibit 11.10

How and What to Discuss in a Performance Appraisal Feedback Session

How to Discuss Performance Feedback

	A	B
	Don't say...	Instead say...
	"What are we stuck on?"	"What are we doing really well?"
	"Nice work."	"You show great promise with…."
	"You need to get better at…."	"This is another way that's been successful."
	"We can't do this."	"We haven't done this yet."

- ✔ Overall progress—an analysis of accomplishments and shortcomings
- ✔ Problems encountered in meeting job requirements
- ✔ Opportunities to improve performance
- ✔ Long-range plans and opportunities—for the job and for the individual's career
- ✔ General discussion of possible plans and goals for the coming year

Source: H. H. Meyer, "A Solution to the Performance Appraisal Feedback Enigma," *Academy of Management Executive* 5, no. 1 (1991): 68–76; R. Feintzeig, "Everything Is Awesome! Why You Can't Tell Employees They're Doing a Bad Job." *Wall Street Journal*, February 10, 2015, accessed May 7, 2015, http://www.wsj.com/articles/everything-is-awesome-why-you-cant-tell-employees-theyre-doing-a-bad-job-1423613936.

Finally, what people do with the performance feedback they receive really matters. A study of 1,361 senior managers found that managers who reviewed their 360-degree feedback with an executive coach (hired by the company) were more likely to set specific goals for improvement, ask their bosses for ways to improve, and subsequently improve their performance.[107]

A five-year study of 252 managers found that their performance improved dramatically if they met with their subordinates to discuss their 360-degree feedback ("You don't listen") and how they were going to address it ("I'll restate what others have said before stating my opinion"). Performance was dramatically lower for managers who never discussed their 360-degree feedback with subordinates and for managers who did not routinely do so. Why is discussing 360-degree feedback with subordinates so effective? These discussions help managers understand their weaknesses better, force them to develop a plan to improve, and demonstrate to the subordinates the managers' public commitment to improving.[108] In short, it helps to have people discuss their performance feedback with others, but it particularly helps to have them discuss their feedback with the people who provided it.

360-degree feedback a performance appraisal process in which feedback is obtained from the boss, subordinates, peers and coworkers, and the employees themselves

Compensation the financial and nonfinancial rewards that organizations give employees in exchange for their work

Employee separation the voluntary or involuntary loss of an employee

 ## 11-6 COMPENSATION AND EMPLOYEE SEPARATION

Regional airlines, which operate 44 percent of all U.S. flights, transport passengers from smaller airports to large hub airports where travelers connect to longer flights on major airlines. Thanks to a wave of baby boomer pilots forced to retire at 65 (a federal requirement), and regulations that raised the minimum number of flight hours for regional pilots from 250 to 1,500 hours, airlines will need 14,500 more pilots over the next decade. Captain Tin Canoll, president of the Air Line Pilots Association union, says, "The marketplace for pilots is pretty tight right now. What we're seeing is the operation of supply and demand economics."[109] Shortages are so severe that some regional airlines increased starting pay for new pilots from $20,000 a year to $50,000 plus travel and training stipends and retention bonuses.[110]

Compensation includes both the financial and the nonfinancial rewards that organizations give employees in exchange for their work. **Employee separation** is a broad term covering the loss of an employee for any reason. *Involuntary separation* occurs when employers terminate or lay off employees. *Voluntary separation* occurs when employees quit or retire. Because employee separations affect recruiting, selection, training, and compensation, organizations should forecast the number of employees they expect to lose through terminations, layoffs, turnover, or retirements when doing human resource planning.

*Let's learn more about compensation by examining the **11-6a compensation decisions that managers must make** as well as **11-6b termination, 11-6c downsizing, 11-6d retirement**, and **11-6e turnover**.*

11-6a Compensation Decisions

There are three basic kinds of compensation decisions: pay level, pay variability, and pay structure.[111] *Pay-level decisions* concern whether to pay workers at a level that is below, above, or at current market wages. Companies use job evaluation to set their pay structures. **Job evaluation** determines the worth of each job by determining the market value of the knowledge, skills, and requirements needed to perform it. After conducting a job evaluation, most companies try to pay the going rate, meaning the current market wage. There are always companies, however, whose financial situation causes them to pay considerably less than current market wages.

Some companies choose to pay above-average wages to attract and keep employees. *Above-market wages* can attract a larger, more qualified pool of job applicants, increase the rate of job acceptance, decrease the time it takes to fill positions, and increase the time that employees stay.[112] While a senior pilot at U.S.-based Delta Airlines makes $209,000 a year, Qindao and Sichuan Airlines, both regional Chinese airlines, are paying $318,000 and $302,000 a year — including the pilots' Chinese income tax! What accounts for the 50 percent premium? Exponential growth in Chinese air travel, where the number of passenger jets has tripled in the last 10 years and the number of airlines has doubled in the last five. Projected growth is so strong that that the only way for Chinese airlines to meet customer demand is to hire 100 new pilots a week for the next 20 years. Dave Ross, president of U.S.-based Wasinc International, is recruiting pilots for over a dozen Chinese airlines. Ross says, "When we ask an airline, 'How many pilots do you need?,' they say, 'Oh, we can take as many as you bring.' It's almost unlimited."[113]

Pay-variability decisions concern the extent to which employees' pay varies with individual and organizational performance. Linking pay to performance is intended to increase employee motivation, effort, and job performance. Piecework, sales commissions, profit sharing, employee stock ownership plans, and stock options are common pay-variability options. For instance, under **piecework** pay plans, employees are paid a set rate for each item produced up to some standard (for example, $3 per item produced for output up to 100 units per day). After productivity exceeds the standard, employees are paid a set amount for each unit of output over the standard (for example, $4.50 for each unit above 100 units). Under a sales **commission** plan, salespeople are paid a percentage of the purchase price of items they sell. The more they sell, the more they earn. At inventory software company **Fishbowl**, every employee's pay is determined in part by how much he or she contributes to company sales. Employees receive a base salary discounted from the market rate, as well as a monthly commission based on how much they were able to directly influence sales. Since a company needs more than just salespeople, the significance of the commission is relative to the function

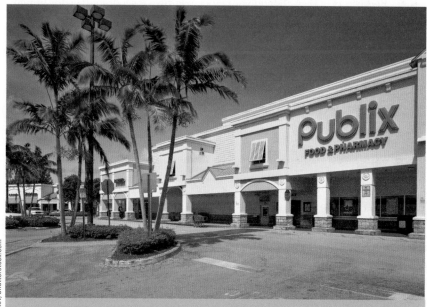

Felix Mizioznikov/Shutterstock.com

Publix Supermarkets ranked number 1 in U.S. ESOPs in 2016, according to the National Center for Employee Ownership.

Job evaluation a process that determines the worth of each job in a company by evaluating the market value of the knowledge, skills, and requirements needed to perform it

Piecework a compensation system in which employees are paid a set rate for each item they produce

Commission a compensation system in which employees earn a percentage of each sale they make within the company. Programmers receive 80 percent of their pay as base salary and 20 percent as commission, whereas salespeople receive 10 percent of their pay as base salary and 90 percent as commission. Even administrative employees earn commission. In lean months, no commissions are paid, but in good months, employees can double their base salaries through commission payouts. Overall, commissions increase Fishbowl employees' compensation by 19 percent per year.[114]

Because pay plans such as piecework and commissions are based on individual performance, they can reduce the incentive that people have to work together. Therefore, companies also use group rewards (discussed in Chapter 10) and organizational incentives, such as profit sharing, employee stock ownership plans, and stock options, to encourage teamwork and cooperation.

With **profit sharing**, employees receive a portion of the organization's profits over and above their regular compensation. Delta Airlines posted a profit of $5.9 billion in 2015. Thanks to the company's generous profit sharing plan, $1.5 billion of that was distributed to employees—the largest payout in the history of U.S. corporate profit sharing.[115]

Employee stock ownership plans (ESOPs) compensate employees by awarding them shares of the company stock in addition to their regular compensation. Central States Manufacturing, a steel-cutting firm in Lowell, Arkansas, is 100 percent owned by its 517 employees. Six and a half percent of each employee's annual pay goes into a tax-deferred ESOP account. Aaron King, a 60-year-old truck driver with the company for 23 years, has accumulated $1.25 million in his ESOP account. Because of the ESOP, he says, "We hold one another accountable. Somebody leaving a bundle of metal where it could be run over—a $3,000 bundle—we go and get that guy and talk to him. [Because] It's going to come out of all of our paychecks."[116] Not all ESOPs are 100 percent employee owned, however. Employees at yogurt company **Chobani** receive stock grants from founder and majority owner Hamdi Ulukaya enabling them to own up to 10 percent of the $3 billion company.[117]

Stock options give employees the right to purchase shares of stock at a set price. Options work like this. Let's say you are awarded the right (or option) to buy 100 shares of stock from the company for $5 a share. If the company's stock price rises to $15 a share, you can exercise your options, sell the stock for $15 a share, come out with $1,000. When you exercise your options, you pay the company $500 (100 shares at $5 a share), but because the stock is selling for $15 in the stock market, you can sell your 100 shares for $1,500 and make $1,000. Of course, as the company's profits and share values increase, stock options become even more valuable to employees. Stock options have no value, however, if the company's stock falls below the option "grant price," the price at which the options have been issued to you. The options you have on 100 shares of stock with a grant price of $5 aren't going to do you a lot of good if the company's stock is worth $2.50. Proponents of stock options argue that this gives employees and managers a strong incentive to work hard to make the company successful. If they do, the company's profits and stock price increase, and their stock options increase in value. If they don't, profits stagnate or turn into losses, and their stock options decrease in value or become worthless. To learn more about ESOPs and stock options, see the National Center for Employee Ownership (www.nceo.org).

The incentive has to be more than just a piece of paper, however. It has to motivate employees with the real opportunity to grow the value of the company and their wealth. **Adworkshop**, a digital marketing agency that does website design and development, search marketing, media buying, and creative work, became an employee-owned company in 2007. Account supervisor Kelly Frady says the ESOP has energized employee commitment. She says, "Everyone knows that you do well, and your stock will rise. It's a driving factor in making the company succeed in the long term."[118] In the United States, 7,000 employee-owned businesses, worth $1.30 trillion, are owned by 14 million employees.[119]

Pay-structure decisions are concerned with internal pay distributions, meaning the extent to which people in the company receive very different levels of pay.[120] With *hierarchical pay structures*, there are big differences from one pay level to another. The highest pay levels are for people near the top of the pay distribution. The basic idea behind hierarchical pay structures is that large differences in pay between jobs or organizational levels should motivate people to work harder to obtain those higher-paying jobs. Many publicly owned companies have hierarchical pay structures, paying huge salaries to their top managers and CEOs. For example, CEOs of the 350 largest U.S. firms, now make an average of $15.6 million per year, which is 271 times salary of the average employee.[121]

By contrast, *compressed pay structures* typically have fewer pay levels and smaller differences in pay

Profit sharing a compensation system in which a company pays a percentage of its profits to employees in addition to their regular compensation

Employee stock ownership plan (ESOP) a compensation system that awards employees shares of company stock in addition to their regular compensation

Stock options a compensation system that gives employees the right to purchase shares of stock at a set price, even if the value of the stock increases above that price between levels. Pay is less dispersed and more similar across jobs in the company. The basic idea behind compressed pay structures is that similar pay levels should lead to higher levels of cooperation, feelings of fairness and a common purpose, and better group and team performance.

So should companies choose hierarchical or compressed pay structures? The evidence isn't straightforward, but studies seem to indicate that there are significant problems with the hierarchical approach. The most damaging finding is that there appears to be little link between organizational performance and the pay of top managers.[122] Furthermore, studies of professional athletes indicate that hierarchical pay structures (for example, paying superstars 40 to 50 times as much as the lowest-paid athlete on the team) hurt the performance of teams and individual players.[123] Likewise, managers are twice as likely to quit their jobs when their companies have very strong hierarchical pay structures (that is, when they're paid dramatically less than the people above them).[124] For now, it seems that hierarchical pay structures work best for independent work, where it's easy to determine the contributions of individual performers, and little coordination with others is needed to get the job done. In other words, hierarchical pay structures work best when clear links can be drawn between individual performance and individual rewards. By contrast, compressed pay structures, in which everyone receives similar pay, seem to work best for interdependent work, which requires employees to work together. Some companies are pursuing a middle ground: combining hierarchical and compressed pay structures by giving ordinary workers the chance to earn more through ESOPs, stock options, and profit sharing.

11-6b Terminating Employees

The words "You're fired!" may have never been directed at you, but lots of people hear them, as more than 400,000 people a year get fired from their jobs. Getting fired is a terrible thing, but many managers make it even worse by bungling the firing process, needlessly provoking the person who was fired

and unintentionally inviting lawsuits. Manager Craig Silverman had to fire the head of a company whom his organization had just acquired. He was specifically instructed to invite her to a meeting, which would require her to travel halfway across the country, and then fire her immediately on arrival. He said, "I literally had to tell the car service to wait. I don't think it ever entered [her] mind that [she] would be terminated."[125] When Zynga terminated almost all of the employees from OMGPOP, a startup company it had acquired a year before, one of the employees tweeted, "I learned via Facebook I was laid off today and @omgpop office is closed. Thanks @zynga for again reminding me how not to operate a business."[126] A computer systems engineer was fired on "Take Your Daughter to Work Day," with his eight-year-old daughter sitting next to him in the human resource manager's office. He and his daughter were both escorted from the building.[127] How would you feel if you had been fired in one of these ways? Though firing is never pleasant (and managers hate firings nearly as much as employees do), managers can do several things to minimize the problems inherent in firing employees.

To start, in most situations, firing should not be the first option. Instead, employees should be given a chance to change their behavior. When problems arise, employees should have ample warning and must be specifically informed as to the nature and seriousness of the trouble they're in. After being notified, they should be given sufficient time to change their behavior. Ron Cohen is CEO and founder of **Acorda Therapeutics**, a company that develops therapies to restore neurological function for people with multiple sclerosis and spinal cord injuries. Cohen first fired an employee when he was 31 years old. He says it was painful, and, "I wound up hugging the employee, and she was crying on my shoulder." Since then, however, when he fires someone, they've had plenty of opportunities to address performance issues. Says Cohen, "I've learned over the

Oleg Golovnev/Shutterstock.com

Dos and Don'ts of Conducting Layoffs in the Digital Age

» **DO** conduct layoffs in person. If that's not possible, conduct the layoff live over the phone or via Skype. Email should only be used as a last resort if the employee is perpetually absent and unresponsive.

» **DON'T** announce a mass layoff via chat, IM, or other collaborative networking platform.

» **DO** shut down access to internal communication systems at the same time employees are being summoned to the meeting or call during which they will learn of the layoff.

» **DON'T** let employees figure out that they've been laid off by seeing that their access to email, Slack, IM, or other digital platforms has been disabled.

» **DO** keep communication brief and to the point to minimize time for speculation and suspense.

» **DON'T** conduct a layoff without a representative from Human Resources present.

» **DO** gather the remaining team and let them know who is no longer with the company. Remember to alert remote employees and freelancers.

» **DON'T** discuss specifics about why an employee was let go with remaining employees.

» Most of all, **DO** be kind, **DO** treat people decently, and **DO** act with integrity.

Source: L. Dishman, "The New Etiquette of Firing in the Digital Age," *Fast Company*, November 19, 2015, accessed May 1, 2016, http://www.fastcompany.com/3053763/the-future-of-work/the-new-etiquette-of-firing-in-the-digital-age.

years that if the employee doesn't expect it and know it's coming, you're not doing your job as a manager."[128]

If problems continue, the employees should again be counseled about their job performance, what could be done to improve it, and the possible consequences if things don't change (such as a written reprimand, suspension without pay, or firing). Sometimes this is enough to solve the problem. If the problem isn't corrected after several rounds of warnings and discussions, however, the employee may be terminated.[129]

Second, employees should be fired only for a good reason. Employers used to hire and fire employees under the legal principle of employment at will, which allowed them to fire employees for a good reason, a bad reason, or no reason at all. (Employees could also quit for a good reason, a bad reason, or no reason whenever they desired.) As employees began contesting their firings in court, however, the principle of wrongful discharge emerged. **Wrongful discharge** is a legal doctrine that requires employers to have a job-related reason to terminate employees. In other words, like other major human resource decisions, termination decisions should be made on the basis of job-related factors such as violating company rules or consistently poor performance. And with former employees winning 68 percent of wrongful discharge cases and the average wrongful termination award at $532,000 and climbing, managers should record the job-related reasons for the termination, document specific instances of rule violations or continued poor performance, and keep notes and documents from the counseling sessions held with employees.[130]

11-6c Downsizing

Downsizing is the planned elimination of jobs in a company (see box "Dos and Don'ts of Conducting Layoffs in the Digital Age"). Two-thirds of companies that downsize will downsize a second time within a year. After struggling to successfully integrate its purchase of cell phone maker Nokia, **Microsoft** announced in January 2015 that it had completed a layoff of roughly

Wrongful discharge a legal doctrine that requires employers to have a job-related reason to terminate employees

Downsizing the planned elimination of jobs in a company

12,500 employees in Nokia's manufacturing division.[131] Six months later, Microsoft CEO Satya Nadella announced that the company would lay off an additional 7,800 employees in the phone division and focus on running "a more effective and focused phone portfolio while retaining capability for long-term reinvention in mobility."[132]

Does downsizing work? In theory, downsizing is supposed to lead to higher productivity and profits, better stock performance, and increased organizational flexibility. However, numerous studies demonstrate that it doesn't. For instance, a 15-year study of downsizing found that downsizing 10 percent of a company's workforce produced only a 1.5 percent decrease in costs; that downsizing firms increased their stock price by only 4.7 percent over three years, compared with 34.3 percent for firms that didn't; and that profitability and productivity were generally not improved by downsizing. Downsizing can also result in the loss of skilled workers who would be expensive to replace when the company grows again. These results make it clear that the best strategy is to conduct effective human resource planning and avoid downsizing altogether. Downsizing should always be a last resort.[133]

If companies do find themselves in financial or strategic situations where downsizing is required for survival, however, they should train managers how to break the news to downsized employees, have senior managers explain in detail why downsizing is necessary, and time the announcement so that employees hear it from the company and not from other sources, such as TV or online reports.[134] Finally, companies should do everything they can to help downsized employees find other jobs. One of the best ways to do this is to use **outplacement services** that provide employment counseling for employees faced with downsizing. Outplacement services often include advice and training in preparing résumés, getting ready for job interviews, and even identifying job opportunities in other companies. Sixty-nine percent of companies provide outplacement services for laid-off employees, 61 percent provide extended health coverage, and most offer up to 26 weeks of severance payments.[135] Offering this kind of assistance can soften the blow from being laid off, preserve goodwill, and lower the risk of future lawsuits.[136]

Companies also need to pay attention to the survivors, the employees remaining after layoffs have occurred. According to author Sylvia Ann Hewlett, the impact of layoffs on remaining employees' morale is severe: 64 percent of employees who survived a layoff felt demotivated,

73 percent felt demoralized, and 74 percent said they simply shut down. "In other words," she says, "just when a company needs its top performers to charge the hill, they retreat to the bunkers."[137] The key to working with layoff survivors, according to Barry Nickerson, president of Dallas-based Marlow Industries, which downsized from 800 to 200 employees, is "Communicate. Communicate. Communicate." Nickerson says, "Every time we had a change we had a meeting to explain exactly what we were doing. We were very open with our employees about where we were financially. We would explain exactly the current status and where we were."[138]

11-6d Retirement

Early retirement incentive programs (ERIPs) offer financial benefits to employees to encourage them to retire early. Companies use ERIPs to reduce the number of employees in the organization, to lower costs by eliminating positions after employees retire, to lower costs by replacing high-paid retirees with lower-paid, less-experienced employees, or to create openings and job opportunities for people inside the company. Fidelity Investments offered early retirement to 3,000 employees 55 or older who had at least 10 years with the company. Depending on tenure and job level, incentives range from 6 to 24 months of salary, and a bonus. Everyone receives 18 months of health-care benefits, with the option to pay for continued coverage beyond that time.[139]

Although ERIPs can save companies money, they can pose a big problem for managers if they fail to accurately predict which employees will retire—the good performers or the poor performers—and how many will retire early. When Progress Energy, in Raleigh, North Carolina, identified 450 jobs it wanted to eliminate with an ERIP, it carefully shared the list of jobs with employees, indicated that layoffs would follow if not enough people took early retirement, and then held 80 meetings with employees to answer questions. Despite this care, an extra 1,000 employees, for a total of 1,450, took the ERIP offer and applied for early retirement![140]

Because of the problems associated with

Outplacement services employment-counseling services offered to employees who are losing their jobs because of downsizing

Early retirement incentive programs (ERIPs) programs that offer financial benefits to employees to encourage them to retire early

Phased retirement employees transition to retirement by working reduced hours over a period of time before completely retiring

ERIPs, 14 percent companies are now offering **phased retirement**, in which employees transition to retirement by working reduced hours over a period of time before completely retiring. The advantage for employees is that they have more free time but continue to earn salaries and benefits without changing companies or careers. The advantage for companies is that it allows them to reduce salaries and hiring and training costs and retain experienced, valuable workers.[141] Paul Irving, chairman of the Milken Institute Center for the Future of Aging, said, "There's a need for more companies to do this if they want to preserve their best practices, innovations, and customer relations. And there's receptivity among older workers, a majority of whom want to stay engaged and keep working, but in new ways."[142]

11-6e Employee Turnover

In 2016, 74 percent of workers with a job were either actively seeking or open to a new job.[143] **Employee turnover** is the loss of employees who voluntarily choose to leave the company. In general, most companies try to keep the rate of employee turnover low to reduce recruiting, hiring, training, and replacement costs. Not all kinds of employee turnover are bad for organizations, however. In fact, some turnover can actually be good. **Functional turnover** is the loss of poor-performing employees who choose to leave the organization.[144] Functional turnover gives the organization a chance to replace poor performers with better workers. In fact, one study found that simply replacing poor-performing workers with average workers would increase the revenues produced by retail salespeople in an upscale department store by $112,000 per person per year.[145] By contrast, **dysfunctional turnover**, the loss of high performers who choose to leave, is a costly loss to the organization. To minimize dysfunctional turnover, **VoloMetrix, Inc.** uses algorithms to identify so-called flight risks—employees who are gearing up to quit. Software examines anonymized data from employee emails and calendars to identify patterns of communication that indicate the employee is spending less time interacting with colleagues and attending only required meetings. The analysis helps the company predict a departure up to a year in advance, which is important, as the median cost of turnover for most jobs is 21 percent of the employee's annual salary.[146]

Employee turnover should be carefully analyzed to determine whether good or poor performers are choosing to leave the organization. If the company is losing too many high performers, managers should determine the reasons and find ways to reduce the loss of valuable employees. The company might have to raise salary levels, offer enhanced benefits, or improve working conditions to retain skilled workers. One of the best ways to influence functional and dysfunctional turnover is to link pay directly to performance. A study of four salesforces found that when pay was strongly linked to performance via sales commissions and bonuses, poor performers were much more likely to leave (that is, functional turnover). By contrast, poor performers were much more likely to stay when paid large, guaranteed monthly salaries and small sales commissions and bonuses.[147]

Employee turnover loss of employees who voluntarily choose to leave the company

Functional turnover loss of poor-performing employees who voluntarily choose to leave a company

Dysfunctional turnover loss of high-performing employees who voluntarily choose to leave a company

STUDY TOOLS 11

LOCATED IN TEXTBOOK
☐ Rip out and review chapter review card.

LOCATED AT WWW.CENGAGEBRAIN.COM
☐ Gain unique perspectives on key concepts with new 4LTR concept videos in the e-book.

☐ Increase your comprehension with Aplia for MGMT11.

☐ Complete interactive content within the e-book.

12 | Managing Individuals and a Diverse Workforce

After you finish this chapter, go to **PAGE 280** for **STUDY TOOLS**

LEARNING OUTCOMES

12-1 Describe diversity and explain why it matters.

12-2 Understand the special challenges that the dimensions of surface-level diversity pose for managers.

12-3 Explain how the dimensions of deep-level diversity affect individual behavior and interactions in the workplace.

12-4 Explain the basic principles and practices that can be used to manage diversity.

Darrin Klimek/Getty Images

12-1 DIVERSITY: DIFFERENCES THAT MATTER

Workplace diversity as we know it is changing. Exhibit 12.1 shows predictions from the U.S. Census Bureau of how the U.S. population will change over the next 40 years. The percentage of white, non-Hispanic Americans in the general population is expected to decline from 61.7 percent in 2015 to 43.7 percent by 2060. By contrast, the percentage of black Americans will increase (from 12.4 to 13%), as will the percentage of Asian Americans (from 5.3 to 9.1%). Meanwhile, the proportion of Native Americans will slightly decline (from 0.7 to 0.6%). The fastest-growing group by far, though, will be Hispanics, who are expected to increase from 17.7 percent of the total population in 2015 to 28.56 percent by 2060. Other significant changes have already occurred. For example, today women hold 46.8 percent of the jobs in the

United States, up from 38.2 percent in 1970.[1] Furthermore, white males, who composed 63.9 percent of the workforce in 1950, hold just 42.8 percent of today's jobs.[2]

These rather dramatic changes have taken place in a relatively short time. And, as these trends clearly show, the workforce of the near future will be increasingly Hispanic, Asian American, and female. It will also be older, as the average baby boomer approaches the age of 70 around 2020. Because many boomers are likely to postpone retirement and work well into their 70s to offset predicted reductions in Social Security and Medicare benefits, the workforce may become even older than expected. For instance, between 1994 and 2024, 16- to 24-year olds (16.5 to 11.3%), 25- to 34-year olds (26.2 to 22.5%), and 35- to 44-year-olds (26.9 to 21.3%) will have become a smaller part of the U.S. labor force. By contrast, those 45- to 54-year-olds (18.6 to 19.4%), 55- to 64-year-olds (6.5 to 16.6%),65- to 74-year-olds (2.4 to 6.5%), and 75 years and older (0.5 to 1.7%) will all have become larger parts of the U.S. labor force.[3]

Diversity means variety. Therefore, **diversity** exists in organizations when there is a variety of demographic, cultural, and personal differences among the people who work there and the customers who do business there. With 5,700 locations in 110 countries, few business have the diversity of locations and customers that Marriott Hotels has.[4] But Marriott's Executive Global Diversity and Inclusion Council still expects each hotel to have diversity in terms of its local workforce, customer, and vendor communities. For instance, the Marriott Marquis Washington, DC, which is just two years old, filled 58 percent of its jobs with applicants from eight inner city neighborhoods, hired 200 disadvantage applicants with limited work experience who completed a

> **Diversity** a variety of demographic, cultural, and personal differences among an organization's employees and customers

Exhibit 12.1
Percent of the Projected Population by Race and Hispanic Origin for the United States: 2015–2060

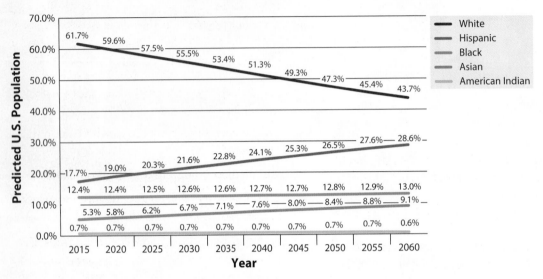

Source: "Table 11. Percent of the Projected Population by Hispanic Origin and Race for the United States: 2015 to 2060 (NP2014-T11)," *U.S. Census Bureau*, accessed April 22, 2017, https://www.census.gov/population/projections/data/national/2014/summarytables.html.

joint Marriott/Goodwill Jobs Training Partnership, and is already doing millions of dollars of business with women- and minority-owned businesses.[5] CEO and Chairman Bill Marriott says that everywhere Marriott does business, "We are broadening how we think about global diversity and inclusion, reaching across cultural borders to compete for customers and talent worldwide."[6] Marriott is regularly recognized as one of the top ten most diverse firms in the world.

You'll begin your exploration of diversity by learning 12-1a that diversity is not affirmative action and 12-1b that diversity makes good business sense.

12-1a Diversity Is Not Affirmative Action

A common misconception is that workplace diversity and affirmative action are the same, yet these concepts differ in several critical ways, including their purpose, how they are practiced, and the reactions they produce. To start, **affirmative action**

Affirmative action purposeful steps taken by an organization to create employment opportunities for minorities and women refers to purposeful steps taken by an organization to create employment opportunities for minorities and women.[7] By contrast, diversity has a broader focus that includes demographic, cultural, and personal differences.

A second difference is that affirmative action is a policy for actively creating diversity, but diversity can exist even if organizations don't take purposeful steps to create it. A local restaurant located near a university in a major city is likely to have a more diverse group of employees than one located in a small town. So, organizations can achieve diversity without affirmative action. Conversely, affirmative action does not guarantee diversity. An organization can create employment opportunities for women and minorities yet not have a diverse workforce.

A third important difference is that affirmative action is required by law for private employers with 50 or more employees, whereas diversity is not. Affirmative action originated with Executive Order 11246 but is also related to the 1964 Civil Rights Act, which bans discrimination in voting, public places, federal government programs, federally supported public education, and employment. Title VII of the Civil Rights Act (www.eeoc.gov/laws/statutes/titlevii.cfm) requires that workers have equal employment opportunities when being hired or promoted. More specifically, Title VII prohibits companies from discriminating on the basis of race, color, religion, sex, or national origin. Title VII also created the

Equal Employment Opportunity Commission, or EEOC (www.eeoc.gov), to administer these laws. By contrast, there is no federal law or agency to oversee diversity. Organizations that pursue diversity goals and programs do so voluntarily.

Fourth, affirmative action programs and diversity programs have different purposes. The purpose of affirmative action programs is to compensate for past discrimination, which was widespread when legislation was introduced in the 1960s; to prevent ongoing discrimination; and to provide equal opportunities to all, regardless of race, color, religion, sex, or national origin. Organizations that fail to uphold affirmative action laws may be required to

» hire, promote, or give back pay to those not hired or promoted;

» reinstate those who were wrongly terminated;

» pay attorneys' fees and court costs for those who bring charges against them; or

» take other actions that make individuals whole by returning them to the condition or place they would have been had it not been for discrimination.[8]

Consequently, affirmative action is basically a punitive approach.[9] By contrast, the general purpose of diversity programs is to create a positive work environment where no one is advantaged or disadvantaged, where "we" is everyone, where everyone can do his or her best work, where differences are respected and not ignored, and where everyone feels comfortable.[10] So, unlike affirmative action, which punishes companies for not achieving specific sex and race ratios in their workforces, diversity programs seek to benefit both organizations and their employees by encouraging organizations to value all kinds of differences.

Despite the overall success of affirmative action in making workplaces much fairer than they used to be, many people argue that some affirmative action programs unconstitutionally offer preferential treatment to females and minorities at the expense of other employees, a view accepted by some courts.[11] The American Civil Rights institute successfully campaigned via state ballot initiatives to ban race- and sex-based affirmative action in college admissions, government hiring, and government contracting programs in California (1996), Washington (1998), and Michigan (2006). Led by Ward Connerly, the institute backed similar efforts in Arizona, Colorado, Missouri, Nebraska, and Oklahoma in 2008. In a 2014 decision, the U.S. Supreme Court ruled 6-2 that state ballot initiatives banning race- and sex-based action are constitutional.[12] Opponents of affirmative action, like Connerly, believe that affirmative action

bikeriderlondon/Shutterstock.com

policies establish only surface-level diversity and, ironically, promote preferential treatment.[13]

Research shows that people who have gotten a job or promotion as a result of affirmative action are commonly viewed as unqualified, even when clear evidence of their qualifications exists.[14] This effect is so robust that those benefitting from affirmative action experience doubts about their competence.[15] So, while affirmative action programs have created opportunities for minorities and women, they unintentionally produce persistent doubts and self-doubts regarding the qualifications of those who are believed to have obtained their jobs as a result of affirmative action.

12-1b Diversity Makes Good Business Sense

Those who support the idea of diversity in organizations often ignore its business aspects altogether, claiming instead that diversity is simply the right thing to do. Yet diversity actually makes good business sense in several ways: cost savings, attracting and retaining talent, and driving business growth.[16]

Diversity helps companies with *cost savings* by reducing turnover, decreasing absenteeism, and avoiding expensive lawsuits.[17] Because of lost productivity and the cost of recruiting and selecting new workers, companies lose substantial amounts of money when employees quit their jobs. In fact, turnover costs typically amount to more than 90 percent of employees' salaries. By this estimate, if an executive who makes $200,000 leaves, the organization will have to spend approximately $180,000 to find a replacement; even the lowest-paid hourly workers can cost the company as much as $10,000 when they quit. Because turnover rates for African Americans average 40 percent higher than for whites, and since women quit their jobs at twice the rate men do, companies that manage diverse workforces well can cut costs by reducing the turnover rates of these employees.[18] And, with women absent from work 60 percent more often than men, primarily because of family responsibilities, diversity programs that address the needs of female workers can also reduce the substantial costs of absenteeism.

Diversity programs also save companies money by helping them avoid discrimination lawsuits, which have increased by a factor of 20 since 1970 and quadrupled just since 1995. In one survey conducted by the Society for Human Resource Management, 78 percent of respondents reported that diversity efforts helped them avoid lawsuits and litigation costs.[19] In fact, because companies lose two-thirds of all discrimination cases that go to trial, the best strategy from a business perspective is not to be sued for discrimination at all. When companies lose, the average individual settlement amounts to more than $600,000.[20] And settlement costs can be substantially higher in class-action lawsuits, in which individuals join together to sue a company as a group. For example Qualcomm, a maker of computer chips, reached a court settlement to pay $19.5 million to 3,300 women in science, technology and engineering positions who accused the company of giving them lower pay and chances for promotion than men.[21]

Diversity also makes business sense by helping companies *attract and retain talented* workers.[22] Female employees at **Google** were once twice as likely as male employees to quit the company. Company data revealed that many of the women who left were young mothers. Google head of human resources Laszlo Bock responded by substantially increasing parental leave at the company. Biological mothers now get 18 weeks of fully paid leave for the birth of a child, and mothers who experience complications during childbirth receive 22 weeks. Primary caregivers, adoptive caregivers, and surrogate caregivers are also eligible for 12 weeks of fully paid time off. Now, a new mother is no more likely to leave Google than the average employee.[23] Diversity-friendly companies tend to attract better *and* more diverse job applicants. Very simply, diversity begets more diversity. Companies that make *Fortune* magazine's list of the 50 best companies for minorities or are recognized by *Working Women* and *Diversity Inc.* magazine have already attracted a diverse and talented pool of job applicants. But, after being recognized for their efforts, they subsequently experience big increases in both the quality and the diversity of people who apply for jobs. Research shows that companies with acclaimed diversity programs not only attract more talented workers but also have higher performance in the stock market.[24]

The third way that diversity makes business sense is by *driving business growth*. In the United States today, there are 43 million African Americans, 57 million Hispanic Americans, and 18 million Asian Americans with, respectively, $1.2 trillion, $1.3 trillion, and $825 billion in purchasing power. Given the size of those markets, it shouldn't be surprising that a survey conducted by the Society for Human Resource Management found that tapping into "diverse customers and markets" was the number-one reason managers gave for implementing diversity programs.[25] Demand for air travel in Asia is exploding as 100 million new passengers fly every year. To meet surging demand, the region's airlines will need to add 226,000 pilots over the next 20 years—far more than the current pool of job candidates. Despite needing more pilots, many Asian airlines won't hire women out

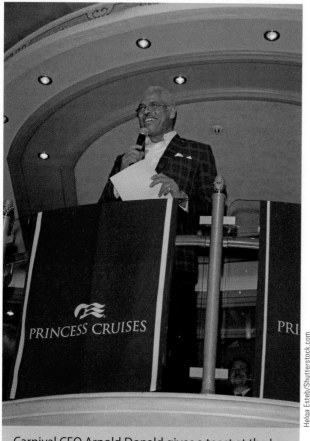

Carnival CEO Arnold Donald gives a toast at the Los Angeles World Cruise Center in 2016.

leadership team is a broader mix of ethnicities, genders, and sexual orientations. Emboldened by Donald's focus on diversity, president of **Princess Cruises** Jan Swartz worked with her team to redesign bedding for its typical customer—a 53-year-old woman going through menopause and suffering from night sweats and hot flashes. While luxurious, the new bedding doesn't trap heat and is layered so that it can easily be taken on and off. Attention to different customers' needs is exactly what Donald was aiming for: "I guarantee if you get a diverse group of people aligned around a common objective with a process to work together, they will out-engineer, out-solution a homogeneous team 90 percent of the time."[29] Carnival's stock price has risen 53 percent under Donald and its profits are up 15 percent to $1.2 billion.

12-2 SURFACE-LEVEL DIVERSITY

A survey that asked managers "What is meant by diversity to decision makers in your organization?" found that they most frequently mentioned race, culture, sex, national origin, age, religion, and regional origin.[30] When managers describe workers this way, they are focusing on surface-level diversity. **Surface-level diversity** consists of differences that are immediately observable, typically unchangeable, and easy to measure.[31] In other words, independent observers can usually agree on dimensions of surface-level diversity, such as another person's age, sex, race/ethnicity, or physical capabilities.

Most people start by using surface-level diversity to categorize or stereotype other people. But those initial categorizations typically give way to deeper impressions formed from knowledge of others' behaviors and psychological characteristics such as personality and attitudes.[32] When you think of others this way, you are focusing on deep-level diversity. **Deep-level diversity** consists of differences that are communicated through verbal and nonverbal behaviors and are learned only through extended interaction with others.[33] Examples of deep-level diversity include personality differences, attitudes, beliefs, and values. In other words,

of concern about male and female pilots sharing bunk space on long flights (which are common in the region). However, some carriers like **Vietnam Airlines** have begun actively recruiting women by creating flexible, family-friendly schedules. Mireille Goyer, founder of the Institute for Women of Aviation Worldwide, believes that refusing to recruit women is shortsighted: "Arbitrarily reducing the potential pool . . . has strangled growth and led to today's situation."[26] **Boeing** executive Sherry Carbary, whose team assists Asian airlines in training pilots, agrees: "There is such an enormous demand that the gender bias will have to be pushed aside."[27]

Diversity also helps companies grow through higher-quality problem solving. Though diverse groups initially have more difficulty working together than homogeneous groups, diverse groups eventually establish a rapport and can a better job of identifying problems and generating alternative solutions, the two most important steps in problem solving.[28] When Arnold Donald became CEO of **Carnival Corporation**, his first mission was to fix operational issues and diversify the customer base. To accomplish this, he hired a wide variety of new executives at seven of the company's 10 cruise lines. Now, Carnival's

Surface-level diversity differences such as age, sex, race/ethnicity, and physical disabilities that are observable, typically unchangeable, and easy to measure

Deep-level diversity differences such as personality and attitudes that are communicated through verbal and nonverbal behaviors and are learned only through extended interaction with others as people in diverse workplaces get to know each other, the initial focus on surface-level differences such as age, race/ethnicity, sex, and physical capabilities is replaced by deeper, more complex knowledge of coworkers.

If managed properly, the shift from surface- to deep-level diversity can accomplish two things.[34] First, 95 percent of studies on this issue show that getting to know and understand each other reduces prejudice and conflict.[35] Second, it can lead to stronger social integration. **Social integration** is the degree to which group members are psychologically attracted to working with each other to accomplish a common objective, or, as one manager put it, "working together to get the job done."

Because age, sex, race/ethnicity, and disabilities are usually immediately observable, many managers and workers use these dimensions of surface-level diversity to form initial impressions and categorizations of co-workers, bosses, customers, or job applicants. While not always immediately known, sexual orientation and gender identity (often referred to as LGBT, meaning lesbian, gay, bisexual, or transgender) may also be a form of surface-level diversity. Whether intentional or not, sometimes those initial categorizations and impressions lead to decisions or behaviors that discriminate. Consequently, these dimensions of surface-level diversity pose special challenges for managers who are trying to create positive work environments where everyone feels comfortable, and no one is advantaged or disadvantaged.

Let's learn more about those challenges and the ways that **12-2a age, 12-2b sex, 12-2c sexual and gender identity, 12-2d race/ethnicity,** *and* **12-2e mental or physical disabilities can affect decisions and behaviors in organizations.**

12-2a Age

Age discrimination is treating people differently (for example, in hiring and firing, promotion, and compensation decisions) because of their age. The victims of age discrimination are almost always older workers, and the discrimination is based on the assumption that "you can't teach an old dog new tricks." Perhaps this is why, according to comedian Bill Maher, "Ageism is the last acceptable prejudice."[36] Indeed, it's commonly believed that older workers are less motivated, less productive, more prone to illness and accidents, not interested in learning new things, cost more, and make

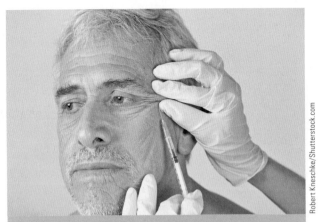

Ageism in the tech sector has caused plastic surgery to surge in Silicon Valley.

greater—more expensive—use of health care benefits.[37] Facebook founder and CEO Mark Zuckerberg once said, "I want to stress the importance of being young and technical . . . Young people are just smarter."[38] Consistent with that stereotype (and the fact that the average age of employees at Google, Facebook, LinkedIn, and Apple are 20, 28, 29, and 31 respectively), Apple and Dropbox are among the companies that have specified preferences for "new grads" in job openings. Because that clearly violates the Age Discrimination in Employment Act, companies such as Zipcar, Panasonic, and, yes, Facebook, now list being a "digital native" as a job requirement.[39] Ingrid Fredeen of **NAVEX Global**, a supplier of ethics and compliance programs, says the term makes her cringe because it implies that "only young applicants need apply."[40] The increase in age discrimination claims filed with the EEOC, 20,857 in 2016, up from 15,785 in 1997, suggests that discriminatory attitudes like this still exist.[41]

So, what's reality and what's myth? Do older employees actually cost more? In some ways, they do. The older people are and the longer they stay with a company, the more the company pays for salaries, pension plans, and vacation time. But older workers cost companies less, too, because they show better judgment, care more about the quality of their work, and are less likely to quit, show up late, or be absent, the cost of which can be substantial.[42] A meta-analysis combining the results of 118 individual studies also found that older workers are more likely to help others at work and are much less likely to use drugs or alcohol at work, engage in workplace aggression, or be involved in accidents. The authors of this study concluded, "The stereotype of older workers as difficult colleagues, then, seems largely unfounded."[43]

As for the widespread belief that job performance declines with age, the scientific evidence clearly refutes this stereotype. Performance does not decline with age, regardless of the type of job.[44]

Social integration the degree to which group members are psychologically attracted to working with each other to accomplish a common objective

Age discrimination treating people differently (for example in hiring and firing, promotion, and compensation decisions) because of their age

ONE IS THE LONELIEST NUMBER

Even as the number of women in the managerial ranks of U.S. companies is growing, in many companies, it seems there is an upper limit. Researchers have found that, if there is a woman on an executive team, then the chances of another woman joining the team drop by 51 percent. Among the 1,500 Standard & Poor's companies, 8.7 percent have a top female manager, but when one of the top five executive positions in the company is held by a woman, she is usually the only one on the team. Researcher Cristian Dezso speculates that top male managers may just want to fill a quota and "check a box. They are one and done."

Source: R. Feintzeig, "One Often Appears to Be the Limit for Women at the Top," *Wall Street Journal*, April 8, 2015, B6.

Rafael Croonen/Shutterstock.com

What can companies do to reduce age discrimination?[45] To start, managers need to recognize that age discrimination is much more pervasive than they probably think. Whereas "old" used to mean mid-50s, in today's workplace "old" is closer to 40. When 773 CEOs were asked, "At what age does a worker's productivity peak?" the average age they gave was 43, which is concerning because the median age (half above, half below) of U.S. workers is 42.[46] Thus, age discrimination may be affecting more workers because perceptions about age have changed. In addition, with the aging of the baby boomers, age discrimination is more likely to occur simply because there are millions more older workers than there used to be. In 1992, 1 in 12 women worked beyond the age of 65. In 2016, 1 in 7 do. By 2024, 1 in 5 women age 65 and older will work.[47] And, because studies show that interviewers rate younger job candidates as more qualified (even when they aren't), companies need to train managers and recruiters to make hiring and promotion decisions on the basis of qualifications, not age.

Companies also need to monitor the extent to which older workers receive training. The U.S. Bureau of Labor Statistics found that the number of training courses and number of hours spent in training drop dramatically after employees reach the age of 44.[48] Finally, companies need to ensure that younger and older workers interact with each other. One study found that younger workers generally hold positive views of older workers and that the more time they spent working with older coworkers, the more positive their attitudes became.[49]

12-2b Sex

Sex discrimination occurs when people are treated differently because of their sex. Sex discrimination and racial/ethnic discrimination (discussed in section 12-2d) are often associated with the so-called **glass ceiling**, the invisible barrier that prevents women and minorities from advancing to the top jobs in organizations.

To what extent do women face sex discrimination in the workplace? Almost every year, the EEOC receives between 23,000 and 30,000 charges of sex-based discrimination.[50] In some ways, there is much less sex discrimination than there used to be. For example, whereas women held only 17 percent of managerial jobs in 1972, today they hold 52 percent of managerial and professional jobs, and they hold 47 percent of all jobs in the workplace.[51] Likewise, women own 38 percent of all U.S. businesses. Although women owned 2.8 million businesses in 1982 and 5.4 million businesses in 1997, today they own 11.3 million businesses, generating $1.6 trillion in sales and employing more than 9 million people![52] Finally, though women still earn less than men on average, the differential is narrowing. Women earned 81 percent of what men did in 2014, up from 63 percent in 1979.[53]

Although progress is being made, sex discrimination continues to operate via the glass ceiling at higher levels in organizations, as

> **Sex discrimination** treating people differently because of their sex
>
> **Glass ceiling** the invisible barrier that prevents women and minorities from advancing to the top jobs in organizations

Scrub Résumés to Remove Bias

In an effort to reduce hiring biases and improve workplace diversity, some companies have begun using a technique called blind hiring. With blind hiring, information such as a person's name and alma mater are redacted from his or her résumé and work sample before reviewing them. This way, the hiring manager can evaluate candidates based solely on their past experiences and actual work performance. The goal is to reduce unconscious biases that may result in giving preferential treatment to a candidate of a particular sex or ethnicity, or with work experience at a prominent company or a degree from an elite school, things that are not always accurate predictors of a good fit.

Source: R. Feintzeig, "Tossing Out the Résumé in Favor of 'Blind Hiring,'" *Wall Street Journal*, January 6, 2016, B1.

Creativa Images/Shutterstock.com

shown in Exhibit 12.2. For instance, while the trends are going upward, women were the top earners in just 9.5 percent of companies in 2016.[54] Likewise, only 18 percent of corporate officers (that is, top management) were women, and the numbers were even lower for women of color. Indra K. Nooyi, PepsiCo's CEO, is the only women of color heading *Fortune* 500 companies.[55] In fact, only 27 of the 500 largest companies in the United States have women CEOs.[56] Similarly, only 20.6 percent of the members of U.S. corporate boards of directors are women.[57]

Finally, a meta-analysis of 97 studies covering 378,850 employees in multiple industries over three decades found that, "Across occupations ranging from bank tellers to accountants, industries ranging from IT to healthcare, and jobs ranging from mundane to challenging, our results show that sex differences in organizational rewards were almost 14 times larger than sex differences in performance evaluations. Moreover, performance differences did not explain reward differences between men and women."[58]

Is sex discrimination the sole reason for the slow rate at which women have been rewarded and promoted to

Exhibit 12.2
Women at *Fortune* 500 and 1000 Companies

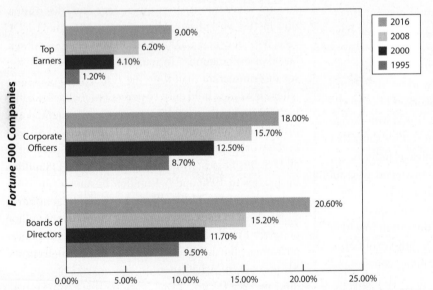

Sources: "Women in S&P 500 Companies," Catalyst, March 1, 2017, accessed April 23, 2017, http://www.catalyst.org/knowledge/women-sp-500-companies; J. Lublin, "Dozens of Boards Excluded Women for Years," *Wall Street Journal*, December 27, 2016, accessed April 23, 2017, https://www.wsj.com/articles/dozens-of-boards-excluded-women-for-years-1482847381; B. Darrow, "Nearly All Fortune 1000 Companies Are Still Led by Men," *Fortune*, September 6, 2016, accessed April 23, 2017, http://fortune.com/2016/09/06/fortune-1000-still-led-by-men/; V. Zarya, "Female Fortune 500 CEOs Set to Break Records in 2017," *Fortune*, December 22, 2016, accessed April 23, 2017, http://fortune.com/2016/12/22/female-fortune-500-ceos-2017/. "U.S. Women in Business," Catalyst, June 10, 2014, accessed July 11, 2014, http://www.catalyst.org/knowledge/us-women-business-0.

middle and upper levels of management and corporate boards? Some studies indicate that it's not.[59] In some instances, the slow progress appears to related to choices of college major, jobs, and careers. After examining 47,000 resumes over seven years, jobs site Glassdoor.com found that, "Many college majors that lead to high-paying roles in tech and engineering are male dominated, while majors that lead to lower-paying roles in social sciences and liberal arts tend to be female dominated, placing men in higher-paying career pathways, on average. Nine of the 10 highest paying majors we examined are male dominated. By contrast, 6 of the 10 lowest-paying majors are female dominated."[60] For, example women earn just 21 percent of engineering degrees, but nearly 78 percent of psychology degrees.[61] Likewise, men's career and job choices are often driven by the search for higher pay and advancement, while women are more likely to choose jobs or careers that also give them a greater sense of accomplishment, more control over their work schedules, and easier movement in and out of the workplace.[62] For instance, 82 percent of women without children are interested in being promoted to the next level, compared to 73 percent of women with two or more children.[63] Likewise, a survey by LeanIn. Org and McKinsey & Co. of 30,000 people in 118 companies found that 78 percent of men and 75 percent of women wanted to be promoted, but just 43 percent of women wanted to be top executives compared to 53 percent for men.[64]

As those numbers suggest, women are historically much more likely than men to prioritize family over work at some time in their careers. Even Indra Nooyi, PepsiCo's CEO, says, "My observation . . . is that the biological clock and the career clock are in total conflict with each other. Total, complete conflict. When you have to have kids you have to build your career. Just as you're rising to middle management, your kids need you because they're teenagers, they need you for the teenage years . . . And as you grow even more, your parents need you because they're aging. So . . . we cannot have it all."[65]

Beyond these reasons, however, it's likely that sex discrimination does play a role in women's slow progress into the higher levels of management. And even if you don't think so, many of the women you work with probably do. In fact, studies indicate that 90 percent of women believe the glass ceiling hurts their careers, and 80 percent said they left their last job because of the glass ceiling and that starting a business allows them to avoid the career limitations of the glass ceiling.[66] Discrimination is believed to be the most significant factor behind the lack of women at top levels of management.[67]

So, what can companies do to make sure that women have the same opportunities for development and advancement as men? One strategy is mentoring, or pairing promising female executives with senior executives from whom they can seek advice and support.[68] **Salesforce**, a leading customer relationship management software company, has a mentoring program for women. So, co-founder Parker Harris, who encourages Salesforce managers to speak up about their ambitions, was surprised when he discovered that Leyla Seka, who ran their mobile apps unit, was preparing to leave. Seka wanted to lead a larger division but thought her bosses didn't think she was capable, so she didn't share her aspirations. In fact, her bosses found her so capable, they hired her to run Desk.com, a company recently acquired by Salesforce, and coached her as she developed her leadership skills. "I've never had more fun at work, and I've never felt more challenged," she says. "I almost missed this opportunity by shutting the doors on myself."[69] In fact, 91 percent of female executives had a mentor at some point and felt their mentor was critical to their advancement.

Another strategy is to make sure that male-dominated social activities don't unintentionally exclude women. Nearly half (47%) of women in the workforce believe that "exclusion from informal networks" makes it more difficult to advance their careers (by contrast, just 18% of male CEOs thought this was a problem). For instance, at company conferences, **Rockwell Automation** has replaced cocktail receptions (that is, hanging out at the bar), which are a traditional social function at conferences, with alternative activities, such as chili cook-offs.[70] Another is to designate a go-to person other than their supervisors that women can talk to if they believe that they are being held back or discriminated against because of their sex. That person, of course, must have the knowledge and authority to conduct a fair, confidential internal investigation.[71]

12-2c Sexual and Gender Identity

Sexual orientation indicates an individual's attraction to people of the same and/or different sex. **Sexual orientation discrimination** occurs when people are treated differently because of their sexual orientation. Usually, sexual orientation discrimination occurs toward lesbians, gays, or bisexuals. Though less frequent, straight or heterosexual people can be discriminated against, too. According to the

> **Sexual orientation** an individual's attraction to people of the same and/or different sex
>
> **Sexual orientation discrimination** treated people differently because of their sexual orientation

EEOC, examples of sexual orientation discrimination include not hiring, not promoting, firing, awarding a lower salary, denying spousal health insurance, or making derogatory, sexually oriented, or disparaging comments because of someone's sexual orientation.[72]

A **transgender person** is someone whose personal and gender identity differ from the person's birth sex—for example, someone born female who identifies as male. **Gender identity discrimination** occurs when people are treated differently because of their gender identity. According to the EEOC, in addition to typical discriminatory acts, examples of gender identity discrimination include firing an employee who is planning, making, or has completed a gender transition, denying equal access to a common restroom corresponding to the employee's gender identity, or intentionally not using the name and gender pronoun corresponding to the person's gender identity.[73]

Federal, state, and city laws regarding workplace discrimination in terms of age, sex, race/ethnicity, and mental or physical disabilities have been in place for 20 to 50 years (See Exhibit 11.2, Summary of Major Federal Employment Laws in Chapter 11). By contrast, laws and regulations regarding sexual orientation and gender identity discrimination are new, in question, or not yet in place. Since Title VII of the Civil Rights Act explicitly prohibits employment discrimination on the basis of race, color, religion, sex, or national origin, a strict interpretation is that Title VII does not cover sexual orientation or gender identity.[74] However, the EEOC has ruled that Title VII's sex discrimination provision prohibits, "discrimination against employees on the basis of sexual orientation and gender identity."[75] In April 2017, a federal appeals court upheld that ruling[76] But, the U.S. Supreme Court has yet to rule on this decision.

Although there is currently some uncertainty regarding federal law, 22 states have laws preventing sexual orientation discrimination, and 17 states have laws addressing gender identity discrimination.[77] Rather than wait for the law to settle, many companies have proactively changed their policies to prohibit sexual orientation and gender identity discrimination. Todd Sears, who founded Out Leadership, a nonprofit organization that partners with companies to develop LGBT-inclusive workplaces, says, "Big business was way out ahead of government when it came to creating domestic partner benefits for their teams—and they remain way out in front when it comes to nondiscrimination policies."[78]

Because of legal uncertainties, many companies have proactively included sexual orientation and gender identity in their nondiscrimination and equal opportunity policies.

To what extent do LGBT individuals face sexual orientation discrimination or gender identity discrimination in the workplace? Twenty-nine states do not prohibit sexual orientation discrimination, and 33 states do not prohibit gender identity discrimination. With federal law being uncertain, that means that in roughly 30 or more U.S. states, LGBT employees can be fired, not promoted, or not hired just because they are LGBT. Not surprisingly, 53 percent of LGBT employees hide their sexual orientation or gender identity at work, while 35 percent lie about their personal lives.[79] Thirty-five percent who were open about their sexual or gender identity have reported being harassed at work.[80] Sixty-two percent of LGBT employees have heard disparaging jokes about gays or lesbians, 42 percent have heard jokes about bisexuals, and 40 percent have heard jokes about transgender people.[81] In 2015, the EEOC received 1,412 charges of sexual identity or gender identity discrimination, up 28 percent from 1,100 charges in 2014.[82] A national survey of nearly 28,000 transgender people found that 27 percent were fired, not promoted, or not hired because of sexual identity; 15 percent were verbally harassed, physically attacked, or sexually assaulted at work; 15 percent were unemployed;13 percent had lost a job because of gender identity; and that 77 percent took steps at work to hide or delay their gender transition.[83]

What can companies do to make sure that LGBT individuals have the same opportunities as others? Start by including sexual orientation and gender identity in nondiscrimination and equal opportunity policies. Ben Hladilek, executive director of human resources at JPMorgan Chase, said, "What we have found in our recruiting efforts is that individuals will often look for signals about what a culture is like; having gender identity protection signals we are a diversity leader and are serious

transgender person someone whose personal and gender identity differ from the person's birth sex—for example, someone born female who identifies as male

Gender identity discrimination treating people differently because of their gender identity about providing an inclusive environment."[84] Organizations can reduce the isolation that LGBT employees often feel at work by connecting LGBT employees to mentors and creating employee resource groups where LGBT employees can learn from and support each other.[85] Most organizations are unable to track whether LGBT employees are treated fairly because they don't ask employees about LGBT status. Companies can fix this by giving LGBT employees the opportunity to confidentially self-identify their sexual orientation or gender identity as part of the normal gathering of demographic information.[86]

A few additional steps are required to be sure that transgender employees are treated the same as other employees. A small but critical step is changing the employee's name on all official records, including badge, office and phone numbers, email, corporate directory, business cards, and anywhere else the employee's name appears. Chloe, a copy writer at the Leo Burnett advertising agency, transitioning from male to female, had to wait five months for a court date to officially change her name. When the human resources department learned of the delay, it changed her name in all company records months before the court made the change official.[87] Companies can also publish guidelines and protocols for gender transitions that make clear the responsibilities for the transitioning employee, as well as their subordinates, colleagues and managers.[88] For example, EY, a global accounting firm, has a set of transition guidelines that specify everything from appearance (dressing consistent with one's new gender and unisex restroom and locker access), to identifying a support team, medical leave, and health benefits.[89] Finally, the World Professional Association for Transgender Health has published Standards of Care to assist companies in providing medical care for transitioning transgender employees.[90]

12-2d Race/Ethnicity

Racial and ethnic discrimination occurs when people are treated differently because of their race or ethnicity. To what extent is racial and ethnic discrimination a factor in the workplace? Every year, the EEOC receives between 26,000 and 36,000 charges of racial discrimination, which is more than any other type of charge of discrimination.[91] However, it is true that since the passage of the 1964 Civil Rights Act and Title VII, there is much less racial and ethnic discrimination than there used to be. For example, 22 *Fortune* 500 firms had an African American (4), Hispanic (9), or Asian (9) CEOs in 2017 whereas none did in 1988.[92]

Nonetheless, strong racial and ethnic disparities still exist. For instance, whereas 11.9 percent of employed Americans are black, only 7.5 percent of managers and 3.4 percent of CEOs are black. Similarly, 16.7 percent of employed Americans are Hispanic, but only 9.9 percent are managers and 6 percent are CEOs. By contrast, Asians, who constitute 6.1 percent of employed workers, are better represented, holding 6.1 percent of management jobs and 5.6 percent of CEO jobs.[93]

What accounts for the disparities between the percentages of minority groups in the general population and their smaller representation in management positions? Some studies have found that the disparities are due to preexisting differences in training, education, and skills. When African Americans, Hispanics, Asian Americans, and whites have similar skills, training, and education, they are much more likely to have similar jobs and salaries.[94]

Other studies, however, provide increasingly strong direct evidence of racial or ethnic discrimination in the workplace. For example, one study directly tested hiring discrimination by sending pairs of black and white males and pairs of Hispanic and non-Hispanic males to apply for the same jobs. Each pair had résumés with identical qualifications, and all were trained to present themselves in similar ways to minimize differences during interviews. The researchers found that the white males got three times as many job offers as the black males, and that the non-Hispanic males got three times as many offers as the Hispanic males.[95] Another study, which used similar methods to test hiring procedures at 149 different companies, found that whites received 10 percent more interviews than blacks. Half of the whites interviewed then received job offers, but only 11 percent of the blacks. And when job offers were made, blacks were much more likely to be offered lower-level positions, while whites were more likely to be offered jobs at higher levels than the jobs they had applied for.[96]

Critics of these studies point out that it's nearly impossible to train different applicants to give identical responses in job interviews and that differences in interviewing skills may have somehow accounted for the results. However, researchers at the University of Chicago mailed thousands of résumés to employers that were identical except for the candidate's name, which was either stereotypically black, such as "Jamal," or stereotypically white, such as "Brendan." Applicants with the "white" name were called back for interviews 50 percent more often those with "black" names.[97] Comparable studies in the United Kingdom with Indian and Pakistani

Racial and ethnic discrimination treating people differently because of their race or ethnicity applicants and in Australia with Greek and Vietnamese applicants produced similar results.[98] In short, the evidence indicates that there is strong and persistent racial and ethnic discrimination in the hiring processes of many organizations.

What can companies do to make sure that people of all racial and ethnic backgrounds have the same opportunities?[99] Start by looking at the numbers. Compare the hiring rates of whites with the hiring rates for racial and ethnic applicants. Do the same thing for promotions within the company. See if nonwhite workers quit the company at higher rates than white workers. Also, survey employees to compare white and nonwhite employees' satisfaction with jobs, bosses, and the company as well as their perceptions concerning equal treatment. Next, if the numbers indicate racial or ethnic disparities, consider employing a private firm to test your hiring system by having applicants of different races with identical qualifications apply for jobs in your company, or by data mining your application criteria.[100] Data analysis software showed **Xerox** that customer-service employees with the shortest daily commutes stayed with the company the longest. Nevertheless, managers stopped screening job applicants for commute times because they thought that doing so would put applicants from minority neighborhoods, which were generally farther from Xerox offices, at a disadvantage.[101]

Another step companies can take is to eliminate unclear selection and promotion criteria. Vague criteria allow decision makers to focus on nonjob-related characteristics that may unintentionally lead to employment discrimination. Instead, selection and promotion criteria should spell out the specific knowledge, skills, abilities, education, and experience needed to perform a job well. Finally, as explained in Chapter 11, "Managing Human Resource Systems," it is also important to train managers and others who make hiring and promotion decisions.

12-2e Mental or Physical Disabilities

According to the Americans with Disabilities Act (www.ada.gov), a **disability** is a mental or physical impairment that substantially limits one or more major life activities.[102]

New apps and software use Braille and speech to "read" computer screens to vision-impaired employees.

zlikovec/123RF

Approximately 40 million Americans—12.6 percent of the population—are disabled.[103] **Disability discrimination** occurs when people are treated differently because of their disabilities. To what extent is disability discrimination a factor in the workplace? Similar to studies examining racial discrimination, researchers sent out 6,000 fictitious résumés and cover letters for jobs (in accounting). One résumé was for a highly qualified candidate with six years of experience, and another was for an inexperienced candidate a year out of college. One of three different cover letters accompanied each résumé: one for an applicant with no disabilities, one for an applicant with an injured spinal cord, and one for an applicant with Asperger's Syndrome, which makes interpersonal relationships and communication difficult. Overall, applicants with disabilities were 26 percent less likely to be contacted by an employer for further steps in the hiring process. Interestingly, experienced applicants were 34 percent less likely to be contacted by employers.[104] Indeed, while 65 percent of the U.S. population was employed in 2015, only 35.2 percent of disabled people had jobs. Individuals with sensory disabilities, such as blindness (42%) or deafness (51.8%), had the highest employment rates; those with self-care disabilities (15.8%), who can't dress or bathe themselves, or with independent living disabilities (16.3%), who can't do basic errands such as shopping or go to the doctor without assistance, were the least likely to work.[105]

What accounts for the disparities between those with and without disabilities? Contrary to popular opinion, it has nothing to do with how well people with disabilities can do their jobs. Studies show that as long as companies

Disability a mental or physical impairment that substantially limits one or more major life activities

Disability discrimination treating people differently because of their disabilities make reasonable accommodations for disabilities (for example, changing procedures or equipment), people with disabilities perform their jobs just as well as people without disabilities. Furthermore, they have better safety records and are not any more likely to be absent or quit their jobs.[106] At a recent disability summit sponsored by the state of Michigan, speakers from Walgreens, Meijer, and Trijicon said that, compared to employees without disabilities, disabled employees were more dependable, took less time off, and had better safety records.[107]

What can companies do to make sure that people with disabilities have the same opportunities as everyone else? Beyond educational efforts to address incorrect stereotypes and expectations, a good place to start is to commit to reasonable workplace accommodations such as changing work schedules, reassigning jobs, acquiring or modifying equipment, or providing assistance when needed. Accommodations for disabilities needn't be expensive. According to the Job Accommodation Network, 59 percent of accommodations don't cost anything at all, while those with costs are typically just $500.[108]

For about $1,000, the JAWS (Job Access With Speech) app uses Braille and speech to "read" the contents of a computer screen to a blind employee. JAWS can also be paired with screen magnification software or a keyboard with large font, boldfaced easy-to-read letters. Color identification apps and currency identification apps also help blind employees. Lee Huffman, editor of *AccessWorld* magazine, says, "You simply wave your phone camera over the piece of clothing [for color identification] or the currency, and it tells you what it is. Five years ago, these programs might have cost $125 or more, but now you can download these apps at low or no cost and have all that accessible technology on one device in your pocket."[109]

Some of the accommodations just described involve *assistive technology* that gives workers with disabilities the tools they need to overcome their disabilities. Providing workers with assistive technology is also an effective strategy to recruit, retain, and enhance the productivity of people with disabilities. According to the National Council on Disability, 92 percent of workers with disabilities who use assistive technology report that it helps them work faster and better, 81 percent indicate that it helps them work longer hours, and 67 percent say that it is critical to getting a job.[110] To learn about assistive technologies that can help workers with disabilities, see AbleData (www.abledata.com), which lists 40,000 products, or the National Rehabilitation Information Center (www.naric.com), which provides information for specific disabilities.

Finally, companies should actively recruit qualified workers with disabilities. Numerous organizations, such as Mainstream, Kidder Resources, the American Council of the Blind (www.acb.org), the National Federation of the Blind (http://nfb.org), the National Association of the Deaf (www.nad.org), the Epilepsy Foundation (www.epilepsy.com), and the National Amputation Foundation (www.nationalamputation.org), actively work with employers to find jobs for qualified people with disabilities. Companies can also place advertisements in publications, such as *Careers and the disABLED*, or on online job boards, such as Recruit AbilityJobs.com or RecruitDisability.org, that specifically target workers with disabilities.

12-3 DEEP-LEVEL DIVERSITY

As you learned in Section 12-2, people often use the dimensions of surface-level diversity to form initial impressions about others. Over time, however, as people have a chance to get to know each other, initial impressions based on age, sex, race/ethnicity, and mental or physical disabilities give way to deeper impressions based on behavior and psychological characteristics. When we think of others this way, we are focusing on deep-level diversity. *Deep-level diversity* represents differences that can be learned only through extended interaction with others. Examples of deep-level diversity include differences in personality, attitudes, beliefs, and values. In short, recognizing deep-level diversity requires getting to know and understand one another better. And that matters, because it can result in less prejudice, discrimination, and conflict in the workplace. These changes can then lead to better *social integration*, the degree to which organizational or group members are psychologically attracted to working with each other to accomplish a common objective.

Stop for a second and think about your boss (or the boss you had in your last job). What words would you use to describe him or her? Is your boss introverted or extraverted? Emotionally stable or unstable? Agreeable or disagreeable? Organized or disorganized? Open or closed to new experiences? When you describe your boss or others in this way, what you're really doing is describing dispositions and personality.

A **disposition** is the tendency to respond to situations and events in a predetermined manner. **Personality** is the relatively stable set of behaviors, attitudes, and emotions displayed over time that

> **Disposition** the tendency to respond to situations and events in a predetermined manner
>
> **Personality** the relatively stable set of behaviors, attitudes, and emotions displayed over time that makes people different from each other

makes people different from each other.[111] For example, which of your aunts or uncles is a little offbeat, a little out of the ordinary? What were they like when you were small? What are they like now? Chances are that she or he is pretty much the same wacky person. In other words, the person's core personality hasn't changed. For example, as a child, Kip Tindell, CEO of the Container Store, would reorganize the pantry or closets when his parents were out of the house. "If your house is unbelievably messy, I probably won't come back to visit. I'll meet you at a restaurant. I'm just not comfortable around mess. You don't have to be obsessive-compulsive about it. Well, OK, maybe just a tiny bit."[112] Research conducted in different cultures, different settings, and different languages has shown that five basic dimensions of personality account for most of the differences in peoples' behaviors, attitudes, and emotions (or why your boss is the way he or she is!). The *Big Five Personality Dimensions* are extraversion, emotional stability, agreeableness, conscientiousness, and openness to experience.[113]

Extraversion is the degree to which someone is active, assertive, gregarious, sociable, talkative, and energized by others. In contrast to extraverts, introverts tend to be focused, thoughtful, quiet, reserved, and energized by ideas. For the best results in the workplace, introverts and extraverts should be correctly matched to their jobs. Research shows that being talkative and assertive is not correlated with greater insight, and that those who speak first and more often (usually extraverts) are not more capable than less talkative people.[114] Professor Stephen Garras is often frustrated by the premium placed on extraversion, saying, "I worry that there are people who are put in positions of authority because they're good talkers, but they don't have good ideas. It's so easy to confuse schmoozing ability with talent . . . we put too much of a premium on presenting and not enough on substance and critical thinking.[115]

Emotional stability is the degree to which someone is not angry, depressed, anxious, emotional, insecure, or excitable. People who are emotionally stable respond well to stress. In other words, they can maintain a calm, problem-solving attitude in even the toughest situations (for example, conflict, hostility, dangerous conditions,or extreme time pressures). By contrast, emotionally unstable people find it difficult to handle the most basic demands of their jobs under only moderately stressful situations and become distraught, tearful, self-doubting, and anxious. Emotional stability is particularly important for high-stress jobs such as police work, firefighting, emergency medical treatment, piloting planes, or commanding Tragically, investigators found emotional stability was a factor in the deliberate crash of a Germanwings flight that killed 150 people. The copilot, who had previously with depression used Google just days before the crash to search for ways to commit suicide.[116] When the pilot left the cabin for a bathroom break, the copilot locked the cabin door and set the plane's auto pilot to descend to a lower altitude where it slammed into a mountain. While most Asian airlines conduct regular psychological assessments of their pilots, U.S. and European airlines only screen for emotional stability issues during initial pilot recruitment and training, or if staff members report unusual behavior.[117]

Agreeableness is the degree to which someone is cooperative, polite, flexible, forgiving, good-natured, tolerant, and trusting. Basically, agreeable people are easy to work with and be around, whereas disagreeable people are distrusting and difficult to work with and be around. A number of companies have made general attitude or agreeableness the most important factor in their hiring decisions.

Conscientiousness is the degree to which someone is organized, hardworking, responsible, persevering, thorough, and achievement oriented. One management consultant wrote about his experiences with a conscientious employee: "He arrived at our first meeting with a typed copy of his daily schedule, a sheet bearing his home and office phone numbers, addresses, and his email address. At his request, we established a timetable for meetings for the next four months. He showed up on time every time, day planner in hand, and carefully listed tasks and due dates. He questioned me exhaustively if he didn't understand an assignment and returned on schedule with the completed work or with a clear explanation as to why it wasn't done."[118] Conscientious employees are also more likely to engage in positive behaviors, such as helping new employees, coworkers, and supervisors, and are less likely to engage

bram janssens/123RF

Extraversion the degree to which someone is active, assertive, gregarious, sociable, talkative, and energized by others

Emotional stability the degree to which someone is not angry, depressed, anxious, emotional, insecure, and excitable

Agreeableness the degree to which someone is cooperative, polite, flexible, forgiving, good-natured, tolerant, and trusting

Conscientiousness the degree to which someone is organized, hardworking, responsible, persevering, thorough, and achievement oriented

DEEP-LEVEL DIVERSITY: THE REAL KEY TO TEAM PROBLEM SOLVING

While diverse groups initially have difficulty working to-gether, they eventually do a better job of identifying problems and generating alternative solutions.

But that doesn't come from surface-level diversity—that is, people of different ages, sexes, or ethnicities. It comes from cognitive diversity, that is, differences in experience, knowledge, and thinking styles (engineers vs. artists). It's the clash of ideas, assumptions, or approaches that makes cognitively diverse teams better at solving problems. Professors Alison Reynolds and David Lewis explain that the difficulty is that, "Someone being from a different culture or of a different generation gives no clue as to how that person might process information, engage with, or respond to change."

So create diverse teams using knowledge of peoples' deep-level diversity, which only comes from working closely with them. Select people with different functional backgrounds, personalities (introverts vs. extroverts), and thinking

Rawpixel.com/Shutterstock.com

styles, and you'll greatly increase the chances of successful team problem solving.

Sources: A. Reynolds and D. Lewis, "Teams Solve Problems Faster When They're More Cognitively Diverse," *Harvard Business Review*, March 30, 2017, accessed April 26, 2017, https://hbr.org/2017/03/teams-solve-problems-faster-when-theyre-more-cognitively-diverse; A. Eagly, "When Passionate Advocates Meet Research on Diversity, Does the Honest Broker Stand a Chance?" *Journal of Social Issues* 72 no. 1 (2016): 199–222.

---

in negative behaviors, such as verbally or physically abusing coworkers or stealing.[119]

Openness to experience is the degree to which someone is curious, broadminded, and open to new ideas, things, and experiences; is spontaneous; and has a high tolerance for ambiguity. Most companies need people who are strong in terms of openness to experience to fill certain positions, but for other positions, this dimension is less important. People in marketing, advertising, research, or other creative jobs need to be curious, open to new ideas, and spontaneous. By contrast, openness to experience is not particularly important to accountants, who need to apply stringent rules and formulas consistently to make sense out of complex financial information.

Which of the Big Five Personality Dimensions has the largest impact on behavior in organizations? The cumulative results of multiple studies indicate that conscientiousness is related to job performance across five different occupational groups (professionals, police, managers, salespeople, and skilled or semiskilled workers).[120] In short, people "who are dependable, persistent, goal directed, and organized tend to be higher performers on virtually any job; viewed negatively, those who are careless, irresponsible, low achievement striving,

and impulsive tend to be lower performers on virtually any job."[121] The results also indicate that extraversion is related to performance in jobs, such as sales and management, that involve significant interaction with others. In people-intensive jobs like these, it helps to be sociable, assertive, and talkative and to have energy and be able to energize others. Finally, people who are extraverted and open to experience seem to do much better in training. Being curious and open to new experiences as well as sociable, assertive, talkative, and full of energy helps people perform better in learning situations.[122]

12-4 MANAGING DIVERSITY

How much should companies change their standard business practices to accommodate the diversity of their workers? What do you do when a talented top executive has a drinking problem that seems to affect his behavior only at company business parties (for entertaining clients), where he has made inappropriate advances toward

> **Openness to experience** the degree to which someone is curious, broad-minded, and open to new ideas, things, and experiences; is spontaneous; and has a high tolerance for ambiguity

female employees? What do you do when, despite aggressive company policies against racial discrimination, employees continue to tell racist jokes and publicly post cartoons displaying racist humor? And, because many people confuse diversity with affirmative action, what do you do to make sure that your company's diversity practices and policies are viewed as benefiting all workers and not just some workers?

No doubt about it, questions like these make managing diversity one of the toughest challenges that managers face. Nonetheless, there are steps companies can take to begin to address these issues.

As discussed earlier, diversity programs try to create a positive work environment where no one is advantaged or disadvantaged, where "we" is everyone, where everyone can do his or her best work, where differences are respected and not ignored, and where everyone feels comfortable.

Let's begin to address those goals by learning about **12-4a different diversity paradigms, 12-4b diversity principles, 12-4c diversity training and practices,** *and* **12-4d what works**

12-4a Diversity Paradigms

There are several different methods or paradigms for managing diversity: the discrimination and fairness paradigm, the access and legitimacy paradigm, and the learning and effectiveness paradigm.[123]

The *discrimination and fairness paradigm*, which is the most common method of approaching diversity, focuses on equal opportunity, fair treatment, recruitment of minorities, and strict compliance with the equal employment opportunity laws. Under this approach, success is usually measured by how well companies achieve recruitment, promotion, and retention goals for women, people of different racial/ethnic backgrounds, or other underrepresented groups. According to a workplace diversity practices survey conducted by the Society for Human Resource Management, 66 to 91 percent of companies use specialized strategies to recruit, retain, and promote talented women and minorities. The percentages increase with company size, and companies of more than 500 employees are the most likely to use these strategies. Of companies with more than 500 employees, 77 percent systematically collect measurements on diversity-related practices.[124] One manager says, "If you don't measure something, it doesn't count. You measure your market share. You measure your profitability. The same should be true for diversity. There has to be some way of measuring whether you did, in fact, cast your net widely and whether the company is better off today in terms of the experience of people of color than it was a few years ago. I measure my market share and my

"We are all on the same team...

profitability. Why not this?"[125] The primary benefit of the discrimination and fairness paradigm is that it generally brings about fairer treatment of employees and increases demographic diversity. The primary limitation is that the focus of diversity remains on the surface-level diversity dimensions of sex, race, and ethnicity.[126]

The *access and legitimacy paradigm* focuses on the acceptance and celebration of differences to ensure that the diversity within the company matches the diversity found among primary stakeholders, such as customers, suppliers, and local communities. This is similar to the *business growth* advantage of diversity discussed earlier in the chapter. The basic idea behind this approach is to create a demographically diverse workforce that attracts a broader customer base. For example, the diversity strategy at Oshkosh, a maker of specialty trucks and truck bodies, states, "We operate and sell our products and services in over 100 countries on six continents, each with its own culture, customs, and business practices. We seek employees who are passionate about serving customers and who reflect our diverse customer base so that we can truly understand our customers to better serve and delight them."[127]

The primary benefit of this approach is that it establishes a clear business reason for diversity. Like the discrimination and fairness paradigm, however, it focuses only on the surface-level diversity dimensions of sex, race, and ethnicity. Furthermore, employees who are assigned responsibility for customers and stakeholders on the basis of their sex, race, or ethnicity may eventually feel frustrated and exploited.

Although the discrimination and fairness paradigm focuses on assimilation (having a demographically representative workforce), and the access and legitimacy paradigm focuses on differentiation (having demographic differences inside the company match those of key customers and stakeholders), the *learning and effectiveness paradigm* focuses on integrating deep-level diversity differences, such as personality, attitudes, beliefs, and values, into the actual work of the organization. One sign that a company hasn't yet created a learning and effectiveness paradigm is that people withhold their opinions for fear of being seen as different. For example, while Helena Morrissey is the CEO of Newton Investment Management, a London firm that invests $71 billion for its clients, she admits to sometimes keeping her business opinions to herself for fear of being seen as "the annoying" woman at the table. She says, "At a recent meeting, I wasn't comfortable with a controversial point and I spoke up, but I also had a different view on the next item on the agenda but instead of speaking up I held back." Says Morrissey, "I have been conscious of feeling that where I did have different views from the rest of the [all-male]

with our differences—not despite them."

iStock.com/Rawpixel Ltd

group, I may be being perceived as the 'difficult woman' rather than being listened to for what I was saying." She felt this way despite there being "no evidence that the men were actually feeling that."[128]

The learning and effectiveness paradigm is consistent with achieving organizational plurality. **Organizational plurality** is a work environment where (1) all members are empowered to contribute in a way that maximizes the benefits to the organization, customers, and themselves, and (2) the individuality of each member is respected by not segmenting or polarizing people on the basis of their membership in a particular group.[129]

The learning and effectiveness diversity paradigm offers four benefits.[130] First, it values common ground. Former Harvard Business School professor David Thomas explains, "Like the fairness paradigm, it promotes equal opportunity for all individuals. And like the access paradigm, it acknowledges cultural differences among people and recognizes the value in those differences. Yet this new model for managing diversity lets the organization internalize differences among employees so that it learns and grows because of them. Indeed, with the model fully in place, members of the organization can say, 'We are all on the same team, with our differences—not despite them.[131]

Second, this paradigm makes a distinction between individual and group differences. When diversity focuses only on differences between groups, such as females versus males, large differences within groups are ignored.[132] For example, think of the women you know at work. Now, think for a second about what they have in common. After that, think about how they're different. If your situation is typical, the list of differences should be just as long as the list of commonalties, if not longer. In short, managers can achieve a greater understanding of diversity and their employees by treating them as individuals and by realizing that not all African Americans, Hispanics, women, or white males want the same things at work.[133]

Third, because the focus is on individual differences, the learning and effectiveness paradigm is less likely to encounter the conflict, backlash, and divisiveness sometimes associated with diversity programs that focus only on group differences. Taylor Cox, one of the leading management writers on diversity, says, "We are concerned here with these more destructive forms of conflict which may be present

DIVERSITY APPS

Information technology has helped us in countless ways, but we're just beginning to discover how it can help us create a workforce that is talented, capable, and diverse. Check out these three new apps developed to increase diversity in the workplace:

» **Textio** is a diversity spell checker that scans job listings for biased language that might discourage a diverse applicant pool. And just like a regular spell checker, Textio suggests different wordings to help increase the number and diversity of applicants.

» **GapJumpers** helps companies review job applications without knowing candidates' sex or race. GapJumpers also provides companies with a number of online performance auditions so they can see how candidates perform tasks that pertain to the job in question.

» **Unitive** is a complete recruiting/hiring platform that tracks job applicants and assesses their fit within the company and job throughout the entire hiring process. Unitive provides visual data for easier analysis and reminds managers to implement best practices at each step to reduce bias and increase the size and quality of the applicant pool.

Source: R. Silverman and L. Gellman, "Apps Take on Workplace Bias," *Wall Street Journal*, September 30, 2015, accessed May 9, 2016, http://www.wsj.com/articles/apps-take-on-workplace-bias-1443601027.

with diverse workforces due to language barriers, cultural clash, or resentment by majority-group members of what they may perceive as preferential and unwarranted treatment of minority-group members."[134] And Ray Haines, a consultant who has helped companies deal with the aftermath of diversity programs that became divisive, says, "There's a large amount of backlash related to diversity training. It stirs up a lot of hostility, anguish, and resentment but doesn't give people tools to deal with [the backlash]. You have people come in and talk about their specific ax to grind."[135] Not all diversity programs are divisive or lead to conflict. But by focusing on individual rather than group differences, the learning and effectiveness paradigm helps minimize these potential problems.

Finally, unlike the other diversity paradigms that simply focus on surface-level diversity, the learning and effectiveness paradigm focuses on bringing different talents and perspectives (that is deep-level diversity) *together* to make the best organizational decisions and to produce innovative, competitive products and services.

12-4b Diversity Principles

Diversity paradigms are general approaches or strategies for managing diversity. Whatever diversity paradigm a manager chooses, diversity principles will help managers do a better job of *managing company diversity programs.*[136]

Begin by *carefully and faithfully following and enforcing federal and state laws regarding equal opportunity employment.* Diversity programs can't and won't succeed if the company is being sued for discriminatory actions and behavior. Faithfully following the law will also reduce the time and expense associated with EEOC investigations or lawsuits. Start by learning more at the EEOC website (www.eeoc.gov). Following the law also means strictly and fairly enforcing company policies.

Treat group differences as important but not special. Surface-level diversity dimensions such as age, sex, gender orientation and sexual identity, and race/ethnicity should be respected but should not be treated as more important than other kinds of differences (that is, deep-level diversity). Remember, the shift in focus from surface- to deep-level diversity helps people know and understand each other better, reduces prejudice and conflict, and leads to stronger social integration with people wanting to work together and get the job done. Also, *find the common ground.* Although respecting differences is important, it's just as important, especially with diverse workforces, to actively find ways for employees to see and share commonalties.

Tailor opportunities to individuals, not groups. Special programs for training, development, mentoring, or promotion should be based on individual strengths and weaknesses, not on group status. Instead of making mentoring available for just one group of workers, create mentoring opportunities for everyone who wants to be mentored. DuPont Corporation's mentoring program, for example, is voluntary and open to all employees. Through candid and confidential conversations, DuPont's mentors help younger workers and managers with problem solving and career and leadership development.[137]

Maintain high standards. Companies have a legal and moral obligation to make sure that their hiring and promotion procedures and standards are fair to all. At the same time, in today's competitive markets, companies should not lower standards to promote diversity. This not only hurts the organizations but also feeds the stereotype that applicants who are hired or promoted in the name of affirmative action or diversity are less qualified. After a knee injury ended the career of WNBA player and Olympic medalist Becky Hammon,

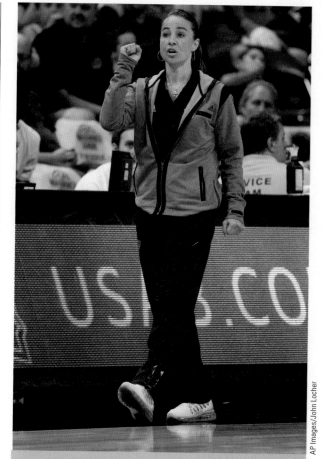

After an injury ended Becky Hammon's pro basketball career, she went on to become the first female NBA head coach to win a summer league title.

she became a coaching intern for the NBA's San Antonio Spurs. While rehabbing her knee, Hammon attended coaches' meetings, gave instructions during practices, and, when asked, willingly shared her opinions with head coach Gregg Popovich, who has led the Spurs to five NBA championships. Popovich told her, "As cool as it would be to hire you [as a full-time assistant coach], you'd have to be qualified, and I'd have to make sure you're qualified." She agreed. When Popovich hired her after the completion of her internship, Hammon said, "Honestly, I don't think he gives two cents that I'm a woman. And, I don't want to be hired because I'm a woman . . . I'm getting hired because I'm capable."[138] In 2015, Hammon became the first female head coach to win the NBA's summer league title. The summer league, which starts after the completion of the regular NBA playoffs, is made up of teams' rookies, second-year players, and unsigned free agents.[139]

Solicit negative as well as positive feedback. Diversity is one of the most difficult management issues. No company or manager gets it right from the start.

Consequently, companies should aggressively seek positive and negative feedback about their diversity programs. One way to do that is to use a series of measurements to see if progress is being made.

Set high but realistic goals. Just because diversity is difficult doesn't mean that organizations shouldn't try to accomplish as much as possible. The general purpose of diversity programs is to try to create a positive work environment where no one is advantaged or disadvantaged, where "we" is everyone, where everyone can do his or her best work, where differences are respected and not ignored, and where everyone feels comfortable. Even if progress is slow, companies should not shrink from these goals.

12-4c Diversity Training and Practices

Organizations use diversity training and several common diversity practices to manage diversity. There are two basic types of diversity training programs, skills-based and awareness. **Skills-based diversity training** teaches employees the practical skills they need for managing a diverse workforce, skills such as flexibility and adaptability, negotiation, problem solving, and conflict resolution.[140] By contrast, **awareness training** is designed to raise employees' awareness of diversity issues and to challenge underlying assumptions or stereotypes we may have about others. **Dell Inc.** enrolled several male executives in a six-month program run by Catalyst, a nonprofit group that tracks and advocates for women's advancement. The program teaches managers to recognize the hurdles facing women in the workplace. As a result of the training, Doug Hillary, a Dell vice president, checked in with a female staff member with two young children and asked her if he was adequately accommodating her family needs. She told him that, actually, he was regularly scheduling staff conference calls at an hour when she was dropping her children off at school. He changed the meeting times, saying that, previously, "He didn't pay as much attention."[141]

Some companies use the Implicit Association Test (IAT) for awareness training.[142] The IAT measures the extent to which people associate positive or negative thoughts (that is underlying assumptions or stereotypes) with blacks or whites, men or women, homosexuals or heterosexuals, young or old, or other groups. For the race IAT (versions also exist for weight, age, sexuality, and other ethnic groups), test takers are shown black or white faces that they must instantly pair with various words. IAT proponents argue that shorter responses generally indicate stronger associations and that the patterns of associations indicate the extent to which people are biased. For example, an early study showed that 88 percent of whites have a more positive mental association toward whites than toward blacks, but surprisingly, 48 percent of blacks showed the same bias. Do the biases measured by the IAT mean we're likely to discriminate against others? Thankfully, no, according to the consistent results of a number of critical studies that indicate that IAT scores are not consistent over time and are not related to discriminatory behavior.[143] But the IAT does can help us become aware of our potential biases so that we monitor our workplace behavior and decision making. So, taking the IAT can increase awareness of diversity issues.

Companies also use diversity audits, diversity pairing, and minority experiences for top executives to better manage diversity. **Diversity audits** are formal assessments that measure employee and management attitudes, investigate the extent to which people are advantaged or disadvantaged with respect to hiring and promotions, and review companies' diversity-related policies and procedures. Writing in *The New York Times* against age discrimination, Ashton Applewhite says that any manager serious about diversity should start with the "shoe test." She says, "Look under the table, and if everyone's wearing the same kind of shoes, whether wingtips or flip-flops, you've got a problem." In other words, measurement and data are at the core of diversity audits.[144] According to Harvard Professor Iris Bohnet, "Using data to learn about the possible disparate treatment of employees shouldn't be controversial. No company runs its finances based just on intuition, and the same should hold for personnel decisions."[145] One manager whose company uses metrics for assessing diversity says that he has asked he team, "'How come, in the last month, you've gone after a large number of new people, and you haven't interviewed one woman for the position?' I started asking questions like this — I am not expecting them to have the answers. I'm expecting them to know that the next time I ask these questions, you better have the answers because I already have the data."[146]

Skills-based diversity training training that teaches employees the practical skills they need for managing a diverse workforce, such as flexibility and adaptability, negotiation, problem solving, and conflict resolution

Awareness training training that is designed to raise employees' awareness of diversity issues and to challenge the underlying assumptions or stereotypes they may have about others

Diversity audits formal assessments that measure employee and management attitudes, investigate the extent to which people are advantaged or disadvantaged with respect to hiring and promotions, and review companies' diversity-related policies and procedure

Mentoring and the newer trend of "reverse mentoring" provides different aged workers with the opportunity of tapping into new resources for learning.

Monkey Business Images/Shutterstock.com

Earlier in the chapter, you learned that *mentoring* is a common strategy for creating learning and promotional opportunities for women. Diversity pairing is a special kind of mentoring. In **diversity pairing**, people of different ages, cultural backgrounds, sexes, or races/ethnicities are paired for mentoring. The hope is that stereotypical beliefs and attitudes will change as people get to know each other as individuals.[147] Phyllis Korkki, a *New York Times* assignment editor in her mid-50s approached Talya Minsberg, age 27, and asked, "Will you mentor me?"[148] Minsberg said, "Korkki is a longtime *Times* employee, an accomplished journalist and an author. So the fact that she was approaching me for mentorship was unexpected."[149] Korkki wanted Minsberg to "reverse mentor" her so she could learn SnapChat. Minsberg leads the *Times'* efforts to attract younger readers via SnapChat stories. Korkki said, "I sought a mentor to help me develop a specific new skill—and something entirely outside my comfort zone—namely, how to use Snapchat, the smartphone-based photo and video service that is popular among teenagers and young adults."[150] While awkward at first, both benefited from the relationship. Minsberg said, "I realized our mentorship provided me with something unexpected: a chance to take what amounts to a leadership position I had not seen coming."[151] Korkki said that being mentored, "…made me realize that organizations and individual workers could do a lot more to bridge the gaps between generations. Each age group has untapped resources that can benefit others at a different stage of life."[152]

Because top managers are still overwhelmingly white and male, a number of companies believe that it is worthwhile to *have top executives experience what it is like to be in the minority.* This can be done by having top managers go to places or events where nearly everyone else is of a different sex or racial/ethnic background. For example, managers at Raytheon are required to spend an entire day in the office in a wheelchair so that they have a better understanding of the challenges faced by their disabled colleagues. Managers and executives at Sodexho Alliance are asked to spend time working with organizations that represent minorities. One male manager became the sponsor of a women employees group at Sodexho and accompanied a female colleague to a meeting of the Women's Food Service Forum. The manager called the experience, in which he was at a conference with 1,500 women, "profound" and said that it taught him what it feels like to be different. He also described how his experiences working with women made him more sensitive to women's feelings and even led him to change the social activities that he plans with coworkers from golf to dinner cruises. Rohini Anand, Sodexho's chief diversity officer, endorses this experiential approach, saying, "To really engage people, you have to create a series of epiphanies and take leaders through those epiphanies.[153]

12-4d Diversity: What Works?

Finally, while there's a wealth of data on what is being done to address diversity issues, there's not much clear, consistent, scientifically rigorous evidence on effectiveness.[154] So what do we know at this time? Let's start with what does *not* work. A review of 985 studies examining ways to reduce prejudice or bias toward others (similar to awareness training) concluded, "Psychologists are a long way from demonstrating the most effective ways to reduce prejudice," and that the evidence, so far, "does not reveal whether, when, and why interventions reduce prejudice in the world."[155] A recent survey of 829 companies suggests that the most popular programs,

> **Diversity pairing** a mentoring program in which people of different ages, cultural backgrounds, sexes, or races/ethnicities are paired together to get to know each other and change stereotypical beliefs and attitudes

diversity training, diversity performance audits (assessing how well managers are addressing diversity issues), and network programs (company sponsored affinity groups for women and minorities) "have no positive effects in the average workplace,"[156]. In fact, not only does diversity training not work, but it may also produce negative effects. According to professors Frank Dobbin and Alexandra Kalev, who studied 30 years of data across 800 companies, "The positive effects of diversity training rarely last beyond a day or two, and a number of studies suggest that it can activate bias or spark a backlash. Nonetheless, nearly half of midsize companies use it, as do nearly all the *Fortune* 500."[157] Why? Because training is required, and the message is, "We don't trust you to treat people fairly." As a result, they say, "Trainers tell us that people often respond to compulsory courses with anger and resistance—and many participants actually report more animosity toward other groups afterward."[158]

So what does work? Ironically, the two least frequently used programs, diversity mentoring and appointing diversity managers responsible for diversity programs, "were among the most effective."[159] Finally, focusing on deep-level diversity appears to have strong positive effects. According to professors Jonathan Haidt and Lee Jussim, "In a review of more than 500 studies, published in the *Journal of Personality and Social Psychology*, authors Thomas Pettigrew and Linda Tropp concluded that when people of different races and ethnicities mix together and get to know each other, the effect is generally to reduce prejudice on all sides. This is a good justification for increasing diversity."[160]

STUDY TOOLS 12

LOCATED IN TEXTBOOK

☐ Rip out and review chapter review card.

LOCATED AT WWW.CENGAGEBRAIN.COM

☐ Gain unique perspectives on key concepts with new 4LTR concept videos in the e-book.

☐ Increase your comprehension with Aplia for MGMT11.

☐ Complete interactive content within the e-book.

13 | Motivation

After you finish this chapter, go to **PAGE 304** for **STUDY TOOLS**

LEARNING OUTCOMES

13-1 Explain the basics of motivation.

13-2 Use equity theory to explain how employees' perceptions of fairness affect motivation.

13-3 Use expectancy theory to describe how workers' expectations about rewards, effort, and the link between rewards and performance influence motivation.

13-4 Explain how reinforcement theory works and how it can be used to motivate.

13-5 Describe the components of goal-setting theory and how managers can use them to motivate workers.

13-6 Discuss how the entire motivation model can be used to motivate workers.

Sergey Nivens/Shutterstock.com

13-1 BASICS OF MOTIVATION

What makes people happiest and most productive at work? Is it money, benefits, opportunities for growth, interesting work, or something else altogether? And if people desire different things, how can a company keep everyone motivated? It takes insight and hard work to motivate workers to join the company, perform well, and then stay with the company. In a 2016 study, Gallup found that only 33 percent of U.S. employees are "engaged" or motivated at work, whereas 63 percent are "not engaged," meaning they are unmotivated, not interested in organizational goals or outcomes, or, as Gallup reports, "they're just there." Even worse, 16 percent of employees are "actively disengaged."

Says Gallup, "They are miserable in the workplace and destroy what the most engaged employees build."[1] Gallup examined the results of 1.9 million people across 49 countries employed in 82,000 work units for 230 companies to see how engagement, or motivation, matters. "Business/work units scoring in the top half on employee engagement nearly double their odds of success compared with those in the bottom half. Those at the 99th percentile have four times the success rate of those at the first percentile. Median differences between top-quartile and bottom-quartile units were 10 percent in customer ratings, 21 percent in profitability, 20 percent in sales production, 17 percent in production records, 24 percent in turnover (high-turnover organizations), 59 percent in turnover (low-turnover organizations), 70 percent in safety incidents, 28 percent in shrinkage, 41 percent in absenteeism, 58 percent in patient safety incidents, and 40 percent in quality (defects)."[2]

So what is motivation? **Motivation** is the set of forces that initiates, directs, and makes people persist in their efforts to accomplish a goal.[3] *Initiation of effort* is concerned with the choices that people make about how much effort to put forth in their jobs. ("Do I really knock myself out or just do a decent job?") *Direction of effort* is concerned with the choices that people make in deciding where to put forth effort in their jobs. ("I should be spending time with my high-dollar accounts instead of learning this new computer system!") *Persistence of effort* is concerned with the choices that people make about how long they will put forth effort in

their jobs before reducing or eliminating those efforts. ("I'm only halfway through the project, and I'm exhausted. Do I plow through to the end, or just call it quits?") Initiation, direction, and persistence are at the heart of motivation.

Bruce Arians coaches the National Football League's Arizona Cardinals, while Pete Carroll coaches the NFL's Seattle Seahawks. Arians, a screamer and a hugger, took the Cardinals to the NFC championship, one game short of the Super Bowl. Cardinals' defensive back Tyrann Mathieu said, "I'll mess up on the practice field and he'll scream and curse at me. Then he'll find me before meetings start—he'll give me a hug, tell me it's all good and ask how my family is."[4] Pete Carroll, by contrast, coaches the Seattle Seahawks. Under Carroll, who never yells, the Seahawks have won one Super Bowl and just barely lost another. When All-Pro tight-end Jimmy Graham dropped a pass in practice, Carroll told him to focus more on what he was doing and not to worry about it. Regarding how Carroll motivates Seahawks players, Graham says, "It's literally all positive reinforcement."[5]

Motivation the set of forces that initiates, directs, and makes people persist in their efforts to accomplish a goal

Under which coach, the Cardinals' Arians or the Seahawks' Carroll, would you be more motivated? Or, in Gallup's terms, are you engaged at work? Are your coworkers? If you and your coworkers are "disengaged" or "actively disengaged," why? Are there parts of the job that interest and energize you? If so, what are they and why? Answering questions like these is at the heart of figuring out how best to motivate people at work.

*Let's learn more about motivation by building a basic model of motivation out of **13-1a effort and performance, 13-1b need satisfaction,** and **13-1c extrinsic and intrinsic rewards** and then discussing **13-1d how to motivate people with this basic model of motivation.***

13-1a Effort and Performance

When most people think of work motivation, they think that working hard (effort) should lead to a good job (performance). Exhibit 13.1 shows a basic model of work motivation and performance, displaying this process. The first thing to notice about Exhibit 13.1 is that this is a basic model of work motivation *and* performance. In practice, it's almost impossible to talk about one without mentioning the other. Not surprisingly, managers often assume motivation is the only determinant of performance, saying things such as "Your performance was really terrible last quarter. What's the matter? Aren't you as motivated as you used to be?" In fact, motivation is just one of three primary determinants of job performance. In industrial psychology, job performance is frequently represented by this equation:

Exhibit 13.1
A Basic Model of Work Motivation and Performance

$$\text{Job Performance} =$$
$$\text{Motivation} \times \text{Ability} \times \text{Situational Constraints}$$

In this formula, *job performance* is how well someone performs the requirements of the job. *Motivation*, as defined previously, is effort, the degree to which someone works hard to do the job well. *Ability* is the degree to which workers possess the knowledge, skills, and talent needed to do a job well. And *situational constraints* are factors beyond the control of individual employees, such as tools, policies, and resources that have an effect on job performance.

Because job performance is a multiplicative function of motivation times ability times situational constraints, job performance will suffer if any one of these components is weak. This doesn't mean that motivation

Exhibit 13.2
A Basic Model of Work Motivation and Performance

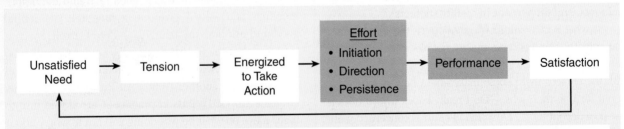

As shown on the left side of this exhibit, a person's unsatisfied need creates an uncomfortable internal state of tension that must be resolved. So, according to needs theories, people are motivated by unmet needs. But after a need is met, it no longer motivates. When this occurs, people become satisfied, as shown on the right side of the exhibit.

doesn't matter. It just means that all the motivation in the world won't translate into high performance when an employee has little ability and high situational constraints. So, even though we will spend this chapter developing a model of work motivation, it is important to remember that ability and situational constraints affect job performance as well.

13-1b Need Satisfaction

In Exhibit 13.1, we started with a very basic model of motivation in which effort leads to job performance. But managers want to know, "What leads to effort?" Determining employee needs is the first step to answering that question.

Needs are the physical or psychological requirements that must be met to ensure survival and well-being.[6] As shown on the left side of Exhibit 13.2, a person's unmet need creates an uncomfortable, internal state of tension that must be resolved. For example, if you normally skip breakfast but then have to work through lunch, chances are you'll be so hungry by late afternoon that the only thing you'll be motivated to do is find something to eat. So, according to needs theories, people are motivated by unmet needs. But a need no longer motivates once it is met. For example, when the author of the Mr. Everyday Dollar financial strategies website (now ChrisReining.com) learned that he had become a millionaire at 35, he described it as a "huge letdown," saying, "You might think when your account rolls over to seven digits that fireworks light up the sky, confetti falls, and champagne starts flowing. I can tell you that doesn't happen, in fact, it's pretty anticlimactic; I was like, 'Oh, cool,' and then went back to work." In other words, once obtained, his need for financial independence, no longer motivated him as much.[7] When this occurs, people become satisfied, as shown on the right side of Exhibit 13.2.

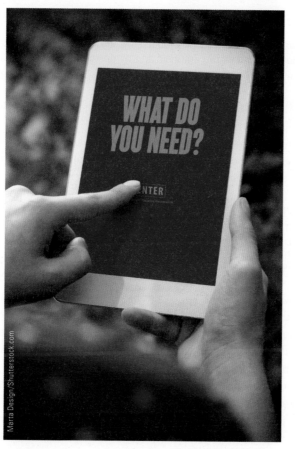

Note: Throughout the chapter, as we build on this basic model, the parts of the model that we've already discussed will appear shaded in color. For example, because we've already discussed the effort → performance part of the model, those components are shown with a colored background. When we add new parts to the model, they will have a white background. We're adding need satisfaction to the model at this step, so the need-satisfaction components of unsatisfied need, tension, energized to take action, and satisfaction are shown with a white background. This shading convention should make it easier to understand the work motivation model as we add to it in each section of the chapter.

Because people are motivated by unmet needs, managers must learn what those unmet needs are and address them. This is not always a straightforward task, however, because different needs theories suggest different needs categories. Consider three well-known needs theories. Maslow's Hierarchy of Needs suggests that people are motivated by *physiological* (food and water), *safety* (physical and economic), *belongingness* (friendship, love, social interaction), *esteem* (achievement and recognition), and *self-actualization* (realizing your full potential) needs.[8] Alderfer's ERG Theory collapses Maslow's five needs into three: *existence* (safety and physiological needs), *relatedness* (belongingness), and *growth* (esteem and self-actualization).[9] McClelland's Learned Needs Theory suggests that people are motivated by the need for *affiliation* (to be liked and accepted), the need for *achievement* (to accomplish challenging goals), or the need for *power* (to influence others).[10]

Things become even more complicated when we consider the different predictions made by these theories. According to Maslow, needs are arranged in a hierarchy from low (physiological) to high (self-actualization). Within this hierarchy, people are motivated by their lowest unsatisfied need. As

Needs the physical or psychological requirements that must be met to ensure survival and well-being

Exhibit 13.3
Adding Rewards to the Model

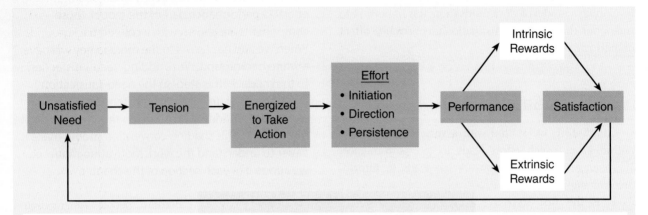

Performing a job well can be rewarding intrinsically (the job itself is fun, challenging, or interesting) or extrinsically (as you receive better pay, promotions, and so on). Intrinsic and extrinsic rewards lead to satisfaction of various needs.

each need is met, they work their way up the hierarchy from physiological to self-actualization needs. By contrast, Alderfer says that people can be motivated by more than one need at a time. Furthermore, he suggests that people are just as likely to move down the needs hierarchy as up, particularly when they are unable to achieve satisfaction at the next higher need level. McClelland argues that the degree to which particular needs motivate varies tremendously from person to person, with some people being motivated primarily by achievement and others by power or affiliation. Moreover, McClelland says that needs are learned, not innate. For instance, studies show that children whose parents own a small business or hold a managerial position are much more likely to have a high need for achievement.[11]

So, with three different sets of needs and three very different ideas about how needs motivate, how do we provide a practical answer to managers who just want to know what leads to effort? Fortunately, the research evidence simplifies things a bit. To start, studies indicate that there are two basic kinds of needs categories.[12] *Lower-order needs* are concerned with safety and with physiological and existence requirements, whereas *higher-order needs* are concerned with relationships (belongingness, relatedness, and affiliation), challenges and accomplishments (esteem, self-actualization, growth, and achievement), and influence (power). Studies generally show that higher-order needs will not motivate people as long as lower-order needs remain unsatisfied.[13]

Extrinsic reward a reward that is tangible, visible to others, and given to employees contingent on the performance of specific tasks or behaviors

For example, imagine that you graduated from college six months ago and are still looking for your first job. With money running short (you're probably living on your credit cards), and the possibility of having to move back in with your parents looming (if this doesn't motivate you, what will?), your basic needs for food, shelter, and security drive your thoughts, behavior, and choices at this point. But after you land that job, find a great place (of your own!) to live, and put some money in the bank, these basic needs should decrease in importance as you begin to think about making new friends and taking on challenging work assignments. In fact, after lower-order needs are satisfied, it's difficult for managers to predict which higher-order needs will motivate behavior.[14] Some people will be motivated by affiliation, while others will be motivated by growth or esteem. Also, the relative importance of the various needs may change over time but not necessarily in any predictable pattern. So, what leads to effort? In part, needs do. After we discuss rewards in Subsection 13-1c, in Subsection 13-1d, we discuss how managers can use what we know from need-satisfaction theories to motivate workers.

13-1c Extrinsic and Intrinsic Rewards

No discussion of motivation would be complete without considering rewards. Let's add two kinds of rewards, extrinsic and intrinsic, to the model in Exhibit 13.3.[15]

Extrinsic rewards are tangible and visible to others and are given to employees contingent on the

Gym members who have a fun workout experience are more likely to exercise longer and stay on goal.

performance of specific tasks or behaviors.[16] External agents (managers, for example) determine and control the distribution, frequency, and amount of extrinsic rewards, such as pay, company stock, benefits, and promotions. For example, 91 percent of large- and medium-sized U.S. companies surveyed by Hewitt Associates, a consulting company based in Lincolnshire, Illinois, offer incentives or bonuses to reward employees.[17]

Lincoln Electric, a manufacturer of arc welding tools and technology, has paid annual profit sharing bonuses to its factory workers for 83 straight years. In 2016, Lincoln paid out 32 percent of its pretax profits, $68 million, to employees who received bonuses of $24,111 each, worth 33 percent of total wages. In the 83 years in which Lincoln has paid profit-sharing bonuses, the percentage has never dropped below 25 percent of total wages and has been as high as 120 percent. Over the past decade, bonuses have averaged 40 percent of total salary.[18]

Why do companies need to offer extrinsic rewards? To get people to do things they wouldn't otherwise do. Companies use extrinsic rewards to motivate people to perform four basic behaviors: join the organization, regularly attend their jobs, perform their jobs well, and stay with the organization.[19] Think about it. Would you show up at work every day to do the best possible job that you could just out of the goodness of your heart? Very few people would.

Intrinsic rewards are the natural rewards associated with performing a task or activity for its own sake. For example, aside from the external rewards management offers for doing something well, employees often find the activities or tasks they perform interesting and enjoyable. Examples of intrinsic rewards include a sense of accomplishment or achievement, a feeling of responsibility, the chance to learn something new or interact

with others, or simply the fun that comes from performing an interesting, challenging, and engaging task.

Across five studies with 449 people, Professors Kaitlin Woolley and Ayelet Fishbach found that the immediate rewards from performing a task (that is, intrinsic rewards) predicted long-term task persistence.[20] For example, people who work out do so to get subsequent rewards, such as losing weight, getting fit, or better health. Woolley and Fishbach found that gym goers kept going to the gym only if they enjoyed their workouts. In other words, people only kept working toward their long-term goals when the tasks or steps to accomplish those goals were intrinsically rewarding. They concluded, "Gym-goers who cared more about having a fun workout exercised longer than those who cared less about having fun."[21]

Which types of rewards are most important to workers in general? A number of surveys suggest that both extrinsic and intrinsic rewards are important and that employee preferences for either intrinsic or extrinsic rewards are relatively stable.[22] A 2016 Society for Human Resource Management national survey found that three extrinsic factors—pay, benefits, and job security/organizational financial stability—and four intrinsic factors—respectful treatment of employees, trust in senior management, relationships with immediate supervisors, and the chance to use one's skills and abilities in your work—were among the top factors rated as "very important" by employees.[23]

13-1d Motivating with the Basics

So, given the basic model of work motivation in Exhibit 13.3, what practical steps can managers take to motivate employees to increase their effort?

The first step is to *start by asking people what their needs are.* Jonathan Robinson, CEO of **Freetextbooks .com**, an online college textbook seller (sorry, the textbooks aren't really free), says the key to motivating employees is finding out what they like and then giving them the rewards they want. To do that, Robinson gives each new hire a brief survey asking them about their favorite candy, restaurant, hobby, or music. Says Robinson, "You just have to know your team. We're pretty small so I have to stay in tune with the preferences and pulse of our employees. The perks are in the details." As a result, he recently gave one employee a free round of golf, another $100 to be used at a great restaurant, and another IMAX theater tickets. Because he asked, all got what they WANTED.[24] So, if you want to meet employees' needs, just ask.

> **Intrinsic reward** a natural reward associated with performing a task or activity for its own sake

Next, *satisfy lower-order needs first*. Because higher-order needs will not motivate people as long as lower-order needs remain unsatisfied, companies should satisfy lower-order needs first. In practice, this means providing the equipment, training, and knowledge to create a safe workplace free of physical risks; paying employees well enough to provide financial security; and offering a benefits package that will protect employees and their families through good medical coverage and health and disability insurance. Indeed, the Society for Human Resource Management study mentioned previously found that three of the most important factors in 2016—compensation/pay (63%), job security (58%), and benefits (60%)—were all lower-order needs.[25] Consistent with the idea of satisfying lower-order needs first, a survey of 12,000 employees found that inadequate compensation is the number-one reason employees leave organizations. This is why The Container Store CEO Kip Tindell pays his employees an average salary of $48,000 per year, twice the average retail salary. As a result, says Tindell, "My employees advance on Maslow's hierarchy [from lower- to higher-order needs]." He says, "I didn't think about this when we started out. But it's the most powerful thing you can do."[26]

Third, managers should *expect people's needs to change*. As needs are satisfied or situations change, what motivated people before may not motivate them now. Likewise, what motivates people to accept a job may not necessarily motivate them after they have the job. For instance, David Stum, president of the Loyalty Institute, says, "The [attractive] power of pay and benefits is only [strong] during the recruitment stage. After employees take the job, pay and benefits become entitlements to them. They think: 'Now that I work here, you owe me that.'"[27] Managers should also expect needs to change as people mature. For older employees, benefits are as important as pay, which is always ranked as more important by younger employees. Older employees also rank job security as more important than personal and family time, which is more important to younger employees.[28]

Finally, *as needs change and lower-order needs are satisfied, create opportunities for employees to satisfy higher-order needs*. Recall that intrinsic rewards such as accomplishment, achievement, learning something new, and interacting with others are the natural rewards associated with performing a task or activity for its own sake. And, with

the exception of influence (power), intrinsic rewards correspond very closely to higher-order needs that are concerned with relationships (belongingness, relatedness, and affiliation) and challenges and accomplishments (esteem, self-actualization, growth, and achievement). Therefore, one way for managers to meet employees' higher-order needs is to create opportunities for employees to experience intrinsic rewards by providing challenging work, encouraging employees to take greater responsibility for their work, and giving employees the freedom to pursue tasks and projects they find naturally interesting.

13-2 EQUITY THEORY

We've seen that people are motivated to achieve intrinsic and extrinsic rewards. However, if employees don't believe that rewards are awarded fairly or don't believe that they can achieve the performance goals the company has set for them, they won't be very motivated.

Fairness, or what people perceive to be fair, is also a critical issue in organizations. **Equity theory** says that people will be motivated at work when they *perceive* that they are being treated fairly. In particular, equity theory stresses the importance of perceptions. So, regardless of the actual level of rewards people receive, they must also perceive that, relative to others, they are being treated fairly. For example, you learned in Chapter 11 that the CEOs of the largest U.S. firms now make $15.6 million per year, which is 271 times their average employee salary.[29] The 10 highest-paid CEOs averaged earnings of $43.2 million per year, led by Thomas Rutledge, the CEO of Charter Communications, who made $98 million.[30] By contrast, in 2016, CEOs of companies with less than $1 billion a year in revenues averaged $230,090 in earnings, or 5.42 times what the average worker makes.[31]

Many people believe that CEO pay is obscenely high and unfair. Others believe that CEO pay is fair because the supply and demand for executive talent largely determine what CEOs are paid. They argue that if it were easier to find good CEOs, then CEOs would be

Equity theory a theory that states that people will be motivated when they perceive that they are being treated fairly

Greg Brave/Shutterstock.com

paid much less. Equity theory doesn't focus on objective equity (that is, that CEOs make 271 times or 5.42 times more than average workers). Instead, equity theory says that equity, like beauty, is in the eye of the beholder.

Let's learn more about equity theory by examining **13-2a the components of equity theory, 13-2b how people react to perceived inequity, and 13-2c how to motivate people using equity theory.**

13-2a Components of Equity Theory

The basic components of equity theory are inputs, outcomes, and referents. **Inputs** are the contributions employees make to the organization. They include education and training, intelligence, experience, effort, number of hours worked, and ability. **Outcomes** are what employees receive in exchange for their contributions to the organization. They include pay, fringe benefits, status symbols, and job titles and assignments. And, because perceptions of equity depend on comparisons, **referents** are other people with whom people compare themselves to determine if they have been treated fairly. The referent can be a single person (comparing yourself with a coworker), a generalized other (comparing yourself with "accountants in general," for example), or even yourself over time ("I was better off last year than I am this year"). Usually, people choose to compare themselves with referents who hold the same or similar jobs or who are otherwise similar in gender, race, age, tenure, or other characteristics.[32]

Copywriter Lucy Bayly says, "You think you're satisfied [with your pay] and then all of a sudden, you find out someone is paid a little more, and it ruins your day."[33] That's what happened to Olivia Wainhouse, an account executive at New York social media analytics firm SumAll. When Wainhouse learned that a new hire was earning $10,000 more than she was, she felt betrayed: "My competitive drive kicked in. I thought, 'What's going on here?'"[34] To see how SumAll dealt with unsanctioned salary disclosures—and the hurt feelings that followed—see the box on "Transparent Pay—Not a Big Deal."

According to equity theory, employees compare their outcomes (the rewards they receive from the organization) with their inputs (their contributions to the organization). This comparison of outcomes with inputs is called the **outcome/input (O/I) ratio**. After an internal comparison in which they compare their outcomes with their inputs, employees then make an external comparison in which they compare their O/I ratio with the O/I ratio of a referent.[35] With "pay secrecy" a

standard organizational policy, how are employees finding the information they need to make these comparisons? Kevin Hallock, dean of Cornell University's School of Industrial and Labor Relations, says, "People are much more willing to talk about pay than they were even 10 years ago."[36] Elle Kaplan, founder of LexION Capital explains that, "Comparing pay stubs by the water cooler isn't the only way to find out your fair market value." Indeed Glassdoor.com, a recruiting website, has extensive salary information. Says Kaplan, "Even if you can't find the exact salaries of your coworkers, you can see the average pay for your skills and position by geography and industry."[37]

When people perceive that their O/I ratio is equal to the referent's O/I ratio, they conclude that they are being treated fairly. But when people perceive that their O/I ratio is different from their referent's O/I ratio, they conclude that they have been treated inequitably or unfairly.

Inequity can take two forms, underreward and overreward. **Underreward** occurs when a referent's O/I ratio is better than your O/I ratio. In other words, you are getting fewer outcomes relative to your inputs than the referent you compare yourself with is getting. When people perceive that they have been underrewarded, they tend to experience anger or frustration. And that tends to happen a lot. A PayScale survey of 71,000 employees found that among people who actually had *higher than average* salaries (above market), 35 percent thought they were underpaid, 45 percent thought they were paid fairly, and 21 percent thought they were overpaid. Among those who actually had *average salaries* (at market), 64 percent thought they were underpaid, 30 percent thought they were paid fairly, and just 6 percent thought they were overpaid.[38]

By contrast, **overreward** occurs when a referent's O/I ratio is worse than your O/I ratio. In this case, you are getting more outcomes relative to your inputs than your referent is. In theory, when people

Inputs in equity theory, the contributions employees make to the organization

Outcomes in equity theory, the rewards employees receive for their contributions to the organization

Referents in equity theory, others with whom people compare themselves to determine if they have been treated fairly

Outcome/input (O/I) ratio in equity theory, an employee's perception of how the rewards received from an organization compare with the employee's contributions to that organization

Underreward a form of inequity in which you are getting fewer outcomes relative to inputs than your referent is getting

Overreward a form of inequity in which you are getting more outcomes relative to inputs than your referent perceive that they have been overrewarded, they experience guilt. But, not surprisingly, people have a very high tolerance for overreward. It takes a tremendous amount of overpayment before people decide that their pay or benefits are more than they deserve.

13-2b How People React to Perceived Inequity

So what happens when people perceive that they have been treated inequitably at work? Exhibit 13.4 shows that perceived inequity affects satisfaction. In the case of underreward, this usually translates into frustration or anger; with overreward, the reaction is guilt. These reactions lead to tension and a strong need to take action to restore equity in some way. At first, a slight inequity may not be strong enough to motivate an employee to take immediate action. If the inequity continues, or there are multiple inequities, however, tension may build over time until a point of intolerance is reached and the person is energized to take action to restore equity by reducing inputs, increasing outcomes, rationalizing inputs or outcomes, changing the referent, or simply leaving. We will discuss these possible responses in terms of the inequity associated with underreward, which is much more common than the inequity associated with overreward.

People who perceive that they have been underrewarded may try to restore equity by *decreasing or withholding their inputs (that is, effort)*. In response to impending budget cuts and layoffs and stalled contract negotiations, all of the teachers at East Baltimore School in Baltimore, Maryland, engaged in a sick-out that canceled a full day of classes. Alan Rebar, a teacher at nearby Sinclair Lane Elementary School said, "You go in,

day-in, day-out, doing your job, and you get told, 'We don't respect you. We don't care about you. We don't care about your future. It's a problem other people caused, and we're going to solve it on you.' It's enough—people have had it. Teachers have had it. It's amazing that there aren't way more people sicking out."[39]

Increasing outcomes is another way people try to restore equity. This might include asking for a raise or pointing out the inequity to the boss and hoping that he or she takes care of it. Sometimes, however, employees may go to external organizations such as labor unions, federal agencies, or the courts for help in increasing outcomes to restore equity. For instance, the U.S. Department of Labor estimates that 10 percent of workers are not getting the extra overtime pay they deserve when they work more than forty hours a week. These are known as Fair Labor Standards Act (FLSA) violations.[40] After a U.S. Department of Labor ruling, Halliburton, a global oil field services company, agreed to pay $18.2 million in back wages to 1,106 oil and gas employees who were at first denied overtime pay after incorrectly being classified as exempt employees (who are ineligible for overtime).[41] In 2016, 10,884 FLSA cases resulted in companies paying $172 million in back wages to 210,000 employees.[42]

Another method of restoring equity is to *rationalize or distort inputs or outcomes*. Instead of decreasing inputs or increasing outcomes, employees restore equity by making mental or emotional adjustments in their O/I ratios or the O/I ratios of their referents. For example, suppose that a company downsizes 10 percent of its workforce. It's likely that the people who still have jobs will be angry or frustrated with company management because of the layoffs. If alternative jobs are difficult to find, however, these survivors may rationalize or distort their O/I ratios and conclude, "Well, things could be worse. At least I still have my job." Rationalizing or distorting outcomes may be used when other ways to restore equity aren't available.

Changing the referent is another way of restoring equity. In this case, people compare themselves with someone other than the referent they had been using for previous O/I ratio comparisons. Because people usually choose to compare themselves with others who hold the same or similar jobs or who are otherwise similar (that is, friends, family members, neighbors who work at

Exhibit 13.4
Adding Equity Theory to the Model

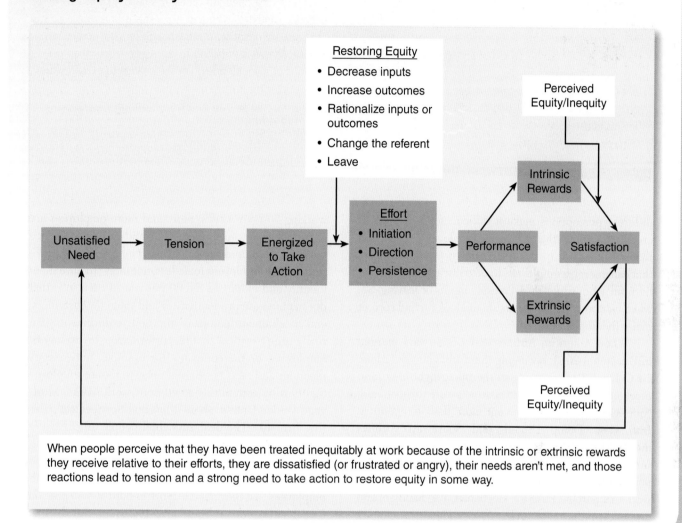

Restoring Equity
- Decrease inputs
- Increase outcomes
- Rationalize inputs or outcomes
- Change the referent
- Leave

Perceived Equity/Inequity

Unsatisfied Need → Tension → Energized to Take Action → **Effort** • Initiation • Direction • Persistence → Performance

Intrinsic Rewards

Satisfaction

Extrinsic Rewards

Perceived Equity/Inequity

When people perceive that they have been treated inequitably at work because of the intrinsic or extrinsic rewards they receive relative to their efforts, they are dissatisfied (or frustrated or angry), their needs aren't met, and those reactions lead to tension and a strong need to take action to restore equity in some way.

other companies), they may change referents to restore equity when their personal situations change, such as a decrease in job status or pay.[43]

13-2c Motivating with Equity Theory

What practical steps can managers take to use equity theory to motivate employees? They can *start by looking for and correcting major inequities*. Among other things, equity theory makes us aware that an employee's sense of fairness is based on subjective perceptions. What one employee considers grossly unfair may not affect another employee's perceptions of equity at all. Although these

People who perceive that they have been underrewarded at the office may withhold their efforts until they feel they are fairly compensated.

TRANSPARENT PAY—NOT A BIG DEAL

Dane Atkison has run almost a dozen companies during his career, often paying different employees vastly different salaries for the same skill set, only because some negotiated better than others. Tired of employee outrage when significant differences are discovered, he adopted a transparent salary system when he took the lead at social media analytics company SumAll. During the hiring process, Atkinson lets candidates know what the job pays—no negotiating allowed—and that everyone knows everyone else's salary.

Sometimes seasoned job candidates balk. Atkison remembers one candidate who told him, "This is unfair because I can't actually negotiate." And although tensions sometimes surface, Atkison says talking to employees about their perceptions of inequity gives him the chance to explain why some people make more money than others.

Source: L. Pollak, "The Company Where Everyone Knows Everyone Else's Salary," *Planet Money* on National Public Radio, July 2, 2014, accessed May 8, 2015. http://www.npr.org/blogs/money/2014/07/02/327758712/the-company-where-everyone-knows-everyone-elses-salary.

different perceptions make it difficult for managers to create conditions that satisfy all employees, it's critical that they do their best to take care of major inequities that can energize employees to take disruptive, costly, or harmful actions such as decreasing inputs or leaving. So, whenever possible, managers should look for and correct major inequities.

When American Airlines and US Airways merged in December 2013, becoming the world's largest airline, CEO Doug Parker promised the pilot, flight crew, and mechanics unions that when contracts were renegotiated, American would pay 3 percent more than competitors. But when Delta, United, and Southwest Airlines increased their pay in 2015, American's employees fell further behind.[44] American eventually corrected the pay inequities *prior* to contract renegotiations, starting with a 22 percent raise for mechanics, bag handlers and ground workers in November 2016, and pay raises of 4.2 to 6.5 percent for flight attendants and 7 to 8.7 percent for pilots in May 2017.[45] CEO Parker said, "Today's news is about doing the right thing and doing so not because we are contractually required to or because we are locked in a contentious contractual battle. We must continue moving past the days of discontent as we build a new American where team members trust each other and work together with our customers' care in mind."[46]

Second, managers can *reduce employees' inputs*. Increasing outcomes is often the first and only strategy that companies use to restore equity, yet reducing employee inputs is just as viable a strategy. In fact, with dual-career couples working 50-hour weeks, more and more employees are looking for ways to reduce stress and restore a balance between work and family. Consequently, it may make sense to ask employees to do less, not more; to have them identify and eliminate the 20 percent of their jobs that doesn't increase productivity or add value for customers; and to eliminate company-imposed requirements that really aren't critical to the performance of managers, employees, or the company (for example, unnecessary meetings and reports). Another way to reduce employee inputs is by committing to 40-hour work weeks. Mortgage lender United Shore Financial Services calls this the "firm 40." The deal, says chief people officer Laura Lawson, is that "You give us 40. Everything else is yours."[47] That means no online shopping at work, and no checking Facebook or Twitter. CEO Mat Isbia tells employees that they need to work as hard at 5:55 p.m. on Friday as they do on Tuesday at 10:55 a.m. But then, at 6 p.m. sharp, the office empties. Ahmed Haider, who works in client relations at USFS, says that "the parking lot is pretty much empty" by 6:05 p.m.[48] At first, Haider doubted whether the commitment to "firm 40" was real. But now, he always leaves at 6 p.m. and rarely sends emails or phones colleagues after work hours. "There's nobody to call. Everyone's at home," he says.[49]

Finally, managers should *make sure decision-making processes are fair*. Equity theory focuses on **distributive justice**, the perceived degree to which outcomes and rewards are fairly distributed or allocated. However, **procedural justice**, the perceived fairness of the procedures used to make reward allocation decisions, is just as important.[50] Procedural justice matters because even when employees are unhappy with their outcomes (that is, low pay), they're much less likely to be unhappy with company management if they believe that the procedures used to allocate outcomes were

Distributive justice the perceived degree to which outcomes and rewards are fairly distributed or allocated

Procedural justice the perceived fairness of the process used to make reward allocation decisions fair. For example, employees who are laid off tend to be hostile toward their employer when they perceive that the procedures leading to the layoffs were unfair. When Air France announced a plan to reduce costs by $2 billion over two years—partly by cutting 2,900 jobs—angry employees interrupted a work council meeting attended by key members of management and leaders representing the workers. Five irate employees stormed into the meeting, knocking a security guard unconscious as they attempted to assault two top managers by ripping the shirts and jackets off their backs. Ultimately, the executives were forced to climb a fence to avoid further harm.[51] By contrast, employees who perceive layoff procedures to be fair tend to continue to support and trust their employers.[52] Also, if employees perceive that their outcomes are unfair (that is, distributive injustice) but that the decisions and procedures leading to those outcomes were fair (that is, procedural justice), they are much more likely to seek constructive ways of restoring equity, such as discussing these matters with their manager. By contrast, if employees perceive both distributive and procedural injustice, they may resort to more destructive tactics, such as withholding effort, absenteeism, tardiness, or even sabotage and theft.[53]

13-3 EXPECTANCY THEORY

One of the hardest things about motivating people is that not everyone is attracted to the same rewards. **Expectancy theory** says that people will be motivated to the extent to which they believe that their efforts will lead to good performance, that good performance will be rewarded, and that they will be offered attractive rewards.[54]

Let's learn more about expectancy theory by examining **13-3a the components of expectancy theory** *and* **13-3b how to use expectancy theory as a motivational tool.**

13-3a Components of Expectancy Theory

Expectancy theory holds that people make conscious choices about their motivation. The three factors that affect those choices are valence, expectancy, and instrumentality.

Valence is simply the attractiveness or desirability of various rewards or outcomes. Expectancy theory recognizes that the same reward or outcome—say, a

promotion—will be highly attractive to some people, will be highly disliked by others, and will not make much difference one way or the other to still others. Accordingly, when people are deciding how much effort to put forth, expectancy theory says that they will consider the valence of all possible rewards and outcomes that they can receive from their jobs. The greater the sum of those valences, each of which can be positive, negative, or neutral, the more effort people will choose to put forth on the job. Imagine you drive for Uber. It's busy. You have one pickup after another and higher peak fares have kicked in because there aren't enough drivers to meet demand. Do you keep driving to make "more" money than usual, or do you stop when you've met your income goal for the day? New drivers stop when they've met their daily goal, knocking off work early. Experienced drivers, however, put in a full day and pocket the extra pay.[55] But Major League Baseball's Nick Franklin, who made $507,500 in 2016, drives for Uber in the off-season because "I wanted to do something on the weekends because I never really do anything."[56] Just as expectancy theory predicts, the same rewards have different valences (or attractiveness) for different people.

Expectancy is the perceived relationship between effort and performance. When expectancies are strong, employees believe that their hard work and efforts will result in good performance, so they work harder. By contrast, when expectancies are weak, employees figure that no matter what they do or how hard they work, they won't be able to perform their jobs successfully, so they don't work as hard.

Instrumentality is the perceived relationship between performance and rewards. When instrumentality is strong, employees believe that improved performance will lead to better and more rewards, so they choose to work harder. When instrumentality is weak, employees don't believe that better performance will result in more or better rewards, so they choose not to work as hard.

Expectancy theory holds that for people to be highly motivated, all three variables—valence, expectancy, and instrumentality—must be

Expectancy theory the theory that people will be motivated to the extent to which they believe that their efforts will lead to good performance, that good performance will be rewarded, and that they will be offered attractive rewards

Valence the attractiveness or desirability of a reward or outcome

Expectancy the perceived relationship between effort and performance

Instrumentality the perceived relationship between performance and rewards

Cut CEO Pay to Raise Worker Pay: Early Results

In 2015, CEO Dan Price of Gravity Payments, a credit-card processing company, cut his salary from $1 million to $70,000 so he could increase employee salaries from $48,000 to $70,000. Although viewed positively by labor activists, others were skeptical. So, 15 months later, what's happened? Early on, two of his best employees quit, believing that paying everyone the same was unfair. But now surveys indicate employees are happier, turnover is at a six-year low, profits have doubled, client retention is up, and new accounts are up 60 percent. Thirty thousand people applied for jobs and 50 new employees were hired. Price's pay cut, however, is temporary. "When I made the announcement, I said I would just put my salary back where it was once the company's profits had gone back to where they were." While business is good and employee salaries will not change, he has yet to increase his salary to $1 million a year. When he does, how will his business and employees be affected?

Sources: P. Cohen, "A Company Copes With Backlash Against the Raise That Roared - The New York," *New York Times*, July 31, 2015, accessed April 28, 2017, https://www.nytimes.com/2015/08/02/business/a-company-copes-with-backlash-against-the-raise-that-roared.html; R. Murray, "Gravity Payments' $70K Minimum Salary: CEO Dan Price Shares Result Over a Year Later," Today, August 11, 2016, accessed April 28, 2017, http://www.today.com/money/gravity-payments-70k-minimum-salary-ceo-dan-price-shares-results-t101678; "The Gravity of 70k," *Gravity Payments*, accessed April 28, 2017, https://gravitypayments.com/thegravityof70k/.

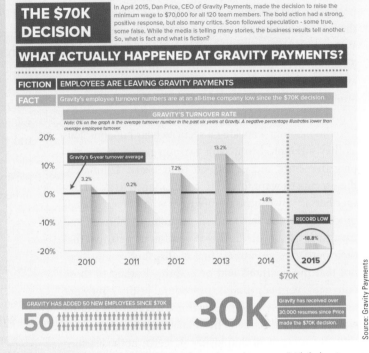

Source: Gravity Payments

---

high. Thus, expectancy theory can be represented by the following simple equation:

$$\text{Motivation} =$$
$$\textbf{Valence} \times \textbf{Expectancy} \times \textbf{Instrumentality}$$

If any one of these variables (valence, expectancy, or instrumentality) declines, overall motivation will decline, too.

Exhibit 13.5 incorporates the expectancy theory variables into our motivation model. Valence and instrumentality combine to affect employees' willingness to put forth effort (that is, the degree to which they are energized to take action), while expectancy transforms intended effort ("I'm really going to work hard in this job") into actual effort. If you're offered rewards that you desire and you believe that you will in fact receive these rewards for good performance, you're highly likely to be energized to take action. However, you're not likely to actually exert effort unless you also believe that you can do the job (that is, that your efforts will lead to successful performance).

13-3b Motivating with Expectancy Theory

What practical steps can managers take to use expectancy theory to motivate employees? First, they can *systematically gather information to find out what employees want from their jobs*. In addition to individual managers directly asking employees what they want from their jobs (see Subsection 13-1d, "Motivating with the Basics"), companies need to survey their employees regularly to determine their wants, needs, and dissatisfactions. Because people consider the valence of all the possible rewards and outcomes that they can receive from their jobs, regular identification of wants, needs, and dissatisfactions gives companies the chance to turn negatively valent rewards and outcomes into positively valent rewards and outcomes, thus raising overall motivation and effort. Mark Peterman, vice president of client solutions at Maritz Incentives, says that individual employees are motivated in vastly different ways: "For some, being honored in front of one's peers is a great award, but for

Exhibit 13.5
Adding Expectancy Theory to the Model

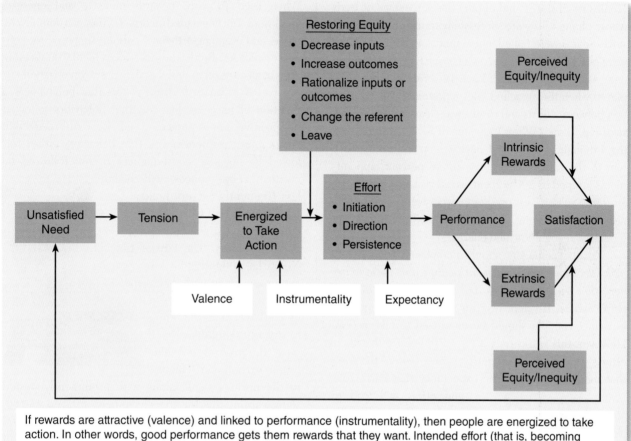

If rewards are attractive (valence) and linked to performance (instrumentality), then people are energized to take action. In other words, good performance gets them rewards that they want. Intended effort (that is, becoming energized to take action) turns into actual effort when people expect that their hard work and efforts will result in good performance. After all, why work hard if that hard work is wasted?

others, the thought of being put on display in front of peers embarrasses them." And companies have a long way to go to ensure that their employees feel valued, Peterman says. A Maritz survey found that only 27 percent of employees who want to be recognized by non-monetary incentives are recognized that way.[57] Such findings suggest that employers should routinely survey employees to identify not only the range of rewards that are valued by most employees but also to understand the preferences of specific employees.

Second, managers can *take specific steps to link rewards to individual performance in a way that is clear and understandable to employees.* Unfortunately, most employees are extremely dissatisfied with the link between pay and performance in their organizations, and

their companies are, too. A survey by compensation consulting firm Willis Towers Watson found that 80 percent of companies report that merit pay, which links pay to performance, does not increase employee performance. Not surprisingly, 68 percent report that pay is not clearly tied to performance difference, either.[58]

One way to establish a clear connection between pay and performance (see Chapter 11 for a discussion of compensation strategies) is for managers to publicize the way in which pay decisions are made. This is especially important given that only 52 percent of employees know how their pay increases are determined.[59] Inspired by fantasy sports leagues, **Clayton Homes** director of inside sales, David Schwall, had his sales managers become team "owners" who drafted sales representatives onto their sales teams, which competed against each other in a rotating schedule, with the best four teams moving on to the "championships." Sales reps (players) scored points by making more calls to sales leads, by increasing the percentage of leads who made appointments at Clayton Homes retail stores, and upping the percentage of leads whose phone calls were successfully transferred to a local store. Scores were tallied in real time, and the best scores were posted on TVs for everyone to see (poor scores were only visible within teams). Each sales rep's theme music played when they reached sales milestones. The connection between efforts and results was clear, prompting one sales rep to say, "When I saw one of my colleagues leaving, I thought—'Yes, now I can catch up and climb above him in the ranks.'" Calls rose by 18 percent, appointments jumped by 200 percent, as did visits to stores. And, after the "season" was over, employees were eager for the next season to begin, saying they missed the immediate feedback, recognition, and energy.[60]

Finally, managers should *empower employees to make decisions if management really wants them to believe that their hard work and effort will lead to good performance.* If valent rewards are linked to good performance, people should be energized to take action. However, this works only if they also believe that their efforts will lead to good performance. One of the ways that managers destroy the expectancy that hard work and effort will lead to good performance is by restricting what employees can do or by ignoring employees' ideas. In Chapter 9, you learned that *empowerment* is a feeling of intrinsic motivation in which workers perceive their work to have meaning and perceive themselves to be competent, to have an impact, and to be capable of self-determination.[61] So, if managers want workers to have strong expectancies, they should empower them to make decisions. Doing so will motivate employees to take active rather than passive roles in their work.

13-4 REINFORCEMENT THEORY

When used properly, rewards motivate and energize employees. But when used incorrectly, they can demotivate, baffle, and even anger them. Goals are supposed to motivate employees. But leaders who focus blindly on meeting goals at all costs often find that they destroy motivation.

Reinforcement theory says that behavior is a function of its consequences, that behaviors followed by positive consequences (that is, reinforced) will occur more frequently, and that behaviors either followed by negative consequences or not followed by positive consequences will occur less frequently.[62] Every holiday season, thousands of Christmas trees are cut down and stolen from private and public property. The city of Lincoln, Nebraska, is fighting back by spraying evergreen trees with fox urine. This urine produces no smell in cold weather, but emits a strong, skunk-like smell once the tree is brought into a warm home. Thanks to the noxious smell, along with prominently posted signs warning that the trees have been sprayed, thieves are no long cutting down Lincoln's evergreen trees.[63] More specifically, **reinforcement** is the process of changing behavior by changing the consequences that follow behavior.[64]

Reinforcement has two parts: reinforcement contingencies and schedules of reinforcement. **Reinforcement contingencies** are the cause-and-effect relationships between the performance of specific behaviors and specific consequences. For example, if you get docked an hour's pay for being late to work, then a reinforcement contingency exists between a behavior (being late to work) and a consequence (losing an hour's pay). A **schedule of reinforcement** is the set of rules regarding reinforcement contingencies such as which behaviors will be reinforced, which consequences will follow those behaviors, and the schedule by which those consequences will be delivered.[65]

Exhibit 13.6 incorporates reinforcement contingencies and reinforcement schedules into our motivation model. First, notice that extrinsic rewards and the schedules of reinforcement used to deliver them are the primary methods for creating reinforcement contingencies

Oleksandr Lytvynenko/Shutterstock.com

in organizations. In turn, those reinforcement contingencies directly affect valences (the attractiveness of rewards), instrumentality (the perceived link between rewards and performance), and effort (how hard employees will work).

*Let's learn more about reinforcement theory by examining **13-4a the components of reinforcement theory, 13-4b the different schedules for delivering reinforcement,** and **13-4c how to motivate with reinforcement theory.***

13-4a Components of Reinforcement Theory

As just described, *reinforcement contingencies* are the cause-and-effect relationships between the performance of specific behaviors and specific consequences. There are four kinds of reinforcement contingencies: positive reinforcement, negative reinforcement, punishment, and extinction.

Positive reinforcement strengthens behavior (that is, increases its frequency) by following behaviors with desirable consequences. Only 25 percent of U.S. employees use all of their paid time off each year. And even when on vacation, one-third work because they fear "getting behind," or because "no one else at my company can do my job." The Latin root of vacation is *vacare*, which means to "be unoccupied." That's impossible if you're working and responding to email while ostensibly on vacation. To prevent employees from working on vacation, Denver software company **Full Contact** pays a $7,500 time-off bonus—but only if employees resist making contact electronically, by phone, or by working in any other way during vacation.[66]

Negative reinforcement strengthens behavior by withholding an unpleasant consequence when employees perform a specific behavior. Negative reinforcement is also called *avoidance learning* because workers perform a behavior to *avoid* a negative consequence. A study at the University of Pennsylvania shows how well negative reinforcement works. Over three months, 281 employees were given a daily walking goal

One-third of U.S. employees work on vacation because they fear "getting behind," or because "no one else at my company can do my job."

of 7,000 steps. Thirty percent of those who were not rewarded for walking (the control group) met the daily goal. Thirty-five percent of those who were positively reinforced with a $1.40 per day for walking 7,000 steps met the goal. Finally, the negative reinforcement group was given $42 at the start of the study and was told they'd lose $1.40 each day they didn't walk 7,000 steps. Achieving the goal avoided the unpleasant consequence of losing money. Fifty-five percent who were negatively reinforced met the daily goal. Professor Mitesh Patel said, "It was surprising how dramatically effective loss aversion [negative reinforcement] was."[67]

By contrast, punishment weakens behavior (that is, decreases its frequency) by following behaviors with undesirable consequences. For example, the standard disciplinary or punishment process in most companies is an oral warning ("Don't ever do that again"), followed by a written warning ("This letter is to discuss the serious problem you're having with . . ."), followed by three days off without pay ("While you're at home not being paid, we want you to think hard about . . ."), followed by being fired ("That was your last chance"). Though punishment can weaken behavior, managers must be careful to avoid the backlash that sometimes occurs when employees are punished at work. In an undoubtedly unique approach, a furniture store in China punishes employees who don't meet daily sale goals by making them eat meal worms. At the end of each day, in public, employees who didn't meet their sales goals are given a cup of liquor containing worms to drink. An employee said, "Today's punishment is eating worms they bought from a pet market. Four worms for losing one customer."[68] A manager explained, "We set sales targets for the next day and everyone signs a guarantee. If anyone fails to achieve the target, he or she will accept the punishment voluntarily. The targets are set by employees, with the purpose of self-motivation."[69] Even though the sales targets are reportedly self-set, the punishment may be

Riccardo Piccinini/Shutterstock.com

Positive reinforcement
that strengthens behavior by following behaviors with desirable consequences

Negative reinforcement
that strengthens behavior by withholding an unpleasant consequence when employees perform a specific behavior

Exhibit 13.6
Adding Reinforcement Theory to the Model

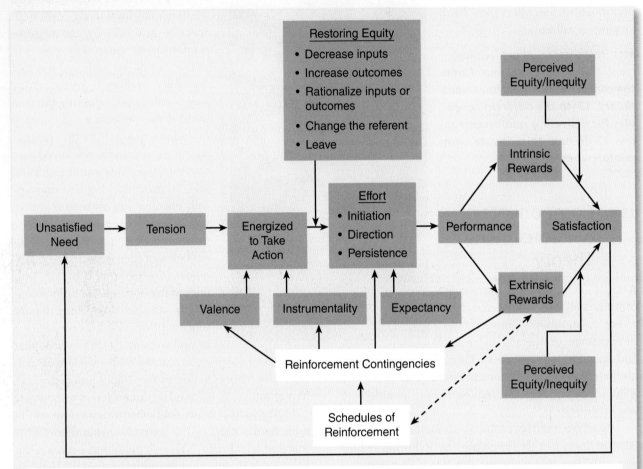

Extrinsic rewards and the schedules of reinforcement used to deliver them are the primary methods for creating reinforcement contingencies in organizations. In turn, those reinforcement contingencies directly affect valence (the attractiveness of rewards), instrumentality (the perceived link between rewards and performance), and effort (how hard employees will work).

short-lived since local officials view it as "a type of physical punishment," which employees can report, "to safeguard their rights and interests."[70]

Extinction is a reinforcement strategy in which a positive consequence is no longer allowed to follow a previously reinforced behavior. By removing the positive consequence, extinction weakens the behavior, making it less likely to occur. Based on the idea of positive reinforcement, most companies give company leaders and managers substantial financial

Extinction reinforcement in which a positive consequence is no longer allowed to follow a previously reinforced behavior, thus weakening the behavior

rewards when the company performs well. Based on the idea of extinction, you would then expect that leaders and managers would not be rewarded (that is, the positive consequence would be removed) when companies perform poorly. That's what happened at Burberry Group, the London-based fashion house at which CEO Christopher Bailey saw his pay cut by 75 percent after the company's revenue and profits dropped by 1 percent and 10 percent, respectively, and the value of its company stock plummeted by 35 percent in 2016.[71] If companies really want pay to reinforce the right kinds of behaviors rewards have to be removed, like at Burberry,

Burberry CEO Christopher Bailey suffered a 75 percent paycut when the company's revenue and profits dropped in 2016.

when company management doesn't produce successful performance.

13-4b Schedules for Delivering Reinforcement

As mentioned earlier, a *schedule of reinforcement* is the set of rules regarding reinforcement contingencies, such as which behaviors will be reinforced, which consequences will follow those behaviors, and the schedule by which those consequences will be delivered. There are two categories of reinforcement schedules: continuous and intermittent.

With **continuous reinforcement schedules**, a consequence follows every instance of a behavior. For example, employees working on a piece-rate pay system earn money (consequence) for every part they manufacture (behavior). The more they produce, the more they earn. By contrast, with **intermittent reinforcement**

schedules, consequences are delivered after a specified or average time has elapsed or after a specified or average number of behaviors has occurred. As Exhibit 13.7 shows, there are four types of intermittent reinforcement schedules. Two of these are based on time and are called *interval reinforcement schedules*; the other two, known as *ratio schedules*, are based on behaviors.

With **fixed interval reinforcement schedules**, consequences follow a behavior only after a fixed time has elapsed. For example, most people receive their paychecks on a fixed interval schedule (for example, once or twice per month). As long as they work (behavior) during a specified pay period (interval), they get a paycheck (consequence). With **variable interval reinforcement schedules**, consequences follow a behavior after different times, some shorter and some longer, that vary around a specified average time. On a 90-day variable interval reinforcement schedule, you might receive a bonus after 80 days or perhaps after 100 days, but the average interval between performing your job well (behavior) and receiving your bonus (consequence) would be 90 days.

With **fixed ratio reinforcement schedules**, consequences are delivered following a specific number of behaviors. For example, a car salesperson might receive a $1,000 bonus after every 10 sales. Therefore, a salesperson with only nine sales would not receive the bonus until finally selling that tenth car.

With **variable ratio reinforcement schedules**, consequences are delivered following a different number of behaviors, sometimes more and sometimes less, that vary around a specified average number of behaviors. With a 10-car variable ratio reinforcement schedule, a salesperson might receive the bonus after seven car

Continuous reinforcement schedule a schedule that requires a consequence to be administered following every instance of a behavior

Intermittent reinforcement schedule a schedule in which consequences are delivered after a specified or average time has elapsed or after a specified or average number of behaviors has occurred

Fixed interval reinforcement schedule an intermittent schedule in which consequences follow a behavior only after a fixed time has elapsed

Variable interval reinforcement schedule an intermittent schedule in which the time between a behavior and the following consequences varies around a specified average

Fixed ratio reinforcement schedule an intermittent schedule in which consequences are delivered following a specific number of behaviors

Variable ratio reinforcement schedule an intermittent schedule in which consequences are delivered following a different number of behaviors, sometimes more and sometimes less, that vary around a specified average number of behaviors

Exhibit 13.7
Intermittent Reinforcement Schedules

	Fixed	**Variable**
INTERVAL (TIME)	Consequences follow behavior after a fixed time has elapsed.	Consequences follow behavior after different times, some shorter and some longer, that vary around a specific average time.
RATIO (BEHAVIOR)	Consequences follow a specific number of behaviors.	Consequences follow a different number of behaviors, sometimes more and sometimes less, that vary around a specified average number of behaviors.

sales, or after 12, 11, or 9 sales, but the average number of cars sold before receiving the bonus would be 10 cars.

Which reinforcement schedules work best? In the past, the standard advice was to use continuous reinforcement when employees were learning new behaviors because reinforcement after each success leads to faster learning. Likewise, the standard advice was to use intermittent reinforcement schedules to maintain behavior after it is learned because intermittent rewards are supposed to make behavior much less subject to extinction.[72] Research shows, however, that except for interval-based systems, which usually produce weak results, the effectiveness of continuous reinforcement, fixed ratio, and variable ratio schedules differs very little.[73] In organizational settings, all three consistently produce large increases over noncontingent reward schedules. So managers should choose whichever of these three is easiest to use in their companies.

13-4c Motivating with Reinforcement Theory

What practical steps can managers take to use reinforcement theory to motivate employees? University of Nebraska business professor Fred Luthans, who has been studying the effects of reinforcement theory in organizations for more than a quarter of a century, says that there are five steps to motivating workers with reinforcement theory: *identify*, *measure*, *analyze*, *intervene*, and *evaluate* critical performance-related behaviors.[74]

Identify means singling out critical, observable, performance-related behaviors. These are the behaviors that are most important to successful job performance. In addition, they must also be easily observed so that they can be accurately measured. *Measure* means determining the baseline frequencies of these behaviors. In

other words, find out how often workers perform them. *Analyze* means studying the causes and consequences of these behaviors. Analyzing the causes helps managers create the conditions that produce these critical behaviors, and analyzing the consequences helps them determine if these behaviors produce the results that they want. *Intervene* means changing the organization by using positive and negative reinforcement to increase the frequency of these critical behaviors. *Evaluate* means assessing the extent to which the intervention actually changed workers' behavior. This is done by comparing behavior after the intervention to the original baseline of behavior before the intervention.

In addition to these five steps, managers should remember three other key things when motivating with reinforcement theory. First, *Don't reinforce the wrong behaviors*. Although reinforcement theory sounds simple, it's actually very difficult to put into practice. One of the most common mistakes is accidentally reinforcing the wrong behaviors. Sometimes organizations reinforce behaviors that they don't want! To encourage green driving in Norway, the national government exempted electric cars from fees for toll roads, tunnels, ferries, and parking. With one of the highest costs of living (30% higher than the United States), not having to pay those fees has resulted in a surge of electric car usage in Norway. For example, Arne Nordbo avoids a $20 one-way fee every time he drives through the 3.5 mile undersea tunnel leading in and out of Finnoy, an island-locked Norwegian town. Finnoy borrowed $70 million to dig the tunnel, expecting drivers like Nordbo to pay off the loan via their $40-a-day tunnel fees. But with electric cars now making up 25 percent of all tunnel traffic, "We won't be able to pay down the tunnel," says Gro Skartveit, head of the company that operates the tunnel.[75] The Norwegian government now loses half a billion dollars a year in forgone tax revenue, and tunnel/ferry fees.

CAN PUNISHMENT GET DOG OWNERS TO PICK UP AFTER FIDO?

Dog owners are doing a terrible job of cleaning up after their pets. Cities have tried dispensing free dog poop baggies and posting signs asking dog owners to "Keep [insert city name here] Clean for All." Since asking nicely didn't work, many cities are becoming more vigilant about punishing dog owners who don't pick up after their dogs. The city of Colmenar Viejo, Spain, began issuing fines after hiring private detectives to video record dogs and their offending owners. Brunete, Spain, used volunteers to identify lazy dog owners who surreptitiously collected dogs' names ("My, what a cute dog! What's her name?"). After dog names were matched to city registration records, offenders were mailed their dogs' droppings. Said Mayor Borja Gutierrez, "It's your dog, it's your dog poop. We are just returning it to you." Incidents of unscooped dog poop are now down by 70 percent.

Source: K. Brulliard, "Cities Go to Extreme Lengths to Tackle a Dog Poop Epidemic," *Washington Post*, April 27, 2016, accessed May 5, 2016, https://www.washingtonpost.com/news/animalia/wp/2016/04/27/madrid-is-the-latest-city-to-fight-a-dog-poop-epidemic-that-just-wont-go-away/.

Likewise, road operator revenues are down $40 million. Be careful what you reward!

Managers should also *correctly administer punishment at the appropriate time.* Many managers believe that punishment can change workers' behavior and help them improve their job performance. Furthermore, managers believe that fairly punishing workers also lets other workers know what is or isn't acceptable.[76] A danger of using punishment is that it can produce a backlash against managers and companies. But, if administered properly, punishment can weaken the frequency of undesirable behaviors without creating a backlash.[77] To be effective, the punishment must be strong enough to stop the undesired behavior and must be administered objectively (same rules applied to everyone), impersonally (without emotion or anger), consistently and contingently (each time improper behavior occurs), and quickly (as soon as possible following the undesirable behavior). In addition, managers should clearly explain what the appropriate behavior is and why the employee is being punished. Employees typically respond well when punishment is administered this way.[78]

Finally, managers should *choose the simplest and most effective schedule of reinforcement.* When choosing a schedule of reinforcement, managers need to balance effectiveness against simplicity. In fact, the more complex the schedule of reinforcement, the more likely it is to be misunderstood and resisted by managers and employees. For example, a forestry and logging company experimented with a unique variable ratio schedule. When tree-planters finished planting a bag of seedlings (about 1,000 seedlings per bag), they got to flip a coin. If they called the coin flip correctly (heads or tails), they were paid $4, double the regular rate of $2 per bag. If they called the coin flip incorrectly, they got nothing. The company began having problems when several workers and a manager, who was a part-time minister, claimed that the coin flip was a form of gambling. Then another worker found that the company was taking out too much money for taxes from workers' paychecks. Because the workers didn't really understand the reinforcement schedule, they blamed the payment plan associated with it and accused the company of trying to cheat them out of their money. After all of these problems, the researchers who implemented the variable ratio schedule concluded that "the results of this study may not be so much an indication of the relative effectiveness of different schedules of reinforcement as they are an indication of the types of problems that one encounters when applying these concepts in an industrial setting."[79] In short, choose the simplest, most effective schedule of reinforcement. Because continuous reinforcement, fixed ratio, and variable ratio schedules are about equally effective, continuous reinforcement schedules may be the best choice in many instances by virtue of their simplicity.

Performance feedback—information about the quality or quantity of past performance—is key to attaining goals.

Rawpixel.com/Shutterstock.com

13-5 GOAL-SETTING THEORY

Goal a target, objective, or result that someone tries to accomplish

Goal-setting theory the theory that people will be motivated to the extent to which they accept specific, challenging goals and receive feedback that indicates their progress toward goal achievement

Goal specificity the extent to which goals are detailed, exact, and unambiguous

Goal difficulty the extent to which a goal is hard or challenging to accomplish

Goal acceptance the extent to which people consciously understand and agree to goals

Performance feedback information about the quality or quantity of past performance that indicates whether progress is being made toward the accomplishment of a goal

The basic model of motivation with which we began this chapter showed that individuals feel tension after becoming aware of an unfulfilled need. When they experience tension, they search for and select courses of action that they believe will eliminate this tension. In other words, they direct their behavior toward something. This something is a goal. A **goal** is a target, objective, or result that someone tries to accomplish. **Goal-setting theory** says that people will be motivated to the extent to which they accept specific, challenging goals and receive feedback that indicates their progress toward goal achievement.

*Let's learn more about goal setting by examining **13-5a the components of goal-setting theory** and **13-5b how to motivate with goal-setting theory**.*

13-5a Components of Goal-Setting Theory

The basic components of goal-setting theory are goal specificity, goal difficulty, goal acceptance, and performance feedback.[80] **Goal specificity** is the extent to which goals are detailed, exact, and unambiguous. Specific goals, such as "I'm going to have a 3.0 average this semester," are more motivating than general goals, such as "I'm going to get better grades this semester."

Goal difficulty is the extent to which a goal is hard or challenging to accomplish. Difficult goals, such as "I'm going to have a 3.5 average and make the dean's list this semester," are more motivating than easy goals, such as "I'm going to have a 2.0 average this semester."

Goal acceptance, which is similar to the idea of goal commitment discussed in Chapter 5, is the extent to which people consciously understand and agree to goals. Accepted goals, such as "I really want to get a 3.5 average this semester to show my parents how much I've improved," are more motivating than unaccepted goals, such as "My parents really want me to get a 3.5 average this semester, but there's so much more I'd rather do on campus than study!"

Performance feedback is information about the quality or quantity of past performance and indicates whether progress is being made toward the accomplishment of a goal. General Electric (GE) managers now use a smartphone app to give employees immediate performance feedback. The app prompts managers to provide detailed feedback using categories such as *Insights* (for current challenges), *Consider* (for changes to make), and *Continue* (for actions to keep doing). Leonardo Baldassarre and Brien Finken, of GE's Oil & Gas Turbomachinery Solutions explain, "For example, an engineer was asked to 'consider' being more open to supplier recommendations and to visit the supplier for a day. He did, and in GE's Real-Time Performance Development the following weeks the change was apparent. He championed a new approach that doubled our overall savings rate on budgeted project costs. Similarly, a procurement specialist was told to 'continue' encouraging volume pricing and other such practices among vendors to increase savings."[81]

Exhibit 13.8
Adding Goal-Setting Theory to the Model

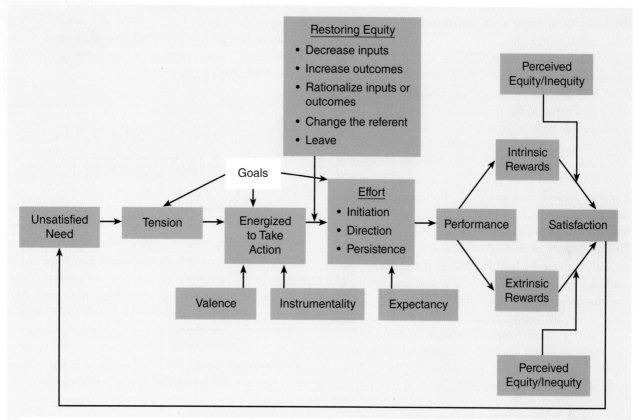

Goals create tension between the goal, which is the desired future state of affairs, and where the employee or company is now, meaning the current state of affairs. This tension can be satisfied only by achieving or abandoning the goal. Goals also energize behavior. When faced with unaccomplished goals, employees typically develop plans and strategies to reach those goals. Finally, goals influence persistence.

How does goal setting work? To start, challenging goals focus employees' attention (that is, direction of effort) on the critical aspects of their jobs and away from unimportant areas. Goals also energize behavior. When faced with unaccomplished goals, employees typically develop plans and strategies to reach those goals. Goals also create tension between the goal, which is the desired future state of affairs, and where the employee or company is now, meaning the current state of affairs. This tension can be satisfied only by achieving or abandoning the goal. Finally, goals influence persistence. Because goals only go away when they are accomplished, employees are more likely to persist in their efforts in the presence of goals, especially with performance feedback. Exhibit 13.8 incorporates goals into the motivation

model by showing how goals directly affect tension, effort, and the extent to which employees are energized to take action.

13-5b Motivating with Goal-Setting Theory

What practical steps can managers take to use goal-setting theory to motivate employees? Managers can do three things, beginning with *assigning specific, challenging goals*. One of the simplest, most effective ways to motivate workers is to give them specific, challenging goals. When the chief of staff of a CEO received feedback that he micromanaged and didn't listen, he and his executive coach set specific, challenging goals to track his progress. Because changing work habits is difficult, he started with just three long-term goals, each accompanied by one short-term goal. For his "listen better" goal, the short-term goal was "attending one meeting a day without devices (smart phone, tablet, or laptop)." The short-term goal then increased to "two meetings a day," and so on, until, after four months, he no longer took devices to meetings.[82]

Second, managers should *make sure workers truly accept organizational goals*. Specific, challenging goals won't motivate workers unless they really accept, understand, and agree to the organization's goals. For this to occur, people must see the goals as fair and reasonable. Employees must also trust management and believe that managers are using goals to clarify what is expected from them rather than to exploit or threaten them ("If you don't achieve these goals . . ."). Participative goal setting, in which managers and employees generate goals together, can help increase trust and understanding and thus acceptance of goals. Furthermore, providing workers with training can help increase goal acceptance, particularly when workers don't believe they are capable of reaching the organization's goals.[83]

Finally, managers should *provide frequent, specific, performance-related feedback*. After employees have accepted specific, challenging goals, they should receive frequent performance-related feedback so that they can track their progress toward goal completion. Feedback leads to stronger motivation and effort in three ways.[84] Receiving specific feedback about the quality of their performance can encourage employees who don't have specific, challenging goals to set goals to improve their performance. After people meet goals, performance feedback often encourages them to set higher, more difficult goals. And feedback lets people know whether they need to increase their efforts or change strategies in order to accomplish their goals.

13-6 MOTIVATING WITH THE INTEGRATED MODEL

We began this chapter by defining motivation as the set of forces that initiates, directs, and makes people persist in their efforts to accomplish a goal. We also asked the basic question that managers ask when they try to figure out how to motivate their workers: What leads to effort? The answer to that question is likely to be somewhat different for each employee. So, if you're having difficulty figuring out why people aren't motivated where you work, check your Review Card for a useful, theory-based starting point.

STUDY TOOLS 13

LOCATED IN TEXTBOOK
☐ Rip out and review chapter review card.

LOCATED AT WWW.CENGAGEBRAIN.COM
☐ Gain unique perspectives on key concepts with new 4LTR concept videos in the e-book.
☐ Increase your comprehension with Aplia for MGMT11.
☐ Complete interactive content within the e-book.

14 | Leadership

After you finish
this chapter, go
to **PAGE 329** for
STUDY TOOLS

LEARNING OBJECTIVES

14-1 Explain what leadership is.

14-2 Describe who leaders are and what effective leaders do.

14-3 Explain Fiedler's contingency theory.

14-4 Describe how path-goal theory works.

14-5 Explain the normative decision theory.

14-6 Explain how visionary (that is, charismatic or transformational) leadership helps leaders achieve strategic leadership.

14-1 LEADERS VERSUS MANAGERS

If you've ever been in charge, or even just thought about it, chances are you've considered questions such as these: Do I have what it takes to lead? What are the most important things leaders do? How can I transform a poorly performing department, division, or company? Do I need to adjust my leadership depending on the situation and the employee? Why doesn't my leadership inspire people? If you feel overwhelmed at the prospect of being a leader, you're not alone—millions of leaders in organizations across the world struggle with these fundamental leadership issues on a daily basis.

Even the world's best leaders have doubts. Theo Epstein is president of baseball operations for Major League Baseball's Chicago Cubs, who, after 108 years since their last championship, rallied from a three games to one deficit against the Cleveland Indians to win game 7 of the 2016 worlds series in extra innings. In 2017, *Fortune* magazine named him "the world's best leader." On being told of this honor, he said, "Um, I can't even get my dog to stop peeing in the house. That is ridiculous. The whole thing is patently ridiculous. It's baseball—a pastime involving a lot of chance. If [Ben] Zobrist's ball is three inches farther off the line, I'm on the hot seat for a failed five-year plan. And I'm not even the best leader in our organization; our players are."[1]

Whether you construct buildings, create and innovate to bring new products to markets, help a company gain competitive advantage and thereby increase profits, or build a historically bad baseball franchise into world champs, **leadership** is the process of influencing others to achieve group or organizational goals. The knowledge and skills you'll learn in this chapter won't make the task of leadership less daunting, but they will help you navigate your journey as a leader.

According to late business professor Warren Bennis, the primary difference between leaders and managers is that leaders are concerned with doing the right thing, while managers are concerned with doing things right.[2] In other words, leaders begin with the question "What should we be doing?" while managers start with "How can we do what we're already doing better?" Before becoming the CEO of open source software company Red Hat, Jim Whitehurst was chief operating officer of Delta Airlines.

When Whitehurst made the switch, he knew that his new job would be different. "Red Hat is a high-growth company with incredible opportunities. My job is a lot more about developing strategies, inspiring people, inspiring creativity," he said. As CEO, Whitehurst found, "The input you receive will often conflict. Some investors may want you to focus more on short-term results than long-term growth. Different customers may want very different things. Even individual board members can have very different opinions . . . That's one of the most challenging things about the job; since you have multiple bosses with multiple agendas, you constantly wonder, 'Am I doing the right things?'"[3]

Leaders focus on vision, mission, goals, and objectives, while managers focus on productivity and efficiency. Managers see themselves as preservers of the status quo, while leaders see themselves as promoters of change and challengers of the status quo in that they encourage creativity and risk taking. The Chicago Cubs had three straight

Leadership the process of influencing others to achieve group or organizational goals losing seasons before Epstein became president of baseball operations in 2012, when he began the process of changing the team's "lovable losers" culture by telling players, coaches, office and behind-the-scenes employees that the Cub would win the World Series within five years (they did). As described by *Sport's Illustrated's* Tom Verducci, "Back in January 2012, Epstein summoned every manager, coach, scout, instructor, trainer, and baseball operations person in the Cubs' organization to a budget hotel in Mesa, Arizona, for a four-day summit. They spent one day on hitting philosophy, one day on pitching philosophy, one day on defense and base-running philosophy—and one day on character: 'What types of human beings we wanted and what our expectations would be for players, how we want them to behave,' says Epstein."[4] Verducci further explained that Epstein, "set about changing the Cubs' culture so that rather than expecting to lose, members of the organization expected to thrive and win through camaraderie and attention to detail. 'That's so Cub' became short hand for playing baseball the right way."[5]

Another difference is that managers have a relatively short-term perspective, while leaders take a long-term view. Managers are concerned with control and limiting the choices of others, while leaders are more concerned with expanding people's choices and options.[6] Managers also solve problems so that others can do their work, while leaders inspire and motivate others to find their own solutions. Finally, managers are also more concerned with *means*, how to get things done, while leaders are more concerned with *ends*, what gets done.

Although leaders are different from managers, organizations need them both. Managers are critical to getting out the day-to-day work, and leaders are critical to inspiring employees and setting the organization's long-term direction. The key issue for any organization is the extent to which it is properly led and properly managed. As Bennis said in summing up the difference between leaders and managers, "American organizations (and probably those in much of the rest of the industrialized world) are underled and overmanaged. They do not pay enough attention

to doing the right thing, while they pay too much attention to doing things right."[7]

bigjom jom/Shutterstock.com

14-2 WHO LEADERS ARE AND WHAT LEADERS DO

Jack Dorsey, Twitter's CEO, once a micromanager, has become a listener who asks questions to facilitate discussion and strategic direction with his leadership team.[8] Mark Donegan, CEO of Precision Castparts, which makes complex parts for aircrafts and aircraft engines, is known for being a hard-nosed businessperson, focused more on tasks than people. His predecessor and mentor, Bill McCormick, says, "I was relatively relentless. But he was a lot more relentless."[9]

Which one is likely to be successful as a CEO? According to a survey of 1,542 senior managers, it's the extrovert. Of those 1,542 senior managers, 47 percent felt that extroverts make better CEOs, while 65 percent said that being an introvert hurts a CEO's chances of success.[10] So clearly, senior managers believe that extroverted CEOs are better leaders. But are they? Not necessarily. In fact, a relatively high percentage of CEOs, 40 percent, are introverts. Elena Lytkina Botelho, a partner at executive consulting firm ghSmart, says, "The biggest aha, overall, is that some of the things that make CEOs attractive to the board have no bearing on their performance. Like most human beings, they get seduced by [extroverts, who are] charismatic, polished presenters. They simply do better in interviews."[11]

So, what makes a good leader? Does leadership success depend on who leaders are, such as introverts or extroverts, or on what leaders do and how they behave?

Let's learn more about who leaders are by investigating 14-2a leadership traits and 14-2b leadership behaviors.

14-2a Leadership Traits

Trait theory is one way to describe who leaders are. **Trait theory** says that effective leaders possess a similar set of traits or characteristics. **Traits** are relatively stable characteristics such as abilities, psychological motives, or consistent patterns of behavior. For example, trait theory holds that leaders are taller and more confident and have greater physical stamina (that is, higher energy levels) than nonleaders. In fact, studies show we perceive those in authority as being taller than they actually are, and that

Trait theory a leadership theory that holds that effective leaders possess a similar set of traits or characteristics

Traits relatively stable characteristics, such as abilities, psychological motives, or consistent patterns of behavior taller people see themselves as more qualified to lead.[12] Indeed, while just 14.5 percent of men are six feet tall, 58 percent of *Fortune* 500 CEOs are six feet or taller. Author Malcolm Gladwell says, "We have a sense, in our minds, of what a leader is supposed to look like, and that stereotype is so powerful that when someone fits it, we simply become blind to other considerations.[13] Likewise, in terms of physical stamina, companies whose CEOs have run and finished a marathon have a stock valuation that is 5 percent larger than those whose CEO had not.[14] Another study found a small relationship between *Fortune* 500 CEO face width (thought to indicate a leader's dominance, ambition, and power) and company profitability.[15] Trait theory is also known as the "great person" theory because early versions of the theory stated that leaders are born, not made. In other words, you either have the right stuff to be a leader, or you don't. And if you don't, there is no way to get it.

For some time, it was thought that trait theory was wrong and that there are no consistent trait differences between leaders and nonleaders, or between effective and ineffective leaders. However, more recent evidence shows that "successful leaders are not like other people," that successful leaders are indeed different from the rest of us.[16] More specifically, leaders are different from nonleaders in the following traits: drive, the desire to lead, honesty/integrity, self-confidence, emotional stability, cognitive ability, and knowledge of the business.[17]

Drive refers to high levels of effort and is characterized by achievement, motivation, initiative, energy, and tenacity. In terms of achievement and ambition, leaders always try to make improvements or achieve success in what they're doing. Because of their initiative, they have strong desires to promote change or solve problems. At Amazon, founder Jeff Bezos calls this "high-velocity decision making." Bezos says, "… most decisions should probably be made with somewhere around 70 percent of the information you wish you had. If you wait for 90 percent, in most cases, you're probably being slow. Plus, either way, you need to be good at quickly recognizing and correcting bad decisions. If you're good at course correcting, being wrong may be less costly than you think, whereas being slow is going to be expensive for sure."[18] Leaders who possess drive typically have more energy—they have to, given the long hours they put in and followers' expectations that they be positive and upbeat. Thus, leaders must have physical, mental, and emotional vitality. Leaders are also more tenacious than nonleaders and are better at overcoming obstacles and problems that would deter most of us.

Successful leaders also have a stronger *desire to lead*. They want to be in charge and think about ways

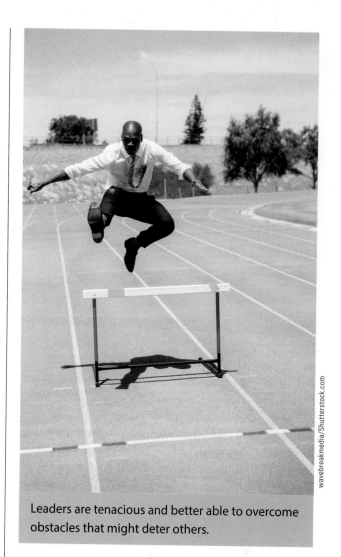

Leaders are tenacious and better able to overcome obstacles that might deter others.

wavebreakmedia/Shutterstock.com

to influence or convince others about what should or shouldn't be done. *Honesty/integrity* is also important to leaders. *Honesty*, being truthful with others, is a cornerstone of leadership. Without it, leaders won't be trusted. When leaders are honest, subordinates are willing to overlook other flaws. Bezos says, "If you have conviction on a particular direction even though there's no consensus, it's helpful to say, 'Look, I know we disagree on this but will you gamble with me on it? Disagree and commit?'"[19] He cites the example of a new Amazon Studios TV show that he didn't like, but which was still approved for funding. "I told the team my [negative] view… They had a completely different opinion and wanted to go ahead. I wrote back right away with, "I disagree and commit and hope it becomes the most watched thing we've ever made."[20] *Integrity* is the extent to which leaders do what they say they will do. Leaders may be honest and have good intentions, but if they don't consistently deliver on what they promise, they won't be trusted.

CONSIDERATE LEADER BEHAVIOR: SHOULD THE BOSS BE A HUGGER?

Receptionist Felicia Flewelling gets a hug and a twirl from her boss each morning. She says, "You go in for like a regular hug and then you just spin in a circle. It makes it a lot easier to come into work." Sam Lavoie got hugged by the same boss during his job interview. "I was like, 'Oh, OK, this is happening… It was two strangers just hugging." Now that he's been hired, he's declared a nonhugging policy, which the boss respects.

Attorney Aaron Goldstein warns his corporate clients against initiating hugs. The only safe hug, he says, is the "HR hug," which is a sideways, one-armed momentary hug across the back of the shoulders to be used when you're "looking not to offend anyone."

Source: R. Feintzeig, "Embraceable You: When the CEO Is a Hugger," *Wall Street Journal*, April 16, 2017, accessed April 30, 2017, https://www.wsj.com/articles/embraceable-you-when-the-ceo-is-a-hugger-1492380506.

Jan Mika/123RF

Self-confidence, or believing in one's abilities, also distinguishes leaders from nonleaders. Self-confident leaders are more decisive and assertive and are more likely to gain others' confidence. Moreover, self-confident leaders will admit mistakes because they view them as learning opportunities rather than as refutations of their leadership capabilities. Krispy Kreme looked for candidates who demonstrated these specific qualities during a recent CEO hunt. According to chair (and former CEO) James Morgan, humility and servant leadership are strong aspects of Krispy Kreme's culture. Morgan says that Tony Thomson, who was selected to succeed him, "exhibited those two characteristics strongly." Not everyone who joins the company understands how integral this philosophy is, however. One senior manager would not collaborate with his team on new product or operation ideas, but would take credit for them and would steal the limelight when they were presented to the executive leadership team. This executive was later fired, said Morgan, because, "He didn't understand the humility part."[21]

Leaders also have *emotional stability*. Even when things go wrong, they remain even-tempered and consistent in their outlook and in the way they treat others. After experiencing disappointing results in its mobile unit, Samsung appointed DJ Koh, who is known for his even-tempered demeanor, to lead the division. Having joined Samsung out of college, Koh quickly rose through the company ranks because he was well-liked and kept a low-profile. In contrast to his hard-charging predecessor, employees describe Koh as a "predictable, realistic, and reasonable executive who is hardworking and direct." One of his close colleagues adds, "He's not a screamer."[22] Leaders who can't control their emotions, who anger quickly or attack and blame others for mistakes, are unlikely to be trusted.

Leaders are also smart—they typically have strong *cognitive abilities*. This doesn't mean that leaders are necessarily geniuses—far from it. But it does mean that leaders have the capacity to analyze large amounts of seemingly unrelated, complex information and see patterns, opportunities, or threats where others might not see them. Finally, leaders also know their stuff, which means they have superior technical knowledge about the businesses they run. Leaders who have a good *knowledge of the business* understand the key technological decisions and concerns facing their companies. More often than not, studies indicate that effective leaders have long, extensive experience in their industries. Emirates Airline CEO Tim Clark has been in the airline industry for four decades. Starting with just two planes 32 years ago, Emirates is the world's largest international carrier thanks to his 30+ years of leadership. Emirates's massive industrial dishwashers clean 3.5 million items a day. All the meals it serves are made in its flight kitchens, which bakes 25,000 muffins a day. And, to keep passengers happy, it owns a wine cellar in Burgundy, France for aging 3.75 million bottles of wine.[23]

14-2b Leadership Behaviors

Thus far, you've read about who leaders *are*. But traits alone are not enough to make a successful leader. They are, however, a precondition for success. After all, it's hard to imagine a truly successful leader who lacks most of these qualities. Leaders who have these traits (or many of them) must then take actions that encourage people to achieve group or organizational goals.[24] Accordingly, we now examine what leaders *do*, meaning the behaviors they perform or the actions they take to influence others to achieve group or organizational goals.

Researchers at the University of Michigan, the Ohio State University, and the University of Texas examined the specific behaviors that leaders use to improve subordinate satisfaction and performance. Hundreds of studies were conducted, and hundreds of leader behaviors were examined. At all three universities, two basic leader behaviors emerged as central to successful leadership: initiating structure (called *job-centered leadership* at the University of Michigan and *concern for production* at the University of Texas) and considerate leader behavior (called *employee-centered leadership* at the University of Michigan and *concern for people* at the University of Texas).[25] These two leader behaviors form the basis for many of the leadership theories discussed in this chapter.

Initiating structure is the degree to which a leader structures the roles of followers by setting goals, giving directions, setting deadlines, and assigning tasks. A leader's ability to initiate structure primarily affects subordinates' job performance. Precision Castparts' CEO Mark Donegan, described earlier as focused more on tasks than people, initiated structure in terms of the performance goals and directions (lower costs) for its 150+ factories. AeroDynamic Advisory's Kevin Michaels says, "They're maniacs about operational improvement. That comes right from Mark Donegan." Donegan has regular on-site reviews at every factory every three months, meeting with the factory's plant manager, head of finance, the business segment president to whom the plant manager reports, and the factory's head of operations. Prior to each meeting, 26 identical charts, used across all 150 factories, are used to track productivity, plant earnings, product market share, and fixed costs per employee. When once asked how the company could keep costs so low, he responded, "We're a different breed. We're kind of a blue-collar, in-your-face, slug-it-out, down-in-the-trenches type of company. And I take great pride in that."[26]

Consideration is the extent to which a leader is friendly, approachable, and supportive and shows concern for employees. Consideration primarily affects subordinates' job satisfaction. Specific leader consideration behaviors include listening to employees' problems and concerns, consulting with employees before making decisions, and treating employees as equals. When Chip Conley joined Airbnb at age 52 as the strategic advisor for hospitality and leadership, he had run a boutique hotel chain for 24 years, but he'd never used Airbnb, didn't know how to code software, was twice as old as most employees, and had a new boss, "a smart guy," 21 years his junior. He

Airbnb's Chip Conley utilizes a considerate leadership style as he learns from those who are younger in age and senior in authority to him.

quickly adopted a considerate leadership style. He says, "More than anything, I listened and watched intently, with as little judgment or ego as possible… Part of my job was to just observe. Often I would leave a meeting and discreetly ask one of my fellow leaders, who might be two decades younger than I was, if they were open to some private feedback on how to read the emotions in the room, or the motivations of a particular engineer, a little more effectively."[27] Often he would say, "I'll offer you some emotional intelligence for your digital intelligence."[28]

Although researchers at all three universities generally agreed that initiating structure and consideration were basic leader behaviors, their interpretation differed on how these two behaviors are related to one another and which are necessary for effective leadership. The University of Michigan studies indicated that initiating structure and consideration were mutually exclusive behaviors on opposite ends of the same continuum. In other words, leaders who wanted to be more considerate would have to do less initiating of structure (and vice versa). The University of Michigan studies also indicated that only considerate leader behaviors (that is, employee-centered behaviors) were associated with successful leadership. By contrast, researchers at the Ohio State University and the University of Texas found that initiating structure and consideration were independent behaviors, meaning that leaders can be considerate and initiate structure at the same time. Additional evidence confirms this finding.[29] The same researchers also

Initiating structure the degree to which a leader structures the roles of followers by setting goals, giving directions, setting deadlines, and assigning tasks

Consideration the extent to which a leader is friendly, approachable, and supportive and shows concern for employees

Exhibit 14.1
Blake/Mouton Leadership Grid

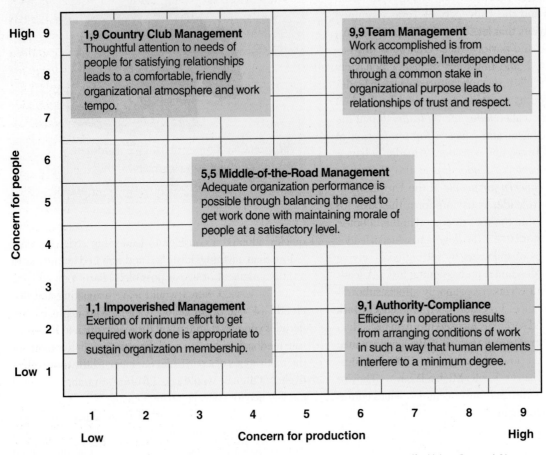

Concern for people

High 9

1,9 Country Club Management
Thoughtful attention to needs of people for satisfying relationships leads to a comfortable, friendly organizational atmosphere and work tempo.

9,9 Team Management
Work accomplished is from committed people. Interdependence through a common stake in organizational purpose leads to relationships of trust and respect.

5,5 Middle-of-the-Road Management
Adequate organization performance is possible through balancing the need to get work done with maintaining morale of people at a satisfactory level.

1,1 Impoverished Management
Exertion of minimum effort to get required work done is appropriate to sustain organization membership.

9,1 Authority-Compliance
Efficiency in operations results from arranging conditions of work in such a way that human elements interfere to a minimum degree.

Low 1

Low   1   2   3   4   5   6   7   8   9   High
Concern for production

Source: R. R. Blake and A. A. McCanse, "The Leadership Grid®," Leadership Dilemmas—Grid Solutions (Houston: Gulf Publishing Company), 21.

concluded that the most effective leaders were strong on both initiating structure and considerate leader behaviors.

This "high-high" approach can be seen in the upper-right corner of the Blake/Mouton leadership grid, as shown in Exhibit 14.1. Blake and Mouton used two leadership behaviors, concern for people (that is, consideration) and concern for production (that is, initiating structure), to categorize five different leadership styles. Both behaviors are rated on a nine-point scale, with 1 representing "low" and 9 representing "high." Blake and Mouton suggest that a "high-high," or 9,9, leadership style is the best. They call this style *team management* because leaders who use it display a high concern for people (9) and a high concern for production (9).

By contrast, leaders use a 9,1 *authority-compliance* leadership style when they have a high concern for production and a low concern for people. A 1,9 *country club* style occurs when leaders care about having a friendly,

enjoyable work environment but don't really pay much attention to production or performance. The worst leadership style, according to the grid, is the 1,1 *impoverished* leader, who shows little concern for people or production and does the bare minimum needed to keep his or her job. Finally, the 5,5 *middle-of-the-road* style occurs when leaders show a moderate amount of concern for both people and production.

Is the team management style, with a high concern for production and a high concern for people, the best leadership style? Logically, it would seem so. Why wouldn't you want to show high concern for both people and production? Nonetheless, nearly 50 years of research indicates that there isn't one best leadership style. The best leadership style depends on the situation. In other words, no one leadership behavior by itself and no one combination of leadership behaviors work well across all situations and employees.

14-3 PUTTING LEADERS IN THE RIGHT SITUATION: FIEDLER'S CONTINGENCY THEORY

After leader traits and behaviors, the situational approach to leadership is the third major method used in the study of leadership. We'll review four major situational approaches to leadership—Fiedler's contingency theory, path-goal theory, Hersey and Blanchard's Situational Leadership theory, and Vroom, Yetton, and Jago's normative decision model. All assume that the effectiveness of any **leadership style**, the way a leader generally behaves toward followers, depends on the situation.[30] A study of 130 restaurants in a pizza franchise examined the interaction between how extroverted store managers were and how involved employees were in trying "to bring about improved procedures [in the store.]" Profits were 16 percent *above* average in stores with extroverted managers and less involved employees. In those instances, the strengths of the more outgoing boss fit well with the less involved employees. By contrast, profits were 14 percent *below* average in stores with extroverted leaders and highly involved employees. Why? Because the extroverted leaders were less comfortable with employees who wanted a say in making improvements. Again, leadership success depends on the situation.[31]

According to situational leadership theories, there is no one best leadership style. But one of these situational theories differs from the other three in one significant way. Fiedler's contingency theory assumes that leadership styles are consistent and difficult to change. Therefore, leaders must be placed in or matched to a situation that fits their leadership style. By contrast, the other three situational theories all assume that leaders are capable of adapting and adjusting their leadership styles to fit the demands of different situations.

Fiedler's **contingency theory** states that in order to maximize work group performance, leaders must be matched to the right leadership situation.[32] More specifically, the first basic assumption of Fiedler's theory is that leaders are effective when the work groups they lead perform well. So, instead of judging leaders' effectiveness by what they do (that is, initiating structure and consideration) or who they are (that is, trait theory), Fiedler assesses leaders by the conduct and performance of the people they supervise. Second, Fiedler assumes that leaders are generally unable to change their leadership styles and that they will be more effective when their styles are matched to the proper situation. This explains why company founders are not always the best suited to lead their companies. Evernote, a software company known for its digital note taking applications, was growing at such a rate that it eventually surpassed founder Phil Libin's ability to lead it. Although the company is valued at roughly $1 billion, Evernote began to stumble as it transitioned from a free app to a paid subscription service for professionals. After cutting about 13 percent of its staff and closing some global operations, Libin brought in a former Google executive to be Evernote's new CEO. At the same time, Evernote's board named Jeff Shotts, a former finance executive from eBay, as its new CFO. Shotts explained the need for different leadership this way: "The company is transitioning from startup mode to a more mature organization.[33]

Let's learn more about Fiedler's contingency theory by examining **14-3a the least preferred coworker and leadership styles, 14-3b situational favorableness,** *and* **14-3c how to match leadership styles to situations**.

14-3a Leadership Style: Least Preferred Coworker

When Fiedler refers to *leadership style*, he means the way that leaders generally behave toward their followers. Do the leaders yell and scream and blame others when things go wrong? Or do they correct mistakes by listening and then quietly but directly make their point? Do they take credit for others' work when things go right? Or do they make sure that those who did the work receive the credit they rightfully deserve? Do they let others make their own decisions

Leadership style the way a leader generally behaves toward followers

Contingency theory a leadership theory states that to maximize work group performance, leaders must be matched to the situation that best fits their leadership style and hold them accountable for the results? Or do they micromanage, insisting that all decisions be approved first by them? Fiedler also assumes that leadership styles are tied to leaders' underlying needs and personalities. Because personalities and needs are relatively stable, he assumes that leaders are generally incapable of changing their leadership styles. In other words, the way that leaders treat people now is probably the way they've always treated others. So, according to Fiedler, if your boss's first instinct is to yell and scream and blame others, chances are he or she has always done that.

Fiedler uses a questionnaire called the Least Preferred Coworker (LPC) scale to measure leadership style. When completing the LPC scale, people are instructed to consider all of the people with whom they have ever worked and then to choose the one person with whom they have worked *least* well. Fiedler explains, "This does not have to be the person you liked least well, but should be the one person with whom you have the most trouble getting the job done."[34]

Would you describe your LPC as pleasant, friendly, supportive, interesting, cheerful, and sincere? Or would you describe the person as unpleasant, unfriendly, hostile, boring, gloomy, and insincere? People who describe their LPC in a positive way (scoring 64 and above) have *relationship-oriented* leadership styles. After all, if they can still be positive about their least preferred coworker, they must be people-oriented. By contrast, people who describe their LPC in a negative way (scoring 57 or below) have *task-oriented* leadership styles. Given a choice, they'll focus first on getting the job done and second on making sure everyone gets along. Finally, those with moderate scores (from 58 to 63) have a more *flexible* leadership style and can be somewhat relationship-oriented or somewhat task-oriented.

14-3b Situational Favorableness

Fiedler assumes that leaders will be more effective when their leadership styles are matched to the proper situation. More specifically, Fiedler defines **situational favorableness** as the degree to which a particular situation either permits or denies a leader the chance to influence the behavior of group members.[35] In highly favorable situations, leaders find that their actions influence followers. But in highly unfavorable situations, leaders have little or no success influencing the people they are trying to lead.

Three situational factors determine the favorability of a situation: leader-member relations, task structure, and position power. The most important situational factor is **leader-member relations**, which refers to how well followers respect, trust, and like their leaders. When leader-member relations are good, followers trust the leader, and there is a friendly work atmosphere.

Situational favorableness the degree to which a particular situation either permits or denies a leader the chance to influence the behavior of group members

Leader-member relations the degree to which followers respect, trust, and like their leaders

How LPC is described	Leadership style
Positively	Relationship-oriented
Negatively	Task-oriented
Moderately	Flexible

Image Source/Getty Images

Task structure is the degree to which the requirements of a subordinate's tasks are clearly specified. With highly structured tasks, employees have clear job responsibilities, goals, and procedures. **Position power** is the degree to which leaders are able to hire, fire, reward, and punish workers. The more influence leaders have over hiring, firing, rewards, and punishments, the greater their power.

Exhibit 14.2 shows how leader-member relations, task structure, and position power can be combined into eight situations that differ in their favorability to leaders. In general, Situation I, on the left side of Exhibit 14.2, is the most favorable leader situation. Followers like and trust their leaders and know what to do because their tasks are highly structured. Also, the leaders have the formal power to influence workers through hiring, firing, rewarding, and punishing them. Therefore, it's relatively easy for a leader to influence followers in Situation I. By contrast, Situation VIII, on the right side of Exhibit 14.2, is the least favorable situation for leaders. Followers don't like or trust their leaders. Plus, followers are not sure what they're supposed to be doing, given that their tasks or jobs are highly unstructured. Finally, leaders find it difficult to influence followers because they don't have the ability to hire, fire, reward, or punish the people who work for them. In short, it's very difficult to influence followers given the conditions found in Situation VIII.

14-3c Matching Leadership Styles to Situations

After studying thousands of leaders and followers in hundreds of different situations, Fiedler found that the performance of relationship- and task-oriented leaders followed the pattern displayed in Exhibit 14.3.

> **Task structure** the degree to which the requirements of a subordinate's tasks are clearly specified
>
> **Position power** the degree to which leaders are able to hire, fire, reward, and punish workers

Exhibit 14.2
Situational Favorableness

Leader-Member Relations	Good	Good	Good	Good	Poor	Poor	Poor	Poor
Task Structure	High	High	Low	Low	High	High	Low	Low
Position Power	Strong	Weak	Strong	Weak	Strong	Weak	Strong	Weak
Situation	I	II	III	IV	V	VI	VII	VIII
	Favorable		**Moderately Favorable**				**Unfavorable**	

Exhibit 14.3
Matching Leadership Styles to Situations

CHAPTER 14: Leadership   315

Relationship-oriented leaders with high LPC scores were better leaders (that is, their groups performed more effectively) under moderately favorable situations. In moderately favorable situations, the leader may be liked somewhat, tasks may be somewhat structured, and the leader may have some position power. In this situation, a relationship-oriented leader improves leader-member relations, which is the most important of the three situational factors. In turn, morale and performance improve.

By contrast, as Exhibit 14.3 shows, task-oriented leaders with low LPC scores are better leaders in highly favorable and unfavorable situations. Task-oriented leaders do well in favorable situations where leaders are liked, tasks are structured, and the leader has the power to hire, fire, reward, and punish. In these favorable situations, task-oriented leaders effectively step on the gas of a well-tuned car. Their focus on performance sets the goal for the group, which then charges forward to meet it. But task-oriented leaders also do well in unfavorable situations where leaders are disliked, tasks are unstructured, and the leader doesn't have the power to hire, fire, reward, and punish. In these unfavorable situations, the task-oriented leader sets goals that focus attention on performance and clarify what needs to be done, thus overcoming low task structure. This is enough to jump-start performance even if workers don't like or trust the leader.

Finally, though not shown in Exhibit 14.3, people with moderate LPC scores, who can be somewhat relationship-oriented or somewhat task-oriented, tend to do fairly well in all situations because they can adapt their behavior. Typically, though, they don't perform quite as well as relationship-oriented or task-oriented leaders whose leadership styles are well matched to the situation.

Recall, however, that Fiedler assumes leaders to be incapable of changing their leadership styles. Accordingly, the key to applying Fiedler's contingency theory in the workplace is to accurately measure and match leaders to situations or to teach leaders how to change situational favorableness by changing leader-member relations, task structure, or position power. Although matching or placing leaders in appropriate situations works particularly well, practicing managers have had little luck reengineering situations to fit their leadership styles. The primary problem, as you've no doubt realized, is the complexity of the theory.

In a study designed to teach leaders how to reengineer their situations to fit their leadership styles, Fiedler found that most of the leaders simply did not understand what they were supposed to do to change their situations. Furthermore, if they didn't like their LPC profile (perhaps they felt they were more relationship-oriented than their scores indicated), they arbitrarily changed it to better suit their view of themselves. Of course, the theory won't work as well if leaders are attempting to change situational factors to fit their perceived leadership style rather than their real leadership style.[36]

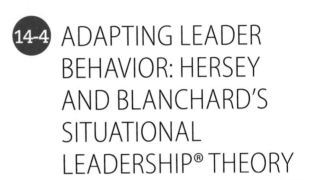

14-4 ADAPTING LEADER BEHAVIOR: HERSEY AND BLANCHARD'S SITUATIONAL LEADERSHIP® THEORY

Have you ever had a new job that you didn't know how to do and your boss was not around to help you learn it? Conversely, have you ever known exactly how to do your job but your boss kept treating you like you didn't? Hersey and Blanchard's Situational Leadership theory is based on the idea of follower readiness. Hersey and Blanchard argue that employees have different levels of readiness for handling different jobs, responsibilities, and work assignments. Accordingly, Hersey and Blanchard's **situational theory** states that leaders need to adjust their leadership styles to match followers' readiness.[37]

*Let's learn more about Hersey and Blanchard's situational theory by examining **14-4a worker readiness** and **14-4b different leadership styles.***

14-4a Worker Readiness

Performance readiness is the ability and willingness to take responsibility for directing one's behavior at work. Readiness is composed of two components. *Job readiness* consists of the amount of knowledge, skill, ability, and experience people have to perform their jobs. As you would expect, people with greater skill, ability, and experience do a better job of supervising their own work. *Psychological readiness*, on the other hand, is a feeling of self-confidence or self-respect. Likewise, confident people do a better job of guiding their own work than do insecure people. Job readiness and psychological readiness are combined to produce four different levels of readiness in Hersey and Blanchard's Situational Leadership theory.

Situational theory theory that says leaders need to adjust their leadership styles to match followers' readiness

Performance readiness the ability and willingness to take responsibility for directing one's behavior at work

Exhibit 14.4
Hersey and Blanchard's Situational Leadership Model

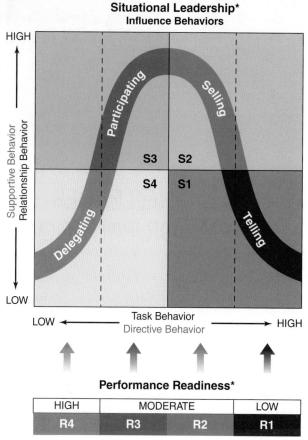

Situational Leadership*
Influence Behaviors

HIGH

Supportive Behavior
Relationship Behavior

Participating

Selling

Delegating

Telling

S3 S2
S4 S1

LOW

LOW ← **Task Behavior**
Directive Behavior → HIGH

Performance Readiness*

HIGH	MODERATE		LOW
R4	R3	R2	R1

Source: https://situational.com/the-cls-difference/situational-leadership-what-we-do/.

The lowest level, R1, represents insecure people who are neither willing nor able to take responsibility for guiding their own work. R2 represents people who are confident and are willing but not able to take responsibility for guiding their own work. R3 represents people who are insecure and are able but not willing to take responsibility for guiding their own work. And R4 represents people who are confident and willing and able to take responsibility for guiding their own work. It's important to note that a follower's readiness is usually task specific. For example, you may be highly confident and capable when it comes to social media marketing, but know nothing about setting up budgets for planning purposes. Thus, you would possess readiness (R4) with respect to social media marketing but not (R1) with respect to budgets.

14-4b Leadership Styles

Similar to Blake and Mouton's managerial grid, situational theory defines leadership styles in terms of task behavior (that is, concern for production) and relationship behavior (that is, concern for people). As shown in Exhibit 14.4, these two behaviors can be combined to form four different leadership styles: telling, selling, participating, and delegating. Leaders choose one of these styles, depending on the readiness a follower has for a specific task.

A *telling* leadership style (high task behavior and low relationship behavior) is based on one-way communication, in which followers are told what, how, when, and where to do particular tasks. Telling is used when people are insecure and neither willing nor able to take responsibility for guiding their own work (R1). For instance, someone using a telling leadership style might say, "We're going to start a company e-newsletter that goes out once a month to our customers, pointing them to new content on our website. I want you to contact bulk email services, like MailChimp for cost estimates. Then get together with each product manager and then get a list of product feature and usability updates. Don't write these yourself. Have the product managers write them and we'll edit them as we see fit. Also, call the CEO's assistant to remind her that we need her comments. Finally, have this all assembled in a draft email for me next Friday."

A *selling* leadership style (high task behavior and high relationship behavior) involves two-way communication and psychological support to encourage followers to "own" or "buy into" particular ways of doing things. Selling is used when confident people are willing but not able to take responsibility for guiding their own work (R2). For instance, someone using a selling leadership style might say, "We're going to start a company e-newsletter that goes out once a month to our customers, pointing them to new content on our website. I really think that's a great idea, don't you? We're going to need some cost estimates from bulk email services, like MailChimp, and a list of product feature and usability updates from each product manager. But that's pretty straightforward. Oh, don't forget that we need the CEO's comments, too. She's expecting you to call. I know that you'll do a great job on this. We'll meet next Tuesday to see if you have any questions once you've dug into this. I'd like to see a draft email at that time. By the way, we need to have this done by next Friday."

A *participating* style (low task behavior and high relationship behavior) is based on two-way communication and shared decision making. Participating is used when insecure people are able but not willing to take responsibility for guiding their own work (R3). Since the problem is with motivation and not ability, someone using a participating leadership style might say, "What do you think about starting a company e-newsletter that goes out once a month to our customers, pointing them to new content on our website? Uh-huh, uh-huh (listening). Ok, I think so, too. What kind of stuff do you hate in company e-newsletters? Un-huh (listening). Ok, I agree. That stuff drives me nuts, too. Well, what do you think we should put in ours? Uh-huh (listening). Those are great ideas. I'd like to see you implement them. We've got about 10 days to put it together. Why don't you put together a first draft, based on what we talked about here today, get the product managers involved to generate web content, touch base with the CEO's assistant, and we can meet on Tuesday to review those ideas. Great!"

A *delegating* style (low task behavior and low relationship behavior) is used when leaders basically let workers "run their own show" and make their own decisions. Delegating is used when people are willing and able to take responsibility for guiding their own work (R4). For instance, someone using a delegating leadership style might say, "We're going to start a company e-newsletter that goes out once a month to our customers, pointing them to new content on our website generated by the product managers. You've got 10 days to do it. Run with it. Let me know when you've got it done. I'll email you a couple of ideas, but other than that, do what you think is best. Thanks."

In general, as people become more "ready," and thus more willing and able to guide their own behavior, leaders should become less task oriented and more relationship oriented. Then, as people become even more "ready," leaders should become both less task oriented and less relationship oriented until people eventually manage their own work with little input from their leaders.

How well does Hersey and Blanchard's situational theory work? Despite its intuitive appeal (managers and consultants tend to prefer it over Fiedler's contingency theory because of its underlying logic and simplicity), most studies don't support situational theory.[38] While managers generally do a good job of judging followers' readiness levels, the theory doesn't seem to work well, except at lower levels, where a telling style is recommended for people who are insecure and neither willing nor able to take responsibility for guiding their own work.[39]

Path-goal theory a leadership theory states that leaders can increase subordinate satisfaction and performance by clarifying and clearing the paths to goals and by increasing the number and kinds of rewards available for goal attainment

Delegating is used when people are willing and able to take responsibility for guiding their own work.

14-5 ADAPTING LEADER BEHAVIOR: PATH-GOAL THEORY

Just as its name suggests, **path-goal theory** states that leaders can increase subordinate satisfaction and performance by clarifying and clearing the paths to goals and by increasing the number and kinds of rewards available for goal attainment. Said another way, leaders need to clarify how followers can achieve organizational goals, take care of problems that prevent followers from achieving goals, and then find more and varied rewards to motivate followers to achieve those goals.[40]

Leaders must meet two conditions for path clarification, path clearing, and rewards to increase followers' motivation and effort. First, leader behavior must be a source of immediate or future satisfaction for followers. The things you do as a leader must either please your followers today or lead to activities or rewards that will satisfy them in the future. One of the key cultural principles followed by Charlie Kim, CEO of New York-based Next Jump, which runs web-based reward programs for 90,000 companies, is "Better Me + Better You = Better Us," Kim says, "The culture we're building is predicated on the concept of long-term, sustained happiness."[41] This is why Next Jump's leadership frequently asks its people what *would* make them happier. Because of the long hours they put in, employees were spending half a day per weekend in a NYC laundromat doing their laundry. So they asked if washers and dryers could be installed at work to be used (and which they would pay for) when working late hours. Recognizing the problem (not

Exhibit 14.5
Path-Goal Theory

effective, and **14-5c the outcomes of path-goal theory in improving employee satisfaction and performance**.

14-5a Leadership Styles

As illustrated in Exhibit 14.5, the four leadership styles in path-goal theory are directive, supportive, participative, and achievement oriented.[43] **Directive leadership** involves letting employees know precisely what is expected of them, giving them specific guidelines for performing tasks, scheduling work, setting standards of performance, and making sure that people follow standard rules and regulations. These activities are especially important during economic downturns and periods during which a company is struggling. Recent research suggests that in more challenging economic environments (such as recessions), a more directive and authoritarian approach to leadership may produce stronger financial results for the company. More directive leaders reinforce discipline, effective coordination, and operational efficiency, so they are more likely to increase revenues during short-term crises and economic downturns.[44] Directive leadership is very similar to initiating structure.

Supportive leadership involves being approachable and friendly to employees, showing concern for them and their welfare, treating them as equals, and creating a friendly climate. Supportive leadership is very similar to considerate leader behavior. Supportive leadership often results in employee satisfaction with the job and with leaders. This leadership style may also result in improved performance when it increases employee confidence, lowers employee job stress, or improves relations and trust between employees and leaders.[45]

laundry, but the secondary effect of long hours resulting in lost weekend time), Next Jump now pays for laundry service. Employees bring in laundry on Fridays and it returns done on Mondays in a bag with Next Jump's logo and this phrase: "My company gets my laundry. I get my weekends back."[42] Next Jump's culture is so positive, rewarding, and satisfying that 18,000 people applied for 35 openings last year. Furthermore, while the quit rate in the tech industry is 22 percent per year, Next Jump has an incredibly low 1 percent quit rate.

Second, while providing the coaching, guidance, support, and rewards necessary for effective work performance, leader behaviors must complement and not duplicate the characteristics of followers' work environments. Thus, leader behaviors must offer something unique and valuable to followers beyond what they're already experiencing as they do their jobs or what they can already do for themselves.

In contrast to Fiedler's contingency theory, path-goal theory assumes that leaders *can* change and adapt their leadership styles. Exhibit 14.5 illustrates this process, showing that leaders change and adapt their leadership styles contingent on their subordinates or the environment in which those subordinates work.

Let's learn more about path-goal theory by examining 14-5a the four kinds of leadership styles that leaders use, 14-5b the subordinate and environmental contingency factors that determine when different leader styles are

Directive leadership a leadership style in which the leader lets employees know precisely what is expected of them, gives them specific guidelines for performing tasks, schedules work, sets standards of performance, and makes sure that people follow standard rules and regulations

Supportive leadership a leadership style in which the leader is friendly and approachable to employees, shows concern for employees and their welfare, treats them as equals, and creates a friendly climate

Participative leadership involves consulting employees for their suggestions and input before making decisions. Participation in decision making should help followers understand which goals are most important and clarify the paths to accomplishing them. Furthermore, when people participate in decisions, they become more committed to making them work. San Antonio, Texas-based H-E-B Grocery regularly is frequently honored as a "best place to work." President and COO Craig Boyan says there is a culture of "restless dissatisfaction" to reduce costs, satisfy customers, and keep employees engaged. Listening to and empowering employees is central to those efforts. Boyan says, "Our store leaders run their business the way they know best, and each store and each department in each store is always looking to improve and evolve how we do things. The key is pushing decision making to those who know best—partners in our stores—and having great leaders and partners to be constantly learning and working to evolve our business."[46] H-E-B employees are even more committed now that the company awarded 15 percent of its stock to 55,000+ employees (who must be over 21 and have worked at least 1,000 hours in the last year). Veronica Solis, who started with H-E-B after high school and manages store payroll, says, "I'm going to retire from here. I'm not going anywhere."[47]

Achievement-oriented leadership means setting challenging goals, having high expectations of employees, and displaying confidence that employees will assume responsibility and put forth extraordinary effort. Psychiatrist Samantha Boardman did her medical internship with two physicians. The first, Dr. M, was clearly an achievement-oriented leader. The second, Dr. F, wasn't. Boardman wrote of the experience, "Dr. M, thought the world of me. 'Dr. Boardman, what do you think?' he asked whenever there was a question about a diagnosis. 'Good work, Dr. Boardman,' he said whenever I reported lab results or presented a new patient. I thrived under his leadership and did my utmost to live up to his high expectations. It motivated me to work harder and to do my best."[48] Dr. F, she says, "thought very little of me. His low expectations became a reality. I made dumb mistakes. My mind went blank whenever he asked me questions. My confidence evaporated along with my motivation. I became a completely different person in his presence."[49]

14-5b Subordinate and Environmental Contingencies

As shown in Exhibit 14.5, path-goal theory specifies that leader behaviors should be adapted to subordinate characteristics. The theory identifies three kinds of subordinate contingencies: perceived ability, experience, and locus of control. *Perceived ability* is simply how much ability subordinates believe they have for doing their jobs well. Subordinates who perceive that they have a great deal of ability will be dissatisfied with directive leader behaviors. Experienced employees are likely to react in a similar way. Because they already know how to do their jobs (or perceive that they do), they don't need or want close supervision. By contrast, subordinates with little experience or little perceived ability will welcome directive leadership.

Participative leadership a leadership style in which the leader consults employees for their suggestions and input before making decisions

Achievement-oriented leadership a leadership style in which the leader sets challenging goals, has high expectations of employees, and displays confidence that employees will assume responsibility and put forth extraordinary effort

Exhibit 14.6
Path-Goal Theory: When to Use Directive, Supportive, Participative, or Achievement-Oriented Leadership

Directive Leadership	Supportive Leadership	Participative Leadership	Achievement-Oriented Leadership
Unstructured tasks	Structured, simple, repetitive tasks Stressful, frustrating tasks	Complex tasks	Unchallenging tasks
Workers with external locus of control	Workers lack confidence	Workers with internal locus of control	
Unclear formal authority system	Clear formal authority system	Workers not satisfied with rewards	
Inexperienced workers		Experienced workers	
Workers with low perceived ability		Workers with high perceived ability	

Locus of control is a personality measure that indicates the extent to which people believe that they have control over what happens to them in life. *Internals* believe that what happens to them, good or bad, is largely a result of their choices and actions. *Externals*, on the other hand, believe that what happens to them is caused by external forces beyond their control. Accordingly, externals are much more comfortable with a directive leadership style, whereas internals greatly prefer a participative leadership style because they like to have a say in what goes on at work.

Path-goal theory specifies that leader behaviors should complement rather than duplicate the characteristics of followers' work environments. There are three kinds of environmental contingencies: task structure, the formal authority system, and the primary work group. As in Fiedler's contingency theory, *task structure* is the degree to which the requirements of a subordinate's tasks are clearly specified. When task structure is low, and tasks are unclear, directive leadership should be used because it complements the work environment. When task structure is high and tasks are clear, however, directive leadership is not needed because it duplicates what task structure provides. Alternatively, when tasks are stressful, frustrating, or dissatisfying, leaders should respond with supportive leadership.

The *formal authority system* is an organization's set of procedures, rules, and policies. When the formal authority system is unclear, directive leadership complements the situation by reducing uncertainty and increasing clarity. But when the formal authority system is clear, directive leadership is redundant and should not be used.

Primary work group refers to the amount of work-oriented participation or emotional support that is provided by an employee's immediate work group. Participative leadership should be used when tasks are complex, and there is little existing work-oriented participation in the primary work group. When tasks are stressful, frustrating, or repetitive, supportive leadership is called for.

Finally, because keeping track of all of these subordinate and environmental contingencies can get a bit confusing, Exhibit 14.6 provides a summary of when directive, supportive, participative, and achievement-oriented leadership styles should be used.

14-5c Outcomes

Does following path-goal theory improve subordinate satisfaction and performance? Preliminary evidence suggests that it does.[50] In particular, people who work for supportive leaders are much more satisfied with their jobs and their bosses. Likewise, people who work for directive leaders are more satisfied with their jobs and bosses (but not quite as much as when their bosses are supportive) and perform their jobs better, too. Does adapting one's leadership style to subordinate

Poor Sleep Is Hurting Your Leadership

Whether due to stress, long hours, or travel, four nights a week 43 percent of leaders don't get enough sleep. That hurts their ability to focus, to be creative and innovative, to learn new things, and to recall what they've learned. Sleep deficiencies make it more difficult for leaders to regulate their emotions and read others' emotions correctly, both of which increase the odds of inappropriately snapping at others. Finally, lack of sleep zaps the charisma from leaders, which hurts their relationship with subordinates. Solutions include reasonable time limits, time off after disruptive travel, true work-free vacations, and nap rooms at work. Get enough sleep each night. You'll be a better leader!

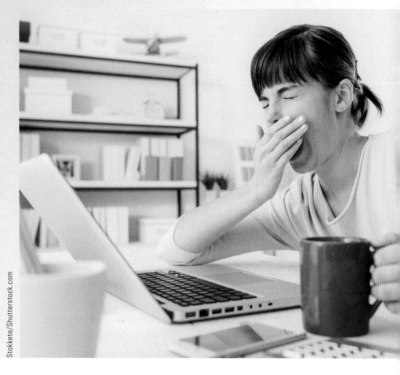

Sources: N. van Dam & E. van der Helm, "There's a Proven Link Between Effective Leadership and Getting Enough Sleep," *Harvard Business Review*, February 16, 2017, accessed April 30, 2017, https://hbr.org/2016/02/theres-a-proven-link-between-effective-leadership-and-getting-enough-sleep; C. Barnes, "Research: Sleep-Deprived Leaders Are Less Inspiring," *Harvard Business Review*, June 15, 2016, accessed April 30, 2017, https://hbr.org/2016/06/research-sleep-deprived-leaders-are-less-inspiring; W. Yakowicz, "Study Links Good Sleep and Great Leadership," *Inc.*, February 18, 2016, accessed April 30, 2017, https://www.inc.com/will-yakowicz/study-finds-connection-between-good-sleep-great-leadership.html.

Stokkete/Shutterstock.com

and environmental characteristics improve subordinate satisfaction and performance? At this point, because it is difficult to completely test this complex theory, it's too early to tell.[51] However, because the data clearly show that it makes sense for leaders to be both supportive *and* directive, it also makes sense that leaders could improve subordinate satisfaction and performance by adding participative and achievement-oriented leadership styles to their capabilities as leaders.

14-6 ADAPTING LEADER BEHAVIOR: NORMATIVE DECISION THEORY

Many people believe that making tough decisions is at the heart of leadership. Yet experienced leaders will tell you that deciding *how* to make decisions is just as important. The **normative decision theory** (also known as the *Vroom-Yetton-Jago model*) helps leaders decide how much employee participation (from none to letting employees make the entire decision) should be used when making decisions.[52]

Let's learn more about normative decision theory by investigating 14-6a decision styles and 14-6b decision quality and acceptance.

14-6a Decision Styles

Unlike nearly all of the other leadership theories discussed in this chapter, which have specified *leadership* styles, that is, the way a leader generally behaves toward followers, the normative decision theory specifies five different *decision* styles, or ways of making decisions. (See Chapter 5 for a more complete review of decision making in organizations.) As shown in Exhibit 14.7, those styles vary from *autocratic decisions* (AI or AII) on the left, in which leaders make the decisions by themselves, to *consultative decisions* (CI or CII), in which leaders share problems with subordinates but still make the decisions themselves, to *group decisions* (GII) on the right, in which leaders share the problems with subordinates and then have the group make the decisions.

> **Normative decision theory**
> a theory that suggests how leaders can determine an appropriate amount of employee participation when making decisions

Exhibit 14.7
Normative Theory, Decision Styles, and Levels of Employee Participation

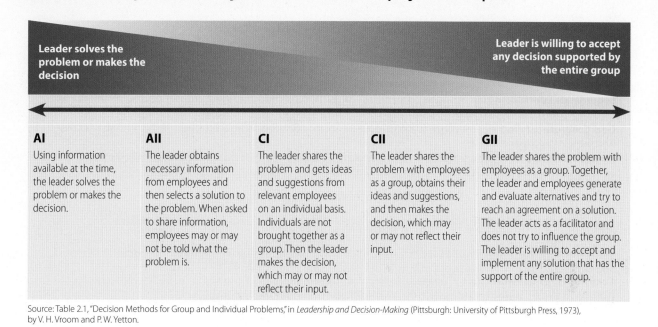

Leader solves the problem or makes the decision				Leader is willing to accept any decision supported by the entire group
AI	**AII**	**CI**	**CII**	**GII**
Using information available at the time, the leader solves the problem or makes the decision.	The leader obtains necessary information from employees and then selects a solution to the problem. When asked to share information, employees may or may not be told what the problem is.	The leader shares the problem and gets ideas and suggestions from relevant employees on an individual basis. Individuals are not brought together as a group. Then the leader makes the decision, which may or may not reflect their input.	The leader shares the problem with employees as a group, obtains their ideas and suggestions, and then makes the decision, which may or may not reflect their input.	The leader shares the problem with employees as a group. Together, the leader and employees generate and evaluate alternatives and try to reach an agreement on a solution. The leader acts as a facilitator and does not try to influence the group. The leader is willing to accept and implement any solution that has the support of the entire group.

Source: Table 2.1, "Decision Methods for Group and Individual Problems," in *Leadership and Decision-Making* (Pittsburgh: University of Pittsburgh Press, 1973), by V. H. Vroom and P. W. Yetton.

GE Aircraft Engines in Durham, North Carolina, uses a similar approach when making decisions. According to *Fast Company* magazine, "At GE/Durham, every decision is either an 'A' decision, a 'B' decision, or a 'C' decision. An 'A' decision is one that the plant manager makes herself, without consulting anyone.[53] One plant manager said, "I don't make very many of those, and when I do make one, everyone at the plant knows it. I make maybe 10 or 12 a year."[54] "B" decisions are also made by the plant manager but with input from the people affected. "C" decisions, the most common type, are made by consensus, by the people directly involved, with plenty of discussion. With "C" decisions, the view of the plant manager doesn't necessarily carry more weight than the views of those affected.[55]

14-6b Decision Quality and Acceptance

Management consultant John Canfield says, "Leaders are responsible for improving the performance of organizations. Two significant components of [a leader's] decisions are the quality of the decision and the level of buy-in associated with it. Effective leaders want them both."[56] According to the normative decision theory, using the right degree of employee participation improves the quality of decisions and the extent to which employees accept and are committed to decisions (that is, buy-in). Exhibit 14.8 lists the decision rules that normative decision theory uses to increase the quality of a decision and the degree to which employees accept and commit to it.

The quality, leader information, subordinate information, goal congruence, and problem structure rules are used to increase decision quality. For example, the leader information rule states that if a leader doesn't have enough information to make a decision on his or her own, then the leader should not use an autocratic decision style. The commitment probability, subordinate conflict, and commitment requirement rules shown in Exhibit 14.8 are used to increase employee acceptance and commitment to decisions. For example, the commitment requirement rule says that if decision acceptance and commitment are important, and the subordinates share the organization's goals, then you shouldn't use an autocratic or consultative style. In other words, if followers want to do what's best for the company, and you need their acceptance and commitment to make a decision work, then use a group decision style and let them make the decision. As you can see, these decision rules help leaders improve decision quality and

Exhibit 14.8
Normative Theory Decision Rules

Decision Rules to Increase Decision Quality

Quality Rule. If the quality of the decision is important, then don't use an autocratic decision style.

Leader Information Rule. If the quality of the decision is important, and if the leader doesn't have enough information to make the decision on his or her own, then don't use an autocratic decision style.

Subordinate Information Rule. If the quality of the decision is important, and if the subordinates don't have enough information to make the decision themselves, then don't use a group decision style.

Goal Congruence Rule. If the quality of the decision is important, and subordinates' goals are different from the organization's goals, then don't use a group decision style.

Problem Structure Rule. If the quality of the decision is important, the leader doesn't have enough information to make the decision on his or her own, and the problem is unstructured, then don't use an autocratic decision style.

Decision Rules to Increase Decision Acceptance

Commitment Probability Rule. If having subordinates accept and commit to the decision is important, then don't use an autocratic decision style.

Subordinate Conflict Rule. If having subordinates accept the decision is important and critical to successful implementation, and subordinates are likely to disagree or end up in conflict over the decision, then don't use an autocratic or consultative decision style.

Commitment Requirement Rule. If having subordinates accept the decision is absolutely required for successful implementation, and subordinates share the organization's goals, then don't use an autocratic or consultative style.

Sources: Adapted from V. H. Vroom, "Leadership," in *Handbook of Industrial and Organizational Psychology*, ed. M. D. Dunnette (Chicago: Rand McNally, 1976); V. H. Vroom and A. G. Jago, *The New Leadership: Managing Participation in Organizations* (Englewood Cliffs, NJ: Prentice Hall, 1988).

follower acceptance and commitment by eliminating decision styles that don't fit the particular decision or situation they're facing. Normative decision theory, like path-goal theory, is situational in nature. The abstract decision rules in Exhibit 14.8 are framed as yes/no questions, which makes the process of applying these rules more concrete. These questions are shown in the decision tree displayed in Exhibit 14.9. You start at the left side of the tree and answer the first question, "How important is the technical quality of this decision?" by choosing "high" or "low." Then you continue by answering each question as you proceed along the decision tree until you get to a recommended decision style.

Let's use the model to make the decision of whether to change from private offices to open offices and cubicles. The problem sounds simple, but it is actually more complex than you might think. Follow the yellow line in Exhibit 14.9 as we work through the decision in the bottom half of the exhibit (see Problem: Change To Open Offices and Cubicles).

How well does the normative decision theory

work? A prominent leadership scholar has described it as the best supported of all leadership theories.[57] In general, the more managers violate the decision rules in Exhibit 14.8, the less effective their decisions are, especially with respect to subordinate acceptance and commitment.[58]

 14-7 VISIONARY LEADERSHIP

Strategic leadership is the ability to anticipate, envision, maintain flexibility, think strategically, and work with others to initiate changes that will create a positive future for an organization.[59] Even though 25 percent of Japanese online purchases are made on Rakuten.com, CEO Hiroshi Mikitani worries about Japan's shrinking population. So he acquired Ebates, the U.S. shopping reward website, and invested in Lyft and Pinterest. But his biggest strategic investment in Rakuten's future was requiring all 8,000 employees to use English in all written and spoken communication. Mikitani said, "To grow, we need to go outside Japan. To do that, we need talented, non-Japanese people, and we need to have a standard of communication, which is spoken English. Therefore, the Japanese staff needs to be able to communicate in English so that we don't alienate

Strategic leadership the ability to anticipate, envision, maintain flexibility, think strategically, and work with others to initiate changes that will create a positive future for an organization

Exhibit 14.9

Normative Decision Theory Tree for Determining the Level of Participation in Decision Making

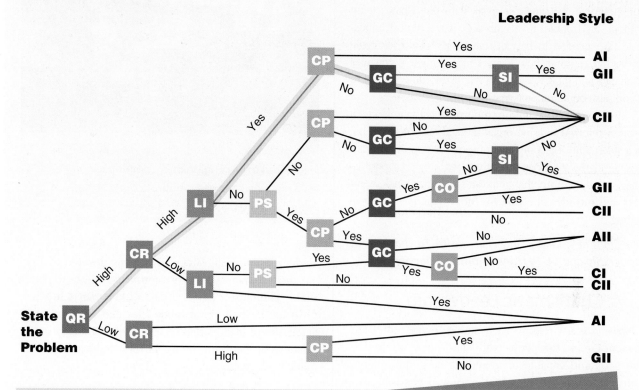

PROBLEM: CHANGE TO OPEN OFFICES AND CUBICLES?

1. *Quality requirement: How important is the technical quality of this decision?* High. This question has to do with whether there are quality differences in the alternatives and whether those quality differences matter. In other words: Is there a lot at stake in this decision? People have incredibly strong reactions to giving up private offices for cubicles. While companies use open offices to increase communication, workers will see this as a loss of privacy and status. Yes, there is a lot at stake.

2. *Commitment requirement: How important is subordinate commitment to the decision?* High. Changes in offices, from private to open settings, require subordinate commitment or they fail. In fact, it's not uncommon for companies to abandon open offices after trying them.

3. *Leader's information: Do you have sufficient information to make a high-quality decision?* Yes. Let's assume that you've done your homework. Much has been written about open offices and cubicles, from how to make the change to the effects it has in companies (which are mixed, sometimes positive and sometimes negative).

4. *Commitment probability: If you were to make the decision by yourself, is it reasonably certain that your subordinate(s) would* be committed to the decision? No. Studies of companies that change from private offices to open offices find that employees' initial reactions are almost uniformly negative. Employees are likely to be angry if you change something as personal as their offices without consulting them.

5. *Goal congruence: Do subordinates share the organizational goals to be attained in solving this problem?* Probably not. The goals that usually accompany a change to open offices are a more informal culture, better communication, and less money spent on renting or buying office space (because open offices and cubicles take less square footage than private offices), none of which will matter much to employees who are losing their private offices.

6. *CII is the answer:* With a CII, or consultative decision process, the leader shares the problem with employees as a group, obtains their ideas and suggestions, and then makes the decision, which may or may not reflect their input. So, given the answers to these questions (remember, different managers won't necessarily answer these questions the same way), the normative decision theory recommends that leaders consult with their subordinates before deciding whether to change from private offices to open offices and cubicles.

Source: "Figure 9.3, Decision-Process Flow Chart for Both Individual and Group Problems," in *Leadership and Decision-Making* (Pittsburgh: University of Pittsburgh Press, 1973), by V. H. Vroom and P. W. Yetton.

non-Japanese speakers. And it is working extremely well. Already, close to 40 percent of our engineers in Japan are non-Japanese. We are hiring from all over the world. Now our e-commerce team can speak with our Ebates team without any trouble. Five years ago, it was almost impossible. We needed to have a translator."[60] Thus, strategic leadership captures how leaders inspire their companies to change and their followers to give extraordinary effort to accomplish organizational goals.

In Chapter 5, we defined a purpose statement, which is often referred to as an organizational mission or vision, as a statement of a company's purpose or reason for existing. Similarly, **visionary leadership** creates a positive image of the future that motivates organizational members and provides direction for future planning and goal setting.[61]

Two kinds of visionary leadership are **14-7a charismatic leadership** *and* **14-7b transformational leadership.**

14-7a Charismatic Leadership

Charisma is a Greek word meaning "divine gift." The ancient Greeks saw people with charisma as inspired by the gods and capable of incredible accomplishments. German sociologist Max Weber viewed charisma as a special bond between leaders and followers.[62] Weber wrote that the special qualities of charismatic leaders enable them to strongly influence followers. Weber also noted that charismatic leaders tend to emerge in times of crisis and that the radical solutions they propose enhance the admiration that followers feel for them. In fact, charismatic leaders tend to have incredible influence over followers who may be inspired by their leaders and become fanatically devoted to them. From this perspective, charismatic leaders are often seen as larger-than-life.

Charismatic leaders have strong, confident, dynamic personalities that attract followers and enable the leaders to create strong bonds with their followers. Followers trust charismatic leaders, are loyal to them, and are inspired to work toward the accomplishment of the

All of Rakuten's Japan-based employees are required to use English in all communication, eliminating the need for translators between Japan staff and the U.S.-based Ebates team.

leader's vision. Followers who become devoted to charismatic leaders may go to extraordinary lengths to please them. Therefore, we can define **charismatic leadership** as the behavioral tendencies and personal characteristics of leaders that create an exceptionally strong relationship between them and their followers. Charismatic leaders also

» articulate a clear vision for the future that is based on strongly held values or morals;

» model those values by acting in a way consistent with the vision;

» communicate high performance expectations to followers; and

» display confidence in followers' abilities to achieve the vision.[63]

Does charismatic leadership work? Studies indicate that it often does. In general, the followers of charismatic leaders are more committed and satisfied, are better performers, are more likely to trust their leaders, and simply work harder.[64] Nonetheless, charismatic leadership also has risks that are at least as large as its benefits. The problems are likely to occur with ego-driven charismatic leaders who take advantage of fanatical followers.

In general, there are two kinds of charismatic leaders, ethical charismatics and unethical charismatics.[65] **Ethical charismatics** provide developmental opportunities for followers, are open to positive and negative feedback, recognize others' contributions, share information, and have moral standards that emphasize the larger interests of the group, organization, or society. Twenty years ago, J. J. Irani, then CEO of Tata Steel, had to close down a money-losing steel plant in Jamshedpur, India. Given that Tata not only

Visionary leadership
leadership that creates a positive image of the future that motivates organizational members and provides direction for future planning and goal setting

Charismatic leadership
the behavioral tendencies and personal characteristics of leaders that create an exceptionally strong relationship between them and their followers

Ethical charismatics
charismatic leaders who provide developmental opportunities for followers, are open to positive and negative feedback, recognize others' contributions, share information, and have moral standards that emphasize the larger interests of the group, organization, or society

guaranteed all employees' jobs but also jobs for their children (after you had worked at Tata 25 years), this was the first time that any Tata employees would lose their jobs. Rather than doing only what was best for Tata, Irani decided that laid-off employees, age 40 or under, would receive full salaries for the remainder of their working lives. Laid-off employees over 40 would get salaries plus a 20–50 percent bonus, depending on how close they were to retirement. Moreover, workers' families would receive the payments even if the workers died prior to retiring. Tata benefited, too, because it no longer had to pay payroll taxes, and part of the deal was that workers' payments would not increase over time. Over time, its labor costs shrunk, but its reputation as a caring employer among Indian managers and workers persisted.[66] As you would expect, ethical charismatics like Irani produce stronger commitment, higher satisfaction, more effort, better performance, and greater trust.

By contrast, **unethical charismatics** control and manipulate followers, do what is best for themselves instead of their organizations, want to hear only positive feedback, share information that is only beneficial to themselves, and have moral standards that put their interests before everyone else's. Steven Cohen, the billionaire owner of SAC Capital Advisors, was renowned

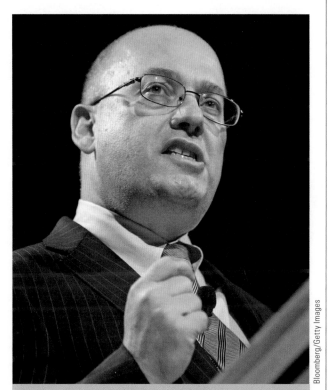

Steven Cohen, founder and chief executive officer of SAC Capital Advisors, speaks during a Robin Hood Veterans Summit in New York City.

Bloomberg/Getty Images

for being acerbic and impatient with his staff of financial analysts and managers. One of his standard responses when portfolio managers couldn't answer a question about a stock was, "Do you even know how to do your f***ing job?" Once, during the first week of January, he yelled at an employee for not having come up with any good trading ideas so far that year. Cohen routinely pitted traders against each other by displaying their profits and losses in real time. He also pushed them to compete to have their picks included in his personal portfolio. Under his leadership, SAC Capital pleaded guilty to insider trading, paying $1.8 billion in fines.[67]

Because followers can become just as committed to unethical charismatics as to ethical charismatics, unethical characteristics pose a tremendous risk for companies. Professor Diane Chandler explains, "By being greatly influenced by charismatic leaders, followers are apt to agree with, feel affection for, and obey them. With charismatic leaders fostering a sense of strong identification with followers, they may likewise curry followers' inordinate allegiance to them in the face of unethical or moral leadership indiscretion."[68]

Exhibit 14.10 shows the stark differences between ethical and unethical charismatics on several leader behaviors: exercising power, creating the vision, communicating with followers, accepting feedback, stimulating followers intellectually, developing followers, and living by moral standards. For example, ethical charismatics account for the concerns and wishes of their followers when creating a vision by having followers participate in the development of the company vision. By contrast, unethical charismatics develop a vision by themselves solely to meet their personal agendas. One unethical charismatic said, "The key thing is that it is my idea; and I am going to win with it at all costs."[69]

14-7b Transformational Leadership

While charismatic leadership involves articulating a clear vision, modeling values consistent with that vision, communicating high performance expectations, and establishing very strong relationships with followers, **transformational leadership** goes further by generating awareness and acceptance of a group's purpose and mission and by getting

Unethical charismatics charismatic leaders who control and manipulate followers, do what is best for themselves instead of their organizations, want to hear only positive feedback, share only information that is beneficial to themselves, and have moral standards that put their interests before everyone else's

Transformational leadership leadership that generates awareness and acceptance of a group's purpose and mission and gets employees to see beyond their own needs and self-interests for the good of the group

Exhibit 14.10
Ethical and Unethical Charismatics

Charismatic Leader Behaviors	Ethical Charismatics ...	Unethical Charismatics ...
Exercising power	... use power to serve others.	... use power to dominate or manipulate others for personal gain.
Creating the vision	... allow followers to help develop the vision.	... are the sole source of vision, which they use to serve their personal agendas.
Communicating with followers	... engage in two-way communication and seek out viewpoints on critical issues.	... engage in one-way communication and are not open to suggestions from others.
Accepting feedback	... are open to feedback and willing to learn from criticism.	... have inflated egos, thrive on attention and admiration of sycophants, and avoid candid feedback.
Stimulating followers intellectually	... want followers to think and question status quo as well as leader's views.	... don't want followers to think but instead want uncritical acceptance of leader's ideas.
Developing followers	... focus on developing people with whom they interact, express confidence in them, and share recognition with others.	... are insensitive and unresponsive to followers' needs and aspirations.
Living by moral standards	... follow self-guided principles that may go against popular opinion and have three virtues: courage, a sense of fairness or justice, and integrity.	... follow standards only if they satisfy immediate self-interests, manipulate impressions so that others think they are doing the right thing, and use communication skills to manipulate others to support their personal agendas.

Source: J. M. Howell and B. J. Avolio, "The Ethics of Charismatic Leadership: Submission or Liberation?" *Academy of Management Executive 6*, no. 2 (1992): 43–54.

employees to see beyond their own needs and self-interest for the good of the group.[70] Like charismatic leaders, transformational leaders are visionary, but they transform their organizations by getting their followers to accomplish more than they intended and even more than they thought possible.

Transformational leaders are able to make their followers feel that they are a vital part of the organization and help them see how their jobs fit with the organization's vision. By linking individual and organizational interests, transformational leaders encourage followers to make sacrifices for the organization because they know that they will prosper when the organization prospers. Transformational leadership has four components: charismatic leadership or idealized influence, inspirational motivation, intellectual stimulation, and individualized consideration.[71]

Charismatic leadership or idealized influence means that transformational leaders act as role models for their followers. Because transformational leaders put others' needs ahead of their own and share risks with their followers, they are admired, respected, and trusted, and followers want to emulate them. When Whole Foods' profit dropped 10 percent and the company needed to trim costs, co-CEO John Mackey voluntarily cut his pay by 67 percent. Likewise, Jay Leno, who hosted the *Tonight Show* for 22 years, voluntarily took a $15 million cut in pay when NBC announced that it needed to cut $20 million in costs for the show. While 20 employees were let go, Leno's voluntary pay cut absorbed 75 percent of the needed cost reduction so that many other long-time staffers on the show could keep their jobs.[72] Thus, in contrast to purely charismatic leaders (especially unethical charismatics), transformational leaders can be counted on to do the right thing and maintain high standards for ethical and personal conduct.

Inspirational motivation means that transformational leaders motivate and inspire followers by providing meaning and challenge to their work. By clearly communicating expectations and demonstrating commitment to goals, transformational leaders help followers envision future states, such as the organizational vision or mission. In turn, this leads to greater enthusiasm and optimism about the future.

Intellectual stimulation means that transformational leaders encourage followers to be creative and innovative, to question assumptions, and to look at problems and situations in new ways even if their ideas are different from those of leaders. Guive Balooch, global vice president for L'Oreal's Technology Incubator, leads a 26-person team charged with marrying beauty products to technology. Says Balooch, "If you put a UX (user experience) designer, a physicist, a biologist and a micro-engineer all together in a room, the tension between their ideas creates really cool things."[73] One of their first products, the MakeupGenius App, combines the camera on a smartphone with software to, "select that new shade of eyeshadow or lipstick and virtually try it on yourself."[74] Just like in a store, the app uses augmented reality technology to virtually "apply" the makeup to your image on your smart phone or tablet, allowing you to see how you look from any angle in real time. Balooch says, "My team has freedom to create, to innovate,

to embrace the very best in industrial design, in science, and technology and adapt it for the beauty industry."[75]

Individualized consideration means that transformational leaders pay special attention to followers' individual needs by creating learning opportunities, accepting and tolerating individual differences, encouraging two-way communication, and being good listeners.

Finally, a distinction needs to be drawn between transformational leadership and transactional leadership. While transformational leaders use visionary and inspirational appeals to influence followers, **transactional leadership** is based on an exchange process in which followers are rewarded for good performance and punished for poor performance. When leaders administer rewards fairly and offer followers the rewards that they want, followers will often reciprocate with effort. A problem, however, is that transactional leaders often rely too heavily on discipline or threats to bring performance up to standards. This may work in the short run, but it's much less effective in the long run. Also, as discussed in Chapters 11 and 13, many leaders and organizations have difficulty successfully linking pay practices to individual performance. As a result, studies consistently show that transformational leadership is much more effective on average than transactional leadership. In the United States, Canada, Japan, and India at all organizational levels, from first-level supervisors to upper-level executives, followers view transformational leaders as much better leaders and are much more satisfied when working for them. Furthermore, companies with transformational leaders have significantly better financial performance.[76]

Transactional leadership leadership based on an exchange process in which followers are rewarded for good performance and punished for poor performance

STUDY TOOLS 14

LOCATED IN TEXTBOOK

☐ Rip out and review chapter review card.

LOCATED AT WWW.CENGAGEBRAIN.COM

☐ Gain unique perspectives on key concepts with new 4LTR concept videos in the e-book.

☐ Increase your comprehension with Aplia for MGMT11.

☐ Complete interactive content within the e-book.

15 | Managing Communication

After you finish this chapter, go to **PAGE 351** for **STUDY TOOLS**

LEARNING OUTCOMES

15-1 Explain the role that perception plays in communication and communication problems.

15-2 Describe the communication process and the various kinds of communication in organizations.

15-3 Explain how managers can manage effective one-on-one communication.

15-4 Describe how managers can manage effective organization-wide communication.

15-1 PERCEPTION AND COMMUNICATION PROBLEMS

It's estimated that managers spend over 80 percent of their day communicating with others.[1] Indeed, much of the basic management process—planning, organizing, leading, and controlling—cannot be performed without effective communication. If this weren't reason enough to study communication, consider that effective oral communication—achieved by listening, following instructions, conversing, and giving feedback—is the most important skill for college graduates who are entering the workforce.[2] **Communication** is the process of transmitting information from one person or place to another. While some bosses sugarcoat bad news, smart managers understand that effective, straightforward communication between managers and employees is essential for success.

Communication the process of transmitting information from one person or place to another

One study found that when *employees* were asked whether their supervisor gave recognition for good work, only 13 percent said their supervisor gave a pat on the back, and a mere 14 percent said their supervisor gave sincere and thorough praise. But when the *supervisors* of these employees were asked if they gave recognition for good work, 82 percent said they gave pats on the back, while 80 percent said that they gave sincere and thorough praise.[3] Given that these managers and employees worked closely together, how could they have had such different perceptions of something as simple as praise?

*Let's learn more about perception and communication problems by examining **15-1a the basic perception process, 15-1b perception problems, 15-1c how we perceive others,** and **15-1d how we perceive ourselves.** We'll also consider how all of these factors make it difficult for managers to communicate effectively.*

15-1a Basic Perception Process

As shown in Exhibit 15.1, **perception** is the process by which individuals attend to, organize, interpret, and retain information from their environments. And because communication is the process of transmitting information from one person or place to another, perception is obviously a key part of communication. Yet perception can also be a key obstacle to communication.

As people perform their jobs, they are exposed to a wide variety of informational stimuli such as emails, direct conversations with the boss or coworkers, rumors heard over lunch, stories about the company in the press, or a video broadcast of a speech from the CEO to all employees. Just being exposed to an informational stimulus, however, is no guarantee that an individual will pay attention or attend to that stimulus. People experience stimuli through their own **perceptual filters**—the personality-, psychology-, or experience-based differences that influence them to ignore or pay attention to particular stimuli. Because of filtering, people exposed to the

> **Perception** the process by which individuals attend to, organize, interpret, and retain information from their environments
>
> **Perceptual filters** the personality-, psychology-, or experience-based differences that influence people to ignore or pay attention to particular stimuli

Exhibit 15.1
Basic Perception Process

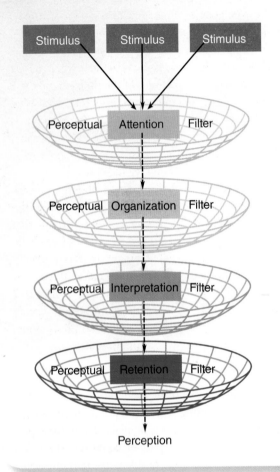

same information will often disagree about what they saw or heard. As shown in Exhibit 15.1, perceptual filters affect each part of the *perception process*: attention, organization, interpretation, and retention.

Attention is the process of noticing, or becoming aware of, particular stimuli. Because of perceptual filters, we attend to some stimuli and not others. For instance, a study at the University of Illinois asked viewers to watch people in black shirts and white shirts toss a basketball back and forth and to count the number of times someone in a black shirt tossed the basketball. Because their perceptual filters had narrowed to track the activities of people in black shirts, half of the viewers did not notice when the experimenters had someone in a gorilla suit walk through the midst of the people tossing the basketball back and forth.[4] *Organization* is the process of incorporating new information (from the stimuli that you notice) into your existing knowledge. Because of perceptual filters, we are more likely to incorporate

new knowledge that is consistent with what we already know or believe. *Interpretation* is the process of attaching meaning to new knowledge. Because of perceptual filters, our preferences and beliefs strongly influence the meaning we attach to new information (for example, "This decision must mean that top management supports our project"). Finally, *retention* is the process of remembering interpreted information. Retention affects what we recall and commit to memory after we have perceived something. Of course, perceptual filters affect retention as much as they do organization and interpretation.

For instance, imagine that you miss the first 10 minutes of a TV show and turn on your TV to see two people talking to each other in a living room. As they talk, they walk around the room, picking up and putting down various items. Some items, such as a ring, watch, and credit card, appear to be valuable, while others appear to be drug-related, such as a water pipe for smoking marijuana. In fact, this situation was depicted on videotape in a well-known study that manipulated people's perceptual filters.[5] Before watching the video, one-third of the study participants were told that the people were there to rob the apartment. Another third were told that police were on their way to conduct a drug raid and that the people in the apartment were getting rid of incriminating evidence. The remaining third of the participants were told that the people were simply waiting for a friend.

After watching the video, participants were asked to list all of the objects from the video that they could remember. Not surprisingly, the different perceptual filters (theft, drug raid, and waiting for a friend) affected what the participants attended to, how they organized the information, how they interpreted it, and ultimately which objects they remembered. Participants who thought a theft was in progress were more likely to remember the valuable objects in the video. Those who thought a drug raid was imminent were more likely to remember the drug-related objects. There was no discernible pattern to the items remembered by those who thought that the people in the video were simply waiting for a friend.

In short, because of perception and perceptual filters, people are likely to pay attention to different things, organize and interpret what they pay attention to differently, and, finally, remember things differently. Consequently, even when people are exposed to the same communications (for example, organizational memos, discussions with managers or customers), they can end up with very different perceptions and understandings. This is why communication can be so difficult and frustrating for managers. Let's review some of the communication problems created by perception and perceptual filters.

THE POWER OF PERCEPTION

Perception is a powerful influence on human behavior. A group of researchers testing the relationship between the size of a wine glass and the amount of wine consumed discovered that people who are served wine in a large glass drink more wine overall in one sitting than do people served the same amount of wine in a smaller wine glass. Why does this happen? Even though they are being served the same amount, the people drinking from the larger glass perceive

Oksana Klimenkova/Shutterstock.com

that there is less wine in the glass. To compensate, they order more glasses throughout the evening.

Source: D. Rowland, "Large Wine Glasses Encourage More Drinking, Study Finds," *Wall Street Journal*, December 13, 2015, accessed May 7, 2016, http://www.wsj.com/articles/larger-wine-glasses-encourage-more-drinking-study-finds-1450696305.

15-1b Perception Problems

Perception creates communication problems for organizations because people exposed to the same communication and information can end up with completely different ideas and understandings. Two of the most common perception problems in organizations are selective perception and closure.

At work, we are constantly bombarded with sensory stimuli: phones ringing, people talking in the background, computers dinging as new email arrives, people calling our names, and so forth. As limited processors of information, we cannot possibly notice, receive, and interpret all of this information. As a result, we attend to and accept some stimuli but screen out and reject others. This isn't a random process. **Selective perception** is the tendency to notice and accept objects and information consistent with our values, beliefs, and expectations, while ignoring or screening out inconsistent information. For example, in a research

study, pedestrians are stopped on a sidewalk by a man who asks for directions. Ten seconds into giving directions, two people carrying a door walk between the man who asked for directions, on the left, and the pedestrian, on the right. When the door goes by, the man who asked for directions quickly switches places with one of the young men carrying the door. The pedestrian, however, doesn't see this switch because the door blocks the view. Like the invisible gorilla example cited earlier, 50 percent of the time people don't even notice that they're talking to a different man and go right back to giving directions. Selective perception, is one of the biggest contributors to misunderstandings and miscommunication, because it strongly influences what people see, hear, read, and understand at work.[6]

After we have initial information about a person, event, or process, **closure** is the tendency to fill in the gaps where information is missing, that is, to assume that what we don't know is consistent with what we already do know. If employees are told that budgets must be cut by 10 percent, they may automatically assume that 10 percent of employees will lose their jobs, too, even if that isn't the case. Not surprisingly, when closure occurs, people sometimes fill in the gaps with inaccurate information, which can create problems for organizations.

15-1c Perceptions of Others

Attribution theory says that we all have a basic need to understand and explain the causes of other people's behavior.[7] In other words, we need to know why people do what they do. According to attribution theory, we use two general reasons or attributions to explain people's behavior: an *internal attribution*, in which behavior is thought to be voluntary or under the control of the individual, and an *external attribution*, in which behavior is thought to be involuntary and outside of the control of the individual.

If you've ever seen someone changing a flat tire on the side of the road and thought to yourself, "What rotten luck—somebody's having a bad day," you perceived the person through an external attribution known as the defensive bias. The **defensive bias** is the tendency for people to perceive

Selective perception the tendency to notice and accept objects and information consistent with our values, beliefs, and expectations, while ignoring or screening inconsistent information

Closure the tendency to fill in gaps of missing information by assuming that what we don't know is consistent with what we already know

Attribution theory the theory that we all have a basic need to understand and explain the causes of other people's behavior

Defensive bias the tendency for people to perceive themselves as personally and situationally similar to someone who is having difficulty or trouble

Exhibit 15.2
Defensive Bias and Fundamental Attribution Error

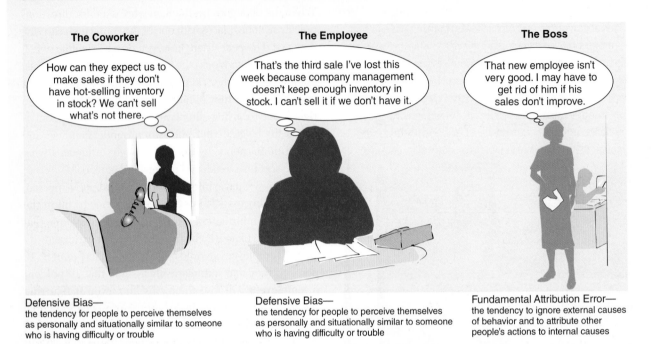

The Coworker

How can they expect us to make sales if they don't have hot-selling inventory in stock? We can't sell what's not there.

The Employee

That's the third sale I've lost this week because company management doesn't keep enough inventory in stock. I can't sell it if we don't have it.

The Boss

That new employee isn't very good. I may have to get rid of him if his sales don't improve.

Defensive Bias— the tendency for people to perceive themselves as personally and situationally similar to someone who is having difficulty or trouble

Defensive Bias— the tendency for people to perceive themselves as personally and situationally similar to someone who is having difficulty or trouble

Fundamental Attribution Error— the tendency to ignore external causes of behavior and to attribute other people's actions to internal causes

themselves as personally and situationally similar to someone who is having difficulty or trouble.[8] When we identify with the person in a situation, we tend to use external attributions (that is, features related to the situation) to explain the person's behavior. For instance, because flat tires are common, it's easy to perceive ourselves in that same situation and put the blame on external causes such as running over a nail.

Now, let's assume a different situation, this time in the workplace:

A utility company worker puts a ladder on a utility pole and then climbs up to do his work. As he's doing his work, he falls from the ladder and seriously injures himself.[9]

Answer this question: Who or what caused the accident? If you thought, "It's not the worker's fault. Anybody could fall from a tall ladder," then you interpreted the incident with a defensive bias in which you saw yourself as personally and situationally similar to someone who is having difficulty or trouble. In other words, you made an external attribution by

Fundamental attribution error the tendency to ignore external causes of behavior and to attribute other people's actions to internal causes

attributing the accident to an external cause or some feature of the situation.

Most accident investigations, however, initially blame the worker (that is, an internal attribution) and not the situation (that is, an external attribution). Typically, 60–80 percent of workplace accidents each year are blamed on "operator error," that is, on the employees themselves. In reality, more complete investigations usually show that workers are responsible for only 30–40 percent of all workplace accidents.[10] Why are accident investigators so quick to blame workers? The reason is that they are committing the **fundamental attribution error**, which is the tendency to ignore external causes of behavior and to attribute other people's actions to internal causes.[11] In other words, when investigators examine the possible causes of an accident, they're much more likely to assume that the accident is a function of the person and not the situation.

Which attribution—the defensive bias or the fundamental attribution error—are workers likely to make when something goes wrong? In general, as shown in Exhibit 15.2, employees and coworkers are more likely to perceive events and explain behavior from a defensive bias. Because they do the work themselves and see themselves as similar to others who make mistakes, have accidents, or are otherwise held responsible for things that go wrong at work, employees and coworkers are likely to attribute problems to external causes such as failed machinery, poor support, or inadequate training. By contrast, because they are typically observers (who don't do the work themselves) and see themselves as situationally and personally different from workers, managers tend to commit the fundamental attribution error and blame mistakes, accidents, and other things that go wrong on workers (that is, an internal attribution).

Consequently, workers and managers in most workplaces can be expected to take opposite views when things go wrong. Therefore, the defensive bias, which is typically used by workers, and the fundamental attribution error, which is typically made by managers, together present a significant challenge to effective communication and understanding in organizations.

15-1d Self-Perception

The **self-serving bias** is the tendency to overestimate our value by attributing successes to ourselves (internal causes) and attributing failures to others or the environment (external causes).[12] The self-serving bias can make it especially difficult for managers to talk to employees about performance problems. In general, people have a need to maintain a positive self-image. This need is so strong that when people seek feedback at work, they typically want

verification of their worth (rather than information about performance deficiencies) or assurance that mistakes or problems weren't their fault.[13] People can become defensive and emotional when managerial communication threatens their positive self-image. They quit listening, and communication becomes ineffective. In the second half of the chapter, which focuses on improving communication, we'll explain ways in which managers can minimize this self-serving bias and improve effective one-on-one communication with employees.

15-2 KINDS OF COMMUNICATION

There are many kinds of communication—formal, informal, coaching/counseling, and nonverbal—but they all follow the same fundamental process.

*Let's learn more about the different kinds of communication by examining **15-2a the communication process**, **15-2b formal communication channels**, **15-2c informal communication channels**, **15-2d coaching and counseling, or one-on-one communication**, and **15-2e nonverbal communication**.*

15-2a The Communication Process

At the beginning of this chapter, we defined *communication* as the process of transmitting information from one person or place to another. Exhibit 15.3 displays a model of the communication process and its major components: the sender (message to be conveyed, encoding the message, transmitting the message); the receiver (receiving message, decoding the message, and the message that was understood); and noise, which interferes with the communication process.

The communication process begins when a *sender* thinks of a message he or she wants to convey to another person. For example, you had a flu shot and a pneumonia shot, and yet you've had an unexplainable fever for nine days, so you visit the doctor. The doctor asks a series of questions regarding your appetite, fatigue, tenderness in your abdomen, and

---

Exhibit 15.3
The Interpersonal Communication Process

Sender

Message to be conveyed

Feedback to Sender

Encode message

Transmit message

Communication Channel

Receiver

Message that was understood

Decode message

Receive message

NOISE

Burke/Triolo Productions/Jupiterimages; TongRo Image Stock/Jupiterimages

---

Self-serving bias the tendency to overestimate our value by attributing successes to ourselves (internal causes) and attributing failures to others or the environment (external causes)

whether your fever comes and goes during the day. The doctor, the sender, runs some tests and then has you, the receiver, come back the next day to give you a diagnosis and recommend a treatment.

The next step is to encode the message. **Encoding** means putting a message into a written, verbal, or symbolic form that can be recognized and understood by the receiver. In our example, this means the doctor has to take the technical language of medicine and lab test results and communicate it in a way that patients can understand. This is not easy to do. And the difficulty of doing this well is compounded by the average doctor's visit lasting less than 15 minutes. And, while your visit might be 15 minutes, you're not getting a full 15 minutes to talk to the doctor. Not surprisingly, 60 percent of patients feel as if their doctor is rushing through their exam. Despite this, 58 percent of surveyed patients say their doctors do a good job of explaining things to them. But, as we'll see in a few steps, that doesn't mean communication has been effective.[14]

The sender then *transmits the message* via *communication channels*. The traditional communication channel for doctors and patients is face-to-face discussion in the doctor's office. Ironically, though, the introduction of electronic health records may be interfering with that. Dr. Rita Redberg, at the University of California San Francisco Medical Center, says, "The recent introduction of electronic health records in the office, for example, requires many doctors to spend much of a patient exam looking at a computer screen instead of the patient in order to record information." Studies show that one-third of the time, doctors forget to give patients critical information. Another critical study found that across 30 different medical conditions, patients only received all the information they needed from their doctors about 55 percent of the time.[15] Why? In an average 15-minute doctor's visit, the doctor will spend just 1.3 minutes telling the patient about his or her condition, prognosis, and treatment. Furthermore, as we will see, that 1.3 minutes is filled with information that is too complex and technical for the typical patient to understand.[16]

With some communication channels such as the telephone and face-to-face communication, the sender receives immediate feedback, whereas with others such as email (or text messages and file attachments), voice mail, memos, and letters, the sender must wait for the receiver to respond. Unfortunately, because of technical difficulties (for example, fax down, dead battery in the cell phone, inability to read email attachments) or people-based transmission problems (for example, forgetting to pass on the message), messages aren't always transmitted.

If the message is transmitted and received, however, the next step is for the receiver to decode it. **Decoding** is the process by which the receiver translates the verbal or symbolic form of the message into an understood message. Surveys indicate that many patients clearly do not understand what their doctors are telling them. Up to 85 percent of hospitalized patients don't even know the name of the doctor in charge of their treatment. As many as 58 percent don't know why they were admitted to the hospital. Likewise, in a typical 15-minute doctor's appointment, half of patients will leave without understanding what their doctor has told to them to do to get better.[17] Unfortunately, even when patients seem to understand what their doctors are telling them in their 15-minute visit, it turns out that they immediately forget 80 percent of that medical information, and then half of what they do remember is wrong![18]

The last step of the communication process occurs when the receiver gives the sender feedback. **Feedback to sender** is a return message to the sender that indicates the receiver's understanding of the message (of what the receiver was supposed to know, to do, or not to do). Feedback makes senders aware of possible miscommunications and enables them to continue communicating until the receiver understands

Ditty_about_summer/Shutterstock.com

Encoding putting a message into a written, verbal, or symbolic form that can be recognized and understood by the receiver

Decoding the process by which the receiver translates the written, verbal, or symbolic form of a message into an understood message

Feedback to sender in the communication process, a return message to the sender that indicates the receiver's understanding of the message the intended message. Because of the difficulties of communicating complex medical information in too little time, many doctors now employ the "teach-back" method at the end of a patient visit, where they ask patients to explain in their own words what they've heard the doctor say regarding their problem (diagnosis), whether they'll get better (prognosis), and what the patient is supposed to do after they leave the doctor's office (that is, treatment plan and managing medications).[19] Even so, much progress needs to be made, as about half of patients are not even asked if they have questions.[20]

Unfortunately, feedback doesn't always occur in the communication process. Complacency and overconfidence about the ease and simplicity of communication can lead senders and receivers to simply assume that they share a common understanding of the message and, consequently, to not use feedback to improve the effectiveness of their communication. This is a serious mistake, especially as messages and feedback are always transmitted with and against a background of noise. Part of the background noise in medicine is how well medical information is communicated between medical professionals. After all, medicine is a "team sport" involving various doctors, physician assistants, nurses, and other care professionals for each patient. Medical mistakes kill 500 people per day, and 80 percent of those deaths are caused by miscommunication that occurs when patients are transferred from one set of caregivers to another, for instance, the night-shift nurses not communicating key information to the day-shift nurses, or one doctor not being aware of the diagnosis and treatment plan of another doctor on a case.[21]

Noise is anything that interferes with the transmission of the intended message. Noise can occur in any of the following situations:

» The sender isn't sure what message to communicate.

» The message is not clearly encoded.

» The wrong communication channel is chosen.

» The message is not received or decoded properly.

» The receiver doesn't have the experience or time to understand the message.

Emotional outbursts are an often unrecognized type of noise. Whether yelling, crying, sulking, or table pounding, strong emotions interfere with the transmission of intended messages. The outburst itself, however, is a signal that what's being discussed touches strongly held beliefs or values. The first step in addressing noise related to strong emotions is spotting early indicators, such as body language not matching words. Acknowledge the difficulty of the issue, and then ask them to share their views. Next, listen to the response, and ask follow-up questions. Finally, work toward resolution by helping them articulate their core issues.[22] We'll cover listening and asking questions in greater detail in section 15-2d on coaching and counseling.

Jargon, which is vocabulary particular to a profession or group, is another form of noise that interferes with communication in the workplace. Jargon is a common cause of misunderstandings between doctors and patients. Brian Jack, chief of family medicine at Boston Medical Center, says, "We throw papers and throw words at patients. It is crazy to think they would understand."[23] The result, says Dr. David Langer, chief of neurosurgery at Lenox Hill Hospital in New York City, is that patients, "would go home and call back and say they didn't understand, and then ask me the same questions . . . Doctors often do a terrible job at educating their patients."[24] To combat this problem, Dr. Langer and his colleagues have begun using digital videos to explain CT scans and MRIs, as well as to provide detailed post-visit medical instructions. While preparing for an upcoming surgery, Emily Monato watched the video of her brain MRI several times to better "grasp these big chunks of information."[25] She had her children, father, and friends watch it, too.

15-2b Formal Communication Channels

An organization's **formal communication channel**, is the system of official channels that carry organizationally approved messages and information. Organizational objectives, rules, policies, procedures, instructions, commands, and requests for information are all transmitted via the formal communication system or channel. There are three formal communication channels: downward communication, upward communication, and horizontal communication.[26]

Downward communication flows from higher to lower levels in an organization. Downward communication is used to issue orders down the organizational hierarchy, to give organizational members job-related information, to give managers and workers performance reviews from upper managers, and to clarify organizational objectives and goals.[27] Michael Beer, professor emeritus at Harvard

Noise anything that interferes with the transmission of the intended message

Jargon vocabulary particular to a profession or group that interferes with communication in the workplace

Formal communication channel the system of official channels that carry organizationally approved messages and information

Downward communication communication that flows from higher to lower levels in an organization

Marc Benioff ✔
@Benioff

[👤+ Follow] ⌄

My favorite internal salesforce group is Airing of Grievances! #salesforce1selfie

Airing of Grievances

4,037 Members • Public • Active

● ● ●

Source:Twitter, Inc.

Salesforce.com CEO Marc Benioff encourages upward communication by regularly participating in the "Airing of Grievances" chat group.

Business School, says, "You can never overcommunicate. When you think you've communicated well, go out three or four more times and communicate again." Beer's consulting firm, TruePoint, studied 40 CEOs whose companies have been above-average performers for more than a decade. He found that those leaders spend an immense amount of time in downward communication. "They have a simple story, and that story gets out every place they go."[28]

Upward communication flows from lower levels to higher levels in an organization. Upward communication is used to give higher-level managers feedback about operations, issues, and problems; to help higher-level managers assess organizational performance and effectiveness; to encourage lower-level managers and employees to participate in organizational decision making; and to give those at lower levels the chance to share their concerns with higher-level authorities. Salesforce.com, the largest customer relationship marketing platform in the world, is used by companies to find, manage, and close more sales leads and to better manage and monitor existing customer relationships. CEO and founder Marc Benioff and his senior leadership team encourage upward communication by regularly participating in the "Airing of Grievances" chat group that is open to everyone in the company.[29] Salesforce's Jody Kohner, vice president of employee marketing and engagement, says that Airing of Grievances is based on a communication philosophy of "'bring it out into the open, let's talk about it and solve it'—because that's what the world's most innovative companies do, they solve problems."[30]

> **Upward communication**
> communication that flows from lower to higher levels in an organization

> **Horizontal communication**
> communication that flows among managers and workers who are at the same organizational level

Horizontal communication flows among managers and workers who are at the same organizational level, such as when a day shift nurse comes in at 7:30 a.m. for a half-hour discussion with the midnight nurse supervisor who leaves at 8:00 a.m. Horizontal communication helps facilitate coordination and cooperation between different parts of a company and allows coworkers to share relevant information. It also helps people at the same level resolve conflicts and solve problems without involving high levels of management. Many hospitals now use bedside shift reports for horizontal communication during shift changes. Both nurses, one leaving and the other coming on, discuss the patient's status at their bedside with family members present. Beverly Johnson, CEO of the Institute for Patient-and-Family-Centered Care, says bedside shift reports, "ensure that complete and accurate information is shared and there is mutual understanding of the care plan and other priorities."[31] Shift reports usually take three to seven minutes per patient and nurses typically hand off three to six patients per shift.

In general, what can managers do to improve formal communication? First, decrease reliance on downward communication. Second, increase chances for upward communication by increasing personal contact with lower-level managers and workers. Third, encourage much better use of horizontal communication.

15-2c Informal Communication Channels

An organization's **informal communication channel**, sometimes called the **grapevine**, is the transmission of messages from employee to employee outside of formal communication channels. The grapevine arises out of curiosity, that is, the need to know what is going on in an organization and how it might affect you or others. To satisfy this curiosity, employees need a consistent supply of relevant, accurate, in-depth information about what is going on in the company and why. Some companies using tracking technology to measure how well informal communication functions in their organizations and how it can be improved. As it prepared to move to new offices, BCG, a global consulting firm, had one in five employees wear badges that tracked where they went in the office and who they talked to (but not their conversations). BCG managing partner Ross Love, who headed the research, said the firm learned that employees were spending too much time with their bosses and subordinates, thus hurting cross-team communication. However, employees who spoke to a wider variety of people within the office spent five fewer hours in meetings each week because, he thinks, they were obtaining and sharing information much more effectively—just as informal grapevines should.[32] As a result of what BCG learned, it created a town-square lounge in its new offices, offering free breakfast, lunch, and snacks to increase informal interactions and reduce formal meetings.[33]

Grapevines arise out of informal communication networks such as the gossip or cluster chains shown in Exhibit 15.4. In a *gossip chain*, one highly connected individual shares information with many other managers and workers. By contrast, in a *cluster chain*, numerous people simply tell a few of their friends. The result in both cases is that information flows freely and quickly through the organization. Some believe that grapevines are a waste of employees' time, that they promote gossip and rumors that fuel political speculation, and that

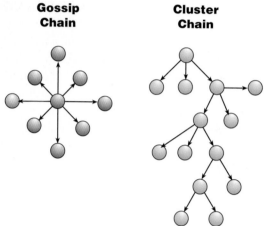

Exhibit 15.4
Grapevine Communication Networks

Gossip Chain

Cluster Chain

Source: K. Davis and J. W. Newstrom, *Human Behavior at Work: Organizational Behavior*, 8th ed. (New York: McGraw-Hill, 1989).

they are sources of highly unreliable, inaccurate information. Yet studies clearly show that grapevines are highly accurate sources of information for a number of reasons.[34] First, because grapevines typically carry "juicy" information that is interesting and timely, information spreads rapidly. During Allstate's annual Leaders Forum, a gathering of 2,000 agents and employees, CEO Thomas Wilson announced plans for reducing the company's sales force and changing sales commission rates. Later that evening, a group of employees were at the hotel bar, complaining about the changes and about Wilson, when the president of Allstate's home and auto insurance division, was allegedly overheard using two expletives in reference to Wilson. By the next day, nearly all conference attendees had heard the critical remarks. The president of that division was abruptly let go just a few weeks later.[35]

Second, because information is typically spread by face-to-face conversation, receivers can send feedback to make sure they understand the message that is being communicated. This reduces misunderstandings and increases accuracy. Third, because most of the information in a company moves along the grapevine rather than through formal communication channels, people can usually verify the accuracy of information by checking it out with others.

What can managers do to manage organizational

There is a fine line between news and gossip. At some point, you might find yourself a target of the rumor mill.

Ollyy/Shutterstock.com

Informal communication channel (grapevine) the transmission of messages from employee to employee outside of formal communication channels grapevines? The very worst thing they can do is withhold information or try to punish those who share information with others. The grapevine abhors a vacuum, so rumors and anxiety will flourish in the absence of information from company management. Why does this occur? According to workplace psychologist Nicholas DiFonzo, "The main focus of rumor is to figure out the truth. It's the group trying to make sense of something that's important to them."[36] A better strategy is to embrace the grapevine and keep employees informed about possible changes and strategies. Failure to do so will just make things worse. And, in addition to using the grapevine to communicate with others, managers should not overlook the grapevine as a tremendous source of valuable information and feedback. In fact, research shows that, contrary to popular belief, grapevines are fast, accurate, and focused on information more than gossip.[37]

15-2d Coaching and Counseling: One-on-One Communication

When the Wyatt Company surveyed 531 U.S. companies undergoing major changes and restructuring, it asked the CEOs, "If you could go back and change one thing, what would it be?" The answer: "The way we communicated with our employees." The CEOs said that instead of flashy videos, printed materials, or formal meetings, they would make greater use of one-on-one communication, especially with employees' immediate supervisors instead of with higher-level executives whom employees didn't know.[38]

Coaching and counseling are two kinds of one-on-one communication. **Coaching** is communicating with someone for the direct purpose of improving the person's on-the-job performance or behavior.[39] Managers tend to make several mistakes when coaching employees. First, they wait for a problem to arise before coaching. Why? Because similar to performance appraisals, most managers also dislike giving employees feedback. Peggy Klaus, an executive trainer, says that managers "worry that the person will go to HR and get into a big kerfuffle."[40] When she told an executive she was working with that he needed to give employees more feedback, he responded, "I'd rather have a colonoscopy."[41] Second, when mistakes *are* made, managers wait much too long before talking to the employee

Coaching communicating with someone for the direct purpose of improving the person's on-the-job performance or behavior

Counseling communicating with someone about non-job-related issues that may be affecting or interfering with the person's performance

about the problem. The late management professor Ray Hilgert said, "A manager must respond as soon as possible after an incident of poor performance. Don't bury your head. . . . When employees are told nothing, they assume everything is okay."[42] Jack Welch, who was CEO at GE for two decades, says, "I've spoken to more than 500,000 people around the world, and I always ask audiences, 'How many of you know where you stand in your organization?'" He says, "Typically no more than 10 percent raise their hands. That's criminal! As a manager, you owe candor to your people. They must not be guessing about what the organization thinks of them. My experience is that most employees appreciate this reality check, and today's 'Millenials' practically demand it."[43] In short, says Welch, "You have no right to be a leader if someone who works for you doesn't know where they stand."[44] So coach your employees about their job performance.

> When one executive was told that he needed to give employees more feedback, he responded, "I'd rather have a colonoscopy."

In contrast to coaching, **counseling** is communicating with someone about non-job-related issues such as stress, child care, health issues, retirement planning, or legal issues that may be affecting or interfering with the person's performance. But counseling does not mean that managers should try to be clinicians, even though an estimated 20 percent of employees are dealing with personal problems at any one time. Dana Kiel, regional director in Account Management at Magellan Health, says, "We call it the quicksand. If you're a good supervisor, you do care about your employees, but it's not your job to be a therapist."[45] Instead, managers should discuss specific performance problems, listen if the employee chooses to share personal issues, and then recommend that the employee call the company's *Employee Assistance Program (EAP)*. EAPs are typically free when provided as part of a company's benefit package. In emergencies or times of crisis, EAPs can offer immediate counseling and support; they can also provide referrals to organizations and professionals that can help employees and their family members address personal issues. On the first day of her new job, Wendy Wolfson

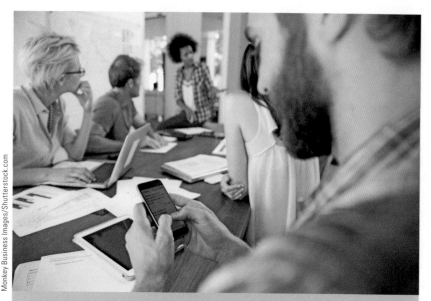

Consultant Suzanne Bates says that some of her CEO clients check their phones so much during meetings, "it's the equivalent of not showing up for half of the meeting."

Kinesics and paralanguage are two kinds of nonverbal communication.[49] **Kinesics** (from the Greek word *kinesis*, meaning "movement") are movements of the body and face.[50] These movements include arm and hand gestures, facial expressions, eye contact, folding arms, crossing legs, and leaning toward or away from another person. For example, people tend to avoid eye contact when they are embarrassed or unsure of the message they are sending. Crossed arms or legs usually indicate defensiveness or that the person is not receptive to the message or the sender. Also, people tend to smile frequently when they are seeking someone's approval.

It turns out that kinesics play an incredibly important role in communication. One of the most powerful ways is *mirroring*, in which people in conversations mimic or mirror physical gestures, facial expressions, or pitch and tone of voice. Brain scanning studies indicate that when mirroring occurs during conversations, peoples' brains react in similar positive ways at the same time. Mirroring, while usually done unconsciously, can be used intentionally by managers as a positive nonverbal behavior. David Hoffied, author of *The Science of Selling*, says, "It's not something you do to someone. It's something you do with someone. The very process of mirroring will help you keep your focus where it should be—on the other person."[51].

Kinesics provide clues about people's true feelings, over and above what they say (or don't say). Unfortunately, not making or maintaining eye contact is an increasingly frequent and negative occurrence in today's workplace. Consultant Suzanne Bates, author of *Speak Like a CEO*, says that some of her CEO clients check their phones so much during appointments that, "it's the equivalent of not showing up for half of the meeting." And that, she says, breeds resentment in others who think, "I'm just as busy as the CEO. I just have different things to juggle."[52] In fact, a survey of business professionals found that strong majorities think it is inappropriate to answer phone calls (86%) or write texts or emails (84%) in meetings or at

was called to pick up her first grader from school. Worried she might have to quit unless she could find childcare, Wolfson called her employer's EAP for help with this problem. Despite their proven effectiveness and a wide variety of assistance services (including mental health, substance abuse, financial counseling, and elder care services), only 4–6 percent of employees use EAPs.[46] According to Wolfson, "The problem is, you're pressed for time and you don't know where to go. It was a resource and another set of options."[47]

15-2e Nonverbal Communication

Nonverbal communication is any communication that doesn't involve words. Nonverbal communication almost always accompanies verbal communication and may either support and reinforce the verbal message or contradict it. The importance of nonverbal communication is well established. Researchers have estimated that as much as 93 percent of any message is transmitted nonverbally, with 55 percent coming from body language and facial expressions, and 38 percent coming from the tone and pitch of the voice.[48] Because many nonverbal cues are unintentional, receivers often consider nonverbal communication to be a more accurate representation of what senders are thinking and feeling than the words they use. If you have ever asked someone out on a date and been told "yes," but realized that the real answer was "no," then you understand the importance of paying attention to nonverbal communication.

Nonverbal communication any communication that doesn't involve words

Kinesics movements of the body and face

What If Your Emotions Were an Open Book?

Over the course of his career, 83-year-old psychologist Dr. Paul Ekman built a catalog of more than 5,000 facial muscle movements that communicate one of six base emotions: anger, disgust, fear, happiness, sadness, or surprise. What started out for Ekman as an anthropological study has recently been transformed by big data, as a host of software start-ups are building programs to uncover people's hidden emotions. One software company, Emotient, has video recorded encounters with hundreds of thousands of people and extracted 90,000 data points from each frame. Rival company Affectiva has measured billions of emotional reactions from 2.4 million face videos taken in 80 countries. Enthusiastic organizations such as Procter & Gamble, Coca-Cola, and others have used the software to gauge consumers' emotional reactions to products and advertisements; law-enforcement agencies have used the software in criminal interrogations; and retailers have used it to determine how people are feeling as they exit their stores. But despite their

foundation on big data, emotional software programs run the risk of misinterpreting emotions or incorrectly labeling people as liars. Critics are wary, however, because people are not always aware they are being recorded. Privacy advocate Ginger McCall says, "I can see few things more invasive than trying to record someone's emotions in a database."

Source: E. Dwoskin and E. M. Rusli, "The Technology That Unmasks Your Hidden Emotions," *Wall Street Journal*, January 28, 2015, accessed May 12, 2015, http://www.wsj.com /articles/startups-see-your-face-unmask-your-emotions-1422472398.

---

business lunches (66%). The kinesics related to checking smartphones in these situations communicate a lack of respect, attention, listening, and self-control.[53] TalentSmart's Travis Bradberry says, "Take a page out of the Old West and put a basket by the conference room door with an image of a smartphone and the message, 'Leave your guns at the door.'"[54]

Paralanguage includes the pitch, rate, tone, volume, and speaking pattern (use of silences, pauses, or hesitations) of one's voice. When people are unsure of what to say, for example, they tend to decrease their communication effectiveness by speaking softly. When people are nervous, they tend to speak faster and louder. How much does paralanguage matter? A study in which 1,000 people listened to 120 different speeches found that the tone of the speaker's voice accounted for 23 percent of the difference in listener's evaluations of the speech, compared to speech content, which accounted for only 11 percent.[55] So paralanguage was twice as important as what was actually said.

In short, because nonverbal communication is so informative, especially when it contradicts verbal communication, managers need to learn how to monitor and control their nonverbal behaviors.

> **Paralanguage** the pitch, rate, tone, volume, and speaking pattern (that is, use of silences, pauses, or hesitations) of one's voice

> **Communication medium** the method used to deliver an oral or written message

15-3 MANAGING ONE-ON-ONE COMMUNICATION

When it comes to improving communication, managers face two primary tasks, managing one-on-one communication and managing organization-wide communication.

On average, first-line managers spend 57 percent of their time with people, middle managers spend 63 percent of their time directly with people, and top managers spend as much as 78 percent of their time dealing with people.[56] These numbers make it clear that managers spend a great deal of time in one-on-one communication with others.

*Let's learn more about managing one-on-one communication by reading how to **15-3a choose the right communication medium**, **15-3b be a good listener**, and **15-3c give effective feedback**.*

15-3a Choosing the Right Communication Medium

Sometimes messages are poorly communicated simply because they are delivered using the wrong **communication medium**, which is the method used to deliver a message. For example, the wrong communication medium is being used when an employee returns from lunch, picks up the note left on her office chair, and learns she has been fired. The wrong communication medium is also being used when an employee pops into your office every 10 minutes with a simple request. (An email would be better.)

There are two general kinds of communication media: oral and written communication. *Oral communication* includes face-to-face interactions and group meetings through telephone calls, videoconferencing, or any other means of sending and receiving spoken messages. Studies show that managers generally prefer oral communication over written because it provides the opportunity to ask questions about parts of the message that they don't understand. Oral communication is also a rich communication medium because it allows managers to receive and assess the nonverbal communication that accompanies spoken messages (that is, body language, facial expressions, and the voice characteristics associated with paralanguage). Furthermore, you don't need a PC and an Internet connection to conduct oral communication. Simply schedule an appointment, track someone down in the hall, or catch someone on the phone. **A&E Network** executive Mel Berning travels two weeks a month, and when he is at headquarters, he forgoes what he calls "antiseptic" formal meetings and instead prefers impromptu informal meetings in which he breezes into the offices of direct reports in the morning. "You have a conversation that is less hurried and less guarded," he says. "Face-to-face encounters are so much more revealing than a text or an email.[57] Amit Singh, president of Google for Work, agrees. He says that because "so much gets lost in translation in emails," companies should make greater use of face-to-face discussions, where there is "a clash of ideas, but a respectful clash."[58]

Former *Wall Street Journal* columnist Jason Fry worries that voice mail and email have made managers less willing to engage in meaningful, face-to-face oral communication than before. In fact, 67 percent of managers admit to using email as a substitute for face-to-face conversations. While there are advantages to email (for example, it creates a record of what's been said), it's often better to talk to people instead of just emailing them. Fry writes, "If you're close enough that the person you're emailing uses the plonk of your return key as a cue to look for the little Outlook envelope, [it's] best [to] think carefully about whether you should be typing instead of talking."[59] But the oral medium should not be used for *all* communication. In general, when the message is simple, such as a quick request or a presentation of straightforward information, a memo or email is often the better communication medium.

Written communication includes letters, email, and memos. Although most managers still like and use oral

communication, email in particular is changing how they communicate with workers, customers, and each other. Email is the dominant form of communication in organizations primarily because of its convenience and speed. The average adult spends more than an hour each day reading and sending emails. In fact, nearly 300 billion emails are sent around the world every year.[60]

Part of the reason for email's dominance is that, as written communication, it is well suited for delivering straightforward messages and information. Furthermore, with email accessible at the office, at home, and on the road (by laptop computer, cell phone, or web-based email), managers can use email to stay in touch from anywhere at almost any time. And, because email and other written communications don't have to be sent and received simultaneously, messages can be sent and stored for reading at any time. Consequently, managers can send and receive many more messages using email than by using oral communication, which requires people to get together in person or by phone or videoconference.

Email has its own drawbacks, however. One is that it lacks the formality of paper memos and letters. It is easy to fire off a rushed email that is not well written or fully thought through. The opportunity to lash out with an angry email reply is incredibly tempting. To avoid that temptation and the damage it does to your work relationships, Pamela Rutledge of the Media Psychology Research Center recommends asking yourself, "Do I want an outcome where someone throws a cup of coffee at me? Or do I want an outcome where we work toward a solution"[61] Another drawback to email is that it lacks nonverbal cues, making emails very easy to misinterpret. A final drawback to email is the sheer volume that employees receive each day. At global IT-services company **Atos**, workers were spending 15 to 20 hours every week corresponding by email—and that just includes emails to and from other Atos employees. According to human resource manager Philippe Mareine, email "was becoming a burden to our employees rather than an enabler." To curb the time spent on emails, management began urging employees to use the company's internal social network, BlueKiwi. Since this move, employees' average email load has dropped to just six messages per day, and the time sales consultants take to resolve queries collaboratively has dropped from two hours (over email) to 45 minutes (using BlueKiwi). Over the past five years, email volume has fallen 70 percent at Atos, while operating margins have increased 60 percent.[62]

Although written communication is well suited for delivering straightforward messages and information, it is not well suited to complex, ambiguous, or emotionally laden messages, which are better delivered through oral communication. At software company **Autodesk**, 62 percent of managers have at least one remote employee. Because of this, all employees are trained to makes sure that the medium fits the message. For sharing information and ideas, employees use email. For brainstorming or problem solving, they use video calls or video conferencing. For making difficult decisions or resolving conflicts, they meet face to face.[63]

15-3b Listening

Are you a good listener? You probably think so. In fact, most people, including managers, are terrible listeners. A recent study from Stanford Graduate School of Business showed that listening was among the least mentioned strengths in CEO performance evaluations.[64] You qualify as a poor listener if you frequently interrupt others, jump to conclusions about what people will say before they've said it, hurry the speaker to finish his or her point, are a passive listener (not actively working at your listening), or simply don't pay attention to what people are saying.[65] On this last point—attentiveness—college students were periodically asked to record their thoughts during a psychology course. On average, 20 percent of the students were paying attention (only 12% were actively working at being good listeners), 20 percent were thinking about sex, 20 percent were thinking about things they had done before, and the remaining 40 percent were thinking about other things unrelated to the class (for example, worries, religion, lunch, daydreaming).[66]

How important is it to be a good listener? In general, about 45 percent of the total time you spend communicating with others is spent listening. Furthermore, listening is important for managerial and business success, even for those at the top of an organization. T-Mobile CEO John Legere says that when he took the top job at the telecommunications company, he needed *Wireless for Dummies*. His response to his lack of familiarity with the industry was simple—listen. He listened to customer service calls, visited stores to listen to customers and employees, and even interacted with users over social media. Legere says, "My business philosophy is to listen to your employees, listen to your customers. Shut up and do what they tell you. And each of our uncarrier moves and the way I run my company is completely aligned with that."[67]

Listening is a more important skill for managers than ever because Generation X and Millennial employees tend to expect a high level of interaction with their supervisors. They want feedback on their performance, but they also want to offer feedback and know that it is heard. In fact, managers with better listening skills are rated more highly by their employees and are much more likely to be promoted.[68]

So, what can you do to improve your listening ability? First, understand the difference between hearing and listening. According to *Webster's New World Dictionary*, **hearing** is the "act or process of perceiving sounds," whereas **listening** is "making a conscious effort to hear." In other words, we react to sounds, such as bottles breaking or music being played too loud, because hearing is an involuntary physiological process. By contrast, listening is a voluntary behavior. So, if you want to be a good listener, you have to choose to be a good listener. Typically, that means choosing to be an active, empathetic listener.[69]

Simon Mulcahy, chief marketing officer at Salesforce, is deliberate in meetings about listening, with "this sort of background music playing all the time: Don't tell. Ask questions. Don't tell. Ask questions."[70]

Active listening means assuming half the responsibility for successful communication by actively giving the speaker nonjudgmental feedback that shows you've accurately heard what he or she said. Active listeners make it clear from their behavior that they are listening carefully to what the speaker has to say. Active listeners put the speaker at ease, maintain eye contact, and show the speaker that they are attentively listening by nodding and making short statements.

Several specific strategies can help you be a better active listener. First, engage in immediacy behaviors, such as putting your phone away, turning off the TV, leaning forward and making eye contact, and using short words such as "yes," "uh-huh," and "okay," to encourage the speaker to continue and to demonstrate that you're listening.[71] In group settings, that means not following the "rule of three," which is that in a group of five or six people, it's acceptable to look at your phone as long as three people have their heads up and appear to be paying attention.[72] The "rule of three" is not active listening. Second, clarify responses by asking the speaker to explain confusing or ambiguous statements. Third, when there are natural breaks in the speaker's delivery, use this time to paraphrase or summarize what has been said. *Paraphrasing* is restating what has been said in your own words. *Summarizing* is reviewing the speaker's main points or emotions. Paraphrasing and summarizing give the speaker the chance to correct the message if the active listener has attached the wrong meaning to it.

Hearing the act or process of perceiving sounds

Listening making a conscious effort to hear

Active listening assuming half the responsibility for successful communication by actively giving the speaker nonjudgmental feedback that shows you've accurately heard what he or she said

Exhibit 15.5
Immediacy Behaviors, and Paraphrasing and Summarizing Responses for Active Listeners

Immediacy Behaviors	Clarifying Responses	Paraphrasing Responses	Summarizing Responses
Put your phone away.	Could you explain that again?	What you're really saying is	Let me summarize . . . .
Turn off the TV.	I don't understand what you mean.	If I understand you correctly	Okay, your main concerns are . . . .
Sit close and lean forward.	I'm not sure how	In other words	To recap, what you've said . . . .
Make eye contact.	I'm confused. Would you run through that again?	So your perspective is that	Thus far, you've discussed . . . .
Use "yes," "uh-huh," "okay," and other short words to encourage the speaker to continue.		Tell me if I'm wrong, but what you seem to be saying is	

Source: E. Atwater, *I Hear You*, rev. ed. (New York: Walker, 1992); E. Bernstein, "How 'Active Listening' Makes Both Participants in a Conversation Feel Better," *Wall Street Journal*, January 12, 2015, accessed May 13, 2015, http://www.wsj.com/articles/how-active-listening-makes-both-sides-of-a-conversation-feel-better-1421082684.

Paraphrasing and summarizing also show the speaker that the active listener is interested in the speaker's message.

Exhibit 15.5 reviews immediacy behaviors and lists specific statements that listeners can use to clarify responses, paraphrase, or summarize what has been said. Active listeners also avoid evaluating the message or being critical until the message is complete. They recognize that their only responsibility during the transmission of a message is to receive it accurately and derive the intended meaning from it. Evaluation and criticism can take place after the message is accurately received. Finally, active listeners recognize that a large portion of any message is transmitted nonverbally and thus pay very careful attention to nonverbal cues (that is, immediacy behaviors) transmitted by the speaker.

Empathetic listening means understanding the speaker's perspective and personal frame of reference and giving feedback that conveys that understanding to the speaker. Empathetic listening goes beyond active listening because it depends on our ability to set aside our own attitudes or relationships to be able to see and understand things through someone else's eyes. Empathetic listening is just as important as active listening, especially for managers, because it helps build rapport and trust with others. Unfortunately, an analysis of 14,000 college students across 72 studies found a 40 percent decrease in empathy over the last 30 years.[73] Since most of that decline occurred between 2000 and today, it's clear that companies need to focus on developing their managers' ability to empathize.

Thankfully, one interesting study suggests that empathy and listening skills can quickly improve. Two groups of children were asked to accurately identify peoples' emotions in pictures and videotapes. The first group attended a five-day device-free camp (no phones, tablets, or computers), while the second group did not. After the camp, the two groups were tested again. There was little difference in the second group's scores, but the first group improved nearly 40 percent. Why? Students at camp weren't watching TV or playing video games five hours a day. Aggie Chamlin who attends a no-device camp, said, "I think a cell phone's a virtual wall that you put up for yourself."[74] Yalda Uhls, lead author of the study and senior researcher with the UCLA's Children's Digital Media Center, Los Angeles, commented, "You can't learn nonverbal emotional cues from a screen in the way you can learn it from face-to-face communication."[75] MIT Professor Sherry Turkle, author of *Reclaiming Conversation: The Power of Talk in a Digital Age*, explained the results this way: "They talked to one another. In conversation, things go best if you pay close attention and learn how to put yourself in someone else's shoes."[76]

The key to being a more empathetic listener is to show your desire to understand and to reflect people's feelings. You can *show your desire to understand* by listening, that is, asking people to talk about what's most important to them and then by giving them sufficient time to talk before responding or interrupting.

Reflecting feelings is also an important part of empathetic listening because it demonstrates that you understand the speaker's emotions. Unlike active listening, in which you

Empathetic listening understanding the speaker's perspective and personal frame of reference and giving feedback that conveys that understanding to the speaker

For feedback to be constructive rather than destructive, it must be immediate and focused on specific behaviors and problems.

B Calkins/Shutterstock.com

restate or summarize the informational content of what has been said, the focus is on the affective part of the message. As an empathetic listener, you can use the following statements to *reflect the speaker's emotions*:

» So, right now it sounds like you're feeling . . . .

» You seem as if you're . . . .

» Do you feel a bit . . . ?

» I could be wrong, but I'm sensing that you're feeling . . . .

In the end, says management consultant Terry Pearce, empathetic listening can be boiled down to these three steps. First, wait 10 seconds before you respond. It will seem an eternity, but waiting prevents you from interrupting others and rushing your response. Second, to be sure you understand what the speaker wants, ask questions to clarify the speaker's intent. Third, only then should you respond first with feelings and then facts (notice that facts *follow* feelings).[77]

A word of caution, however: Not everyone appreciates having what they said repeated back to them. Manager Candy Friesen says that whenever she did that, "I seemed to engender animosity or hostility. . . . the person to whom you're speaking may not appreciate having his thoughts paraphrased one little bit."[78] So, when applying these listening techniques, pay attention to the body language and tone of voice of the person you're communicating

Destructive feedback feedback that disapproves without any intention of being helpful and almost always causes a negative or defensive reaction in the recipient

Constructive feedback feedback intended to be helpful, corrective, and/or encouraging

with to make sure they appreciate your attempts to be a better listener.

15-3c Giving Feedback

In Chapter 11, you learned that performance appraisal feedback (that is, judging) should be separated from developmental feedback (that is, coaching).[79] We can now focus on the steps needed to communicate feedback one-on-one to employees.

To start, managers need to recognize that feedback can be constructive or destructive. **Destructive feedback** is disapproving without any intention of being helpful and almost always causes a negative or defensive reaction in the recipient. By contrast, **constructive feedback** is intended to be helpful, corrective, and/or encouraging. It is aimed at correcting performance deficiencies and motivating employees. But finding the fine line between the two can be difficult. Ranstad, a global HR services company, adopted a philosophy of radical candor out of concerns that managers and employees were not having honest, constructive discussions about performance. A recipient of radically candid feedback said it "cut me to the bone." Wendy Finlason Seymour, a director of talent management, said the candid feedback is "not there to destroy," but "sometimes the truth can hurt."[80]

For feedback to be constructive rather than destructive, it must be immediate, focused on specific behaviors, and problem-oriented. *Immediate feedback* is much more effective than delayed feedback because manager and worker can recall the mistake or incident more accurately and discuss it in detail before it's too late to have a meaningful conversation. Employees at **PwC** use an app called Snapshot to request short, immediate assessments from their managers on everything from overall business acumen to specific technical capabilities. The feedback is visible to the employee, career coach, direct supervisor, HR manager, and the partner in charge of the team, and analytics tools assess the quality of the feedback and how quickly the manager responded. PwC vice chairman Tim Ryan says that the goal is to develop employees in real time: "We analogize it to athletes. They get feedback every time they come off the court."[81]

Specific feedback focuses on particular acts or incidents that are clearly under the control of the employee. For instance, instead of telling an employee that he or she is "always late for work," it's much more constructive to say, "In the last three weeks, you have been 30 minutes late on four occasions and more than an hour late on two others." Furthermore, specific feedback isn't very helpful unless employees have control over the problems that the feedback addresses. Giving negative feedback about behaviors beyond someone's control is likely to be seen as unfair. Similarly, giving positive feedback about behaviors beyond someone's control may be viewed as insincere.

Last, *problem-oriented feedback* focuses on the problems or incidents associated with the poor performance rather than on the worker or the worker's personality. Giving feedback does not give managers the right to personally attack workers. Although managers may be frustrated by a worker's poor performance, the point of problem-oriented feedback is to draw attention to the problem in a nonjudgmental way so that the employee has enough information to correct it. Executive coach Deborah Bright says, "As an example, consider someone who cares about being respected by peers but is habitually 10 minutes late to weekly staff meetings and often blames her tardiness on her busy schedule. A manager might simply reprimand her—either nicely ("Please make more of an effort to be on time") or sharply ("Do we need to get you a new watch?"). But a more effective strategy is to say something like: "How do you think coming in late affects your reputation with your colleagues?"[82]

15-4 MANAGING ORGANIZATION-WIDE COMMUNICATION

Although managing one-on-one communication is important, managers must also know how to communicate effectively with a larger number of people throughout an organization.

Learn more about organization-wide communication by reading the following sections about 15-4a improving transmission by getting the message out and 15-4b improving reception by finding ways to hear what others feel and think.

15-4a Improving Transmission: Getting the Message Out

Several methods of electronic communication—email, collaborative discussion sites, streamed or video-shared speeches and conferences, and broadcast voice mail—now make it easier for managers to communicate with people throughout the organization and get the message out.

Although we normally think of email, the transmission of messages via computers, as a means of one-on-one communication, it also plays an important role in organization-wide communication. With the click of a button, managers can send an email to everyone in the company via distribution lists. John Rae-Grant, lead product manager for Gmail, says, "People have been forecasting the death of email for the last 25 years," yet, "there's no sign that email usage is abating. It's certainly changing, but in the working world, email is still the baseline glue that pretty much carries everything."[83] But, as a communication tool, email is a huge burden for most managers and employees, with 40 percent of white-collar employees devoting a minimum of three hours per workday to email. Forty-three percent of employees have felt so controlled by their email that they've put themselves in "detox," completely avoiding touching their email for three to four days.[84] The most overwhelmed emailers declare email bankruptcy by deleting all their unanswered email. Via an email blast to all of their contacts, or using auto reply, they communicate that they've deleted all email and that if you urgently needed something from them, you should send your message again. With a now-empty inbox and the likelihood that most deleted emails won't be resent to them, they can start over.[85]

Collaborative communication tools are another means of electronically promoting organization-wide communication. **Discussion channels and chat rooms** use web- or app-based communication tools to hold company-wide, department-based, topic-based, team, or private discussions. The Salesforce "airing of grievances" chat mentioned earlier is an example of a company-wide channel or chat room. Public questions posed to human resources (HR) about, say, medical insurance coverage, that HR answers publicly would be a department- or topic-based channel or chat room. Team room channels are often restricted to team members working together, while private discussions are typically invitation-only for teams or for one-to-one work sessions. Discussion channels and chat rooms allow the sharing of expertise, avoid duplicating solutions already discovered by others, and provide a historical database for people dealing with particular problems. They promote collaborative discussion via participant comments and through document sharing and editing (see Chapter 17, "Managing Information," for further explanation).

Slack is a robust group communication platform (on computers, smartphones, and tablets) that includes automatic archiving, a powerful search engine, and more informal and accessible online collaboration. Slack's "open channels" increase communication transparency by making messages, files, comments,

> **Discussion channels and chat rooms**
> the use of web- or app-based communication tools to hold company-wide, department-based, topic-based, team, or private discussions

The Right to Disconnect from Email?

France's right to disconnect law requires companies with 50 or more employees to "switch off" after-hours email and communication. The goal is to protect employees from unpaid work that constantly intrudes on their home lives. France has long had a 35-hour work week, but in reality, most managers and a third of employees get around the law that by working at home on evenings or weekends. While noble in intent, can it work in the real world? Professor Anna Cox says, "Some people want to work for two hours every evening, but want to be able to switch off between 3 and 5 p.m. when they pick their kids up and are cooking dinner. Others are happy to use their daily commute to get ahead before they arrive in the office." Under a similar law, German companies such as Volkswagen only allow emails to be received during work hours. Is this enforceable, or would companies and their employees "cheat?" Would this policy increase or decrease email stress in your life?

Source: A. Levitt, "France Is Forcing Its Employees to Power Down: Will It Work?" *QuickBase*, February 14, 2017, accessed May 2, 2017, http://www.quickbase.com/blog/france-is-forcing-its-employees-to-power-down-will-it-work.

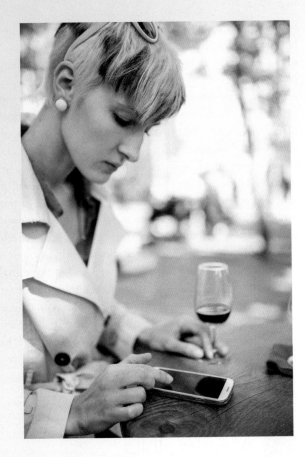

images, and video visible to everyone else in the team (or company). And with everything searchable, anyone can quickly catch up to find out where projects or discussions stand. Technology guru Walt Mossberg says, "It's sort of like a combination of Facebook, Twitter, iMessage, and Dropbox, but just for you and your co-workers.[86] Companies have adopted Slack primarily because it increases communication effectiveness so much that email usage within teams or companies often drops by 70 or 80 percent. *New York Times* reporter Farhad Manjoo is based in California and has found that Slack helps him stay connected to "the mother ship in New York. Using Slack, I can peer into discussions that would never have been accessible to me. I can see how the producers and editors who are handling my column are discussing how to present it, and how the team overseeing the home page is thinking about my work."[87]

Livestreamed/videotaped speeches and meetings are a third electronic method of organization-wide communication.

Streamed/videotaped speeches and meetings speeches and meetings originally made to a smaller audience that are either simultaneously streamed to other locations in the company or recorded for subsequent distribution and viewing

Streamed/videotaped speeches and meetings are simply speeches and meetings originally made to a small audience that are either simultaneously streamed to other locations in the company or recorded for subsequent distribution and viewing by a broader audience.

Voice messaging, or voice mail, is a telephone answering system that records audio messages. In one survey, 89 percent of respondents said that voice messaging is critical to business communication, 78 percent said that it improves productivity, and 58 percent said they would rather leave a message on a voice messaging system than with a receptionist.[88] Nonetheless, most people are unfamiliar with the ability to *broadcast voice mail* by sending a recorded message to everyone in the company. Broadcast voice mail gives top managers a quick, convenient way to address their workforces via oral communication—but only if people actually listen to the message, and that turns out to be a challenge with today's workers, who are much more likely to use their smartphones for social media rather than phone calls. Consequently, company leaders are increasingly using real-time messaging tools like Yammer, a Facebook-like social media platform for companies, or Skype for Business, to broadcast text or video-based messages to their workforces.

Organization silence can isolate a manager if employees are reluctant to tell managers things they don't think they will want to hear.

Syda Productions/Shutterstock.com

When Poojan Kumar, CEO of data storage manufacturer PernixData, wanted to change how employees received internal communications, he blocked company-wide emails and insisted that messages intended for all employees be posted to Yammer instead. To encourage use, Kumar began posting snapshots of the company's equipment in action that he took during his travels. Human resources also put up a company directory with employees' photos. Getting employees to embrace a new communication platform, Kumar says, "will only happen if there's enough interesting content."[89]

15-4b Improving Reception: Hearing What Others Feel and Think

When people think of "organization-wide" communication, they think of the CEO and top managers getting their message out to people in the company. But organization-wide communication also means finding ways to hear what people throughout the organization are thinking and feeling. This is important because most employees and managers are reluctant to share their thoughts and feelings with top managers. Surveys indicate that only 29 percent of first-level managers feel that their companies encourage employees to express their opinions openly. Another study of 22 companies found that 70 percent of the people surveyed were afraid to speak up about problems they knew existed at work.

Withholding information about organizational problems or issues is called **organizational silence**. Organizational silence occurs when employees believe that telling management about problems won't make a difference or that they'll be punished or hurt in some way for sharing such information.[90] A survey of executives found that 85 percent had at some point kept quiet when they saw a serious problem at work.[91] Financial company Charles Schwab CEO Walt Bettinger explains that organizational silence isolates managers in two ways: "people telling you what they think you want to hear, and people being fearful to tell you things they believe you don't want to hear."[92] Nandan Nilekani, a co-founder of Infosys, the India-based global information technology consulting firm, agrees, saying, "If you're a leader, you can put yourself in a cocoon—a good-news cocoon," he notes. "Everyone tells you, 'It's all right—there's no problem.' And the next day, everything's wrong."[93]

Company hotlines, survey feedback, frequent informal meetings, surprise visits, and blogs are additional ways of overcoming organizational silence. **Company hotlines** are phone numbers that anyone in the company can call anonymously to leave information for upper management. Company hotlines are incredibly useful, as 41 percent of the calls placed to them result in an investigation and some form of corrective action within the organization. Anonymity is critical, too, because as those investigations proceeded, 59 percent of the callers did not want their identities revealed.[94]

Survey feedback is information that is collected by survey from organization members and then compiled, disseminated, and used to develop action plans for improvement. Many organizations make use of survey feedback by surveying their managers and employees several times a year. **Sunovian**

Organizational silence when employees withhold information about organizational problems or issues

Company hotlines phone numbers that anyone in the company can call anonymously to leave information for upper management

Survey feedback information that is collected by surveys from organizational members and then compiled, disseminated, and used to develop action plans for improvement

TAKE A MEMO: THE RISE IN ANONYMOUS VENTING

A new app called Memo allows employees to vent about their employers by posting anonymous "memos" (vents). Users of the app can post new memos, comment on existing memos, and even upload photos and documents to support their memos. Employees at companies such as Delta Airline, Ernst & Young, and Hasbro are using Memo to vent about compensation, managerial inefficiency, and working from home. After a user is verified, Memo removes all identifiable data about the person's activity, making that person's posts completely anonymous. Memos (posts) are organized onto public message boards that can be seen by all users and private boards organized by company. Not all companies are thrilled at the availability of Memo. Visa, Boeing, and Hewlett-Packard have all circulated internal corporate memos (the traditional kind) discouraging employees from using the app and reminding them of the risk of proprietary information being released to the public.

Source: L. Gellman, "App Lets Workers Vent Anonymously," *Wall Street Journal*, January 20, 2015, accessed May 12, 2015, http://www.wsj.com/articles/memo-app-lets-workers-vent-anonymously-1421805377.

Ben Schonewille/Shutterstock.com

Pharmaceuticals, a small drug maker in Massachusetts, which had a divided office, with employees on the second floor and executives two floors up, discovered through its annual survey that employees felt walled off from their leaders. So, chief commercial officer Rick Russell, who managed 1,100 people, put a desk in a glass-walled office in the middle of the second floor, which employees quickly dubbed "the fish bowl," where he worked every Friday without an assistant. Soon, the company's chief medical officer joined him, and the following year, survey feedback showed that employee trust in senior leadership improved. Russell says, "You have to rally the troops. You can't do it from a memo."[95]

Frequent *informal meetings* between top managers and lower-level employees are one of the best ways for top managers to hear what others think and feel. Many people assume that top managers are at the center of everything that goes on in organizations, but top managers commonly feel isolated from most of their lower-level managers and employees.[96] Consequently, more and more top managers are scheduling frequent informal meetings with people throughout their companies.

The World Bank, with 10,000 people in 120 offices worldwide, is a non-governmental organization that aims to end extreme poverty and promote "income growth for the bottom 40 percent of every country."[97] When James Wolfensohn became president of the World Bank, "he went on fact-finding trips to developing countries to understand the kinds of projects that the bank was doing. After several visits he realized that he was only being shown successful projects, smiling villagers, and grateful government officials." He told consultant and author Ron Ashkenas that "he eventually learned to stray from his tour guides so that he could meet people who hadn't been prepped for his visit, to see what was really happening. This dramatically changed his assessment of how much of the bank's aid was getting through the local government, to the people who really needed it."[98]

Have you ever been around when a supervisor learns that upper management is going to be paying a visit? First, there's shock. Next, there's anxiety. And then there's panic, as everyone is told to drop what he or she is doing to polish, shine, and spruce up the workplace so that it looks perfect for the visit. Of course, when visits are conducted under these conditions, top managers don't get a realistic look at what's going on in the company. Consequently, one of the ways to get an accurate picture is to pay *surprise visits* to various parts of the organization. These visits should not just be surprise inspections but should also be used as opportunities to encourage meaningful upward communication from those who normally don't get a chance to communicate with upper management.

Blogs are another way to hear what people are thinking and saying, both inside and outside the organization. A **blog** is a personal website that provides personal opinions or recommendations, news summaries, and reader comments. When the 2.0 version of popular time-tracking app **Hours** was released with new functionality, it was featured on the Apple App Store. Within days, the app had tens of thousands of new customers. However, Hours' tech support team soon received hundreds of complaints about the app's new team functions. Company founder Jeremy Olson used the corporate blog to candidly admit the problems and how the company was trying to solve them. He also announced that Hours 2.0 would be free until a fixed version was released, and that all who had purchased a yearly subscription would get a free second year. In response, customers rallied around the company, including Aaron Whitney, who commented on Olson's post, "I've been one of the people struggling with issues since launch day . . . and, admittedly, after three weeks, was frustrated almost to the point of bailing out. This post changed my perspective. Anyone who wants to know how a company should properly handle a less than stellar customer experience should read your post. It's perfect."[99]

Monitoring social media, such as blogs, Twitter, and Facebook, written by people outside the company can be a good way to find out what others are saying or thinking about your organization or its products or actions. McDonald's put together a social media plan called "Our Food. Your Questions." to monitor and engage with both customers and critics. Laney Garcia, McDonald's manager of brand reputation and public relations, said, "What we did was audit the conversations that were happening from a social perspective. We looked at conversations that were happening on Twitter, Facebook, and we really scrubbed the data to find out when consumers have questions about our brand."[94] Common questions included, "Is your meat 100 percent beef?" "Are your eggs real?" "Does your meat include pink slime?" McDonald's prepared answers to questions already posted on social media and assembled a team of rapid responders to address new questions. The result, says Garcia, was a sizable increase in traffic, both to the company's website and to the videos where questions were answered. And, she says, "For the first time, we've seen customers really responding in the sense that they're *defending* us."[100]

Finally, in addition to being a way to deliver organizational communication, so-called *town hall meetings* can be an effective way for companies to hear feedback from employees. In 2016, Dubai-based **Emirates Airline** carried 51.9 million passengers, and by 2020, it expects that number to rise to 70 million. To meet growing demand, Emirates Airline will hire 5,000 additional cabin staff, but in the meantime, the 20,000 current cabin crew employees are working more hours on shorter layovers. Crew members who had worked their way to first-class assignments, a prestigious posting, are having to return to economy class to cover staff shortages. Many staff members have had annual leave allocations deferred. To better understand crew member complaints, the airline held three town hall meetings—the first of which lasted four hours—during which staff aired grievances to senior management. Terry Daly, Emirates' senior vice president of service delivery, announced the meetings in an email, writing that he was "aware that there are a number of subjects that are causing concern at the moment" and that the meetings would be "an opportunity to talk about these directly with me."[101]

Blog a personal website that provides personal opinions or recommendations, news summaries, and reader comments

STUDY TOOLS 15

LOCATED IN TEXTBOOK
☐ Rip out and review chapter review card.

LOCATED AT WWW.CENGAGEBRAIN.COM
☐ Gain unique perspectives on key concepts with new 4LTR concept videos in the e-book.

☐ Increase your comprehension with Aplia for MGMT11.

☐ Complete interactive content within the e-book.

16 | Control

LEARNING OBJECTIVES

16-1 Describe the basic control process.

16-2 Discuss the various methods that managers can use to maintain control.

16-3 Describe the behaviors, processes, and outcomes that today's managers are choosing to control in their organizations.

After you finish this chapter, go to **PAGE 371** for **STUDY TOOLS**

16-1 THE CONTROL PROCESS

For all companies, past success is no guarantee of future success. Even successful companies fall short or face challenges and thus have to make changes. **Control** is a regulatory process of establishing standards to achieve organizational goals, comparing actual performance to the standards, and taking corrective action when necessary to restore performance to those standards. Control is achieved when behavior and work procedures conform to standards and when company goals are accomplished.[1] Control is not just an after-the-fact process, however. Preventive measures are also a form of control.

In a factory setting, fluorescent lighting costs $9 to $10 per square meter every year. So for a typical 600,000 square foot factory, annual lighting costs can run half a million dollars each year. This is why Quality Bicycle Products installed energy-efficient light emitting diode (LED) lighting in its new 122,000 square foot distribution facility in Lancaster, Pennsylvania. While the LED lights are two to three times more expensive to install than fluorescent lighting, they're 90 percent more efficient and can last up to 25 years, reducing the costs of changing burned-out bulbs. Quality Bicycle also outfitted its LED lights with motion sensors that only activate the

Control a regulatory process of establishing standards to achieve organizational goals, comparing actual performance against the standards, and taking corrective action when necessary lights when someone is present and daylight sensors that reduce lighting when natural light is present. San Marks of Greenearth Energy says, "It's effectively [like] having a laptop computer under each light."[2] According to Dave Smith, who runs the distribution facility for Quality Bicycle, the savings are so great that, "The payoff for our investment was a year and a half."[3]

LED lights are two to three times more expensive than fluorescent lights, but they're 90 percent more efficient and can last up to 25 years.

The basic control process 16-1a begins with the establishment of clear standards of performance; 16-1b involves a comparison of performance to those standards; 16-1c takes corrective action, if needed, to repair performance deficiencies; 16-1d is a dynamic, cybernetic process; and 16-1e consists of three basic methods: feedback control, concurrent control, and feedforward control. However, as much as managers would like, 16-1f control isn't always worthwhile or possible.

16-1a Standards

The control process begins when managers set goals such as satisfying 90 percent of customers or increasing sales by 5 percent. Companies then specify the performance standards that must be met to accomplish those goals. **Standards** are a basis of comparison for measuring the extent to which organizational performance is satisfactory or unsatisfactory. For example, many pizzerias use 30 to 40 minutes as the standard for delivery

> **Standards** a basis of comparison for measuring the extent to which various kinds of organizational performance are satisfactory or unsatisfactory

tarczas/Shutterstock.com

PHONE-FREE PERFORMANCES! THANKS YONDR!

Comedian Dave Chappelle hates it when people in the audience record him on their smartphones. Fan-posted videos on Facebook and YouTube also limit his ability to develop new material. Comedians like Chappelle can take months to craft, edit, and finely hone new material in small venues before playing larger performance halls.

Chappelle, however, now has his audiences put their smartphones in Yondr pouches, which fans hold onto during performance. Yondr automatically locks, preventing access and recording. If your phone buzzes, indicating a call, you leave the performance area and unlock the Yondr pouch by tapping it on an unlocking pod in the lobby.

Chappelle says, "I know my show is protected, and it empowers me to be more honest and open with the audience." Most fans find that without the distraction of their phones they enjoy the performance much more, except for a drunk fan at one performance who chewed off the bottom of his Yondr pouch.

Source: J. Morrissey, "Your Phone's on Lockdown. Enjoy the Show," *New York Times*, October 15, 2016, accessed May 5, 2017, https://www.nytimes.com/2016/10/16/technology/your-phones-on-lockdown-enjoy-the-show.html' J. Stern, "The Night They Locked Up All the Smartphones," *Wall Street Journal*, February 28, 2017, accessed May 5, 2017, https://www.wsj.com/articles/the-night-they-locked-up-all-the-smartphones-1488306868.

time. Because anything longer is viewed as unsatisfactory, they'll typically reduce the price if they can't deliver a hot pizza to you within that time period.

So how do managers set standards? How do they decide which levels of performance are satisfactory and which are unsatisfactory? The first criterion for a good standard is that it must enable goal achievement. If you're meeting the standard but still not achieving company goals, then the standard may have to be changed. Credit card use has skyrocketed in the last 20 years because consumers like the convenience of not carrying cash and retailers like the convenience of guaranteed payment. Credit card issuers, however, have lost billions from stolen credit card numbers hacked via the credit card swipe machines used in retail stores. Credit card issuers changed the standard from convenience to security when they informed retailers that they would need to pay for new, more secure pin and chip swipe machines by October 2016.

Benchmarking the process of identifying outstanding practices, processes, and standards in other companies and adapting them to your company

Credit card issuers would continue to pay for fraudulent credit card charges as long as retailers used the pin and chip swipe machines. But retailers who continued using the older insecure swipe machines would now, for the first time, have to pay for fraudulent charges themselves.[5]

Companies also determine standards by listening to customers' comments, complaints, and suggestions or by observing competitors. By January 2017, one-third of retailers used pin and chip credit card swipe machines. But customers hated them! The *Wall Street Journal's* Joanna Stern described using the new swipe machines like this: "1. Swipe card. 2. Get scolded by cashier to use the chip reader. 3. Insert chip and cancel all foreseeable plans. 4. Wait. 5. Wait some more. 6. Celebrate once you hear that joyless "Remove card" sound."[6] Stern found the pin and chip machines took 13 seconds to approve payment! As a result, some retailers continued using the less-secure swipe machines, despite liability for fraudulent charges, just to avoid long cash register lines.[7] Fortunately, the new swipe machines also process even more secure smartphone payments (using Apple Pay, Samsung Pay, and Android Pay) in 6 seconds or less. So, thanks to customers, the more secure standard for credit card payments will also be fast *and* convenient.

Standards can also be determined by benchmarking other companies. **Benchmarking** is the process of determining how well other companies (not just competitors) perform business functions or tasks. In other words, benchmarking is the process of determining other companies' standards. When setting standards by benchmarking, the first step is to determine what to benchmark. Organizations can benchmark anything from cycle time (how fast) to quality (how well) to price (how much). For example, based on national benchmarking studies of thousands of fire departments, many firefighters are expected to respond to an alarm within 15 seconds 95 percent of the time. Additionally, 90 percent of the time, it should take no more than 60 seconds to leave the firehouse, and then no more than four minutes to arrive at the scene.[8]

After setting standards, the next step is to identify the companies *against which* to benchmark those standards. The last step is to collect data to determine other companies' performance standards. Intuit, maker of financial software and websites such as QuickBooks, Intuit Payroll, and TurboTax, gets nearly 40 percent of its revenues by selling its products and services to tens of thousands of small- to medium-sized businesses in different industries. Fred Shilmover, CEO of InsightSquared, which sells data-analytic tools to those businesses, says, "Intuit figured out how to leverage its internal data team for their customers, when those companies couldn't gather enough data on their own to understand the bigger [industry and business] trends."[9] And because Intuit also sells add-on products and services to help manage payroll, inventory, financing, customers, point of sale trends, and online/social media marketing, he says those businesses "can now benchmark their costs [and organizational performance in all of those areas] against each other." This benchmarking shows them whether they perform at, above, or below thousands of other companies on a number of critical dimensions.

16-1b Comparison to Standards

The next step in the control process is to compare actual performance to performance standards. Although this sounds straightforward, the quality of the comparison depends largely on the measurement and information systems a company uses to keep track of performance. The better the system, the easier it is for companies to track their progress and identify problems that need to be fixed.

On average, 5 percent of hospital patients catch an infection at the hospital. It costs an average of $15,000 per incident to treat such infections, and 100,000 patients will die each year from them. Why? Because in most hospitals, health care workers wash their hands only 50 percent of the time before examining or touching a patient. Because of the risks, the Center for Disease Control created a video, "Hand Hygiene Saves Lives," to be shown to patients admitted to hospitals. In the video, a patient's wife asks her husband's doctor, on entering the hospital room, to wash his hands before beginning the medical exam.[10]

So, how can a hospital measure the rate at which its employees wash their hands so it can compare the actual rate of handwashing to its goal for handwashing? At the University Health Network in Toronto, researchers electronically monitored the hand-hygiene system. Pushing the lever on a soap dispenser sends a signal time-stamping the handwashing event and logging it into a central database. Even though the hospital was able to measure the rate of handwashing digitally, it found that with the presence of an auditor—a person in a white lab coat (who did not know the purpose of the study)—the rate of handwashing nearly tripled to 3.75 washes per hour versus 1.07 washes per hour when no auditor was present.[11]

16-1c Corrective Action

The next step in the control process is to identify performance deviations, analyze those deviations, and then develop and implement programs to correct them. This is similar to the planning process discussed in Chapter 5. Regular, frequent performance feedback allows workers and managers to track their performance and make adjustments in effort, direction, and strategies.

Travelers to China have long encountered public bathrooms with no toilet and no toilet paper (bring your own). But after investing $3.6 billion to modernize public bathrooms, Chinese officials have a new problem—senior citizens stealing toilet paper for home use. At Beijing's Temple of Heaven, one of China's most popular sites, toilet paper is dispensed by machines with facial recognition cameras that only permit two feet of paper every nine minutes. Lei Zhenshan, marketing director for Shoulian Zhineng, which makes the dispensers said, "We brainstormed many options: fingerprints, infrared, and facial recognition. We went with facial recognition, because it's the most hygienic way."[12]

16-1d Dynamic, Cybernetic Process

As shown in Exhibit 16.1, control is a continuous, dynamic, cybernetic process. Control begins by setting standards, measuring performance, and then comparing performance to the standards. If the performance deviates from the standards, then managers and employees analyze the deviations and develop and implement corrective programs that (they hope) achieve the desired performance by meeting the standards. Managers must repeat the entire process again and again in an endless feedback loop (a continuous process). Thus, control is not a one-time achievement or result. It continues over time (that is, it is dynamic) and requires daily, weekly, and monthly attention from managers to maintain performance

WANG ZHAO/ AFP/ Getty Images

Chinese officials warded off theft of toilet paper at public sites by installing dispensers with control features that use facial recognition technology.

Exhibit 16.1
Cybernetic Control Process

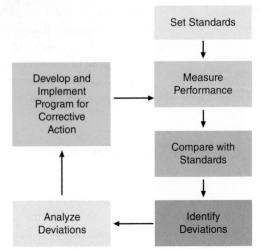

Source: H. Koontz and R. W. Bradspies, "Managing through Feedforward Control: A Future Directed View," *Business Horizons*, June 1972, pp. 25–36.

levels at the standard (that is, it is cybernetic). **Cybernetic** derives from the Greek word *kubernetes*, meaning "steersman," that is, one who steers or keeps on course.[13] The control process shown in Exhibit 16.1 is cybernetic because constant attention to the feedback loop is necessary to keep the company's activity on course.

16-1e Feedback, Concurrent, and Feedforward Control

Cybernetic the process of steering or keeping on course

Feedback control a mechanism for gathering information about performance deficiencies after they occur

Concurrent control a mechanism for gathering information about performance deficiencies as they occur, thereby eliminating or shortening the delay between performance and feedback

Feedforward control a mechanism for monitoring performance inputs rather than outputs to prevent or minimize performance deficiencies before they occur

The three basic control methods are feedback control, concurrent control, and feedforward control. **Feedback control** is a mechanism for gathering information about performance deficiencies *after* they occur. This information is then used to correct or prevent performance deficiencies. Study after study has clearly shown that feedback improves both individual and organizational performance. In most instances, any feedback is better than no feedback.

If feedback has a downside, it's that feedback always comes after the fact. Within minutes of rescuing a snow-mobiler stranded in a whiteout, an Alaska Department of Public Safety helicopter crashed, killing all on board. Video footage from a cockpit camera recovered from the rubble revealed that the pilot had incorrectly reset the device that indicates that the craft is flying level. National Transportation Safety Board chief aviation investigator John DeLisi said, "Without that video, we would have been looking at a pile of burned-up wreckage, trying to figure out what caused the erratic flight path that led to this crash."[14] The black box data and voice recorder required on all jets and helicopters could not have provided that information. Because of this video footage, the Alaska Department of Public Safety now requires pilots to receive instrument training every 90 days. This better prepares pilots to navigate in whiteout conditions, which are common in the state. By contrast, the pilot of the crashed helicopter hadn't received instrument training in more than 10 years.[15]

Concurrent control addresses the problems inherent in feedback control by gathering information about performance deficiencies *as* they occur. Thus, it is an improvement over feedback because it attempts to eliminate or shorten the delay between performance and feedback about the performance. The year after the failed launch of the Windows 8 operating system, Microsoft began developing Windows 10 by asking corporate partners to comment on the software as it was being developed. An aggressive beta-testing program involved roughly 5 million individuals, 30 percent of whom were information technology workers at large companies. An advisory board of managers from large firms (typically Microsoft's biggest customers) was formed to make recommendations and discuss the company's plans. By asking for feedback concurrently, as development occurred, Microsoft was able to fix bugs earlier and add features recommended by key customers and software developers. Asking so many people for feedback also created a high level of interest in the new operating system. Seventy-three percent of information technology managers indicated that their company planned to adopt Windows 10 within two years of its launch.[16]

Feedforward control is a mechanism for gathering information about performance deficiencies *before* they occur. In contrast to feedback and concurrent control, which provide feedback on the basis of outcomes and results, feedforward control provides information about performance deficiencies by monitoring inputs rather than outputs. Thus, feedforward control seeks to prevent or minimize performance deficiencies

Though Windows 10 has been met with critical and public acclaim, some feel that Microsoft has exhibited *too much* control in pressuring customers to upgrade to the new operating system. Users with older versions faced persistent pop-ups and reminders, and some were even upgraded without their consent. In May 2016, Teri Goldstein was awarded $10,000 after suing Microsoft for an unwanted and unauthorized update to Windows 10.

16-1f Control Isn't Always Worthwhile or Possible

Control is achieved when behavior and work procedures conform to standards, and goals are accomplished. By contrast, **control loss** occurs when behavior and work procedures do not conform to standards.[19] Despite strict preventive procedures, control loss occurred when bird flu was discovered in a flock of commercial chickens used for breeding. Tyson, the largest producer of chicken meat in the United States, in cooperation with the U.S. and Tennessee Departments of Agriculture, destroyed 73,500 birds to prevent the disease from spreading. Tennessee State Veterinarian Dr. Charles Hatcher said, "With this [avian influenza] detection, we are moving quickly and aggressively to prevent the virus from spreading."[20] Thirty additional poultry farms within a six-mile radius have been temporarily quarantined.

Maintaining control is important because control loss prevents organizations from achieving their goals. When control loss occurs, managers need to find out what, if anything, they could have done to prevent it. Usually, that means identifying deviations from standard performance, analyzing the causes of those deviations, and taking corrective action. Even so, implementing controls isn't always worthwhile or possible. Let's look at regulation costs and cybernetic feasibility to see why this is so.

To determine whether control is worthwhile, managers need to carefully assess **regulation costs**, that is, whether the costs and unintended consequences of control exceed its benefits. If a control process costs more than it benefits, it may not be worthwhile. For several decades, city and state recycling programs paid for themselves as the cost of collecting recyclables was exceeded by the revenue from reselling millions of tons of glass, aluminum, and plastic. However, in the last two years, recycled aluminum can prices have dropped 28 percent, while prices for recycled plastic bottles are down 44 percent. The major consequence of lower prices is that the cost of collecting recyclable materials now exceeds revenues. Because regulation costs now exceed regulation benefits, 700 of California's 2,400 recycling centers have closed. Fewer recycling centers also means that consumers have to drive further to get paid 5 cents

before they happen. Power companies have traditionally relied on consumers to call in power outages. Then, when repair crews arrive, fault detectors displaying a flag or a light can tell them which line is out, but the crews still have to visually inspect miles of power lines, often in weather with poor visibility, to find the precise cause of the outage. Tollgrade, however, is making sensors the size of a loaf of bread, which sit on and are powered by the electricity flowing through the wires, that can notify power companies about problems before they happen (that is, feedforward). With Global Positioning System (GPS) (location) and wireless (communication) capabilities, the sensors monitor the fluctuations in the flow of electricity—from outages to drops to normal transmissions to surge overloads—and instantaneously send text alerts to power company engineers when there are problems.[17] Pennsylvania's Orange & Rockland Utilities were alerted to an electrical line problem over a Fourth of July weekend, and the advanced notice of the outage offered ample time for repair crews to fix the issue before a single customer could complain. Haukur Asgeirsson, technology manager at DTE Energy, says, "You can actually go out there and do some preemptive work before a permanent outage occurs. It looks actually very promising."[18]

> **Control loss** the situation in which behavior and work procedures do not conform to standards
>
> **Regulation costs** the costs associated with implementing or maintaining control

Josep Curto/Shutterstock.com

per recycled bottle or can. Californian Hiro Tani said, "It kind of defeats the purpose if you have to drive that far."[21] Jose Ponce, who runs six recycling businesses, says, "If it keeps going the way it is, I don't know if I'm going to make it. That would be bad for the environment and also bad for people."[22] Likewise, at this rate, California's Beverage Container Recycling Fund will run out of money in 2018.

Another factor to consider is **cybernetic feasibility**, the extent to which it is possible to implement each of the three steps in the control process. If one or more steps cannot be implemented, then maintaining effective control may be difficult or impossible.

16-2 CONTROL METHODS

When taking college entrance exams such as the SAT, applicants present a photo ID and are warned that sharing information is prohibited, as is "the use of phones and certain other electronic devices."[23] But that hasn't stopped time zone cheating, where students in eastern time zones share test information with those taking the same exam in western time zones later that day; physical theft of tests from supposedly secure lock boxes; or online discussion following each test administration (the College Board reuses questions several times for cost and reliability reasons).[24] Chinese authorities have begun using security drones during China's National Higher Education Entrance Exam. The drones fly over testing centers, scanning for electronic signals used to transmit copies of the exam and/or provide real-time help to test takers. The Chinese education ministry arrests cheaters and bans them from taking the test for three years.[25]

Cybernetic feasibility the extent to which it is possible to implement each step in the control process

Bureaucratic control the use of hierarchical authority to influence employee behavior by rewarding or punishing employees for compliance or noncompliance with organizational policies, rules, and procedures

Managers can use five different methods to achieve control in their organizations: ***16-2a bureaucratic, 16-2b objective, 16-2c normative, 16-2d concertive,*** *and* ***16-2e self-control.***

16-2a Bureaucratic Control

When most people think of managerial control, what they have in mind is bureaucratic control. **Bureaucratic control** is top-down control, in which managers try to influence employee behavior by rewarding or punishing employees for compliance or noncompliance with organizational policies, rules, and procedures. Most employees, however, would argue that bureaucratic managers emphasize punishment of noncompliance much more than rewards for compliance.

As you learned in Chapter 2, bureaucratic management and control were created to prevent just this type of managerial behavior. By encouraging managers to apply well-thought-out rules, policies, and procedures in an impartial, consistent manner to everyone in the organization, bureaucratic control is supposed to make companies more efficient, effective, and fair. Ironically, it frequently has just the opposite effect. Managers who use bureaucratic control often emphasize following the rules above all else.

Another characteristic of bureaucratically controlled companies is that, due to their rule- and policy-driven decision making, they are highly resistant to change and slow to respond to customers and competitors. Recall from Chapter 2 that even Max Weber, the German philosopher who is largely credited with popularizing bureaucratic ideals in the late nineteenth century, referred to bureaucracy as the "iron cage." He said, "Once fully established, bureaucracy is among those social structures which are the hardest to destroy."[26] Of course, the national government, with hundreds of bureaus, agencies, and departments, is typically the largest bureaucracy in most countries. Under new U.S. Department of Transportation rules for long-haul truckers, drivers can now drive only 70 hours per week, down from 82. And, they must take a 34 hour break over two nights between work weeks. Intended to increase safety by preventing tired truck drivers from getting behind the wheel, the changes are instead increasing driver turnover (ironically, putting less experienced drivers on the road), putting more trucks on the road during rush hour, and forcing drivers to try to sleep when they're not tired and to drive when they are. Manny Hernandez, who has driven trucks for three decades, says the new rules prevent him from getting home to see his family. Wherever he is when the 70 hour limit kicks in, he has to stop for 34 hours over two nights. Says Hernandez, "It can be a nightmare of having to sit for 48 hours, tired, when all you want to do is get home . . . . Who made up these rules?" he asks. "Did they have any experience in driving truck[s], and traffic and dealing with customers and [the time lost from] your [truck] breakdowns? Sometimes I think they're trying to choke out the trucking industry."[27]

16-2b Objective Control

In many companies, bureaucratic control has evolved into **objective control**, which is the use of observable measures of employee behavior or output to assess performance and influence behavior. However, bureaucratic control focuses on whether policies and rules are followed, objective control focuses on observing and measuring worker behavior or output. Cyberloafing, wasting time online while at work, costs U.S. companies $85 billion a year due to decreased worker productivity, reduced available bandwidth, and damage from viruses and malware. Rather than blocking websites, an agricultural company uses software to divide the Internet into sites that employees can always, sometimes, or never visit. Sites that eat up too much bandwidth (such as YouTube) and those that may cause legal problems for the company (such as pornography) are forbidden. Otherwise, an on-screen warning alerts employees that a site may not be work related. Employees can browse nonwork-related sites for 10 minutes at a time—up to 90 minutes per day. If they exceed this amount, they must explain to their managers why they need more time on such sites. Lead developer Jeremy Glassman says that the software "provided [employees] with a reminder of the acceptable uses for Internet resources while at work and what is expected of them."[28]

There are two kinds of objective control: behavior control and output control. **Behavior control** is regulating behaviors and actions that workers perform on the job. The basic assumption of behavior control is that if you do the right things (that is, the right behaviors) every day, then those things should lead to goal achievement. Behavior control is still management-based, however, which means that managers are responsible for monitoring and then rewarding or punishing workers for exhibiting desired or undesired behaviors.

Instead of measuring what managers and workers do, **output control** measures the results of their efforts. In addition behavior control regulates, guides, and measures how workers behave on the job, output control gives managers and workers the freedom to behave as they see fit as long as they accomplish prespecified, measurable results. Output control is often coupled with rewards and incentives.

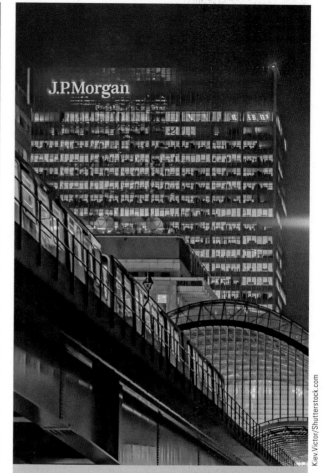

JPMorgan Chase realizes that culture has as much to do with control as algorithms, so it has added and designated more than 300 executives as "cultural ambassadors."

Three things must occur for output control to lead to improved business results. First, output control measures must be reliable, fair, and accurate. Second, employees and managers must believe that they can produce the desired results. If they don't, then the output controls won't affect their behavior. Third, the rewards or incentives tied to output control measures must truly be dependent on achieving established standards of performance. In a unique form of output control, Aetna will reward employees who get extra sleep. CEO Mark Bertolini said, "If they can prove they get 20 nights of sleep for seven hours or more in a row [via Fitbit fitness trackers], we will give them $25 a night, up [to] $500 a year." Bertolini

> **Objective control** the use of observable measures of worker behavior or outputs to assess performance and influence behavior
>
> **Behavior control** the regulation of the behaviors and actions that workers perform on the job
>
> **Output control** the regulation of workers' results or outputs through rewards and incentives

Protecting Smartphone Zombies from Distracted Walking

You're walking, ear buds in, listening to music. You stop at an intersection and wait for the green light indicating it's safe to cross the street. But, as a distracted, smartphone zombie who never looks up, you're a prime candidate for accidentally walking into traffic. Which is why the city of Bodegraven in the Netherlands has installed LED lights into sidewalks where pedestrians wait to cross the road. Town council member Kees Oskam said, "People are increasingly distracted by the smartphone. The attraction of social media, games, WhatsApp, and music is great, and comes at the expense of attention to traffic. As a government, we cannot easily reverse this trend, but we can anticipate it."

Source: T. Ricker, "Lightlines Are Humanity's Latest Attempt to Protect Smartphone Zombies," *The Verge*, February 15, 2017, accessed May 5, 2017, https://www.theverge.com/2017/2/15/14621968/lightlines-protect-distracted-smartphone-users; A. Wang, "The Clever Thing One Dutch Town Is Doing to Protect 'Smartphone Zombies," *Washington Post*, February 16, 2017, accessed May 5, 2017, https://www.washingtonpost.com/news/worldviews/wp/2017/02/16/the-clever-thing-one-dutch-town-is-doing-to-protect-smartphone-zombies/?utm_term=.51dc6dca4823.

urbazon/Shutterstock.com

says, "If we can make … business fundamentals better by investing in our people, then that's going to show up in our revenue."[29] Arianna Huffington, cofounder of the *Huffington Post*, said, "It really changes the cultural delusion that most businesses have been operating under, which has been … the more exhausted and burned out the employees are, the more productive they are."[30]

16-2c Normative Control

Rather than monitoring rules, behavior, or output, another way to control what goes on in organizations is to use normative control to shape the beliefs and values of the people who work there. With **normative controls**, a company's widely shared values and beliefs guide workers' behavior and decisions.

JPMorgan Chase realizes that culture has as much to do with control as algorithms, so it has designated more than 300 executives as "cultural ambassadors" who focus on standards.

> **Normative control** the regulation of workers' behavior and decisions through widely shared organizational values and beliefs

The company published a memo that encouraged employees to flag any compliance concerns and emphasized that poor compliance and scandals damage the bank's reputation and affect everyone, both professionally and financially. The goal of the program is to reshape the beliefs and values of the bank's employees so that compliance and ethical financial stewardship are part of the company culture.[31]

Normative controls are created in two ways. First, companies that use normative controls are very careful about who they hire. While many companies screen potential applicants on the basis of their abilities, normatively controlled companies are just as likely to screen potential applicants based on their attitudes and values. Mark Fitzsimmons, president of Psychometrics Canada, which is in the business of helping organizations select and develop their workforces, says, "Finding a suitable employee is not simply about adequate performance. It involves selecting a candidate who also upholds the carefully fostered organizational climate. An employee who doesn't quite gel can be detrimental to these efforts and can in some cases equate to damaging toxicity in the workplace. To avoid this, [we] use time-saving and objective personality assessments that measure a candidate's organizational values early in the selection process."[32]

Second, with normative controls, managers and employees learn what they should and should not do by observing experienced employees and by listening to the stories they tell about the company. We learned the importance of storytelling and organizational culture in Chapter 3. For normative controls to work, however, managers must not only select the right people, they must reward employees who honor those attitudes and values, and deal with those who don't. Elite SEM is a New York City-based search engine marketing firm that helps *Fortune* 500 companies increase their profile when potential customers do web searches. Elite SEM values hiring people with advanced technical skills and cooperative attitudes. More specifically, the company prides itself on being a "jerk-free workplace." So, there are consequences for employees and managers who, as CEO Ben Kirshner says, "don't embrace our core values." When a new employee refused to work late his first week on the job, he was let go. Kirshner says, "He was a bad seed!" And, because of the long hours people put in to meet client needs, Elite SEM has a free meal policy. So when another new employee ordered himself groceries and $30 breakfasts, Kirshner says, "Everyone jumped on him."[33]

16-2d Concertive Control

Although normative controls are based on beliefs that are strongly held and widely shared throughout a company, **concertive controls** are based on beliefs that are shaped and negotiated by work groups.[34] While normative controls are driven by strong organizational cultures, concertive controls usually arise when companies give work groups complete autonomy and responsibility for task completion (see Chapter 10, "Managing Teams," for a complete discussion of the role of autonomy in teams and groups). The most autonomous groups operate without managers and are completely responsible for controlling work group processes, outputs, and behavior. Such groups do their own hiring, firing, worker discipline, scheduling, materials ordering, budget making and meeting, and decision making.

Concertive control is not established overnight. Highly autonomous work groups evolve through two phases as they develop concertive control. In phase one, group members learn to work with each other,

supervise each other's work, and develop the values and beliefs that will guide and control their behavior. And because they develop these values and beliefs themselves, work group members feel strongly about following them.

An active form of concertive control is used by the teams at The Other Side Movers (TOSM), a moving company run by The Other Side Academy, a nonprofit in Salt Lake City, Utah, that "helps former felons, substance-abusers, and others get clean, stay clean, and learn how to live successful, productive lives."[35] Team members at TOSM are to be "200 percent accountable," meaning 100 percent accountable for their own work and—here's the concertive control—100 percent accountable for the work of everyone else on the team. TOSM team member enforce accountability through "pull-ups." When they see a mistake being made, they're expected to stop, "pull up" the person making the mistake by explaining how to correct the mistake, and then inform the crew leader about the mistake. Team members on the receiving end of a pull-up are expected to be open to the feedback by responding, "OK."[36] Finally, after owning up to a mistake, other team members "patch up" with the "pulled-up" team member by expressing their support and respect for them and their efforts. In its first year, TOSM will do $1 million in business and has become the top-ranked moving company in Salt Lake City.[37]

The second phase in the development of concertive control is the emergence and formalization of objective rules to guide and control behavior. The beliefs and values developed in phase one usually develop into more objective rules as new members join teams. The clearer those rules, the easier it becomes for new members to figure out how and how not to behave.

Ironically, concertive control may lead to even more stress for workers to conform to expectations than bureaucratic control. Under bureaucratic control, most workers only have to worry about pleasing the boss. But with concertive control, their behavior has to satisfy the rest of their team members. For example, one team member says, "I don't have to sit there and look for the boss to be around; and if the boss is not around, I can sit there and talk to my neighbor or do what I want. Now the whole team is around me and the whole team is observing what I'm doing."[38] Plus, with concertive control, team members have a second, much more stressful role to perform: that of making sure that their team members adhere to team values and rules.

Concertive control the regulation of workers' behavior and decisions through work group values and beliefs

16-2e Self-Control

Self-control, also known as **self-management**, is a control system in which managers and workers control their own behavior.[39] Self-control does not result in anarchy, in which everyone gets to do whatever he or she wants. In self-control, or self-management, leaders and managers provide workers with clear boundaries within which they may guide and control their own goals and behaviors.[40] Leaders and managers also contribute to self-control by teaching others the skills they need to maximize and monitor their own work effectiveness. In turn, individuals who manage and lead themselves establish self-control by setting their own goals, monitoring their own progress, rewarding or punishing themselves for achieving or for not achieving their self-set goals, and constructing positive thought patterns that remind them of the importance of their goals and their ability to accomplish them.[41]

For example, let's assume you need to do a better job of praising and recognizing the good work that your staff does for you. You can use goal setting, self-observation, and self-reward to manage this behavior on your own. For self-observation, write "praise/recognition" on a three-by-five-inch card. Put the card in your pocket. Put a check on the card each time you praise or recognize someone. (Wait until the person has left before

you do this.) Keep track for a week. This serves as your baseline, or starting point. Simply keeping track will probably increase how often you do this. After a week, assess your baseline, or starting point, and then set a specific goal. For instance, if your baseline was twice a day, you might set a specific goal to praise or recognize others' work five times a day. Continue monitoring your performance with your cards. After you've achieved your goal every day for a week, give yourself a reward (perhaps a movie or lunch with a friend at a new restaurant) for achieving your goal.[42]

As you can see, the components of self-management, self-set goals, self-observation, and self-reward have their roots in the motivation theories you read about in Chapter 13. The key difference, though, is that the goals, feedback, and rewards originate from employees themselves and not from their managers or organizations.

16-3 WHAT TO CONTROL?

In the first section of this chapter, we discussed the basics of the control process and the fact that control isn't always worthwhile or possible. In the second section, we looked at the various ways in which control can be achieved. In this third and final section, we address an equally important issue: What should managers control? Costs? Quality? Customer satisfaction? The way managers answer this question has critical implications for most businesses.

If you control for just one thing, such as costs, then other dimensions such as marketing, customer service, and quality are likely to suffer. But if you try to control for too many things, then managers and employees become confused about what's really important. In the end, successful companies find a balance that comes from doing three or four things right, such as managing costs, providing value, and keeping customers and employees satisfied.

Walmart's three key areas right now are making stores friendlier, keeping them well stocked, and reducing theft. To keep stores friendlier, the company moved its blue-vested greeters further back from entrances so they could walk customers to the products they were looking for, direct customers to open registers, or lend a hand restocking shelves. Focusing on customers and restocking, however, resulted in an increase in theft. Barb Gertz, an overnight stocker at one Colorado store, said that once the greeters were no longer posted at the doors, "people started walking out with cartloads of stuff." One person even rode a bike out of the store.[43] Walmart lost $375 million due to theft in 2015, so the retailer reposted greeters to the front doors and gave them specialized hand-held scanners. Now, greeters can keep an eye on the doors, but also check in items being returned, track merchandise, and randomly verify the receipts of people leaving the store.[44]

Self-control (self-management) a control system in which managers and workers control their own behavior by setting their own goals, monitoring their own progress, and rewarding themselves for goal achievement

Exhibit 16.2
Barclays Bank–Balanced Scorecard

Balanced Scorecard	Barclays Bank	Objectives	Measures	Targets	Initiatives
Financial	Company	Sustainable Returns above Cost of Equity	Return on Equity	5%	Invest and Grow, Reposition, Transition, or Exit Key Businesses
		Understand and Manage Risks	Capital Requirements (Financial Strength)	10.50%	Reduce costs, Lower Debt, Increase Capital
Customer	Customer & Client	Bank of Choice	Net Promoter Score (Ratio of Delighted vs. Dissatisfied Customers)	#1	Improve Customer Exerience via Technology
			Wallet Share	Top 3	Simplify Products and Services
Internal	Colleague & Conduct	Colleagues Fully Engaged	Sustained Engagement Scores	87–91%	Purpose and Value Program
		Diverse, Inclusive Environment	% of Women in Senior Leadership	26%	Barclays Leadership Academy
Learning	Citizenship	Positively Impact on Our Communities	# of Initiatives Meeting/Exceeding Target	11 of 11	Employee Stock Option Plan, Ground Crew Training
			Conduct Reputation Score (YouGov Survey)	6.5/10	Align Business Practices with Society, Environmental Considerations

Source: "Balanced Scorecard," Barclays, accessed May 4, 2017, https://www.home.barclays/about-barclays/balanced-scorecard.html#metrics.

After reading this section, you should be able to explain **16-3a the balanced scorecard approach to control** *and how companies can achieve balanced control of company performance by choosing to control* **16-3b budgets, cash flows, and economic value added; 16-3c customer defections; 16-3d quality;** *and* **16-3e waste and pollution.**

16-3a The Balanced Scorecard

Most companies measure performance using standard financial and accounting measures such as return on capital, return on assets, return on investments, cash flow, net income, and net margins. The **balanced scorecard** encourages managers to look beyond such traditional financial measures to four different perspectives on company performance. How do customers see us (the customer perspective)? At what must we excel (the internal perspective)? Can we continue to improve and create value (the innovation and learning perspective)? How do we look to shareholders (the financial perspective)?[45]

The balanced scorecard has several advantages over traditional control processes that rely solely on financial measures. First, it forces managers at each level of the company to set specific goals and measure performance in each of the four areas. For example, Exhibit 16.2 shows that the UK-based Barclays Bank uses eight different measures in its balanced scorecard to determine whether it is meeting the standards it has set for itself in the control process. Of those, only one—return on equity—is a standard financial measure of performance. In addition, Barclays measures its financial strength via capital requirements (financial perspective); the ratio of delighted versus dissatisfied customers and wallet share, the percentage of client funds handled by Barclays (customer perspective); employee engagement over time and the percentage of women in senior leadership positions (internal perspective); and the number of community initiatives that are meeting or exceeding their targets, as well as the bank's reputation measured by the Conduct Reputation Score on the YouGov survey, a reliable and reputable UK pollster (innovation and learning perspective).

The second major advantage of the balanced scorecard approach to control is that it minimizes the chances of **suboptimization**, which occurs when performance improves in one area at the expense of decreased performance in others. Jon Meliones, medical director of pediatric cardio ICU at Duke Children's Hospital, says, "We explained the [balanced scorecard] theory to clinicians and administrators like this: if you sacrifice too much in one quadrant to satisfy another, your organization as a whole is thrown out

Balanced scorecard
measurement of organizational performance in four equally important areas: finances, customers, internal operations, and innovation and learning

Suboptimization
performance improvement in one part of an organization but only at the expense of decreased performance in another part

of balance. We could, for example, cut costs to improve the financial quadrant by firing half the staff, but that would hurt quality of service, and the customer quadrant would fall out of balance. Or we could increase productivity in the internal business quadrant by assigning more patients to a nurse, but doing so would raise the likelihood of errors—an unacceptable trade-off.[46]

Let's examine some of the ways in which companies are controlling the four basic parts of the balanced scorecard: the financial perspective (budgets, cash flows, and economic value added), the customer perspective (customer defections), the internal perspective (total quality management), and the innovation and learning perspective (sustainability).

16-3b The Financial Perspective: Controlling Budgets, Cash Flows, and Economic Value Added

The traditional approach to controlling financial performance focuses on accounting tools such as cash flow analysis, balance sheets, income statements, financial ratios, and budgets. **Cash flow analysis** predicts how changes in a business will affect its ability to take in more cash than it pays out. **Balance sheets** provide a snapshot of a company's financial position at a particular time (but not the future). **Income statements**, also called profit and loss statements, show what has happened to an organization's income, expenses, and net profit (income less expenses) over a period of time. **Financial ratios** are typically used to track a business's liquidity (cash), efficiency, and profitability over time compared with other businesses in its industry. For example, Aetna, a health insurance

provider, uses a metric called the medical loss ratio. This financial ratio expresses the percentage of premiums used to pay patient medical costs—the lower the ratio, the higher the company's profits. So when the ratio dropped from 82.3–81.1 percent, it represented a 1.2 percent increase in profitability.[47] Finally, **budgets** are used to project costs and revenues, prioritize and control spending, and ensure that expenses don't exceed available funds and revenues. In a typical budgeting process, a manager uses the previous year's budget and adjusts it to reflect the current situation, but **zero-based budgeting** requires managers to outline a budget from scratch each year. In doing so, they must justify every expenditure—down to the number of color photocopies and garbage bags used—every year. Campbell Soup, Kellogg, and Mondelez (Oreo cookies) all use zero-based budgeting, as does chicken-processor Pilgrim's Pride, which zealously monitors the amount of paper used to print documents, the soap employees use in washrooms, and the Gatorade workers drink each shift. According to one plant manager, the budgeting process has transformed the culture. When one worker said to him, "Hey, I need a flashlight," he responded, "Do you really need a flashlight?"[48]

By themselves, none of these tools—cash flow analyses, balance sheets, income statements, financial ratios, or budgets—tell the whole financial story of a business. They must be used together when assessing a company's financial performance. Because these tools are reviewed in detail in your accounting and finance classes, only a brief overview is provided here. Still, these are necessary tools for controlling organizational finances and expenses, and they should be part of your business toolbox. Unfortunately, most managers don't have a good understanding of these accounting tools even though they should.[49]

Though no one would dispute the importance of cash flow analyses, balance sheets, income statements, financial ratios, or budgets for determining the financial health of a business, accounting research also indicates that the complexity and sheer amount of information contained in these accounting tools can shut down the brain and glaze over the eyes of even the most experienced manager.[50] Sometimes there's simply too much information to make sense of. The balanced scorecard simplifies things by focusing on one simple question when it comes to finances: How do we look to shareholders? One way to answer that question is through something called economic value added.

Cash flow analysis a type of analysis that predicts how changes in a business will affect its ability to take in more cash than it pays out

Balance sheets accounting statements that provide a snapshot of a company's financial position at a particular time

Income statements accounting statements, also called "profit and loss statements," that show what has happened to an organization's income, expenses, and net profit over a period of time

Financial ratios calculations typically used to track a business's liquidity (cash), efficiency, and profitability over time compared to other businesses in its industry

Budgets quantitative plans through which managers decide how to allocate available money to best accomplish company goals

Zero-based budgeting a budgeting technique that requires managers to justify every expenditure every year

Exhibit 16.3
Calculating Economic Value Added (EVA)

1. Calculate net operating profit after taxes (NOPAT).	$ 3,500,000	
2. Identify how much capital the company has invested (that is, spent).	$16,800,000	
3. Determine the cost (that is, rate) paid for capital (usually between 5 and 8%).	10%	
4. Multiply capital used (Step 2) times cost of capital (Step 3).	(10% × $16,800,000) = $1,680,000	
5. Subtract the total dollar cost of capital from net profit after taxes.	$3,500,000 − $1,680,000 $1,820,000	NOPAT Total cost of capital EVA

Conceptually, **economic value added (EVA)** is not the same thing as profits. It is the amount by which profits exceed the cost of capital in a given year. It is based on the simple idea that capital is necessary to run a business and that capital comes at a cost. Although most people think of capital as cash, after it is invested (that is, spent), capital is more likely to be found in a business in the form of computers, manufacturing plants, employees, raw materials, and so forth. And just like the interest that a homeowner pays on a mortgage or that a college student pays on a student loan, there is a cost to that capital.

The most common costs of capital are the interest paid on long-term bank loans used to buy all those resources, the interest paid to bondholders (who lend organizations their money), and the dividends (cash payments) and growth in stock value that accrue to shareholders. EVA is positive when company profits (revenues minus expenses minus taxes) exceed the cost of capital in a given year. In other words, if a business is to truly grow, its revenues must be large enough to cover both short-term costs (annual expenses and taxes) and long-term costs (the cost of borrowing capital from bondholders and shareholders). If you're a bit confused, the late Roberto Goizueta, the former CEO of Coca-Cola, explained it this way: "You borrow money at a certain rate and invest it at a higher rate and pocket the difference. It is simple. It is the essence of banking."[51]

Exhibit 16.3 shows how to calculate EVA. First, starting with a company's income statement, you calculate the net operating profit after taxes (NOPAT) by subtracting taxes owed from income from operations. (Remember, a quick review of an income statement is on the Financial Review Card found at the back of your book.) The NOPAT shown in Exhibit 16.3 is $3,500,000. Second, identify how much capital the company has invested (that is, spent). Total liabilities (what the company owes) less accounts payable and less accrued expenses, neither of which you pay interest on, provides a rough approximation of this amount. In Exhibit 16.3, total capital invested is $16,800,000. Third, calculate the cost (that is, rate) paid for capital by determining the interest paid to bondholders (who lend organizations their money), which is usually somewhere between 5 and 8 percent, and the return that stockholders want in terms of dividends and stock price appreciation, which is historically about 13 percent. Take a weighted average of the two to determine the overall cost of capital. In Exhibit 16.3, the cost of capital is 10 percent. Fourth, multiply the total capital ($16,800,000) from Step 2 by the cost of capital (10%) from Step 3. In Exhibit 16.3, this amount is $1,680,000. Fifth, subtract the total dollar cost of capital in Step 4 from the NOPAT in Step 1. In Exhibit 16.3, this value is $1,820,000, which means that our example company has created economic value or wealth this year. If our EVA number had been negative, meaning that the company didn't make enough profit to cover the cost of capital from bondholders and shareholders, then the company would have destroyed economic value or wealth by taking in more money than it returned.[52]

Economic value added (EVA) the amount by which company profits (revenues minus expenses minus taxes) exceed the cost of capital in a given year

Why is EVA so important? First and most importantly, because it includes the cost of capital, it shows whether a business, division, department, profit center, or product is really paying for itself. The key is to make sure that managers and employees can see how their choices and behaviors affect the company's EVA. For example, because of EVA training and information systems, factory workers at Herman Miller, a leading office furniture manufacturer, understand that using more efficient materials, such as less expensive wood-dust board instead of real wood sheeting, contributes an extra dollar of EVA from each desk the company makes. On its website, Herman Miller explains, "Under the terms of the EVA plan, we shifted our focus from budget performance to long-term continuous improvements and the creation of economic value. When we make plans for improvements around here, we include an EVA analysis. When we make decisions to add or cut programs, we look at the impact on EVA. Every month, we study our performance in terms of EVA, and this measurement system is one of the first things new recruits to the company learn."[53] "The result is a highly motivated and business-literate workforce that challenges convention and strives to create increasingly greater value for both customers and owners. Every month the company and all employees review performance in terms of EVA, which has proven to be a strong corollary to shareholder value."[54]

Second, because EVA can easily be determined for subsets of a company such as divisions, regional offices, manufacturing plants, and sometimes even departments, it makes managers and workers at all levels pay much closer attention to their segment of the business. In other words, EVA motivates managers and workers to think like small-business owners who must scramble to contain costs and generate enough business to meet their bills each month. And, unlike many kinds of financial controls, EVA doesn't specify what should or should not be done to improve performance. Thus, it encourages managers and workers to be creative in looking for ways to improve EVA performance.

Remember that EVA is the amount by which profits exceed the cost of capital in a given year. So the more that EVA exceeds the total dollar cost of capital, the better a company has used investors' money that year. For example, Apple had an EVA of $41.9 billion in 2016, by far the largest EVA in the world. The next-closest company was Alphabet (parent company of Google) at $10.1 billion. Apple's EVA financial performance in 2016 was extraordinary and the third largest ever achieved by any company.[55]

Customer defections a performance assessment in which companies identify which customers are leaving and measure the rate at which they are leaving

> Apple had an EVA of $41.9 billion in 2016—by far the largest in the world.

Rose Carson/Shutterstock.com

16-3c The Customer Perspective: Controlling Customer Defections

The second aspect of organizational performance that the balanced scorecard helps managers monitor is customers. It does so by forcing managers to address the question, "How do customers see us?" Unfortunately, most companies try to answer this question through customer satisfaction surveys, but these are often misleadingly positive. Most customers are reluctant to talk about their problems because they don't know who to complain to or think that complaining will not do any good. In fact, a study by the Australian Federal Office of Consumer Affairs found that 96 percent of unhappy customers never complain to anyone in the company.[56]

One reason that customer satisfaction surveys can be misleading is that sometimes even very satisfied customers will leave to do business with competitors. Rather than poring over customer satisfaction surveys from current customers, studies indicate that companies may do a better job of answering the question, "How do customers see us?" by closely monitoring **customer defections**, that is, by identifying which customers are leaving the company and measuring the rate at which they are leaving. Unlike the results of customer satisfaction surveys, customer defections and retention have a great effect on profits.

Because most accounting systems measure the financial impact of a customer's current activity (sales), rather than the lifetime value of each customer, few managers realize the financial impact that even a low rate of customer defection can have on a business. Businesses frequently lose 15 to 20 percent of their customers each year, so even a small improvement in retention can have a significant impact on profits. In fact, retaining just 5 percent more customers per year can increase annual profits 25 to 100 percent. Managers, therefore, should pay closer attention to customer defections. John Tschohl, an author and business consultant, worked with a network of 17 blood plasma donation centers to determine the financial impact of defections. With 40,600 donors each year, analysis of the network showed that the "lifetime" of a typical donor—the time when the donor was active—was 3.4 years. During that time, each lifetime donor contributed roughly $6,000 in profits to the company. Each year, however, a cohort of 2,340 donors defected, making the network's annual customer defection rate 6 percent. While the defection rate was modest, the financial impact was considerable, resulting in more than $100 million in lost revenue and $60 million less in profits each year, or $200 million in profits over the lifetime (3.4 years) of a single cohort (2,430 people) of defectors.[57]

Beyond the clear benefits to the bottom line, the second reason to study customer defections is that customers who have left are much more likely than current customers to tell you what you are doing wrong. Perhaps the best way to tap into this source of good feedback is to have top-level managers from various departments talk directly to customers who have left. It's also worthwhile to have top managers talk to dissatisfied customers who are still with the company. Finally, companies that understand why customers leave not only can take steps to fix ongoing problems but also can identify which customers are likely to leave and can make changes to prevent them from leaving.

16-3d The Internal Perspective: Controlling Quality

The third part of the balanced scorecard, the internal perspective, consists of the processes, decisions, and actions that managers and workers make within the organization. In contrast to the financial perspective of EVA and the outward-looking customer perspective, the internal perspective focuses on internal processes and systems that add value to the organization. For McDonald's, it could be processes and systems that enable the company to provide consistent, quick, low-cost food. For Toyota, it could be reliability—when you turn on your car, it starts, regardless of whether it has 20,000 or 200,000 miles on it. Yet, no matter what area a company chooses, the key is to excel in that area. Consequently, the internal perspective of the balanced scorecard usually leads managers to a focus on quality.

Quality is typically defined and measured in three ways: excellence, value, and conformance to expectations.[58] When the company defines its quality goal as

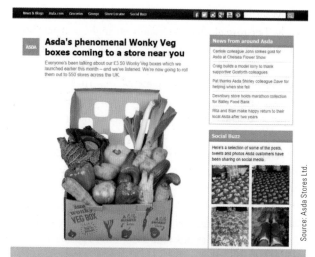

British supermarket chain Asda recently began packaging misshapen, cracked, blemished, and unusually sized vegetables into reduced-price Wonky Veg Boxes.

excellence, managers must try to produce a product or service of unsurpassed performance and features. *Condé Nast Traveler* magazine has been ranking global airlines for 27 years. For 26 of those years, Singapore Airlines was named the best airline in the world.[59] Although many airlines try to cram passengers into every available inch on a plane, Singapore Airlines delivers creature comforts to encourage repeat business and lure customers willing to pay premium prices. On its newer planes, the first-class cabin is divided into eight private mini-rooms, each with an unusually wide leather seat that folds down flat for sleeping, a 23-inch LCD TV that doubles as a computer monitor, and an adjustable table.

These amenities and services are common for private jets but truly unique in the commercial airline industry. Singapore Airlines was the first airline, in the 1970s, to introduce a choice of meals, complimentary drinks, and earphones in coach class. It was the first to introduce worldwide video, news, telephone, and fax services; was the first to feature personal video monitors for movies, news, and documentaries; and has had AC power outlets and on-board high-speed Internet for some time—well ahead of other airlines.

Value is the customer perception that the product quality is excellent for the price offered. At a higher price, for example, customers may perceive the product to be less of a value. When a company emphasizes value as its quality goal, managers must simultaneously control

Value customer perception that the product quality is excellent for the price offered excellence, price, durability, and any other features of a product or service that customers strongly associate with value. Fresh fruits and vegetables are categorized according to size, uniformity, and appearance. The most attractive produce (about 85%) goes to supermarkets, while the nonconforming produce ends up in processed foods, animal feed, and landfills. British supermarket chain **Asda** recently loosened its produce appearance specifications and began packaging misshapen, cracked, blemished, and unusually sized vegetables into five kilogram boxes. Asda's so-called Wonky Veg Box sells for £3.50 (about $5.00), a 30 percent discount, which 95 percent of Asda's customers think is a tremendous value. Sales quadrupled in the first two months after the box launched.[60] Ian Harrison, Asda's produce technical director, said that the Wonky Veg Box "was always meant as a trial to see how customers reacted to slightly scruffier produce, but this has also enabled us to flex our specifications across a wide variety of our standard produce lines. For example, we're taking 340 more tonnes of standard and organic carrots which would previously have been out of spec."[61] Harrison adds, "We've got a real hit on our hands with Wonky!"[62]

When a company defines its quality goal as conformance to specifications, employees must base decisions and actions on whether services and products measure up to the standard. In contrast to excellence and value-based definitions of quality that can be somewhat ambiguous, measuring whether products and services are "in spec" is relatively easy. Furthermore, while conformance to specifications (for example, precise tolerances for a part's weight or thickness) is usually associated with

manufacturing, it can be used equally well to control quality in nonmanufacturing industries like supermarkets. Exhibit 16.4 shows a checklist that a cook or restaurant owner would use to ensure quality when buying fresh fish.

The way in which a company defines quality affects the methods and measures that workers use to control quality. Accordingly, Exhibit 16.5 shows the advantages and disadvantages associated with the excellence, value, and conformance to specification definitions of quality.

16-3e The Innovation and Learning Perspective: Sustainability

The last part of the balanced scorecard, the innovation and learning perspective, addresses the question, "Can we continue to improve and create value?" Thus, the innovation and learning perspective involves continuous improvement in ongoing products and services (discussed in Chapter 18), as well as relearning and redesigning the processes by which products and services are created (discussed in Chapter 7). Because these are discussed in more detail elsewhere in the text, this section reviews an increasingly important topic, sustainability. Exhibit 16.6 shows the four levels of sustainability, ranging from waste disposal, which produces the smallest minimization of waste, to waste prevention and reduction, which produces the greatest minimization.[63]

The goals of the top level, *waste prevention and reduction*, are to prevent waste and pollution before they occur or to reduce them when they do occur. Denmark's Maersk Tankers is reducing pollution and fuel usage

Exhibit 16.4
Conformance to Specifications Checklist for Buying Fresh Fish

Fresh Whole Fish	Acceptable	Not Acceptable
Gills	✓ bright red, free of slime, clear mucus	✗ brown to grayish, thick, yellow mucus
Eyes	✓ clear, bright, bulging, black pupils	✗ dull, sunken, cloudy, gray pupils
Smell	✓ inoffensive, slight ocean smell	✗ ammonia, putrid smell
Skin	✓ opalescent sheen, scales adhere tightly to skin	✗ dull or faded color, scales missing or easily removed
Flesh	✓ firm and elastic to touch, tight to the bone	✗ soft and flabby, separating from the bone
Belly cavity	✓ no viscera or blood visible, lining intact, no bone protruding	✗ incomplete evisceration, cuts or protruding bones, off-odor

iStock.com/Valeriy Evlakhov

Sources: "A Closer Look: Buy It Fresh, Keep It Fresh," *Consumer Reports Online*, accessed June 20, 2005, http://www.seagrant.sunysb.edu/SeafoodTechnology /SeafoodMedia/CR02-2001/CR-SeafoodII020101.htm; "How to Purchase: Buying Fish," *About Seafood*, accessed June 20, 2005, http://www.aboutseafood.com/faqs /purchase1.html.

Exhibit 16.5
Advantages and Disadvantages of Different Measures of Quality

Quality Measure	Advantages	Disadvantages
Excellence	Promotes clear organizational vision.	Provides little practical guidance for managers.
	Being/providing the "best" motivates and inspires managers and employees.	Excellence is ambiguous. What is it? Who defines it?
Value	Appeals to customers who know excellence "when they see it."	Difficult to measure and control.
	Customers recognize differences in value.	Can be difficult to determine what factors influence whether a product/service is seen as having value.
	Easier to measure and compare whether products/services differ in value.	Controlling the balance between excellence and cost (that is, affordable excellence) can be difficult.
Conformance to Specifications	If specifications can be written, conformance to specifications is usually measurable.	Many products/services cannot be easily evaluated in terms of conformance to specifications.
	Should lead to increased efficiency.	Promotes standardization, so may hurt performance when adapting to changes is more important.
	Promotes consistency in quality.	May be less appropriate for services, which are dependent on a high degree of human contact.

Source: Briar Cliff Manor, NY, 10510-8020; C. A. Reeves and D. A. Bednar, "Defining Quality: Alternatives and Implications," *Academy of Management Review* 19 (1994): 419–445.

on its massive ships using wind power obtained from rotor sails (imagine a five-story-tall spinning barber's pole without the stripes) that create the Magnus effect in which a spinning object drags air around itself. With wind to the side of the ship (just like a sailboat), a spinning rotor sail creates higher wind speeds and lower pressure at the front, and slower wind speeds and higher pressure in the back, which together move a ship forward. Jorgan Mansnerus, vice president of Bore Ltd., a shipping firm, says, "If you have good wind, you save 6 percent on fuel," without reducing speed.[64]

There are three strategies for waste prevention and reduction:

1. *Good housekeeping*—performing regularly scheduled preventive maintenance for offices, plants, and equipment. Examples of good housekeeping include fixing leaky valves quickly to prevent wasted water and making sure machines are running properly so that they don't use more fuel than necessary. Likewise, companies are also beginning to apply good housekeeping practices to their cloud computing services. Companies tend to overestimate their capacity needs, but because cloud computing charges work similarly to a taxicab (the meter is always running), companies can end up spending a lot of money on unused computing power. Aquarium Spectrum, in

Tel Aviv, Israel, uses thousands of sensors to listen to the sounds water creates as it passes through or leaks from pipes. Cloud servers analyzing the data pinpoint leaks to within 1 foot of their actual location. CEO Oded Fruchtman says, "We can tell if the leak's in an office building or a flat, or if the problem is with the water meter, a pressure reduce valve—anything that creates a noise that should not be creating a noise. When you can find leaks that small, you don't have to react in an emergency manner, or work on weekends or holidays."[65]

2. *Material/product substitution*—replacing toxic or hazardous materials with less harmful materials.

3. *Process modification*—changing steps or procedures to eliminate or reduce waste.

At the second level of sustainability, *recycle and reuse*, wastes are reduced by reusing materials as long as possible or by collecting materials for on- or off-site recycling. Primark, a worldwide clothing retailer based in the United Kingdom, has an annual revenue of £5.35 billion and is growing roughly 25 percent per year. The company's flagship store has 44 fitting rooms, 104 cash registers, and can—and often does—hold 3,200 customers. When delivery trucks arrive at the back of the store, merchandise is unpacked and sent straight onto the floor. The cardboard boxes used to ship the merchandise go right back onto the truck to be recycled and later return to the store as Primark's iconic brown paper shopping bags.[66]

A growing trend in recycling is *design for disassembly*, where products are designed from the start for easy disassembly, recycling, and reuse after they are no longer usable. Samsung Electronics used design for disassembly principles to redesign a 55-inch TV with a curved screen, replacing 30 out of 38 screws with plastic snaps so that it only takes 10 minutes to disassemble the TV. Likewise, Apple has built robots with 29 arms. Each Robot, which Apple has named "Liam," is capable of disassembling and recycling every part in 1.2 million iPhones a year. Apple's vice president of environment, policy, and social initiatives, Lisa Jackson, said, "We think as much now about the recycling and end of life of products as the design of products itself."[67]

At the third level of sustainability, waste treatment, companies use biological, chemical, or other processes to turn potentially harmful waste into harmless compounds or useful by products. A third of food produced is wasted, ending up in landfills where its decomposition produces harmful methane gas. Restaurants, however, can use biodigesters from BioHiTech to turn food waste into harmless wastewater that is disposed via standard

Siri explains that Liam, Apple's new robot, is busy disassembling iPhones for recycling.

Source: Apple Inc.

sewer lines. Biodigesters, which are about the size of an industrial dishwasher, process 800 to 2,500 pounds of food waste per day using aerobic processes, all without chopping, grinding, chemicals, or odors. Companies save on hauling, landfill, and janitorial costs by simply dumping food waste into on site biodigesters.[68]

The fourth and lowest level of sustainability is *waste disposal*. Wastes that cannot be prevented, reduced, recycled, reused, or treated should be safely disposed of in processing plants or in environmentally secure landfills that prevent leakage and contamination of soil and underground water supplies. Contrary to common belief, all businesses, not just manufacturing firms, have waste disposal problems. For example, with the average computer lasting just three years, approximately 60 million computers come out of service each year, creating disposal problems for offices all over the world. But organizations can't just throw old computers away because they have lead-containing cathode ray tubes in the monitors, toxic metals in the circuit boards, paint-coated plastic, and

Exhibit 16.6 Four Levels of Sustainability

Waste Prevention & Reduction
Recycle & Reuse
Waste Treatment
Waste Disposal

iStock.com/Og-vision

Source: D. R. May and B. L. Flannery, "Cutting Waste with Employee Involvement Teams," *Business Horizons*, September–October 1995, pp. 28–38.

MAKING LEGO BRICKS OUT OF AGRICULTURAL WASTE

Since 1963, LEGO has made its iconic plastic bricks from the same petroleum-based formulation—acrylonitrile butadiene styrene (ABS). In 2015, however, LEGO announced that it was launching a research and development effort to reformulate its plastic using biodegradable plant-based materials. Ideally, says senior director for environmental sustainability Tim Guy Brooks, the new plastic will be derived from agricultural waste that doesn't have any other apparent potential use, such as corn stalk. Even though oil prices have plummeted in recent years, LEGO remains committed to replacing its petroleum-based plastics with bio-plastic. The company estimates that it will take 15 years to develop a bio-based alternative to replace the 77,000 metric tons of petroleum granules it currently uses to make bricks every year—a main contributor to the company's overall carbon footprint. "This is the right thing

to do for LEGO—fossil fuels are a finite resource and we know that," says Brooks.

Source: L. Chao, "Lego Tries to Build a Better Brick," *Wall Street Journal*, July 14, 2015, B4.

ESOlex/Shutterstock.com

metal coatings that can contaminate groundwater.[69] Many companies give old computers and computer equipment to local computer recycling centers that distribute usable computers to nonprofit organizations or safely dispose of lead and other toxic materials. A number of retailers and electronics manufacturers operate recycling programs to keep electronics out of landfills. Dell's Reconnect program partners with Goodwill Industries. Find your local Goodwill location (https://www.dellreconnect.com) and drop off all of your electronics for recycling.[70] Best Buy recycles everything from TVs to ink and toner cartridges for printers to digital cameras, no matter where you bought them or how old the items.[71] Finally, the U.S. Environmental Protection Agency has an online database (https://www.epa.gov/recycle/electronics-donation-and-recycling) to find out what companies have recycling programs for a variety of electronic items.

STUDY TOOLS 16

LOCATED IN TEXTBOOK

☐ Rip out and review chapter review card.

LOCATED AT WWW.CENGAGE.COM/LOGIN

☐ Gain unique perspectives on key concepts with new 4LTR concept videos in the e-book.

☐ Increase your comprehension with Aplia for MGMT11.

☐ Complete interactive content within the e-book.

17 | Managing Information

LEARNING OBJECTIVES

17-1 Explain the strategic importance of information.

17-2 Describe the characteristics of useful information (that is, its value and costs).

17-3 Explain the basics of capturing, processing, and protecting information.

17-4 Describe how companies can access and share information and knowledge.

After you finish this chapter, go to **PAGE 395** for **STUDY TOOLS**

17-1 STRATEGIC IMPORTANCE OF INFORMATION

A generation ago, computer hardware and software had little to do with managing business information. Rather than storing information on hard drives, managers stored it in filing cabinets. Instead of uploading daily sales and inventory levels by high-speed broadband to corporate headquarters, they mailed hard-copy summaries to headquarters at the end of each month. Instead of graphical displays of real-time company data, reports were typed on electric typewriters. Instead of auto-updating spreadsheets that pull live data from internal or external sources, calculations were made by hand on adding machines. Managers communicated by sticky notes, not email or group chat. Phone messages were written down by assistants and coworkers, not forwarded in your email as a sound file with the message converted to text. Workers did not use desktop, laptop, or tablet computers or smartphones as daily tools to get work done. Instead, they scheduled limited access time to run batch jobs on the mainframe computer (and prayed that the batch job computer code they wrote would work).

Today, computer hardware and software are an integral part of managing business information. This is due mainly to something called **Moore's law**. Gordon Moore is one of the founders of Intel Corporation, which makes 75 percent of the integrated processors used in PCs. In 1965, Moore predicted that computer-processing power would double and that its cost would drop by 50 percent every two years.[1] As Exhibit 17.1 shows, Moore was right. Computer power, as measured by the number of transistors per computer chip, *has* more than doubled every few years, as have hard drive sizes and pixel density (that is, screen resolution). Consequently, the computer sitting in your lap or on your desk (or in your hand!) is not only smaller but also much cheaper and more powerful than the large mainframe computers used by *Fortune* 500 companies 30 years ago. For instance, your iPhone replaces 13 of the 15 items, such as a desktop computer, mobile phone, CD player, camcorder, and so on, commonly sold by Radio Shack in 1991, items that would have cost you $3,071.21 then, or, after adjusting for inflation, $5,497.53 today. So your $600 iPhone not only replaces a trunkful of 1991 electronics gear, it does so for only 11 percent of the cost.[2] That's Moore's law in action. Likewise, in 2001, the cost of sequencing one human genome was $100 million. Thanks to Moore's law, that cost dropped to just below $1,000 in 2016.[3] Will Moore's law eventually fail and technological progress eventually slow? Perhaps, as the physics and costs of developing faster, more powerful chips (today's chips are already based

> **Moore's law** the prediction that about every two years, computer processing power would double and its cost would drop by 50 percent

Exhibit 17.1

Moore's Law

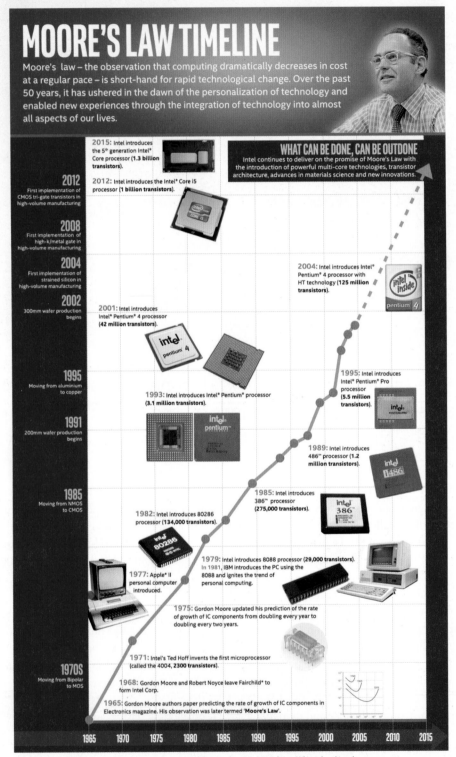

MOORE'S LAW TIMELINE

Moore's law – the observation that computing dramatically decreases in cost at a regular pace – is short-hand for rapid technological change. Over the past 50 years, it has ushered in the dawn of the personalization of technology and enabled new experiences through the integration of technology into almost all aspects of our lives.

2015: Intel introduces the 5th generation Intel® Core processor (**1.3 billion transistors**).

2012: Intel introduces the Intel® Core i5 processor (**1 billion transistors**).

WHAT CAN BE DONE, CAN BE OUTDONE
Intel continues to deliver on the promise of Moore's Law with the introduction of powerful multi-core technologies, transistor architecture, advances in materials science and new innovations.

2012
First implementation of CMOS tri-gate transistors in high-volume manufacturing

2008
First implementation of high-k/metal gate in high-volume manufacturing

2004
First implementation of strained silicon in high-volume manufacturing

2004: Intel introduces Intel® Pentium® 4 processor with HT technology (**125 million transistors**).

2002
300mm wafer production begins

2001: Intel introduces Intel® Pentium® 4 processor (**42 million transistors**).

1995
Moving from aluminium to copper

1995: Intel introduces Intel® Pentium® Pro processor (**5.5 million transistors**).

1993: Intel introduces Intel® Pentium® processor (**3.1 million transistors**).

1991
200mm wafer production begins

1989: Intel introduces 486™ processor (**1.2 million transistors**).

1985
Moving from NMOS to CMOS

1985: Intel introduces 386™ processor (**275,000 transistors**).

1982: Intel introduces 80286 processor (**134,000 transistors**).

1979: Intel introduces 8088 processor (**29,000 transistors**). In 1981, IBM introduces the PC using the 8088 and ignites the trend of personal computing.

1977: Apple® II personal computer introduced.

1975: Gordon Moore updated his prediction of the rate of growth of IC components from doubling every year to doubling every two years.

1971: Intel's Ted Hoff invents the first microprocessor (called the 4004, **2300 transistors**).

1970S
Moving from Bipolar to MOS

1968: Gordon Moore and Robert Noyce leave Fairchild® to form Intel Corp.

1965: Gordon Moore authors paper predicting the rate of growth of IC components in Electronics magazine. His observation was later termed '**Moore's Law**'.

1965 1970 1975 1980 1985 1990 1995 2000 2005 2010 2015

"Adapted from Moore's Law Timeline," Intel, accessed September 27, 2015, http://download.intel.com.

on circuitry 1 billionth of a meter thin) may eventually slow the rate of development. For now, chip producers are meeting Moore's law by offloading tasks from the main CPU to dedicated chips that only handle video, photography, or security. Qualcomm's Keith Kressin says, "Our goal is to minimize the amount of software running in the CPU." For that reason, a typical smartphone uses a dozen or more specialized chips.[4]

Raw data are facts and figures. For example, 11, $762, 128, and 26,100 are some data that I used the day I wrote this section of the chapter. However, facts and figures aren't particularly useful unless they have meaning. For example, you probably can't guess what these four pieces of raw data represent, can you? If you can't, these data are useless. That's why researchers make the distinction between raw data and information. However, raw data consist of facts and figures, **information** is useful data that can influence someone's choices and behavior. One way to think about the difference between data and information is that information has context. When starting a new car, the computers controlling acceleration, braking, safety systems, and navigation update 100,000 data points. Those data are valuable to car companies—and Google and Apple and insurance companies—because of the information they communicate about drivers and passengers, such as where they shop, daily route, driving patterns, and so on. Tony Posawatz, CEO of Invictus iCar, says, "There is tremendous value in the data, and they are trying to figure out how to get it."[5]

So what did those four pieces of data mean to me? Well, 11 stands for Channel 11, the local CBS affiliate on which I watched part of the men's PGA golf tournament; $762 is how much it would cost me to rent a minivan for a week if I go skiing over spring break; 128 is for the 128-gigabyte storage card that I want to add to my digital camera (prices are low, so I'll probably buy it); and 26,100 means that it's time to get the oil changed in my car.

In today's hypercompetitive business environments, information is as important as capital (that is, money) for business success, whether it's about product inventory, pricing, or costs. It takes money to get businesses started, but businesses can't survive and grow without the right information.

Tony Posawatz, CEO of Invictus iCar, notes that computer data from car systems has tremendous value for car companies, as well as technology and insurance companies.

> The key to sustaining a competitive advantage is using information technology to continuously improve and support the core functions of a business.

Information has strategic importance for organizations because it can be used to **17-1a obtain first-mover advantage** and **17-1b sustain competitive advantage after it has been created.**

17-1a First-Mover Advantage

First-mover advantage is the strategic advantage that companies earn by being the first in an industry to use new information technology to substantially lower costs or to differentiate a product or service from that of competitors. Pandora, for example, pioneered music streaming and leads this highly competitive market. Free to listeners because it makes money via advertising, Pandora has 77.9 million active listeners, slightly up from 79.4 million in 2016, and just 4.2 million paying subscribers.[6]

While first-mover advantage typically leads to above average profits and market share, it doesn't immunize a company from competition. Pandora faces four primary competitors: Spotify (50 million

Raw data facts and figures

Information useful data that can influence people's choices and behavior

First-mover advantage the strategic advantage that companies earn by being the first to use new information technology to substantially lower costs or to make a product or service different from that of competitors

iStock.com/ManuelBurgos

Third, is it difficult for another company to create or buy the information technology used by the firm? If so, then the firm has established a sustainable competitive advantage over competitors through information technology. If not, then the competitive advantage is just temporary, and competitors should eventually be able to duplicate the advantages the leading firm has gained from information technology.

In short, the key to sustaining a competitive advantage is not faster computers, more memory, or larger hard drives. The key is using information technology to

subscribers), Deezer (6.9 million subscribers), Apple Music (20 million subscribers), and Amazon's Prime Music, which is free for Amazon's estimated 80 million Prime members (who pay $99 a year for Prime membership, which includes two-day shipping and a number of other benefits).[7]

Many first-movers have failed to capitalize on their strategic advantages. BlackBerry lost first-mover advantage in smartphones (to Apple and Android), as did Taxi Magic (to Uber and Lyft) and HomeAway (to Airbnb).[8] A study of 30 first-movers found two key factors mattered in terms of sustaining first-mover advantage: the pace at which product technology is changing and how fast the market is growing.[9] As these examples show, if better technology is quickly being introduced by new market entrants, and the market is quickly growing (which attracts new competitors who want a share of that growing market), it can be difficult to sustain first-mover advantage.

17-1b Sustaining Competitive Advantage

As described earlier, companies that use information technology to establish first-mover advantage usually have higher market shares and profits. According to the resource-based view of information technology shown in Exhibit 17.2, companies need to address three critical questions to sustain a competitive advantage through information technology. First, does the information technology create value for the firm by lowering costs or providing a better product or service? If an information technology doesn't add value, then investing in it would put the firm at a competitive disadvantage relative to companies that choose information technologies that do add value.

Second, is the information technology the same or different across competing firms? If all the firms have access to the same information technology and use it in the same way, then no firm has an advantage over another (that is, there is competitive parity).

Exhibit 17.2
Using Information Technology to Sustain a Competitive Advantage

Source: Adapted from F. J. Mata, W. L. Fuerst, and J. B. Barney, "Information Technology and Sustained Competitive Advantage: A Resource-Based Analysis," *MIS Quarterly* 19, no. 4 (December 1995): 487–505.

continuously improve and support the core functions of a business.

17-2 CHARACTERISTICS AND COSTS OF USEFUL INFORMATION

Information and data are more abundant today than ever before. For example, modern Major League Baseball (MLB) teams use iPad Pros loaded with baseball-related software to analyze data and make decisions. MLB Commissioner Rob Manfred says, "I started in this game 25 years ago and the single biggest change has been the emergence and predominance of analytics. It affects the way we judge players, make decisions on the field and the way fans consume the game."[10] Phil Schiller, Apple's senior vice president of marketing, says about the MLB's adoption of iPads, "We're not just replacing binders with tablets, we're actually helping them do things that weren't possible before."[11] Teams can pull up statistics, explore pitching match-ups against specific batters, study game videos, and examine real time spray charts indicating where batters usually hit the ball. While all teams have access to the MLB Dugout App, each team's data are proprietary and are not shared league-wide. New York Mets third base coach Tim Teufel says, "Managers have plans and positions laid out before the game even starts. This won't change that much. But when a relief pitcher comes in, when a pinch hitter comes up, when the game changes in unexpected ways, that's when it'll be really useful [to use the iPads]."[12] Likewise, radio frequency identification tags (discussed in Section 17-3a) in shoulder pads indicate how fast NFL players run, whether they consistently work hard in practice, or how many calories they burn. Pittsburgh Steelers general manager Kevin Colbert is excited about the possibilities, saying, "To be able to tell a quarterback where he should be, to be able to show a defense what an offense looks like at ground level would be great. That would be more realistic."

As the MLB's use of iPads, data, and analytics demonstrates, information is useful when it is **17-2a accurate, 17-2b complete, 17-2c relevant,** and **17-2d timely.** However, there can be significant **17-2e acquisition, 17-2f processing, 17-2g storage, 17-2h retrieval,**

PHISHING ATTACK: DON'T CLICK THAT GOOGLE DOC!

Google Docs is an online file-sharing app for presentation, spreadsheet, and word-processing files. Google Docs users received a highly convincing email from someone they knew, who "has invited you to view the following document." The only problem is that it was a phishing attack using fake but real-looking emails to trick users into providing unauthorized account access. Normally, phishing attacks send people to fake but authentic-looking websites that can be detected if you closely examine the URL.

This time, however, clicking on "Open in Docs," took people to Google's real sign-in screen, where they unknowingly gave hackers access to their Gmail and Gmail contacts. Although Google stopped the attack within four hours, a white-hat hacker duplicated a similar version within a day. How could 1 million people have avoided the fast-spreading attack? Don't click on email attachments that you're not expecting, even if they appear to be from people you know.

Source: A. Robertson, "Google Docs Users Hit with Sophisticated Phishing Attack," *The Verge*, May 3, 2017, accessed May 7, 2017, https://www.theverge.com/2017/5/3/15534768/google-docs-phishing-attack-share-this-document-with-you-spam; R. McMillan, "Phishing Attack Hits Google Docs," *Wall Street Journal*, May 4, 2017, accessed May 7, 2017, https://www.wsj.com/articles/phishing-attack-hits-google-docs-1493853168.

and **17-2i communication costs** *associated with useful information.*

17-2a Accurate Information

Information is useful when it is accurate. Before relying on information to make decisions, you must know that the information is correct. But what if it isn't?

In the next 25 years, the world's population will grow from 7 billion to 9 billion people. Many of those 9 billion will be moving into the middle class, drastically increasing demand for meat, dairy, and other foods dense with protein and calories. To produce the 70 percent more calories needed to feed everyone in 2050, farmers will need to plant, irrigate, and feed their crops much more efficiently. Ohioan Mark Bryant is one of a growing number of farmers using data-driven technologies to do just that. Bryant uses Google's Granular app, which collects data on moisture and soil quality from aircrafts, drones, self-driving tractors, and other sensors. Agricultural machinery manufacturer John Deere produces wireless sensors that map fields and provide farmers with information on which acres need more (or less) water and nutrients. According to Mississippi farmer Jeremy Jack, "If we're really going to be professional farmers and feed everybody in the world, we really have to utilize this technology to do the job."[13]

17-2b Complete Information

Information is useful when it is complete. Incomplete or missing information makes it difficult to recognize problems and identify potential solutions. In 2016, Samsung suspected that Apple's iPhone 7, planned for release in September, would have a limited number of improvements. So it rushed the launch of its Galaxy Note 7, pushing engineers and suppliers to get its new phone to market one month before Apple. With a wrap-to-the-edges screen, a faster charging battery, and iris recognition for security, Samsung was confident they could take market share from Apple. The Note 7 was released on August 7, but by the beginning of September, dozens of online videos showed Note 7's on fire. On September 2, wanting to act quickly to take care of customers, mobile phone chief D.J. Koh announced that Samsung would replace 2.5 million Note 7's with batteries made by another supplier.[14]

Unfortunately, Koh and his team had incomplete information that only showed problems with batteries made by one of their two battery suppliers. Two weeks later, customers began having problems with replacement phones containing the other supplier's batteries.

The decisive event that killed the Galaxy Note 7 occurred on October 5, 2016 when a Southwest Airlines flight was evacuated on the runway after a passenger's replacement Note 7 caught fire.[15] On October 11, 2016, Koh announced Samsung was discontinuing the Note 7, promising refunds or replacements for customers. It made sure that Note 7s would not work by pushing a software program to the phones which "bricked" them by preventing charging and access to mobile data.[16]

17-2c Relevant Information

You can have complete, accurate information, but it's not very useful if it doesn't pertain to the problems you're facing. The dairy industry is a low-margin, highly competitive industry where small changes in productivity make a big difference. Keeping cows healthy and managing pregnancies so that each cow has a calf every year are fundamental to a well run dairy farm. Austin Knowles, a dairy farmer in Worcestershire, England, in the United Kingdom, has relevant information thanks to sensors inserted in his cow's stomachs. The sensors, which last about four years, act as an early warning signal by letting him know the cow's temperature, how much she's had to drink, how many steps she's taken, and the pH content of her stomach. Stefan Rosenkranz, cofounder of SmaXtec, which makes the devices that upload information to cloud servers for analysis, said, "It's easier, after all, to look at the situation from inside the cow than

In 2016, Samsung recalled all of its Galaxy Note 7 phones due to potential fire hazards.

in the lab."[17] The real-time data save farmers from having a vet examine the cows for vital signs. And, that information is 95 percent accurate in predicting when calves will be born. Farmer Knowles said, "The crux of any dairy farm is fertility. We are trying to have a calf per cow every year. Everything we do on the farm comes back to that."[18]

17-2d Timely Information

Finally, information is useful when it is timely. To be timely, the information must be available when needed to define a problem or to begin to identify possible solutions. If you've ever thought, "I wish I had known that earlier," then you understand the importance of timely information and the opportunity cost of not having it.

Feeding America, a nonprofit organization with more than 200 food banks, collects 4 billion pounds of food every year and distributes it to 46 million people. Until recently, the organization struggled to manage its food inventory because it could not anticipate what types or quantities of food donations it would receive. This uncertainty made it extremely difficult to distribute perishable food items before they spoiled. The problem always got much worse during November and December, when the volume of food donations was twice that donated during the other 10 months combined. To reduce the large amount of wasted food, Feeding America uses inventory software made by Exact Macola to track when and where goods are received. Workers are then sent automated alerts indicating which foods are approaching their use-by dates, their locations in the warehouse, and a recommended action (distribute or destroy). Since Feeding America has begun using the software, food waste has declined by more than 50 percent. Kathy Fulton, executive director of the American Logistics Aid Network, which donates logistics services to nonprofits like Feeding America, says, "The last thing you want is this fabulous donation that you can't use quickly enough."[19]

17-2e Acquisition Costs

Acquisition cost is the cost of obtaining data that you don't have. Firms with gigantic databases, like Amazon, Facebook, and Google, have a tremendous advantage over other retailers because they have so much direct data about consumer interests, product searches, and purchase behaviors. Smaller retailers and publishers can overcome this advantage, in part, by banding together to lower the acquisition cost of information. Bombora is a New York data co-op of more than 2,500 publishers that pool their subscriber and website visitor data, demographics, and purchase histories. Any company can purchase information about the consumers in the Bombora database, but co-op members receive

a 50 percent discount. Similarly, Skimlinks is a UK-based data co-op of 55,000 digital publishers and 20,000 retailers that have combined their proprietary customer information into a database of 1.3 billion unique users. Advertisers of everything from computers to shoes to toothpaste pay on a cost-per-thousand basis to access information about consumers' intent to purchase. Participating companies get a royalty any time their data is purchased by another firm, which ends up offsetting their own acquisition costs.[20]

17-2f Processing Costs

Companies often have massive amounts of data but not in the form or combination they need. **Processing cost** is the cost of turning raw data into usable information. A **data silo** is an isolated data set that is difficult to obtain, combine or use with other company data.[21] Data silos often have high processing costs because of **data variety**, that is, data that are formatted or structured in different ways. Making differently formatted and structured data, such as numbers, words, pictures, and social media, compatible is difficult and costly.[22] For example, after declining for several years, the number of accidents at railroad crossings is now increasing. The Federal Railroad Administration is partnering with Google Maps to add data on 210,000 railroad crossings to the Google Maps database. Previously, Google did not have access to those data. Google will need to process those data into formats compatible with the Google Maps database so that drivers using its turn-by-turn navigation are warned when approaching a rail crossing. Sara Feinberg, acting director of the Federal Railroad Administration, said, "We have some really good data on these crossings, but we have to put the data where people are using it."[23]

17-2g Storage Costs

Storage cost is the cost of physically or electronically archiving information for later retrieval and use. TV and movie footage is digital these days, rather than polyester film or videotape. Digital recording makes it easier to edit and add special effects, is cheaper, and directors don't have to wait for it to be chemically developed

Acquisition cost the cost of obtaining data that you don't have

Processing cost the cost of turning raw data into usable information

Data silo is an isolated data set that is difficult to obtain, combine or use with other company data.

Data variety that is, data that are formatted or structured in different ways.

Storage cost the cost of physically or electronically archiving information for later retrieval and use

Talk to Your Bar Code Scanner Like a Smart Phone

Logistic and warehouse workers scan up to 3,000 bar codes every day as they move, pack, and track items, so anything that speeds up the process or reduces the number of steps involved has value. With this in mind, Exel Logistics, a unit of delivery company **Deutsche Post DHL**, recently began testing a new bar code scanner that looks and operates sort of like a smartphone. Holding the scanner in front of your face like a magnifying glass, you can see the bar code on a small screen, allowing more precise aiming and reducing uncomfortable wrist angles. Between this scanner's point-and-shoot operation and its ability to use voice confirmations instead of physical buttons, Exel found that the new scanner increased worker productivity by 10 to 20 percent. James Bonner, Exel Logistics' general manager, said, "In the big scheme of the world, it sounds like nothing. But when you take away three [button] touches, that's like three halves of a second. And you're shipping thousands of shipments a day."

vectorfusionart/Shutterstock.com

Source: L. Chao, "Bar-Code Readers Get Makeover to Spur Bustling Warehouses," *Wall Street Journal*, January 8, 2016, http://www.wsj.com/articles/bar-code -readers-get-makeover-to-spur-bustling-warehouses-1452162601.

for viewing, like film. Distribution is inexpensive, too, as digital movies are sent to theaters using high-speed broadband. But storing a digital, feature-length movie costs about $20,000 a year, while storing an hour-long TV show costs about $12,000 a year. Since the standard LTO (linear tape-open) digital storage technology is only backward compatible for two versions, each movie or TV show needs to copied from an old LTO format to the new LTO format every two to three years at a cost that is typically twice as much as the cost of annual storage. Dino Everett, a film archivist at the University of Southern California, says LTO is "archive heroin—the first taste doesn't cost much, but once you start, you can't stop. And the habit is expensive."[24]

17-2h Retrieval Costs

Retrieval cost is the cost of accessing already-stored and processed information. One of the most common misunderstandings about information is that it is easy and cheap to retrieve after the company has it. Not so. First, you have to find the information. Then, you've got to convince whoever has it to share it with you. Then the information has to be processed into a form that is useful for you. By the time you get the information you need, it may not be timely anymore.

For example, as companies move toward paperless office systems, how will employees quickly and easily retrieve archived emails, file records, website information, word processing documents, or images? Likewise, how will managers and employees quickly and easily retrieve information about costs, inventory, and sales?

Retrieval cost is also a big factor for firms moving their data to the cloud. Which is why Amazon Web Services (AWS), the largest cloud service in the world, is offering its new Snowmobile service to transport huge amounts of corporate data to its AWS servers. Despite the name, Amazon's Snowmobile uses a long-haul truck trailer, 45 feet long, that is stuffed with hard drives and servers capable of holding 100 petabytes of data (a petabyte is 1 million gigabytes). Since it's not uncommon for large firms to have exabyte-sized amounts of data (an exabyte is 1 billion gigabytes), Amazon already has firms using the trucks to transfer data. Amazon estimates that it would take 26 years to transfer an exabyte of data from a corporate data warehouse to AWS servers using a 10 gigabyte-per-second broadband connection. However, it takes just under six months using ten Snowmobile data trucks. At a cost of $500,000 per month per truck, the total cost of retrieval from one system to another would be $30 million for an exabyte of data.[25]

Retrieval cost the cost of accessing already-stored and processed information

Amazon Web Services estimate it would take 26 years to transfer an exabyte of data from a corporate data warehouse to AWS servers using a 10 gigabyte per second broadband connection. It takes just under six months using 10 of the company's Snowmobile data trucks.

17-2i Communication Costs

Communication cost is the cost of transmitting information from one place to another. For example, a small business with 20 people needing phone lines, a hosted website, and high-speed Internet access pays Comcast about $1,300 a month for that access. Sixty dollars per line for a smartphone with unlimited data and voice services adds another $1,200 for a total of $2,500 per month, and that's without high-speed options needed for data-intensive companies like design, engineering, or manufacturing firms. Costs would, of course, be much higher for the Virtual Care Center at Mercy Health System in St. Louis, Missouri, that uses high-speed data, voice, and video to support intensive care units and emergency rooms in 38 small hospitals. Critical care specialist Vinaya Sermadevi said, "It's almost like being at the bedside—I can't shock a patient [restart his heart with electrical paddles], but I can give an order to the nurses there."[26]

17-3 CAPTURING, PROCESSING, AND PROTECTING INFORMATION

In 1907, Metropolitan Life Insurance built a huge office building in New York City for its brand-new, state-of-the-art information technology system. What was this great breakthrough in information management? Card files. That's right, the same card file system that every library in America used before computers. Metropolitan Life's information technology consisted of 20,000 separate file drawers that sat in hundreds of file cabinets more than 15 feet tall. This filing system held 20 million insurance applications, 700,000 accounting books, and 500,000 death certificates. Metropolitan Life employed 61 workers who did nothing but sort, file, and climb ladders to pull files as needed.[27]

How we get and share information has clearly changed. The cost, inefficiency, and ineffectiveness of using this formerly state-of-the-art system would put an insurance company out of business within months. Today, if storms, fire, or accidents damage a policyholder's property, he or she can use the insurance company's smartphone app to photograph and describe the damage. A company representative will then show up and write a check on the spot to cover the losses. As the claims process unfolds, the policyholder can ask questions, fill out forms, and access documents on the company's personalized web portal. From card files to Internet files in just under a century, the rate of change in information technology is spectacular.

*In this section, you will learn about the information technologies that companies use to **17-3a capture, 17-3b process, and 17-3c protect information.***

17-3a Capturing Information

There are two basic methods of capturing information: manual and electronic. Manual capture of information is a slow, costly, labor-intensive, and often inaccurate process, which entails recording and entering data by hand into a data storage device. For example, when you applied for a driver's license, you probably recorded personal information about yourself by filling out a form. Then, after you passed your driver's test, someone typed your handwritten information into the department of motor vehicles' computer database so that local and state police could access it from their patrol cars in the event they pulled you over for speeding. (Isn't information great?) To avoid the problems inherent in such a system, companies are relying more on electronic capture. They use electronic storage devices such as bar codes, radio frequency identification (RFID) tags, and document scanners to capture and record data electronically.

> **Communication cost** the cost of transmitting information from one place to another

Bar codes represent numerical data by varying the thickness and pattern of vertical bars. The primary advantage of bar codes is that the data they represent can be read and recorded in an instant with a handheld or pen-type scanner. One pass of the scanner (okay, sometimes several) and "beep!" the information has been captured. Bar codes cut checkout times in half, reduce data entry errors by 75 percent, and save stores money because stockers don't have to go through the labor-intensive process of putting a price tag on each item in the store.[28] And, with mobile phone apps, bar codes are becoming ubiquitous in travel (mobile boarding passes), for customer loyalty and payment programs (Starbucks), and in entertainment, such as movies (Fandango) and live events (LiveNation or TicketMaster). QR (quick response) codes are bar codes with black and white patterns scanned with your smartphone. Chinese consumers can quickly pay for taxi rides by scanning the taxi driver's QR code using Alipay Wallet (China-based Alibaba's PayPal equivalent).[29] Replicon's CloudClock system works by having employees scan a QR code that prompts a camera to take and time-stamp their picture, indicating when they started and stopped work.[30] Finally, BMO Harris Bank is launching cardless ATM machines where customers use their bank app to indicate how much money they want to withdraw. The app generates a QR code that the ATM machine scans and authorizes before dispensing cash in just 15 seconds, or just one-third of the time of a card-based transaction. Also, QR codes eliminate the risk of card skimming in which hackers tap into the card-reading device in the ATM machine.[31]

Radio frequency identification (RFID) tags contain minuscule microchips and antennas that transmit information via radio waves.[32] Unlike bar codes, which require direct line-of-sight scanning, RFID tags are read by turning on an RFID reader that, like a radio, tunes into a specific frequency to determine the number *and* location of products, parts, or anything else to which the RFID tags are

With mobile phone apps, bar codes are becoming ubiquitous in travel (mobile boarding passes), for customer loyalty, payment programs and in entertainment, such as movies (Fandango), and live events (TicketMaster).

attached. Turn on an RFID reader, and every RFID tag within the reader's range (from several hundred to several thousand feet) is accounted for.

Because they are now so inexpensive, RFID tags and readers are being put to thousands of uses in all kinds of businesses. When Johnson Controls, a $37 billion manufacturer, realized that it was missing thousands of shipping containers and racks used to transport parts and finished products, it bought 830,000 RFID tags and attached them to its remaining equipment. Thanks to the RFID tag readers installed in all of its factories and warehouses, Johnson Controls can now track the location of its 830,000 containers and racks—down to which door they exited the factory from and which customers they got shipped to. Brian Kelly, Johnson Controls' director of supply-chain management, said, "We could get to a point that we not only know where all of our containers are but what is in each one without ever opening them up."[33]

Electronic scanners, which convert printed text and pictures into digital images, have become an increasingly popular method of capturing data electronically because they are inexpensive and easy to use. The first requirement for a good scanner is a document feeder that automatically feeds document pages into the scanner or turns the pages (often with a puff of air) when scanning books or bound documents. Text that has been digitized cannot be searched or edited like the regular text in your word processing software, however; so the second requirement for a good scanner is **optical character recognition** software to

---

Bar code a visual pattern that represents numerical data by varying the thickness and pattern of vertical bars

Radio frequency identification (RFID) tags tags containing minuscule microchips that transmit information via radio waves and can be used to track the number and location of the objects into which the tags have been inserted

Electronic scanner an electronic device that converts printed text and pictures into digital images

Optical character recognition the ability of software to convert digitized documents into ASCII (American Standard Code for Information Interchange) text that can be searched, read, and edited by word processing and other kinds of software scan and convert original or digitized documents into ASCII (American Standard Code for Information Interchange) text or Adobe PDF documents. ASCII text can be searched, read, and edited with standard word processing, email, desktop publishing, database management, and spreadsheet software, and PDF documents can be searched and edited with Adobe's Acrobat software.

17-3b Processing Information

Processing information means transforming raw data into meaningful information that can be applied to business decision making. Evaluating sales data to determine the best- and worst-selling products, examining repair records to determine product reliability, and monitoring the cost of long-distance phone calls are all examples of processing raw data into meaningful information. And with automated, electronic capture of data, increased processing power, and cheaper and more plentiful ways to store data, managers no longer worry about getting data. Instead, they scratch their heads about how to use the overwhelming amount of data that pours into their businesses every day. Furthermore, most managers know little about statistics and have neither the time nor the inclination to learn how to use them to analyze data.

One promising tool to help managers dig out from under the avalanche of data is data mining. **Data mining** is the process of discovering patterns and relationships in large amounts of data.[34] Data mining is carried out using complex algorithms such as neural networks, rule induction, and decision trees. If you don't know what those are, that's okay. With data mining, you don't have to. Most managers only need to know that data mining looks for patterns that are already in the data but are too complex for them to spot on their own. Many Airbnb hosts who rent their rooms or homes to travelers have trouble deciding how much to charge per night. Data mining showed Airbnb that adjusting prices for *similarity, recency,* and *location* could maximize profits and occupancy rates. Similarity measured factors such as a home versus a private room, the number of bedrooms, the uniqueness of the property (are you renting a room in a castle or in an apartment?) and the number of reviews. Why reviews? They give potential renters confidence regarding the property and its host. Travel is seasonal, and demand for rentals is affected by major events like holidays, trade shows, and sporting events. Taking these and other recency factors into consideration, Airbnb can decide whether last week's, last month's, or last year's pricing

> Data mining is carried out using complex algorithms such as neural networks, rule induction, and decision trees. If you don't know what those are, that's okay. With data mining, you don't have to.

should guide how much to charge today. Finally, data mining revealed that a rental's location was critical to renters. Is it safe? Is it near transportation, restaurants, and tourist sites? To measure the value of rentals' locations, Airbnb hired cartographers to "map the boundaries of every neighborhood in our top cities all over the world."[35]

Data mining typically splits a data set in half, finds patterns in one half, and then tests the validity of those patterns by trying to find them again in the second half of the data set. The data typically come from a **data warehouse**, which stores huge amounts of data that have been prepared for data mining analysis by being cleaned of errors and redundancy. The data in a data warehouse can then be analyzed using two kinds of data mining. **Supervised data mining** usually begins with the user telling the data mining software to look and test for specific patterns and relationships in a data set. Typically, this is done through a series of "what-if?" questions or statements. For instance, a grocery store manager might instruct the data mining software to determine if coupons placed in the Sunday paper increase or decrease sales. By contrast, with **unsupervised data mining**, the user simply tells the data mining software to uncover whatever patterns and relationships

Processing information transforming raw data into meaningful information

Data mining the process of discovering unknown patterns and relationships in large amounts of data

Data warehouse a database that stores huge amounts of data that have been prepared for data mining analysis by being cleaned of errors and redundancy

Supervised data mining the process when the user tells the data mining software to look and test for specific patterns and relationships in a data set

Unsupervised data mining the process when the user simply tells the data mining software to uncover whatever patterns and relationships it can find in a data set it can find in a data set. Castlight Healthcare conducts unsupervised data mining to identify nonmedical data that are related to employees having diabetes, or heart disease, etc. Harry Greenspun, director of Deloitte LLP's Center for Health Solutions, which does health-related data mining like Castlight, says, "I bet I could better predict your risk of a heart attack by where you shop and where you eat than by your genome."[36] Someone who regularly buys things at a bike shop will likely be in better shape than someone who regularly buys video games online or at GameStop. Castlight then "nudges" employees with personalized messages regarding medical services or healthier behavior related to their medical issues.[37] Unsupervised data mining is particularly good at identifying association or affinity patterns, sequence patterns, and predictive patterns. It can also identify what data mining technicians call data clusters.[38]

Association or affinity patterns occur when two or more database elements tend to occur together in a significant way. Castlight Healthcare has a new data mining tool that it uses to determine which female employees are likely to get pregnant. The idea is to identify them early in their pregnancy to make sure mothers and babies are healthy from the start. It typically finds that the earliest predictors of pregnancy are whether women have searched for pregnancy-related information on the Castlight Healthcare website (which helps employees search for medical information and providers) and if they have stopped filling birth-control prescriptions. When those two pieces of data are combined with a woman's age and ages of her children (if any), Castlight can accurately predict whether a woman is pregnant. At that point, unbeknown to employers who are not privy to this information to protect confidentiality, Castlight sends female employees information to help them choose an obstetrician and begin prenatal care. And, if the data mining was wrong, they can opt out of receiving the messages.[39]

Sequence patterns appear when two or more database elements occur together in a significant pattern in which one of the elements precedes the other. Hospitals employ the Modified Early Warning Score (MEWS), which uses commonly measured vital signs, such as blood pressure, temperature, and heart rate, to predict the likelihood of a patient going Code Blue, that is, respiratory or cardiac arrest. Patients with higher MEWS scores are monitored more closely. Doctors at Chicago's NorthShore University HealthSystem used data mining to see how well 72 medical variables predicted the likelihood of a patient going Code Blue. On a data set of 133,000 patients, data mining correctly predicted Code Blues 72 percent of the time—four hours before they happened. By contrast, MEWS scores accurately predicted Code Blues just 30 percent of the time.[40]

Predictive patterns are just the opposite of association or affinity patterns. While association or affinity patterns look for database elements that seem to go together, **predictive patterns** help identify database elements that are different. Banks and credit card companies use data mining to find predictive patterns that distinguish customers who are good credit risks from those who are less likely to pay their loans and monthly bills. Lending money to people with poor credit or without bank accounts (one out of four adults worldwide) is risky. To better assess that risk, some startup companies are going beyond standard credit scores and are using social media to separate good borrowers from bad ones. For example, you're a better candidate if you access the Internet via an expensive smartphone (versus an Internet cafe where you pay by the hour); don't let your phone battery run down; and you get more phone calls than you make. You are also more likely to get a loan if your phone stays in the same place every day (indicating that you're at work) and you regularly interact with a group of close friends who are good credit risks (meaning that you probably are as well).[41]

Data clusters are the last kind of pattern found by data mining. **Data clusters** occur when three or more database elements occur together (that is, cluster) in a significant way. For example, after analyzing several years' worth of repair and warranty claims, Ford Motor Company might find that, compared with cars built in its Chicago plant, the cars it builds in Kansas City (first element) are more likely to have problems with over-tightened fan belts (second element) that break (third element) and result in overheated engines (fourth element), ruined radiators (fifth element), and payments for tow trucks (sixth element), which are paid for by Ford's five-year, 60,000-mile power train warranty.

Traditionally, data mining has been very expensive and very complex. Today, however, data mining services and analyses are much more affordable and within reach of most companies' budgets. And, if it follows the path of most technologies, data mining will become even easier and cheaper to use in the future.

Association or affinity patterns when two or more database elements tend to occur together in a significant way

Sequence patterns when two or more database elements occur together in a significant pattern in which one of the elements precedes the other

Predictive patterns patterns that help identify database elements that are different

Data clusters when three or more database elements occur together (that is, cluster) in a significant way

17-3c Protecting Information

Protecting information is the process of ensuring that data are reliably and consistently retrievable in a usable format for authorized users but no one else. Unfortunately, data breaches are occurring at record levels. According to IBM, 4 billion records, such as credit cards, personal identification, passwords and health information, were compromised via hacking in 2016, a 566 percent increase over 2015.[42] Cash ranging from $10,000 to $50,000 was stolen from Amazon third-party sellers. Amazon deposits customer payments in the third-party sellers Amazon accounts after customer receive delivery. Hackers likely used stolen emails and passwords to access the business accounts and transfer funds to inaccessible offshore accounts.[43] Tax returns, Hyatt, Starwood and Hilton hotels, Yahoo! accounts, and Google Docs accounts were all hacked to steal credentials, credit card information, or cash.[44] And, if hackers can get to Facebook founder and CEO Mark Zuckerberg's social media accounts—and they did—they can get to anyone.[45]

> If hackers can get to Facebook founder and CEO Mark Zuckerberg's social media accounts— and they did—they can get to anyone.

People inside and outside companies can steal or destroy company data in various ways, including denial-of-service web server attacks that can bring down some of the busiest and best-run sites on the Internet; viruses and malware, spyware, or adware that spread quickly and can result in data loss and business disruption; keystroke monitoring, in which every mouse click and keystroke you make is monitored, stored, and sent to unauthorized users; password-cracking software that steals supposedly secure passwords; and phishing, where fake but real-looking emails and websites trick users into sharing personal information (user names, passwords, account numbers) leading to unauthorized account access; and ransomware in which data are encrypted and made unusable until a ransom is paid to hackers to unlock the data. On average, 32 percent of computers are infected with malware. Of those, 57 percent are infected with

Protecting information the process of ensuring that data are reliably and consistently retrievable in a usable format for authorized users but no one else

Rawpixel.com/Shutterstock.com

WHAT HAPPENED WHEN CHRISTOPHER MIMS GAVE THE WORLD HIS TWITTER PASSWORD

Wall Street Journal reporter Christopher Mims published his Twitter password, "christophermims," in one of his columns. Mims wrote, "Knowing that won't help you hack it, however." And he was right. Despite hundreds of attempts, no one accessed his account.

The reason they couldn't? Mims had enabled two-factor authentication, a second form of authentication, which in this case was based on codes good for just 60 seconds that were randomly generated by the Google Authenticator app linked to his Twitter account.

Mims concluded, "I think I proved my point: Even when I exposed my password in as public a fashion as possible, my account remained secure."

So, protect your accounts. Enable two-factor authentication. But, don't give the world your password.

Sources: C. Mims, "The Password Is Finally Dying. Here's Mine," *Wall Street Journal*, July 13, 2014, accessed May 7, 2017, https://www.wsj.com/articles/the-password-is-finally-dying-heres-mine-1405298376; C. Mims, "Commentary: What I Learned, and What You Should Know, After I Published My Twitter Password," Digits, *Wall Street Journal*, July 15, 2014, accessed May 7, 2017, https://blogs.wsj.com/digits/2014/07/15/commentary-what-i-learned-and-what-you-should-know-after-i-published-my-twitter-password/.

viruses, and 21 percent are infected with Trojans, which is malware disguised to look like a normal file or program.[46] Studies show that the threats listed in Exhibit 17.3 are so widespread that automatic attacks will begin on an unprotected computer, which will be infected with Malware or viruses 60 seconds after it connecting to the Internet.[47]

As shown in the right-hand column of Exhibit 17.3, numerous steps can be taken to secure data and data networks. Some of the most important are authentication and authorization, firewalls, antivirus software for PCs and email servers, data encryption, virtual private networks, and updating and patching outdated software.[48] We will review those steps and then finish this section with a brief review of the dangers of wireless networks.

Two critical steps are required to make sure that data can be accessed by authorized users and no one else. One is **authentication**, that is, making sure users are who they claim to be.[49] The other is **authorization**, that is, granting authenticated users approved access to data, software, and systems.[50] When an ATM prompts you to enter your personal identification number (PIN), the bank is authenticating that you are you. After you've been authenticated, you are authorized to access your funds and no one else's. Of course, as anyone who has lost a PIN or password or had

one stolen knows, user authentication systems are not foolproof. In particular, users create security risks by not changing their default account passwords (such as birth dates) or by using weak passwords such as names ("Larry") or complete words ("football") that are quickly guessed by password-cracking software.[51]

This is why many companies are now turning to **two-factor authentication**, which is based on what users know, such as a password, and what they have, in their possession, such as a secure ID card, their phones, or unique information that only they would know.[52] When logging in, users are first asked for their passwords. But then they must provide a second authentication factor, such as an answer to a security question (that is, unique information) or a validation code that has been sent to their mobile phone. Google, for example, requires two-factor authentication for its Google Apps (Gmail, Calendar, Drive, Docs, and so on). After entering their passwords, users can either use the code sent via text to their phone, or a code generated by Google's Authenticator app. Google Authenticator, which requires a mobile phone or Internet connection, gives you the ability to generate authentication codes for multiple accounts (including non-Google accounts), and generates codes that are only good for 60 seconds.[53]

Unfortunately, stolen or cracked passwords are not the only way for hackers and electronic thieves to gain access to an organization's computer resources. Unless special safeguards are put in place, every time corporate users are online, there's literally nothing between their PCs and the Internet (home users with high-speed Internet access face the same risks). Hackers can access files, run programs, and control key parts of computers if precautions aren't taken. To reduce these risks, companies use **firewalls**, hardware or software devices that

Authentication making sure potential users are who they claim to be

Authorization granting authenticated users approved access to data, software, and systems

Two-factor authentication authentication based on what users know, such as a password and what they have in their possession, such as a secure ID card or key

Firewall a protective hardware or software device that sits between the computers in an internal organizational network and outside networks, such as the Internet

Exhibit 17.3
Security Threats to Data and Data Networks

Security Problem	Source	Affects	Severity	The Threat	The Solution
Denial of service; web server attacks and corporate network attacks	Internet hackers	All servers	High	Loss of data, disruption of service, and theft of service.	Implement firewall, password control, server-side review, threat monitoring, and bug fixes; turn PCs off when not in use.
Password cracking software and unauthorized access to PCs	Local area network, Internet	All users, especially digital subscriber line and cable Internet users	High	Hackers take over PCs. Privacy can be invaded. Corporate users' systems are exposed to other machines on the network.	Close ports and firewalls, disable file and print sharing, and use strong passwords.
Viruses, worms, Trojan horses, and rootkits	Email, downloaded and distributed software	All users	Moderate to high	Monitor activities and cause data loss and file deletion; compromise security by sometimes concealing their presence.	Use antivirus software and firewalls; control Internet access.
Malware, spyware, adware, malicious scripts, and applets	Rogue web pages	All users	Moderate to high	Invade privacy, intercept passwords, and damage files or file system.	Disable browser script support; use security, blocking, and spyware/adware software.
Email snooping	Hackers on your network and the Internet	All users	Moderate to high	People read your email from intermediate servers or packets, or they physically access your machine.	Encrypt messages, ensure strong password protection, and limit physical access to machines.
Keystroke monitoring	Trojan horses, people with direct access to PCs	All users	High	Records everything typed at the keyboard and intercepts keystrokes before password masking or encryption occurs.	Use antivirus software to catch Trojan horses, control Internet access to transmission, and implement system monitoring and physical access control.
Phishing	Hackers on your network and the Internet	All users, including customers	High	Fake but real-looking emails and websites that trick users into sharing personal information on what they wrongly think is a company's website. This leads to unauthorized account access.	Educate and warn users and customers about the dangers. Encourage both not to click on potentially fake URLs, which might take them to phishing websites. Instead, have them type your company's URL into the web browser.
Spam	Email	All users and corporations	Mild to high	Clogs and overloads email servers and inboxes with junk mail. HTML-based spam may be used for profiling and identifying users.	Filter known spam sources and senders on email servers; have users create further lists of approved and unapproved senders on their PCs.
Ransomware	Hackers on your network and the Internet	All users and corporations	High	Encrypts personal or corporate data so it can't be accessed. Attacked individuals or corporations must pay a ransom of hundreds to tens of thousands of dollars using Bitcoin (an anonymous method of payment) within a specified time or the data will be permanently locked or destroyed.	Educate managers and employees about phishing, close open ports, patch and update unpatched and outdated applications.

Sources: M. Ali, "Is Your Company Ready for a Ransomware Attack?," *Harvard Business Review*, October 3, 2016, accessed May 6, 2017, https://hbr.org/2016/10/is-your-company-ready-for-a-ransomware-attack; "The 11 Most Common Computer Security Threats . . . And What You Can Do to Protect Yourself from Them," *Symantec-Norton*, accessed May 12, 2015, http://www.symantec-norton.com/11-most-common-computer-security-threats_k13.aspx; K. Bannan, "Look Out: Watching You, Watching Me," *PC Magazine*, July 2002, 99; A. Dragoon, "Fighting Phish, Fakes, and Frauds," *CIO*, September 1, 2004, 33; B. Glass, "Are You Being Watched?" *PC Magazine*, April 23, 2002, 54; K. Karagiannis, "DDoS: Are You Next?" *PC Magazine*, January 2003, 79; B. Machrone, "Protect & Defend," *PC Magazine*, June 27, 2000, 168–181; "Top 10 Security Threats," *PC Magazine*, April 10, 2007, 66; M. Sarrel, "Master End-User Security," *PC Magazine*, May 2008, 101.

In 2016, Home Depot announced that it would pay as much as $19.5 million to settle a class-action lawsuit brought by customers affected by a massive online security breach at the company.

sit between the computers in an internal organizational network and outside networks such as the Internet. Firewalls filter and check incoming and outgoing data. They prevent company insiders from accessing unauthorized sites or from sending confidential company information to people outside the company. Firewalls also prevent outsiders from identifying and gaining access to company computers and data. If a firewall is working properly, the computers behind the company firewall literally cannot be seen or accessed by outsiders.

A **virus** is a program or piece of code that, without your knowledge, attaches itself to other programs on your computer and can trigger anything from a harmless flashing message to the reformatting of your hard drive to a system-wide network shutdown. You used to have to do something or run something to get a virus, such as double-clicking an infected email attachment. Today's viruses are much more threatening. In fact, with some viruses, just being connected to a network can infect your computer. *Antivirus software for PCs* scans email, downloaded files, and computer hard drives, disk drives, and memory to detect and stop computer viruses from doing damage. However, this software is effective only to the extent that users of individual computers have and use up-to-date versions. With new viruses appearing all the time, users should update their antivirus software

weekly or, even better, configure their virus software to automatically check for, download, and install updates. By contrast, *corporate antivirus software* automatically scans email attachments such as Microsoft Word documents, graphics, or text files as they come across the company email server. It also monitors and scans all file downloads across company databases and network servers. So, while antivirus software for PCs prevents individual computers from being infected, corporate antivirus software for email servers, databases, and network servers adds another layer of protection by preventing infected files from multiplying and being sent to others.

Another way of protecting information is to encrypt sensitive data. **Data encryption** transforms data into complex, scrambled digital codes that can be decrypted only by authorized users who possess unique decryption keys. One method of data encryption is to use products by Symantec to encrypt the files stored on PCs or network servers and databases. This is especially important with laptop computers, which are easily stolen, and with sensitive data like customer credit card numbers. Indeed, after being hit by a major security breach in which 56 million customers' unencrypted credit card numbers were stolen by hackers, The Home Depot now spends $7 million a year to encrypt data at its 2,200 stores.[54]

With people increasingly gaining unauthorized access to email messages—email snooping—it's also important to encrypt sensitive email messages and file attachments. You can use a system called "public key encryption" to do so. First, give copies of your "public key" to anyone who sends you files or email. Have the sender use the public key, which is actually a piece of software, to encrypt files, before sending them to you. The only way to decrypt the files is with a companion "private key" that you keep to yourself.

Although firewalls can protect PCs and network servers connected to the corporate network, people away from their offices (for example, salespeople, business travelers, telecommuters) who interact with their company networks via the Internet face a security risk. Because Internet data are not encrypted, "packet sniffer" software easily allows hackers to read everything sent or received except files that have been encrypted before sending.

Previously, the only practical solution was to have employees dial in to secure company phone lines for direct access to the company network. Of course, with international and long-distance phone calls, the costs quickly

Virus a program or piece of code that, without your knowledge, attaches itself to other programs on your computer and can trigger anything from a harmless flashing message to the reformatting of your hard drive to a system-wide network shutdown

Data encryption the transformation of data into complex, scrambled digital codes that can be decrypted only by authorized users who possess unique decryption keys

Uber Hires White Hat Hackers

If you own a car, chances are you've got a wireless key fob that lets you lock and unlock the vehicle at the touch of a button. While convenient, keyless entry systems are highly susceptible to hacking attacks. German researchers found that at least 24 different models from 19 auto manufacturers could be unlocked, started, and driven away as long as the car owner's key fob was within several hundred meters. In other words, your car keys could be in your house and hackers could drive away with your supposedly locked car. Two hackers, Charlier Miller and Chris Valasek, recently demonstrated that they could remotely control a Jeep Cherokee from 10 miles away. They were able to adjust the air conditioning, change the radio, flip on the windshield wipers, and scariest of all, shift the transmission into neutral in the middle of a busy highway. They were also able to kill the engine and slam on the brakes—or disable them altogether. Uber, a ride sharing company that may ultimately become a provider of driverless services, is a common target of hackers. To combat

Kamira/Shutterstock.com

this, the company hired Miller and Valesek to "continue building out a world-class safety and security program at Uber."

Sources: A. Greenberg, "Radio Attack Lets Hackers Steal 24 Different Car Models," *Wired*, March 21, 2016, accessed May 12, 2016, https://www.wired.com/2016/03/study-finds-24-car-models-open-unlocking-ignition-hack/; A. Greenberg, "Hackers Remotely Kill a Jeep on the Highway—With Me in It," *Wired*, July 21, 2015, accessed May 12, 2016, https://www.wired.com/2015/07/hackers-remotely-kill-jeep-highway/; M. Isaac and N. Perlroth, "Uber Hires Two Engineers Who Showed Cars Could Be Hacked," *New York Times*, August 28, 2015, accessed May 12, 2016, http://www.nytimes.com/2015/08/29/technology/uber-hires-two-engineers-who-showed-cars-could-be-hacked.html.

---

added up. Now, **virtual private networks (VPNs)** have solved this problem by using software to encrypt all Internet data at both ends of the transmission process. Instead of making long-distance calls, employees connect to the Internet. But, unlike typical Internet connections in which data packets are decrypted, the VPN encrypts the data sent by employees outside the company computer network, decrypts the data when they arrive within the company network, and does the same when data are sent back to the computer outside the network. VPN connections provide secure access to everything on a company's network. If your employer or university doesn't provide a VPN, you can purchase VPN services for personal use and protection from well-known providers, such as AnchorFree Hotspot Shield or Cloak VPN, for about $3 a month. VPN services should be used when connected to public Wi-Fi systems, such as in hotels, airports, or coffee shops, where anyone on the public network can monitor or spy on what you're doing.

Alternatively, many companies are now adopting web-based **secure sockets layer (SSL) encryption** to provide secure off-site access to data and programs. If you've ever entered your credit card in a web browser to make an online purchase, you've used SSL technology to encrypt and protect that information.

You can tell if SSL encryption is being used on a website if you see a padlock icon or if the URL begins with "https." SSL encryption works the same way in the workplace. Managers and employees who aren't at the office simply connect to the Internet, open a web browser, and then enter a user name and password to gain access to SSL-encrypted data and programs.

Finally, while wireless networks come equipped with security and encryption capabilities that, in theory, permit only authorized users to access the wireless network, those capabilities are easily bypassed with the right tools. Compounding the problem, many wireless network routers are shipped with outdated firmware susceptible to hacking and with encryption capabilities turned off for ease of installation.[55] To stay safe, organizations should regularly update their wireless network routers' firmware. Also, caution is important even when encryption is turned on, because the WEP (Wired Equivalent Privacy) security protocol is easily compromised. If you work at home or are working on the go, extra care is critical because Wi-Fi networks in homes and public places such as hotel lobbies are among the most targeted by hackers.[56] See the Wi-Fi Alliance site at www.wi-fi.org for the latest information on

Virtual private network (VPN) software that securely encrypts data sent by employees outside the company network, decrypts the data when they arrive within the company computer network, and does the same when data are sent back to employees outside the network

Secure sockets layer (SSL) encryption Internet browser–based encryption that provides secure off-site web access to some data and programs wireless security and encryption protocols that provide much stronger protection for your company's wireless network.

Finally, companies are combating security threats by hiring *white hat hackers*, so-called good guys, who test security weak points in information systems so that they can be fixed. While this is typically done using traditional hacking tools, as discussed in Exhibit 17.3, white hat hackers also test security via *social engineering*, in which they trick people into giving up passwords and authentication protocols or unknowingly providing unauthorized access to company computers. One test involves emailing a picture of a cat with a purple mohawk and this subject line, "Check out these kitties!" to employees with a link to more cute kitty photos. When you click an embedded link to "more cute kitty photos," you're taken to a company website warning about the dangers of phishing scams. Think that you wouldn't fall for this? Forty-eight percent of employees receiving this email click the link.[57] Another test involves "lost or left-behind" USB thumb drives, ostensibly belonging to competitors. When the person who picked up the thumb drive inserts it into a computer, it installs software that uses the webcam to snap a picture of the employee, who then receives a visit from the IT security team.[58]

17-4 ACCESSING AND SHARING INFORMATION AND KNOWLEDGE

Today, information technologies are letting companies communicate data, share data, and provide data access to workers, managers, suppliers, and customers in ways that were unthinkable just a few years ago.

*After reading this section, you should be able to explain how companies use information technology to improve **17-4a internal access and sharing of information, 17-4b external access and sharing of information,** and **17-4c the sharing of knowledge and expertise.***

Daniel Koh, chief of staff for Boston Mayor Marty Walsh, updates the mayor and staff on City Score performances.

17-4a Internal Access and Sharing

Executives, managers, and workers inside the company use three kinds of information technology to access and share information: executive information systems, intranets, and portals. An **executive information system (EIS)** uses internal and external sources of data to provide managers and executives the information they need to monitor and analyze organizational performance.[59] The goal of an EIS is to provide accurate, complete, relevant, and timely information to managers. With just a few mouse clicks and basic commands such as *find*, *compare*, and *show*, the EIS displays costs, sales revenues, and other kinds of data in color-coded charts and graphs. Managers can drill down to view and compare data by global region, country, state, time period, and product. Boston Mayor Marty Walsh tracks the performance of the city's various departments on a huge display in his office. The dashboard, called City Score, monitors 21 quality of life measures, from response time on 911 calls, to cleaning up graffiti, and collecting trash to crime. Every measure is scaled so a score of 1.00 or above, shown in white, indicates meeting or exceeding goals. A score below 1.00, shown in red, indicates below targeted performance. Daniel Koh, the mayor's chief of staff, says, "Everybody knows that he is looking at this."[60] For instance, says Koh, "the mayor could see over and over that EMS [Emergency Medical Services] response time was in the red." Mayor Walsh's phone call with the head of EMS revealed that the number of ambulances had not increased as Boston's population had grown. So, the city bought 10 more. Says Koh, "It's not a stretch to say… [this] will save lives because of improved response times."[61] City Score can be viewed at https://www.boston.gov/cityscore.

Intranets are private company networks that allow employees to easily access, share, and publish information using Internet software. Intranet websites are just like external websites, but the firewall separating the internal company network from the Internet permits only authorized internal access.[62] Companies typically use intranets to share information (for example, about benefits) and to replace paper forms with online forms. Many company intranets are built on the web model as it existed a decade ago. Intranets are evolving to include:

» collaboration tools, such as wikis, where team members can post all relevant information for a project they're working on together

» customizable email accounts

» presence awareness (information on whether someone you are looking for on the network is in the office, in a meeting, working from home, and so on)

» instant messaging

» simultaneous access to files for virtual team members

Dorma+kaba, a global provider of security and business access solutions (keys, locks, automatic doors, door and controls), recently launched a company intranet that was recognized in 2015 as one of the world's 10 best. With 16,000 employees in 50 countries speaking multiple languages, Dorma+kaba needed an intranet that promoted collaboration and sharing of information. The new intranet's communication platform was designed so that employees could easily create corporate blogs, disseminate company news and videos, and promote events and announcements. What's more, it made all of this content readily accessible in each user's native language. Dorma+kaba's intranet has other advanced features as well. SmartFeed, which sits on the intranet home page, automatically finds the most important and relevant news for each user. Collaboration is facilitated by building Yammer, a corporate social networking function, directly into the intranet. Within months of launch, more than 500 conversations on new products had taken place on Yammer, allowing global sales and operational teams to answer questions and share best practices. To reach employees no matter where they're located or what devices they're using, Dorma+kaba's intranet is synchronized across PCs and Macs and there are native applications for iOS, Android, and Windows phones and tablets.[63]

Finally, **corporate portals** are a hybrid of executive information systems and intranets. While an EIS provides managers and executives with the information they need to monitor and analyze organizational performance, and intranets help companies distribute and publish information and forms within the company, corporate portals allow company managers and employees to access customized information *and* complete specialized transactions using a web browser.

17-4b External Access and Sharing

Historically, companies have been unable or reluctant to let outside groups have access to corporate information. Now, however, a number of information technologies—electronic data interchange, extranets, web services, and the Internet—are making it easier to share company data with external groups such as suppliers and customers. They're also reducing costs, increasing productivity by eliminating manual information processing (70% of the data output from one company, such as a purchase order, ends up as data input at another company, such as a sales invoice or shipping order), reducing data entry errors, improving customer service, and speeding communications. As a result, managers are scrambling to adopt these technologies.

With **electronic data interchange, or EDI,** two companies convert purchase and ordering information to a standardized format to enable direct electronic transmission of that information from one company's computer

> A number of information technologies--electronic data interchange, extranets, web services, and the Internet— are making it easier to share company data with external groups such as suppliers and customers.

Corporate portal a hybrid of executive information systems and intranets that allows managers and employees to use a web browser to gain access to customized company information and to complete specialized transactions

Electronic data interchange (EDI) when two companies convert their purchase and ordering information to a standardized format to enable the direct electronic transmission of that information from one company's computer system to the other company's computer system

Self-service kiosks have sped up check-in times for the more than 34 million passengers who pass through Gatwick Airport every year.

system to the other company's system. For example, when a Walmart checkout clerk drags an Apple iPad across the checkout scanner, Walmart's computerized inventory system automatically reorders another iPad through the direct EDI connection that its computer has with Apple's manufacturing and shipping computer. No one at Walmart or Apple fills out paperwork. No one makes phone calls. There are no delays to wait to find out whether Apple has the iPad in stock. The transaction takes place instantly and automatically because the data from both companies were translated into a standardized, shareable, compatible format.

Web services are another way for companies to directly and automatically transmit purchase and ordering data from one company's computer system to another company's computer system. **Web services** use standardized protocols to describe and transfer data from one company in such a way that those data can automatically be read, understood, transcribed, and processed by different computer systems in another company.[64] Route One, which helps automobile dealers process loans for car buyers, was started by the financing companies of DaimlerChrysler, Ford, General Motors, and Toyota. Not surprisingly, each auto company had a different computer system with different operating systems, different programs, and

Web services software that uses standardized protocols to describe data from one company in such a way that those data can automatically be read, understood, transcribed, and processed by different computer systems in another company

Extranets networks that allow companies to exchange information and conduct transactions with outsiders by providing them direct, web-based access to authorized parts of a company's intranet or information system

different data structures. RouteOne relies on web services to connect these different computer systems to 135+ different databases and software used by various auto dealers, credit bureaus, banks, and other auto financing companies. Without web services, there's no way these different companies and systems could share information.[65]

Now, what's the difference between web services and EDI? For EDI to work, the data in different companies' computer, database, and network systems must adhere to a particular set of standards for data structure and processing. For example, company X, which has a seven-digit parts numbering system, and company Y, which has an eight-digit parts numbering system, would agree to convert their internal parts numbering systems to identical ten-digit parts numbers when their computer systems talk to each other. By contrast, the tools underlying web services such as extensible markup language (or XML) automatically do the describing and transcribing so that data with different structures can be shared across very different computer systems in different companies. (Don't worry if you don't understand how this works, just appreciate what it does.) As a result, by automatically handling those differences, web services allow organizations to communicate data without special knowledge of each other's computer information systems.

In EDI and web services, the different purchasing and ordering applications in each company interact automatically without any human input. No one has to lift a finger to click a mouse, enter data, or hit the Enter key. An **extranet**, by contrast, allows companies to exchange information and conduct transactions by purposely providing outsiders with direct, password-protected, web browser–based access to authorized parts of a company's intranet or information system.[66]

General Electric (GE) is a global, U.S.-based conglomerate that makes products for a wide variety of markets, including software controlled factory automation. GE Intelligent Platform's customer portal allows customers to create and track a case when experiencing product problems. The customer portal also allows customers to search the knowledge base for product documentation and software updates, to pose questions in the discussion forum to other product users, to suggest product improvements and ideas, to order maintenance products or service, and to manage and keep track of the products purchased from GE Intelligent Platforms.[67]

Finally, companies are reducing paperwork and manual information processing by using the Internet to electronically automate transactions with customers; this is similar to the way in which extranets are used to handle transactions with suppliers and distributors. For example, most airlines have automated the ticketing process by eliminating paper tickets altogether. Simply buy an e-ticket via the Internet, and then check yourself in online via an app on your smart phone, or by printing your boarding pass from your PC or an airport kiosk. Internet purchases, ticketless travel, and automated check-ins have together fully automated the purchase of airline tickets. Use of self-service kiosks is expanding, too.

At London's Gatwick airport, self-service kiosks now offer "self bag drop," which travelers use to check in, weigh, and tag their luggage—all without the help of an agent. The self-service kiosks can process excess, oversized, and overweight baggage, even taking credit card payments for modified or extra charges. After check-in and bag tagging, customers place their luggage on baggage conveyor belts immediately adjacent to the kiosks. While the kiosks are speeding up check-in, some customers still prefer checking bags with gate agents.[68] New Yorker Mark Rosenthal says, "I don't work for the airline. Why should I do their job? If something goes wrong or I have a question, the self-tagging machine isn't going to have an answer."[69]

In the long run, the goal is to link customer Internet sites with company intranets (or EDI) and extranets so that everyone—all the employees and managers within a company as well as the suppliers and distributors outside the company—involved in providing a service or making a product for a customer is automatically notified when a purchase is made. Companies that use EDI, web services, extranets, and the Internet to share data with customers and suppliers achieve increases in productivity 2.7 times larger than those that don't.[70]

17-4c Sharing Knowledge and Expertise

At the beginning of the chapter, we distinguished between raw data, which consist of facts and figures, and information, which consists of useful data that influence someone's choices and behavior. One more important distinction needs to be made, namely, that data and information are not the same as knowledge. **Knowledge** is the understanding that one gains from information. Importantly, knowledge does not reside in information. Historically, knowledge has resided in people. That's why companies hire consultants and why family doctors refer patients to specialists. Unfortunately, it can be quite expensive to employ consultants, specialists, and experts. So companies have used two information technologies to capture and share the knowledge of consultants, specialists, and experts with other managers and workers: decision support systems and expert systems. Thanks to cheap computing power and the availability of "big data," companies are now in the early stages of using systems in which knowledge resides in machines or computers via artificial intelligence.

Although an executive information system speeds up and simplifies the acquisition of information, a **decision support system (DSS)** helps

Knowledge the understanding that one gains from information

Decision support system (DSS) an information system that helps managers understand specific kinds of problems and potential solutions managers understand problems and potential solutions by acquiring and analyzing information with sophisticated models and tools.[71] Furthermore, whereas EIS programs are broad in scope and permit managers to retrieve all kinds of information about a company, DSS programs are usually narrow in scope and targeted toward helping managers solve specific kinds of problems. DSS programs have been developed to help managers pick the shortest and most efficient routes for delivery trucks, select the best combination of stocks for investors, and schedule the flow of inventory through complex manufacturing facilities. It's important to understand that DSS programs don't replace managerial decision making; they *improve* it by furthering managers' and workers' understanding of the problems they face and the solutions that might work.

IBM's Watson has been used in myriad industries, from finance to cancer research.

Sean Gallup/Getty Images

Expert systems are created by capturing the specialized knowledge and decision rules used by experts and experienced decision makers. They permit nonexpert employees to draw on this expert knowledge base to make decisions. Most expert systems work by using a collection of "if–then" rules to sort through information and recommend a course of action. For example, let's say that you're using your American Express card to help your spouse celebrate a promotion. After dinner and a movie, the two of you stroll by a travel office with a Las Vegas poster in its window. Thirty minutes later, caught up in the moment, you find yourselves at the airport ticket counter trying to purchase last-minute tickets to Vegas. But there's just one problem. American Express didn't approve your purchase. In fact, the ticket counter agent is now on the phone with an American Express customer service agent. So what put a temporary halt to your weekend escape to Vegas? An expert system that American Express calls Authorizer's Assistant.[72]

The first "if–then" rule that prevented your purchase was the rule "*if* a purchase is much larger than the cardholder's regular spending habits, *then* deny approval of the purchase." This if–then rule, just one of 3,000, is built into American Express's transaction-processing system that handles thousands of purchase requests per second. Now that the American Express customer service agent is on the line, he or she is prompted by the Authorizer's Assistant to ask the ticket counter agent to examine your identification. You hand over your driver's license and another credit card to prove you're you. Then the ticket agent asks for your address, phone number, and your mother's maiden name and relays the information to American Express. Finally, your ticket purchase is approved. Why? Because you met the last series of "if–then" rules. *If* the purchaser can provide proof of identity and *if* the purchaser can provide personal information that isn't common knowledge, *then* approve the purchase.

Artificial intelligence, or **AI**, is the capability of computerized systems to learn and adapt through experience.[73] Devices and applications that have this capability are said to possess artificial intelligence. A common way to develop AI is to feed information into an AI system, have it analyze that information for patterns, and then have the AI system make decisions (do this or that) or categorical distinctions (this is a picture of a wolf, not a dog), letting the system know when it was wrong or right. That feedback helps the AI system "learn" and become more accurate over time.

For example, H&R Block is using IBM's "Watson" AI system to analyze tax returns for 11 million people at 10,000 branch offices. CEO Bill Cobb says that when H&R Block approached IBM with the idea to use Watson in its business, they told him, "This is not magic. You have to teach Watson over time."[74] To do that, they started by feeding Watson 74,000 pages of the U.S. federal tax code, along with thousands of tax questions that H&R Block's tax preparers asked clients over 60 years of business. Watson was eventually given thousands of tax filings, already handled by H&R Block tax preparers, from which to learn. Watson would

Expert system an information system that contains the specialized knowledge and decision rules used by experts and experienced decision makers so that nonexperts can draw on this knowledge base to make decisions

Artificial intelligence, or **AI** the capability of computerized systems to learn and adapt through experience suggest a question for a particular tax situation and then learn, via feedback from H&R Block's tax specialists, who indicated whether the question was appropriate or not. The advantage of using Watson, says H&R Block's George Gaustello, is that it makes their people better. Gaustello said, "We have 70,000 experts, but let's say 500 of those are very knowledgeable about firefighters, or they know every credit deduction a farmer can get." If Watson learns what those 500 experts know, then, he says, we're "making our experts even smarter."[75] CEO Bill Cobb said, "Our clients will benefit from an enhanced experience and our tax pros will have the latest technology to help them ensure every deduction and credit is found."[76]

STUDY TOOLS 17

LOCATED IN TEXTBOOK
☐ Rip out and review chapter review card.

LOCATED AT WWW.CENGAGE.COM/LOGIN
☐ Gain unique perspectives on key concepts with new 4LTR concept videos in the e-book.

☐ Increase your comprehension with Aplia for MGMT11.
☐ Complete interactive content within the e-book.

18 | Managing Service and Manufacturing Operations

LEARNING OBJECTIVES

18-1 Discuss the kinds of productivity and their importance in managing operations.

18-2 Explain the role that quality plays in managing operations.

18-3 Explain the essentials of managing a service business.

18-4 Describe the different kinds of manufacturing operations.

18-5 Explain why and how companies should manage inventory levels.

After you finish this chapter, go to **PAGE 417** for **STUDY TOOLS**

18-1 PRODUCTIVITY

Furniture manufacturers, hospitals, restaurants, automakers, airlines, and many other kinds of businesses struggle to find ways to produce quality products and services efficiently and then deliver them in a timely manner. Managing the daily production of goods and services, or **operations management**, is a key part of a manager's job. But an organization depends on the quality of its products and services as well as its productivity.

On turnaround day, Royal Caribbean's *Oasis of the Seas* cruise ship sails into port at 6:00 a.m., dropping off 6,000 passengers, restocking supplies, taking on 6,000 new passengers, and departing by 4:30 p.m. Provision master Rodolfo Corrales says, "Embarkation day is frantic. It's not just busy, it's crazy busy."[1] Corrales and other crewmembers will load 12,000 bags, 24,000 beer bottles, 1,400 champagne bottles, 15,000 pounds of potatoes, 9,000 pounds of tomatoes, and 9,000 cans of soft drinks onto the ship. In 2,700 rooms, attendants will strip the beds and towels, which go into green and red bags (for easier handling of 93,000 pounds of laundry). One hundred eighty-nine housekeepers clean 2,700 cabins and bathrooms. Precisely choreographed jobs and tasks, as well as a service corridor (which passengers never see) nicknamed I-95 because it runs the length of the ship to quickly get anything anywhere, make all of this happen. None of it is

Operations management managing the daily production of goods and services accidental. In fact, Royal Caribbean brought in productivity experts from Porsche, the German carmaker, and DHL, the delivery logistics firm to learn how to best manage the flow of goods, people, and luggage. The ship's hotel director, Martin Rissley, says, "The minute efficiencies you can create in the process make a big difference in the end."[2]

At their core, organizations are production systems. Companies combine inputs such as labor, raw materials, capital, and knowledge to produce outputs in the form of finished products or services. **Productivity** is a measure of performance that indicates how many inputs it takes to produce or create an output.

$$Productivity = \frac{Outputs}{Inputs}$$

The fewer inputs it takes to create an output (or the greater the output from one input), the higher the productivity.

On calm weather days, London's Heathrow airport lands 40 to 45 planes every hour. Strong headwinds drop that rate to just 32 to 38 planes per hour, however. How could Heathrow be more productive on windy days? Arriving planes are typically spaced three to seven miles apart depending on jet size. Heathrow, however, now uses time-based plane separation to improve arrival efficiency.

The *Wall Street Journal's* Scott McCartney explains: "If a plane normally needs to be five miles behind the one it's following, but the headwind at 3,000 feet above sea level is 50 knots, or 58 miles an hour, now the plane might move a mile closer. Time between touchdowns remains the same, even with the headwinds slowing down the flight." How well does this work? On a blustery March day with nearly 60-miles-per-hour headwinds, 60 more planes than normal landed at Heathrow. Indeed, delays and circling patterns have dropped significantly, and the airport reports a 50 percent increase in landing productivity on windy days.[3]

Let's examine **18-1a why productivity matters, 18-1b the different kinds of productivity,** *and* **18-1c productivity and automation.**

18-1a Why Productivity Matters

Why does productivity matter? For companies, higher productivity—that is, doing more with less—results in lower costs for the company, lower prices, faster service, higher market share, and higher profits. In 1989, 85 percent of the items on a UPS delivery truck were shipped to businesses.

> **Productivity** a measure of performance that indicates how many inputs it takes to produce or create an output

PACKAGING AND PRODUCTIVITY: "WE HATE AIR AT IKEA"

Ikea, famous for its low prices and assemble-ready furniture, is striving to grow by 10 percent a year. The Swedish retailer expects much of that growth to come from lower prices driving higher sales volumes. And, lower prices will likely come from increasing productivity. When Ikea hollowed out the solid wood legs of its Bjursta dining table, it reduced the table's weight and shipping costs, allowing it to cut the price from $360 to $260. When it cut the number of parts in its Textur lamp from 33 to 9, the lamp was 28 percent lighter and could be packed in smaller boxes. Now, 128 Textur boxes can fit on one pallet instead of 80.

That enabled Ikea to drop the Textur's price by 28 percent. The Ektrop sofa used to be one piece, but redesigning it to have a hinged back and removable arms allowed Ikea to cut the sofa's package size in half, resulting in 7,500 fewer truck loads per year and a 14 percent lower price. CEO Peter Agnefjall says, "We are engineering costs out of our value chain that don't contribute anything . . . We hate [shipping] air at Ikea."

Source: S. Chaudhuri, "IKEA Can't Stop Obsessing About Its Packaging, *Wall Street Journal*, June 17, 2015, accessed May 6, 2016, http://www.wsj.com/articles/ikea-cant-stop-obsessing-about-its-packaging-1434533401.

Today, 60 percent of those items are delivered to consumers, with one-third shipping from Amazon.com. Although UPS earns $11 billion a year from e-commerce deliveries, revenues per package are dropping, while per-package delivery costs are rising, all thanks to rising home deliveries. Consequently, UPS is intensifying its already strong focus on productivity by spending $500 million in preparation for the holiday season where, at its peak, it will deliver 34 million packages in one day (double an average day). It is getting large productivity increases, however, from its "Next Generation Sort Aisle," where sorters scan a package barcode (just like in stores), hear a beep (indicating a successful scan), and then read the name of a color-coded chute to which the packages needs to go. Before the scanning system, employees trained for two weeks on computers to memorize 120 ZIP codes. Now, new employees can be trained in two or three days. Rosemary Etheredge, who has worked at UPS for 10 years, says, "For new employees, it is much better."[4] In fact, with the Next Generation scanning system, sorters can process 15 percent more packages per day, which means that UPS can hire the same number of temporary holiday season workers as it did two years ago, even though product volumes are rising more than 10 percent per year.[5]

Productivity matters because it results in a higher standard of living in terms of higher wages, charitable giving, and making products more affordable. When companies can do more with less, they can raise employee wages without increasing prices or sacrificing normal profits. For instance, recent government economic data indicated that U.S. companies were paying workers 2.4 percent more than in the previous year. But because workers were only producing 1.1 percent more than they had the year before, real labor costs actually increased.[6]

The median U.S. family income was $70,697 in 2015. If productivity grows 1 percent per year, that family's income will increase to $90,664 in 2040. But if productivity grows 2 percent per year, their income in 2040 will be $115,985, an increase of $25,321, and that's without working longer hours.[7]

Thanks to long-term increases in business productivity, the typical American family today earns 22.7 percent more than the average family in 1980 and 43.6 percent more than the average family in 1967—and that's after accounting for inflation.[8] Productivity increased an average of 1.5 percent from 1979 to 1990, 2.2 percent from 1990 to 2000, 2.6 percent from 2000 to 2007, and 1.2 percent from 2007 to 2016.[9] And, from 2007 to 2017, the U.S. economy created nearly 7.1 million new jobs.[10]

And when more people have jobs that pay more, they give more to charity. For example, in 2015 Americans donated more than $373 billion to charities, compared to $358 million in 2014, $261 billion in 2009 and $230 billion in 2000.[11] Did Americans become more thoughtful, caring, conscientious, and giving? Probably not. Yet, because of increases in productivity during this time, the average American's income (which is different from family income) increased by 57.3 percent, from $36,433 in 2000 to $57,300 in 2016.[12] Because people earned more money, they were able to share their good fortune with others by giving more to charity.[13]

For instance, in 1964, a 21-inch color TV sold for $750, or $5,800 in 2016 dollars. According to economist Mark Perry, "An American consumer or household spending that same amount of inflation-adjusted dollars today ($5,800) would be able to furnish their entire kitchen with five brand-new appliances (refrigerator, gas stove and oven, washer, dryer, and freezer) and buy seven state-of-the-art electronic items for their home (a Toshiba Satellite 15.6" laptop computer, a Garmin 5 Inch GPS, a Canon EOS Rebel T5i DSLR Camera, a Sony 1,000 Watt, 5.1-Channel 3-D Smart Blu-Ray Home Theater System, a Samsung 55 inch Smart HDTV, an Apple iPod Touch, 64GB MP3 Player (6th generation), and an Apple iPhone 7 Plus."[14] And while the average American would work 293 hours in 1964 to pay off a $5,800 bill, it would take just 266 hours in 2016.[15] People like to reminisce about the "good 'ol days," when things were "cheaper." But, mostly, they really weren't. Thanks to steady increases in productivity, most goods become better and more affordable over time.

18-1b Kinds of Productivity

Two common measures of productivity are partial productivity and multifactor productivity. **Partial productivity** indicates how much of a particular kind of input it takes to produce an output.

$$\text{Partial Productivity} = \frac{\text{Outputs}}{\text{Single Kind of Inputs}}$$

Labor is one kind of input that is frequently used when determining partial productivity. *Labor productivity* typically indicates the cost or number of hours of labor it takes to produce an output. In other words, the lower the cost of the labor to produce a unit of output, or the less time it takes to produce a unit of output, the higher the labor productivity. Labor cost as a percentage of revenue is a basic measure of labor productivity used in the airline industry. The lower the percentage of revenue attributable to labor costs, the more productively an airline uses labor to generate a unit of revenue (that is, dollars, euros, and so on). In Europe, for example, Wizz Air (6.5%), Ryanair (9.5%), and easyJet (12.4%) have some of the lowest labor costs per unit of revenue, especially when compared to major carriers such as British Airways (21.7%), Lufthansa (23.4%), Air France (29.9%), and Scandinavian Airlines (32.1%).[16]

Partial productivity assesses how efficiently companies use only one input, such as labor, when creating outputs. Multifactor productivity is an overall measure of productivity that assesses how efficiently companies use all the inputs it takes to make outputs. More specifically, **multifactor productivity** indicates how much labor, capital, materials, and energy it takes to produce an output.[17]

$$\frac{\text{Multifactor}}{\text{Productivity}} = \frac{\text{Outputs}}{(\text{Labor} + \text{Capital} + \text{Materials} + \text{Energy})}$$

Exhibit 18.1 shows the trends in multifactor productivity across a number of U.S. industries since 1987.

With a 7.2-fold increase since 1987, the growth in multifactor productivity in the computer and electronic products industry far exceeded the productivity growth in mining, utilities, auto manufacturing, retail stores, air transportation, and financial and insurance services, as well as most other industries tracked by the U.S. government.

Should managers use multiple or partial productivity measures? In general, they should use both. Multifactor productivity indicates a company's overall level of productivity relative to its competitors. In the end, that's what counts most. However, multifactor productivity measures don't indicate the specific contributions that labor, capital, materials, or energy make to overall productivity. To analyze the contributions of these individual components, managers need to use partial productivity measures. Doing so can help them determine what factors need to be adjusted or in what areas adjustment can make the most difference in overall productivity.

18-1c Productivity and Automation

Automation isn't new. Consider these jobs that no longer exist: Bowling alley pinsetter, window knockers (who used long poles to tap on windows to wake people up for work before alarm clocks), ice cutters, street lamplighters, and switchboard operators. All have long been automated.[18] At home, would you give up your dishwasher, clothes dryer and washing machine, and furnace to wash dishes, wash and dry clothes, and cut logs for the wood stove to heat your house? Indeed, thanks to productivity-enhancing automation, we spend roughly 13 hours a week on housework compared to 26 hours in 1965.[19] From the Industrial Revolution, to the telegraph, to the car, to the Internet, computers and, yes, home appliances, automation has long made life easier and tasks more productive.

Thanks to advances in robotics design and artificial intelligence, we are at the beginning of another surge in automation, this one driven by **robots**, which are machines or programs capable of completing complex tasks. The McKinsey Global Institute estimates that robot-driven automation could raise global productivity 0.8 to 1.4 percent a year.[20] Let's look at the three ways in which work can be automated with robots: robotic process automation, intelligent recognition, and collaborative/social robotics.[21]

Partial productivity a measure of performance that indicates how much of a particular kind of input it takes to produce an output

Multifactor productivity an overall measure of performance that indicates how much labor, capital, materials, and energy it takes to produce an output

Robots machines or programs capable of completing complex tasks

Exhibit 18.1
Multifactor Productivity Growth Across Industries

Source: "Nonmanufacturing Sectors and NIPA-level Nonmanufacturing Industries KLEMS Multifactor Productivity Tables by Industry: Table Multifactor Productivity and Related KLEMS Measures from the NIPA Industry Database, 1987 to 2014," Bureau of Labor Statistics, Division of Industry Productivity Studies, June 22, 2016, accessed May 8, 2017. http://www.bls.gov/mfp/special_requests/klemsmfpxg.zip; "Manufacturing Sector and NIPA-level Manufacturing Industries KLEMS Multifactor Productivity Tables by Industry: Table Multifactor Productivity and Related KLEMS Measures from the NIPA Industry Database, 1987 to 2014," Bureau of Labor Statistics, Division of Industry Productivity Studies, June 22, 2016, accessed May 8, 2017. http://www.bls.gov/mfp/special_requests/prod3.klemsmfp.zip.

Process automation is using robots to automate routine, highly repetitive, low complexity or single-purpose tasks. This works well in work environments such as factories where a robot is dedicated to one task or a limited set of tasks, or in the automation of data collection and processing.[22] The robot barista used at Café X in San Francisco is example of process automation. Order and pay for your latte using a kiosk or smartphone app and the six-arm robot grabs a cup, grinds beans, steams and foams milk, and places your order on a hydraulic pedestal. Café X founder Henry Hu says, "The art part of coffee is the expertise in creating the beverage, not how well you can repeatedly do it."[23] Creating great coffee drinks every time, he says, "That is repetition a robot can do."[24]

Intelligent recognition is using automation programming to recognize and react to patterns of speech, written language, images, and other items. When you say, "Hey Google," or "Hey Siri," to your smartphone, followed by a command such as finding something on the Web, figuring out when your next appointment is, or getting directions, you're using intelligent recognition automation. Target is using Tally, a 30-pound, 38-inch-tall robot built by Simbe Robotics to analyze product inventory on retail store shelves. Tally rolls down store aisles, even when customers are shopping, using its camera and software to determine how many of each product are on the shelf, whether items are misplaced on the wrong shelves or not facing toward the aisle, and whether items need to be restocked or reordered. According to Simbe, Tally can inventory all of the items in a medium-sized store in 30 minutes with 95 percent accuracy, compared to a person who would take 25 hours at 65 percent accuracy.[25]

Collaborative/social automation is using robots to automate tasks while working directly with or near people. Worker safety was one of the earliest concerns with using robots in factories. Because robots were typically used for physically demanding tasks requiring high levels of force, they were surrounded by steel cages or industrial fencing so that people couldn't be harmed by walking into the robot's workspace. By contrast,

Process automation using robots to automate routine, highly repetitive, low-complexity, or single-purpose tasks

Intelligent recognition using automation programming to recognize and react to patterns of speech, written language, images, and other items

Collaborative/social automation using robots to automate tasks while working directly with or near people

Exhibit 18.2
2017 J. D. Power Initial Quality Survey

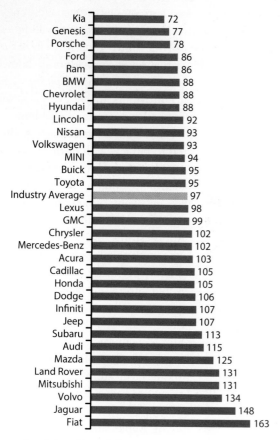

Problems per 100 Vehicles (PP100)

Brand	PP100
Kia	72
Genesis	77
Porsche	78
Ford	86
Ram	86
BMW	88
Chevrolet	88
Hyundai	88
Lincoln	92
Nissan	93
Volkswagen	93
MINI	94
Buick	95
Toyota	95
Industry Average	97
Lexus	98
GMC	99
Chrysler	102
Mercedes-Benz	102
Acura	103
Cadillac	105
Honda	105
Dodge	106
Infiniti	107
Jeep	107
Subaru	113
Audi	115
Mazda	125
Land Rover	131
Mitsubishi	131
Volvo	134
Jaguar	148
Fiat	163

Source: Press Release, "New-Vehicle Initial Quality is Best Ever, J.D. Power Finds," J.D. Power, June 21, 2017, accessed August 31, 2017, http://www.jdpower.com/press-releases/2017-us-initial-quality-study-iqs.

collaborative/social automation puts workers and robots side by side. Rick Faulk, CEO of Locus, which makes robots that work with warehouse workers, said, "The first trend was to try to replace humans. Now it's about humans and robots working collaboratively." [26] Amazon, which bought Kiva several years ago, has Kiva robots zip down the aisles of its massive warehouse to retrieve and deliver packages directly to warehouse workers, who used to walk 15 to 20 miles a day finding the items needed to complete orders. With the help of Kiva robots (which will slow as they get near people and stop if they make contact), Amazon warehouse employees can now fill an order in 15 minutes instead of 90 minutes. Overall, thanks to its collaborative/social robots, warehouse productivity is up 20 percent and Amazon can put 50 percent more items in each warehouse. [27]

18-2 QUALITY

With the average car costing $34,721 car buyers want to make sure that they're getting good quality for their money. [28] Fortunately, as indicated by the number of problems per 100 cars (PP100), today's cars are of much higher quality than earlier models. In 1981, Japanese cars averaged 240 PP100. GM's cars averaged 670, Ford's averaged 740, and Chrysler's averaged 870 PP100! In other words, as measured by PP100, the quality of American cars was two to three times worse than that of Japanese cars. By 1992, however, U.S. carmakers had made great strides, significantly reducing the number of problems to an average of 155 PP100. Japanese vehicles had improved, too, averaging just 125 PP100. According to the 2016 J. D. Power and Associates survey of initial car quality, as shown in Exhibit 18.2, however, overall quality improved to 97 problems per 100 vehicles, and even the worst rated cars easily beat the scores of the Japanese cars of decades ago. Fourteen car brands, including Kia, Genesis, Porsche, Ford, Ram (trucks), BMW and Chevrolet, came in with scores under 100. That means less than one problem per car! [29]

The American Society for Quality gives two meanings for **quality**. It can mean a product or service free of deficiencies, such as the number of problems per 100 cars, or it can mean the characteristics of a product or service that satisfy customer needs. [30] Today's cars are of higher quality than those produced 20 years ago in both senses. Not only do they have fewer problems per 100 cars, they also have a number of additional standard features (power brakes and steering, Bluetooth connectivity, power windows and locks, keyless entry, cruise control).

*In this part of the chapter, you will learn about **18-2a quality-related characteristics for products and services, 18-2b ISO 9000, 14000, and 27000, 18-2c the Baldrige National Quality Award,** and **18-2d total quality management.***

18-2a Quality-Related Characteristics for Products and Services

Quality products usually possess three characteristics: reliability, serviceability, and durability. [31] A breakdown occurs when a product quits working or doesn't do what it was designed to do. The longer it takes for a product to break down, or the longer the time between breakdowns, the

> **Quality** a product or service free of deficiencies, or the characteristics of a product or service that satisfy customer needs

more reliable the product. Consequently, many companies define *product reliability* in terms of the average time between breakdowns. *Serviceability* refers to how easy or difficult it is to fix a product. The easier it is to maintain a working product or fix a broken product, the more serviceable that product is.

A product breakdown assumes that a product can be repaired. However, some products don't break down; they fail. *Product failure* means products can't be repaired. They can only be replaced. *Durability* is defined as the mean time to failure. A typical incandescent lightbulb, for example, has a mean time of failure of 1,000 hours. By contrast, LED bulbs, which use the same technology that lights up HDTVs and cell phone screens, have a mean time to failure of between 20 and 25 years. Furthermore, the energy savings from one $10 LED bulb means it will pay for itself within two years and then provide 20 more years of lighting while saving $149 in energy costs over the longer lifetime of the bulb.[32]

While high-quality products are characterized by reliability, serviceability, and durability, services are different. There's no point in assessing the durability of a service because services are consumed the minute they're performed. For example, after a lawn service has mowed your lawn, the job is done until the mowers come back next week to do it again. Services also don't have serviceability. You can't maintain or fix a service. If a service wasn't performed correctly, all you can do is perform it again. Rather than serviceability and durability, the quality of service interactions often depends on how the service provider interacts with the customer. Was the service provider friendly, rude, or helpful? Five characteristics typically distinguish a quality service: reliability, tangibles, responsiveness, assurance, and empathy.[33]

Service reliability is the ability to consistently perform a service well. Studies clearly show that reliability matters more to customers than anything else when buying services. When you take your clothes to the dry cleaner, you don't want them returned with cracked buttons or wrinkles down the front. If your dry cleaner gives you perfectly clean and pressed clothes every time, it's providing a reliable service.

Also, although services themselves are not tangible (you can't see or touch them), services are provided in

Video game manufacturer Nintendo has long been known for high-quality games and hardware. Knowing that its products are used largely by children and teens, Nintendo designs its hand held devices, controllers, and consoles to be incredibly durable.

tangible places. Thus, *tangibles* refer to the appearance of the offices, equipment, and personnel involved with the delivery of a service. One of the best examples of the effect of tangibles on the perception of quality is the restroom. When you eat at a fancy restaurant, you expect clean, upscale restrooms. How different is your perception of a business, say a gas station, if it has clean restrooms rather than filthy ones?

Responsiveness is the promptness and willingness with which service providers give good service. *Assurance* is the confidence that service providers are knowledgeable, courteous, and trustworthy. *Empathy* is the extent to which service providers give individual attention and care to customers' concerns and problems.

When Apple first launched its retail stores, they were widely predicted to fail given all of the locations where consumers could already buy computer and electronics equipment. Those predictions were wrong, however, as more than 400 million people visit Apple stores every year. Apple's average annual revenue tops $50 million per store, and malls with Apple Stores average 10 percent more overall customer traffic than those without.[34] Why have Apple Stores achieved these extraordinary results? In addition to great products, the stores are great at delivering responsiveness, assurance, and empathy.

At Apple stores, responsiveness manifests itself in a sales philosophy of not selling. Instead, Apple store employees are trained to help customers solve problems. An Apple training manual says, "Your job is to understand all of your customers' needs— some of which they may not even realize they have." David Ambrose, a former Apple store employee, says, "You were never trying to close a sale. It was about finding solutions for a customer and finding their pain points."

Apple store employees demonstrate assurance through the high level of training that they receive. Apple "geniuses," who staff the Genius Bar in each Apple store, are trained at Apple headquarters and, according to Apple's website, "can take care of everything from troubleshooting your problems to actual repairs." Geniuses are regularly tested on their knowledge and problem-solving skills to maintain their certification. Other Apple store employees are highly trained, too, and are not allowed to help customers until they've spent two to four weeks shadowing experienced store employees.

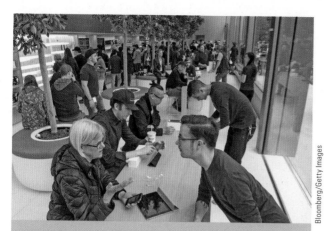

To improve customer service at its retail stores, Apple recently redesigned the Genius Bar customer service desk to be more welcoming and rebranded it as the Genius Grove. Here, Genius Grove employees help customers solve problems at the company's new flagship store in San Francisco.

The acronym APPLE instructs employees on how to empathetically engage with customers: "Approach customers with a personalized warm welcome," "Probe politely to understand all the customer's needs," "Present a solution for the customer to take home today," "Listen for and resolve any issues or concerns," and "End with a fond farewell and an invitation to return." And when customers are frustrated and become emotional, the advice is to "listen and limit your responses to simple reassurances that you are doing so. 'Uh-huh,' 'I understand,' etc."

The results from Apple's retail approach speak for themselves, as Apple retail sales average $5,546 per square foot, higher than Tiffany & Co. jewelry stores ($2,951), Lululemon Athletica ($1,560), or Michael Kors ($1,466).[35]

18-2b 9000, 14000, and 27000

ISO, pronounced *eye-so*, comes from the Greek word *isos*, meaning "equal, similar, alike, or identical" and is also an acronym for the International Organization for Standardization, which helps set standards for 163 countries. The purpose of this agency is to develop and publish standards that facilitate the international exchange of goods and services.[36] **ISO 9000** is a series of five international standards, from ISO 9000 to ISO 9004, for achieving consistency in quality management and quality assurance in companies throughout the world. **ISO 14000** is a series of international standards for managing, monitoring, and minimizing an organization's harmful effects on the environment.[37] (For more on environmental quality and issues, see subsection 16-3e of Chapter 16 on

sustainability.) **ISO 27000** is a series of 12 international standards for managing and monitoring security techniques for information technology.[38] (For more in information technology security issues, see subsection 17-3c of Chapter 17 on protecting information.)

The ISO 9000, 14000, and 27000 standards publications, which are available from the American National Standards Institute (see the end of this section), are general and can be used for manufacturing any kind of product or delivering any kind of service. Importantly, the ISO 9000 standards don't describe how to make a better-quality car, computer, or widget. Instead, they describe how companies can extensively document (and thus standardize) the steps they take to create and improve the quality of their products. Why should companies go to the trouble to achieve ISO 9000 certification? Because their customers increasingly want them to. In fact, studies show that customers clearly prefer to buy from companies that are ISO 9000 certified. Companies, in turn, believe that being ISO 9000 certified helps them keep customers who might otherwise switch to an ISO 9000–certified competitor.[38]

To become ISO certified, a process that can take months, a company must show that it is following its own procedures for improving production, updating design plans and specifications, keeping machinery in top condition, educating and training workers, and satisfactorily dealing with customer complaints.[39] An accredited third party oversees the ISO certification process, just as a certified public accountant verifies that a company's financial accounts are up to date and accurate. After a company has been certified as ISO 9000 compliant, the accredited third party will issue an ISO 9000 certificate that the company can use in its advertising and publications. This is the quality equivalent of the *Good Housekeeping* Seal of Approval. But continued ISO 9000 certification is not guaranteed. Accredited third parties typically conduct periodic audits to make sure the company is still following quality procedures. If it is not, its certification is suspended or canceled.

To get additional information on ISO 9000 guidelines and procedures, see the American National Standards Institute (www.webstore.ansi.org; the ISO 9000, 14000, and 27000 (27000, 27001, and 27002) standards publications are

ISO 9000 a series of five international standards, from ISO 9000 to ISO 9004, for achieving consistency in quality management and quality assurance in companies throughout the world

ISO 14000 a series of international standards for managing, monitoring, and minimizing an organization's harmful effects on the environment

ISO 27000 a series of 12 international standards for managing and monitoring security techniques for information technology

For a Lighter, More Fuel-Efficient Car: Superglue?

With some cars, instead of being welded to a steel frame, steel body panels are welded to each other to create a "unibody," which forms the interior frame and exterior structure of the car. But the unibody of the 2017 GMC Acadia, a mid-sized SUV, is held together with welds and superglue! The 2017 Acadia is 700 pounds lighter than the 2016 model, which helped increase its gas mileage 28 percent from 18 to 23 miles per gallon. The superglue GMC is using is similar to the "advanced adhesives" that plane manufacturers, like Boeing, use to construct a plane's outer shell. As explained in the *New York Times*, "Since this ultra-superglue bonds parts together all along the seam where they connect, not just in certain spots, the parts become stiffer." That let's GM use a lighter, thinner steel. And GMC's customers get a higher-quality, more efficient car.

Source: N. Boudette, "The Superglue Diet: How to Make a Lighter, Fuel-Sipping Car," *New York Times*, August 11, 2016, accessed May 9, 2017, https://www.nytimes.com/2016/08/12/automobiles/the-superglue-diet-how-to-make-a-lighter-fuel-sipping-car.html.

available here for about $599, $575, and $462, respectively), the American Society for Quality (www.asq.org), and the IOS (www.iso.org).

18-2c Baldrige National Quality Award

The Malcolm Baldrige National Quality Award, which is administered by the U.S. government's National Institute of Standards and Technology, is given "to recognize U.S. companies for their achievements in quality and business performance and to raise awareness about the importance of quality and performance excellence as a competitive edge."[40] Each year, up to three awards may be given in the categories of manufacturing, education, health care, service, small business, and nonprofit.

The cost of applying for the Baldrige Award includes a $400 eligibility fee, an application fee of $19,800 for manufacturing firms and $10,500 for small businesses, and a site visitation fee of $55,000 to $60,000 for manufacturing firms and $33,000 to $38,500 for small businesses.[41] Why does it cost so much? Because you get a great deal of useful information about your business even if you don't win. At a minimum, each company that applies receives an extensive report based on 300 hours of assessment from at least eight business and quality experts. At $128 an hour for small businesses and about $200 an hour for manufacturing and service businesses, the *Journal for Quality and Participation* called the Baldrige feedback report "the best bargain in consulting in America."[42] Arnold Weimerskirch, former chair of the

Baldrige Award panel of judges and former vice president of quality at Honeywell, says, "The application and review process for the Baldrige Award is the best, most cost-effective and comprehensive business health audit you can get."[43]

Businesses that apply for the Baldrige Award are judged on the seven criteria shown in Exhibit 18.3: leadership; strategy; customers; measurement, analysis, and knowledge management; workforce; operations; and results.[44] Results are typically the most important category. In other words, in addition to the six other criteria, companies must show that they have achieved superior quality when it comes to products and process, its customers, workforce, leadership, governance (social responsibility), and financial and market results. This emphasis on results is what differentiates the Baldrige Award from the ISO 9000 standards. The Baldrige Award indicates the extent to which companies have actually achieved world-class quality. The ISO 9000 standards simply indicate whether a company is following the management system it put into place to improve quality. In fact, ISO 9000 certification covers less than 10 percent of the requirements for the Baldrige Award.[45]

Why should companies go to the trouble of applying for the Baldrige National Quality Award? Baldrige program examiner Betsy Beam explains that it's not just about winning the award; it's about the opportunity to improve. "Ritz-Carlton has won the Baldrige Award twice," Beam says. "Even in … the years they won, there were 35 opportunities for improvement identified. This is a very difficult journey for any organization, but it's well worth it as changes [that are needed] become obvious."[46]

Exhibit 18.3
Criteria for the Baldrige National Quality Award

2015–2016 Categories/Items

1 Leadership
1.1 Senior Leadership
1.2 Governance and Social Responsibilities

2 Strategy
2.1 Strategy Development
2.2 Strategy Implementation

3 Customers
3.1 Voice of the Customer
3.2 Customer Engagement

4 Measurement, Analysis, and Knowledge Management
4.1 Measurement, Analysis, and Improvement of Organizational Performance
4.2 Information and Knowledge Management

5 Workforce
5.1 Workforce Environment
5.2 Workforce Engagement

6 Operations
6.1 Work Processes
6.2 Operational Effectiveness

7 Results
7.1 Product and Process Results
7.2 Customer-Focused Results
7.3 Workforce-Focused Results
7.4 Leadership and Governance Results
7.5 Financial and Market Results

Source: "Baldrige Criteria Commentary," Baldrige Performance Excellence Program, December 14, 2016, accessed May 8, 2017, https://www.nist.gov/baldrige/baldrige-criteria-commentary.

18-2d Total Quality Management

Total quality management (TQM) is an integrated, organization-wide strategy for improving product and service quality.[47] TQM is not a specific tool or technique. Rather, TQM is a philosophy or overall approach to management that is characterized by three principles: customer focus and satisfaction, continuous improvement, and teamwork.[48]

Although most economists, accountants, and financiers argue that companies exist to earn profits for shareholders, TQM suggests that customer focus and customer satisfaction should be a company's primary goals. **Customer focus** means that the entire organization, from top to bottom, should be focused on meeting customers' needs. The result of that customer focus should be **customer satisfaction**, which occurs when the company's products or services meet or exceed customers' expectations.

At companies where customer satisfaction is taken seriously, such as **Alaska Airlines**, paychecks depend on keeping customers satisfied. Everyone at Alaska Airlines, from the CEO to pilots to people who handle baggage, gets a monthly bonus, 70 percent of which is based on earnings, with the remaining 30 percent split among costs, safety, and customer satisfaction. J.D. Power and Associates rates Alaska Airlines as the highest in customer satisfaction among traditional U.S. airlines from 2008 to 2015. Likewise, according to FlightStats, Alaska Airlines was the best North American airline in terms of on-time arrivals, a key issue in terms of customer satisfaction, from 2010 to 2015.[49]

Continuous improvement is an ongoing commitment to increase product and service quality by constantly assessing and improving the processes and procedures used to create those products and services. How do companies know whether they're achieving continuous improvement? Invented in 1885, Dr Pepper is the oldest soft drink in the United States. While soft drink sales have dropped 11 years in a row, Dr Pepper is increasing profits and lowering costs through rapid continuous improvement (RCI). Chief Financial Officer Marty Ellen says, "RCI is about taking the existing baseline and improving it by finding the waste. We walk by waste every day. A team watched the process of fountain-syrup bags being assembled and packed into the cardboard boxes used to ship the bags. Somebody asked, 'Why does that box have the maroon Dr Pepper logo on it when the box isn't a consumer package?' You immediately call on the box supplier and ask, if we took that off, how much could we save a year? They said $60,000, and we said great. Put it in the bank."[50]

Besides higher customer satisfaction, continuous improvement is usually associated with a

Total quality management (TQM) an integrated, principle-based, organization-wide strategy for improving product and service quality

Customer focus an organizational goal to concentrate on meeting customers' needs at all levels of the organization

Customer satisfaction an organizational goal to provide products or services that meet or exceed customers' expectations

Continuous improvement an organization's ongoing commitment to constantly assess and improve the processes and procedures used to create products and services

Everyone at Alaska Airlines, from the CEO to the pilots to the people who handle baggage, gets a monthly bonus based, in part, on customer satisfaction.

reduction in variation. **Variation** is a deviation in the form, condition, or appearance of a product from the quality standard for that product. The less a product varies from the quality standard, or the more consistently a company's products meet a quality standard, the higher the quality. Beyond safety, the quality standard for an airline is on-time departure and arrival. Variation from that standard means delays, and even worse, cancellations. On average, 1.7 percent of flights are cancelled each year, sometimes because of weather, but often because of poor management decisions. Delta Airlines, however, cancels only 0.3 percent of its flights because it stocks extra parts (engine starters) that often cause delays, maintains 20 extra planes that are brought into service when a jet encounters mechanical problems, and gets around flight hour limitations for flight crews (typically 8 hours within 24 hours) by having planes make interim stops (meaning less than 8 hours) with new crews taking over. With 15,000 daily flights, Delta cancels just 45 flights per day. But if Delta had an average cancellation rate, it would cancel 255 flights per day, or more than five times as many.[51] Delta did even better in 2016, when it canceled no flights on 241 days, twice as good as 2014, which was its previous best year.[52]

The third principle of TQM is teamwork. **Teamwork** means collaboration between managers and nonmanagers, across business functions, and between the company and its customers and suppliers. In short, quality improves when everyone in the company is given the incentive to work together and the responsibility and authority to make improvements and solve problems. ArcellorMittal's Gent, Belgium, plant needs only needs 1.3 man-hours to make a ton of steel, or one-third less than average. One of ArcellorMittal's practices is to "twin" its best plants, such as Gent, with its poor performing plants, such as its Burns Harbor, Indiana, plant. Then, it uses teamwork—and competition—to improve both. So it flew 100 Burns Harbor engineers and managers to Gent and told them, "Do as the Belgians do," whereas the Belgians were told to maintain their advantage. Founder Lakshmi Mittal says, "The process doesn't change: melt iron, cast, roll [steel]. But there are always incremental improvements you can make. We wanted Burns Harbor to be more like Gent."[53] Teamwork comes into play as teams from both plants meet regularly to discuss plant performance and share the steps they're taking to improve it. Following practices at Gent, Burns Harbor began using a different high pressure water nozzle to remove flakes (that is, imperfections) from super-heated steel. Not only did steel quality improve, the nozzle used less water and power, saving $1.4 million in annual energy costs. Likewise, Burns Harbor workers began trimming less steel off the sides of steel coils, saving 725 coils of steel per year, the equivalent of 17,000 cars. Today, thanks to twinning and teamwork, Burns Harbor now produces 900 tons of steel per employee each year, close to Gent's 950.

Customer focus and satisfaction, continuous improvement, and teamwork mutually reinforce each other to improve quality throughout a company. Customer-focused, continuous improvement is necessary to increase customer satisfaction. At the same time, continuous improvement depends on teamwork from different functional and hierarchical parts of the company.

18-3 SERVICE OPERATIONS

At the start of this chapter, you learned that operations management means managing the daily production of goods and services. Then you learned that to manage production, you must oversee the factors that affect productivity and quality. In this half of the chapter, you will learn about managing operations in service and manufacturing businesses. The chapter ends with a discussion of inventory management, a key factor in a company's profitability.

Imagine that your trusty TiVo digital video recorder (DVR) breaks down as you try to record your

Variation a deviation in the form, condition, or appearance of a product from the quality standard for that product

Teamwork collaboration between managers and nonmanagers, across business functions, and between companies, customers, and suppliers

Exhibit 18.4
Service-Profit Chain

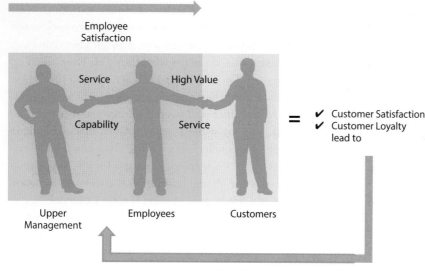

Sources: R. Hallowell, L. A. Schlesinger, and J. Zornitsky, "Internal Service Quality, Customer and Job Satisfaction: Linkages and Implications for Management," *Human Resource Planning* 19 (1996): 20–31; J. L. Heskett, T. O. Jones, G. W. Loveman, W. E. Sasser Jr., and L. A. Schlesinger, "Putting the Service-Profit Chain to Work," *Harvard Business Review* (March–April 1994): 164–174.

favorite TV show. You've got two choices. You can run to Walmart and spend $250 to purchase a new DVR, or you can spend less (you hope) to have it fixed at a repair shop. Either way, you end up with the same thing, a working DVR. However, the first choice, getting a new DVR, involves buying a physical product (a good), while the second, dealing with a repair shop, involves buying a service.

Services differ from goods in several ways. First, goods are produced or made, but services are performed. In other words, services are almost always labor-intensive in that someone typically has to perform the service for you. A repair shop could give you the parts needed to repair your old DVR, but you're still going to have a broken DVR without the technician to perform the repairs. Second, goods are tangible, but services are intangible. You can touch and see that new DVR, but you can't touch or see the service provided by the technician who fixed your old DVR. All you can "see" is that the DVR works. Third, services are perishable and unstorable. If you don't use them when they're available, they're wasted. For example, if your DVR repair shop is backlogged on repair jobs, then you'll just have to wait until next week to get your DVR repaired. You can't store an unused

service and use it when you like. By contrast, you can purchase a good, such as motor oil, and store it until you're ready to use it.

Because services are different from goods, managing a service operation is different from managing a manufacturing or production operation.

*Let's look at **18-3a the service-profit chain** and **18-3b service recovery and empowerment**.*

18-3a The Service-Profit Chain

One of the key assumptions in the service business is that success depends on how well employees—that is, service providers—deliver their services to customers. But success actually begins with how well management treats service employees, as the service-profit chain, depicted in Exhibit 18.4, demonstrates.[54]

The key concept behind the service-profit chain is **internal service quality**, meaning the quality of treatment that employees receive from a company's internal service providers, such as management, payroll and benefits, human resources, and so forth. An employee at Adobe, a global software company, says, "The company has great perks for their employees that include company parties, outdoor activities, indoor pool and ping-pong tables, and a computer gaming room." Netflix gives new parents a year of *paid* maternity leave. Facebook gives parents $4,000 of "baby cash." Spotify pays for infertility treatments, such as egg freezing. Airbnb gives employees $2,000 a year to stay at any of its listings, anywhere in the world. Burton, which makes snowboarding equipment and outdoor gear, pays for season-long ski passes, plus "snow days" to use them. Finally, if a Google employee dies, the surviving spouse or partner gets half of his or her annual salary for 10 years.[55] These extraordinary benefits are clearly signs of companies with internal service quality orientations.

As depicted in Exhibit 18.4, good internal service leads to employee satisfaction and service capability. *Employee satisfaction*

Internal service quality the quality of treatment employees receive from management and other divisions of a company occurs when companies treat employees in a way that meets or exceeds their expectations. In other words, the better employees are treated, the more satisfied they are, and the more likely they are to give high-value service that satisfies customers. How employers treat employees is important because it affects service capability. *Service capability* is an employee's perception of his or her ability to serve customers well. When an organization serves its employees in ways that help them to do their jobs well, employees, in turn, are more likely to believe that they can and ought to provide high-value service to customers.

Finally, according to the service-profit chain shown in Exhibit 18.4, *high-value service* leads to *customer satisfaction* and *customer loyalty*, which, in turn, lead to *long-term profits and growth.*[56] What's the link between customer satisfaction and loyalty and profits? To start, the average business keeps only 70 to 90 percent of its existing customers each year. No big deal, you say? Just replace leaving customers with new customers. Well, there's one significant problem with that solution. It costs ten times as much to find a new customer as it does to keep an existing customer. Also, new customers typically buy only 20 percent as much as established customers. In fact, keeping existing customers is so cost-effective that most businesses could double their profits by simply keeping 5 percent more customers per year![57] How does this work? Imagine that keeping more of your customers turns some of those customers into customers for life. How much of a difference would that make to company profits? Consider that just one lifetime customer spends $8,000 on pizza and over $330,000 on luxury cars![58]

18-3b Service Recovery and Empowerment

When mistakes are made, when problems occur, and when customers become dissatisfied with the service they've received, service businesses must switch from the process of service delivery to the process of **service recovery**, or restoring customer satisfaction to strongly dissatisfied customers.[59] Or as business consultant Barry Moltz explains, "When a customer says they are dissatisfied, the company gets a chance to fix it and turn them into a more loyal customer."[60] Service recovery sometimes requires service employees to not only fix whatever mistake was made but also perform heroic service acts that delight highly dissatisfied customers by far surpassing their expectations of fair treatment. Jason Friend, co-founder of 37signals.com, which provides web-based collaboration software such as Basecamp and Campfire, bought a custom bike via the Web from Mission Bicycle Company in San Francisco. When the bike arrived, he found a large gash on the side of the bike's frame. He described what happened when he contacted Mission: "They said sending the whole bike back would be overkill since the only thing that was damaged was the frame. Further, the bike was rideable—it was just a paint problem—so sending the bike back would mean I didn't have a bike for a week or so. They didn't feel good about that. So here's what they did: They called up a local shop (On The Route) and arranged to ship a new frame to them. Then one of their bike techs would drive down to my office and swap the frames and reassemble the bike for me while I waited. All of this at Mission's expense." He concluded by saying, "That's incredible customer service. I'm a happy customer for life. If you're in the market for a great custom bike, check out the good people and products at Mission Bicycle Company."[61]

Unfortunately, when mistakes occur, service employees often don't have the discretion to resolve customer complaints. Customers who want service employees to correct or make up for poor service are frequently told, "I'm not allowed to do that," "I'm just following company rules," or "I'm sorry, only managers are allowed to make changes of any kind." In other words, company rules prevent them from engaging in acts of service recovery meant to turn dissatisfied customers back into satisfied customers. The result is frustration for customers and service employees and lost customers for the company.

Now, however, many companies are empowering their service employees.[62] In Chapter 9, you learned that *empowering workers* means permanently passing decision-making authority and responsibility from managers to workers. With respect to service recovery, empowering workers means giving service employees the authority and responsibility to make decisions that immediately solve customer problems.[63] For example, when customers call into Nicor National, an energy utility, to ask for credits to their accounts, they are not transferred to a billing department. They are not put on hold while the operator looks for a supervisor or manager. Instead, the operator, who is empowered to make this decision, simply awards the credit without having to check with anyone. According to Barbara Porter, the company's vice president of business development and customer service, empowering the call centers in this way results in a quick, easy resolution. "They're professionals and we trust them to make the right decisions," says Porter.[64]

When things go wrong for customers, how well does service recovery work? Sixty-nine percent of customers see quick resolution of their problems as central to good customer service. Furthermore, about half of customers

Service recovery restoring customer satisfaction to strongly dissatisfied customers will stop buying from a company when bad customer service is not resolved. Either way, roughly nine out of ten customers will tell others about their poor customer service or how you fixed their problem.[65]

18-4 MANUFACTURING OPERATIONS

Ford makes cars, and Dell does computers. BP produces gasoline, whereas Sherwin-Williams makes paint. Boeing makes jet planes, but Budweiser makes beer. Seagate makes hard drives, and Maytag makes appliances. The *manufacturing operations* of these companies all produce physical goods. But not all manufacturing operations, especially these, are the same.

Let's learn how various manufacturing operations differ in terms of 18-4a the amount of processing that is done to produce and assemble a product and 18-4b the flexibility to change the number, kind, and characteristics of products that are produced.

18-4a Amount of Processing in Manufacturing Operations

Manufacturing operations can be classified according to the amount of processing or assembly that occurs after a customer order is received. The highest degree of processing occurs in **make-to-order operations**. A make-to-order operation does not start processing or assembling products until it receives a customer order. In fact, some make-to-order operations may not even order parts until a customer order is received. Not surprisingly, make-to-order operations produce or assemble highly specialized or customized products for customers. At 6:03 p.m. on "Selection Sunday," the Northwestern University's men's basketball team learned it was in the NCAA tournament. At 6:07 p.m., Fanatics posted a Northwestern make-to-order T-shirt, "Chicago is Dancin': The Road to the Final Four," on its website. Fanatics can design a T-shirt, get it approved by a college or professional team, and post the design on its website in 15 minutes. Apparel division president Raphael Peck says, "To fully monetize that opportunity, you want to be up and running as close as possible to that highest level of passion."[66] Furthermore, if only 10 people want the T-shirt, it will make and sell 10 T-shirts.

A moderate degree of processing occurs in **assemble-to-order operations**. A company using an assemble-

Within minutes of the 2017 NCAA Selection Sunday party announcement at Northwestern University, above, Fanatics posted a "Chicago is Dancin': The Road to the Final Four" T-shirt for sale on its website.

David Banks/Getty Images

to-order operation divides its manufacturing or assembly process into separate parts or modules. The company orders parts and assembles modules ahead of customer orders. Then, based on actual customer orders or on research forecasting what customers will want, those modules are combined to create semicustomized products. For example, when a customer orders a new car, GM may have already ordered the basic parts or modules it needs from suppliers. In other words, based on sales forecasts, GM may already have ordered enough tires, air-conditioning compressors, brake systems, and seats from suppliers to accommodate nearly all customer orders on a particular day. Special orders from customers and car dealers are then used to determine the final assembly checklist for particular cars as they move down the assembly line.

The lowest degree of processing occurs in **make-to-stock operations** (also called build-to-stock). Because the products are standardized, meaning each product is exactly the same as the next, a company using a make-to-stock operation starts ordering parts and assembling finished products before receiving customer orders. Customers then purchase these standardized products—such as Rubbermaid storage containers, microwave ovens, and vacuum

Make-to-order operation a manufacturing operation that does not start processing or assembling products until a customer order is received

Assemble-to-order operation a manufacturing operation that divides manufacturing processes into separate parts or modules that are combined to create semicustomized products

Make-to-stock operation a manufacturing operation that orders parts and assembles standardized products before receiving customer orders cleaners—at retail stores or directly from the manufacturer. Because parts are ordered and products are assembled before customers order the products, make-to-stock operations are highly dependent on the accuracy of sales forecasts. If sales forecasts are incorrect, make-to-stock operations may end up building too many or too few products, or they may make products with the wrong features or without the features that customers want.

18-4b Flexibility of Manufacturing Operations

A second way to categorize manufacturing operations is by **manufacturing flexibility**, meaning the degree to which manufacturing operations can easily and quickly change the number, kind, and characteristics of products they produce. Flexibility allows companies to respond quickly to changes in the marketplace (that is, in response to competitors and customers) and to reduce the lead time between ordering and final delivery of products. There is often a trade-off between flexibility and cost, however, with the most flexible manufacturing operations frequently having higher costs per unit, and the least flexible operations having lower costs per unit. Some common manufacturing operations, arranged in order from the least flexible to the most flexible, are continuous-flow production, line-flow production, batch production, and job shops.

Most production processes generate finished products at a discrete rate. A product is completed, and then—perhaps a few seconds, minutes, or hours later—another is completed, and so on. For instance, if you stood at the end of an automobile assembly line, nothing much would seem to be happening for 55 seconds of every minute. In that last 5 seconds, however, a new car would be started and driven off the assembly line, ready for its new owner. By contrast, in **continuous-flow production**, products are produced continuously rather than at a discrete rate. Like a water hose that is never turned off and just keeps on flowing, production of the final product never stops. Until recently, drug companies used discrete production operations to make drugs, mixing ingredients in huge vats at separate factories. But to cut costs and increase quality, many are switching to continuous-flow production where the raw materials used to make drugs are "fed into a single, continuously running process."[67] Johnson & Johnson, GlaxoSmithKline, and Novartis are building continuous-flow factories, which should reduce operating costs by 30 percent and increase quality because corrections can be made immediately and not after large batches have been produced. Furthermore, continuous-flow pharmaceutical factories are much smaller at 4,000 square feet compared to the typical 100,000 square foot drug making facility, and thus, much less costly to build. Finally, production speeds and output can be dramatically higher. For instance, while it takes four to six weeks to make 100,000 tablets of Vertex's new cystic-fibrosis drug, its new continuous-flow factory will be able to make that many tablets in an hour![68] Despite

---

Manufacturing flexibility the degree to which manufacturing operations can easily and quickly change the number, kind, and characteristics of products they produce

Continuous-flow production a manufacturing operation that produces goods at a continuous, rather than a discrete, rate their many advantages, continuous-flow production processes are the most standardized and least flexible manufacturing operations. In other words, a continuous-flow factory dedicated to making cystic-fibrosis drugs could not be used to make another kind of drug.

Line-flow production processes are preestablished, occur in a serial or linear manner, and are dedicated to making one type of product. In this way, the 10 different steps required to make product X can be completed in a separate manufacturing process (with separate machines, parts, treatments, locations, and workers) from the 12 different steps required to make product Y. Line-flow production processes are inflexible because they are typically dedicated to manufacturing one kind of product. Space satellites used for communication typically take five years to make, cost about $150 million, and last about 15 years. Historically, each satellite is different, customized to the buyer's needs, and handcrafted with every component and process tested at every production step. But OneWeb, in a joint venture with Airbus, the European maker of passenger jets, is using an automated, line-flow assembly process to manufacture hundreds of satellites a year at a cost of just $1 million each.[69] Startup Planet Labs is producing even smaller satellites, called cubesats, which weigh 9 pound each, with line-flow production. By simplifying parts so they can only connect in one way, which prevents manufacturing mistakes, it produced 120 satellites in just six weeks.[70]

The next most flexible manufacturing operation is **batch production**, which involves the manufacture of large batches of different products in standard lot sizes. A worker in a batch production operation will perform the same manufacturing process on 100 copies of product X, followed by 200 copies of product Y, and then 50 copies of product Z. Furthermore, these batches move through each manufacturing department or process in identical order. So, if the paint department follows chemical treatment, and chemical treatment is now processing a batch of 50 copies of product Z, then the paint department's next task will be to paint 50 copies of product Z. Batch production is finding increasing use among restaurant chains. To ensure consistency in the taste and quality of their products, many restaurant chains have central kitchens, or commissaries, that produce batches of food such as mashed potatoes, stuffing, macaroni and cheese, rice, quiche filling, and chili, in volumes ranging from 10 to 200 gallons. These batches are then delivered to the individual restaurant locations, which in turn serve the food to customers.

Next in terms of flexibility is the job shop. **Job shops** are typically small manufacturing operations that

CubeSats deployed from the International Space Station fly free after being deployed in 2016. These are two Dove satellites, part of the constellation designed, built and operated by Planet Labs Inc.

handle special manufacturing processes or jobs. In contrast to batch production, which handles large batches of different products, job shops typically handle very small batches, some as small as one product or process per batch. Basically, each job in a job shop is different, and after a job is done, the job shop moves on to a completely different job or manufacturing process for, most likely, a different customer. Kenworthy Machine LLC in Duvall, Washington, is a job shop with six employees that uses CNC (computer numerical control) machine tools to make high-quality parts from plastics to the hardest carbon, alloy tool steels. Owner Mark Kenworthy

Line-flow production manufacturing processes that are preestablished, occur in a serial or linear manner, and are dedicated to making one type of product

Batch production a manufacturing operation that produces goods in large batches in standard lot sizes

Job shops manufacturing operations that handle custom orders or small batch jobs says, "When it comes to part design, we have various types of customers."[71] It made 90,000 parts last year, with orders as small as just two parts to as large as several thousand of the same parts.[72] The addition of a new 3-D printer has allowed the company to expand its business by "printing" one-off parts when needed. For example, it used 3-D printing to make metal shelf brackets, a metal kitchen wall rack, and replacement plastic buttons for the machines it runs in its job shop.

18-5 INVENTORY

Inventory is the amount and number of raw materials, parts, and finished products that a company has in its possession. Inventory issues have plagued fast-growing furniture retailer Restoration Hardware (RH) for years. Customers who purchased a $4,800 desk often waited up to seven months for delivery. The wait for a $1,260 lamp was often more than two months. RH says that many of its expensive items are custom made, and thus take longer to manufacture and ship. However, analysts at BB&T Capital found that 29 of 50 noncustomized RH items were out of stock, with an average delivery of 63 days. In an age of free two-day shipping, many customers were turned off by the company's frequent delays. With more than 90 percent of its items in stock, RH is making progress. But, it's inability to manage inventory contributed to a 22 percent decline in profits.[73]

*In this section, you will learn about **18-5a the different types of inventory, 18-5b how to measure inventory levels, 18-5c the costs of maintaining an inventory, and 18-5d the systems for managing inventory.***

18-5a Types of Inventory

Exhibit 18.5 shows the four kinds of inventory a manufacturer stores: raw materials, component parts, work-in-process, and finished goods. The flow of inventory through a manufacturing plant begins when the purchasing department buys raw materials from vendors. **Raw material inventories** are the basic inputs in the manufacturing process. For example, to begin making a car, automobile manufacturers purchase raw materials such

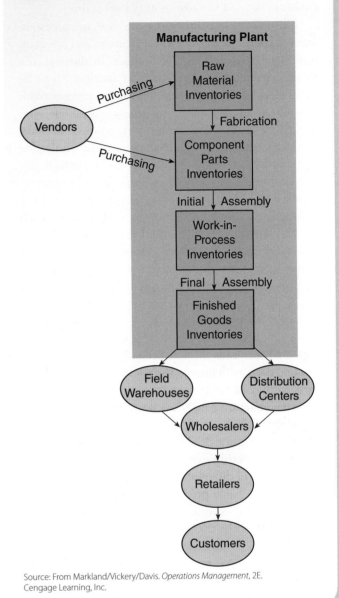

Exhibit 18.5
Types of Inventory

Source: From Markland/Vickery/Davis. *Operations Management*, 2E. Cengage Learning, Inc.

as steel, iron, aluminum, copper, rubber, and unprocessed plastic.

Next, raw materials are fabricated or processed into **component parts inventories**, meaning the basic parts used in manufacturing a product. For example, in an automobile plant, steel is fabricated or processed into a car's body panels, and steel and iron are melted and shaped into engine parts such as pistons or engine blocks. Some component parts are purchased from vendors rather than fabricated in-house.

Inventory the amount and number of raw materials, parts, and finished products that a company has in its possession

Raw material inventories the basic inputs in a manufacturing process

Component parts inventories the basic parts used in manufacturing that are fabricated from raw materials

McDonald's McFlurry Stockouts? Nooooooooooo!!!

McDonald's is best known for its Big Mac hamburgers and golden fries, but people throughout the world love the McDonald's McFlurry, a soft-serve, low-fat, ice cream concoction made with M&M's candies or Oreo cookies. But the McFlurry machines keep breaking. College student Matt Laliberte, who tweeted his frustration, said, "I'm convinced there's no way an ice cream machine would be down all the time with no replacement or repair of the machine. It's getting to the point where I won't bother going back." New Zealander Caitlin Davidson got so mad after being repeatedly told that she couldn't get a McFlurry because the machines were broken that she posted a rant against McDonald's on Facebook, which over a million people have seen. She says, "I've stopped asking for ice cream unless I see people walk out with it."

Part of the problem is the daily four-hour, 11-step process required to kill bacteria and clean the McFlurry machines. But with many McDonald's open 24 hours, it's inevitable that some customers will ask for a McFlurry when the machine is being cleaned. What's the solution to the global McFlurry stockouts angering McDonald's customers? A new McFlurry machine with fewer parts that is easier and faster to maintain. McDonald's McFlurry lovers can finally rejoice, especially those who like to dip their Chicken McNuggets or French fries in it.

Sources: J. Jargon, "Why Is the McFlurry Machine Down Again?," *Wall Street Journal*, January 19, 2017, accessed May 9, 2017, https://www.wsj.com/articles/six-horrifying-words-the-mcflurry-machine-is-down-again-1484840520; J. Jargon, "McDonald's Customers Scream, and Get New Ice Cream Machines," *Wall Street Journal*, March 2, 2017, accessed May 9, 2017, https://www.wsj.com/articles/mcdonalds-customers-scream-and-get-new-ice-cream-machines-1488476862.

The component parts are then assembled to make unfinished **work-in-process inventories**, which are also known as partially finished goods. This process is also called *initial assembly*. For example, steel body panels are welded to each other and to the frame of the car to make a "unibody," which comprises the unpainted interior frame and exterior structure of the car. Likewise, pistons, camshafts, and other engine parts are inserted into the engine block to create a working engine.

Next, all the work-in-process inventories are assembled to create **finished goods inventories**, which are the final outputs of the manufacturing process. This process is also called *final assembly*. For a car, the engine, wheels, brake system, suspension, interior, and electrical system are assembled into a car's painted unibody to make the working automobile, which is the factory's finished product. In the last step in the process, the finished goods are sent to field warehouses, distribution centers, or wholesalers, and then to retailers for final sale to customers.

18-5b Measuring Inventory

As you'll learn next, uncontrolled inventory can lead to huge costs for a manufacturing operation. Consequently, managers need good measures of inventory to prevent inventory costs from becoming too large. Three basic measures of inventory are average aggregate inventory, weeks of supply, and inventory turnover.

If you've ever worked in a retail store and had to take inventory, you probably weren't too excited about the process of counting every item in the store and storeroom. It's an extensive task that's a bit easier today because of bar codes that mark items and computers that can count and track them. Nonetheless, inventories still differ from day to day. An inventory count taken at the beginning of the month will likely be different from a count taken at the end of the month. Similarly, an inventory count taken on a Friday will differ from a count taken on a Monday. Because of such differences, companies often measure **average aggregate inventory**, which is the average overall inventory during a particular time period. Average aggregate inventory for a month can be determined by simply averaging the inventory counts at the end of each business day for that

---

Work-in-process inventories partially finished goods consisting of assembled component parts

Finished goods inventories the final outputs of manufacturing operations

Average aggregate inventory average overall inventory during a particular time period

"IN THEORY, MAKE-TO-ORDER COMPANIES HAVE NO INVENTORY. IN FACT, THEY'VE GOT INVENTORY, BUT YOU HAVE TO MEASURE IT IN HOURS."

B Calkins/Shutterstock.com

month. One way companies know whether they're carrying too much or too little inventory is to compare their average aggregate inventory with the industry average for aggregate inventory. For example, 72 days of inventory is the average for the automobile industry.

The automobile industry records inventory in terms of days of supply, but most other industries measure inventory in terms of *weeks of supply*, meaning the number of weeks it would take for a company to run out of its current supply of inventory. In general, there is an acceptable number of weeks of inventory for a particular kind of business. Too few weeks of inventory on hand, and a company risks a **stockout**—running out of inventory. With low interest rates, fast growth in Asia, and aging jet fleets needing replacement, the largest makers of passenger jets, Airbus and Boeing, are experiencing record orders that will raise production 30 percent a year by 2020. Pratt & Whitney, which makes jet engines, and Zodiac, which makes $100,000 business-class seats, have experienced stockouts as they've struggled to keep up with rising production levels. Airbus, in particular, has so many finished planes—without engines—that a frustrated Qatar Airlines canceled its orders.[74]

Another common inventory measure, **inventory turnover**, is the number of times per year that a company sells, or "turns over," its average inventory. For example, if a company keeps an average of 100 finished widgets in inventory each month, and it sold 1,000 widgets this year, then it turned its inventory ten times this year.

In general, the higher the number of inventory turns, the better. In practice, a high turnover means that a company can continue its daily operations with just a small amount of inventory on hand. For example, let's take two companies, A and B, which have identical inventory levels of 520,000 widget parts and raw materials over the course of a year. If company A turns its inventories 26 times a year, it will completely replenish its inventory every two weeks and have an average inventory of 20,000 widget parts and raw materials. By contrast, if company B turns its inventories only two times a year, it will completely replenish its inventory every 26 weeks and have an average inventory of 260,000 widget parts and raw materials. So, by turning its inventory more often, company A has 92 percent less inventory on hand at any one time than company B.

The average number of inventory turns across all kinds of manufacturing plants is approximately eight per year, although the average can be higher or lower for different industries.[75] For example, whereas the average automobile or truck manufacturer turns its entire inventory 7.8 times per year, truck manufacturer Paccar turns its inventory 17.64 times a year—roughly once every three weeks.[76] Turning inventory more frequently than the industry average can cut an auto company's costs by several hundred million dollars per year.

18-5c Costs of Maintaining Inventory

Maintaining an inventory incurs four kinds of costs: ordering, setup, holding, and stockout. **Ordering cost** is not the cost of the inventory itself but the costs associated with ordering the inventory. It includes the costs of completing paperwork, manually entering data into a computer, making phone calls, getting competing bids, correcting mistakes, and simply determining when and how much new inventory should be reordered. For example, ordering costs are relatively high in the restaurant business because 80 percent of foodservice orders (in which restaurants reorder food supplies) are processed manually. A report, *Enabling Profitable Growth in the Food-Prepared-Away-From-Home Industries*, estimated that the food industry could save $14.3 billion if all restaurants converted to electronic data interchange (see Chapter 17), in which purchase and ordering information from one company's computer system is automatically relayed to another company's computer system. Toward that end, an industry-wide

Stockout the point when a company runs out of finished product

Inventory turnover the number of times per year that a company sells, or "turns over," its average inventory

Ordering cost the costs associated with ordering inventory, including the cost of data entry, phone calls, obtaining bids, correcting mistakes, and determining when and how much inventory to order

CEO David Brandon has eliminated stockouts at Toys'R'Us and says stores are now "full and chunky."

cost of spending money on inventory that could have been spent elsewhere in the company. With $19 billion of parts on the shelf at any one time, it's estimated that the holding costs for parts inventory for U.S. airlines is approximately $5 billion a year.[79] Amazon charges for holding costs when it bills sellers $11.25 per cubic foot for products stored in Amazon's warehouses, until they ship to customers.[80]

Stockout cost is the cost incurred when a company runs out of a product. There are two basic kinds of stockout costs. First, the company incurs the transaction costs of overtime work, shipping, and the like in trying to quickly replace out-of-stock inventories with new inventories. The second and perhaps more damaging cost is the loss of customers' goodwill when a company cannot deliver the products it promised. Before David Brandon became CEO at Toys'R'Us, the company had only three units per toy at each store. Brandon said, "If someone came in and bought those three items, we'd be out of stock, which meant we were out of stock a lot," which cost them millions.[81] So Brandon is eliminating stockouts, explaining that, "If a customer can't find what they're looking for at your store 60% of the time, they will shop somewhere else and never come back. We want our stores to be bulkier. We call it full and chunky."[82] It's estimated that stockouts cost retailers $634 billion a year in lost sales.[83]

effort, Efficient Foodservice Response (EFR), is underway to improve efficiencies in the foodservice supply chain.[77]

Setup cost is the cost of changing or adjusting a machine so that it can produce a different kind of inventory.[78] For example, 3M uses the same production machinery to make several kinds of industrial tape, but it must adjust the machines whenever it switches from one kind of tape to another. There are two kinds of setup costs: downtime and lost efficiency. *Downtime* occurs whenever a machine is not being used to process inventory. If it takes five hours to switch a machine from processing one kind of inventory to another, then five hours of downtime have occurred. Downtime is costly because companies earn an economic return only when machines are actively turning raw materials into parts or parts into finished products. The second setup cost is *lost efficiency*. Recalibrating a machine to its optimal settings after a switchover typically takes some time. It may take several days of fine-tuning before a machine finally produces the number of high-quality parts that it is supposed to. So, each time a machine has to be changed to handle a different kind of inventory, setup costs (downtime and lost efficiency) rise.

Holding cost, also known as *carrying* or *storage cost*, is the cost of keeping inventory until it is used or sold. Holding cost includes the cost of storage facilities, insurance to protect inventory from damage or theft, inventory taxes, the cost of obsolescence (holding inventory that is no longer useful to the company), and the opportunity

18-5d Managing Inventory

Inventory management has two basic goals. The first is to avoid running out of stock and thus angering and dissatisfying customers. This goal seeks to increase inventory to a safe level that won't risk stockouts. The second is

Setup cost the costs of downtime and lost efficiency that occur when a machine is changed or adjusted to produce a different kind of inventory

Holding cost the cost of keeping inventory until it is used or sold, including storage, insurance, taxes, obsolescence, and opportunity costs

Stockout cost the cost incurred when a company runs out of a product, including transaction costs to replace inventory and the loss of customers' goodwill to efficiently reduce inventory levels and costs as much as possible without impairing daily operations. This goal seeks a minimum level of inventory. The following inventory management techniques—economic order quantity (EOQ), just-in-time inventory (JIT), and materials requirement planning (MRP)—are different ways of balancing these competing goals.

Economic order quantity (EOQ) is a system of formulas that helps determine how much and how often inventory should be ordered. EOQ takes into account the overall demand (D) for a product while trying to minimize ordering costs (O) and holding costs (H). The formula for EOQ is

$$EOQ = \sqrt{\frac{2DO}{H}}$$

For example, if a factory uses 40,000 gallons of paint a year (D), ordering costs (O) are \$75 per order, and holding costs (H) are \$4 per gallon, then the optimal quantity to order is 1,225 gallons:

$$EOQ = \sqrt{\frac{2(40,000(75)}{4}} = 1,225$$

With 40,000 gallons of paint being used per year, the factory uses approximately 110 gallons per day:

$$\frac{4,000 \text{ gallons}}{365 \text{ days}} = 110$$

Consequently, the factory would order 1,225 new gallons of paint approximately every 11 days:

$$\frac{1,225 \text{ gallons}}{110 \text{ gallons per days}} = 11.1 \text{ days}$$

In general, EOQ formulas do a good job of letting managers know what size or amount of inventory they should reorder to minimize ordering and holding costs. Mark Lore, former founder of (Diapers.com, now an Amazon brand), explains how it used EOQ formulas to decide precisely how much inventory to keep on hand. He says, "We built software with computational algorithms to determine what the optimal number of boxes to have in the warehouse is and what the sizes of those boxes should be. Should we stock five different kinds of boxes to ship product in? Twenty kinds? Fifty kinds? And what size should those boxes be? Right now, it's 23 box sizes, given what we sell, in order to minimize the cost of dunnage (those little plastic air-filled bags or peanuts), the cost of corrugated boxes, and the cost of shipping. We rerun the simulation every quarter."[84] As this example makes clear, EOQ formulas and models can become much more complex as adjustments are made for price changes, quantity discounts, setup costs, and many other factors.[85]

While EOQ formulas try to minimize holding and ordering costs, the just-in-time (JIT) approach to inventory management attempts to eliminate holding costs by reducing inventory levels to near zero. With a **just-in-time (JIT) inventory system**, component parts arrive from suppliers just as they are needed at each stage of production. By having parts arrive just in time, the manufacturer has little inventory on hand and thus avoids the costs associated with holding inventory. Thanks to its strict JIT inventory system, Apple carries the smallest amount of inventory among technology companies, averaging just 6.1 days of inventory of iPhones, iPad Pro tablets, and Mac computers waiting to be shipped. That six days of inventory is equivalent to an inventory turn of 60.05 times a year (remember, more turns is better). Samsung Electronics was next with 17.7 turns a year, followed by Cisco Systems with 12.6 turns a year and Amazon with 8.7.[86]

To have just the right amount of inventory arrive at just the right time requires a tremendous amount of coordination between manufacturing operations and suppliers. One way to promote tight coordination under JIT is close proximity. Most parts suppliers for Toyota's JIT system at its Georgetown, Kentucky, plant are located within 200 miles of the plant. Furthermore, parts are picked up from suppliers and delivered to Toyota as often as 16 times a day.[87] A second way to promote close coordination under JIT is to have a shared information system that allows a manufacturer and its suppliers to know the quantity and kinds of parts inventory the other has in stock. Generally, factories and suppliers facilitate information sharing by using the same part numbers and names. Ford's seat supplier accomplishes this by sticking a bar code on each seat, and Ford then uses the sticker to route the seat through its factory.

Manufacturing operations and their parts suppliers can also facilitate close coordination by using the system of kanban. **Kanban**, which is Japanese for "sign," is a simple ticket-based system that indicates when it is time to reorder inventory. Suppliers attach kanban

Economic order quantity (EOQ) a system of formulas that minimizes ordering and holding costs and helps determine how much and how often inventory should be ordered

Just-in-time (JIT) inventory system an inventory system in which component parts arrive from suppliers just as they are needed at each stage of production

Kanban a ticket-based JIT system that indicates when to reorder inventory cards to batches of parts. Then, when an assembly-line worker uses the first part out of a batch, the kanban card is removed. The cards are then collected, sorted, and quickly returned to the supplier, who begins re-supplying the factory with parts that match the order information on the kanban cards. Glenn Uminger, former manager of production control and logistics at Toyota's Georgetown, Kentucky, plant, said they would place, "orders for new parts as the first part is used out of a box." Because prices and batch sizes are typically agreed to ahead of time, kanban tickets greatly reduce paperwork and ordering costs.[88]

A third method for managing inventory is **materials requirement planning (MRP)**. MRP is a production and inventory system that, from beginning to end, precisely determines the production schedule, production batch sizes, and inventories needed to complete final products. The three key parts of MRP systems are the master production schedule, the bill of materials, and the inventory records. The *master production schedule* is a detailed schedule that indicates the quantity of each item to be produced, the planned delivery dates for those items, and the time by which each step of the production process must be completed to meet those delivery dates. Based on the quantity and kind of products set forth in the master production schedule, the *bill of materials* identifies all the necessary parts and inventory, the quantity or volume of inventory to be ordered, and the order in which the parts and inventory should be assembled. *Inventory records* indicate the kind, quantity, and location of inventory that is on hand or that has been ordered. When inventory records are combined with the bill of materials, the resulting report indicates what to buy, when to buy it, and what it will cost to order. Today, nearly all MRP systems are available in the form of powerful, flexible computer software.[89]

Which inventory management system should you use? Economic order quantity (EOQ) formulas are intended for use with **independent demand systems**, in which the level of one kind of inventory does not depend on another. For example, because inventory levels for automobile tires are unrelated to the inventory levels of women's dresses, Sears could use EOQ formulas to calculate separate optimal order quantities for dresses and tires. By contrast, JIT and MRP are used with **dependent demand systems**, in which the level of inventory depends on the number of finished units to be produced. For example, if Yamaha makes 1,000 motorcycles a day, then it will need 1,000 seats, 1,000 gas tanks, and 2,000 wheels and tires each day. So, when optimal inventory levels depend on the number of products to be produced, use a JIT or MRP management system.

> **Materials requirement planning (MRP)** a production and inventory system that determines the production schedule, production batch sizes, and inventory needed to complete final products
>
> **Independent demand system** an inventory system in which the level of one kind of inventory does not depend on another
>
> **Dependent demand system** an inventory system in which the level of inventory depends on the number of finished units to be produced

STUDY TOOLS 18

LOCATED IN TEXTBOOK
- [ ] Rip out and review chapter review card.

LOCATED AT WWW.CENGAGEBRAIN.COM
- [ ] Gain unique perspectives on key concepts with new 4LTR concept videos in the e-book.

- [ ] Increase your comprehension with Aplia for MGMT11.
- [ ] Complete interactive content within the e-book.

Endnotes

1

1. S. Kapner & I. Moise, "Sears Vows to Cut $1 Billion in Expenses," *Wall Street Journal*, February 10, 2017, accessed March 2, 2017, https://www.wsj.com/articles /sears-shares-surge-on-new-restructuring-plan-1486733935; "Sears Holdings Reports Third Quarter 2016 Results And Other Corporate Developments," Sears Holdings, December 8, 2016, accessed March 2, 2017, Corporation, https://searsholdings.com/press -releases/pr/1971; "Sears Holdings Reports Second Quarter 2016 Results And Other Corporate Developments," Sears Holdings, August 25, 2016, accessed March 2, 2017, Corporation, https://searsholdings.com /press-releases/pr/1971; "Sears Holdings Reports First Quarter 2016 Results And Other Corporate Developments," Sears Holdings, May 26, 2016, accessed March 2, 2017, Corporation, https://searsholdings.com /press-releases/pr/1971; "Sears Is Now Closing Nearly 250 Stores In 2017," *Seeking Alpha*, June 16, 2017, accessed July 30, 2017, https://seekingalpha.com /article/4082101-sears-now-closing-nearly-250 -stores-2017.

2. S. Kapner, "Sears Buys Time With Craftsman Brand Sale, Store Closures," *Wall Street Journal*, January 5, 2017, accessed March 2, 2017, https:// www.wsj.com/articles/sears-sells-craftsman-brand -to-stanley-black-decker-1483623215; A. Steele, "Sears Revenue Drops 20%," *Wall Street Journal*, December 4, 2015, B3; A. Steele, "Sears Holdings Revenue Slides," *Wall Street Journal*, December 3, 2015, accessed April 15, 2016, http://www.wsj .com/articles/sears-narrows-loss-1449144707; S. Kapner and L. Beilfuss, "Sears Looks to Sell More Assets After Weak Holiday Quarter," *Wall Street Journal*, February 9, 2016, accessed April 15, 2016, http://www.wsj.com/articles /sears-holdings-warns -on-fourth-quarter-sales-moves-to-cut-more-costs -1455019066; S. Kapner, "Sears Bets Big on Tech-nology, but at the Expense of Its Stores," *Wall Street Journal*, December 16, 2014, accessed April 24, 2015, http://www.wsj.com /articles/sears-bets-big-on-tech nology-but-at-the-expense-of-its-stores-1418787001; K. Gustafson, "Sears to Accelerate Closings, Shutter 235 Stores," CNBC, December 4, 2014, accessed April 24, 2015, http://www.cnbc.com/id/102237069.

3. "Industry Snapshot: Management, Scientific, and Technical Consulting Services (NAICS 5416)," *US Census Bureau*, accessed March 2, 2017, http://thedataweb.rm.census.gov/TheDataWeb _HotReport2/econsnapshot/2012/snapshot .hrml?NAICS=5416.

4. "What Do Managers Do?" Adapted from "The Wall Street Journal Guide to Management" by Alan Murray. *Wall Street Journal*, accessed March 2, 2017, http://guides.wsj.com/management/developing-a -leadership-style/what-do-managers-do/.

5. D. Michaels and R. Wall, "Airbus-Boeing Speed Race Increasingly Takes Place on the Ground," *Wall Street Journal*, June 12, 2015, A1.

6. N. Safo, "'Greedy,' 'Heartless,'...but Also 'On-time,'" *Marketplace*, February 10, 2016, accessed April 15, 2016, http://www.marketplaceorg /2016/02/09/world/greedy-heartless-also-time.

7. N. Safo, "'Greedy,' 'Heartless,'...but Also 'On-time,'" *Marketplace*, February 10, 2016, accessed April 15, 2016, http://www.marketplace .org/2016/02/09/world/greedy-heartless-also-time; B. Hill, "Time Warner Cable Combats Dreadful Customer Service with One-Hour Service Windows and Self-Deprecating Humor," *HotHardware*, October 5, 2015, accessed April 15, 2016, http:// hothardware.com/news/time-warner-cable-combats -dreadful-customer-service-with-one-hour-service -windows-and-self-deprecating-humor; "Time Warner Cable Responds to Its Customers During Customer Service Week: We Hear You Loud and Clear. We're Changing," *BusinessWire*, October 5, 2015, accessed April 15, 2016, http://www.businesswire.com/news /home/20151005005324/en/Time-Warner-Cable -Responds-Customers-Customer-Service; A. Russell, "Read TWC's Open Letter to Customers (Hint: We Get Your Frustration)," *Untangled*, October 5, 2015, accessed April 15, 2016, http://www.twcableuntangled .com/2015/10/read-twcs-open-letter-to-customers-hint -we-get-your-frustration/.

8. D. A. Wren, A. G. Bedeian, and J. D. Breeze, "The Foundations of Henri Fayol's Administrative Theory," *Management Decision* 40 (2002): 906–918.

9. A. Bryant, "Google's Quest to Build a Better Boss," *New York Times*, March 12, 2011, accessed February 23, 2012, http://www.nytimes.com /2011/03/13/business/13hire.html?_r=0; B. Hall, "Google's Project Oxygen Pumps Fresh Air into Management," *The Street*, February 11, 2014, accessed June 11, 2014, http://www.thestreet.com /story/12328981/1/googles-project-oxygen-pumps -fresh-air-into-management.html.

10. H. Fayol, *General and Industrial Management* (London: Pittman & Sons, 1949).

11. R. Stagner, "Corporate Decision Making," *Journal of Applied Psychology* 53 (1969): 1–13.

12. D. W. Bray, R. J. Campbell, and D. L. Grant, *Formative Years in Business: A Long-Term AT&T Study of Managerial Lives* (New York: Wiley, 1993).

13. H. Tabuchi, "Backpack Makers Rethink Student Staple," *New York Times*, September 2, 2015, B1.

14. Ibid.

15. "Our Story," Walmart, accessed March 14, 2016, http://corporate.walmart.com/; J. Fox, "Retailers Discover That Labor Isn't Just a Cost," *Bloomberg View*, November 16, 2015, accessed April 16, 2016, http:// www.bloombergview.com /articles/2015-11-16 /retailers-discover-that-labor-isn-t-just-a-cost; L. DePillis, "Walmart Is Rolling Out Big Changes to Worker Schedules This Year," *Washington Post*, February 17, 2016, accessed April 16, 2016, https:// www.washingtonpost.com/news /wonk/wp/2016/02/17 /walmart-is-rolling-out-big -changes-to-worker-schedules-this-year/.

16. E. Martinson, "Corner Office: Eileen Martinson of Sparta Systems on Clarity of Leadership," inter-view by A. Bryant, *New York Times*, January 9, 2014, accessed June 3, 2014, http://www.nytimes.com /2014/01/10/business/eileen-martinson-of-sparta -systems-on-clarity-of-leadership.html.

17. Ibid.

18. A. Narayan, "An App Gives India's Hotels a Closer Look," *Bloomberg Businessweek*, October 19–25, 2015, 39–40; "How We Do Hotel Audits," Official OYO Blog, April 12, 2016, accessed April 16, 2016, https://www.oyorooms.com/officialoyoblog /2016/04/12/how-we-do-hotel-audits.

19. Ibid.

20. H. S. Jonas III, R. E. Fry, and S. Srivastva, "The Office of the CEO: Understanding the Executive Experience," *Academy of Management Executive* 4 (1990): 36–47.

21. A. Ignatius, "We Need People to Lean into the Future," *Harvard Business Review*, March-April 2017, accessed March 8, 2017, https://hbr .org/2017/03/we-need-people-to-lean-into-the-future.

22. Ibid.

23. Jonas et al., "The Office of the CEO."

24. D. Bass, "Beyond Windows," *Bloomberg Businessweek*, February 2–8, 2015, pp. 30–31.

25. Jonas et al., "The Office of the CEO."

26. M. Porter, J. Lorsch, and N. Nohria, "Seven Surprises for New CEOs," *Harvard Business Review* (October 2004): 62.

27. C. Rogers, "CEO Mark Fields Sets Ford on a Dual Track," *Wall Street Journal*, October 17, 2016, accessed March 8, 2017, https://www.wsj.com/articles /ceo-fields-sets-ford-on-a-dual-track-1476696604.

28. B. Pope, "Mulally Plans to Stay the Course," *Ward's AutoWorld*, December 2008, 22–24.

29. D. Newcomb, "Ford Eyes its Biggest Car Inno-vation Since the Model T," *PC Magazine*, December 18, 2015, accessed March 8, 2017, http://www.pcmag .com/article2/0,2817,2496787,00.asp.

30. Q. Huy, "In Praise of Middle Managers," *Harvard Business Review*. September 2001, 72–79.

31. "Using Their Own Words, Middle Managers Describe the Nature of Their Jobs," *Wall Street Journal*, August 6, 2013, accessed June 12, 2014, www.wsj.com/articles/SB100014241278873234206 04578652110485397972.

32. R. Feintzeig, "Radical New Idea: Middle Man-agers," *Wall Street Journal*, August 19, 2015, B5.

33. "Using Their Own Words, Middle Managers Describe the Nature of Their Jobs."

34. R. Silverman, "Some Tech Firms Ask: Who Needs Managers?" *Wall Street Journal*, August 6, 2013, accessed June 12, 2014, http://www.wsj.com/articles /SB10001424127887323420604578652051466314748.

35. R. Feintzeig, "Radical New Idea: Middle Man-agers," *Wall Street Journal*, August 19, 2015, B5.

36. S. Tully, "What Team Leaders Need to Know," *Fortune*, February 20, 1995, 93.

37. B. Francella, "In a Day's Work," *Convenience Store News*, September 25, 2001, 7.

38. L. Liu and A. McMurray, "Frontline Leaders: The Entry Point for Leadership Development in the Manufacturing Industry," *Journal of European Industrial Training* 28, no. 2–4 (2004): 339–352.

39. A. Nowogrodski, "Corner Office: Avinoam No-wogrodski of Clarizen, on the Rewards of Listening," interview by A. Bryant, *New York Times*, March 13, 2014, accessed June 3, 2014, http://www.nytimes .com/2014/03/14/business/avinoam-nowogrodski-of -clarizen-on-the-rewards-of-listening.html.

40. K. Hultman, "The 10 Commandments of Team Leadership," *Training & Development*, February 1, 1998, 12–13.

41. A. Nowogrodski, "Corner Office: Avinoam No-wogrodski of Clarizen, on the Rewards of Listening ".

42. Ibid.

43. C. Porath, "How Rudeness Stops People from Working Together," *Harvard Business Review*, January 20, 2017, accessed March 8, 2017, https://hbr.org/2017/01/how-rudeness-stops-people-from-working-together.

44. N. Steckler and N. Fondas, "Building Team Leader Effectiveness: A Diagnostic Tool," *Organizational Dynamics*, Winter 1995, 20–34.

45. H. Mintzberg, *The Nature of Managerial Work* (New York: Harper & Row, 1973).

46. K. Bowers, "Corner Office: Kim Bowers of CST Brands, on Managing Up vs. Managing Down," interview by A. Bryant, *New York Times*, April 5, 2014, accessed June 3, 2014, http://www.nytimes.com/2014/04/06/business/kim-bowers-of-cst-brands-on-managing-up-vs-managing-down.html.

47. C. P. Hales, "What Do Managers Do? A Critical Review of the Evidence," *Journal of Management Studies* 23, no. 1 (1986): 88–115.

48. B. Kilkha, "FENDI Celebrates the Opening of the New York Flagship Store," *Forbes*, February 14, 2015, accessed April 24, 2015, http://www.forbes.com/sites/bettinazilkha/2015/02/14/fendi-celebrates-the-opening-of-the-new-york-flagship-store/.

49. E. Chasan, "Marco's Pizza CFO: Using Corporate Culture to Enhance Profitability - CFO Journal," *Wall Street Journal*, May 18, 2015, accessed March 8, 2017, http://blogs.wsj.com/cfo/2015/05/18/marcos-pizza-cfo-using-corporate-culture-to-enhance-profitability/.

50. M. Murphy and E. Chasan, "A Boardroom with a View—Outside Directorships Can Offer CFOs Fresh Perspective, Add to Financial Toolbox," *Wall Street Journal*, May 7, 2013, B7.

51. J. Light, "Study Points to Benefits of Outside Board Seats," *Wall Street Journal*, May 23, 2011, B6.

52. "News by Industry," *Business Wire*, accessed April 16, 2016, http://www.businesswire.com/portal/site/home/news/industries/.

53. "Media Monitoring and Analysis Services," Glean.info, accessed March 8, 2017, http://glean.info/glean-info-media-monitoring-service-stores-all-media-clips-in-an-online-digital-clip-archive-with-a-full-featured-dashboard-to-manage-your-stored-clips/.

54. "CQ: Legislative Tracking, Custom Alerts and Policy Analysis," CQ Roll Call, accessed March 8, 2017, http://cqrollcall.com/cq/.

55. A. Bryant, "Transparency Is Much More Than a Buzzword," *New York Times*, March 2, 2013, accessed May 14, 2013, http://www.nytimes.com/2013/03/03/business/ryan-smith-of-qualtrics-on-building-a-transparent-culture.html.

56. T. Mochizuki, "Sharp Aims to Restore Image," *Wall Street Journal*, August 23, 2016, B4.

57. Ibid.

58. E. Warnock, "You Know What Banks Need? Slot Machines, Miniskirts and Chocolate," *Wall Street Journal*, January 12, 2017, accessed March 9, 2017, https://www.wsj.com/articles/with-loan-rates-in-the-tank-a-lender-turns-its-atms-into-slot-machines-1484244143.

59. Ibid.

60. Fox News, "Waffle House Won't Stop Slinging Waffles During Hurricane Matthew," Fox News, October 5, 2016, accessed March 9, 2017, http://www.foxnews.com/food-drink/2016/10/05/waffle-house-wont-stop-slinging-waffles-during-hurricane-matthew.html.

61. Ibid.

62. L. Rao, "The Wall Street Veteran Who's Helping Google Get Disciplined," *Fortune*, September 12, 2016, accessed March 9, 2017, http://fortune.com/google-cfo-ruth-porat-most-powerful-women/.

63. Ibid.

64. Press Release, "Leading US Companies Announce Plan to Transform the Corporate Health Care System," Health Transformation Alliance, February 5, 2016, accessed March 9, 2017, http://htahealth.com/docs/press/Leading_US_Companies_Announce_Plan_to_Transform_the_Corporate_Health_Care_System.pdf.

65. J. Walker, "Health Costs Get a Rethink," *Wall Street Journal*, March 8, 2017, B8.

66. L. A. Hill, *Becoming a Manager: Mastery of a New Identity* (Boston: Harvard Business School Press, 1992).

67. R. L. Katz, "Skills of an Effective Administrator," *Harvard Business Review*, September–October 1974, 90–102.

68. C. A. Bartlett and S. Ghoshal, "Changing the Role of Top Management: Beyond Systems to People," *Harvard Business Review*, May–June 1995, 132–142.

69. F. L. Schmidt and J. E. Hunter, "Development of a Causal Model of Process Determining Job Performance," *Current Directions in Psychological Science* 1 (1992): 89–92.

70. J. B. Miner, "Sentence Completion Measures in Personnel Research: The Development and Validation of the Miner Sentence Completion Scales," in *Personality Assessment in Organizations*, ed. H. J. Bernardin and D. A. Bownas (New York: Praeger, 1986), 145–176.

71. M. W. McCall, Jr., and M. M. Lombardo, "What Makes a Top Executive?" *Psychology Today*, February 1983, 26–31; E. van Velsor and J. Brittain, "Why Executives Derail: Perspectives Across Time and Cultures," *Academy of Management Executive*, November 1995, 62–72.

72. Ibid.

73. J. Lublin, "How to Delegate the Right Way," *Wall Street Journal*, March 13, 2014, accessed June 3, 2014, http://www.wsj.com/articles/SB10001424052702304185104579435640803345898.

74. A. K. Naj, "Corporate Therapy: The Latest Addition to Executive Suite Is Psychologist's Couch," *Wall Street Journal*, August 29, 1994, A1.

75. Ibid.

76. P. Wallington, "Leadership: How to Spot a Toxic Boss," *CIO*, April 26, 2006, accessed June 13, 2014, http://www.cio.com/article/20139/Leadership_How_to_Spot_a_Toxic_Boss; P. Wallington, "Management2 Toxic!" *Financial Mail*, July 28, 2006, 48.

77. R. Ashkenas, "First-Time Managers, Don't Do Your Team's Work for Them," *Harvard Business Review*, September 21, 2015, accessed April 16, 2016, https://hbr.org/2015/09/first-time-managers-dont-do-your-teams-work-for-them.

78. J. Sandberg, "Overcontrolling Bosses Aren't Just Annoying: They're Also Inefficient," *Wall Street Journal*, March 30, 2005, B1.

79. P. Drexler, "Managing Up: When Your Boss Is an Obsessive Micromanager," *Forbes*, June 13, 2013, accessed June 3, 2014, http://www.forbes.com/sites/peggydrexler/2013/06/13/managing-up-when-your-boss-is-an-obsessive-micromanager/.

80. Hill, *Becoming a Manager*, p. 17.

81. Ibid., p. 55.

82. Ibid., p. 57.

83. Ibid., p. 64.

84. Ibid., p. 67.

85. Ibid., p. 161.

86. J. McGregor, "Tim Cook, the Interview: Running Apple 'Is Sort of a Lonely Job,'" *Washington Post*, August 13, 2016, accessed March 2, 2017, http://www.washingtonpost.com/sf/business/2016/08/13/tim-cook-the-interview-running-apple-is-sort-of-a-lonely-job/?utm_term=.0fe4524234b2.

87. J. Pfeffer, *The Human Equation: Building Profits by Putting People First* (Boston: Harvard Business School Press, 1996); J. Pfeffer, *Competitive Advantage Through People: Unleashing the Power of the Work Force* (Boston: Harvard Business School Press, 1994)..

88. M. A. Huselid, "The Impact of Human Resource Management Practices on Turnover, Productivity, and Corporate Financial Performance," *Academy of Management Journal* 38 (1995): 635–672.

89. D. McDonald and A. Smith, "A Proven Connection: Performance Management and Business Results," *Compensation & Benefits Review* 27, no. 6 (January 1, 1995): 59.

90. J. Combs, Y. Liu, A. Hall, and D. Ketchen, "How Much Do High-Performance Work Practices Matter? A Meta-Analysis of Their Effects on Organizational Performance," *Personnel Psychology* 59 (2006): 501–528.

91. B. Becker & M. Huselid, "Strategic Human Resources Management: Where Do We Go From Here?" *Journal of Management* 32 (2006): 898–925; M. Huselid & B. Becker, "Comment On "measurement Error in Research on Human Resources and Firm Performance: How Much Error Is There And How Does It Influence Effect Size Estimates?" *Personnel Psychology* 53 (2000): 835–854.

92. I. Fulmer, B. Gerhart, and K. Scott, "Are the 100 Best Better? An Empirical Investigation of the Relationship between Being a 'Great Place to Work' and Firm Performance," *Personnel Psychology*, Winter 2003, 965–993.

93. B. Schneider and D. E. Bowen, "Employee and Customer Perceptions of Service in Banks: Replication and Extension," *Journal of Applied Psychology* 70 (1985): 423–433; B. Schneider, J. J. Parkington, and V. M. Buxton, "Employee and Customer Perceptions of Service in Banks," *Administrative Science Quarterly* 25 (1980): 252–267.

94. "How Investing in Intangibles—Like Employee Satisfaction—Translates into Financial Returns," *Knowledge@Wharton*, January 9, 2008, accessed January 24, 2010, http://knowledge.wharton.upenn.edu/article.cfm?articleid=1873.

2

1. C. S. George, Jr., *The History of Management Thought* (Englewood Cliffs, NJ: Prentice-Hall, 1972).

2. D. Schmandt-Besserat, *How Writing Came About* (Austin: University of Texas Press, 1997).

3. A. Erman, *Life in Ancient Egypt* (London: Macmillan & Co., 1984).

4. J. Burke, *The Day the Universe Changed* (Boston: Little, Brown, 1985).

5. S. A. Epstein, *Wage Labor and Guilds in Medieval Europe* (Chapel Hill: University of North Carolina Press, 1991).

6. R. Braun, *Industrialization and Everyday Life*, trans. S. Hanbury-Tenison (Cambridge: Cambridge University Press, 1990).

7. J. B. White, "The Line Starts Here: Mass-Production Techniques Changed the Way People Work and Live Throughout the World," *Wall Street Journal*, January 11, 1999, R25.

8. R. B. Reich, *The Next American Frontier* (New York: Time Books, 1983).

9. J. Mickelwait and A. Wooldridge, *The Company: A Short History of a Revolutionary Idea* (New York: Modern Library, 2003).

10. H. Kendall, "Unsystematized, Systematized, and Scientific Management," in *Scientific Management: A Collection of the More Significant Articles Describing the Taylor System of Management*, ed. C. Thompson (Easton, PA: Hive Publishing, 1972), 103–131.

11. United States Congress, House, Special Committee, *Hearings to Investigate the Taylor and Other Systems of Shop Management*, vol. 3 (Washington, DC: Government Printing Office, 1912).

12. Ibid.

13. Ibid.

14. A. Derickson, "Physiological Science and Scientific Management in the Progressive Era: Frederic S. Lee and the Committee on Industrial Fatigue," *Business History Review* 68 (1994): 483–514.

15. U.S. Congress, House, Special Committee, 1912.

16. F. W. Taylor, *The Principles of Scientific Management* (New York: Harper, 1911).

17. C. D. Wrege and R. M. Hodgetts, "Frederick W. Taylor's 1899 Pig Iron Observations: Examining Fact, Fiction, and Lessons for the New Millennium," *Academy of Management Journal* 43 (December 2000): 1283; J. R. Hough and M. A. White, "Using Stories to Create Change: The Object Lesson of Frederick Taylor's 'Pig-tale,'" *Journal of Management* 27, no. 5 (October 2001): 585–601; E. A. Locke, "The Ideas of Frederick W. Taylor: An Evaluation," *Academy of Management Review* 7, no. 1 (1982) 14–24.

18. Locke, "The Ideas of Frederick W. Taylor."

19. George, *The History of Management Thought*.

20. F. Gilbreth and L. Gilbreth, "Applied Motion Study," in *The Writings of the Gilbreths*, ed. W. R. Spriegel and C. E. Myers (1917; reprint, Homewood, IL: Irwin, 1953), 207–274.

21. Ibid.

22. D. Ferguson, "Don't Call It 'Time and Motion Study,'" *IIE Solutions* 29, no. 5 (1997): 22–23.

23. H. Gantt, "A Graphical Daily Balance in Manufacture," *Transactions of the American Society of Mechanical Engineers* 24 (1903): 1325.

24. P. Peterson, "Training and Development: The View of Henry L. Gantt (1861–1919)," *SAM Advanced Management Journal*, Winter 1987, 20–23.

25. H. Gantt, "Industrial Efficiency," *National Civic Federation Report of the 11th Annual Meeting*, New York, January 12, 1991, 103.

26. Ibid.

27. M. Weber, *The Theory of Social and Economic Organization*, trans. A. Henderson and T. Parsons (New York: Free Press, 1947).

28. M. Weber, *The Protestant Ethic and the Spirit of Capitalism* (New York: Scribner's, 1958).

29. George, *The History of Management Thought*.

30. D. A. Wren, "Henri Fayol as Strategist: A Nineteenth Century Corporate Turnaround," *Management Decision* 39, no. 6 (2001): 475–487; D. Reid, "Fayol: From Experience to Theory," *Journal of Management History* (Archive) 1, no. 3 (1995): 21–36.

31. Ibid.

32. Ibid.

33. Ibid.

34. F. Blancpain, "Les cahiers inédits d'Henri Fayol," trans. D. Wren, *Extrait du bulletin de l'institut international d'administration publique* 28–29 (1974): 1–48.

35. D. A. Wren, A. G. Bedeian, and J. D. Breeze, "The Foundations of Henri Fayol's Administrative Theory," *Management Decision* 40 (2002): 906–918.

36. H. Fayol, *General and Industrial Management* (London: Pittman & Sons, 1949); Wren, Bedeian, and Breeze, "Foundations."

37. P. Graham, ed., *Mary Parker Follett—Prophet of Management: A Celebration of Writings from the 1920s* (Boston: Harvard Business School Press, 1995).

38. D. Linden, "The Mother of Them All," *Forbes*, January 16, 1995, 75.

39. J. H. Smith, "The Enduring Legacy of Elton Mayo," *Human Relations* 51, no. 3 (1998): 221–249.

40. E. Mayo, *The Human Problems of an Industrial Civilization* (New York: Macmillan, 1933).

41. Ibid.

42. "Hawthorne Revisited: The Legend and the Legacy," *Organizational Dynamics*, Winter 1975, 66–80.

43. E. Mayo, *The Social Problems of an Industrial Civilization* (Boston: Harvard Graduate School of Business Administration, 1945).

44. "Hawthorne Revisited: The Legend and the Legacy."

45. Mayo, *The Social Problems of an Industrial Civilization*, 45.

46. George, *The History of Management Thought*.

47. C. I. Barnard, *The Functions of the Executive* (Cambridge, MA: Harvard University Press, 1938), 4.

48. C. I. Barnard, *The Functions of the Executive: 30th Anniversary Edition* (Cambridge, MA: Harvard University Press, 1968), 5.

49. J. Fuller and A. Mansour, "Operations Management and Operations Research: A Historical and Relational Perspective," *Management Decision* 41 (2003): 422–426.

50. D. Wren and R. Greenwood, "Business Leaders: A Historical Sketch of Eli Whitney," *Journal of Leadership & Organizational Studies* 6 (1999): 131.

51. "Monge, Gaspard, comte de Péluse," *Britannica Online*, accessed January 9, 2005, http://www.britannica.com/biography/Gaspard-Monge-comte-de-Peluse.

52. M. Schwartz and A. Fish, "Just-in-Time Inventories in Old Detroit," *Business History* 40, no. 3 (July 1998): 48.

53. D. Ashmos and G. Huber, "The Systems Paradigm in Organization Theory: Correcting the Record and Suggesting the Future," *Academy of Management Review* 12 (1987): 607–621; F. Kast and J. Rosenzweig, "General Systems Theory: Applications for Organizations and Management," *Academy of Management Journal* 15 (1972): 447–465; D. Katz and R. Kahn, *The Social Psychology of Organizations* (New York: Wiley, 1966).

54. R. Mockler, "The Systems Approach to Business Organization and Decision Making," *California Management Review* 11, no. 2 (1968): 53–58.

55. F. Luthans and T. Stewart, "A General Contingency Theory of Management," *Academy of Management Review* 2, no. 2 (1977): 181–195.

3

1. H. Haddon, "Grocers Feel Chill From Millennials," *Wall Street Journal*, October 27, 2016, accessed March 5, 2017, https://www.wsj.com/articles/grocers-feel-chill-with-millennials-1477579072.

2. G. Bensinger & L. Stevens, "Amazon to Expand Grocery Business With New Convenience Stores," *Wall Street Journal*, October 12, 2016, accessed March 5, 2017, https://www.wsj.com/articles/amazon-to-expand-grocery-business-with-new-convenience-stores-1476189657.

3. A. Dizzy, "Amazon to Expand Grocery Business With New Convenience Stores," *Wall Street Journal*, July 12, 2016, accessed March 5, 2017, https://www.wsj.com/articles/amazon-to-expand-grocery-business-with-new-convenience-stores-1476189657.

4. H. Haddon, "Grocers Feel Chill From Millennials," *Wall Street Journal*, October 27, 2016, accessed March 5, 2017, https://www.wsj.com/articles/grocers-feel-chill-from-millennials-147757907.

5. "NFDA Releases Results of 2015 Member General Price List Survey," National Funeral Directors Association (NFDA), October 1, 2015, http://www.nfda.org/news/media-center/nfda-news-releases/id/840/nfda-releases-results-of-2015-member-general-price-list-survey; D. Herbert "Rest in Peace for Less with Caskets Made in China," *Bloomberg Businessweek*, February 20, 2015, accessed April 24, 2015, http://www.bloomberg.com/news/features/2015-02-20/casket-industry-fends-off-chinese-imports-favored-by-vegas-entrepreneur; P. Cain, "The Living Dead: New Embalming Method Aids Surgical Training," BBC News, June 15, 2013, accessed April 24, 2015, http://www.bbc.com/news/health-22908661.

6. B. Sisario, "SiriusXM Fights to Dominate the Dashboard of the Connected Car," *New York Times*, February 20, 2016, accessed March 5, 2017, https://www.nytimes.com/2016/02/21/business/media/siriusxm-fights-to-dominate-the-dashboard-of-the-connected-car.html.

7. "The Infinite Dial 2016," Edison Research, March 10, 2016, accessed March 5, 2017, http://www.edisonresearch.com/the-infinite-dial-2016/.

8. E. Romanelli and M. L. Tushman, "Organizational Transformation as Punctuated Equilibrium: An Empirical Test," *Academy of Management Journal* 37 (1994): 1141–1166.

9. H. Banks, "A Sixties Industry in a Nineties Economy," *Forbes*, May 9, 1994, 107–112.

10. L. Cowan, "Cheap Fuel Should Carry Many Airlines to More Record Profits for 1st Quarter," *Wall Street Journal*, April 4, 1998, B17A.

11. "Annual Revenues and Earnings: US Airlines—All Services," Air Transport Association, accessed January 15, 2005, http://www.airlines.org; S. Carey, "Carrier Makes Deeper Cuts as It Seeks Federal Backing Needed to Exit Chapter 11," *Wall Street Journal*, November 27, 2002, A3; S. Carey, "UAL Will Lay Off 1,500 Workers as Part of Cost-Cutting Strategy," *Wall Street Journal*, January 6, 2003, A3; D. Carty, "Oral Testimony of Mr. Donald J. Carty, Chairman and CEO, American Airlines: United States Senate, Committee on Commerce, Science, and Transportation," accessed January 9, 2003, http://www.amrcorp.com; S. McCartney, M. Trottman, and S. Carey, "Northwest, Continental, America West Post Losses as Delta Cuts Jobs," *Wall Street Journal*, November 18, 2002, B4.

12. "Airlines Still in Upheaval, 5 Years after 9/11," *CNNMoney.com*, September 8, 2006, accessed July 25, 2008, http://money.cnn.com/2006/09/08/news/companies/airlines_sept11/?postversion=2006090813&eref=yahoo.

13. "Economic Performance of the Airline Industry," International Air Transport Association (IATA), 2016 End-Year Report, accessed March 5, 2017, http://www.iata.org/whatwedo/Documents/economics/IATA-Economic-Performance-of-the-Industry-end-year-2016-report.pdf; "Net Income In Thousands of Dollars $000 All U.S. Carriers - All Regions," Bureau of Transportation Statistics, accessed March 5, 2017, Data Elements - Financial, https://www.transtats.bts.gov/Data_Elements_Financial.aspx?Data=6.

14. J. Mouawad, "Airlines Reap Record Profits, and Passengers Get Peanuts," *New York Times*, February 6, 2016, accessed August 4, 2016, http://www.nytimes.com/2016/02/07/business/energy-environment/airlines-reap-record-profits-and-passengers-get-peanuts.html.

15. B. Sumers, "How Cozy: Airlines Add an Extra Seat to Each Row," *Condé Nast Traveler*, March 10, 2016, accessed March 5, 2017, http://www.cntraveler.com/stories/2016-03-10/airlines-add-an-extra-seat-to-each-row.

16. J. Mouawad, "Airlines Reap Record Profits, and Passengers Get Peanuts," *New York Times*, February 6, 2016, accessed August 4, 2016, http://www.nytimes.com/2016/02/07/business/energy-environment/airlines-reap-record-profits-and-passengers-get-peanuts.html.

17. "National Statistics for Milk: Production, Measured in LB/Head," USDA - National Agricultural Statistics Service, April 29, 2016, accessed March 5, 2017, https://www.nass.usda.gov/Statistics_by_Subject/result.php?4B229587-F308-34B9-8E3F-A02380B426BD&sector=ANIMALS%20%26%20PRODUCTS&group=DAIRY&comm=MILK; A. Madrigal, "The Perfect Milk Machine: How Big Data Transformed the Dairy Industry," *The Atlantic*, May 1, 2012, accessed April 25, 2015, http://www.theatlantic.com/technology/archive/2012/05/the-perfect-milk-machine-how-big-data-transformed-the-dairy-industry/256423/; "U.S. Dairy: Milk Produced Per Cow in the United States from 1999 to 2015 (in Pounds)," *Statistica*, accessed April 17, 2016, http://www.statista.com.ezproxy.butler.edu/statistics/194935/quantity-of-milk-produced-per-cow-in-the-us-since-1999/.

18. "National Statistics for Milk: Production, Measured in LB/Head," USDA - National Agricultural Statistics Service, April 29, 2016, accessed March 5, 2017, https://www.nass.usda.gov/Statistics_by_Subject/result.php?4B229587-F308-34B9-8E3F-A02380B426BD&sector=ANIMALS%20%26%20PRODUCTS&group=DAIRY&comm=MILK; "US Dairy: Total Milk Production 2015," *Statista*, accessed April 17, 2016, http://www.statista.com/statistics/194937/total-us-milk-production-since-1999/.

19. B. Morris, "E-Commerce Boom Roils Trucking Industry," *Wall Street Journal*, March 31, 2016, accessed March 5, 2017, https://www.wsj.com/articles/e-commerce-boom-roils-trucking-industry-1459442027.

20. Ibid.

21. B. Wexler, "Chocolate Makers Fight a Melting Supply of Cocoa," *Wall Street Journal*, January 13, 2016, accessed March 5, 2017, https://www.wsj.com/articles/chocolate-makers-fight-a-melting-supply-of-cocoa-1452738616.

22. G. Wearden, "Chinese Economic Boom Has Been 30 Years in the Making," *The Guardian*, August 16, 2016, accessed April 17, 2016, http://www.theguardian.com/business/2010/aug/16/chinese-economic-boom; "The Economist Explains: Why China's Economy Is Slowing," *The Economist*, March 11, 2015, accessed April 17, 2016, http://www.economist.com/blogs/economist-explains/2015/03/economist-explains-8.

23. C. Paris, "Dry-Bulk Shipping Firms Face Unprecedented Crisis; Companies Selling Vessels to Survive," *Wall Street Journal*, January 20, 2016, accessed April 17, 2016, http://www.wsj.com/articles/dry-bulk-shipping-firms-face-unprecedented-crisis-1453293892.

24. C. Paris, "Economic Slump Sends Big Ships to Scrap Heap," *Wall Street Journal*, August 14, 2016, accessed March 5, 2017, https://www.wsj.com/articles/economic-slump-sends-big-ships-to-scrap-heap-1471192256.

25. B. Einhorn and C. Matlack, "The Shipping Industry Is Suffering From China's Trade Slowdown," *Bloomberg BusinessWeek*, February 11, 2016, accessed April 17, 2016, http://www.bloomberg.com/news/articles/2016-02-11/shipping-industry-suffering-from-china-s-trade-slowdown; "Baltic Dry Index," accessed April 17, 2016, http://www|.bloomberg.com/quote/BDIY:IND.

26. C. Paris, "Dry-Bulk Shipping Firms Face Unprecedented Crisis; Companies Selling Vessels to Survive," *Wall Street Journal*, January 20, 2016, accessed April 17, 2016, http://www.wsj.com/articles/dry-bulk-shipping-firms-face-unprecedented-crisis-1453293892.

27. C. Paris, "Dry-Bulk Shipping Firms Face Unprecedented Crisis; Companies Selling Vessels to Survive," *Wall Street Journal*, January 20, 2016, accessed April 17, 2016, http://www.wsj.com/articles/dry-bulk-shipping-firms-face-unprecedented-crisis-1453293892.

28. R. Silverman, J. Lublin & R. Fentzeig, "In Uncertain Times, CEOs Lose Faith in Forecasts," *Wall Street Journal*, July 12, 2016, accessed March 5, 2017, https://www.wsj.com/articles/in-uncertain-times-ceos-lose-faith-in-forecasts-1468315801.

29. Ibid.

30. "CEO Confidence Rebounds Sharply," The Conference Board, January 5, 2017, accessed March 5, 2017, https://www.conference-board.org/data/ceoconfidence.cfm.

31. "CEOs Remain Optimistic," *WSJ/Vistage Small Business CEO Survey*, February 2017, accessed March 5, 2017, http://1y573z2ztctoalc2f2fja0kj.wpengine.netdna-cdn.com/wp-content/uploads/2017/02/WSJ-CEO-Survey-0217.pdf.

32. L. Scism, "Driverless Cars Threaten to Crash Insurers' Earnings - WSJ," *Wall Street Journal*, July 26, 2016, accessed March 5, 2017, https://www.wsj.com/articles/driverless-cars-threaten-to-crash-insurers-earnings-1469542958.

33. C. Paris, "Carnival Sails Toward China Growth," *Wall Street Journal*, January 22, 2015, B7.

34. S. Daneshkhu and L. Whipp, "Hipster Dollar Carries Heavy Weight as Millennials Come to Market," *Financial Times*, January 20, 2016, accessed April 17, 2016, http://www.ft.com/cms/s/0/bfce2878-c691-11e5-b3b1-7b2481276e45.html.

35. Ibid.

36. "The Civil Rights Act of 1991," US Equal Employment Opportunity Commission, accessed April 17, 2016, http://www.eeoc.gov/policy/cra91.html.

37. "Compliance Assistance—Family and Medical Leave Act (FMLA)," U.S. Department of Labor: Employment Standards Administration, Wage and Hour Division, accessed April 17, 2016, http://www.dol.gov/.

38. A Loten, "Small Business Owners Scramble to Prepare for New Tax Form," *Wall Street Journal*, March 4, 2015, B5.

39. R. J. Bies and T. R. Tyler, "The Litigation Mentality in Organizations: A Test of Alternative Psychological Explanations," *Organization Science* 4 (1993): 352–366.

40. M. Orey, "Fear of Firing," *BusinessWeek*, April 23, 2007, 52–62.

41. S. Gardner, G. Gomes, and J. Morgan, "Wrongful Termination and the Expanding Public Policy Exception: Implications and Advice," *SAM Advanced Management Journal* 65 (2000): 38.

42. "Bases by Issue: FY 2010 - FY 2016," U.S. Equal Employment Opportunity Commission, accessed March 6, 2017, https://www.eeoc.gov/eeoc/statistics/enforcement/bases_by_issue.cfm.

43. J. Mundy, "Wrongful Termination Lawsuits on the Rise," *LawyersandSettlements.com*, January 5, 2011, accessed June 4, 2014, http://www.lawyersandsettlements.com/articles/wrongful-termination/wrongful-termination-law-11-15747.html#.U48_GvldWSp.

44. Orey, "Fear of Firing."

45. Ibid.

46. "Little Gym Case Study," Listen360, April 2014, accessed April 4, 2015, http://listen360.com/assets/case_studies/LittleGym_4-2014.pdf.

47. R. Johnston and S. Mehra, "Best-Practice Complaint Management," *Academy of Management Experience* 16 (November 2002): 145–154.

48. D. Smart and C. Martin, "Manufacturer Responsiveness to Consumer Correspondence: An Empirical Investigation of Consumer Perceptions," *Journal of Consumer Affairs* 26 (1992): 104.

49. "Spotify Launches Tool to Let Artists Track their Biggest Fans," *Fact*, November 18, 2015, accessed April 17, 2016, http://www.factmag.com/2015/11/18/spotify-fan-insights-tool-artists-track-biggest-fans/.

50. Ibid.

51. S. A. Zahra and S. S. Chaples, "Blind Spots in Competitive Analysis," *Academy of Management Executive* 7 (1993): 7–28.

52. T. Corrigan, "San Francisco's Biggest Taxi Operator Seeks Bankruptcy Protection," *Wall Street Journal*, January 24, 2016, accessed March 6, 2017, https://www.wsj.com/articles/san-franciscos-biggest-taxi-operator-seeks-bankruptcy-protection-1453677177.

53. Ibid.

54. K. G. Provan, "Embeddedness, Interdependence, and Opportunism in Organizational Supplier-Buyer Networks," *Journal of Management* 19 (1993): 841–856.

55. Opinion, "China's Rare-Earths Bust," *Wall Street Journal*, July 18, 2016, accessed March 6, 2017, https://www.wsj.com/articles/chinas-rare-earths-bust-1468860856; Press Release, "Rare Earth Metals Market Forecast By End-use Industry 2016-2026," openPR, February 27, 2017, accessed March 6, 2017, http://www.openpr.com/news/449519/Rare-Earth-Metals-Market-Forecast-By-End-use-Industry-2016-2026.html.

56. V. Dudau, "Samsung Will Reportedly Supply Apple with 100 million OLED Displays in 2017," Neowin, April 15, 2016, accessed March 6, 2017, https://www.neowin.net/news/samsung-will-reportedly-supply-apple-with-100-million-oled-displays-in-2017; T. Mochizuki, "Apple's Next iPhone Will Have a Curved Screen," *Wall Street Journal*, February 28, 2017, accessed March 6, 2017, https://www.wsj.com/articles/apples-next-iphone-will-have-a-curved-screen-1488260583; M. Wuerthele, "Supply Constraints Will Limit OLED to Just iPhone 8,' Benefiting Apple in Long Run - report, Apple Insider, February 28, 2017, accessed March 6, 2017, http://appleinsider.com/articles/17/02/28/supply-constraints-will-limit-oled-to-just-iphone-8-benefitting-apple-in-long-run---report.

57. M. Geuss, "Honda Engineers Scaled Back Rare Earth Metals in Hybrid Engines Significantly," *Ars Technica*, July 13, 2016, accessed March 6, 2017, https://arstechnica.com/cars/2016/07/honda-engineers-scaled-back-rare-earth-metals-in-hybrid-engines-significantly/.

58. "Viewpoint: Antecedents and Outcomes of Employee Perspective Taking," *Academy of Management Journal* 44 (2001): 1085–1100; B. K. Pilling, L. A. Crosby, and D. W. Jackson, "Relational Bonds in Industrial Exchange: An Experimental Test of the Transaction Cost

Economic Framework," *Journal of Business Research* 30 (1994): 237–251.

59. J. Bennett, "GM Loosens Terms for Some Parts Suppliers," June 17, 2016, accessed March 6, 2017, https://www.wsj.com/articles/gm-loosens -terms-for-some-suppliers-1466185855.

60. Ibid.

61. K. Benner, "Airbnb Sues Over New Law Regulating New York Rentals," *New York Times* October 21, 2016, accessed March 6, 2017, https: //www.nytimes.com/2016/10/22/technology/new-york passes-law-airbnb.html; S. Schlechter & G. Bensinger, "Airbnb to Enforce Limits on Rentals in London, Amsterdam," *Wall Street Journal*, December 1, 2016, accessed March 6, 2017, https://www.wsj.com /articles/airbnb-agrees-to-enforce-amsterdam-limit -on-rentals-1480580233.

62. "Following an Additional Child Fatality, IKEA Recalls 29 Million MALM and Other Models of Chests and Dressers Due to Serious Tip-Over Hazard; Consumers Urged to Anchor Chests and Dressers or Return for Refund," U.S. Consumer Product Safety Commission, June 28, 2016, accessed March 6, 2017, https://www.cpsc.gov/Recalls/2016 /following-an-additional-child-fatality-ikea-recalls -29-million-malm-and-other-models-of.

63. J. Hansegard, "Lego Builds Stronger Bridges to Girls: Danish Toy Maker Finally Is Succeeding after Several Failed Attempts to Span the Gender Gap," *Wall Street Journal*, December 30, 2015, B1.

64. SPARKsummit, "Our Letter to LEGO," January 20, 2012, accessed February 17, 2016, http://www.sparksummit.com/2012/01/20/our -letter-to-lego/.

65. J. Hansegard, "Lego Builds Stronger Bridges to Girls: Danish Toy Maker Finally Is Succeeding After Several Failed Attempts to Span the Gender Gap," *Wall Street Journal*, December 30, 2015, B1.

66. Ibid.

67. E. Brown, "WeWork's Biggest Competitor: Anyone and Everyone," *Wall Street Journal*, July 12, 2016, accessed March 7, 2017, https://www.wsj .com/articles/weworks-biggest-competitor-anyone -and-everyone-1468333187.

68. D. F. Jennings and J. R. Lumpkin, "Insights Between Environmental Scanning Activities and Porter's Generic Strategies: An Empirical Analysis," *Journal of Management* 4 (1992): 791–803.

69. J. Adamy, "Baby Lull Promises Growing Pains for Economy," *Wall Street Journal*, May 10, 2016, accessed March 7, 2017, https://www.wsj.com /articles/baby-lull-promises-growing-pains-for -economy-1462894211.

70. Ibid.

71. Ibid.

72. E. Jackson and J. E. Dutton, "Discerning Threats and Opportunities," *Administrative Science Quarterly* 33 (1988): 370–387.

73. B. Thomas, S. M. Clark, and D. A. Gioia, "Strategic Sensemaking and Organizational Performance: Linkages Among Scanning, Interpretation, Action, and Outcomes," *Academy of Management Journal* 36 (1993): 239–270.

74. R. Daft, J. Sormunen, and D. Parks, "Chief Executive Scanning, Environmental Characteristics, and Company Performance: An Empirical Study," *Strategic Management Journal* 9 (1988): 123–139; V. Garg, B. Walters, and R. Priem, "Chief Executive Scanning Emphases, Environmental Dynamism, and Manufacturing Firm Performance," *Strategic Management Journal* 24 (2003): 725–744; D. Miller and P. H. Friesen, "Strategy-Making and Environment: The Third Link," *Strategic Management Journal* 4 (1983): 221–235.

75. A. Gasparro and A. Prior, "Kellogg's Profit Falls 16% as Cereal Sales Drop," *Wall Street Journal*, July 31, 2014, accessed April 25, 2015, http://www .wsj.com/articles/kelloggs-profit-pressured-by-cereal -sales-1406809902.

76. D. Leonard, "Bad News in Cereal City—Will Kellogg Ever Catch a Break?" *Bloomberg Businessweek*, March 2–8, 2015, pp. 42–47.

77. J. Bunge, "Tastes Like Chicken: The Race Is On to Breed Better Birds as Chicken Emerges as the Protein of the Masses," *Wall Street Journal*, December 4, 2015, 2016, accessed April 17, 2016, http://www.wsj.com/articles/how-to-satisfy-the-worlds -surging-appetite-for-meat-1449238059.

78. K. Paris, "How Cargill Plans to Help Feed the World," *Foodonline.com*, September 25, 2014, accessed April 17, 2016, http://www.foodonline.com /doc/how-cargill-plans-to-help-feed-the-world-0001; S. Lewis, "Cargill's New Poultry Processing Facility Is Up and Running, September 16, 2014, 2016, accessed April 17, 2016, http://www.foodonline.com /doc/cargill-s-new-poultry-processing-facility-is-up -and-running-0001.

79. J. Bunge, "Tastes Like Chicken: The Race Is On to Breed Better Birds as Chicken Emerges as the Protein of the Masses," *Wall Street Journal*, December 4, 2015, accessed April 17, 2016, http://www.wsj.com/articles/how-to-satisfy-the worlds-surging-appetite-for-meat-1449238059.

80. A. Dizik, "The Relationship Between Corporate Culture and Performance," *Wall Street Journal*, February 21, 2016, accessed March 7, 2017, WSJ, https://www.wsj.com/articles/the -relationship-between-corporate-culture-and -performance-1456110320.

81. Ibid.

82. A. Boyce, L. Nieminen, M. Gillespie, A. Ryan & D. Denison, "Which Comes First, Organizational Culture or Performance? A Longitudinal Study of Causal Priority with Automobile Dealerships," *Journal of Organizational Behavior* 36 (2015): 339-359.

83. A. Dizik, "The Relationship Between Corporate Culture and Performance," *Wall Street Journal*, February 21, 2016, accessed March 7, 2017, WSJ, https://www.wsj.com/articles /the-relationship-between-corporate-culture -and-performance-1456110320.

84. S. Berfield, "Container Store: Conscious Capitalism and the Perils of Going Public," Bloomberg Business, February 19, 2015, accessed April 25, 2015, http://www.bloomberg.com/news /articles/2015-02-19/container-store-conscious -capitalism-and-the-perils-of-going-public.

85. Ibid.; K. Gustafson, "Retail's Turnover a Plus for Economy But Challenge for Stores," CNBC, September 23, 2014, accessed April 25, 2015, http://www.cnbc.com/id/102021496.

86. D. M. Boje, "The Storytelling Organization: A Study of Story Performance in an Office-Supply Firm," *Administrative Science Quarterly* 36 (1991): 106–126.

87. E. Chasan, "Marco's Pizza CFO: Using Corporate Culture to Enhance Profitability," *Wall Street Journal*, May 18, 2015, accessed March 7, 2017, http://blogs.wsj.com/cfo/2015/05/18/marcos -pizza-cfo-using-corporate-culture-to-enhance -profitability/.

88. Ibid.

89. P. Sanchez, "Why Your Company Needs More Ceremonies," *Harvard Business Review*, July 27, 2016, accessed March 7, 2017, https:// hbr.org/2016/07/why-your-company-needs -more-ceremonies.

90. Ibid.

91. D. R. Denison and A. K. Mishra, "Toward a Theory of Organizational Culture and Effectiveness," *Organization Science* 6 (1995): 204–223.

92. P. Ziobro, "Floundering Mattel Tries to Make Things Fun Again," *Wall Street Journal*, December 22, 2014, accessed April 26, 2015, http://www.wsj .com/articles/floundering-mattel-tries-to-make -things-fun-again-1419305830.

93. P. Ziobro & J. Lublin, "Mattel Finds Its New CEO at Google," *Wall Street Journal*, January 18, 2017, B2; Anonymous, "Business News: Mattel Gets a Boost From Dolls," *Wall Street Journal*, October 20, 2016, B3; P. Ziobro, "Barbie Stalls on the Road to Comeback," *Wall Street Journal*, April 21, 2016, B1; R. Feintzeig & J. Lublin, "Business News: It Can Be a Tough Road for Interim CEOs," *Wall Street Journal*, January 8, 2016, B4.

94. "Our Philosophy," *BPV Capital Management*, June 18, 2014, accessed June 18, 2014, http://www .backporchvista.com/about-bpv/our-philosophy/.

95. D. Roberts, "Why U.S. Olympic Swimming Is So Dominant," *Fortune*, April 17, 2015, accessed February 17, 2016, http://fortune.com/2015/04/17 /usa-olympic-swimming-gold/.

96. "Swimming: Medal Count," NBC Olympics, August 12, 2016, accessed March 7, 2017, http: //www.nbcolympics.com/swimming/.

97. A. Zuckerman, "Strong Corporate Cultures and Firm Performance: Are There Tradeoffs?" *Academy of Management Executive*, November 2002, 158–160.

98. E. Schein, *Organizational Culture and Leadership*, 2nd ed. (San Francisco: Jossey-Bass, 1992).

99. S. Albert & D.A. Whetten, "Organizational Identity," *Research in Organizational Behavior* 7 (1985): 263–295. C.M. Fiol, "Managing Culture as a Competitive Resource: An Identity-Based View of Sustainable Competitive Advantage," *Journal of Management* 17 (1991): 191–211.

100. R. Fentzeig, "Companies Rethink Sales Rewards," *Wall Street Journal*, November 8, 2016, accessed March 8, 2017, https://www.wsj.com /articles/companies-rethink-sales-rewards -1478602745.

101. E. Glazer & C. Rexrode, "Wells Fargo CEO Defends Bank Culture, Lays Blame With Bad Employees," *Wall Street Journal*, September 13, 2016, accessed March 8, 2017, https://www.wsj.com /articles/wells-fargo-ceo-defends-bank-culture -lays-blame-with-bad-employees-1473784452.

102. Ibid.

103. E. Glazer, "Wells Fargo to Roll Out New Compensation Plan to Replace Sales Goals," *Wall Street Journal*, January 6, 2017, accessed March 8, 2017, https://www.wsj.com/articles/wells-fargo-to -roll-out-new-compensation-plan-to-replace-sales -goals-1483719468.

104. Ibid.

105. "Michael O'Leary's Most Memorable Quotes," *The Telegraph*, September 5, 2012, accessed April 17, 2016, http://www.telegraph.co.uk/travel/lists /Michael-OLearys-most-memorable-quotes/.

106. Ryanair: How the Airline Is Trying to Change Its Image," *The Telegraph*, February 4, 2016, accessed April 17, 2016, http://www.telegraph.co.uk /travel/galleries/Ryanair-how-the-airline-is-trying -to-change-its-image/ryanair4/; C. Osborne, "Ryanair CEO Admits His Loudmouth Ways Are Affecting Carrier's Growth," ZDNet, November 22, 2013, accessed April 17, 2016, http://www.zdnet .com/article /ryanair-ceo-admits-personal-behavior-is -affecting -carriers-growth/#!; A. Tovey, "Being Nice Pays Off for Ryanair as Passenger Numbers Soar," *The Telegraph*, September 2, 2015, accessed April

17, 2016, http://www.telegraph.co.uk/finance/newsbysector /transport/11839609/Being-nice-pays-off-for-Ryanair as-passenger-numbers-soar.html.

107. Tovey, "Being Nice Pays Off for Ryanair as Passenger Numbers Soar."

108. G. Bensinger, "Amazon Recruits Face 'Bar Raisers,'" *Wall Street Journal*, January 8, 2014, B1.

4

1. "Executive Summary: 2016 Edelman Trust Barometer Annual Global Study," Edelman Berland, accessed March 18, 2017, https://www.scribd.com /document/336621519/2017-Edelman -Trust-Barometer-Executive-Summary#download; "2016 Edelman Trust Barometer Annual Global Study," Edelman Berland, accessed April 18, 2016, http://www.edelman.com/insights/intellectual -property/2014-edelman-trust-barometer/.

2. D. Meinhert, "Creating an Ethical Workplace," *HR Magazine* 59 (April 2014): 4, accessed June 4, 2014, https://www.shrm.org/Publications /hrmagazine/EditorialContent/2014/0414 /Pages/0414-ethical-workplace-culture.aspx.

3. "2016 Global Business Ethics Survey: Measuring Risk and Promoting Workplace Integrity," Ethics Research Center of the Ethics & Compliance Initiative, accessed March 18, 2017, http://www.ethics.org/research/ethics.org/gbes/gbes-form.

4. "2013 National Business Ethics Survey of the U.S. Workforce," Ethics Research Center of the Ethics & Compliance Initiative, accessed March 18, 2017, http://www.ethics.org/research/nbes/nbes -reports/nbes-2013.

5. C. Smith, "The Ethical Workplace," *Association Management* 52 (2000): 70–73.

6. "Trust in the Workplace: 2010 Ethics & Workplace Survey," Deloitte LLP, 2010, accessed June 4, 2014, http://www.deloitte.com/assets/Dcom-United -States/Local%20Assets/Documents/us_2010 _Ethics_and_Workplace_Survey_report_071910.pdf.

7. "Communication, Honesty among Traits Most Desired and Lacking in Corporate Leaders, ASQ Survey Says," *Reuters.com*, February 11, 2014, accessed April 11, 2015, http://www.reuters.com /article/2014/02/11/idUSnGNX91ymYv+1c2 +GNW20140211.

8. A. Bryant, "Michael Gould of Bloomingdale's, on Passion and Compassion," *New York Times*, October 5, 2013, accessed March 18, 2017, http://www.nytimes.com/2013/10/06/business/michael-gould -of-bloomingdales-on-passion-and-compassion .html?smid=tw-share&_r=0.

9. Association of Certified Fraud Examiners, "Report to the Nations on Occupational Fraud and Abuse: 2016 Global Fraud Study," Association of Certified Fraud Examiners, accessed March 18, 2017, http://www.acfe.com/rttn2016/docs/2016-report-to-the-nations.pdf; K. Gibson, "Excuses, Excuses: Moral Slippage in the Workplace," *Business Horizons* 43, no. 6 (2000): 65; S. L. Robinson and R. J. Bennett, "A Typology of Deviant Workplace Behaviors: A Multidimensional Scaling Study," *Academy of Management Journal* 38 (1995): 555–572.

10. Harvard Management Update, "Learn by 'Failing Forward,'" *Globe & Mail*, October 31, 2000, B17.

11. A. Gouveia, "2014 Wasting Time at Work Survey," Salary.com, accessed March 18, 2017, http://www.salary.com/2014-wasting-time-at-work/slide/2/.

12. C. Conner, "Wasting Time At Work: The Epidemic Continues," *Forbes*, July 31, 2015, accessed March 18, 2017, https://www.forbes.com /sites/cherylsnappconner/2015/07/31/wasting-time -at-work-the-epidemic-continues/#13c222031d94.

13. C. Zakrzewski, "Workplace Technology (A Special Report) — The Key to Getting Workers To Stop Wasting Time Online," *Wall Street Journal*, March 14, 2016, R4.

14. C. Mele, "Self-Service Checkouts Can Turn Customers Into Shoplifters, Study Says," *New York Times*, August 10, 2016, accessed March 18, 2017, https://www.nytimes.com/2016/08/11/business/self -service-checkouts-can-turn-customers-into -shoplifters-study-says.html.

15. A. Fisher, "U.S. Retail Workers are No. 1 ... In Employee Theft," *Fortune*, January 26, 2015, accessed March 18, 2017, http://fortune .com/2015/01/26/us-retail-worker-theft/; Global Retail Theft Barometer 2014, accessed April 11, 2015, http://globalretailtheftbarometer.com/.

16. J.L. Hayes, "28th Annual Retail Theft Survey," *Hayes International* press release, June 2016, accessed March 18, 2017, http://hayesinternational .com/wp-content/uploads/2016/06/28th-Annual -Retail-Theft-Survey-PR-Stats-Thoughts1.pdf.

17. A. Wren, "Sweethearting: A Bottom Line Drain for Retailers," *Chain Store Age*, June 21, 2012, accessed April 11, 2015, http://www .chainstoreage.com/article/sweethearting-bottom -line-drain-retailers; M. K. Brady, C. M. Voorhees, and M. J. Brusco, "Service Sweethearting: Its Antecedents and Customer Consequences," *Journal of Marketing* 76 (2012): 81–98.

18. J. Norman, "Cultivating a Culture of Honesty," *The Orange County [California] Register*, October 23, 2006.

19. News Release, "Nonfatal Occupational Injuries and Illnesses Requiring Days Away from Work, 2015," U.S. Bureau of Labor Statistics, November 10, 2016, accessed March 18, 2017, http://www.bls .gov/news.release/pdf/osh2.pdf; Economic News Release, "Fatal Occupational Injuries by Major Event, 2015, in Census of Fatal Occupations Injuries Charts, 1992–2015 (final data)," U.S. Bureau of Labor Statistics, accessed March 18, 2017, https:// www.bls.gov/iif/oshwc/cfoi/cfch0014.pdf.

20. D. Palmer and A. Zakhem, "Bridging the Gap Between Theory and Practice: Using the 1991 Federal Sentencing Guidelines as a Paradigm for Ethics Training," *Journal of Business Ethics* 29, no. 1/2 (2001): 77–84.

21. K. Tyler, "Do the Right Thing: Ethics Training Programs Help Employees Deal with Ethical Dilemmas," *HR Magazine*, February 2005, accessed March 13, 2009, http://www.shrm.org/publications /hrmagazine/editorialcontent/pages/0205tyler .aspx.

22. D. R. Dalton, M. B. Metzger, and J. W. Hill, "The 'New' US Sentencing Commission Guidelines: A Wake-up Call for Corporate America," *Academy of Management Executive* 8 (1994): 7–16.

23. G. Marcias, "Q&A: Gayle Macias, World Vision," interview by B. DiPietro, *Wall Street Journal*, June 12, 2013, accessed June 4, 2014, http://blogs .wsj.com/riskandcompliance/2013/06/12/qa-gayle -macias-world-vision/.

24. B. Ettore, "Crime and Punishment: A Hard Look at White-Collar Crime," *Management Review* 83 (1994): 10–16.

25. F. Robinson and C. C. Pauze, "What Is a Board's Liability for Not Adopting a Compliance Program?" *Healthcare Financial Management* 51, no. 9 (1997): 64.

26. "Quick Facts: Organizational Offenders," United States Sentencing Commission, accessed March 19, 2017, http://www.ussc.gov/sites/default /files/pdf/research-and-publications/quick-facts /DELETE-Organizational-Offenders_FY15.pdf.

27. Robinson and Pauze, "What Is a Board's Liability?"

28. B. Schwartz, "The Nuts and Bolts of an Effective Compliance Program," *HR Focus* 74, no. 8 (1997): 13–15.

29. C. Chen, "The CEO Who Saved a Life and Lost His Job," *Bloomberg Businessweek*, January 22, 2015, accessed April 18, 2016, http://www .bloomberg.com /news/articles/2015-01-22/biotech -drug-approvals -social-media-storm-hits-chimerix.

30. S. Morris and R. McDonald, "The Role of Moral Intensity in Moral Judgments: An Empirical Investigation," *Journal of Business Ethics* 14 (1995): 715–726; B. Flannery and D. May, "Environmental Ethical Decision Making in the US Metal-Finishing Industry," *Academy of Management Journal* 43 (2000): 642–662.

31. L. Kohlberg, "Stage and Sequence: The Cognitive-Developmental Approach to Socialization," in *Handbook of Socialization Theory and Research*, ed. D. A. Goslin (Chicago: Rand McNally, 1969); L. Trevino, "Moral Reasoning and Business Ethics: Implications for Research, Education, and Management," *Journal of Business Ethics* 11 (1992): 445–459.

32. L. Trevino and M. Brown, "Managing to be Ethical: Debunking Five Business Ethics Myths," *Academy of Management Executive* 18 (May 2004): 69–81.

33. L. T. Hosmer, "Trust: The Connecting Link Between Organizational Theory and Philosophical Ethics," *Academy of Management Review* 20 (1995): 379–403.

34. A. Edney, "Cost to Develop a Drug More Than Doubles to $2.56 Billion," *Bloomberg BusinessWeek*, November 18, 2014, accessed April 18, 2016, http://www.bloomberg.com/news /articles/2014-11-18 /cost-to-develop-a-drug -more-than-doubles-to -2-56-billion.

35. C. Chen, "The CEO Who Saved a Life and Lost His Job," *Bloomberg BusinessWeek*, January 22, 2015, accessed April 18, 2016, http://www .bloomberg.com/news/articles/2015-01-22/biotech -drug-approvals-social-media-storm-hits-chimerix.

36. Ibid; "Chimerix Announces Final Data from AdVise Trial of Brincidofovir at BMT Tandem Meetings," Chimeriz, February 22, 2017, accessed March 19, 2017, http://ir.chimerix.com/releasedetail .cfm?ReleaseID=1013907.

37. C. Chen, "The CEO Who Saved a Life and Lost His Job," *Bloomberg BusinessWeek*, January 22, 2015, accessed April 18, 2016, http://www. bloomberg.com/news/articles/2015-01-22/biotech -drug-approvals-social-media-storm-hits-chimerix.

38. Ibid.

39. "Josh Hardy, Va. Boy Who Inspired Social Media Campaign, Dies," NBC4 Washington, October 22, 2016, accessed March 19, 2017, http:// www.nbcwashington.com/news/local/Josh-Hardy -Va-Boy-Who-Inspired-Social-Media-Campaign -Dies-394586831.html.

40. "2013 National Business Ethics Survey of the U.S. Workforce."

41. H. J. Bernardin, "Validity of an Honesty Test in Predicting Theft Among Convenience Store Employees," *Academy of Management Journal* 36 (1993): 1097–1108.

42. J. M. Collins and F. L. Schmidt, "Personality, Integrity, and White Collar Crime: A Construct Validity Study," *Personnel Psychology* (1993): 295–311.

43. W. C. Borman, M. A. Hanson, and J. W. Hedge, "Personnel Selection," *Annual Review of Psychology* 48 (1997): 299–337.

44. "303A.10 Code of Business Conduct and Ethics," *NYSE Listed Company Manual*, November 25, 2009, accessed April 18, 2016, http://nysemanual

.nyse.com/lcm/Help/mapContent.asp?sec=lcm -sections&title=sx-ruling-nyse-policymanual_303A .09&id=chp_1_4_3_11.

45. P. E. Murphy, "Corporate Ethics Statements: Current Status and Future Prospects," *Journal of Business Ethics* 14 (1995): 727–740.

46. "ADP's Code of Business Conduct & Ethics," ADP, April 6, 2016, accessed March 19, 2017, https://www.adp.com/who-we-are/corporate-social -responsibility/working-with-adp/ethics.aspx#C.

47. "More Corporate Boards Involved in Ethics Programs; Ethics Training Becoming Standard Practice," *PR Newswire*, October 16, 2006.

48. S. J. Harrington, "What Corporate America Is Teaching About Ethics," *Academy of Management Executive* 5 (1991): 21–30.

49. L. A. Berger, "Train All Employees to Solve Ethical Dilemmas," *Best's Review–Life-Health Insurance Edition* 95 (1995): 70–80.

50. Meinhert, "Creating an Ethical Workplace."

51. L. Trevino, G. Weaver, D. Gibson, and B. Toffler, "Managing Ethics and Legal Compliance: What Works and What Hurts," *California Management Review* 41, no. 2 (1999): 131–151.

52. J. Katz, "Making Compliance Training Stick," *Compliance Week*, November 5, 2013, accessed March 19, 2017, https://www.complianceweek.com /news/news-article/making-compliance-training -stick#.WM73NBiZNhE.

53. "Leader's Guide: A Culture of Trust 2008," *Lockheed Martin*, accessed July 17, 2008, http:// www.lockheedmartin.com/data/assets/corporate /documents/ethics/2008_EAT_Leaders_Guide .pdf.

54. Meinhert, "Creating an Ethical Workplace."

55. E. White, "Theory & Practice: What Would You Do? Ethics Courses Get Context; Beyond Checking Boxes, Some Firms Start Talking About Handling Gray Areas," *Wall Street Journal*, June 12, 2006, B3.

56. "The State of Ethics in Large Companies: A Research Report from the National Business Ethics Survey (NBES)," Ethic Research Center of the Ethics & Compliance Initiative, 2015, accessed April 11, 2015, http://www.ethics .org/nbes/wp-content/uploads/2015/03 /LargeCompaniesExecSummary.pdf.

57. Ibid.

58. G. Weaver and L. Trevino, "Integrated and Decoupled Corporate Social Performance: Man- agement Commitments, External Pressures, and Corporate Ethics Practices," *Academy of Manage- ment Journal* 42 (1999): 539–552; Trevino, et al., "Managing Ethics and Legal Compliance."

59. "2013 National Business Ethics Survey of the U.S. Workforce."

60. J. Salopek, "Do the Right Thing," *Training & Development* 55 (July 2001): 38–44.

61. M. Gundlach, S. Douglas, and M. Martinko, "The Decision to Blow the Whistle: A Social Information Processing Framework," *Academy of Management Executive* 17 (2003): 107–123.

62. R. Carucci, "Why Ethical People Make Unethical Choices," *Harvard Business Review*, December 16, 2016, accessed March 19, 2017, https:// hbr.org/2016/12/why-ethical-people-make-unethical -choices.

63. "2013 National Business Ethics Survey of the U.S. Workforce"; "The State of Ethics in Large Companies: A Research Report from the National Business Ethics Survey (NBES)."

64. N. Popper, "JPMorgan Ordered to Pay Dam- ages for Firing Whistle-Blower," *New York Times*, January 11, 2017, accessed March 20, 2017, https://

www.nytimes.com/2017/01/11/business/dealbook /jpmorgan-chase-johnny-burris-whistleblower.html.

65. S. Craig and J. Silver-Greenberg, "Selling the Home Brand: A Look Inside an Elite JPMorgan Unit," *New York Times*, March 2, 2013, accessed March 20, 2017, https://dealbook.nytimes .com/2013/03/02/selling-the-home-brand-a-look -inside-an-elite-jpmorgan-unit-2/?_r=0.

66. N. Popper, "JPMorgan Ordered to Pay Dam- ages for Firing Whistle-Blower."

67. J. Deschenaux, "High Court Extends Employ- ee Whistle-blower Protections," *Society for Human Resource Management*, March 5, 2014, accessed June 4, 2014, http://www.shrm.org/LegalIssues /FederalResources/Pages/High-Court-Extends -Employee-Whistle-blower-Protections.aspx.

68. "Reporting Ethical Violations Globally (except Europe), ADP, accessed March 20, 2017, https:// www.adp.com/who-we-are/corporate-social -responsibility/ethics-and-compliance/reporting -ethical-violations.aspx; "EthicsPoint - ADP," EthicsPoint, accessed March 20, 2017, https:// secure.ethicspoint.com/domain/media/en /gui/48099/index.html.

69. "2016 Global Business Ethics Survey: Measur- ing Risk and Promoting Workplace Integrity," Eth- ics Research Center of the Ethics & Compliance Initiative, accessed March 18, 2017, http://www .ethics.org/research/ethics.org/gbes/gbes-form.

70. M. P. Miceli and J. P. Near, "Whistleblowing: Reaping the Benefits," *Academy of Management Executive* 8 (1994): 65–72.

71. M. Mucci, "Compliance Without Compliance Officer."

72. Ibid.

73. M. Master and E. Heresniak, "The Disconnect in Ethics Training," *Across the Board* 39 (Septem- ber 2002): 51–52.

74. H. R. Bower, *Social Responsibilities of the Businessman* (New York: Harper & Row, 1953).

75. M. Apuzzo, J. Goldstein, and E. Lichtblau, "Apple's Line in the Sand Was Over a Year in the Making," *New York Times*, February 18, 2016, accessed March 20, 2017, https://www.nytimes .com/2016/02/19/technology/a-yearlong-road-to-a -standoff-with-the-fbi.html.

76. S. L. Wartick and P. L. Cochran, "The Evolu- tion of the Corporate Social Performance Model," *Academy of Management Review* 10 (1985): 758–769.

77. J. Nocera, "The Paradox of Businesses as Do-Gooders," *New York Times*, November 11, 2006, C1.

78. S. Waddock, C. Bodwell, and S. Graves, "Responsibility: The New Business Imperative," *Academy of Management Executive* 16 (2002): 132–148.

79. T. Donaldson and L. E. Preston, "The Stakeholder Theory of the Corporation: Concepts, Evidence, and Implications," *Academy of Manage- ment Review* 20 (1995): 65–91.

80. R. King, "The Week Ahead: At Tech Confab, a Social Component," *Wall Street Journal*, October 3, 2016, B2.

81. M. Langley, "The Many Stakeholders Of Salesforce.Com: They Go Well Beyond Sharehold- ers, Says the Company's CEO, Marc Benioff," *Wall Street Journal*, October 27, 2015, R2.

82. Press Release, "Adoption of Salesforce.com's 1/1/1 Model Accelerates Around the World, Febru- ary 23, 2010, accessed March 20, 2017, http:// www.prnewswire.com/news-releases/adoption -of-salesforcecoms-111-model-accelerates-around -the-world-85034902.html.

83. Q. Hardy, "Marc Benioff, SalesForce Chief, on the Strategic Benefits of Corporate Giving," *New York Times*, November 2, 2015, accessed March 20, 2017, https://www.nytimes.com/2015/11/08/giving /marc-benioff-salesforce-chief-on-the-strategic -benefits-of-corporate-giving.html.

84. M. B. E. Clarkson, "A Stakeholder Framework for Analyzing and Evaluating Corporate Social Performance," *Academy of Management Review* 20 (1995): 92–117.

85. B. Agle, R. Mitchell, and J. Sonnenfeld, "Who Matters to CEOs? An Investigation of Stakeholder Attributes and Salience, Corporate Performance, and CEO Values," *Academy of Management Jour- nal* 42 (1999): 507–525.

86. K. Pullen, "Just Below the Surface - The Hidden Side of Triclosan," June 27, 2014, accessed April 18, 2016, https://www.nrdc.org/experts/kristi -pullen/just-below-surface-hidden-side-triclosan.

87. L. Landro, "Antibacterial Soaps Go under the Microscope," *Wall Street Journal*, February 16, 2016, R1.

88. E. W. Orts, "Beyond Shareholders: Interpret- ing Corporate Constituency Statutes," *George Washington Law Review* 61 (1992): 14–135.

89. A. B. Carroll, "A Three-Dimensional Concep- tual Model of Corporate Performance," *Academy of Management Review* 4 (1979): 497–505.

90. S. Carey, "Spirit Air Abruptly Replaces CEO," *Wall Street Journal*, January 6, 2016, B1.

91. J. Lublin and M. Murrary, "CEOs Leave Faster Than Ever Before as Boards, Investors Lose Patience," *Wall Street Journal Interactive*, October 27, 2000.

92. "CEO Dismissals in the US at the Lowest Level in a Decade, The Conference Board Finds," The Conference Board, April 14, 2015, accessed April 18, 2016, http://www.prnewswire.com/news -releases/ceo-dismissals-in-the-us-at-the -lowest-level-in-a-decade-the-conference-board -finds-300065351.html.

93. J. Ewing and N. Boudette, "As VW Pleads Guilty in U.S. Over Diesel Scandal, Trouble Looms in Europe," *New York Times*, March 10, 2017, accessed March 20, 2017, https://www.nytimes .com/2017/03/10/business/volkswagen-europe -diesel-car-owners.html.

94. P. Ziobro, "How Do Companies Quietly Raise Prices? They Do This," *Wall Street Journal*, June 11, 2015, accessed March 20, 2017, https://www .wsj.com/articles/how-do-companies-quietly-raise -prices-they-do-this-1434041940.

95. P. Ziobro, "Same Package, Same Price, Less Product," *Wall Street Journal*, June 12, 2015, B1; S. Ng, "P&G Settles Suit on Puffed-Up Packaging," *Wall Street Journal*, July 7, 2015, accessed February 23, 2016, http://www.wsj.com/articles/p-g -settles-suit-on-puffed-up-packaging-1436305037.

96. Ibid.

97. B. Weber, "Costs of Alberta Wildfire Reach $9.5 Billion: Study," BNN, January 17, 2017, accessed March 20, 2017, http://www.bnn.ca/costs-of-alberta -wildfire-reach-9-5-billion-study-1.652292.

98. S. Horwitz, "In Natural Disasters, Companies Operate Like Neighbors," *Wall Street Journal*, June 7, 2016, accessed March 20, 2017, https://www.wsj.com /articles/in-natural-disasters-companies-operate-like -neighbors-1465338881.

99. Ibid.

100. A. Pasztor, "Helicopter Industry Moves to Improve Safety," *Wall Street Journal*, December 31, 2015, B5.

101. H. Tabuchi, "Automakers Still Selling Cars with Defective Takata Airbags," *New York Times*, June 1, 2016, accessed March 20, 2017, https://

www.nytimes.com/2016/06/02/business/
automakers-still-selling-cars-with-riskiest-takata
-airbags.html.

102. J. Stewart, "Chipotle's New Mantra: Safe Food, Not Just Fresh," *The New York Times*, January 15, 2016, B1.

103. J. Jargon and J. Newman, "Chipotle Revamps Following E. coli Crisis," *Wall Street Journal*, February 3, 2016, B1.

104. D. Kesmodel, J. Bunge, and A. Gasparro, "McDonald's to Curb Antibiotics Use," *Wall Street Journal*, March 5, 2015, B1, B2.

105. A. McWilliams and D. Siegel, "Corporate Social Responsibility: A Theory of the Firm Perspective," *Academy of Management Review* 26, no.1 (2001): 117–127; H. Haines, "Noah Joins Ranks of Socially Responsible Funds," *Dow Jones News Service*, October 13, 1995. A meta-analysis of 41 different studies also found no relationship between corporate social responsibility and profitability. Though not reported in the meta-analysis, when confidence intervals are placed around its average sample-weighted correlation of .06, the lower confidence interval includes zero, leading to the conclusion that there is no relationship between corporate social responsibility and profitability. See M. Orlitzky, "Does Firm Size Confound the Relationship Between Corporate Social Responsibility and Firm Performance?" *Journal of Business Ethics* 33 (2001): 167–180; S. Ambec and P. Lanoie, "Does It Pay to Be Green? A Systematic Overview," *Academy of Management Perspectives*, 22 (2008): 45–62.

106. M. Orlitzky, "Payoffs to Social and Environmental Performance," *Journal of Investing* 14 (2005): 48–51.

107. M. Orlitzky, F. Schmidt, and S. Rynes, "Corporate Social and Financial Performance: A Meta-analysis," *Organization Studies* 24 (2003): 403–441.

108. Orlitzky, "Payoffs to Social and Environmental Performance."

109. D. Kesmodel, "Beef's Meaty Profits Slow Effort to Boost Antibiotic-Free Production," *Wall Street Journal*, September 15, 2015, accessed March 20, 2017, https://www.wsj.com/articles/beefs -meaty-profits-slow-effort-to-boost-antibiotic-free -production-1442309400.

110. Orlitzky, et al., "Corporate Social and Financial Performance."

111. S. Russolillo, "The Great Mystery Behind Tesla's Rally," *Wall Street Journal*, February 21, 2017, accessed March 21, 2017, https://www.wsj .com/articles/the-great-mystery-behind-teslas- rally-1487709262.

112. T. Higgins, "Tesla Sets Aggressive Production Plan for Model 3," *Wall Street Journal*, February 22, 2017, accessed March 21, 2017, https://www.wsj.com/articles/tesla-loss -narrows-in-fourth-quarter-1487798522.

113. J. Lippert, "Will Tesla Ever Make Money?" Bloomberg, March 4, 2015, accessed March 21, 2017, https://www.bloomberg.com/news/articles/2015-03-04 /as-tesla-gears-up-for-suv-investors-ask-where-the -profits-are.

5

1. L. A. Hill, *Becoming a Manager: Master a New Identity* (Boston: Harvard Business School Press, 1992).

2. L. Cook, S. Kent, and P. Kiernan, "Shell Makes a Titanic Bet on Offshore Oil," *Wall Street Journal*, March 21, 2017, A1./vre-kicks-off-major -expansion-plan-with-a-new-spotsylvania-county

-stop/2015/04/18/63576394-e1f8-11e4-b510 -962fcfabc310_story.html.

3. E. A. Locke and G. P. Latham, *A Theory of Goal Setting & Task Performance* (Englewood Cliffs, NJ: Prentice Hall, 1990).

4. M. E. Tubbs, "Goal-Setting: A Meta-Analytic Examination of the Empirical Evidence," *Journal of Applied Psychology* 71 (1986): 474–483.

5. J. Bavelas and E. S. Lee, "Effect of Goal Level on Performance: A Trade-Off of Quantity and Quality," *Canadian Journal of Psychology* 32 (1978): 219–240.

6. D. Turner, "Ability, Aspirations Fine, But Persistence Is What Gets Results," *Seattle Times*, February 13, 2005, http://community.seattletimes .nwsource.com/archive/?date=20030215&slug=d ale15m.

7. J. Jargon, "Burger King Returns to Its Roots," *Wall Street Journal*, March 9, 2016, accessed March 23, 2017, https://www.wsj.com/articles/burger-king -returns-to-its-roots-1457519402.

8. Ibid.

9. C. C. Miller, "Strategic Planning and Firm Performance: A Synthesis of More Than Two Decades of Research," *Academy of Management Performance* 37 (1994): 1649–1665.

10. H. Mintzberg, "Rethinking Strategic Planning: Part I: Pitfalls and Fallacies," *Long Range Planning* 27 (1994): 12–21, and "Part II: New Roles for Planners," 22–30; H. Mintzberg, "The Pitfalls of Strategic Planning," *California Management Review* 36 (1993): 32–47.

11. W. Duggan, "Swiss Watch Makers Aren't Worried About The Apple Watch," *Benzinga*, May 18, 2015, accessed March 23, 2017, https: //www.benzinga.com/analyst-ratings/analyst -color/15/05/5520111/swiss-watch-makers-arent -worried-about-the-apple-watch.

12. "The Swiss and World Watchmaking Industries in 2016," Federation of the Swiss Watch Industry FH, accessed March 23, 2017, http://www.fhs.swiss /file/59/Watchmaking_2016.pdf.

13. S. Wilmot, "No Time for Joy in Swiss Watches," *Wall Street Journal*, December 21, 2016.

14. D. Reisinger, "Here's How Popular Apple Watch Was Last Quarter," *Fortune*, February 8, 2017, accessed March 23, 2017, http://fortune .com/2017/02/08/apple-watch-2016-sales/.

15. K. Chu, "Changing Tastes Hit Luxury-Watch Dealers," *Wall Street Journal*, August 8, 2016, B3.

16. K. Wiggers, "New Android Wear Watches Could Motivate Sales," *Digital Trends*, March 15, 2017, accessed March 23, 2017, http://www .digitaltrends.com/wearables/smartwatch-industry -2017-projections/.

17. G. Ip, "China, Oil Show Peril of Faulty Assumptions," *Wall Street Journal*, January 13, 2016, accessed May 7, 2016, http://www.wsj.com /articles/china-oil-show-peril-of-faulty-assumptions -1452705708.

18. Mintzberg, "The Pitfalls of Strategic Planning."

19. M. Esterl, "Pepsi Learns Consumers Mostly Want Chips," *Wall Street Journal*, December 12, 2016, accessed March 23, 2017, A1.

20. Ibid.

21. Ibid.

22. Locke and Latham, *A Theory of Goal Setting & Task Performance*.

23. A. King, B. Oliver, B. Sloop, and K. Vaverek, *Planning & Goal Setting for Improved Performance: Participant's Guide* (Cincinnati, OH: Thomson Executive Press, 1995).

24. M. Prior, "Lafly: P&G Getting into Shape," *WWD*, February 20, 2015, 9, *P&G 2014 Annual Report*, accessed April 26, 2015, http://www .pginvestor.com/interactive/lookandfeel/4004124 /PG_Annual_Report_2014.pdf; J. Hawkins, "Procter & Gamble Looking to Trim Its Brand Portfolio by Exiting Over 100 Brands," *Mainenewsonline*, February 23, 2015, accessed April 26, 2015, http://mainenewsonline.com /content/15022993-procter-gamble-looking-trim -its -brand-portfolio-exiting-over.

25. Ibid.

26. Ibid; A. Steele, "Coty Profits Hit by Costs of Merger with PG Brands," *Market Watch*, February 4, 2016, accessed May 7, 2016, http://www .marketwatch.com/story/coty-profit-hit-by-costs-of- merger-with-pg-brands-2016-02-04; "P&G Accepts Coty's Offer of $12.5 Billion to Merge 43 P&G Beauty Brands with Coty," *Business Wire*, July 9, 2015, accessed May 7, 2016, http://www .businesswire.com/news/home/20150709005357/en /PG-Accepts-Coty%e2%80%99s-Offer-12.5-Billion -Merge.

27. C. Loomis, J. Schlosser, J. Sung, M. Boyle, and P. Neering, "The 15% Delusion: Brash Predictions about Earnings Growth Often Lead to Missed Targets, Battered Stock, and Creative Accounting —and That's When Times Are Good," *Fortune*, February 5, 2001, 102; H. Paster, "Manager's Journal: Be Prepared," *Wall Street Journal*, September 24, 2001, A24; P. Sellers, "The New Breed: The Latest Crop of CEOs Is Disciplined, Deferential, Even a Bit Dull," *Fortune*, November 18, 2002, 66; H. Klein and M. Wesson, "Goal and Commitment and the Goal-Setting Process: Conceptual Clarification and Empirical Synthesis," *Journal of Applied Psychology* 84 (1999): 885–896.

28. Locke and Latham, *A Theory of Goal Setting & Task Performance*.

29. J. Jargon, "Wendy's Three-Year Quest to Find Blackberries," *Wall Street Journal*, August 19, 2015, B1; C. Beach. "Wendy's Needs 2 Million Pounds of Blackberries," *The Packer*, August 20, 2015, accessed May 7, 2016, http://www.thepacker .com/news/wendy%E2%80%99s-needs-2-million -pounds-blackberries.

30. A. Bandura and D. H. Schunk, "Cultivating Competence, Self-Efficacy, and Intrinsic Interest Through Proximal Self-Motivation," *Journal of Personality & Social Psychology* 41 (1981): 586–598.

31. Naughton, K., "Driverless in Detroit: Even General Motors Thinks the Age of Autonomous Cars Is Inevitable," *Bloomberg Businessweek*, November 2–8, 2015, 53.

32. Locke and Latham, *A Theory of Goal Setting & Task Performance*.

33. M. J. Neubert, "The Value of Feedback and Goal Setting over Goal Setting Alone and Potential Moderators of This Effect: A Meta-Analysis," *Human Performance* 11 (1998): 321–335.

34. E. H. Bowman and D. Hurry, "Strategy Through the Option Lens: An Integrated View of Resource Investments and the Incremental-Choice Process," *Academy of Management Review* 18 (1993): 760–782.

35. S. Nassauer, "Wal-Mart Seals Deal for jet. com," *Wall Street Journal*, August 9, 2016, B1; S. Nassauer, "Wal-Mart Pulls Back on New Stores," *Wall Street Journal*, October 7, 2016, B1; S. Nassauer, "Wal-Mart to Scrap Its Amazon Prime Rival," *Wall Street Journal*, January 31, 2017, accessed March 24, 2017, http://www.wsj .com/articles/wal-mart-to-scrap-its-amazon-prime -rival-1485838861; S. Nassauer, "With Niche Sites, Wal-Mart Tries Selling to Hipsters," *Wall Street*

Journal, March 24, 2017, accessed March 24, 2017, https://www.wsj.com/articles/with-niche-sites-wal-mart-tries-selling-to-hipsters-1490347802; L. Picker & R. Abrams, "Walmart Rewrites Its E-Commerce Strategy With $3.3 Billion Deal for jet.com," *New York Times*, August 8, 2016, accessed March 24, 2017, https://www.nytimes.com/2016/08/09/business/dealbook/walmart-jet-com.html.

36. M. Lawson, "In Praise of Slack: Time Is of the Essence," *Academy of Management Executive* 15 (2000): 125–135.

37. R. Smith, "Utilities Seek to Stockpile Essential Parts for Disasters," *Wall Street Journal*, April 7, 2016, accessed May 7, 2016, http://www.wsj.com/articles/utilities-seek-to-stockpile-essential-parts-for-disasters-1460076194.

38. M. Prior, "Lafley: P&G Getting Into Shape," *WWD*, February 20, 2015, p. 9; C. Hymowitz and L. Coleman-Lochner, "Lafley Pivots from Builder to Demolition Man as He Shrinks P&G," *Bloomberg News*, April 14, 2015, accessed April 27, 2015, http://www.bloomberg.com/news/articles/2015-04-14/lafley-pivots-from-builder-to-demolition-man-as-he-shrinks-p-g.

39. J. C. Collins and J. I. Porras, "Organizational Vision and Visionary Organizations," *California Management Review*, Fall 1991: 30–52.

40. "About Avon," *Avon*, accessed May 7, 2016, http://www.avoncompany.com/aboutavon/index.html.

41. Collins and Porras, "Organizational Vision and Visionary Organization."; "About Us," *Highlights for Children*, accessed March 24, 2017, https://www.highlights.com/about-us.

42. Collins and Porras, "Organizational Vision and Visionary Organizations"; J. A. Pearce II, "The Company Mission as a Strategic Goal," *Sloan Management Review*, Spring 1982: 15–24.

43. J. Jargon, "Sbarro Seeks New Life Outside the Mall," *Wall Street Journal*, October 2, 2015, accessed May 7, 2016, http://www.wsj.com/articles/sbarro-seeks-new-life-outside-the-mall-1443778202.

44. Ibid.

45. "Corporate Profile: Innovating. Empowering. Delighting," Intuit, accessed March 24, 2017, https://www.intuit.com/company/profile/; V. Goel, "Intuit Sheds Its PC Roots and Rises as a Cloud Software Company," *New York Times*, April 10, 2016, accessed March 24, 2017, https://www.nytimes.com/2016/04/11/technology/intuit-sheds-its-pc-roots-and-rises-as-a-cloud-software-company.html; K. Kokalitcheva, "Intuit to Sell Off Quicken, Demandforce, QuickBase," *Fortune*, August 20, 2015, accessed March 24, 2017, http://fortune.com/2015/08/20/intuit-quicken-sale-turbotax/.

46. J. Jargon, "New Plan at Hostess: Cupcakes Everywhere," *Wall Street Journal*, September 18, 2015, B1.

47. Ibid.

48. L. Weber, "At Kimberly-Clark, 'Dead Wood' Workers Have Nowhere to Hide," *Wall Street Journal*, August 21, 2016, accessed March 24, 2017, https://www.wsj.com/articles/focus-on-performance-shakes-up-stolid-kimberly-clark-1471798944.

49. Ibid.

50. T. Mann, and V. McGrane, "GE to Cash Out of Banking Business," *Wall Street Journal*, April 11, 2015, A1.

51. S. McCartney, "Inside an Airline's Winter War Room," *Wall Street Journal*, February 5, 2015, D1.

52. J. Paterson, "Presenteeism on the Rise Among UK Workforce," *Employee Benefits*, May 2013, 3.

53. J. Weed, "Airlines, Now More Proactive on Weather, Allow Fliers to Shift Own Travel Plans," *New York Times*, January 2, 2017, accessed March 23, 2017, https://www.nytimes.com/2017/01/02/business/flight-weather-delay-change-itinerary.html.

54. S. McCartney, "The Trouble with Keeping Commercial Flights Clean," *Wall Street Journal*, September 18, 2014, D1.

55. "Volume VII, Book A Medical Staff, Chapter 1: Medical Staff Approved Policies," The University of Texas MD Anderson Cancer Center, accessed March 24, 2017, www.palliativedrugs.com/download/med%20brought%20into%20hospital3.pdf.

56. K. R. MacCrimmon, R. N. Taylor, and E. A. Locke, "Decision Making and Problem Solving," in *Handbook of Industrial & Organizational Psychology*, ed. M. D. Dunnette (Chicago: Rand McNally, 1976), 1397–1453.

57. M. Evans, "Hospitals Alter Routines to Control Drug Spending," *Wall Street Journal*, December 18, 2016, accessed March 24, 2017, https://www.wsj.com/articles/hospitals-alter-routines-to-control-drug-spending-1482062403.

58. MacCrimmon, et al., "Decision Making and Problem Solving."

59. G. Kress, "The Role of Interpretation in the Decision Process," *Industrial Management* 37 (1995): 10–14.

60. M. Esterl, "Coke Chief's Solution for Lost Fizz: More Soda," *Wall Street Journal*, March 19, 2015, A1, A12.

61. M. Evans, "Hospitals Alter Routines to Control Drug Spending," *Wall Street Journal*, December 18, 2016, accessed March 24, 2017, https://www.wsj.com/articles/hospitals-alter-routines-to-control-drug-spending-1482062403.

62. J. Bartlett & G. Shenhar, "How Consumer Reports Tests Cars," *Consumer Reports*, February 14, 2017, accessed March 24, 2017, http://www.consumerreports.org/cars-how-consumer-reports-tests-cars/; M. Rechtin, "A Better Way to Find Your Next Car," *Consumer Reports*, February 23, 2016, accessed March 24, 2017, http://www.consumerreports.org/new-car-buying/a-better-way-to-find-your-next-car/.

63. P. Djang, "Selecting Personal Computers," *Journal of Research on Computing in Education* 25 (1993): 327.

64. J. Ellenberg, "How Not to Be Misled by Data," *Wall Street Journal*, June 26, 2015, accessed March 25, 2017, https://www.wsj.com/articles/how-not-to-be-misled-by-data-1435258933.

65. "European Cities Monitor," Cushman & Wakefield, 2010, http://www.europeancitiesmonitor.eu/wp-content/uploads/2010/10/ECM-2010-Full-Version.pdf.

66. J. Stiff, "6 Tips to Build Your Social Media Strategy," *CIO*, May 8, 2013, accessed May 26, 2013, http://www.cio.com/article/732975/6_Tips_to_Build_Your_Social_Media_Strategy; D. Steiner, "How to Choose the Right Social Media for your ecommerce Business," *CIO*, October 19, 2016, accessed March 25, 2017, http://www.cio.com/article/3132468/social-networking/how-to-choose-the-right-social-media-for-your-ecommerce-business.html.

67. "The Critical Role of Teams," The Ken Blanchard Companies, March 23, 2006, accessed June 5, 2014, http://www.kenblanchard.com/img/pub/pdf_critical_role_teams.pdf.

68. I. L. Janis, *Groupthink* (Boston: Houghton Mifflin, 1983).

69. C. P. Neck and C. C. Manz, "From Groupthink to Teamthink: Toward the Creation of Constructive Thought Patterns in Self-Managing Work Teams," *Human Relations* 47 (1994): 929–952; J. Schwartz and M. L. Wald, "'Groupthink' Is 30 Years Old, and Still Going Strong," *New York Times*, March 9, 2003, 5.

70. J. Almandoz & A. Tilcsik, "When Experts Become Liabilities: Domain Experts on Boards and Organizational Failure," *Academy of Management Journal* 59 no. 4 (2016): 1124-1149.

71. J. McIntosh, "Assumptions of Quality Could Hinder Group Decision-Making Ability," Medical News Today, March 10, 2015, accessed April 27, 2015, http://www.medicalnewstoday.com/articles/290618.php.

72. A. Mason, W.A. Hochwarter, and K.R. Thompson, "Conflict: An Important Dimension in Successful Management Teams," *Organizational Dynamics* 24 (1995): 20.

73. B. Taylor, "True Leaders Believe Dissent Is an Obligation," *Harvard Business Review*, January 12, 2017, accessed March 25, 2017, https://hbr.org/2017/01/true-leaders-believe-dissent-is-an-obligation.

74. A. Bryant, "Amit Singh of Google for Work: A Respectful Clash of Ideas," *New York Times*, January 22, 2016, accessed March 25, 2017, https://www.nytimes.com/2016/01/24/technology/amit-singh-of-google-for-work-a-respectful-clash-of-ideas.html.

75. A. Mason, et al., "Conflict: An Important Dimension in Successful Management Teams."

76. R. Cosier and C. R. Schwenk, "Agreement and Thinking Alike: Ingredients for Poor Decisions," *Academy of Management Executive* 4 (1990): 69–74.

77. K. Jenn and E. Mannix, "The Dynamic Nature of Conflict: A Longitudinal Study of Intragroup Conflict and Group Performance," *Academy of Management Journal* 44, no. 2 (2001): 238–251; R. L. Priem, D. A. Harrison, and N. K. Muir, "Structured Conflict and Consensus Outcomes in Group Decision Making," *Journal of Management* 21 (1995): 691–710.

78. Priem, Harrison, & Muir, "Structured Conflict and Consensus Outcomes in Group Decision Making."

79. A. Van De Ven and A. L. Delbecq, "Nominal versus Interacting Group Processes for Committee Decision Making Effectiveness," *Academy of Management Journal* 14 (1971): 203–212.

80. P. Gilbert, "Hearing Every Voice in the Room: How IBM Brings Ideas Forward from Its Teams," *New York Times*, December 6, 2014, BU8.

81. A. R. Dennis and J. S. Valicich, "Group, Sub-Group, and Nominal Group Idea Generation: New Rules for a New Media?" *Journal of Management* 20 (1994): 723–736.

82. R. B. Gallupe, W. H. Cooper, M. L. Grise, and L. M. Bastianutti, "Blocking Electronic Brainstorms," *Journal of Applied Psychology* 79 (1994): 77–86.

83. A. Fisher, "Shy at Work? 7 Ways to Speak Up," *Fortune*, May 31, 2013, accessed March 25, 2017, http://fortune.com/2013/05/31/shy-at-work-7-ways-to-speak-up/.

84. R. B. Gallupe and W. H. Cooper, "Brainstorming Electronically," *Sloan Management Review*, Fall 1993, 27–36.

85. Ibid.

86. G. Kay, "Effective Meetings through Electronic Brainstorming," *Management Quarterly* 35 (1995): 15.

6

1. "iPhone, iPad and iPod sales from 1st quarter 2006 to 1st quarter 2017 (in million units)," Statista, accessed March 25, 2017, https://www -statista-com.ezproxy.butler.edu /statistics/253725 /iphone-ipad -and-ipod-sales -comparison /; "• Tablet vendor unit shipments worldwide 2011-2016 | Statista, accessed March 25, 2017, https://www-statista-com.ezproxy.butler.edu /statistics/276651/global-media -tablet -shipments -since-3rd-quarter-2011-by -vendor/; D. Van Boom, "Apple and Amazon were tablet standouts in 2016," CNET, February 15, 2017, accessed March 25, 2017, https://www.cnet.com /news /apple-and-amazon-were-tablet-sales -standouts -in-2016/#ftag=CAD590a51e.

2. J. Barney, "Firm Resources and Sustained Competitive Advantage," *Journal of Management* 17 (1991): 99–120; J. Barney, "Looking Inside for Competitive Advantage," *Academy of Management Executive* 9 (1995): 49–61.

3. D. Bailey, "Is It Time to Say Goodbye to Netbooks?," *The Motley Fool*, April 30, 2011, accessed March 1, 2012, http://www.fool.com /investing/general/2011/04/30/is-it-time-to -say -goodbye-to-netbooks.aspx; S. Lohr, "Netbooks Lose Status as Tablets Like the iPad Rise," *New York Times*, February 13, 2011, accessed March 1, 2012, http://www.nytimes.com/2011/02/14/technology /14netbook.html?pagewanted=all.

4. C. Arther, "Netbooks Plummet While Tablets and Smartphones Soar, Says Canalys," *The Guardian* (technology blog), February 3, 2012 (5:38), accessed June 5, 2014, http://www.theguardian.com/technology /blog/2012/feb/03/netbooks-pc-canalys-tablet.

5. M. Muchmore, "Microsoft Windows 10 Review & Rating," *PC Magazine*, February 24, 2017, accessed March 26, 2017, PCMag.com, http://www .pcmag.com/article2/0,2817,2488631,00.asp; N. Ralph, "Microsoft Windows 10 Review: Microsoft Gets It Right," CNet.com, July 28, 2015, accessed April 20, 2016, http://www.cnet.com /products/microsoft -windows-10/; E. Price, "Here's How Nokia Creates Its Maps," Mashable.com, November 12, 2012, accessed March 10, 2016, http://mashable .com/2012/11/20/nokia-here-map-car.

6. K. Carlon, "Why Apple's A10 chip 'Blows Away the Competition'" *AndroidAuthority*, October 22, 2016, accessed March 26, 2017, http://www .androidauthority.com/apple-a10-fusion-chip -performance-723918/; V. Savov, "The iPhone's New Chip Should Worry Intel," *The Verge*, September 16, 2016, accessed March 26, 2017, http://www .theverge.com/2016/9/16/12939310 /iphone-7-a10 -fusion-processor-apple-intel-future.

7. S. Cheney, "On Apple's Insurmountable Platform Advantage," *Steve Cheney - Technology, Business & Strategy*, October 10, 2015, accessed March 26, 2017, http://stevecheney.com/on-apples -incredible-platform-advantage/.

8. "U.S. Market Reach of the Most Popular iPhone Apps in March 2012," Statista, accessed April 20, 2016, http://www.statista.com/statistics/243757/us -market-reach-of-the-most-popular-iphone-app/.

9. N. Carlson, "Apple Has ~7,000 Fewer People Working On Maps Than Google," *Business Insider*, September 21, 2012, accessed April 20, 2016, http: //www.businessinsider.com/apple-has-7000-fewer -people-working-on-maps-than-google-2012 -9?op=1.

10. D. Goldman, "Apple CEO: 'We are extremely sorry' for Maps Frustration," *CNN Money*, September 28, 2012, accessed April 20, 2016, http: //money .cnn.com/2012/09/28/technology/apple -maps-apology /index.html.

11. P. Elmer-DeWitt, "How Apple Maps Overtook Google Maps," *Fortune*, June 16, 2015, accessed April 20, 2016, http://fortune.com/2015/06/16 /apple-google-maps-ios/.

12. S. Hart and C. Banbury, "How Strategy -Making Processes Can Make a Difference," *Strategic Management Journal* 15 (1994): 251–269.

13. R. A. Burgelman, "Fading Memories: A Process Theory of Strategic Business Exit in Dynamic Environments," *Administrative Science Quarterly* 39 (1994): 24–56; R. A. Burgelman and A. S. Grove, "Strategic Dissonance," *California Management Review* 38 (Winter 1996): 8–28.

14. "U.S. Computer and Video Game Sales -Digital vs. Physical 2015," Statista, accessed March 26, 2017, https://www-statista-com.ezproxy.butler. edu/statistics/190225/digital-and-physical-game-sales -in-the-us-since-2009/.

15. A. Kharpal, "Mobile Game Revenue to Pass Console, PC for First Time," CNBC, April 22, 2016, accessed March 26, 2017, http://www.cnbc .com/2016/04/22/mobile-game-revenue-to-pass -console-pc-for-first-time.html.

16. D. Gallagher, "Nintendo Switch May Not Flip GameStop's Prospects," March 24, 2017, accessed March 26, 2017, *WSJ*, https://www.wsj.com /articles/nintendo-switch-may-not-flip-gamestops -prospects-1490376229; M. Armental, "GameStop Closing at Least 150 Stores Amid Sales Decline," *Wall Street Journal*, March 23, 2017, accessed March 26, 2017, https://www.wsj.com/articles /gamestop-closing-at-least-150-stores-amid-sales -declines-1490305703.

17. R. A. Burgelman and A. S. Grove, "Strategic Dissonance," *California Management Review* 38 (Winter 1996): 8–28.

18. D. Wakabayashi & N. Wingfield, "Google, Lagging Amazon, Races Across the Threshold Into the Home," *New York Times*, October 2, 2016, accessed March 26, 2017, https://www.nytimes .com/2016/10/03 /technology /google -lagging -amazon-races-across-the-threshold -into-the -home.html.

19. Ibid.

20. R. Wall, "Airbus Cuts A380 Production Plans in 2017," *Wall Street Journal*, December 27, 2016, accessed March 26, 2017, *WSJ*, https://www.wsj .com/articles/airbus-cuts-a380-production-plans -in-2017-1482860279.

21. A. Fiegenbaum, S. Hart, and D. Schendel, "Strategic Reference Point Theory," *Strategic Management Journal* 17 (1996): 219–235.

22. S. Salomon, "'Consumer Reports' Names the 10 Best (and Worst) Cars of 2016," *Boston.com*, March 17, 2016, accessed April 25, 2016, http://www.boston.com/cars/news-and -reviews/2016/03/17/consumer-reports -names-the-best-and-worst-cars /arJvxL2UNGXRyRH2Qxt2AI/story.html.

23. K. Yakal, "The Best Online Tax Preparation Software for 2016," *PC Magazine*, March 4, 2016, accessed April 25, 2016, http://www.pcmag.com /article2/0,2817,2498447,00.asp.

24. S. Pettypiece, "Wal-Mart Loses Everyday Low Price Edge as Aldi Opens Across U.S." *Bloomberg*, March 22, 2016, accessed March 28, 2017, https: //www.bloomberg.com/news/articles /2016-03-22/wal -mart-loses-everyday-low -price-edge-as-aldi-opens -across-u-s; L. Patton, "Aldi Grocery Chain Tries High-End Food and Discounts, Too," *Bloomberg*, August 6, 2015, accessed March 28, 2017, https://www.bloomberg.com/news /articles/2015-08-06 /aldi-grocery-chain-tries-high -end-food-and -discounts-too.

25. A. Fiegenbaum and H. Thomas, "Strategic Groups as Reference Groups: Theory, Modeling and Empirical Examination of Industry and Competitive Strategy," *Strategic Management Journal* 16 (1995): 461–476.

26. "Home Improvement Market Expects Growth of 5.9% in 2016," Home Improvement Research Institute, March 6, 2017, accessed March 28, 2017, https://www.hiri.org/news/334015/Home -Improvement-Market-Expects-Growth-of-5.9 -in-2016.htm.

27. R. K. Reger and A. S. Huff, "Strategic Groups: A Cognitive Perspective," *Strategic Management Journal* 14 (1993): 103–124.

28. "Home Depot At-A-Glance," Home Depot, accessed March 28, 2017, https: //corporate. homedepot.com/sites/default/files /newsroom_ presskit_02_21_2017.pdf; "Lowe's Reports Fourth Quarter Sales And Earnings Results," Lowe's, March 1, 2017, accessed March 28,2017,https: //newsroom .lowes.com/news-releases /lowesreportsfourthquater -salesandearningsresults-3/.

29. "About Ace Hardware," Ace Corporate, accessed March 28, 2017, https://www.myace .com/invest/about-ace.

30. "About Aubuchon Hardware," Aubuchon Hardware, accessed March 28, 2017, https://www .hardwarestore.com/about-us.

31. "Frequently Asked Questions," Ace Hardware, accessed July 29, 2008, http://www .acehardware.com/corp/index.jsp?page=faq; "Company History: 2010s," Ace Hardware, accessed June 5, 2014, http://www.acehardware .com/category/index.jsp?categoryId=34641526.

32. "History of 84 Lumber," accessed March 28, 2017, http://www.84lumber.com/About/History.aspx.

33. C. Morran, "Here Is Comcast's 10-Point Action Plan For Winning Over Customers," Consumerist, May 6, 2015, accessed March 28, 2017, https: //consumerist.com/2015/05/06/here-is-comcasts-10 -point-action-plan-for-winning-over-customers/.

34. S. Ramachandran, "Comcast Results Show Cable's Comeback," *Wall Street Journal*, February 3, 2016, accessed March 28, 2017, https://www.wsj .com/articles/comcast-profit-buoyed-by-growth-in -video-and-broadband-subscribers-1454500891.

35. C. Morran, "Here Is Comcast's 10-Point Action Plan For Winning Over Customers."

36. R. Blumenstein, "How IBM Plans to Thrive as a Digital Company," *Wall Street Journal*, October 27, 2015, R3.

37. "Vision," Dr. Pepper Snapple Group, accessed April 25, 2016, http://www.drpeppersnapplegroup .com/company/vision/.

38. M. Lubatkin, "Value-Creating Mergers: Fact or Folklore?" *Academy of Management Executive* 2 (1988): 295–302; M. Lubatkin and S. Chatterjee, "Extending Modern Portfolio Theory Into the Domain of Corporate Diversification: Does It Apply?" *Academy of Management Journal* 37 (1994): 109–136; M. H. Lubatkin and P. J. Lane, "Psst ... The Merger Mavens Still Have It Wrong!" *Academy of Management Executive* 10 (1996): 21–39.

39. "Science Applied to Life, Annual Report 2016," *3M*, accessed March 29, 2017, http://s2.q4cdn .com/974527301/files/doc_downloads/2017 /Annual/2016_3M_Annual_Report.pdf.

40. P. Morris, "Why Warren Buffett Just Bought Duracell," *Money*, November 14, 2014, accessed April 28, 2015, http://time.com/money/3585592 /warren-buffett-duracell/; P. Ziobro and E. Byron, "P7G to Unload Duracell as CEO Lafley Focuses on Best Sellers," *Wall Street Journal*, October 14, 2014, accessed April 28, 2015, http://online.wsj.com /articles/p-g-to-exit-duracell-battery-ops-1414149781; "Mars to Buy Most of P&G's Pet Food Business for

$2.9 Billion," *Reuters.com*, April 9, 2014, accessed April 28, 2015, http://uk.reuters.com /article/2014/04/09/uk-mars-pgpetcare-acquisition -idUKBREA3813B20140409.

41. C. Alessis, "Germany's Merck Builds Up Non -Drug Businesses," *Wall Street Journal*, August 25, 2016, accessed March 29, 2017, https://www.wsj .com/articles/germanys-merck-builds-up-non-drug -businesses-1472117402.

42. M. Reeves, S. Moose, and T. Venema, "BCG Classics Revisited: The Growth Share Matrix," *BCG Perspectives*, June 4, 2014, accessed April 25, 2016, https://www.bcgperspectives.com/content/articles /corporate_strategy_portfolio_management _strategic_planning_growth_share_matrix_bcg _classics_revisited/.

43. M. Lubatkin & P.J. Lane, "Psst! . . . The Merger Mavens Still Have it Wrong,"*Academy of Management Executive* 10 (1996) 21–39; L. Palich, L. Cardinal & C. Miller, "Curvilinearity in the Diversification–Performance Linkage: An Examination of Over Three Decades of Research," *Strategic Management Journal* 21 (2000): 155-174; G. Ahuja & E. Novelli, "Redirecting Research Efforts on the Diversification-Performance Linkage: The Search for Synergy," *Academy of Management Annals* v. 11 no. 1 (2017): 342-390.

44. D. Hambrick, I. MacMillan, and D. Day, "Strategic Attributes and Performance in the BCG Matrix—A PIMS-based Analysis of Industrial Product Businesses," *Academy of Management Journal* 25 (1982): 510–531.

45. J. Armstrong and R. Brodie, "Effects of Portfolio Planning Methods on Decision Making: Experimental Results," *International Journal of Research in Marketing* 11 (1994): 73–84.

46. M. Rogowsky, "Microsoft Office: Could the Cash Cow's Long-Awaited Death Finally Be Imminent," *Forbes*, May 5, 2014, accessed April 28, 2015, http: //www.forbes.com/sites/markrogowsky/2014/05/05 /microsoft-office-could-the-cash-cows-long-awaited -death-finally-be-imminent/.

47. "Up-to-Date Program for Pages, Numbers, and Keynote," *Apple*, accessed April 28, 2015, https://www.apple.com/creativity-apps/mac/up-to -date/; T. Green, "What did Microsoft's Earnings Reveal about Its Biggest Cash Cow?" *The Motley Fool*, April 30, 2014, accessed April 28, 2015, http://www.fool.com/investing/general/2014/04/30 /microsofts-stellar-quarter-was-driven-by -office.aspx.

48. S. Ovide, "Microsoft Outperforms Its Low Growth Expectations," *Wall Street Journal*, April 24, 2015, B4.

49. J. A. Pearce II, "Selecting Among Alternative Grand Strategies," *California Management Review* (Spring 1982): 23–31.

50. Associated Press, "Marriott Buys Starwood, Becoming World's Largest Hotel Chain," CNBC, September 23, 2016, accessed March 29, 2017, http://www.cnbc.com/2016/09/23/marriott-buys -starwood-becoming-worlds-largest-hotel-chain .html.

51. A. Bhattaria, "'Size Matters': Marriott to Buy Starwood, Creating the World's Largest Hotel Company," *Washington Post*, November 16, 2015, accessed March 29, 2017,https://www.washingtonpost. com/business/capitalbusiness/marriott-to-buy -starwood-creating-the-worlds-largest-hotel -company/2015/11/16/acb40a20-8c6f-11e5 -acff-673ae92ddd2b_story.html?utm_term=. e8bc5773d6b5.

52. G. Bensinger, "Amazon Plans Hundreds of Brick-and-Mortar Bookstores, Mall CEO Says," *Wall Street Journal*, February 2, 2016, B1; H. Tabuchi, "Amazon Challenges Etsy with Strictly Handmade Marketplace," *New York Times*, October 8, 2015, B3.

53. "Vanguard Reports Lower Expense Ratios Resulting in Nearly $75 Million in Savings for Clients," Vanguard, January 28, 2016, accessed March 30, 2017, https://pressroom.vanguard.com /news/Vanguard_reports_lower_expense_ratios _saving_75_million_for_clients_012816.html; "Benefits of Lower Costs at Vanguard," Vanguard, accessed March 30, 2017, https://about.vanguard. com/what-sets-vanguard-apart/the-benefits-of-lower -costs/; "Why Ownership Matters at Vanguard," Vanguard, accessed March 30, 2017, https://about .vanguard.com/what-sets-vanguard-apart/why -ownership-matters/.

54. J. A. Pearce II, "Retrenchment Remains the Foundation of Business Turnaround," *Strategic Management Journal* 15 (1994): 407–417.

55. L. Johnson, "Here's a Timeline of Yahoo's 22 -Year History as a Digital Pioneer," *Adweek*, July 25, 2016, accessed March 30, 2017, http://www .adweek.com/digital/heres-timeline-yahoo-s-22-year -history-digital-pioneer-172663/.

56. S. Austin, "Yahoo Writes Down Tumblr's Value by $230 Million," *Wall Street Journal*, February 2, 2016, accessed March 30, 2017, http://blogs.wsj .com/digits/2016/02/02/yahoo-writes-down -tumblrs-value-by-230-million/; V. Goel & M. de la Merced, "Yahoo's Sale to Verizon Ends an Era for a Web Pioneer," *New York Times*, July 24, 2016, accessed March 30, 2017, https://www .nytimes.com/2016/07/25/business/yahoo-sale.html; D. MacMillan, "Yahoo Cuts Digital Magazines, Closes Burbank, Calif., Office," *Wall Street Journal*, February 17, 2016, accessed March 30, 2017, https: //www.wsj.com/articles/yahoo-cuts-digital -magazines-closes-burbank-calif-office-1455753291; D. MacMillan & D. Mattiolo, "Yahoo to Cut 15% of Workforce, Explore Strategic Options," *Wall Street Journal*, February 2, 2016, accessed March 30, 2017, https://www.wsj.com/articles/yahoo-plans -to-say-it-is-exploring-strategic -options-1454444977. C. Smith, "After Verizon Acquires Yahoo, 'Altaba' Will Be Left Behind," BGR, January 10, 2017, accessed March 30, 2017, http://bgr.com/2017/01/10/verizon-yahoo -purchase-altaba/.

57. J. Jargon, "McDonald's Gets Some Sizzle Back," *Wall Street Journal*, October 23, 2015, B1.

58. J. Jargon, "McDonald's Profit Climbs, Showing Turnaround Is Sustainable," *Wall Street Journal*, April 22, 2016, accessed April 25, 2016, http://www .wsj.com/articles/mcdonalds-profit-climbs-above -expectations-1461327646.

59. M. Ramsey, "Tesla Is Hiring Fast as Rivals Loom," *Wall Street Journal*, December 29, 2015, B1; M. Ramsey, "Tesla Rival Plans $1 Billion Plant," *Wall Street Journal*, November 6, 2015, B6; D. Wakabayashi and M. Ramsey, "Apple Secretly Gears Up to Create Car," *Wall Street Journal*, February 14–16, 2015, A1; "Best Cars: 2015 Tesla Model S," *U.S. News and World Report*, April 25, 2016, http://usnews.rankingsandreviews.com/cars -trucks/Tesla_Model-S/.

60. L. Ellis and L. Stevens, "UPS Tries On 3-D Printing in Bet to Stem New Threat," *Wall Street Journal*, September 19–20, 2015, B1.

61. Ibid.

62. D. Leonard, "Will Amazon Kill FedEx?" *BloombergBusinessweek*, August 31, 2016, accessed March 30, 2017, https://www.bloomberg.com /features/2016-amazon-delivery/.

63. G. Bensinger & L. Stevens, "Amazon's Newest Ambition: Competing Directly With UPS and FedEx," *Wall Street Journal*, September 27, 2016, accessed March 30, 2017, https://www.wsj.com /articles/amazons-newest-ambitioncompeting -directly-with-ups-and-fedex-1474994758; D. Leonard, "Will Amazon Kill FedEx?" *BloombergBusinessweek*, August 31, 2016, https: //www.bloomberg.com/features/2016-amazon -delivery/.

64. D. Sax, "A $99.99 Surfboard Upends the Industry," *Bloomberg Businessweek*, October 29, 2015, April 26, 2016, http://www.bloomberg.com /news/articles/2015-10-29/wavestorm-s-99-99 -surfboard-upends-the-industry.

65. Ibid.

66. D. Hardawar, "Kindle Oasis review: The Perfect E-Reader for the 1 Percent," Engadget, May 2, 2016, accessed March 30, 2017, https: //www.engadget.com/2016/05/02/amazon-kindle -oasis-review/.

67. J. Perlow, "With Kindle Oasis, Amazon's Apple Moment Arrives," ZDNet, April 14, 2016, accessed March 30, 2017, http://www.zdnet.com/article/with -kindle-oasis-amazons-apple-moment-arrives/.

68. J. Snell, "Which Kindle Should You Buy?" Six Colors, July 15, 2016, accessed March 30, 2017, https://sixcolors.com/post/2016/07/which-kindle -should-you-buy/.

69. G. Smith, "HGTV Will Never Upset You: How the Network Beat CNN in 2016," *Bloomberg*, December 28, 2016, accessed March 30, 2017, https: //www.bloomberg.com/news/articles/2016-12-28 /hgtv-will-never-upset-you-how -the-network-beat -cnn-in-2016.

70. R. E. Miles and C. C. Snow, *Organizational Strategy, Structure, & Process* (New York: McGraw -Hill, 1978); S. Zahra and J. A. Pearce, "Research Evidence on the Miles-Snow Typology," *Journal of Management* 16 (1990): 751–768; W. L. James and K. J. Hatten, "Further Evidence on the Validity of the Self Typing Paragraph Approach: Miles and Snow Strategic Archetypes in Banking," *Strategic Management Journal* 16 (1995): 161–168.

71. W. Boston, "Porsche Tries to Remain Exclusive as Luxury Demand Surges," *Wall Street Journal*, March 17, 2015, http://www.wsj.com/articles /porsche-tries-to-keep-itself-exclusive-as-luxury -demand-surges-1426591087.

72. S. Frier, "Facebook Mimics Snapchat Stories In Its Main Application, Copying Snap for a Fourth Time," *Bloomberg*, March 28, 2017, accessed March 31, 2017, https://www.bloomberg.com/news /articles/2017-03-28/facebook-mimics-snapchat -stories-in-its-main-application-copying-snap-for-a -fourth-time; C. Newton, "Facebook Launches Stories to Complete Its All-Out Assault on Snapchat," *The Verge*, March 28, 2017, accessed March 31, 2017, http://www.theverge .com/2017/3/28/15081398/facebook-stories -snapchat-camera-direct; D. Seetharaman, "Facebook, Eye on Snapchat, Adds Camera Features," *Wall Street Journal*, March 28, 2017, accessed March 31, 2017, Facebook launches stories to complete its all-out assault on Snapchathttps://www.wsj.com/articles/facebook -eye-on-snapchat-adds-camera-features- 1490702404.

73. W. Boston, "In Luxury Race, Profits Get Dented," *Wall Street Journal*, March 13, 2015, B1.

74. M. Chen, "Competitor Analysis and Interfirm Rivalry: Toward a Theoretical Integration," *Academy of Management Review* 21 (1996): 100–134; J. C. Baum and H. J. Korn, "Competitive Dynamics of Interfirm Rivalry," *Academy of Management Journal* 39 (1996): 255–291.

75. M. Chen, "Competitor Analysis and Interfirm Rivalry: Toward a Theoretical Integration," *Academy of Management Review* 21 (1996): 100–124.

76. J. Jargon, "McDonald's Decides to Embrace Fast-Food Identity," *Wall Street Journal*, March 1, 2017, accessed March 31, 2017, https://www.wsj.com/articles/mcdonalds-to-expand-mobile-delivery-as-it-plots-future-1488390702; K. Samuelson, "McDonald's to Test UberEATS Delivery Service in Three Florida Cities," *Fortune*, December 16, 2016, accessed March 31, 2017, http://fortune.com/2016/12/16/mcdonalds-delivery-service-florida-cities/.

77. J. White, "Wendy's Wendy Gets a Makeover," *Wall Street Journal*, October 11, 2012, accessed June 5, 2014. http://blogs.wsj.com/corporate-intelligence/2012/10/11/wendy/?KEYWORDS=wendy%27s+strategy.

78. "Wendy's Plans to Double Pace of Image Activation Reimages in 2014," *Yahoo! Finance*, February 27, 2014, accessed June 5, 2014, http://finance.yahoo.com/news/wendys-plans-double-pace-image-123613973.html.

79. J. Jargon, "McDonald's to Switch to Fresh Beef in Quarter Pounders," *Wall Street Journal*, March 30, 2017, accessed March 31, 2017, https://www.wsj.com/articles/mcdonalds-to-switch-to-fresh-beef-in-quarter-pounders-1490878800; R. Leadem, "Wendy's Trolls McDonald's Over Its Fresh Beef Announcement," *Entrepreneur*, March 31, 2017, accessed March 31, 2017, https://www.entrepreneur.com/article/292265.

80. L. Lavelle, "The Chickens Come Home to Roost, and Boston Market Is Prepared to Expand," *The Record*, October 6, 1996.

81. "2017 Franchise 500—Subway," *Entrepreneur*, accessed March 31, 2017, http://www.entrepreneur.com/franchises/subway/282839; "2017 Franchise 500—McDonald's," *Entrepreneur*, accessed March 31, 2017, https://www.entrepreneur.com/franchises/mcdonalds/282570; "Discover McDonald's Around the Globe," McDonald's, accessed March 31, 2017, http://corporate.mcdonalds.com/mcd/country/map.html.

82. "Our People, Our Communities: Heart Health & Childhood Obesity," *Subway*, accessed April 26, 2016, http://www.subway.com/subwayroot/about_us/Social_Responsibility/OurPeopleOurCommunities.aspx#joy.

83. S. Bertoni, "Razor Wars: Harry's Raises $75 Million to Fight Gillette and Dollar Shave Club," *Forbes*, July 7, 2015, accessed March 9, 2016 http://www.forbes.com/sites/stevenbertoni/2015/07/07/razor-wars-harrys-raises-75-million-to-fight-gillette-and-dollar-shave-club/2/#5ff774d832c9; S. Ng and P. Ziobro, "Razor Sales Move Online, Away from Gillette," *Wall Street Journal*, June 23, 2015, B1.

84. S. Terlep & K. Safdar, "Online Upstart Harry's Razor Jumps Into Gillette's Turf," *Wall Street Journal*, November 9, 2016, accessed March 31, 2017, https://www.wsj.com/articles/online-upstart-harrys-razor-jumps-into-gillettes-turf-1478707250.

85. D. Ketchen Jr., C. Snow, and V. Street, "Improving Firm Performance by Matching Strategic Decision—Making Process to Competitive Dynamics," *Academy of Management Executive* 18 (2004) 29–43.

86. D. Harwell, "Razor Lawsuit: Gillette Takes on Online Service," *New Zealand Herald*, December 21, 2016, accessed April 26, 2016, http://www.nzherald.co.nz/business/news/article.cfm?c_id=3&objectid=11564163; S. Terlep & K. Safdar, "Online Upstart Harry's Razor Jumps Into Gillette's Turf," *Wall Street Journal*, November 9, 2016, accessed March 31, 2017, https://www.wsj.com/articles/online-upstart-harrys-razor-jumps-into-gillettes-turf-1478707250.

87. M. Gottfried, "T-Mobile's Shine Dims Sprint's Deal Hopes," *Wall Street Journal*, March 1, 2014, B14.

88. "Investor Factbook: Q4 and Full-Year 2016," T-Mobile, accessed March 31, 2017, http://investor.t-mobile.com/Cache/1001220063.PDF?O=PDF&T=&Y=&D=&FID=1001220063&iid=4091145; "US Wireless Carrier Market Share 2016," Statista, accessed March 31, 2017, https://www-statista-com.ezproxy.butler.edu/statistics/199359/market-share-of-wireless-carriers-in-the-us-by-subscriptions/; R. Karpinski, "Un-Carrier at Three Years: Assessing T-Mobile's Disruptive Impact," 451 Research, March 28, 2016, accessed April 26, 2016, https://newsroom.t-mobile.com/content/1020/files/NEWImpactReport.pdf.

89. "Investor Factbook: Q4 and Full-Year 2016," T-Mobile, accessed March 31, 2017, http://investor.t-mobile.com/Cache/1001220063.PDF?O=PDF&T=&Y=&D=&FID=1001220063&iid=4091145."US Wireless Carrier Market Share 2016," Statista, accessed March 31, 2017, https://www-statista-com.ezproxy.butler.edu/statistics/199359/market-share-of-wireless-carriers-in-the-us-by-subscriptions/; "Now More Than 100 Services Stream Free with T-Mobile's Binge On and Music Freedom," *T-Mobile*, April 5, 2016, accessed April 26, 2016, https://newsroom.t-mobile.com/news-and-blogs/binge-on-music-freedom-new-services.htm; "T-Mobile Introduces 'Mobile without Borders': Extends Coverage & Calling Across North America at No Extra Charge," T-Mobile, July 9, 2015, accessed April 26, 2016, https://newsroom.t-mobile.com/media-kits/mobile-without-borders.htm; M. Gottfried, "T-Mobile Takes Toll on Verizon," *Wall Street Journal*, April 25, 2014, C8; E. Mason, "T-Mobile's Loss Widens as Costs Press Higher," *Wall Street Journal*, February 26, 2014, B4; T Gryta and B. Rubin, "T-Mobile Posts Big Gain in Subscribers," *Wall Street Journal*, May 1, 2014, accessed June 26, 2014, http://www.wsj.com/articles/SB10001424052702304677904579535291254065308; Z. Epstein, "The Most Important Wireless Carrier in America," *BGR*, October 10, 2013, accessed June 26, 2014, http://bgr.com/2013/10/10/t-mobile-free-international-roaming-analysis/; T. Gryta, "T-Mobile will Waive Data Fees for Music Services," *Wall Street Journal*, June 18, 2014, accessed June 26, 2014, http://online.wsj.com/articles/t-mobile-will-waive-data-fees-for-music-service-1403142678.

90. R. Wall and J. Chow, "Europe's Top Airlines to Spend Billions in Battle to Win Back Passengers," *Wall Street Journal*, June 4, 2015, accessed April 26, 2016, http://www.wsj.com/articles/europes-top-airlines-to-spend-billions-in-battle-to-win-back-passengers-1433425762.

91. Ibid.

92. S. Nassauer & L. Stevens, "Star Shower Price War Shakes Up Retailers," *Wall Street Journal*, December 14, 2016, accessed April 1, 2017, https://www.wsj.com/articles/star-shower-price-war-shakes-up-retailers-1481657498.

93. J. Del Rey, "Amazon and Walmart are in an All-Out Price War that is Terrifying America's Biggest Brands," *Recode*, March 30, 2017, accessed April 1, 2017, https://www.recode.net/2017/3/30/14831602/amazon-walmart-cpg-grocery-price-war.

94. Ibid.

7

1. T. Randall, "Inside the Connected Future of Architecture," *Bloomberg Businessweek*, September 23, 2015, 72–77.

2. P. Anderson and M. L. Tushman, "Managing Through Cycles of Technological Change," *Research/Technology Management* 34(3) (May–June 1991): 26–31.

3. R. N. Foster, *Innovation: The Attacker's Advantage* (New York: Summit, 1986).

4. "The Silicon Engine: A Timeline of Semiconductors in Computers," *Computer History Museum*, accessed April 22, 2001, http://www.computerhistory.org/semi-conductor/; "Transistor Count," *Wikipedia*, March 3, 2017, accessed April 2, 2017, https://en.wikipedia.org/wiki/Transistor_count; T. Smith, "Inside Intel's Haswell: What do 1.4 BEELION Transistors Get You?" *The Register*, June 3, 2013, accessed June 13, 2014, http://www.theregister.co.uk/2013/06/03/feature_inside_haswell_intel_4g_core/; P. Alcorn, "Intel Xeon E5-2600 v4 Broadwell-EP Review," *Tom's Hardware*, March 31, 2016, accessed May 12, 2016, http://www.tomshardware.com/reviews/intel-xeon-e5-2600-v4-broadwell-ep,4514-2.html.

5. J. Burke, *The Day the Universe Changed* (Boston: Little, Brown, 1985).

6. "Total Shipments of Digital Still Cameras (Classified by Type)," Camera & Imaging Products Association, www.cipa.jp/stats/documents/common/cr300.pdf.

7. D. Wakabayashi, "The Point-and-Shoot Camera Faces Its Existential Moment," *Wall Street Journal*, July 30, 2013, accessed June 30, 2014, http://online.wsj.com/news/articles/SB10001424127887324251504578580263719432252.

8. J. Osawa, "Phones Imperil Fancy Cameras," *Wall Street Journal*, November 7, 2013, accessed June 13, 2014, http://online.wsj.com/news/articles/SB10001424052702304672404579183643696236868?KEYWORDS=high-end+camera&mg=reno64-wsj.

9. L. Hutchinson, "Shootout Redux: Smartphone Camera vs Tricked-out DSLR, One Year Later," *Ars Technica*, January 31, 2016, accessed April 2, 2017, https://arstechnica.com/gadgets/2016/01/shootout-redux-smartphone-camera-vs-tricked-out-dslr-one-year-later/; E. Kypreos, "iPhone 7 Plus review – Camera," *Trusted Reviews*, February 2, 2017, accessed April 2, 2017, http://www.technologyreview.com/iphone-7-plus-review-camera-page-3.

10. M. L. Tushman, P. C. Anderson, and C. O'Reilly, "Technology Cycles, Innovation Streams, and Ambidextrous Organizations: Organization Renewal Through Innovation Streams and Strategic Change," in *Managing Strategic Innovation and Change*, ed. M. L. Tushman and P. Anderson (New York: Oxford Press, 1997), 3–23.

11. L. Grush, "Magnetically Levitating Elevators Could Reshape Skylines—They Go Up, Down, and All Around," *Popular Science*, April 14, 2015, accessed April 26, 2015, http://www.popsci.com/elevator-will-reshape-skylines; "ThyssenKrupp Develops the World's First Rope-Free Elevator System to Enable the Building Industry to Face the Challenges of Global Urbanization," *ThyssenKrupp*, November 27, 2014, accessed May 4, 2015, http://www.thyssenkrupp-elevator.com/Show-article.104.0.html?&L=1&cHash=08b38cb686f00ec874ad82c44c737427&tx_ttnews%5Btt_news%5D=546.

12. S. J. Blumberg and J. V. Luke, "Wireless Substitution: Early Release of Estimates from the National Health Interview Survey, July–December 2015," U.S. Department of Health and Human Services, Centers for Disease Control and Prevention, May 2016, accessed April 3, 2017, https://www.cdc.gov/nchs/data/nhis/earlyrelease/wireless201605.pdf.

13. Staff, "Landline Phone Penetration Dwindles as Cell-Only Households Grow," *Marketing Charts*, June 6, 2012, accessed June 2, 2013, http://www.marketingcharts.com/direct/landline-phone-penetra-tion-dwindles-as-cell-only-households-grow-22577/.

14. Blumberg and Luke, "Wireless Substitution."

15. "AT&T, Verizon Are Leaving Landlines Behind," *Wall Street Journal News Hub*, online video, 17:27, April 8, 2014, accessed June 13, 2014, http://live.wsj .com/video/att-verizon-are-leaving -landlines-behind/7874152B-A635-4092-9B7B -69EB86AE3787.html?KEYWORDS=milestone s#!7874152B-A635-4092-9B7B-69EB86AE3787; R. Knutson, "Verizon Union Says Company Is Not Fixing Landline Phones," *Wall Street Journal*, June 10, 2015, B3.

16. R. Knutson, "Who Needs a Wireless Carrier? Go Wi-Fi Only," *Wall Street Journal*, March 2, 2015, B1.

17. E. Schlossberg, *Interactive Excellence: Defining and Developing New Standards for the Twenty-First Century* (New York: Ballantine, 1998).

18. W. Abernathy and J. Utterback, "Patterns of Industrial Innovation," *Technology Review* 2 (1978): 40–47.

19. R. Triggs, "Wireless Charging Technology: What You Need to Know," *Android Authority*, January 11, 2017, accessed April 3, 2017, http: //www.androidauthority.com/wireless-charging -qi-pad-technology-580015/.

20. "Revenue of the Wireless Power Market Worldwide from 2014 to 2024 (in Billion U.S. dollars)°" Statista, 2017, accessed April 3, 2017, https://www -statista-com.ezproxy.butler.edu/statis -tics/681398/wireless-power-market-size-world-wide/.

21. C. Reichert, "5G standards Updated Ahead of Industry Freeze," *ZDNet*, February 26, 2017, accessed April 3, 2017, http://www.zdnet.com /article/5g-standards-updated-ahead-of-industry -freeze/.

22. T. Gryta, "Wireless Players Tout 5G as They Await Next Smartphone Wave," *Wall Street Journal*, February 26, 2017, accessed April 3, 2017, https: //www.wsj.com/articles/wireless-players-tout-5g-as -they-await-next-smartphone-wave-1488024006.

23. M. Schilling, "Technological Lockout: An Integrative Model of the Economic and Strategic Factors Driving Technology Success and Failure," *Academy of Management Review* 23 (1998): 267–284; M. Schilling, "Technology Success and Failure in Winner-Take-All Markets: The Impact of Learning Orientation, Timing, and Network Externalities," *Academy of Management Journal* 45 (2002): 387–398.

24. R. McMillan, "Tech World Prepares Obituary for Adobe Flash," *Wall Street Journal*, July 20, 2015, B1.

25. "Chromium Blog: Roll-out plan for HTML5 by Default," *Chromium Blog*, December 9, 2016, accessed April 3, 2017, https://blog.chromium. org/2016/12/roll-out-plan-for-html5-by-default. html.

26. N. Tadena, "Agencies Ready for the Move Away From Flash Ad—CMO Today," *Wall Street Journal*, September 14, 2015, accessed April 3, 2017, http: //blogs.wsj.com/cmo/2015/09/14/agen -cies-ready-for -the-move-away-from-flash-ads/.

27. "Usage Statistics of Flash for Websites," *W³Techs*, April 3, 2017, accessed April 3, 2017, https://w3techs.com/technologies/details/cp-flash /all/all.

28. T. M. Amabile, R. Conti, H. Coon, J. Lazenby, and M. Herron, "Assessing the Work Environment for Creativity," *Academy of Management Journal* 39 (1996): 1154–1184.

29. Ibid.

30. M. Csikszentmihalyi, *Flow: The Psychology of Optimal Experience* (New York: Harper & Row, 1990).

31. R. Feintzeig, "Can Furniture Help Workers Stay Focused?" *Wall Street Journal*, April 22, 2015, B7.

32. R. Silverman, "GE Re-Engineers Perfor -mance Reviews, Pay Practices," *Wall Street Jour -nal*, June 8, 2016, accessed April 3, 2017, https: //www.wsj.com /articles/ge-re-engineers-perfor -mance-reviews-pay -practices-1465358463.

33. C. Dougherty, "They Promised Us Jet Packs. They Promised the Bosses Profit," *New York Times*, July 23, 2016, accessed April 3, 2017, https://www .nytimes.com/2016/07/24/technology /they-promised -us-jet-packs-they-promised-the -bosses -profit.html?_r=0.

34. A. Teller, "More Moonshot Secrets: Making Audacity the Path of Least Resistance," *Back Channel*, April 15, 2016, accessed April 3, 2017, https://backchannel.com/the-head-of-x-explains -how-to-make-audacity-the-path-of-least-resistance -fac53c3338d.

35. A. Ahrendts, "The Experts: How Should Leaders Spur Innovation?" interview by C. Wiens, March 12, 2013, accessed June 13, 2014, http: //online.wsj.com/news/articles/SB100014241278873 2382670457835292147382531 6?mg=reno64 -wsj&url=http%3A%2F%2Fonline.wsj.com%2 Farticle%2FSB10001424127887323826704 578352921473825316.html.

36. R. Tetzeli, "9 Ways GE Executed Its Radical Green Reinvention," *FastCoexist.com*, December 11, 2015, accessed April 27, 2016, http://www. fast-coexist .com/3054441/9-ways-ge-executed-its -radical-green -reinvention.

37. Ibid.

38. T. Higgins, "Distressed Denim: At 162 Years Old, Levi Strauss Confronts the Yoga Pant," *Bloomberg Businessweek*, July 27–August 2, 2015, 48–55.

39. K. M. Eisenhardt, "Accelerating Adaptive Processes: Product Innovation in the Global Computer Industry," *Administrative Science Quarterly* 40 (1995): 84–110.

40. Ibid.

41. M. Belfiore, "Ultrasonic X-rays," *Bloomberg*, July 7, 2016, accessed April 3, 2017, https: //www.bloomberg.com/news /articles/2016-07-07 /ultrasonic-x-rays; "About Us," S-Ray, accessed April 3, 2017, http://s-rayinc.com/about-us/.

42. K. Naughton and J. Green, "Crash Test City," *Bloomberg Businessweek*, April 6–12, 2015, pp. 19–20.

43. Teller, "More Moonshot Secrets: Making Audacity the Path of Least Resistance."

44. M. Gurman and G. De Vynck, "Apple Said to Develop Car Operating System in BlackBerry Country," *Bloomberg*, October 25, 2016, accessed April 4, 2017, https://www.bloomberg.com/news /articles/2016-10-25/apple-develops-car-operating -system-in-blackberry-country; M. Gurman & A. Webb, "How Apple Scaled Back Its Titanic Plan to Take on Detroit," *Bloomberg*, October 17, 2016, accessed April 4, 2017, https://www.bloom -berg.com /news/articles/2016-10-17/how-apple -scaled-back-its -titanic-plan-to-take-on-detroit.

45. D. Gates, "McNerney: No More 'Moonshots' as Boeing Develops New Jets," *The Seattle Times*, May 22, 2014, accessed May 4, 2015, http://www .seattletimes.com/business/mcnerney-no-more -lsquomoonshotsrsquo-as-boeing-develops-new jets/.

46. Ibid.; J. Ostrower, "At Boeing, Innovation Means Small Steps, Not Giant Leap," *Wall Street Journal*, April 3, 2015, B1.

47. L. Kraar, "25 Who Help the US Win: Innovators Everywhere are Generating Ideas to Make America a Stronger Competitor. They Range from a Boss Who Demands the Impossible to a Mathematician with a Mop," *Fortune*, March 22, 1991.

48. M. W. Lawless and P. C. Anderson, "Generational Technological Change: Effects of Innovation and Local Rivalry on Performance," *Academy of Management Journal* 39 (1996): 1185–1217.

49. "USB.org—Hi-Speed FAQ," *USB Implementers Forum*, accessed April 4, 2017, http://www .usb.org/developers/usb20/faq20/; "USB.org—SuperSpeed USB," USB Implementers Forum, accessed April 4, 2017, http://www.usb. org/developers/ssusb/.

50. A. Satariano, "Apple Gets More Bank for Its R&D Buck," *Bloomberg BusinessWeek*, November 30–December 6, 2015, 38–39.

51. "Micromax Unite 4 Plus/Unite 4 Android Smartphone in India," Micromax Mobiles, accessed April 4, 2017, http://www.micromaxinfo.com /mobile -phones/smartphones/canvas-mobiles /unite-4-plus' E. Bellman and J. Jai Krishna, "Churning Out Smartphones Like Fast Fashion," *Wall Street Journal*, June 5, 2015, B1.

52. J. Brustein, "Inside RadioShack's Collapse— How Did the Electronics Retailer Go Broke? Gradually, Then All at Once," *Bloomberg Businessweek*, February 9–15, 2015, 56. "Table 13–AT&T Interstate Residential Tariff Rates for 10-Minute Calls," *The Industry Analysis Division's Reference Book of Rates, Price Indices, and Household Expenditures for Telephone Service*, March 1997, Federal Trade Commission, 69, accessed April 25, 2015, http://transition .fcc. gov/Bureaus/Common_Carrier/Reports/FCC -State_Link/IAD/ref97.pdf.

53. Brustein, "Inside RadioShack's Collapse."

54. P. Strebel, "Choosing the Right Change Path," *California Management Review* 36(2) (Winter 1994): 29–51.

55. E. Steel, "Netflix Refines Its DVD Business, Even as Streaming Unit Booms," *New York Times*, July 27, 2015, B1.

56. D. Fitzgeral and M. Jarzemsky, "Besieged RadioShack Spirals Into Bankruptcy," *Wall Street Journal*, February 6, 2015, accessed May 4, 2015, http://www.wsj.com/articles/SB21810972877477764 69470458044181413975 1730.

57. P. Brickley and D. FitzGerald, "RadioShack Is Dead, Long Live RadioShack," *Wall Street Journal*, April 2, 2015, B1.

58. D. Fitzgerald and R. Knutson, "RadioShack to Seek Bankruptcy Protection, Again," *Wall Street Journal*, March 6, 2017, accessed April 4, 2017, https://www.wsj.com/articles/radioshack-to -seek-bankruptcy-protection-again-1488843485; "Bankruptcy Announcement – RadioShack," General Wireless Operations, March 8, 2017, accessed April 4, 2017, https://www.radioshack. com/pages /bankruptcy-announcement.

59. K. Lewin, *Field Theory in Social Science: Selected Theoretical Papers* (New York: Harper & Brothers, 1951).

60. J. Owen, "Film is Finished–This Could Be Its Last Oscars," *The Independent*, February 24, 2013, accessed June 13, 2014, http://www.independent. co.uk/arts-entertainment /films /news/film-is -fin-ished—this-could-be-its -last-oscars-8508257 .html?printService=print.

61. Lewin, *Field Theory in Social Science*.

62. A. B. Fisher, "Making Change Stick," *Fortune*, April 17, 1995, 121.

63. J. P. Kotter and L. A. Schlesinger, "Choosing Strategies for Change," *Harvard Business Review* (March–April 1979): 106–114.

64. S. Giessner, G. Viki, T. Otten, S. Terry, and D. Tauber, "The Challenge of Merging: Merger Patterns, Premerger Status, and Merger Support," *Personality and Social Psychology Bulletin* 32, no. 3 (2006): 339–352.

65. E. Cassano, "How Vince Donnelly Led PMA Companies Through an Acquisition by Involving Everyone," *Smart Business*, February 1, 2012, accessed March 7, 2012, http://www.sbnonline.com/article/how-vince-donnelly-led-pma-companies-through-an-acquisition-by-involving-everyone/.

66. J. Dean, "Why Digital Transformations Are Hard," *Wall Street Journal*, March 6, 2017, accessed April 4, 2017, https://www.wsj.com/articles/why-digital-transformations-are-hard-1488856200.

67. D. Meinert, "An Open Book," *HR Magazine*, April 2013, 42–46.

68. J. P. Kotter, "Leading Change: Why Transformation Efforts Fail," *Harvard Business Review* 73, no. 2 (March–April 1995): 59.

69. "Nordstrom Company History," Nordstrom, accessed March 23, 2016, http://shop.nordstrom.com/c/company-history.

70. S. Kapner, "Macy's Seeks Answers as Sales Slide," *Wall Street Journal*, November 12, 2015, A1, A14.

71. R. Tetzeli, "9 Ways GE Executed Its Radical Green Reinvention," *FastCoexist.com*, December 11, 2015, accessed March 22, 2016, http://www.fastcoexist.com/3054441/9-ways-ge-executed-its-radical-green-reinvention.

72. Ibid.

73. D. Newcomb, "Ford Eyes its Biggest Car Innovation Since the Model T," *PC Magazine*, December 18, 2015, accessed March 8, 2017, http://www.pcmag.com/article2/0,2817,2496787,00.asp.

74. "Mark Fields" 2015 Consumer Electronics Show," Ford Media Center, January 6, 2015, accessed April 5, 2017, https://media.ford.com/content/dam/fordmedia/North%20America/US/2015/01/06/MarkFieldsCESRemarks.pdf.

75. "Ford Smart Mobility Experiments," Ford Media Center, accessed April 5, 2017, https://media.ford.com/content/dam/fordmedia/North%20America/US/2015/01/07/FordSmart-MobilityMap.pdf.

76. J. Stoll, "Ford CEO Paid $2.5 Million 'Strategic Incentive' Grant for 2016," *Wall Street Journal*, March 31, 2017, accessed April 5, 2017, https://www.wsj.com/articles/ford-ceo-paid-22-1-million-total-compensation-in-2016-up-19-1490966481.

77. S. Cramm, "A Change of Hearts," *CIO*, April 1, 2003, May 20, 2003, http://www.cio.com/archive/040103/hsleadership.html.

78. K. Safdar, "As Gap Struggles, Its Analytical CEO Prizes Data Over Design," *Wall Street Journal*, November 27, 2016, accessed April 5, 2017, https://www.wsj.com/articles/as-gap-struggles-its-analytical-ceo-prizes-data-over-design-1480282911.

79. S. Baker, "Zara's Recipe for Success: More Data, Fewer Bosses," *Bloomberg*, November 23, 2016, accessed April 5, 2017, https://www.bloomberg.com/news/articles/2016-11-23/zara-s-recipe-for-success-more-data-fewer-bosses.

80. R. Clough, "General Electric Wants to Act Like a Startup," *BloombergBusinessweek*, August 11, 2014, pp. 22-24.

81. "General Electric Empowers Employees To Act Like Entrepreneurs," *Business Because*, November 24, 2014, accessed April 5, 2017, http://www.businessbecause.com/news/mba-careers/2933/general-electric-empowers-employees-to-act-like-entrepreneurs.

82. B. Power, "How GE Applies Lean Startup Practices," *Harvard Business Review Digital Articles*, April 23, 2014, pp. 2-4.

83. W. J. Rothwell, R. Sullivan, and G. M. McLean, *Practicing Organizational Development: A Guide for Consultants* (San Diego, CA: Pfeiffer & Co., 1995).

84. Ibid.

8

1. D. Barboza, "An iPhone's Journey, From the Factory Floor to the Retail Store," *New York Times*, December 29, 2016, accessed April 6, 2017, https://www.nytimes.com/2016/12/29/technology/iphone-china-apple-stores.html.

2. S. McLain & A. Tangel, "Harley-Davidson Is Doing Pretty Well Overseas," *Wall Street Journal*, March 1, 2017, accessed April 6, 2017, https://www.wsj.com/articles/trump-puts-spotlight-on-harley-davidsons-overseas-sales-challenges-1488372741; "Facility Locations," Harley-Davidson, , accessed April 6, 2017, http://www.harley-davidson.com/content/h-d/en_US/company/locations.html.

3. "World Investment Report, 2016: Investor Nationality - Policy Challenges," United Nations Conference on Trade and Development, accessed April 6, 2017, http://unctad.org/en/PublicationsLibrary/wir2016_en.pdf; "Web Table 34. Number of Parent Corporations and Foreign Affiliates, by Region and Economy," World Investment Report 2011, United Nations Conference on Trade and Development, accessed April 28, 2016, http://unctad.org/Sections/dite_dir /docs/WIR11_web tab 34.pdf.

4. S. Strom & C. Bray, "A Coffee Empire Grows, as Panera Is Sold to JAB Holding Company," *New York Times*, April 5, 2017, accessed April 6, 2017, https://www.nytimes.com/2017/04/05/business/dealbook/panera-bread-jab-.html.

5. C. Bray & Q. Hardy, "Qualcomm to Acquire NXP Semiconductors for $38.5 Billion," *New York Times*, October 27, 2016, accessed April 6, 2017, https://www.nytimes.com/2016/10/28/business/dealbook/qualcomm-acquire-nxp-semiconductors.html?_r=0.

6. I King, "Qualcomm to Buy NXP Semiconductors in $47 Billion Deal," *Bloomberg*, October 27, 2016, accessed April 6, 2017, https://www.bloomberg.com/news/articles/2016-10-27/qualcomm-to-buy-nxp-semiconductors-for-47-billion-in-cash.

7. T. Moss, C. Dawson & W. Mauldin, "Auto Makers Target China as New U.S. Trade Rules Loom," *Wall Street Journal*," March 22, 2017, accessed April 6, 2017, https://www.wsj.com/articles/auto-makers-target-china-as-new-u-s-trade-rules-loom-1490175002.

8. B. Davis & J. Hilsenrath, "Whatever Happened to Free Trade?" Wall Street Journal, March 29, 2017, accessed April 7, 2017, https://www.wsj.com/articles/whatever-happened-to-free-trade-1490800293.

9. T. Turner & P. Kiernan, "How Latin America Pays the Price of Protectionism," *Wall Street Journal*, November 25, 2016, accessed April 6, 2017, https://www.wsj.com/articles/how-latin-america-pays-the-price-of-protectionism-1480089781.

10. G. Kantchev and E. Ballard, "Ground Shifts under Wheat Export Market," *Wall Street Journal*, February 7, 2016, accessed May 19, 2016, http://www.wsj.com/articles/ground-shifts-under-wheat-export-market-1454754785; "Argentina Cuts Tariffs, Affects Grain Markets," *WHOTV.com*, December 16, 2015, accessed April 8, 2016, http://whotv.com/2015/12/16/argentina-cuts-tariffs-affects-grain-markets/; "Macri Eliminates Argentine Farm Export Taxes on Wheat, Corn," *AgWeb.com*, December 14, 2015, accessed April 8, 2016, http://www.agweb.com/article/macri-eliminates-argentine-farm-export-taxes-on-wheat-corn-blmg/.

11. P. Prengaman, "Argentine President's Decision to Lift Agricultural Export Taxes Puts Country on New Course," *Canada.com*, December 14, 2015, accessed April 8, 2016, http://www.canada.com/business/argentine+president+eliminates+export+taxes+corn+wheat+meat+products/11588534/story.html.

12. L. Lin & E. Schwartzel, "China Lets More Foreign Films Slip In," *Wall Street Journal*, November 2, 2016, accessed April 6, 2017, https://www.wsj.com/articles/china-lets-more-foreign-films-slip-in-1478083587; B. Fritz and L. Burkitt, "Chinese Film Company Takes Role in Hollywood," *Wall Street Journal*, April 20, 2015, B1.

13. Reuters, "Mexico Bows to Brazilian Pressure on Auto Exports," *Reuters*, March 15, 2012, accessed June 8, 2013, http://www.reuters.com/article/2012/03/16/mexico-brazil-autos-idUSL2E8EF3G420120316.

14. "Understanding the WTO," World Trade Organization, accessed April 28, 2016, http://www.wto.org/english/thewto_e/whatis_e/tif_e/agrm9_e.htm.

15. C. Tate, "Dispute Over Europe's Ban on US Beef Could Mean Tariffs on Imports," *McClatchy DC*, December 22, 2016, accessed April 6, 2017, http://www.mcclatchydc.com/news/nation-world/national/economy/article122427524.html.

16. R. Wall & D. Cameron, "EU Failed to Cut Off Illegal Subsidies to Airbus, WTO Rules," *Wall Street Journal*, September 22, 2016, accessed April 6, 2017, https://www.wsj.com/articles/eu-gave-billions-in-illegal-subsidies-to-airbus-wto-rules-1474554683.

17. Ibid.

18. "EU Rapped by WTO for $10bn a Year Airbus Subsidies," BBC News, September 22, 2016, accessed April 6, 2017, http://www.bbc.com/news/business-37444780.

19. T. Shields, "'Costumes or Clothes?' H.R. 3128 Department of Homeland Security Appropriations, 2016," *Bloomberg Businessweek*, October 19–25, 2015, 35.

20. "GATT/WTO," Duke Law: Library & Technology, June 2014, accessed April 7, 2017, https://law.duke.edu/lib/researchguides/gatt/.

21. R. Azevêdo, "WTO Press Conference — Entry into Force of Trade Facilitation Agreement," World Trade Organization, February 27, 2017, accessed April 7, 2017, https://www.wto.org/english/news_e/spra_e/spra157_e.htm.

22. "IFPI Digital Music Report 2015," International Federation of the Phonographic Industry, January 2015, accessed April 28, 2016, http://www.ifpi.org/downloads/Digital-Music-Report-2015.pdf.

23. "Seizing Opportunity Through License Compliance: BSA Global Software Survey," BSA The Software Alliance, May 2016, accessed April 7, 2017, globalstudy.bsa.org/2016/downloads/studies/BSA_GSS_US.pdf.

24. C. Bialik, "Putting a Price Tag on Film Piracy," *Wall Street Journal*, April 5, 2013, accessed June 8, 2013, http://blogs.wsj.com/numbersguy/putting-a-price-tag-on-film-piracy-1228/.

25. "From 6 to 28 members - European Commission," European Union, June 12, 2016, accessed April 7, 2017, https://ec.europa.eu/neighbourhood-enlargement/policy/from-6-to-28-members_en.

26. L. Hughes, K. McCann & G. Rayner, "Theresa May Triggers Article 50 with Warning Over Security as EU Leaders Rule Out Key Brexit Demand," *Telegraph*, March 30, 2017, accessed April 7, 2017, http://www.telegraph.co.uk/news/2017/03/29/article-50-triggered-brexit-eu-theresa-may-watch-live/.

27. M. Villarreal and I. Ferguson, "The North American Free Trade Agreement (NAFTA)," Congressional Research Service, February 22, 2017, accessed April 7, 2017, https://fas.org/sgp/crs/row/R42965.pdf.

28. "CAFTA-DR (Dominican Republic-Central America FTA)," United States Trade Representative, accessed April 7, 2017, https://ustr.gov/trade-agreements/free-trade-agreements/cafta-dr-dominican-republic-central-america-fta; "Trade in Goods with CAFTA-DR," U.S. Census Bureau, accessed April 7, 2017, https://www.census.gov/foreign-trade/balance/c0017.html.

29. "La Región en Cifras: UNASUR: Espacio de Cooperación e Integración para al Desarrollo," accessed April 28, 2016, http://unasursg.org/; "Union of South American Nations - Wikipedia," *Wikipedia*, April 5, 2017, accessed April 7, 2017, https://en.wikipedia.org/wiki/Union_of_South_American_Nations.

30. "Selected Key Basic ASEAN Indicators," ASEANstats, August 2016, accessed April 7, 2017, http://data.aseanstats.org/static/SelectedKey/table1.xls. "Almost $100 Billion of US Goods and Services Exports Go to ASEAN," *US-ASEAN*, September 16, 2016, accessed April 7, 2017, https://www.usasean.org/why-asean/trade.

31. "Almost $100 Billion of US Goods and Services Exports Go to ASEAN," *US-ASEAN*, accessed April 7, 2017, https://www.usasean.org/why-asean/trade; "ASEAN 2025—Forging Ahead Together," *US-ASEAN*, November 2015, accessed April 28, 2016, http://asean.org/?static_post=asean-2025-forging-ahead-together

32. "Trade Raises Living Standards in APEC Region: Report," *Asia-Pacific Economic Cooperation*, accessed April 7, 2017, http://www.apec.org/Press/News-Releases/2016/0331_development.aspx; "StatsAPEC—Data for the Asia-Pacific Region—Economic and Social Statistics & Bilateral Trade and Investment Flows," *StatsAPEC*, accessed April 7, 2017, http://statistics.apec.org/index.php/apec_psu/index.

33. "Member Economies," *Asia Pacific Economic Cooperation*, accessed August 6, 2008, http://www.apec.org/About-Us/About-APEC/Member-Economies.aspx; "Frequently Asked Questions (FAQs)," *Asia-Pacific Economic Cooperation*, accessed August 6, 2008, http://www.apec.org/FAQ.aspx.

34. "African integration: Facing up to Emerging Challenges," Tralac Trade Law Centre, January 9, 2017, accessed April 8, 2017, https://www.tralac.org/news/article/11045-african-integration-facing-up-to-emerging-challenges.html; C. Ligami, "East African Countries to Ratify TFTA Agreement before March," *The East African*, December 20, 2016, accessed April 8, 2017, http://www.theeastafrican.co.ke/business/East-African-countries-to-ratify-TFTA-agreement-before-March/2560-3493016-as7c5xz/index.html.

35. "Gross National Income (GNI) per Capita 2015, Atlas Method and PPP," The World Bank, February 1, 2017, accessed April 8, 2017, http://databank.worldbank.org/data/download/GNIPC.pdf.

36. Ibid.

37. Ibid.

38. "The Global Competitiveness Report: 2016–2017," World Economic Forum, accessed April 8, 2017, http://www3.weforum.org/docs/GCR2016-2017/05FullReport/TheGlobalCompetitivenessReport2016-2017_FINAL.pdf.

39. M. Yamaguchi, "Japan-US Talks on Pacific Trade Accord Get Push from 'Fast-Track' Proposal in US Congress," *US News & World Report*, April 17, 2015, accessed April 28, 2015, http://www.usnews.com/news/business/articles/2015/04/17/trade-talks-in-tokyo-get-push-from-fast-track-deal-in-us; "Commodity Policies," US Department of Agriculture, Economic Research Service, August 7, 2014, accessed April 28, 2015, http://www.ers.usda.gov/topics/international-markets-trade/countries-regions/japan/policy.aspx.

40. J. Furman, "Ten Facts about U.S. Trade," The White House, May 1, 2015, accessed April 8, 2017, https://obamawhitehouse.archives.gov/blog/2015/05/01/ten-facts-about-us-trade; B. Lomborg, "The Free-Trade Miracle," *Project Syndicate*, October 21, 2016, accessed April 8, 2017, https://www.project-syndicate.org/commentary/free-trade-benefits-for-global-poor-by-bjorn-lomborg-2016-10.

41. J. Boak & E. Swanson, "AP-GfK Poll: Americans Prefer Low Prices to Items 'Made in the USA,'" *Associated Press GfK Poll*, April 14, 2016, accessed April 8, 2017, http://ap-gfkpoll.com/featured/ap-gfk-poll-americans-prefer-low-prices-to-items-made-in-the-usa.

42. L. Lockwood, "Ralph's Brazilian Vibe," *WWD*, April 13, 2015, p. 2.

43. S. Ramachandran, "Netflix, Amazon Take Divergent Paths to Reach Indian Audience," *Wall Street Journal*, November 1, 2016, accessed April 8, 2017, https://www.wsj.com/articles/netflix-amazon-take-divergent-paths-to-reach-indian-audience-1477954726.

44. Ibid.

45. S. Pearson & S. Nassauer, "Wal-Mart Doubles Down in Brazil Despite Sluggish Sales," *Wall Street Journal*, March 12, 2017, accessed April 8, 2017, WSJ, https://www.wsj.com/articles/wal-mart-doubles-down-in-brazil-despite-sluggish-sales-1489327201.

46. Ibid.

47. A. Sundaram and J. S. Black, "The Environment and Internal Organization of Multinational Enterprises," *Academy of Management Review* 17 (1992): 729–757.

48. S. Ramachandran, "Netflix, Amazon Take Divergent Paths to Reach Indian Audience," *Wall Street Journal*, November 1, 2016, accessed April 8, 2017, https://www.wsj.com/articles/netflix-amazon-take-divergent-paths-to-reach-indian-audience-1477954726.

49. H. S. James, Jr. and M. Weidenbaum, *When Businesses Cross International Borders: Strategic Alliances & Their Alternatives* (Westport, CT: Praeger Publishers, 1993).

50. Staff Reports, "BMW Reports Record Production Year at Spartanburg Plant, Go Upstate, January 9, 2017, accessed April 8, 2017, http://www.goupstate.com/news/20170109/bmw-reports-record-production-year-at-spartanburg-plant; B. Davis & V. Bauerlien, "South Carolina GOP Voters Feel the Benefits of Free Trade—but Also the Scars," *Wall Street Journal*, February 17, 2016, accessed April 8, 2017, https://www.wsj.com/articles/south-carolina-gop-voters-feel-the-benefits-of-free-tradebut-also-the-scars-1455663542.

51. A. Whitley, "Giving a New Meaning to Cattle Class," *Bloomberg Businessweek*, November 23–29, 2015, 24–25.

52. A. Sharma, "TV Studios Court Licensing Deals in Bustling Foreign Markets: For Warner Bros. and Other U.S. Studios, the International TV-Licensing Bazaar Has Never Been More Lucrative," *Wall Street Journal*, November 19, 2014, accessed April 28, 2016 http://www.wsj.com/articles/tv-studios-court-licensing-deals-in-bustling-foreign-markets-1416454383.

53. M. Willens, "NBCUniversal to Produce American TV Shows for European Broadcasters," *International Business Times*, April 14, 2015, accessed April 28, 2016, http://www.ibtimes.com/nbcuniversal-produce-american-tv-shows-european-broadcasters-1881835.

54. K. Chu and M. Fujikawa, "Burberry Gets Grip on Brand in Japan," *Wall Street Journal*, August 15–16, 2015, B4.

55. "2016 Franchise 500—McDonald's at a Glance," Entrepreneur.com, accessed April 7, 2017, http://www.entrepreneur.com/franchises/mcdonalds/282570-0.html; "New Restaurants," *McDonald's.com*, accessed April 28, 2016, http://www.aboutmcdonalds.com/mcd/franchising/us_franchising/acquiring_a_franchise.html.

56. B. Gruley and L. Patton, "McRevolt: The Frustrating Life of the McDonald's Franchisee—Not Lovin' it," *Bloomberg BusinessWeek*, September 16, 2015, accessed April 28, 2016, http://www.bloomberg.com/features/2015-mcdonalds-franchises/.

57. K. Le Mesurier, "Overseas and Overwhelmed," *BRW*, January 25, 2007, 51.

58. L. Stampler, "16 Bizarre Fast Food Items That Should Have Never Been," *Time*, March 25, 2015, accessed April 9, 2017, http://time.com/3752903/ridiculous-fast-food-items/; People Staff, "The Weirdest International Fast Foods," *People*, December 8, 2016, accessed April 9, 2017, http://people.com/food/weirdest-international-fast-foods/black-burger/.

59. O. Zaleski & L. Yilun Chen, "Airbnb Inches Its Way Into China," *Bloomberg*, December 6, 2016, accessed April 9, 2017, https://www.bloomberg.com/news/articles/2016-12-06/airbnb-inches-its-way-into-china; "China's mobile Internet: WeChat's World," *Economist*, August 6, 2016, accessed April 9, 2017, http://www.economist.com/news/business/21703428-chinas-wechat-shows-way-social-medias-future-wechats-world.

60. E. Fung, "U.S. Mall Developers Face Hurdles in China," *Wall Street Journal*, January 3, 2017, accessed April 9, 2017, https://www.wsj.com/articles/u-s-mall-developers-face-hurdles-in-china-1483459559.

61. J. Hagerty, "In Alabama, Chinese Firm Struggles to Fit In," *Wall Street Journal*, February 29, 2016, B1.

62. K. Chu, "Garment Maker Retreats as China Shifts Policy," *Wall Street Journal*, December 2, 2015, accessed April 28, 2016, http://www.wsj.com/articles/garment-maker-succumbs-to-shift-in-chinas-policy-1449082802.

63. W. Hordes, J. A. Clancy, and J. Baddaley, "A Primer for Global Start-Ups," *Academy of Management Executive*, May 1995, 7–11.

64. P. Dimitratos, J. Johnson, J. Slow, and S. Young, "Micromultinationals: New Types of Firms for the Global Competitive Landscape," *European Management Journal* 21, no. 2 (April 2003): 164; B. M. Oviatt and P. P. McDougall, "Toward a Theory of International New Ventures," *Journal of International Business Studies*, Spring 1994, 45–64; S. Zahra, "A Theory of International New Ventures: A Decade of Research," *Journal of International Business Studies*, January 2005, 20–28.

65. B. Keplesky, "MakerBot's Bre Pettis on the Next P. Rudegeair, "Startup Trov Finds New Funding for Insurance On Demand," *Wall Street Journal*, April 6, 2017, accessed April 9, 2017, https://www.wsj.com/articles/startup -trov-finds-new-funding-for-insurance-on -demand-1491484119.

66. M. Meltzer, "What a Starbucks Latte Costs in 30 Countries," *Thrillist*, March 1, 2016, accessed April 9, 2017, https://www.thrillist.com/travel/na tion/what-a-starbucks-caffe-latte-costs-in-china -japan-france-and-italy/travel.

67. J. Qian, "Forget Love: In China, I'll Marry You for Your License Plate," *Wall Street Journal*, March 20, 2017, accessed April 9, 2017, https://www.wsj .com/articles/forget-love-in-china-ill-marry-you-for -your-license-plate-1490001303; "New PC Registr ations or Sales," The International Organization of Motor Vehicle Manufacturers, accessed April 9, 2017, www.oica.net/wp-content/uploads//pc -sales-2016.pdf; "Global Sector Report: Autom otive," Euler Hermes Economic Research, February 2017, accessed April 9, 2017, www.eulerhermes.com/economic-research/blog/ EconomicPublications/automotive-global-sector -report-feb17.pdf.

68. L. Craymer, "China's Changing Tastes Offer Upside for Coffee," *Wall Street Journal*, September 6, 2015, accessed April 28, 2016, http://www.wsj .com/articles/chinas-changing-tastes-offer-upside -for-coffee-1442431980; D. Harashima, "China's Coffee Market: Cafe Competition Perks Up Amid Slowdown," *Nikkei Asian Review*, October 31, 2015, accessed April 28, 2016, http://asia.nikkei.com /Business/Trends/Cafe-competition-perks-up-amid -slowdown.

69. A. Tangel, "South Korea's LG Electronics to Build U.S. Factory in Tennessee," *Wall Street Journal*, February 28, 2017, accessed April 9, 2017, https://www.wsj.com/articles/south-koreas-lg-ele ctronics-to-build-u-s-factory-in-tennessee -1488315600.

70. "Tax Environment," *NFIA*, accessed April 28, 2016, http://www.nfia.com/tax.html; D. Dzombak, "The Highest Corporate Tax Rates in the World," *The Motley Fool*, March 1, 2014, accessed April 28, 2016, http://www.fool.com/investing/ general/2014/03/01/the-highest-corporate-tax-rates -in-the-world.aspx.

71. "Special Eurobarometer 386: Europeans and Their Languages," European Commission, June 2012, accessed April 28, 2016, http://ec.europa.eu /public_opinion/archives/ebs/ebs_386_en.pdf.

72. "IMD World Talent Report 2014," *IMD World Competitiveness Center*, November 2014, accessed April 28, 2016, http://www.imd.org/uupload/imd .website/wcc/NewTalentReport/IMD_World _Talent_Report_2014bis.pdf.

73. C. Passariello and S. Kapner, "Search for Cheaper Labor Leads to Africa," *Wall Street Jour nal*, July 13, 2015, B1.

74. S. Adams, "2015's Most and Least Reliable Countries to Do Business In," *Forbes*, March 31, 2015, accessed April 28, 2016, http://www.forbes .com/sites/susanadams/2015/03/31/2015s-most- and-least-reliable-countries-to-do-business-in/; "Resilience Index," FM Global, http://www .fmglobal.com/assets/pdf/Resilience _Methodology.pdf.

75. J. Oetzel, R. Bettis, and M. Zenner, "How Risky Are They?" *Journal of World Business* 36, no. 2 (Summer 2001): 128–145.

76. K. D. Miller, "A Framework for Integrated Risk Management in International Business," *Journal of International Business Studies*, 2nd Quarter 1992, 311.

77. M. Colchester, "J.P. Morgan Scours Europe for Best Post-Brexit Home," *Wall Street Journal*, March 29, 2017, accessed April 9, 2017, https:// www.wsj.com/articles/j-p-morgan-scours -europe-for-best-post-brexit-home-1490779804.

78. N. Trentmann, "U.K. Airlines Face Bumpy Post-Brexit Path," *Wall Street Journal*, March 29, 2017, accessed April 9, 2017, https://www.wsj.com /articles/turbulence-ahead-for-u-k-airlines-post -brexit-1490811448.

79. J. Bennett and J. Stoll, "GM's Hopes for Russia Go in Reverse," *Wall Street Journal*, March 19, 2015, B1, B2; D. Levin, "GM Exits Russia," *Fortune*, March 27, 2015, accessed April 28, 2016, http://fortune.com/2015/03/27/gm-exits-russia/.

80. Levin, "GM Exits Russia."

81. "United Arab Emirates Country Risk Report, 2016, 2nd Quarter," *Business Monitor Interna tional*, March 8, 2016, 1-37.

82. A. Irrera, "Uber Hires Uber-Lobbyist for Eur opean Expansion," *Wall Street Journal*, September 5, 2014, accessed April 28, 2016, http://blogs.wsj .com/digits/2014/09/05/uber-hires-uber-lobbyist-for -european-expansion/.

83. D. Kerr, "Uber Fights Back in Europe, Files Complaints Against Governments," *Cnet*, April 10, 2015, accessed April 28, 2016, http://www.cnet.com /news/uber-fights-back-in-europe-files-complaints -against-governments/; S. Schechner, "Uber's Europe Policy Chief Exits," *Wall Street Journal*, November 16, 2015, B4.

84. C. Alessi, "India Invests in Germany's Family Firms," *Wall Street Journal*, April 11–12, 2015, B4.

85. G. Hofstede, "The Cultural Relativity of the Quality of Life Concept," *Academy of Manag ement Review* 9 (1984): 389–398; G. Hofstede, "The Cultural Relativity of Organizational Practices and Theories," *Journal of International Business Studies*, Fall 1983, 75–89; G. Hofstede, "The Interaction Between National and Organizational Value Systems," *Journal of Management Studies*, July 1985, 347–357; M. Hoppe, "An Interview with Geert Hofstede," *Academy of Management Executive*, February 2004, 75–79.

86. Alessi, "India Invests in Germany's Family Firms."

87. Ibid.

88. Ibid.

89. R. Hodgetts, "A Conversation with Geert Hofstede," *Organizational Dynamics*, Spring 1993, 53–61.

90. T. Lenartowicz and K. Roth, "Does Subculture within a Country Matter? A Cross-Cultural Study of Motivational Domains and Business Performance in Brazil," *Journal of International Business Studies* 32 (2001): 305–325.

91. K. Lahrichi, "An Expat's Guide to the Latin American Concept of Time," *Wall Street Journal*, September 26, 2016, accessed April 10, 2017, http: //blogs.wsj.com/expat/2016/09/06/an-expats-guide- to-the-latin-american-concept-of-time.

92. Ibid.

93. Ibid.

94. J. S. Black, M. Mendenhall, and G. Oddou, "Toward a Comprehensive Model of International Adjustment: An Integration of Multiple Theoretical Perspectives," *Academy of Management Review* 16 (1991): 291–317; R. L. Tung, "American Expatriates Abroad: From Neophytes to Cosmopolitans," *Columbia Journal of World Business*, June 22, 1998, 125; A. Harzing, "The Persistent Myth of High Expatriate Failure Rates," *International Journal of Human Resource Management* 6 (1995): 457–475; A. Harzing, "Are Our Referencing Errors Undermining Our Scholarship and Credibility?

The Case of Expatriate Failure Rates," *Journal of Organizational Behavior* 23 (2002): 127–148; N. Fo rster, "The Persistent Myth of High Expatriate Fai lure Rates: A Reappraisal," *International Journal of Human Resource Management* 8 (1997): 414–433.

95. J. Black, "The Right Way to Manage Expats," *Harvard Business Review* 77 (March–April 1999): 52; C. Joinson, "No Returns," *HR Magazine*, November 1, 2002, 70.

96. "International Assignment Perspectives: Criti cal Issues Facing the Globally Mobile Workforce," *PricewaterhouseCoopers*, Vol. 5, November 2011, accessed June 13, 2014, http://www.pwc.com/ en_US/us/hr-international-assignment-services/ publications/assets/ny-12-0258_ias_journal_vol ume_5_new_images.pdf.

97. R. Feintzeig, "After Stints Abroad, Re-Entry Can be Hard," *Wall Street Journal*, September 17, 2013, accessed June 14, 2014, http://online.wsj.com /news/articles/SB100014241278873233424045790 81382781895274?KEYWORDS=after+stints+abroad &mg=reno64-wsj.

98. B. Fritz, "At Shanghai Disneyland, Crowds Line Up for 'Colorful Magical Fanciful Transforma tion,'" *Wall Street Journal*, June 22, 2016, accessed April 10, 2017, https://www.wsj.com/articles/at- shanghai-disneyland-crowds-line-up-for -magical-fanciful-transformation-1466530253.

99. Ibid.

100. J. S. Black and M. Mendenhall, "Cross-Cul tural Training Effectiveness: A Review and Theoret ical Framework for Future Research," *Academy of Management Review* 15 (1990): 113–136.

101. K. Essick, "Executive Education: Transferees Prep for Life, Work in Far-Flung Lands," *Wall Street Journal*, November 12, 2004, A6.

102. Ibid.

103. E. Meyer, "When Culture Doesn't Translate," *Harvard Business Review*, October 2015, accessed April 10, 2017, https://hbr.org/2015/10/when -culture-doesnt-translate.

104. S. Hamm, "Aperian: Helping Companies Bridge Cultures," *BusinessWeek*, September 8, 2008, 16.

105. W. Arthur, Jr. and W. Bennett, Jr., "The International Assignee: The Relative Importance of Factors Perceived to Contribute to Success," *Personnel Psychology* 48 (1995): 99–114; B. Cheng, "Home Truths About Foreign Post ings; To Make an Overseas Assignment Work, Employers Need More Than an Eager Exec with a Suitcase. They Must Also Motivate the Staffer's Spouse," *BusinessWeek Online*, accessed March 20, 2009, http://www.businessweek.com/careers /content/jul2002/ca20020715_9110.htm.

106. B. Groysberg and R. Abrahams, "A Successful International Assignment Depends on These Factors," *Harvard Business Review* (blog), February 13, 2014, 10:00, accessed June 15, 2014, http://blogs.hbr.org/2014/02/a-successful -international-assignment-depends-on-these -factors/.

107. "OAI: Overseas Assignment Inventory," *Prude ntial Real Estate and Relocation Services Intercu ltural Group*, accessed April 10, 2017,, http://www .performance programs.com/self-assessments/work -across-cultures/overseas-assignment-inventory/.

108. S. P. Deshpande and C. Visweswaran, "Is Cross-Cultural Training of Expatriate Managers Effective? A Meta-Analysis," *International Journal of Intercultural Relations* 16, no. 3 (1992): 295–310.

109. D. M. Eschbach, G. Parker, and P. Stoeberl, "American Repatriate Employees' Retrospective Assessments of the Effects of Cross-Cultural Train ing on Their Adaptation to International Assign-

ments," *International Journal of Human Resource Management* 12 (2001): 270–287; "Culture Training: How to Prepare Your Expatriate Employees for Cross-Cultural Work Environments," *Managing Training & Development,* February 1, 2005.

110. I. Driscoll, "You Love Going Abroad for Work. Your Spouse Hates It." *BBC,* November 11, 2014, accessed May 5, 2015, http://www.bbc.com/capital /story/20141110-the-reluctant-expat-spouse.

111. Ibid.

9

1. "Letter to Shareholders: 2016 Annual Report," *Thomson Reuters,* March 9, 2017, accessed April 11, 2017, https://annual-report.thomsonreuters.com /letter-to-shareholders.html

2. M. Hammer and J. Champy, *Reengineering the Corporation: A Manifesto for Business Revolution* (New York: Harper & Row, 1993).

3. D. Halfin, "Windows Insider Program for Business Frequently Asked Questions," Microsoft, April 7, 2017, accessed April 11, 2017, https: //technet.microsoft.com/en-us/itpro/windows/up-date/waas-windows-insider-for-business-faq; A. Patrizio, "Microsoft's Windows Insider Program Surpasses 10 Million Users," *Network World,* March 28, 2017, accessed April 11, 2017, http://www.networkworld.com/article/3185461/windows /windows-insider-program-surpasses-10-million -users.html.

4. J. G. March and H. A. Simon, *Organizations* (New York: John Wiley & Sons, 1958).

5. M. Isaac, "EBay to Cut 2,400 Jobs, and Weighs 2nd Spinoff," *New York Times,* January 22, 2015, B4.

6. "Global Human Capital Trends 2016-The New Organization: Different by Design," *Deloitte University Press,* accessed April 29, 2016, http: //www2.deloitte.com/content/dam/Deloitte/global /Documents/HumanCapital/gx-dup-global-human -capital-trends-2016.pdf.

7. "At a Glance," *UTC,* accessed April 11, 2017, http://www.utc.com/Our-Businesses/Pages/At-A -Glance.aspx.

8. Ibid.

9. "Annual Report 2016," Swisscomm, accessed April 11, 2017, http://reports.swisscom.ch/en/2016 /; "Swisscom Company Structure," Swisscomm, accessed April 11, 2017, https://www.swisscom .ch/content/dam/swisscom/en/about/governance /documents/swisscom-company-structure.pdf.res /swisscom-company-structure.pdf.

10. "Our Story," *AB InBev,* accessed April 11, 2017, http://www.ab-inbev.com/our-story.html; "Peru Fact Sheet," ABInBev, accessed April 11, 2017, www.ab-inbev.com/content/dam/universaltemplate/ ab-inbev/News/Press%20kit/ABI_FS16_Peru.PDF; "Ecuador Fact Sheet," ABInBev, accessed April 11, 2017, http://www.ab-inbev.com/content/dam /universaltemplate/ab-inbev/News/Press%20kit /ABI_FS16_Ecuador.pdf; "Colombia Fact Sheet," ABInBev.com/content/dam/universaltemplate/ab -inbev.com/content/dam/universaltemplate/ab -inbev/News/Press%20kit/ABI_FS16_Colombia .pdf; "Annual Report 2016," SABMiller, accessed April 11, 2017, http://www.ab-inbev.com/content /dam/universaltemplate/ab-inbev/investors /sabmiller/reports/annual-reports/annual -report-2016.pdf.

11. "Our Brands," AB InBev, accessed April 11, 2017, http://www.ab-inbev.com/our-brands.html.

12. "Anheuser Busch InBev Annual Report 2015," Anheuser Busch InBev, accessed April 14, 2016, http://annualreport.ab-inbev.com.

13. "P&G 2016 Annual Report," *Procter & Gamble,* accessed April 11, 2017, http://www .pginvestor.com/Cache/1500090608.PDF?O=PDF &T=&Y=&D=&FID=1500090608&iid=4004124.

14. "Corporate Structure," *Procter & Gamble,* accessed April 12, 2016, http://us.pg.com/who_we _are/structure_governance/corporate_structure.

15. L. R. Burns, "Adoption and Abandonment of Matrix Management Programs: Effects of Organizational Characteristics and Interorganizational Networks," *Academy of Management Journal* 36 (1993): 106–138.

16. H. Fayol, *General and Industrial Management,* trans. C. Storrs (London: Pitman Publishing, 1949).

17. M. Weber, *The Theory of Social and Economic Organization,* trans. and ed. A. M. Henderson and T. Parsons (New York: Free Press, 1947).

18. Fayol, *General and Industrial Management.*

19. C. Zillman, "With Co-CEOs, Companies Flirt with Disaster," *Fortune,* September 20, 2014, accessed April 29, 2016, http://fortune .com/2014/09/20 /oracle-two-ceos-disaster/.

20. A. Gasparro, "CEO Revamp Raises Questions About Whole Foods' Strategy," *Wall Street Journal,* November 3, 2016, accessed April 12, 2017, https: //www.wsj.com/articles/ceo-revamp-raises-questions -about-whole-foods-strategy-1478197430.

21. E. Henning, D. Enrich, & J. Strasburg, "Deutsche Bank Co-CEOs Jain and Fitschen Resign," *Wall Street Journal,* June 7, 2016, accessed April 12, 2017, https://www.wsj.com /articles/deutsche-bank-co-ceos-to-announce -resignations-1433674815.

22. J. Jargon, "Chipotle Drops Dual-CEO Model," *Wall Street Journal,* December 12, 2016, accessed April 12, 2017, https://www.wsj.com/articles /chipotle-drops-dual-ceo-model-1481554627.

23. A. Lashinsky, "Inside Apple, from Steve Jobs Down to the Janitor: How America's Most Successful—and Most Secretive—Big Company Really Works," *Fortune,* May 23, 2011, 125–134.

24. M. Mamet, "Directly Responsible Individuals," *Medium,* November 13, 2016, accessed April 12, 2017, https://medium.com/@mmamet/directly -responsible-individuals-f5009f465da4.

25. B. Borzykowski, "Why You Can't Delegate and How to Fix It," *BBC Capital,* April 2, 2015, accessed April 18, 2015, http://www.bbc.com/capital /story/20150401-why-you-find-it-hard-to-delegate.

26. Ibid.

27. I. Brat, "Whole Foods Reworks Approach," *Wall Street Journal,* February 16, 2016, B2.

28. K. Safdar, "As Gap Struggles, Its Analytical CEO Prizes Data over Design," *Wall Street Journal,* November 27, 2016, accessed April 12, 2017, https: //www.wsj.com/articles/as-gap-struggles-its -analytical-ceo-prizes-data-over-design -1480282911.

29. E. E. Lawler, S. A. Mohrman, and G. E. Ledford, *Creating High Performance Organizations: Practices and Results of Employee Involvement and Quality Management in Fortune 1000 Companies* (San Francisco: Jossey-Bass, 1995).

30. C. Rauwald & C. Reiter, "At Volkswagen, Engineering Change in the Eye of the Diesel Storm," *Bloomberg,* December 8, 2016, accessed April 12, 2017, https://www.bloomberg.com/news /articles/2016-12-08/at-volkswagen-engineering -change-in-the-eye-of-the-diesel-storm.

31. "Employee Turnover Rate Tops 70% in 2015," National Restaurant Association, March 22, 2016, accessed April 29, 2016, http://www.restaurant.org /News-Research/News/Employee-turnover-rate -tops-70-in-2015.

32. R. W. Griffin, *Task Design* (Glenview, IL: Scott, Foresman, 1982).

33. F. Herzberg, *Work and the Nature of Man* (Cleveland, OH: World Press, 1966).

34. R. Hackman and G. R. Oldham, *Work Redesign* (Reading, MA: Addison-Wesley, 1980).

35. T. Burns and G. M. Stalker, *The Management of Innovation* (London: Tavistock, 1961).

36. Hammer and Champy, *Reengineering the Corporation.*

37. Ibid.

38. J. D. Thompson, *Organizations in Action* (New York: McGraw-Hill, 1967).

39. G. James, "World's Worst Management Fads," *Inc.,* May 10, 2013, accessed May 1, 2015 http:// www.inc.com/geoffrey-james/worlds-worst -management-fads.html.

40. J. B. White, "'Next Big Thing': Re-Engineering Gurus Take Steps to Remodel Their Stalling Vehicles," *Wall Street Journal Interactive,* November 26, 1996.

41. C. Tuna, "Remembrances: Champion of 'Re-Engineering' Saved Companies, Challenged Thinking," *Wall Street Journal,* September 6, 2008, A12.

42. G. M. Spreitzer, "Individual Empowerment in the Workplace: Dimensions, Measurement, and Validation," *Academy of Management Journal* 38 (1995): 1442–1465.

43. O. Stanley, "Warby Parker is Getting Better Results by Getting Better Results," *Quartz,* September 15, 2016, accessed April 12, 2017, https: //qz.com/749863/warby-parker-is-getting-better -results-by-reducing-managers-control-over -workers/.

44. K. W. Thomas and B. A. Velthouse, "Cognitive Elements of Empowerment," *Academy of Management Review* 15 (1990): 666–681.

45. C. Gallo, "How Wegmans, Apple Store and Ritz-Carlton Empower Employees to Offer Best-in-Class Service," Retail Customer Experience, December 27, 2012, accessed June 12, 2013, http://www.retailcustomerexperience.com /article/205849/How-Wegmans-Apple-Store-and -Ritz-Carlton-empower-employees-to-offer-best -in-class-service.

46. R. Nelsen, "Why Giving Your Employees More Freedom Will Improve Your Customer Experience," *Qualtrics,* October 26, 2015, accessed April 12, 2017, https://www.qualtrics.com/blog/why-giving-your-employees-more-freedom-will -improve-your-customer-experience/.

47. J. Lee, "Finding Gooey Goodness in Nutella's Huge Supply Chain," *Triple Pundit,* January 10, 2014, accessed April 29, 2016, http://www .triplepundit.com/2014/01/nutella-supply-chain/; D. Mitzman, "Nutella, How the World Went Nuts for a Hazelnut Spread," *BBC News,* May 18, 2014, accessed May 19, 2016; http://www.bbc.com/news /magazine-27438001.

48. L. Weber, "The End of Employees," *Wall Street Journal,* February 2, 2017, accessed April 13, 2017, https://www.wsj.com/articles/the-end-of -employees-1486050443.

49. A. Satariano and S. Soper, "Yuletemps," *Bloomberg Businessweek,* December 14–20, 2015, 30–31; "Amazon.com Announces Fourth Quarter Sales up 22% to $35.7 Billion," *Business Wire,* January 28, 2016, accessed April 29, 2016, http://www .businesswire.com/news/home/20160128006357 /en/Amazon.com-Announces-Fourth-Quarter -Sales-22-35.7.

50. C. C. Snow, R. E. Miles, and H. J. Coleman, Jr., "Managing 21st Century Network Organizations," *Organizational Dynamics* 20 (Winter 1992): 5–20.

51. J. H. Sheridan, "The Agile Web: A Model for the Future?" *Industry Week*, March 4, 1996, 31.

10

1. B. Dumaine, "The Trouble with Teams," *Fortune*, September 5, 1994, 86–92.

2. K. C. Stag, E. Salas, and S. M. Fiore, "Best Practices in Cross Training Teams," in *Workforce Cross Training Handbook*, ed. D. A. Nembhard (Boca Raton, FL: CRC Press), 156–175.

3. M. Marks, "The Science of Team Effectiveness," *Psychological Science in the Public Interest* 7 (December 2006): pi–i.

4. J. R. Katzenbach and D. K. Smith, *The Wisdom of Teams* (Boston: Harvard Business School Press, 1993).

5. S. G. Cohen and D. E. Bailey, "What Makes Teams Work: Group Effectiveness Research from the Shop Floor to the Executive Suite," *Journal of Management* 23, no. 3 (1997): 239–290.

6. S. E. Gross, *Compensation for Teams* (New York: American Management Association, 1995); B. L. Kirkman and B. Rosen, "Beyond Self-Management: Antecedents and Consequences of Team Empowerment," *Academy of Management Journal* 42 (1999): 58–74; G. Stalk and T. M. Hout, *Competing Against Time: How Time-Based Competition Is Reshaping Global Markets* (New York: Free Press, 1990); S. C. Wheelwright and K. B. Clark, *Revolutionizing New Product Development* (New York: Free Press, 1992).

7. D. A. Harrison, S. Mohamed, J. E. McGrath, A. T. Florey, and S. W. Vandersteep, "Time Matters in Team Performance: Effects of Member Familiarity, Entrainment, and Task Discontinuity on Speed and Quality," *Personnel Psychology* 56, no. 3 (August 2003): 633–669.

8. R. Cross, R. Rebele, and A. Grant, "Collaborative Overload," *Harvard Business Review*, January–February 2016, accessed April 30, 2016, https://hbr.org/2016/01/collaborative-overload.

9. L. Chao, "Auto Makers, Others Explore New Roles for 3-D Printing," *Wall Street Journal*, April 25, 2016, accessed April 30, 2016, http://www.wsj.com/articles/auto-makers-others-explore-new-roles-for-3-d-printing-1461626635; "Hunton & Williams Launches 3D Printing Team to Guide Clients Through Emerging Technology's Legal Complexities," *Business Wire*, April 30, 2016, accessed May 19, 2016, http://www.businesswire.com/news/home/20160420006044/en/Hunton-Williams-Launches-3D-Printing-Team-Guide.

10. R. D. Banker, J. M. Field, R. G. Schroeder, and K. K. Sinha, "Impact of Work Teams on Manufacturing Performance: A Longitudinal Field Study," *Academy of Management Journal* 39 (1996): 867–890.

11. L. Chao, "Trucker Teams Drive to the Rescue of Online Shipping," *Wall Street Journal*, December 24, 2015, accessed April 30, 2016, http://www.wsj.com/articles/trucker-teams-drive-to-the-rescue-of-online-shipping-1450953001.

12. Ibid.

13. J. L. Cordery, W. S. Mueller, and L. M. Smith, "Attitudinal and Behavioral Effects of Autonomous Group Working: A Longitudinal Field Study," *Academy of Management Journal* 34 (1991):464–476; T. D. Wall, N. J. Kemp, P. R. Jackson, and C. W. Clegg, "Outcomes of Autonomous Workgroups: A Long-Term Field Experiment," *Academy of Management Journal* 29 (1986): 280–304.

14. S. Crowley, "Open-Book Management at Atomic," Atomic Objects, March 14, 2016, accessed April 13, 2017, Object, https://spin.atomicobject.com/2016/03/14/open-book-management/.

15. L. Tjapkes, "Atoms on 'Give a Shit' – the Quintessential Atomic Value," Atomic Objects, January 31, 2015, accessed April 13, 2017, https://spin.atomicobject.com/2015/01/31/atomic-values-part-5-give-a-shit/.

16. R. Silverman, "At Zappos, Some Employees Find Offer to Leave Too Good to Refuse," *Wall Street Journal*, May 7, 2015, accessed May 8, 2015, http://www.wsj.com/articles/at-zappos-some-employees-find-offer-to-leave-too-good-to-refuse-1431047917?KEYWORDS=zappos; D. Gelles, "The Zappos Exodus Continues after a Radical Management Experiment," *New York Times*, January 13, 2016,accessed April 30, 2016, http://bits.blogs.nytimes.com/2016/01/13/after-a-radical-management-experiment-the-zappos-exodus-continues/.

17. R. Liden, S. Wayne, R. Jaworski, and N. Bennett, "Social Loafing: A Field Investigation," *Journal of Management* 30 (2004): 285–304.

18. J. George, "Extrinsic and Intrinsic Origins of Perceived Social Loafing in Organizations," *Academy of Management Journal* 35 (1992): 191–202.

19. T. T. Baldwin, M. D. Bedell, and J. L. Johnson, "The Social Fabric of a Team-Based M.B.A. Program: Network Effects on Student Satisfaction and Performance," *Academy of Management Journal* 40 (1997): 1369–1397.

20. S. Perry, N. Lorinkova, E. Hunter, A Hubbard, and J. McMahon, "When Does Virtuality Really Work? Examining the Role of Work-Family and Virtuality in Social Loafing," *Journal of Management* 42 (2016), 449–479.

21. K. H. Price, D. A. Harrison, and J. H. Gavin, "Withholding Inputs in Team Contexts: Member Composition, Interaction Processes, Evaluation Structure and Social Loafing," *Journal of Applied Psychology* 91(6) (2006): 1375–1384.

22. L. P. Tost, F. Gino, and R. P. Larrick, "When Power Makes Others Speechless: The Negative Impact of Leader Power on Team Performance," *Academy of Management Journal* 35, no. 5 (October 1, 2013): 1465–1486.

23. C. Joinson, "Teams at Work," *HR Magazine*, May 1, 1999, 30.

24. R. Wageman, "Critical Success Factors for Creating Superb Self-Managing Teams," *Organizational Dynamics* 26, no. 1 (1997): 49–61.

25. R. Etherington, "Audi Announces New Design Strategy," *Dezeen*, December 19, 2012, accessed June 13, 2013, http://www.dezeen.com/2012/12/19/audi-announces-new-car-design-strategy/.

26. Kirkman and Rosen, "Beyond Self-Management: B. L. Kirkman and B. Rosen, "Beyond Self-Management: Antecedents and Consequences of Team Empowerment," *Academy of Management Journal* 42 (1999): 58–74;

27. K. Kelly, "Managing Workers Is Tough Enough in Theory. When Human Nature Enters the Picture, It's Worse," *BusinessWeek*, October 21, 1996, 32.

28. S. Easton and G. Porter, "Selecting the Right Team Structure to Work in Your Organization," in *Handbook of Best Practices for Teams*, vol. 1, ed. G. M. Parker (Amherst, MA: Irwin, 1996).

29. S. Wilhelm, "Quadrupling 787 Production Won't Be Easy for Boeing, Just Necessary," *Puget Sound Business Journal*, February 10, 2012, accessed March 12, 2012, http://www.bizjournals.com/seattle/print-edition/2012/02/10/quadrupling-787-production-wont-be.html?page=all.

30. R. M. Yandrick, "A Team Effort: The Promise of Teams Isn't Achieved Without Attention to Skills and Training," *HR Magazine* 46, no. 6 (June 2001): 136–144.

31. M. Mankins & E. Garton, "How Spotify Balances Employee Autonomy and Accountability," *Harvard Business Review*, February 9, 2017, accessed April 14, 2017, https://hbr.org/2017/02/how-spotify-balances-employee-autonomy-and-accountability; AC. Hardy, "Agile Team Organisation: Squads, Chapters, Tribes and Guilds," *Full-Stack Agile*, February 14, 2016, accessed April 14, 2017, http://www.full-stackagile.com/2016/02/14/team-organisation-squads-chapters-tribes-and-guilds/.

32. R. Williams, "Self-Directed Work Teams: A Competitive Advantage," *Quality Digest*, accessed November 18, 2009, http://www.qualitydigest.com.

33. Yandrick, "A Team Effort."

34. "Valve: Handbook for New Employees," *Valve*, accessed May 8, 2015, http://media.steampowered.com/apps/valve/Valve_Handbook_LowRes.pdf.

35. Ibid.

36. R. Silverman, "Who's the Boss? There Isn't One," *Wall Street Journal*, June 19, 2012, accessed May 8, 2015, http://www.wsj.com/articles/SB10001424052702303379204577474953586383604.

37. R. J. Recardo, D. Wade, C. A. Mention, and J. Jolly, *Teams* (Houston: Gulf Publishing Co., 1996).

38. D. R. Denison, S. L. Hart, and J. A. Kahn, "From Chimneys to Cross-Functional Teams: Developing and Validating a Diagnostic Model," *Academy of Management Journal* 39, no. 4 (1996): 1005–1023.

39. A. M. Townsend, S. M. DeMarie, and A. R. Hendrickson, "Virtual Teams: Technology and the Workplace of the Future," *Academy of Management Executive* 13, no. 3 (1998): 17–29.

40. F. Rendón, "Understanding the Proliferation of Virtual Teams in the Global Economy," *Huffington Post*, April 28, 2014, accessed June 16, 2014, http://www.huffingtonpost.com/frankie-rendon/understanding-the-prolife_b_5212366.html.

41. M.E. Slater, "How to Effectively Delegate to Your Remote Team," Startup Collective, accessed May 8, 2015, http://startupcollective.com/effectively-delegate-remote-team/.

42. C. Kane, "Virtual offices: What Happens When All Employees Telecommute," *Fortune*, May 15, 2015, accessed April 14, 2017, http://fortune.com/2015/05/15/office-less-virtual-companies/.

43. N. Radley, "Survey: How Team Members Prefer to Communicate on Virtual Projects," *Software Ad-vice*, July 17, 2014, accessed May 8, 2015, http://blog.softwareadvice.com/articles/project-manage-ment/survey-communication-virtual-projects-0714/.

44. Slater, "How to Effective Delegate to Your Remote Team."

45. Ibid.

46. D. Mankin, S. G. Cohen, and T. K. Bikson, *Teams and Technology: Fulfilling the Promise of the New Organization* (Boston: Harvard Business School Press, 1996).

47. A. P. Ammeter and J. M. Dukerich, "Leadership, Team Building, and Team Member Characteristics in High Performance Project Teams," *Engineering Management* 14, no. 4 (December 2002): 3–11.

48. K. Lovelace, D. Shapiro, and L. Weingart, "Maximizing Cross-Functional New Product

Teams' Innovativeness and Constraint Adherence: A Conflict Communications Perspective," *Academy of Management Journal* 44 (2001): 779–793.

49. L. Holpp and H. P. Phillips, "When Is a Team Its Own Worst Enemy?" *Training*, September 1, 1995, 71.

50. S. Asche, "Opinions and Social Pressure," *Scientific American* 193 (1995): 31–35.

51. J. Corsello & D. Minor, "Want to Be More Productive? Sit Next to Someone Who Is," *Harvard Business Review*, February 14, 2017, accessed April 14, 2017, https://hbr.org/2017/02/want-to-be-more -productive-sit-next-to-someone-who-is.

52. S. G. Cohen, G. E. Ledford, and G. M. Spreitzer, "A Predictive Model of Self-Managing Work Team Effectiveness," *Human Relations* 49, no. 5 (1996): 643–676.

53. C. Duhigg, "Group Study: What Google Learned from Its Quest to Build the Perfect Team," *New York Times*, February 28, 2016, MM20.

54. A. Edmondson, "Psychological Safety and Learning Behavior in Work Teams," *Administrative Science Quarterly* 44 (1999): 350–383.

55. A. Wooley, C. Chabris, A. Pentland, N. Hashmi, and T. Malone, "Evidence for a Collective Intelli -gence Factor in the Performance of Human Groups," *Science* 330 (2010): 686–688.

56. K. Bettenhausen and J. K. Murnighan, "The Emergence of Norms in Competitive Decision -Making Groups," *Administrative Science Quarterly* 30 (1985): 350–372.

57. M. E. Shaw, *Group Dynamics* (New York: McGraw Hill, 1981).

58. F. Rees, *Teamwork from Start to Finish* (San Francisco: Josey-Bass, 1997).

59. R. E. Silverman, "Tracking Sensors Invade the Workplace," *Wall Street Journal*, March 7, 2013, accessed June 16, 2014, http://online.wsj.com/news /articles/SB10001424127887324034804578344303 429080678.

60. S. M. Gully, D. S. Devine, and D. J. Whitney, "A Meta-Analysis of Cohesion and Performance: Effects of Level of Analysis and Task Interdependence," *Small Group Research* 26, no. 4 (1995): 497–520.

61. K. Kahler, "Vikings' Donut Club Is NFL Tradition Like No Other," *The MMQB with Peter King*, October 20, 2015, accessed April 14, 2017, http://mmqb.si.com/mmqb/2015/10/20 /nfl-minnesota-vikings-donut-club.

62. J. Bersin, J. Geller, N. Wakefield & B. Walsh, *Global Human Capital Trends 2016—The New Organization: Different by Design*, eds. B. Pelster and J. Schwartz (Deloitte University Press), 20.

63. Gully, et al., "A Meta-Analysis of Cohesion and Performance." F. Tschan and M. V. Cranach, "Group Task Structure, Processes and Outcomes," in *Handbook of Work Group Psychology*, ed. M. A. West (Chichester, UK: Wiley, 1966).

64. D. E. Yeatts and C. Hyten, High-Performing Self-Managed Work Teams (Thousand Oaks, CA: Sage Publications, 1998).

65. S. Shellenbarger, "A Manifesto to End Boring Meetings," December 20, 2016, accessed April 14, 2017, https://www.wsj.com/articles/a-manifesto-to -end-boring-meetings-1482249683.

66. Ibid.

67. J. Lublin, "Smaller Boards Get Bigger Returns," *Wall Street Journal*, August 26, 2014, accessed April 30, 2016, 8, 2015, http://www.wsj. com/articles /smaller-boards-get-bigger-returns-1409078628.

68. Yeatts and Hyten, *High-Performing Self-Managed Work Teams*; J. Colquitt, R. Noe, and

C. Jackson, "Justice in Teams: Antecedents and Consequences of Procedural Justice Climate," *Personnel Psychology*, April 1, 2002, 83.

69. D. S. Kezsbom, "Re-Opening Pandora's Box: Sources of Project Team Conflict in the '90s," *Indu strial Engineering* 24, no. 5 (1992): 54–59.

70. A. C. Amason, W. A. Hochwarter, and K. R. Thompson, "Conflict: An Important Dimension in Successful Management Teams," *Organizational Dynamics* 24 (1995): 20.

71. A. C. Amason, "Distinguishing the Effects of Functional and Dysfunctional Conflict on Strategic Decision Making: Resolving a Paradox for Top Management Teams," *Academy of Management Journal* 39, no. 1 (1996): 123–148.

72. K. M. Eisenhardt, J. L. Kahwajy, and L. J. Bourgeois III, "How Management Teams Disagree," *California Management Review* 39, no. 2 (Winter 1997): 42–62.

73. K. M. Eisenhardt, J. L. Kahwajy, and L. J. Bourgeois III, "How Management Teams Can Have a Good Fight," *Harvard Business Review* 75, no. 4 (July–August 1997): 77–85.

74. S. Shellenbarger, "Meet the Meeting Killers," *Wall Street Journal*, May 15, 2012, accessed May 8, 2015, http://www.wsj.com/articles/SB100014240527 02304192704577404434001058726.

75. C. Nemeth and P. Owens, "Making Work Groups More Effective: The Value of Minority Dissent," in *Handbook of Work Group Psychology*, ed. M. A. West (Chichester, UK: Wiley, 1996).

76. J. M. Levin and R. L. Moreland, "Progress in Small Group Research," *Annual Review of Psychology* 9 (1990): 72–78; S. E. Jackson, "Team Composition in Organizational Settings: Issues in Managing a Diverse Work Force," in *Group Processes and Productivity*, ed. S. Worchel, W. Wood, and J. Simpson (Beverly Hills, CA: Sage, 1992).

77. Eisenhardt, et al., "How Management Teams Can Have a Good Fight."

78. Ibid.

79. J. Lublin, "Arguing with the Boss: A Winning Career Strategy," *Wall Street Journal*, August 9, 2012, accessed May 8, 2015, http://www.wsj.com/ articles/SB1000087239639044399170457757920 1122821724.

80. Eisenhardt, et al., "How Management Teams Can Have a Good Fight."

81. B. W. Tuckman, "Development Sequence in Small Groups," *Psychological Bulletin* 63, no. 6 (1965): 384–399.

82. Gross, *Compensation for Teams.*

83. J. F. McGrew, J. G. Bilotta, and J. M. Deeney, "Software Team Formation and Decay: Extending the Standard Model for Small Groups," *Small Group Research* 30, no. 2 (1999): 209–234.

84. Ibid.

85. J. Case, "What the Experts Forgot to Mention: Management Teams Create New Difficulties, But Succeed for XEL Communication," *Inc.*, September 1, 1993, 66.

86. J. R. Hackman, "The Psychology of Self-Man -agement in Organizations," in *Psychology and Work: Productivity, Change, and Employment*, ed. M. S. Pallak and R. Perloff (Washington, DC: American Psychological Association, 1986), 85–136.

87. A. O'Leary-Kelly, J. J. Martocchio, and D. D. Frink, "A Review of the Influence of Group Goals on Group Performance," *Academy of Management Journal* 37, no. 5 (1994): 1285–1301.

88. A. Zander, "The Origins and Consequences of Group Goals," in *Retrospections on Social Psychology*, ed. L. Festinger (New York: Oxford University Press, 1980), 205–235.

89. M. Erez and A. Somech, "Is Group Productivity Loss the Rule or the Exception? Effects of Culture and Group-Based Motivation," *Academy of Management Journal* 39, no. 6 (1996): 1513–1537.

90. S. Sherman, "Stretch Goals: The Dark Side of Asking for Miracles," *Fortune*, November 13, 1995.

91. S. Ramakrishnan & S. John, "We Don't Want to Waste a Crisis: Tata Steel MD TV Narendran," *The Economic Times*, February 29, 2016, accessed April 14, 2017, http://economictimes.indiatimes.com/opi nion/interviews/we-dont-want-to-waste-a-crisis-tata -steel-md-tv-narendran/articleshow/51180585.cms.

92. K. Leigh, "At Hormel, Growth Means Doing Deals," *Star Tribune*, November 27, 2016, 1D.

93. K. R. Thompson, W. A. Hochwarter, and N. J. Mathys, "Stretch Targets: What Makes Them Effective?" *Academy of Management Executive* 11, no. 3 (1997): 48–60.

94. J. Baskin, "Innovation At Experian: Build, Don't Just Buy," *Forbes*, March 2, 2016, accessed April 14, 2017, https://www.forbes.com/sites /jonathansalem-baskin/2016/03/02/innovation-at -experian-build-dont-just-buy/#34c1a22f520e.

95. Ibid.

96. M. Freeman, "How Experian is Turning Big Data Into Big Dollars," *Los Angeles Times*, September 28, 2016, http://www.latimes.com /business/la-fi-experian-big-data-20160928-snap -story.html.

97. B. Dumaine, "The Trouble with Teams," *Fortune*, 5 September 1994, 86–92.

98. G. A. Neuman, S. H. Wagner, and N. D. Chri stiansen, "The Relationship Between Work-Team Personality Composition and the Job Performance of Teams," *Group & Organization Management* 24, no. 1 (1999): 28–45.

99. M. A. Campion, G. J. Medsker, and A. C. Higgs, "Relations Between Work Group Characteristics and Effectiveness: Implications for Designing Effective Work Groups," *Personnel Psychology* 46, no. 4 (1993): 823–850.

100. B. L. Kirkman and D. L. Shapiro, "The Impact of Cultural Values on Employee Resistance to Teams: Toward a Model of Globalized Self-Managing Work Team Effectiveness," *Academy of Management Review* 22, no. 3 (1997): 730–757.

101. J. Pavlus, "SAP Looks to XRX for R&D Inspiration," *Bloomberg Businessweek*, February 2–8, 2015, p. 32.

102. A. Galinsky, "Is Your Team Too Talented," *Columbia Ideas at Work*, October 30, 2014, accessed May 8, 2015, http://www8.gsb.columbia .edu/ideas-at-work/publication/1700.

103. J. Bunderson and K. Sutcliffe, "Comparing Alternative Conceptualizations of Functional Diversity in Management Teams: Process and Performance Effects," *Academy of Management Journal* 45 (2002): 875–893.

104. S. Woo, "In Search of a Perfect Team at Work," *Wall Street Journal*, April 4, 2017, accessed April 15, 2017, https://www.wsj.com/articles /in-search-of-a-perfect-team-at-work-1489372003.

105. "Rebel Alliance: To Develop Star Wars and Jurassic World, in VR, Industrial Light & Magic Has Formed a Supergroup," *Bloomberg Businessweek*, April 11–24, 2016, 48.

106. J. Hackman, "New Rules for Team Building— The Times Are Changing—And So Are the Guide -lines for Maximizing Team Performance," *Optimize*, July 1, 2002, 50.

107. Joinson, "Teams at Work."

108. Strozniak, "Teams at Work."

109. Ibid.

110. L. Davey, "If Your Team Agrees on Everything, Working Together Is Pointless," *Harvard Business Review*, January 31, 2017, accessed April 15, 2017, https://hbr.org/2017/01/if-your-team-agrees-on-everything-working-together-is-pointless.

111. Wellins, et al., *Inside Teams*.

112. E. Salas, D. DiazGranados, C. Klein, C. Burke, K. Stagl, G. Goodwin, and S. Halpin, "Does Team Training Improve Team Performance? A Meta-Analysis," *Human Factors* 50, no. 6 (2008): 903–933.

113. S. Caudron, "Tie Individual Pay to Team Success," *Personnel Journal* 73, no. 10 (October 1994): 40.

114. Ibid.

115. A. Mitra, N. Gupta, & J. Shaw, "A Comparative Examination of Traditional and Skill-Based Pay Plans," *Journal of Managerial Psychology* 26, no. 4 (2011): 278-296.

116. G. Ledford, "Three Case Studies on Skill-Based Pay: An Overview," *Compensation & Benefits Review* 23, no. 2 (1991): 11–24.

117. T. Law, "Where Loyalty Is Rewarded," *The Press*, September 29, 2008, *Business Day* 4.

118. J. R. Schuster and P. K. Zingheim, *The New Pay: Linking Employee and Organizational Performance* (New York: Lexington Books, 1992).

119. Cohen and Bailey, "What Makes Teams Work."

120. R. Allen and R. Kilmann, "Aligning Reward Practices in Support of Total Quality Management," *Business Horizons* 44 (May 2001): 77–85.

11

1. L. Weber, "High Salaries Haunt Some Job Hunters," Wall Street Journal, February 4, 2016, accessed April 16, 2017, https://www.wsj.com/articles/high-salaries-haunt-some-job-hunters-1454634475.

2. Ibid.

3. Ibid.

4. K. Gee, "Cities Push Employers to Ignore Pay History," Wall Street Journal, April 15, 2017, accessed April 16, 2017, https://www.wsj.com/articles/cities-push-employers-to-ignore-pay-history-1492254003.

5. "Genetic Information Discrimination," *U.S. Equal Employment Opportunity Commission*, accessed May 6, 2016, http://www.eeoc.gov/laws/types/genetic.cfm.

6. K. McGowan, "Barring Male Guards for Female Inmates Might Violate Title VII, Ninth Circuit Rules," *Bloomberg BNA*, July 8, 2014, accessed May 6, 2016, http://www.bna.com/barring-male-guards-n17179891923/.

7. J. Hyman, "No Matter What the Producers of #Hamilton Tell You, Race is Never a BFOQ," Ohio Employer's Law Blog, April 5, 2016, http://www.ohioemployerlawblog.com/2016/04/no-matter-what-producers-of-hamilton.html, accessed August 25, 2017.

8. P. S. Greenlaw and J. P. Kohl, "Employer 'Business' and 'Job' Defenses in Civil Rights Actions," *Public Personnel Management* 23, no. 4 (1994): 573.

9. M. Miller, "SeaWorld Fined for Improperly Protecting Employees from Killer Whales," *Washington Post*, May 1, 2015, accessed May 1, 2016, http://www.washingtonpost.com/news/morning-mix/wp/2015/05/01/seaworld-fined-for-improperly-protecting-employees-from-killer-whales/.

10. Greenlaw and Kohl, "Employer 'Business' and 'Job' Defenses in Civil Rights Actions."

11. City News Service, "66-Year-Old Man Awarded $26 Million in Age Discrimination Lawsuit," *Los Angeles Daily News*, February 27, 2014, accessed May 6, 2016, http://www.dailynews.com/general-news/20140227/66-year-old-man-awarded-26-million-in-age-discrimination-lawsuit-against-staples.

12. P. Lee and C. Hymowitz, "No Place for Old Waiters at Texas Roadhouse?" *Bloomberg Businessweek*, September 28–October 4, 2015, 23–24.

13. E. Coe, "Steakhouse Chain Says EEOC Age Bias Suit Too Vague," *Law 360*, accessed April 30, 2016, http://www.law360.com/articles/305259/steakhouse-chain-says-eeoc-age-bias-suit-too-vague.

14. W. Peirce, C. A. Smolinski, and B. Rosen, "Why Sexual Harassment Complaints Fall on Deaf Ears," *Academy of Management Executive* 12, no. 3 (1998): 41–54.

15. "Jury Awards $2,323,505.48 to Former Employee In Her Tennessee State Action Alleging Quid Pro Quo Sexual Harassment and Sexual Discrimination," LexisNexis, February 16, 2017, accessed April 17, 2017, https://www.lexisnexis.com/jvsubmission/b/case_of_week/archive/2017/02/16/jury-awards-2-323-505-48-to-former-employee-in-her-tennessee-state-action-alleging-quid-pro-quo-sexual-harassment-and-sexual-discrimination.aspx.

16. B. Frank, "Zillow accused of 'adult frat house' culture, sales manager fired after sexual harassment investigation," *Geek Wire*, December 2, 2014, accessed April 17, 2017, http://www.geekwire.com/2014/zillow-accused-adult-frat-house-culture-sales-manager-fired-sexual-harassment-investigation/.

17. R. Smith, "Zillow Settles Several Suits Alleging Sexual Harassment, Discrimination," *Mortgage Professional America*, June 7, 2016, accessed April 17, 2017, http://www.mpamag.com/news/zillow-settles-several-suits-alleging-sexual-harassment-discrimination-32939.aspx.

18. Peirce, et al., "Why Sexual Harassment Complaints Fall on Deaf Ears."

19. Ibid.

20. E. Larson, "The Economic Costs of Sexual Harassment," *The Freeman* 46, August 1996, accessed May 6, 2016, http://fee.org/freeman/the-economic-costs-of-sexual-harassment.

21. L. Weber, "Firms Flock to Cities with Top Talent," *Wall Street Journal*, April 13, 2016, B11.

22. R. D. Gatewood and H. S. Field, *Human Resource Selection* (Fort Worth, TX: Dryden Press, 1998).

23. Ibid.

24. "Machine Learning," SAP, accessed April 17, 2017, https://www.sap.com/solution/machine-learning.what-is-machine-learning.html#benefits.

25. T. Greenwald, "How AI Is Transforming the Workplace," *Wall Street Journal*, March 10, 2017, accessed April 17, 2017, https://www.wsj.com/articles/how-ai-is-transforming-the-workplace-1489371060.

26. *Griggs v. Duke Power Co.*, 401 US 424, 436 (1971); *Albemarle Paper Co. v. Moody*, 422 US 405 (1975).

27. R. E. Silverman and N. Waller, "The Algorithm That Tells the Boss Who Might Quit," *Wall Street Journal*, March 13, 2015, accessed May 6, 2016, http://www.wsj.com/articles/the-algorithm-that-tells-the-boss-who-might-quit-1426287935.

28. J. A. Breaugh, *Recruitment: Science and Practice* (Boston: PWSKent, 1992).

29. R. Albergotti, "LinkedIn Wants to Help You Stay at Your Company," *Wall Street Journal* (blog), April 10, 2014, accessed May 6, 2016, http://blogs.wsj.com/atwork/2014/04/10/linkedin-wants-to-help-you-stay-at-your-company/.

30. Ibid.

31. J. Lublin, "The Danger of Being Too Good at Your Job," *Wall Street Journal*, April 11, 2017, April 17, 2017, https://www.wsj.com/articles/the-danger-of-being-too-good-at-your-job-1491912000.

32. L. Klaff, "New Internal Hiring Systems Reduce Cost and Boost Morale," *Workforce Management* 83 (March 2004): 76–79.

33. R. Silverman and L. Weber, "An Inside Job: More Firms Opt to Recruit from Within," *Wall Street Journal*, May 29, 2012, accessed May 6, 2016, http://online.wsj.com/article/SB10001424052702303395604577434563715828218.html.

34. R. E. Silverman, "Climbing the Career Ladder with Help," *Wall Street Journal*, January 14, 2015, B6.

35. Ibid.

36. C. Hymowitz, "Diebold's New Executive Suite," *Bloomberg Businessweek*, August 10–23, 2015, 21–22.

37. J. Breaugh and M. Starke, "Research on Employee Recruitment: So Many Studies, So Many Remaining Questions," *Journal of Management* 26 (2000): 405–434.

38. J. J. Colao, "The Facebook Job Board Is Here: Recruiting Will Never Look the Same," *Forbes*, November 14, 2012, accessed May 6, 2016, http://www.forbes.com/sites/jjcolao/2012/11/14/the-facebook-job-board-is-here-recruiting-will-never-look-the-same/; J. Zappe, "Now Almost Gone: The Decline of Print-Based Help-Wanted Ads," *Source Con*, March 20, 2012, accessed May 5, 2015, http://www.sourcecon.com/news/2012/03/20/now-almost-gone-the-decline-of-print-based-help-wanted-ads/.

39. "2016 Jobvite Job Seeker Nation Study," *Jobvite*, accessed May 1, 2016, http://www.jobvite.com/wp-content/uploads/2016/03/Jobvite_Jobseeker_Nation_2016.pdf.

40. R. E. Silverman, "New Year, New Job? Read This First," *Wall Street Journal*, January 2, 2015, B1, B4.

41. T. Greenwald, "How AI Is Transforming the Workplace."

42. N. Buhayar, "Be a Grand Pooh-Bah of Probability," *Bloomberg Businessweek*, March 16–22, 2015, 34–35.

43. S. Shellenbarger, "How to Deal with a Long Hiring Process," *Wall Street Journal*, January 19, 2016, B1; R. Feintzeig, "Hiring on the Fast Track," *Wall Street Journal*, September 17, 2015, B1.

44. Feintzeig, "Hiring on the Fast Track."

45. C. Camden and B. Wallace, "Job Application Forms: A Hazardous Employment Practice," *Personnel Administrator* 28 (1983): 31–32.

46. J. Valentino-Devries, "Bosses May Use Social Media to Discriminate Against Job Seekers," *Wall Street Journal*, November 20, 2013, accessed May 6, 2016, http://online.wsj.com/news/articles/SB10001424052702303755504579208304255139392.

47. "Fifty-Eight Percent of Employers Have Caught a Lie on a Résumé, According to a New Career-Builder Survey," *CareerBuilder.com*, August 7, 2014, accessed May 6, 2016, http://www.careerbuilder.com/share/aboutus/pressreleasesdetail.aspx?sd=8%2F7%2F2014&id=pr837&ed=12%2F31%2F2014.

48. R. Feintzeig & R. Silverman, "In the Uber Age, a Boom in Background Checks," *Wall Street Journal*, May 11, 2016, accessed April 18, 2017, https://www.wsj.com/articles/background-checks-are-booming-1462926915.

49. L. Chao, "Driver-Screening Firms Draw Scrutiny," *Wall Street Journal*, October 19, 2016, accessed April 18, 2017, https://www.wsj.com/articles/driver-screening-firms-draw-scrutiny-1476869402.

50. S. Adler, "Verifying a Job Candidate's Background: The State of Practice in a Vital Human Resources Activity," *Review of Business* 15, no. 2 (1993/1994): 3–8.

51. W. Woska, "Legal Issues for HR Professionals: Reference Checking/Background Investigations," *Public Personnel Management* 36 (Spring 2007): 79–89.

52. "More Than 70 Percent of HR Professionals Say Reference Checking Is Effective in Identifying Poor Performers," *Society for Human Resource Management*, accessed May 6, 2016, http://www.shrm.org/press_published/CMS_011240.asp.

53. P. Babcock, "Spotting Lies: The High Cost of Careless Hiring," *HR Magazine* 48, no. 10 (October 2003).

54. E. Leizerman, "Oregon Jury Renders $5.2M Verdict Against Trucking Broker and Driver in Negligent Hiring Case," *PRWeb*, March 6, 2012, accessed May 6, 2016, http://www.prweb.com/releases/2012/3/prweb9258166.htm.

55. M. Le, T. Nguyen, and B. Kleiner, "Legal Counsel: Don't Be Sued for Negligent Hiring," *Nonprofit World*, May 1, 2003, 14–15.

56. B. Goldberg, "Majority of Employers Background Check Employees … Here's Why," *CareerBuilder*, November 17, 2016, accessed April 19, 2017, http://www.careerbuilder.com/advice/majority-of-employers-background-check-employees.

57. J. Calmes, "Hiring Hurdle: Finding Workers Who Can Pass a Drug Test," *New York Times*, May 17, 2016, accessed April 19, 2017, https://www.nytimes.com/2016/05/18/business/hiring-hurdle-finding-workers-who-can-pass-a-drug-test.html?_r=0.

58. Emshwiller and Fields, "Decadeslong Arrest Wave Vexes Employers."; S. Thurm, "Background Checks Fuel Jobs Debate," *Wall Street Journal*, June 11, 2013, accessed May 6, 2016, http://www.wsj.com/articles/SB10001424127887323495604578539283518855020.

59. "Reference Search – No Longer Supported | LinkedIn Help," LinkedIn, June 9, 2015, accessed April 19, 2017, https://www.linkedin.com/help/linkedin/answer/135?query=references.

60. C. Brooks, "The Pros and Cons of Social Media Background Checks," Business News Daily, August 2, 2016, accessed April 19, 2017, http://www.businessnewsdaily.com/9289-social-media-background-checks.html; J. Segal, "LEGAL TRENDS Social Media Use in Hiring: Assessing the Risks," Society for Human Resource Management, September 2014, accessed April 19, 2017, https://www.shrm.org/hr-today/news/hr-magazine/pages/0914-social-media-hiring.aspx.

61. C. Cohen, "Reference Checks," *CA Magazine*, November 2004, 41.

62. Keith J. Winstein, "Inflated Credentials Surface in Executive Suite," *Wall Street Journal*, November 13, 2008, accessed May 6, 2016, http://online.wsj.com/article/SB122652836844922165.html.

63. B. Ellis, "For Hire: Professional Liars for Job Seekers," *CNN Money*, July 17, 2013, accessed May 6, 2016, http://money.cnn.com/2013/07/17/pf/professional-liars/.

64. L. Weber, "To Get a Job, New Hires Are Put to the Test," *Wall Street Journal*, April 15, 2015, A1, A10.

65. J. Piereson and N. Schaefer Riley, "Here's Why Tests Matter," *Wall Street Journal*, March 31, 2016, accessed May 6, 2016, http://www.wsj.com/articles/heres-why-tests-matter-1459379670.

66. J. Hunter, "Cognitive Ability, Cognitive Aptitudes, Job Knowledge, and Job Performance," *Journal of Vocational Behavior* 29 (1986): 340–362.

67. F. L. Schmidt, "The Role of General Cognitive Ability and Job Performance: Why There Cannot Be a Debate," *Human Performance* 15 (2002): 187–210.

68. "D. Hambrick and C. Chabris, "Yes, IQ Really Matters," *Slate*, April 14, 2014, accessed July 10, 2014, http://www.slate.com/articles/health_and_science/science/2014/04/what_do_sat_and_iq_tests_measure_general_intelligence_predicts_school_and.html.

69. E. E. Cureton, "Comment," in *Research Conference on the Use of Autobiographical Data as Psychological Predictors*, ed. E. R. Henry (Greensboro, NC: The Richardson Foundation, 1965), 13.

70. J. R. Glennon, L. E. Albright, and W. A. Owens, *A Catalog of Life History Items* (Greensboro, NC: The Richardson Foundation, 1966).

71. Gatewood and Field, *Human Resource Selection*.

72. J. M. Digman, "Personality Structure: Emergence of the Five-Factor Model," *Annual Review of Psychology* 41 (1990): 417–440; M. R. Barrick and M. K. Mount, "The Big Five Personality Dimensions and Job Performance: A Meta-Analysis," *Personnel Psychology* 44 (1991): 1–26.

73. N. Schmitt, "Beyond the Big Five: Increases in Understanding and Practical Utility," *Human Performance* 17 (2004): 347–357.

74. L. Weber, "Today's Personality Tests Raise the Bar for Job Seekers," *Wall Street Journal*, April 15, 2015, accessed April 19, 2017, https://www.wsj.com/articles/a-personality-test-could-stand-in-the-way-of-your-next-job-1429065001.

75. Ibid.

76. R. Feintzeig, "The Boss Doesn't Want Your Résumé," *Wall Street Journal*, January 5, 2016, accessed April 19, 2017, https://www.wsj.com/articles/the-boss-doesnt-want-your-resume-1452025908.

77. L. Weber, "Today's Personality Tests Raise the Bar for Job Seekers," *Wall Street Journal*, April 14, 2015, accessed May 6, 2016, http://www.wsj.com/articles/a-personality-test-could-stand-in-the-way-of-your-next-job-1429065001.

78. M. S. Taylor and J. A. Sniezek, "The College Recruitment Interview: Topical Content and Applicant Reactions," *Journal of Occupational Psychology* 57 (1984): 157–168.

79. M. Harris, "Reconsidering the Employment Interview: A Review of Recent Literature and Suggestions for Future Research," *Personnel Psychology* 42 (Winter 1989): 691–726.

80. Taylor and Sniezek, "The College Recruitment Interview."

81. M. Wilson, "Here's Google's Secret to Hiring the Best People," *Wired*, April 7, 2015, accessed April 19, 2017, https://www.wired.com/2015/04/hire-like-google/.

82. R. Burnett, C. Fan, S. J. Motowidlo, and T. DeGroot, "Interview Notes and Validity," *Personnel Psychology* 51, (1998): 375–396; M. A. Campion, D. K. Palmer, and J. E. Campion, "A Review of Structure in the Selection Interview," *Personnel Psychology* 50, no. 3 (1997): 655–702.

83. T. Judge, "The Employment Interview: A Review of Recent Research and Recommendations for Future Research," *Human Resource Management Review* 10, no. 4 (2000): 383–406.

84. J. Cortina, N. Goldstein, S. Payne, K. Davison, and S. Gilliland, "The Incremental Validity of Interview Scores Over and Above Cognitive Ability and Conscientiousness Scores," *Personnel Psychology* 53, no. 2 (2000): 325–351; F. L. Schmidt and J. E. Hunter, "The Validity and Utility of Selection Methods in Personnel Psychology: Practical and Theoretical Implications of 85 Years of Research Findings," *Psychological Bulletin* 124, no. 2 (1998): 262–274.

85. K. Tyler, "Training Revs Up," *HR Magazine* (April 2005), *Society for Human Resource Management*, accessed March 23, 2009, http://www.shrm.org.

86. 2016 Training Industry Report," Trainingmag, November/December 2016, accessed April 19, 2017, https://trainingmag.com/sites/default/files/images/Training_Industry_Report_2016.pdf; "2014 State of the Industry Report," TD: Talent Development 68 no. 11 (November 2014): 30–35.

87. S. Lupkin, "Texas Health Workers Use Tabasco to Help Train for Ebola," *Good Morning America*, October 23, 2014, accessed May 7, 2015, http://abcnews.go.com/Health/texas-health-workers-tabasco-train-ebola/story?id=26385702.

88. Ibid.

89. T. Jacoby, "Wal-Mart Tries to Skill Up," *Wall Street Journal*, September 5–6, 2015, C3.

90. L. Kolodny, "The Latest Approach to Employee Training," *Wall Street Journal*, March 13, 2016, accessed May 6, 2016, http://www.wsj.com/articles/the-latest-approach-to-employee-training-1457921560.

91. D. L. Kirkpatrick, "Four Steps to Measuring Training Effectiveness," *Personnel Administrator* 28 (1983): 19–25.

92. L. Bassi, J. Ludwig, D. McMurrer, and M. Van Buren, "Profiting from Learning: Do Firms' Investments in Education and Training Pay Off?" *American Society for Training and Development*, accessed August 14, 2008, https://www.td.org/Publications/Research-Reports/2000/Profiting-from-Learning

93. Daley, "It's Shaping Up to Be a Good Year," *Entrepreneur*, January 2014, 92.

94. D. Meinert, "Is It Time to Put the Performance Appraisal on a PIP?," Society of Human Resource Management, April 1, 2015, accessed May 6, 2016, https://www.shrm.org/publications/hrmagazine/editorialcontent/2015/0415/pages/0415-qualitative-performance-reviews.aspx; J. McGregor, "This Big Change Was Supposed To Make Performance Reviews Better. Could It Be Making Them Worse?" Washington Post, June 7, 2016, accessed April 19, 2017, https://www.washingtonpost.com/news/on-leadership/wp/2016/06/07/this-big-change-was-supposed-to-make-performance-reviews-better-could-it-be-making-them-worse/?utm_term=.9476cc57671d.

95. M. Nisen, "Why GE Had to Kill Its Annual Performance Reviews after More than Three Decades," *Quartz*, August 13, 2015, accessed May 6, 2016, http://qz.com/428813/ge-performance-review-strategy-shift/

96. Ibid.

97. J. McGregor, "This Big Change Was Supposed To Make Performance Reviews Better. Could It Be Making Them Worse?"

98. K. R. Murphy and J. N. Cleveland, *Understanding Performance Appraisal: Social, Organizational and Goal-Based Perspectives* (Thousand Oaks, CA: Sage, 1995).

99. L. Goler, J. Gale & A. Grant, "Let's Not Kill Performance Reviews Yet," *Harvard Business Review*, November 2016, accessed April 20, 2017, https://hbr.org/2016/11/lets-not-kill-performance-evaluations-yet.

100. U. J. Wiersma and G. P. Latham, "The Practicality of Behavioral Observation Scales, Behavioral Expectation Scales, and Trait Scales," *Personnel Psychology* 39 (1986): 619–628; U. J. Wiersma, P. T. Van Den Berg, and G. P. Latham, "Dutch Reactions to Behavioral Observation, Behavioral Expectation, and Trait Scales," *Group & Organization Management* 20 (1995): 297–309.

101. D. J. Schleicher, D. V. Day, B. T. Mayes, and R. E. Riggio, "A New Frame for Frame-of-Reference Training: Enhancing the Construct Validity of Assessment Centers," *Journal of Applied Psychology* (August 2002): 735–746.

102. R. Feintzeig, "Everything Is Awesome! Why You Can't Tell Employees They're Doing a Bad Job," *Wall Street Journal*, February 10, 2015, accessed May 6, 2016, http://www.wsj.com/articles/everything-is-awesome-why-you-cant-tell-employees-theyre-doing-a-bad-job-1423613936.

103. R. Feintzeig, "The Trouble with Grading Employees," *Wall Street Journal*, April 22, 2015, B1, B7.

104. H. H. Meyer, "A Solution to the Performance Appraisal Feedback Enigma," *Academy of Management Executive* 5, no. 1 (1991): 68–76; G. C. Thornton, "Psychometric Properties of Self-Appraisals of Job Performance," *Personnel Psychology* 33 (1980): 263–271.

105. Thornton, "Psychometric Properties of Self-Appraisals of Job Performance."

106. K. Mullaney, "It's Not OK to 'Rate' Employees," *CNBC*, April 18, 2016, accessed May 6, 2016, http://www.cnbc.com/2016/04/18/its-not-ok-to-rate-employees-commentary.html.

107. J. Smither, M. London, R. Flautt, Y. Vargas, and I. Kucine, "Can Working with an Executive Coach Improve Multisource Feedback Ratings Over Time? A Quasi-Experimental Field Study," *Personnel Psychology* (Spring 2003): 21–43.

108. A. Walker and J. Smither, "A Five-Year Study of Upward Feedback: What Managers Do with Their Results Matters," *Personnel Psychology* 52 (Summer 1999): 393–422.

109. S. Carey, "Pilot Shortage Prompts Regional Airlines to Boost Starting Wages," *Wall Street Journal*, November 11, 2016, accessed April 20, 2017, https://www.wsj.com/articles/pilot-shortage-prompts-regional-airlines-to-boost-starting-wages-1478473042.

110. Ibid.

111. G. T. Milkovich and J. M. Newman, *Compensation*, 4th ed. (Homewood, IL: Irwin, 1993).

112. M. L. Williams and G. F. Dreher, "Compensation System Attributes and Applicant Pool Characteristics," *Academy of Management Journal* 35, no. 3 (1992): 571–595.

113. A. Whitley, "Chinese Airlines Wave Wads of Cash to Lure Foreign Pilots," *Bloomberg*, August 17, 2016, accessed April 20, 2017, https://www.bloomberg.com/news/articles/2016-08-17/chinese-airlines-lure-expat-pilots-with-lucrative-pay-perks.

114. D. K. Williams and M. M. Scott, "Why We Pay All Our Employees a Commission," *Harvard Business Review*, March 26, 2013, accessed May 6, 2016, https://hbr.org/2013/03/why-we-pay-all-our-employees-a/.

115. R. Solomon, "Delta Pays Out Biggest Profit Sharing in U.S. History," *Delta*, February 12, 2016, accessed May 6, 2016, http://news.delta.com/delta-pays-out-biggest-profit-sharing-us-history.

116. M. Josephs, "The Millionaire Truck Driver and Other ESOP Miracles," *Forbes,* April 30, 2014, accessed May 6, 2016, http://www.forbes.com/sites/maryjosephs/2014/04/30/the-millionaire-truck-driver-and-other-esop-miracles/.

117. S. Strom, "At Chobani, Now It's Not Just the Yogurt That's Rich," *New York Times*, April 26, 2016, accessed July 26, 2016, http://www.nytimes.com/2016/04/27/business/a-windfall-for-chobani-employees-stakes-in-the-company.html?_r=0.

118. Y. Naguchi, "Why Chobani Gave Employees a Financial Stake in Company's Future," *All Things Considered, NPR*, April 28, 2016, accessed May 6, 2016, http://www.npr.org/templates/transcript/transcript.php?storyId=476021520.

119. "ESOPs by the Numbers, "National Center for Employee Ownership," March 2017, accessed April 20, 2017, http://www.nceo.org/articles/esops-by-the-numbers.

120. M. Bloom, "The Performance Effects of Pay Dispersion on Individuals and Organizations," *Academy of Management Journal* 42, no. 1 (1999): 25–40.

121. L. Mischel & J. Scheider, "Ceo Pay Remains High Relative to the Pay of Typical Workers and High-Wage Earners," Economic Policy Institute, July 20, 2017, accessed August 26, 2017, http://www.epi.org/publication/ceo-pay-remains-high-relative-to-the-pay-of-typical-workers-and-high-wage-earners/.

122. W. Grossman and R. E. Hoskisson, "CEO Pay at the Crossroads of Wall Street and Main: Toward the Strategic Design of Executive Compensation," *Academy of Management Executive* 12, no. 1 (1998): 43–57.

123. Bloom, "The Performance Effects of Pay Dispersion."

124. M. Bloom and J. Michel, "The Relationships Among Organizational Context, Pay Dispersion, and Managerial Turnover," *Academy of Management Journal* 45 (2002): 33–42.

125. S. Needleman, "Bad Firings Can Hurt Firm's Reputation," *Wall Street Journal*, July 8, 2008, D4.

126. J. Strickland, "Zynga Layoffs: The Aftermath," *Inc*, June 3, 2013, accessed May 6, 2016, http://www.inc.com/julie-strickland/zynga-lay-off-eighteen-percent-staff-close-three-offices.html.

127. A. Rupe, "Horrors from the Bad-Firing File," *Workforce Management*, November 2003, 16.

128. D. Mattel, J. Lublin, and R. Silverman, "Bad Call: How Not to Fire a Worker," *Wall Street Journal*, September 9, 2011, B2.

129. P. Michal-Johnson, *Saying Good-Bye: A Manager's Guide to Employee Dismissal* (Glenview, IL: Scott, Foresman & Co., 1985).

130. M. Bordwin, "Employment Law: Beware of Time Bombs and Shark-Infested Waters," *HR Focus*, April 1, 1995, 19; D. Jones, "Fired Workers Fight Back ... and Win; Laws, Juries Shift Protection to Terminated Employees," *USA Today*, April 2, 1998, 01B.

131. J. Bort, "Microsoft's Layoffs Are Not *Yet* Done," *Business Insider*, January 27, 2015, accessed May 6, 2016, http://www.businessinsider.com/microsofts-layoffs-are-not-yet-done-2015-1.

132. B. Brown, "Microsoft, Blackberry, and NetApp among Those Trimming Workforces," *Network World*, July 22, 2015, accessed May 6, 2016, http://www.networkworld.com/article/2951484/microsoft-subnet/biggest-tech-industry-layoffs-of-2015.

133. W. F. Cascio, "Employment Downsizing and Its Alternatives: Strategies for Long-Term Success," *SHRM Foundation's Effective Practice Guideline Series, Society for Human Resource Management Foundation,* accessed May 6, 2016, http://www.shrm.org/about/foundation/products/Documents/Downsizing%20EPG-%20Final.pdf.

134. K. E. Mishra, G. M. Spreitzer, and A. K. Mishra, "Preserving Employee Morale During Downsizing," *Sloan Management Review* 39, no. 2 (1998): 83–95.

135. K. Frieswick, "Until We Meet Again?" *CFO*, October 1, 2001, 41; Cascio, "Employment Downsizing and Its Alternatives: Strategies for Long-Term Success"; L. Weber and R. Feintzeig, "Assistance for Laid-Off Workers Gets Downsized," *Wall Street Journal*, February 18, 2013, accessed May 6, 2016, http://www.wsj.com/news/articles/SB10001424052702304899704579391254047535652

136. Cascio, "Employment Downsizing and Its Alternatives: Strategies for Long-Term Success."

137. C. Jones and L. Scott, "Layoffs Are Awful, but Don't Forget the Survivors," *Oilweek*, January 14, 2016, accessed May 6, 2016, http://www.oilweek.com/index.php/columnists/699-layoffs-are-awful-but-don-t-forget-the-survivors.

138. J. Ackerman, "Helping Layoff Survivors Cope: Companies Strive to Keep Morale High," *Boston Globe*, December 30, 2001, H1.

139. S. Krouse, "Fidelity Investments Offers Buyouts to 3,000 Older Workers," *Wall Street Journal*, February 28, 2017, accessed April 20, 2017, https://www.wsj.com/articles/fidelity-investments-offers-buyouts-to-3-000-older-workers-1488297272.

140. J. Lublin and S. Thurm, "How Companies Calculate Odds in Buyout Offers," *Wall Street Journal*, March 27, 2009, B1.

141. M. Willett, "Early Retirement and Phased Retirement Programs for the Public Sector," *Benefits & Compensation Digest*, April 2005, 31.

142. C. Hymowitz, "American Firms Want to Keep Older Workers a Bit Longer," *Bloomberg*, December 16, 2016, accessed April 20, 2017, https://www.bloomberg.com/news/articles/2016-12-16/american-firms-want-to-keep-older-workers-a-bit-longer.

143. "2016 Jobvite Job Seeker Nation Study," *Jobvite*, accessed May 6, 2016, http://www.jobvite.com/wp-content/uploads/2016/03/Jobvite_Jobseeker_Nation_2016.pdf.

144. D. R. Dalton, W. D. Todor, and D. M. Krackhardt, "Turnover Overstated: The Functional Taxonomy," *Academy of Management Review* 7 (1982): 117–123.

145. J. R. Hollenbeck and C. R. Williams, "Turnover Functionality versus Turnover Frequency: A Note on Work Attitudes and Organizational Effectiveness," *Journal of Applied Psychology* 71 (1986): 606–611.

146. Silverman and Waller, "The Algorithm That Tells the Boss Who Might Quit."

147. C. R. Williams, "Reward Contingency, Unemployment, and Functional Turnover," *Human Resource Management Review* 9 (1999): 549–576.

12

1. "Table 11. Percent of the Projected Population by Hispanic Origin and Race for the United States: 2015 to 2060 (NP2014-T11)," Census Bureau, accessed May 8, 2016, https://www.census.gov

/population/projections/data/national/2014
/summarytables.html.

2. "Table 3.4. Continued—Civilian Labor Force, by Age, Gender, Race, and Ethnicity, 1994, 2004, 2014, and Projected 2024," Bureau of Labor Statistics, December 2015, accessed May 8, 2016, http://www.bls.gov/emp/ep_table_304.htm; "Labor Force Projections to 2020: A More Slowly Growing Workforce," *Monthly Labor Review*, January 2012, 43–64.

3. "Table 3.4. Continued- Civilian Labor Force, by Age, Gender, Race, and Ethnicity, 1994, 2004, 2014, and Projected 2024," Bureau of Labor Statistics, December 2015, accessed May 8, 2016, http://www.bls.gov/emp/ep_table_304.htm.

4. "Marriott Facts: Prepare for your Interview and Learn about Marriott," Marriott, accessed April 22, 2017, http://www.marriott.com/careers/business-facts.mi.

5. B. Marriott, "Diversity & Inclusion Matters," *Marriott on the Move*, February 6, 2017, accessed April 22, 2017, http://www.blogs.marriott.com/marriott-on-the-move/2017/02/diversity-matters.html.

6. "Diversity & Inclusion Global Fact Sheet, Marriott International, Spirit To Serve Our Diverse World," Marriott, accessed April 22, 2017, www.marriott.com/Multimedia/PDF/Corporate/DiversityFactSheet.pdf.

7. Equal Employment Opportunity Commission, "Affirmative Action Appropriate Under Title VII of the Civil Rights Act of 1964, as Amended. Chapter XIV—Equal Employment Opportunity Commission, Part 1608," *Government Publishing Office*, accessed May 8, 2016, http://www.access.gpo.gov/nara/cfr/waisidx_04/29cfr1608_04.html.

8. Equal Employment Opportunity Commission, "Federal Laws Prohibiting Job Discrimination: Questions and Answers," *Equal Employment Opportunity Commission*, accessed May 8, 2016, http://www.eeoc.gov/facts/qanda.html.

9. A. P. Carnevale and S. C. Stone, *The American Mosaic: An In-Depth Report on the Future of Diversity at Work* (New York: McGraw-Hill, 1995).

10. T. Roosevelt, "From Affirmative Action to Affirming Diversity," *Harvard Business Review* 68, no. 2 (1990): 107–117.

11. A. M. Konrad and F. Linnehan, "Formalized HRM Structures: Coordinating Equal Employment Opportunity or Concealing Organizational Practices?" *Academy of Management Journal* 38, no. 3 (1995): 787–820; see, for example, *Hopwood v. Texas*, 78 F.3d 932 (5th Cir., March 18, 1996). The U.S. Supreme Court has upheld the principle of affirmative action but has struck down some specific programs.

12. J. Bravin, "Court Backs Affirmative Action Ban—Justices Uphold State Initiative to End Race-Based Admissions, But Are Divided on Broader Issue," *Wall Street Journal*, April 23, 2014, A1.

13. P. Schmidt, "5 More States May Curtail Affirmative Action," *The Chronicle of Higher Education*, October 19, 2007, A1.

14. M. E. Heilman, C. J. Block, and P. Stathatos, "The Affirmative Action Stigma of Incompetence: Effects of Performance Information Ambiguity," *Academy of Management Journal* 40, no. 3 (1997): 603–625; D. Evans, "A Comparison of the Other Directed Stigmatization Produced by Legal and Illegal Forms of Affirmative Action," *Journal of Applied Psychology* 88, no. 1 (2003): 121–130.

15. L. Leslie, D. Mayer, and D. Kravitz, "The Stigma of Affirmative Action: A Stereotyping-Based Theory and Meta-Analytic Test of the Consequences for Performance." *Academy of Management Journal* 57, no. 4 (2014): 964–989.

16. E. Orenstein, "The Business Case for Diversity," *Financial Executive*, May 2005, 22–25; G. Robinson and K. Dechant, "Building a Business Case for Diversity," *Academy of Management Executive* 11, no. 3 (1997): 21–31.

17. E. Esen, "2005 Workplace Diversity Practices: Survey Report," *Society for Human Resource Management*, accessed March 24, 2009, http://www.shrm.org/research.

18. Orenstein, "Business Case for Diversity."

19. Esen, "2005 Workplace Diversity Practices: Survey Report."

20. Orenstein, "Business Case for Diversity."

21. S. Randazzo, "Qualcomm to Pay $19.5 Million to Settle Claims of Bias Against Women," *Wall Street Journal*, July 26, 2016, accessed April 22, 2017, https://www.wsj.com/articles/qualcomm-to-pay-19-5-million-to-settle-claims-of-bias-against-women-1469571756.

22. P. Wright and S. P. Ferris, "Competitiveness Through Management of Diversity: Effects on Stock Price Valuation," *Academy of Management Journal* 38 (1995): 272–285.

23. I. Bohnet, "Real Fixes for Workplace Bias," *Wall Street Journal*, March 12–13, 2016, C3; K. Lachance Shandrow, "10 U.S. Companies with Radically Awesome Parental Leave Policies," *Entrepreneur*, August 11, 2015, accessed May 8, 2016, https://www.entrepreneur.com/slideshow/249467.

24. P. Wright and S. P. Ferris, "Competitiveness Through Management of Diversity: Effects on Stock Price Valuation."

25. "QuickFacts: United States," Census Bureau, July 1, 2015, accessed April 22, 2017, https://www.census.gov/quickfacts/table/RHI125215/00#headnote-js-a; M. Weeks & J. Humphreys, "Asians, Hispanics Driving U.S. Economy Forward, According to UGA Study," *UGA Today*, September 24, 2015, accessed April 22, 2017, http://news.uga.edu/releases/article/2015-multicultural-economy-report/.

26. J. Boudreau and N. Kieu Giang, "More Women May Sit in the Front of the Plane," *Bloomberg Businessweek*, April 11–25, 2016, 20–21.

27. Anonymous, "Bumpkin Bosses; Schumpeter," *The Economist*, May 10, 2014, 70.

28. W. W. Watson, K. Kumar, and L. K. Michaelsen, "Cultural Diversity's Impact on Interaction Process and Performance: Comparing Homogeneous and Diverse Task Groups," *Academy of Management Journal* 36 (1993): 590–602; K. A. Jehn, G. B. Northcraft, and M. A. Neale, "Why Differences Make a Difference: A Field Study of Diversity, Conflict, and Performance in Workgroups," *Administrative Science Quarterly* 44 (1999): 741–763; E. Kearney, D. Gebert, and S. Voelpel, "When and How Diversity Benefits Teams: The Importance of Team Members' Need for Cognition," *Academy of Management Journal* 52 (2009): 581–598.

29. C. Palmieri, "Carnival Rocks the Boat," *Bloomberg Businessweek*, November 16–22, 2015, 22–23.

30. M. R. Carrell and E. E. Mann, "Defining Workplace Diversity Programs and Practices in Organizations," *Labor Law Journal* 44 (1993): 743–764.

31. D. A. Harrison, K. H. Price, and M. P. Bell, "Beyond Relational Demography: Time and the Effects of Surface- and Deep-Level Diversity on Work Group Cohesion," *Academy of Management Journal* 41 (1998): 96–107.

32. D. Harrison, K. Price, J. Gavin, and A. Florey, "Time, Teams, and Task Performance: Changing Effects of Surface- and Deep-Level Diversity on Group Functioning," *Academy of Management Journal* 45 (2002): 1029–1045.

33. Harrison, et al., "Beyond Relational Demography."

34. Ibid.

35. J. Haidt and L. Jussim, "Hard Truths About Race on Campus," *Wall Street Journal*, May 6, 2016, accessed May 8, 2016, http://www.wsj.com/articles/hard-truths-about-race-on-campus-1462544543; T. Pettigrew and L. Tropp, "A Meta-Analytic Test of Intergroup Contact Theory," *Journal of Personality and Social Psychology* 90 (2006): 751–783.

36. S. Levy, "How Can We Achieve Age Diversity in Silicon Valley?" *BackChannel*, October 19, 2015, accessed April 23, 2017, https://backchannel.com/how-can-we-achieve-age-diversity-in-silicon-valley-11a847.

37. R. Alsop, "Why Your Grandfather Might Land a Job Before You Do," BBC, October 25, 2013, accessed May 8, 2016, http://www.bbc.com/capital/story/20131024-older-workers-fogey-or-find; E. White, "The New Recruits: Older Workers," *Wall Street Journal*, January 14, 2008, B3.

38. M. Kane, "Say What? Young People are Just Smarter,'" *CNET*, March 28, 2007, accessed May 9, 2015, http://www.cnet.com/news/say-what-young-people-are-just-smarter/.

39. V. Giang, "This Is the Latest Way Employers Mask Age Bias, Lawyers Say," *Fortune*, May 4, 2015, http://fortune.com/2015/05/04/digital-native-employers-bias/, accessed May 9, 2015;

40. Ibid.

41. "Age Discrimination in Employment Act (Charges filed with EEOC) (includes Concurrent Charges with Title VII, ADA and EPA) FY 1997–FY 2016," *US Equal Employment Opportunity Commission*, accessed April 23, 2017, http://www.eeoc.gov/eeoc/statistics/enforcement/adea.cfm.

42. S. R. Rhodes, "Age-Related Differences in Work Attitudes and Behavior," *Psychological Bulletin* 92 (1983): 328–367.

43. T. Ng and D. Feldman, "The Relationship of Age to Ten Dimensions of Job Performance," *Journal of Applied Psychology* 93, no. 2 (2008): 392–423.

44. G. M. McEvoy and W. F. Cascio, "Cumulative Evidence of the Relationship Between Employee Age and Job Performance," *Journal of Applied Psychology* 74 (1989): 11–17; T. Ng and D. Feldman, "The Relationship of Age to Ten Dimensions of Job Performance," *Journal of Applied Psychology* 93, no. 2 (2008): 392–423; A. Tergesen, "Why Everything You Think about Aging May Be Wrong," *Wall Street Journal*, November 30, 2014, accessed May 9, 2015, http://www.wsj.com/articles/why-everything-you-think-about-aging-may-be-wrong-1417408057; A. Tergesen, "Five Myths About Landing a Good Job Later in Life," *Wall Street Journal*, November 29, 2016, accessed April 23, 2017, tell application "Safari" to return URL of front dochttps://www.wsj.com/articles/five-myths-about-landing-a-good-job-later-in-life-1480302842.

45. S. E. Sullivan and E. A. Duplaga, "Recruiting and Retaining Older Workers for the Millennium," *Business Horizons* 40 (November 12, 1997): 65; E. Townsend, "To Keep Older Workers, Consider New Responsibilities and Guard Against Discrimination," SHRM Foundation, accessed

May 3, 2016, http://www.shrm.org/about/foundation/pages/researchthatmatters.aspx.

46. C. Hymowitz and R. Burnson, "It's Tough Being Over 40 in Silicon Valley," *Bloomberg*, September 8, 2016, accessed April 23, 2017, https://www.bloomberg.com/news/articles/2016-09-08/silicon-valley-s-job-hungry-say-we-re-not-to-old-for-this.

47. N. Timiraos, "How Older Women Are Reshaping U.S. Job Market," *Wall Street Journal*, February 22, 2016, accessed May 8, 2016, http://www.wsj.com/articles/older-women-reshape-u-s-job-market-1456192536?mod=djem10point.

48. T. Maurer and N. Rafuse, "Learning, Not Litigating: Managing Employee Development and Avoiding Claims of Age Discrimination," *Academy of Management Executive* 15, no. 4 (2001): 110–121.

49. D. Brady, "The Bottom-Line Reasons for \Mixing the Young and Old at Work," *Bloomberg Businessweek*, April 10, 2014, accessed July 11, 2014, http://www.businessweek.com/articles/2014-02-10/workplaces-boost-profits-when-young-and-old-workers-mentor-each-other; B. L. Hassell and P. L. Perrewe, "An Examination of Beliefs About Older Workers: Do Stereotypes Still Exist?" *Journal of Organizational Behavior* 16 (1995): 457–468.

50. "Charge Statistics: FY 1997 Through FY 2016," *Equal Employment Opportunity Commission*, accessed April 23, 2017, http://eeoc.gov/eeoc/statistics/enforcement/charges.cfm.

51. "Women in the Labor Force: A Databook," Bureau of Labor Statistics, April 2017, accessed April 23, 2017, https://www.bls.gov/opub/reports/womens-databook/2016/pdf/home.pdf.

52. "The 2016 State of Women-Owned Businesses Report: A Summary of Important Trends 1997–2016," *Commissioned by American Express OPEN*, with the assistance of the Economic Census Branch of the Company Statistics Division of the U.S. Census Bureau, May 2016, accessed April 23, 2017, http://www.womenable.com/content/userfiles/2016_State_of_Women-Owned_Businesses_Executive_Report.pdf.

53. "Women in the Labor Force: A Databook," Bureau of Labor Statistics.

54. "Women in S&P 500 Companies," Catalyst, March 1, 2017, accessed April 23, 2017, http://www.catalyst.org/knowledge/women-sp-500-companies.

55. B. Darrow, "Nearly All Fortune 1000 Companies Are Still Led by Men," *Fortune*, September 6, 2016, accessed April 23, 2017, http://fortune.com/2016/09/06/fortune-1000-still-led-by-men/; 1 MORE CITATION HERE FEMAIL CEOS OF COLOR

56. V. Zarya, "Female Fortune 500 CEOs Set to Break Records in 2017," *Fortune*, December 22, 2016, accessed April 23, 2017, http://fortune.com/2016/12/22/female-fortune-500-ceos-2017/.

57. J. Lublin, "Women Make Gains Toward Winning CEO Job," *Wall Street Journal*, January 17, 2017, accessed April 23, 2017, https://www.wsj.com/articles/women-make-gains-toward-winning-ceo-job-1484665381.

58. A. Joshi, J. Son, and H. Roh, "When Can Women Close the Gap? A Meta-Analytic Test of Sex Differences in Performance and Rewards," *Academy of Management Journal* 58 (2015): 1516–1545.

59. M. Bertrand and K. Hallock, "The Gender Gap in Top Corporate Jobs," *Industrial & Labor Relations Review* 55 (2001): 3–21.

60. A. Chamberlain & J. Jayaraman, "The Pipeline Problem: How College Majors Contribute to the Gender Pay Gap - Glassdoor Economic Research," Glassdoor, April 19, 2017, accessed April 23, 2017, https://www.glassdoor.com/research/studies/pipeline-problem-college-majors-gender-pay-gap/.

61. M. Korn, "Science, Engineering Studies Are Still a Hard Sell to Women," *Wall Street Journal*, April 11, 2017, accessed April 23, 2017, https://www.wsj.com/articles/science-engineering-studies-are-still-a-hard-sell-to-women-1491883260.

62. J. R. Hollenbeck, D. R. Ilgen, C. Ostroff, and J. B. Vancouver, "Sex Differences in Occupational Choice, Pay, and Worth: A Supply-Side Approach to Understanding the Male-Female Wage Gap," *Personnel Psychology* 40 (1987): 715–744.

63. S. Shellenbarger, "Does Having Kids Dull Career Opportunities?" WSJ Blogs: The Juggle, *Wall Street Journal*, April 6, 2011, accessed May 28, 2011, http://blogs.wsj.com/juggle/2011/04/06/does-having-kids-dull-job-ambition/.

64. N. Waller and J. Lublin, "What's Holding Women Back in the Workplace?," *Wall Street Journal*, September 30, 2015, accessed April 23, 2017, https://www.wsj.com/articles/whats-holding-women-back-in-the-workplace-1443600242.

65. C. Friedersdorf, "Why PepsiCo CEO Indra K. Nooyi Can't Have It All," *The Atlantic*, July 1, 2014, accessed July 12, 2014, http://www.theatlantic.com/business/archive/2014/07/why-pepsico-ceo-indra-k-nooyi-cant-have-it-all/373750/.

66. Department of Industry, Labor and Human Relations, Report of the Governor's Task Force on the Glass Ceiling Commission (Madison, WI: State of Wisconsin, 1993); S. Devillard, S. Sancier, C. Werner, I. Maller, and C. Kossoff, "Women Matter 2013, Gender Diversity in Top Management: Moving Corporate Culture, Moving Boundaries," *McKinsey & Company*, November 2013, 10–11; E. O. Wright and J. Baxter, "The Glass Ceiling Hypothesis: A Reply to Critics," *Gender & Society* 14 (2000): 814–821.

67. M. Fix, G. C. Galster, and R. J. Struyk, "An Overview of Auditing for Discrimination," in *Clear and Convincing Evidence: Measurement of Discrimination in America*, ed. M. Fix and R. Struyk (Washington, DC: Urban Institute Press, 1993), 1–68.

68. S. Devillard, S. Sancier, C. Werner, I. Maller, and C. Kossoff, "Women Matter 2013, Gender Diversity in Top Management: Moving Corporate Culture, Moving Boundaries," *McKinsey & Company*, November 2013, 13–14.

69. S. Shellenbarger, "One Way to Get Unstuck and Move Up? All You Have to Do Is Ask" *Wall Street Journal*, April 15, 2015, D3.

70. J. Lublin, "Men Enlist in Fight for Gender Equality," *Wall Street Journal*, March 11, 2015, B7.

71. "How to Report Sexual Harassment at Work," *Schwin Law*, accessed August 17, 2016, http://www.schwinlaw.com/uncategorized/how-to-report-sexual-harassment-at-work.

72. "What You Should Know: EEOC and Enforcement Protections for LGBT Workers," U.S. Equal Employment Opportunity Commission, accessed April 24, 2017, https://www.eeoc.gov/eeoc/newsroom/wysk/enforcement_protections_lgbt_workers.cfm.

73. Ibid.

74. K. Sangha, "LGBT Protection in the Workplace—A Survey of State and Local Laws," *Employment Relations Today* 42 no. 2 (2015): 57–68.

75. "What You Should Know: EEOC and Enforcement Protections for LGBT Workers," U.S. Equal Employment Opportunity Commission.

76. J. Palazzolo, "Court Says Gay Employees Can Sue Under 1964 Civil Rights Act," *Wall Street Journal*, April 4, 2017, accessed April 24, 2017, https://www.wsj.com/articles/court-says-gay-employees-can-sue-under-1964-civil-rights-act-1491360550.

77. "Non-Discrimination Laws," Movement Advancement Project, April 21, 2017, accessed April 25, 2017, http://www.lgbtmap.org/equality-maps/non_discrimination_laws; N. Scheiber, "U.S. Agency Rules for Gays in Workplace Discrimination," *New York Times*, July 17, 2015, accessed April 24, 2017, https://www.nytimes.com/2015/07/18/business/us-agency-rules-for-gays-in-workplace-discrimination.html.

78. M. Bianco, "Pride 2016: The Simple Reason More and More Businesses Openly Support LGBT Rights," *Quartz*, June 26, 2016, accessed April 24, 2017, https://qz.com/710643/the-business-sense-of-supporting-lgbt-rights/.

79. D. Fidas and L. Cooper, The Cost of the Closet and the Rewards of Inclusion: Why the Workplace Environment for LGBT People Matters to Employees," Human Rights Campaign, May 2015, accessed April 24, 2017, http://hrc-assets.s3-website-us-east-1.amazonaws.com//files/assets/resources/Cost_of_the_Closet_May2014.pdf.

80. B. Sears and C. Mallory, "Documented Evidence of Employment Discrimination & Its Effects on LGBT People," The Williams Institute, UCLA Law School, July 2011, accessed April 24, 2017, https://williamsinstitute.law.ucla.edu/wp-content/uploads/Sears-Mallory-Discrimination-July-20111.pdf.

81. D. Fidas and L. Cooper, The Cost of the Closet and the Rewards of Inclusion: Why the Workplace Environment for LGBT People Matters to Employees," Human Rights Campaign, May 2015, accessed April 24, 2017, http://hrc-assets.s3-website-us-east-1.amazonaws.com//files/assets/resources/Cost_of_the_Closet_May2014.pdf.

82. What You Should Know: EEOC and Enforcement Protections for LGBT Workers," U.S. Equal Employment Opportunity Commission.

83. "The Report of the 2015 U.S. Transgender Survey," National Center for Transgender Equality, December 2016, accessed April 24, 2017, http://www.transequality.org/sites/default/files/docs/usts/Executive%20Summary%20-%20FINAL%201.6.17.pdf.

84. "Building LGBT-Inclusive Workplaces: Engaging Organizations And Individuals In Change," Catalyst, 2009, accessed April 24, 2017, http://www.catalyst.org/system/files/Building_LGBT_Inclusive_Workplaces_Engaging_Organizations_and_Individuals_in_Change.pdf.

85. "Building LGBT-Inclusive Workplaces: Engaging Organizations And Individuals In Change," Catalyst.

86. "Transgender Inclusion in the Workplace: A Toolkit for Employers," Human Rights Campaign Foundation, 2016, accessed April 24, 2017, http://assets.hrc.org//files/assets/resources/Transgender_Inclusion_in_the_Workplace_A_Toolkit_for_Employers_Version_10_14_2016.pdf?_ga=1.40958882.1697316505.1493052696.

87. Elejalde-Ruiz, "How Companies Accommodate Transgender Employees — and their Colleagues," *Chicago Tribune*, January 9, 2016, accessed April 24, 2017, http://www.chicagotribune.com/business/ct-transgender-workplace-0110-biz-20160109-story.html.

88. "First Step: Gender Identity in the Workplace," *Catalyst*, June 22, 2015, accessed April 24, 2017, http://www.catalyst.org/knowledge/first-step-gender-identity-workplace.

89. "Workplace Gender Transition Guidelines at Ernst & Young," EY, accessed April 24, 2017, hrc

-assets.s3-website-us-east-1.amazonaws.com//files/assets/resources/ErnstYoung-TransitionGuidelines.pdf.

90. Standards of Care for the Health of Transsexual, Transgender, and Gender Nonconforming People, Version 7," The World Professional Association for Transgender Health, September 14, 2011, accessed April 24, 2017, https://s3.amazonaws.com/amo_hub_content/Association140/files/Standards%20of%20Care%20V7%20-%202011%20WPATH%20(2)(1).pdf.

91. "Charge Statistics: FY1997 Through FY 2014," Equal Employment Opportunity Commission, accessed April 26, 2017, https://www.eeoc.gov/eeoc/statistics/enforcement/charges.cfm.

92. V. Zarya, "Female Fortune 500 CEOs Set to Break Records in 2017,"; G. Wallace, "Only 5 Black CEOs at 500 Biggest Companies," CNN, January 29, 2015, accessed May 8, 2016, http://money.cnn.com/2015/01/29/news/economy/mcdonalds-ceo-diversity/?iid=EL; A. Garcia, "Only 9 Hispanic CEOs at Top 500 Companies," CNN, September 9, 2015, accessed May 8, 2016, http://money.cnn.com/2015/09/09/news/hispanic-ceo-fortune-500-companies/index.html.

93. "Household Data Annual Averages: Table 11. Employed Persons by Detailed Occupation, Sex, Race, and Hispanic or Latino Ethnicity," Bureau of Labor Statistics, Department of Labor, February 8, 2017, accessed April 25, 2017, http://www.bls.gov/cps/cpsaat11.htm.

94. D. A. Neal and W. R. Johnson, "The Role of Premarket Factors in Black-White Wage Differences," Journal of Political Economy 104, no. 5 (1996): 869–895.

95. Fix, et al., "An Overview of Auditing for Discrimination."

96. M. Bendick, Jr., C. W. Jackson, and V. A. Reinoso, "Measuring Employment Discrimination through Controlled Experiments," in African-Americans and Post-Industrial Labor Markets, ed. James B. Stewart (New Brunswick, NJ: Transaction Publishers, 1997), 77–100.

97. S. Mullainathan, "Racial Bias Even When We Have Good Intentions," New York Times, January 3, 2015, BU6.

98. P. B. Riach and J. Rich, "Measuring Discrimination by Direct Experimental Methods: Seeking Gunsmoke," Journal of Post Keynesian Economics 14, no. 2 (Winter 1991–1992): 143–150.

99. A. P. Brief, R. T. Buttram, R. M. Reizenstein, and S. D. Pugh, "Beyond Good Intentions: The Next Steps Toward Racial Equality in the American Workplace," Academy of Management Executive 11 (1997): 59–72.

100. L. E. Wynter, "Business & Race: Federal Agencies, Spurred on by Nonprofit Groups, Are Increasingly Embracing the Use of Undercover Investigators to Identify Discrimination in the Marketplace," Wall Street Journal, July 1, 1998, B1; E. Dwoskin, "Social Bias Creeps Into New Web Technology," Wall Street Journal, August 21, 2015, B1, B4.

101. E. Dwoskin, "Social Bias Creeps into New Web Technology," Wall Street Journal, August 21, 2015, B1, B4.

102. "Americans with Disabilities Act Questions and Answers," US Department of Justice, accessed April 25, 2017, http://www.ada.gov/qandaeng.htm.

103. "Disability Statistics," Disability Statistics, accessed April 25, 2017, https://www.disabilitystatistics.org/reports/acs.cfm?statistic=1.

104. N. Scheiber, "Fake Cover Letters Expose Discrimination Against Disabled," New York Times, November 2, 2015, accessed May 8, 2016, http://www.nytimes.com/2015/11/02/upshot/fake-cover-letters-expose-discrimination-against-disabled.html.

105. "Disability Statistics," Disability Statistics; Economic News Release, "Persons with a Disability: Labor Force Characteristics Summary," Bureau of Labor Statistics, June 21, 2016, accessed April 25, 2017, https://www.bls.gov/news.release/disabl.nr0.htm.

106. R. Greenwood and V. A. Johnson, "Employer Perspectives on Workers with Disabilities," Journal of Rehabilitation 53 (1987): 37–45.

107. M. Zelley and R. Keys, "Give Michigan's Disabled a Chance to Work," Detroit News, November 14, 2014, accessed May 3, 2016, http://www.detroitnews.com/story/opinion/2014/11/06/give-disabled-workers-chance/18553557/. http://www.washingtonpost.com/blogs/on-leadership/wp/2015/04/06/microsoft-launches-a-pilot-program-for-hiring-autistic-workers/.

108. B. Loy, "Accommodation and Compliance Series Workplace Accommodations: Low Cost, High Impact," Job Accommodation Network, September 1, 2016, accessed April 25, 2017, https://askjan.org/media/downloads/LowCostHighImpact.pdf.

109. D. Zielinski, "New Assistive Technologies Aid Employees with Disabilities," Society for Human Resource Management, December 20, 2016, accessed April 25, 2017, https://www.shrm.org/resourcesandtools/hr-topics/technology/pages/new-assistive-technologies-aid-employees-with-disabilities.aspx.

110. "Study on the Financing of Assistive Technology Devices and Services for Individuals with Disabilities: A Report to the President and the Congress of the United States," National Council on Disability, accessed May 8, 2016, http://www.ncd.gov/newsroom/publications/assistive.html.

111. R. B. Cattell, "Personality Pinned Down," Psychology Today 7 (1973): 40–46; C. S. Carver and M. F. Scheier, Perspectives on Personality (Boston, MA: Allyn & Bacon, 1992).

112. S. Berfield, "Will Investors Put the Lid on the Container Store's Generous Wages," Bloomberg BusinessWeek, February 19, 2015, accessed May 8, 2016, http://www.bloomberg.com/news/articles/2015-02-19/container-store-conscious-capitalism-and-the-perils-of-going-public.

113. J. M. Digman, "Personality Structure: Emergence of the Five-Factor Model," Annual Review of Psychology 41 (1990): 417–440; M. R. Barrick and M. K. Mount, "The Big Five Personality Dimensions and Job Performance: A Meta-Analysis," Personnel Psychology 44 (1991): 1–26.

114. C. Anderson and G. Kilduff, "Why Do Dominant Personalities Attain Influence in Face-to-Face Groups? The Competence Signaling Effects of Trait Dominance," Journal of Personal and Social Psychology 96, no. 2 (2001): 1160–1175.

115. K. D. Lassila, "A Brief History of Groupthink: Why Two, Three, or Many Heads Aren't Always Better Than One," Yale Alumni Magazine, January/February 2008, accessed May 8, 2016, http://yalealumnimagazine.com/articles/1947.

116. R. Wall, "Germanwings Co-Pilot Andreas Lubitz Appeared to Rehearse Crash, Investigators Say," Wall Street Journal, May 6, 2015, accessed May 9, 2015, http://www.wsj.com/articles/germanwings-co-pilot-andreas-lubitz-altered-settings-of-earlier-flight-investigators-say-1430908536.

117. A. George, "How Airlines Screen Their Pilots and Watch Out for Warning Signs," Popular Mechanics, April 10, 2015, accessed May 8, 2016, http://www.popularmechanics.com/flight/a14776/how-airlines-screen-pilots-germanwings-9525/.

118. O. Behling, "Employee Selection: Will Intelligence and Conscientiousness Do the Job?" Academy of Management Executive 12 (1998): 77–86.

119. R. S. Dalal, "A Meta-Analysis of the Relationship Between Organizational Citizenship Behavior and Counterproductive Work Behavior," Journal of Applied Psychology 90 (2005): 1241–1255.

120. Barrick and Mount, "The Big Five Personality Dimensions and Job Performance"; M. K. Mount and M. R. Barrick, "The Big Five Personality Dimensions: Implications for Research and Practice in Human Resource Management," Research in Personnel & Human Resources Management 13 (1995): 153–200; M. K. Mount and M. R. Barrick, "Five Reasons Why the 'Big Five' Article Has Been Frequently Cited," Personnel Psychology 51 (1998): 849–857; D. S. Ones, M. K. Mount, M. R. Barrick, and J. E. Hunter, "Personality and Job Performance: A Critique of the Tett, Jackson, and Rothstein (1991) Meta-Analysis," Personnel Psychology 47 (1994): 147–156.

121. Mount and Barrick, "Five Reasons Why the 'Big Five' Article Has Been Frequently Cited."

122. J. A. Lopez, "Talking Desks: Personality Types Revealed in State Workstations," Arizona Republic, January 7, 1996, D1.

123. D. A. Thomas and R. J. Ely, "Making Differences Matter: A New Paradigm for Managing Diversity," Harvard Business Review 74 (September–October 1996): 79–90.

124. Esen, "2005 Workplace Diversity Practices."

125. D. A. Thomas and S. Wetlaufer, "A Question of Color: A Debate on Race in the U.S. Workplace," Harvard Business Review 75 (September–October 1997): 118–132.

126. E. Esen, "2007 State of Workplace Diversity Management. A Survey Report by the Society for Human Resource Management," 2008.

127. "Oshkosh Corporation—Diversity & Inclusion," Oshkosh, accessed July 12, 2014, http://www.oshkoshcorporation.com/about/diversity.html.

128. J. Espinoza, "Working to Prove Benefits of More Women at the Top," Wall Street Journal, February 27, 2011, accessed March 15, 2011, http://www.wsj.com/articles/SB1000142405274870415060457616648301282135.

129. J. R. Norton and R. E. Fox, The Change Equation: Capitalizing on Diversity for Effective Organizational Change (Washington, DC: American Psychological Association, 1997).

130. Ibid.

131. Thomas and Ely, "Making Differences Matter."

132. R. Thomas, Jr., Beyond Race and Gender: Unleashing the Power of Your Total Workforce by Managing Diversity (New York: AMACOM, 1991).

133. Ibid.

134. T. Cox, Jr., "The Multicultural Organization," Academy of Management Executive 5 (1991): 34–47.

135. S. Lubove, "Damned If You Do, Damned If You Don't: Preference Programs Are on the Defensive in the Public Sector, but Plaintiffs' Attorneys and Bureaucrats Keep Diversity Inc. Thriving in Corporate America," Forbes, December 15, 1997, 122.

136. L. S. Gottfredson, "Dilemmas in Developing Diversity Programs," in Diversity in the

Workplace, ed. S. E. Jackson and Associates (New York: Guilford Press, 1992).

137. J. Graham and S. Kerr, "Mentoring," in *Diversity in Engineering: Managing the Workforce of the Future* (Washington, DC: National Academies Press, 2002), accessed June 16, 2013, http://www.nap.edu/openbook .php?record_id=10377&page=99.

138. J. Longman, "Pioneer of a Crossover Move: How Becky Hammon Became NBA's First Full -Time Female Assistant Coach," *New York Times*, August 12, 2014, B8.

139. B. Hammon, "Becky's Biography," *The Official Website of Becky Hammon*, accessed April 25, 2017, http://beckyhammon25.com/index.php/ about-becky/becky-s-biography; NBA.com Staff, "Blogtable: Who Might Be the NBA's First Female Head Coach?" *NBA.com*, March 29, 2017, accessed April 25, 2017, http://www.nba.com /article/2017/03/29/blogtablefemale-nba-head -coach.

140. Carnevale and Stone, *The American Mosaic*.

141. J. Lublin, "Men Enlist in Fight for Gender Equality," *Wall Street Journal*, March 11, 2015, B7.

142. A. Greenwald, B. Nosek, and M. Banaji, "Understanding and Using the Implicit Association Test: I. An Improved Scoring Algorithm," *Journal of Personality & Social Psychology* (August 2003): 197–206; J. S. Lublin, "Bringing Hidden Biases Into the Light," *Wall Street Journal*, January 9, 2014, accessed May 9, 2016, http://online.wsj.com/news/articles/SB100014 24052702303754404579308562690896896; "The IAT | The Blind Spot," *The Blind Spot*, accessed July 13, 2014, http://spottheblindspot .com/the-iat/.

143. H. Blanton, J. Jaccard, E. Strauts, G. Mitchell and P. Tetlock, "Toward a Meaningful Metric of Implicit Prejudice," *Journal of Applied Psychology* 100 (2015): 1468–1481; F. Oswald, G. Mitchell, H. Blanton, J. Jaccard, and P. Tetlock, "Predicting Ethnic and Racial Discrimination: A Meta-Analysis of IAT Criterion Studies," *Journal of Personality and Social Psychology* 105 (2013): 171–192; H. Blanton, J. Jaccard, J. Klick, B. Mellers, G. Mitchell, and P. Tetlock, "Strong Claims and Weak Evidence: Reassessing the Predictive Validity of the IAT," *Journal of Applied Psychology* 94 (2009): 567–582; T. Bartlett, "Can We Really Measure Implicit Bias? Maybe Not," *Chronicle of Higher Education*, January 5, 2017, accessed April 25, 2017, http://www.chronicle .com/article/Can-We-Really-Measure -Implicit/238807.

144. A. Applewhite, "You're How Old? We'll Be in Touch - The New York," *New York Times*, September 3, 2016, accessed April 25, 2017, https:// www.nytimes.com/2016/09/04/opinion /sunday/youre-how-old-well-be-in-touch.html.

145. Bohnet, "Real Fixes for Workplace Bias.'"

146. A. Valerio and K. Sawyer, "The Men Who Mentor," *Harvard Business Review*, December 7, 2016, accessed April 25, 2017, https://hbr.org/2016 /12/the-men-who-mentor-women.

147. R. Joplin and C. S. Daus, "Challenges of Leading a Diverse Workforce," *Academy of Management Executive* 11 (1997): 32–47.

148. Korkki, "What Could I Possibly Learn From a Mentor Half My Age? Plenty," *New York Times*, September 10, 2016, accessed April 25, 2017, https://www.nytimes.com/2016/09/11/business /what-could-i-possibly-learn-from-a-mentor-half -my-age.html?_r=0.

149. T. Minsberg, "In a Reverse Mentorship, Seeing Age Though a New Lens," *New York Times*,

September 10, 2016, accessed April 25, 2017, https://www.nytimes.com/2016/09/11 /business/in-a-reverse-mentorship-seeing-age -though-a-new-lens.html.

150. Korkki, "What Could I Possibly Learn From a Mentor Half My Age? Plenty."

151. Minsberg, "In a Reverse Mentorship, Seeing Age Though a New Lens."

152. Korkki, "What Could I Possibly Learn From a Mentor Half My Age? Plenty."

153. P. Dvorak, "How Executives Are Pushed to Foster Diversity," *Wall Street Journal*, December 18, 2006, accessed May 8, 2016, http://online.wsj .com/article/SB116640764543853102.html?mod =rss_build.

154. A. Kalev, F. Dobbin, and E. Kelly. "Best Practices or Best Guesses? Diversity Management and the Remediation of Inequality." *American Sociological Review* 71 (2006): 589–617; A. Eagly, "When Passionate Advocates Meet Research on Diversity, Does the Honest Broker Stand a Chance," *Journal of Social Issues* 72 (2016): 199–122; C. Moss-Racusin, J. van der Toorn, J. Dovidio, V. Brescoll, M. Graham, and J. Handelsman, "Scientific Diversity Interventions," *Science* 343 (2014): 615–616.

155. F. Dobbin, A. Kalev, and E. Kelley, "Diversity Management in Corporate America," *Contexts* 6 (2007): 21–27.

156. E. Paluck and D. Green, "Prejudice Reduction: What Works? A Review and Assessment of Research and Practice," Annual Review of Psychology 60 (2009): 339–367.

157. F. Dobbin and A. Kalev, "Why Diversity Program," *Harvard Business Review*, July-August 2016, accessed April 25, 2017, https://hbr .org/2016/07/why-diversity-programs-fail.

158. Ibid.

159. Dobbin, A. Kalev, and E. Kelley, "Diversity Management in Corporate America."

160. Haidt and Jussim, "Hard Truths About Race on Campus."

13

1. "State of the American Workplace," Gallup, April 12, 2017, accessed April 26, 2017, http: //www.gallup.com/reports/199961/state-american -workplace-report-2017.aspx.

2. J. Harter, F. Schmidt, Ph.D., S. Agrawal, S. Plowman, M.A., and A. Blue, "The Relationship Between Engagement at Work and Organizational Outcomes 2016 Q 12® Meta-Analysis: Ninth Edition," Gallup, April 2016, http://www.gallup.com /services/191558/q12-meta-analysis-ninth-edition -2016.aspx.

3. P. Campbell and R. D. Pritchard, "Motivation Theory in Industrial and Organizational Psychology," in *Handbook of Industrial and Organizational Psychology*, ed. M. D. Dunnette (Chicago: Rand McNally, 1976).

4. K. Clark, "The Cardinals Way: Yell, Hug, Repeat," *Wall Street Journal*, October 20, 2015, accessed May 4, 2016, http://www.wsj.com/ articles/the-cardinals-way-yell-hug-repeat -1445371413.

5. K. Belson, "No Foul Mouths on This Field: Football With a New Age Twist," *New York Times*, September 6, 2015, accessed May 4, 2016, http://www.nytimes.com/2015/09/07/sports/football /no-foul-mouths-on-pete-carrolls-field-football-with -a-new-age-twist.html?_r=0.

6. A. Locke, "The Nature and Causes of Job Satisfaction," in *Handbook of Industrial and*

Organizational Psychology, ed. M. D. Dunnette (Chicago: Rand McNally, 1976).

7. Mr. Everyday Dollar, "I Just Became a Millionaire at Age 35, and It's a Huge Letdown," *Business Insider*, March 27, 2015, accessed May 10, 2015, http://www.businessinsider.com/i-just-became -a-millionaire-at-age-35-and-its-a-huge-letdown -2015-3.

8. H. Maslow, "A Theory of Human Motivation," *Psychological Review* 50 (1943): 370–396.

9. P. Alderfer, *Existence, Relatedness, and Growth: Human Needs in Organizational Settings* (New York: Free Press, 1972).

10. C. McClelland, "Toward a Theory of Motive Acquisition," *American Psychologist* 20 (1965): 321–333; D. C. McClelland and D. H. Burnham, "Power Is the Great Motivator," *Harvard Business Review* 54, no. 2 (1976): 100–110.

11. J. H. Turner, "Entrepreneurial Environments and the Emergence of Achievement Motivation in Adolescent Males," *Sociometry* 33 (1970): 147–165.

12. L. W. Porter, E. E. Lawler III, and J. R. Hackman, *Behavior in Organizations* (New York: McGraw-Hill, 1975).

13. C. Ajila, "Maslow's Hierarchy of Needs Theory: Applicability to the Nigerian Industrial Setting," *IFE Psychology* 5 (1997): 162–174.

14. M. A. Wahba and L. B. Birdwell, "Maslow Reconsidered: A Review of Research on the Need Hierarchy Theory," *Organizational Behavior & Human Performance* 15 (1976): 212–240; J. Rauschenberger, N. Schmitt, and J. E. Hunter, "A Test of the Need Hierarchy Concept by a Markov Model of Change in Need Strength," *Administrative Science Quarterly* 25 (1980): 654–670.

15. E. E. Lawler III and L. W. Porter, "The Effect of Performance on Job Satisfaction," *Industrial Relations* 7 (1967): 20–28.

16. Porter, et al., *Behavior in Organizations*.

17. P. Cohen, "One-Time Bonuses and Perks Muscle Out Pay Raises for Workers," *New York Times*, May 25, 2016, accessed May 4, 2016, http://www.nytimes.com/2015/05/26/business/one -time-bonuses-and-perks-muscle-out-pay-raises -for-workers.html?_r=0.

18. F. Koller, "2016 Ends at Lincoln Electric, No Layoffs for, now, 68 years and 83 Years of Amazing Profit-Sharing Bonuses « Frank ," *Frank Koller*, December 9, 2016, accessed April 26, 2017, http: //www.frankkoller.com/2016/12/2016-ends-at -lincoln-electric-no-layoffs-for-now-68-years-and -83-years-of-amazing-profit-sharing-bonuses/.

19. Porter, et al., *Behavior in Organizations*.

20. K. Woolley and A. Fishbach, "Immediate Rewards Predict Adherence to Long-Term Goals," *Personality and Social Psychology Bulletin* 43 no. 2 (2017): 151–162.

21. K. Woolley and A. Fishbach, "What Separates Goals We Achieve from Goals We Don't," *Harvard Business Review*, April 26, 2017, accessed April 27, 2017, https://hbr.org/2017/04/what-separates-goals -we-achieve-from-goals-we-dont.

22. C. Caggiano, "What Do Workers Want?" *Inc.*, November 1992, 101–104; "National Study of the Changing Workforce," *Families & Work Institute*, accessed May 31, 2005, http://www.familiesandwork .org/summary/nscw.pdf.

23. C. Lee, A. Alonso, E. Esen, J. Coombs, T. Mulvey, K. Wessels, and H. Ng, "Employee Job Satisfaction and Engagement: Revitalizing a Changing Workforce," *Society for Human Resource Management*, April 18, 2016, accessed May 4, 2016, https://www.shrm.org/Research/SurveyFindings /Articles/Documents/2016-Employee-Job -Satisfaction-and-Engagement-Report.pdf.

24. N. Jackson, "5 Ways to Reward Employees When Raises Aren't an Option," *Entrepreneur*, August 24, 2012, accessed June 16, 2013, http://www.entrepreneur.com/article/224249.

25. Lee, et. al., "Employee Job Satisfaction and Engagement."

26. S. Berfield, "Will Investors Put the Lid on the Container Store's Generous Wages," *Bloomberg Businessweek*, February 19, 2015, accessed May 9, 2015, http://www.bloomberg.com/news/articles/2015-02-19/container-store-conscious-capitalism-and-the-perils-of-going-public.

27. J. Laabs, "Satisfy Them with More Than Money," *Personnel Journal* 77, no. 11 (1998): 40.

28. R. Kanfer and P. Ackerman, "Aging, Adult Development, and Work Motivation," *Academy of Management Review* (2004): 440–458.

29. L. Mishel and J. Schieder, "CEO Pay Remains High Relative to the Pay of Typical Workers and High-Wage Earners," *Economic Policy Institute*, July 20, 2017, accessed August 26, 2017, http://www.epi.org/publication/ceo-pay-remains-high-relative-to-the-pay-of-typical-workers-and-high-wage-earners/.

30. S. Choe (Associated Press), "CEO pay: Top 10 Highest Paid CEOs in 2016," USA Today, May 23, 2017, accessed August 26, 2017, https://www.usatoday.com/story/money/2017/05/23/ceo-pay-highest-paid-chief-executive-officers-2016/339079001/.

31. "Occupational Employment and Wages, May 2016: 11-1011 Chief Executives," *Bureau of Labor Statistics*, March 31, 2017, accessed August 26, 2017, http://www.bls.gov/oes/current/oes111011.htm.

32. C. T. Kulik and M. L. Ambrose, "Personal and Situational Determinants of Referent Choice," *Academy of Management Review* 17 (1992): 212–237.

33. L. Weber and R. Silverman, "Worker Share Their Secret Salaries," *Wall Street Journal*, April 6, 2013, accessed May 4, 2016, http://www.wsj.com/articles/SB10001424127887324345804578426744168583824.

34. S. Shellenbarger, "Open Salaries: The Good, the Bad and the Awkward," *Wall Street Journal*, January 12, 2016, accessed May 4, 2016, http://www.wsj.com/articles/open-salaries-the-good-the-bad-and-the-awkward-1452624480.

35. J. S. Adams, "Toward an Understanding of Inequity," *Journal of Abnormal Social Psychology* 67 (1963): 422–436.

36. S. Shellenbarger, "Open Salaries: The Good, the Bad and the Awkward," *Wall Street Journal*, January 12, 2016, accessed May 4, 2016, http://www.wsj.com/articles/open-salaries-the-good-the-bad-and-the-awkward-1452624480.

37. J. Kramer, "Should You Ever Ask What Your Coworkers Make?" Glamour, April 17, 2017, accessed April 27, 2017, http://www.glamour.com/story/why-we-need-to-talk-to-our-coworkers-about-our-salaries.

38. D. Burkus, "Why Being Transparent About Pay Is Good for Business," *Wall Street Journal*, May 30, 2016, accessed April 27, 2017, https://www.wsj.com/articles/why-being-transparent-about-pay-is-good-for-business-1464660062.

39. T. Prudente, "Teachers at Baltimore elementary school report sick en masse," *Baltimore Sun*, February 22, 2017, accessed April 27, 2017, http://www.baltimoresun.com/news/maryland/education/k-12/bs-md-ci-schools-sick-out-20170222-story.html.

40. "General Information on the Fair Labor Standards Act (FLSA)," *Department of Labor*, July 2009, accessed April 27, 2017, https://www.dol.gov/whd/regs/compliance/mwposter.htm; "Overtime Pay—Wage and Hour Division (WHD)," *Department of Labor*, accessed May 4, 2016, https://www.dol.gov/whd/overtime_pay.htm.

41. News Release, "Halliburton Pays Nearly $18.3 Million in Overtime Owed to More Than 1,000 Employees Nationwide After US Labor Department Investigation, *Department of Labor*, September 22, 2015, accessed May 4, 2016, https://www.dol.gov/opa/media/press/whd/whd20151647.htm.

42. "Fair Labor Standards Act Enforcement Statistics," United States Department of Labor Wage and Hour Division, accessed April 27, 2017, https://www.dol.gov/whd/data/xls/FairLabor_MinWage.xlsx; "Data - Wage and Hour Division (WHD) - U.S. Department of Labor Wage and Hour Division," accessed April 27, 2017, https://www.dol.gov/whd/data/datatables.htm#panel2.

43. C. Chen, J. Choi, and S. Chi, "Making Justice Sense of Local-Expatriate Compensation Disparity: Mitigation by Local Referents, Ideological Explanations, and Interpersonal Sensitivity in China - Foreign Joint Ventures," *Academy of Management Journal* 45 (2002): 807–817.

44. M. Schlangenstein, "American Air's Labor Discord Stymies CEO Push to Change Culture - Blo," Bloomberg, January 26, 2017, accessed April 27, 2017, https://www.bloomberg.com/news/articles/2017-01-26/american-air-s-labor-discord-stymies-ceo-push-to-change-culture.

45. C. Shine, "American Airlines Offering Raises of Up to 8 Percent for Pilots, Flight Attendants," Dallas News, April 26, 2017, accessed April 27, 2017, https://www.dallasnews.com/business/american-airlines/2017/04/26/american-airlines-offering-raises-8-percent-pilots-flight-attendants.

46. Ibid.

47. R. Feintzeig, "Radical Idea at the Office: A 40-Hour Workweek," *Wall Street Journal*, October 13, 2015, accessed May 4, 2016, http://www.wsj.com/articles/radical-idea-at-the-office-a-40-hour-workweek-1444754956.

48. Ibid.

49. Ibid.

50. R. Folger and M. A. Konovsky, "Effects of Procedural and Distributive Justice on Reactions to Pay Raise Decisions," *Academy of Management Journal* 32 (1989): 115–130; M. A. Konovsky, "Understanding Procedural Justice and Its Impact on Business Organizations," *Journal of Management* 26 (2000): 489–512.

51. "Four Air France Employees Sacked Over Violent Protest," *BBC News*, November 12, 2015, accessed May 4, 2016, http://www.bbc.com/news/world-europe-34804611.

52. E. Barret-Howard and T. R. Tyler, "Procedural Justice as a Criterion in Allocation Decisions," *Journal of Personality & Social Psychology* 50 (1986): 296–305; Folger and Konovsky, "Effects of Procedural and Distributive Justice on Reactions to Pay Raise Decisions."

53. R. Folger and J. Greenberg, "Procedural Justice: An Interpretive Analysis of Personnel Systems," in *Research in Personnel and Human Resources Management*, vol. 3, ed. K. Rowland and G. Ferris (Greenwich, CT: JAI, 1985); R. Folger, D. Rosenfield, J. Grove, and L. Corkran, "Effects of 'Voice' and Peer Opinions on Responses to Inequity," *Journal of Personality & Social Psychology* 37 (1979): 2253–2261; E. A. Lind and T. R. Tyler, *The Social Psychology of Procedural Justice* (New York: Plenum, 1988); Konovsky, "Understanding Procedural Justice and Its Impact on Business Organizations."

54. V. H. Vroom, *Work and Motivation* (New York: John Wiley & Sons, 1964); L. W. Porter and E. E. Lawler III, *Managerial Attitudes and Performance* (Homewood, IL: Dorsey & Richard D. Irwin, 1968).

55. N. Scheiber, "How Uber Drivers Decide How Long to Work - The New York," *New York Times*, September 4, 2016, accessed April 27, 2017, https://www.nytimes.com/2016/09/05/business/economy/how-uber-drivers-decide-how-long-to-work.html.

56. M. Murphy, "This Uber driver made $507,500 last year (but not by driving)," *Market Watch*, February 20, 2017, accessed April 27, 2017, http://www.marketwatch.com/(S(rnrsydaynixa5x55oiibxm45))/story/this-uber-driver-made-507500-last-year-but-not-by-driving-2017-02-16?link=MW_latest_news.

57. S. Miller, "Countering the Employee Recognition Gap," SHRM Library, *Society for Human Resource Management*, February 2006, accessed March 25, 2009, http://www.shrm.org.

58. Press Release, "North American Employers Give Pay-for-Performance Programs Low Marks, Willis Towers Watson Survey Finds," Willis Towers Watson, February 4, 2016, accessed April 27, 2017, https://www.willistowerswatson.com/en/press/2016/02/north-american-employers-give-pay-for-performance-programs-low-marks.

59. E. Bernstein and H. Blunden, "The Sales Director Who Turned Work Into a Fantasy Sports Competition," *Harvard Business Review*, March 27, 2015, accessed May 10, 2015, https://hbr.org/2015/03/the-sales-director-who-turned-work-into-a-fantasy-sports-competition.

60. Ibid.

61. K. W. Thomas and B. A. Velthouse, "Cognitive Elements of Empowerment," *Academy of Management Review* 15 (1990): 666–681.

62. E. L. Thorndike, *Animal Intelligence* (New York: Macmillan, 1911).

63. "Fox Urine and Christmas Tree Theft," Today I Found Out, December 7, 2015, accessed May 4, 2016, http://www.todayifoundout.com/index.php/2015/12/fox-urine-stops-christmas-tree-theft/.

64. B. F. Skinner, *Science and Human Behavior* (New York: Macmillan, 1954); B. F. Skinner, *Beyond Freedom and Dignity* (New York: Bantam, 1971); B. F. Skinner, *A Matter of Consequences* (New York: New York University Press, 1984).

65. A. M. Dickinson and A. D. Poling, "Schedules of Monetary Reinforcement in Organizational Behavior Management: Latham and Huber Revisited," *Journal of Organizational Behavior Management* 16, no. 1 (1992): 71–91.

66. M. Jamrisko, "Bosses Bribe Workers to Take Vacation in Healing U.S. Job Market," *Bloomberg Business*, October 1, 2015, accessed May 4, 2016, http://www.bloomberg.com/news/articles/2015-10-01/bosses-bribe-workers-to-take-vacation-in-healing-u-s-job-market.

67. R. Greenfield, "Why Pay Employees to Exercise When You Can Threaten Them?" *Bloomberg*, February 15, 2016, accessed April 27, 2017, https://www.bloomberg.com/news/articles/2016-02-15/why-pay-employees-to-exercise-when-you-can-threaten-them.

68. "Chinese Company Makes Underperforming Employees Eat Live Worms as Punishment," *Straits Times*, November 15, 2016, accessed April 28, 2017, http://www.straitstimes.com/asia/east-asia/chinese-company-makes

-underperforming-employees-eat-live-worms-as
-punishment.

69. Ibid.

70. G. Marks, "A Chinese Firm Makes Its Employees Eat Worms If They Don't Meet Their Sales Targets," *Washington Post*, November 16, 2016, accessed April 28, 2017, https://www .washingtonpost.com/news/on-small-business /wp/2016/11/16/a-chinese-firm-makes-its -employees-eat-worms-if-they-dont-meet-their -sales-targets/?utm_term=.a1a217608d8c.

71. S. Chaudhuri, "Burberry CEO Christopher Bailey Gets 75% Pay Cut after Disappointing Results," *Wall Street Journal*, June 6, 2016, accessed April 28, 2017, http://www.wsj.com /articles/burberry-ceo-christopher-bailey-gets -75-pay-cut-1465208025.

72. J. B. Miner, *Theories of Organizational Behavior* (Hinsdale, IL: Dryden, 1980).

73. Dickinson and Poling, "Schedules of Monetary Reinforcement in Organizational Behavior Management."

74. F. Luthans and A. D. Stajkovic, "Reinforce for Performance: The Need to Go Beyond Pay and Even Rewards," *Academy of Management Executive* 13, no. 2 (1999): 49–57.

75. K. Hovland, "Electric-Car Perks Put Norway in a Pinch," *Wall Street Journal*, September 18, 2015, accessed May 5, 2016, http://www.wsj.com/articles /electric-car-perks-put-norway-in-a-pinch-1442601936.

76. K. D. Butterfield, L. K. Trevino, and G. A. Ball, "Punishment from the Manager's Perspective: A Grounded Investigation and Inductive Model," *Academy of Management Journal* 39 (1996): 1479–1512.

77. R. D. Arvey and J. M. Ivancevich, "Punishment in Organizations: A Review, Propositions, and Research Suggestions," *Academy of Management Review* 5 (1980): 123–132.

78. R. D. Arvey, G. A. Davis, and S. M. Nelson, "Use of Discipline in an Organization: A Field Study," *Journal of Applied Psychology* 69 (1984): 448–460; M. E. Schnake, "Vicarious Punishment in a Work Setting," *Journal of Applied Psychology* 71 (1986): 343–345.

79. G. A. Yukl and G. P. Latham, "Consequences of Reinforcement Schedules and Incentive Magnitudes for Employee Performance: Problems Encountered in a Field Setting," *Journal of Applied Psychology* 60 (1975): 294–298.

80. E. A. Locke and G. P. Latham, *Goal Setting: A Motivational Technique That Works* (Englewood Cliffs, NJ: Prentice Hall, 1984); E. A. Locke and G. P. Latham, *A Theory of Goal Setting and Task Performance* (Englewood Cliffs, NJ: Prentice Hall, 1990).

81. L. Baldassarre and Brian Finken, "GE's Real -Time Performance Development," *Harvard Business Review*, August 12, 2015, accessed May 5, 2016, https://hbr.org/2015/08/ges-real-time -performance-development.

82. S. Nawaz, "Break Bad Habits with a Simple Checklist," *Harvard Business Review*, February 10, 2017, accessed April 28, 2017, https://hbr.org/2017 /02/break-bad-habits-with-a-simple-checklist.

83. G. P. Latham and E. A. Locke, "Goal Setting— A Motivational Technique That Works," *Organizational Dynamics* 8, no. 2 (1979): 68.

84. Ibid.

14

1. T. Verducci, "Why Theo Epstein and the Chicago Cubs Are Fortune's MVPs This Year,"

Fortune, March 23, 2017, accessed April 28, 2017, http://fortune.com/2017/03/23/theo-epstein -chicago-cubs-worlds-greatest-leaders/.

2. W. Bennis, "Why Leaders Can't Lead," *Training & Development Journal* 43, no. 4 (1989): 35–39.

3. J. Haden, "What No One Ever Tells You About Being the Boss," *LinkedIn Pulse*, August 18, 2015, accessed May 9, 2016, https://www.linkedin.com /pulse/inside-story-what-being-boss-really-means -jeff-haden.

4. T. Verducci, "Theo Epstein: How Cubs' Boss Ended Team's World Series Drought," *Sports Illustrated*, December 14, 2016, accessed April 28, 2017, https://www.si.com/mlb/2016/12/14/theo -epstein-chicago-cubs-world-series-rainmaker.

5. T. Verducci, "World Series: Cubs Beat Indians in Epic and Historic World Series Game 7," *Sports Illustrated*, November 3, 2016, accessed April 28, 2017, https://www.si.com/mlb/2016/11/03/world -series-cubs-indians-game-7.

6. A. Zaleznik, "Managers and Leaders: Are They Different?" *Harvard Business Review* 55 (1977): 76–78; A. Zaleznik, "The Leadership Gap," *Washington Quarterly* 6 (1983): 32–39.

7. Bennis, "Why Leaders Can't Lead."

8. S. Frier, "Jack Dorsey Is Losing Control of Twitter," *Bloomberg*, October 5, 2016, accessed April 29, 2017, https://www.bloomberg.com /features/2016-twitter-dorsey-strategy/.

9. N. Buhayar, "Warren Buffett Made a Big Bet on an 'In-Your-Face' CEO," *Wall Street Journal*, August 3, 2016, accessed April 29, 2017, https: //www.bloomberg.com/news/features/2016-08-03 /buffett-s-bet-on-a-relentless-ceo.

10. D. Jones, "Not All Successful CEOs Are Extroverts," *USA Today*, June 7, 2006, B.1.

11. J. McGregor, "Introverts Tend to Be Better CEOs—and Other Surprising Traits of Top-Performing Executives," *Washington Post*, April 17, 2017, accessed April 29, 2017, https://www .washingtonpost.com/news/on-leadership /wp/2017/04/17/introverts-tend-to-be-better-ceos -and-other-surprising-traits-of-top-performing -executives/.

12. G. Murray, "Caveman Politics," *Psychology Today*, December 15, 2011, accessed May 9, 2016, http://www.psychologytoday.com/blog/caveman -politics/201112/are-you-sure-we-prefer-taller -leaders; G. Murray and J. Schmitz, "Caveman Politics: Evolutionary Leadership Preferences and Physical Stature," *Social Science Quarterly* 92 (2011): 1215–1235.

13. M. Gladwell, "Why Do We Love Tall Men?" Gladwell.com, accessed July 16, 2014, http: //gladwell.com/blink/why-do-we-love-tall-men/.

14. Schumpeter, "The Look of a Leader," *The Economist*, September 27, 2014, accessed May 6, 2016, http://www.economist.com/news/business /21620197-getting-top-much-do-how-you-look-what -you-achieve-look-leader.

15. E. Wong, M. Ormiston, and M. Haselhuhn, "A Face Only an Investor Could Love: CEO's Facial Structure Predicts Their Firms' Financial Performance," *Psychological Science* 22 (2011): 1478–1483; S. Knapton, "Successful Male Leaders Have Wider Faces than Average Man," *Telegraph*, August 16, 2015, accessed May 9, 2016, http: //www.telegraph.co.uk/news/science/science-news /11806360/Successful-male-leaders-have-wider -faces-than-average-man.html.

16. S. Zaccaro, "Trait-Based Perspectives of Leadership," *American Psychologist* 62 (2007): 6-16; R. J. House and R. M Aditya, "The Social Scientific Study of Leadership: Quo Vadis?" *Journal of Management* 23 (1997): 409–473; T. Judge,

R. Illies, J. Bono, and M. Gerhardt, "Personality and Leadership: A Qualitative and Quantitative Review," *Journal of Applied Psychology* 89 (August 2002): 765–782; S. A. Kirkpatrick and E. A. Locke, "Leadership: Do Traits Matter?" *Academy of Management Executive* 5, no. 2 (1991): 48–60.

17. House and Aditya, "The Social Scientific Study of Leadership"; Kirkpatrick and Locke, "Leadership: Do Traits Matter?"

18. J. McGregor, "Introverts Tend To Be Better CEOs — and Other Surprising Traits of Top -Performing Executives."

19. About Amazon - 2016 Letter to Shareholders," Amazon, April 12, 2017, accessed April 29, 2017, https://www.amazon.com/p/feature/z6o9g6sysx- ur57t.

20. Ibid.

21. J. Lublin, "The Case for Humble Executives," *Wall Street Journal*, October 20, 2015, accessed May 9, 2016, http://www.wsj.com/articles/the-case -for-humble-executives-1445385076.

22. J. Cheng, "Samsung Picks New Mobile Lead-er," *Wall Street Journal*, December 2, 2015, B4.

23. M. Campbell, "Is Emirates Airline Running Out of Sky?" *Bloomberg*, January 5, 2017, accessed April 29, 2017, https://www.bloomberg.com/news /features/2017-01-05/is-emirates-airline-running -out-of-sky.

24. Kirkpatrick and Locke, "Leadership: Do Traits Matter?"

25. E. A. Fleishman, "The Description of Supervisory Behavior," *Journal of Applied Psychology* 37 (1953): 1–6; L. R. Katz, *New Patterns of Management* (New York: McGraw-Hill, 1961).

26. N. Buhayar, "Warren Buffett Made a Big Bet on an 'In-Your-Face' CEO."

27. C. Conley, "I Joined Airbnb at 52, and Here's What I Learned About Age, Wisdom, and the Tech Industry," *Harvard Business Review*, April 18, 2017, accessed April 29, 2017, https://hbr.org/2017/04/i -joined-airbnb-at-52-and-heres-what-i-learned -about-age-wisdom-and-the-tech-industry.

28. Ibid.

29. P. Weissenberg and M. H. Kavanagh, "The Independence of Initiating Structure and Consideration: A Review of the Evidence," *Personnel Psychology* 25 (1972): 119–130.

30. R. J. House and T. R. Mitchell, "Path-Goal Theory of Leadership," *Journal of Contemporary Business* 3 (1974): 81–97; F. E. Fiedler, "A Contingency Model of Leadership Effectiveness," in *Advances in Experimental Social Psychology*, ed. L. Berkowitz (New York: Academic Press, 1964); V. H. Vroom and P. W. Yetton, *Leadership and Decision Making* (Pittsburgh: University of Pittsburgh Press, 1973); P. Hersey and K. H. Blanchard, The *Management of Organizational Behavior*, 4th ed. (Englewood Cliffs, NJ: Prentice Hall, 1984); S. Kerr and J. M. Jermier, "Substitutes for Leadership: Their Meaning and Measurement," *Organizational Behavior & Human Performance* 22 (1978): 375–403.

31. A. Grant, F. Gino, and D. Hofmann, "The Hidden Advantage of Quiet Bosses," *Harvard Business Review* 88, no. 12 (2010): 28.

32. F. E. Fiedler and M. M. Chemers, *Leadership and Effective Management* (Glenview, IL: Scott, Foresman, 1974); F. E. Fiedler and M. M. Chemers, *Improving Leadership Effectiveness: The Leader Match Concept*, 2nd ed. (New York: Wiley, 1984).

33. E. Chasan, "A Startup in Transition: The CFO of Evernote on Where It Is," *Wall Street Journal*, October 29, 2015, R9.

34. Fiedler and Chemers, *Improving Leadership Effectiveness*.

35. F. E. Fiedler, "The Effects of Leadership Training and Experience: A Contingency Model Interpretation," *Administrative Science Quarterly* 17, no. 4 (1972): 455; F. E. Fiedler, *A Theory of Leadership Effectiveness* (New York: McGraw-Hill, 1967).

36. L. S. Csoka and F. E. Fiedler, "The Effect of Military Leadership Training: A Test of the Contingency Model," *Organizational Behavior & Human Performance* 8 (1972): 395–407.

37. P. Hersey and K. Blanchard, *Management of Organizational Behavior: Leading Human Resources*, 8th ed. (Escondido, CA: Center for Leadership Studies, 2001).

38. W. Blank, J. Weitzel, and S. Green, "A Test of the Situational Leadership Theory," *Personnel Psychology* 43, no. 3 (1990): 579–597; W. Norris and R. Vecchio, "Situational Leadership Theory: A Replication," *Group & Organization Management* 17, no. 3 (1992): 331–342.

39. Ibid.

40. House and Mitchell, "Path-Goal Theory of Leadership."

41. "Up and Coming Leaders," *Entrepreneur*, March 26, 2014, accessed July 17, 2014, http://www.entrepreneur.com/article/231531.

42. M. Tenney, "More Than Money," *Collector*, October 2013, 26–28.

43. House and Mitchell, "Path-Goal Theory of Leadership."

44. X. Huang, E. Xu, W. Chiu, C. Lam, and J. Farh, "When Authoritarian Leaders Outperform Transformational Leaders: Firm Performance in a Harsh Economic Environment," *Academy of Management Discoveries* 1, no. 2 (2015): 180–200.

45. B. M. Fisher and J. E. Edwards, "Consideration and Initiating Structure and Their Relationships with Leader Effectiveness: A Meta-Analysis," *Proceedings of the Academy of Management*, August 1988, 201–205.

46. Z. Ton and S. Kalloch, "How 4 Retailers Became "Best Places to Work," *Harvard Business Review*, January 2, 2017, accessed April 29, 2017, https://hbr.org/2017/01/how-4-retailers-became-best-places-to-work.

47. H. Tabuchi, "HEB Grocery Chain to Give Stock to 55,000 Employees," *New York Times*, November 2, 2015, accessed April 29, 2017, https://www.nytimes.com/2015/11/03/business/heb-grocery-chain-to-give-stock-to-55000-employees.html.

48. S. Boardman, "The Pygmalion Effect: Do Expectations Shape Reality?" *Huffington Post*, May 21, 2015, accessed May 9, 2016, http://www.huffingtonpost.com/samantha-boardman-md/the-pygmalion-effect-do-expectations-shape-reality_b_7322780.html.

49. Ibid.

50. J. C. Wofford and L. Z. Liska, "Path-Goal Theories of Leadership: A Meta-Analysis," *Journal of Management* 19 (1993): 857–876.

51. House and Aditya, "The Social Scientific Study of Leadership."

52. V. H. Vroom and A. G. Jago, *The New Leadership: Managing Participation in Organizations* (Englewood Cliffs, NJ: Prentice Hall, 1988).

53. C. Fishman, "How Teamwork Took Flight: This Team Built a Commercial Engine—and Self-Managing GE Plant—from Scratch," *Fast Company*, October 1, 1999, 188.

54. Ibid.

55. Ibid.

56. N. Fallon, "Is Your Management Style Hurting Your Team?" *Business News Daily*, May 14, 2014, accessed May 9, 2016, http://www.businessnewsdaily.com/6409-management-styles-strategies.html.

57. G. A. Yukl, *Leadership in Organizations*, 3rd ed. (Englewood Cliffs, NJ: Prentice Hall, 1995).

58. B. M. Bass, *Bass & Stogdill's Handbook of Leadership: Theory, Research, and Managerial Applications* (New York: Free Press, 1990).

59. R. D. Ireland and M. A. Hitt, "Achieving and Maintaining Strategic Competitiveness in the 21st Century: The Role of Strategic Leadership," *Academy of Management Executive* 13, no. 1 (1999): 43–57.

60. P. Haggin, "Why a Japanese E-Tailer Requires Workers to Speak English," *Wall Street Journal*, October 2, 2016, accessed April 29, 2017, https://www.wsj.com/articles/why-a-japanese-e-tailer-requires-workers-to-speak-english-1475460061.

61. P. Thoms and D. B. Greenberger, "Training Business Leaders to Create Positive Organizational Visions of the Future: Is It Successful?" *Academy of Management Journal*, Best Papers & Proceedings 1995, 212–216.

62. M. Weber, *The Theory of Social and Economic Organizations*, trans. R. A. Henderson and T. Parsons (New York: Free Press, 1947).

63. D. A. Waldman and F. J. Yammarino, "CEO Charismatic Leadership: Levels-of-Management and Levels-of-Analysis Effects," *Academy of Management Review* 24, no. 2 (1999): 266–285.

64. K. B. Lowe, K. G. Kroeck, and N. Sivasubram aniam, "Effectiveness Correlates of Transformation-al and Transactional Leadership: A Meta-Analytic Review of the MLQ Literature," *Leadership Quarterly* 7 (1996): 385–425.

65. J. M. Howell and B. J. Avolio, "The Ethics of Charismatic Leadership: Submission or Liberation?" *Academy of Management Executive* 6, no. 2 (1992): 43–54.

66. G. Colvin, "The Greatest Business Decisions of All Time: Tata Steel," *Fortune*, October 1, 2012, accessed May 9, 2016, http://money.cnn.com/gallery/news/companies/2012/10/01/greatest-business-decisions.fortune/4.html.

67. H. Perlberg and K. Burton, "The Softer Side of Stevie Cohen" *Bloomberg BusinessWeek*, November 6–December 15, 2015, 41–43; A. Viswanatha and J. Chung, "Deal Ends SEC's Pursuit of Steven Cohen," *Wall Street Journal*, January 8, 2016, accessed October 20, 2016, http://www.wsj.com/articles/sec-bars-steven-cohen-from-supervising-hedge-funds-for-two-years-1452278527.

68. D. J. Chandler, "The Perfect Storm of Leaders' Unethical Behavior: A Conceptual Framework," *International Journal of Leadership Studies* 5, no.1 (2009): 69–93.

69. Howell and Avolio, "The Ethics of Charismatic Leadership."

70. B. M. Bass, "From Transactional to Transformational Leadership: Learning to Share the Vision," *Organizational Dynamics* 18 (1990): 19–36.

71. B. M. Bass, *A New Paradigm of Leadership: An Inquiry into Transformational Leadership* (Alexandra, VA: US Army Research Institute for the Behavioral and Social Sciences, 1996).

72. CNN Wire Staff, "Network: Leno Took 50% Pay Cut to Reduce 'Tonight Show' Layoffs," CNN, September 8, 2012, accessed May 9, 2016, http://www.cnn.com/2012/09/07/showbiz/jay-leno-tonight-show/; A. Farnham, "Bosses Who Volunteer for Pay Cuts," ABC News, September 11, 2012, accessed May 9, 2016, http://abcnews.go.com/Business/bosses-pay-cuts/story?id=17209062.

73. V. Gomelsky, "L'Oréal's Technology Incubator: Creating the Future of Beauty," *New York Times*, March 30, 2017, accessed April 30, 2017, https://www.nytimes.com/2017/03/30/fashion/craft smanship-loreal-beauty-technology.html.

74. "MakeupGenius App - Virtual Makeup Application Tool," L'Oréal Paris, accessed April 30, 2017, http://www.lorealparisusa.com/beauty-magazine/makeup/makeup-looks/makeupgenius-changes-makeup-application-forever.aspx.

75. M. Hawthorne, "Lipstick on an App: L'Oreal Incubator Blends Science, Electronics and Beauty," *Sydney Morning Herald*, February 11, 2017, accessed April 30, 2017, http://www.smh.com.au/business/retail/from-bad-hair-days-to-sun-smarts-loreal-has-skin-in-the-game-20170210-gua55x.html.

76. Bass, "From Transactional to Transformational Leadership."

15

1. E. E. Lawler III, L. W. Porter, and A. Tannenbaum, "Manager's Attitudes Toward Interaction Episodes," *Journal of Applied Psychology* 52 (1968): 423–439; H. Mintzberg, *The Nature of Managerial Work* (New York: Harper & Row, 1973).

2. J. D. Maes, T. G. Weldy, and M. L. Icenogle, "A Managerial Perspective: Oral Communication Competency Is Most Important for Business Students in the Workplace," *Journal of Business Communication* 34 (1997): 67–80.

3. E. E. Jones and K. E. Davis, "From Acts to Dispositions: The Attribution Process in Person Perception," in *Advances in Experimental and Social Psychology*, vol. 2, ed. L. Berkowitz (New York: Academic Press, 1965), 219–266; R. G. Lord and J. E. Smith, "Theoretical, Information -Processing, and Situational Factors Affecting Attribution Theory Models of Organizational Behavior," *Academy of Management Review* 8 (1983): 50–60.

4. D. Simons and C. Chabris, "Gorillas in Our Midst: Sustained Inattentional Blindness for Dynamic Events," *Perception* 28 (1999): 1059–1074.

5. J. Zadney and H. B. Gerard, "Attributed Intentions and Informational Selectivity," *Journal of Experimental Social Psychology* 10 (1974): 34–52.

6. M. Beck, "What Cocktail Parties Teach Us," *Wall Street Journal*, April 23, 2012, D1.

7. H. H. Kelly, *Attribution in Social Interaction* (Morristown, NJ: General Learning Press, 1971).

8. J. M. Burger, "Motivational Biases in the Attribution of Responsibility for an Accident: A Meta-Analysis of the Defensive-Attribution Hypothesis," *Psychological Bulletin* 90 (1981): 496–512.

9. D. A. Hofmann and A. Stetzer, "The Role of Safety Climate and Communication in Accident Interpretation: Implications for Learning from Negative Events," *Academy of Management Journal* 41, no. 6 (1998): 644–657.

10. C. Perrow, *Normal Accidents: Living with High-Risk Technologies* (New York: Basic Books, 1984).

11. A. G. Miller and T. Lawson, "The Effect of an Informational Opinion on the Fundamental Attribution Error," *Journal of Personality & Social*

Psychology 47 (1989): 873–896; J. M. Burger, "Changes in Attribution Errors Over Time: The Ephemeral Fundamental Attribution Error," *Social Cognition* 9 (1991): 182–193.

12. F. Heider, *The Psychology of Interpersonal Relations* (New York: Wiley, 1958); D. T. Miller and M. Ross, "Self-Serving Biases in Attribution of Causality: Fact or Fiction?" *Psychological Bulletin* 82 (1975): 213–225.

13. J. R. Larson, Jr., "The Dynamic Interplay Between Employees' Feedback-Seeking Strategies and Supervisors' Delivery of Performance Feedback," *Academy of Management Review* 14, no. 3 (1989): 408–422.

14. R. C. Rabin, "15-Minute Visits Take a Toll on the Doctor-Patient Relationship," *Kaiser Health News*, April 21, 2014, accessed May 10, 2016, http://www.kaiserhealthnews.org/Stories/2014/April/21/15-minute-doctor-visits.aspx; S. Wilkins, "The Truth About Those High Patient Satisfaction Scores for Doctor-Patient Communication," *Center For Advancing Health* (Prepared Patient Blog), April 11, 2013, accessed May 10, 2016, http://www.cfah.org/blog/2013/the-truth-about-those-high-patient-satisfaction-scores-for-doctor-patient-communication.

15. Ibid.

16. S. Brownlee, "The Doctor Will See You—If You're Quick," *The Daily Beast*, April 16, 2012, accessed May 10, 2016, http://www.thedailybeast.com/newsweek/2012/04/15/why-your-doctor-has-no-time-to-see-you.html.

17. S. Wilkins, "The Truth About Those High Patient Satisfaction Scores for Doctor-Patient Communication."

18. "The Experts: How to Improve Doctor-Patient Communication," *Wall Street Journal*, April 12, 2013, accessed May 10, 2016, http://www.wsj.com/articles/SB10001424127887324050304578411251805908228.

19. Ibid.

20. S. Wilkins, "The Truth About Those High Patient Satisfaction Scores for Doctor-Patient Communication," Center for Advancing Health (Prepared Patient Blog), April 11, 2013, accessed May 10, 2016, http://www.cfah.org/blog/2013/the-truth-about-those-high-patient-satisfaction-scores-for-doctor-patient-communication.

21. "The Experts: How to Improve Doctor-Patient Communication."

22. L. Davey, "Managing Emotional Outbursts on Your Team," *Harvard Business Review*, April 30, 2015, accessed May 13, 2015, https://hbr.org/2015/04/handling-emotional-outbursts-on-your-team.

23. L. Lagnado, "What Patients Need to Remember after Leaving the Hospital," *Wall Street Journal*, November 30, 2015, accessed May 10, 2016, http://www.wsj.com/articles/what-patients-need-to-remember-after-leaving-the-hospital-1448908354.

24. Ibid.

25. Ibid.

26. G. L. Kreps, *Organizational Communication: Theory and Practice* (New York: Longman, 1990).

27. Ibid.

28. J. Jusko, "A Little More Communication," *Industry Week*, March 1, 2010, 19.

29. H. Gregersen, "Bursting Out of the CEO Bubble," *Harvard Business Review*, March–April 2017, accessed April 30, 2017, https://hbr.org/2017/03/bursting-the-ceo-bubble.

30. "Employee Engagement in a Digital Business—Technology's Role in Fostering Culture," *Dimension Data*, accessed April 30, 2017, http://www2.dimensiondata.com/en/insights/ambitious-thinking/culture-as-a-business-accelerator/employee-engagement-in-a-digital-business.

31. L. Landro, "The Most Crucial Half-Hour at a Hospital: The Shift Change," *Wall Street Journal*, October 26, 2015, accessed May 1, 2017, https://www.wsj.com/articles/the-most-crucial-half-hour-at-a-hospital-the-shift-change-1445887115.

32. K. Gee, "The Not-So-Creepy Reason More Bosses Are Tracking Employees," *Wall Street Journal*, March 21, 2017, accessed May 1, 2017, https://www.wsj.com/articles/the-not-so-creepy-reason-more-bosses-are-tracking-employees-1490101200.

33. K. Gee (Dow Jones), "Companies Tracking Employees' Emails, Conversations 'to improve collaboration,'" *Australian Business Review*, March 22, 2017, accessed May 1, 2017, http://www.theaustralian.com.au/business/technology/companies-tracking-employees-emails-conversations-to-improve-collaboration/news-story/1190680b8305cac0a9446884d47285b3.

34. J. Sandberg, "Ruthless Rumors and the Managers Who Enable Them," *Wall Street Journal*, October 29, 2003, B1.

35. E. Holm and J. S. Lublin, "Loose Lips Trip Up a Good Hands Executive," *Wall Street Journal*, August 1, 2011, C1.

36. K. Voight, "Office Intelligence," *Asian Wall Street Journal*, January 21, 2005, P1.

37. A. Aschale, "Review of the Grapevine Communication," June 2013, accessed May 10, 2016, http://www.academia.edu/4362950/Review_of_the_Grapevine_Communication.

38. W. C. Redding, *Communication within the Organization: An Interpretive View of Theory and Research* (New York: Industrial Communication Council, 1972).

39. D. T. Hall, K. L. Otazo, and G. P. Hollenbeck, "Behind Closed Doors: What Really Happens in Executive Coaching," *Organizational Dynamics* 27, no. 3 (1999): 39–53.

40. Shellenbarger, "How to Find Out What the Boss Really Thinks of You," *Wall Street Journal*, June 28, 2016, accessed May 1, 2017, https://www.wsj.com/articles/how-to-find-out-what-the-boss-really-thinks-of-you-1467138157.

41. Ibid.

42. R. McGarvey, "Lords of Discipline," *Entrepreneur Magazine*, January 1, 2000, page number not available.

43. Jack Welch, "'Rank-and-Yank'? That's Not How It's Done," *Wall Street Journal*, November 15, 2013, A.15.

44. N. Goodman, "Jack Welch on How to Manage Employees," *Entrepreneur*, October 5, 2012, accessed May 10, 2016, http://www.entrepreneur.com/blog/224604.

45. C. Hirschman, "Firm Ground: EAP Training for HR and Managers Improves Supervisor-Employee Communication and Helps Organizations Avoid Legal Quagmires," *Employee Benefit News*, June 13, 2005, accessed May 10, 2016, http://www.highbeam.com/doc/1G1-121455684.html.

46. L. Zamosky, "A Little-Known Worker Benefit: Employee Assistance Programs," *Los Angeles Times*, June 15, 2014, accessed May 10, 2016, http://www.latimes.com/business/la-fi-healthcare-watch-20140615-story.html.

47. Ibid.

48. A. Mehrabian, "Communication without Words," *Psychology Today* 3 (1968): 53; A. Mehrabian, *Silent Messages* (Belmont, CA: Wadsworth, 1971); R. Harrison, *Beyond Words: An Introduction to Nonverbal Communication* (Upper Saddle River, NJ: Prentice Hall, 1974); A. Mehrabian, *Non-Verbal Communication* (Chicago: Aldine, 1972).

49. M. L. Knapp, *Nonverbal Communication in Human Interaction*, 2nd ed. (New York: Holt, Rinehart & Winston, 1978).

50. H. M. Rosenfeld, "Instrumental Affiliative Functions of Facial and Gestural Expressions," *Journal of Personality & Social Psychology* 24 (1966): 65–72; P. Ekman, "Differential Communication of Affect by Head and Body Cues," *Journal of Personality & Social Psychology* 23 (1965): 726–735; A. Mehrabian, "Significance of Posture and Position in the Communication of Attitude and Status Relationships," *Psychological Bulletin* 71 (1969): 359–372.

51. S. Shellenbarger, "Use Mirroring to Connect With Others," *Wall Street Journal*, September 20, 2016, accessed May 1, 2017, https://www.wsj.com/articles/use-mirroring-to-connect-with-others-1474394329.

52. T. Bradberry and K. Kruse, "Why Successful People Never Bring Smartphones Into Meetings," *LinkedIn*, September 22, 2014, accessed May 10, 2016, https://www.linkedin.com/pulse/20140922000612-50578967-why-successful-people-never-bring-smartphones-into-meetings.

53. Ibid.

54. Ibid.

55. S. Shellenbarger, "Is This How You Really Talk?" *Wall Street Journal*, accessed May 10, 2016, accessed June 20, 2014, http://www.wsj.com/news/articles/SB10001424127887323735604578440851083674898.

56. C. A. Bartlett and S. Ghoshal, "Changing the Role of Top Management: Beyond Systems to People," *Harvard Business Review*, May–June 1995, 132–142.

57. J. Lublin, "Managers Need to Make Time for Face Time," *Wall Street Journal*, March 18, 2015, B6.

58. A. Bryant, "Amit Singh of Google for Work: A Respectful Clash of Ideas," *New York Times*, January 22, 2016, BU2.

59. J. Fry, "When Talk Isn't Cheap: Is Emailing Colleagues Who Sit Feet Away a Sign of Office Dysfunction, or a Wise Move?" *Wall Street Journal*, November 28, 2005, accessed May 10, 2016, http://www.wsj.com/articles/SB113293718044406629.

60. "Email Statistics Report, 2017–2021—Executive Summary," London: The Radicati Group, Inc., copyright 2017. http://www.radicati.com/wp/wp-content/uploads/2017/01/Email-Statistics-Report-2017-2021-Executive-Summary.pdf.

61. E. Bernstein, "Thou Shalt Not Send in Anger: Recovering from a Snippy Email to Friends, Even the Boss, Is Possible If You Grovel," *Wall Street Journal*, October 14, 2014, D1, D4.

62. C. Matlack, "One Company Tries Life Without (Much) E-mail," *Bloomberg BusinessWeek*, October 12–18, 2015, 36–37.

63. S. Shellenbarger, "The Challenge of Managing a Long-Distance Relationship with Your Boss," *Wall Street Journal*, March 15, 2016, http://www.wsj.com/articles/the-challenge-of-managing-a-long-distance-relationship-with-your-boss-1458065121.

64. D. F. Larcker, S. Miles, B. Tayan, and M. E. Gutman, "2013 CEO Performance Evaluation Survey," *Stanford Graduate School of Business*, accessed May 10, 2016, http://www.gsb.stanford.edu/cldr/research/surveys/performance.html.

65. E. Atwater, *I Hear You*, revised ed. (New York: Walker, 1992).

66. R. G. Nichols, "Do We Know How to Listen? Practical Helps in a Modern Age," in *Communication Concepts and Processes*, ed. J. DeVitor (Englewood Cliffs, NJ: Prentice Hall, 1971); P. V. Lewis, *Organizational Communication: The Essence of Effective Management* (Columbus, OH: Grid Publishing Company, 1975); S. Khan, "Why Long Lectures Are Ineffective," *Time*, October 2, 2012, accessed May 10, 2016, http://ideas.time.com/2012/10/02/why-lectures-are-ineffective/.

67. A. Stevenson, "T-Mobile CEO to Cramer: 'Shut Up and Listen,'"*CNBC*, April 28, 2015, accessed May 10, 2016, http://www.cnbc.com/id/102628529.

68. D. A. Kaplan, "Undercover Employee: A Day on the Job at Three Best Companies," *CNNMoney*, January 20, 2011, accessed May 10, 2016, 2012, http://features.blogs.fortune.cnn.com/2011/01/20/undercover-employee-a-day-on-the-job-at-three-best-companies/.

69. L. Gurkow, "The Art of Active Listening," *Jerusalem Post*, May 11, 2014, accessed June 20, 2014, http://www.jpost.com/Jewish-World/Judaism/Active-listening-351878.

70. Gregersen, "Bursting Out of the CEO Bubble."

71. E. Bernstein, "How 'Active Listening' Makes Both Participants in a Conversation Feel Better," *Wall Street Journal*, January 12, 2015, accessed May 10, 2016, http://www.wsj.com/articles/how-active-listening-makes-both-sides-of-a-conversation-feel-better-1421082684.

72. S. Turkle, "Stop Googling. Let's Talk," *New York Times*, September 26, 2015, accessed May 10, 2016, http://www.nytimes.com/2015/09/27/opinion/sunday/stop-googling-lets-talk.html?_r=0.

73. S. Konrath, E. O'Brien, and C. Hsing, "Changes in Dispositional Empathy in American College Students Over Time: A Meta-Analysis," *Personality and Social Psychology Review* 15 (2011): 180–198.

74. T. Smith, "Summer Camps Struggle To Enforce Bans On Screen Time," *NPR*, August 11, 2016, accessed May 1, 2017, http://www.npr.org/2016/08/11/489661961/summer-camps-struggle-to-enforce-bans-on-screen-time.

75. S. Wolpert, "In Our Digital World, Are Young People Losing the Ability to Read Emotions?," *UCLA Newsroom*, August 21, 2014, accessed May 10, 2016, http://newsroom.ucla.edu/releases/in-our-digital-world-are-young-people-losing-the-ability-to-read-emotions; Y. Uhls, M Michikyan, J. Morris, D. Garcia, G. Small, E. Zgourou, and P. Greenfield, "Five Days at Outdoor Education Camp Without Screens Improves Preteen Skills with Nonverbal Emotion Cues," *Computers in Human Behavior* 39 (2014): 387–392.

76. Turkle, "Stop Googling. Let's Talk."

77. Atwater, *I Hear You*.

78. C. Edwards, "Death of a Pushy Salesman," *BusinessWeek*, July 3, 2006, 108.

79. J. Sandberg, "Not Communicating with Your Boss? Count Your Blessings," *Wall Street Journal*, May 22, 2007, B1.

80. R. Feintzeig, "'Nice' Is a Four-Letter Word at Companies Practicing Radical Candor," *Wall Street Journal*, December 30, 2015, accessed May 1, 2017, https://www.wsj.com/articles/nice-is-a-four-letter-word-at-companies-practicing-radical-candor-1451498192.

81. L. Weber and R.E. Silverman, "Workers Get New Tools for Airing Their Gripes," *Wall Street Journal*, August 26, 2015, B1, B4.

82. D. Bright, "How to Deliver Criticism So Employees Pay Attention," *Harvard Business Review*, January 17, 2017, accessed May 1, 2017, https://hbr.org/2017/01/how-to-deliver-criticism-so-employees-pay-attention.

83. Bellis, "Point-Counterpoint: Will Email Ever Disappear From The Workplace?" *Fast Company*, March 29, 2016, accessed May 1, 2017, https://www.fastcompany.com/3058312/point-counterpoint-will-email-ever-disappear-from-the-workplace.

84. R. Holmes, "Why You Should Declare Email Bankruptcy for 2015," *Hootsuite*, January 12, 2015, accessed May 1, 2017, https://blog.hootsuite.com/why-you-should-declare-email-bankruptcy-for-2015/.

85. A. Samuel, "How I Tamed the Email Beast at Work," *Wall Street Journal*, March 14, 2016, accessed May 1, 2017, https://www.wsj.com/articles/how-i-tamed-the-email-beast-at-work-1457921533.

86. W. Mossberg, "Slack Beats EMail, But Still Needs to Get Better," *The Verge*, April 13, 2016, accessed May 10, 2016, http://www.theverge.com/2016/4/13/11417726/slack-app-walt-mossberg-stewart-butterfield-interview.

87. F. Manjoo, "Slack, the Office Messaging App That May Finally Sink Email," *New York Times*, March 22, 2015, B1.

88. A. Bryant, "The Memo List: Where Everyone Has an Opinion," *New York Times*, March 10, 2012, accessed May 10, 2016, http://www.nytimes.com/2012/03/11/business/jim-whitehurst-of-red-hat-on-merits-of-an-open-culture.html.

89. S. Ovide, "Companies Get the Message on Chatting," *Wall Street Journal*, October 14, 2015, R7.

90. E. W. Morrison, "Organizational Silence: A Barrier to Change and Development in a Pluralistic World," *Academy of Management Review* 25 (2000): 706–725.

91. M. Heffernan, "Encourage Employees to Speak Up," *Inc*, April 9, 2014, accessed July 21, 2014, http://www.inc.com/margaret-heffernan/encourage-employees-to-speak-up.html.

92. H. Gregersen, "Bursting Out of the CEO Bubble."

93. Ibid.

94. E. O'Mara, "Three Key Findings from Our 2016 Hotline Benchmark Report," *JD Supra Business Advisor*, April 25, 2016, http://www.jdsupra.com/legalnews/three-key-findings-from-our-2016-67770/. Full NAVEXGlobal 2016 Hotline Benchmark Report available http://trust.navexglobal.com/rs/852-MYR-807/images/NAVEX-Global_2016_Hotline_BenchmarkReport.pdf.

95. Lublin, "Managers Need to Make Time for Face Time."

96. C. Hymowitz, "Sometimes, Moving Up Makes It Harder to See What Goes on Below," *Wall Street Journal*, October 15, 2007, B1.

97. R. Ashkenas, "How to Overcome Executive Isolation," *Harvard Business Review*, February 2, 2017, accessed May 2, 2017, https://hbr.org/2017/02/how-to-overcome-executive-isolation.

98. Ibid.

99. G. Kane, "How McDonalds Cooked Up More Transparency," *MIT Sloan Management Review* 57 (Winter 2016), accessed May 11, 2016, http://sloan-review.mit.edu/article/how-mcdonalds-cooked-up-more-transparency/.

100. Ibid.

101. R. Jones, "Labor Strife at Emirates Air," *Wall Street Journal*, March 23, 2015, B3.

16

1. R. Leifer and P. K. Mills, "An Information Processing Approach for Deciding Upon Control Strategies and Reducing Control Loss in Emerging Organizations," *Journal of Management* 22 (1996): 113–137.

2. D. Winning, "More Companies Are Outfitting Warehouses With 'Smart' Lights," *Wall Street Journal*, September 13, 2015, accessed May 11, 2016, http://www.wsj.com/articles/more-companies-are-outfitting-1442197722.

3. Ibid.

4. J. Dunn, "Criminals Steal Money from ATMs by Gluing Down Keys," *TechWorld* March 18, 2011, accessed May 11, 2016, http://www.techworld.com/news/security/criminals-steal-money-from-atms-by-gluing-down-keys-3265904/.

5. R. Abrams, "Chip-Card Payment System Delays Frustrate Retailers," *New York Times*, March 22, 2016, accessed May 3, 2017, https://www.nytimes.com/2016/03/23/business/chip-card-payment-system-delays-frustrate-retailers.html.

6. J. Stern, "Chip Card Nightmares? Help Is on the Way," *Wall Street Journal*, August 2, 2016, accessed May 3, 2017, https://www.wsj.com/articles/chip-card-nightmares-help-is-on-the-way-1470163865.

7. Ibid.

8. R. Upson and K. Notarianni, "Quantitative Evaluaton of Fire and EMS Mobilization Times," The Fire Protection Research Foundation, May 2010, p. 1.

9. D. Robb, "Is Big Data Right for Small Business?" *Tech Page One*, June 26, 2014, accessed May 11, 2016, http://techpageone.dell.com/technology/is-big-data-right-for-small-business/.

10. "Handwashing - Clean Hands Save Lives," Centers for Disease Control and Prevention, January 27, 2016, accessed May 3, 2017, https://www.cdc.gov/handwashing/; L. Landro, "Why Hospitals Want Patients to Ask Doctors, 'Have You Washed Your Hands?'" *Wall Street Journal*, September 30, 2013, accessed May 11, 2016, http://wsj.com/news/articles/SB10001424052702303918804579107202360565642.

11. University Health Network, "HealthCare Worker Hand Hygiene Rates Increase Three-Fold When Auditors Visible," *Science Daily*, July 8, 2014, accessed May 11, 2016, http://www.sciencedaily.com/releases/2014/07/140708165727.htm.

12. J. Hernández, "China's High-Tech Tool to Fight Toilet Paper Bandits," *New York Times*, March 20, 2017, accessed May 3, 2017, https://www.nytimes.com/2017/03/20/world/asia/china-toilet-paper-theft.html.

13. N. Wiener, *Cybernetics; Or Control and Communication in the Animal and the Machine* (New York: Wiley, 1948).

14. A. Levin, "Pilots Can't Stop Cockpit Video Forever," *Bloomberg Businessweek*, October 12–18, 2015, 27–28.

15. Ibid.

16. S. Ovide, "Microsoft Hopes Sneak Peaks Will Pay Off," *Wall Street Journal*, July 29, 2015, B6.

17. M. Griggs, "In Nasty Weather, High-Tech Sensors Get the Lights Back on Faster," *Popular Science*, December 23, 2014, accessed May 11, 2016, http://www.popsci.com/high-tech-power-line-sensors-get-lights-turned-faster.

18. D. Cardwell, "Grid Sensors Could Ease Disruptions of Power," *New York Times*, February 3, 2015, B4.

19. Leifer and Mills, "An Information Processing Approach."

20. J. Bunge, "Bird Flu Found at Tennessee Chicken Farm Affiliated with Tyson Foods," *Wall Street Journal*, March 6, 2017, accessed May 3, 2017, https://www.wsj.com/articles/usda

-confirms-bird-flu-found-at-tennessee-chicken
-farm-1488745861.

21. J. Nash, "California's Recycling Crisis Sends
Billions of Bottles and Cans into Landfills,"
Bloomberg, October 6, 2016, accessed May 3, 2017,
https://www.bloomberg.com/news
/articles/2016-10-06/california-s-recycling-crisis
-sends-billions-of-bottles-and-cans-into-landfills.

22. Ibid.

23. "Test Security and Fairness: Know Your Rights
and Responsibilities," accessed May 11, 2016,
College Board, https://collegereadiness
.collegeboard.org/sat/taking-the-test/test-security
-fairness.

24. R. Dudley, S. Stecklow, A. Harney, and I. Liu,
"College Board Gave Sat Tests That It Knew Had
Been Compromised in Asia," Reuters, March 28,
2016, accessed May 11, 2016, http://www.reuters
.com/investigates/special-report/college-sat-one/.

25. J. Koffler, "China Uses a Drone to Curb
Cheating on College Placement Exams," *Time*,
June 9, 2015, accessed May 11, 2016, http://time
.com/3914087/china-drones-cheating-exams/.

26. M. Weber, *The Protestant Ethic and the Spirit
of Capitalism* (New York: Scribner's, 1958).

27. B. Morris, "Truckers Tire of Government Sleep
Rules," *Wall Street Journal*, accessed May 11, 2016,
http://wsj.com/news/articles/SB10001424052702304
6724045791852252881942740.

28. C. Zakrzewski, "The Key to Getting Workers
to Stop Wasting Time Online," *Wall Street Journal*,
March 13, 2016, accessed May 11, 2016, http://www
.wsj.com/articles/the-key-to-getting-workers-to-stop
-wasting-time-online-1457921545.

29. M. Belvedere, "Why Aetna's CEO Pays
Workers up to $500 to Sleep," CNBC, April 5,
2016, accessed May 3, 2017, http://www.cnbc.
com/2016/04/05/why-aetnas-ceo-pays-workers-up
-to-500-to-sleep.html.

30. Ibid.

31. H. Son, "'Bob in Accounting Is Going to Fix
Currency Rates.'—'I'll tell Jamie Dimon,'"
Bloomberg Businessweek, April 13–19, 2015, pp.
34–35.

32. "Capital Question: How Do You Hire People
Who Fit Your Company Culture?"
Edmonton Journal (Alberta), January 29, 2014, C11.

33. A. Kadet, "City News—Metro Money/Jerks
Need Not Apply," *Wall Street Journal*, January 18,
2014, accessed May 11, 2016, http://www.wsj.com
/articles/SB10001424052702304149404579326730
931946454.

34. J. R. Barker, "Tightening the Iron Cage:
Concertive Control in Self-Managing Teams,"
Administrative Science Quarterly 38 (1993):
408–437.

35. "The Other Side Movers—We Move Lives,"
The Other Side Movers, accessed May 3, 2017,
http://theothersidemovers.com/.

36. J. Grenny, "How to Make Feedback Feel
Normal," *Harvard Business Review*, August 19,
2016, accessed May 3, 2017, https://hbr
.org/2016/08/how-to-make-feedback-feel-normal.

37. Ibid.

38. Barker, "Tightening the Iron Cage."

39. C. Manz and H. Sims, "Leading Workers to
Lead Themselves: The External Leadership of Self-
Managed Work Teams," *Administrative Science
Quarterly* 32 (1987): 106–128.

40. J. Slocum and H. A. Sims, "Typology for
Integrating Technology, Organization and Job
Design," *Human Relations* 33 (1980): 193–212.

41. C. C. Manz and H. P. Sims, Jr., "Self-
Managment as a Substitute for Leadership: A Social

Learning Perspective," *Academy of Management
Review* 5 (1980): 361–367.

42. C. Manz and C. Neck, *Mastering Self-
Leadership*, 3rd ed. (Upper Saddle River, NJ:
Pearson, Prentice Hall, 2004).

43. S. Nassauer, "Welcome Back, Wal-Mart
Greeters," *Wall Street Journal*, June 19, 2015, B1.
S. Nassauer, "Welcome Back, Wal-Mart Greeters,"
Wall Street Journal, June 19, 2015, accessed May
11, 2016, http://www.wsj.com/articles/wal-mart
-ushers-greeters-back-to-the-front-1434651944.

44. Ibid.

45. R. S. Kaplan and D. P. Norton, "Using the Balanced Scorecard as a Strategic Management System,"
Harvard Business Review (January–February 1996):
75–85; R. S. Kaplan and D. P. Norton, "The Balanced
Scorecard: Measures That Drive Performance,"
Harvard Business Review (January–February 1992):
71–79.

46. J. Meliones, "Saving Money, Saving Lives,"
Harvard Business Review (November–December
2000): 57–65.

47. A. Wilde Mathews and A. Steele, "Aetna Lifts
Forecast; Net Tops Expectations as Key Measure
Falls," *Wall Street Journal*, October 30, 2015, B4.

48. D. Kesmodel and A. Gasparro, "Lean Recipe
Fuels Food Deals," *Wall Street Journal*, March 26,
2015, A1, A6; T. McLaughlin, "Back to Zero:
Companies Use 1970s Budget Tool to Cut Costs as
They Hunt for Growth," *Reuters*, January 30, 2017,
accessed May 4, 2017, http://www.reuters.com
/article/us-usa-companies-budget
-idUSKBN15E0CF.

49. S. L. Fawcett, "Fear of Accounts: Improving
Managers' Competence and Confidence Through
Simulation Exercises," *Journal of European
Industrial Training* (February 1996): 17.

50. M. H. Stocks and A. Harrell, "The Impact of
an Increase in Accounting Information Level on
the Judgment Quality of Individuals and Groups,"
Accounting, Organizations & Society (October–
November 1995): 685–700.

51. B. Morris, "Roberto Goizueta and Jack Welch:
The Wealth Builders," *Fortune*, December 11,
1995, 80–94.

52. G. Colvin, "America's Best & Worst Wealth
Creators: The Real Champions Aren't Always Who
You Think. Here's an Eye-Opening Look at Which
Companies Produce and Destroy the Most Money
for Investors—Plus a New Tool for Spotting Future
Winners," *Fortune*, December 18, 2000, 207.

53. "About Herman Miller: Operational
Excellence," *Herman Miller*, accessed June 20,
2011, http://www.hermanmiller.com/About-Us
/About-Herman-Miller/Operational-Excellence.

54. M. Schurman, "A Herman Miller Primer,"
Herman Miller, accessed June 20, 2011, http://www
.hermanmiller.com/MarketFacingTech/hmc/about
_us/News_Events_Media/Corporate_Backgrounder
.pdf.

55. B. Stewart, *Best-Practice EVA: The Definitive
Guide to Measuring and Maximizing Shareholder
Value* (New York: Wiley Finance, 2013); "Apple,
Inc.: Economic Value Added," Stock *Analysis on
Net*, accessed May 4, 2017, https://www.stock
-analysis-on.net/NASDAQ/Company/Apple-Inc
/Performance-Measure/Economic-Value-Added;
"Alphabet, Inc.: Economic Value Added," *Stock
Analysis on Net*, accessed May 4, 2017, https:
//www.stock-analysis-on.net/NASDAQ/Company
/Alphabet-Inc/Performance-Measure/Economic
-Value-Added.

56. "Welcome Complaints," *Office of Consumer
and Business Affairs*, Government of South
Australia, accessed June 20, 2005, http://www.ocba

.sa.gov.au/businessadvice/complaints/03_welcome
.html.

57. J. Tschohl, "Cultivate Loyal Customers: The
Value of Defection Management," Desk.com, May
23, 2013, accessed May 11, 2016, http://www.desk
.com/blog/loyal-customers/.

58. C. A. Reeves and D. A. Bednar, "Defining
Quality: Alternatives and Implications," *Academy of
Management Review* 19 (1994): 419–445.

59. "The Best Airlines in the World: Readers'
Choice Awards 2015," *Condé Nast Traveler*,
October 19, 2015, accessed May 10, 2016, http:
//www.cntraveler.com/galleries/2015-10-07/top
-international-airlines-readers-choice-awards;
"About Us: *Singapore Airlines*—Our Awards,"
Singapore Airlines, accessed May 10, 2016, http:
// www.singaporeair.com/en_UK/about-us/sia
-history/sia-awards/.

60. R. Smithers, "Asda Puts UK's First
Supermarket Wonky Veg Box on Sale," *The
Guardian*, February 5, 2016, accessed May 11,
2016, http://www.theguardian.com
/environment/2016/feb/05/asda-puts-uks-first
-supermarket-wonky-veg-box-on-sale.

61. L. Neel, "Wonky Veg Introduced in Ongoing
Supermarket Price War," *Fresh Business* Thinking,
February 9, 2016, accessed May 11, 2016 http:
//www.freshbusinessthinking.com/wonky-veg
-introduced-in-ongoing-supermarket-price-war/.

62. Ibid.

63. D. R. May and B. L. Flannery, "Cutting Waste
with Employee Involvement Teams," *Business
Horizons*, September–October 1995, 28–38.

64. C. Paris, "The Next Innovation in Shipping:
Wind Power," *Wall Street Journal*, March 15, 2017,
accessed May 4, 2017, https://www.wsj.com
/articles/the-next-innovation-in-shipping-wind
-power-1489511445; "Norsepower—Installation
Requirements," Norsepower, accessed May 4, 2017,
http://www.norsepower.com/rotor-sail-solution
/installation_requirements.

65. L. Kaye, "Israeli Startup Prevents Water Leaks
Before They Happen," *Triple Pundit*, March 31,
2017, accessed May 4, 2017, http://www
.triplepundit.com/2017/03/israeli-startups
-advanced-technology-prevent-water-leaks
-occur/.

66. M. Campbell, "The Fastest Pants on Earth:
Primark Makes Fast-Fashion Look Slow,"
Bloomberg Businessweek, December 21–27, 2015,
46–50.

67. D. Wakabayashi, "Why Tech Companies
Design Products with Their Destruction in Mind,"
Wall Street Journal, June 7, 2016, accessed May 4,
2017, https://www.wsj.com/articles/why-tech
-companies-design-products-with-their-destruction
-in-mind-1465351202.

68. "Eco-Safe Digester," BioHiTech, accessed
May 5, 2017, http://biohitech.com/ecosafe; O.
Kharif, "Better Business From Dumpster Diving,"
Bloomberg, May 26, 2016, accessed May 5, 2017,
https://www.bloomberg.com/news
/articles/2016-05-26/better-business-from-dumpster
-diving.

69. "The End of the Road: Schools and Computer
Recycling," *Intel*, accessed September 5, 2008,
http://www.intel.com/education/recycling_
computers/recycling.htm.

70. "Goodwill | Donate Computers, Laptops &
Electronics | Recycle," Goodwill, accessed May 5,
2017, http://www.goodwillsc.org/donate/computers.

71. "Electronics and Appliances Recycling at Best
Buy," Best Buy, accessed May 5, 2017, http://www
.bestbuy.com/site/clp/recycling/pcmcat149900050025
.c?id=pcmcat149900050025.

17

1. R. Lenzner, "The Reluctant Entrepreneur," *Forbes*, September 11, 1995, 162–166.

2. "Inflation Calculator | Find US Dollar's Value from 1913-2014," US Inflation Calculator, accessed May 5, 2017, http://www.usinflationcalculator.com/; T. Lee, "Today's iPhone Is More Useful Than $3,000 Worth of Gadgets from a 1991 Radio Shack," *The Washington Post*, January 31, 2014, accessed July 24, 2014, http://www.washingtonpost.com/blogs/the-switch/wp/2014/01/31/todays-iphone-is-more-useful-than-3000-worth-of-gadgets-from-a-1991-radio-shack/.

3. "The Cost of Sequencing a Human Genome," National Human Genome Research Institute, July 6, 2016, accessed May 5, 2017, https://www.genome.gov/sequencingcosts/.

4. C. Mims, "How Chip Designers Are Breaking Moore's Law," *Wall Street Journal*, March 19, 2017, accessed May 5, 2017, https://www.wsj.com/articles/how-chip-designers-are-breaking-moores-law-1489924804.

5. D. Welch, "Your Car's Been Studying You Closely and Everyone Wants the Data," *Bloomberg*, July 12, 2016, accessed May 5, 2017, https://www.bloomberg.com/news/articles/2016-07-12/your-car-s-been-studying-you-closely-and-everyone-wants-the-data.

6. "Number of Pandora's Paying Subscribers from 2008 to 2022 (In Millions)," Statista, accessed May 5, 2017, https://www-statista-com.ezproxy.butler.edu/statistics/253850/number-of-pandoras-paying-subscribers/.

7. "Number of Deezer's Paying Subscribers Worldwide as of January 2017," Statista, accessed May 5, 2017, https://www-statista-com.ezproxy.butler.edu/statistics/321559/deezer-paying-subscribers/; "Number of Apple Music Subscribers Worldwide from October 2015 to December 2016 (in millions)," Statista, accessed May 5, 2017, https://www-statista-com.ezproxy.butler.edu/statistics/604959/number-of-apple-music-subscribers/; "Number of Paying Spotify Subscribers Worldwide from July 2010 to March 2017 (in millions) (in millions)," Statista, accessed May 5, 2017, https://www-statista-com.ezproxy.butler.edu/statistics/604959/number-of-apple-music-subscribers/; "Number of Amazon Prime Members in the United States as of March 2017 (In Millions)," Statista, accessed May 5, 2017, https://www-statista-com.ezproxy.butler.edu/statistics/546894/number-of-amazon-prime-paying-members/.

8. A. Tabarrok, "How Uber and Airbnb Won," *Wall Street Journal*, January 30, 2017, accessed May 5, 2017, https://www.wsj.com/articles/how-uber-and-airbnb-won-1485821086.

9. F. Suarez and G. Lanzolla, "The Half-Truth of First Mover Advantage," *Harvard Business Review*, April 2005, accessed May 12, 2016, http://hbr.org/2005/04/the-half-truth-of-first-mover-advantage/ar/1.

10. N. Olivarez-Giles, "Baseball's Latest Recruit Is an iPad," *Wall Street Journal*, March 29, 2016, accessed May 12, 2016, http://www.wsj.com/articles/baseballs-latest-recruit-is-an-ipad-1459310403.

11. Ibid.

12. Ibid.

13. C. Mims, "To Feed Billions, Farms Are about Data as Much as Dirt," *Wall Street Journal*, April 9, 2015, accessed May 12, 2016, http://www.wsj.com/articles/to-feed-billions-farms-are-about-data-as-much-as-dirt-1439160264.

14. Y. Lee and M. J. Lee, "Rush to Take Advantage of a Dull iPhone Started Samsung's Battery Crisis - Bloomberg," Bloomberg, September 18, 2016, accessed May 5, 2017, https://www.bloomberg.com/news/articles/2016-09-18/samsung-crisis-began-in-rush-to-capitalize-on-uninspiring-iphone.

15. J. Bromwich, "Southwest Flight Evacuated After Samsung Phone Catches Fire, Airline Says," New York Times, October 5, 2016, accessed May 5, 2017, https://www.nytimes.com/2016/10/06/business/southwest-samsung.html.

16. C. Warren, "Samsung Is About to Brick Every Galaxy Note 7 in America," Gizmodo, December 9, 2016, accessed May 5, 2017, http://gizmodo.com/samsung-is-about-to-brick-every-galaxy-note-7-in-americ-1789913643.

17. M. Scaturro, "These Cows Will Text You When They're in Heat," Bloomberg, November 4, 2016, accessed May 6, 2017, https://www.bloomberg.com/news/articles/2016-11-04/these-cows-will-text-you-when-they-re-in-heat.

18. Ibid.

19. E. Phillips, "Technology Helps Food Banks Handle Holiday Surge," *Wall Street Journal*, December 3, 2015, accessed May 12, 2016, http://www.wsj.com/articles/technology-helps-food-banks-handle-holiday-surge-1449101555.

20. B. Levine, "Facing Facebook, Google, and Amazon, Brands Pool Their Data: Sharing Data in Cooperatives Is Becoming a Way for the Non-Giants to Survive," *Marketing Land*, May 2, 2016, accessed May 12, 2016, http://marketingland.com/facing-facebook-google-amazon-brands-pool-data-175424.

21. E. Wilder-James, "Breaking Down Data Silos," Harvard Business Review, December 5, 2016, accessed May 6, 2017, https://hbr.org/2016/12/breaking-down-data-silos.

22. R. Bean, "Variety, Not Volume, Is Driving Big Data Initiatives," Sloan Management Review, March 28, 2016, accessed May 6, 2017, http://sloanreview.mit.edu/article/variety-not-volume-is-driving-big-data-initiatives/.

23. J. Mouawad, "Agency Taps Mapping Technology to Curb Rail Crossing Accidents," New York Times, June 29, 2015, accessed May 6, 2017, https://www.nytimes.com/2015/06/29/technology/agency-taps-mapping-technology-to-curb-rail-crossing-accidents.html.

24. M. Perlmutter, "The Lost Picture Show: Hollywood Archivists Can't Outpace Obsolescence," IEEE Spectrum, April 28, 2017, accessed May 6, 2017, http://spectrum.ieee.org/computing/it/the-lost-picture-show-hollywood-archivists-cant-outpace-obsolescence.

25. J. Greene and L. Stevens, "Amazon Uses Trucks to Drive Data Faster," *Wall Street Journal*, November 30, 2016, accessed May 6, 2017, https://www.wsj.com/articles/amazon-extends-web-based-artificial-intelligence-1480529802.

26. M. Beck, "How Telemedicine Is Transforming Health Care," *Wall Street Journal*, June 26, 2016, accessed May 6, 2017, https://www.wsj.com/articles/how-telemedicine-is-transforming-health-care-1466993402.

27. S. Lubar, *Infoculture: The Smithsonian Book of Information Age Inventions* (Boston, MA: Houghton Mifflin, 1993).

28. Ibid.

29. P. Mozur and J. Osawa, "Can Alibab's Taxi App Be New Growth Driver," *Wall Street Journal*, March 17, 2014, B4.

30. Anonymous, "Home & Digital: #ASKWSJD," *Wall Street Journal*, March 5, 2014, D3.

31. R. Trichur, "Global Finance: No Cards Necessary with New ATM Grid," *Wall Street Journal*, March 16, 2015, C3.

32. B. Worthen, "Bar Codes on Steroids," *CIO*, December 15, 2002, 53.

33. J. Bennett, "Johnson Controls Unravels Riddle of Missing Crates," Wall Street Journal, April 29, 2016, accessed May 12, 2016, http://www.wsj.com/articles/johnson-controls-unravels-riddle-of-missing-crates-1461943710.

34. N. Rubenking, "Hidden Messages," *PC Magazine*, May 22, 2001, 86.

35. D. Hill, "The Secret of Airbnb's Pricing Algorithm, *IEEE Spectrum*, August 20, 2015, accessed May 12, 2016, http://spectrum.ieee.org/computing/software/the-secret-of-airbnbs-pricing-algorithm.

36. R. Emma Silverman, "Bosses Tap Outside Firms to Predict Which Workers Might Get Sick," Wall Street Journal, February 17, 2016, accessed May 6, 2017, https://www.wsj.com/articles/bosses-harness-big-data-to-predict-which-workers-might-get-sick-1455664940.

37. Ibid.

38. Rubenking, "Hidden Messages."

39. Silverman, "Bosses Tap Outside Firms to Predict Which Workers Might Get Sick."

40. A. Rutkin, "Machine Predicts Heart Attacks 4 Hours before Doctors," *NewScientist*, August 11, 2014, accessed May 12, 2016, http://www.newscientist.com/article/mg22329814.400-machine-predicts-heart-attacks-4-hours-before-doctors.html#.VVKi5mBtEkE.

41. S. Yoon, "Lot of Contacts in Your Mobile Phone May Get You Loans," *BloombergBusiness Week*, November 15, 2015, accessed May 12, 2016, http://www.bloomberg.com/news/articles/2015-11-15/lot-of-contacts-in-your-mobile-phone-you-may-qualify-for-a-loan; S. Armour, "Lenders Use Social Media to Screen Borrowers," *Wall Street Journal*, January 8, 2014, accessed May 12, 2016, http://www.wsj.com/articles/SB10001424052702304773104579266423512930050.

42. A. McLean, "Leaked Records up 566 Percent to 4 Billion in 2016: IBM Security," ZDNet, accessed May 6, 2017, March 30, 2017, http://www.zdnet.com/article/leaked-records-up-566-percent-to-4-billion-in-2016-ibm-security/.

43. L. Stevens and R. McMillan, "Amazon's Third-Party Sellers Hit by Hackers," Wall Street Journal, April 10, 2017, accessed May 6, 2017, https://www.wsj.com/articles/amazon-coms-third-party-sellers-hit-by-hackers-1491816600.

44. R. Sidel, "Cyberthieves' Latest Target: Your Tax Forms," Wall Street Journal, April 3, 2016, accessed May 6, 2017, https://www.wsj.com/articles/online-thieves-target-employee-tax-information-1459715329; R. Sidel and C. Karmin, "Checking In at a Hotel? Hackers May Be, Too," Wall Street Journal, January 14, 2016, accessed May 6, 2017, https://www.wsj.com/articles/checking-in-at-a-hotel-hackers-may-be-too-1452793763.

45. R. McMillan, "Password Hacking Forces Big Tech Companies to Act," Wall Street Journal, August 7, 2016, accessed May 6, 2017, https://www.wsj.com/articles/password-hacking-forces-big-tech-companies-to-act-1470562202.

46. "Cloud Infographic: Computer Virus Facts and Stats, CloudTweaks, April 11, accessed May 12, 2016, http://cloudtweaks.com/2014/04/cloud-infographic-computer-virus-facts-stats/.

47. "Survival Time," Internet Storm Center, May 5, 2016, accessed May 6, 2017, https://isc.sans.edu/survivaltime.html.

48. D. Yadron, "Five Simple Steps to Protect Corporate Data," *Wall Street Journal*, April 19, 2015, accessed May 6, 2017, https://www.wsj.com

/articles/five-simple-steps-to-protect-corporate
-data-1429499477.

49. "Authentication," *PC Magazine*, accessed May 12, 2016, http://www.pcmag.com/encyclopedia/term/38192/authentication.

50. "Authorization," *PC Magazine*, accessed May 12, 2016, http://www.pcmag.com/encyclopedia/term/38202/authorization.

51. K. Olmstead and A. Smith, "Americans and Cybersecurity," *Pew Research Center*, January 26, 2017, accessed May 6, 2017, http://www.pewinternet.org/2017/01/26/americans-and-cybersecurity/.

52. "Two-Factor Authentication," *Information Security Glossary*, accessed May 12, 2016, http://www.rsa.kz/node/glossary/default4b75.html?id=1056.

53. "Google 2-Step Verification," Google, accessed May 6, 2017, https://www.google.com/landing/2step/#tab=how-it-protects; "Install Google Authenticator—Google Account Help," Google, accessed May 6, 2017, https://support.google.com/accounts/answer/1066447?hl=en.

54. D. Yadron, "Five Simple Steps to Protect Corporate Data."

55. J. Valentino-Devries, "Rarely Patched Software Bugs in Home Routers Cripple Security," *Wall Street Journal*, accessed May 12, 2016, http://www.wsj.com/articles/rarely-patched-software-bugs-in-home-routers-cripple-security-1453136285.

56. J. DeAvila, "Wi-Fi Users, Beware: Hot Spots Are Weak Spots," *Wall Street Journal*, January 16, 2008, D1; J. Vijayan, "Hotel Router Vulnerability a Reminder of Untrusted WiFi Risks," March 27, 2015, Information Week Dark Reading, accessed May 12, 2016, http://www.darkreading.com/perimeter/hotel-router-vulnerability-a-reminder-of-untrusted-wifi-risks/d/d-id/1319668.

57. G. A. Fowler, "You Won't Believe How Adorable This Kitty Is! Click For More!" *Wall Street Journal*, March 26, 2013, accessed May 12, 2016, http://online.wsj.com/news/articles/SB10001424127887324373204578373011392662962?mg=reno64-wsj.

58. Ibid.

59. J. van den Hoven, "Executive Support Systems & Decision Making," *Journal of Systems Management* 47, no. 8 (March–April 1996): 48.

60. "Local Government: How Cities Score," *Economist*, March 23, 2016, accessed May 7, 2017, http://www.economist.com/news/special-report/21695194-better-use-data-could-make-cities-more-efficientand-more-democratic-how-cities-score.

61. C. Mims, "Yelp, Google Hold Pointers to Fix Governments," *Wall Street Journal*, May 9, 2016, accessed May 7, 2017, https://www.wsj.com/articles/yelp-google-hold-pointers-to-fix-governments-1462766463.

62. "Intranet," *PC Magazine*, accessed May 13, 2016, http://www.pcmag.com/encyclopedia/term/45310/intranet.

63. "2016 Intranet Design Annual Winners," Nielsen Norman Group, January 9, 2016, accessed May 12, 2016, https://www.nngroup.com/news/item/2016-intranet-design-awards/; "DORMA Delivers Access To Innovation For 7000 Global Users With a Unily intranet," Unily, accessed May 12, 2016, https://www.unily.com/insights/dorma-delivers-access-to-innovation-for-7000-global-users-with-unily; "Dorma-Supporting Employees with Access to Innovation," Unily, accessed May 12, 2016, https://www.unily.com/media/23157/unily-dorma-case-study-2.pdf; M. Gibson, "dorma+kaba Pan-European Intranet Wins Nielsen Norman Best

Intranet 2016," Unily, January 11, 2016, accessed May 12, 2016, https://www.unily.com/insights/dormakaba-wins-nielsen-norman-award-for-best-intranet-of-2016.

64. "Web Services," *PC Magazine*, accessed May 13, 2016, http://www.pcmag.com/encyclopedia/term/54345/web-services.

65. "Integration Services | RouteOne," RouteOne, accessed May 7, 2017, https://www.routeone.com/dealers/integration-services; S. Overby, "This Could Be the Start of Something Small," *CIO*, February 15, 2003, 54.

66. "Extranet," *PC Magazine*, accessed May 13, 2016, http://www.pcmag.com/encyclopedia/term/42945/extranet.

67. "GE Customer Center," GE Intelligent Platforms, accessed May 7, 2017, https://ge-ip.force.com/communities/.

68. "Travellers Embracing Efficiencies of Self-Service Bag Drop," *Airport Business*, April 14, 2016, accessed May 12, 2016, http://www.airport-business.com/2016/04/travellers-embracing-efficiencies-self-service-bag-drop/.

69. J. Nicas and T. Shukla, "The Next Frontier in Airline Baggage: Digital Bag Tags," *Wall Street Journal*, July 1, 2015, accessed May 12, 2016, http://www.wsj.com/articles/bag-tags-1435340070.

70. S. Hamm, D. Welch, W. Zellner, F. Keenan, and F. Engardio, "Down But Hardly Out: Downturn Be Damned, Companies Are Still Anxious to Expand Online," *BusinessWeek*, March 26, 2001, 126.

71. K. C. Laudon and J. P. Laudon, *Management Information Systems: Organization and Technology* (Upper Saddle River, NJ: Prentice Hall, 1996).

72. R. Hernandez, "American Express Authorizer's Assistant," *Business Rules Journal*, August 2001, accessed May 13, 2016, http://bizrules.info/page/art_amexaa.htm.

73. "AI Definition from PC Magazine Encyclopedia," *PC Magazine*, accessed May 7, 2017, http://www.pcmag.com/encyclopedia/term/37613/ai.

74. S. Lohr, "IBM Gives Watson a New Challenge: Your Tax Return," *New York Times*, February 1, 2017, accessed May 7, 2017, https://www.nytimes.com/2017/02/01/technology/ibm-watson-tax-return.html.

75. J. Vincent, "H&R Block Will Use IBM'S Watson to Help Quiz Clients about Their Taxes," *The Verge*, February 1, 2017, accessed May 7, 2017, https://www.theverge.com/2017/2/1/14475054/ibm-watson-hr-block-tax-preparation.

76. A. Moscaritolo, "H&R Block Enlists IBM Watson to Find Tax Deductions," *PC magazine*, February 7, 2017, accessed May 7, 2017, http://www.pcmag.com/news/351508/h-r-block-enlists-ibm-watson-to-find-tax-deductions.

18

1. J. Mouawad, "A Luxury Liner Docks, and the Countdown's On," *The New York Times*, March 22, 2015, BU1.

2. Ibid.

3. S. McCartney, "How Heathrow Airport Cut Down on Flight Delays," *Wall Street Journal*, September 16, 2015, accessed May 5, 2016, http://www.wsj.com/articles/how-heathrow-airport-cut-down-on-flight-delays-1442423115.

4. L. Stevens, "For UPS, E-Commerce Brings Big Business and Big Problems," *Wall Street Journal*, September 11, 2014, accessed May 11, 2015, http://www.wsj.com/articles/for-ups-e-commerce-brings-big-business-and-big-problems-1410489642.

5. Ibid.

6. "Employment Cost Index - March 2017," Bureau of Labor Statistics, April 28, 2017, accessed May 8, 2017, http://www.bls.gov/news.release/eci.nr0.htm; "Productivity and Costs: First Quarter 2017, Preliminary," Bureau of Labor Statistics, May 4, 2017, accessed May 8, 2017, http://www.bls.gov/news.release/prod2.nr0.htm.

7. "Historical Income Tables—Families: Table F-23—Families by Total Money Income, Race, and Hispanic Origin of Householder: 1967 to 2015," U.S. Census Bureau, Current Population Survey, Annual Social and Economic Supplements, accessed May 8, 2017, http://www.census.gov/hhes/www/income/data/historical/families/2014/f23.xls.

8. Ibid.

9. "Labor Productivity and Costs: Productivity Change in the Nonfarm Business Sector, 1947-2016," Bureau of Labor Statistics, May 4, 2017, accessed May 8, 2017, https://www.bls.gov/lpc/prodybar.htm.

10. "Databases, Tables & Calculators by Subject: Labor Force Statistics from the Current Population Survey, 2007 to 2017 (Employment Level, Employed, Number in Thousands, 16 Years and Over," Bureau of Labor Statistics, May 8, 2017, accessed May 8, 2017, https://data.bls.gov/pdq/SurveyOutputServlet.

11. "Charitable Giving Statistics," *National Philanthropic Trust*, accessed accessed May 8, 2017, http://www.nptrust.org/philanthropic-resources/charitable-giving-statistics/; C. Lourosa-Ricardo, "How America Gives to Charity," Wall Street Journal, December 14, 2014, http://www.wsj.com/articles/how-america-gives-to-charity-1418619046, accessed May 11, 2015.

12. "North America: United States," The World Factbook, January 12, 2017, accessed May 8, 2017, https://www.cia.gov/library/publications/the-world-factbook/geos/us.html.

13. "Philanthropy in the American Economy," *Council of Economic Advisers*, February 19, 2002, accessed April 13, 2009, http://clinton4.nara.gov/media/pdf/philanthropy.pdf.

14. M. Perry, "Global Trade Is Why Your Television Did Not Cost $6,200 Like It Did in 1964," Foundation for Economic Education, December 26, 2016, accessed May 8, 2017, https://fee.org/articles/global-trade-is-why-your-television-did-not-cost-6-200-like-it-did-in-1964/.

15. Ibid.

16. "European Airline Labor Productivity: CAPA Rankings," CAPA Centre for Aviation, April 9, 2013, accessed May 11, 2015, http://centreforaviation.com/analysis/european-airline-labour-productivity-capa-rankings-104204.

17. "Multifactor Productivity: Frequently Asked Questions," Bureau of Labor Statistics, accessed May 5, 2016, http://www.bls.gov/mfp/mprfaq.htm#1.

18. C. Jandreau, "Jobs That No Longer Exist," Ranker, accessed May 8, 2017, http://www.ranker.com/list/jobs-that-no-longer-exist/coy-jandreau.

19. G. Reynolds, "What Housework Has to Do With Waistlines," *New York Times*, February 27, 2013, accessed May 8, 2017, https://well.blogs.nytimes.com/2013/02/27/what-housework-has-to-do-with-waistlines/.

20. J. Manyika, M. Chui, M. Miremadi, J. Bughin, K. George, P. Willmott, and M. Dewhurst, "Harnessing Automation for a Future That Works," McKinsey Global Institute, January 2017, accessed May 8, 2017, http://www.mckinsey.com/global

-themes/digital-disruption/harnessing-automation
-for-a-future-that-works.

21. G. Zarkadakis, R. Jesuthasan, and T. Malcolm, "The 3 Ways Work Can Be Automated," *Harvard Business Review*, October 13, 2016, accessed May 8, 2017, https://hbr.org/2016/10/the-3-ways-work -can-be-automated.

22. "Harnessing Automation for a Future That Works," McKinsey Global Institute.

23. G. Fowler, "Robot Baristas Serve Up the Future of Coffee at Cafe X," *Wall Street Journal*, January 30, 2017, accessed May 8, 2017, https: //www.wsj.com/articles/robot-baristas-serve-up-the -future-of-coffee-at-cafe-x-1485781201.

24. Ibid.

25. B. Brown, "The Robots Are Coming to Help, May Take Jobs," *Digital Trends*, June 11, 2016, accessed May 8, 2017, https://www.digitaltrends. com/cool-tech/mit-robots-stores-hotels-parking -lots/.

26. P. Clark and K. Bhasin, "Amazon's Robot War Is Spreading," *Bloomberg*, April 5, 2017, accessed May 8, 2017, https://www.bloomberg.com/news /articles/2017-04-05/robots-enlist-humans-to-win -the-warehouse-war-amazon-started.

27. "Harnessing Automation for a Future That Works," McKinsey Global Institute.

28. Press Release, "New-Car Transaction Prices Rise Nearly 2 Percent Year-Over-Year in July 2017, According To Kelley Blue Book, Kelley Blue Book, August 1, 2017, accessed August 31, 2017, https:// mediaroom.kbb.com/2017-08-01-New-Car -Transaction-Prices-Rise-Nearly-2-Percent-Year- Over-Year-in-July-2017-According-To-Kelley-Blue- Book.

29. Press Release, "New-Vehicle Initial Quality is Best Ever, J.D. Power Finds," J.D. Power, June 21, 2017, accessed August 31, 2017, http://www. jdpower.com/press-releases/2017-us-initial-quality- study-iqs.

30. "Basic Quality Concepts," *American Society for Quality*, accessed May 8, 2017, http://www.asq.org/learn-about-quality/basic -concepts.html.

31. R. E. Markland, S. K. Vickery, and R. A. Davis, "Managing Quality" (Chapter 7), in *Operations Management: Concepts in Manufacturing and Services* (Cincinnati, OH: South-Western College Publishing, 1998).

32. J. Ewoldt, "A Brighter Day for LED Bulbs," *StarTribune*, April 3, 2013, accessed June 23, 2013, http://www.startribune.com/business/201357281. html?refer=y; M. White, "Light Switch: Why You'll Start Using LED Bulbs This Year," *Time*, April 25, 2013, accessed June 23, 2013, http://business.time .com/2013/04/25/light-switch-why-youll-start-using -led-bulbs-this-year/.

33. L. L. Berry and A. Parasuraman, *Marketing Services* (New York: Free Press, 1991).

34. S. Kapner, "Apple Gets Sweet Deals From Mall Operators," *Wall Street Journal*, March 10, 2015, accessed May 5, 2016, http://www.wsj.com/articles /apple-gets-sweet-deals-from-mall-operators -1426007804; S. Kovach, "10 Mind-Blowing Facts about the Apple Store," *Business Insider*, March 13, 2015, accessed May 5, 2016, http://www .businessinsider.com/apple-store-facts -2015-3?op=1.

35. L. Eadicicco, "Apple Stores Make Over $5,000 Per Square Foot in Sales," *Time*, accessed May 8, 2017, http://time.com/4339170/apple-store-sales- comparison/.

36. "About ISO," *International Organization for Standardization*, accessed May 5, 2016, 2014, http://www.iso.org/iso/home/about.htm.

37. "ISO 9000 Essentials," and "ISO 14000 Essentials," *International Organization for Standardization*, accessed May 5, 2016, http: //www.iso.org/iso/iso_catalogue/management _standards/iso_9000_iso_14000.htm; "ISO/IEC 27000," International Organization for Standardiza- tion, February 15, 2016, accessed May 8, 2017, https://www.iso.org/obp/ui/#iso:std:iso-iec:27000:ed- 4:v1:en.

38. J. Briscoe, S. Fawcett, and R. Todd, "The Implementation and Impact of ISO 9000 Among Small Manufacturing Enterprises," *Journal of Small Business Management* 43 (July 1, 2005): 309.

39. R. Henkoff, "The Hot New Seal of Quality (ISO 9000 Standard of Quality Management)," *Fortune*, June 28, 1993, 116.

40. "Baldrige Frequently Asked Questions: Baldrige Performance Excellence Program," *National Institute of Standards and Technology*, accessed May 5, 2016, http://www.nist.gov /baldrige/about/baldrige_faqs.cfm.

41. "Baldrige Award Process Fees," *National Institute of Standards and Technology*, accessed May 8, 2017, http://www.nist.gov/baldrige/enter /award_fees.cfm.

42. "Frequently Asked Questions About the Malcolm Baldrige National Quality Award."

43. Ibid.

44. "Baldrige Criteria Commentary," Baldrige Performance Excellence Program, December 14, 2016, accessed May 8, 2017, https://www.nist.gov /baldrige/baldrige-criteria-commentary.

45. Ibid.

46. D. C. Moody, "Beam Integral Part of Prestigious Baldridge Program," *theeasleyprogress. com*, June 4, 2014, accessed June 25, 2014, http: //www.theeasleyprogress.com/news/home_top -news/4915403/Beam-integral-part-of-prestigious -Baldridge-Program.

47. J. W. Dean, Jr., and J. Evans, *Total Quality: Management, Organization, and Strategy* (St. Paul, MN: West, 1994).

48. J. W. Dean, Jr., and D. E. Bowen, "Management Theory and Total Quality: Improving Research and Practice Through Theory Development," *Academy of Management Review* 19 (1994): 392–418.

49. "7th Annual On-time Performance Service Awards," FlightStats, accessed May 5, 2016, http: //www.flightstats.com/company/media/on-time -performance-awards/; Press Release, "2015 North America Airline Satisfaction Study," J.D. Power, May 13, 2015, accessed May 5, 2016, http://www .jdpower.com/press-releases/2015-north-america -airline-satisfaction-study. "Alaska Airlines Awards and Recognition," Alaska Airlines, accessed May 11, 2015, http://www.alaskaair.com/content/about-us /newsroom/alaska-awards.aspx; M. Kaminsky, "The Weekend Interview with Bill Ayer: An Airline That Makes Money—Really," *Wall Street Journal*, February 4, 2012, A13; T. Maxon, "JetBlue Leads American Customer Satisfaction Index for Second Year," *Dallas Morning News*, June 18, 2012, accessed June 23, 2013, http://aviationblog .dallasnews.com/2013/06/jetblue-leads-american -consumer-satisfaction-index-for-second-year.html/.

50. M. Esterl, "How Dr Pepper Cuts Costs. And Keeps Cutting," *Wall Street Journal*, February 21, 2016, accessed May 6, 2016, http://www.wsj.com /articles/how-dr-pepper-cuts-costs-and-keeps -cutting-1456110339.

51. S. McCartney, "A World Where Flights Aren't Canceled," *Wall Street Journal*, April 2, 2014, accessed July 28, 2014, https://www.wsj.com/articles /a-world-where-flights-arent-canceled-1396480202.

52. M. Thomas, "Airline Goes Two-Thirds of 2016 Without Mainline Canceled Flight," *Delta News Hub*, January 9, 2017, accessed May 8, 2017, http: //news.delta.com/airline-goes-two-thirds-2016-with- out-mainline-canceled-flight.

53. J. Miller, "Remade in the USA: Indiana Steel Mill Revived with Lessons from Abroad," *Wall Street Journal*, May 21, 2012, A1.

54. R. Hallowell, L. A. Schlesinger, and J. Zornitsky, "Internal Service Quality, Customer and Job Satisfaction: Linkages and Implications for Management," *Human Resource Planning* 19 (1996): 20–31; J. L. Heskett, T. O. Jones, G. W. Loveman, W. E. Sasser, Jr., and L. A. Schlesinger, "Putting the Service-Profit Chain to Work," *Harvard Business Review* (March–April 1994): 164–174.

55. L. Dishman, "These are the Best Employee Benefits and Perks," *Fast Company*, February 3, 2016, accessed May 5, 2016, http://www .fastcompany.com/3056205/the-future-of-work /these-are-the-best-employee-benefits-and-perks.

56. J. Paravantis, N. Bouranta, and L. Chitiris, "The Relationship Between Internal and External Service Quality," *International Journal of Contem- porary Hospital Management* 21 (2009): 275–293.

57. G. Brewer, "The Ultimate Guide to Winning Customers: The Customer Stops Here," *Sales & Marketing Management* 150 (March 1998): 30; F. F. Reichheld, *The Loyalty Effect: The Hidden Force Behind Growth, Profits, and Lasting Value* (Cambridge, MA: Harvard Business School Press, 2001).

58. J. Heskett, T. Jones, G. Loveman, E. Sasser, and L. Schlesinger, "Putting the Service-Profit Chain to Work," *Harvard Business Review* 86 (July–August 2008): 118–129.

59. L. L. Berry and A. Parasuraman, "Listening to the Customer—The Concept of a Service-Quality Information System," *Sloan Management Review* 38, no. 3 (Spring 1997): 65; C. W. L. Hart, J. L. Heskett, and W. E. Sasser, Jr., "The Profitable Art of Service Recovery," *Harvard Business Review* (July–August 1990): 148–156.

60. A. L. Rodgers, "A 5-Point Plan for Making the Most of Customer Complaints," *Inc.*, January 14, 2014, accessed June 25, 2014, http://www.inc.com /the-build-network/a-5-point-plan-for-making-the -most-of-customer-complaints.html.

61. "Great Customer Service from the Mission Bicycle Company," *37signals.com*, August 16, 2011, accessed April 9, 2012, http://37signals.com/svn /posts/2989-great-customer-service-from-the -mission-bicycle-company.

62. D. E. Bowen and E. E. Lawler III, "The Empowerment of Service Workers: What, Why, How, and When," *Sloan Management Review* 33 (Spring 1992): 31–39; D. E. Bowen and E. E. Lawler III, "Empowering Service Employees," *Sloan Management Review* 36 (Summer 1995): 73–84.

63. Bowen and Lawler, "The Empowerment of Service Workers: What, Why, How, and When."

64. J. Shelly, "Empowering Employees," *Human Resource Executive*, October 2, 2011, accessed April 9, 2012, http://www.hreonline.com/HRE/view /story.jhtml?id=533341639.

65. "Customer Service and Business Results: A Survey of Customer Service from Mid-Size Companies," *ZenDesk*, April 2013, accessed July 28, 2014, http://cdn.zendesk.com/resources /whitepapers/Zendesk_WP_Customer_Service_ and_Business_Results.pdf.

66. E. Novy-Williams, "Sports Champion T-Shirts, Delivered Just after the Buzzer," *Bloomberg*,

March 15, 2017, accessed May 9, 2017, https://www.bloomberg.com/news/articles/2017-03-15/sports-champion-t-shirts-delivered-just-after-the-buzzer.

67. J. Rockoff, "Drug Making Breaks Away from Its Old Ways," *Wall Street Journal*, February 8, 2015, accessed May 11, 2015, http://www.wsj.com/articles/drug-making-breaks-away-from-its-old-ways-1423444049.

68. Ibid.

69. A. Pasztor, "Boeing Looks to Build Satellites More Quickly, With Fewer Workers," *Wall Street Journal*, February 21, 2017, accessed May 9, 2017, https://www.wsj.com/articles/boeing-looks-to-build-satellites-more-quickly-with-fewer-workers-1487692416.

70. A. Pasztor, "How to Build Satellites Much Faster—and Cheaper," *Wall Street Journal*, June 7, 2016, accessed May 9, 2017, https://www.wsj.com/articles/how-to-build-satellites-much-fasterand-cheaper-1465351261.

71. P. Zelinski, "Desktop 3D Printer as Job Shop Resource," *Modern Machine Shop*, March 26, 2015, accessed May 9, 2017, http://www.mmsonline.com/articles/desktop-3d-printer-as-job-shop-resource.

72. "About Us: Kenworthy Machine LLC – CNC Production Services," Kenworthy Machine LLC, accessed May 9, 2017, http://www.kenworthymachine.com/.

73. K. Safdar & L. Chao, "Logistics Woes Crimp Restoration Hardware's Modern Collection," *Wall Street Journal*, March 28, 2016, accessed May 9, 2017, https://www.wsj.com/articles/logistics-woes-crimp-restoration-hardwares-modern-collection-1459207483; K. Safdar, "Restoration Hardware

Warns Shipping Problems Will Hurt Profit," *Wall Street Journal*, March 30, 2016, accessed May 9, 2017, https://www.wsj.com/articles/restoration-hardware-warns-shipping-problems-will-hurt-profit-1459294902.

74. R. Wall and D. Cameron, "Where Are the Toilets? Order Glut Stretches Giant Jet Makers to Limit," *Wall Street Journal*, February 23, 2017, accessed May 9, 2017, https://www.wsj.com/articles/where-are-the-toilets-order-glut-stretches-giant-jet-makers-to-limit-1487885428.

75. "Warehouse & Wholesale Inventory Turnover Data," *Strategos*, May 2017, accessed May 9, 2017, http://www.strategosinc.com/articles/inventory/warehouse_inventory_turns.htm.

76. "Paccar Inc., Efficiency Comparisons," CSIMarket, accessed May 6, 2016, http://csimarket.com/stocks/PCAR-Efficiency-Comparisons.html; "GM's Management Effectiveness versus its Competition," CSIMarket, accessed May 6, 2016, http://csimarket.com/stocks/competitionNO6.php?code=GM.

77. "Efficient Foodservice Response (EFR)," accessed August 3, 2009, http://www.ifdaonline.org/webarticles.

78. J. R. Henry, "Minimized Setup Will Make Your Packaging Line S.M.I.L.E.," *Packaging Technology & Engineering*, February 1, 1998, 24.

79. C. Spafford, T. Cleary, and M. Poitras, "Spare Parts as Insurance," Oliver Wyman, 2013, accessed May 9, 2017, www.oliverwyman.com/content/dam/oliver-wyman/global/en/files/archive/2013/final_spare_parts_as_insurance.pdf.

80. "Amazon.com Help: Inventory Storage Fees," Amazon.com, accessed May 9, 2017, https://www.amazon.com/gp/help/customer/display.html?nodeId=200627230.

81. S. Kapner, "Struggling Toys 'R' Us Tries Fuller Stores," *Wall Street Journal*, December 15, 2015, accessed May 9, 2017, https://www.wsj.com/articles/toys-r-us-plays-with-a-fresh-strategy-1450141526.

82. Ibid.

83. IHL Group, "How to Lose Your Customer's in 1 Easy Step: Retail'S $634 Billion Out-of-Stock Problem," Dynamic Action, accessed May 9, 2017, http://engage.dynamicaction.com/WS-2015-08-IHL-Haunting-of-Out-of-Stocks-AR_LP.html.

84. "The Way I Work: Marc Lore of Diapers.com," *Inc.*, September 1, 2009, accessed March 15, 2010, http://www.inc.com/magazine/20090901/the-way-i-work-marc-lore-of-diaperscom.html.

85. E. Powell, Jr., and F. Sahin, "Economic Production Lot Sizing with Periodic Costs and Overtime," *Decision Sciences* 32 (2001): 423–452.

86. Apple Inc's Management Effectiveness Versus Its Competition, CSIMarket, accessed May 6, 2016, http://csimarket.com/stocks/competitionNO6.php?code=AAPL; 63. Press Release, "Gartner Announces Rankings of Its 2015 Supply Chain Top 25," May 14, 2015, accessed May 6, 2016, http://www.gartner.com/newsroom/id/3053118.

87. N. Shirouzu, "Why Toyota Wins Such High Marks on Quality Surveys," *Wall Street Journal*, March 15, 2001, A1.

88. Ibid.

89. G. Gruman, "Supply on Demand; Manufacturers Need to Know What's Selling Before They Can Produce and Deliver Their Wares in the Right Quantities," *InfoWorld*, April 18, 2005, accessed April 15, 2009, http://www.infoworld.com/article/2669692/database/supply-on-demand.html.

Index

A

financial perspective, 364–366
innovation and learning perspective, 368–371
internal perspective, 367–368
methods, 358–362
normative control, 360–361
objective control, 359–360
self-control, 362
standards, 353–355
Controlling, 6, 33
budgets, 364–366
quality, 367–368
Control loss, 357–358
Conventional level of moral development, 76
Cook, Tim, 19, 83
Coolidge, Calvin, 92
Coon, H., 144
Cooperation, 38, 177
necessities of management, 34
Cooperative contracts, 169–171
Coordination, 35
Core and secondary firms in home improvement industry, 119
Core businesses of Thomson Reuters, 184
Core capabilities, 118
Core change coalition, 153
Core firms, 119
Corporate antivirus software, 388
Corporate cultures, 67
Corporate-level strategy, 121
grand strategies, 125–127
portfolio strategy, 121–125
Corporate portals, 391
Corrales, Rodolfo, 396
Corrective action, 355
Cort's puddling and rolling process, 25
Cost-cutting program, 59
Costa, Rosario, 58
Cost leadership, 129
Cost savings, 262
Costs of maintaining inventory, 414–415
Counseling, 340–341
Country club style, 312
Cox, Kevin, 14
Cox, Taylor, 276
Creative work environments, 143–144
Credit card issuers, 354
Crisis stage, 150
Cross-functional teams, 211, 214
Cross-training, 208, 224
C-type conflict, 107–108, 218
Cubesats, 411
Culpability score, 72, 74
Cultural differences, aware of, 178–180
Cultural simulations, 181–182
Cultures, 63, 66
Cummins Engine, 206
Customer defections, 366
Customer departmentalization, 189–190

Customer focus, 405
Customer loyalty, 408
Customer satisfaction, 207, 405, 408
Customs classification, 162
Customs valuation/classification, 161
CyberAlert Social, 12
Cyberloafing, 71, 359
Cybernetic feasibility, 358
Cybernetic process, dynamic, 355–356
Cyrus, 24

D

Dalton, D. R., 74
Daly, Terry, 351
Darby's coke-smelting process, 25
Darrow, B., 266
Data clusters, 384
Data encryption, 388
Data mining, 383
Data silo, 379
Data variety, 379
Data warehouse, 383
Davis, K., 339
Decentralization, 195
Decision
quality, 323–324
roles, 13–14
styles, 322–323
trees algorithm, 383
Decision criteria, 103
Decision making, 102, 105–107, 188, 224
Decision support system (DSS), 393–394
Declaring victory too soon, 153–154
Decoding, 336
Deeney, J. M., 220
Deep-level diversity, 263, 271–273. *See also* Surface-level diversity
Deep cleanings, 101
Deere, John, 377
De-forming, 220
Defenders, 130
Defensive bias, 333–334
Defensive strategy, 87
Degree of centralization, 195–196
Delegating style, 318
Delegation of authority, 194–195
DeLisi, John, 356
Dell Inc., 278
Dell's Reconnect program, 371
Delphi technique, 109
Delta Airlines, 101, 252, 406
Demand (D), 416
Denial-of-service web server attacks, 385
Dennis, Craig, 9
De-norming, 220
Departmentalization, 184, 186
customer, 189–190

functional, 186–187
geographic, 190–191
matrix, 191–193
product, 187–188
Department of Labor (DOL), 56, 227
Dependent demand systems, 417
Descriptive Geometry, 39
Design competition, 140–141
Design iteration, 146
De-storming, 220
Destructive feedback, 346
Detractors, customer responses, 53
Deutsche Post DHL, 380
Devil's advocacy, 108
Dialectical inquiry, 108
Diebold, 234
Differentiation, 129
DiFonzo, Nicholas, 340
Digital music services, 47
Digital recording, 380
Digital single-lens reflex cameras (DSLRs), 139
Digital video recorder (DVR), 406–407
Diocletian, 24
Direct competition, 131–133
strategic moves of, 133–135
Direct foreign investment, 160
Direction of effort, 283
Directive leadership, 319
Directly responsible individual (DRI), 194
Disability, 270
Disability discrimination, 270
Disagreements, 218, 219, 220
Discontinuous change, 140
managing innovation during, 145–147
Discretionary responsibilities, 86
Discrimination and fairness paradigm, 274
Discussion channels, 347
Dishman, L., 254
Disney, Walt, 62
Disparate treatment, 229
Disposition, 271
Disseminator role, 12
Dissolution stage, 150
Distal goals, 95
Distinctive competence, 118, 139
Distracted walking, protecting Smartphone zombies from, 360
Distributive justice, 292
Disturbance handler role, 13
Diversification, 121–122
Diversity, 259, 263, 273. *See also* Workplace diversity
paradigms, 274–276
principles, 277–278
programs, 262
training and practices, 278–279
working, 279–280

Social engineering, 390
Social integration, 264, 271
Social loafing, 209
Social media (SM), 238
Social responsibility, 82–89
    and economic performance, 88–89
    organizations, 82–83, 85–86
    responses to demands for, 87–88
    stakeholder, 83–85
Social responsiveness, 87
Society of Industrial Engineers, 29
Soldiering, 26
Sparta Systems, 6
Spaulding, C. C., 34
Specific ability tests, 238
Specific environment, 44, 49, 51, 53
    advocacy groups, 57–58
    competitor component, 54–55
    customer component, 53–54
    industry regulation component, 57
    supplier component, 55–56
Specific feedback, 346
Specific, measurable, attainable,
    realistic, and timely (S.M.A.R.T.),
    93–94, 221
Specific team goals, 221
Spectrum, 4
Spectrum Health Care, 194
Spirit Airlines, 85
Spokesperson role, 13
Spotify, 46, 47, 54
Spotify Fan Insights, 54
Spouse, 182–183
Spreadsheet, 110
Sqwiggle, 213
Stability strategy, 126
Stable environments, 46, 225
Staff authority, 194
Staff function, 194
Stakeholder model, 83
    of corporate social responsibility, 84
Stakeholders, 83–84
Stamp, Benedikte Schinkel, 58
Standardization, 196
Standards, 353–355
    comparison to, 355
Standing plans, 100–101
Staples, 55
Stars, 122–123
Star Wars: The Force Awakens, 223
State-of-the-art information technology
    system, 381
Steelcase, 144
Stein, Joel, 64, 86
Stern, Joanna, 354
Stevens, L., 243
Stock options, 252
Stockout, 414
Stockout cost, 415
Stock price appreciation, 365
Stockton, Bryan, 63

Storage cost. *See* Holding cost
Storage costs, 379–380
Storming, 220
Strategic alliances, 171
Strategic alternatives, 120–121
Strategic change, assessing for, 116–117
Strategic change assessment, 116–117
Strategic dissonance, 117
Strategic group, 118
Strategic leadership, 324
Strategic Management Journal, 25
Strategic moves of direct competition,
    133–135
Strategic objective, 99
Strategic planning, 129
Strategic plans, 98
Strategic reference points, 120, 121
Strategic reference point theory, 120
Strategy-making process, 113, 116
    assessing for strategic change,
        116–117
    situational analysis, 117–120
    strategic alternatives, 120–121
Strauss, Levi, 145
Streamed/videotaped speeches and
    meetings, 348
Stretch goals, 221
Structural accommodation, 222
Structured conflict, 107–108
Structured interviews, 241
Subjective performance appraisal scales,
    247
Subjective performance measures, 248
Suboptimization, 363
Subordinate contingencies, 320–321
Subsidies, 162
Subsystems, 41
Sullivan, R., 155, 156
Summarizing, 344, 345
Sun Design Home Remodeling
    Specialists, 152
Sunovian Pharmaceuticals, 349–350
Sun Tzu, 24
Superglue, 404
Supervised data mining, 383
Supervisory encouragement, 144–145
Supplier, 55–56
Supplier dependence, 55
Supportive leadership, 319
Surface-level diversity, 263
    age, 264–265
    mental or physical disabilities,
        270–271
    race/ethnicity, 269–270
    sex, 265–267
    sexual and gender identity, 267–269
Surprise visits, 350
Survey feedback, 349
Sustainability, 368
    four levels, 370
    waste disposal, 368

Sustainable competitive advantage,
    112–114
Sustaining competitive advantage,
    376–377
Swartz, Jan, 263
"Sweethearting," 71
Swisscom AG, 189
Switzer, Ken, 11, 62
SWOT analysis. *See* Situational analysis
Symonds, Scott, 142
Synergy, 41
System, 41
    management, 41–42
    view of organizations, 42
Systema Naturae, 40

T

Tactical plans, 99–100
Tai Jeng-wu, 13
TAL Group, 172
Tangibles, 402
Tani, Hiro, 358
Tankers, Maersk, 368–369
Tariff, 161
Tariff barriers, 161
Task identity, 197–198
Task interdependence, 201
Task-oriented leadership styles, 314
Task significance, 198
Task structure, 315, 321
Tata, Zeniz, 143
Taylor, Frederick W., 25–28, 196
Tayra, Flavio, 168
"Teach-back" method, 337
Team diversity, 223
Team leaders, 9–10
Team level, 222
Team(s), 206
    advantages, 207–209
    autonomy continuum, 212
    autonomy, 211–214
    cohesiveness, 216–217
    collaboration tool overload, 208
    compensation and recognition, 225
    conflict, 218–219
    disadvantages, 209–210
    enhancing work team effectiveness,
        221
    goals and priorities setting, 221–222
    good and bad of using, 206
    individualism-collectivism, 222
    kinds, 211
    management, 312
    norms, 215–216
    player inventory, 223
    room channels, 347
    size, 217–218
    special kinds, 214–215
    stages of team development,
        219–221

A GUIDE FOR NEW MANAGERS: SIX STEPS TO BECOME A SUCCESSFUL MANAGER

—ED MUZIO

If you've recently been hired as a manager, you know the dirty secret: Management positions come with surprisingly little guidance. Whether you were promoted internally or brought in from outside, you were probably expected to hit the ground running, toward only the vaguest of goals.

Many of the problems new managers experience stem from that secret. They are faced with an ill-defined job and equally intense pressure from above and below. In addition, as the pivot points in the information revolution, they are barraged with queries about the work of their groups.

It's easy to see why capable, well-meaning managers resort to micromanagement, detachment, grandstanding, or sheer blockheadedness in an effort to find some sort of stability for themselves and their employees.

How can you avoid these pitfalls? The following six steps will help you define your purpose as manager:

1. DEFINE YOUR OWN JOB CLEARLY.

If you're a new manager, this is your first and most important step. You need a memorable, meaningful definition, something that you can figuratively (or literally) write across your bathroom mirror so that you see it every morning.

I suggest "engender useful output." Your primary responsibility as a manager is to maximize the likelihood that your employees will be productive; your task is to create an environment in which employee output is clearly defined and realistically achievable. If you're not doing that, then it doesn't matter what data you're gathering, which employees you're monitoring, or whose ear you're bending. You may be busy, you may be stressed, and you may look managerial, but you're not doing your job.

2. DEFINE YOUR GROUP'S OUTPUT.

To engender output, you must first define it. This task is easier said than done. Today's workplace changes quickly, and managers at all levels are expected to turn the work of their groups on a dime. Your own manager may not be terribly clear on long-range company plans, so neither of you may fully understand how the work of your group will change in the next quarter, month, or even week.

Uncertainty about the future is not an excuse for lack of productivity in the present. If your plan is to wait around until everything is known before doing anything, you might as well lock the doors and go home for good! Things will change again and again, and only by delivering on current plans will you and your company learn what works, and what changes to make next. Besides, the definition of your group's required output is the definition of YOUR required output as manager. Defining it is one part good management practice and one part career survival.

3. SEEK MOMENTARY CLARITY RATHER THAN PERMANENT ANSWERS.

Speak with your leaders about what your group can reasonably produce right now and then agree to task your group with producing it right now. Make it clear that unless you hear otherwise, until the next scheduled check-in you will follow the current plan. Then, verbally summarize the output you are committing to engender in about 90 seconds. During follow-up discussions with your management, use that mini-commercial as a way to gently remind them what you are working on so that they can edit your understanding if needed.

When changes do come, don't fight them. Welcome the new information, openly revise your understanding of what you need to produce, and clearly explain the time and resources you need to accomplish the change. If you can't turn the boat in an hour, say so. It's far better to be up front when something isn't possible than to agree to it under duress but fail to deliver.

4. BECOME AN EXPERT IN DEFINING AND COMMUNICATING EXPECTATIONS.

Of course, your definition is only half the story. To engender output from your group, you need to convert from the commitment you made as manager into what each of your employees must do individually.

Contrary to popular opinion, this doesn't mean telling your employees what to do. It means teaching them to discuss what they are doing themselves—to create their own 90-second mini-commercials—and then working with them on a shared understanding of what's needed. You haven't successfully taught an employee his or her expected output until you hear that person say it to you spontaneously, in a way that matches your own understanding. Then you know it's happening.

This also means your employees must be in the habit of speaking openly about what they are doing. To get honesty, avoid using discussions about current objectives as pop quizzes! When you need to adjust an employee's understanding of his or her work, frame your conversation as being about expectations for the future and defining how to succeed. Don't let it degrade into how the employee should already know these things. Remember: When your employees don't know what they're supposed to be doing, it's at least as likely to be your fault as theirs.

5. KEEP TALKING ABOUT OUTPUT.

A VSO, or *verbalized summary objective statement*, is a kind of mini-commercial in which you state the output you're trying to deliver at the moment. It should take about 90 seconds and should list about five to seven output goals that together cover about 80 percent of what you are working on. It's yours to change, adjust, and modify whenever you see fit. It's also yours to use as your introduction whenever you're talking to people in or about your workplace. Use VSOs with your management and teach your employees to use them with you.

Why? Your VSO trains people as to what to expect—and not expect—from you. It provides an avenue for a manager to edit an employee's understanding of the job, and a basis for you to accept or decline requests for additional work. As time goes by, and you deliver on your VSO, you also increase your credibility within the organization as people see that you are following through on your commitments.

6. KEEP AT IT.

Management is like exercise: It's often difficult, you're never done, and it requires self-discipline.

Get in the habit of having conversations with superiors about the output needed from your group and discussions with your employees about their individual contributions to that output. Then remind yourself that your job is to maximize the chances that your employees will produce. This won't make management easy, but it's the first step in making you better at it.

AUTHOR BIO

Edward G. Muzio, CEO of Group Harmonics, is the author of the award-winning books *Make Work Great: Supercharge Your Team, Reinvent the Culture, and Gain Influence One Person at a Time* and *Four Secrets to Liking Your Work: You May Not Need to Quit to Get the Job You Want*. An expert in workplace improvement and its relationship to individual enjoyment, Muzio has been featured on Fox Business Network, CBS, and other national media. For more information, visit *Make Work Great* and follow the author on Facebook.

CHAPTER 1 LEARNING OUTCOMES / KEY TERMS

1-1 Describe what management is. Good management is working through others to accomplish tasks that help fulfill organizational objectives as efficiently as possible.

Management getting work done through others (p. 3)

Efficiency getting work done with a minimum of effort, expense, or waste (p. 3)

Effectiveness accomplishing tasks that help fulfill organizational objectives (p. 4)

1-2 Explain the four functions of management. Henri Fayol's classic management functions are known today as planning, organizing, leading, and controlling. Planning is determining organizational goals and a means for achieving them. Organizing is deciding where decisions will be made, who will do what jobs and tasks, and who will work for whom. Leading is inspiring and motivating workers to work hard to achieve organizational goals. Controlling is monitoring progress toward goal achievement and taking corrective action when needed. Studies show that performing the management functions well leads to better managerial performance.

Planning determining organizational goals and a means for achieving them (p. 5)

Organizing deciding where decisions will be made, who will do what jobs and tasks, and who will work for whom (p. 5)

Leading inspiring and motivating workers to work hard to achieve organizational goals (p. 6)

Controlling monitoring progress toward goal achievement and taking corrective action when needed (p. 6)

1-3 Describe different kinds of managers. There are four different kinds of managers. Top managers are responsible for creating a context for change, developing attitudes of commitment and ownership, creating a positive organizational culture through words and actions, and monitoring their companies' business environments. Middle managers are responsible for planning and allocating resources, coordinating and linking groups and departments, monitoring and managing the performance of subunits and managers, and implementing the changes or strategies generated by top managers. First-line managers are responsible for managing the performance of nonmanagerial employees, teaching entry-level employees how to do their jobs, and making detailed schedules and operating plans based on middle management's intermediate-range plans. Team leaders are responsible for facilitating team performance, fostering good relationships among team members, and managing external relationships.

Top managers executives responsible for the overall direction of the organization (p. 7)

Middle managers responsible for setting objectives consistent with top management's goals and for planning and implementing subunit strategies for achieving these objectives (p. 7)

First-line managers responsible for training and supervising the performance of nonmanagerial employees who are directly responsible for producing the company's products or services (p. 9)

Team leaders managers responsible for facilitating team activities toward goal accomplishment (p. 9)

1-4 Explain the major roles and subroles that managers perform in their jobs. Managers perform interpersonal, informational, and decisional roles in their jobs. In fulfilling interpersonal roles, managers act as figureheads by performing ceremonial duties, as leaders by motivating and encouraging workers, and as liaisons by dealing with people outside their units. In performing informational roles, managers act as monitors by scanning their environment for information, as disseminators by sharing information with others in their companies, and as spokespeople by sharing information with people outside their departments or companies. In fulfilling decisional roles, managers act as entrepreneurs by adapting their units to change, as disturbance handlers by responding to larger problems that demand immediate action, as resource allocators by deciding resource recipients and amounts, and as negotiators by bargaining with others about schedules, projects, goals, outcomes, and resources.

Figurehead role the interpersonal role managers play when they perform ceremonial duties (p. 11)

Leader role the interpersonal role managers play when they motivate and encourage workers to accomplish organizational objectives (p. 11)

Liaison role the interpersonal role managers play when they deal with people outside their units (p. 11)

Monitor role the informational role managers play when they scan their environment for information (p. 11)

Disseminator role the informational role managers play when they share information with others in their departments or companies (p. 12)

Spokesperson role the informational role managers play when they share information with people outside their departments or companies (p. 13)

Entrepreneur role the decisional role managers play when they adapt themselves, their subordinates, and their units to change (p. 13)

Disturbance handler role the decisional role managers play when they respond to severe pressures and problems that demand immediate action (p. 13)

Resource allocator role the decisional role managers play when they decide who gets what resources and in what amounts (p. 13)

Negotiator role the decisional role managers play when they negotiate schedules, projects, goals, outcomes, resources, and employee raises (p. 14)

1-5

Explain what companies look for in managers.
Companies do not want one-dimensional managers. They want managers with a balance of skills. Managers need to have the knowledge and abilities to get the job done (technical skills), must be able to work effectively in groups and be good listeners and communicators (human skills), must be able to assess the relationships between the different parts of their companies and the external environment and position their companies for success (conceptual skills), and should want to assume positions of leadership and power (motivation to manage). Technical skills are most important for team leaders and lower-level managers, human skills are equally important at all levels of management, and conceptual skills as well as motivation to manage both increase in importance as managers rise through the managerial ranks.

Technical skills the specialized procedures, techniques, and knowledge required to get the job done (p. 14)

Human skills the ability to work well with others (p. 15)

Conceptual skills the ability to see the organization as a whole, understand how the different parts affect each other, and recognize how the company fits into or is affected by its environment (p. 15)

Motivation to manage an assessment of how enthusiastic employees are about managing the work of others (p. 16)

1-6

Discuss the top mistakes that managers make in their jobs. Another way to understand what it takes to be a manager is to look at the top mistakes managers make. Five of the most important mistakes made by managers are being abrasive and intimidating; being cold, aloof, or arrogant; betraying trust; being overly ambitious; and being unable to delegate, build a team, and staff effectively.

1-7

Describe the transition that employees go through when they are promoted to management. Managers often begin their jobs by using more formal authority and less people management skills. However, most managers find that being a manager has little to do with "bossing" their subordinates. According to a study of managers in their first year, after six months on the job, the managers were surprised by the fast pace and heavy workload and by the fact that "helping" their subordinates was viewed as interference. After a year on the job, most of the managers had come to think of themselves not as doers but as managers who get things done through others. Because they finally realized that people management was the most important part of their job, most of them had abandoned their authoritarian approach for one based on communication, listening, and positive reinforcement.

Exhibit 1.6
Stages in the Transition to Management

MANAGERS' INITIAL EXPECTATIONS			AFTER SIX MONTHS AS A MANAGER			AFTER A YEAR AS A MANAGER					
JAN	FEB	MAR	APR	MAY	JUN	JUL	AUG	SEP	OCT	NOV	DEC

MANAGERS' INITIAL EXPECTATIONS	AFTER SIX MONTHS AS A MANAGER	AFTER A YEAR AS A MANAGER
⊙ Be the boss	⊙ Initial expectations were wrong	⊙ No longer a doer
⊙ Formal authority	⊙ Fast pace	⊙ Communication, listening, and positive reinforcement
⊙ Manage tasks	⊙ Heavy workload	⊙ Learning to adapt to and control stress
⊙ Job is not managing people	⊙ Job is to be problem solver and troubleshooter for subordinates	⊙ Job is people development

Source: L. A. Hill, *Becoming a Manager: Mastery of a New Identity* (Boston: Harvard Business School Press, 1992).

1-8

Explain how and why companies can create competitive advantage through people. Why does management matter? Well-managed companies are competitive because their workforces are smarter, better trained, more motivated, and more committed. Furthermore, companies that practice good management consistently have greater sales revenues, profits, and stock market performance than companies that don't. Finally, good management matters because it leads to satisfied employees who, in turn, provide better service to customers. Because employees tend to treat customers the same way that their managers treat them, good management can improve customer satisfaction.

2-1 Explain the origins of management. Management as a field of study is just 125 years old, but management ideas and practices have actually been used since 5000 BCE. From ancient Sumer to sixteenth-century Europe, there are historical antecedents for each of the functions of management discussed in this textbook: planning, organizing, leading, and controlling. However, there was no compelling need for managers until systematic changes in the nature of work and organizations occurred during the past two centuries. As work shifted from families to factories; from skilled laborers to specialized, unskilled laborers; from small, self-organized groups to large factories employing thousands under one roof; and from unique, small batches of production to standardized mass production; managers were needed to impose order and structure, to motivate and direct large groups of workers, and to plan and make decisions that optimized overall performance by effectively coordinating the different parts of an organizational system.

2-2 Explain the history of scientific management. Scientific management involves studying and testing different work methods to identify the best, most efficient way to complete a job. According to Frederick W. Taylor, the father of scientific management, managers should follow four scientific management principles. First, study each element of work to determine the one best way to do it. Second, scientifically select, train, teach, and develop workers to reach their full potential. Third, cooperate with employees to ensure that the scientific principles are implemented. Fourth, divide the work and the responsibility equally between management and workers. Above all, Taylor believed these principles could be used to align managers and employees by determining a fair day's work (what an average worker could produce at a reasonable pace) and a fair day's pay (what management should pay workers for that effort). Taylor believed that incentives were one of the best ways to align management and employees.

Frank and Lillian Gilbreth are best known for their use of motion studies to simplify work. While Taylor used time study to determine a fair day's work based on how long it took a "first-class man" to complete each part of his job, Frank Gilbreth used motion-picture films and microchronometers to conduct motion studies to improve efficiency by eliminating unnecessary or repetitive motions. Henry Gantt is best known for the Gantt chart, which graphically indicates when a series of tasks must be completed in order to complete a job or project, but he also developed ideas regarding worker training, specifically, that all workers should be trained and their managers should be rewarded for training them.

Scientific management thoroughly studying and testing different work methods to identify the best, most efficient way to complete a job (p. 25)

Soldiering when workers deliberately slow their pace or restrict their work output (p. 26)

Rate buster a group member whose work pace is significantly faster than the normal pace in his or her group (p. 26)

Motion study breaking each task or job into its separate motions and then eliminating those that are unnecessary or repetitive (p. 28)

Time study timing how long it takes good workers to complete each part of their jobs (p. 29)

Gantt chart a graphical chart that shows which tasks must be completed at which times in order to complete a project or task (p. 29)

2-3 Discuss the history of bureaucratic and administrative management. Today, we associate bureaucracy with inefficiency and red tape. Yet German sociologist Max Weber thought that bureaucracy—that is, running organizations on the basis of knowledge, fairness, and logical rules and procedures—would accomplish organizational goals much more efficiently than monarchies and patriarchies, where decisions were based on personal or family connections, personal gain, and arbitrary decision making. Bureaucracies are characterized by seven elements: qualification-based hiring; merit-based promotion; chain of command; division of labor; impartial application of rules and procedures; recording rules, procedures, and decisions in writing; and separating managers from owners. Nonetheless, bureaucracies are often inefficient and can be highly resistant to change.

The Frenchman Henri Fayol, whose ideas were shaped by his more than 20 years of experience as a CEO, is best known for developing five management functions (planning, organizing, coordinating, commanding, and controlling) and 14 principles of management (division of work, authority and responsibility, discipline, unity of command, unity of direction, subordination of individual interests to the general interest, remuneration, centralization, scalar chain, order, equity, stability of tenure of personnel, initiative, and *esprit de corps*).

Bureaucracy the exercise of control on the basis of knowledge, expertise, or experience (p. 31)

2-4 Explain the history of human relations management. Unlike most people who view conflict as bad, Mary Parker Follett believed that it should be embraced rather than avoided. Of the three ways of dealing with conflict—domination, compromise, and integration—she argued that the latter was the best because it focuses on developing creative methods for meeting conflicting parties' needs.

Elton Mayo is best known for his role in the Hawthorne Studies at the Western Electric Company. In the first stage of the Hawthorne Studies, production went up because both the increased attention paid to the workers in the study and their development into a cohesive work group led to significantly higher levels of job satisfaction and productivity. In the second stage, productivity dropped because the workers had already developed strong negative norms. The Hawthorne Studies demonstrated that workers' feelings and attitudes affect their work, that financial incentives aren't necessarily the most important motivator for workers, and that group norms and behavior play a critical role in behavior at work.

Chester Barnard, president of New Jersey Bell Telephone, emphasized the critical importance of willing cooperation in organizations. In general, Barnard argued that people will be indifferent to managerial directives or orders if they (1) are understood, (2) are consistent with the purpose of the organization, (3) are compatible with the people's personal interests, and (4) can actually be carried out by those people. Acceptance of managerial authority (that is, cooperation) is not automatic, however.

Domination an approach to dealing with conflict in which one party satisfies its desires and objectives at the expense of the other party's desires and objectives (p. 35)

Compromise an approach to dealing with conflict in which both parties give up some of what they want in order to

reach agreement on a plan to reduce or settle the conflict (p. 35)

Integrative conflict resolution an approach to dealing with conflict in which both parties indicate their preferences and then work together to find an alternative that meets the needs of both (p. 35)

Organization a system of consciously coordinated activities or forces created by two or more people (p. 38)

2-5 **Discuss the history of operations, information, systems, and contingency management.** Operations management uses a quantitative or mathematical approach to find ways to increase productivity, improve quality, and manage or reduce costly inventories. The manufacture of standardized, interchangeable parts; the graphical and computerized design of parts; and the accidental discovery of just-in-time inventory systems were some of the most important historical events in operations management.

Throughout history, organizations have pushed for and quickly adopted new information technologies that reduce the cost or increase the speed with which they can acquire, store, retrieve, or communicate information. Historically, some of the most important technologies that have revolutionized information management were the invention of machines to produce pulp for paper and the printing press in the fourteenth and fifteenth centuries,

the manual typewriter in 1850, the telephone in the 1880s, the personal computer in the 1980s, and the Internet in the 1990s.

A system is a set of interrelated elements or parts (subsystems) that function as a whole. Organizational systems obtain inputs from both general and specific environments. Managers and workers then use their management knowledge and manufacturing techniques to transform those inputs into outputs that, in turn, provide feedback to the organization. Organizational systems must also address the issues of synergy and open versus closed systems.

Finally, the contingency approach to management clearly states that there are no universal management theories. The most effective management theory or idea depends on the kinds of problems or situations that managers or organizations are facing at a particular time. This means that management is much harder than it looks.

System a set of interrelated elements or parts that function as a whole (p. 41)

Subsystems smaller systems that operate within the context of a larger system (p. 41)

Synergy when two or more subsystems working together can produce more than they can working apart (p. 41)

Closed systems systems that can sustain themselves without interacting with their environments (p. 41)

Open systems systems that can sustain themselves only by interacting with their environments, on which they depend for their survival (p. 41)

Contingency approach holds that there are no universal management theories and that the most effective management theory or idea depends on the kinds of problems or situations that managers are facing at a particular time and place (p. 42)

Exhibit 2.7
Systems View of Organizations

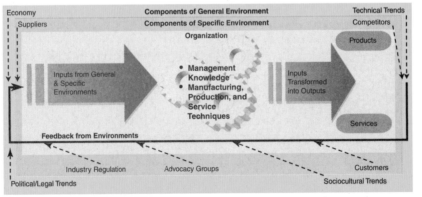

3-1 **Discuss how changing environments affect organizations.** Environmental change, environmental complexity, and resource scarcity are the basic components of external environments. Environmental change is the rate of variation in a company's general and specific environments. Environmental complexity is the number and intensity of factors in the external environment. Resource scarcity is the abundance or shortage of critical resources in the external environment. As the rate of environmental change increases, as the environment becomes more complex, and as resources become more scarce, managers become less confident that they can understand, predict, and effectively react to the trends affecting their businesses. According to punctuated equilibrium theory, companies experience long periods of stability followed by short periods of dynamic, fundamental change, followed by a return to stability.

External environments all events outside a company that have the potential to influence or affect it (p. 45)

Environmental change the rate at which a company's general and specific environments change (p. 46)

Stable environment an environment in which the rate of change is slow (p. 46)

Dynamic environment an environment in which the rate of change is fast (p. 46)

Punctuated equilibrium theory the theory that companies go through long periods of stability (equilibrium), followed by short periods of dynamic, fundamental change (revolutionary periods), and then a new equilibrium (p. 46)

Environmental complexity the number and the intensity of external factors in the environment that affect organizations (p. 48)

Simple environment an environment with few environmental factors (p. 48)

Complex environment an environment with many environmental factors (p. 48)

Resource scarcity the abundance or shortage of critical organizational resources in an organization's external environment (p. 48)

Uncertainty extent to which managers can understand or predict which environmental changes and trends will affect their businesses (p. 48)

3-2 **Describe the four components of the general environment.** The general environment consists of trends that affect all organizations. Because the economy influences basic business decisions, managers often use economic statistics and business confidence indices to predict future economic activity. Changes in technology, which transforms inputs into outputs, can be a benefit or a threat to a business. Sociocultural trends, such as changing demographic characteristics, affect how companies staff their businesses. Similarly, sociocultural changes in behavior, attitudes, and beliefs affect the demand for businesses' products and services. Court decisions and new federal and state laws have imposed much greater political/legal responsibility on companies. The best way to manage legal responsibilities is to educate managers and employees about laws and regulations as well as potential lawsuits that could affect a business.

Exhibit 3.3
General and Specific Environments

General environment the economic, technological, sociocultural, and political/legal trends that indirectly affect all organizations (p. 48)

Specific environment the customers, competitors, suppliers, industry regulations, and advocacy groups that are unique to an industry and directly affect how a company does business (p. 49)

Business confidence indices indices that show managers' level of confidence about future business growth (p. 51)

Technology the knowledge, tools, and techniques used to transform inputs into outputs (p. 51)

3-3 **Explain the five components of the specific environment.** The specific environment is made up of five components: customers, competitors, suppliers, industry regulations, and advocacy groups. Companies can monitor customers' needs by identifying customer problems after they occur or by anticipating problems before they occur. Because they tend to focus on well-known competitors, managers often underestimate their competition or do a poor job of identifying future competitors. Suppliers and buyers are very dependent on each other, and that dependence sometimes leads to opportunistic behavior in which one party benefits at the expense of the other. Regulatory agencies affect businesses by creating rules and then enforcing them. Advocacy groups cannot regulate organizations' practices. Nevertheless, through public communications, media advocacy, and product boycotts, they try to convince companies to change their practices.

Competitors companies in the same industry that sell similar products or services to customers (p. 54)

Competitive analysis a process for monitoring the competition that involves identifying competition, anticipating their moves, and determining their strengths and weaknesses (p. 54)

Suppliers companies that provide material, human, financial, and informational resources to other companies (p. 55)

Supplier dependence the degree to which a company relies on a supplier because of the importance of the supplier's product to the company and the difficulty of finding other sources of that product (p. 55)

Buyer dependence the degree to which a supplier relies on a buyer because of the

importance of that buyer to the supplier and the difficulty of finding other buyers for its products (p. 55)

Opportunistic behavior a transaction in which one party in the relationship benefits at the expense of the other (p. 56)

Relationship behavior the establishment of mutually beneficial, long-term exchanges between buyers and suppliers (p. 56)

Industry regulation regulations and rules that govern the business practices and procedures of specific industries, businesses, and professions (p. 57)

Advocacy groups concerned citizens who band together to try to influence the business practices of specific industries, businesses, and professions (p. 57)

Public communications an advocacy group tactic that relies on voluntary participation by the news media and the advertising industry to get the advocacy group's message out (p. 57)

Media advocacy an advocacy group tactic that involves framing issues as public issues; exposing questionable, exploitative, or unethical practices; and forcing media coverage by buying media time or creating controversy that is likely to receive extensive news coverage (p. 57)

Product boycott an advocacy group tactic that involves protesting a company's actions by persuading consumers not to purchase its product or service (p. 57)

3-4 **Describe the process that companies use to make sense of their changing environments.** Managers use a three-step process to make sense of external environments: environmental scanning, interpreting information, and acting on threats and opportunities. Managers scan their environments in order to keep up to date on factors influencing their industries, to reduce uncertainty, and to detect potential problems. When managers

identify environmental events as threats, they take steps to protect their companies from harm. When managers identify environmental events as opportunities, they formulate alternatives for taking advantage of them to improve company performance. Using cognitive maps can help managers visually summarize the relationships between environmental factors and the actions they might take to deal with them.

Environmental scanning searching the environment for important events or issues that might affect an organization (p. 59)

Cognitive maps graphic depictions of how managers believe environmental factors relate to possible organizational actions (p. 61)

3-5 **Explain how organizational cultures are created and how they can help companies be successful.** Organizational culture is the set of key values, beliefs, and attitudes shared by members of an organization. Organizational cultures are often created by company founders and then sustained through repetition of organizational stories and recognition of organizational heroes. Companies with adaptable cultures that promote employee involvement, make clear the organization's strategic purpose and direction, and actively define and teach organizational values and beliefs can achieve higher sales growth, return on assets, profits, quality, and employee satisfaction. Organizational

cultures exist on three levels: the surface level, where visible artifacts and behaviors can be observed; just below the surface, where values and beliefs are expressed; and deep below the surface, where unconsciously held assumptions and beliefs exist. Managers can begin to change company cultures by focusing on the top two levels. Techniques for changing organizational cultures include using behavioral substitution and behavioral addition, changing visible artifacts, and selecting job applicants who have values and beliefs consistent with the desired company culture.

Internal environment the events and trends inside an organization that affect management, employees, and organizational culture (p. 61)

Organizational culture the values, beliefs, and attitudes shared by organizational members (p. 61)

Organizational stories stories told by organizational members to make sense of organizational events and changes and to emphasize culturally consistent assumptions, decisions, and actions (p. 62)

Organizational heroes people celebrated for their qualities and achievements within an organization (p. 62)

Organizational ceremonies gatherings in which symbolic acts commemorate or celebrate notable achievements or changes (p. 62)

Company mission a company's purpose or reason for existing (p. 63)

Consistent organizational culture a company culture in which the company actively defines and teaches organizational values, beliefs, and attitudes (p. 63)

Behavioral addition the process of having managers and employees perform new behaviors that are central to and symbolic of the new organizational culture that a company wants to create (p. 64)

Behavioral substitution the process of having managers and employees perform new behaviors central to the new organizational culture in place of behaviors that were central to the old organizational culture (p. 65)

Visible artifacts visible signs of an organization's culture, such as the office design and layout, company dress code, and company benefits and perks, such as stock options, personal parking spaces, or the private company dining room (p. 66)

CHAPTER 4 LEARNING OUTCOMES / KEY TERMS

4-1 **Identify common kinds of workplace deviance.** Ethics is the set of moral principles or values that define right and wrong. Workplace deviance is behavior that violates organizational norms about right and wrong and harms the organization or its workers. There are four different types of workplace deviance. Production deviance and property deviance harm the company, whereas political deviance and personal aggression harm individuals within the company.

Ethics the set of moral principles or values that defines right and wrong for a person or group (p. 69)

Ethical behavior behavior that conforms to a society's accepted principles of right and wrong (p. 70)

Workplace deviance unethical behavior that violates organizational norms about right and wrong (p. 70)

Production deviance unethical behavior that hurts the quality and quantity of work produced (p. 71)

Property deviance unethical behavior aimed at the organization's property or products (p. 71)

Employee shrinkage employee theft of company merchandise (p. 71)

Political deviance using one's influence to harm others in the company (p. 71)

Personal aggression hostile or aggressive behavior toward others (p. 71)

4-2 **Describe the U.S. Sentencing Commission Guidelines for Organizations, and explain how they both encourage ethical behavior and punish unethical behavior by businesses.** Under the U.S. Sentencing Commission guidelines, companies can be prosecuted and fined up to $600 million for employees' illegal actions. Fines are computed by multiplying the base fine by a culpability score. Companies that establish compliance programs to encourage ethical behavior can reduce their culpability scores and their fines.

4-3 **Describe what influences ethical decision making.** Three factors influence ethical decisions: the ethical intensity of the decision, the moral development of the manager, and the ethical principles used to solve the problem. Ethical intensity is high when decisions have large, certain, immediate consequences and when the decision maker is physically or psychologically close to those affected by the decision. There are three levels of moral development. At the preconventional level, decisions are made for selfish reasons. At the conventional level, decisions conform to societal expectations. At the postconventional level, internalized principles are used to make ethical decisions. Each of these levels has two stages. Managers can use a number of different principles when making ethical decisions: long-term self-interest, religious injunctions, government requirements, individual rights, personal virtue, distributive justice, and utilitarian benefits.

Ethical intensity the degree of concern people have about an ethical issue (p. 75)

Magnitude of consequences the total harm or benefit derived from an ethical decision (p. 75)

Social consensus agreement on whether behavior is bad or good (p. 75)

Probability of effect the chance that something will happen that results in harm to others (p. 75)

Temporal immediacy the time between an act and the consequences the act produces (p. 75)

Proximity of effect the social, psychological, cultural, or physical distance between a decision maker and those affected by his or her decisions (p. 75)

Concentration of effect the total harm or benefit that an act produces on the average person (p. 76)

Preconventional level of moral development the first level of moral development, in which people make decisions based on selfish reasons (p. 76)

Conventional level of moral development the second level of moral development, in which people make decisions that conform to societal expectation (p. 76)

Postconventional level of moral development the third level of moral development, in which people make decisions based on internalized principles (p. 76)

Principle of long-term self-interest an ethical principle that holds that you should never take any action that is not in your or your organization's long-term self-interest (p. 77)

Principle of religious injunctions an ethical principle that holds that you should never take any action that is not kind and that does not build a sense of community (p. 77)

Principle of government requirements an ethical principle that holds that you should never take any action that violates the law, for the law represents the minimal moral standard (p. 77)

Principle of individual rights an ethical principle that holds that you should never take any action that infringes on others' agreed-upon rights (p. 77)

Principle of personal virtue an ethical principle that holds that you should never do anything that is not honest, open, and truthful and that you would not be glad to see reported in the newspapers or on TV (p. 78)

Principle of distributive justice an ethical principle that holds that you should never take any action that harms the least fortunate among us: the poor, the uneducated, the unemployed (p. 78)

Principle of utilitarian benefits an ethical principle that holds that you should never take any action that does not result in greater good for society (p. 78)

4-4 **Explain what practical steps managers can take to improve ethical decision making.** Employers can increase their chances of hiring ethical employees by testing all job applicants. Most large companies now have corporate codes of ethics. In addition to offering general rules, ethics codes must also provide specific, practical advice. Ethics training seeks to increase employees' awareness of ethical issues; make ethics a serious, credible factor in organizational decisions; and teach employees a practical model of ethical decision making. The most important factors in creating an ethical business climate are the personal examples set by company managers, the involvement of management in the company ethics program, a reporting system that encourages whistle-blowers to report potential ethics violations, and fair but consistent punishment of violators.

Overt integrity test a written test that estimates job applicants' honesty by directly asking them what they think or feel about theft or about punishment of unethical behaviors (p. 79)

Personality-based integrity test a written test that indirectly estimates job applicants' honesty by measuring psychological traits, such as dependability and conscientiousness (p. 79)

Whistle-blowing reporting others' ethics violations to management or legal authorities (p. 82)

4-5 Explain to whom organizations are socially responsible. Social responsibility is a business's obligation to benefit society. According to the shareholder model, a company's only social responsibility is to maximize shareholder wealth by maximizing company profits. According to the stakeholder model, companies must satisfy the needs and interests of multiple corporate stakeholders, not just shareholders. The needs of primary stakeholders, on which the organization relies for its existence, take precedence over those of secondary stakeholders.

Social responsibility a business's obligation to pursue policies, make decisions, and take actions that benefit society (p. 82)

Shareholder model a view of social responsibility that holds that an organization's overriding goal should be profit maximization for the benefit of shareholders (p. 83)

Stakeholder model a theory of corporate responsibility that holds that management's most important responsibility, long-term survival, is achieved by satisfying the interests of multiple corporate stakeholders (p. 83)

Stakeholders persons or groups with a stake, or legitimate interest, in a company's actions (p. 83)

Primary stakeholder any group on which an organization relies for its long-term survival (p. 84)

Secondary stakeholder any group that can influence or be influenced by a company and can affect public perceptions about the company's socially responsible behavior (p. 84)

4-6 Explain for what organizations are socially responsible. Companies can best benefit their stakeholders by fulfilling their economic, legal, ethical, and discretionary responsibilities. Being profitable, or meeting its economic responsibility, is a business's most basic social responsibility. Legal responsibility consists of following a society's laws and regulations. Ethical responsibility means not violating accepted principles of right and wrong when doing business. Discretionary responsibilities are social responsibilities beyond basic economic, legal, and ethical responsibilities.

Economic responsibility a company's social responsibility to make a profit by producing a valued product or service (p. 85)

Legal responsibility a company's social responsibility to obey society's laws and regulations (p. 85)

Ethical responsibility a company's social responsibility not to violate accepted principles of right and wrong when conducting its business (p. 85)

Discretionary responsibilities the social roles that a company fulfills beyond its economic, legal, and ethical responsibilities (p. 86)

4-7 Explain how organizations can respond to societal demands for social responsibility. Social responsiveness is a company's response to stakeholders' expectations concerning socially responsible behavior. There are four social responsiveness strategies. When a company uses a reactive strategy, it denies responsibility for a problem. When it uses a defensive strategy, a company takes responsibility for a problem but does the minimum required to solve it. When a company uses an accommodative strategy, it accepts responsibility for problems and does all that society expects to solve them. Finally, when a company uses a proactive strategy, it does much more than expected to solve social responsibility problems.

Social responsiveness a company's strategy to respond to stakeholders' economic, legal, ethical, or discretionary expectations concerning social responsibility (p. 87)

Reactive strategy a social responsiveness strategy in which a company does less than society expects (p. 87)

Defensive strategy a social responsiveness strategy in which a company admits responsibility for a problem but does the least required to meet societal expectations (p. 87)

Accommodative strategy a social responsiveness strategy in which a company accepts responsibility for a problem and does all that society expects to solve that problem (p. 87)

Proactive strategy a social responsiveness strategy in which a company anticipates a problem before it occurs and does more than society expects to take responsibility for and address the problem (p. 87)

4-8 Explain whether social responsibility hurts or helps an organization's economic performance. Does it pay to be socially responsible? Studies show that there is generally no trade-off between social responsibility and economic performance. In most circumstances, there is generally a small positive relationship between social responsibility and economic performance that becomes stronger when a company or its products have a positive reputation. Social responsibility, however, does not guarantee profitability, as socially responsible companies experience the same ups and downs as other companies.

WWW.CENGAGEBRAIN.COM

5-1 **Discuss the benefits and pitfalls of planning.** Planning is choosing a goal and developing a method or strategy for achieving it. Planning is one of the best ways to improve organizational and individual performance. It encourages people to work harder (intensified effort), to work hard for extended periods (persistence), to engage in behaviors directly related to goal accomplishment (directed behavior), and to think of better ways to do their jobs (task strategies). However, planning also has three potential pitfalls. Companies that are overly committed to their plans may be slow to adapt to environmental changes. Planning can create a false sense of security: planning is based on assumptions about the future, and when those assumptions are wrong, plans can fail. Finally, planning can fail when planners are detached from the implementation of their plans.

Planning choosing a goal and developing a strategy to achieve that goal (p. 90)

5-2 **Describe how to make a plan that works.** There are five steps to making a plan that works: (1) Set S.M.A.R.T. goals—goals that are **S**pecific, **M**easurable, **A**ttainable, **R**ealistic, and **T**imely. (2) Develop commitment to the goals. Managers can increase workers' goal commitment by encouraging their participation in goal setting, making goals public, and getting top management to show support for goals. (3) Develop action plans for goal accomplishment. (4) Track progress toward goal achievement by setting both proximal and distal goals and by providing workers with regular performance feedback. (5) Maintain flexibility by keeping options open.

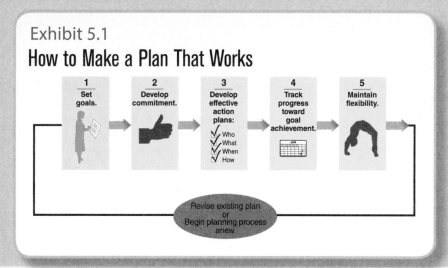

Exhibit 5.1
How to Make a Plan That Works

1 Set goals. → 2 Develop commitment. → 3 Develop effective action plans: ✓Who ✓What ✓When ✓How → 4 Track progress toward goal achievement. → 5 Maintain flexibility.

Revise existing plan or Begin planning process anew.

S.M.A.R.T. goals goals that are specific, measurable, attainable, realistic, and timely (p. 93)

Goal commitment the determination to achieve a goal (p. 94)

Action plan a plan that lists the specific steps, people, resources, and time period needed to attain a goal (p. 95)

Proximal goals short-term goals or subgoals (p. 95)

Distal goals long-term or primary goals (p. 95)

Options-based planning maintaining planning flexibility by making small, simultaneous investments in many alternative plans (p. 97)

Slack resources a cushion of extra resources that can be used with options-based planning to adapt to unanticipated changes, problems, or opportunities (p. 97)

5-3 **Discuss how companies can use plans at all management levels, from top to bottom.** Proper planning requires that the goals at the bottom and middle of the organization support the objectives at the top of the organization. The goals at the top will be longer range than those at the bottom. Top management develops strategic plans, which start with the creation of an organizational purpose statement and strategic objectives. Middle managers use techniques such as management by objectives to develop tactical plans that direct behavior, efforts, and priorities. Finally, lower-level managers develop operational plans that guide daily activities in producing or delivering an organization's products and services. There are three kinds of operational plans: single-use plans, standing plans (policies, procedures, and rules and regulations), and budgets.

Strategic plans overall company plans that clarify how the company will serve customers and position itself against competitors over the next two to five years (p. 98)

Purpose statement a statement of a company's purpose or reason for existing (p. 98)

Strategic objective a more specific goal that unifies company-wide efforts, stretches and challenges the organization, and possesses a finish line and a time frame (p. 99)

Tactical plans plans created and implemented by middle managers that direct behavior, efforts, and attention over the next six months to two years (p. 99)

Management by objectives a four-step process in which managers and employees discuss and select goals, develop tactical plans, and meet regularly to review progress toward goal accomplishment (p. 100)

Operational plans day-to-day plans, developed and implemented by lower-level managers, for producing or delivering the organization's products and services over a 30-day to six-month period (p. 100)

Single-use plans plans that cover unique, one-time-only events (p. 100)

Standing plans plans used repeatedly to handle frequently recurring events (p. 100)

Policies standing plans that indicate the general course of action that should be taken in response to a particular event or situation (p. 101)

Procedures standing plans that indicate the specific steps that should be taken in response to a particular event (p. 101)

Rules and regulations standing plans that describe how a particular action

should be performed or what must happen or not happen in response to a particular event (p. 101)

Budgeting quantitative planning through which managers decide how to allocate available money to best accomplish company goals (p. 102)

5-4 **Explain the steps and limits to rational decision making.** Rational decision making is a six-step process in which managers define problems, evaluate alternatives, and compute optimal solutions. Step 1 is identifying and defining the problem. Problems are gaps between desired and existing states. Managers won't begin the decision-making process unless they are aware of a gap, are motivated to reduce it, and possess the necessary resources to fix it. Step 2 is defining the decision criteria used to judge alternatives. In Step 3, an absolute or relative comparison process is used to rate the importance of the decision criteria. Step 4 involves generating many alternative courses of action (that is,

solutions). Potential solutions are assessed in Step 5 by systematically gathering information and evaluating each alternative against each criterion. In Step 6, criterion ratings and weights are used to compute the weighted average for each alternative course of action. Rational managers then choose the alternative with the highest value.

The rational decision-making model describes how decisions should be made in an ideal world without constraints. However, managers' limited resources, incomplete and imperfect information, and limited decision-making capabilities restrict their decision-making processes in the real world.

Decision making the process of choosing a solution from available alternatives (p. 102)

Rational decision making a systematic process of defining problems, evaluating alternatives, and choosing optimal solutions (p. 102)

Problem a gap between a desired state and an existing state (p. 102)

Decision criteria the standards used to guide judgments and decisions (p. 103)

Absolute comparisons a process in which each decision criterion is compared to a standard or ranked on its own merits (p. 103)

Relative comparisons a process in which each decision criterion is

compared directly with every other criterion (p. 104)

Maximize choosing the best alternative (p. 106)

Satisficing choosing a "good-enough" alternative (p. 106)

5-5 **Explain how group decisions and group decision-making techniques can improve decision making.**
When groups view problems from multiple perspectives, use more information, have a diversity of knowledge and experience, and become committed to solutions they help choose, they can produce better solutions than do individual decision makers. However, group decisions can suffer from several disadvantages: groupthink, slowness, discussions dominated by just a few individuals, and unfelt responsibility for decisions. Group decision making works

best when group members encourage c-type (cognitive) conflict. Group decision making doesn't work as well when groups become mired in a-type (affective) conflict. The devil's advocacy approach improves group decisions because it brings structured c-type conflict into the decision-making process. By contrast, the nominal group technique improves decision making by reducing a-type conflict. Because it overcomes the problems of production blocking and evaluation apprehension, electronic brainstorming is more effective than face-to-face brainstorming.

Groupthink a barrier to good decision making caused by pressure within the group for members to agree with each other (p. 107)

C-type conflict (cognitive conflict) disagreement that focuses on problem- and issue-related differences of opinion (p. 107)

A-type conflict (affective conflict) disagreement that focuses on individuals or personal issues (p. 108)

Devil's advocacy a decision-making method in which an individual or a subgroup is assigned the role of critic (p. 108)

Dialectical inquiry a decision-making method in which decision makers state

the assumptions of a proposed solution (a thesis) and generate a solution that is the opposite (antithesis) of that solution (p. 108)

Nominal group technique a decision-making method that begins and ends by having group members quietly write down and evaluate ideas to be shared with the group (p. 108)

Delphi technique a decision-making method in which members of a panel of experts respond to questions and to each other until reaching agreement on an issue (p. 109)

Brainstorming a decision-making method in which group members build

on each others' ideas to generate as many alternative solutions as possible (p. 109)

Electronic brainstorming a decision-making method in which group members use computers to build on each others' ideas and generate as many alternative solutions as possible (p. 109)

Production blocking a disadvantage of face-to-face brainstorming in which a group member must wait to share an idea because another member is presenting an idea (p. 109)

Evaluation apprehension fear of what others will think of your ideas (p. 109)

6-1 Specify the components of sustainable competitive advantage, and explain why it is important.

Firms can use their resources to create and sustain a competitive advantage, that is, to provide greater value for customers than competitors can. A competitive advantage becomes sustainable when other companies cannot duplicate the benefits it provides and have, for now, stopped trying. Four conditions must be met if a firm's resources are to be used to achieve a sustainable competitive advantage. The resources must be valuable, rare, imperfectly imitable, and nonsubstitutable.

Resources the assets, capabilities, processes, employee time, information, and knowledge that an organization uses to improve its effectiveness and efficiency and create and sustain competitive advantage (p. 113)

Competitive advantage providing greater value for customers than competitors can (p. 114)

Sustainable competitive advantage a competitive advantage that other companies have tried unsuccessfully to duplicate and have, for the moment, stopped trying to duplicate (p. 114)

Valuable resource a resource that allows companies to improve efficiency and effectiveness (p. 114)

Rare resource a resource that is not controlled or possessed by many competing firms (p. 114)

Imperfectly imitable resource a resource that is impossible or extremely costly or difficult for other firms to duplicate (p. 115)

Nonsubstitutable resource a resource that produces value or competitive advantage and has no equivalent substitutes or replacements (p. 115)

6-2 Describe the steps involved in the strategy-making process.

The first step in strategy making is determining whether a strategy needs to be changed to sustain a competitive advantage. The second step is to conduct a situational (SWOT) analysis that examines internal strengths and weaknesses as well as external opportunities and threats. The third step involves choosing a strategy. Strategic reference point theory suggests that when companies are performing better than their strategic reference points, top management will typically choose a risk-averse strategy. When performance is below strategic reference points, risk-seeking strategies are more likely to be chosen.

Competitive inertia a reluctance to change strategies or competitive practices that have been successful in the past (p. 117)

Strategic dissonance a discrepancy between a company's intended strategy and the strategic actions managers take when implementing that strategy (p. 117)

Situational (SWOT) analysis an assessment of the strengths and weaknesses in an organization's internal environment and the opportunities and threats in its external environment (p. 117)

Shadow-strategy task force a committee within a company that analyzes the company's own weaknesses to determine how competitors could exploit them for competitive advantage (p. 118)

Distinctive competence what a company can make, do, or perform better than its competitors (p. 118)

Core capabilities the internal decision-making routines, problem-solving processes, and organizational cultures that determine how efficiently inputs can be turned into outputs (p. 118)

Strategic group a group of companies within an industry against which top managers compare, evaluate, and benchmark strategic threats and opportunities (p. 118)

Core firms the central companies in a strategic group (p. 119)

Secondary firms the firms in a strategic group that follow strategies related to but somewhat different from those of the core firms (p. 119)

Strategic reference points the strategic targets managers use to measure whether a firm has developed the core competencies it needs to achieve a sustainable competitive advantage (p. 120)

6-3 Explain the different kinds of corporate-level strategies.

Corporate-level strategies, consisting of portfolio strategies and grand strategies, help managers determine what businesses they should be in. Portfolio strategy focuses on lowering business risk by being in multiple, unrelated businesses and by investing the cash flows from slow-growing businesses into faster-growing businesses. One portfolio strategy is based on the BCG matrix. The most successful way to use the portfolio approach to corporate strategy is to reduce risk through related diversification. The three kinds of grand strategies are growth, stability, and retrenchment/recovery. Companies can grow externally by merging with or acquiring other companies, or they can grow internally through direct expansion or creating new businesses. Companies choose a stability strategy when their external environment changes very little or after they have dealt with periods of explosive growth. Retrenchment strategy, shrinking the size or scope of a business, is used to turn around poor performance. If retrenchment works, it is often followed by a recovery strategy that focuses on growing the business again.

Corporate-level strategy the overall organizational strategy that addresses the question, "What business or businesses are we in or should we be in?" (p. 121)

Diversification a strategy for reducing risk by buying a variety of items (stocks or, in the case of a corporation, types of businesses) so that the failure of one stock or one business does not doom the entire portfolio (p. 121)

Portfolio strategy a corporate-level strategy that minimizes risk by diversifying investment among various businesses or product lines (p. 122)

Acquisition the purchase of a company by another company (p. 122)

Unrelated diversification creating or acquiring companies in completely unrelated businesses (p. 122)

BCG matrix a portfolio strategy developed by the Boston Consulting Group that categorizes a corporation's businesses by growth rate and relative market share and helps managers decide how to invest corporate funds (p. 122)

Star a company with a large share of a fast-growing market (p. 122)

Question mark a company with a small share of a fast-growing market (p. 123)

Cash cow a company with a large share of a slow-growing market (p. 123)

Dog a company with a small share of a slow-growing market (p. 123)

Related diversification creating or acquiring companies that share similar products, manufacturing, marketing, technology, or cultures (p. 124)

Grand strategy a broad corporate-level strategic plan used to achieve strategic goals and guide the strategic alternatives that managers of individual businesses or subunits may use (p. 125)

Growth strategy a strategy that focuses on increasing profits, revenues, market

share, or the number of places in which the company does business (p. 125)

Stability strategy a strategy that focuses on improving the way in which the company sells the same products or services to the same customers (p. 126)

Retrenchment strategy a strategy that focuses on turning around very poor company performance by shrinking the size or scope of the business (p. 126)

Recovery the strategic actions taken after retrenchment to return to a growth strategy (p. 126)

6-4 **Describe the different kinds of industry-level strategies.** The five industry forces determine an industry's overall attractiveness to corporate investors and its potential for long-term profitability. Together, a high level of these elements combine to increase competition and decrease profits. Industry-level strategies focus on how companies choose to compete in their industries. The three positioning strategies can help companies protect themselves from the negative effects of industry-wide competition. The four adaptive strategies help companies adapt to changes in the external environment. Defenders want to defend their current strategic positions. Prospectors look for new market opportunities to bring innovative new products to market. Analyzers minimize risk by following the proven successes of prospectors. Reactors do not follow a consistent adaptive strategy but instead react to changes in the external environment after they occur.

Industry-level strategy a corporate strategy that addresses the question, "How should we compete in this industry?" (p. 127)

Character of the rivalry a measure of the intensity of competitive behavior between companies in an industry (p. 127)

Threat of new entrants a measure of the degree to which barriers to entry make it easy or difficult for new companies to get started in an industry (p. 127)

Threat of substitute products or services a measure of the ease with which customers can find substitutes for an industry's products or services (p. 128)

Bargaining power of suppliers a measure of the influence that suppliers of parts, materials, and services to firms in an industry have on the prices of these inputs (p. 128)

Bargaining power of buyers a measure of the influence that customers have on a firm's prices (p. 128)

Cost leadership the positioning strategy of producing a product or service of acceptable quality at consistently lower production costs than competitors can, so that the firm can offer the product or service at the lowest price in the industry (p. 129)

Differentiation the positioning strategy of providing a product or service that is sufficiently different from competitors' offerings that customers are willing to pay a premium price for it (p. 129)

Focus strategy the positioning strategy of using cost leadership or differentiation to produce a specialized product or service for a limited, specially targeted group of customers in a particular geographic region or market segment (p. 129)

Defenders companies using an adaptive strategy aimed at defending strategic positions by seeking moderate, steady growth and by offering a limited range of high-quality products and services to a well-defined set of customers (p. 130)

Prospectors companies using an adaptive strategy that seeks fast growth by searching for new market opportunities, encouraging risk taking, and being the first to bring innovative new products to market (p. 130)

Analyzers companies using an adaptive strategy that seeks to minimize risk and maximize profits by following or imitating the proven successes of prospectors (p. 131)

Reactors companies that do not follow a consistent adaptive strategy but instead react to changes in the external environment after they occur (p. 131)

6-5 **Explain the components and kinds of firm-level strategies.** Firm-level strategies are concerned with direct competition between firms. Market commonality and resource similarity determine whether firms are in direct competition and thus likely to attack each other and respond to each other's attacks. In general, the more markets in which there is product, service, or customer overlap and the greater the resource similarity between two firms, the more intense the direct competition between them will be.

Firm-level strategy a corporate strategy that addresses the question, "How should we compete against a particular firm?" (p. 131)

Direct competition the rivalry between two companies that offer similar products and services, acknowledge each other as rivals, and act and react to each other's strategic actions (p. 132)

Market commonality the degree to which two companies have overlapping products, services, or customers in multiple markets (p. 132)

Resource similarity the extent to which a competitor has similar amounts and kinds of resources (p. 132)

Attack a competitive move designed to reduce a rival's market share or profits (p. 133)

Response a competitive countermove, prompted by a rival's attack, to defend or improve a company's market share or profit (p. 133)

CHAPTER 7 LEARNING OUTCOMES / KEY TERMS

7-1

Explain why innovation matters to companies.

Technology cycles typically follow an S-curve pattern of innovation. Early in the cycle, technological progress is slow, and improvements in technological performance are small. As a technology matures, however, performance improves quickly. Finally, as the limits of a technology are reached, only small improvements occur. At this point, significant improvements in performance must come from new technologies. The best way to protect a competitive advantage is to create a stream of innovative ideas and products. Innovation streams begin with technological discontinuities that create significant breakthroughs in performance or function. Technological discontinuities are followed by discontinuous change, in which customers purchase new technologies, and companies compete to establish the new dominant design. Dominant designs emerge because of critical mass, because they solve a practical problem, or because of the negotiations of independent standards bodies. Because technological innovation both enhances and destroys competence, companies that bet on the wrong design often struggle, while companies that bet on the eventual dominant design usually prosper. When a dominant design emerges, companies focus on incremental change, lowering costs, and making small but steady improvements in the dominant design. This focus continues until the next technological discontinuity occurs.

Organizational innovation the successful implementation of creative ideas in organizations (p. 137)

Technology cycle a cycle that begins with the birth of a new technology and ends when that technology reaches its limits and is replaced by a newer, substantially better technology (p. 138)

S-curve pattern of innovation a pattern of technological innovation characterized by slow initial progress, then rapid progress, and then slow progress again as a technology matures and reaches its limits (p. 138)

Innovation streams patterns of innovation over time that can create sustainable competitive advantage (p. 139)

Technological discontinuity the phase of an innovation stream in which a scientific advance or unique combination of existing technologies creates a significant breakthrough in performance or function (p. 139)

Discontinuous change the phase of a technology cycle characterized by technological substitution and design competition (p. 140)

Technological substitution the purchase of new technologies to replace older ones (p. 140)

Design competition competition between old and new technologies to establish a new technological standard or dominant design (p. 140)

Dominant design a new technological design or process that becomes the accepted market standard (p. 141)

Technological lockout the inability of a company to competitively sell its products because it relies on old technology or a nondominant design (p. 142)

Incremental change the phase of a technology cycle in which companies innovate by lowering costs and improving the functioning and performance of the dominant technological design (p. 142)

7-2

Discuss the different methods that managers can use to effectively manage innovation in their organizations.

To successfully manage innovation streams, companies must manage the sources of innovation and learn to manage innovation during both discontinuous and incremental change. Because innovation begins with creativity, companies can manage the sources of innovation by supporting a work environment in which creative thoughts and ideas are welcomed, valued, and encouraged. Creative work environments provide challenging work; offer organizational, supervisory, and work group encouragement; allow significant freedom; and remove organizational impediments to creativity. Discontinuous and incremental change require different strategies. Companies that succeed in periods of discontinuous change typically follow an experiential approach to innovation. The experiential approach assumes that intuition, flexible options, and hands-on experience can reduce uncertainty and accelerate learning and understanding. A compression approach to innovation works best during periods of incremental change. This approach assumes that innovation can be planned using a series of steps and that compressing the time it takes to complete those steps can speed up innovation.

Creative work environments workplace cultures in which workers perceive that new ideas are welcomed, valued, and encouraged (p. 143)

Flow a psychological state of effortlessness, in which you become completely absorbed in what you're doing, and time seems to pass quickly (p. 144)

Experiential approach to innovation an approach to innovation that assumes a highly uncertain environment and uses intuition, flexible options, and hands-on experience to reduce uncertainty and accelerate learning and understanding (p. 145)

Design iteration a cycle of repetition in which a company tests a prototype of a new product or service, improves on that design, and then builds and tests the improved prototype (p. 146)

Product prototype a full-scale, working model that is being tested for design, function, and reliability (p. 146)

Testing the systematic comparison of different product designs or design iterations (p. 146)

Milestones formal project review points used to assess progress and performance (p. 147)

Multifunctional teams work teams composed of people from different departments (p. 147)

Compression approach to innovation an approach to innovation that assumes that incremental innovation can be planned using a series of steps and that compressing those steps can speed innovation (p. 148)

Generational change change based on incremental improvements to a dominant technological design such that the improved technology is fully backward compatible with the older technology (p. 148)

7-3 **Discuss why not changing can lead to organizational decline.** The five-stage process of organizational decline begins when organizations don't recognize the need for change. In the blinded stage, managers fail to recognize the changes that threaten their organization's survival. In the inaction stage, management recognizes the need to change but doesn't act, hoping that the problems will correct themselves. In the faulty action stage, management focuses on cost cutting and efficiency rather than facing up to the fundamental changes needed to ensure survival. In the crisis stage, failure is likely unless fundamental reorganization occurs. Finally, in the dissolution stage, the company is dissolved through bankruptcy proceedings; by selling assets to pay creditors; or through the closing of stores, offices, and facilities. If companies recognize the need to change early enough, however, dissolution may be avoided.

Organizational decline a large decrease in organizational performance that occurs when companies don't anticipate, recognize, neutralize, or adapt to the internal or external pressures that threaten their survival (p. 149)

7-4 **Discuss the different methods that managers can use to better manage change as it occurs.** The basic change process involves unfreezing, change intervention, and refreezing. Resistance to change stems from self-interest, misunderstanding, and distrust as well as a general intolerance for change. Resistance can be managed through education and communication, participation, negotiation, top management support, and coercion. Knowing what not to do is as important as knowing what to do to achieve successful change. Managers should avoid these errors when leading change: not establishing a sense of urgency, not creating a guiding coalition, lacking a vision, undercommunicating the vision, not removing obstacles to the vision, not creating short-term wins, declaring victory too soon, and not anchoring changes in the corporation's culture. Finally, managers can use a number of change techniques. Results-driven change and the General Electric fastworks reduce resistance to change by getting change efforts off to a fast start. Organizational development is a collection of planned change interventions (large-system, small-group, person-focused), guided by a change agent, that are designed to improve an organization's long-term health and performance.

Change forces forces that produce differences in the form, quality, or condition of an organization over time (p. 150)

Resistance forces forces that support the existing conditions in organizations (p. 150)

Resistance to change opposition to change resulting from self-interest, misunderstanding and distrust, and a general intolerance for change (p. 150)

Unfreezing getting the people affected by change to believe that change is needed (p. 151)

Change intervention the process used to get workers and managers to change their behaviors and work practices (p. 151)

Refreezing supporting and reinforcing new changes so that they stick (p. 151)

Coercion the use of formal power and authority to force others to change (p. 152)

Results-driven change change created quickly by focusing on the measurement and improvement of results (p. 154)

General Electric fastworks quickly experimenting with new ideas to solve customer problems and learn from repeated tests and improvements (p. 154)

Organizational development a philosophy and collection of planned change interventions designed to improve an organization's long-term health and performance (p. 155)

Change agent the person formally in charge of guiding a change effort (p. 155)

Exhibit 7.6
Different Kinds of Organizational Development Interventions

Large-System Interventions	
Sociotechnical systems	An intervention designed to improve how well employees use and adjust to the work technology used in an organization.
Survey feedback	An intervention that uses surveys to collect information from the members of the system, reports the results of that survey to the members, and then uses those results to develop action plans for improvement.

Small-Group Interventions	
Team building	An intervention designed to increase the cohesion and cooperation of work group members.
Unit goal setting	An intervention designed to help a work group establish short- and long-term goals.

Person-Focused Interventions	
Counseling/coaching	An intervention designed so that a formal helper or coach listens to managers or employees and advises them on how to deal with work or interpersonal problems.
Training	An intervention designed to provide individuals with the knowledge, skills, or attitudes they need to become more effective at their jobs.

Source: W. J. Rothwell, R. Sullivan, and G. M. McLean, *Practicing Organizational Development: A Guide for Consultants* (San Diego: Pfeiffer & Co., 1995).

CHAPTER 8 LEARNING OUTCOMES / KEY TERMS

8-1 **Discuss the impact of global business and the trade rules and agreements that govern it.** Today, there are more than 30,000 multinational corporations worldwide; the United States is the second-largest base for multinationals. Global business affects the United States in two ways: through direct foreign investment in the United States by foreign companies and through U.S. companies' investment in businesses in other countries. U.S. direct foreign investment throughout the world amounts to more than $4.9 trillion per year, whereas direct foreign investment by foreign companies in the United States amounts to more than $2.9 trillion per year. Historically, tariffs and nontariff trade barriers such as quotas, voluntary export restraints, government import standards, government subsidies, and customs classifications have made buying foreign goods much harder or more expensive than buying domestically produced products. In recent years, however, worldwide trade agreements such as GATT and the WTO, along with regional trading agreements such as the Maastricht Treaty of Europe, NAFTA, CAFTA-DR, UNASUR, ASEAN, APEC, and TFTA have substantially reduced tariffs and nontariff barriers to international trade. Companies have responded by investing in growing markets in Asia, Eastern Europe, and Latin America. Consumers have responded by purchasing products based on value rather than geography.

Global business the buying and selling of goods and services by people from different countries (p. 158)

Multinational corporation a corporation that owns businesses in two or more countries (p. 159)

Direct foreign investment a method of investment in which a company builds a new business or buys an existing business in a foreign country (p. 160)

Trade barriers government-imposed regulations that increase the cost and restrict the number of imported goods (p. 161)

Protectionism a government's use of trade barriers to shield domestic companies and their workers from foreign competition (p. 161)

Tariff a direct tax on imported goods (p. 161)

Nontariff barriers nontax methods of increasing the cost or reducing the volume of imported goods (p. 161)

Quota a limit on the number or volume of imported products (p. 161)

Voluntary export restraints voluntarily imposed limits on the number or volume of products exported to a particular country (p. 161)

Government import standard a standard ostensibly established to protect the health and safety of citizens but, in reality, is often used to restrict imports (p. 161)

Subsidies government loans, grants, and tax deferments given to domestic companies to protect them from foreign competition (p. 162)

Customs classification a classification assigned to imported products by government officials that affects the size of the tariff and the imposition of import quotas (p. 162)

General Agreement on Tariffs and Trade (GATT) a worldwide trade agreement that reduced and eliminated tariffs, limited government subsidies, and established protections for intellectual property (p. 162)

World Trade Organization (WTO) the successor to GATT; the only international organization dealing with the global rules of trade between nations; its main function is to ensure that trade flows as smoothly, predictably, and freely as possible (p. 162)

Regional trading zones areas in which tariff and nontariff barriers on trade between countries are reduced or eliminated (p. 163)

Maastricht Treaty of Europe a regional trade agreement among most European countries (p. 163)

North American Free Trade Agreement (NAFTA) a regional trade agreement among the United States, Canada, and Mexico (p. 165)

Dominican Republic-Central America Free Trade Agreement (CAFTA-DR) a regional trade agreement among Costa Rica, the Dominican Republic, El Salvador, Guatemala, Honduras, Nicaragua, and the United States (p. 165)

Union of South American Nations (UNASUR) a regional trade agreement among Argentina, Brazil, Paraguay, Uruguay, Venezuela, Bolivia, Colombia, Ecuador, Peru, Guyana, Suriname, and Chile (p. 165)

Association of Southeast Asian Nations (ASEAN) a regional trade agreement among Brunei Darussalam, Cambodia, Indonesia, Laos, Malaysia, Myanmar, the Philippines, Singapore, Thailand, and Vietnam (p. 165)

Asia-Pacific Economic Cooperation (APEC) a regional trade agreement among Australia, Canada, Chile, the People's Republic of China, Hong Kong, Japan, Mexico, New Zealand, Papua New Guinea, Peru, Russia, South Korea, Taiwan, the United States, and all the members of ASEAN except Cambodia, Lao PDR, and Myanmar (p. 165)

Tripartite Free Trade Agreement (TFTA) a regional trade agreement among 27 African countries (p. 166)

8-2 **Explain why companies choose to standardize or adapt their business procedures.** Global business requires a balance between global consistency and local adaptation. Global consistency means using the same rules, guidelines, policies, and procedures in each location. Managers at company headquarters like global consistency because it simplifies decisions. Local adaptation means adapting standard procedures to differences in markets. Local managers prefer a policy of local adaptation because it gives them more control. Not all businesses need the same combination of global consistency and local adaptation. Some thrive by emphasizing global consistency and ignoring local adaptation. Others succeed by ignoring global consistency and emphasizing local adaptation.

Global consistency when a multinational company has offices, manufacturing plants, and distribution facilities in different countries and runs them all using the same rules, guidelines, policies, and procedures (p. 167)

Local adaptation modifying rules, guidelines, policies, and procedures to adapt to differences in foreign customers, governments, and regulatory agencies (p. 167)

8-3 **Explain the different ways that companies can organize to do business globally.** The phase model of globalization says that, as companies move from a domestic to a global orientation, they use these organizational forms in sequence: exporting, cooperative contracts (licensing and franchising), strategic alliances, and wholly owned affiliates. Yet, not all companies follow the phase model. For example, global new ventures are global from their inception.

Exporting selling domestically produced products to customers in foreign countries (p. 168)

Cooperative contract an agreement in which a foreign business owner pays a company a fee for the right to conduct that business in his or her country (p. 169)

Licensing an agreement in which a domestic company, the licensor, receives royalty payments for allowing another company, the licensee, to produce the licensor's product, sell its service, or use its brand name in a specified foreign market (p. 169)

Franchise a collection of networked firms in which the manufacturer or marketer of a product or service, the franchisor, licenses the entire business to another person or organization, the franchisee (p. 170)

Strategic alliance an agreement in which companies combine key resources, costs, risks, technology, and people (p. 170)

Joint venture a strategic alliance in which two existing companies collaborate to form a third, independent company (p. 171)

Wholly owned affiliates foreign offices, facilities, and manufacturing plants that are 100 percent owned by the parent company (p. 171)

Global new ventures new companies that are founded with an active global strategy and have sales, employees, and financing in different countries (p. 172)

8-4 **Explain how to find a favorable business climate.** The first step in deciding where to take your company global is finding an attractive business climate. Be sure to look for a growing market where consumers have strong purchasing power, and foreign competitors are weak. When locating an office or manufacturing facility, consider both qualitative and quantitative factors. In assessing political risk, be sure to examine both political uncertainty and policy uncertainty. If the location you choose has considerable political risk, you can avoid it, try to control the risk, or use a cooperation strategy.

Purchasing power the relative cost of a standard set of goods and services in different countries (p. 172)

Political uncertainty the risk of major changes in political regimes that can result from war, revolution, death of political leaders, social unrest, or other influential events (p. 175)

Policy uncertainty the risk associated with changes in laws and government policies that directly affect the way foreign companies conduct business (p. 175)

8-5 **Discuss the importance of identifying and adapting to cultural differences.** National culture is the set of shared values and beliefs that affects the perceptions, decisions, and behavior of the people from a particular country. The first step in dealing with culture is to recognize meaningful differences such as power distance, individualism, masculinity, uncertainty avoidance, and short-term/long-term orientation. Cultural differences should be interpreted carefully because they are based on generalizations rather than specific individuals. Adapting managerial practices to cultural differences is difficult because policies and practices can be perceived differently in different cultures.

National culture the set of shared values and beliefs that affects the perceptions, decisions, and behavior of the people from a particular country (p. 177)

8-6 **Explain how to successfully prepare workers for international assignments.** Many expatriates return prematurely from international assignments because of poor performance. This is much less likely to happen if employees receive language and cross-cultural training, such as documentary training, cultural simulations, or field experiences, before going on assignment. Adjustment of expatriates' spouses and families, which is the most important determinant of success in international assignments, can be improved through adaptability screening and language and cross-cultural training.

Expatriate someone who lives and works outside his or her native country (p. 180)

9-1 Describe the departmentalization approach to organizational structure. There are five traditional departmental structures: functional, product, customer, geographic, and matrix. Functional departmentalization is based on the different business functions or types of expertise used to run a business. Product departmentalization is organized according to the different products or services a company sells. Customer departmentalization focuses its divisions on the different kinds of customers a company has. Geographic departmentalization is based on different geographic areas or markets in which the company does business. Matrix departmentalization is a hybrid form that combines two or more forms of departmentalization, the most common being the product and functional forms. There is no single best departmental structure. Each structure has advantages and disadvantages.

Organizational structure the vertical and horizontal configuration of departments, authority, and jobs within a company (p. 184)

Organizational process the collection of activities that transforms inputs into outputs that customers value (p. 185)

Departmentalization subdividing work and workers into separate organizational units responsible for completing particular tasks (p. 186)

Functional departmentalization organizing work and workers into separate units responsible for particular business functions or areas of expertise (p. 187)

Product departmentalization organizing work and workers into separate units responsible for producing particular products or services (p. 187)

Customer departmentalization organizing work and workers into separate units responsible for particular kinds of customers (p. 189)

Geographic departmentalization organizing work and workers into separate units responsible for doing business in particular geographic areas (p. 190)

Matrix departmentalization a hybrid organizational structure in which two or more forms of departmentalization, most often product and functional, are used together (p. 190)

Simple matrix a form of matrix departmentalization in which managers in different parts of the matrix negotiate conflicts and resources (p. 193)

Complex matrix a form of matrix departmentalization in which managers in different parts of the matrix report to matrix managers, who help them sort out conflicts and problems (p. 193)

9-2 Explain organizational authority. Organizational authority is determined by the chain of command, line versus staff authority, delegation, and the degree of centralization in a company. The chain of command vertically connects every job in the company to higher levels of management and makes clear who reports to whom. Managers have line authority to command employees below them in the chain of command but have only staff, or advisory, authority over employees not below them in the chain of command. Managers delegate authority by transferring to subordinates the authority and responsibility needed to do a task; in exchange, subordinates become accountable for task completion. In centralized companies, most authority to make decisions lies with managers in the upper levels of the company. In decentralized companies, much of the authority is delegated to the workers closest to the problems, who can then make the decisions necessary for solving the problems themselves.

Authority the right to give commands, take action, and make decisions to achieve organizational objectives (p. 193)

Chain of command the vertical line of authority that clarifies who reports to whom throughout the organization (p. 193)

Unity of command a management principle that workers should report to just one boss (p. 193)

Line authority the right to command immediate subordinates in the chain of command (p. 194)

Staff authority the right to advise, but not command, others who are not subordinates in the chain of command (p. 194)

Line function an activity that contributes directly to creating or selling the company's products (p. 194)

Staff function an activity that does not contribute directly to creating or selling the company's products but instead supports line activities (p. 194)

Delegation of authority the assignment of direct authority and responsibility to a subordinate to complete tasks for which the manager is normally responsible (p. 194)

Centralization of authority the location of most authority at the upper levels of the organization (p. 195)

Decentralization the location of a significant amount of authority in the lower levels of the organization (p. 195)

Standardization solving problems by consistently applying the same rules, procedures, and processes (p. 196)

9-3 Discuss the different methods for job design. Companies use specialized jobs because they are economical, easy to learn, and don't require highly paid workers. However, specialized jobs aren't motivating or particularly satisfying for employees. Companies have used job rotation, job enlargement, job enrichment, and the job characteristics model to make specialized jobs more interesting and motivating. The goal of the job characteristics model is to make jobs intrinsically motivating. For this to happen, jobs must be strong on five core job characteristics (skill variety, task identity, task significance, autonomy, and feedback), and workers must experience three critical psychological states (knowledge of results, responsibility for work outcomes, and meaningful work). If jobs aren't internally motivating, they can be redesigned by combining tasks, forming natural work units, establishing client relationships, using vertical loading, and opening feedback channels.

Job design the number, kind, and variety of tasks that individual workers perform in doing their jobs (p. 196)

Job specialization a job composed of a small part of a larger task or process (p. 196)

Job rotation periodically moving workers from one specialized job to another to give them more variety and the opportunity to use different skills (p. 197)

Job enlargement increasing the number of different tasks that a worker performs within one particular job (p. 197)

Job enrichment increasing the number of tasks in a particular job and giving workers the authority and control to make meaningful decisions about their work (p. 197)

Job characteristics model (JCM) an approach to job redesign that seeks to formulate jobs in ways that motivate workers and lead to positive work outcomes (p. 197)

Internal motivation motivation that comes from the job itself rather than from outside rewards (p. 197)

Skill variety the number of different activities performed in a job (p. 197)

Task identity the degree to which a job, from beginning to end, requires the completion of a whole and identifiable piece of work (p. 197)

Task significance the degree to which a job is perceived to have a substantial impact on others inside or outside the organization (p. 198)

Autonomy the degree to which a job gives workers the discretion, freedom, and independence to decide how and when to accomplish the job (p. 198)

Feedback the amount of information the job provides to workers about their work performance (p. 198)

9-4 **Explain the methods that companies are using to redesign internal organizational processes (that is, intraorganizational processes).** Today, companies are using reengineering and empowerment to change their intraorganizational processes. Reengineering changes an organization's orientation from vertical to horizontal and changes its work processes by decreasing sequential and pooled interdependence and by increasing reciprocal interdependence. Reengineering promises dramatic increases in productivity and customer satisfaction, but it has been criticized as simply an excuse to cut costs and lay off workers. Empowering workers means taking decision-making authority and responsibility from managers and giving it to workers. Empowered workers develop feelings of competence and self-determination and believe that their work has meaning and impact.

Mechanistic organization an organization characterized by specialized jobs and responsibilities; precisely defined, unchanging roles; and a rigid chain of command based on centralized authority and vertical communication (p. 199)

Organic organization an organization characterized by broadly defined jobs and responsibilities; loosely defined, frequently changing roles; and decentralized authority and horizontal communication based on task knowledge (p. 199)

Intraorganizational process the collection of activities that take place within an organization to transform inputs into outputs that customers value (p. 199)

Reengineering fundamental rethinking and radical redesign of business processes to achieve dramatic improvements in critical measures of performance, such as cost, quality, service, and speed (p. 199)

Task interdependence the extent to which collective action is required to complete an entire piece of work (p. 201)

Pooled interdependence work completed by having each job or department independently contribute to the whole (p. 201)

Sequential interdependence work completed in succession, with one group's or job's outputs becoming the inputs for the next group or job (p. 201)

Reciprocal interdependence work completed by different jobs or groups working together in a back-and-forth manner (p. 201)

Empowering workers permanently passing decision-making authority and responsibility from managers to workers by giving them the information and resources they need to make and carry out good decisions (p. 202)

Empowerment feeling of intrinsic motivation in which workers perceive their work to have impact and meaning and perceive themselves to be competent and capable of self-determination (p. 202)

9-5 **Describe the methods that companies are using to redesign external organizational processes (that is, interorganizational processes).** Organizations are using modular and virtual organizations to change interorganizational processes. Because modular organizations outsource all noncore activities to other businesses, they are less expensive to run than traditional companies. However, modular organizations require extremely close relationships with suppliers, may result in a loss of control, and could create new competitors if the wrong business activities are outsourced. Virtual organizations participate in a network in which they share skills, costs, capabilities, markets, and customers. Virtual organizations can reduce costs, respond quickly, and, if they can successfully coordinate their efforts, produce outstanding products and services.

Interorganizational process a collection of activities that take place among companies to transform inputs into outputs that customers value (p. 203)

Modular organization an organization that outsources noncore business activities to outside companies, suppliers, specialists, or consultants (p. 203)

Virtual organization an organization that is part of a network in which many companies share skills, costs, capabilities, markets, and customers to collectively solve customer problems or provide specific products or services (p. 204)

10-1 Explain the good and bad of using teams. In many industries, teams are growing in importance because they help organizations respond to specific problems and challenges. Teams have been shown to increase customer satisfaction (specific customer teams), product and service quality (direct responsibility), and employee job satisfaction (cross-training, unique opportunities, and leadership responsibilities). Although teams can produce significant improvements in these areas, using teams does not guarantee these positive outcomes. Teams and teamwork have the disadvantages of initially high turnover and social loafing (especially in large groups). Teams also share many of the advantages (multiple perspectives, generation of more alternatives, and more commitment) and disadvantages (groupthink, time, poorly run meetings, domination by a few team members, and weak accountability) of group decision making. Teams should be used for a clear purpose, when the work requires that people work together, when rewards can be provided for both teamwork and team performance, and when ample resources can be provided.

Exhibit 10.1
When to Use and When Not to Use Teams

Use Teams When . . .
- ✓ there is a clear, engaging reason or purpose.
- ✓ the job can't be done unless people work together.
- ✓ rewards can be provided for teamwork and team performance.
- ✓ ample resources are available.

Don't Use Teams When . . .
- ✗ there isn't a clear, engaging reason or purpose.
- ✗ the job can be done by people working independently.
- ✗ rewards are provided for individual effort and performance.
- ✗ the necessary resources are not available.

Source: R. Wageman, "Critical Success Factors for Creating Superb Self-Managing Teams," *Organizational Dynamics* 26, no. 1 (1997): 49–61.

Work team a small number of people with complementary skills who hold themselves mutually accountable for pursuing a common purpose, achieving performance goals, and improving interdependent work processes (p. 206)

Cross-training training team members to do all or most of the jobs performed by the other team members (p. 208)

Social loafing behavior in which team members withhold their efforts and fail to perform their share of the work (p. 209)

10-2 Recognize and understand the different kinds of teams. Companies use different kinds of teams to make themselves more competitive. Autonomy is the key dimension that makes teams different. Traditional work groups (which execute tasks) and employee involvement groups (which make suggestions) have the lowest levels of autonomy. Semi-autonomous work groups (which control major direct tasks) have more autonomy, while self-managing teams (which control all direct tasks) and self-designing teams (which control membership and how tasks are done) have the highest levels of autonomy. Cross-functional, virtual, and project teams are common but are not easily categorized in terms of autonomy. Cross-functional teams combine employees from different functional areas to help teams attack problems from multiple perspectives and generate more ideas and solutions. Virtual teams use telecommunications and information technologies to bring coworkers together, regardless of physical location or time zone. Virtual teams reduce travel and work time, but communication may suffer because team members don't work face-to-face. Finally, project teams are used for specific, one-time projects or tasks that must be completed within a limited time. Project teams reduce communication barriers and promote flexibility; teams and team members are reassigned to their departments or to new projects as their current projects are completed.

Traditional work group a group composed of two or more people who work together to achieve a shared goal (p. 211)

Employee involvement team team that provides advice or makes suggestions to management concerning specific issues (p. 211)

Semi-autonomous work group a group that has the authority to make decisions and solve problems related to the major tasks of producing a product or service (p. 213)

Self-managing team a team that manages and controls all of the major tasks of producing a product or service (p. 213)

Self-designing team a team that has the characteristics of self-managing teams but also controls team design, work tasks, and team membership (p. 214)

Cross-functional team a team composed of employees from different functional areas of the organization (p. 214)

Virtual team a team composed of geographically and/or organizationally dispersed coworkers who use telecommunication and information technologies to accomplish an organizational task (p. 214)

Project team a team created to complete specific, one-time projects or tasks within a limited time (p. 215)

10-3 **Understand the general characteristics of work teams.**
The most important characteristics of work teams are team norms, cohesiveness, size, conflict, and development. Norms let team members know what is expected of them and can influence team behavior in positive and negative ways. Positive team norms are associated with organizational commitment, trust, and job satisfaction. Team cohesiveness helps teams retain members, promotes cooperative behavior, increases motivation, and facilitates team performance. Attending team meetings and activities, creating opportunities to work together, and engaging in nonwork activities can increase cohesiveness. Team size has a curvilinear relationship with team performance: teams that are very small or very large do not perform as well as moderate-sized teams of six to nine members. Teams of this size are cohesive and small enough for team members to get to know each other and contribute in a meaningful way but are large enough to take advantage of team members' diverse skills, knowledge, and perspectives. Conflict and disagreement are inevitable in most teams. The key to dealing with team conflict is to maximize cognitive conflict, which focuses on issue-related differences, and minimize affective conflict, the emotional reactions that occur when disagreements become personal rather than professional. As teams develop and grow, they pass through four stages of development: forming, storming, norming, and performing. If a team is not managed well, its performance may decline after a period of time as the team regresses through the stages of de-norming, de-storming, and de-forming.

Norms informally agreed-on standards that regulate team behavior (p. 215)

Cohesiveness the extent to which team members are attracted to a team and motivated to remain in it (p. 216)

Forming the first stage of team development, in which team members meet each other, form initial impressions, and begin to establish team norms (p. 219)

Storming the second stage of development, characterized by conflict and disagreement, in which team members disagree over what the team should do and how it should do it (p. 220)

Norming the third stage of team development, in which team members begin to settle into their roles, group cohesion grows, and positive team norms develop (p. 220)

Performing the fourth and final stage of team development, in which performance improves because the team has matured into an effective, fully functioning team (p. 220)

De-norming a reversal of the norming stage, in which team performance begins to decline as the size, scope, goal, or members of the team change (p. 220)

De-storming a reversal of the storming phase, in which the team's comfort level decreases, team cohesion weakens, and angry emotions and conflict may flare (p. 220)

De-forming a reversal of the forming stage, in which team members position themselves to control pieces of the team, avoid each other, and isolate themselves from team leaders (p. 221)

10-4 **Explain how to enhance work team effectiveness.**
Companies can make teams more effective by setting team goals and managing how team members are selected, trained, and compensated. Team goals provide a clear focus and purpose, reduce the incidence of social loafing, and lead to higher team performance 93 percent of the time. Extremely difficult stretch goals can be used to motivate teams as long as teams have autonomy, control over resources, structural accommodation, and bureaucratic immunity. Not everyone is suited for teamwork. When selecting team members, companies should select people who have a preference for teamwork (that is, are more collectivists than individualists) and should consider team level (average ability of a team) and team diversity (different abilities of a team). Organizations that use teams successfully provide thousands of hours of training to make sure that teams work. The most common types of team training are for interpersonal skills, decision-making and problem-solving skills, conflict resolution, technical training to help team members learn multiple jobs (that is, cross-training), and training for team leaders. Employees can be compensated for team participation and accomplishments in three ways: skill-based pay, gainsharing, and nonfinancial rewards.

Structural accommodation the ability to change organizational structures, policies, and practices in order to meet stretch goals (p. 222)

Bureaucratic immunity the ability to make changes without first getting approval from managers or other parts of an organization (p. 222)

Individualism-collectivism the degree to which a person believes that people should be self-sufficient and that loyalty to one's self is more important than loyalty to team or company (p. 222)

Team level the average level of ability, experience, personality, or any other factor on a team (p. 222)

Team diversity the variances or differences in ability, experience, personality, or any other factor on a team (p. 223)

Interpersonal skills skills, such as listening, communicating, questioning, and providing feedback, that enable people to have effective working relationships with others (p. 224)

Skill-based pay compensation system that pays employees for learning additional skills or knowledge (p. 225)

Gainsharing a compensation system in which companies share the financial value of performance gains, such as increased productivity, cost savings, or quality, with their workers (p. 225)

11-1 **Explain how different employment laws affect human resource practice.** Human resource management is subject to numerous major federal employment laws and subject to review by several federal agencies. In general, these laws indicate that sex, age, religion, color, national origin, race, disability, and genetic history may not be considered in employment decisions unless these factors reasonably qualify as BFOQs. Two important criteria, disparate treatment (intentional discrimination) and adverse impact (unintentional discrimination), are used to decide whether companies have wrongly discriminated against someone. The two kinds of sexual harassment are quid pro quo sexual harassment and hostile work environment.

Human resource management (HRM) the process of finding, developing, and keeping the right people to form a qualified workforce (p. 226)

Bona fide occupational qualification (BFOQ) an exception in employment law that permits sex, age, religion, and the like to be used when making employment decisions, but only if they are "reasonably necessary to the normal operation of that particular business." BFOQs are strictly monitored by the Equal Employment Opportunity Commission (p. 228)

Disparate treatment intentional discrimination that occurs when people are purposely not given the same hiring, promotion, or membership opportunities because of their race, color, sex, age, ethnic group, national origin, or religious beliefs (p. 229)

Adverse impact unintentional discrimination that occurs when members of a particular race, sex, or ethnic group are unintentionally harmed or disadvantaged because they are hired, promoted, or trained (or any other employment decision) at substantially lower rates than others (p. 230)

Four-fifths (or 80%) rule a rule of thumb used by the courts and the EEOC to determine whether there is evidence of adverse impact; a violation of this rule occurs when the impact ratio (calculated by dividing the decision ratio for a protected group by the decision ratio for a nonprotected group) is less than 80 percent, or four-fifths (p. 230)

Sexual harassment a form of discrimination in which unwelcome sexual advances, requests for sexual favors, or other verbal or physical conduct of a sexual nature occurs while performing one's job (p. 230)

Quid pro quo sexual harassment a form of sexual harassment in which employment outcomes, such as hiring, promotion, or simply keeping one's job, depend on whether an individual submits to sexual harassment (p. 231)

Hostile work environment a form of sexual harassment in which unwelcome and demeaning sexually related behavior creates an intimidating and offensive work environment (p. 231)

11-2 **Explain how companies use recruiting to find qualified job applicants.** Recruiting is the process of finding qualified job applicants. The first step in recruiting is to conduct a job analysis, which is used to write a job description of basic tasks, duties, and responsibilities and to write job specifications indicating the knowledge, skills, and abilities needed to perform the job. Whereas internal recruiting involves finding qualified job applicants from inside the company, external recruiting involves finding qualified job applicants from outside the company.

Recruiting the process of developing a pool of qualified job applicants (p. 232)

Job analysis a purposeful, systematic process for collecting information on the important work-related aspects of a job (p. 232)

Job description a written description of the basic tasks, duties, and responsibilities required of an employee holding a particular job (p. 232)

Job specifications a written summary of the qualifications needed to successfully perform a particular job (p. 232)

Internal recruiting the process of developing a pool of qualified job applicants from people who already work in the company (p. 233)

External recruiting the process of developing a pool of qualified job applicants from outside the company (p. 234)

11-3 **Describe the selection techniques and procedures that companies use when deciding which applicants should receive job offers.** Selection is the process of gathering information about job applicants to decide who should be offered a job. Accurate selection procedures are valid, are legally defensible, and improve organizational performance. Application forms and résumés are the most common selection devices. Managers should check references and conduct background checks even though previous employers are often reluctant to provide such information for fear of being sued for defamation. Unfortunately, without this information, other employers are at risk of negligent hiring lawsuits. Selection tests generally do the best job of predicting applicants' future job performance. The three kinds of job interviews are unstructured, structured, and semistructured.

Selection the process of gathering information about job applicants to decide who should be offered a job (p. 235)

Validation the process of determining how well a selection test or procedure predicts future job performance; the better or more accurate the prediction of future job performance, the more valid a test is said to be (p. 236)

Human resource information system (HRIS) a computerized system for gathering, analyzing, storing, and disseminating information related to the HRM process (p. 236)

Employment references sources such as previous employers or coworkers who can provide job-related information about job candidates (p. 237)

Background checks procedures used to verify the truthfulness and accuracy of information that applicants provide about themselves and to uncover negative, job-related background information not provided by applicants (p. 237)

Specific ability tests (aptitude tests) tests that measure the extent to which an applicant possesses the particular kind of ability needed to do a job well (p. 238)

Cognitive ability tests tests that measure the extent to which applicants have abilities in perceptual speed, verbal comprehension, numerical aptitude, general reasoning, and spatial aptitude (p. 239)

Biographical data (biodata) extensive surveys that ask applicants questions about their personal backgrounds and life experiences (p. 239)

Personality test an assessment that measures the extent to which an applicant possesses different kinds of job-related personality dimensions (p. 239)

Work sample tests tests that require applicants to perform tasks that are actually done on the job (p. 240)

Assessment centers a series of managerial simulations, graded by trained observers, that are used to determine applicants' capability for managerial work (p. 240)

Interview a selection tool in which company representatives ask job applicants job-related questions to determine whether they are qualified for the job (p. 241)

Unstructured interviews interviews in which interviewers are free to ask the applicants anything they want (p. 241)

Structured interviews interviews in which all applicants are asked the same set of standardized questions, usually including situational, behavioral, background, and job-knowledge questions (p. 241)

11-4 Describe how to determine training needs, and select the appropriate training methods.
Training is used to give employees the job-specific skills, experience, and knowledge they need to do their jobs or improve their job performance. To make sure training dollars are well spent, companies need to determine specific training needs, select appropriate training methods, and then evaluate the training.

Training developing the skills, experience, and knowledge employees need to perform their jobs or improve their performance (p. 243)

Needs assessment the process of identifying and prioritizing the learning needs of employees (p. 243)

11-5 Discuss how to use performance appraisal to give meaningful performance feedback.
The keys to successful performance appraisals are accurately measuring job performance and effectively sharing performance feedback with employees. Organizations should develop good performance appraisal scales; train raters how to accurately evaluate performance; and impress upon managers the value of providing feedback in a clear, consistent, and fair manner, as well as setting goals and monitoring progress toward those goals.

Performance appraisal the process of assessing how well employees are doing their jobs (p. 246)

Objective performance measures measures of job performance that are easily and directly counted or quantified (p. 248)

Subjective performance measures measures of job performance that require someone to judge or assess a worker's performance (p. 248)

Behavior observation scales (BOSs) rating scales that indicate the frequency with which workers perform specific behaviors that are representative of the job dimensions critical to successful job performance (p. 248)

Rater training training performance appraisal raters in how to avoid rating errors and increase rating accuracy (p. 248)

360-degree feedback a performance appraisal process in which feedback is obtained from the boss, subordinates, peers and coworkers, and the employees themselves (p. 249)

11-6 Describe basic compensation strategies, and discuss the four kinds of employee separations.
Compensation includes both the financial and the nonfinancial rewards that organizations provide employees in exchange for their work. There are three basic kinds of compensation decisions: pay level, pay variability, and pay structure. Employee separation is the loss of an employee, which can occur voluntarily or involuntarily. Companies use downsizing and early retirement incentive programs (ERIPs) to reduce the number of employees in the organization and lower costs. However, companies generally try to keep the rate of employee turnover low to reduce costs associated with finding and developing new employees. Functional turnover, on the other hand, can be good for organizations.

Compensation the financial and nonfinancial rewards that organizations give employees in exchange for their work (p. 250)

Employee separation the voluntary or involuntary loss of an employee (p. 250)

Job evaluation a process that determines the worth of each job in a company by evaluating the market value of the knowledge, skills, and requirements needed to perform it (p. 251)

Piecework a compensation system in which employees are paid a set rate for each item they produce (p. 251)

Commission a compensation system in which employees earn a percentage of each sale they make (p. 251)

Profit sharing a compensation system in which a company pays a percentage of its profits to employees in addition to their regular compensation (p. 252)

Employee stock ownership plan (ESOP) a compensation system that awards employees shares of company stock in addition to their regular compensation (p. 252)

Stock options a compensation system that gives employees the right to purchase shares of stock at a set price, even if the value of the stock increases above that price (p. 252)

Wrongful discharge a legal doctrine that requires employers to have a job-related reason to terminate employees (p. 254)

Downsizing the planned elimination of jobs in a company (p. 254)

Outplacement services employment-counseling services offered to employees who are losing their jobs because of downsizing (p. 255)

Early retirement incentive programs (ERIPs) programs that offer financial benefits to employees to encourage them to retire early (p. 255)

Phased retirement employees transition to retirement by working reduced hours over a period of time before completely retiring (p. 255)

Employee turnover loss of employees who voluntarily choose to leave the company (p. 256)

Functional turnover loss of poor-performing employees who voluntarily choose to leave a company (p. 256)

Dysfunctional turnover loss of high-performing employees who voluntarily choose to leave a company (p. 256)

CHAPTER REVIEW

CHAPTER 12 LEARNING OUTCOMES / KEY TERMS

12-1 Describe diversity and explain why it matters. Diversity exists in organizations when there are demographic, cultural, and personal differences among the employees and the customers. A common misconception is that workplace diversity and affirmative action are the same. However, affirmative action is more narrowly focused on demographics; is required by law; and is used to punish companies that discriminate on the basis of race/ethnicity, religion, sex, or national origin. By contrast, diversity is broader in focus (going beyond demographics); voluntary; more positive in that it encourages companies to value all kinds of differences; and, at this time, substantially less controversial than affirmative action. Thus, affirmative action and diversity differ in purpose, practice, and the reactions they produce. Diversity also makes good business sense in terms of reducing costs (decreasing turnover and absenteeism and avoiding lawsuits), attracting and retaining talent, and driving business growth (improving marketplace understanding and promoting higher-quality problem solving).

Diversity a variety of demographic, cultural, and personal differences among an organization's employees and customers (p. 259)

Affirmative action purposeful steps taken by an organization to create employment opportunities for minorities and women (p. 260)

12-2 Understand the special challenges that the dimensions of surface-level diversity pose for managers. Age, sex, race/ethnicity, and physical and mental disabilities are dimensions of surface-level diversity. Because those dimensions are (usually) easily observed, managers and workers tend to rely on them to form initial impressions and stereotypes. Sometimes this can lead to age, sex, racial/ethnic, or disability discrimination (that is, treating people differently) in the workplace. In general, older workers, women, people of color or different national origins, and people with disabilities may be less likely to be hired or promoted than are white males. This disparity is often due to incorrect beliefs or stereotypes such as "job performance declines with age," or "women aren't willing to travel on business," or "workers with disabilities aren't as competent as able workers." To reduce discrimination, companies can determine the hiring and promotion rates for different groups, train managers to make hiring and promotion decisions on the basis of specific criteria, and make sure that everyone has equal access to training, mentors, reasonable work accommodations, and assistive technology. Finally, companies need to designate a go-to person to whom employees can talk if they believe they have suffered discrimination.

Surface-level diversity differences such as age, sex, race/ethnicity, and physical disabilities that are observable, typically unchangeable, and easy to measure (p. 263)

Deep-level diversity differences such as personality and attitudes that are communicated through verbal and nonverbal behaviors and are learned only through extended interaction with others (p. 263)

Social integration the degree to which group members are psychologically attracted to working with each other to accomplish a common objective (p. 264)

Age discrimination treating people differently (for example, in hiring and firing, promotion, and compensation decisions) because of their age (p. 264)

Sex discrimination treating people differently because of their sex (p. 265)

Glass ceiling the invisible barrier that prevents women and minorities from advancing to the top jobs in organizations (p. 265)

Sexual orientation an individual's attraction to people of the same and/or different sex (p. 267)

Sexual orientation discrimination treating people differently because of their sexual orientation (p. 267)

transgender person someone whose personal and gender identity differs from the person's birth sex—for example, someone born female who identifies as male (p. 268)

Gender identity discrimination treating people differently because of their gender identity (p. 268)

Racial and ethnic discrimination treating people differently because of their race or ethnicity (p. 269)

Disability a mental or physical impairment that substantially limits one or more major life activities (p. 270)

Disability discrimination treating people differently because of their disabilities (p. 270)

12-3 Explain how the dimensions of deep-level diversity affect individual behavior and interactions in the workplace. Deep-level diversity matters because it can reduce prejudice, discrimination, and conflict while increasing social integration. It consists of dispositional and personality differences that can be recognized only through extended interaction with others. Research conducted in different cultures, settings, and languages indicates that there are five basic dimensions of personality: extraversion, emotional stability, agreeableness, conscientiousness, and openness to experience. Of these, conscientiousness is perhaps the most important because conscientious workers tend to be better performers on virtually any job. Extraversion is also related to performance in jobs that require significant interaction with others.

Disposition the tendency to respond to situations and events in a predetermined manner (p. 271)

Personality the relatively stable set of behaviors, attitudes, and emotions displayed over time that makes people different from each other (p. 271)

Extraversion the degree to which someone is active, assertive, gregarious, sociable, talkative, and energized by others (p. 272)

Emotional stability the degree to which someone is not angry, depressed, anxious, emotional, insecure, and excitable (p. 272)

Agreeableness the degree to which someone is cooperative, polite, flexible, forgiving, good-natured, tolerant, and trusting (p. 272)

Conscientiousness the degree to which someone is organized, hardworking, responsible, persevering, thorough, and achievement oriented (p. 272)

© Cengage Learning   **WWW.CENGAGEBRAIN.COM**

Openness to experience the degree to which someone is curious, broadminded, and open to new ideas, things, and experiences; is spontaneous; and has a high tolerance for ambiguity (p. 273)

12-4 **Explain the basic principles and practices that can be used to manage diversity.** The three paradigms for managing diversity are the discrimination and fairness paradigm (equal opportunity, fair treatment, strict compliance with the law), the access and legitimacy paradigm (matching internal diversity to external diversity), and the learning and effectiveness paradigm (achieving organizational plurality by integrating deep-level diversity into the work of the organization). Unlike the other paradigms that focus on surface-level differences, the learning and effectiveness paradigm values common ground, distinguishes between individual and group differences, minimizes conflict and divisiveness, and focuses on bringing different talents and perspectives together. What principles can companies use when managing diversity? Follow and enforce federal and state laws regarding equal employment opportunity. Treat group differences as important but not special. Find the common ground. Tailor opportunities to individuals, not groups. Solicit negative as well as positive feedback. Set high but realistic goals. The two types of diversity training are awareness training and skills-based diversity training. Companies also manage diversity through diversity audits and diversity pairing and by having top executives experience what it is like to be in the minority.

Organizational plurality a work environment where (1) all members are empowered to contribute in a way that maximizes the benefits to the organization, customers, and themselves, and (2) the individuality of each member is respected by not segmenting or polarizing people on the basis of their membership in a particular group (p. 276)

Skills-based diversity training training that teaches employees the practical skills they need for managing a diverse workforce, such as flexibility and adaptability, negotiation, problem solving, and conflict resolution (p. 278)

Awareness training training that is designed to raise employees' awareness of diversity issues and to challenge the underlying assumptions or stereotypes they may have about others (p. 278)

Diversity audits formal assessments that measure employee and management attitudes, investigate the extent to which people are advantaged or disadvantaged with respect to hiring and promotions, and review companies' diversity-related policies and procedures (p. 278)

Diversity pairing a mentoring program in which people of different cultural backgrounds, sexes, or races/ethnicities are paired together to get to know each other and change stereotypical beliefs and attitudes (p. 279)

Paradigms for Managing Diversity

Diversity Paradigm	Focus	Success Measured By	Benefits	Limitations
Discrimination & Fairness	Equal opportunity / Fair treatment / Recruitment of minorities / Strict compliance with laws	Recruitment, promotion, and retention goals for underrepresented groups	Fairer treatment / Increased demographic diversity	Focus on surface-level diversity
Access & Legitimacy	Acceptance and celebration of differences	Diversity in company matches diversity of primary stakeholders	Establish a clear business reason for diversity	Focus on surface-level diversity
Learning & Effectiveness	Integrating deep-level differences into organization	Valuing people on the basis of individual knowledge, skills, and abilities	Values common ground / Distinction between individual and group differences / Less conflict, backlash, and divisiveness / Bringing different talents and perspectives together	Focus on deep-level diversity, which is more difficult to measure and quantify

© Cengage Learning

WWW.CENGAGEBRAIN.COM

CHAPTER 13 LEARNING OUTCOMES / KEY TERMS

13-1 Explain the basics of motivation. Motivation is the set of forces that initiates, directs, and makes people persist in their efforts over time to accomplish a goal. Managers often confuse motivation and performance, but job performance is a multiplicative function of motivation times ability times situational constraints. Needs are the physical or psychological requirements that must be met to ensure survival and well-being. Different motivational theories (Maslow's Hierarchy of Needs, Alderfer's ERG Theory, and McClelland's Learned Needs Theory) specify a number of different needs. However, studies show that there are only two general kinds of needs: lower-order needs and higher-order needs. Both extrinsic and intrinsic rewards motivate people.

Motivation the set of forces that initiates, directs, and makes people persist in their efforts to accomplish a goal (p. 283)

Needs the physical or psychological requirements that must be met to ensure survival and well-being (p. 285)

Extrinsic reward a reward that is tangible, visible to others, and given to employees contingent on the performance of specific tasks or behaviors (p. 286)

Intrinsic reward a natural reward associated with performing a task or activity for its own sake (p. 287)

13-2 Use equity theory to explain how employees' perceptions of fairness affect motivation. The basic components of equity theory are inputs, outcomes, and referents. After an internal comparison in which employees compare their outcomes to their inputs, they then make an external comparison in which they compare their O/I ratio with the O/I ratio of a referent, a person who works in a similar job or is otherwise similar. When their O/I ratio is equal to the referent's O/I ratio, employees perceive that they are being treated fairly. But, when their O/I ratio is lower than or higher than their referent's O/I ratio, they perceive that they have been treated inequitably or unfairly. There are two kinds of inequity: underreward and overreward. Underreward, which occurs when a referent's O/I ratio is higher than the employee's O/I ratio, leads to anger or frustration. Overreward, which occurs when a referent's O/I ratio is lower than the employee's O/I ratio, can lead to guilt but only when the level of overreward is extreme.

Equity theory a theory that states that people will be motivated when they perceive that they are being treated fairly (p. 288)

Inputs in equity theory, the contributions employees make to the organization (p. 289)

Outcomes in equity theory, the rewards employees receive for their contributions to the organization (p. 289)

Referents in equity theory, others with whom people compare themselves to determine if they have been treated fairly (p. 289)

Outcome/input (O/I) ratio in equity theory, an employee's perception of how the rewards received from an organization compare with the employee's contributions to that organization (p. 289)

Underreward a form of inequity in which you are getting fewer outcomes relative to inputs than your referent is getting (p. 289)

Overreward a form of inequity in which you are getting more outcomes relative to inputs than your referent (p. 289)

Distributive justice the perceived degree to which outcomes and rewards are fairly distributed or allocated (p. 292)

Procedural justice the perceived fairness of the process used to make reward allocation decisions (p. 292)

13-3 Use expectancy theory to describe how workers' expectations about rewards, effort, and the link between rewards and performance influence motivation. Expectancy theory holds that three factors affect the conscious choices people make about their motivation: valence, expectancy, and instrumentality. Expectancy theory holds that all three factors must be high for people to be highly motivated. If any one of these factors declines, overall motivation will decline, too.

Expectancy theory the theory that people will be motivated to the extent to which they believe that their efforts will lead to good performance, that good performance will be rewarded, and that they will be offered attractive rewards (p. 293)

Valence the attractiveness or desirability of a reward or outcome (p. 293)

Expectancy the perceived relationship between effort and performance (p. 293)

Instrumentality the perceived relationship between performance and rewards (p. 293)

13-4 Explain how reinforcement theory works and how it can be used to motivate. Reinforcement theory says that behavior is a function of its consequences. Reinforcement has two parts: reinforcement contingencies and schedules of reinforcement. The four kinds of reinforcement contingencies are positive reinforcement and negative reinforcement, which strengthen behavior, and punishment and extinction, which weaken behavior. There are two kinds of reinforcement schedules—continuous and intermittent; intermittent schedules, in turn, can be divided into fixed and variable interval schedules and fixed and variable ratio schedules.

Reinforcement theory the theory that behavior is a function of its consequences, that behaviors followed by positive consequences will occur more frequently, and that behaviors followed by negative consequences, or not followed by positive consequences, will occur less frequently (p. 296)

Reinforcement the process of changing behavior by changing the consequences that follow behavior (p. 296)

Reinforcement contingencies cause-and-effect relationships between the performance of specific behaviors and specific consequences (p. 296)

Schedule of reinforcement rules that specify which behaviors will be reinforced, which consequences will follow those behaviors, and the schedule by which those consequences will be delivered (p. 296)

Positive reinforcement reinforcement that strengthens behavior by following behaviors with desirable consequences (p. 297)

Negative reinforcement reinforcement that strengthens behavior by withholding an unpleasant consequence when employees perform a specific behavior (p. 297)

Extinction reinforcement in which a positive consequence is no longer allowed to follow a previously reinforced behavior, thus weakening the behavior (p. 298)

Continuous reinforcement schedule a schedule that requires a consequence to be administered following every instance of a behavior (p. 299)

Intermittent reinforcement schedule a schedule in which consequences are delivered after a specified or average time has elapsed or after a specified or average number of behaviors has occurred (p. 299)

Fixed interval reinforcement schedule an intermittent schedule in which consequences follow a behavior only after a fixed time has elapsed (p. 299)

Variable interval reinforcement schedule an intermittent schedule in which the time between a behavior and the following consequences varies around a specified average (p. 299)

Fixed ratio reinforcement schedule an intermittent schedule in which consequences are delivered following a specific number of behaviors (p. 299)

Variable ratio reinforcement schedule an intermittent schedule in which consequences are delivered following a different number of behaviors, sometimes more and sometimes less, that vary around a specified average number of behaviors (p. 299)

13-5 **Describe the components of goal-setting theory and how managers can use them to motivate workers.**
A goal is a target, objective, or result that someone tries to accomplish. Goal-setting theory says that people will be motivated to the extent to which they accept specific, challenging goals and receive feedback that indicates their progress toward goal achievement. The basic components of goal-setting theory are goal specificity, goal difficulty, goal acceptance, and performance feedback. Goal specificity is the extent to which goals are detailed, exact, and unambiguous. Goal difficulty is the extent to which a goal is hard or challenging to accomplish. Goal acceptance is the extent to which people consciously understand and agree to goals. Performance feedback is information about the quality or quantity of past performance and indicates whether progress is being made toward the accomplishment of a goal.

Goal a target, objective, or result that someone tries to accomplish (p. 302)

Goal-setting theory the theory that people will be motivated to the extent to which they accept specific, challenging goals and receive feedback that indicates their progress toward goal achievement (p. 302)

Goal specificity the extent to which goals are detailed, exact, and unambiguous (p. 302)

Goal difficulty the extent to which a goal is hard or challenging to accomplish (p. 302)

Goal acceptance the extent to which people consciously understand and agree to goals (p. 302)

Performance feedback information about the quality or quantity of past performance that indicates whether progress is being made toward the accomplishment of a goal (p. 302)

13-6 **Discuss how the entire motivation model can be used to motivate workers.**

Motivating with the Integrated Model

Motivating with	Managers should . . .
The Basics	• Ask people what their needs are. • Satisfy lower-order needs first. • Expect people's needs to change. • As needs change and lower-order needs are satisfied, satisfy higher-order needs by looking for ways to allow employees to experience intrinsic rewards.
Equity Theory	• Look for and correct major inequities. • Reduce employees' inputs. • Make sure decision-making processes are fair.
Expectancy Theory	• Systematically gather information to find out what employees want from their jobs. • Take specific steps to link rewards to individual performance in a way that is clear and understandable to employees. • Empower employees to make decisions if management really wants them to believe that their hard work and efforts will lead to good performance.
Reinforcement Theory	• Identify, measure, analyze, intervene, and evaluate critical performance-related behaviors. • Don't reinforce the wrong behaviors. • Correctly administer punishment at the appropriate time. • Choose the simplest and most effective schedules of reinforcement.
Goal-Setting Theory	• Assign specific, challenging goals. • Make sure workers truly accept organizational goals. • Provide frequent, specific, performance-related feedback.

14-1 Explain what leadership is. Management is getting work done through others; leadership is the process of influencing others to achieve group or organizational goals. Leaders are different from managers. The primary difference is that leaders are concerned with doing the right thing, while managers are concerned with doing things right. Organizations need both managers and leaders. But, in general, companies are overmanaged and underled.

Leadership the process of influencing others to achieve group or organizational goals (p. 307)

14-2 Describe who leaders are and what effective leaders do. Trait theory says that effective leaders possess traits or characteristics that differentiate them from nonleaders. Those traits are drive, the desire to lead, honesty/integrity, self-confidence, emotional stability, cognitive ability, and knowledge of the business. These traits alone aren't enough for successful leadership; leaders who have many or all of them must also behave in ways that encourage people to achieve group or organizational goals. Two key leader behaviors are initiating structure, which improves subordinate performance, and consideration, which improves subordinate satisfaction. There is no ideal combination of these behaviors. The best leadership style depends on the situation.

Trait theory a leadership theory that holds that effective leaders possess a similar set of traits or characteristics (p. 308)

Traits relatively stable characteristics, such as abilities, psychological motives, or consistent patterns of behavior (p. 308)

Initiating structure the degree to which a leader structures the roles of followers by setting goals, giving directions, setting deadlines, and assigning tasks (p. 311)

Consideration the extent to which a leader is friendly, approachable, and supportive and shows concern for employees (p. 311)

14-3 Explain Fiedler's contingency theory. Fiedler's contingency theory assumes that leaders are effective when their work groups perform well, that leaders are unable to change their leadership styles, that leadership styles must be matched to the proper situations, and that favorable situations permit leaders to influence group members. According to the Least Preferred Coworker (LPC) scale, there are two basic leadership styles. People who describe their LPC in a positive way have a relationship-oriented leadership style. By contrast, people who describe their LPC in a negative way have a task-oriented leadership style. Situational favorableness, which occurs when leaders can influence followers, is determined by leader-member relations, task structure, and position power. In general, relationship-oriented leaders with high LPC scores are better leaders under moderately favorable situations, whereas task-oriented leaders with low LPC scores are better leaders in highly favorable and highly unfavorable situations. Because Fiedler assumes that leaders are incapable of changing their leadership styles, the key is to accurately measure and match leaders to situations or to teach leaders how to change situational factors. Though matching or placing leaders in appropriate situations works well, reengineering situations to fit leadership styles doesn't because the complexity of the model makes it difficult for people to understand.

Leadership style the way a leader generally behaves toward followers (p. 313)

Contingency theory a leadership theory states that to maximize work group performance, leaders must be matched to the situation that best fits their leadership style (p. 313)

Situational favorableness the degree to which a particular situation either permits or denies a leader the chance to influence the behavior of group members (p. 314)

Leader-member relations the degree to which followers respect, trust, and like their leaders (p. 314)

Task structure the degree to which the requirements of a subordinate's tasks are clearly specified (p. 315)

Position power the degree to which leaders are able to hire, fire, reward, and punish workers (p. 315)

14-4 Explain Hersey and Blanchard's leadership theory Job readiness and psychological readiness are combined to produce four different levels of readiness in Hersey and Blanchard's Situational Leadership theory. A *telling* leadership style (high task behavior and low relationship behavior) is based on one-way communication, in which followers are told what, how, when, and where to do particular tasks. A *selling* leadership style (high task behavior and high relationship behavior) involves two-way communication and psychological support to encourage followers to "own" or "buy into" particular ways of doing things. A *participating* style (low task behavior and high relationship behavior) is based on two-way communication and shared decision making. A *delegating* style (low task behavior and low relationship behavior) is used when leaders basically let workers "run their own show" and make their own decisions.

Situational theory theory that says leaders need to adjust their leadership styles to match followers' readiness (p. 316)

Performance readiness the ability and willingness to take responsibility for directing one's behavior at work (p. 316)

14-5 Describe how path-goal theory works. Path-goal theory states that leaders can increase subordinate satisfaction and performance by clarifying and clearing the paths to goals and by increasing the number and kinds of rewards available for goal attainment. For this to work, however, leader behavior must be a source of immediate or future satisfaction for followers and must complement and not duplicate the characteristics of followers' work environments. In contrast to Fiedler's contingency theory, path-goal theory assumes that leaders can and do change their leadership styles (directive, supportive, participative, and achievement-oriented), depending on their subordinates (experience, perceived ability, and internal or external locus of control) and the environment in which those subordinates work (task structure, formal authority system, and primary work group).

Path-goal theory a leadership theory states that leaders can increase subordinate satisfaction and performance by clarifying and clearing the paths to goals and by increasing the number and kinds of rewards available for goal attainment (p. 318)

Directive leadership a leadership style in which the leader lets employees know precisely what is expected of them, gives them specific guidelines for performing tasks, schedules work, sets standards of performance, and makes sure that people follow standard rules and regulations (p. 319)

Supportive leadership a leadership style in which the leader is friendly and approachable to employees, shows concern for employees and their welfare, treats them as equals, and creates a friendly climate (p. 319)

Participative leadership a leadership style in which the leader consults employees for their suggestions and input before making decisions (p. 320)

Achievement-oriented leadership a leadership style in which the leader sets challenging goals, has high expectations of employees, and displays confidence that employees will assume responsibility and put forth extraordinary effort (p. 320)

14-6 Explain the normative decision theory. The normative decision theory helps leaders decide how much employee participation should be used when making decisions. Using the right degree of employee participation improves the quality of decisions and the extent to which employees accept and are committed to decisions. The theory specifies five different decision styles or ways of making decisions: autocratic decisions (AI or AII), consultative decisions (CI or CII), and group decisions (GII). The theory improves decision quality via decision rules concerning quality, leader information, subordinate information, goal congruence, and problem structure. The theory improves employee commitment and acceptance via decision rules related to commitment probability, subordinate conflict, and commitment requirement. These decision rules help leaders improve decision quality and follower acceptance and commitment by eliminating decision styles that don't fit the decision or situation the group or organization is facing. Normative decision theory operationalizes these decision rules in the form of yes/no questions.

Normative decision theory a theory that suggests how leaders can determine an appropriate amount of employee participation when making decisions (p. 322)

14-7 Explain how visionary (that is, charismatic or transformational) leadership helps leaders achieve strategic leadership. Strategic leadership requires visionary leadership, which can be charismatic or transformational. Visionary leadership creates a positive image of the future that motivates organizational members and provides direction for future planning and goal setting. Charismatic leaders have strong, confident, and dynamic personalities that attract followers, enable the leader to create strong bonds, and inspire followers to accomplish the leader's vision. Followers of ethical charismatic leaders work harder, are more committed and satisfied, are better performers, and are more likely to trust their leaders. Followers can be just as supportive and committed to unethical charismatics, but these leaders can pose a tremendous risk for companies. Unethical charismatics control and manipulate followers and do what is best for themselves instead of their organizations. Transformational leadership goes beyond charismatic leadership by generating awareness and acceptance of a group's purpose and mission and by getting employees to see beyond their own needs and self-interests for the good of the group. The four components of transformational leadership are charismatic leadership or idealized influence, inspirational motivation, intellectual stimulation, and individualized consideration.

Strategic leadership the ability to anticipate, envision, maintain flexibility, think strategically, and work with others to initiate changes that will create a positive future for an organization (p. 324)

Visionary leadership leadership that creates a positive image of the future that motivates organizational members and provides direction for future planning and goal setting (p. 326)

Charismatic leadership the behavioral tendencies and personal characteristics of leaders that create an exceptionally strong relationship between them and their followers (p. 326)

Ethical charismatics charismatic leaders who provide developmental opportunities for followers, are open to positive and negative feedback, recognize others' contributions, share information, and have moral standards that emphasize the larger interests of the group, organization, or society (p. 326)

Unethical charismatics charismatic leaders who control and manipulate followers, do what is best for themselves instead of their organizations, want to hear only positive feedback, share only information that is beneficial to themselves, and have moral standards that put their interests before everyone else's (p. 327)

Transformational leadership leadership that generates awareness and acceptance of a group's purpose and mission and gets employees to see beyond their own needs and self-interests for the good of the group (p. 327)

Transactional leadership leadership based on an exchange process in which followers are rewarded for good performance and punished for poor performance (p. 329)

CHAPTER 15 LEARNING OUTCOMES / KEY TERMS

15-1 **Explain the role that perception plays in communication and communication problems.** Perception is the process by which people attend to, organize, interpret, and retain information from their environments. Perception is not a straightforward process. Because of perceptual filters such as selective perception and closure, people exposed to the same information or stimuli often end up with very different perceptions and understandings. Perception-based differences can also lead to differences in the attributions (internal or external) that managers and workers make when explaining workplace behavior. In general, workers are more likely to explain behavior from a defensive bias, in which they attribute problems to external causes (that is, the situation).

Managers, on the other hand, tend to commit the fundamental attribution error, attributing problems to internal causes (that is, the worker made a mistake or error). Consequently, when things go wrong, it's common for managers to blame workers and for workers to blame the situation or context in which they do their jobs. Finally, this problem is compounded by a self-serving bias that leads people to attribute successes to internal causes and failures to external causes. So, when workers receive negative feedback from managers, they may become defensive and emotional and not hear what their managers have to say. In short, perceptions and attributions represent a significant challenge to effective communication and understanding in organizations.

Communication the process of transmitting information from one person or place to another (p. 330)

Perception the process by which individuals attend to, organize, interpret, and retain information from their environments (p. 331)

Perceptual filters the personality-, psychology-, or experience-based differences that influence people to ignore or pay attention to particular stimuli (p. 331)

Selective perception the tendency to notice and accept objects and information consistent with our values, beliefs, and expectations, while ignoring or screening inconsistent information (p. 333)

Closure the tendency to fill in gaps of missing information by assuming that what we don't know is consistent with what we already know (p. 333)

Attribution theory the theory that we all have a basic need to understand and explain the causes of other people's behavior (p. 333)

Defensive bias the tendency for people to perceive themselves as personally and situationally similar to someone who is having difficulty or trouble (p. 333)

Fundamental attribution error the tendency to ignore external causes of behavior and to attribute other people's actions to internal causes (p. 334)

Self-serving bias the tendency to overestimate our value by attributing successes to ourselves (internal causes) and attributing failures to others or the environment (external causes) (p. 335)

15-2 **Describe the communication process and the various kinds of communication in organizations.** Organizational communication depends on the communication process, formal and informal communication channels, one-on-one communication, and nonverbal communication. The major components of the communication process are the sender, the receiver, noise, and feedback. Senders often mistakenly assume that they can pipe their intended messages directly into receivers' heads with perfect clarity. Formal communication channels such as downward, upward, and horizontal communication carry organizationally approved messages and information. By contrast, the informal communication channel, called the *grapevine*, arises out of curiosity and is carried out through gossip or cluster chains. There are two kinds of one-on-one communication. Coaching is used to improve on-the-job performance, while counseling is used to communicate about nonjob-related issues affecting job performance. Nonverbal communication, such as kinesics and paralanguage, accounts for as much as 93 percent of the transmission of a message's content.

Exhibit 15.3

The Interpersonal Communication Process

Encoding putting a message into a written, verbal, or symbolic form that can be recognized and understood by the receiver (p. 336)

Decoding the process by which the receiver translates the written, verbal, or symbolic form of a message into an understood message (p. 336)

Feedback to sender in the communication process, a return message to the sender

that indicates the receiver's understanding of the message (p. 336)

Noise anything that interferes with the transmission of the intended message (p. 337)

Jargon vocabulary particular to a profession or group that interferes with communication in the workplace (p. 337)

Formal communication channel the system of official channels that carry organizationally approved messages and information (p. 337)

Downward communication communication that flows from higher to lower levels in an organization (p. 337)

Upward communication communication that flows from lower to higher levels in an organization (p. 338)

Horizontal communication communication that flows among managers and workers who are at the same organizational level (p. 338)

Informal communication channel (grapevine) the transmission of messages from employee to employee outside of formal communication channels (p. 339)

Coaching communicating with someone for the direct purpose of improving the person's on-the-job performance or behavior (p. 340)

Counseling communicating with someone about non-job-related issues that may be affecting or interfering with the person's performance (p. 340)

Nonverbal communication any communication that doesn't involve words (p. 341)

Kinesics movements of the body and face (p. 341)

Paralanguage the pitch, rate, tone, volume, and speaking pattern (that is, use of silences, pauses, or hesitations) of one's voice (p. 342)

15-3 Explain how managers can manage effective one-on-one communication. One-on-one communication can be managed by choosing the right communication medium, being a good listener, and giving effective feedback. Managers generally prefer oral communication because it provides the opportunity to ask questions and assess nonverbal communication. Oral communication is best suited to complex, ambiguous, or emotionally laden topics. Written communication is best suited for delivering straightforward messages and information. Listening is important for managerial success, but most people are terrible listeners. To improve your listening skills, choose to be an active listener (clarify responses, paraphrase, and summarize) and an empathetic listener (show your desire to understand, reflect feelings). Feedback can be constructive or destructive. To be constructive, feedback must be immediate, focused on specific behaviors, and problem oriented.

Communication medium the method used to deliver an oral or written message (p. 342)

Hearing the act or process of perceiving sounds (p. 344)

Listening making a conscious effort to hear (p. 344)

Active listening assuming half the responsibility for successful communication by actively giving the speaker nonjudgmental feedback that shows you've accurately heard what he or she said (p. 344)

Empathetic listening understanding the speaker's perspective and personal frame of reference and giving feedback that conveys that understanding to the speaker (p. 345)

Destructive feedback feedback that disapproves without any intention of being helpful and almost always causes a negative or defensive reaction in the recipient (p. 346)

Constructive feedback feedback intended to be helpful, corrective, and/or encouraging (p. 346)

15-4 Describe how managers can manage effective organization-wide communication. Managers need methods for managing organization-wide communication and for making themselves accessible so that they can hear what employees throughout their organizations are feeling and thinking. Email, collaborative discussion sites, streamed/videotaped speeches and conferences, and broadcast voice mail make it much easier for managers to improve message transmission and get the message out. By contrast, anonymous company hotlines, survey feedback, frequent informal meetings, town halls and surprise visits help managers avoid organizational silence and improve reception by giving them the opportunity to hear what others in the organization think and feel. Monitoring internal and external blogs is another way to find out what people are saying and thinking about your organization.

Discussion channels and chat rooms the use of web- or app-based communication tools to hold company-wide, department-based, topic-based, team, or private discussions (p. 347)

Streamed/videotaped speeches and meetings speeches and meetings originally made to a smaller audience that are either simultaneously broadcast to other locations in the company or videotaped for subsequent distribution and viewing (p. 348)

Organizational silence when employees withhold information about organizational problems or issues (p. 349)

Company hotlines phone numbers that anyone in the company can call anonymously to leave information for upper management (p. 349)

Survey feedback information that is collected by surveys from organizational members and then compiled, disseminated, and used to develop action plans for improvement (p. 349)

Blog a personal website that provides personal opinions or recommendations, news summaries, and reader comments (p. 351)

CHAPTER 16 LEARNING OUTCOMES / KEY TERMS

16-1 **Describe the basic control process.** The control process begins by setting standards and then measuring performance and comparing performance to the standards. The better a company's information and measurement systems, the easier it is to make these comparisons. The control process continues by identifying and analyzing performance deviations and then developing and implementing programs for corrective action. Control is a continuous, dynamic, cybernetic process, not a one-time achievement or result. Control requires frequent managerial attention. The three basic control methods are feedback control (after-the-fact performance information), concurrent control (simultaneous performance information), and feedforward control (preventive performance information). Control has regulation costs and unanticipated consequences and therefore isn't always worthwhile or possible.

Exhibit 16.1
Cybernetic Control Process

Source: From *Business Horizons*, June 1972, H. Koontz and R. W. Bradspies, "Managing through Feedforward Control: A Future Directed View," pp. 25–36.

Control a regulatory process of establishing standards to achieve organizational goals, comparing actual performance against the standards, and taking corrective action when necessary (p. 352)

Standards a basis of comparison for measuring the extent to which various kinds of organizational performance are satisfactory or unsatisfactory (p. 353)

Benchmarking the process of identifying outstanding practices, processes, and standards in other companies and adapting them to your company (p. 354)

Cybernetic the process of steering or keeping on course (p. 356)

Concurrent control a mechanism for gathering information about performance deficiencies as they occur,

thereby eliminating or shortening the delay between performance and feedback (p. 356)

Feedback control a mechanism for gathering information about performance deficiencies after they occur (p. 356)

Feedforward control a mechanism for monitoring performance inputs rather than outputs to prevent or minimize performance deficiencies before they occur (p. 356)

Control loss the situation in which behavior and work procedures do not conform to standards (p. 357)

Regulation costs the costs associated with implementing or maintaining control (p. 357)

Cybernetic feasibility the extent to which it is possible to implement each step in the control process (p. 358)

16-2 **Discuss the various methods that managers can use to maintain control.** There are five methods of control: bureaucratic, objective, normative, concertive, and self-control (self-management). Bureaucratic and objective controls are top down, management based, and measurement based. Normative and concertive controls represent shared forms of control because they evolve from company-wide or team-based beliefs and values. Self-control, or self-management, is a control system in which managers and workers control their own behavior.

Bureaucratic control is based on organizational policies, rules, and procedures. Objective control is based on reliable measures of

behavior or outputs. Normative control is based on strong corporate beliefs and careful hiring practices. Concertive control is based on the development of values, beliefs, and rules in autonomous work groups. Self-control is based on individuals setting their own goals, monitoring themselves, and rewarding or punishing themselves with respect to goal achievement.

Each of these control methods may be more or less appropriate, depending on the circumstances.

Bureaucratic control the use of hierarchical authority to influence employee behavior by rewarding or punishing employees for compliance or noncompliance with organizational policies, rules, and procedures (p. 358)

Objective control the use of observable measures of worker behavior or outputs to assess performance and influence behavior (p. 359)

Behavior control the regulation of the behaviors and actions that workers perform on the job (p. 359)

Output control the regulation of workers' results or outputs through rewards and incentives (p. 359)

Normative control the regulation of workers' behavior and decisions through widely shared organizational values and beliefs (p. 360)

Concertive control the regulation of workers' behavior and decisions through work group values and beliefs (p. 361)

Self-control (self-management) a control system in which managers and workers control their own behavior by setting their own goals, monitoring their own progress, and rewarding themselves for goal achievement (p. 362)

16-3 Describe the behaviors, processes, and outcomes that today's managers are choosing to control in their organizations. Deciding what to control is just as important as deciding whether to control or how to control. In most companies, performance is measured using financial measures alone. However, the balanced scorecard encourages managers to measure and control company performance from four perspectives: financial, customer, internal, and innovation and learning. Traditionally, financial control has been achieved through cash flow analysis, balance sheets, income statements, financial ratios, and budgets. (For a refresher on these traditional financial control tools, see the Financial Review Card.) Another way to measure and control financial performance is to evaluate economic value added (EVA). Unlike traditional financial measures, EVA helps managers assess whether they are performing well enough to pay the cost of the capital needed to run the business. Instead of using customer satisfaction surveys to measure performance, companies should pay attention to customer defections, as customers who leave are more likely to speak up about what the company is doing wrong. From the internal perspective, performance is often measured in terms of quality, which is defined in three ways: excellence, value, and conformance to specifications. Sustainability has become an important part of innovation and learning in companies. The four levels of sustainability are waste prevention and reduction, recycling and reuse, waste treatment, and waste disposal.

Exhibit 16.5

Advantages and Disadvantages of Different Measures of Quality

Quality Measure	Advantages	Disadvantages
Excellence	Promotes clear organizational vision.	Provides little practical guidance for managers.
	Being/providing the "best" motivates and inspires managers and employees.	Excellence is ambiguous. What is it? Who defines it?
Value	Appeals to customers who know excellence "when they see it."	Difficult to measure and control.
	Customers recognize differences in value.	Can be difficult to determine what factors influence whether a product/service is seen as having value.
	Easier to measure and compare whether products/services differ in value.	Controlling the balance between excellence and cost (that is, affordable excellence) can be difficult.
Conformance to Specifications	If specifications can be written, conformance to specifications is usually measurable.	Many products/services cannot be easily evaluated in terms of conformance to specifications.
	Should lead to increased efficiency.	Promotes standardization, so may hurt performance when adapting to changes is more important.
	Promotes consistency in quality.	May be less appropriate for services, which are dependent on a high degree of human contact.

Source: Briar Cliff Manor, NY, 10510-8020; C. A. Reeves and D. A. Bednar, "Defining Quality: Alternatives and Implications," *Academy of Management Review* 19 (1994): 419–445.

Balanced scorecard measurement of organizational performance in four equally important areas: finances, customers, internal operations, and innovation and learning (p. 363)

Suboptimization performance improvement in one part of an organization but only at the expense of decreased performance in another part (p. 363)

Cash flow analysis a type of analysis that predicts how changes in a business will affect its ability to take in more cash than it pays out (p. 364)

Balance sheets accounting statements that provide a snapshot of a company's financial position at a particular time (p. 364)

Income statements accounting statements, also called "profit and loss statements," that show what has happened to an organization's income, expenses, and net profit over a period of time (p. 364)

Financial ratios calculations typically used to track a business's liquidity (cash), efficiency, and profitability over time compared to other businesses in its industry (p. 364)

Budgets quantitative plans through which managers decide how to allocate available money to best accomplish company goals (p. 364)

Zero-based budgeting a budgeting technique that requires managers to justify every expenditure every year (p. 364)

Economic value added (EVA) the amount by which company profits (revenues minus expenses minus taxes) exceed the cost of capital in a given year (p. 365)

Customer defections a performance assessment in which companies identify which customers are leaving and measure the rate at which they are leaving (p. 366)

Value customer perception that the product quality is excellent for the price offered (p. 367)

Basic Accounting Tools for Controlling Financial Performance

Steps for a Basic Cash Flow Analysis

1. Forecast sales (steady, up, or down).

2. Project changes in anticipated cash inflows (as a result of changes).

3. Project anticipated cash outflows (as a result of changes).

4. Project net cash flows by combining anticipated cash inflows and outflows.

Parts of a Basic Balance Sheet (Assets 5 Liabilities 1 Owner's Equity)

1. Assets
   a. Current assets (cash, short-term investment, marketable securities, accounts receivable, and so on)
   b. Fixed assets (land, buildings, machinery, equipment, and so on)

2. Liabilities
   a. Current liabilities (accounts payable, notes payable, taxes payable, and so on)
   b. Long-term liabilities (long-term debt, deferred income taxes, and so on)

3. Owner's Equity
   a. Preferred stock and common stock
   b. Additional paid-in capital
   c. Retained earnings

Basic Income Statement

   SALES REVENUE
− sales returns and allowances
+ other income
= NET REVENUE
− cost of goods sold (beginning inventory, costs of goods purchased, ending inventory)
= GROSS PROFIT
− total operating expenses (selling, general, and administrative expenses)
= INCOME FROM OPERATIONS
− interest expense
= PRETAX INCOME
− income taxes
= NET INCOME

Common Kinds of Budgets

Revenue Budgets—used to project or forecast future sales.	• Accuracy of projection depends on economy, competitors, sales force estimates, and so on • Determined by estimating future sales volume and sales prices for all products and services.
Expense Budgets—used within departments and divisions to determine how much will be spent on various supplies, projects, or activities.	• One of the first places that companies look for cuts when trying to lower expenses.
Profit Budgets—used by profit centers, which have "profit and loss" responsibility.	• Combine revenue and expense budgets into one budget. • Typically used in large businesses with multiple plants and divisions.
Cash Budgets—used to forecast how much cash a company will have on hand to meet expenses.	• Similar to cash-flow analyses. • Used to identify cash shortfalls, which must be covered to pay bills, or cash excesses, which should be invested for a higher return.
Capital Expenditure Budgets—used to forecast large, long-lasting investments in equipment, buildings, and property.	• Help managers identify funding that will be needed to pay for future expansion or strategic moves designed to increase competitive advantage.
Variable Budgets—used to project costs across varying levels of sales and revenues.	• Important because it is difficult to accurately predict sales revenue and volume. • Lead to more accurate budgeting with respect to labor, materials, and administrative expenses, which vary with sales volume and revenues. • Build flexibility into the budgeting process.

Common Financial Ratios

Ratios	Formula	What It Means	When to Use
Liquidity Ratios			
Current Ratio	$\dfrac{\text{Current Assets}}{\text{Current Liabilities}}$	• Whether you have enough assets on hand to pay for short-term bills and obligations. • Higher is better. • Recommended level is two times as many current assets as current liabilities.	• Track monthly and quarterly. • Basic measure of your company's health.
Quick (Acid Test) Ratio	$\dfrac{€\ \text{Current Assets} - \text{Inventories}\ €}{\text{Current Liabilities}}$	• Stricter than current ratio. • Whether you have enough (that is, cash) to pay short-term bills and obligations. • Higher is better. • Recommended level is one or higher.	• Track monthly. • Also calculate quick ratio with potential customers to evaluate whether they're likely to pay you in a timely manner.
Leverage Ratios			
Debt to Equity	$\dfrac{\text{Total Liabilities}}{\text{Total Equity}}$	• Indicates how much the company is leveraged (in debt) by comparing what is owed (liabilities) to what is owned (equity). • Lower is better. A high debt-to-equity ratio could indicate that the company has too much debt. • Recommended level depends on industry.	• Track monthly. • Lenders often use this to determine the creditworthiness of a business (that is, whether to approve additional loans).
Debt Coverage	$\dfrac{€\ \text{Net Profit} + \text{Noncash Expense}\ €}{\text{Debt}}$	• Indicates how well cash flow covers debt payments. • Higher is better.	• Track monthly. • Lenders look at this ratio to determine if there is adequate cash to make loan payments.
Efficiency Ratios			
Inventory Turnover	$\dfrac{\text{Cost of Goods Sold}}{\text{Average Value of Inventory}}$	• Whether you're making efficient use of inventory. • Higher is better, indicating that inventory (dollars) isn't purchased (spent) until needed. • Recommended level depends on industry.	• Track monthly by using a 12-month rolling average.
Average Collections Period	$\dfrac{\text{Accounts Receivable}}{€\ \text{Annual Net Credit Sales} \div 365\ €}$	• Shows on average how quickly your customers are paying their bills. • Recommended level is no more than 15 days longer than credit terms. If credit is net 30 days, then average should not be longer than 45 days.	• Track monthly. • Use to determine how long company's money is being tied up in customer credit.
Profitability Ratios			
Gross Profit Margin	$\dfrac{\text{Gross Profit}}{\text{Total Sales}}$	• Shows how efficiently a business is using its materials and labor in the production process. • Higher is better, indicating that a profit can be made if fixed costs are controlled.	• Track monthly. • Analyze when unsure about product or service pricing. • Low margin compared to competitors means you're underpricing.
Return on Equity	$\dfrac{\text{Net Income}}{\text{Owner's Equity}}$	• Shows what was earned on your investment in the business during a particular period. Often called "return on investment." • Higher is better.	• Track quarterly and annually. • Use to compare to what you might have earned on the stock market, bonds, or government Treasury bills during the same period.

CHAPTER 17 LEARNING OUTCOMES / KEY TERMS

17-1 Explain the strategic importance of information. The first company to use new information technology to substantially lower costs or differentiate products or services often gains a first-mover advantage, higher profits, and a larger market share. Creating a first-mover advantage can be difficult, expensive, and risky, however. According to the resource-based view of information technology, sustainable competitive advantage occurs when information technology adds value, is different across firms, and is difficult to create or acquire.

Moore's law the prediction that about every two years, computer processing power would double and its cost would drop by 50 percent (p. 373)

Raw data facts and figures (p. 375)

Information useful data that can influence people's choices and behavior (p. 375)

First-mover advantage the strategic advantage that companies earn by being the first to use new information technology to substantially lower costs or to make a product or service different from that of competitors (p. 375)

17-2 Describe the characteristics of useful information (that is, its value and costs). Raw data are facts and figures. Raw data do not become information until they are in a form that can affect decisions and behavior. For information to be useful, it has to be reliable and valid (accurate), of sufficient quantity (complete), pertinent to the problems you're facing (relevant), and available when you need it (timely). Useful information is not cheap. The five costs of obtaining good information are: the costs of acquiring, processing, storing, retrieving, and communicating information.

Acquisition cost the cost of obtaining data that you don't have (p. 379)

Processing cost the cost of turning raw data into usable information (p. 379)

data silo an isolated data set that is difficult to obtain, combine, or use with other company data (p. 379)

data variety data that are formatted or structured in different ways (p. 379)

Storage cost the cost of physically or electronically archiving information for later retrieval and use (p. 379)

Retrieval cost the cost of accessing already-stored and processed information (p. 380)

Communication cost the cost of transmitting information from one place to another (p. 381)

17-3 Explain the basics of capturing, processing, and protecting information. Electronic data capture (using bar codes, radio frequency identification [RFID] tags, scanners, or optical character recognition), is much faster, easier, and cheaper than manual data capture. Processing information means transforming raw data into meaningful information that can be applied to business decision making. Data mining helps managers with this transformation by discovering unknown patterns and relationships in data. Supervised data mining looks for patterns specified by managers, while unsupervised data mining looks for four general kinds of data patterns: association or affinity patterns, sequence patterns, predictive patterns, and data clusters. Protecting information ensures that data are reliably and consistently retrievable in a usable format by authorized users but no one else. Authentication and authorization, firewalls, antivirus software for PCs and corporate email and network servers, data encryption, virtual private networks (VPNs), and web-based secure sockets layer (SSL) encryption are some of the best ways to protect information. Be careful when using wireless networks, which are easily compromised even when security and encryption protocols are in place.

Exhibit 17.3
Security Threats to Data and Data Networks

Security Problem	Source	Affects	Severity	The Threat	The Solution
Denial of service; web server attacks and corporate network attacks	Internet hackers	All servers	High	Loss of data, disruption of service, and theft of service.	Implement firewall, password control, server-side review, threat monitoring, and bug fixes; turn PCs off when not in use.
Password cracking software and unauthorized access to PCs	Local area network, Internet	All users, especially digital subscriber line and cable Internet users	High	Hackers take over PCs. Privacy can be invaded. Corporate users' systems are exposed to other machines on the network.	Close ports and firewalls, disable file and print sharing, and use strong passwords.
Viruses, worms, Trojan horses, and rootkits	Email, downloaded and distributed software	All users	Moderate to high	Monitor activities and cause data loss and file deletion; compromise security by sometimes concealing their presence.	Use antivirus software and firewalls; control Internet access.
Malware, spyware, adware, malicious scripts, and applets	Rogue web pages	All users	Moderate to high	Invade privacy, intercept passwords, and damage files or file system.	Disable browser script support; use security, blocking, and spyware/adware software.
Email snooping	Hackers on your network and the Internet	All users	Moderate to high	People read your email from intermediate servers or packets, or they physically access your machine.	Encrypt messages, ensure strong password protection, and limit physical access to machines.
Keystroke monitoring	Trojan horses, people with direct access to PCs	All users	High	Records everything typed at the keyboard and intercepts keystrokes before password masking or encryption occurs.	Use antivirus software to catch Trojan horses, control Internet access to transmission, and implement system monitoring and physical access control.
Phishing	Hackers on your network and the Internet	All users, including customers	High	Fake but real-looking emails and websites that trick users into sharing personal information on what they wrongly think is a company's website. This leads to unauthorized account access.	Educate and warn users and customers about the dangers. Encourage both not to click on potentially fake URLs, which might take them to phishing websites. Instead, have them type your company's URL into the web browser.
Spam	Email	All users and corporations	Mild to high	Clogs and overloads email servers and inboxes with junk mail. HTML-based spam may be used for profiling and identifying users.	Filter known spam sources and senders on email servers; have users create further lists of approved and unapproved senders on their PCs.
Cookies	Websites you visit	Individual users	Mild to moderate	Trace web usage and permit the creation of personalized web pages that track behavior and interest profiles.	Use cookie managers to control and edit cookies, and use ad blockers.

Sources: "The 11 Most Common Computer Security Threats … And What You Can Do to Protect Yourself from Them," Symantec-Norton, accessed May 12, 2015. http://www.symantec-norton.com/11-most-common-computer-security-threats_k13.aspx; K. Bannan, "Look Out: Watching You, Watching Me," *PC Magazine*, July 2002, 99; A. Dragoon, "Fighting Phish, Fakes, and Frauds," *CIO*, September 1, 2004, 33; B. Glass, "Are You Being Watched?" *PC Magazine*, April 23, 2002, 54; K. Karagiannis, "DDoS: Are You Next?" *PC Magazine*, January 2003, 79; B. Machrone, "Protect & Defend," *PC Magazine*, June 27, 2000, 168–181; "Top 10 Security Threats," *PC Magazine*, April 10, 2007, 66; M. Sarrel, "Master End-User Security," *PC Magazine*, May 2008, 101.

Bar code a visual pattern that represents numerical data by varying the thickness and pattern of vertical bars (p. 382)

Radio frequency identification (RFID) tags tags containing minuscule microchips that transmit information via radio waves and can be used to track the number and location of the objects into which the tags have been inserted (p. 382)

Electronic scanner an electronic device that converts printed text and pictures into digital images (p. 382)

Optical character recognition the ability of software to convert digitized documents into ASCII (American Standard Code for Information Interchange) text that can be searched, read, and edited by word processing and other kinds of software (p. 382)

Processing information transforming raw data into meaningful information (p. 383)

Data mining the process of discovering unknown patterns and relationships in large amounts of data (p. 383)

Data warehouse a database that stores huge amounts of data that have been prepared for data mining analysis by being cleaned of errors and redundancy (p. 383)

Supervised data mining the process when the user tells the data mining software to look and test for specific patterns and relationships in a data set (p. 383)

Unsupervised data mining the process when the user simply tells the data mining software to uncover whatever patterns and relationships it can find in a data set (p. 383)

Association or affinity patterns when two or more database elements tend to occur together in a significant way (p. 384)

Sequence patterns when two or more database elements occur together in a significant pattern in which one of the elements precedes the other (p. 384)

Predictive patterns patterns that help identify database elements that are different (p. 384)

Data clusters when three or more database elements occur together (that is, cluster) in a significant way (p. 384)

Protecting information the process of ensuring that data are reliably and consistently retrievable in a usable format for authorized users but no one else (p. 385)

Authentication making sure potential users are who they claim to be (p. 386)

Authorization granting authenticated users approved access to data, software, and systems (p. 386)

Two-factor authentication authentication based on what users know, such as a password and what they have in their

possession, such as a secure ID card or key (p. 386)

Firewall a protective hardware or software device that sits between the computers in an internal organizational network and outside networks, such as the Internet (p. 386)

Virus a program or piece of code that, without your knowledge, attaches itself to other programs on your computer and can trigger anything from a harmless flashing message to the reformatting of your hard drive to a system-wide network shutdown (p. 388)

Data encryption the transformation of data into complex, scrambled digital codes that can be decrypted only by authorized users who possess unique decryption keys (p. 388)

Virtual private network (VPN) software that securely encrypts data sent by employees outside the company network, decrypts the data when they arrive within the company computer network, and does the same when data are sent back to employees outside the network (p. 389)

Secure sockets layer (SSL) encryption Internet browser–based encryption that provides secure off-site web access to some data and programs (p. 389)

17-4 **Describe how companies can access and share information and knowledge.** Executive information systems, intranets, and corporate portals facilitate internal sharing and access to company information and transactions. Electronic data interchange and the Internet allow external groups such as suppliers and customers to easily access company information. Both decrease costs by reducing or eliminating data entry, data errors, and paperwork and by speeding up communication. Organizations use decision support systems and expert systems to capture and share specialized knowledge with nonexpert employees.

Executive information system (EIS) a data processing system that uses internal and external data sources to provide the information needed to monitor and analyze organizational performance (p. 390)

Intranets private company networks that allow employees to easily access, share, and publish information using Internet software (p. 390)

Corporate portal a hybrid of executive information systems and intranets that allows managers and employees to use a web browser to gain access to customized company information and to complete specialized transactions (p. 391)

Electronic data interchange (EDI) when two companies convert their purchase and ordering information to a

standardized format to enable the direct electronic transmission of that information from one company's computer system to the other company's computer system (p. 391)

Web services software that uses standardized protocols to describe data from one company in such a way that those data can automatically be read, understood, transcribed, and processed by different computer systems in another company (p. 392)

Extranets networks that allow companies to exchange information and conduct transactions with outsiders by providing them direct, web-based access to authorized parts of a company's intranet or information system (p. 392)

Knowledge the understanding that one gains from information (p. 393)

Decision support system (DSS) an information system that helps managers understand specific kinds of problems and potential solutions (p. 393)

Expert system an information system that contains the specialized knowledge and decision rules used by experts and experienced decision makers so that nonexperts can draw on this knowledge base to make decisions (p. 394)

Artificial intelligence, or AI the capability of computerized systems to learn and adapt through experience (p. 394)

CHAPTER 18 LEARNING OUTCOMES / KEY TERMS

18-1

Discuss the kinds of productivity and their importance in managing operations. Productivity is a measure of how many inputs it takes to produce or create an output. The greater the output from one input, or the fewer inputs it takes to create an output, the higher the productivity. Partial productivity measures how much of a single kind of input, such as labor, is needed to produce an output. Multifactor productivity is an overall measure of productivity that indicates how much labor, capital, materials, and energy are needed to produce an output.

$$\text{Partial Productivity} = \frac{\text{Outputs}}{\text{Single Kind of Input}}$$

Operations management managing the daily production of goods and services (p. 396)

Productivity a measure of performance that indicates how many inputs it takes to produce or create an output (p. 397)

Partial productivity a measure of performance that indicates how much of a particular kind of input it takes to produce an output (p. 399)

Multifactor productivity an overall measure of performance that indicates how much labor, capital, materials, and energy it takes to produce an output (p. 399)

Robots machines or programs capable of completing complex tasks (p. 399)

Process automation using robots to automate routine, highly repetitive, low-complexity, or single-purpose tasks (p. 400)

Intelligent recognition using automation programming to recognize and react to patterns of speech, written language, images, and other items (p. 400)

Collaborative/social automation using robots to automate tasks while working directly with or near people (p. 400)

18-2

Explain the role that quality plays in managing operations. Quality can mean that a product or service is practically free of deficiencies or has characteristics that satisfy customer needs. Quality products usually possess three characteristics: reliability, serviceability, and durability. Quality service includes reliability, tangibles, responsiveness, assurance, and empathy. ISO 9000 is a series of five international standards for achieving consistency in quality management and quality assurance, while ISO 14000 is a set of standards for minimizing an organization's harmful effects on the environment. The Baldrige Performance Excellence Program recognizes U.S. companies for their achievements in quality and business performance. Each year, up to three Baldrige National Quality Awards may be given in the categories of manufacturing, service, small business, education, nonprofit, and health care. Total quality management (TQM) is an integrated organization-wide strategy for improving product and service quality. TQM is based on three mutually reinforcing principles: customer focus and satisfaction, continuous improvement, and teamwork.

Quality a product or service free of deficiencies, or the characteristics of a product or service that satisfy customer needs (p. 401)

ISO 9000 a series of five international standards, from ISO 9000 to ISO 9004, for achieving consistency in quality management and quality assurance in companies throughout the world (p. 403)

ISO 14000 a series of international standards for managing, monitoring, and minimizing an organization's harmful effects on the environment (p. 403)

ISO 27000 a series of 12 international standards for managing and monitoring security techniques for information technology (p. 403)

Total quality management (TQM) an integrated, principle-based, organization-wide strategy for improving product and service quality (p. 405)

Customer focus an organizational goal to concentrate on meeting customers' needs at all levels of the organization (p. 405)

Customer satisfaction an organizational goal to provide products or services that meet or exceed customers' expectations (p. 405)

Continuous improvement an organization's ongoing commitment to constantly assess and improve the processes and procedures used to create products and services (p. 405)

Variation a deviation in the form, condition, or appearance of a product from the quality standard for that product (p. 406)

Teamwork collaboration between managers and nonmanagers, across business functions, and between companies, customers, and suppliers (p. 406)

18-3

Explain the essentials of managing a service business. Services are different from goods. Goods are produced, tangible, and storable. Services are performed, intangible, and perishable. Likewise, managing service operations is different from managing production operations. The service-profit chain indicates that success begins with internal service quality, meaning how well management treats employees. Internal service quality leads to employee satisfaction and service capability, which, in turn, lead to high-value service to customers, customer satisfaction, customer loyalty, and long-term profits and growth. Keeping existing customers is far more cost-effective than finding new ones. Consequently, to prevent disgruntled customers from leaving, some companies are empowering service employees to perform service recovery—restoring customer satisfaction to strongly dissatisfied customers—by giving employees the authority and responsibility to immediately solve customer problems. The hope is that empowered service recovery will prevent customer defections.

Internal service quality the quality of treatment employees receive from management and other divisions of a company (p. 407)

Service recovery restoring customer satisfaction to strongly dissatisfied customers (p. 408)

18-4 **Describe the different kinds of manufacturing operations.** Manufacturing operations produce physical goods. Manufacturing operations can be classified according to the amount of processing or assembly that occurs after receiving an order from a customer.

Manufacturing operations can also be classified in terms of flexibility, the degree to which the number, kind, and characteristics of products can easily and quickly be changed. Flexibility allows companies to respond quickly to competitors and customers and to reduce order lead times, but it can also lead to higher unit costs.

Make-to-order operation a manufacturing operation that does not start processing or assembling products until a customer order is received (p. 409)

Assemble-to-order operation a manufacturing operation that divides manufacturing processes into separate parts or modules that are combined to create semicustomized products (p. 409)

Make-to-stock operation a manufacturing operation that orders parts and assembles standardized products before receiving customer orders (p. 409)

Manufacturing flexibility the degree to which manufacturing operations can easily and quickly change the number,

kind, and characteristics of products they produce (p. 410)

Continuous-flow production a manufacturing operation that produces goods at a continuous, rather than a discrete, rate (p. 410)

Line-flow production manufacturing processes that are preestablished, occur in a serial or linear manner, and are dedicated to making one type of product (p. 411)

Batch production a manufacturing operation that produces goods in large batches in standard lot sizes (p. 411)

Job shops manufacturing operations that handle custom orders or small batch jobs (p. 411)

18-5 **Explain why and how companies should manage inventory levels.** There are four kinds of inventory: raw materials, component parts, work-in-process, and finished goods. Because companies incur ordering, setup, holding, and stockout costs when handling inventory, inventory costs can be enormous. To control those costs, companies measure and track inventory in three ways: average aggregate inventory, weeks of supply, and turnover. Companies meet the basic goals of inventory management (avoiding stockouts and reducing inventory

without hurting daily operations) through economic order quantity (EOQ) formulas, just-in-time (JIT) inventory systems, and materials requirement planning (MRP). The formula for EOQ is

$$EOQ = \sqrt{\frac{2DO}{H}}$$

Use EOQ formulas when inventory levels are independent, and use JIT and MRP when inventory levels are dependent on the number of products to be produced.

Inventory the amount and number of raw materials, parts, and finished products that a company has in its possession (p. 412)

Raw material inventories the basic inputs in a manufacturing process (p. 412)

Component parts inventories the basic parts used in manufacturing that are fabricated from raw materials (p. 412)

Work-in-process inventories partially finished goods consisting of assembled component parts (p. 413)

Finished goods inventories the final outputs of manufacturing operations (p. 413)

Average aggregate inventory average overall inventory during a particular time period (p. 413)

Stockout the point when a company runs out of finished product (p. 414)

Inventory turnover the number of times per year that a company sells, or "turns over," its average inventory (p. 414)

Ordering cost the costs associated with ordering inventory, including the cost of data entry, phone calls, obtaining bids, correcting mistakes, and determining when and how much inventory to order (p. 414)

Setup cost the costs of downtime and lost efficiency that occur when a machine is changed or adjusted to produce a different kind of inventory (p. 415)

Holding cost the cost of keeping inventory until it is used or sold, including storage, insurance, taxes, obsolescence, and opportunity costs (p. 415)

Stockout cost the cost incurred when a company runs out of a product, including transaction costs to replace inventory and the loss of customers' goodwill (p. 415)

Economic order quantity (EOQ) a system of formulas that minimizes ordering and holding costs and helps determine how much and how often inventory should be ordered (p. 416)

Just-in-time (JIT) inventory system an inventory system in which component parts arrive from suppliers just as they are needed at each stage of production (p. 416)

Kanban a ticket-based JIT system that indicates when to reorder inventory (p. 416)

Materials requirement planning (MRP) a production and inventory system that determines the production schedule, production batch sizes, and inventory needed to complete final products (p. 417)

Independent demand system an inventory system in which the level of one kind of inventory does not depend on another (p. 417)

Dependent demand system an inventory system in which the level of inventory depends on the number of finished units to be produced (p. 417)